INTERNATIONAL YEARBOOK OF INDUSTRIAL STATISTICS
2019

INTERNATIONAL YEARBOOK
OF
INDUSTRIAL STATISTICS
2019

UNITED NATIONS INDUSTRIAL DEVELOPMENT ORGANIZATION
VIENNA
2019

Published by
Edward Elgar Publishing Limited
The Lypiatts
15 Lansdown Road
Cheltenham
Glos GL50 2JA
UK

Edward Elgar Publishing, Inc.
The William Pratt House
9 Dewey Court
Northampton
Massachusetts 01060-3815
USA

A catalogue record for this book
is available from the British Library

This book is available electronically in the **Elgar**online
Economics subject collection
DOI 10.4337/9781788977890

The description and classification of countries, economies and territories in this publication and the arrangement of the material do not imply the expression of any opinion whatsoever on the part of the Secretariat of the United Nations Industrial Development Organization concerning the legal status of any country, territory, city or area, or of its authorities, or concerning the delimitation of its frontiers or boundaries, or regarding its economic system or degree of development. The designation "country, economy or area" covers countries, economies, territories, cities and areas. The designation "region, country, economies or area" extends the preceding one by including groupings of entities designated as "country, economy or area". Designations such as "industrialized" and "developing and emerging industrial" economies are intended for statistical convenience and do not necessarily express a judgement about the stage reached by a particular country, economy or area in the development process.

ISBN 978 1 78897 788 3 (cased)
ISBN 978 1 78897 789 0 (eBook)
ISSN 1025-8493

Printed and bound in Great Britain by TJ International Ltd, Padstow, Cornwall

Acknowledgements

The 2019 edition of the International Yearbook of Industrial Statistics was prepared by a team of statistical staff under the supervision of Shyam Upadhyaya, Chief Statistician of UNIDO. Overall IT support was provided by Valentin Todorov, who managed the integrated statistical databases and produced the final PDF/digital manuscript. Dong Guo contributed to production of selected statistical tables for part I. Romana Bauer, Anja Boukhari, Kateryna Gumeniuk, Martin Haitzmann, P.Y.Rita Liang, Jürgen Muth and Romana Ransmayr were involved in the collection of data and the compilation of the regional and country tables. Nelson Correa Fernandez contributed to the final checking of statistical tables. Fernando Russo provided administrative support to the team.

The team members wish to express their sincere thanks to Cecilia Ugaz Estrada, Director of the Department of Policy Research and Statistics of UNIDO, for her support of the preparation of this publication.

The co-operation of national statistical offices, the United Nations Statistics Division (UNSD), the Organisation for Economic Co-operation and Development (OECD), the International Monetary Fund, the World Bank and other international and regional agencies in providing the information that has served as the basis of the current publication is gratefully acknowledged.

Explanatory notes

Unless otherwise indicated, "manufacturing" includes the industry groups listed under section C (Revision 4) of the *International Standard Industrial Classification of All Economic Activities* (ISIC) [Statistical Papers, Series M, No.4/Rev.4 (United Nations publication, Sales No. E.08.XVII.25)] or category D (Revision 3) of ISIC [Statistical Papers, Series M, No.4/Rev.3 (United Nations publication, Sales No. E.90.XVII.II)].

ISIC code numbers are accompanied by a descriptive title (for example in the case of Revision 4 of ISIC, ISIC 2023: "Manufacture of soap and detergents, cleaning and polishing preparations, perfumes and toilet preparations"). For considerations of space, however, the description is sometimes shortened (that is, ISIC 2023 may be described simply as "Soap, cleaning and cosmetic preparations"). For Revision 3 and 4 of ISIC, all 2-, 3- and 4-digit codes and their corresponding descriptive titles are listed in appendix II to the introduction.

In the presentation of several statistical tables in part I, individual countries and areas are presented by economies. They are listed alphabetically whenever appropriate, within two successive categories: "industrialized economies" and "developing and emerging industrial economies". Designation of economies as "industrialized" or "developing and emerging industrial" is based on adjusted manufacturing value added (MVA) per capita, which is a statistical measure derived from the share of MVA in gross domestic product (GDP) at 2010 current prices and GDP per capita in 2010 at the purchasing power parity (PPP) rate. This measure reflects an approximate value of MVA per capita by PPP. An economy is considered to be "industrialized" if its adjusted MVA per capita is higher than 2,500 international dollars or its GDP per capita is higher than 20,000 international dollars by PPP. Similarly, an "emerging industrial economy" corresponds to an economy with an adjusted MVA per capita ranging between 1,000 and 2,500 international dollars or an economy whose share of world MVA is higher than 0.5 per cent. All remaining economies fall in the category of "other developing economies". The list of least developed countries (LDCs) is based on decisions of the United Nations General Assembly. Users are advised to note that MVA per capita presented in the *Yearbook* is in United States dollars, not in PPP.

Data are also presented by income groups: high income, upper middle income, lower middle income and low income. These four country groups correspond to the World Bank's definition for each income category. The list of economies by all country groups used in the *Yearbook* is provided in appendix I to the introduction. Owing to a lack of data, some economies could not be included in their respective groups in some tables.

In the present publication, unless otherwise stated, data for China do not include data for Hong Kong SAR, for Macao SAR or for Taiwan Province of China, which are presented separately under China (Hong Kong SAR), China (Macao SAR) and China (Taiwan Province).

Data for Ireland indicate a substantial increase in manufacturing output and value added from 2015 onwards, as presented in part I and II of this *Yearbook*. This increase is primarily attributable to the relocation of a limited number of multinational companies to Ireland, in particular their intellectual property rights. Users are advised to exercise extra caution when interpreting these data and be aware of limited data availability by ISIC due to statistical disclosure control measures of the Central Statistics Office of Ireland.

In part I, references to dollars ($) are to United States dollars. National currencies have been converted to dollar equivalents by using period average exchange rates as published in *International Financial Statistics* (International Monetary Fund publication) and other sources.

Data converted to dollars by using current exchange rates are liable to be strongly influenced by fluctuations in exchange rates. Annual variations of data converted in that manner may not reflect movements in the national data.

Unless otherwise noted, average annual growth rates are calculated from the data available for each year of a given period (for example, 2010-2017), using a semi-log regression over time. Growth rates are expressed in percentages.

Periods set off by a hyphen (for instance, 2010-2017) include the beginning and end years.

Apparent arithmetic discrepancies, such as percentages that do not add up to precise totals, result from the rounding of basic data or figures known to different degrees of precision.

Three dots (...) indicate that data are not available or are not separately reported.

A dash (-) indicates that an amount is nil or negligible.

The letter "x" designates the item applicable to an economy when several options exist.

To avoid ambiguity, the letters "l", "o" and "O" are not used to designate footnotes.

The following abbreviations and acronyms are used:

ASEAN	Association of Southeast Asian Nations
CACM	Central American Common Market
CARICOM	Caribbean Community
CEMAC	Central African Economic and Monetary Community
CIS	Commonwealth of Independent States
ECOWAS	Economic Community of West African States
EIE	emerging industrial economy
EU	European Union
GCC	Cooperation Council for the Arab States of the Gulf
GDP	gross domestic product
IIP	index of industrial production
ISIC	International Standard Industrial Classification of All Economic Activities
LAIA	Latin American Integration Association
LDC	Least Developed Country
MERCOSUR	Common Market of the South/ Mercado Común del Sur
MVA	manufacturing value added
NACE	statistical classification of economic activities in the European Community/ Nomenclature statistique des activités économiques dans la Communauté européenne
n.e.c.	not elsewhere classified
n.e.s.	not elsewhere specified
NSO	national statistical office
OECD	Organisation for Economic Co-operation and Development
PPP	purchasing power parity
SAARC	South Asian Association for Regional Cooperation
SADC	Southern African Development Community
UNIDO	United Nations Industrial Development Organization
UNSD	United Nations Statistics Division
VAT	value added tax
WAEMU/UEMOA	West African Economic and Monetary Union

CONTENTS

Page

PART II. COUNTRY TABLES [a/]

[a/] For information on the countries/areas that are not presented, please see page 87.

DATA AVAILABLE ONLINE AND ON CD-ROM

Database	Description
INDSTAT2: UNIDO Industrial Statistics Database at the 2-digit level of ISIC code (Revision 3)	Long time series data for more than 170 countries/areas compiled on eight principle indicators (number of establishments, total employment, female employment, wages and salaries paid to employees, output, value added, gross fixed capital formation and index numbers of industrial production) starting from 1963 onwards. The data are arranged at the 2-digit level of ISIC (Revision 3) pertaining to the manufacturing sector, which comprises 23 manufacturing divisions.
INDSTAT4: UNIDO Industrial Statistics Database at the 3- and 4-digit levels of ISIC code (Revision 3 & 4)	Time series data for more than 130 (Revision 3)/90 (Revision 4) countries/areas on seven selected data items including number of establishments, total employment, female employment, wages and salaries paid to employees, output, value added and gross fixed capital formation. The data are arranged at the 3- and 4-digit levels of ISIC (Revision 3 & 4) pertaining to the manufacturing sector.
MINSTAT: UNIDO Mining & Utilities Statistics Database at the 2- and 3-digit levels of ISIC code (Revision 3 & 4)	Time series data for more than 110 (Revision 3)/80 (Revision 4) countries/areas on seven selected data items including number of establishments, total employment, female employment, wages and salaries paid to employees, output, value added and gross fixed capital formation. The data are arranged at the 2- and 3-digit levels of ISIC (Revision 3 & 4) pertaining to the mining and utilities sectors.
IDSB: UNIDO Industrial Demand-Supply Balance Database at the 4-digit level of ISIC code (Revision 3 & 4)	Time series data for more than 120 (Revision 3)/90 (Revision 4) countries/ areas on output, imports, exports and apparent consumption (all in current United States dollars) at the 4-digit level of ISIC Revision 3 & 4.
UNIDO Manufacturing Value Added (MVA) Database	Country data on GDP, MVA and population for various regions and groups of economies displayed at constant 2010 and at current United States dollars prices.
UNIDO CIP Database	Country data on ranks and values of Competitive Industrial Performance (CIP) index and its component indicators.

Further details on above products may be obtained from:
Statistics Division
UNIDO
Email: stat@unido.org
Internet: http://www.unido.org/statistics

INTRODUCTION

This is the twenty-fifth issue of UNIDO's annual publication, the *International Yearbook of Industrial Statistics*. The *Yearbook* succeeded the *Handbook of Industrial Statistics* which was published biennially by UNIDO up to 1992. At the same time, it replaced the United Nations' *Industrial Statistics Yearbook,* volume I (General Industrial Statistics), which was discontinued after its 1991 edition published in 1993. These changes were in accordance with the recommendations of the United Nations Statistical Commission at its twenty-seventh session, namely that UNIDO, in collaboration with the Organisation for Economic Co-operation and Development (OECD), assumes responsibility for the collection and dissemination of world-wide general industrial statistics, effective 1994. The present *Yearbook* pertains to the manufacturing sector only. UNIDO has also released a separate biennial publication *World Statistics on Mining and Utilities 2018*.

The main purpose of the *Yearbook* is to provide statistical indicators to facilitate international comparisons relating to the manufacturing sector. The data presented were compiled bearing in mind the requirements of international comparability and the standards for this work promulgated by the United Nations. Concepts and definitions are drawn from the *International Recommendations for Industrial Statistics* 2008 (Statistical Papers, Series M, No.90; United Nations publication, Sales No.E.08.XVII.8) and the classification by industry follows the *International Standard Industrial Classification of All Economic Activities.*

The present *Yearbook* consists of two parts. Part I deals with the manufacturing sector as a whole (section 1.1) and with its divisions (section 1.2). Statistical indicators are presented in terms of percentage distributions, cross-country averages, ratios and real growth rates that facilitate international comparison among selected country groups and/or economies. Graphical presentations followed by a brief description of the overall trend of world industrial growth are also displayed here. In the present publication data for manufacturing divisions are arranged according to Revision 4 of ISIC at the two-digit level.

Part II consists of a series of country/area-specific tables showing detailed data on selected basic statistics that were reported by national statistical offices (NSOs) and are presented in accordance with Revision 3 or Revision 4 of ISIC.

Sources and methods

In section 1.1 of part I, manufacturing value added (MVA) was estimated in accordance with the national accounting concept, which represents the net contribution of the manufacturing sector to gross domestic product (GDP). The data on MVA and GDP were obtained from various national and international sources including the World Bank, OECD, the United Nations Statistics Division (UNSD), the International Monetary Fund and regional development banks. These sources were supplemented with estimates generated by UNIDO.

Data reported in accordance with Revision 3 of ISIC have been converted to Revision 4 of ISIC to facilitate long time series comparison and are displayed in various tables of part I. Therefore, differences may arise from the conversion and users might find discrepancies when comparing converted data of later years with data of earlier years, published in the present edition of the *Yearbook.*

Due to the revision of data received from external sources, there might also be differences between the data presented in the current edition of the *Yearbook* and those shown in previous editions. Figures with respect to population are based on the 2017 revision of data compiled by the Population Division of the United Nations Secretariat.

The information in section 1.2 is drawn from the UNIDO Industrial Statistics Databases, as well as data communicated to the United Nations by official national sources. With regard to the member countries of OECD, data were compiled by that organization. Information is solicited through a questionnaire issued jointly by the two organizations.

To facilitate the comparability of the data over time and across economies, see "Explanatory notes", UNIDO has supplemented originally reported data with information obtained from various other sources. The latter include: industrial censuses, statistics supplied by national and international organizations, unpublished data collected in the field by UNIDO as well as estimates made by the UNIDO secretariat.[1]

---

[1] UNIDO's procedures for estimation are described in "Nowcasting manufacturing value added for cross-country comparison", Statistical Journal of the International Association for Official Statistics Volume 26 (2009).

The indicators presented in tables 1.5 to 1.9 of section 1.2 were derived from estimates of value added at constant 2010 prices. For each economy and industrial division, these value-added estimates were generated by applying production indices to the 2010 value added base weights, which in turn were generated by UNIDO from various national and international sources.

Except for index numbers of industrial production (IIP), the information for the countries and areas other than the OECD member countries presented in part II were compiled from: (i) the 2016 edition of the UNIDO General Industrial Statistics Questionnaires completed by NSOs; and (ii) relevant publications issued by NSOs. Information referring to OECD member countries is based on: (a) data compiled by OECD and incorporated in OECD's Information System on Industrial Statistics as well as in the UNIDO database; and (b) data derived from official sources of NSOs. With respect to production indices, data were either supplied by UNSD which compiles these data regularly from national sources through the quarterly United Nations Index of Industrial Production Questionnaires, or derived from UNIDO estimates based on the quarterly IIP, which were obtained from national sources. In some cases annual IIP figures were obtained from official websites of NSOs.

In part II, the measures generally used are census output and census value added. Thus, the costs of non-industrial services are included in value added, whereas the receipts for these services are excluded from output. For a quick reference, appendix III to this introduction provides notes on certain aspects of the data used, and it is recommended that the reader consult them when using the *Yearbook*. A detailed version appears in the individual country notes in part II, which also covers deviations from the standards applied. In general, these notes are also applicable to the estimates that supplement the officially reported data.

PART I. SUMMARY TABLES

Section 1.1: The manufacturing sector
Section 1.1 comprises tables 1.1 to 1.4. Table 1.1 shows the distribution of world MVA for various regions and groups of economies at constant 2010 prices as well as at current prices.

The readers should be aware that due to variation in official exchange rates, the world distribution may change considerably, depending on the choice of the base year.

To maintain comparability over time, composition of each group of economies was

kept the same throughout the period. However, due to data limitations, a number of economies listed in appendix I are not included.

China belongs to the group of emerging industrial economies. However, because of the large size of its economy, China is presented separately in tables 1.2 to 1.4.

Table 1.2 presents the shares of selected groups of economies in world MVA and population including industrialized economies.

Table 1.3 shows real growth rates and index numbers (2010=100) of total and per-capita MVA as well as values of per-capita MVA for the latest year 2017 for individual economies and for selected country groups. Data referring to country groups were based on cross-country aggregates of MVA in constant 2010 U.S. dollars.

Table 1.4 shows the percentage shares of MVA in GDP estimated at both constant 2010 prices and current prices. The data are presented by individual economies as well as by selected country groups. With respect to the selected country groups, common country samples were taken for both indicators and for all reference years.

Section 1.2: The manufacturing divisions/ branches
Section 1.2 comprises tables 1.5 to 1.10. It focuses on the divisions of the manufacturing sector. The ISIC (Revision 4) definition of manufacturing consists of 24 divisions reported in accordance with a two-digit code.

In (i) tables 1.5 to 1.9, Repair and installation of machinery (ISIC 33) and (ii) table 1.7, Tobacco products (ISIC 12), had to be excluded from the presentation due to data limitations. Data for China and China (Taiwan Province) are UNIDO estimates. Furthermore, a number of estimates at the country level were also generated to enable regional aggregation or to derive world totals for the latest years.

Table 1.5 shows the world distribution of the respective value added of selected divisions among selected country groups.

Table 1.6 shows the shares of developing regions and the least developed countries in the value added of all developing and emerging economies in selected divisions.

Table 1.7 shows the world's major producers in various industrial divisions as well as the major developing and emerging industrial economies in terms of value added.

China, which is an emerging industrial economy, is presented only among major 'World' economies. However, due to data limitations, it is not presented in all industrial divisions.

Table 1.8 shows the shares of individual divisions in total MVA by country groups.

Table 1.9 shows real growth rates of value added of individual divisions, calculated for selected country groups. The reference periods are 2005-2010 and 2010-2017.

Table 1.10 presents the share of female employees in total employment in individual divisions. For some economies, employment refers to number of persons engaged instead of number of employees (see appendix III of the present introduction). Only a limited number of economies have reported data on female employment at the division level.

PART II. COUNTRY TABLES

Part II comprises country/area-specific tables presenting the following selected industrial statistics: number of establishments, number of employees (or, if not reported, number of persons engaged), wages and salaries paid to employees, output, value added, gross fixed capital formation and index numbers of industrial production. All value data are presented in current national currencies. The data on these items (except gross fixed capital formation and index numbers of industrial production) relate to the last four years for which data were reported. Gross fixed capital formation refers to the last two years for which data were reported. Index numbers of industrial production refer to the period 2005-2016.

Coverage of countries/areas

The countries/areas that are presented in part II are those which reported data during the current round of the UNIDO annual compilation programme of global industrial statistics. Those countries/areas, which reported data only in previous rounds of the UNIDO compilation programme, are not included in the present *Yearbook* but were included in previous editions. At the beginning of part II, those countries/areas are listed together with a reference to the respective editions of the *Yearbook* in which their latest data were presented.

Industrial classification

The classification of industrial activity set out in the tables follows either Revision 3 or Revision 4 of ISIC, at the two-, three- and/or four-digit levels depending on the individual country's data reporting scheme. Where information was not provided in this form, the estimates are shown in the most applicable ISIC category. Aggregates for total manufacturing are included. With regard to production indices, data are arranged either in accordance with the 2-digit level of Revision 3 or Revision 4 of ISIC.

It should be noted that in several cases a figure presented for a 3-digit group does not agree with the sum of data given for the corresponding 4-digit categories. As far as possible, UNIDO resolved these discrepancies with the help of available supplementary information.

Reference unit

For most countries and areas represented, the data shown relate to the activity of "establishments" in the specified industries. Others follow the concepts of "kind-of-activity unit", "local unit" or "enterprise". An "establishment" is ideally a production unit that engages, under a single ownership or control, in one, or predominantly one, kind of activity at a single location; for example, workshop or factory. A "kind-of-activity unit" differs from the establishment in that there is no restriction with respect to the geographical area in which a given kind of activity is carried out by a single legal entity. A "local unit", on the other hand, comprises all activities carried out under a single ownership or control at a single location and differs from the establishment-type of unit in that there is no restriction on the range of these activities. An "enterprise" is a legal entity possessing the right to conduct business in its own name; for example, to enter into contracts, own property, incur liability for debts, and establish bank accounts. An enterprise may own one or more establishments.

Specific information on the character of the units covered in the tables for each country is set out in the corresponding country note.

Reference period

The statistics in the tables relate, in general, to the calendar year. It should be noted, however, that in many cases where the basic reference period of the industrial inquiry is the calendar year, returns covering proximate fiscal years may be accepted for reporting purposes and the data for these years incorporated in the calendar-year aggregate without adjustment. In a few countries, fiscal years normally used for public accounting purposes have been adopted as the basic reference periods. In the case of fiscal-year coverage, the year indicated in the tables refers to the calendar year in which the major part of the fiscal year falls. In the case of fiscal years from 1 July to 30 June, the year referred to is normally the one in which the fiscal year ends.

Concepts and definitions of the items

The United Nations standards that have been applied in preparing the tables are set out below. All values are in national currency units and are at current prices unless otherwise indicated. Deviations from these concepts and definitions are described in the respective country notes.

(1) Number of persons engaged and number of employees

The number of persons engaged is defined as the total number of persons who worked in or for the establishment during the reference year. However, home workers are excluded. The concept covers working proprietors, active business partners and unpaid family workers as well as employees. The figures reported refer normally to the average number of persons engaged during the reference year, obtained as the sum of the "average number of employees" during the year and the total number of other persons engaged measured for a single period of the year. The category "employees" is intended to include all persons engaged other than working proprietors, active business partners and unpaid family workers. In this publication, preference has been given, whenever possible, to employees over persons engaged.

(2) Wages and salaries

Estimates of wages and salaries include all payments in cash or in kind made to "employees" during the reference year in relation to work done for the establishment. Payments include: (a) direct wages and salaries; (b) remuneration for time not worked; (c) bonuses and gratuities; (d) housing allowances and family allowances paid directly by the employer; and (e) payments in kind.

Compensation of employees is equivalent to wages and salaries plus employers' contributions on behalf of their employees paid to social security, pension and insurance schemes, as well as the benefits received by employees under these schemes and severance and termination pay.

(3) Output

The measure of output for many countries is based on census concept that covers only activities of an industrial nature. The value of output in the case of estimates compiled on a production basis comprises: (a) the value of sale of all products of the establishment; (b) the net change between the beginning and the end of the reference period in the value of work in progress and stocks of goods to be shipped in the same condition as received; (c) the value of industrial work done or industrial services rendered to others; (d) the value of goods shipped in the same condition as received less the amount paid for these goods; and (e) the value of fixed assets produced during the period by the unit for its own use. In the case of estimates compiled on a shipment basis, the net change in the value of stocks of finished goods between the beginning and the end of the reference period is also included.

Gross output is equivalent to census output plus the revenue from activities of a non-industrial nature. Valuation methods differ from country to country. An increasing number of countries are reporting at basic prices, which exclude taxes on commodity and include commodity related subsidies. Other methods of reporting valuation are: (a) at factor costs, which exclude all indirect taxes falling on production and include all current subsidies received in support of production activities; and (b) at producers' prices, which include all indirect taxes except VAT, or any other deductible taxes and exclude all subsidies.

(4) Value added

Value added is defined as the value of output less the value of input. Items covered in the latter include: (a) value of materials and supplies for production (including cost of all fuels and electricity purchased); and (b) cost of services received (mainly payments for contract and commission work and repair and maintenance work). If input estimates are compiled on a "received" rather than on a "consumed" basis, the result is adjusted for the net change between the beginning and the end of the period in the value of stocks of materials, fuel and other supplies.

Total value added is the national accounting concept. It is ideally represented by the contribution of the establishments in each branch of activity to the gross domestic product. Whenever census concept is applied, for the measure of total value added, the cost of non-industrial services is deducted and the receipts for non-industrial services are added to census value added.

The estimates, whether in terms of census value added or total value added, are gross of depreciation and other provisions for capital consumption, unless otherwise stated. The valuation may be at factor costs, at basic prices or at producers' prices, depending on the treatment of indirect taxes and subsidies as described above.

(5) Gross fixed capital formation

Gross fixed capital formation refers to the value of acquisition of fixed assets including the work done on own-account during the reference year, less the value of corresponding disposals. The fixed assets covered are those (whether new or used) with a productive life of one year or more. Major additions, alterations and improvements to existing assets, which extend their normal economic life or raise their productivity, are also included.

New fixed assets include all those that have not been previously used in the country. Thus, newly imported fixed assets are considered new whether or not used before they were imported. Used fixed assets include all those that have been previously used within the country.

Transactions in fixed assets include: (a) cost of land purchase and land improvement; (b) dwellings, other buildings and structures; (c) machinery and equipment including transport and ICT equipment; and (d) intellectual property products, such as products of research and development, computer software, databases, etc. However, national practice may vary in terms of including these items. For example, data derived from OECD's database refer to Gross investment in tangible goods only.

Assets acquired from others are valued at purchasers' prices, which cover all costs directly connected with the acquisition and installation of the items for use. Imported assets are included only after it is acquired by the establishment which intends to use it.

In principle, assets produced on own account are also valued in this manner. However, it may frequently be necessary to value such own-account production at explicit cost, including any imputations that may be required in respect of the employed own-account labour.

Assets produced by one establishment of a multi-establishment enterprise, for the use of another establishment of the same enterprise, should be valued by the receiving establishment as though purchased from outside the enterprise. Sales of assets should be valued at the actual amounts realized rather than at book values.

(6) Index numbers of industrial production
Most of the national indices are calculated using the Laspeyres formula and a combination of volume extrapolation and deflation methods. These methods are described in the International Recommendations for the Index of Industrial Production 2010, United Nations. In the present *Yearbook* the base year for comparison is 2010. However, if any country uses different base years, the national indices are converted to the comparison base year. The theoretical aim of the IIP is to reflect the volume movements of goods or services produced over time.

Appendix I

LIST OF COUNTRIES AND AREAS INCLUDED IN SELECTED GROUPINGS
Industrialized Economies

EU a/

Austria
Belgium
Czechia
Denmark
Estonia
Finland
France
Germany
Hungary
Ireland
Italy
Lithuania
Luxembourg
Malta
Netherlands
Portugal
Slovakia
Slovenia
Spain
Sweden
United Kingdom

East Asia

China, Hong Kong SAR
China, Macao SAR
China, Taiwan Province
Japan
Malaysia
Republic of Korea
Singapore

West Asia

Bahrain
Kuwait
Qatar
United Arab Emirates

Others

Aruba
Australia
British Virgin Islands
Cayman Islands
Curaçao
French Guiana
French Polynesia
Guam
Israel
New Caledonia
New Zealand
Puerto Rico
Trinidad and Tobago
United States Virgin Islands

Other Europe

Andorra
Belarus
Iceland
Liechtenstein
Monaco
Norway
Russian Federation
San Marino
Switzerland

North America

Bermuda
Canada
Greenland
United States of America

---

a/ Excluding non-industrialized EU economies.

(continued)

Appendix I

LIST OF COUNTRIES AND AREAS INCLUDED IN SELECTED GROUPINGS
Developing and Emerging Industrial Economies by Region

AFRICA

Central Africa

Cameroon
Central African Republic
Chad
Congo
Equatorial Guinea
Gabon
Sao Tome and Principe

Eastern Africa

Burundi
Comoros
Djibouti
Eritrea
Ethiopia
Kenya
Réunion
Rwanda
Somalia
Uganda

North Africa

Algeria
Egypt
Libya
Morocco
South Sudan
Sudan
Tunisia

Southern Africa

Angola
Botswana
Democratic Rep of the Congo
Lesotho
Madagascar
Malawi
Mauritius
Mozambique
Namibia
Seychelles
South Africa
Swaziland
United Republic of Tanzania
Zambia
Zimbabwe

Western Africa

Benin
Burkina Faso
Cabo Verde
Côte d'Ivoire
Gambia
Ghana
Guinea
Guinea-Bissau
Liberia
Mali
Mauritania
Niger
Nigeria
Senegal
Sierra Leone
Togo

ASIA & PACIFIC

China

Central Asia

Kazakhstan
Kyrgyzstan
Mongolia
Tajikistan
Turkmenistan
Uzbekistan

South Asia

Afghanistan
Bangladesh
Bhutan
India
Maldives
Nepal
Pakistan
Sri Lanka

South East Asia

Brunei Darussalam
Cambodia
Indonesia
Lao People's Dem Rep
Myanmar
Philippines
Thailand
Viet Nam

West Asia

Armenia
Azerbaijan
Iran (Islamic Republic of)
Iraq
Jordan
Lebanon
Oman
Saudi Arabia
State of Palestine
Syrian Arab Republic
Yemen

Other Asia & Pacific

Cook Islands
Democratic People's Rep of Korea
Fiji
Kiribati
Marshall Islands
Micronesia, Federated States of
Palau
Papua New Guinea
Samoa
Solomon Islands
Timor-Leste
Tonga
Tuvalu
Vanuatu

EUROPE

Albania
Bosnia and Herzegovina
Bulgaria
Croatia
Cyprus
Georgia
Greece
Latvia
Montenegro
Poland
Republic of Moldova
Romania
Serbia
The f. Yugosl. Rep of Macedonia
Turkey
Ukraine

LATIN AMERICA

Caribbean

Anguilla
Antigua and Barbuda
Bahamas
Barbados
Cuba
Dominica
Dominican Republic
Grenada
Guadeloupe
Haiti
Jamaica
Martinique
Montserrat
Saint Kitts and Nevis
Saint Lucia
Saint Vincent and the Grenadines

Central America

Belize
Costa Rica
El Salvador
Guatemala
Honduras
Mexico
Nicaragua
Panama

South America

Argentina
Bolivia (Plurinational State of)
Brazil
Chile
Colombia
Ecuador
Guyana
Paraguay
Peru
Suriname
Uruguay
Venezuela (Bolivarian Republic of)

Appendix I

LIST OF COUNTRIES AND AREAS INCLUDED IN SELECTED GROUPINGS
Developing and Emerging Industrial Economies by Development

Emerging Industrial Economies

Argentina
Brazil
Brunei Darussalam
Bulgaria
Chile
Colombia
Costa Rica
Croatia
Cyprus
Egypt
Greece
India
Indonesia
Iran (Islamic Republic of)
Kazakhstan
Latvia
Mauritius
Mexico
Oman
Peru
Poland
Romania
Saudi Arabia
Serbia
South Africa
Suriname
Thailand
The f. Yugosl. Rep of Macedonia
Tunisia
Turkey
Ukraine
Uruguay
Venezuela (Bolivarian Republic of)

China

Other Developing Economies

Albania
Algeria
Angola
Anguilla
Antigua and Barbuda
Armenia
Azerbaijan
Bahamas
Barbados
Belize
Bolivia (Plurinational State of)
Bosnia and Herzegovina
Botswana
Cabo Verde
Cameroon
Congo
Cook Islands
Côte d'Ivoire
Cuba
Democratic People's Rep of Korea
Dominica
Dominican Republic
Ecuador
El Salvador
Equatorial Guinea
Fiji

Gabon
Georgia
Ghana
Grenada
Guadeloupe
Guatemala
Guyana
Honduras
Iraq
Jamaica
Jordan
Kenya
Kyrgyzstan
Lebanon
Libya
Maldives
Marshall Islands
Martinique
Micronesia, Federated States of
Mongolia
Montenegro
Montserrat
Morocco
Namibia
Nicaragua
Nigeria
Pakistan
Palau
Panama
Papua New Guinea
Paraguay
Philippines
Republic of Moldova
Réunion
Saint Kitts and Nevis
Saint Lucia
Saint Vincent and the Grenadines
Seychelles
Sri Lanka
State of Palestine
Swaziland
Syrian Arab Republic
Tajikistan
Tonga
Turkmenistan
Uzbekistan
Viet Nam
Zimbabwe

Least Developed Countries

Afghanistan
Bangladesh
Benin
Bhutan
Burkina Faso
Burundi
Cambodia
Central African Republic
Chad
Comoros
Democratic Rep of the Congo
Djibouti
Eritrea
Ethiopia
Gambia
Guinea
Guinea-Bissau
Haiti
Kiribati
Lao People's Dem Rep
Lesotho
Liberia
Madagascar
Malawi
Mali
Mauritania
Mozambique
Myanmar
Nepal
Niger
Rwanda
Samoa
Sao Tome and Principe
Senegal
Sierra Leone
Solomon Islands
Somalia
South Sudan
Sudan
Timor-Leste
Togo
Tuvalu
Uganda
United Republic of Tanzania
Vanuatu
Yemen
Zambia

(continued)

Appendix I

LIST OF COUNTRIES AND AREAS INCLUDED IN SELECTED GROUPINGS
Country Groups by Income Categories

High Income

Andorra
Anguilla
Antigua and Barbuda
Aruba
Australia
Austria
Bahamas
Bahrain
Barbados
Belgium
Bermuda
Brunei Darussalam
Canada
Cayman Islands
Chile
China, Hong Kong SAR
China, Macao SAR
China, Taiwan Province
Croatia
Curaçao
Cyprus
Czechia
Denmark
Equatorial Guinea
Estonia
Finland
France
French Polynesia
Germany
Greece
Greenland
Guam
Iceland
Ireland
Israel
Italy
Japan
Kuwait
Latvia
Liechtenstein
Lithuania
Luxembourg
Malta
Monaco
Netherlands
New Caledonia
New Zealand
Norway
Oman
Poland
Portugal
Puerto Rico
Qatar
Republic of Korea
Russian Federation
Saint Kitts and Nevis
San Marino
Saudi Arabia
Singapore
Slovakia
Slovenia
Spain
Sweden
Switzerland
Trinidad and Tobago
United Arab Emirates

United Kingdom
United States of America
United States Virgin Islands
Uruguay

Upper Middle Income

Albania
Algeria
American Samoa
Angola
Argentina
Azerbaijan
Belarus
Belize
Bosnia and Herzegovina
Botswana
Brazil
Bulgaria
China
Colombia
Costa Rica
Cuba
Dominica
Dominican Republic
Ecuador
Fiji
Gabon
Grenada
Hungary
Iran (Islamic Republic of)
Iraq
Jamaica
Jordan
Kazakhstan
Lebanon
Libya
Malaysia
Maldives
Marshall Islands
Mauritius
Mexico
Montenegro
Namibia
Palau
Panama
Peru
Romania
Saint Lucia
Saint Vincent and the Grenadines
Serbia
Seychelles
South Africa
Suriname
Thailand
The f. Yugosl. Rep of Macedonia
Tonga
Tunisia
Turkey
Turkmenistan
Tuvalu
Venezuela (Bolivarian Republic of)

Lower Middle Income

Armenia
Bhutan
Bolivia (Plurinational State of)
Cabo Verde
Cameroon
Congo
Côte d'Ivoire
Djibouti
Egypt
El Salvador
Georgia
Ghana
Guatemala
Guyana
Honduras
India
Indonesia
Kiribati
Kyrgyzstan
Lao People's Dem Rep
Lesotho
Mauritania
Micronesia, Federated States of
Mongolia
Morocco
Nicaragua
Nigeria
Pakistan
Papua New Guinea
Paraguay
Philippines
Republic of Moldova
Samoa
Sao Tome and Principe
Senegal
Solomon Islands
South Sudan
Sri Lanka
State of Palestine
Sudan
Swaziland
Syrian Arab Republic
Timor-Leste
Ukraine
Uzbekistan
Vanuatu
Viet Nam
Yemen
Zambia

Low Income

Afghanistan
Bangladesh
Benin
Burkina Faso
Burundi
Cambodia
Central African Republic
Chad
Comoros
Democratic People's Rep of Korea
Democratic Rep of the Congo
Eritrea
Ethiopia
Gambia
Guinea
Guinea-Bissau
Haiti
Kenya
Liberia
Madagascar
Malawi
Mali
Mozambique
Myanmar
Nepal
Niger
Rwanda
Sierra Leone
Somalia
Tajikistan
Togo
Uganda
United Republic of Tanzania
Zimbabwe

Appendix I

LIST OF COUNTRIES AND AREAS INCLUDED IN SELECTED GROUPINGS
Other Common Country Groups

ASEAN

Brunei Darussalam
Cambodia
Indonesia
Lao People's Dem Rep
Malaysia
Myanmar
Philippines
Singapore
Thailand
Viet Nam

CACM

Costa Rica
El Salvador
Guatemala
Honduras
Nicaragua

CARICOM

Antigua and Barbuda
Bahamas
Barbados
Belize
Dominica
Grenada
Guyana
Haiti
Jamaica
Montserrat
Saint Kitts and Nevis
Saint Lucia
Saint Vincent and the Grenadines
Suriname
Trinidad and Tobago

CEMAC

Cameroon
Central African Republic
Chad
Congo
Equatorial Guinea
Gabon

CIS

Armenia
Azerbaijan
Belarus
Georgia
Kazakhstan
Kyrgyzstan
Republic of Moldova
Russian Federation
Tajikistan
Turkmenistan
Ukraine
Uzbekistan

ECOWAS

Benin
Burkina Faso
Cabo Verde
Côte d'Ivoire
Gambia
Ghana
Guinea
Guinea-Bissau
Liberia
Mali
Niger
Nigeria
Senegal
Sierra Leone
Togo

EU

Austria
Belgium
Bulgaria
Croatia
Cyprus
Czechia
Denmark
Estonia
Finland
France
Germany
Greece
Hungary
Ireland
Italy
Latvia
Lithuania
Luxembourg
Malta
Netherlands
Poland
Portugal
Romania
Slovakia
Slovenia
Spain
Sweden
United Kingdom

GCC

Bahrain
Kuwait
Oman
Qatar
Saudi Arabia
United Arab Emirates

LAIA

Argentina
Bolivia (Plurinational State of)
Brazil
Chile
Colombia
Cuba
Ecuador
Mexico
Paraguay
Peru
Uruguay
Venezuela (Bolivarian Republic of)

OECD

Australia
Austria
Belgium
Canada
Chile
Czechia
Denmark
Estonia
Finland
France
Germany
Greece
Hungary
Iceland
Ireland
Israel
Italy
Japan
Latvia
Lithuania
Luxembourg
Mexico
Netherlands
New Zealand
Norway
Poland
Portugal
Republic of Korea
Slovakia
Slovenia
Spain
Sweden
Switzerland
Turkey
United Kingdom
United States of America

MERCOSUR

Argentina
Bolivia (Plurinational State of)
Brazil
Chile
Colombia
Ecuador
Paraguay
Peru
Uruguay
Venezuela (Bolivarian Republic of)

SAARC

Afghanistan
Bangladesh
Bhutan
India
Maldives
Nepal
Pakistan
Sri Lanka

SADC

Angola
Botswana
Democratic Rep of the Congo
Lesotho
Madagascar
Malawi
Mauritius
Mozambique
Namibia
Seychelles
South Africa
Swaziland
United Republic of Tanzania
Zambia
Zimbabwe

WAEMU/UEMOA

Benin
Burkina Faso
Côte d'Ivoire
Guinea-Bissau
Mali
Niger
Senegal
Togo

Appendix II

DETAILED DESCRIPTION OF INTERNATIONAL STANDARD INDUSTRIAL CLASSIFICATION OF ALL ECONOMIC ACTIVITIES (ISIC) REVISION 3 AND 4

ISIC REVISION 3

ISIC		Description

D   **MANUFACTURING**

Division 15   **Manufacture of food products and beverages**

151   Production, processing and preservation of meat, fish, fruit, vegetables, oils and fats
       1511   Production, processing and preserving of meat and meat products
       1512   Processing and preserving of fish and fish products
       1513   Processing and preserving of fruit and vegetables
       1514   Manufacture of vegetable and animal oils and fats

152   1520   Manufacture of dairy products

153   Manufacture of grain mill products, starches and starch products, and prepared animal feeds
       1531   Manufacture of grain mill products
       1532   Manufacture of starches and starch products
       1533   Manufacture of prepared animal feeds

154   Manufacture of other food products
       1541   Manufacture of bakery products
       1542   Manufacture of sugar
       1543   Manufacture of cocoa, chocolate and sugar confectionery
       1544   Manufacture of macaroni, noodles, couscous and similar farinaceous products
       1549   Manufacture of other food products n.e.c.

155   Manufacture of beverages
       1551   Distilling, rectifying and blending of spirits; ethyl alcohol production from fermented materials
       1552   Manufacture of wines
       1553   Manufacture of malt liquors and malt
       1554   Manufacture of soft drinks; production of mineral waters

Division 16   **Manufacture of tobacco products**

160   1600   Manufacture of tobacco products

Division 17   **Manufacture of textiles**

171   Spinning, weaving and finishing of textiles
       1711   Preparation and spinning of textile fibres; weaving of textiles
       1712   Finishing of textiles

172   Manufacture of other textiles
       1721   Manufacture of made-up textile articles, except apparel
       1722   Manufacture of carpets and rugs
       1723   Manufacture of cordage, rope, twine and netting
       1729   Manufacture of other textiles n.e.c.

ISIC REVISION 3 (continued)

ISIC		Description
173	1730	Manufacture of knitted and crocheted fabrics and articles

Division 18   **Manufacture of wearing apparel; dressing and dyeing of fur**

181	1810	Manufacture of wearing apparel, except fur apparel
182	1820	Dressing and dyeing of fur; manufacture of articles of fur

Division 19   **Tanning and dressing of leather; manufacture of luggage, handbags, saddlery, harness and footwear**

191		Tanning and dressing of leather; manufacture of luggage, handbags, saddlery and harness
	1911	Tanning and dressing of leather
	1912	Manufacture of luggage, handbags and the like, saddlery and harness
192	1920	Manufacture of footwear

Division 20   **Manufacture of wood and of products of wood and cork, except furniture; manufacture of articles of straw and plaiting materials**

201	2010	Sawmilling and planing of wood
202		Manufacture of products of wood, cork, straw and plaiting materials
	2021	Manufacture of veneer sheets; manufacture of plywood, laminboard, particle board and other panels and boards
	2022	Manufacture of builders' carpentry and joinery
	2023	Manufacture of wooden containers
	2029	Manufacture of other products of wood; manufacture of articles of cork, straw and plaiting materials

Division 21   **Manufacture of paper and paper products**

210		Manufacture of paper and paper products
	2101	Manufacture of pulp, paper and paperboard
	2102	Manufacture of corrugated paper and paperboard and of containers of paper and paperboard
	2109	Manufacture of other articles of paper and paperboard

Division 22   **Publishing, printing and reproduction of recorded media**

221		Publishing
	2211	Publishing of books, brochures, musical books and other publications
	2212	Publishing of newspapers, journals and periodicals
	2213	Publishing of recorded media
	2219	Other publishing
222		Printing and service activities related to printing
	2221	Printing
	2222	Service activities related to printing
223	2230	Reproduction of recorded media

ISIC REVISION 3 (continued)

ISIC		Description
Division 23		**Manufacture of coke, refined petroleum products and nuclear fuel**
231	2310	Manufacture of coke oven products
232	2320	Manufacture of refined petroleum products
233	2330	Processing of nuclear fuel
Division 24		**Manufacture of chemicals and chemical products**
241		Manufacture of basic chemicals
	2411	Manufacture of basic chemicals, except fertilizers and nitrogen compounds
	2412	Manufacture of fertilizers and nitrogen compounds
	2413	Manufacture of plastics in primary forms and of synthetic rubber
242		Manufacture of other chemical products
	2421	Manufacture of pesticides and other agro-chemical products
	2422	Manufacture of paints, varnishes and similar coatings, printing ink and mastics
	2423	Manufacture of pharmaceuticals, medicinal chemicals and botanical products
	2424	Manufacture of soap and detergents, cleaning and polishing preparations, perfumes and toilet preparations
	2429	Manufacture of other chemical products n.e.c.
243	2430	Manufacture of man-made fibres
Division 25		**Manufacture of rubber and plastics products**
251		Manufacture of rubber products
	2511	Manufacture of rubber tyres and tubes; retreading and rebuilding of rubber tyres
	2519	Manufacture of other rubber products
252	2520	Manufacture of plastics products
Division 26		**Manufacture of other non-metallic mineral products**
261	2610	Manufacture of glass and glass products
269		Manufacture of non-metallic mineral products n.e.c.
	2691	Manufacture of non-structural non-refractory ceramic ware
	2692	Manufacture of refractory ceramic products
	2693	Manufacture of structural non-refractory clay and ceramic products
	2694	Manufacture of cement, lime and plaster
	2695	Manufacture of articles of concrete, cement and plaster
	2696	Cutting, shaping and finishing of stone
	2699	Manufacture of other non-metallic mineral products n.e.c.
Division 27		**Manufacture of basic metals**
271	2710	Manufacture of basic iron and steel
272	2720	Manufacture of basic precious and non-ferrous metals

ISIC		Description
273		Casting of metals
	2731	Casting of iron and steel
	2732	Casting of non-ferrous metals

Division 28   **Manufacture of fabricated metal products, except machinery and equipment**

281		Manufacture of structural metal products, tanks, reservoirs and steam generators
	2811	Manufacture of structural metal products
	2812	Manufacture of tanks, reservoirs and containers of metal
	2813	Manufacture of steam generators, except central heating hot water boilers
289		Manufacture of other fabricated metal products; metal working service activities
	2891	Forging, pressing, stamping and roll-forming of metal; powder metallurgy
	2892	Treatment and coating of metals; general mechanical engineering on a fee or contract basis
	2893	Manufacture of cutlery, hand tools and general hardware
	2899	Manufacture of other fabricated metal products n.e.c.

Division 29   **Manufacture of machinery and equipment n.e.c.**

291		Manufacture of general purpose machinery
	2911	Manufacture of engines and turbines, except aircraft, vehicle and cycle engines
	2912	Manufacture of pumps, compressors, taps and valves
	2913	Manufacture of bearings, gears, gearing and driving elements
	2914	Manufacture of ovens, furnaces and furnace burners
	2915	Manufacture of lifting and handling equipment
	2919	Manufacture of other general purpose machinery
292		Manufacture of special purpose machinery
	2921	Manufacture of agricultural and forestry machinery
	2922	Manufacture of machine tools
	2923	Manufacture of machinery for metallurgy
	2924	Manufacture of machinery for mining, quarrying and construction
	2925	Manufacture of machinery for food, beverage and tobacco processing
	2926	Manufacture of machinery for textile, apparel and leather production
	2927	Manufacture of weapons and ammunition
	2929	Manufacture of other special purpose machinery
293	2930	Manufacture of domestic appliances n.e.c.

Division 30   **Manufacture of office, accounting and computing machinery**

300	3000	Manufacture of office, accounting and computing machinery

Division 31   **Manufacture of electrical machinery and apparatus n.e.c.**

311	3110	Manufacture of electric motors, generators and transformers
312	3120	Manufacture of electricity distribution and control apparatus
313	3130	Manufacture of insulated wire and cable
314	3140	Manufacture of accumulators, primary cells and primary batteries

ISIC REVISION 3 (continued)

ISIC		Description
315	3150	Manufacture of electric lamps and lighting equipment
319	3190	Manufacture of other electrical equipment n.e.c.

Division 32 — Manufacture of radio, television and communication equipment and apparatus

ISIC		Description
321	3210	Manufacture of electronic valves and tubes and other electronic components
322	3220	Manufacture of television and radio transmitters and apparatus for line telephony and line telegraphy
323	3230	Manufacture of television and radio receivers, sound or video recording or reproducing apparatus, and associated goods

Division 33 — Manufacture of medical, precision and optical instruments, watches and clocks

ISIC		Description
331		Manufacture of medical appliances and instruments and appliances for measuring, checking, testing, navigating and other purposes, except optical instruments
	3311	Manufacture of medical and surgical equipment and orthopaedic appliances
	3312	Manufacture of instruments and appliances for measuring, checking, testing, navigating and other purposes, except industrial process control equipment
	3313	Manufacture of industrial process control equipment
332	3320	Manufacture of optical instruments and photographic equipment
333	3330	Manufacture of watches and clocks

Division 34 — Manufacture of motor vehicles, trailers and semi-trailers

ISIC		Description
341	3410	Manufacture of motor vehicles
342	3420	Manufacture of bodies (coachwork) for motor vehicles; manufacture of trailers and semi-trailers
343	3430	Manufacture of parts and accessories for motor vehicles and their engines

Division 35 — Manufacture of other transport equipment

ISIC		Description
351		Building and repairing of ships and boats
	3511	Building and repairing of ships
	3512	Building and repairing of pleasure and sporting boats
352	3520	Manufacture of railway and tramway locomotives and rolling stock
353	3530	Manufacture of aircraft and spacecraft
359		Manufacture of transport equipment n.e.c.
	3591	Manufacture of motorcycles
	3592	Manufacture of bicycles and invalid carriages
	3599	Manufacture of other transport equipment n.e.c.

ISIC REVISION 3 (continued)

ISIC		Description

Division 36   **Manufacture of furniture; manufacturing n.e.c.**

| 361 | 3610 | Manufacture of furniture |

369		Manufacturing n.e.c.
	3691	Manufacture of jewellery and related articles
	3692	Manufacture of musical instruments
	3693	Manufacture of sports goods
	3694	Manufacture of games and toys
	3699	Other manufacturing n.e.c.

Division 37   **Recycling**

| 371 | 3710 | Recycling of metal waste and scrap |
| 372 | 3720 | Recycling of non-metal waste and scrap |

* * * * * * * * * *

ISIC REVISION 4

ISIC		Description

C   **MANUFACTURING**

Division 10   **Manufacture of food products**

101	1010	Processing and preserving of meat
102	1020	Processing and preserving of fish, crustaceans and molluscs
103	1030	Processing and preserving of fruit and vegetables
104	1040	Manufacture of vegetable and animal oils and fats
105	1050	Manufacture of dairy products
106		Manufacture of grain mill products, starches and starch products
	1061	Manufacture of grain mill products
	1062	Manufacture of starches and starch products
107		Manufacture of other food products
	1071	Manufacture of bakery products
	1072	Manufacture of sugar
	1073	Manufacture of cocoa, chocolate and sugar confectionery
	1074	Manufacture of macaroni, noodles, couscous and similar farinaceous products
	1075	Manufacture of prepared meals and dishes
	1079	Manufacture of other food products n.e.c.
108	1080	Manufacture of prepared animal feeds

Division 11   **Manufacture of beverages**

	1101	Distilling, rectifying and blending of spirits
	1102	Manufacture of wines
	1103	Manufacture of malt liquors and malt
	1104	Manufacture of soft drinks; production of mineral waters and other bottled waters

Division 12   **Manufacture of tobacco products**

| 120 | 1200 | Manufacture of tobacco products |

Division 13   **Manufacture of textiles**

131		Spinning, weaving and finishing of textiles
	1311	Preparation and spinning of textile fibres
	1312	Weaving of textiles
	1313	Finishing of textiles
139		Manufacture of other textiles
	1391	Manufacture of knitted and crocheted fabrics
	1392	Manufacture of made-up textile articles, except apparel
	1393	Manufacture of carpets and rugs
	1394	Manufacture of cordage, rope, twine and netting
	1399	Manufacture of other textiles n.e.c.

ISIC		Description

Division 14   **Manufacture of wearing apparel**

141	1410	Manufacture of wearing apparel, except fur apparel
142	1420	Manufacture of articles of fur
143	1430	Manufacture of knitted and crocheted apparel

Division 15   **Manufacture of leather and related products**

151		Tanning and dressing of leather; manufacture of luggage, handbags, saddlery and harness; dressing and dyeing of fur
	1511	Tanning and dressing of leather; dressing and dyeing of fur
	1512	Manufacture of luggage, handbags and the like, saddlery and harness
152	1520	Manufacture of footwear

Division 16   **Manufacture of wood and of products of wood and cork, except furniture; manufacture of articles of straw and plaiting materials**

161	1610	Sawmilling and planing of wood
162		Manufacture of products of wood, cork, straw and plaiting materials
	1621	Manufacture of veneer sheets and wood-based panels
	1622	Manufacture of builders' carpentry and joinery
	1623	Manufacture of wooden containers
	1629	Manufacture of other products of wood; manufacture of articles of cork, straw and plaiting materials

Division 17   **Manufacture of paper and paper products**

	1701	Manufacture of pulp, paper and paperboard
	1702	Manufacture of corrugated paper and paperboard and of containers of paper and paperboard
	1709	Manufacture of other articles of paper and paperboard

Division 18   **Printing and reproduction of recorded media**

181		Printing and service activities related to printing
	1811	Printing
	1812	Service activities related to printing
182	1820	Reproduction of recorded media

Division 19   **Manufacture of coke and refined petroleum products**

| 191 | 1910 | Manufacture of coke oven products |
| 192 | 1920 | Manufacture of refined petroleum products |

ISIC REVISION 4 (continued)

ISIC		Description

Division 20   **Manufacture of chemicals and chemical products**

201   Manufacture of basic chemicals, fertilizers and nitrogen compounds, plastics and synthetic rubber in primary forms
    2011   Manufacture of basic chemicals
    2012   Manufacture of fertilizers and nitrogen compounds
    2013   Manufacture of plastics and synthetic rubber in primary forms

202   Manufacture of other chemical products
    2021   Manufacture of pesticides and other agrochemical products
    2022   Manufacture of paints, varnishes and similar coatings, printing ink and mastics
    2023   Manufacture of soap and detergents, cleaning and polishing preparations, perfumes and toilet preparations
    2029   Manufacture of other chemical products n.e.c.

203   2030   Manufacture of man-made fibres

Division 21   **Manufacture of pharmaceuticals, medicinal chemical and botanical products**

210   2100   Manufacture of pharmaceuticals, medicinal chemical and botanical products

Division 22   **Manufacture of rubber and plastics products**

221   Manufacture of rubber products
    2211   Manufacture of rubber tyres and tubes; retreading and rebuilding of rubber tyres
    2219   Manufacture of other rubber products

222   2220   Manufacture of plastics products

Division 23   **Manufacture of other non-metallic mineral products**

231   2310   Manufacture of glass and glass products

239   Manufacture of non-metallic mineral products n.e.c.
    2391   Manufacture of refractory products
    2392   Manufacture of clay building materials
    2393   Manufacture of other porcelain and ceramic products
    2394   Manufacture of cement, lime and plaster
    2395   Manufacture of articles of concrete, cement and plaster
    2396   Cutting, shaping and finishing of stone
    2399   Manufacture of other non-metallic mineral products n.e.c.

Division 24   **Manufacture of basic metals**

241   2410   Manufacture of basic iron and steel
242   2420   Manufacture of basic precious and other non-ferrous metals

243   Casting of metals
    2431   Casting of iron and steel
    2432   Casting of non-ferrous metals

ISIC REVISION 4 (continued)

ISIC		Description
Division 25		**Manufacture of fabricated metal products, except machinery and equipment**
251		Manufacture of structural metal products, tanks, reservoirs and steam generators
	2511	Manufacture of structural metal products
	2512	Manufacture of tanks, reservoirs and containers of metal
	2513	Manufacture of steam generators, except central heating hot water boilers
252	2520	Manufacture of weapons and ammunition
259		Manufacture of other fabricated metal products; metalworking service activities
	2591	Forging, pressing, stamping and roll-forming of metal; powder metallurgy
	2592	Treatment and coating of metals; machining
	2593	Manufacture of cutlery, hand tools and general hardware
	2599	Manufacture of other fabricated metal products n.e.c.
Division 26		**Manufacture of computer, electronic and optical products**
261	2610	Manufacture of electronic components and boards
262	2620	Manufacture of computers and peripheral equipment
263	2630	Manufacture of communication equipment
264	2640	Manufacture of consumer electronics
265		Manufacture of measuring, testing, navigating and control equipment; watches and clocks
	2651	Manufacture of measuring, testing, navigating and control equipment
	2652	Manufacture of watches and clocks
266	2660	Manufacture of irradiation, electromedical and electrotherapeutic equipment
267	2670	Manufacture of optical instruments and photographic equipment
268	2680	Manufacture of magnetic and optical media
Division 27		**Manufacture of electrical equipment**
271	2710	Manufacture of electric motors, generators, transformers and electricity distribution and control apparatus
272	2720	Manufacture of batteries and accumulators
273		Manufacture of wiring and wiring devices
	2731	Manufacture of fibre optic cables
	2732	Manufacture of other electronic and electric wires and cables
	2733	Manufacture of wiring devices
274	2740	Manufacture of electric lighting equipment
275	2750	Manufacture of domestic appliances
279	2790	Manufacture of other electrical equipment

ISIC REVISION 4 (continued)

ISIC		Description

Division 28   **Manufacture of machinery and equipment n.e.c.**

281		Manufacture of general-purpose machinery
	2811	Manufacture of engines and turbines, except aircraft, vehicle and cycle engines
	2812	Manufacture of fluid power equipment
	2813	Manufacture of other pumps, compressors, taps and valves
	2814	Manufacture of bearings, gears, gearing and driving elements
	2815	Manufacture of ovens, furnaces and furnace burners
	2816	Manufacture of lifting and handling equipment
	2817	Manufacture of office machinery and equipment (except computers and peripheral equipment)
	2818	Manufacture of power-driven hand tools
	2819	Manufacture of other general-purpose machinery
282		Manufacture of special-purpose machinery
	2821	Manufacture of agricultural and forestry machinery
	2822	Manufacture of metal-forming machinery and machine tools
	2823	Manufacture of machinery for metallurgy
	2824	Manufacture of machinery for mining, quarrying and construction
	2825	Manufacture of machinery for food, beverage and tobacco processing
	2826	Manufacture of machinery for textile, apparel and leather production
	2829	Manufacture of other special-purpose machinery

Division 29   **Manufacture of motor vehicles, trailers and semi-trailers**

291	2910	Manufacture of motor vehicles
292	2920	Manufacture of bodies (coachwork) for motor vehicles; manufacture of trailers and semi-trailers
293	2930	Manufacture of parts and accessories for motor vehicles

Division 30   **Manufacture of other transport equipment**

301		Building of ships and boats
	3011	Building of ships and floating structures
	3012	Building of pleasure and sporting boats
302	3020	Manufacture of railway locomotives and rolling stock
303	3030	Manufacture of air and spacecraft and related machinery
304	3040	Manufacture of military fighting vehicles
309		Manufacture of transport equipment n.e.c.
	3091	Manufacture of motorcycles
	3092	Manufacture of bicycles and invalid carriages
	3099	Manufacture of other transport equipment n.e.c.

Division 31   **Manufacture of furniture**

310	3100	Manufacture of furniture

ISIC REVISION 4 (continued)

ISIC		Description

Division 32 **Other manufacturing**

321		Manufacture of jewellery, bijouterie and related articles
	3211	Manufacture of jewellery and related articles
	3212	Manufacture of imitation jewellery and related articles
322	3220	Manufacture of musical instruments
323	3230	Manufacture of sports goods
324	3240	Manufacture of games and toys
325	3250	Manufacture of medical and dental instruments and supplies
329	3290	Other manufacturing n.e.c.

Division 33 **Repair and installation of machinery and equipment**

331		Repair of fabricated metal products, machinery and equipment
	3311	Repair of fabricated metal products
	3312	Repair of machinery
	3313	Repair of electronic and optical equipment
	3314	Repair of electrical equipment
	3315	Repair of transport equipment, except motor vehicles
	3319	Repair of other equipment
332	3320	Installation of industrial machinery and equipment

* * * * * * * * * *

Country or area	Value added					Output					Employment		
	Basic prices	Factor values	Producers' prices	Unspecified	Mixed	Basic prices	Factor values	Producers' prices	Unspecified	Mixed	Persons engaged	Employees	Mixed
Afghanistan									X			X	
Albania	X					X						X	
Algeria			X							X		X	
Angola									X		X		
Argentina		X							X			X	
Armenia					X					X		X	
Australia			X						X		X		
Austria		X							X			X	
Azerbaijan		X						X				X	
Bahamas												X	
Bahrain		X							X			X	
Bangladesh		X					X					X	
Belarus	X					X						X	
Belgium		X							X			X	
Bermuda	X					X					X		
Bolivia (Plurinational State of)		X						X				X	
Bosnia and Herzegovina		X						X				X	
Botswana	X					X						X	
Brazil					X					X			X
Brunei Darussalam								X				X	
Bulgaria					X					X		X	
Burundi	X					X						X	
Cabo Verde												X	
Cambodia		X						X			X		
Cameroon									X			X	
Canada			X						X			X	
Chile			X						X			X	
China					X					X		X	
China, Hong Kong SAR		X						X				X	
China, Macao SAR		X						X			X		
China, Taiwan Province			X						X			X	
Colombia					X					X		X	
Costa Rica					X					X		X	
Croatia		X							X			X	
Cyprus		X						X				X	
Czechia		X							X			X	
Denmark		X							X			X	
Dominican Republic											X		
Ecuador					X					X		X	
Egypt		X					X						X
Eritrea			X					X				X	
Estonia		X								X		X	
Ethiopia					X					X		X	
Fiji					X					X		X	
Finland		X								X		X	
France		X								X		X	
Georgia	X					X							X
Germany		X							X			X	
Ghana			X					X				X	
Greece		X							X		X		
Guatemala									X			X	
Hungary		X							X			X	
Iceland				X					X				X
India				X						X			X
Indonesia				X				X				X	
Iran (Islamic Republic of)		X						X				X	
Iraq			X						X			X	
Ireland		X							X				X
Israel	X					X						X	
Italy		X							X			X	
Japan	X								X				X
Jordan		X						X				X	
Kazakhstan	X					X						X	
Kenya	X					X							X
Kuwait		X						X				X	
Kyrgyzstan			X					X				X	
Lao People's Dem Rep	X					X						X	

DESCRIPTION OF DATA USED IN SECTION 1.2

Country or area	Value added					Output					Employment		
	Basic prices	Factor values	Producers' prices	Unspecified	Mixed	Basic prices	Factor values	Producers' prices	Unspecified	Mixed	Persons engaged	Employees	Mixed
Latvia		X								X		X	
Lebanon					X					X		X	
Liechtenstein													X
Lithuania		X								X		X	
Luxembourg		X						X				X	
Malawi			X					X				X	
Malaysia					X					X		X	
Maldives			X					X					X
Malta		X					X					X	
Mauritius	X					X						X	
Mexico			X					X					X
Mongolia					X					X			X
Montenegro	X					X						X	
Morocco		X					X					X	
Namibia				X				X				X	
Nepal					X					X		X	
Netherlands		X								X		X	
New Zealand					X					X			X
Niger				X				X				X	
Nigeria							X				X		
Norway		X								X		X	
Oman					X					X		X	
Pakistan			X				X					X	
Panama			X				X					X	
Paraguay					X					X			X
Peru	X					X					X		
Philippines			X				X					X	
Poland		X								X		X	
Portugal		X						X				X	
Qatar			X				X					X	
Republic of Korea					X			X				X	
Republic of Moldova				X						X		X	
Romania					X					X		X	
Russian Federation	X					X						X	
Saudi Arabia					X					X		X	
Senegal			X				X					X	
Serbia	X					X						X	
Singapore	X					X					X		
Slovakia		X						X					X
Slovenia		X								X		X	
South Africa	X									X		X	
Spain		X						X				X	
Sri Lanka					X					X		X	
State of Palestine					X					X			X
Suriname	X							X				X	
Swaziland	X					X						X	
Sweden		X								X			X
Switzerland					X				X		X		
Syrian Arab Republic				X						X		X	
Tajikistan									X			X	
Thailand				X						X		X	
The f. Yugosl. Rep of Macedonia					X				X			X	
Tonga							X					X	
Trinidad and Tobago					X				X			X	
Tunisia					X					X		X	
Turkey					X				X			X	
Turkmenistan										X	X		
Uganda			X									X	
Ukraine					X					X		X	
United Arab Emirates					X		X				X		
United Kingdom		X								X		X	
United Republic of Tanzania		X					X					X	
United States of America				X						X		X	
Uruguay					X				X		X		
Viet Nam			X							X		X	
Yemen				X					X			X	
Zimbabwe	X					X							

Part I
SUMMARY TABLES

Section 1.1
THE MANUFACTURING SECTOR

Major trends of growth and distribution of manufacturing in the world

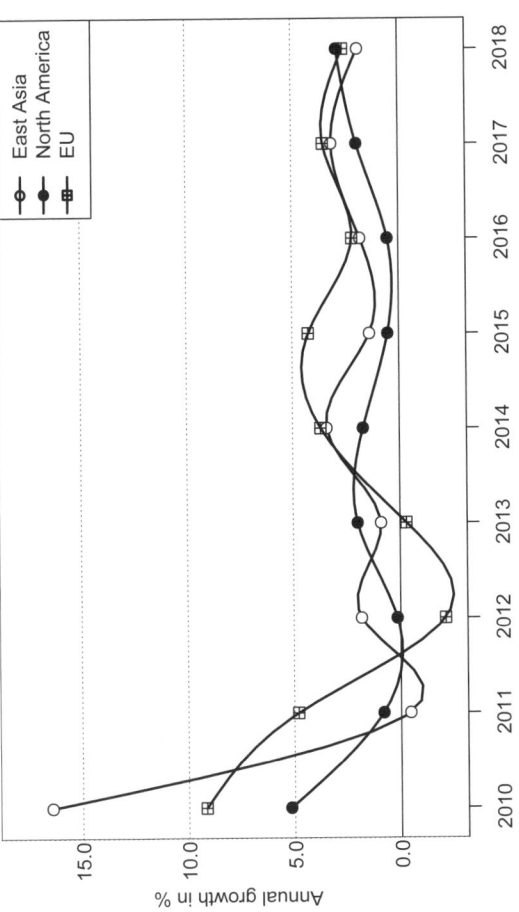

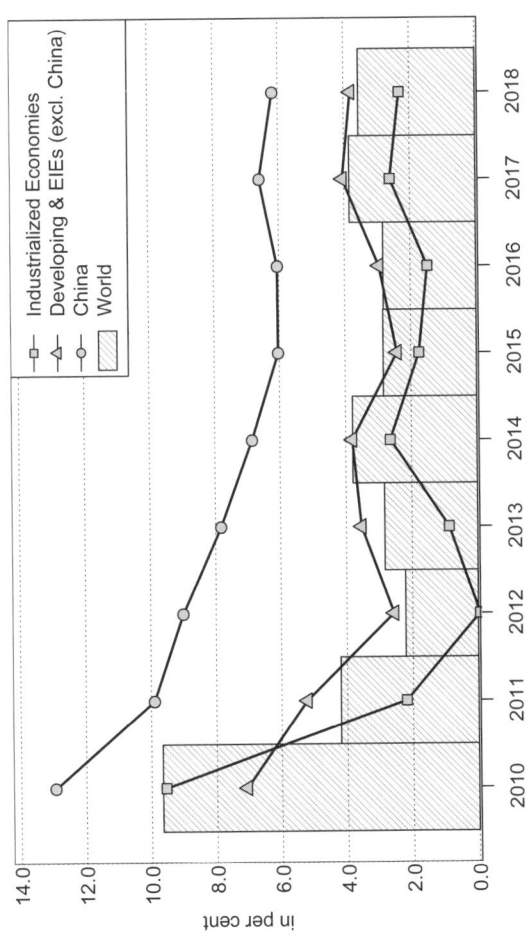

Figure 1: Annual manufacturing growth rates in per cent by country group (at 2010 constant prices)

Figure 2: Annual manufacturing growth in per cent in East Asia, EU and North America (at 2010 constant prices)

Global manufacturing value added rose by 3.6 per cent in 2018, which was slightly lower than in the previous year. The slowdown is mainly attributed to emerging trade and tariff barriers involving USA and China as well as the US and the EU, which has exposed the markets to a significant amount of uncertainty, limiting investment and future growth. China, the EU and the US account for over half of global manufacturing production. The trade instability and tariff relations between these countries is likely to have a serious impact on overall global manufacturing growth. A slowdown in production was observed in all major country groups (Figure 1). China's growth remained strong and stable with a 6.2 per cent increase in MVA, albeit at a lower rate than in 2017 (6.6 per cent). The MVA growth rate of developing and emerging industrial economies was 3.8 per cent in 2018, lower than the rate of 4.1 per cent in the previous year. A manufacturing slowdown was also observed in industrialized economies, where the MVA growth rate rose by 2.3 per cent compared to 2.6 per cent in 2017.

With a relatively slow manufacturing growth, industrialized economies have been trying to get an edge ahead of their competitors and increase their industry's competitiveness. These efforts have led to recurring trade frictions in the industrialized world. These frictions may result in short-term advantages for the country that initially establishes trade barriers, but at the cost of a loss in long-term prosperity for all countries, once the other countries respond by introducing protectionist measures. While the majority of industrialized countries has registered a slight drop in 2018, North America's manufacturing sector recorded a slight increase, from 2.0 per cent annual growth in 2017 to 2.9 per cent in 2018. The opposite has been the case in EU and East Asian countries - for example, Japan, the Republic of Korea, Malaysia and Singapore - where the annual manufacturing growth rate decreased from 3.5 per cent to 2.6 per cent and from 3.1 per cent to 1.9 per cent, respectively.

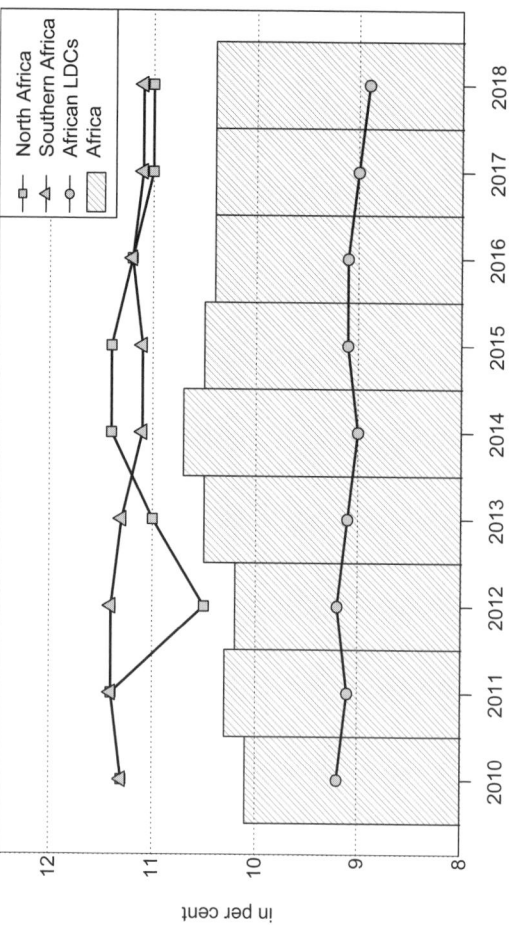

Figure 3: Annual manufacturing growth in the BRICS countries (at 2010 constant prices)

Over the entire decade, the BRICS countries have been able to take advantage of market opportunities and their manufacturing growth has therefore remained strong. One of the major contributors to the BRICS's successful industrial performance has undoubtedly been China. The country's manufacturing growth in the last decade is only matched by India, which, like China, registered an annual manufacturing growth rate of over 7 per cent between 2010 and 2018. China and India's performance lies in stark contrast to Brazil's, Latin America's largest manufacturer, which recorded a growth rate of -1.6 per cent for the same period. Thus, despite the slowdown of China's annual manufacturing growth from 12.9 per cent in 2010 to 6.2 per cent in 2018, it has consistently exceeded the BRICS's average growth rate (5.7 per cent in 2018) as well as that of other emerging industrial economies (3.5 per cent in 2018) every year for the last decade.

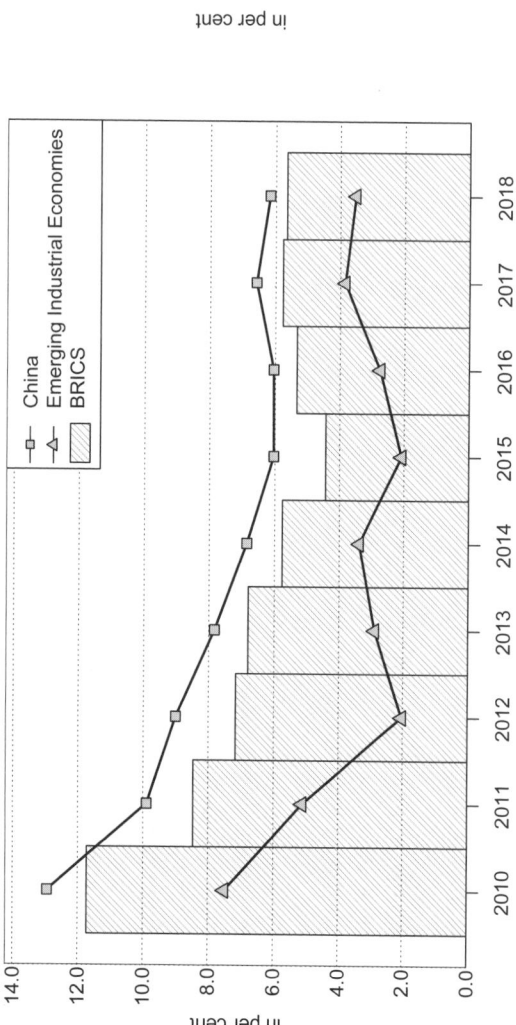

Figure 4: Share of MVA in GDP in Africa (at 2010 constant prices)

The African continent has faced major obstacles in its efforts to develop and catch up with the rest of the world. Of the 47 least developed countries (LDCs), 33 are located in sub-Saharan Africa, and they are afflicted by widespread poverty, low income per capita, weak institutional capacities and other major challenges impeding economic development. Northern and Southern African countries provide a more mixed picture of the continent, with the growth rate in Egypt, Morocco and South Africa bolstering the regions' average economic growth. The industrialization paths followed by Northern and Southern African countries have resulted in an MVA share of GDP of around 11 per cent in 2018, clearly above the African continent's average (Figure 4). While Africa's share of MVA in GDP declined from 10.6 per cent in 2014 to 10.3 per cent in 2018, that of African LDCs dropped from 9.1 per cent in 2016 to 8.9 per cent in 2018.

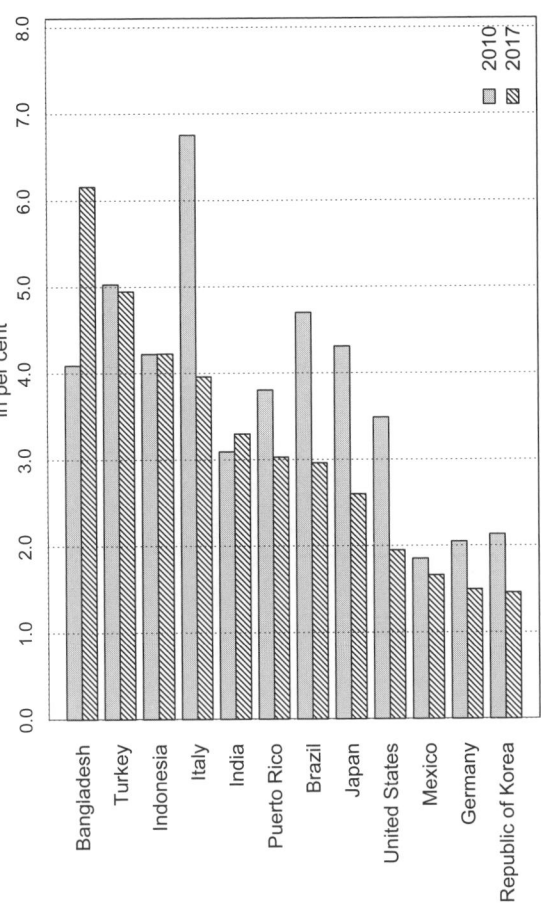

Figure 6: Leading economies in the wearing apparel industry by share in the industry's world value added (excluding China)

Developing economies dominate global production in the wearing apparel industry, which is one of the most essential consumer goods and also the first step up the technology ladder. Many developing countries that have successfully transformed and developed their industrial sector often reinforced their position in low-tech industries—such as textile and apparel—and continued adding value to manufacturing to eventually move into more medium- and high-tech industries. A classic example of a country that has followed this path of structural change is China. China continues to be the world leader in textile and apparel, with its share in world value added increasing from 28.1 per cent in 2010 to 39.8 per cent in 2017. Figure 6 excludes China to more accurately illustrate the contribution of other countries to this industry's world value added. Remarkably, Bangladesh has managed to surpass other much larger economies and now contributes the second largest share to the wearing apparel industry's world added value (4.1 per cent in 2010 to 6.2 per cent in 2018).

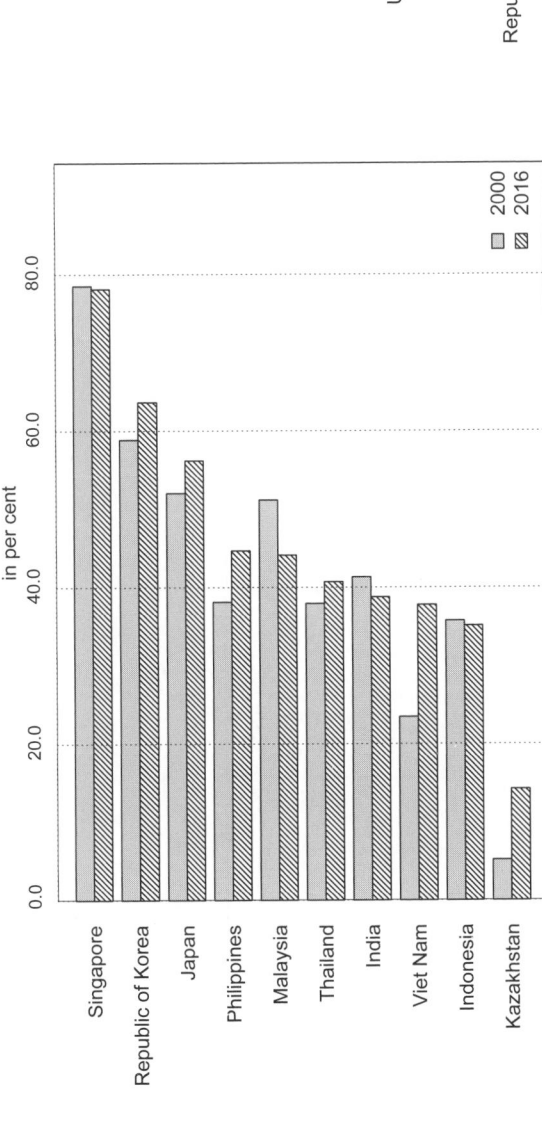

Figure 5: Share of medium high- and high-tech value added in total manufacturing value added for selected countries, in per cent

Medium high- and high-tech (MHT) refers to the technological intensity of a group of industries. It includes, for example, the production of machinery, motor vehicles, computers, electronic, communication and optical products.

Asian countries have made considerable strides in developing strong industries, particularly in industries producing MHT products. A closer look at this region reveals that Singapore continues to maintain its lead in technological innovation, with the highest share of medium- and high-tech industries worldwide (78.1 per cent in 2016) in total manufacturing value added. Figure 5 compares Singapore's and Asian economies' share of medium high- and high-tech industries' value added in total MVA. Kazakhstan and Viet Nam have also intensified their efforts in technological upgrading in recent years.

Table 1.1

DISTRIBUTION OF WORLD MVA AMONG SELECTED COUNTRY GROUPS, 2005-2018

Year	Industrialized Economies						Developing and Emerging Industrial Economies							
	Europe		East Asia	West Asia	North America	Others	Regional groups				Development groups			
	EU a/	Other					Africa	Asia and Pacific	Europe	Latin America	Emerging Industrial Economies	China	Other Developing Economies	Least Developed Countries
Percentage share in world total MVA (at constant 2010 prices)														
2005	24.3	3.7	17.3	0.4	22.1	2.1	1.7	18.4	2.8	7.2	15.8	11.5	2.3	0.5
2010	20.9	3.4	16.4	0.4	19.1	1.9	1.8	26.5	2.8	6.8	16.5	18.3	2.5	0.6
2011	21.1	3.4	15.7	0.5	18.4	1.8	1.8	27.6	2.9	6.8	16.6	19.3	2.6	0.6
2012	20.2	3.5	15.6	0.4	18.1	1.7	1.9	29.0	3.0	6.6	16.6	20.6	2.6	0.7
2013	19.5	3.5	15.3	0.5	17.9	1.7	1.9	30.1	3.0	6.6	16.6	21.6	2.7	0.7
2014	19.5	3.3	15.3	0.4	17.6	1.6	2.0	30.9	3.1	6.3	16.6	22.2	2.8	0.7
2015	19.7	3.2	15.0	0.5	17.2	1.5	2.0	31.9	3.1	5.9	16.4	22.9	2.8	0.8
2016 b/	19.6	3.1	14.9	0.5	16.8	1.5	1.9	32.9	3.1	5.7	16.4	23.7	2.8	0.7
2017 c/	19.5	3.0	14.8	0.4	16.5	1.5	1.9	33.7	3.2	5.5	16.4	24.3	2.8	0.8
2018 c/	19.3	3.0	14.5	0.5	16.4	1.4	1.9	34.6	3.2	5.2	16.4	24.9	2.8	0.8
Percentage share in world total MVA (at current prices)														
2009	22.9	3.3	15.3	0.4	20.2	1.8	1.8	25.0	3.0	6.3	15.5	17.4	2.6	0.6
2010	20.9	3.4	16.4	0.4	19.1	1.9	1.8	26.5	2.8	6.8	16.5	18.3	2.5	0.6
2011	20.6	3.6	15.3	0.5	17.9	1.8	1.8	29.0	2.8	6.7	16.4	20.7	2.6	0.6
2012	18.9	3.6	14.3	0.6	18.3	1.8	1.9	31.3	2.8	6.5	16.3	22.7	2.8	0.7
2013	19.3	3.7	12.4	0.6	18.3	1.7	1.9	32.7	2.9	6.5	16.1	24.3	3.0	0.6
2014	19.4	3.4	11.8	0.6	18.3	1.6	2.1	33.7	2.9	6.2	15.6	25.5	3.1	0.7
2015	18.5	2.8	11.7	0.5	19.7	1.5	2.0	34.7	2.7	5.9	15.2	26.2	3.1	0.8
2016 b/	18.7	2.7	12.4	0.5	19.5	1.6	1.8	34.6	2.7	5.5	14.9	25.8	3.0	0.9

a/ Excluding non-industrialized EU economies.
b/ Provisional.
c/ Estimate.

Table 1.2

DISTRIBUTION OF WORLD MVA AND POPULATION, SELECTED YEARS
(Percentage)

Country group	MVA at constant 2010 prices					MVA at current prices					Population				
	2005	2010	2016 a/	2017 b/	2018 b/	2012	2013	2014	2015	2016 a/	2005	2010	2016	2017	2018
Industrialized Economies	69.9	62.1	56.4	55.7	55.1	57.5	56.0	55.1	54.7	55.4	18.1	17.6	16.9	16.8	16.7
Emerging Industrial Economies	15.8	16.5	16.4	16.4	16.4	16.3	16.1	15.6	15.2	14.9	36.1	36.1	36.1	36.1	36.1
China	11.5	18.3	23.7	24.3	24.9	22.7	24.3	25.5	26.2	25.8	20.2	19.6	18.8	18.7	18.6
Other Developing Economies	2.3	2.5	2.8	2.8	2.8	2.8	3.0	3.1	3.1	3.0	14.4	14.9	15.6	15.7	15.8
Least Developed Countries	0.5	0.6	0.7	0.8	0.8	0.6	0.7	0.7	0.8	0.8	11.1	11.7	12.6	12.7	12.9
World	100.0	100.0	100.0	100.0	100.0	100.0	100.0	100.0	100.0	100.0	100.0	100.0	100.0	100.0	100.0
Low Income	0.5	0.6	0.7	0.7	0.8	0.6	0.7	0.7	0.7	0.8	11.0	11.6	12.4	12.5	12.6
Lower Middle Income	5.6	6.5	7.5	7.7	7.9	6.7	6.7	6.8	7.1	7.1	34.9	35.6	36.2	36.3	36.4
Upper Middle Income (excl.China)	11.7	11.5	10.6	10.4	10.2	11.4	11.3	10.8	10.1	9.7	14.8	14.8	14.8	14.8	14.8
China	11.5	18.3	23.7	24.3	24.9	22.7	24.3	25.5	26.2	25.8	20.2	19.6	18.8	18.7	18.6
High Income	70.8	63.1	57.5	56.8	56.2	58.6	57.0	56.2	55.9	56.6	19.1	18.5	17.8	17.7	17.5
World	100.0	100.0	100.0	100.0	100.0	100.0	100.0	100.0	100.0	100.0	100.0	100.0	100.0	100.0	100.0
Africa	1.7	1.9	1.9	1.9	1.9	1.9	2.0	2.1	2.0	1.8	14.0	14.9	16.3	16.5	16.7
Asia & Pacific	37.6	44.7	49.4	50.1	50.7	47.5	46.9	47.3	48.0	48.7	60.1	59.8	59.3	59.2	59.1
Europe	30.8	27.1	25.8	25.7	25.5	25.3	25.9	25.7	24.0	24.0	12.3	11.7	11.1	11.0	10.9
Latin America	7.7	7.2	6.1	5.8	5.6	6.9	6.9	6.6	6.3	6.0	8.6	8.6	8.5	8.5	8.5
North America	22.1	19.1	16.8	16.5	16.4	18.3	18.3	18.3	19.7	19.5	5.0	4.9	4.8	4.8	4.8
World	100.0	100.0	100.0	100.0	100.0	100.0	100.0	100.0	100.0	100.0	100.0	100.0	100.0	100.0	100.0

a/ Provisional.
b/ Estimate.

Table 1.3

ANNUAL GROWTH OF MVA, 2005-2017 AND PER-CAPITA MVA, 2017 a/ b/

Country group or economy	Total MVA						Per-capita MVA						
	Growth rate (percentage)		Index (2010 = 100)				Growth rate (percentage)		Index (2010 = 100)				Value (US dollars)
	2005-2010	2010-2017	2014	2015	2016 c/	2017 d/	2005-2010	2010-2017	2014	2015	2016 c/	2017 d/	2017 d/
Industrialized Economies	-0.5	1.6	106	108	109	112	-1.1	1.1	104	105	106	109	5770
EU	-1.2	2.0	106	110	112	116	-1.7	1.7	105	109	111	114	5987
Austria	0.6	2.1	112	113	115	121	0.2	1.6	110	110	111	116	8913
Belgium	-0.6	2.1	108	112	112	114	-1.3	1.5	105	108	108	109	6362
Czechia	4.9	3.7	110	116	124	135	4.3	3.6	109	115	123	134	5607
Denmark	-1.5	3.0	115	116	122	126	-2.0	2.5	113	114	119	122	7733
Estonia	-1.9	3.8	127	129	129	137	-1.6	4.1	128	131	131	139	2799
Finland	-1.9	-1.3	88	87	89	93	-2.3	-1.7	87	85	87	91	7154
France	-1.0	1.3	106	107	109	112	-1.6	0.9	104	104	106	108	4604
Germany	-0.9	2.4	112	115	117	121	-0.7	2.2	111	113	115	119	10064
Hungary	-1.2	3.0	104	114	114	123	-0.9	3.3	105	116	116	125	3007
Ireland	-0.9	16.1	122	237	242	264	-2.8	15.7	120	234	237	257	24077
Italy	-2.7	0.3	98	100	101	103	-3.0	0.4	98	100	102	104	5248
Lithuania	0.2	4.6	126	130	134	141	1.6	5.8	133	139	144	153	3065
Luxembourg	-8.4	4.3	118	120	119	117	-10.3	2.2	108	107	105	101	5574
Malta	0.0	-1.6	91	89	90	96	-0.5	-2.1	89	86	87	92	2202
Netherlands	-0.9	1.1	103	104	107	110	-1.3	0.8	101	102	105	108	5739
Portugal	-1.6	1.1	101	103	105	107	-1.7	1.5	102	106	107	110	2856
Slovakia	5.6	7.4	121	135	149	159	5.6	7.2	120	134	148	158	4951
Slovenia	-0.1	2.3	104	107	112	119	-0.6	2.0	103	105	110	117	4828
Spain	-2.4	1.7	96	103	107	110	-3.6	1.9	97	104	108	111	4139
Sweden	-0.8	-1.2	96	91	93	96	-1.5	-2.0	93	87	89	91	7766
United Kingdom	-1.8	0.3	103	103	103	102	-2.8	-0.3	100	99	99	98	3371
Other Europe	0.5	1.3	114	111	111	113	0.5	1.2	113	110	110	112	2381
Andorra	-2.2	-1.9	83	85	85	85	-3.5	-0.4	88	92	93	93	1371
Belarus	8.5	-0.1	111	104	103	108	8.8	-0.1	111	104	103	108	1468
Iceland	2.8	2.8	121	127	119	123	1.1	2.2	118	123	115	117	6281
Liechtenstein	0.5	3.0	114	107	113	112	-0.2	2.2	111	103	108	107	...
Norway	0.3	0.2	111	105	101	102	-0.7	-1.0	105	99	94	94	5909
Russian Federation	-0.4	1.6	118	113	114	115	-0.4	1.5	117	112	113	115	1561
San Marino	-4.9	-1.4	78	84	86	87	-6.1	-2.4	74	79	81	81	15462
Switzerland	1.5	1.3	109	109	111	113	0.4	0.1	104	103	103	105	14688
East Asia	0.6	1.8	106	107	109	113	0.2	1.5	104	105	107	110	7814
China, Hong Kong SAR	-3.2	-0.8	100	98	98	94	-3.8	-1.5	97	95	94	89	498
China, Macao SAR	...	-2.7	91	99	77	71	...	-4.8	83	89	67	61	177

a/ At constant 2010 prices.
b/ See Explanatory notes for more details on data for Ireland from 2015 onwards.
c/ Provisional.
d/ Estimate.

Table 1.3
(continued)

ANNUAL GROWTH OF MVA, 2005-2017 AND PER-CAPITA MVA, 2017 a/ b/

Country group or economy	Total MVA						Per-capita MVA						
	Growth rate (percentage)		Index (2010 = 100)				Growth rate (percentage)		Index (2010 = 100)				Value (US dollars)
	2005-2010	2010-2017	2014	2015	2016 c/	2017 d/	2005-2010	2010-2017	2014	2015	2016 c/	2017 d/	2017 d/
China, Taiwan Province	0.8	-0.4	98	97	96	95	0.4	-0.7	97	95	94	93	4525
Japan	-0.6	1.5	103	104	106	109	-0.7	1.6	103	105	107	110	10191
Malaysia	1.4	5.0	121	127	133	142	-0.4	3.2	112	116	120	126	2682
Republic of Korea	5.7	3.2	117	119	122	127	5.4	2.7	115	117	119	123	7548
Singapore	4.7	1.2	113	107	111	113	2.1	-0.5	105	98	100	100	9437
West Asia	3.5	4.0	123	129	132	132	-6.7	1.0	106	109	109	107	3359
Bahrain	6.1	4.2	117	121	127	133	-0.8	1.7	109	109	111	110	3315
Kuwait	0.4	-2.6	120	109	101	93	-5.1	-7.0	96	83	75	67	1544
Qatar	12.6	4.8	135	139	138	140	-2.7	-0.9	101	100	96	95	5961
United Arab Emirates	0.9	5.4	119	132	140	140	-10.6	3.8	108	119	125	123	3434
North America	-0.8	1.1	105	105	106	108	-1.7	0.4	102	101	101	102	5965
Bermuda	-2.6	-6.0	69	69	67	65	-2.3	-5.5	71	71	69	68	795
Canada	-4.5	1.5	108	109	110	113	-5.6	0.5	104	104	103	106	5157
Greenland	-11.2	5.0	143	169	146	145	-11.1	5.1	143	169	147	145	1884
United States of America	-0.4	1.1	104	105	105	107	-1.3	0.3	101	101	101	102	6058
Others	0.0	-0.3	97	96	99	98	-1.5	-1.5	92	90	92	90	4455
Aruba	-0.6	1.0	109	108	108	109	-0.8	0.5	106	105	104	105	1016
Australia	-0.1	-0.5	94	92	99	98	-1.9	-1.9	89	85	90	88	3833
British Virgin Islands	-0.8	4.3	109	114	123	123	-3.9	2.3	100	103	109	108	813
Cayman Islands	0.5	1.5	106	107	108	108	-2.1	0.0	100	99	99	98	504
Curaçao	1.3	8.2	179	171	162	165	-1.4	6.9	168	160	150	152	1884
French Polynesia	-2.5	0.9	101	104	105	104	-3.4	0.1	98	100	100	98	1019
Israel	4.4	0.8	103	103	104	106	2.0	-0.8	96	95	94	94	4098
New Caledonia	-5.9	0.9	111	113	118	99	-7.3	-0.5	105	105	108	90	4096
New Zealand	-3.4	1.4	104	105	108	109	-4.5	0.3	99	100	101	102	3696
Puerto Rico	-1.3	-0.9	97	97	94	92	-1.0	-0.7	98	98	96	94	11745
Trinidad and Tobago	5.3	-3.3	91	89	82	77	4.8	-3.8	89	87	80	74	2428
Developing & EIEs	7.7	5.4	127	132	138	146	6.2	4.0	120	124	128	133	923
Emerging Industrial Economies	3.4	2.9	114	116	120	124	2.1	1.8	109	110	112	115	789
Argentina	3.6	-1.1	101	102	96	97	2.6	-2.1	97	96	90	91	1487
Brazil	1.6	-2.1	102	91	90	89	0.6	-2.9	98	87	85	83	1189
Brunei Darussalam	-2.0	-0.9	96	98	97	99	-3.2	-2.3	90	91	89	89	4697

a/ At constant 2010 prices.
b/ See Explanatory notes for more details on data for Ireland from 2015 onwards.
c/ Provisional.
d/ Estimate.

Table 1.3
(continued)

ANNUAL GROWTH OF MVA, 2005-2017 AND PER-CAPITA MVA, 2017 a/ b/

Country group or economy	Total MVA						Per-capita MVA						
	Growth rate (percentage)		Index (2010 = 100)				Growth rate (percentage)		Index (2010 = 100)				Value (US dollars)
	2005-2010	2010-2017	2014	2015	2016 c/	2017 d/	2005-2010	2010-2017	2014	2015	2016 c/	2017 d/	2017 d/
Bulgaria	2.7	3.6	116	123	126	133	3.5	4.3	118	126	131	139	1113
Chile	0.7	1.3	113	114	113	112	-0.3	0.4	109	109	107	105	1461
Colombia	2.0	1.5	107	109	112	112	0.8	0.5	103	104	106	105	835
Costa Rica	-0.4	1.9	108	108	114	116	-1.8	0.8	103	102	107	107	1273
Croatia	-1.1	1.1	96	101	105	107	-0.9	1.6	98	103	108	111	1852
Cyprus	-1.0	-3.0	70	74	78	78	-2.5	-3.7	67	71	74	74	867
Egypt	6.1	2.3	107	110	111	116	4.2	0.2	98	99	98	100	410
Greece	-3.6	-0.5	84	87	94	94	-3.8	-0.1	86	89	96	97	1829
India	9.2	7.5	128	142	154	165	7.6	6.2	122	134	143	152	330
Indonesia	3.8	4.9	123	128	134	141	2.4	3.6	117	121	124	130	888
Iran (Islamic Republic of)	5.7	1.0	104	99	106	112	4.5	-0.3	99	93	98	103	868
Kazakhstan	3.2	2.2	115	116	116	119	2.1	0.6	108	107	106	107	1099
Latvia	-4.8	1.8	108	108	114	117	-3.6	3.0	113	115	123	127	1719
Mauritius	2.3	1.7	110	110	110	112	1.8	1.5	109	109	108	110	1252
Mexico	-0.8	2.4	112	115	116	118	-2.3	1.0	106	107	107	107	1501
Oman	9.2	1.8	105	108	110	115	5.2	-4.3	81	78	76	75	1537
Peru	5.4	1.1	114	112	110	111	4.1	-0.2	108	105	102	102	795
Poland	9.2	5.2	121	129	134	146	9.2	5.2	121	129	134	146	2848
Romania	2.8	3.7	110	115	116	125	3.8	4.3	113	118	120	130	2281
Saudi Arabia	6.6	5.6	128	137	141	146	3.7	2.9	114	119	120	121	2576
Serbia	2.1	2.5	113	116	118	119	2.5	2.9	115	118	121	122	728
South Africa	0.9	0.9	106	106	107	107	-0.2	-0.5	101	99	98	98	927
Suriname	1.8	-2.1	83	84	87	87	0.7	-3.1	80	80	82	81	1416
Thailand	3.8	1.7	104	106	107	111	3.3	1.3	102	103	104	108	1704
The f. Yugosl. Rep of Macedonia	-1.1	7.8	148	155	161	159	-1.2	7.7	147	154	161	158	709
Tunisia	3.0	0.9	102	102	103	105	1.9	-0.3	97	96	96	97	665
Turkey	2.2	7.0	142	150	156	170	0.9	5.3	133	139	141	152	2460
Ukraine	-3.2	-5.7	83	70	73	75	-2.7	-5.2	85	72	75	78	305
Uruguay	6.2	1.6	103	108	109	110	5.9	1.3	102	107	107	108	1742
Venezuela (Bolivarian Republic of)	0.2	-4.1	98	91	87	73	-1.4	-5.4	93	85	80	67	1168
China	13.1	7.3	138	146	155	165	12.5	6.7	135	142	150	160	2254
Other Developing Economies	4.9	4.9	125	129	134	139	2.9	3.0	116	118	119	122	311
Albania	5.5	3.6	112	121	121	126	6.5	3.6	113	121	122	127	280
Algeria	5.0	3.7	116	121	126	127	3.3	1.7	107	110	112	111	207
Angola	13.2	9.6	196	192	196	204	9.2	5.8	170	161	159	160	257
Anguilla	-2.3	2.1	114	115	108	110	-4.0	1.0	108	108	101	102	483

a/ At constant 2010 prices.
b/ See Explanatory notes for more details on data for Ireland from 2015 onwards.
c/ Provisional.
d/ Estimate.

Table 1.3
(continued)

ANNUAL GROWTH OF MVA, 2005-2017 AND PER-CAPITA MVA, 2017 [a/] [b/]

Country group or economy	Total MVA						Per-capita MVA						
	Growth rate (percentage)		Index (2010 = 100)				Growth rate (percentage)		Index (2010 = 100)				Value (US dollars)
	2005-2010	2010-2017	2014	2015	2016 [c/]	2017 [d/]	2005-2010	2010-2017	2014	2015	2016 [c/]	2017 [d/]	2017 [d/]
Antigua and Barbuda	2.2	1.9	106	108	108	109	1.0	0.8	102	102	102	101	265
Armenia	0.5	4.3	134	126	133	141	1.3	3.9	132	125	130	138	435
Azerbaijan	3.1	3.4	120	129	127	125	2.0	2.2	114	122	118	115	323
Bahamas	-3.7	0.3	113	86	108	110	-5.4	-1.0	107	80	99	101	599
Barbados	-4.4	-1.4	89	87	91	88	-4.8	-1.7	87	85	89	86	777
Belize	10.6	-4.4	67	59	82	79	7.8	-6.5	61	53	72	68	360
Bolivia (Plurinational State of)	4.9	4.9	120	125	133	138	3.2	3.3	113	116	121	124	277
Bosnia and Herzegovina	5.7	3.7	109	116	121	126	6.0	4.7	113	122	128	134	672
Botswana	9.2	3.7	124	128	129	133	7.4	1.8	115	116	115	117	474
Cabo Verde	5.5	3.2	120	118	122	126	4.3	2.0	114	111	114	116	208
Cameroon	2.7	4.1	122	126	131	135	0.0	1.3	110	110	111	112	212
Congo	7.1	3.4	141	133	130	122	3.6	0.7	127	117	112	102	102
Cook Islands	-1.1	-2.0	86	86	87	87	0.2	-1.0	90	92	93	92	416
Côte d'Ivoire	-1.2	9.8	132	152	154	170	-3.3	7.1	120	134	132	143	237
Cuba	4.5	1.5	105	111	112	112	4.4	1.3	104	110	111	110	980
Democratic People's Rep of Korea	0.1	0.2	100	97	102	100	-0.4	-0.3	98	95	99	97	120
Dominica	-4.3	-5.8	96	87	69	65	-4.5	-6.2	95	85	67	63	103
Dominican Republic	2.3	3.8	113	119	124	129	0.9	2.6	108	112	116	119	976
Ecuador	3.8	1.4	113	112	112	114	2.0	-0.1	106	103	102	102	638
El Salvador	1.1	2.5	109	113	115	119	0.6	2.0	107	110	112	115	749
Fiji	-0.6	1.6	108	110	108	112	-1.5	0.9	104	106	104	106	479
Gabon	4.8	4.2	124	122	127	132	1.6	1.1	108	104	105	107	403
Georgia	5.1	5.1	136	135	141	148	6.3	6.4	145	144	152	160	466
Ghana	2.0	2.4	118	120	124	128	-0.6	0.1	107	107	107	109	91
Grenada	-1.9	1.3	99	103	105	111	-2.3	0.8	97	100	103	107	273
Guatemala	2.0	3.3	114	117	122	124	-0.2	1.1	104	106	107	108	567
Guyana	1.2	3.8	131	138	124	126	1.4	3.2	128	134	120	121	217
Honduras	1.3	3.2	113	117	120	126	-0.8	1.4	105	107	108	111	356
Iraq	12.4	...	76	56	59	57	9.6	...	66	48	49	46	47
Jamaica	-1.9	0.3	100	102	104	102	-2.4	0.0	99	100	102	100	362
Jordan	5.7	1.7	110	112	113	113	1.0	-2.6	90	88	86	84	504
Kenya	2.6	3.4	115	120	124	128	-0.2	0.7	104	105	106	107	116
Kyrgyzstan	3.5	1.9	108	101	107	110	2.2	0.3	101	94	97	99	147
Lebanon	6.7	-4.5	101	96	74	75	5.2	-9.2	78	71	53	53	361
Libya	2.9	...	13	10	7	9	1.6	...	13	10	7	9	64
Maldives	-5.0	4.2	120	121	132	141	-7.5	1.5	107	106	112	118	191
Marshall Islands	1.3	-2.2	90	93	88	90	1.2	-2.4	90	92	87	89	47
Mongolia	6.8	4.5	135	138	134	135	5.3	2.7	125	126	120	119	215

a/ At constant 2010 prices.
b/ See Explanatory notes for more details on data for Ireland from 2015 onwards.
c/ Provisional.
d/ Estimate.

Table 1.3
(continued)

ANNUAL GROWTH OF MVA, 2005-2017 AND PER-CAPITA MVA, 2017 [a/] [b/]

Country group or economy	Total MVA							Per-capita MVA							Value (US dollars)
	Growth rate (percentage)		Index (2010 = 100)					Growth rate (percentage)		Index (2010 = 100)					
	2005-2010	2010-2017	2014	2015	2016 [c/]	2017 [d/]		2005-2010	2010-2017	2014	2015	2016 [c/]	2017 [d/]	2017 [d/]
Montenegro	-14.6	0.3	101	107	102	105		-14.8	0.2	100	106	102	104	315
Montserrat	0.0	-2.1	109	93	91	91		-0.6	-2.7	106	90	87	87	150
Morocco	6.0	4.4	115	124	128	131		4.7	3.0	109	116	117	119	534
Namibia	5.1	0.4	103	98	101	108		3.7	-1.8	94	88	89	93	600
Nicaragua	2.0	6.0	139	140	145	154		0.7	4.8	132	132	135	142	309
Nigeria	8.7	8.9	187	184	176	179		5.9	6.1	168	161	150	149	223
Pakistan	4.0	4.4	116	120	126	135		1.9	2.3	107	108	112	117	156
Palau	-1.6	7.5	143	155	166	165		-2.1	6.6	139	149	158	155	117
Panama	3.4	1.5	117	115	112	114		1.6	-0.2	109	106	101	101	577
Papua New Guinea	5.8	2.9	116	118	121	125		3.3	0.7	106	106	107	108	54
Paraguay	1.3	5.0	122	126	130	133		-0.1	3.6	115	117	120	122	439
Philippines	2.9	7.2	132	139	149	159		1.2	5.4	123	128	135	142	651
Republic of Moldova	-4.7	5.9	136	141	145	150		-4.3	6.0	137	142	146	151	220
Saint Kitts and Nevis	0.2	-4.1	78	80	73	73		-0.9	-5.1	75	76	69	68	850
Saint Lucia	1.9	-2.2	91	93	86	86		0.8	-2.7	89	90	83	83	184
Saint Vincent and the Grenadines	-3.4	0.6	102	104	106	105		-3.5	0.6	102	104	106	104	313
Seychelles	-3.7	1.3	108	116	115	124		-4.2	0.8	106	113	111	120	1021
Sri Lanka	5.3	3.1	112	117	119	124		4.6	2.6	110	114	116	120	608
State of Palestine	8.9	1.5	113	104	114	112		6.2	-1.3	101	91	97	92	268
Swaziland	6.9	4.0	108	116	131	129		5.1	2.1	100	106	117	114	1361
Syrian Arab Republic	10.5	-14.9	36	35	34	34		7.3	-13.0	40	39	39	40	55
Tajikistan	-4.9	5.0	92	104	123	129		-7.0	2.7	84	93	108	110	120
Tonga	-2.6	2.2	110	114	116	116		-3.2	1.7	108	112	113	112	244
Turkmenistan	19.4	9.4	166	175	186	196		17.8	7.5	154	160	167	173	2818
Uzbekistan	6.3	4.8	126	130	134	138		4.7	3.2	118	120	122	124	346
Viet Nam	4.0	9.6	143	158	177	197		3.0	8.4	137	150	166	182	309
Zimbabwe	2.2	0.7	113	113	114	113		0.5	-1.6	103	101	99	96	76
Least Developed Countries	9.1	6.9	131	140	150	161		6.6	4.5	119	125	130	136	104
Afghanistan	3.9	1.9	109	110	111	119		1.1	-1.1	96	94	93	97	66
Bangladesh	8.3	10.2	145	160	179	198		7.0	8.9	139	151	167	183	222
Benin	-4.2	4.2	112	119	125	128		-6.9	1.4	100	104	105	105	110
Bhutan	13.8	4.1	119	124	127	137		11.5	2.5	111	114	116	123	235
Burkina Faso	-3.1	6.1	138	145	149	151		-5.9	3.0	122	125	125	122	48
Burundi	2.4	3.9	121	116	129	127		-0.9	0.7	107	99	107	103	24
Cambodia	5.0	8.8	145	159	169	188		3.4	7.1	136	146	154	168	194
Central African Republic	6.6	-0.1	96	99	99	104		5.0	-0.7	95	96	96	99	79
Chad	11.0	...	98	113	110	102		7.4	...	86	96	91	81	48

a/ At constant 2010 prices.
b/ See Explanatory notes for more details on data for Ireland from 2015 onwards.
c/ Provisional.
d/ Estimate.

Table 1.3
(continued)

ANNUAL GROWTH OF MVA, 2005-2017 AND PER-CAPITA MVA, 2017 a/ b/

Country group or economy	Total MVA Growth rate (percentage) 2005-2010	2010-2017	Total MVA Index (2010 = 100) 2014	2015	2016 c/	2017 d/	Per-capita MVA Growth rate (percentage) 2005-2010	2010-2017	Per-capita MVA Index (2010 = 100) 2014	2015	2016 c/	2017 d/	Value (US dollars) 2017 d/
Comoros	1.7	9.2	125	136	140	146	-0.8	6.6	113	120	121	124	97
Democratic Rep of the Congo	-1.6	8.2	130	147	160	160	-4.7	4.6	113	125	131	127	69
Djibouti	3.8	5.5	118	127	135	141	2.1	3.7	110	117	122	125	52
Eritrea	-3.7	4.9	126	132	137	143	-5.6	2.8	117	119	121	124	35
Ethiopia	9.8	16.3	180	213	252	283	6.9	13.3	162	187	216	237	28
Gambia	-1.7	2.4	113	115	116	118	-4.8	-0.7	100	98	96	95	25
Guinea	-1.0	3.7	120	120	123	127	-3.1	1.3	110	107	107	108	73
Guinea-Bissau	1.5	2.2	111	113	115	118	-0.9	-0.4	100	99	98	99	61
Haiti	-0.8	4.4	132	138	140	141	-2.3	3.0	125	129	129	128	76
Kiribati	-0.1	-0.7	90	92	92	92	-2.2	-2.4	83	84	82	81	69
Lao People's Dem Rep	10.3	7.3	143	149	154	167	8.5	5.9	136	140	142	153	193
Lesotho	0.8	1.0	86	104	103	105	-0.1	-0.3	82	98	95	96	140
Liberia	9.8	4.5	131	143	136	132	5.6	1.9	118	125	116	110	16
Madagascar	1.5	4.5	110	124	127	133	-1.3	1.7	98	108	108	110	57
Malawi	15.9	3.5	113	118	119	124	12.4	0.5	100	102	100	101	46
Mali	...	5.3	141	138	142	151	-3.0	2.2	125	119	119	122	129
Mauritania	-0.2	0.5	118	118	114	116	-3.0	-2.3	105	102	95	95	81
Mozambique	0.8	3.8	109	119	124	127	-2.1	0.8	97	103	104	104	46
Myanmar	19.9	9.5	144	158	173	189	19.1	8.5	139	151	164	178	292
Nepal	0.8	2.4	119	119	110	122	-0.2	1.2	113	113	102	112	40
Niger	2.9	10.0	179	178	188	192	-0.9	5.9	154	147	149	147	24
Rwanda	5.4	6.7	129	140	149	157	2.7	4.1	117	123	128	132	46
Samoa	-6.9	-1.4	83	83	89	89	-7.6	-2.2	81	80	85	84	368
Sao Tome and Principe	7.0	2.1	108	108	117	120	4.6	-0.1	98	97	102	103	99
Senegal	1.9	1.3	113	109	111	114	-0.9	-1.7	101	94	93	93	112
Sierra Leone	2.5	1.4	114	114	119	119	-0.2	-0.9	104	102	104	101	9
Solomon Islands	...	1.4	102	104	106	108	...	-0.7	93	93	93	93	102
Somalia	2.4	1.8	107	108	110	115	-0.6	-1.1	95	94	93	94	2
Sudan	5.6	2.3	105	109	113	114	3.3	-0.1	95	97	98	97	149
Timor-Leste	-6.6	1.0	97	99	99	103	-8.0	-1.3	89	89	87	88	7
Togo	4.5	9.1	160	165	169	181	1.7	6.3	144	145	144	151	61
Tuvalu	7.4	1.3	91	102	110	112	6.3	0.4	88	98	104	106	35
Uganda	6.0	3.4	110	121	121	127	2.4	0.0	96	103	99	101	55
United Republic of Tanzania	9.1	6.5	127	135	145	155	5.7	3.2	112	115	121	125	58
Vanuatu	4.3	-2.5	74	78	80	81	1.8	-4.7	68	70	70	70	98
Yemen	5.3	-13.2	93	67	40	39	2.4	-15.4	84	59	35	32	31
Zambia	3.7	5.5	131	138	142	146	0.9	2.4	116	119	118	118	131

a/ At constant 2010 prices.
b/ See Explanatory notes for more details on data for Ireland from 2015 onwards.
c/ Provisional.
d/ Estimate.

Table 1.3
(continued)

ANNUAL GROWTH OF MVA, 2005-2017 AND PER-CAPITA MVA, 2017 a/ b/

Country group or economy	Total MVA — Growth rate (percentage) 2005-2010	2010-2017	Total MVA — Index (2010 = 100) 2014	2015	2016 c/	2017 d/	Per-capita MVA — Growth rate (percentage) 2005-2010	2010-2017	Per-capita MVA — Index (2010 = 100) 2014	2015	2016 c/	2017 d/	Value (US dollars) 2017 d/
Africa	5.1	3.6	120	122	124	127	2.5	1.0	108	108	106	106	200
Central Africa	13.0	2.0	116	114	118	122	9.8	-0.6	104	100	100	101	217
Eastern Africa	4.1	5.8	123	133	141	149	1.2	2.9	110	116	119	123	50
North Africa	7.4	2.2	103	107	109	112	5.6	0.2	95	97	97	98	351
Southern Africa	2.0	2.4	114	116	118	119	-0.7	-0.3	102	101	100	99	242
Western Africa	5.7	7.9	167	167	163	167	2.9	5.0	150	146	138	138	161
Asia & Pacific (excl. China)	6.1	5.3	122	129	136	144	4.5	4.0	115	120	126	132	448
China	13.1	7.3	138	146	155	165	12.5	6.7	135	142	150	160	2254
Central Asia	6.8	4.9	129	133	137	142	5.2	3.1	121	122	124	126	675
South Asia	8.5	7.3	128	141	152	163	6.9	5.9	121	131	140	149	294
South East Asia	3.9	4.6	119	125	130	138	2.7	3.4	114	118	121	127	773
West Asia	6.4	2.5	112	113	117	121	4.2	0.6	104	102	104	107	755
Other Asia & Pacific	0.5	0.6	102	100	104	103	-0.5	-0.3	98	95	98	97	111
Europe	2.7	4.7	122	128	132	142	2.5	4.5	121	126	130	140	1793
Latin America	1.3	-0.2	106	102	101	101	0.0	-1.3	101	96	95	93	1119
Caribbean	2.8	2.4	108	114	117	119	1.9	1.6	105	109	111	112	649
Central America	-0.5	2.4	112	115	117	118	-2.1	1.0	106	107	107	107	1253
South America	2.0	-1.3	103	97	95	93	0.8	-2.3	99	92	89	87	1105
World	2.2	3.1	114	117	120	125	1.0	1.9	108	110	112	115	1736
Low Income	5.9	7.3	132	142	153	165	3.6	4.9	120	127	134	141	104
Lower Middle Income	6.0	5.9	125	133	140	149	4.3	4.3	118	124	129	135	368
Upper Middle Income (excl.China)	2.1	1.5	110	109	110	113	0.9	0.2	105	103	102	104	1221
China	13.1	7.3	138	146	155	165	12.5	6.7	135	142	150	160	2254
High Income	-0.3	1.6	106	108	109	112	-1.0	1.1	104	105	106	109	5586
African LDCs	8.9	5.0	121	129	135	140	5.8	2.0	108	112	114	114	62
ASEAN	3.7	4.3	119	123	128	136	2.4	3.1	113	116	120	125	943
CACM	1.1	3.0	113	116	120	123	-0.6	1.4	106	107	109	111	591
CARICOM	2.5	-1.6	95	94	92	89	1.3	-2.6	91	89	86	82	380
CEMAC	...	2.0	116	114	118	122	...	-0.6	104	100	100	101	217
CIS	0.6	1.6	117	112	114	116	0.4	1.3	115	110	111	113	1067
ECOWAS	5.8	7.9	167	167	163	168	2.9	5.1	150	146	139	139	162
EU	-0.9	2.1	106	111	113	117	-1.3	1.9	105	110	112	116	5387
GCC	5.4	4.8	125	132	136	138	0.3	1.7	109	112	113	112	2739
LAIA	1.3	-0.3	105	101	100	99	0.1	-1.4	101	96	94	92	1194
MERCOSUR	2.0	-1.3	103	97	95	93	0.8	-2.3	99	92	89	87	1106
OECD	-0.5	1.8	106	109	110	114	-1.2	1.2	104	105	107	109	5600

a/ At constant 2010 prices.
b/ See Explanatory notes for more details on data for Ireland from 2015 onwards.
c/ Provisional.
d/ Estimate.

Table 1.3
(continued)

ANNUAL GROWTH OF MVA, 2005-2017 AND PER-CAPITA MVA, 2017 [a/] [b/]

Country group or economy	Total MVA						Per-capita MVA						
	Growth rate (percentage)		Index (2010 = 100)				Growth rate (percentage)		Index (2010 = 100)				Value (US dollars)
	2005-2010	2010-2017	2014	2015	2016 [c/]	2017 [d/]	2005-2010	2010-2017	2014	2015	2016 [c/]	2017 [d/]	2017 [d/]
SAARC	8.5	7.3	128	141	152	163	6.9	5.9	121	131	140	149	294
SADC	2.0	2.4	114	116	118	119	-0.7	-0.3	102	101	100	99	242
WAEMU/UEMOA	0.9	6.6	131	138	142	151	-2.0	3.5	116	119	118	123	110

a/ At constant 2010 prices.
b/ See Explanatory notes for more details on data for Ireland from 2015 onwards.
c/ Provisional.
d/ Estimate.

Table 1.4

SHARE OF MVA IN GDP, SELECTED YEARS
(Percentage)

Country group or economy	At constant 2010 prices						At current prices					
	2005	2010	2014	2015	2016 a/	2017 b/	2011	2012	2013	2014	2015	2016 a/
Industrialized Economies	14.6	14.3	14.2	14.1	14.1	14.2	14.2	13.9	13.7	13.7	13.9	13.8
EU	14.3	13.8	14.1	14.4	14.4	14.5	14.1	13.8	13.8	13.9	14.3	14.4
Austria	16.2	16.5	17.8	17.7	17.7	18.0	16.6	16.7	16.5	16.6	16.6	16.2
Belgium	14.1	13.2	13.7	14.0	13.8	13.9	12.8	12.6	12.5	12.6	12.8	12.7
Czechia	17.6	21.2	22.6	22.6	23.6	24.7	22.1	22.2	22.2	24.2	24.1	24.4
Denmark	11.4	10.9	12.1	12.0	12.4	12.5	11.0	11.4	11.8	11.9	12.4	13.3
Estonia	13.1	13.7	14.8	14.8	14.5	14.7	14.5	13.9	13.6	14.1	13.8	13.5
Finland	18.0	17.1	15.1	15.0	14.9	15.3	16.3	14.5	14.6	14.6	14.8	14.5
France	10.8	10.1	10.3	10.3	10.4	10.4	10.2	10.2	10.2	10.1	10.3	10.2
Germany	20.0	20.0	21.0	21.1	21.1	21.3	20.6	20.4	20.2	20.6	20.8	20.6
Hungary	17.8	18.2	17.8	18.9	18.5	19.1	18.6	18.7	18.9	19.5	20.5	19.9
Ireland	20.3	19.5	21.0	32.6	31.6	32.2	21.4	20.4	19.8	19.7	34.3	32.1
Italy	15.0	14.2	14.4	14.6	14.7	14.7	14.2	13.8	13.8	13.9	14.4	14.6
Lithuania	16.6	16.9	18.1	18.3	18.4	18.6	18.3	18.7	17.6	17.4	17.4	17.0
Luxembourg	8.5	5.2	5.5	5.4	5.2	5.0	4.9	4.8	4.9	5.0	4.9	5.1
Malta	12.7	11.4	8.8	8.0	7.7	7.7	11.5	11.0	9.5	8.8	8.0	7.7
Netherlands	11.4	10.6	10.7	10.6	10.7	10.7	10.9	10.7	10.2	10.3	10.7	10.9
Portugal	12.4	11.6	12.4	12.5	12.5	12.4	11.3	11.4	11.6	11.8	12.2	12.1
Slovakia	16.5	18.9	20.9	22.5	24.1	24.9	19.1	19.0	18.4	19.7	19.8	20.4
Slovenia	18.3	17.6	18.4	18.4	18.7	18.9	18.2	18.7	19.2	19.8	20.0	20.1
Spain	14.1	12.2	12.2	12.7	12.8	12.7	12.4	12.1	12.3	12.5	12.9	12.9
Sweden	16.4	16.3	14.8	13.4	13.3	13.4	16.1	15.2	14.9	14.6	13.7	13.5
United Kingdom	9.6	8.9	8.5	8.3	8.1	8.0	8.9	8.8	9.1	8.9	9.0	9.0
Other Europe	14.4	13.4	14.1	13.8	13.9	13.8	12.6	12.4	12.5	12.8	13.4	13.4
Andorra	3.5	3.7	3.2	3.2	3.2	3.2	3.6	3.4	3.2	3.2	3.2	3.2
Belarus	20.9	22.5	22.6	22.0	22.6	23.0	26.4	24.8	22.0	21.1	20.6	19.6
Iceland	11.8	12.9	14.2	14.3	12.5	12.4	12.9	11.4	11.3	10.7	10.1	8.8
Liechtenstein	26.4	26.6	29.0	27.0	28.3	28.1	24.5	25.7	28.8	29.0	27.0	28.3
Norway	7.3	7.2	7.4	7.0	6.6	6.5	6.7	6.6	6.6	6.8	6.9	6.7
Russian Federation	14.7	12.8	13.7	13.5	13.6	13.6	11.4	11.5	11.7	11.9	12.7	12.8
San Marino	30.5	27.7	26.7	28.7	29.3	29.0	27.4	26.7	27.8	26.7	28.7	29.3
Switzerland	18.7	18.8	19.2	18.9	19.0	19.1	19.2	18.7	18.6	18.3	18.0	17.8
East Asia	20.6	21.5	21.3	21.3	21.4	21.6	20.6	20.3	20.2	20.4	20.8	20.3
China, Hong Kong SAR	2.3	1.7	1.5	1.5	1.4	1.3	1.6	1.5	1.4	1.2	1.1	1.1
China, Macao SAR	3.3	0.6	0.3	0.5	0.4	0.3	0.5	0.5	0.4	0.4	0.6	0.5

a/ Provisional.
b/ Estimate.

Table 1.4
(continued)

SHARE OF MVA IN GDP, SELECTED YEARS
(Percentage)

Country group or economy	At constant 2010 prices						At current prices					
	2005	2010	2014	2015	2016 a/	2017 b/	2011	2012	2013	2014	2015	2016 a/
China, Taiwan Province	26.6	26.1	23.5	22.9	22.5	21.9	24.7	...	...	...	...	...
Japan	20.1	20.9	20.6	20.7	20.9	21.1	19.7	19.7	19.4	19.7	20.4	19.8
Malaysia	25.7	23.4	23.0	23.0	23.1	23.3	23.3	23.1	22.8	22.9	22.8	22.8
Republic of Korea	24.8	27.8	28.8	28.5	28.4	28.6	28.4	28.1	28.3	27.5	27.1	26.6
Singapore	19.8	20.2	19.0	17.7	17.9	17.6	19.0	18.8	17.4	17.8	18.3	18.4
West Asia	8.6	8.1	8.1	8.3	8.2	8.2	8.0	8.3	8.1	8.2	9.1	9.1
Bahrain	14.0	14.5	14.6	14.6	14.9	15.0	15.0	14.9	14.8	14.9	17.3	18.1
Kuwait	6.3	6.0	6.1	5.4	4.9	4.6	5.6	6.0	5.9	5.5	6.7	6.1
Qatar	11.7	9.1	9.5	9.5	9.2	9.2	9.5	10.5	10.2	10.1	9.7	9.0
United Arab Emirates	8.4	8.0	7.8	8.3	8.5	8.5	7.7	7.7	7.5	7.8	8.8	9.2
North America	12.5	12.0	11.6	11.4	11.3	11.2	12.1	12.1	12.0	11.9	11.9	11.5
Bermuda	1.5	1.3	1.0	1.0	0.9	0.9	1.2	0.9	0.9	0.8	0.8	0.8
Canada	13.1	10.4	10.2	10.1	10.0	10.1	10.3	10.4	9.6	9.5	9.9	9.6
Greenland	6.3	3.2	4.6	5.3	4.6	4.6	3.4	3.3	2.4	3.0	2.6	2.7
United States of America	12.4	12.2	11.8	11.5	11.4	11.4	12.3	12.3	12.2	12.1	12.1	11.7
Others	12.0	10.8	9.5	9.1	9.2	8.9	10.2	9.8	9.6	9.7	9.9	9.9
Aruba	3.7	4.1	4.2	4.1	4.1	4.1	4.2	4.1	4.1	4.2	4.1	4.1
Australia	8.4	7.4	6.3	5.9	6.2	6.1	7.1	6.6	6.4	6.3	6.1	6.3
British Virgin Islands	2.4	2.3	2.5	2.6	2.8	2.8	2.1	2.3	2.2	2.6	2.4	2.4
Cayman Islands	0.9	0.9	0.9	0.9	0.9	0.9	0.9	0.9	0.9	0.9	0.9	0.9
Curaçao	6.0	6.2	11.3	10.8	10.3	10.5	7.1	6.7	11.2	11.3	10.8	10.3
French Polynesia	5.4	4.6	4.7	4.8	4.8	4.7	4.6	4.9	4.9	4.8	4.9	4.8
Israel	13.0	13.8	12.2	11.9	11.6	11.4	13.2	13.5	12.3	12.1	11.8	11.7
New Caledonia	14.7	12.2	12.1	11.9	12.0	10.1	12.7	11.4	12.1	12.1	11.9	12.0
New Zealand	13.5	10.8	10.2	10.0	9.9	9.8	10.9	10.6	10.2	11.1	11.4	10.9
Puerto Rico	46.8	47.3	46.7	47.2	47.3	47.4	46.6	46.2	46.4	46.7	47.2	47.3
Trinidad and Tobago	17.5	19.6	17.4	17.0	16.2	15.4	21.4	18.7	15.9	15.9	15.3	14.2
Developing & EIEs	17.9	19.4	20.1	20.1	20.3	20.4	19.6	19.7	19.6	19.9	19.7	19.6
Emerging Industrial Economies	15.3	15.0	14.9	14.8	14.9	15.0	14.6	14.5	14.3	14.4	14.9	14.8
Argentina	16.1	15.8	15.2	15.0	14.4	14.3	15.9	15.2	15.0	14.8	14.5	13.8
Brazil	14.3	12.7	11.8	11.0	11.2	11.0	11.8	10.7	10.5	10.3	10.1	10.7
Brunei Darussalam	16.7	14.9	14.3	14.7	15.0	14.9	16.4	16.6	16.5	16.1	14.5	11.5

a/ Provisional.
b/ Estimate.

Table 1.4
(continued)

SHARE OF MVA IN GDP, SELECTED YEARS
(Percentage)

Country group or economy	At constant 2010 prices						At current prices					
	2005	2010	2014	2015	2016 a/	2017 b/	2011	2012	2013	2014	2015	2016 a/
Bulgaria	12.1	11.7	13.0	13.3	13.2	13.4	13.7	13.7	12.6	13.2	13.6	13.9
Chile	12.2	10.8	10.3	10.1	9.8	9.7	11.0	10.8	11.1	11.2	11.4	11.0
Colombia	14.2	12.8	11.2	11.1	11.2	11.0	12.3	12.2	11.8	11.5	11.4	11.5
Costa Rica	17.8	14.5	13.5	12.9	13.0	12.8	14.0	13.5	12.6	12.2	12.0	12.1
Croatia	13.0	12.1	12.1	12.3	12.4	12.4	12.4	12.3	11.9	12.4	12.6	12.7
Cyprus	6.2	5.1	3.9	4.1	4.2	4.1	4.6	4.1	3.8	4.1	4.3	4.4
Egypt	16.3	16.1	15.9	15.4	14.8	14.9	14.5	16.3	16.8	17.0	16.7	16.8
Greece	8.7	7.2	7.4	7.7	8.3	8.2	7.8	8.0	8.4	8.6	8.3	8.6
India	15.3	16.2	16.2	16.6	16.8	16.9	16.1	15.8	15.2	15.2	15.1	14.9
Indonesia	24.0	22.0	21.7	21.6	21.4	21.5	21.7	21.5	21.0	21.1	21.0	20.5
Iran (Islamic Republic of)	11.5	12.8	13.4	12.9	12.2	12.5	12.2	14.4	13.7	13.8	12.4	11.9
Kazakhstan	12.3	11.3	10.4	10.3	10.2	10.1	11.1	11.1	10.6	10.3	10.3	11.1
Latvia	13.4	12.0	11.2	11.0	11.3	11.1	11.8	11.7	11.2	10.8	10.5	10.7
Mauritius	16.1	14.2	13.4	13.0	12.5	12.3	13.9	13.6	13.9	13.6	13.1	12.4
Mexico	16.5	15.6	15.6	15.4	15.2	15.1	15.3	16.3	15.9	15.9	17.1	16.8
Oman	8.6	10.6	9.6	9.4	9.3	9.7	11.4	10.7	10.8	9.7	9.7	10.1
Peru	16.4	15.6	14.5	13.8	13.1	12.9	15.1	15.2	14.8	13.9	13.2	12.7
Poland	12.3	15.6	16.8	17.3	17.5	18.2	15.9	16.3	15.9	16.8	17.6	18.1
Romania	21.1	21.3	21.6	21.7	21.0	21.1	21.5	19.8	20.3	20.9	19.3	18.8
Saudi Arabia	9.1	11.0	11.5	11.7	11.9	12.4	10.0	9.8	9.9	10.8	12.4	12.6
Serbia	14.2	13.6	15.3	15.5	15.4	15.2	14.1	15.1	16.1	15.7	15.6	15.6
South Africa	14.0	13.1	12.6	12.4	12.5	12.4	12.0	11.7	11.6	12.0	12.0	11.9
Suriname	23.4	21.0	15.6	16.1	17.7	17.3	20.8	21.3	18.8	16.4	9.8	12.5
Thailand	29.9	31.1	28.8	28.4	27.5	27.6	29.1	28.2	27.8	27.8	27.6	27.5
The f. Yugosl. Rep of Macedonia	12.0	9.9	13.4	13.5	13.7	13.5	11.4	10.2	9.9	11.0	11.8	12.2
Tunisia	17.7	16.5	15.8	15.7	15.7	15.7	16.6	16.2	15.9	15.6	16.3	...
Turkey	15.1	15.2	16.2	16.2	16.2	16.5	16.5	15.9	16.2	16.8	16.7	16.6
Ukraine	14.8	13.2	11.1	10.4	10.6	10.6	11.9	12.4	11.3	12.2	11.9	12.0
Uruguay	13.6	13.5	11.9	12.4	12.3	12.2	12.7	12.2	11.3	12.1	13.2	12.7
Venezuela (Bolivarian Republic of)	15.1	12.9	11.9	11.7	13.4	13.1	12.7	12.7	12.3	12.6	16.2	13.7
China	29.0	31.6	32.0	31.7	31.4	31.3	32.2	31.4	30.5	30.2	27.8	27.5
Other Developing Economies	11.3	11.0	11.7	11.6	11.6	11.7	11.1	11.0	11.2	11.5	11.7	11.6
Albania	5.1	5.5	5.7	6.0	5.8	5.9	5.7	4.6	5.1	5.3	5.7	5.5
Algeria	3.8	4.2	4.3	4.3	4.3	4.3	3.7	3.6	3.7	3.9	4.3	4.4
Angola	3.4	4.5	7.2	6.9	7.1	7.6	4.1	4.3	4.8	4.9	5.2	5.0
Anguilla	3.4	2.4	2.7	2.7	2.5	2.5	1.8	2.0	1.9	2.0	2.0	1.7

a/ Provisional.
b/ Estimate.

Table 1.4
(continued)

SHARE OF MVA IN GDP, SELECTED YEARS
(Percentage)

Country group or economy	At constant 2010 prices						At current prices					
	2005	2010	2014	2015	2016 a/	2017 b/	2011	2012	2013	2014	2015	2016 a/
Antigua and Barbuda	1.9	2.2	2.2	2.1	2.0	2.0	2.2	2.0	2.7	2.7	2.6	2.4
Armenia	10.4	9.2	10.2	9.4	9.8	9.7	10.0	9.4	9.7	9.7	9.2	9.2
Azerbaijan	8.5	4.8	5.3	5.7	5.7	5.6	4.0	4.2	4.2	4.7	5.0	5.2
Bahamas	2.3	2.1	2.4	1.8	2.3	2.3	2.2	2.9	2.7	2.9	2.4	2.8
Barbados	7.4	5.8	5.1	4.9	5.0	4.9	5.9	5.5	5.7	5.8	5.6	5.6
Belize	8.4	12.2	7.4	6.3	8.8	8.4	13.5	12.0	10.0	8.6	6.9	6.0
Bolivia (Plurinational State of)	11.0	11.3	10.8	10.8	11.0	11.0	10.3	10.2	9.9	9.7	10.2	11.0
Bosnia and Herzegovina	9.2	10.9	11.4	11.8	12.0	12.1	10.9	10.5	10.9	10.9	11.7	12.4
Botswana	5.0	6.4	6.1	6.5	6.2	6.3	5.8	5.9	5.8	5.3	5.8	5.2
Cabo Verde	5.4	5.4	6.1	6.0	5.9	5.9	5.4	5.7	5.8	6.4	5.9	5.7
Cameroon	14.8	14.5	14.5	14.2	14.1	14.0	14.7	15.1	15.0	14.4	14.7	14.7
Congo	3.3	3.6	4.2	3.9	3.9	3.8	3.5	3.8	4.3	5.0	3.3	3.2
Cook Islands	3.6	3.3	2.5	2.5	2.4	2.4	3.1	2.8	2.9	2.8	2.8	3.0
Côte d'Ivoire	16.5	13.6	14.3	15.1	14.0	14.4	12.8	14.0	16.2	16.9	16.1	15.6
Cuba	16.5	15.6	14.9	15.1	15.4	15.4	15.3	16.1	15.7	15.1	14.9	15.4
Democratic People's Rep of Korea	21.7	21.9	21.1	20.6	20.8	20.5	21.9	21.9	22.1	21.3	20.4	20.6
Dominica	3.3	2.4	2.2	2.1	1.6	1.6	2.7	3.0	3.0	3.0	2.7	2.2
Dominican Republic	18.1	15.3	14.5	14.3	14.0	13.9	15.1	15.0	14.8	14.5	14.2	13.6
Ecuador	13.3	13.4	12.2	12.0	12.3	12.2	13.0	13.0	13.0	13.8	14.5	13.8
El Salvador	19.0	18.8	19.0	19.3	19.2	19.4	18.5	18.5	18.8	18.8	19.1	19.0
Fiji	12.6	12.4	11.6	11.4	11.2	11.2	11.9	11.6	11.6	11.1	10.6	10.1
Gabon	4.0	4.8	4.8	4.5	4.5	4.7	5.5	5.9	5.9	6.5	6.3	6.2
Georgia	9.9	10.6	11.7	11.2	11.4	11.4	11.3	11.0	11.6	11.4	10.9	10.8
Ghana	7.6	6.4	5.4	5.3	5.3	5.0	6.4	5.7	5.1	4.7	4.5	4.3
Grenada	3.6	3.5	3.1	3.0	3.1	3.1	3.4	3.2	3.4	3.4	3.6	3.7
Guatemala	20.0	18.6	18.3	18.1	18.2	18.1	18.6	19.1	19.1	18.8	18.5	18.3
Guyana	6.8	5.9	6.4	6.6	5.7	5.7	5.7	5.3	5.9	5.5	5.8	5.1
Honduras	18.1	16.5	16.3	16.3	16.2	16.2	17.2	17.7	17.3	17.3	17.3	17.1
Iraq	2.0	2.7	1.3	0.9	0.9	0.9	3.3	3.2	2.6	2.2	1.9	2.0
Jamaica	8.4	7.7	7.6	7.7	7.7	7.5	7.9	8.0	8.1	8.1	7.9	7.6
Jordan	16.7	16.4	16.1	16.0	15.8	15.6	16.6	16.1	16.7	16.3	16.3	16.0
Kenya	12.4	11.3	10.5	10.3	10.1	9.9	11.8	11.0	10.5	10.0	9.4	9.2
Kyrgyzstan	18.7	16.9	15.0	13.5	13.7	13.5	18.3	12.1	15.8	13.7	14.1	14.8
Lebanon	8.1	7.6	7.1	6.7	5.1	5.1	7.6	7.5	7.8	7.8	8.3	4.7
Libya	6.5	5.7	2.3	1.9	1.3	1.0	2.0	3.7	3.7	3.7	3.0	3.4
Maldives	3.9	2.3	2.1	2.1	2.2	2.2	2.6	2.6	2.1	2.0	1.9	2.0
Marshall Islands	1.8	1.7	1.4	1.5	1.3	1.3	2.9	1.1	0.9	1.3	1.0	1.1
Mongolia	6.6	6.8	5.8	5.8	5.6	5.3	7.1	7.5	8.7	8.8	7.6	6.7

a/ Provisional.
b/ Estimate.

Table 1.4
(continued)

SHARE OF MVA IN GDP, SELECTED YEARS
(Percentage)

Country group or economy	At constant 2010 prices						At current prices					
	2005	2010	2014	2015	2016 a/	2017 b/	2011	2012	2013	2014	2015	2016 a/
Montenegro	10.9	4.6	4.3	4.4	4.1	4.1	5.0	4.1	4.0	3.9	4.1	3.8
Montserrat	1.6	1.5	1.4	1.2	1.2	1.2	1.3	1.6	1.7	1.7	1.5	1.6
Morocco	15.0	15.6	15.2	15.5	15.5	15.3	15.5	15.2	15.5	16.5	16.1	15.8
Namibia	12.0	12.5	10.3	9.3	9.5	10.2	13.7	12.2	11.0	10.0	9.9	11.0
Nicaragua	14.2	14.3	15.9	15.3	15.1	15.3	14.1	14.2	14.5	14.7	14.1	13.5
Nigeria	5.9	6.5	9.8	9.4	9.2	9.3	7.1	7.7	8.9	9.6	9.4	8.7
Pakistan	12.7	13.1	13.0	12.9	12.8	13.0	13.8	14.0	13.6	13.5	12.8	12.0
Palau	0.8	0.8	1.1	1.0	1.1	1.1	0.9	1.0	1.0	1.0	0.9	0.9
Panama	8.6	7.2	6.1	5.7	5.3	5.1	6.4	6.4	6.2	5.9	5.5	5.2
Papua New Guinea	2.5	2.5	2.4	2.3	2.3	2.4	2.6	2.6	2.6	2.6	2.6	2.6
Paraguay	13.1	11.2	11.1	11.1	11.1	10.8	11.0	11.0	10.5	10.9	10.8	10.6
Philippines	22.9	21.4	22.5	22.4	22.4	22.5	21.1	20.6	20.4	20.6	20.0	19.6
Republic of Moldova	14.4	10.2	11.4	11.9	11.7	11.6	10.7	10.8	11.2	11.6	11.9	11.9
Saint Kitts and Nevis	10.2	9.1	6.2	6.1	5.5	5.4	8.6	8.4	7.9	7.0	6.6	5.9
Saint Lucia	3.2	3.1	2.8	2.8	2.6	2.5	3.2	3.1	2.6	2.3	2.3	2.2
Saint Vincent and the Grenadines	6.1	4.8	4.7	4.7	4.8	4.7	4.3	4.3	4.4	4.9	4.8	4.6
Seychelles	11.0	8.0	7.2	7.3	7.2	7.3	7.7	8.4	7.2	6.5	6.0	5.6
Sri Lanka	18.8	18.1	15.7	15.7	15.4	15.4	18.4	19.4	18.0	17.0	16.4	15.5
State of Palestine	13.1	13.3	12.3	11.0	11.6	11.3	12.3	14.2	12.8	12.0	10.6	11.8
Swaziland	27.5	32.5	29.5	30.6	34.4	34.0	31.7	31.7	30.0	29.8	30.3	30.0
Syrian Arab Republic	3.7	4.8	3.2	3.2	3.3	3.3	4.6	4.7	4.7	4.7	4.7	4.7
Tajikistan	24.2	14.7	10.8	11.4	12.7	12.4	14.5	13.7	12.6	12.1	13.3	15.1
Tonga	7.1	6.1	6.5	6.5	6.4	6.3	5.9	5.7	6.3	6.2	6.2	6.2
Turkmenistan	28.9	36.8	39.3	39.1	39.0	38.5	39.9	39.3	38.6	39.3	39.1	39.0
Uzbekistan	22.3	20.3	18.7	17.9	17.4	17.0	20.3	20.1	19.9	19.7	19.6	19.6
Viet Nam	15.7	12.9	14.8	15.4	16.2	16.8	13.4	13.3	13.3	13.2	13.7	14.3
Zimbabwe	16.3	11.0	8.7	8.6	8.6	8.2	10.7	10.1	9.6	9.2	8.7	8.7
Least Developed Countries	11.5	11.4	12.2	12.5	12.7	13.0	11.4	11.2	11.0	11.2	11.6	11.9
Afghanistan	15.8	12.2	10.1	10.3	10.1	10.5	13.1	12.0	10.9	11.1	11.1	11.0
Bangladesh	14.5	16.1	18.3	19.0	19.8	20.5	16.0	15.9	16.4	16.6	16.8	17.0
Benin	19.8	13.8	12.6	12.8	12.7	12.4	13.3	12.6	12.9	12.7	13.9	13.4
Bhutan	7.1	8.7	8.4	8.3	7.8	7.9	8.3	8.8	8.3	8.1	8.0	7.5
Burkina Faso	10.3	6.8	7.5	7.6	7.4	7.0	7.0	6.8	5.3	6.3	6.6	9.9
Burundi	11.1	10.2	10.4	10.0	10.9	10.8	10.0	10.5	10.7	11.0	9.3	10.3
Cambodia	14.1	14.7	16.2	16.5	16.4	17.1	15.2	15.1	15.3	15.3	16.0	16.0
Central African Republic	14.9	17.4	25.0	24.4	23.5	23.6	17.3	17.0	22.4	21.5	18.8	19.1
Chad	6.0	7.1	6.0	6.6	6.7	6.4	6.9	9.6	7.1	7.3	9.3	9.5

a/ Provisional.
b/ Estimate.

Table 1.4
(continued)

SHARE OF MVA IN GDP, SELECTED YEARS
(Percentage)

Country group or economy	At constant 2010 prices						At current prices					
	2005	2010	2014	2015	2016 a/	2017 b/	2011	2012	2013	2014	2015	2016 a/
Comoros	5.1	5.0	5.1	5.6	5.6	5.7	5.5	5.4	5.3	7.5	8.9	8.9
Democratic Rep of the Congo	23.5	16.2	15.5	16.5	17.5	16.8	15.4	15.4	15.4	15.6	17.1	18.9
Djibouti	3.8	3.3	3.2	3.3	3.3	3.2	3.2	3.2	3.0	2.1	2.1	2.2
Eritrea	6.8	5.8	5.8	5.8	5.8	5.8	5.9	5.8	5.8	5.8	5.8	5.8
Ethiopia	4.1	3.9	4.7	5.0	5.5	5.6	3.7	3.4	3.7	4.0	4.4	4.0
Gambia	6.2	4.7	5.0	4.8	4.8	4.7	5.5	5.7	5.5	5.2	4.8	4.5
Guinea	12.5	10.6	10.6	10.1	9.7	9.3	10.5	10.5	10.8	11.1	10.9	5.0
Guinea-Bissau	12.4	11.3	11.4	11.1	10.7	10.4	11.1	12.2	12.7	12.7	12.5	12.6
Haiti	10.0	8.8	10.0	10.4	10.4	10.3	9.9	10.3	10.0	10.0	10.4	10.4
Kiribati	5.6	5.7	4.6	4.4	4.2	4.1	6.0	5.1	4.6	4.7	3.9	4.4
Lao People's Dem Rep	10.1	10.8	11.4	11.1	10.7	10.9	10.7	9.0	8.4	8.4	8.2	7.8
Lesotho	14.6	12.5	9.1	10.4	10.0	10.4	12.0	10.8	10.6	10.2	11.1	10.6
Liberia	5.1	4.4	4.4	4.4	4.2	3.9	4.0	4.6	5.3	6.5	6.5	5.9
Madagascar	11.3	10.6	10.7	11.7	11.5	11.6	11.8	9.0	8.8	5.9	6.1	4.3
Malawi	7.0	9.9	9.5	9.7	9.5	9.5	10.1	7.4	8.6	8.2	8.1	8.3
Mali	13.8	14.9	15.1	13.8	13.1	13.2	14.1	15.9	13.8	14.1	12.8	12.2
Mauritania	10.0	7.1	6.8	6.6	6.2	6.1	6.8	7.5	6.8	8.0	8.0	7.6
Mozambique	14.1	10.5	8.6	8.8	8.8	8.8	10.3	9.1	8.6	9.0	9.1	8.7
Myanmar	13.5	19.9	21.5	22.1	22.9	23.5	19.7	20.1	19.9	19.9	20.8	22.4
Nepal	7.0	5.9	5.9	5.7	5.3	5.4	5.9	6.0	5.9	5.8	5.6	5.3
Niger	5.3	4.8	6.6	6.3	6.3	6.2	4.8	6.0	6.7	6.3	5.7	5.9
Rwanda	6.8	6.2	6.0	6.0	6.1	6.0	6.0	6.0	5.9	5.9	5.9	5.8
Samoa	17.7	12.0	9.6	9.3	9.4	9.2	10.8	10.9	10.8	10.1	9.9	9.8
Sao Tome and Principe	8.2	8.5	7.6	7.3	7.9	7.9	8.3	7.4	7.3	6.5	6.2	7.0
Senegal	13.2	12.1	12.0	10.8	10.3	9.9	12.8	12.2	12.0	11.5	10.6	9.9
Sierra Leone	2.3	2.2	1.6	2.0	2.0	1.9	2.3	2.0	1.6	1.5	1.8	1.8
Solomon Islands	3.7	8.0	7.1	7.1	7.0	6.9	7.9	8.9	8.4	9.1	8.8	8.8
Somalia	2.2	2.2	2.1	2.1	2.1	2.1	2.2	2.2	2.2	2.2	2.2	2.2
Sudan	...	9.7	9.7	9.7	9.7	9.7	8.9	9.2	7.8	8.7	8.6	8.4
Timor-Leste	0.5	0.2	0.3	0.2	0.2	0.2	0.2	0.1	0.2	0.3	0.4	0.3
Togo	7.2	7.6	9.6	9.4	9.1	9.3	7.2	6.4	7.9	7.4	6.8	6.6
Tuvalu	0.9	1.1	0.9	1.0	1.0	1.0	1.0	1.2	0.9	0.9	0.9	1.0
Uganda	10.5	9.4	8.6	9.0	8.8	8.8	10.5	9.5	9.0	8.2	8.9	9.0
United Republic of Tanzania	6.0	6.9	6.7	6.7	6.7	6.8	7.6	7.5	6.4	5.6	5.2	5.1
Vanuatu	3.6	4.8	3.3	3.4	3.4	3.3	4.2	3.6	3.2	3.3	3.5	3.3
Yemen	7.7	7.9	9.6	9.7	6.5	6.6	7.7	8.5	8.1	8.4	10.2	8.9
Zambia	9.6	7.6	8.0	8.2	8.1	8.0	7.5	7.1	6.2	6.8	7.5	7.3

a/ Provisional.
b/ Estimate.

Table 1.4
(continued)

SHARE OF MVA IN GDP, SELECTED YEARS
(Percentage)

Country group or economy	At constant 2010 prices						At current prices					
	2005	2010	2014	2015	2016 a/	2017 b/	2011	2012	2013	2014	2015	2016 a/
Africa	10.4	10.1	10.7	10.5	10.4	10.4	9.7	9.7	9.9	10.3	10.5	10.0
Central Africa	8.5	11.7	11.5	11.1	11.5	11.9	12.2	11.7	11.9	12.1	11.9	12.0
Eastern Africa	9.3	8.2	7.8	7.9	7.9	7.8	8.5	7.7	7.5	7.2	7.1	6.9
North Africa	11.1	11.3	11.4	11.4	11.2	11.0	10.3	10.6	11.1	11.9	12.3	11.7
Southern Africa	12.4	11.3	11.1	11.1	11.2	11.1	10.5	10.0	9.7	9.8	10.1	10.0
Western Africa	7.5	7.3	9.8	9.5	9.2	9.2	7.7	8.1	9.1	9.7	9.5	8.8
Asia & Pacific (excl. China)	16.0	16.4	16.3	16.5	16.4	16.7	15.9	15.9	15.5	15.6	15.7	15.7
China	29.0	31.6	32.0	31.7	31.4	31.3	32.2	31.4	30.5	30.2	27.8	27.5
Central Asia	15.6	15.5	15.2	15.1	15.2	15.0	15.5	15.6	15.2	15.0	15.6	17.1
South Asia	15.0	15.9	15.9	16.3	16.5	16.6	15.9	15.6	15.1	15.0	14.9	14.7
South East Asia	24.2	23.1	22.6	22.5	22.3	22.4	22.3	21.9	21.6	21.5	21.3	21.0
West Asia	9.2	10.4	10.3	10.2	10.0	10.4	9.8	10.4	10.0	10.1	10.6	10.6
Other Asia & Pacific	11.8	10.4	9.8	9.2	9.3	9.1	9.8	9.2	9.6	9.7	9.4	9.8
Europe	13.5	14.0	15.0	15.2	15.3	15.7	14.7	14.6	14.7	15.4	15.6	15.6
Latin America	15.0	13.7	12.9	12.5	12.7	12.5	13.1	12.9	12.6	12.6	13.2	12.9
Caribbean	13.9	13.0	12.6	12.7	12.7	12.7	13.0	13.3	13.2	12.9	12.7	12.8
Central America	16.5	15.5	15.4	15.2	15.1	14.9	15.2	16.1	15.6	15.6	16.5	16.2
South America	14.4	13.1	12.1	11.6	11.8	11.5	12.5	11.8	11.7	11.5	11.9	11.7
World	15.5	15.9	16.2	16.2	16.3	16.4	16.0	15.9	15.8	15.9	16.1	15.9
Low Income	12.7	12.5	12.9	13.2	13.5	13.7	12.7	12.3	12.1	12.0	12.3	12.6
Lower Middle Income	16.0	15.7	16.1	16.2	16.3	16.4	15.6	15.6	15.3	15.3	15.3	15.2
Upper Middle Income (excl.China)	15.3	14.5	14.1	13.9	13.9	13.9	14.1	13.8	13.7	13.8	14.2	14.1
China	29.0	31.6	32.0	31.7	31.4	31.3	32.2	31.4	30.5	30.2	27.8	27.5
High Income	14.4	14.1	14.0	14.0	14.0	14.0	14.0	13.7	13.5	13.6	13.8	13.7
African LDCs	10.6	9.2	9.0	9.1	9.1	9.0	9.1	8.8	8.2	8.2	8.4	8.3
ASEAN	23.9	22.8	22.2	22.0	21.9	22.0	22.1	21.7	21.2	21.2	21.1	20.9
CACM	18.5	16.8	16.5	16.3	16.3	16.2	16.7	16.7	16.5	16.3	16.1	16.0
CARICOM	10.6	11.3	10.2	10.0	9.9	9.5	12.2	11.5	10.4	10.2	9.3	8.8
CEMAC	8.5	11.7	11.5	11.2	11.6	11.9	12.2	11.7	11.9	12.1	11.9	12.1
CIS	14.8	13.2	13.8	13.6	13.7	13.7	12.1	12.1	12.2	12.5	13.2	13.4
ECOWAS	7.4	7.3	9.8	9.5	9.2	9.3	7.7	8.1	9.1	9.7	9.5	8.8
EU	14.2	13.8	14.2	14.4	14.5	14.6	14.1	13.8	13.8	13.9	14.4	14.5
GCC	8.8	9.6	9.7	9.9	10.0	10.2	9.1	9.1	9.1	9.5	10.7	10.8
LAIA	15.0	13.7	12.9	12.5	12.6	12.4	13.1	12.8	12.6	12.5	13.2	13.0
MERCOSUR	14.4	13.1	12.1	11.6	11.8	11.5	12.5	11.8	11.6	11.5	11.9	11.7
OECD	14.4	14.2	14.2	14.1	14.1	14.2	14.2	14.1	13.9	13.9	14.1	13.9

a/ Provisional.
b/ Estimate.

Table 1.4
(continued)

SHARE OF MVA IN GDP, SELECTED YEARS
(Percentage)

Country group or economy	At constant 2010 prices						At current prices						
	2005	2010	2014	2015	2016 [a]	2017 [b]	2011	2012	2013	2014	2015	2016 [a]
SAARC	15.0	15.9	15.9	16.3	16.5	16.6	15.9	15.6	15.1	15.0	14.9	14.7
SADC	12.4	11.3	11.1	11.1	11.2	11.1	10.5	10.0	9.7	9.8	10.1	10.0
WAEMU/UEMOA	13.9	11.7	12.2	12.1	11.6	11.6	11.4	11.9	12.3	12.6	12.2	12.2

a/ Provisional.
b/ Estimate.

Section 1.2

THE MANUFACTURING DIVISIONS

Table 1.5

DISTRIBUTION OF WORLD VALUE ADDED, SELECTED DIVISIONS AND YEARS a/
(Percentage)

| ISIC Division | Year | Industrialized Economies | | | | | | | Developing & Emerging Industrial Economies | | | | World |
| | | All Economies | Europe | | East Asia | West Asia | North America | Others | All Economies | Emerging Industrial c/ Economies | Other Developing Economies | Least Developing Countries | |
			EU b/	Other									
10 Food products	2005	66.5	22.2	3.5	13.4	0.3	24.1	3.0	33.5	28.3	4.9	0.3	100.0
	2010	60.5	20.3	3.6	12.0	0.4	21.6	2.6	39.5	33.9	5.0	0.6	100.0
	2017	54.0	17.7	3.4	10.4	0.5	19.8	2.2	46.0	38.5	6.4	1.1	100.0
11 Beverages	2005	63.4	22.8	2.1	14.6	0.4	20.6	2.9	36.6	30.3	5.7	0.6	100.0
	2010	56.0	19.6	2.3	12.7	0.4	18.5	2.5	44.0	37.1	6.2	0.7	100.0
	2017	49.8	16.5	2.2	10.8	0.4	17.8	2.1	50.2	41.5	7.8	0.9	100.0
12 Tobacco products	2005	52.9	8.5	1.8	6.6	0.0	34.1	1.9	47.1	41.4	4.1	1.6	100.0
	2010	38.8	6.1	2.0	6.4	0.0	22.6	1.7	61.2	53.9	5.4	1.9	100.0
	2017	29.0	3.5	2.1	6.8	0.0	15.1	1.5	71.0	61.0	6.7	3.3	100.0
13 Textiles	2005	48.1	18.1	1.4	8.8	0.0	18.7	1.1	51.9	45.1	5.1	1.7	100.0
	2010	33.8	13.6	1.2	7.3	0.1	10.7	0.9	66.2	57.9	5.7	2.6	100.0
	2017	26.1	10.6	0.9	5.8	0.0	8.1	0.7	73.9	64.1	6.4	3.4	100.0
14 Wearing apparel	2005	47.0	20.7	1.7	9.7	0.3	9.4	5.2	53.0	45.4	4.7	2.9	100.0
	2010	34.6	15.9	1.7	7.5	0.5	4.2	4.8	65.4	56.7	4.5	4.2	100.0
	2017	24.0	11.0	1.4	4.9	0.5	2.4	3.8	76.0	64.3	5.4	6.3	100.0
15 Leather and related products	2005	50.6	35.0	1.3	7.5	0.0	4.4	2.4	49.4	45.3	3.6	0.5	100.0
	2010	37.4	25.2	1.5	5.4	0.1	3.1	2.1	62.6	57.4	4.6	0.6	100.0
	2017	29.0	20.7	1.1	3.5	0.0	2.1	1.6	71.0	63.7	6.2	1.1	100.0
16 Wood products, excluding furniture	2005	78.1	30.4	5.6	9.0	0.4	29.3	3.4	21.9	20.0	1.7	0.2	100.0
	2010	69.7	28.2	6.4	9.2	0.4	22.1	3.4	30.3	28.0	2.0	0.3	100.0
	2017	64.1	23.9	5.4	7.9	0.5	23.8	2.6	35.9	33.3	2.3	0.3	100.0
17 Paper and paper products	2005	74.3	21.6	2.3	13.7	0.2	34.7	1.8	25.7	24.5	1.1	0.1	100.0
	2010	65.8	20.9	2.2	12.6	0.1	28.4	1.6	34.2	32.8	1.3	0.1	100.0
	2017	58.5	18.5	1.9	11.5	0.2	25.0	1.4	41.5	39.8	1.5	0.2	100.0
18 Printing and reproduction of recorded media	2005	84.8	27.2	3.9	21.0	1.0	28.2	3.5	15.2	13.9	1.1	0.2	100.0
	2010	79.5	26.0	4.1	21.4	1.2	23.5	3.3	20.5	18.8	1.3	0.4	100.0
	2017	72.8	22.3	4.1	18.5	1.8	23.1	3.0	27.2	24.8	2.0	0.4	100.0
19 Coke and refined petroleum products	2005	54.2	8.6	8.6	10.1	2.0	22.8	2.1	45.8	39.9	5.9	0.0	100.0
	2010	50.8	7.2	9.5	9.0	2.3	20.9	1.9	49.2	43.6	5.5	0.1	100.0
	2017	48.5	6.2	9.7	8.4	2.5	19.9	1.8	51.5	46.5	5.0	0.0	100.0

a/ At constant 2010 prices.
b/ Excluding non-industrialized EU economies.
c/ Including China.

Table 1.5
(continued)

DISTRIBUTION OF WORLD VALUE ADDED, SELECTED DIVISIONS AND YEARS [a]
(Percentage)

| ISIC Division | Year | Industrialized Economies | | | | | | | Developing & Emerging Industrial Economies | | | | World |
		All Economies	Europe EU [b]	Europe Other	East Asia	West Asia	North America	Others	All Economies	Emerging Industrial [c] Economies	Other Developing Economies	Least Developing Countries	
20 Chemicals and chemical products	2005	72.7	21.9	3.6	15.4	0.6	29.9	1.3	27.3	25.7	1.5	0.1	100.0
	2010	63.9	19.5	3.5	14.5	0.8	24.5	1.1	36.1	34.5	1.5	0.1	100.0
	2017	54.4	16.8	3.8	12.8	1.0	19.2	0.8	45.6	43.7	1.7	0.2	100.0
21 Pharmaceuticals, medicinal chemicals, etc.	2005	80.6	24.6	3.9	14.7	0.1	33.8	3.5	19.4	18.1	1.2	0.1	100.0
	2010	75.1	25.0	5.4	14.4	0.0	26.8	3.5	24.9	23.6	1.2	0.1	100.0
	2017	66.2	25.3	6.3	13.0	0.0	19.0	2.6	33.8	32.2	1.3	0.3	100.0
22 Rubber and plastics products	2005	76.4	26.9	1.6	20.2	0.4	25.2	2.1	23.6	22.1	1.4	0.1	100.0
	2010	68.7	25.1	2.1	19.0	0.5	20.0	2.0	31.3	29.8	1.4	0.1	100.0
	2017	64.1	23.6	2.3	16.4	0.5	19.7	1.6	35.9	34.1	1.6	0.2	100.0
23 Other non-metallic mineral products	2005	66.4	27.7	3.2	13.9	1.3	17.9	2.4	33.6	29.4	3.6	0.6	100.0
	2010	53.0	21.2	2.9	12.9	1.5	12.4	2.1	47.0	42.1	4.2	0.7	100.0
	2017	44.6	16.6	2.4	10.7	1.6	11.6	1.7	55.4	50.1	4.2	1.1	100.0
24 Basic metals	2005	56.6	16.6	5.8	15.9	0.7	16.0	1.6	43.4	41.4	1.6	0.4	100.0
	2010	46.5	13.0	5.3	13.0	0.8	12.8	1.6	53.5	51.5	1.6	0.4	100.0
	2017	38.3	10.9	4.4	10.5	0.8	10.5	1.2	61.7	59.4	1.7	0.6	100.0
25 Fabricated metal products, except machinery	2005	83.1	35.6	2.4	15.4	1.2	26.1	2.4	16.9	16.2	0.6	0.1	100.0
	2010	75.6	32.2	2.9	13.7	1.3	22.9	2.6	24.4	23.5	0.8	0.1	100.0
	2017	68.8	30.4	2.3	11.5	1.5	20.9	2.2	31.2	30.1	1.0	0.1	100.0
26 Computer, electronic and optical products	2005	79.2	17.1	3.6	34.3	0.0	20.6	3.6	20.8	19.4	1.3	0.1	100.0
	2010	74.1	13.9	3.1	31.8	0.0	22.4	2.9	25.9	24.7	1.2	0.0	100.0
	2017	63.7	11.2	2.6	26.1	0.0	21.6	2.2	36.3	34.3	1.9	0.1	100.0
27 Electrical equipment	2005	76.6	34.1	2.8	21.5	0.1	16.2	1.9	23.4	22.1	1.2	0.1	100.0
	2010	66.0	30.2	2.9	18.8	0.1	12.3	1.7	34.0	32.7	1.1	0.2	100.0
	2017	57.0	25.9	2.6	15.9	0.2	11.1	1.3	43.0	41.4	1.3	0.3	100.0
28 Machinery and equipment n.e.c.	2005	84.0	36.2	3.7	20.8	0.1	22.0	1.2	16.0	15.5	0.4	0.1	100.0
	2010	74.5	32.0	3.7	19.1	0.1	18.4	1.2	25.5	25.1	0.4	0.0	100.0
	2017	68.4	29.5	2.9	19.0	0.0	16.1	0.9	31.6	31.1	0.5	0.0	100.0
29 Motor vehicles, trailers and semi-trailers	2005	78.0	30.3	0.8	25.9	0.1	20.1	0.8	22.0	21.4	0.6	0.0	100.0
	2010	67.5	27.3	0.8	23.3	0.0	15.2	0.9	32.5	31.7	0.8	0.0	100.0
	2017	63.2	26.9	0.8	18.3	0.1	16.6	0.5	36.8	36.0	0.8	0.0	100.0

a/ At constant 2010 prices.
b/ Excluding non-industrialized EU economies.
c/ Including China.

Table 1.5
(continued)

DISTRIBUTION OF WORLD VALUE ADDED, SELECTED DIVISIONS AND YEARS a/
(Percentage)

ISIC Division	Year	Industrialized Economies							Developing & Emerging Industrial Economies				World
		All Economies	Europe		East Asia	West Asia	North America	Others	All Economies	Emerging Industrial c/ Economies	Other Developing Economies	Least Developing Countries	
			EU b/	Other									
30 Other transport equipment	2005	81.0	21.8	2.3	14.0	0.0	41.1	1.8	19.0	17.4	1.5	0.1	100.0
	2010	77.4	20.3	2.4	13.6	0.0	39.5	1.6	22.6	21.1	1.4	0.1	100.0
	2017	74.2	21.6	2.3	11.5	0.1	37.3	1.4	25.8	23.7	1.9	0.2	100.0
31 Furniture	2005	80.0	33.5	2.8	6.5	0.9	33.8	2.5	20.0	17.1	2.7	0.2	100.0
	2010	70.5	32.3	3.3	6.7	1.1	24.3	2.8	29.5	25.3	3.9	0.3	100.0
	2017	63.7	27.3	2.8	6.1	1.3	23.7	2.5	36.3	30.0	5.9	0.4	100.0
32 Other manufacturing	2005	84.1	26.3	2.3	13.2	0.1	41.1	1.1	15.9	15.0	0.9	0.0	100.0
	2010	79.6	26.4	2.5	11.4	0.1	38.3	0.9	20.4	19.3	1.0	0.1	100.0
	2017	73.4	28.1	2.3	10.4	0.0	31.8	0.8	26.6	25.0	1.3	0.3	100.0

a/ At constant 2010 prices.
b/ Excluding non-industrialized EU economies.
c/ Including China.

Table 1.6

DISTRIBUTION OF VALUE ADDED OF SELECTED DIVISIONS AMONG DEVELOPING REGIONS, 2010 AND 2017 [a]
(Percentage)

ISIC Division	All Developing & Emerging Industrial Economies												Least Developed Countries	
	Africa		Asia and Pacific [b]		Europe		Latin America		All Economies					
	2010	2017	2010	2017	2010	2017	2010	2017	2010	2017			2010	2017
10 Food products	9.1	9.4	46.6	54.9	10.8	9.3	33.5	26.4	100.0	100.0			1.6	2.4
11 Beverages	10.5	11.1	37.7	47.3	9.7	6.9	42.1	34.7	100.0	100.0			1.5	1.8
12 Tobacco products	3.2	2.3	76.5	79.3	4.1	4.0	16.2	14.4	100.0	100.0			3.1	4.7
13 Textiles	4.1	4.0	77.9	83.1	8.8	7.5	9.2	5.4	100.0	100.0			4.0	4.6
14 Wearing apparel	4.5	3.5	68.8	77.8	13.3	10.3	13.4	8.4	100.0	100.0			6.5	8.2
15 Leather and related products	3.4	3.5	69.2	78.4	7.3	5.1	20.1	13.0	100.0	100.0			0.9	1.5
16 Wood products, excluding furniture	9.6	8.7	51.0	60.3	17.7	15.7	21.7	15.3	100.0	100.0			0.9	0.7
17 Paper and paper products	4.5	3.3	60.8	65.5	7.6	8.0	27.1	23.2	100.0	100.0			0.4	0.5
18 Printing and reproduction of recorded media	8.0	6.5	48.5	60.8	14.8	13.4	28.7	19.3	100.0	100.0			1.5	1.8
19 Coke and refined petroleum products	9.2	8.0	51.6	62.4	2.6	2.8	36.6	26.8	100.0	100.0			0.1	0.0
20 Chemicals and chemical products	4.4	3.4	71.8	80.3	5.2	4.0	18.6	12.3	100.0	100.0			0.4	0.4
21 Pharmaceuticals, medicinal chemicals, etc.	3.0	2.1	62.2	76.4	7.2	6.4	27.6	15.1	100.0	100.0			0.6	0.9
22 Rubber and plastics products	3.3	2.8	60.4	66.2	13.4	13.7	22.9	17.3	100.0	100.0			0.5	0.6
23 Other non-metallic mineral products	7.7	5.1	62.3	72.1	11.8	9.9	18.2	12.9	100.0	100.0			1.6	2.1
24 Basic metals	2.5	1.5	77.9	85.0	4.8	3.9	14.8	9.6	100.0	100.0			0.9	1.0
25 Fabricated metal products, except machinery	3.7	2.9	59.2	69.9	14.6	13.9	22.5	13.3	100.0	100.0			0.5	0.4
26 Computer, electronic and optical products	0.5	0.5	89.7	94.4	3.6	2.5	6.2	2.6	100.0	100.0			0.1	0.1
27 Electrical equipment	2.7	1.6	70.7	78.0	12.0	11.3	14.6	9.1	100.0	100.0			0.5	0.8
28 Machinery and equipment n.e.c.	2.7	1.9	72.9	81.5	8.6	7.6	15.8	9.0	100.0	100.0			0.1	0.1
29 Motor vehicles, trailers and semi-trailers	2.0	1.5	58.5	67.5	8.7	9.4	30.8	21.6	100.0	100.0			0.1	0.1
30 Other transport equipment	2.2	4.5	71.0	73.8	12.3	11.4	14.5	10.3	100.0	100.0			0.4	0.6
31 Furniture	8.0	8.2	44.0	51.5	23.7	24.0	24.3	16.3	100.0	100.0			0.8	1.1
32 Other manufacturing	5.9	5.0	63.9	71.7	8.8	7.9	21.4	15.4	100.0	100.0			0.6	1.0

a/ At constant 2010 prices.
b/ Including China.

Table 1.7

MAJOR PRODUCERS IN SELECTED DIVISIONS, 2010 AND 2017 [a/]

Food products (ISIC 10)

World — 2010 Economy	Share [b/] (percentage)	World — 2017 Economy	Share [b/] (percentage)	Developing & emerging industrial economies — 2010 Economy	Share [c/] (percentage)	Developing & emerging industrial economies — 2017 Economy	Share [c/] (percentage)
United States of America	19.7	United States of America	17.9	Brazil	14.8	Indonesia	14.4
Japan	10.3	China	13.5	Indonesia	10.1	Brazil	11.4
China	8.8	Japan	8.8	Mexico	9.0	Mexico	8.0
Brazil	4.5	Indonesia	4.7	Thailand	5.5	Nigeria	6.3
Germany	4.1	Brazil	3.7	India	5.3	Thailand	5.1
France	3.3	Germany	3.5	Nigeria	4.5	Turkey	4.6
Indonesia	3.1	France	2.7	Turkey	4.5	India	4.3
Mexico	2.8	Mexico	2.6	Argentina	4.3	Poland	3.7
United Kingdom	2.7	United Kingdom	2.5	Venezuela (Bolivarian Republic of)	4.3	Venezuela (Bolivarian Republic of)	3.5
Italy	2.7	Russian Federation	2.3	Poland	3.5	Argentina	3.2
Russian Federation	2.4	Italy	2.3	Colombia	2.7	Colombia	2.5
Spain	2.3	Nigeria	2.0	South Africa	2.6	South Africa	2.3
Nigeria	2.3	Spain	2.0	Philippines	2.1	Philippines	1.9
Canada	2.0	Canada	1.9	Chile	1.9	Chile	1.8
Thailand	1.7	Thailand	1.6	Greece	1.7	Iran (Islamic Republic of)	1.8
India	1.6						
Sum of above	**72.0**	**Sum of above**	**72.0**	**Sum of above**	**76.8**	**Sum of above**	**74.8**

Beverages (ISIC 11)

World — 2010 Economy	Share [b/] (percentage)	World — 2017 Economy	Share [b/] (percentage)	Developing & emerging industrial economies — 2010 Economy	Share [c/] (percentage)	Developing & emerging industrial economies — 2017 Economy	Share [c/] (percentage)
United States of America	16.2	China	16.5	Mexico	14.3	Mexico	15.1
Japan	11.2	United States of America	15.8	Brazil	13.9	Brazil	10.7
China	10.0	Japan	9.2	Venezuela (Bolivarian Republic of)	7.4	Venezuela (Bolivarian Republic of)	6.4
Mexico	4.8	Mexico	5.1	Colombia	4.6	Colombia	5.1
Brazil	4.7	Brazil	3.6	Argentina	4.4	Thailand	4.7
United Kingdom	3.7	United Kingdom	3.1	Thailand	4.0	Philippines	4.2
France	3.0	France	2.6	South Africa	4.0	Nigeria	4.2
Spain	3.0	Spain	2.4	India	3.6	South Africa	4.0
Germany	2.8	Germany	2.3	Chile	3.3	Argentina	3.4
Venezuela (Bolivarian Republic of)	2.5	Venezuela (Bolivarian Republic of)	2.2	Philippines	3.2	Chile	3.3
Canada	2.4	Canada	2.1	Poland	3.2	India	3.1
Italy	2.3	Italy	1.9	Nigeria	2.8	Poland	2.7
Australia	2.0	Colombia	1.7	Turkey	2.2	Dominican Republic	2.7
Colombia	1.6	Australia	1.7	Dominican Republic	2.0	Turkey	2.0
Argentina	1.5	Thailand	1.6	Romania	1.9	Angola	1.7
Sum of above	**71.7**	**Sum of above**	**71.8**	**Sum of above**	**74.8**	**Sum of above**	**73.3**

a/ China is presented only among "World", depending on data availability.
b/ In world total value added at constant 2010 prices.
c/ In total value added of developing and emerging industrial economies at constant 2010 prices.

Table 1.7

MAJOR PRODUCERS IN SELECTED DIVISIONS, 2010 AND 2017 [a]

Textiles (ISIC 13)

	World 2010		World 2017		Developing & emerging industrial economies 2010		Developing & emerging industrial economies 2017	
	Economy	Share [b] (percentage)	Economy	Share [b] (percentage)	Economy	Share [c] (percentage)	Economy	Share [c] (percentage)
	China	32.7	China	44.7	India	21.1	India	23.2
	United States of America	8.4	India	6.7	Turkey	14.0	Turkey	15.0
	India	7.0	United States of America	6.4	Indonesia	11.7	Pakistan	10.6
	Japan	4.8	Turkey	4.3	Brazil	8.6	Indonesia	7.7
	Turkey	4.7	Japan	4.0	Pakistan	8.2	Nigeria	6.1
	Italy	4.2	Pakistan	3.1	Thailand	4.6	Brazil	5.3
	Indonesia	3.9	Italy	2.9	Nigeria	3.6	Bangladesh	4.5
	Brazil	2.9	Indonesia	2.2	Bangladesh	3.5	Mexico	3.1
	Pakistan	2.7	Germany	2.1	Mexico	3.2	Thailand	2.8
	Germany	2.5	Canada	1.9	Argentina	3.1	Poland	2.6
	Canada	2.4	Nigeria	1.7	Iran (Islamic Republic of)	1.8	Argentina	2.5
	Thailand	1.5	Brazil	1.5	Egypt	1.6	Iran (Islamic Republic of)	2.0
	United Kingdom	1.4	Bangladesh	1.3	Poland	1.5	Egypt	1.3
	France	1.3	France	1.1	Syrian Arab Republic	1.4	Viet Nam	1.3
	Republic of Korea	1.2	Spain	1.0	Peru	1.2	Syrian Arab Republic	1.3
	Sum of above	81.6	Sum of above	84.9	Sum of above	89.1	Sum of above	89.3

Wearing apparel (ISIC 14)

	World 2010		World 2017		Developing & emerging industrial economies 2010		Developing & emerging industrial economies 2017	
	Economy	Share [b] (percentage)	Economy	Share [b] (percentage)	Economy	Share [c] (percentage)	Economy	Share [c] (percentage)
	China	28.1	China	39.8	Turkey	13.4	Bangladesh	17.0
	Italy	6.8	Bangladesh	6.2	Brazil	12.6	Turkey	13.7
	Turkey	5.0	Turkey	4.9	Indonesia	11.3	Indonesia	11.7
	Brazil	4.7	Indonesia	4.2	Bangladesh	10.9	India	9.1
	Japan	4.3	Italy	4.0	India	8.3	Brazil	8.2
	Indonesia	4.2	India	3.3	Thailand	5.4	Mexico	4.6
	Bangladesh	4.1	Puerto Rico	3.0	Mexico	5.0	Viet Nam	3.8
	Puerto Rico	3.8	Brazil	3.0	Romania	3.0	Thailand	3.4
	United States of America	3.5	Japan	2.6	Tunisia	2.7	Poland	2.4
	India	3.1	United States of America	1.9	Viet Nam	2.5	Sri Lanka	2.4
	Republic of Korea	2.1	Mexico	1.7	Sri Lanka	2.3	Romania	2.3
	Germany	2.0	Germany	1.5	Colombia	2.3	Tunisia	2.3
	Republic of Korea	2.0	Republic of Korea	1.5	Poland	2.2	Colombia	1.9
	Spain	1.9	Spain	1.4	Peru	2.1	Jordan	1.8
	Viet Nam	1.8	Viet Nam	1.4	Pakistan	1.4	Pakistan	1.7
	Sum of above	77.4	Sum of above	80.4	Sum of above	85.4	Sum of above	86.3

a/ China is presented only among "World", depending on data availability.
b/ In world total value added at constant 2010 prices.
c/ In total value added of developing and emerging industrial economies at constant 2010 prices.

Table 1.7

MAJOR PRODUCERS IN SELECTED DIVISIONS, 2010 AND 2017 [a]

Leather and related products (ISIC 15)

World 2010		World 2017		Developing & emerging industrial economies 2010		Developing & emerging industrial economies 2017	
Economy	Share [b] (percentage)	Economy	Share [b] (percentage)	Economy	Share [c] (percentage)	Economy	Share [c] (percentage)
China	30.7	China	40.5	Brazil	26.7	Indonesia	21.8
Italy	13.9	Italy	11.3	Indonesia	16.2	Brazil	18.3
Brazil	8.5	Indonesia	6.6	India	8.0	Viet Nam	10.3
Indonesia	5.2	Brazil	5.6	Mexico	5.6	India	8.0
Japan	3.0	Viet Nam	3.1	Thailand	5.5	Mexico	4.6
France	2.9	India	2.4	Turkey	4.9	Thailand	3.5
United States of America	2.9	France	2.1	Viet Nam	4.9	Turkey	3.5
India	2.6	United States of America	2.0	Romania	3.4	Romania	2.8
Spain	2.5	Spain	1.8	Tunisia	2.3	Poland	2.7
Mexico	1.8	Japan	1.8	Poland	2.0	Nicaragua	2.3
Thailand	1.8	Germany	1.6	Nicaragua	1.8	Bangladesh	2.2
Germany	1.8	Mexico	1.4	Colombia	1.6	Tunisia	1.9
Turkey	1.6	Portugal	1.2	South Africa	1.6	Egypt	1.6
Viet Nam	1.6	Thailand	1.1	Bangladesh	1.2	Colombia	1.5
Portugal	1.5	Turkey	1.1	Dominican Republic	1.2	Dominican Republic	1.4
Sum of above	**82.1**	**Sum of above**	**83.6**	**Sum of above**	**86.9**	**Sum of above**	**86.4**

Wood products, excluding furniture (ISIC 16)

World 2010		World 2017		Developing & emerging industrial economies 2010		Developing & emerging industrial economies 2017	
Economy	Share [b] (percentage)	Economy	Share [b] (percentage)	Economy	Share [c] (percentage)	Economy	Share [c] (percentage)
United States of America	16.3	China	16.3	Brazil	12.5	Brazil	11.8
China	10.8	United States of America	10.8	Argentina	11.8	Poland	11.6
Japan	7.4	Canada	7.4	Indonesia	10.8	Argentina	10.2
Germany	6.1	Japan	6.1	Poland	9.3	South Africa	8.1
Canada	5.9	Germany	5.8	South Africa	7.7	Indonesia	7.5
Russian Federation	4.4	Russian Federation	2.8	Turkey	6.2	Turkey	7.1
Italy	3.1	Italy	2.7	Thailand	4.8	Thailand	4.7
Brazil	2.7	Brazil	2.1	Chile	4.4	Romania	4.4
Poland	2.7	Poland	2.1	Romania	4.0	Chile	3.9
United Kingdom	2.4	United Kingdom	2.0	Latvia	2.7	Latvia	3.6
France	2.4	France	2.0	Nigeria	2.2	Nigeria	3.4
Australia	2.3	Australia	1.9	Tunisia	1.9	Viet Nam	2.1
Austria	2.3	Austria	1.9	Greece	1.9	Tunisia	1.9
Argentina	2.3	Argentina	1.8	India	1.7	India	1.7
Indonesia	2.1	Sweden	1.8	Viet Nam	1.2	Ukraine	1.3
Sum of above	**73.2**	**Sum of above**	**74.7**	**Sum of above**	**82.9**	**Sum of above**	**83.0**

a/ China is presented only among "World", depending on data availability.
b/ In world total value added at constant 2010 prices.
c/ In total value added of developing and emerging industrial economies at constant 2010 prices.

Table 1.7

MAJOR PRODUCERS IN SELECTED DIVISIONS, 2010 AND 2017 [a]

Paper and paper products (ISIC 17)

World 2010 Economy	Share [b] (percentage)	World 2017 Economy	Share [b] (percentage)	Developing & emerging industrial economies 2010 Economy	Share [c] (percentage)	Developing & emerging industrial economies 2017 Economy	Share [c] (percentage)
United States of America	23.9	United States of America	21.2	Brazil	19.2	Brazil	17.8
China	14.0	China	20.8	Indonesia	16.8	Indonesia	13.2
Japan	10.5	Japan	9.5	Mexico	8.4	Mexico	8.8
Germany	5.1	Germany	4.4	India	6.5	Poland	6.2
Canada	4.5	Canada	3.8	Chile	5.6	India	6.0
Brazil	3.9	Brazil	3.7	Poland	4.8	Turkey	5.9
Indonesia	3.4	Indonesia	2.7	Turkey	4.5	Chile	5.6
Italy	2.6	Italy	2.3	South Africa	4.4	Venezuela (Bolivarian Republic of)	4.5
Spain	2.0	Spain	1.9	Thailand	3.9	South Africa	3.9
France	1.9	Mexico	1.8	Argentina	3.8	Thailand	3.8
Sweden	1.9	Sweden	1.7	Venezuela (Bolivarian Republic of)	2.8	Argentina	3.0
United Kingdom	1.8	United Kingdom	1.7	Colombia	2.0	Peru	1.9
Finland	1.7	Finland	1.4	Peru	1.6	Saudi Arabia	1.9
Mexico	1.7	France	1.4	Saudi Arabia	1.5	Viet Nam	1.8
Russian Federation	1.5	Russian Federation	1.4	Pakistan	1.2	Colombia	1.7
Sum of above	**80.4**	**Sum of above**	**79.7**	**Sum of above**	**87.0**	**Sum of above**	**86.0**

Printing and reproduction of recorded media (ISIC 18)

World 2010 Economy	Share [b] (percentage)	World 2017 Economy	Share [b] (percentage)	Developing & emerging industrial economies 2010 Economy	Share [c] (percentage)	Developing & emerging industrial economies 2017 Economy	Share [c] (percentage)
United States of America	22.7	United States of America	22.4	Brazil	13.1	Indonesia	10.9
Japan	19.2	Japan	16.5	Argentina	11.3	Brazil	10.8
Germany	6.6	China	10.6	India	10.9	India	10.4
China	5.3	Germany	6.0	Indonesia	8.6	Argentina	9.9
United Kingdom	4.2	United Kingdom	3.7	Turkey	6.5	Turkey	8.0
France	3.4	France	2.6	South Africa	6.3	Poland	7.7
Russian Federation	2.8	Russian Federation	2.3	Poland	5.2	South Africa	5.2
Italy	2.7	Italy	2.2	Thailand	3.9	Thailand	4.0
Spain	2.2	Spain	2.0	Mexico	3.3	Philippines	3.1
Australia	2.1	Australia	1.9	Chile	3.2	Mexico	2.8
Indonesia	1.9	Indonesia	1.8	Peru	3.2	Peru	2.2
Brazil	1.7	Brazil	1.8	Greece	2.8	Romania	1.8
Argentina	1.6	India	1.7	Colombia	2.0	Chile	1.7
India	1.5	Argentina	1.6	Romania	1.7	Colombia	1.5
Netherlands	1.5	Netherlands	1.5	Egypt	1.3	Egypt	1.5
Switzerland	1.5						
Sum of above	**79.4**	**Sum of above**	**78.6**	**Sum of above**	**83.3**	**Sum of above**	**81.5**

a/ China is presented only among "World", depending on data availability.
b/ In world total value added at constant 2010 prices.
c/ In total value added of developing and emerging industrial economies at constant 2010 prices.

Table 1.7

MAJOR PRODUCERS IN SELECTED DIVISIONS, 2010 AND 2017 [a/]

World 2010 Economy	World 2010 Share [b/] (percentage)	World 2017 Economy	World 2017 Share [b/] (percentage)	Developing & emerging industrial economies 2010 Economy	Developing & emerging 2010 Share [c/] (percentage)	Developing & emerging 2017 Economy	Developing & emerging 2017 Share [c/] (percentage)
Coke and refined petroleum products (ISIC 19)							
United States of America	18.9	United States of America	18.1	Brazil	20.5	India	21.8
China	10.4	China	14.2	India	17.6	Brazil	17.8
Russian Federation	9.4	Russian Federation	9.6	Mexico	14.3	Mexico	8.3
Brazil	8.0	India	8.1	Egypt	6.8	Egypt	7.2
India	6.8	Brazil	6.6	Philippines	5.4	Iran (Islamic Republic of)	6.1
Mexico	5.6	Mexico	3.1	Saudi Arabia	3.9	Saudi Arabia	5.2
Malaysia	3.6	Malaysia	2.8	Colombia	3.7	Philippines	4.0
Japan	2.7	Japan	2.8	Venezuela (Bolivarian Republic of)	3.4	Colombia	3.7
Egypt	2.6	Egypt	2.7	Iran (Islamic Republic of)	2.7	Viet Nam	3.3
Germany	2.2	Iran (Islamic Republic of)	2.3	South Africa	2.4	Venezuela (Bolivarian Republic of)	2.9
Philippines	2.1	Saudi Arabia	1.9	Viet Nam	1.8	Thailand	2.3
Canada	2.1	Germany	1.9	Ecuador	1.6	South Africa	2.2
Saudi Arabia	1.5	Canada	1.8	Greece	1.6	Greece	2.0
Colombia	1.4	Republic of Korea	1.6	Thailand	1.6	Ecuador	1.9
Republic of Korea	1.4	Philippines	1.5	Oman	1.5	Turkey	1.6
Sum of above	**78.7**	**Sum of above**	**79.0**	**Sum of above**	**88.8**	**Sum of above**	**90.3**
Chemicals and chemical products (ISIC 20)							
United States of America	22.9	China	23.1	Saudi Arabia	17.5	Saudi Arabia	19.9
China	14.6	United States of America	17.7	Brazil	15.9	India	14.5
Japan	10.3	Japan	8.8	India	13.5	Brazil	12.7
Germany	7.0	Germany	5.6	Indonesia	10.4	Indonesia	11.1
Saudi Arabia	3.7	Saudi Arabia	4.5	Mexico	4.0	Iran (Islamic Republic of)	5.5
Brazil	3.4	India	3.3	Thailand	3.5	Turkey	3.4
India	2.9	Brazil	2.8	Turkey	3.3	Thailand	3.1
Russian Federation	2.5	Russian Federation	2.7	South Africa	3.0	Mexico	2.8
France	2.3	France	2.5	Poland	2.7	South Africa	2.8
Indonesia	2.2	Indonesia	2.5	Argentina	2.7	Poland	2.5
United Kingdom	2.0	United Kingdom	1.8	Iran (Islamic Republic of)	2.4	Argentina	2.2
Italy	1.8	Canada	1.5	Colombia	2.3	Colombia	1.9
Canada	1.6	Republic of Korea	1.4	Egypt	2.0	Philippines	1.8
Republic of Korea	1.6	Italy	1.4	Chile	2.0	Egypt	1.7
Spain	1.5	Netherlands	1.3	Venezuela (Bolivarian Republic of)	1.8	Pakistan	1.5
Sum of above	**80.3**	**Sum of above**	**80.9**	**Sum of above**	**87.0**	**Sum of above**	**87.4**

a/ China is presented only among "World", depending on data availability.
b/ In world total value added at constant 2010 prices.
c/ In total value added of developing and emerging industrial economies at constant 2010 prices.

Table 1.7

MAJOR PRODUCERS IN SELECTED DIVISIONS, 2010 AND 2017[a]

Pharmaceuticals, medicinal chemicals, etc. (ISIC 21)

World				Developing & emerging industrial economies			
2010		2017		2010		2017	
Economy	Share [b] (percentage)	Economy	Share [b] (percentage)	Economy	Share [c] (percentage)	Economy	Share [c] (percentage)
United States of America	26.4	United States of America	18.6	Mexico	20.2	India	18.8
Japan	12.3	China	14.4	India	19.5	Iran (Islamic Republic of)	17.6
China	7.7	Japan	10.7	Indonesia	11.6	Indonesia	16.1
Germany	5.6	Ireland	6.5	Brazil	11.0	Mexico	12.9
Ireland	4.6	Germany	5.7	Iran (Islamic Republic of)	8.5	Turkey	6.8
Switzerland	4.5	Switzerland	5.1	Turkey	5.2	Brazil	6.7
India	3.5	India	3.7	Argentina	3.0	Argentina	2.2
Iran (Islamic Republic of)	3.5	Iran (Islamic Republic of)	3.4	Poland	3.0	Poland	2.1
United Kingdom	3.4	Indonesia	3.1	Egypt	2.4	Egypt	1.9
Italy	3.3	Italy	3.1	Colombia	2.1	Philippines	1.6
France	2.9	France	2.8	Pakistan	1.4	Colombia	1.6
Puerto Rico	2.1	Mexico	2.5	Philippines	1.3	Pakistan	1.4
Indonesia	2.0	Singapore	2.0	Peru	1.3	Bangladesh	1.1
Brazil	1.9	United Kingdom	2.0	Romania	0.9	Romania	1.0
Singapore	1.8	Puerto Rico	1.5	Thailand	0.7	Thailand	0.8
Sum of above	**85.5**	**Sum of above**	**85.1**	**Sum of above**	**92.1**	**Sum of above**	**92.6**

Rubber and plastics products (ISIC 22)

World				Developing & emerging industrial economies			
2010		2017		2010		2017	
Economy	Share [b] (percentage)	Economy	Share [b] (percentage)	Economy	Share [c] (percentage)	Economy	Share [c] (percentage)
United States of America	17.7	United States of America	17.2	Brazil	13.7	Indonesia	11.4
China	15.5	China	15.2	India	11.9	Thailand	10.4
Japan	9.8	Japan	12.9	Indonesia	11.8	India	10.2
Germany	7.9	Germany	7.6	Thailand	11.3	Brazil	10.0
Italy	3.7	Italy	3.3	Turkey	7.9	Poland	9.3
France	3.4	France	3.0	Mexico	7.1	Turkey	8.9
Brazil	3.0	Indonesia	2.6	Poland	6.7	Mexico	7.2
Indonesia	2.6	Canada	2.5	Argentina	4.8	Argentina	4.4
United Kingdom	2.6	India	2.4	South Africa	2.2	Venezuela (Bolivarian Republic of)	2.4
Thailand	2.5	Thailand	2.3	Venezuela (Bolivarian Republic of)	1.9	Saudi Arabia	2.3
India	2.4	United Kingdom	2.1	Saudi Arabia	1.8	Romania	2.2
Canada	2.2	Brazil	1.9	Colombia	1.7	South Africa	2.0
Spain	2.1	Spain	1.9	Romania	1.7	Iran (Islamic Republic of)	1.9
Poland	1.7	Poland	1.8	Iran (Islamic Republic of)	1.4	Colombia	1.4
Turkey	1.6	Turkey	1.6	Greece	1.2	Philippines	1.2
Sum of above	**78.7**	**Sum of above**	**78.3**	**Sum of above**	**87.1**	**Sum of above**	**85.2**

a/ China is presented only among "World", depending on data availability.
b/ In world total value added at constant 2010 prices.
c/ In total value added of developing and emerging industrial economies at constant 2010 prices.

Table 1.7

MAJOR PRODUCERS IN SELECTED DIVISIONS, 2010 AND 2017 [a/]

	World				Developing & emerging industrial economies			
	2010		2017		2010		2017	
Economy	Share [b/] (percentage)	Economy	Share [b/] (percentage)	Economy	Share [c/] (percentage)	Economy	Share [c/] (percentage)
Other non-metallic mineral products (ISIC 23)								
China	17.2	China	26.0	India	11.5	Iran (Islamic Republic of)	10.3
United States of America	10.3	United States of America	9.8	Brazil	10.4	India	10.0
Japan	9.7	Japan	7.9	Turkey	7.7	Indonesia	7.3
Germany	5.1	Germany	4.4	Mexico	6.3	Turkey	7.3
Italy	4.1	Iran (Islamic Republic of)	3.0	Indonesia	6.0	Brazil	6.9
India	3.4	India	2.9	Saudi Arabia	5.2	Saudi Arabia	6.2
Brazil	3.1	Italy	2.6	Poland	4.7	Mexico	5.8
Spain	2.8	Indonesia	2.2	Iran (Islamic Republic of)	4.6	Poland	5.4
France	2.6	Turkey	2.2	Thailand	3.8	Argentina	3.6
Turkey	2.3	Brazil	2.0	Argentina	3.6	Thailand	2.9
Russian Federation	2.3	France	2.0	Egypt	3.5	Romania	2.5
Canada	2.1	Russian Federation	1.9	Colombia	2.5	Bangladesh	2.4
Mexico	1.9	Saudi Arabia	1.8	Peru	2.0	Colombia	2.2
Indonesia	1.8	Spain	1.8	Pakistan	1.7	Peru	1.9
United Kingdom	1.7	Canada	1.8	South Africa	1.6	Pakistan	1.8
Sum of above	**70.4**	**Sum of above**	**72.3**	**Sum of above**	**75.1**	**Sum of above**	**76.5**
Basic metals (ISIC 24)								
China	30.2	China	39.7	India	21.6	India	26.1
United States of America	10.8	United States of America	8.6	Brazil	12.9	Brazil	8.8
Japan	9.7	Japan	7.6	Mexico	9.1	Mexico	8.4
India	5.0	India	5.7	Kazakhstan	5.4	Kazakhstan	5.9
Russian Federation	4.6	Russian Federation	3.9	Iran (Islamic Republic of)	5.1	Indonesia	5.1
Germany	4.1	Germany	3.5	Turkey	4.6	Turkey	5.0
Brazil	3.0	Brazil	1.9	Indonesia	4.5	Iran (Islamic Republic of)	4.9
Mexico	2.1	Canada	1.9	Venezuela (Bolivarian Republic of)	4.5	Saudi Arabia	4.0
Canada	2.1	Mexico	1.8	Argentina	3.6	Thailand	3.4
Italy	2.0	Republic of Korea	1.6	Thailand	3.6	Venezuela (Bolivarian Republic of)	3.2
Republic of Korea	1.8	Italy	1.5	Saudi Arabia	3.2	Argentina	2.8
Australia	1.4	Kazakhstan	1.3	South Africa	2.2	Bangladesh	2.6
Kazakhstan	1.2	Indonesia	1.1	Poland	1.8	Philippines	2.5
France	1.2	Turkey	1.1	Ukraine	1.7	Poland	2.0
Spain	1.2	Iran (Islamic Republic of)	1.1	Bangladesh	1.7	South Africa	1.9
Sum of above	**80.4**	**Sum of above**	**82.3**	**Sum of above**	**85.5**	**Sum of above**	**86.6**

a/ China is presented only among "World", depending on data availability.
b/ In world total value added at constant 2010 prices.
c/ In total value added of developing and emerging industrial economies at constant 2010 prices.

Table 1.7

MAJOR PRODUCERS IN SELECTED DIVISIONS, 2010 AND 2017 [a/]

	World				Developing & emerging industrial economies			
	2010		2017		2010		2017	
Economy	Share b/ (percentage)	Economy	Share b/ (percentage)	Economy	Share c/ (percentage)	Economy	Share c/ (percentage)	

Fabricated metal products, except machinery (ISIC 25)

Economy	Share b/	Economy	Share b/	Economy	Share c/	Economy	Share c/
United States of America	20.2	United States of America	18.3	Brazil	14.7	Poland	12.5
Japan	10.7	China	16.7	India	12.0	India	9.9
Germany	9.8	Germany	10.2	Argentina	8.8	Turkey	9.6
China	9.7	Japan	8.6	Poland	8.3	Indonesia	8.8
Italy	6.0	Italy	5.1	Turkey	7.8	Brazil	8.7
France	3.6	France	3.1	Mexico	6.7	Argentina	7.3
Spain	2.9	United Kingdom	2.6	Indonesia	6.4	Thailand	6.4
United Kingdom	2.8	Canada	2.5	Thailand	5.9	Mexico	6.3
Canada	2.7	Spain	2.2	South Africa	3.3	South Africa	3.0
Brazil	2.2	Poland	1.8	Greece	2.7	Iran (Islamic Republic of)	2.6
India	1.8	India	1.4	Chile	2.0	Saudi Arabia	2.3
Australia	1.6	Turkey	1.4	Saudi Arabia	1.8	Greece	2.0
Switzerland	1.4	United Arab Emirates	1.4	Romania	1.8	Romania	1.9
Republic of Korea	1.4	Indonesia	1.3	Venezuela (Bolivarian Republic of)	1.8	Chile	1.8
Netherlands	1.3	Brazil	1.3	Iran (Islamic Republic of)	1.7	Philippines	1.8
Sum of above	**78.1**	**Sum of above**	**77.9**	**Sum of above**	**85.7**	**Sum of above**	**84.9**

Computer, electronic and optical products (ISIC 26)

Economy	Share b/	Economy	Share b/	Economy	Share c/	Economy	Share c/
United States of America	21.1	China	29.5	Thailand	31.0	Thailand	27.6
China	17.9	United States of America	20.9	Brazil	13.6	Philippines	18.9
Japan	16.7	Japan	11.3	Philippines	13.0	Indonesia	9.0
China, Taiwan Province	6.0	China, Taiwan Province	6.2	India	11.2	Brazil	8.1
Republic of Korea	5.2	Republic of Korea	4.7	Indonesia	8.5	India	6.8
Germany	4.4	Germany	4.3	Argentina	4.5	Turkey	6.0
Switzerland	2.5	Thailand	2.1	Turkey	3.9	Viet Nam	4.1
Singapore	2.4	Switzerland	2.0	Poland	3.8	Argentina	4.0
Malaysia	2.3	Singapore	2.0	Romania	1.4	Poland	3.7
Thailand	1.8	Malaysia	1.8	Mexico	1.3	Romania	2.1
United Kingdom	1.6	United Kingdom	1.4	South Africa	1.1	Mexico	1.8
France	1.6	France	1.3	Viet Nam	1.1	South Africa	1.4
Philippines	1.6	Philippines	1.2	Ukraine	0.7	Iran (Islamic Republic of)	0.9
Puerto Rico	1.4	Puerto Rico	1.1	Greece	0.6	Egypt	0.8
Italy	1.2	Italy	0.9	Iran (Islamic Republic of)	0.5	Greece	0.6
Sum of above	**87.7**	**Sum of above**	**90.7**	**Sum of above**	**96.2**	**Sum of above**	**95.8**

a/ China is presented only among "World", depending on data availability.
b/ In world total value added at constant 2010 prices.
c/ In total value added of developing and emerging industrial economies at constant 2010 prices.

Table 1.7

MAJOR PRODUCERS IN SELECTED DIVISIONS, 2010 AND 2017 [a]

	World			Developing & emerging industrial economies			
	2010		2017		2010		2017
Economy	Share [b] (percentage)	Economy	Share [b] (percentage)	Economy	Share [c] (percentage)	Economy	Share [c] (percentage)
Electrical equipment (ISIC 27)							
China	16.5	China	26.9	India	17.1	Turkey	14.8
Japan	15.6	Japan	13.2	Brazil	13.5	Indonesia	11.6
Germany	13.8	Germany	12.5	Turkey	11.9	Mexico	11.3
United States of America	11.4	United States of America	10.4	Mexico	10.8	Brazil	9.0
Italy	4.0	Italy	2.4	Indonesia	8.9	India	8.4
India	3.0	Turkey	2.4	Thailand	7.1	Poland	8.2
France	2.7	France	2.0	Poland	5.8	Thailand	7.1
Brazil	2.4	Indonesia	1.9	Iran (Islamic Republic of)	2.5	Romania	3.6
Turkey	2.1	Mexico	1.8	Philippines	2.3	Iran (Islamic Republic of)	3.6
Mexico	1.9	Austria	1.5	Argentina	1.9	Philippines	2.8
Spain	1.9	Brazil	1.4	Egypt	1.7	Saudi Arabia	2.1
Republic of Korea	1.8	United Kingdom	1.4	Romania	1.6	Bangladesh	1.8
United Kingdom	1.7	Spain	1.4	Saudi Arabia	1.6	Viet Nam	1.7
Indonesia	1.6	Republic of Korea	1.4	Ukraine	1.3	Argentina	1.7
Austria	1.5	India	1.3	South Africa	1.2	Ukraine	1.1
Sum of above	**81.9**	**Sum of above**	**81.9**	**Sum of above**	**89.2**	**Sum of above**	**88.8**
Machinery and equipment n.e.c. (ISIC 28)							
United States of America	16.6	China	16.6	Brazil	22.0	India	20.8
Japan	15.9	Japan	15.9	India	16.2	Brazil	19.5
China	14.9	United States of America	14.9	Turkey	14.1	Turkey	7.2
Germany	13.6	Germany	13.6	Mexico	12.9	Mexico	7.0
Italy	5.7	Italy	5.7	Poland	4.8	Poland	6.0
United Kingdom	2.4	Canada	2.4	Argentina	2.0	Iran (Islamic Republic of)	6.0
Brazil	2.2	United Kingdom	2.2	Thailand	1.8	Thailand	5.4
India	2.1	France	2.1	South Africa	1.7	Argentina	4.1
France	2.0	India	2.0	Indonesia	1.7	Indonesia	3.0
Canada	1.9	Republic of Korea	1.9	Ukraine	1.4	South Africa	2.8
Russian Federation	1.6	Netherlands	1.6	Iran (Islamic Republic of)	1.3	Saudi Arabia	2.5
Republic of Korea	1.5	Brazil	1.5	Saudi Arabia	1.3	Romania	2.3
Switzerland	1.4	Russian Federation	1.4	Romania	1.2	Ukraine	1.9
Netherlands	1.3	Spain	1.3	Venezuela (Bolivarian Republic of)	1.2	Algeria	1.8
Spain	1.3	Austria	1.3	Algeria	1.1	Greece	1.5
Sum of above	**84.4**	**Sum of above**	**84.7**	**Sum of above**	**84.7**	**Sum of above**	**90.6**

a/ China is presented only among "World", depending on data availability.
b/ In world total value added at constant 2010 prices.
c/ In total value added of developing and emerging industrial economies at constant 2010 prices.

Table 1.7

MAJOR PRODUCERS IN SELECTED DIVISIONS, 2010 AND 2017 [a/]

World				Developing & emerging industrial economies			
2010		2017		2010		2017	
Economy	Share b/ (percentage)	Economy	Share b/ (percentage)	Economy	Share c/ (percentage)	Economy	Share c/ (percentage)
Motor vehicles, trailers and semi-trailers (ISIC 29)							
Japan	20.4	Japan	15.9	Brazil	21.4	Mexico	23.0
United States of America	14.0	United States of America	15.4	Mexico	17.0	Indonesia	16.8
Germany	13.8	China	15.2	Indonesia	14.1	Brazil	10.3
China	9.7	Germany	12.7	Thailand	9.4	India	8.7
Mexico	4.9	Mexico	5.0	India	9.4	Thailand	8.3
Indonesia	3.9	Indonesia	3.6	Turkey	5.6	Turkey	7.2
United Kingdom	3.2	United Kingdom	2.5	Iran (Islamic Republic of)	4.9	Iran (Islamic Republic of)	7.1
Brazil	2.5	Brazil	2.2	Poland	4.3	Poland	5.1
Italy	2.2	Italy	2.0	Venezuela (Bolivarian Republic of)	2.6	Romania	3.1
France	2.1	France	2.0	Argentina	2.2	Philippines	1.9
India	2.1	India	1.9	Romania	2.0	Venezuela (Bolivarian Republic of)	1.8
Thailand	2.1	Thailand	1.8	South Africa	1.9	South Africa	1.6
Republic of Korea	2.1	Republic of Korea	1.8	Philippines	1.6	Argentina	1.1
Spain	1.8	Spain	1.7	Pakistan	0.7	Pakistan	0.8
Turkey	1.3	Turkey	1.6	Colombia	0.5	Viet Nam	0.7
Sum of above	**86.1**	**Sum of above**	**85.3**	**Sum of above**	**97.6**	**Sum of above**	**97.5**
Other transport equipment (ISIC 30)							
United States of America	39.4	United States of America	37.4	Indonesia	22.4	India	21.6
China	8.3	China	11.6	India	17.4	Indonesia	15.1
Japan	7.3	Japan	6.7	Brazil	12.2	Brazil	8.6
Germany	4.5	Germany	5.7	Argentina	7.0	Turkey	7.7
United Kingdom	4.4	United Kingdom	4.9	Turkey	5.7	Philippines	7.1
France	4.1	France	4.8	Philippines	5.3	Poland	6.2
India	3.6	India	3.0	Ukraine	5.0	Argentina	6.2
Italy	3.2	Italy	2.5	Poland	3.9	Romania	3.5
Indonesia	2.8	Indonesia	2.1	Thailand	3.8	Viet Nam	3.4
Republic of Korea	2.5	Republic of Korea	2.0	Romania	2.4	Thailand	3.1
Singapore	1.8	Singapore	1.5	Viet Nam	2.2	Mexico	3.1
Spain	1.7	Spain	1.3	Mexico	2.0	Ukraine	2.3
Brazil	1.7	Brazil	1.2	South Africa	1.4	Iran (Islamic Republic of)	1.5
Turkey	1.1	Turkey	1.1	Croatia	1.2	Angola	1.5
Argentina	1.0	Philippines	1.0	Iran (Islamic Republic of)	0.9	South Africa	1.1
Sum of above	**87.4**	**Sum of above**	**86.8**	**Sum of above**	**92.8**	**Sum of above**	**92.0**

a/ China is presented only among "World", depending on data availability.
b/ In world total value added at constant 2010 prices.
c/ In total value added of developing and emerging industrial economies at constant 2010 prices.

Table 1.7

MAJOR PRODUCERS IN SELECTED DIVISIONS, 2010 AND 2017[a/]

Furniture (ISIC 31)

World 2010 Economy	Share [b/] (percentage)	World 2017 Economy	Share [b/] (percentage)	Developing & emerging 2010 Economy	Share [c/] (percentage)	Developing & emerging 2017 Economy	Share [c/] (percentage)
United States of America	21.2	United States of America	20.8	Brazil	16.4	Poland	16.9
Germany	8.3	China	12.3	Poland	12.1	Turkey	11.1
China	7.4	Germany	7.1	Turkey	10.0	Brazil	10.7
Italy	6.5	Italy	4.8	Indonesia	8.2	Indonesia	7.6
Japan	5.3	Japan	4.7	Thailand	5.5	Nigeria	7.4
Brazil	3.6	Poland	4.1	Nigeria	5.2	Philippines	5.7
United Kingdom	3.6	United Kingdom	3.6	Mexico	3.9	Dominican Republic	3.6
Spain	3.3	Canada	2.8	Dominican Republic	3.5	Romania	3.4
Canada	3.1	Turkey	2.7	Argentina	3.3	Mexico	2.9
Poland	2.7	Brazil	2.6	Romania	3.2	India	2.9
France	2.6	Spain	2.2	India	3.1	Thailand	2.8
Turkey	2.2	France	2.0	Viet Nam	3.0	Argentina	2.5
Indonesia	1.8	Indonesia	1.8	Greece	2.4	Viet Nam	2.3
Russian Federation	1.5	Nigeria	1.8	South Africa	2.0	South Africa	1.6
Austria	1.4	Philippines	1.4	Colombia	1.5	Chile	1.4
Sum of above	**74.5**	**Sum of above**	**74.7**	**Sum of above**	**83.3**	**Sum of above**	**82.8**

Other manufacturing (ISIC 32)

World 2010 Economy	Share [b/] (percentage)	World 2017 Economy	Share [b/] (percentage)	Developing & emerging 2010 Economy	Share [c/] (percentage)	Developing & emerging 2017 Economy	Share [c/] (percentage)
United States of America	38.3	United States of America	31.8	Brazil	14.5	Mexico	14.9
Japan	9.2	China	14.5	Mexico	13.4	Thailand	12.8
China	8.9	Germany	9.7	India	11.9	India	12.0
Germany	8.8	Japan	7.5	Thailand	10.5	Brazil	10.7
Italy	3.7	Italy	3.3	Turkey	7.2	Poland	6.8
France	2.9	Ireland	3.0	Indonesia	6.7	Turkey	6.7
United Kingdom	2.7	France	2.8	South Africa	5.2	Indonesia	4.4
Ireland	2.3	United Kingdom	2.8	Argentina	4.5	Nigeria	4.3
Brazil	1.7	Mexico	1.8	Poland	4.4	Argentina	3.7
Mexico	1.6	Thailand	1.5	Nigeria	2.8	South Africa	3.6
India	1.4	India	1.4	Saudi Arabia	2.7	Saudi Arabia	3.4
Thailand	1.2	Brazil	1.3	Peru	1.9	Viet Nam	2.0
Spain	1.2	Denmark	1.3	Colombia	1.7	United Republic of Tanzania	1.9
Switzerland	1.2	Spain	1.2	Greece	1.5	Peru	1.5
Russian Federation	0.9	Switzerland	1.2	Viet Nam	1.2	Colombia	1.4
Sum of above	**86.0**	**Sum of above**	**85.1**	**Sum of above**	**90.1**	**Sum of above**	**90.1**

a/ China is presented only among "World", depending on data availability.
b/ In world total value added at constant 2010 prices.
c/ In total value added of developing and emerging industrial economies at constant 2010 prices.

Table 1.8

STRUCTURE OF MVA IN SELECTED COUNTRY GROUPS, SELECTED YEARS [a]
(Percentage)

| ISIC Division | Year | Industrialized Economies | | | | | | | Developing & Emerging Industrial Economies | | | |
| | | Europe | | East Asia | West Asia | North America | Others | All Economies | Emerging Industrial Economies [c] | Other Developing Economies | Least Developed Countries | All Economies |
		EU [b]	Other									
10 Food products	2005	9.8	11.7	8.5	8.4	10.9	15.0	10.1	14.9	24.6	15.8	13.4
	2010	10.6	12.2	8.7	7.8	12.1	14.9	10.8	15.3	24.9	18.9	12.7
	2017	10.2	12.4	8.6	8.0	12.2	15.8	10.7	16.0	26.8	22.2	12.2
11 Beverages	2005	2.3	1.6	2.1	2.1	2.1	3.2	2.2	3.5	6.4	5.3	3.3
	2010	2.3	1.7	2.1	2.0	2.3	3.2	2.2	3.7	6.9	4.3	3.2
	2017	2.1	1.8	2.0	2.0	2.5	3.4	2.2	3.6	7.3	4.0	3.0
12 Tobacco products	2005	0.5	0.7	0.5	0.0	1.8	1.1	0.9	1.5	2.4	7.6	2.2
	2010	0.4	0.7	0.5	0.0	1.4	1.1	0.8	1.5	3.0	6.4	2.2
	2017	0.2	0.8	0.6	0.0	1.0	1.1	0.6	1.4	3.0	7.1	2.0
13 Textiles	2005	1.8	1.0	1.3	0.1	1.9	1.3	1.6	3.6	5.7	14.8	4.6
	2010	1.4	0.8	1.1	0.1	1.2	1.1	1.2	3.2	5.8	15.8	4.3
	2017	1.2	0.7	1.0	0.1	1.0	0.9	1.1	2.6	5.4	13.9	4.0
14 Wearing apparel	2005	1.5	1.0	1.0	1.2	0.7	4.3	1.2	3.2	3.9	18.8	3.5
	2010	1.2	0.8	0.8	1.3	0.3	4.0	0.9	2.5	3.3	18.4	3.0
	2017	0.9	0.7	0.5	1.4	0.2	3.8	0.7	2.2	3.2	17.4	2.8
15 Leather and related products	2005	1.0	0.3	0.4	0.0	0.2	0.8	0.5	1.1	1.2	1.2	1.3
	2010	0.8	0.3	0.3	0.1	0.1	0.7	0.4	1.0	1.4	1.1	1.2
	2017	0.7	0.2	0.1	0.1	0.0	0.7	0.3	0.9	1.6	1.3	1.1
16 Wood products, excluding furniture	2005	2.3	3.3	1.0	1.4	2.3	3.0	2.1	1.8	1.5	1.5	1.5
	2010	2.0	2.9	0.9	1.3	1.6	2.6	1.7	1.4	1.3	1.1	1.3
	2017	1.8	2.6	0.9	1.4	2.0	2.5	1.7	1.3	1.3	0.6	1.3
17 Paper and paper products	2005	2.6	2.1	2.4	0.8	4.3	2.5	3.1	2.9	1.5	1.2	2.8
	2010	2.7	1.9	2.3	0.8	4.0	2.3	2.9	2.9	1.6	1.1	2.7
	2017	2.5	1.6	2.2	0.8	3.6	2.2	2.7	2.8	1.5	0.9	2.5

a/ Percentage shares of individual divisions in total MVA at constant 2010 prices
b/ Excluding non-industrialized EU economies.
c/ Excluding China.

Table 1.8
(continued)

STRUCTURE OF MVA IN SELECTED COUNTRY GROUPS, SELECTED YEARS [a/]
(Percentage)

| ISIC Division | Year | Industrialized Economies | | | | | | | Developing & Emerging Industrial Economies | | | |
| | | Europe | | East Asia | West Asia | North America | Others | All Economies | Emerging Industrial Economies [c/] | Other Developing Economies | Least Developed Countries | All Economies |
		EU [b/]	Other									
18 Printing and reproduction of recorded media	2005	2.3	2.6	2.6	4.7	2.5	3.4	2.5	1.4	1.1	2.1	1.2
	2010	2.2	2.3	2.5	4.4	2.2	3.0	2.3	1.4	1.1	1.5	1.1
	2017	1.7	1.9	2.0	4.6	1.9	2.8	1.9	1.2	1.1	1.3	0.9
19 Coke and refined petroleum products	2005	1.5	11.5	2.6	18.4	4.1	4.3	3.3	8.1	12.0	0.4	7.3
	2010	1.4	12.1	2.4	19.2	4.4	4.1	3.4	7.6	10.3	0.3	5.9
	2017	1.3	12.4	2.4	17.1	4.3	4.5	3.4	7.2	7.4	0.1	4.8
20 Chemicals and chemical products	2005	7.0	8.8	7.1	11.0	9.8	4.7	8.0	8.0	5.5	2.9	7.9
	2010	7.4	8.5	7.5	12.6	9.9	4.3	8.2	8.7	5.5	3.1	8.4
	2017	7.0	10.0	7.6	13.3	8.6	4.1	7.8	9.5	5.3	2.9	8.8
21 Pharmaceuticals, medicinal chemicals, etc.	2005	4.0	4.9	3.5	0.1	5.7	6.6	4.6	3.3	2.3	1.4	2.9
	2010	4.9	6.8	3.9	0.1	5.6	7.4	5.1	3.7	2.3	1.7	3.0
	2017	5.7	8.8	4.2	0.1	4.6	7.1	5.1	4.4	2.2	2.3	3.5
22 Rubber and plastics products	2005	5.0	2.3	5.5	4.5	4.8	4.4	4.9	4.6	2.9	2.0	4.0
	2010	5.0	2.7	5.2	4.2	4.3	4.2	4.7	4.6	2.6	2.0	3.8
	2017	5.1	3.1	5.0	4.3	4.6	4.2	4.8	4.5	2.5	1.6	3.6
23 Other non-metallic mineral products	2005	4.8	4.3	3.5	11.8	3.2	4.7	4.0	5.4	7.2	8.9	5.3
	2010	4.0	3.5	3.4	11.7	2.5	4.2	3.4	5.5	7.6	8.1	5.5
	2017	3.6	3.2	3.3	11.8	2.7	4.4	3.3	5.7	6.6	8.6	5.5
24 Basic metals	2005	4.2	11.2	5.8	9.3	4.1	4.7	4.9	8.5	4.7	7.9	9.9
	2010	4.0	10.4	5.5	10.1	4.2	5.3	4.9	7.6	4.6	8.2	10.1
	2017	3.8	9.5	5.2	10.2	3.9	5.0	4.6	7.5	4.4	7.7	9.9
25 Fabricated metal products, except machinery	2005	10.5	5.5	6.6	18.7	7.9	8.2	8.5	5.0	2.0	2.6	4.5
	2010	9.9	5.7	5.8	17.0	7.5	8.7	7.9	4.9	2.3	2.2	4.6
	2017	10.0	4.7	5.4	17.3	7.4	8.8	7.8	4.9	2.4	1.5	4.8

a/ Percentage shares of individual divisions in total MVA at constant 2010 prices
b/ Excluding non-industrialized EU economies.
c/ Excluding China.

Table 1.8
(continued)

STRUCTURE OF MVA IN SELECTED COUNTRY GROUPS, SELECTED YEARS [a]
(Percentage)

| ISIC Division | Year | Industrialized Economies | | | | | | | Developing & Emerging Industrial Economies | | | |
| | | Europe | | East Asia | West Asia | North America | Others | All Economies | Emerging Industrial Economies [c] | Other Developing Economies | Least Developed Countries | All Economies |
		EU [b]	Other									
26 Computer, electronic and optical products	2005	4.8	7.6	13.9	0.5	5.9	11.6	7.6	3.1	4.1	0.4	5.3
	2010	5.2	7.5	16.4	0.5	9.0	12.2	9.5	3.0	4.3	0.3	5.9
	2017	5.1	7.6	17.1	0.5	10.7	12.3	10.1	2.5	6.4	0.3	7.7
27 Electrical equipment	2005	5.6	3.5	5.1	1.1	2.8	3.5	4.3	3.2	2.2	1.5	3.5
	2010	5.7	3.6	4.9	1.1	2.5	3.4	4.3	3.6	2.1	1.9	4.0
	2017	5.3	3.4	4.7	1.2	2.5	3.4	4.1	3.3	1.9	2.5	4.1
28 Machinery and equipment n.e.c.	2005	11.6	9.0	9.7	1.2	7.3	4.4	9.3	4.0	1.6	0.7	4.7
	2010	11.8	8.7	9.7	1.1	7.3	4.7	9.4	4.4	1.4	0.6	5.8
	2017	12.3	7.6	11.4	1.2	7.2	4.6	9.9	4.2	1.4	0.4	6.1
29 Motor vehicles, trailers and semi-trailers	2005	9.9	2.1	12.3	1.2	6.8	3.1	8.8	8.2	2.4	0.5	6.5
	2010	9.5	1.8	11.2	1.1	5.7	3.3	8.0	8.9	2.5	0.7	6.9
	2017	11.5	2.1	11.2	1.1	7.6	2.9	9.3	9.8	2.5	0.7	7.3
30 Other transport equipment	2005	2.5	2.0	2.3	0.3	4.9	2.3	3.2	2.2	1.9	0.9	2.0
	2010	3.0	2.3	2.8	0.5	6.3	2.5	3.9	2.2	2.0	0.8	2.1
	2017	3.4	2.3	2.6	0.5	6.3	2.7	4.0	2.1	2.2	0.8	1.9
31 Furniture	2005	2.1	1.4	0.6	2.9	2.2	1.8	1.8	1.3	2.0	1.2	1.1
	2010	1.9	1.2	0.5	2.7	1.5	1.8	1.4	1.2	2.2	0.8	1.0
	2017	1.7	1.1	0.5	2.7	1.6	1.8	1.3	1.2	2.6	0.9	1.0
32 Other manufacturing	2005	2.4	1.6	1.7	0.3	3.8	1.1	2.6	1.2	0.9	0.4	1.3
	2010	2.7	1.6	1.6	0.3	4.1	1.0	2.7	1.2	1.0	0.7	1.3
	2017	2.9	1.5	1.5	0.3	3.6	1.0	2.6	1.2	1.0	1.0	1.2
C Total manufacturing	2005	100.0	100.0	100.0	100.0	100.0	100.0	100.0	100.0	100.0	100.0	100.0
	2010	100.0	100.0	100.0	100.0	100.0	100.0	100.0	100.0	100.0	100.0	100.0
	2017	100.0	100.0	100.0	100.0	100.0	100.0	100.0	100.0	100.0	100.0	100.0

a/ Percentage shares of individual divisions in total MVA at constant 2010 prices
b/ Excluding non-industrialized EU economies.
c/ Excluding China.

Table 1.9

ANNUAL GROWTH OF VALUE ADDED OF DIVISIONS, SELECTED COUNTRY GROUPS, 2005-2010 AND 2010-2017 [a]
(Percentage)

ISIC Division	Industrialized Economies		Developing & Emerging Industrial Economies						World	
			Emerging Industrial Economies [b]		Other Developing Economies		Least Developed Countries			
	2005-2010	2010-2017	2005-2010	2010-2017	2005-2010	2010-2017	2005-2010	2010-2017	2005-2010	2010-2017
10 Food products	0.3	1.1	3.3	2.6	3.2	6.3	13.2	11.9	2.2	2.7
11 Beverages	-0.3	1.1	3.8	1.7	4.1	6.2	6.6	7.6	2.3	2.7
12 Tobacco products	-5.1	-2.1	3.3	1.1	7.3	5.1	4.7	10.0	1.5	2.0
13 Textiles	-7.6	-0.8	-0.5	-0.4	2.9	4.6	10.0	6.6	-0.1	3.0
14 Wearing apparel	-7.0	-3.0	-3.4	0.1	-0.6	4.7	8.1	7.8	-1.1	2.1
15 Leather and related products	-6.1	-1.3	-1.5	0.4	5.4	7.6	6.3	10.0	0.0	2.5
16 Wood products, excluding furniture	-6.3	1.4	-2.5	1.4	0.4	5.3	3.2	1.3	-3.9	2.7
17 Paper and paper products	-2.5	0.0	2.7	1.8	3.7	3.9	6.0	5.4	0.1	1.6
18 Printing and reproduction of recorded media	-2.8	-1.7	2.4	-0.2	1.1	6.8	2.1	6.1	-1.6	-0.5
19 Coke and refined petroleum products	-0.2	0.9	1.8	1.7	-1.0	0.3	0.7	-1.0	1.0	1.8
20 Chemicals and chemical products	-1.2	0.3	4.3	3.4	2.6	6.7	10.0	6.6	1.6	2.8
21 Pharmaceuticals, medicinal chemicals, etc.	0.7	1.4	5.3	4.8	2.9	6.4	12.3	14.6	2.3	3.2
22 Rubber and plastics products	-3.1	1.4	2.9	1.4	1.5	4.1	14.2	6.0	-0.8	2.4
23 Other non-metallic mineral products	-5.2	0.6	2.5	2.7	3.9	2.9	6.8	10.2	-0.4	3.1
24 Basic metals	-3.0	-0.1	-0.2	1.5	1.2	4.9	9.3	8.8	1.6	3.0
25 Fabricated metal products, except machinery	-3.3	0.6	1.6	1.4	5.2	5.4	5.5	2.7	-1.4	2.0
26 Computer, electronic and optical products	2.2	2.0	1.7	-0.9	3.3	10.5	7.4	12.9	3.8	4.1
27 Electrical equipment	-2.6	0.1	5.0	1.3	1.5	4.2	13.2	14.9	0.8	2.4
28 Machinery and equipment n.e.c.	-2.6	0.9	3.6	1.0	-0.1	5.5	4.7	4.5	0.1	2.2
29 Motor vehicles, trailers and semi-trailers	-5.3	3.5	3.8	2.8	3.1	5.4	12.8	12.4	-2.0	4.3
30 Other transport equipment	3.0	1.6	3.9	0.7	3.2	5.9	5.5	14.7	4.0	2.1
31 Furniture	-6.3	0.6	1.6	1.7	4.3	7.9	-0.2	8.8	-3.7	2.0
32 Other manufacturing	-0.8	0.8	2.7	2.2	4.3	5.0	20.8	13.0	0.4	2.0

a/ At constant 2010 prices.
b/ Excluding China.
c/ Including China.

Table 1.9
(continued)

ANNUAL GROWTH OF VALUE ADDED OF DIVISIONS, SELECTED COUNTRY GROUPS, 2005-2010 AND 2010-2017 [a]
(Percentage)

ISIC Division	All Economies		Developing & Emerging Industrial Economies							
			Africa		Asia and Pacific [c]		Europe		Latin America	
	2005-2010	2010-2017	2005-2010	2010-2017	2005-2010	2010-2017	2005-2010	2010-2017	2005-2010	2010-2017
10 Food products	5.6	4.9	5.7	5.8	9.2	7.2	3.3	2.5	2.2	1.4
11 Beverages	6.2	4.6	5.1	5.6	10.9	7.8	1.8	-0.3	4.1	2.0
12 Tobacco products	7.4	4.1	2.6	-0.7	9.8	4.6	-2.2	4.6	2.2	2.2
13 Textiles	5.3	4.6	4.1	3.7	8.0	5.7	-5.0	1.9	-1.3	-3.0
14 Wearing apparel	3.1	4.2	-0.9	0.6	6.5	6.0	-5.9	0.8	0.6	-2.7
15 Leather and related products	5.0	4.4	-1.1	3.9	10.0	6.2	-3.6	-0.9	-2.8	-1.5
16 Wood products, excluding furniture	3.5	5.2	-1.5	4.1	8.1	7.8	2.8	3.4	-2.0	-0.2
17 Paper and paper products	6.6	4.3	3.3	0.9	9.4	5.4	3.6	4.9	2.7	2.0
18 Printing and reproduction of recorded media	4.5	3.4	-1.0	0.8	8.1	6.7	2.8	2.1	2.0	-2.3
19 Coke and refined petroleum products	2.5	2.7	3.4	1.0	4.8	5.3	-2.3	4.6	-0.1	-1.5
20 Chemicals and chemical products	7.8	6.5	4.3	3.1	10.5	8.3	2.1	2.0	2.0	0.3
21 Pharmaceuticals, medicinal chemicals, etc.	7.9	7.8	5.0	4.0	11.2	10.9	6.8	6.5	2.6	-1.2
22 Rubber and plastics products	5.9	4.3	4.1	1.9	8.1	5.8	4.0	4.3	2.1	-0.1
23 Other non-metallic mineral products	7.2	5.5	0.2	0.6	11.8	7.7	-0.1	2.6	3.2	0.3
24 Basic metals	6.7	5.4	-1.7	-1.3	11.3	6.8	-1.2	1.1	-5.3	-1.8
25 Fabricated metal products, except machinery	6.5	5.7	1.1	3.2	10.8	8.4	2.2	4.4	1.2	-2.1
26 Computer, electronic and optical products	9.0	9.1	3.0	5.5	10.9	9.9	-5.7	4.9	-1.1	-4.6
27 Electrical equipment	9.8	6.1	-4.7	-1.1	13.9	7.6	7.2	4.7	0.7	-0.8
28 Machinery and equipment n.e.c.	11.0	5.6	-2.4	0.4	16.4	7.4	1.2	3.2	1.7	-2.7
29 Motor vehicles, trailers and semi-trailers	7.5	5.8	-1.0	3.0	11.5	8.2	4.5	6.7	2.8	-0.1
30 Other transport equipment	8.3	3.7	-0.7	10.8	10.9	4.7	-0.7	1.6	8.9	-1.3
31 Furniture	4.5	4.8	3.2	5.7	8.0	7.2	1.7	5.1	2.1	-1.2
32 Other manufacturing	6.1	5.8	2.8	3.3	9.2	7.8	2.7	3.1	1.0	0.5

a/ At constant 2010 prices.
b/ Excluding China.
c/ Including China.

Table 1.10

SHARE OF FEMALES IN TOTAL EMPLOYMENT BY DIVISION, SELECTED YEARS
(Percentage)

ISIC Revision 4	Armenia 2013	Armenia 2016	Azerbaijan 2012	Azerbaijan 2016	Bulgaria 2012	Bulgaria 2016	China 2013	China 2016	Colombia 2012	Colombia 2016
10 Food products	45.1	50.3	28.2	28.1	51.6	52.8	43.8	45.4	31.7	34.0
11 Beverages	31.7	32.6	23.4	23.5	37.8	37.9	35.8	36.4	36.1	21.5
12 Tobacco products	55.0	50.0	18.4	20.5	46.7	47.5	35.9	33.5	25.0	...
13 Textiles	58.1	70.7	45.1	32.4	65.7	64.0	60.0	61.2	40.0	35.9
14 Wearing apparel	70.5	86.8	52.0	54.8	88.5	88.1	66.6	68.2	75.7	70.8
15 Leather and related products	37.6	36.5	37.1	30.3	81.1	81.1	56.6	57.1	52.6	50.7
16 Wood products, excluding furniture	5.9	16.4	25.4	36.4	23.5	22.1	40.2	43.0	16.7	18.4
17 Paper and paper products	44.5	40.6	34.6	29.5	46.4	44.3	37.5	38.7	22.5	24.6
18 Printing and reproduction of recorded media	37.8	47.4	33.1	31.2	45.1	45.2	43.5	43.6	43.5	41.4
19 Coke and refined petroleum products	...	...	34.0	33.6	22.0	18.7	25.3	25.9	16.4	18.7
20 Chemicals and chemical products	29.2	28.4	36.7	27.8	43.1	44.4	30.8	31.8	44.1	42.2
21 Pharmaceuticals, medicinal chemicals, etc.	56.0	61.8	49.7	47.8	55.3	54.8	45.4	46.5	55.8	54.6
22 Rubber and plastics products	15.8	22.4	18.7	22.2	39.6	39.6	40.9	41.3	37.8	36.5
23 Other non-metallic mineral products	17.7	17.2	14.7	11.6	27.7	26.9	27.9	28.8	12.8	13.7
24 Basic metals	13.1	11.5	12.5	15.0	22.5	21.7	20.2	20.8	13.3	13.2
25 Fabricated metal products, except machinery	29.5	22.6	18.7	15.5	28.6	31.1	29.8	31.1	18.7	18.3
26 Computer, electronic and optical products	34.9	33.9	30.4	30.7	54.3	52.4	48.1	45.8	50.7	...
27 Electrical equipment	27.1	29.6	17.5	11.2	42.3	43.8	40.7	41.1	33.1	25.4
28 Machinery and equipment n.e.c.	19.9	31.6	9.8	22.7	24.7	24.3	25.5	26.7	19.1	19.8
29 Motor vehicles, trailers and semi-trailers	...	...	20.0	14.0	65.8	60.5	27.2	27.8	15.5	21.3
30 Other transport equipment	...	9.1	21.1	28.1	21.0	22.8	24.8	26.8	21.8	23.9
31 Furniture	38.5	22.3	19.2	18.8	32.7	32.2	34.2	34.7	27.0	27.2
32 Other manufacturing	28.5	34.3	14.2	25.2	52.6	49.9	55.2	55.5	56.6	39.9
33 Repair and installation of machinery/equipment	21.3	19.6	12.7	8.7	17.2	17.8	18.9	16.5	...	...
C Total manufacturing	34.4	39.5	23.9	23.1	50.5	49.3	39.2	39.8	36.6	35.9

Table 1.10

SHARE OF FEMALES IN TOTAL EMPLOYMENT BY DIVISION, SELECTED YEARS
(Percentage)

ISIC Revision 4	Cyprus		Ecuador		Egypt		Georgia		India	
	2012	2016	2012	2016	2012	2015	2012	2016	2012	2015
10 Food products	51.3	49.7	31.1	29.4	11.3	10.2	42.4	46.4	16.4	14.6
11 Beverages	20.0	24.7	12.6	17.7	8.1	8.0	32.7	32.5	5.4	5.7
12 Tobacco products	...	...	11.1	9.1	12.8	12.7	32.8	35.5	14.5	34.3
13 Textiles	60.6	43.9	22.8	16.7	13.1	12.8	39.6	53.2	13.2	13.7
14 Wearing apparel	89.9	95.4	70.9	61.7	51.2	49.4	83.6	86.8	36.6	39.2
15 Leather and related products	65.6	45.8	21.9	16.3	13.2	12.7	21.9	31.9	24.5	29.6
16 Wood products, excluding furniture	9.9	12.4	10.2	7.8	2.7	2.2	12.8	15.8	3.7	5.3
17 Paper and paper products	31.3	37.7	26.5	24.1	4.5	3.5	31.4	27.3	6.5	7.2
18 Printing and reproduction of recorded media	33.5	31.7	36.2	35.2	7.9	10.0	40.4	39.0	4.4	6.2
19 Coke and refined petroleum products	...	...	19.9	20.0	10.5	12.4	...	...	1.2	0.9
20 Chemicals and chemical products	33.8	31.1	28.4	28.2	7.2	8.6	29.2	33.7	8.6	7.6
21 Pharmaceuticals, medicinal chemicals, etc.	61.1	58.8	43.0	41.7	32.6	31.3	61.8	66.8	5.0	4.5
22 Rubber and plastics products	27.7	26.7	14.8	13.4	9.6	6.0	19.1	22.5	4.8	4.5
23 Other non-metallic mineral products	15.9	15.3	17.4	16.2	5.2	4.5	10.5	10.5	3.2	3.2
24 Basic metals	18.4	20.6	15.6	9.5	2.1	1.9	11.8	11.4	0.8	0.9
25 Fabricated metal products, except machinery	12.5	13.2	10.7	9.2	7.4	6.6	9.5	12.2	1.8	2.1
26 Computer, electronic and optical products	...	...	25.5	19.0	30.1	21.1	31.2	24.6	10.8	8.3
27 Electrical equipment	...	...	11.0	17.7	7.2	6.9	16.5	16.9	5.2	5.3
28 Machinery and equipment n.e.c.	25.1	28.2	14.4	13.2	6.5	7.7	13.2	12.7	1.3	1.2
29 Motor vehicles, trailers and semi-trailers	9.5	15.4	13.7	10.3	4.5	3.2	...	...	2.6	2.3
30 Other transport equipment	29.4	21.6	...	12.8	3.5	6.1	22.5	24.8	1.0	1.2
31 Furniture	27.9	25.2	25.7	22.0	3.2	4.0	16.6	15.9	2.7	3.2
32 Other manufacturing	57.1	45.8	50.0	48.5	22.1	20.3	48.9	48.7	11.7	12.3
33 Repair and installation of machinery/equipment	14.1	8.6	...	11.2	5.2	6.4	18.4	20.6	1.7	1.5
C Total manufacturing	35.0	35.1	26.8	25.3	13.6	12.9	30.0	34.8	9.8	10.9

Table 1.10

SHARE OF FEMALES IN TOTAL EMPLOYMENT BY DIVISION, SELECTED YEARS
(Percentage)

ISIC Revision 4	Iran (Islamic Republic of) 2012	Iran (Islamic Republic of) 2015	Jordan 2012	Jordan 2016	Kazakhstan 2012	Kazakhstan 2016	Kuwait 2012	Kuwait 2016	Kyrgyzstan 2012	Kyrgyzstan 2016
10 Food products	16.2	14.8	7.7	8.5	51.8	49.6	7.2	6.7	37.2	41.8
11 Beverages	8.0	7.5	9.3	8.7	41.0	36.3	1.1	1.7	35.2	29.2
12 Tobacco products	12.1	13.6	28.9	18.6	33.9	35.5	...	...	46.6	41.5
13 Textiles	11.8	12.1	6.9	8.9	37.3	34.4	0.9	0.9	43.7	59.0
14 Wearing apparel	51.5	59.1	55.2	42.4	85.4	82.8	10.6	7.9	61.9	83.1
15 Leather and related products	12.8	13.5	4.0	4.4	63.5	62.1	0.9	4.2	35.5	30.4
16 Wood products, excluding furniture	5.4	5.2	0.4	0.6	20.5	25.1	0.3	0.3	4.2	10.5
17 Paper and paper products	14.7	15.7	12.9	14.2	35.1	31.0	2.0	1.8	27.2	25.4
18 Printing and reproduction of recorded media	11.4	13.3	15.5	9.2	51.9	51.5	6.7	6.4	36.1	37.8
19 Coke and refined petroleum products	5.6	5.2	10.8	4.2	23.2	23.7	3.2	9.6	21.2	15.4
20 Chemicals and chemical products	9.9	9.5	12.0	12.8	30.5	28.7	4.1	4.6	24.8	29.2
21 Pharmaceuticals, medicinal chemicals, etc.	22.8	22.3	36.3	25.8	66.1	62.1	...	...	31.6	48.8
22 Rubber and plastics products	12.0	12.4	7.4	6.9	26.3	23.5	1.3	1.6	20.4	23.6
23 Other non-metallic mineral products	5.7	5.8	2.9	1.8	21.8	20.9	1.0	1.0	19.3	19.4
24 Basic metals	3.4	3.8	2.6	1.6	29.9	28.3	0.8	1.6	8.6	8.1
25 Fabricated metal products, except machinery	6.4	6.8	1.7	2.4	24.3	22.9	1.2	0.8	36.2	42.4
26 Computer, electronic and optical products	24.2	22.8	20.3	12.2	37.4	34.3	0.5	0.6	...	11.0
27 Electrical equipment	22.4	15.9	5.1	4.7	26.6	24.9	4.1	1.3	44.5	48.8
28 Machinery and equipment n.e.c.	7.5	9.6	3.7	4.1	28.0	29.6	1.3	1.1	16.2	24.0
29 Motor vehicles, trailers and semi-trailers	5.3	9.0	4.4	4.1	22.5	24.5	1.3	0.8	37.8	21.6
30 Other transport equipment	4.4	5.7	...	...	28.1	28.2	1.3	1.3	...	...
31 Furniture	9.5	7.9	2.1	1.8	32.7	39.2	0.8	1.0	46.7	29.4
32 Other manufacturing	21.6	19.4	13.9	13.3	48.1	46.2	0.3	0.3	68.9	51.3
33 Repair and installation of machinery/equipment	...	...	0.8	0.8	20.6	18.3	...	...	...	21.1
C Total manufacturing	10.2	10.5	20.0	14.4	32.8	31.1	4.0	3.7	30.6	31.0

Table 1.10

SHARE OF FEMALES IN TOTAL EMPLOYMENT BY DIVISION, SELECTED YEARS
(Percentage)

ISIC Revision 4	Lithuania		Malaysia		Mexico		Oman		Philippines	
	2012	2016	2012	2015	2012	2016	2012	2016	2012	2015
10 Food products	58.9	59.3	32.2	33.1	33.1	35.1	8.3	8.0	38.3	36.5
11 Beverages	38.4	36.9	29.9	30.8	12.4	11.6	2.2	3.8	20.4	24.3
12 Tobacco products	...	...	30.8	34.9	22.8	21.7	...	...	34.0	25.0
13 Textiles	68.0	68.4	37.4	33.8	30.4	29.6	14.2	12.1	49.1	46.9
14 Wearing apparel	88.4	88.7	71.6	68.9	57.6	56.3	32.5	41.7	68.4	66.7
15 Leather and related products	65.5	66.4	38.1	32.4	38.9	39.1	30.8	25.0	50.5	54.1
16 Wood products, excluding furniture	23.5	25.5	24.0	22.9	15.1	16.1	0.8	2.5	20.8	23.4
17 Paper and paper products	43.8	42.6	28.0	28.9	22.9	22.4	7.1	4.6	30.5	25.8
18 Printing and reproduction of recorded media	43.0	45.6	34.3	32.9	40.4	39.2	10.1	12.3	33.7	37.2
19 Coke and refined petroleum products	...	...	11.7	16.4	19.1	19.6	6.8	8.8	26.8	23.8
20 Chemicals and chemical products	32.7	35.7	25.9	26.7	25.7	25.3	5.9	6.3	31.5	29.9
21 Pharmaceuticals,medicinal chemicals, etc.	63.3	...	47.9	41.2	43.5	45.5	11.8	22.4	45.1	42.1
22 Rubber and plastics products	31.8	33.8	33.1	31.1	38.5	39.2	5.4	7.4	31.9	38.2
23 Other non-metallic mineral products	24.8	23.7	18.8	18.1	14.5	16.1	2.1	3.0	16.8	19.0
24 Basic metals	21.2	20.7	17.3	18.9	10.2	12.3	2.3	3.7	19.3	20.2
25 Fabricated metal products, except machinery	18.0	17.5	22.1	21.9	17.4	19.1	2.7	3.8	25.2	26.6
26 Computer, electronic and optical products	36.1	36.8	58.2	55.7	52.9	51.5	5.7	4.3	73.3	70.2
27 Electrical equipment	50.0	48.3	42.5	38.0	37.1	36.0	4.4	3.5	50.7	56.9
28 Machinery and equipment n.e.c.	27.2	25.3	26.0	23.0	21.4	24.4	5.6	3.0	30.2	33.7
29 Motor vehicles, trailers and semi-trailers	48.7	58.9	20.9	21.8	35.4	38.0	9.8	13.4	55.8	56.1
30 Other transport equipment	24.4	23.8	17.5	17.4	27.9	29.0	0.0	2.8	30.4	25.8
31 Furniture	39.3	41.9	18.0	20.3	24.6	27.7	3.9	4.7	28.3	24.5
32 Other manufacturing	50.7	52.6	49.9	43.8	56.0	55.7	18.4	5.3	53.2	56.6
33 Repair and installation of machinery/equipment	15.4	15.5	15.6	18.9	...	...	1.2	1.7	11.2	12.2
C Total manufacturing	44.6	44.8	34.7	33.0	33.9	35.0	4.6	5.2	47.3	47.1

Table 1.10

SHARE OF FEMALES IN TOTAL EMPLOYMENT BY DIVISION, SELECTED YEARS
(Percentage)

ISIC Revision 4	Qatar		Sri Lanka		Turkey		United Republic of Tanzania		Viet Nam	
	2012	2016	2012	2015	2012	2015	2012	2016	2012	2016
10 Food products	3.0	6.7	43.1	48.7	25.5	29.2	32.9	27.4	50.8	49.6
11 Beverages	...	2.3	29.0	28.9	14.3	15.4	25.2	27.5	37.9	36.6
12 Tobacco products	...	...	...	62.8	25.9	23.8	42.2	33.4	40.1	35.1
13 Textiles	...	0.2	52.3	52.2	25.7	27.3	44.9	41.5	53.0	55.3
14 Wearing apparel	2.3	1.2	75.5	69.9	44.8	49.7	32.4	71.4	81.0	79.9
15 Leather and related products	4.8	...	51.8	51.4	17.7	20.5	26.8	34.1	79.0	78.5
16 Wood products, excluding furniture	0.5	0.5	38.4	5.7	8.4	10.1	10.6	17.0	39.5	40.4
17 Paper and paper products	0.6	0.4	29.6	21.4	16.2	18.9	23.8	15.5	41.3	38.8
18 Printing and reproduction of recorded media	4.3	4.5	22.8	35.6	21.9	23.5	34.0	32.2	46.0	45.6
19 Coke and refined petroleum products	3.9	3.1	15.2	14.0	14.0	14.0	22.1	8.6	21.9	21.9
20 Chemicals and chemical products	4.6	4.8	36.1	21.7	23.0	24.0	44.1	42.9	31.3	30.7
21 Pharmaceuticals, medicinal chemicals, etc.	...	10.2	...	44.4	31.6	33.7	42.9	44.8	54.2	52.1
22 Rubber and plastics products	1.0	0.7	32.3	35.7	14.9	18.3	26.1	25.9	46.8	45.9
23 Other non-metallic mineral products	0.9	0.7	21.5	23.9	10.5	12.6	9.5	21.0	31.5	29.9
24 Basic metals	1.7	1.2	11.7	25.3	6.7	7.7	7.5	3.1	20.8	19.6
25 Fabricated metal products, except machinery	0.3	0.7	29.2	33.6	11.0	12.5	9.7	19.0	29.3	27.4
26 Computer, electronic and optical products	4.5	...	49.7	54.9	27.5	31.4	...	11.1	77.1	76.8
27 Electrical equipment	1.3	0.5	34.9	44.1	19.3	21.5	16.0	24.6	61.6	58.1
28 Machinery and equipment n.e.c.	0.8	0.3	9.9	11.5	11.4	12.0	5.6	24.8	32.8	35.4
29 Motor vehicles, trailers and semi-trailers	...	...	6.9	30.2	15.7	15.9	14.6	20.5	55.0	56.3
30 Other transport equipment	3.3	2.8	35.4	49.8	10.0	11.3	14.6	16.7	26.8	27.5
31 Furniture	0.6	0.7	10.2	25.0	10.3	12.3	14.8	15.3	42.3	41.7
32 Other manufacturing	...	6.9	59.3	59.4	23.8	27.9	20.5	43.5	72.4	72.2
33 Repair and installation of machinery/equipment	...	3.8	...	40.5	7.6	7.3	9.2	10.4	15.4	15.4
C Total manufacturing	1.8	1.7	55.4	54.5	21.5	23.5	30.5	29.8	58.7	60.1

Part II
COUNTRY TABLES

Countries/areas for which data were presented in previous editions of the *Yearbook* but not in part II of the current edition

Country/area	Latest edition in which data were presented	Country/area	Latest edition in which data were presented	Country/area	Latest edition in which data were presented
Afghanistan	2016	Fiji	2018	Pakistan	2010
Algeria	2018	Gabon	1998	Papua New Guinea	2006
Angola	2018	Gambia	2012	Puerto Rico	2009
Argentina	2007	Ghana	2007	Rwanda	2002
Aruba	2004	Grenada	1999	Saint Lucia	2001
Bahamas	2018	Guatemala	2009	Saint Vincent and the Grenadines	2004
Bahrain	2018	Haiti	2001	Senegal	2015
Bangladesh	2015	Honduras	1999	Serbia and Montenegro	2005
Barbados	2001	Jamaica	2009	Sierra Leone	2011
Belize	1995	Kenya	2018	Solomon Islands	1999
Benin	2003	Lebanon	2012	Sudan	2006
Brazil	2018	Lesotho	2012	Swaziland	2016
Brunei Darussalam	2014	Madagascar	2009	Syrian Arab Republic	2013
Burkina Faso	2001	Malawi	2014	Tajikistan	2018
Burundi	2017	Malaysia	2018	Thailand	2015
Cambodia	2004	Maldives	2018	Tonga	2007
Cameroon	2012	Montenegro	2018	Trinidad and Tobago	2010
Central African Republic	1998	Morocco	2016	Turkmenistan	2003
Chad	1998	Mozambique	2003	Uganda	2009
Congo	2012	Myanmar	2016	Uruguay	2018
Cook Islands	2010	Namibia	2016	Venezuela (Bolivarian Republic of)	2002
Côte d'Ivoire	2000	Nepal	2015	Yemen	2017
El Salvador	2001	Netherlands Antilles	2011	Zimbabwe	2018
Ethiopia	2016	Nigeria	2007		

Albania

Supplier of information:
Institute of Statistics, Tirana.

Basic source of data:
Annual survey.

Major deviations from ISIC (Revision 4):
None reported.

Reference period:
Fiscal year.

Scope:
All enterprises.

Method of data collection:
Direct interview in the field.

Type of enumeration:
Sample survey for enterprises with 1-9 employees; exhaustive survey for enterprises with 10 or more employees.

Adjusted for non-response:
Yes.

Concepts and definitions of variables:
Wages and salaries includes employers' contributions (in respect of their employees) paid to social security, pension and insurance schemes as well as the benefits received by employees under these schemes and severance and termination pay.
Output includes revenue from non-industrial activities.

Related national publications:
Structural Survey Economic Enterprises, published by the Institute of Statistics, Tirana.

Albania

ISIC Revision 4

ISIC	Industry	Note	Number of enterprises (number)				Note	Number of employees (number)				Note	Wages and salaries paid to employees (millions of Albanian Leks)			
			2013	2014	2015	2016		2013	2014	2015	2016		2013	2014	2015	2016
10	Food products		3105	2456	3011	3667		7033	7197	9244	12265		2406	2183	2613	3747
11	Beverages	a/	169	163	193	165	a/	1895	2047	2043	2317	a/	868	1007	1017	1155
12	Tobacco products	a/	...	...	...	...	a/	...	...	...	...	a/	...	...	...	...
13	Textiles		79	131	180	156		376	889	981	991		115	267	313	308
14	Wearing apparel		658	560	641	732		15498	17595	19550	23083		4460	4896	5649	7052
15	Leather and related products		167	210	257	301		13910	16509	19203	21661		4136	4681	5833	6890
16	Wood products, excluding furniture		442	358	476	433		1031	1160	1167	1240		320	341	331	409
17	Paper and paper products		62	61	96	65		1566	2145	2526	2526		500	548	728	783
18	Printing and reproduction of recorded media		168	169	164	202		1112	1216	1198	1419		554	603	667	786
19	Coke and refined petroleum products		11	9	13	8		2038	1495	1365	1258		1332	1486	1134	811
20	Chemicals and chemical products	b/	75	109	102	96	b/	1042	1142	1137	1055	b/	508	546	525	557
21	Pharmaceuticals, medicinal chemicals, etc.	b/	...	...	...	...	b/	...	...	...	...	b/	...	...	...	...
22	Rubber and plastics products		118	91	120	128		1405	1038	989	1367		431	315	287	402
23	Other non-metallic mineral products		747	676	724	834		4145	4390	4186	5171		2133	2148	2105	2442
24	Basic metals		34	32	59	65		1300	1362	1150	1119		613	804	762	672
25	Fabricated metal products, except machinery	c/	1120	1006	1019	1396	c/	3786	4178	4124	5171	c/	1375	1486	1533	1959
26	Computer, electronic and optical products	c/	22	20	35	34	c/	517	525	376	643	c/	316	247	184	292
27	Electrical equipment	c/	...	...	...	...	c/	...	...	...	...	c/	...	...	...	...
28	Machinery and equipment n.e.c.	d/	14	25	61	87	d/	103	229	382	527	d/	53	100	141	239
29	Motor vehicles, trailers and semi-trailers	d/	...	...	...	...	d/	...	...	...	...	d/	...	...	...	...
30	Other transport equipment	d/	...	...	...	...	d/	...	...	...	...	d/	...	...	...	...
31	Furniture		825	841	893	892		2014	2339	2924	3218		624	648	884	1020
32	Other manufacturing		97	99	96	76		837	835	1000	995		255	272	317	332
33	Repair and installation of machinery/equipment		16	23	294	523		70	54	411	414		25	15	201	141
C	Total manufacturing	e/	7929	7039	8431	9860	e/	59678	66345	73958	86437	e/	21024	22593	25226	30000

a/ 11 includes 12.
b/ 20 includes 21.
c/ 26 includes 27.
d/ 28 includes 29 and 30.
e/ Sum of available data.

Albania

ISIC Revision 4		Output at basic prices (millions of Albanian Leks)					Value added at basic prices (millions of Albanian Leks)					Gross fixed capital formation (millions of Albanian Leks)		
ISIC	Industry	Note	2013	2014	2015	2016	Note	2013	2014	2015	2016	Note	2015	2016
10	Food products		29179	25456	29470	38053		6653	6509	7131	9316		4257	3903
11	Beverages	a/	11004	10522	11938	12129	a/	2477	3009	3727	3559	a/	1220	1659
12	Tobacco products	a/	...	...	...	...	a/	...	...	...	...	a/	...	...
13	Textiles		735	1607	1596	1372		354	816	809	670		185	382
14	Wearing apparel		14167	15887	16252	20643		9074	10475	9833	11462		1870	1660
15	Leather and related products		16820	19396	20153	23480		8118	10176	10104	11893		3424	2641
16	Wood products, excluding furniture		3707	3056	3028	3862		1030	1160	822	1153		463	152
17	Paper and paper products		2748	3808	5312	5632		859	1044	1638	1935		898	327
18	Printing and reproduction of recorded media		4988	5253	7528	7158		1883	2302	3881	3204		500	1482
19	Coke and refined petroleum products		4398	4417	2465	1265		-183	995	397	343		43	38
20	Chemicals and chemical products	b/	4322	5470	5404	4975	b/	1270	1733	2120	1639	b/	510	2351
21	Pharmaceuticals,medicinal chemicals, etc.	b/	...	...	...	...	b/	...	...	...	...	b/	...	917
22	Rubber and plastics products		4469	4467	4842	5792		1191	1105	1075	1362		636	917
23	Other non-metallic mineral products		33975	33657	32217	32057		8530	10227	8809	8879		3202	1652
24	Basic metals		25935	30026	21273	19756		6925	6876	3989	5220		737	16915
25	Fabricated metal products, except machinery		19518	18012	19925	22454		4753	5053	5145	5699		2210	2756
26	Computer, electronic and optical products	c/	1966	1220	1226	1168	c/	1032	720	527	536	c/	303	766
27	Electrical equipment	c/	...	...	...	...	c/	...	...	...	...	c/	...	...
28	Machinery and equipment n.e.c.	d/	432	659	669	677	d/	151	299	261	362	d/	159	704
29	Motor vehicles, trailers and semi-trailers	d/	...	...	...	...	d/	...	...	...	...	d/	...	...
30	Other transport equipment	d/	...	...	...	...	d/	...	...	...	...	d/	...	...
31	Furniture		6679	7047	8504	8994		1753	2384	2275	2418		499	444
32	Other manufacturing		797	887	1158	1200		502	656	702	908		82	117
33	Repair and installation of machinery/equipment		210	122	1414	1166		90	52	810	644		46	139
C	Total manufacturing	e/	186049	190969	194374	211834	e/	56462	65591	64056	71203	e/	21244	39006

a/ 11 includes 12.
b/ 20 includes 21.
c/ 26 includes 27.
d/ 28 includes 29 and 30.
e/ Sum of available data.

Albania

Index numbers of industrial production

ISIC Revision 4

(2010=100)

ISIC	Industry	Note	2005	2006	2007	2008	2009	2010	2011	2012	2013	2014	2015	2016
10	Food products	a/	63	77	79	94	94	100	102	117	107	107	123	117
11	Beverages	a/	...	...	...	...	...	...	...	...	...	...	...	...
12	Tobacco products	a/	...	...	...	...	...	...	...	...	...	...	...	...
13	Textiles	b/	75	80	77	86	87	100	114	101	114	133	134	148
14	Wearing apparel	b/	...	...	...	...	...	...	...	...	...	...	...	...
15	Leather and related products		42	52	47	61	89	100	93	87	103	124	118	127
16	Wood products, excluding furniture		52	55	66	75	95	100	139	128	119	129	138	137
17	Paper and paper products	c/	39	34	35	47	45	100	103	102	76	67	98	104
18	Printing and reproduction of recorded media	c/	...	...	...	...	...	...	...	...	...	...	...	...
19	Coke and refined petroleum products	d/	129	101	90	95	158	100	154	122	89	58	48	42
20	Chemicals and chemical products	d/	...	...	...	...	...	...	...	...	...	...	...	...
21	Pharmaceuticals,medicinal chemicals, etc.	d/	...	...	...	...	...	...	...	...	...	...	...	...
22	Rubber and plastics products	d/	...	...	...	...	...	...	...	...	...	...	...	...
23	Other non-metallic mineral products	e/	40	51	59	71	88	100	101	78	82	78	84	69
24	Basic metals	e/	69	56	78	87	75	100	115	141	150	142	160	141
25	Fabricated metal products, except machinery	e/	...	...	...	...	...	...	...	...	...	...	...	...
26	Computer, electronic and optical products	e/	...	...	...	...	...	...	...	...	...	...	...	...
27	Electrical equipment	e/	...	...	...	...	...	...	...	...	...	...	...	...
28	Machinery and equipment n.e.c.	e/	...	...	...	...	...	...	...	...	...	...	...	...
29	Motor vehicles, trailers and semi-trailers	e/	...	...	...	...	...	...	...	...	...	...	...	...
30	Other transport equipment	e/	...	...	...	...	...	...	...	...	...	...	...	...
31	Furniture	f/	76	76	95	107	95	100	92	88	89	114	108	120
32	Other manufacturing	f/	...	...	...	...	...	...	...	...	...	...	...	...
33	Repair and installation of machinery/equipment		...	...	...	...	...	...	...	...	...	...	...	...
C	Total manufacturing		54	57	61	72	82	100	109	107	106	113	122	119

a/ 10 includes 11 and 12.
b/ 13 includes 14.
c/ 17 includes 18.
d/ 19 includes 20, 21 and 22.
e/ 24 includes 25, 26, 27, 28, 29 and 30.
f/ 31 includes 32.

Armenia

Supplier of information:
National Statistical Service of the Republic of Armenia, Yerevan.

Basic source of data:
Annual survey; administrative source.

Major deviations from ISIC (Revision 4):
None reported.

Reference period:
Calendar year.

Scope:
All registered establishments.

Method of data collection:
Direct interview in the field and statistical reports from large and medium establishments.

Type of enumeration:
Complete enumeration for medium and large establishments; sample survey for small establishments.

Adjusted for non-response:
No.

Concepts and definitions of variables:
Figures for wages and salaries were computed by UNIDO from the reported monthly average wages and salaries per employee. They include employers' contributions (in respect of their employees) paid to social security, pension and insurance schemes as well as the benefits received by employees under these schemes and severance and termination pay.

Related national publications:
The Statistical Yearbook of Armenia; Socio-economic Situation of the Republic of Armenia, both published by the National Statistical Service of the Republic of Armenia, Yerevan.

Armenia

ISIC Revision 4

ISIC	Industry	Number of establishments (number)					Number of employees (number)					Wages and salaries paid to employees (millions of Armenian Drams)				
		Note	2013	2014	2015	2016	Note	2013	2014	2015	2016	Note	2013	2014	2015	2016
1010	Processing/preserving of meat		73	68	65	76		2057	2040	1940	1874		14884a/	18641a/	21498a/	2586
1020	Processing/preserving of fish, etc.		8	8	5	6		35	79	70	118		..a/	..a/	..a/	211
1030	Processing/preserving of fruit,vegetables		29	32	40	51		1418	1433	1539	1614		..a/	..a/	..a/	2692
1040	Vegetable and animal oils and fats		5	5	5	5		83	101	96	74		..a/	..a/	..a/	95
1050	Dairy products		61	66	69	81		1656	1746	1900	1927		..a/	..a/	..a/	2682
106	Grain mill products,starches and starch products		21	20	20	20		1449	1403	1336	909		..a/	..a/	..a/	1112
1061	Grain mill products		21	20	20	20		1449	1403	1336	909		...	...	...	...
1062	Starches and starch products		...	...	...	...		...	...	...	...		...	...	...	...
107	Other food products		501	598	614	618		4215	7352	7657	7322		..a/	..a/	..a/	21079
1071	Bakery products		481	493	505	504		3475	4162	4468	4372		...	...	...	...
1072	Sugar		7	3	3	3		601	220	220	221		...	...	...	...
1073	Cocoa, chocolate and sugar confectionery		13	15	15	15		139	1881	1885	1628		...	...	...	...
1074	Macaroni, noodles, couscous, etc.		...	9	8	8		...	144	148	150		...	...	...	...
1075	Prepared meals and dishes		...	17	14	14		...	29	51	74		...	...	...	...
1079	Other food products n.e.c.		...	61	69	74		...	916	885	877		...	...	...	...
1080	Prepared animal feeds		100	4	3	5		2987	169	149	237		..a/	..a/	..a/	300
110	Beverages		128	135	134	128		5874	6089	5829	5431		12236	13624	14670	14462
1101	Distilling, rectifying and blending of spirits		37	37	38	34		2192	2247	2136	1892		...	...	...	...
1102	Wines		21	23	25	25		822	903	844	829		...	...	...	...
1103	Malt liquors and malt		...	6	6	6		...	1012	902	894		...	...	...	...
1104	Soft drinks,mineral waters,other bottled waters		...	69	65	63		...	1927	1947	1816		...	...	...	...
1200	Tobacco products		4	4	4	4		1936	2330	2746	3140		4060	4640	5742	6779
131	Spinning, weaving and finishing of textiles		1	4	4	4		7	49	37	29		416b/	229b/	272b/	30
1311	Preparation and spinning of textile fibres		...	1	1	1		...	10	4	1		...	...	...	...
1312	Weaving of textiles		...	3	3	3		...	39	33	28		...	...	...	...
1313	Finishing of textiles		...	...	...	...		...	...	...	...		...	...	...	...
139	Other textiles		13	14	18	21		241	170	161	179		..b/	..b/	..b/	224
1391	Knitted and crocheted fabrics		4	4	4	4		124	65	48	46		...	...	...	...
1392	Made-up textile articles, except apparel		...	...	2	2		-	...	3	3		...	...	...	...
1393	Carpets and rugs		5	4	5	6		111	92	90	96		...	...	...	...
1394	Cordage, rope, twine and netting		...	...	...	...		...	...	...	...		...	...	...	...
1399	Other textiles n.e.c.		2	6	7	9		3	13	20	34		...	...	...	...
1410	Wearing apparel, except fur apparel		63	67	66	75		2102	2489	2525	2763		1932c/	3026c/	3187c/	3206
1420	Articles of fur		...	...	...	...		...	...	...	...		..c/	..c/	..c/	...
1430	Knitted and crocheted apparel		19	20	21	18		537	477	498	574		..c/	..c/	..c/	566
151	Leather;luggage,handbags,saddlery,harness;fur		16	17	16	14		160	155	42	111		384d/	269d/	486d/	182
1511	Tanning/dressing of leather; dressing of fur		3	4	4	3		18	43	17	45		...	...	...	...
1512	Luggage,handbags,etc.;saddlery/harness		13	13	12	11		142	112	25	66		...	...	...	...
1520	Footwear		31	30	30	35		215	264	303	281		..d/	..d/	..d/	290
1610	Sawmilling and planing of wood		18	17	15	18		610	583	589	431		330e/	572e/	1087e/	402

Code		1	2	3	4	5	6	7	8	9	10	11	12
162	Wood products, cork, straw, plaiting materials	520	…e/	…e/	…e/	368	390	407	404	58	62	59	54
1621	Veneer sheets and wood-based panels	…	…	…	…	12	13	15	14	3	4	4	3
1622	Builders' carpentry and joinery	…	…	…	…	284	312	327	1	34	37	37	34
1623	Wooden containers	…	…	…	…	32	25	32	334	3	3	3	3
1629	Other wood products;articles of cork,straw	…	…	…	…	40	40	33	21	18	18	15	13
170	Paper and paper products	2749	1579	1133	872	1037	901	932	767	49	49	47	54
1701	Pulp, paper and paperboard	…	…	…	…	256	106	110	107	4	4	3	3
1702	Corrugated paper and paperboard	…	…	…	…	432	421	353	660	13	13	12	12
1709	Other articles of paper and paperboard	…	…	…	…	349	374	469	…	32	32	32	32
181	Printing and service activities related to printing	1776	1737f/	1905f/	1560f/	1094	1090	1153	1326	120	111	112	118
1811	Printing	…	…	…	…	972	972	1025	313	103	93	94	16
1812	Service activities related to printing	…	…f/	…f/	…f/	122	118	128	883	17	18	18	84
1820	Reproduction of recorded media	…	…	…	…	1	3	4	10	1	1	1	2
1910	Coke oven products	…	…	…	…	…	…	…	…	…	…	…	…
1920	Refined petroleum products	849	…	…	…	…	…	…	…	…	…	…	…
201	Basic chemicals,fertilizers, etc.	849	3203g/	6505g/	7847g/	627	900	3043	3479	25	24	24	22
2011	Basic chemicals	…	…	…	…	184	461	744	104	19	18	17	5
2012	Fertilizers and nitrogen compounds	…	…	…	…	17	16	14	2	1	2	1	1
2013	Plastics and synthetic rubber in primary forms	…	…	…	…	426	423	2285	807	5	4	5	7
202	Other chemical products	2236	…g/	…g/	…g/	558	552	566	…	62	55	52	…
2021	Pesticides and other agrochemical products	…	…	…	…	244	262	275	…	11	13	14	…
2022	Paints,varnishes;printing ink and mastics	…	…	…	…	232	224	235	…	37	30	27	…
2023	Soap,cleaning and cosmetic preparations	…	…	…	…	82	66	56	…	14	12	11	…
2029	Other chemical products n.e.c.	…	…g/	…g/	…g/	-	93	283	…	14	1	-	…
2030	Man-made fibres	…	…	…	…	…	…	…	…	…	…	…	…
2100	Pharmaceuticals,medicinal chemicals, etc.	3051	1425	1077	899	651	609	564	527	23	21	22	19
221	Rubber products	108	3628h/	2099h/	1942h/	79	86	73	82	13	13	13	13
2211	Rubber tyres and tubes	…	…	…	…	…	…	…	…	…	…	…	…
2219	Other rubber products	…	…	…	…	79	86	73	82	13	13	13	13
2220	Plastics products	3320	…h/	…h/	…h/	2365	2478	2281	2310	195	199	193	188
2310	Glass and glass products	1312	7141i/	6736i/	8342i/	498	689	927	1028	15	15	12	13
239	Non-metallic mineral products n.e.c.	32354	…i/	…i/	…i/	3583	3719	3703	50	226	216	218	8
2391	Refractory products	…	…	…	…	18	22	27	…	3	3	2	…
2392	Clay building materials	…	…	…	…	9	15	21	…	6	6	5	…
2393	Other porcelain and ceramic products	…	…	…	…	9	8	7	…	5	5	3	…
2394	Cement, lime and plaster	…	…	…	…	1740	1814	1759	…	10	9	10	…
2395	Articles of concrete, cement and plaster	…	…	…	…	996	1118	1109	…	98	98	99	…
2396	Cutting, shaping and finishing of stone	…	…	…	…	783	705	740	…	98	89	92	…
2399	Other non-metallic mineral products n.e.c.	…	…	…	…	28	37	40	50	6	6	7	8
2410	Basic iron and steel	5510	13917j/	14066j/	12692j/	960	1202	1328	1106	12	12	11	5
2420	Basic precious and other non-ferrous metals	8253	…j/	…j/	…j/	1732	1699	1787	25	8	8	9	2
243	Casting of metals	1953	…j/	…j/	…j/	864	1138	1256	111	9	9	11	5
2431	Casting of iron and steel	…	…	…	…	862	1136	1253	…	9	7	9	…
2432	Casting of non-ferrous metals	…	…	…	…	2	2	3	…	2	2	2	…
251	Struct.metal products, tanks, reservoirs	829	1689k/	3288k/	3680k/	341	274	240	291	39	35	36	41

continued

Armenia

		Number of establishments (number)					Number of employees (number)					Wages and salaries paid to employees (millions of Armenian Drams)				
ISIC	Industry	Note	2013	2014	2015	2016	Note	2013	2014	2015	2016	Note	2013	2014	2015	2016
2511	Structural metal products		27	36	35	38		136	274	240	336		...	...	...	...
2512	Tanks, reservoirs and containers of metal		14	...	...	1		155	...	...	5		...	...	...	...
2513	Steam generators, excl. hot water boilers		...	...	...	...		...	...	...	...		...	...	...	...
2520	Weapons and ammunition		...	...	...	...		...	...	...	...		..k/	..k/	..k/	...
259	Other metal products;metal working services		59	78	77	89		598	800	634	597		..k/	..k/	..k/	3624
2591	Forging,pressing,stamping,roll-forming of metal		2	9	10	12		22	49	39	43		...	...	...	...
2592	Treatment and coating of metals; machining		4	4	4	5		47	63	44	30		...	...	...	...
2593	Cutlery, hand tools and general hardware		4	9	9	12		61	182	152	119		...	...	...	...
2599	Other fabricated metal products n.e.c.		49	56	54	60		468	506	399	405		...	...	...	...
2610	Electronic components and boards		10	8	11	12		264	228	231	242		1591m/	1701m/	1887m/	357
2620	Computers and peripheral equipment		7	6	6	7		21	16	90	112		...m/	...m/	...m/	218
2630	Communication equipment		8	7	6	7		291	280	262	235		...m/	...m/	...m/	334
2640	Consumer electronics		...	...	...	...		...	...	...	...		...m/	...m/	...m/	...
265	Measuring,testing equipment; watches, etc.		15	13	13	14		483	429	462	431		...m/	...m/	...m/	901
2651	Measuring/testing/navigating equipment,etc.		11	9	9	10		368	305	343	341		...	...	...	...
2652	Watches and clocks		4	4	4	4		115	124	119	90		...	...	...	...
2660	Irradiation/electromedical equipment,etc.		...	...	...	...		...	...	...	...		...	...	...	...
2670	Optical instruments and photographic equipment		3	3	3	4		136	132	124	117		...m/	...m/	...m/	251
2680	Magnetic and optical media		...	...	...	...		...	...	...	...		...m/	...m/	...m/	...
2710	Electric motors,generators,transformers,etc.		9	10	12	12		506	450	374	294		1698n/	1567n/	1954n/	439
2720	Batteries and accumulators		1	1	1	1		136	132	119	76		...n/	...n/	...n/	208
273	Wiring and wiring devices		11	11	11	16		64	63	69	113		...n/	...n/	...n/	134
2731	Fibre optic cables		...	...	...	...		...	...	...	...		...	...	...	...
2732	Other electronic and electric wires and cables		10	10	9	15		61	60	63	111		...	...	...	...
2733	Wiring devices		1	1	2	1		3	3	6	2		...	...	...	...
2740	Electric lighting equipment		3	3	5	7		11	7	16	26		...n/	...n/	...n/	50
2750	Domestic appliances		11	11	12	11		328	297	311	303		...n/	...n/	...n/	684
2790	Other electrical equipment		12	13	12	14		337	291	228	252		...n/	...n/	...n/	357
281	General-purpose machinery		9	25	23	24		118	196	154	146		1747p/	1482p/	1617p/	447
2811	Engines/turbines,excl.aircraft,vehicle engines		1	1	1	1		7	7	5	5		...	...	...	...
2812	Fluid power equipment		3	3	3	3		46	41	23	16		...	...	...	...
2813	Other pumps, compressors, taps and valves		1	1	1	1		23	21	22	12		...	...	...	...
2814	Bearings, gears, gearing and driving elements		1	3	3	3		24	18	11	8		...	...	...	...
2815	Ovens, furnaces and furnace burners		3	3	3	3		18	19	18	13		...	...	...	...
2816	Lifting and handling equipment		...	...	...	1		...	...	...	9		...	...	...	...
2817	Office machinery, excl.computers,etc.		...	7	7	6		...	42	41	33		...	...	...	...
2818	Power-driven hand tools		...	2	2	2		...	33	29	24		...	...	...	...
2819	Other general-purpose machinery		...	5	3	3		...	15	5	5		...	...	...	...
282	Special-purpose machinery		20	25	24	23		141	719	800	722		...p/	...p/	...p/	3443
2821	Agricultural and forestry machinery		4	1	1	1		25	3	3	2		...	...	...	...
2822	Metal-forming machinery and machine tools		...	5	4	4		...	137	122	84		...	...	...	...

ISIC	Activity												
2823	Machinery for metallurgy	9	3	2	2	43	47	45	31	...	...	...	...
2824	Mining, quarrying and construction machinery	2	1	1	-	38	5	4	-	...	...	...	...
2825	Food/beverage/tobacco processing machinery	1	...	...	...	28	...	...	...	...	...	...	...
2826	Textile/apparel/leather production machinery	...	...	...	...	...	...	...	...	...	...	...	...
2829	Other special-purpose machinery	4	15	16	16	7	527	626	605	...	...	...	...
2910	Motor vehicles	...	...	...	...	...	...	...	...	-q/	-q/	-q/	-q/
2920	Automobile bodies, trailers and semi-trailers	...	...	...	...	...	...	...	...	...q/	...q/	...q/	...q/
2930	Parts and accessories for motor vehicles	...	...	...	...	...	...	...	...	...q/	...q/	...q/	...q/
301	Building of ships and boats	...	...	...	...	...	...	...	...	...	31r/	...	...
3011	Building of ships and floating structures	...	...	...	...	...	...	...	...	...	...	...	...
3012	Building of pleasure and sporting boats	...	...	...	...	...	...	...	...	...	...	...	...
3020	Railway locomotives and rolling stock	...	...	...	...	...	...	...	...	...	...r/	...	...
3030	Air and spacecraft and related machinery	...	...	...	...	...	...	...	...	...	...r/	...	...
3040	Military fighting vehicles	...	...	...	...	...	...	...	...	...	...r/	...	...
309	Transport equipment n.e.c.	1	2	3	4	6	7	9	33	...	...r/	...	49
3091	Motorcycles	...	...	...	...	...	...	...	...	...	...	...	...
3092	Bicycles and invalid carriages	1	1	1	1	6	6	6	3	...	...	...	3
3099	Other transport equipment n.e.c.	...	1	2	3	-	1	3	30	...	...	...	30
3100	Furniture	151	156	161	161	631	657	702	683	1153	857	896	943
321	Jewellery, bijouterie and related articles	35	38	46	51	784	781	776	864	1512s/	1830s/	1783s/	1405
3211	Jewellery and related articles	29	32	38	45	732	771	758	852	...s/	...s/	...s/	...
3212	Imitation jewellery and related articles	6	6	8	6	...	10	18	12	...s/	...s/	...s/	...
3220	Musical instruments	1	1	...	1	6	5	3	3	...s/	...s/	...s/	...
3230	Sports goods	1	1	1	1	6	5	3	3	...s/	...s/	...s/	3
3240	Games and toys	3	4	7	9	8	9	13	18	...s/	...s/	...s/	17
3250	Medical and dental instruments and supplies	6	7	9	8	86	91	83	86	...s/	...s/	...s/	149
3290	Other manufacturing n.e.c.	32	35	35	32	135	187	176	180	...s/	...s/	...s/	206
331	Repair of fabricated metal products/machinery	31	31	28	30	680	660	629	583	1213t/	1485t/	1367t/	1238
3311	Repair of fabricated metal products	6	5	4	4	10	8	7	6	...	...	...	...
3312	Repair of machinery	13	13	11	10	399	396	374	339	...	...	...	...
3313	Repair of electronic and optical equipment	2	2	2	1	11	6	11	13	...	...	...	...
3314	Repair of electrical equipment	10	11	11	15	260	250	237	225	...	...	...	...
3315	Repair of transport equip., excl. motor vehicles	...	...	...	...	...	...	...	...	...	...	...	...
3319	Repair of other equipment	...	...	...	...	...	...	...	...	...	...	...	...
3320	Installation of industrial machinery/equipment	...	...	...	...	...	...	...	...	...t/	...t/	...t/	...t/
C	Total manufacturing	2405	2414	2466	2571	51221	51664	49471	47888	85475	90805	92346	137378

a/ 1010 includes 1020, 1030, 1040, 1050, 106, 107 and 1080.
b/ 131 includes 139.
c/ 1410 includes 1420 and 1430.
d/ 151 includes 1520.
e/ 1610 includes 162.
f/ 181 includes 1820.
g/ 201 includes 202 and 2030.
h/ 221 includes 2220.
i/ 2310 includes 239.
j/ 2410 includes 2420 and 243.
k/ 251 includes 2520 and 259.
m/ 2610 includes 2620, 2630, 2640, 265, 2660, 2670 and 2680.
n/ 2710 includes 2720, 273, 2740, 2750 and 2790.
p/ 281 includes 282.
q/ 2910 includes 2920 and 2930.
r/ 301 includes 3020, 3030, 3040 and 309.
s/ 321 includes 3220, 3230, 3240, 3250 and 3290.
t/ 331 includes 3320.

Armenia

ISIC Revision 4			Output at basic prices (millions of Armenian Drams)					Value added at basic prices (millions of Armenian Drams)					Gross fixed capital formation (millions of Armenian Drams)	
ISIC	Industry	Note	2013	2014	2015	2016	Note	2013	2014	2015	2016	Note	2015	2016
1010	Processing/preserving of meat		16458	23166	18875	22840		...	...	7633	3745		697	1686
1020	Processing/preserving of fish, etc.		358	1060	968	2568		...	...	719	773		2	88
1030	Processing/preserving of fruit,vegetables		12636	14760	14786	13253		...	...	7134	4555		2408	1509
1040	Vegetable and animal oils and fats		2190	1952	988	767		...	...	361	64		70	74
1050	Dairy products		42401	51225	52134	51947		...	...	20099	15896		944	1105
106	Grain mill products,starches and starch products		49189	52788	43524	40594		...	...	24650	8981		2960	-722
1061	Grain mill products		49189	52788	43524	40594							2960	-722
1062	Starches and starch products		...	...	...	...				...	...		...	...
107	Other food products		92532	160767	154236	152950		...	...	49784	41863		4075	4358
1071	Bakery products		90235	97120	102341	99758				...	...		329	264
1072	Sugar		1465	24677	13361	13446				...	...		-	-
1073	Cocoa, chocolate and sugar confectionery		832	23671	22245	22463				...	...		3103	3106
1074	Macaroni, noodles, couscous, etc.		...	1241	1411	1575				...	...		73	-12
1075	Prepared meals and dishes		...	195	276	191				...	...		41	33
1079	Other food products n.e.c.		...	13863	14602	15517				...	...		528	966
1080	Prepared animal feeds		57586	2722	2274	2447		...	...	22675	1171		186	24
110	Beverages		126272	125119	103336	111444		...	...	50740	36147		9137	11355
1101	Distilling, rectifying and blending of spirits		86509	76560	57949	67869		...	...	...	...		3569	2439
1102	Wines		7962	7678	7527	9029				...	...		5264	3064
1103	Malt liquors and malt		...	8762	7953	7370				...	...		246	-84
1104	Soft drinks,mineral waters,other bottled waters		...	32119	29908	27177				...	...		59	5936
1200	Tobacco products		38307	63112	111544	136289		...	...	53531	40887		6678	9514
131	Spinning, weaving and finishing of textiles		8	92	103	71				1	33		1	1
1311	Preparation and spinning of textile fibres		...	3	1	...				...	...		-	-
1312	Weaving of textiles		...	89	102	71				...	...		1	-
1313	Finishing of textiles		...	...	...	...				...	...		-	1
139	Other textiles		441	452	404	428		...	...	221	160		-9	3
1391	Knitted and crocheted fabrics		291	229	124	74				...	...		1	1
1392	Made-up textile articles, except apparel		...	...	-	3				...	...		-	-
1393	Carpets and rugs		134	164	177	234				...	...		-10	3
1394	Cordage, rope, twine and netting		...	...	...	...				...	...		-	-
1399	Other textiles n.e.c.		8	59	103	116				...	...		-	-
1410	Wearing apparel, except fur apparel		4601	6164	7547	8577		...	...	4432	4425		694	4406
1420	Articles of fur		...	...	...	...				-	...		-	-
1430	Knitted and crocheted apparel		1320	1166	1948	2907				819	1240		737	249
151	Leather;luggage,handbags,saddlery,harness;fur		710	498	283	602		...	...	179	367		1	33
1511	Tanning/dressing of leather; dressing of fur		48	143	36	354				...	...		-	33
1512	Luggage,handbags,etc.;saddlery/harness		662	355	246	248				...	...		1	-
1520	Footwear		503	729	1036	1137				542	453		-31	49
1610	Sawmilling and planing of wood		92	83	86	134				52	134		39	-38

Code	Description								
162	Wood products, cork, straw, plaiting materials	1031	1431	1439	1671	615	697	15	639
1621	Veneer sheets and wood-based panels	15	53	47	34	...	...	-	-
1622	Builders' carpentry and joinery	2	917	1033	1017	...	...	15	630
1623	Wooden containers	803	173	113	341	...	...	-	10
1629	Other wood products;articles of cork,straw	24	288	246	279	...	...	-	-
170	Paper and paper products	11486	16443	20280	21093	12339	6688	2542	1914
1701	Pulp, paper and paperboard	...	1212	1273	2129	...	...	7	402
1702	Corrugated paper and paperboard	...	11276	15305	15336	...	...	2200	1373
1709	Other articles of paper and paperboard	...	3956	3703	3628	...	...	334	139
181	Printing and service activities related to printing	14144	14129	14364	13483	7070	6010	2487	2226
1811	Printing	2591	12012	12446	11297	...	...	2394	2226
1812	Service activities related to printing	9485	2118	1918	2186	...	...	93	1
1820	Reproduction of recorded media	35	23	20	3	18	3	-	-
1910	Coke oven products	...	...	...	...	-	...	...	...
1920	Refined petroleum products	...	...	...	...	522	765	-510	34
201	Basic chemicals,fertilizers, etc.	1004	915	1300	1280	...	...	-512	34
2011	Basic chemicals	246	863	1183	1219	...	...	...	-
2012	Fertilizers and nitrogen compounds	8	7	26	17	...	...	2	...
2013	Plastics and synthetic rubber in primary forms	424	45	91	45	...	...	654	94
202	Other chemical products	...	7218	7616	7462	...	...	...	...
2021	Pesticides and other agrochemical products	...	...	...	...	...	...	538	-20
2022	Paints,varnishes;printing ink and mastics	...	4051	3905	3305	...	...	8	-5
2023	Soap,cleaning and cosmetic preparations	1333	1333	1473	1606	...	...	108	119
2029	Other chemical products n.e.c.	3779	1834	2237	2551	...	...	...	...
2030	Man-made fibres	...	...	234	-	1435	...	...	...
2100	Pharmaceuticals,medicinal chemicals, etc.	5283	5987	7634	8219	4337	4226	238	356
221	Rubber products	764	819	901	548	511	315	11	27
2211	Rubber tyres and tubes	...	...	...	...	...	...	...	...
2219	Other rubber products	764	819	901	548	...	...	11	27
2220	Plastics products	19805	25583	24778	27269	9793	8558	2142	1531
2310	Glass and glass products	13848	12326	8440	6091	4613	1614	451	181
239	Non-metallic mineral products n.e.c.	730	40336	34795	28261	703	11549	2435	2585
2391	Refractory products	...	42	24	26	...	...	-	-
2392	Clay building materials	...	48	40	15	...	...	-	-
2393	Other porcelain and ceramic products	...	8	21	42	...	...	-	-
2394	Cement, lime and plaster	...	18278	18380	12916	...	...	671	597
2395	Articles of concrete, cement and plaster	...	18198	12357	11463	...	...	626	1526
2396	Cutting, shaping and finishing of stone	...	3186	3013	3439	...	...	1132	462
2399	Other non-metallic mineral products n.e.c.	730	575	959	362	...	...	7	-
2410	Basic iron and steel	49128	62448	30433	20482	9526	8651	563	728
2420	Basic precious and other non-ferrous metals	2082	92103	107704	119310	609	115438	11699	4715
243	Casting of metals	6145	17271	15066	12759	1558	5659	1012	1108
2431	Casting of iron and steel	...	17264	15066	12759	...	...	1012	1108
2432	Casting of non-ferrous metals	...	7	...	...	...	...	-	-
251	Struct.metal products, tanks, reservoirs	6800	6554	5737	5029	1473	1661	152	100

continued

Armenia

ISIC	Industry	Output Note	Output 2013	Output 2014	Output 2015	Output 2016	VA Note	VA 2013	VA 2014	VA 2015	VA 2016	GFCF Note	GFCF 2015	GFCF 2016
			(millions of Armenian Drams)					(millions of Armenian Drams)					(millions of Armenian Drams)	
2511	Structural metal products		5756	6554	5737	5029		...	...	...	...		152	100
2512	Tanks, reservoirs and containers of metal		1044	...	...	...		...	...	...	...		-	-
2513	Steam generators, excl. hot water boilers		...	...	...	...		...	...	...	...		...	...
2520	Weapons and ammunition		...	...	...	...		...	...	-	...		...	...
259	Other metal products;metal working services		5229	6010	4824	5591		...	...	1734	2300		226	-38
2591	Forging,pressing,stamping,roll-forming of metal		313	197	139	144							3	-2
2592	Treatment and coating of metals; machining		1130	695	394	215							1	-111
2593	Cutlery, hand tools and general hardware		500	372	295	343							-3	-190
2599	Other fabricated metal products n.e.c.		3285	4746	3996	4888							225	265
2610	Electronic components and boards		1270	1101	879	899				379	396		51	-1
2620	Computers and peripheral equipment		459	312	540	704				517	389		117	-12
2630	Communication equipment		552	650	630	563				215	330		59	22
2640	Consumer electronics		...	...	...	...				-	...		...	...
265	Measuring;testing equipment; watches, etc.		3380	2983	2811	3633		...	...	1698	1443		3	-14
2651	Measuring/testing/navigating equipment,etc.		1927	1868	2012	2860				-	...		-13	-17
2652	Watches and clocks		1453	1115	799	773				...	...		16	3
2660	Irradiation/electromedical equipment,etc.		...	...	...	...				-	...		...	...
2670	Optical instruments and photographic equipment		383	264	400	453				243	248		20	-32
2680	Magnetic and optical media		...	...	...	...				-	...		...	...
2710	Electric motors,generators,transformers,etc.		1237	991	714	842				169	521		-96	-20
2720	Batteries and accumulators		786	1077	766	503				94	202		-2	-9
273	Wiring and wiring devices		810	865	979	1508				192	500		78	3
2731	Fibre optic cables		...	...	...	...		...	...	...	...		...	...
2732	Other electronic and electric wires and cables		804	853	950	1504		...	...	...	...		78	3
2733	Wiring devices		6	12	29	4							-	-
2740	Electric lighting equipment		17	32	83	118				83	43		-	-
2750	Domestic appliances		607	710	1365	1571				869	1108		124	-26
2790	Other electrical equipment		2084	1519	875	2719				454	1344		1	229
281	General-purpose machinery		282	635	572	576				125	80		1	-3
2811	Engines/turbines,excl.aircraft,vehicle engines		93	64	28	35							...	-
2812	Fluid power equipment		136	104	146	51							-1	-8
2813	Other pumps, compressors, taps and valves		29	4	4	20							...	-
2814	Bearings, gears, gearing and driving elements		4	30	16	15							...	...
2815	Ovens, furnaces and furnace burners		19	31	63	42							...	...
2816	Lifting and handling equipment		...	...	...	1							...	...
2817	Office machinery, excl.computers,etc.		...	326	271	313							2	5
2818	Power-driven hand tools		...	14	34	66							...	...
2819	Other general-purpose machinery		...	62	10	29							...	...
282	Special-purpose machinery		944	2713	3458	3316				176	270		49	2
2821	Agricultural and forestry machinery		80	16	10	11							-	-
2822	Metal-forming machinery and machine tools		...	217	236	141				...	...		-17	9

2823	Machinery for metallurgy	484	607	660	250	…	…	3	13
2824	Mining, quarrying and construction machinery	47	1	1	-	…	…	-	-
2825	Food/beverage/tobacco processing machinery	322	…	…	…	…	…	…	…
2826	Textile/apparel/leather production machinery	…	…	…	…	…	…	…	…
2829	Other special-purpose machinery	11	1873	2551	2913	…	…	40	-21
2910	Motor vehicles	…	…	…	…	-	…	…	…
2920	Automobile bodies, trailers and semi-trailers	…	…	…	…	-	…	…	…
2930	Parts and accessories for motor vehicles	…	…	…	…	-	…	…	…
301	Building of ships and boats	…	…	…	…	-	…	…	…
3011	Building of ships and floating structures	…	…	…	…	…	…	…	…
3012	Building of pleasure and sporting boats	…	…	…	…	…	…	…	…
3020	Railway locomotives and rolling stock	…	…	…	…	…	…	…	…
3030	Air and spacecraft and related machinery	…	…	…	…	-	…	…	…
3040	Military fighting vehicles	-	-	…	…	-	…	…	9
309	Transport equipment n.e.c.	7	10	12	200	9	127	-	9
3091	Motorcycles	…	…	…	…	…	…	…	…
3092	Bicycles and invalid carriages	7	6	6	3	…	…	-	-
3099	Other transport equipment n.e.c.	…	4	197	197	…	…	-	9
3100	Furniture	3294	3019	3311	3102	1803	772	14	142
321	Jewellery, bijouterie and related articles	19439	10919	18110	36361	9319	6696	-59	43
3211	Jewellery and related articles	19383	10909	18087	36339	…	…	-59	43
3212	Imitation jewellery and related articles	…	10	24	22	…	…	-	-
3220	Musical instruments	…	…	…	…	-	…	…	…
3230	Sports goods	5	2	239	…	239	…	-	-
3240	Games and toys	37	35	48	86	46	35	-	2
3250	Medical and dental instruments and supplies	805	816	924	937	557	376	29	2
3290	Other manufacturing n.e.c.	602	568	667	637	232	197	40	124
331	Repair of fabricated metal products/machinery	2688	3075	2453	2066	1756	1045	-863	-2
3311	Repair of fabricated metal products	15	18	18	16	…	…	…	-
3312	Repair of machinery	1499	2077	1456	1338	…	…	-48	11
3313	Repair of electronic and optical equipment	31	7	80	18	…	…	-878	-
3314	Repair of electrical equipment	1144	973	899	694	…	…	62	-14
3315	Repair of transport equip., excl. motor vehicles	…	…	…	…	…	…	…	…
3319	Repair of other equipment	…	…	…	…	…	…	…	…
3320	Installation of industrial machinery/equipment	…	…	…	…	…	…	…	…
C	Total manufacturing	777017	847750	839474	888302	370828	353246	52253	50349

Armenia

ISIC	Industry	Note						Index numbers of industrial production (2010=100)						
			2005	2006	2007	2008	2009	2010	2011	2012	2013	2014	2015	2016
10	Food products		...	...	...	89	91	100	115	116	119	130	118	121
11	Beverages		...	...	...	99	76	100	122	139	165	161	131	139
12	Tobacco products		...	...	...	76	89	100	74	117	140	181	288	358
13	Textiles		...	...	...	277	116	100	276	193	135	47	40	42
14	Wearing apparel		...	...	...	109	89	100	139	123	134	154	178	206
15	Leather and related products		...	...	...	81	75	100	119	93	92	94	86	103
16	Wood products, excluding furniture		...	...	...	72	56	100	80	76	65	81	79	93
17	Paper and paper products		...	...	...	66	60	100	128	167	209	277	327	324
18	Printing and reproduction of recorded media		...	...	...	110	98	100	97	87	90	84	82	82
19	Coke and refined petroleum products		...	...	...	...	...	...	...	...	...	...	...	...
20	Chemicals and chemical products		...	...	...	189	114	100	85	79	74	78	86	79
21	Pharmaceuticals,medicinal chemicals, etc.		...	...	...	79	85	100	104	114	143	151	189	203
22	Rubber and plastics products		...	...	...	81	98	100	120	124	114	145	137	151
23	Other non-metallic mineral products		...	...	...	117	89	100	103	103	110	107	88	70
24	Basic metals		...	...	...	78	94	100	111	120	131	143	123	126
25	Fabricated metal products, except machinery		...	...	...	82	76	100	189	186	204	185	134	139
26	Computer, electronic and optical products		...	...	...	190	86	100	107	102	107	104	99	125
27	Electrical equipment		...	...	...	103	76	100	139	125	116	115	77	112
28	Machinery and equipment n.e.c.		...	...	...	148	126	100	86	124	102	81	98	91
29	Motor vehicles, trailers and semi-trailers		...	...	...	...	...	...	...	...	...	...	...	...
30	Other transport equipment		...	...	...	67	140	100	139	332	300	409	532	...
31	Furniture		...	...	...	117	107	100	93	122	120	108	137	174
32	Other manufacturing		...	...	...	155	87	100	111	113	129	75	119	223
33	Repair and installation of machinery/equipment		...	...	...	91	110	100	86	108	115	124	128	155
C	Total manufacturing		...	...	...	98	90	100	113	119	128	136	130	140

ISIC Revision 4

Australia

Supplier of information:
Australian Bureau of Statistics, Canberra.

Basic source of data:
Economic activity survey; business register.

Major deviations from ISIC (Revision 4):
Data presented in accordance with ISIC (Revision 4) were originally classified according to the Australian and New Zealand Standard Industrial Classification (ANZSIC 2006) system.

Reference period:
Fiscal year ending 30 June of the year indicated.

Scope:
All enterprises.

Method of data collection:
Not reported.

Type of enumeration:
Not reported.

Adjusted for non-response:
Yes.

Concepts and definitions of variables:
No deviations from the standard UN concepts and definitions are reported.

Related national publications:
Australian System of National Accounts, published by the Australian Bureau of Statistics, Canberra.

Australia

ISIC	Industry	Ent. Note	Enterprises 2013	2014	2015	2016	Pers. Note	Persons 2013	2014	2015	2016	Wages Note	Wages 2013	2014	2015	2016
			(number)					(thousands)					(millions of Australian Dollars)			
1010	Processing/preserving of meat		604	617	594	...		61	60	63	62		2922	3013	3170	3292
1020	Processing/preserving of fish, etc.		76	72	68	...		3	3	3	3		110	94	88	93
1030	Processing/preserving of fruit,vegetables		537	564	604	...		15	15	14	15		760	...	698	738
1040	Vegetable and animal oils and fats		64	61	62	...		1	1	2	2		116	99	106	121
1050	Dairy products		360	388	419	...		18	18	18	19		1314	1345	1362	1522
106	Grain mill products,starches and starch products		406	400	407	...		...	...	...	...		...	...	...	...
1061	Grain mill products		323	322	326	...		9	9	9	9		628	630	645	576
1062	Starches and starch products		82	79	81	...		...	...	...	...		...	...	...	...
107	Other food products		9357	9351	9445	...		...	...	...	...		...	...	...	...
1071	Bakery products		6023	5958	5986	...		68	66	68	70		2073	2074	2148	2283
1072	Sugar		33	23	28	...		5	5	5	5		401	421	414	450
1073	Cocoa, chocolate and sugar confectionery		403	409	405	...		12	12	11	11		800	801	847	906
1074	Macaroni, noodles, couscous, etc.		120	123	130	...		...	...	...	...		...	...	...	...
1075	Prepared meals and dishes	b/	1139	1174	1179	...	b/	15	14	14	15	b/	797	747	793	902
1079	Other food products n.e.c.	b/	1639	1664	1718	...	b/	...	...	...	...	b/	...	...	...	...
1080	Prepared animal feeds		323	296	289	...		5	5	...	...		...	...	...	...
110	Beverages		1448	1503	1585	...		31c/	32c/	31c/	30	c/	2138	2175	2289	2181
1101	Distilling, rectifying and blending of spirits		56	54	49	...		...	...	...	1		...	...	...	...
1102	Wines		1053	1044	1052	...		16	16	16	17		938	960	965	931
1103	Malt liquors and malt		248	313	383	...		4	4	...	5		336	360	...	530
1104	Soft drinks,mineral waters,other bottled waters		91	92	101	...		9	9	8	7		571	579	634	656
1200	Tobacco products		6	3	3	...	c/	...c/	...c/	...c/	-	c/	...	...	...	...
131	Spinning, weaving and finishing of textiles		3055	2943	2852	...		1	1	1	1		88	89	81	77
1311	Preparation and spinning of textile fibres		59	55	60	...		...	...	...	...		...	...	...	...
1312	Weaving of textiles		51	46	53	...		...	...	...	...		...	...	...	...
1313	Finishing of textiles		2945	2842	2739	...		...	...	...	...		...	...	...	...
139	Other textiles		2763	2695	2677	...		16	15	14	13		677	649	633	644
1391	Knitted and crocheted fabrics		35	29	29	...		1	1	1	1		28	23	19	19
1392	Made-up textile articles, except apparel		1037	1017	1021	...		...	...	...	...		116	112	111	115
1393	Carpets and rugs		102	97	87	...		2	2	2	1		23	22	23	23
1394	Cordage, rope, twine and netting		74	76	77	...		-	-	-	-		...	...	...	...
1399	Other textiles n.e.c.		1515	1476	1464	...		...	12	11	11		...	491	481	487
1410	Wearing apparel, except fur apparel	d/	662	633	614	...	d/	18	17	17	15	d/	593	549	552	500
1420	Articles of fur	d/	579	551	529	...	d/	...	...	...	...	d/	...	...	...	...
1430	Knitted and crocheted apparel	d/	35	29	29	...	d/	...	...	...	...	d/	...	...	...	...
151	Leather;luggage,handbags,saddlery,harness;fur	e/	178	170	163	...		2	2	2	2		88	92	90	77
1511	Tanning/dressing of leather; dressing of fur	e/	89	85	82	...	e/	2	2	2	2	e/	88	92	90	77
1512	Luggage,handbags,etc.;saddlery/harness	e/	89	85	82	...	e/	...	...	...	...	e/	...	...	...	...
1520	Footwear		42	39	38	...		2	2	2	2		79	89	90	103
1610	Sawmilling and planing of wood		930	885	889	...		12	11	11	11		615	564	604	627

ISIC Revision 4

a/ Number of enterprises

162	Wood products, cork, straw, plaiting materials	2958	2989	3028	...		33	30	30	32		1520	1443	1562	1662
1621	Veneer sheets and wood-based panels	137	144	126	...		3	3	3	3		230	232	249	244
1622	Builders' carpentry and joinery	2047	2108	2167	...		25	23	23	25		1107	1042	1139	1228
1623	Wooden containers	269	255	252	...		...	...	...	...		...	...	...	...
1629	Other wood products;articles of cork,straw	506	483	483	...		4	4	4	4		182	170	176	190
170	Paper and paper products	1104	1075	1107	...		18	17	16	16		1467	1464	1495	1506
1701	Pulp, paper and paperboard	362	341	353	...		4	4	3	4		353	380	379	396
1702	Corrugated paper and paperboard	146	150	151	...		7	7	7	7		552	580	604	608
1709	Other articles of paper and paperboard	596	584	603	...		7	7	7	6		562	504	512	501
181	Printing and service activities related to printing	3364	3312	3184	...		34	35	38	33		1947	1964	2309	2024
1811	Printing	2808	2703	2599	...		32	33	35	31		1874	1884	2220	1937
1812	Service activities related to printing	556	609	585	...		2	2	2	2		73	80	89	88
1820	Reproduction of recorded media	249	268	264	...		2	1	2	1		100	87	102	98
1910	Coke oven products	117	114	116	...		2	2	2	5f/		170	179	204	631f/
1920	Refined petroleum products	193	186	188	...		3	3	2	...f/		512	444	426	...f/
201	Basic chemicals,fertilizers, etc.	762	768	758	...	g/	29	28	29	30	g/	2585	2566	2609	2586
2011	Basic chemicals	317	316	321	...		8	6	7	7		756	686	642	644
2012	Fertilizers and nitrogen compounds	185	187	187	...		4	4	4	4		371	361	364	352
2013	Plastics and synthetic rubber in primary forms	260	265	251	...		4	5	4	5		363	394	403	386
202	Other chemical products	1574	1629	1630	...	g/	...	...	...	...	g/	...	...	...	...
2021	Pesticides and other agrochemical products	77	84	78	...		1	1	1	1		146	121	111	101
2022	Paints,varnishes;printing ink and mastics	113	109	111	...		...	...	...	...		...	...	...	...
2023	Soap,cleaning and cosmetic preparations	1127	1177	1184	...		7	8	9	10		429	453	570	624
2029	Other chemical products n.e.c.	257	259	258	...		5	5	5	4		519	552	520	479
2030	Man-made fibres	15	19	19	...	g/	...	...	...	...	g/	...	...	...	...
2100	Pharmaceuticals,medicinal chemicals, etc.	545	567	598	...		16	15	15	15		1474	1416	1363	1376
221	Rubber products	1155	1110	1088	...		2	2	2	2		180	180	161	163
2211	Rubber tyres and tubes	91	87	79	...		...	...	...	...		...	...	...	...
2219	Other rubber products	1064	1023	1009	...		...	...	...	...		...	...	...	...
2220	Plastics products	1498	1462	1447	...		40	38	35	35		2430	2426	2287	2404
2310	Glass and glass products	897	874	861	...		9	9	9	9		690	684	723	769
239	Non-metallic mineral products n.e.c.	2245	2253	2272	...		...	...	...	...		...	...	...	...
2391	Refractory products	144	142	136	...		...	...	...	...		...	...	...	...
2392	Clay building materials	194	199	190	...		2	2	2	2		163	157	163	180
2393	Other porcelain and ceramic products	144	142	136	...		2	2	2	2		100	92	101	99
2394	Cement, lime and plaster	117	119	113	...		4	5	5	5		431	480	483	463
2395	Articles of concrete, cement and plaster	1270	1258	1286	...		17	17	17	16		1203	1150	1204	1260
2396	Cutting, shaping and finishing of stone	172	180	189	...		...	...	...	...		...	...	...	...
2399	Other non-metallic mineral products n.e.c.	204	212	221	...		5	6	6	7		307	318	355	368
2410	Basic iron and steel	931	877	866	...		18	19	18	16		1406	1490	1502	1463
2420	Basic precious and other non-ferrous metals	337	304	297	...		21	19	15	14		2568	2467	2022	1865
243	Casting of metals	138	129	126	...		...	...	...	...		...	...	...	...
2431	Casting of iron and steel	68	64	59	...		8	8	7	6		638	599	489	460
2432	Casting of non-ferrous metals	70	65	67	...		4	4	4	4		266	281	240	249
251	Struct.metal products, tanks, reservoirs	8101	8104	8083	...	h/	110	111	107	99	h/	6612	6778	6360	5966

continued

Australia

ISIC Revision 4		Number of enterprises a/ (number)					Number of persons engaged (thousands)					Wages and salaries paid to employees (millions of Australian Dollars)				
ISIC	Industry	2013	2014	2015	2016	Note	2013	2014	2015	2016	Note	2013	2014	2015	2016	Note
2511	Structural metal products	6346	6476	6535	...		56	55	54	52		3565	3420	3285	3116	
2512	Tanks, reservoirs and containers of metal	838	773	733	...		9	9	8	8		554	549	532	493	
2513	Steam generators, excl. hot water boilers	917	855	816	...		...	...	...	...		...	...	...	...	
2520	Weapons and ammunition	446	458	455	...	h/	...	...	...	...	h/	...	...	...	...	h/
259	Other metal products;metal working services	6090	5992	5882	...	h/	...	...	...	...	h/	...	...	...	...	h/
2591	Forging,pressing,stamping,roll-forming of metal	634	626	595	...		2	2	2	1		101	132	135	127	
2592	Treatment and coating of metals; machining	1574	1529	1504	...		10	11	11	8		531	634	585	433	
2593	Cutlery, hand tools and general hardware	984	1015	1026	...		...	...	...	...		...	...	...	...	
2599	Other fabricated metal products n.e.c.	2898	2822	2757	...		24	25	25	22		1390	1525	1373	1375	
2610	Electronic components and boards	369	362	357	...		...	...	...	...		...	...	...	...	
2620	Computers and peripheral equipment	130	127	124	...		2	2	2	2		117	131	120	132	
2630	Communication equipment	241	237	237	...		5	5	4	4		347	333	336	340	
2640	Consumer electronics	174	170	167	...	i/	6	5	5	5	i/	397	392	439	476	i/
265	Measuring,testing equipment; watches, etc.	994	991	996	...		7	8	6	...		535	644	495	481	
2651	Measuring/testing/navigating equipment,etc.	908	902	905	...		...	...	...	...		...	...	...	...	
2652	Watches and clocks	86	88	91	...		...	...	...	...		...	...	...	...	
2660	Irradiation/electromedical equipment,etc.	431	433	438	...		11	11	10	10		678	682	704	772	
2670	Optical instruments and photographic equipment	505	503	502	...		1	1	1	...		61	43	59	52	
2680	Magnetic and optical media	71	71	71	...	i/	...	...	...	...	i/	...	...	...	...	i/
2710	Electric motors,generators,transformers,etc.	101	100	100	...		...	...	...	...		...	...	...	...	
2720	Batteries and accumulators	101	100	100	...		...	...	...	...		...	...	...	...	
273	Wiring and wiring devices	721	731	734	...		3	2	2	2		209	213	201	208	
2731	Fibre optic cables	111	115	115	...		...	...	...	...		...	...	...	...	
2732	Other electronic and electric wires and cables	25	27	24	...		...	...	...	...		...	...	...	...	
2733	Wiring devices	585	590	595	...		...	...	...	...		...	...	...	...	
2740	Electric lighting equipment	316	306	300	...		4	4	3	3		232	222	195	200	
2750	Domestic appliances	216	205	210	...		6	6	4	4		368	387	291	307	
2790	Other electrical equipment	761	754	752	...		9	8	8	8		656	529	514	516	
281	General-purpose machinery	4501	4575	4636	...	j/	51	51	43	45	j/	3402	3467	3344	3428	j/
2811	Engines/turbines,excl.aircraft,vehicle engines	1285	1288	1301	...		...	...	...	...		...	...	...	...	
2812	Fluid power equipment	630	645	637	...	k/	4	4	3	3	k/	293	300	310	317	k/
2813	Other pumps, compressors, taps and valves	750	763	755	...	k/	...	...	...	...	k/	...	...	...	...	k/
2814	Bearings, gears, gearing and driving elements	79	82	84	...		...	...	...	...		...	...	...	...	
2815	Ovens, furnaces and furnace burners	299	299	302	...		...	...	...	...		...	...	...	...	
2816	Lifting and handling equipment	466	468	494	...		7	7	5	6		515	553	486	494	
2817	Office machinery, excl.computers,etc.	228	223	221	...		...	...	...	...		...	...	...	...	
2818	Power-driven hand tools	193	212	225	...		...	...	...	...		...	...	...	...	
2819	Other general-purpose machinery	570	595	618	...		4	5	5	5		324	321	413	394	
282	Special-purpose machinery	2699	2731	2742	...	j/	...	...	...	...	j/	...	...	...	...	j/
2821	Agricultural and forestry machinery	441	432	425	...		7	7	6	6		327	350	325	345	
2822	Metal-forming machinery and machine tools	272	294	308	...		6	6	5	5		302	304	292	320	

2823	Machinery for metallurgy	193	212	225	..	..	..	..	..	..	..	..
2824	Mining, quarrying and construction machinery	774	773	754	11	11	8	8	872	904	773	746
2825	Food/beverage/tobacco processing machinery	534	528	525	..	..	..	..	..	..	..	..
2826	Textile/apparel/leather production machinery	208	213	220	..	..	..	..	..	..	..	..
2829	Other special-purpose machinery	277	278	285	5	5	4	5	283	283	318	326
2910	Motor vehicles	777	745	752	16	13	12	12	1153	1073	1126	978
2920	Automobile bodies, trailers and semi-trailers	1371	1394	1325	14	15	14	13	797	796	804	681
2930	Parts and accessories for motor vehicles	1279	1304	1327	17	16	14	14	1084	1052	988	868
301	Building of ships and boats	1754	1726	1742	..	..	..	..	..	..	..	..
3011	Building of ships and floating structures	1330	1320	1332	9	10	10	8	782	836	987	678
3012	Building of pleasure and sporting boats	424	406	411	6	5	5	5	201	238	248	206
3020	Railway locomotives and rolling stock	883	895	904	6	5	5	5	474	353	369	433
3030	Air and spacecraft and related machinery	951	959	968	13	13	13	14	1214	1271	1269	1367
3040	Military fighting vehicles	18	18	18	..	..	..	..	..	..	..	..
309	Transport equipment n.e.c.	333	322	319	1	1	1	1	42	45	57	57
3091	Motorcycles	18	18	18	..	..	..	..	..	..	..	..
3092	Bicycles and invalid carriages	107	103	100	..	..	..	..	..	..	..	..
3099	Other transport equipment n.e.c.	209	201	201	..	..	..	..	..	..	..	..
3100	Furniture	1259	1261	1273	22	22	23	21	844	851	988	1023
321	Jewellery, bijouterie and related articles	2171	2121	2105	4 m/	4	4	4 m/	105 m/	132	131	129 m/
3211	Jewellery and related articles	1698	1662	1652	..	..	..	..	..	..	..	..
3212	Imitation jewellery and related articles	473	459	453	..	..	..	..	..	..	..	..
3220	Musical instruments	195	189	194	..	..	..	..	..	..	..	..
3230	Sports goods	934	903	890	2 n/	2	2	2 n/	66 n/	70	75	83 n/
3240	Games and toys	738	718	723	..	..	..	..	..	..	..	..
3250	Medical and dental instruments and supplies	381	383	380	..	..	..	..	..	..	..	..
3290	Other manufacturing n.e.c.	2398	2366	2347	7	7	8	7	298	319	344	352
331	Repair of fabricated metal products/machinery	10469	10573	10665	..	..	..	..	..	..	..	..
3311	Repair of fabricated metal products	1384	1425	1444	..	..	..	..	..	..	..	..
3312	Repair of machinery	2668	2672	2691	..	..	..	..	..	..	..	..
3313	Repair of electronic and optical equipment	1231	1214	1214	..	..	..	..	..	..	..	..
3314	Repair of electrical equipment	1998	2015	2027	..	..	..	..	..	..	..	..
3315	Repair of transport equip., excl. motor vehicles	1804	1822	1845	..	..	..	..	..	..	..	..
3319	Repair of other equipment	1384	1425	1444	..	..	..	..	..	..	..	..
3320	Installation of industrial machinery/equipment	30126	30516	31397	..	..	..	..	..	..	..	..
C	Total manufacturing	122512	122480	123338	896	879	854	838	55489	55341	55329	54994

a/ Data were derived from OECD's databases.
b/ 1075 includes 1079.
c/ 110 includes 1200.
d/ 1410 includes 1420 and 1430.
e/ 1511 includes 1512.
f/ 1910 includes 1920.
g/ 201 includes 202 and 2030.
h/ 251 includes 2520 and 259.
i/ 2640 includes 2680.
j/ 281 includes 282.
k/ 2812 includes 2813.
m/ 3211 includes 3212.
n/ 3230 includes 3240.

Australia

ISIC	Industry	Note	Output (valuation not defined) (millions of Australian Dollars) 2013	2014	2015	2016	Note	Value added (valuation not defined) (millions of Australian Dollars) 2013	2014	2015	2016	Note	Gross fixed capital formation (millions of Australian Dollars) 2015	2016
1010	Processing/preserving of meat		22842	25530	29320	29615		4753	5569	6395	5822	a/	2167	2417
1020	Processing/preserving of fish, etc.		1100	944	916	964		214	185	177	202	a/	...	...
1030	Processing/preserving of fruit,vegetables		5601	...	5370	5219		1359	...	1406	1408	a/	...	...
1040	Vegetable and animal oils and fats		1634	1626	1765	1880		240	201	232	227	a/	...	...
1050	Dairy products		13132	13570	13694	13749		2449	2381	2233	2704	a/	...	...
106	Grain mill products,starches and starch products		...	...	...	...		...	...	...	...	a/	...	...
1061	Grain mill products		5548	5661	6050	5848		1316	1233	1333	1300		...	...
1062	Starches and starch products		...	...	...	...		...	...	...	...		...	...
107	Other food products		...	...	...	...		...	...	...	...	a/	...	...
1071	Bakery products		8007	8610	8144	8064		3516	3044	2988	3124		...	...
1072	Sugar		3093	3023	2896	3426		710	741	634	710		...	...
1073	Cocoa, chocolate and sugar confectionery		5220	5971	6317	5776		1420	1577	1497	1626		...	...
1074	Macaroni, noodles, couscous, etc.		...	...	...	...		...	...	...	...		...	...
1075	Prepared meals and dishes	b/	5898	5629	6035	6648	b/	1547	1387	1471	1824		...	...
1079	Other food products n.e.c.	b/	...	...	...	...	b/	...	...	...	...		...	...
1080	Prepared animal feeds		...	...	...	...		...	...	...	...	a/	...	...
110	Beverages	c/	18373	18598	18222	17279	c/	7425	7670	7016	5896	c/	540	409
1101	Distilling, rectifying and blending of spirits		...	...	...	...		...	...	125	98		...	...
1102	Wines		5273	5110	5338	6005		1660	1591	1655	1703		...	...
1103	Malt liquors and malt		...	...	...	4611		...	...	...	...		...	...
1104	Soft drinks,mineral waters,other bottled waters		5713	5715	5754	6019		2049	1981	1935	2099		...	...
1200	Tobacco products	c/	...	...	...	...	c/	...	...	...	...	c/	...	...
131	Spinning, weaving and finishing of textiles		542	485	507	557		134	146	134	130	d/	141	132
1311	Preparation and spinning of textile fibres		...	...	...	...		...	...	...	...		...	...
1312	Weaving of textiles		...	...	...	...		...	...	...	...		...	...
1313	Finishing of textiles		...	...	...	...		...	...	...	...		...	...
139	Other textiles		3581	3433	3517	3540		1165	1101	1134	...	d/	...	...
1391	Knitted and crocheted fabrics		136	135	102	108		61	46	34	...		...	...
1392	Made-up textile articles, except apparel		...	...	...	...		...	...	...	...		...	...
1393	Carpets and rugs		802	808	751	785		206	204	193	205		...	...
1394	Cordage, rope, twine and netting		167	162	163	135		41	43	51	44		...	...
1399	Other textiles n.e.c.		...	2328	2500	2512		...	808	856	830		...	...
1410	Wearing apparel, except fur apparel	e/	3016	2683	2859	2640	e/	1005	931	1046	910	d/	...	...
1420	Articles of fur	e/	...	...	...	...	e/	...	...	...	...	d/	...	...
1430	Knitted and crocheted apparel	e/	...	...	...	...	e/	...	...	...	...	d/	...	...
151	Leather;luggage,handbags,saddlery,harness;fur	f/	557	534	523	467	f/	156	176	167	140	d/	...	...
1511	Tanning/dressing of leather; dressing of fur	f/	557	534	523	467	f/	156	176	167	140		...	...
1512	Luggage,handbags,etc.;saddlery/harness		...	...	...	...		...	...	...	...		...	...
1520	Footwear		509	530	579	621		163	163	173	183	d/	...	...
1610	Sawmilling and planing of wood		3393	3288	3727	4108		1064	1002	1154	1228	g/	289	281

162	Wood products, cork, straw, plaiting materials	6829	6934	8314	9087		2411	2639	2640	3060		…	…
1621	Veneer sheets and wood-based panels	1255	1334	1464	1565		383	417	427	474		…	…
1622	Builders' carpentry and joinery	4788	4859	5922	6490		1739	1911	1918	2237		…	…
1623	Wooden containers	…	…	…	…		…	…	…	…		…	…
1629	Other wood products;articles of cork,straw	787	741	928	1032		288	311	296	349	g/	275	320
170	Paper and paper products	9892	9788	10128	10479		2534	2733	2710	2571		…	…
1701	Pulp, paper and paperboard	3061	3168	2941	3057		718	789	769	778		…	…
1702	Corrugated paper and paperboard	2993	3049	3548	3634		803	873	929	785		…	…
1709	Other articles of paper and paperboard	3839	3571	3639	3788		1013	1071	1013	1008		…	…
181	Printing and service activities related to printing	7790	7898	8774	7969		3371	3173	3971	3325	h/	182	393
1811	Printing	7555	7656	8501	7692		3254	3054	3811	3185		…	…
1812	Service activities related to printing	235	242	273	277		117	120	160	140		…	…
1820	Reproduction of recorded media	457	367	433	417		194	140	192	178	h/	…	…
1910	Coke oven products	1875	1816	1874	15807 i/		373	421	1101 i/	…	i/	317	271
1920	Refined petroleum products	36839	25310	21181	… i/		763	1292	…	…	i/	…	…
201	Basic chemicals,fertilizers, etc.	21165	20901	21505	22685	j/	5799	6133	6470	6838	k/	1067	1244
2011	Basic chemicals	7509	7655	7373	7988		1550	1703	1663	1981		…	…
2012	Fertilizers and nitrogen compounds	3666	3234	3800	3916		1118	1154	1359	1301		…	…
2013	Plastics and synthetic rubber in primary forms	2777	2781	2684	2809	i/	545	573	631	689		…	…
202	Other chemical products	…	…	…	…		…	…	…	…		…	…
2021	Pesticides and other agrochemical products	1007	1037	1031	1035		216	193	194	187		…	…
2022	Paints,varnishes;printing ink and mastics	…	…	…	…		…	…	…	…		…	…
2023	Soap,cleaning and cosmetic preparations	2593	2616	3204	3521		755	880	1078	1193		…	…
2029	Other chemical products n.e.c.	3614	3577	3413	3415		1616	1630	1545	1487	k/	…	…
2030	Man-made fibres	…	…	…	…	j/	…	…	…	…	k/	…	…
2100	Pharmaceuticals,medicinal chemicals, etc.	9903	9222	10287	9486		2450	2563	2669	2492	m/	272	240
221	Rubber products	836	814	803	814		294	323	300	323		…	…
2211	Rubber tyres and tubes	…	…	…	…		…	…	…	…		…	…
2219	Other rubber products	…	…	…	…		…	…	…	…		…	…
2220	Plastics products	12743	13203	13132	13466		4192	4179	4105	4315	m/	772	728
2310	Glass and glass products	3139	3173	3506	3740		1203	1226	1201	1358	n/	…	…
239	Non-metallic mineral products n.e.c.	…	…	…	…		…	…	…	…	n/	…	…
2391	Refractory products	735	811	882	1045		256	272	324	433		…	…
2392	Clay building materials	491	464	535	506		179	160	187	175		…	…
2393	Other porcelain and ceramic products	3770	4239	4353	4491		1190	1376	1412	1481		…	…
2394	Cement, lime and plaster	8054	7649	8183	8160		2287	2092	2250	2049		…	…
2395	Articles of concrete, cement and plaster	…	…	…	…		…	…	…	…		…	…
2396	Cutting, shaping and finishing of stone	1619	1653	1867	1896		561	605	686	674		…	…
2399	Other non-metallic mineral products n.e.c.	…	…	…	…		…	…	…	…		…	…
2410	Basic iron and steel	10719	11132	10403	9774		1690	2159	2310	2042	p/	1349	675
2420	Basic precious and other non-ferrous metals	35080	32189	31343	35795		2949	2345	4387	5338	p/	…	…
243	Casting of metals	3300	3126	2579	2581		…	…	…	…	p/	…	…
2431	Casting of iron and steel	2389	2213	1528	1650		797	830	525	645		…	…
2432	Casting of non-ferrous metals	…	…	…	…		396	339	379	402		…	…
251	Struct.metal products, tanks, reservoirs	29932 q/	32307	29588	28598 q/		10932	10715	10499	9968	q/	292	376

continued

Australia

ISIC	Industry	Output (valuation not defined) (millions of Australian Dollars)					Value added (valuation not defined) (millions of Australian Dollars)					Gross fixed capital formation (millions of Australian Dollars)		
		Note	2013	2014	2015	2016	Note	2013	2014	2015	2016	Note	2015	2016
2511	Structural metal products		16506	17423	16108	16011		5860	5329	5507	5202		…	…
2512	Tanks, reservoirs and containers of metal		2770	2678	2619	2565		964	917	883	862		…	…
2513	Steam generators, excl. hot water boilers		…	…	…	…		…	…	…	…		…	…
2520	Weapons and ammunition	q/	…	…	…	…	q/	…	…	…	…	q/	…	…
259	Other metal products;metal working services	q/	…	…	…	…	q/	…	…	…	…	q/	…	…
2591	Forging,pressing,stamping,roll-forming of metal		653	618	617	572		150	166	173	218		…	945
2592	Treatment and coating of metals;machining		2100	2630	2163	1540		852	1019	902	635		…	…
2593	Cutlery, hand tools and general hardware		…	…	…	…		…	…	…	…		…	…
2599	Other fabricated metal products n.e.c.		6066	6924	6305	6317		2354	2463	2302	2395		…	…
2610	Electronic components and boards		741	816	961	989		211	218	242	211	r/	727	…
2620	Computers and peripheral equipment		1363	1437	1399	1451		516	514	532	521		…	…
2630	Communication equipment													
2640	Consumer electronics	s/	1540	1565	1795	2158	s/	744	726	819	1096		…	…
265	Measuring,testing equipment; watches, etc.		2134	2264	1701	…		816	918	649	…		…	…
2651	Measuring/testing/navigating equipment,etc.		…	…	…	…		…	…	…	…		…	…
2652	Watches and clocks		…	…	…	…		…	…	…	…		…	…
2660	Irradiation/electromedical equipment,etc.		3034	3192	3400	3808		1362	1525	1556	1815		…	…
2670	Optical instruments and photographic equipment		264	167	216	…		108	57	65	106		…	…
2680	Magnetic and optical media	s/	…	…	…	…	s/	…	…	…	…		…	…
2710	Electric motors,generators,transformers,etc.		…	…	…	…		…	…	…	…		…	…
2720	Batteries and accumulators		…	…	…	…		…	…	…	…		…	…
273	Wiring and wiring devices		1840	1696	1738	1864		313	290	322	250		…	…
2731	Fibre optic cables		…	…	…	…		…	…	…	…		…	…
2732	Other electronic and electric wires and cables		…	…	…	…		…	…	…	…		…	…
2733	Wiring devices		…	…	…	…		…	…	…	…		…	…
2740	Electric lighting equipment		1037	894	833	805		380	304	301	310		…	…
2750	Domestic appliances		2149	2131	1801	1975		660	675	462	784		…	…
2790	Other electrical equipment		3229	2350	2330	2365		1021	815	794	…		…	…
281	General-purpose machinery	t/	17318	16575	15670	14910	t/	5502	5215	5123	5375		…	…
2811	Engines/turbines,excl.aircraft,vehicle engines		…	…	…	…		…	…	…	…		…	…
2812	Fluid power equipment	u/	1377	1327	1279	1208	u/	525	521	498	504		…	…
2813	Other pumps, compressors, taps and valves	u/	…	…	…	…	u/	…	…	…	…		…	…
2814	Bearings, gears, gearing and driving elements		…	…	…	…		…	…	…	…		…	…
2815	Ovens, furnaces and furnace burners		…	…	…	…		…	…	…	…		…	…
2816	Lifting and handling equipment		2316	2326	2159	1959		822	822	738	755		…	…
2817	Office machinery, excl.computers,etc.		…	…	…	…		…	…	…	…		…	…
2818	Power-driven hand tools		…	…	…	…		…	…	…	…		…	…
2819	Other general-purpose machinery	t/	1398	1434	1804	1728	t/	527	501	681	645		…	…
282	Special-purpose machinery		…	…	…	…		…	…	…	…		…	…
2821	Agricultural and forestry machinery		2234	2124	1920	1910		603	577	615	587		…	…
2822	Metal-forming machinery and machine tools		1186	1225	1148	1227		474	463	437	551		…	…

Code	Description	(1)	(2)	(3)	(4)	(5)	(6)	(7)	(8)	(9)	(10)	Notes
2823	Machinery for metallurgy	:	:	:	:	1323	1171	952	:	:	1050	
2824	Mining, quarrying and construction machinery	5128	4706	3802	3219	:	:	:	:	:	:	
2825	Food/beverage/tobacco processing machinery	:	:	:	:	:	:	:	:	:	:	
2826	Textile/apparel/leather production machinery	:	:	:	:	:	:	:	:	:	:	
2829	Other special-purpose machinery	1495	1463	1559	1529	507	479	531	501	593	840	
2910	Motor vehicles	10241	10184	9389	9005	1580	991	859	1008	:	:	v/
2920	Automobile bodies, trailers and semi-trailers	4020	4236	3867	3862	1321	1357	1212	1191	:	:	v/
2930	Parts and accessories for motor vehicles	5465	5632	4749	4780	1820	1823	1593	1476	:	:	v/
301	Building of ships and boats	:	:	:	:	:	:	:	:	:	:	v/
3011	Building of ships and floating structures	3098	2966	3238	2251	1106	1234	1271	1023	:	:	v/
3012	Building of pleasure and sporting boats	1048	1235	1152	1154	388	429	384	358	:	:	v/
3020	Railway locomotives and rolling stock	3064	2554	2585	2567	763	543	517	577	:	:	v/
3030	Air and spacecraft and related machinery	3707	3719	3951	4730	1618	1623	1710	1768	:	:	v/
3040	Military fighting vehicles	:	:	:	:	:	:	:	:	:	:	
309	Transport equipment n.e.c.	221	246	252	303	82	94	99	112	:	:	v/
3091	Motorcycles	:	:	:	:	:	:	:	:	:	:	
3092	Bicycles and invalid carriages	:	:	:	:	:	:	:	:	:	:	
3099	Other transport equipment n.e.c.	:	:	:	:	:	:	:	:	:	:	
3100	Furniture	3898	3644	4057	4539	1526	1326	1516	1720	93	226	w/
321	Jewellery, bijouterie and related articles	2207	2146	769	829	253	290	247	272	:	:	w/ x/
3211	Jewellery and related articles	:	:	:	:	:	:	:	:	:	:	x/
3212	Imitation jewellery and related articles	:	:	:	:	:	:	:	:	:	:	
3220	Musical instruments	:	:	:	:	:	:	:	:	:	:	w/
3230	Sports goods	409	385	411	476	157	134	146	175	:	:	w/ y/
3240	Games and toys	:	:	:	:	:	:	:	:	:	:	w/ y/
3250	Medical and dental instruments and supplies	:	:	:	:	:	:	:	:	:	:	w/
3290	Other manufacturing n.e.c.	1351	1441	1381	1498	603	535	545	597	:	:	w/
331	Repair of fabricated metal products/machinery	:	:	:	:	:	:	:	:	:	:	
3311	Repair of fabricated metal products	:	:	:	:	:	:	:	:	:	:	
3312	Repair of machinery	:	:	:	:	:	:	:	:	:	:	
3313	Repair of electronic and optical equipment	:	:	:	:	:	:	:	:	:	:	
3314	Repair of electrical equipment	:	:	:	:	:	:	:	:	:	:	
3315	Repair of transport equip., excl. motor vehicles	:	:	:	:	:	:	:	:	:	:	
3319	Repair of other equipment	:	:	:	:	:	:	:	:	:	:	
3320	Installation of industrial machinery/equipment	:	:	:	:	:	:	:	:	:	:	
C	Total manufacturing	387545	377425	374024	372681	97324	97131	99512	101616	9072	9498	

a/ 1010 includes 1020, 1030, 1040, 1050, 106, 107 and 1080.
b/ 1075 includes 1079.
c/ 110 includes 1200.
d/ 131 includes 139, 1410, 1420, 1430, 151 and 1520.
e/ 1410 includes 1420 and 1430.
f/ 1511 includes 1512.
g/ 1610 includes 162.
h/ 181 includes 1820.
i/ 1910 includes 1920.
j/ 201 includes 202 and 2030.

k/ 201 includes 202, 2030 and 2100.
m/ 221 includes 2220.
n/ 2310 includes 239.
p/ 2410 includes 2420 and 243.
q/ 251 includes 2520 and 259.
r/ 26 includes 27 and 28.
s/ 2640 includes 2680.
t/ 281 includes 282.
u/ 2812 includes 2813.
v/ 2910 includes 2920, 2930, 301, 3020, 3030, 3040 and 309.

w/ 3100 includes 321, 3220, 3230, 3240, 3250 and 3290.
x/ 3211 includes 3212.
y/ 3230 includes 3240.

Australia

Index numbers of industrial production

ISIC Revision 4

ISIC	Industry	Note	2005	2006	2007	2008	2009	2010	2011	2012	2013	2014	2015	2016
								(2010=100)						
10	Food products	a/	100	99	100	100	97	100	100	102	104	104	101	99
11	Beverages	a/	...	...	...	...	...	...	...	...	...	...	...	...
12	Tobacco products	a/	...	...	...	...	...	...	...	...	...	...	...	...
13	Textiles	e/	...	...	...	...	...	...	...	...	...	...	...	...
14	Wearing apparel	e/	...	...	...	...	...	...	...	...	...	...	...	...
15	Leather and related products	e/	...	...	...	...	...	...	...	...	...	...	...	...
16	Wood products, excluding furniture	e/	...	...	...	...	...	...	...	...	...	...	...	...
17	Paper and paper products	e/	...	...	...	...	...	...	...	...	...	...	...	...
18	Printing and reproduction of recorded media	e/	...	...	...	...	...	...	...	...	...	...	...	...
19	Coke and refined petroleum products	b/	110	106	104	107	96	100	100	102	96	96	93	91
20	Chemicals and chemical products	b/	...	...	...	...	...	...	...	...	...	...	...	...
21	Pharmaceuticals,medicinal chemicals, etc.	b/	...	...	...	...	...	...	...	...	...	...	...	...
22	Rubber and plastics products	b/	...	...	...	...	...	...	...	...	...	...	...	...
23	Other non-metallic mineral products	e/	...	...	...	...	...	...	...	...	...	...	...	...
24	Basic metals	c/	87	86	95	106	104	100	105	107	98	100	97	92
25	Fabricated metal products, except machinery	c/	...	...	...	...	...	...	...	...	...	...	...	...
26	Computer, electronic and optical products		...	...	...	...	...	...	...	...	...	...	...	...
27	Electrical equipment		...	...	...	...	...	...	...	...	...	...	...	...
28	Machinery and equipment n.e.c.	d/	92	96	95	99	94	100	98	102	98	92	91	88
29	Motor vehicles, trailers and semi-trailers	d/	...	...	...	...	...	...	...	...	...	...	...	...
30	Other transport equipment	d/	...	...	...	...	...	...	...	...	...	...	...	...
31	Furniture		...	...	...	...	...	...	...	...	...	...	...	...
32	Other manufacturing	e/	116	114	113	115	106	100	97	90	89	89	91	91
33	Repair and installation of machinery/equipment		...	...	...	...	...	...	...	...	...	...	...	...
C	Total manufacturing		100	99	101	105	100	100	100	101	97	96	95	93

a/ 10 includes 11 and 12.
b/ 19 includes 20, 21 and 22.
c/ 24 includes 25.
d/ 28 includes 29 and 30.
e/ 32 includes 13-18 and 23.

Austria

Supplier of information:
Statistics Austria, Vienna.
Industrial statistics for the OECD countries are compiled by the OECD secretariat, which supplies them to UNIDO.

Basic source of data:
Annual survey; secondary statistics data; administrative data; business register.

Major deviations from ISIC (Revision 4):
Data presented in ISIC (Revision 4) were originally classified according to the national NACE-related classification system (ÖNACE).

Reference period:
Calendar year; however, data given for a financial year are accepted and incorporated into the calendar year in which the financial year ends.

Scope:
All enterprises.

Method of data collection:
Mainly electronic questionnaire and administrative data.

Type of enumeration:
Cut-off survey for enterprises exceeding legal thresholds; model based estimation for enterprises below thresholds.

Adjusted for non-response:
Not reported.

Concepts and definitions of variables:
No deviations from the standard UN concepts and definitions are reported.

Related national publications:
Structural Business Statistics, Statistical Yearbook of Austria, both published by Statistics Austria, Vienna.

Austria

ISIC	Industry	Note	Number of enterprises (number) 2013	2014	2015	2016	Note	Number of employees (number) 2013	2014	2015	2016	Note	Wages and salaries paid to employees (millions of Euros) 2013	2014	2015	2016
1010	Processing/preserving of meat		956	951	947	937		17002	17147	17468	17436		456	471	491	503
1020	Processing/preserving of fish, etc.		6	9	10	9		129	122	…	145		4	4	…	5
1030	Processing/preserving of fruit,vegetables		130	132	138	135		3884	3769	3739	3729		157	153	152	158
1040	Vegetable and animal oils and fats		69	70	73	72		764	799	857	888		30	32	35	36
1050	Dairy products		151	151	155	155		5115	5180	5302	5401		193	199	208	210
106	Grain mill products,starches and starch products		121	116	119	121		2237	2319	2415	2480		82	86	97	96
1061	Grain mill products		120	115	118	120	a/	2237	2319	2415	2480		82	86	97	96
1062	Starches and starch products		1	1	1	1	a/	…	…	…	…		…	…	…	…
107	Other food products		1958	2015	2025	1995		37524	39404	39800	40088		959	1029	1065	1069
1071	Bakery products		1695	1740	1739	1699		28872	29459	29499	29899		637	664	680	702
1072	Sugar		1	1	1	1		…	…	…	…		…	…	…	…
1073	Cocoa, chocolate and sugar confectionery		36	35	38	41		1969	1984	2010	1980		69	70	74	72
1074	Macaroni, noodles, couscous, etc.		48	49	53	57		589	610	625	614		15	16	17	16
1075	Prepared meals and dishes		23	26	25	23		923	1949	1998	2030		28	55	58	61
1079	Other food products n.e.c.		155	164	169	174		2056	2072	…	2202		79	84	…	94
1080	Prepared animal feeds		63	64	72	76		…	…	…	…		…	…	…	…
110	Beverages		364	364	388	399		8609	8589	8793	8921		364	394	387	413
1101	Distilling, rectifying and blending of spirits		147	144	149	147		736	741	782	772		20	22	23	24
1102	Wines		63	66	70	74		…	…	…	…		…	…	…	…
1103	Malt liquors and malt		80	85	98	106		…	…	…	…		…	…	…	…
1104	Soft drinks,mineral waters,other bottled waters		74	69	71	72		3194	3135	3391	3481		144	144	153	171
1200	Tobacco products		-	-	-	-		-	-	-	-		-	-	-	-
131	Spinning, weaving and finishing of textiles		176	177	166	118		3924	3762	3291	2946		136	134	119	110
1311	Preparation and spinning of textile fibres		17	16	16	16		951	899	811	678		35	33	30	25
1312	Weaving of textiles		39	38	34	34		2124	2037	1718	1733		76	77	65	67
1313	Finishing of textiles		120	123	116	68		849	826	762	535		25	25	24	17
139	Other textiles		434	434	428	402		4509	4634	4883	4790		146	152	166	169
1391	Knitted and crocheted fabrics		21	23	25	24		364	512	510	507		13	19	19	19
1392	Made-up textile articles, except apparel		112	120	123	117		1536	1546	1595	1573		42	44	48	47
1393	Carpets and rugs		17	16	16	17		305	312	327	347		10	11	12	14
1394	Cordage, rope, twine and netting		14	15	15	14		41	40	104	103		1	1	5	5
1399	Other textiles n.e.c.		270	260	249	230		2263	2224	2347	2260		79	77	83	85
1410	Wearing apparel, except fur apparel		655	645	620	589		5386	5028	4674	4277		134	126	124	115
1420	Articles of fur		42	41	40	38		63	64	…	…		1	1	…	…
1430	Knitted and crocheted apparel		27	26	28	27		1109	964	…	…		41	39	…	…
151	Leather;luggage,handbags,saddlery,harness;fur		90	93	92	100		2741	2776	2633	2450		68	71	67	65
1511	Tanning/dressing of leather; dressing of fur		31	30	29	29		2307	2341	2167	2032		57	60	55	55
1512	Luggage,handbags,etc.;saddlery/harness		59	63	63	71		434	435	466	418		11	11	12	11
1520	Footwear		86	84	83	87		1323	1383	1364	1355		44	44	46	46
1610	Sawmilling and planing of wood		1052	1057	1045	1005		9893	9642	9605	9786		317	320	327	347

ISIC Revision 4

162	Wood products, cork, straw, plaiting materials	1698	1717	1684	1684	21320	21041	20823	20961	716	723	745	762
1621	Veneer sheets and wood-based panels	27	28	30	31	3943	3812	3965	4109	181	177	194	195
1622	Builders' carpentry and joinery	1224	1243	1210	1196	15576	15463	15027	14942	490	502	503	516
1623	Wooden containers	114	113	109	113	1071	1037	1083	1126	29	28	30	32
1629	Other wood products;articles of cork,straw	333	333	335	344	730	729	748	784	17	17	17	19
170	Paper and paper products	137	141	140	135	16662	16856	16789	16637	786	815	818	835
1701	Pulp, paper and paperboard	31	32	30	28	7185	...	...	...	379	...	...	...
1702	Corrugated paper and paperboard	61	62	61	57	5436	5598	5577	5463	232	240	242	240
1709	Other articles of paper and paperboard	45	47	49	50	4041	4205	4218	4251	175	188	189	190
181	Printing and service activities related to printing	854	854	842	856	10679	10625	10391	10389	440	443	451	444
1811	Printing	641	642	640	661	9551	9543	9314	9272	402	407	415	405
1812	Service activities related to printing	213	212	202	195	1128	1082	1077	1117	38	36	36	39
1820	Reproduction of recorded media	20	23	22	22	1162	926	840	814	58	47	48	34
1910	Coke oven products	-	-	-	-	-	-	-	-	-	-	-	-
1920	Refined petroleum products	4	5	5	5	1123	1144	1179	1216	100	106	109	118
201	Basic chemicals,fertilizers, etc.	86	83	75	76	6506	6466	6661	6796	403	421	443	468
2011	Basic chemicals	45	43	39	40	...	...	...	...	...	...	...	...
2012	Fertilizers and nitrogen compounds	17	16	17	17	969	963	974	980	54	57	53	57
2013	Plastics and synthetic rubber in primary forms	24	24	19	19	...	...	...	...	...	...	...	...
202	Other chemical products	260	274	280	279	8417	8174	7981	8194	397	398	388	419
2021	Pesticides and other agrochemical products	10	12	9	9	362	360	363	373	20	21	21	21
2022	Paints,varnishes;printing ink and mastics	42	43	42	41	2734	2771	2720	2720	127	133	129	132
2023	Soap,cleaning and cosmetic preparations	135	144	154	155	2750	2515	2483	2529	128	118	117	129
2029	Other chemical products n.e.c.	73	75	75	74	2571	2528	...	...	123	126	...	...
2030	Man-made fibres	5	5	7	5	2511	2507	2643	2791	167	155	162	192
2100	Pharmaceuticals,medicinal chemicals, etc.	87	88	84	88	13079	13549	14121	14652	670	728	770	825
221	Rubber products	44	44	43	44	1998	1989	1989	1964	85	93	92	91
2211	Rubber tyres and tubes	6	5	5	4	96	95	82	77	2	3	3	3
2219	Other rubber products	38	39	38	40	1902	1894	1907	1887	83	90	89	88
2220	Plastics products	550	551	557	559	26603	27113	27235	27644	1019	1079	1097	1145
2310	Glass and glass products	159	152	146	115	9388	9070	8602	8386	380	380	370	373
239	Non-metallic mineral products n.e.c.	1183	1188	1185	1179	21632	21636	21753	21638	909	959	952	971
2391	Refractory products	13	13	14	14	1497	1463	1462	1411	74	83	72	71
2392	Clay building materials	24	23	24	22	968	877	...	...	43	43	...	...
2393	Other porcelain and ceramic products	156	153	142	137	...	...	...	...	...	...	...	...
2394	Cement, lime and plaster	11	11	11	11	1193	1167	1139	1131	61	64	62	64
2395	Articles of concrete, cement and plaster	348	346	342	337	10887	10720	10802	10857	461	477	478	492
2396	Cutting, shaping and finishing of stone	553	563	570	577	3024	2964	2948	2927	87	88	88	89
2399	Other non-metallic mineral products n.e.c.	78	79	82	81	2999	3038	3096	3053	142	146	151	155
2410	Basic iron and steel	48	49	45	46	20805	21104	21286	21513	1102	1094	1218	1126
2420	Basic precious and other non-ferrous metals	55	53	53	52	7491	7648	7796	7995	357	368	381	408
243	Casting of metals	51	52	50	49	6308	6446	6638	6746	283	291	303	310
2431	Casting of iron and steel	15	15	13	13	2176	2217	2197	2141	102	101	105	99
2432	Casting of non-ferrous metals	36	37	37	36	4132	4229	4441	4605	180	190	198	211
251	Struct.metal products, tanks, reservoirs	1611	1678	1677	1689	26339	25616	25870	25561	995	977	1019	1023

continued

Austria

ISIC	Industry	Number of enterprises (number)				Note	Number of employees (number)				Note	Wages and salaries paid to employees (millions of Euros)				Note
		2013	2014	2015	2016		2013	2014	2015	2016		2013	2014	2015	2016	
2511	Structural metal products	1556	1619	1620	1630		22700	21796	22031	21841		824	801	836	847	
2512	Tanks, reservoirs and containers of metal	50	53	51	53		3337	3533	3521	3398		155	162	165	158	
2513	Steam generators, excl. hot water boilers	5	6	6	6		302	287	318	322		16	14	18	17	
2520	Weapons and ammunition	49	49	45	42		1229	1262	1289	1469		53	51	56	71	
259	Other metal products;metal working services	2136	2145	2088	2109		43751	44467	45060	46301		1786	1852	1905	1984	
2591	Forging,pressing,stamping,roll-forming of metal	422	421	418	404		6137	6247	6336	6484		249	252	262	273	
2592	Treatment and coating of metals;machining	838	894	842	855		13117	13265	13219	13657		483	503	511	538	
2593	Cutlery, hand tools and general hardware	459	406	406	409		17150	17469	17981	18485		766	798	825	861	
2599	Other fabricated metal products n.e.c.	417	424	422	441		…	7486	…	…		…	299	…	…	
2610	Electronic components and boards	126	131	129	133		8231	8499	8851	9122		435	462	511	530	
2620	Computers and peripheral equipment	37	37	37	35		884	889	869	885		42	43	42	41	
2630	Communication equipment	64	66	67	65		1935	1956	2023	1988		95	94	97	98	
2640	Consumer electronics	33	37	31	32		770	612	329	339		46	47	19	19	
265	Measuring,testing equipment; watches, etc.	252	257	238	241		5423	5668	5823	6112		246	258	270	282	
2651	Measuring/testing/navigating equipment,etc.	223	227	226	230		5364	5601	5778	6087		244	256	269	281	
2652	Watches and clocks	29	30	12	11		59	67	45	25		2	2	2	1	
2660	Irradiation/electromedical equipment,etc.	49	51	55	61		2373	2269	2298	2445		113	111	109	127	
2670	Optical instruments and photographic equipment	20	20	22	22		1025	…	1032	1120		44	…	47	52	
2680	Magnetic and optical media	-	1	-	-		-	…	…	-		-	…	…	-	
2710	Electric motors,generators,transformers,etc.	193	202	199	188		24155	23783	23751	23948		1345	1292	1315	1410	
2720	Batteries and accumulators	4	5	6	8		651	677	717	851		34	36	35	50	
273	Wiring and wiring devices	46	45	46	42		3417	3461	3587	3627		133	147	150	156	
2731	Fibre optic cables	1	1	1	1		…	…	…	…		…	…	…	…	
2732	Other electronic and electric wires and cables	28	27	29	24		1682	1697	1811	1818		63	70	75	76	
2733	Wiring devices	17	17	16	17		…	…	…	…		…	…	…	…	
2740	Electric lighting equipment	104	108	103	93		4779	4948	5087	5261		201	215	224	222	
2750	Domestic appliances	51	49	46	44		4226	4023	3968	3864		182	178	173	169	
2790	Other electrical equipment	69	74	72	79		7777	7941	8135	7835		346	373	385	369	
281	General-purpose machinery	645	663	651	634		38673	39724	39640	39999		1805	1872	1879	1931	
2811	Engines/turbines,excl.aircraft,vehicle engines	27	27	26	25		2103	2058	2018	2041		100	102	100	103	
2812	Fluid power equipment	46	48	46	45		1874	1884	1870	1895		78	80	82	84	
2813	Other pumps, compressors, taps and valves	46	47	44	43		5635	6038	5538	5506		288	298	278	276	
2814	Bearings, gears, gearing and driving elements	35	36	33	33		4386	4447	4411	4266		209	217	219	212	
2815	Ovens, furnaces and furnace burners	74	75	71	65		2406	2303	2164	2063		112	109	106	103	
2816	Lifting and handling equipment	138	142	141	138		10504	10947	11300	11672		517	540	574	598	
2817	Office machinery, excl.computers,etc.	6	7	5	5		199	154	145	152		5	4	4	5	
2818	Power-driven hand tools	14	14	14	13		105	105	108	101		4	4	5	5	
2819	Other general-purpose machinery	259	267	271	267		11461	11788	12086	12303		492	518	512	546	
282	Special-purpose machinery	682	694	715	707		39637	39672	40147	40149		2005	2004	2070	2137	
2821	Agricultural and forestry machinery	117	120	120	120		6271	6339	6260	6066		273	274	273	275	
2822	Metal-forming machinery and machine tools	150	151	155	155		6325	6408	6552	6731		294	305	316	324	

ISIC Revision 4

2823	Machinery for metallurgy	164	154	148	161	2139	2140	2253	2306	19	20	18	15
2824	Mining, quarrying and construction machinery	226	227	229	228	4563	4671	4636	4735	53	55	53	52
2825	Food/beverage/tobacco processing machinery	76	73	74	71	1577	1534	1564	1552	55	54	53	52
2826	Textile/apparel/leather production machinery	25	23	23	25	535	504	517	513	20	21	22	21
2829	Other special-purpose machinery	1047	1005	951	953	18538	18486	17955	17935	285	290	277	275
2910	Motor vehicles	730	700	651	640	13227	13099	12766	12476	12	12	15	15
2920	Automobile bodies, trailers and semi-trailers	159	148	149	133	4014	3803	4040	3850	144	153	226	217
2930	Parts and accessories for motor vehicles	714	671	643	628	14649	14239	13892	13804	66	64	71	69
301	Building of ships and boats	8	6	6	5	231	199	194	169	39	38	40	38
3011	Building of ships and floating structures	8	6	6	5	231	199	194	169	39	38	40	38
3012	Building of pleasure and sporting boats	-	-	-	-	-	-	-	-	-	-	-	-
3020	Railway locomotives and rolling stock	66	61	55	52	1202	1133	1003	945	18	19	18	20
3030	Air and spacecraft and related machinery	…	…	…	…	…	…	…	…	…	…	…	…
3040	Military fighting vehicles	…	…	…	…	…	…	…	…	…	…	…	…
309	Transport equipment n.e.c.	127	109	95	84	2900	2541	2277	2104	16	16	26	22
3091	Motorcycles	…	…	…	…	…	…	…	…	6	6	12	8
3092	Bicycles and invalid carriages	16	14	14	24	469	435	424	696	9	9	13	13
3099	Other transport equipment n.e.c.	…	…	…	…	…	…	…	…	1	1	1	1
3100	Furniture	741	749	738	733	24062	24797	25109	25655	3171	3201	3200	3147
321	Jewellery, bijouterie and related articles b/	44	44	44	44	1283	1311	1336	1333	431	434	440	430
3211	Jewellery and related articles	44	44	44	44	1283	1311	1336	1333	374	375	384	383
3212	Imitation jewellery and related articles b/	…	…	…	…	…	…	…	…	57	59	56	47
3220	Musical instruments	23	22	22	22	661	629	651	671	204	215	213	206
3230	Sports goods	128	126	125	127	2942	3018	2982	3075	81	85	81	81
3240	Games and toys	81	75	76	70	1771	1778	1833	1732	92	89	82	78
3250	Medical and dental instruments and supplies	265	256	247	250	7929	7931	7908	7999	850	895	905	896
3290	Other manufacturing n.e.c.	48	48	48	48	1462	1474	1515	1540	169	172	178	180
331	Repair of fabricated metal products/machinery	532	519	508	499	12279	12253	12081	11985	1549	1555	1550	1510
3311	Repair of fabricated metal products	14	20	21	22	336	469	451	487	64	65	63	67
3312	Repair of machinery	188	174	170	169	4953	4791	4683	4685	1147	1151	1145	1109
3313	Repair of electronic and optical equipment	116	120	118	116	2222	2277	2298	2255	70	72	70	70
3314	Repair of electrical equipment	34	33	33	28	782	810	816	679	126	131	129	126
3315	Repair of transport equip., excl. motor vehicles	177	170	165	162	3911	3839	3764	3802	97	96	97	95
3319	Repair of other equipment	2	2	2	2	75	67	69	77	45	40	46	43
3320	Installation of industrial machinery/equipment	576	551	568	574	10759	10213	10289	10585	502	493	447	418
C	Total manufacturing	27131	26371	25686	25106	609610	604870	601505	598340	25037	25323	25524	25129

a/ 1061 includes 1062.
b/ 3211 includes 3212.

Austria

ISIC	Industry	Output Note	Output 2013	2014	2015	2016	VA Note	VA 2013	2014	2015	2016	GFCF Note	GFCF 2015	2016
			Output (valuation not defined) (millions of Euros)					**Value added at factor values** (millions of Euros)					**Gross fixed capital formation** (millions of Euros)	
1010	Processing/preserving of meat		4124	4113	4126	4118		792	841	857	911		90	101
1020	Processing/preserving of fish, etc.		36	38	...	44		9	9	...	12		...	1
1030	Processing/preserving of fruit,vegetables		1489	1385	1275	1288		356	315	345	360		53	75
1040	Vegetable and animal oils and fats		494	452	503	519		49	66	81	78		13	17
1050	Dairy products		2375	2485	2302	2293		373	375	409	435		123	135
106	Grain mill products,starches and starch products		798	851	1069	1084		179	226	258	263		45	57
1061	Grain mill products	a/	798	851	1069	1084	a/	179	226	258	263		45	57
1062	Starches and starch products	a/					a/							
107	Other food products		4505	4656	4749	4790		1770	1850	1900	1937		252	257
1071	Bakery products		2272	2315	2393	2467		1120	1156	1172	1231		148	135
1072	Sugar		...	...	...	...		...	...	...	...		...	...
1073	Cocoa, chocolate and sugar confectionery		294	308	326	325		118	129	141	139		25	14
1074	Macaroni, noodles, couscous, etc.		92	87	93	99		31	31	32	31		5	4
1075	Prepared meals and dishes		156	254	267	282		49	92	99	107		7	12
1079	Other food products n.e.c.													
1080	Prepared animal feeds		968	955	...	1011		194	196	...	227		...	26
110	Beverages		5136	5275	6007	6149		1331	1226	1461	1649		195	215
1101	Distilling, rectifying and blending of spirits		159	169	162	175		58	55	56	56		6	12
1102	Wines		...	...	...	...		...	...	...	...		...	...
1103	Malt liquors and malt		...	...	...	...		...	...	...	...		...	...
1104	Soft drinks,mineral waters,other bottled waters		3600	3696	4461	4604		729	600	838	1020		91	107
1200	Tobacco products		-	-	-	-		-	-	-	-		-	-
131	Spinning, weaving and finishing of textiles		656	647	598	579		214	228	207	202		39	65
1311	Preparation and spinning of textile fibres		213	189	184	169		52	44	39	36		11	6
1312	Weaving of textiles		350	363	322	353		126	143	127	142		25	58
1313	Finishing of textiles		93	95	92	57		36	41	40	24		3	1
139	Other textiles		713	749	835	821		260	272	290	304		18	18
1391	Knitted and crocheted fabrics		82	121	116	105		20	29	27	26		1	-
1392	Made-up textile articles, except apparel		190	197	215	218		76	77	83	89		4	5
1393	Carpets and rugs		76	77	80	83		18	17	17	21		3	2
1394	Cordage, rope, twine and netting		4	4	21	24		2	3	8	11		-	-
1399	Other textiles n.e.c.		361	350	404	392		143	147	155	157		10	10
1410	Wearing apparel, except fur apparel		657	669	642	558		220	213	198	186		12	8
1420	Articles of fur		5	4	...	...		2	2	...	...		...	...
1430	Knitted and crocheted apparel		110	98	...	...		55	46	...	...		...	...
151	Leather;luggage,handbags,saddlery,harness;fur		432	475	464	410		112	119	118	114		7	8
1511	Tanning/dressing of leather; dressing of fur		395	434	424	373		93	98	99	97		7	8
1512	Luggage,handbags,etc.;saddlery/harness		37	41	40	37		19	21	18	17		-	-
1520	Footwear		403	405	414	393		128	131	134	122		7	4
1610	Sawmilling and planing of wood		3229	3191	3350	3383		649	617	717	796		131	109

Code		C1	C2	C3	C4	C5	C6	C7	C8	C9	C10
162	Wood products, cork, straw, plaiting materials	4214	4263	4406	4579	1311	1367	1447	1513	141	162
1621	Veneer sheets and wood-based panels	1360	1348	1436	1481	370	404	445	462	69	61
1622	Builders' carpentry and joinery	2633	2688	2730	2831	857	877	908	950	66	90
1623	Wooden containers	151	160	169	170	53	56	62	63	4	8
1629	Other wood products;articles of cork,straw	70	68	71	97	31	31	32	37	2	3
170	Paper and paper products	5700	5762	5791	5881	1652	1776	1773	1903	301	272
1701	Pulp, paper and paperboard	3436	...	...	...	767	...	...	...	...	...
1702	Corrugated paper and paperboard	1280	1338	1337	1321	453	466	452	463	69	62
1709	Other articles of paper and paperboard	984	1026	1049	1058	432	457	465	489	37	36
181	Printing and service activities related to printing	1837	1830	1841	1871	791	743	740	734	78	82
1811	Printing	1703	1689	1699	1724	728	676	674	663	73	77
1812	Service activities related to printing	134	142	143	148	63	67	66	71	4	4
1820	Reproduction of recorded media	371	318	309	297	109	124	132	125	4	3
1910	Coke oven products	-	-	-	-	-	-	-	-	-	-
1920	Refined petroleum products	7841	7433	5778	5350	199	168	435	625	126	152
201	Basic chemicals,fertilizers, etc.	10341	9983	9377	9239	956	963	1394	2093	191	200
2011	Basic chemicals	...	...	...	...	...	...	...	...	...	...
2012	Fertilizers and nitrogen compounds	543	518	511	461	129	133	142	136	25	28
2013	Plastics and synthetic rubber in primary forms	...	...	...	...	...	...	...	...	...	...
202	Other chemical products	2690	2704	2426	2613	872	919	919	1025	76	112
2021	Pesticides and other agrochemical products	166	177	187	173	40	45	52	49	10	7
2022	Paints,varnishes;printing ink and mastics	618	640	631	639	234	254	255	247	22	44
2023	Soap,cleaning and cosmetic preparations	735	700	696	773	331	326	342	391	23	24
2029	Other chemical products n.e.c.	1171	1187	...	...	267	293	...	...	...	...
2030	Man-made fibres	954	965	1004	1151	306	350	344	447	65	98
2100	Pharmaceuticals,medicinal chemicals, etc.	3667	3758	3907	3952	1510	1851	1796	1839	419	275
221	Rubber products	409	382	354	383	161	150	153	196	14	12
2211	Rubber tyres and tubes	17	10	10	9	9	5	5	5	-	2
2219	Other rubber products	391	371	345	374	153	146	148	191	14	9
2220	Plastics products	5353	5684	5662	5806	1851	2050	1978	2059	256	286
2310	Glass and glass products	1285	1314	1242	1267	636	651	589	610	124	132
239	Non-metallic mineral products n.e.c.	4732	4887	4841	4827	1645	1743	1728	1765	221	242
2391	Refractory products	404	442	406	373	128	159	123	130	19	21
2392	Clay building materials	165	156	...	...	61	61	...	...	...	...
2393	Other porcelain and ceramic products	...	...	...	...	...	...	...	...	...	...
2394	Cement, lime and plaster	377	386	390	394	156	159	162	158	22	24
2395	Articles of concrete, cement and plaster	2501	2484	2538	2590	841	841	858	893	115	129
2396	Cutting, shaping and finishing of stone	316	314	314	310	163	157	159	149	11	11
2399	Other non-metallic mineral products n.e.c.	843	895	849	813	233	275	275	278	37	38
2410	Basic iron and steel	9397	9355	9510	8663	2222	2247	2526	2376	538	498
2420	Basic precious and other non-ferrous metals	4119	4169	4642	4554	737	814	809	858	143	205
243	Casting of metals	1252	1272	1392	1393	441	479	549	573	108	112
2431	Casting of iron and steel	417	416	427	421	158	161	168	170	24	18
2432	Casting of non-ferrous metals	835	856	966	972	283	318	381	403	84	95
251	Struct.metal products, tanks, reservoirs	4579	4335	4413	4517	1772	1652	1745	1827	142	114

continued

Austria

ISIC Revision 4		Note	Output (valuation not defined) (millions of Euros)				Note	Value added at factor values (millions of Euros)				Note	Gross fixed capital formation (millions of Euros)	
ISIC	Industry		2013	2014	2015	2016		2013	2014	2015	2016		2015	2016
2511	Structural metal products		3682	3441	3569	3714		1414	1318	1404	1510		113	102
2512	Tanks, reservoirs and containers of metal		812	816	755	722		337	321	312	297		26	12
2513	Steam generators, excl. hot water boilers		86	78	89	82		21	14	29	21		2	-
2520	Weapons and ammunition		367	325	371	513		164	137	172	235		22	57
259	Other metal products;metal working services		8668	8962	9163	9474		3277	3446	3591	3826		456	504
2591	Forging,pressing,stamping,roll-forming of metal		1412	1406	1482	1516		412	438	486	453		45	73
2592	Treatment and coating of metals; machining		2659	2725	2742	2768		899	908	892	1032		104	140
2593	Cutlery, hand tools and general hardware		3224	3374	3471	3653		1453	1539	1646	1769		229	222
2599	Other fabricated metal products n.e.c.		…	1458	…	…		…	561	…	…		…	…
2610	Electronic components and boards		2169	2456	2692	3192		980	929	1015	1087		185	221
2620	Computers and peripheral equipment		191	186	243	220		67	72	85	78		3	1
2630	Communication equipment		321	317	362	365		163	147	170	172		23	11
2640	Consumer electronics		211	168	121	115		84	55	34	49		2	4
265	Measuring,testing equipment; watches, etc.		1017	1064	1111	1138		506	536	561	590		48	47
2651	Measuring/testing/navigating equipment,etc.		1005	1053	1105	1135		501	533	559	589		48	47
2652	Watches and clocks		11	11	6	3		6	3	3	2		-	-
2660	Irradiation/electromedical equipment,etc.		662	675	752	777		291	221	192	237		12	15
2670	Optical instruments and photographic equipment		195	…	192	205		83	…	86	98		12	12
2680	Magnetic and optical media		-	…	-	-		-	…	-	-		-	-
2710	Electric motors,generators,transformers,etc.		5891	5907	6013	6673		2177	2141	2251	2414		107	98
2720	Batteries and accumulators		234	257	277	447		46	47	60	109		13	12
273	Wiring and wiring devices		985	1045	1054	1093		275	291	308	312		44	28
2731	Fibre optic cables		…	…	…	…		…	…	…	…		…	…
2732	Other electronic and electric wires and cables		554	584	608	625		115	121	133	153		30	12
2733	Wiring devices		…	…	…	…		…	…	…	…		…	…
2740	Electric lighting equipment		1096	1224	1147	1284		398	416	421	461		84	73
2750	Domestic appliances		881	780	771	727		367	348	321	307		37	33
2790	Other electrical equipment		1613	1717	1831	1695		602	684	740	716		49	142
281	General-purpose machinery		9778	9879	9946	9681		3328	3499	3578	3304		247	219
2811	Engines/turbines,excl.aircraft,vehicle engines		503	432	476	428		163	142	178	149		29	14
2812	Fluid power equipment		314	306	303	326		133	127	126	136		5	9
2813	Other pumps, compressors, taps and valves		1313	1336	1268	1231		490	481	447	425		43	45
2814	Bearings, gears, gearing and driving elements		1053	1046	1045	966		505	508	509	460		44	26
2815	Ovens, furnaces and furnace burners		551	535	471	468		201	194	171	169		12	9
2816	Lifting and handling equipment		3336	3461	3702	3315		1019	1158	1236	958		53	47
2817	Office machinery, excl.computers,etc.		20	21	22	21		7	8	7	7		1	-
2818	Power-driven hand tools		18	20	18	17		9	9	8	8		1	5
2819	Other general-purpose machinery		2671	2725	2640	2908		801	871	897	992		61	65
282	Special-purpose machinery		10620	10488	11011	11004		3451	3419	3614	3813		226	253
2821	Agricultural and forestry machinery		1830	1847	1758	1784		524	530	480	520		48	48
2822	Metal-forming machinery and machine tools		1362	1411	1441	1489		498	502	557	546		30	37

Code	Description										
2823	Machinery for metallurgy	762	794	784	838	189	221	224	267	5	6
2824	Mining, quarrying and construction machinery	1639	1595	1614	1504	466	385	455	446	31	26
2825	Food/beverage/tobacco processing machinery	341	367	345	377	136	138	132	143	9	6
2826	Textile/apparel/leather production machinery	86	91	86	110	42	43	38	45	2	5
2829	Other special-purpose machinery	4600	4383	4983	4903	1596	1599	1727	1847	102	124
2910	Motor vehicles	8213	8648	8532	8532	1197	1557	1492	1480	228	373
2920	Automobile bodies, trailers and semi-trailers	663	724	756	847	206	231	239	278	17	14
2930	Parts and accessories for motor vehicles	4202	4420	4788	5012	1349	1435	1499	1559	247	218
301	Building of ships and boats	26	30	33	41	11	14	16	19	2	1
3011	Building of ships and floating structures	-	-	-	-	-	-	-	-	-	-
3012	Building of pleasure and sporting boats	26	30	33	41	11	14	16	19	2	1
3020	Railway locomotives and rolling stock	...	...	...	...	...	...	...	...	...	...
3030	Air and spacecraft and related machinery	197	212	259	294	84	86	123	125	16	11
3040	Military fighting vehicles	...	...	...	...	...	...	...	...	...	...
309	Transport equipment n.e.c.	904	966	1068	1252	233	179	226	252	30	29
3091	Motorcycles	...	...	...	...	...	...	...	...	1	...
3092	Bicycles and invalid carriages	219	139	163	199	49	38	40	46	1	...
3099	Other transport equipment n.e.c.	...	...	...	...	...	...	...	...	...	...
3100	Furniture	2845	2845	2867	2994	1211	1262	1282	1373	88	79
321	Jewellery, bijouterie and related articles b/	1975	1299	1771	1286	115	146	145	131	12	6
3211	Jewellery and related articles b/	1975	1299	1771	1286	115	146	145	131	12	6
3212	Imitation jewellery and related articles	...	...	...	...	...	...	...	...	...	...
3220	Musical instruments	65	65	69	76	44	43	46	49	3	3
3230	Sports goods	607	617	627	636	193	197	203	218	34	26
3240	Games and toys	521	538	491	519	154	181	186	180	18	21
3250	Medical and dental instruments and supplies	852	842	909	914	438	433	458	469	24	28
3290	Other manufacturing n.e.c.	182	185	192	190	84	94	94	91	9	6
331	Repair of fabricated metal products/machinery	2006	1792	1880	1868	835	868	896	925	38	38
3311	Repair of fabricated metal products	78	56	66	39	32	28	32	25	1	1
3312	Repair of machinery	713	699	712	736	352	351	363	379	19	18
3313	Repair of electronic and optical equipment	403	393	411	415	175	174	180	182	2	3
3314	Repair of electrical equipment	222	149	165	137	48	61	62	58	2	2
3315	Repair of transport equip., excl. motor vehicles	581	485	517	529	225	248	256	277	14	14
3319	Repair of other equipment	9	11	10	11	4	5	5	5	-	-
3320	Installation of industrial machinery/equipment	2213	2330	2067	2164	836	842	794	851	33	45
C	Total manufacturing	166674	167256	168797	170206	47493	49257	51585	54390	6373	6706

a/ 1061 includes 1062.
b/ 3211 includes 3212.

Austria

Index numbers of industrial production

ISIC Revision 4				(2010=100)										
ISIC	Industry	Note	2005	2006	2007	2008	2009	2010	2011	2012	2013	2014	2015	2016
10	Food products		95	101	101	101	99	100	103	102	105	106	108	108
11	Beverages		97	99	107	105	102	100	105	108	107	107	107	112
12	Tobacco products		...	...	...	...	...	...	...	...	...	...	...	...
13	Textiles		112	111	116	107	89	100	98	94	94	95	105	105
14	Wearing apparel		119	125	121	112	103	100	83	78	71	71	68	75
15	Leather and related products		226	166	145	142	115	100	104	109	114	120	125	116
16	Wood products, excluding furniture		97	105	108	101	91	100	107	104	104	102	105	111
17	Paper and paper products		95	98	102	103	92	100	103	104	104	108	108	112
18	Printing and reproduction of recorded media		92	97	104	104	96	100	97	88	86	85	83	84
19	Coke and refined petroleum products		71	83	82	114	103	100	122	113	103	100	92	83
20	Chemicals and chemical products		87	93	103	108	95	100	103	106	106	109	108	108
21	Pharmaceuticals,medicinal chemicals, etc.		68	71	84	80	90	100	105	109	112	122	131	132
22	Rubber and plastics products		91	100	106	106	96	100	110	111	114	116	118	123
23	Other non-metallic mineral products		107	112	117	112	93	100	101	96	95	97	97	99
24	Basic metals		93	102	108	109	80	100	112	108	109	111	114	114
25	Fabricated metal products, except machinery		98	103	108	111	92	100	106	111	112	113	114	118
26	Computer, electronic and optical products		72	75	96	96	84	100	103	103	108	111	115	129
27	Electrical equipment		84	90	97	106	98	100	106	102	97	102	103	112
28	Machinery and equipment n.e.c.		89	101	111	119	94	100	112	115	117	117	129	130
29	Motor vehicles, trailers and semi-trailers		118	125	123	114	86	100	113	113	123	126	128	133
30	Other transport equipment		104	113	120	135	134	100	110	99	96	92	76	82
31	Furniture		102	107	111	107	100	100	101	101	98	97	95	103
32	Other manufacturing		89	95	99	103	100	100	104	96	111	95	104	102
33	Repair and installation of machinery/equipment		78	78	90	99	92	100	105	107	108	107	107	103
C	Total manufacturing		93	99	105	107	93	100	106	106	107	108	111	114

Azerbaijan

Supplier of information:
State Statistical Committee of the Republic of Azerbaijan, Baku.

Basic source of data:
Annual survey.

Major deviations from ISIC (Revision 4):
None reported.

Reference period:
Calendar year.

Scope:
All enterprises.

Method of data collection:
Mail questionnaires.

Type of enumeration:
Complete enumeration.

Adjusted for non-response:
No.

Concepts and definitions of variables:
Wages and salaries excludes housing and family allowances paid directly by the employer and payments in kind.

Related national publications:
Statistical Yearbook "Industry of Azerbaijan", published by State Statistical Committee of the Republic of Azerbaijan, Baku.

Azerbaijan

ISIC	Industry	Enterprises Note	Enterprises 2013	Enterprises 2014	Enterprises 2015	Enterprises 2016	Employees Note	Employees 2013	Employees 2014	Employees 2015	Employees 2016	Wages Note	Wages 2013	Wages 2014	Wages 2015	Wages 2016
		Number of enterprises (number)					**Number of employees (number)**					**Wages and salaries paid to employees (thousands of Azerbaijani Manat)**				
1010	Processing/preserving of meat		22	22	25	26		2138	2176	2233	2888		8871	11819	9925	11099
1020	Processing/preserving of fish, etc.		6	8	7	8		296	290	320	377		1317	1924	1003	1463
1030	Processing/preserving of fruit,vegetables		64	59	71	72		2976	2872	2105	2354		12925	13271	9389	11247
1040	Vegetable and animal oils and fats		7	9	9	9		649	866	921	888		4007	5294	7547	7199
1050	Dairy products		32	34	33	35		1494	2248	2136	2251		4116	6184	7971	9404
106	Grain mill products,starches and starch products		51	53	56	57		1981	2140	2018	1745		5050	5733	7507	6764
1061	Grain mill products		50	52	55	56		1966	2128	2006	1733		4837	5494	7142	6020
1062	Starches and starch products		1	1	1	1		15	12	12	12		213	239	365	744
107	Other food products		253	198	173	176		9186	9962	9003	8604		23903	33665	31654	31097
1071	Bakery products		208	144	118	119		5257	6158	5041	4754		8989	9683	12339	13275
1072	Sugar		10	11	10	11		1611	1736	1778	1755		9027	16642	11829	9999
1073	Cocoa, chocolate and sugar confectionery		12	15	14	14		1048	1030	1060	996		2106	4460	3233	3749
1074	Macaroni, noodles, couscous, etc.		3	4	4	4		297	233	151	63		795	446	475	191
1075	Prepared meals and dishes		-	1	1	1		-	23	17	8		-	25	26	101
1079	Other food products n.e.c.		20	23	26	27		973	782	956	1028		2986	2409	3752	3782
1080	Prepared animal feeds		4	6	8	8		82	66	52	175		112	137	155	311
110	Beverages		110	118	120	119		5607	5815	6047	6039		24662	32630	30122	33596
1101	Distilling, rectifying and blending of spirits		19	22	25	25		993	1037	1118	1300		2473	7763	4497	5916
1102	Wines		18	19	22	21		806	860	672	775		3018	3121	2375	2673
1103	Malt liquors and malt		21	24	20	20		588	568	552	527		5946	5900	6448	6480
1104	Soft drinks,mineral waters,other bottled waters		52	53	53	53		3220	3350	3705	3437		13225	15849	16802	18527
1200	Tobacco products		8	6	7	8		482	314	320	341		1843	1362	1456	1695
131	Spinning, weaving and finishing of textiles		40	44	42	41		3324	3710	2763	3946		10323	12138	8885	12990
1311	Preparation and spinning of textile fibres		35	36	35	35		2539	2623	1927	2560		8591	9836	6579	9224
1312	Weaving of textiles		5	5	6	5		785	1075	827	1386		1732	2291	2295	3766
1313	Finishing of textiles		...	1	1	1		...	12	9	-		...	11	11	-
139	Other textiles		32	24	26	24		449	443	430	430		1146	1202	1308	1552
1391	Knitted and crocheted fabrics		8	2	2	2		13	13	11	4		23	23	20	8
1392	Made-up textile articles, except apparel		8	7	7	7		98	100	101	85		162	171	158	149
1393	Carpets and rugs		14	12	14	12		79	97	94	87		106	151	201	218
1394	Cordage, rope, twine and netting		1	1	2	2		227	213	214	247		818	829	916	1108
1399	Other textiles n.e.c.		1	2	1	1		32	20	10	7		37	28	13	69
1410	Wearing apparel, except fur apparel		69	52	43	50		2582	2535	2372	2582		9536	10210	9574	10408
1420	Articles of fur		-	...	1	-		-	2	1	1		-	...	...	-
1430	Knitted and crocheted apparel		6	5	8	10		27	46	39	32		46	58	78	95
151	Leather;luggage,handbags,saddlery,harness;fur		11	12	11	9		414	339	355	270		3206	2318	2099	1308
1511	Tanning/dressing of leather; dressing of fur		9	10	9	7		371	292	313	238		2918	2212	1888	1148
1512	Luggage,handbags,etc.;saddlery/harness		2	2	2	2		43	47	42	32		288	106	211	160
1520	Footwear		12	10	12	12		814	525	562	516		2955	2203	2154	2206
1610	Sawmilling and planing of wood		7	5	7	6		133	124	13	63		296	299	18	58

Code	Description												
162	Wood products, cork, straw, plaiting materials	44	43	28	28	1617	1841	1530	1145	7535	9137	8321	6922
1621	Veneer sheets and wood-based panels	3	3	2	2	17	16	6	21	27	26	7	10
1622	Builders' carpentry and joinery	33	34	22	22	1212	1452	1334	1039	7116	8675	7797	6080
1623	Wooden containers	2	2	3	3	143	170	110	85	192	291	442	832
1629	Other wood products;articles of cork,straw	6	4	1	1	245	203	80	-	200	145	75	-
170	Paper and paper products	20	19	23	22	1286	1290	1263	1172	6879	7838	7881	7396
1701	Pulp, paper and paperboard	5	5	6	6	225	174	160	134	1282	1359	1318	900
1702	Corrugated paper and paperboard	2	5	7	7	985	1054	1052	993	5437	6352	6423	6373
1709	Other articles of paper and paperboard	13	9	10	9	76	62	51	45	160	127	140	123
181	Printing and service activities related to printing	142	146	155	138	1920	2009	2121	1748	6765	9010	9785	8396
1811	Printing	120	119	132	116	1693	1728	1806	1546	6015	8139	8034	7452
1812	Service activities related to printing	22	27	23	22	227	281	315	202	750	871	1751	944
1820	Reproduction of recorded media	-	1	2	2	44	38	18	57	17	14	9	153
1910	Coke oven products	-	-	-	-	-	-	-	-	-	-	-	-
1920	Refined petroleum products	4	4	3	3	5170	5009	4266	4048	45192	46082	41891	42859
201	Basic chemicals,fertilizers, etc.	28	28	28	33	5821	4769	4546	4301	35845	30716	37435	42085
2011	Basic chemicals	25	25	23	27	1967	1510	1732	1777	9640	7853	17746	21796
2012	Fertilizers and nitrogen compounds	1	1	1	1	132	57	147	33	377	165	124	94
2013	Plastics and synthetic rubber in primary forms	2	2	4	5	3722	3202	2667	2491	25828	22698	19565	20195
202	Other chemical products	42	44	41	42	1704	1730	1680	1639	6183	7025	7782	7566
2021	Pesticides and other agrochemical products	:	1	1	1	24	22	24	25	75	73	74	27
2022	Paints,varnishes;printing ink and mastics	19	19	19	18	613	615	700	697	2331	2643	3106	3099
2023	Soap,cleaning and cosmetic preparations	13	14	11	11	404	371	279	258	1101	1119	891	921
2029	Other chemical products n.e.c.	10	10	10	12	663	722	677	659	2676	3190	3711	3519
2030	Man-made fibres	-	-	-	-	-	-	-	-	-	-	-	-
2100	Pharmaceuticals,medicinal chemicals, etc.	8	8	11	10	240	243	222	184	1042	1183	977	1207
221	Rubber products	7	7	9	9	67	50	33	255	165	157	142	729
2211	Rubber tyres and tubes	2	2	2	2	32	28	24	215	:	:	:	151
2219	Other rubber products	5	5	7	7	35	22	9	40	113	96	83	578
2220	Plastics products	82	88	89	83	4312	5569	4994	5239	17597	23572	23751	24155
2310	Glass and glass products	20	24	24	23	814	949	772	942	3078	:	2511	3997
239	Non-metallic mineral products n.e.c.	189	206	215	201	9885	12249	12311	10337	61622	76213	79173	71965
2391	Refractory products	4	3	2	2	71	59	29	21	431	258	67	19
2392	Clay building materials	29	33	32	31	1648	1517	1285	984	14390	6590	4209	2687
2393	Other porcelain and ceramic products	2	1	2	2	79	23	5	14	190	108	9	8
2394	Cement, lime and plaster	28	37	35	31	1541	3185	2939	2453	18821	32571	42393	39256
2395	Articles of concrete, cement and plaster	73	78	89	87	4107	4270	4795	4153	21181	28075	22056	19149
2396	Cutting, shaping and finishing of stone	40	40	43	38	1138	1426	1196	802	2399	2238	3272	2760
2399	Other non-metallic mineral products n.e.c.	13	14	12	10	1301	1769	2062	1910	4210	6373	7165	8086
2410	Basic iron and steel	7	9	8	8	4007	3317	2879	2443	31751	27461	20147	20507
2420	Basic precious and other non-ferrous metals	13	17	18	20	2741	1672	1490	1405	7551	8868	7521	7027
243	Casting of metals	-	1	1	1	-	7	7	6	-	3	16	10
2431	Casting of iron and steel	-	-	1	1	-	3	3	3	-	1	11	8
2432	Casting of non-ferrous metals	-	1	-	1	-	4	4	3	-	2	5	2
251	Struct.metal products, tanks, reservoirs	57	59	50	57	2057	2879	3039	2568	8895	13363	11545	12022

continued

Azerbaijan

ISIC	Industry	Number of enterprises (number) 2013	2014	2015	2016	Note	Number of employees (number) Note	2013	2014	2015	2016	Wages and salaries paid to employees (thousands of Azerbaijani Manat) Note	2013	2014	2015	2016
2511	Structural metal products	51	54	46	53			1969	2788	2953	2469		8773	13208	11383	11863
2512	Tanks, reservoirs and containers of metal	5	5	4	4			68	91	86	99		122	155	162	159
2513	Steam generators, excl. hot water boilers	1	-	-	-			20	-	-	-		...	-	-	-
2520	Weapons and ammunition	-	-	-	-			-	-	-	-		-	-	-	-
259	Other metal products;metal working services	29	26	25	26			1064	1184	942	965		4955	6625	12169	9445
2591	Forging,pressing,stamping,roll-forming of metal	-	1	1	2			13	2	2	20		68	...	...	24
2592	Treatment and coating of metals;machining	2	2	4	5			186	279	303	340		2302	4270	10218	7607
2593	Cutlery, hand tools and general hardware	2	1	1	1			40	12	12	8		143	37	37	17
2599	Other fabricated metal products n.e.c.	25	22	19	18			825	891	625	597		2442	2318	1914	1797
2610	Electronic components and boards	9	8	8	7			226	143	98	70		457	400	307	270
2620	Computers and peripheral equipment	-	-	-	2			-	-	-	20		-	-	-	75
2630	Communication equipment	5	4	5	5			519	518	421	427		2179	2253	1988	2386
2640	Consumer electronics	1	-	-	2			1	-	-	14		3	-	-	122
265	Measuring,testing equipment; watches, etc.	7	11	11	8			911	891	896	1002		4489	4451	4750	6063
2651	Measuring/testing/navigating equipment,etc.	7	11	11	8			911	891	896	1002		4489	4451	4750	6063
2652	Watches and clocks	-	-	-	-			-	-	-	-		-	-	-	-
2660	Irradiation/electromedical equipment,etc.	-	-	-	-			-	-	-	-		-	-	-	-
2670	Optical instruments and photographic equipment	1	1	-	1			8	1	-	-		4	1	-	-
2680	Magnetic and optical media	-	-	-	-			-	-	-	-		-	-	-	-
2710	Electric motors,generators,transformers,etc.	23	17	18	19			1241	1336	1443	1444		3129	3332	6567	8388
2720	Batteries and accumulators	...	1	1	1			10	3	2	2		12	4	7	126
273	Wiring and wiring devices	7	9	10	11			...	3963	3039	1914		...	34958	25117	15820
2731	Fibre optic cables	4	4	5	6			99	46	53	48		161	114	268	199
2732	Other electronic and electric wires and cables	3	5	5	5			...	3917	2986	1866		...	34844	24849	15621
2733	Wiring devices	-	-	-	-			-	-	-	-		-	-	-	-
2740	Electric lighting equipment	-	-	-	-			-	-	-	-		-	-	-	-
2750	Domestic appliances	6	10	10	10			163	300	329	275		517	904	1362	1062
2790	Other electrical equipment	3	3	2	2			63	63	60	60			241	246	323
281	General-purpose machinery	42	46	38	38			2952	2894	2696	2598		10350	10850	10424	9448
2811	Engines/turbines,excl.aircraft,vehicle engines	...	...	2	2			12	12	30	18		19	27	60	38
2812	Fluid power equipment	-	-	-	-			-	-	-	-		-	-	-	-
2813	Other pumps, compressors, taps and valves	10	10	8	8			795	806	794	732		3548	3704	3735	3288
2814	Bearings, gears, gearing and driving elements	5	6	6	6			239	281	262	292		923	1042	1045	1262
2815	Ovens, furnaces and furnace burners	...	1	-	-			45	48	-	-		144	148	-	-
2816	Lifting and handling equipment	6	8	4	4			597	528	491	479		1379	1378	1194	739
2817	Office machinery, excl.computers,etc.	...	1	-	-			24	14	-	-		63	34	-	-
2818	Power-driven hand tools	1	1	1	1			38	38	38	37		152	163	178	180
2819	Other general-purpose machinery	20	19	17	17			1202	1167	1081	1040		4122	4354	4212	3941
282	Special-purpose machinery	17	15	21	20			1901	1430	1270	1269		9634	7811	6005	6014
2821	Agricultural and forestry machinery	7	6	6	4			514	42	8	10		1960	139	16	19
2822	Metal-forming machinery and machine tools	1	1	2	3			7	12	13	9		18	36	22	9

2823	Machinery for metallurgy	3	-	-	1	85	81	48	50	266	305	209	126
2824	Mining, quarrying and construction machinery	2	4	4	4	379	357	237	206	2141	2064	531	256
2825	Food/beverage/tobacco processing machinery	...	...	2	1	12	8	13	9	29	15	24	19
2826	Textile/apparel/leather production machinery	-	-	-	-	-	-	-	-	-	-	-	-
2829	Other special-purpose machinery	4	4	7	7	904	930	951	985	5220	5252	5203	5585
2910	Motor vehicles	4	5	4	4	96	586	603	624	302	1988	2932	3094
2920	Automobile bodies, trailers and semi-trailers	-	-	-	-	-	-	-	-	-	-	-	-
2930	Parts and accessories for motor vehicles	2	1	1	1	26	25	14	6	36	68	33	19
301	Building of ships and boats	-	3	3	3	-	43	166	138	-	...	...	395
3011	Building of ships and floating structures	-	3	3	3	-	43	166	138	-	...	...	395
3012	Building of pleasure and sporting boats	-	-	-	-	-	-	-	-	-	-	-	-
3020	Railway locomotives and rolling stock	7	5	6	6	2621	2404	2165	1950	9222	12820	11871	10965
3030	Air and spacecraft and related machinery	1	1	-	-	8	...	-	-	115	...	-	-
3040	Military fighting vehicles	-	-	-	-	-	-	-	-	-	-	-	-
309	Transport equipment n.e.c.	-	-	-	-	-	-	-	-	-	-	-	-
3091	Motorcycles	-	-	-	-	-	-	-	-	-	-	-	-
3092	Bicycles and invalid carriages	-	-	-	-	-	-	-	-	-	-	-	-
3099	Other transport equipment n.e.c.	-	-	-	-	-	-	-	-	-	-	-	-
3100	Furniture	84	94	97	97	4206	4432	4062	3959	14965	16270	14370	15295
321	Jewellery, bijouterie and related articles	6	5	4	3	130	130	111	111	282	394	1170	1357
3211	Jewellery and related articles	5	4	3	3	127	128	110	110	278	392	1170	1357
3212	Imitation jewellery and related articles	1	1	1	-	3	2	1	1	4	2	-	-
3220	Musical instruments	1	1	1	1	49	49	49	49	82	...	95	203
3230	Sports goods	-	-	-	-	-	-	-	-	-	-	-	-
3240	Games and toys	...	-	1	-	3	-	3	-	8	-	...	-
3250	Medical and dental instruments and supplies	7	5	6	6	290	202	218	222	1088	759	911	947
3290	Other manufacturing n.e.c.	22	20	22	22	916	474	373	300	1722	670	748	260
331	Repair of fabricated metal products/machinery	72	90	104	111	4922	5399	7365	6698	37800	48781	68225	82795
3311	Repair of fabricated metal products	2	3	2	3	104	151	951	139	395	...	721	968
3312	Repair of machinery	18	20	19	18	548	547	528	360	2398	1665	1568	1784
3313	Repair of electronic and optical equipment	4	4	8	9	114	171	181	178	251	274	618	6142
3314	Repair of electrical equipment	12	19	24	25	248	335	390	371	1154	1481	2007	5803
3315	Repair of transport equip., excl. motor vehicles	32	35	37	41	3888	4158	5140	5430	33272	44831	62857	67607
3319	Repair of other equipment	4	9	14	15	20	37	175	220	330	53	454	491
3320	Installation of industrial machinery/equipment	11	14	16	19	612	586	498	574	...	3398	3428	3650
C	Total manufacturing	1764	1764	1778	1776	101535	105153	99684	95682	490618	567849	563285	578011

Azerbaijan

ISIC	Industry	Output Note	Output 2013	Output 2014	Output 2015	Output 2016	VA Note	VA 2013	VA 2014	VA 2015	VA 2016	GFCF Note	GFCF 2015	GFCF 2016
	ISIC Revision 4		(thousands of Azerbaijani Manat)					(thousands of Azerbaijani Manat)					(thousands of Azerbaijani Manat)	
1010	Processing/preserving of meat		886349	876120	793558	822555		134617	136034	97134	102390		688	203
1020	Processing/preserving of fish, etc.		...	11587	3924	3639		283	6355	3148	2871		2294	1124
1030	Processing/preserving of fruit,vegetables		86856	115961	121213	203337		33273	43273	46637	77473		14443	470
1040	Vegetable and animal oils and fats		56525	67155	67643	248882		11444	13161	13330	46948		-	-
1050	Dairy products		352906	399842	507311	539890		66682	72559	130818	138417		-	15053
106	Grain mill products,starches and starch products		448106	388981	363397	476976		110419	97134	86294	113198		22256	1708
1061	Grain mill products		446841	388746	363284	472410		109696	96987	86224	110377		836	1603
1062	Starches and starch products		1265	235	...	4566		723	147	70	2821		21420	105
107	Other food products		684292	736502	689936	961311		219503	227617	206908	267645		7662	744
1071	Bakery products		527906	554468	548184	553516		185896	180273	177485	179888		3884	133
1072	Sugar		122772	140350	111130	324605		20782	24523	11600	34319		1529	611
1073	Cocoa, chocolate and sugar confectionery		18938	12709	12309	20148		6563	3764	3596	5727		1312	-
1074	Macaroni, noodles, couscous, etc.		1199	991	34	46		700	592	16	22		-	-
1075	Prepared meals and dishes		-	113	83	126		-	43	36	56		-	-
1079	Other food products n.e.c.		13444	27871	18196	62870		5549	18422	14175	47632		937	-
1080	Prepared animal feeds		605	506	252	409		222	183	66	100		-	10987
110	Beverages		207691	232099	194693	208010		93698	104425	88793	93262		76261	12195
1101	Distilling, rectifying and blending of spirits		17238	18935	16089	35172		5398	7152	5801	12947		46217	-
1102	Wines		24023	30153	23775	24174		12012	13270	10293	10512		717	5487
1103	Malt liquors and malt		48565	51412	36224	36690		26911	31765	26177	26405		5879	-
1104	Soft drinks,mineral waters,other bottled waters		117865	131600	118605	111974		49377	52239	46521	43399		23448	6708
1200	Tobacco products		13084	24551	27155	41541		3729	7082	7982	12053		-	1063
131	Spinning, weaving and finishing of textiles		49362	46761	29243	95869		22622	21485	13000	41730		338	97648
1311	Preparation and spinning of textile fibres		45674	36603	21517	79644		20687	16277	9311	34083		-	94604
1312	Weaving of textiles		3679	10104	7644	16225		1931	5182	3650	7647		338	3044
1313	Finishing of textiles		9	54	82	-		4	26	39	-		-	-
139	Other textiles		1881	1947	1425	1141		977	726	504	403		-	533
1391	Knitted and crocheted fabrics		10	...	...	...		6	...	...	-		-	-
1392	Made-up textile articles, except apparel		727	1626	1226	905		228	499	366	247		-	-
1393	Carpets and rugs		122	174	115	67		93	132	84	49		-	435
1394	Cordage, rope, twine and netting		47	51	29	52		35	39	21	36		-	99
1399	Other textiles n.e.c.		975	96	55	117		615	57	34	71		-	-
1410	Wearing apparel, except fur apparel		39423	54056	51789	60900		7352	10292	9660	11788		157	-
1420	Articles of fur		-	4	4	-		-	1	1	-		-	2
1430	Knitted and crocheted apparel		561	483	785	201		86	76	334	86		-	-
151	Leather;luggage,handbags,saddlery,harness;fur		12406	17886	10424	8609		3115	4628	2589	1869		30	-
1511	Tanning/dressing of leather; dressing of fur		11910	17374	10092	8383		2940	4456	2507	1816		30	-
1512	Luggage,handbags,etc.;saddlery/harness		496	512	332	226		175	172	82	53		-	-
1520	Footwear		8935	1258	1793	4954		2347	372	627	1688		181	42
1610	Sawmilling and planing of wood		325	333	124	147		123	139	36	42		-	-

Code	Description	1	2	3	4	5	6	7	8	9	10
162	Wood products, cork, straw, plaiting materials	14726	18878	16256	11997	4362	5569	4838	3555	1126	34169
1621	Veneer sheets and wood-based panels	69	80	74	55	22	19	16	12	19	33877
1622	Builders' carpentry and joinery	9639	13902	11827	5794	3233	4045	3239	1405	1107	292
1623	Wooden containers	1783	1478	2020	4020	373	303	712	1373		
1629	Other wood products;articles of cork,straw	3235	3418	2335	2128	734	1201	872	765		
170	Paper and paper products	19804	28071	32043	55767	4278	6133	6892	12225	2530	10344
1701	Pulp, paper and paperboard	1194	878	3137	726	273	198	755	183	2429	755
1702	Corrugated paper and paperboard	18254	26903	28586	53476	3915	5859	6137	11596	101	27555
1709	Other articles of paper and paperboard	356	290	320	1565	90	76	91	445		245
181	Printing and service activities related to printing	45670	33830	37342	60053	21012	15643	17411	28021	4330	245
1811	Printing	38777	28000	31006	53883	18835	13626	15246	25911	3384	224
1812	Service activities related to printing	6893	5830	6336	6170	2177	2017	2164	2111	946	
1820	Reproduction of recorded media	2356	219	300	113	1128	105	130	48		22
1910	Coke oven products									282115	40686
1920	Refined petroleum products	2434204	2852704	2473645	2472755	1027633	1218105	1061945	1051290	19927	16146
201	Basic chemicals,fertilizers, etc.	178255	224520	297051	346680	63082	79247	103070	124041	19927	9954
2011	Basic chemicals	36528	45251	138055	131067	14661	18123	55049	52184		
2012	Fertilizers and nitrogen compounds	141718	179269	158996	215613	48418	61124	48020	71857	19927	6192
2013	Plastics and synthetic rubber in primary forms	22021	22648	56167	27565	7415	8741	22851	9324	7963	2433
202	Other chemical products										
2021	Pesticides and other agrochemical products	4218	3606	2959	8675	950	986	694	2013	115	1109
2022	Paints,varnishes;printing ink and mastics	1247	2296	4089	6101	597	1072	1754	2488		240
2023	Soap,cleaning and cosmetic preparations	16556	16746	12320	12789	5868	6683	4621	4822	7848	1083
2029	Other chemical products n.e.c.										
2030	Man-made fibres										
2100	Pharmaceuticals,medicinal chemicals, etc.	3160	2730	2981	1027	1037	900	995	342		94
221	Rubber products	319	457	121	1557	81	112	39	484		94
2211	Rubber tyres and tubes	34	39	25	129	16	17	11	56		
2219	Other rubber products	285	418	96	1428	65	95	29	428		94
2220	Plastics products	73719	68561	94042	180445	17021	16088	22135	42501	27674	3962
2310	Glass and glass products	11987	6780	3519	30179	4716	2059	1050	9272	554	12966
239	Non-metallic mineral products n.e.c.	378228	493538	428325	366973	151329	198995	171703	151143	31713	15681
2391	Refractory products	477	354	78		257	180	39	3273	332	975
2392	Clay building materials	12617	12121	11709	8624	4049	4570	4298	7	860	
2393	Other porcelain and ceramic products	811			14	267					
2394	Cement, lime and plaster	210725	290487	266209	257758	99995	141903	131301	126001	9808	11790
2395	Articles of concrete, cement and plaster	103502	125044	79341	58284	31899	33334	12509	8661	13331	17
2396	Cutting, shaping and finishing of stone	21422	22291	35632	13727	4947	4474	12528	4531	7382	2899
2399	Other non-metallic mineral products n.e.c.	28674	43238	35356	28566	9915	14534	11028	8670		20226
2410	Basic iron and steel	192736	171200	108698	129323	74479	58673	33657	38054	8864	20226
2420	Basic precious and other non-ferrous metals	112474	109994	103914	158178	61339	65600	62618	91997		
243	Casting of metals		4	11	4		3	7	3		
2431	Casting of iron and steel										
2432	Casting of non-ferrous metals		4	11	4		3	7	3		
251	Struct.metal products, tanks, reservoirs	22125	37148	49303	55864	9198	12518	15840	18568	299	2707

continued

Azerbaijan

ISIC Revision 4		Output at factor values (thousands of Azerbaijani Manat)					Value added at factor values (thousands of Azerbaijani Manat)					Gross fixed capital formation (thousands of Azerbaijani Manat)		
ISIC	Industry	Note	2013	2014	2015	2016	Note	2013	2014	2015	2016	Note	2015	2016
2511	Structural metal products		21405	36809	49015	54872		8871	12348	15699	18082		-	2707
2512	Tanks, reservoirs and containers of metal		419	339	288	992		199	170	141	485		299	-
2513	Steam generators, excl. hot water boilers		301	-	-	-		128	-	-	-		-	-
2520	Weapons and ammunition		-	-	-	-		-	-	-	-		-	-
259	Other metal products;metal working services		81322	94433	97414	77348		29285	36539	39186	31209		2337	291
2591	Forging,pressing,stamping,roll-forming of metal		...	22	10	894		4	6	3	267		-	-
2592	Treatment and coating of metals;machining		5036	18832	65708	47549		3313	10745	28972	21776		2337	121
2593	Cutlery, hand tools and general hardware		2050	803	50	212		572	231	36	153		-	-
2599	Other fabricated metal products n.e.c.		74226	74776	31646	28693		25396	25557	10175	9014		-	170
2610	Electronic components and boards		1054	569	313	480		398	220	97	203		-	-
2620	Computers and peripheral equipment		-	-	-	468		-	-	-	108		-	-
2630	Communication equipment		53181	34427	23903	14655		20826	14304	9415	8163		-	-
2640	Consumer electronics		11	-	-	23		3	-	-	10		49	41
265	Measuring,testing equipment; watches, etc.		52020	30359	50573	73738		24467	13653	23674	30363		347	9627
2651	Measuring/testing/navigating equipment,etc.		52020	30359	50573	73738		24467	13653	23674	30363		347	9627
2652	Watches and clocks		-	-	-	-		-	-	-	-		-	-
2660	Irradiation/electromedical equipment,etc.		-	-	-	-		-	-	-	-		-	-
2670	Optical instruments and photographic equipment		20	10	-	-		6	3	-	-		-	-
2680	Magnetic and optical media		-	-	-	-		-	-	-	-		-	-
2710	Electric motors,generators,transformers,etc.		95712	112717	59268	62203		19896	23639	11170	12468		2700	5062
2720	Batteries and accumulators		17	15	-	-		6	5	-	-		-	-
273	Wiring and wiring devices		80846	45704	39436	16814		20546	12401	10990	5297		185754	-
2731	Fibre optic cables		773	221	166	376		200	43	36	80		-	-
2732	Other electronic and electric wires and cables		-	45483	39270	16438		20346	12357	10954	5217		185754	-
2733	Wiring devices		-	-	-	-		-	-	-	-		-	-
2740	Electric lighting equipment		-	-	-	-		-	-	-	-		-	-
2750	Domestic appliances		3786	2732	3399	3135		1071	556	979	875		1467	-
2790	Other electrical equipment		132	1149	402	410		40	395	141	144		-	-
281	General-purpose machinery		81439	79459	41430	34362		21380	18464	7120	5096		309	1510
2811	Engines/turbines,excl.aircraft,vehicle engines		...	...	...	414		...	...	...	216		-	-
2812	Fluid power equipment		-	-	-	-		-	-	-	-		-	-
2813	Other pumps, compressors, taps and valves		36832	33159	11947	11978		9972	8470	1006	1063		-	-
2814	Bearings, gears, gearing and driving elements		4819	3834	4357	2026		3260	2638	2898	1318		8	-
2815	Ovens, furnaces and furnace burners		-	-	-	-		-	...	-	-		-	-
2816	Lifting and handling equipment		14459	20678	8509	5031		1716	3039	1100	672		81	13
2817	Office machinery, excl.computers,etc.		6	99	-	-		2	26	-	-		-	-
2818	Power-driven hand tools		1983	881	943	965		276	168	180	190		-	1
2819	Other general-purpose machinery		23340	20806	15674	13948		6154	4122	1936	1637		220	1496
282	Special-purpose machinery		175594	199037	157340	120557		52217	54891	38779	25436		32834	95137
2821	Agricultural and forestry machinery		53416	...	10	...		14952	...	8	...		-	-
2822	Metal-forming machinery and machine tools		43	126	37	...		9	22	11	...		-	-

2823	Machinery for metallurgy	866	…	311	–	455	…	–	128	–	–
2824	Mining, quarrying and construction machinery	2875	2180	1944	1455	1817	1148	723	926	–	–
2825	Food/beverage/tobacco processing machinery	…	…	–	–	–	…	–	–	–	–
2826	Textile/apparel/leather production machinery	118366	196731	155838	118302	34968	53721	38038	24383	32834	95137
2829	Other special-purpose machinery	3593	82333	105547	155083	1366	31040	42767	59857	1180	588
2910	Motor vehicles	–	–	–	–	–	–	–	–	–	–
2920	Automobile bodies, trailers and semi-trailers	–	–	–	–	–	–	–	–	–	–
2930	Parts and accessories for motor vehicles	1054	114	3	13	487	52	2	10	–	–
301	Building of ships and boats	–	388	166	468	193	193	68	193	–	193
3011	Building of ships and floating structures	–	388	166	468	193	193	68	193	–	193
3012	Building of pleasure and sporting boats	–	–	–	–	–	–	–	–	–	–
3020	Railway locomotives and rolling stock	12390	12926	11004	10721	8102	8564	7302	7225	848	101315
3030	Air and spacecraft and related machinery	93	109	–	–	62	73	–	–	–	–
3040	Military fighting vehicles	–	–	–	–	–	–	–	–	–	–
309	Transport equipment n.e.c.	–	–	–	–	–	–	–	–	–	–
3091	Motorcycles	–	–	–	–	–	–	–	–	–	–
3092	Bicycles and invalid carriages	–	–	–	–	–	–	–	–	–	–
3099	Other transport equipment n.e.c.	–	–	–	–	–	–	–	–	–	–
3100	Furniture	43880	42745	45225	58450	12506	12000	12778	16503	5482	2482
321	Jewellery, bijouterie and related articles	986	1142	3808	2459	619	656	2217	1447	2126	10209
3211	Jewellery and related articles	956	1111	3800	2448	600	638	2213	1441	2126	10209
3212	Imitation jewellery and related articles	30	31	8	11	19	18	4	6	–	–
3220	Musical instruments	1386	7	103	18	795	4	58	11	–	–
3230	Sports goods	–	–	–	–	–	–	–	–	–	–
3240	Games and toys	…	…	…	…	…	1	1	…	12	359
3250	Medical and dental instruments and supplies	2703	2947	2399	2913	1786	1788	1480	1816	–	332
3290	Other manufacturing n.e.c.	4470	2080	2709	3144	2232	1050	1366	1538	–	–
331	Repair of fabricated metal products/machinery	183957	267127	667306	684155	75177	110198	270937	277903	30581	38484
3311	Repair of fabricated metal products	19785	423	808	1181	1971	43	171	251	2833	620
3312	Repair of machinery	13354	7220	14017	11658	5020	2470	5605	4850	158	–
3313	Repair of electronic and optical equipment	2225	1440	3147	1655	428	275	406	229	–	229
3314	Repair of electrical equipment	3247	4306	9197	9631	719	925	3202	3333	13888	57
3315	Repair of transport equip., excl. motor vehicles	145295	253452	638945	656062	67031	106421	261086	267677	13700	37807
3319	Repair of other equipment	51	286	1192	3968	8	63	468	1563	2	–
3320	Installation of industrial machinery/equipment	2544	11771	…	906	914	3027	99	302	–	–
C	Total manufacturing	7243808	8071615	7880434	8899376	2452790	2777749	2713757	2979008	777431	598037

Azerbaijan

ISIC Revision 4 — Index numbers of industrial production (2010=100)

ISIC	Industry	Note	2005	2006	2007	2008	2009	2010	2011	2012	2013	2014	2015	2016
10	Food products		88	90	94	95	98	100	104	107	112	114	118	123
11	Beverages		70	88	109	103	90	100	100	110	124	136	121	114
12	Tobacco products		220	203	154	119	105	100	93	80	56	93	84	77
13	Textiles		361	277	196	148	106	100	115	184	140	147	66	172
14	Wearing apparel		97	89	94	77	91	100	153	181	164	221	123	174
15	Leather and related products		85	68	106	80	84	100	63	95	89	52	54	37
16	Wood products, excluding furniture		94	92	144	249	84	100	109	71	65	198	332	579
17	Paper and paper products		25	37	39	44	90	100	396	164	152	130	139	143
18	Printing and reproduction of recorded media		76	73	98	98	99	100	119	212	282	224	417	454
19	Coke and refined petroleum products		86	88	95	103	92	100	101	96	102	94	89	81
20	Chemicals and chemical products		122	139	93	118	74	100	122	100	119	153	220	195
21	Pharmaceuticals, medicinal chemicals, etc.		129	190	122	105	116	100	84	81	91	116	45	55
22	Rubber and plastics products		115	91	122	134	113	100	119	159	168	117	92	115
23	Other non-metallic mineral products		112	114	145	131	110	100	104	121	147	183	194	175
24	Basic metals		233	268	177	204	69	100	190	220	223	239	230	230
25	Fabricated metal products, except machinery		87	75	142	204	107	100	96	137	78	81	125	151
26	Computer, electronic and optical products		359	233	215	96	84	100	128	167	130	88	181	183
27	Electrical equipment		60	106	118	70	55	100	73	125	121	136	139	463
28	Machinery and equipment n.e.c.		24	37	59	63	53	100	125	90	114	102	73	61
29	Motor vehicles, trailers and semi-trailers		...	...	...	...	...	100	94	26	34	53	56	65
30	Other transport equipment		84	89	120	150	138	100	105	130	302	1025	970	1001
31	Furniture		311	377	395	416	415	100	134	290	307	328	361	394
32	Other manufacturing		504	350	250	211	131	100	102	84	118	127	258	171
33	Repair and installation of machinery/equipment		172	181	171	219	194	100	142	198	261	367	974	1078
C	Total manufacturing		81	87	93	99	91	100	107	113	119	122	131	132

Belarus

Concepts and definitions of variables:
Wages and salaries includes employers' contributions (in respect of their employees) paid to social security, pension and insurance schemes as well as the benefits received by employees under these schemes and severance and termination pay.

Related national publications:
Statistical Yearbook "Industry in the Republic of Belarus", published by National Statistical Committee of the Republic of Belarus, Minsk.

Supplier of information:
National Statistical Committee of the Republic of Belarus, Minsk.

Basic source of data:
Annual survey of registered enterprises.

Major deviations from ISIC (Revision 4):
Data presented in ISIC (Revision 4) were originally classified according to NACE (Revision 2.1).

Reference period:
Calendar year.

Scope:
All enterprises.

Method of data collection:
Mail questionnaires, online survey.

Type of enumeration:
Complete enumeration.

Adjusted for non-response:
No.

Belarus

ISIC	Industry	Number of enterprises (number)					Number of employees (number)					Wages and salaries paid to employees (thousands of Belarusian Roubles)				
		Note	2013	2014	2015	2016	Note	2013	2014	2015	2016	Note	2013	2014	2015	2016
10	Food products		857a/	858a/	774a/	667		150877a/	150218a/	145427a/	126345		1005649a/	1178863a/	1215042a/	1122853
11	Beverages		...a/	...a/	...a/	92b/		...a/	...a/	...a/	15363b/		...a/	...a/	...a/	164151b/
12	Tobacco products		...a/	...a/	...a/	...b/		...a/	...a/	...a/	...b/		...a/	...a/	...a/	...b/
13	Textiles		1869c/	1825c/	1620c/	419		110703c/	103866c/	90437c/	27483		508895c/	548767c/	499770c/	182806
14	Wearing apparel		...c/	...c/	...c/	1024		...c/	...c/	...c/	44011		...c/	...c/	...c/	253609
15	Leather and related products		...c/	...c/	...c/	128		...c/	...c/	...c/	14035		...c/	...c/	...c/	93962
16	Wood products, excluding furniture		2305d/	2287d/	2256d/	1508		66222d/	62937d/	58236d/	38742		338539d/	382006d/	380454d/	253838
17	Paper and paper products		...d/	...d/	...d/	215		...d/	...d/	...d/	12336		...d/	...d/	...d/	94444
18	Printing and reproduction of recorded media		...d/	...d/	...d/	433		...d/	...d/	...d/	6993		...d/	...d/	...d/	61603
19	Coke and refined petroleum products		39	38	36	34		13939	13282	13007	12778		147731	162308	171835	177302
20	Chemicals and chemical products		364	360	345	343		53036	49474	47957	48018		504490	583413	667995	703214
21	Pharmaceuticals, medicinal chemicals, etc.		66	66	64	72		8750	8545	8650	9907		60367	71879	89826	108589
22	Rubber and plastics products		2139e/	2145e/	1921e/	1034		107839e/	103539e/	92328e/	34672		710207e/	774146e/	706408e/	300149
23	Other non-metallic mineral products		...e/	...e/	...e/	884		...e/	...e/	...e/	50154		...e/	...e/	...e/	395896
24	Basic metals		1647f/	1698f/	1588f/	100		75156f/	73840f/	662234f/	17292		537434f/	597651f/	559636f/	162994
25	Fabricated metal products, except machinery		...f/	...f/	...f/	1312		...f/	...f/	...f/	44099		...f/	...f/	...f/	379163
26	Computer, electronic and optical products		326	337	446	264		21723	19798	19212	19767		128706	146265	168078	201623
27	Electrical equipment		387	398	461	326		39622	37169	33736	33351		264274	281422	268627	305482
28	Machinery and equipment n.e.c.		608	656	734	491		117216	107278	99503	86756		803940	808176	775730	751446
29	Motor vehicles, trailers and semi-trailers		186g/	187g/	131g/	133		58453g/	53215g/	47559g/	38855		420520g/	417207g/	390952g/	338178
30	Other transport equipment		...g/	...g/	...g/	45		...g/	...g/	...g/	5899		...g/	...g/	...g/	64707
31	Furniture		2545h/	2592h/	2287h/	979		74036h/	72090h/	66789h/	29690		447376h/	508039h/	512553h/	207034
32	Other manufacturing		...h/	...h/	...h/	320		...h/	...h/	...h/	8864		...h/	...h/	...h/	76393
33	Repair and installation of machinery/equipment		...h/	...h/	...h/	800		...h/	...h/	...h/	28040		...h/	...h/	...h/	300443
C	Total manufacturing		13338	13447	12663	11623		897572	855251	789075	753450		5878129	6460143	6406908	6699677

a/ 10 includes 11 and 12.
b/ 11 includes 12.
c/ 13 includes 14 and 15.
d/ 16 includes 17 and 18.
e/ 22 includes 23.
f/ 24 includes 25.
g/ 29 includes 30.
h/ 31 includes 32 and 33.

Belarus

ISIC	Industry	Note	Output at basic prices (thousands of Belarusian Roubles)				Note	Value added at basic prices (thousands of Belarusian Roubles)				Note	Gross fixed capital formation (thousands of Belarusian Roubles)	
			2013	2014	2015	2016		2013	2014	2015	2016		2015	2016
10	Food products		...	16210850a/	17740501a/	18481885		...	4026773a/	3878299a/	4286743		1105565a/	731907
11	Beverages		...	...a/	...a/	2309683b/		...	...a/	...a/	876572b/		...a/	55611b/
12	Tobacco products		...	...a/	...a/	...b/		...	...a/	...a/	...b/		...a/	...b/
13	Textiles		...	2686098c/	2651839c/	1356028		...	1078112c/	1061963c/	485630		184111c/	200594
14	Wearing apparel		...	...c/	...c/	1312872		...	...c/	...c/	579345		...c/	30192
15	Leather and related products		...	...c/	...c/	651961		...	...c/	...c/	278493		...c/	35795
16	Wood products, excluding furniture		...	2181787d/	2537445d/	2103318		...	661960d/	760930d/	774353		1543074d/	200486
17	Paper and paper products		...	...d/	...d/	802341		...	...d/	...d/	210944		...d/	214045
18	Printing and reproduction of recorded media		...	...d/	...d/	376924		...	...d/	...d/	133104		...d/	25596
19	Coke and refined petroleum products		...	10915199	12189175	10517475		...	1082303	1174043	545054		912400	743139
20	Chemicals and chemical products		...	6218518	7730928	6687196		...	3374255	4190861	2622116		922303	1018080
21	Pharmaceuticals,medicinal chemicals, etc.		...	516106	848745	1002283		...	276324	452908	525253		203120	130347
22	Rubber and plastics products		...	6148427e/	5567248e/	2945027		...	2156633e/	1872858e/	825032		417793e/	271917
23	Other non-metallic mineral products		...	...e/	...e/	3298843		...	...e/	...e/	1188604		...e/	88111
24	Basic metals		...	4542814f/	4789355f/	2457070		...	906947f/	1073745f/	171115		472155f/	107294
25	Fabricated metal products, except machinery		...	...f/	...f/	2666975		...	...f/	...f/	725175		...f/	77086
26	Computer, electronic and optical products		...	834690	995699	1297965		...	316491	452778	550108		100852	121636
27	Electrical equipment		...	1599058	1798967	2279886		...	420670	541479	630177		64363	60217
28	Machinery and equipment n.e.c.		...	3984046	3621793	4548502		...	1196496	1335959	1695250		334874	315283
29	Motor vehicles, trailers and semi-trailers		...	2401492g/	2239985g/	2069003		...	562245g/	644850g/	488985		97196g/	430337
30	Other transport equipment		...	...g/	...g/	526967		...	...g/	...g/	189390		...g/	14696
31	Furniture		...	2358961h/	2669325h/	1326660		...	932980h/	1120575h/	398597		151739h/	71930
32	Other manufacturing		...	...h/	...h/	535382		...	...h/	...h/	225780		...h/	12654
33	Repair and installation of machinery/equipment		...	...h/	...h/	1417397		...	...h/	...h/	728501		...h/	54610
C	Total manufacturing		55207469	60598045	65381005	70971643		14752226	16992187	18561248	19134321		6509545	5011563

a/ 10 includes 11 and 12.
b/ 11 includes 12.
c/ 13 includes 14 and 15.
d/ 16 includes 17 and 18.
e/ 22 includes 23.
f/ 24 includes 25.
g/ 29 includes 30.
h/ 31 includes 32 and 33.

Belarus

- 136 -

Index numbers of industrial production

ISIC Revision 4

ISIC	Industry	Note	2005	2006	2007	2008	2009	2010	2011	2012	2013	2014	2015	2016
								(2010=100)						
10	Food products	a/	...	...	...	...	...	100	109	114	116	114	113	116
11	Beverages	a/	...	...	...	...	...	...	...	...	...	...	...	...
12	Tobacco products	a/	...	...	...	...	...	...	...	...	...	...	...	...
13	Textiles	b/	...	...	...	...	...	100	107	108	106	102	86	90
14	Wearing apparel	b/	...	...	...	...	...	...	...	...	...	...	...	...
15	Leather and related products	b/	...	...	...	...	...	...	...	...	...	...	...	...
16	Wood products, excluding furniture	c/	...	...	...	...	...	100	109	107	109	113	105	116
17	Paper and paper products	c/	...	...	...	...	...	...	...	...	...	...	...	...
18	Printing and reproduction of recorded media	c/	...	...	...	...	...	...	...	...	...	...	...	...
19	Coke and refined petroleum products		...	...	...	...	...	100	118	129	103	111	112	93
20	Chemicals and chemical products		...	...	...	...	...	100	103	123	107	138	146	141
21	Pharmaceuticals,medicinal chemicals, etc.		...	...	...	...	...	100	119	129	146	149	206	215
22	Rubber and plastics products	d/	...	...	...	...	...	100	102	105	108	101	85	81
23	Other non-metallic mineral products	d/	...	...	...	...	...	...	...	...	...	...	...	...
24	Basic metals	e/	...	...	...	...	...	100	106	111	104	106	96	96
25	Fabricated metal products, except machinery	e/	...	...	...	...	...	...	...	...	...	...	...	...
26	Computer, electronic and optical products		...	...	...	...	...	100	111	120	131	137	144	148
27	Electrical equipment		...	...	...	...	...	100	111	116	122	97	78	86
28	Machinery and equipment n.e.c.		...	...	...	...	...	100	113	115	115	91	68	72
29	Motor vehicles, trailers and semi-trailers	f/	...	...	...	...	...	100	132	150	143	110	96	107
30	Other transport equipment	f/	...	...	...	...	...	...	...	...	...	...	...	...
31	Furniture		...	...	...	...	...	...	...	...	...	...	...	...
32	Other manufacturing	g/	...	...	...	...	...	100	112	118	122	109	103	106
33	Repair and installation of machinery/equipment	g/	...	...	...	...	...	...	...	...	...	...	...	...
C	Total manufacturing		...	...	...	...	...	100	111	118	112	112	104	104

a/ 10 includes 11 and 12.
b/ 13 includes 14 and 15.
c/ 16 includes 17 and 18.
d/ 22 includes 23.
e/ 24 includes 25.
f/ 29 includes 30.
g/ 32 includes 33.

Belgium

Supplier of information:
National Institute of Statistics (Institut National de Statistique), Brussels.
Industrial statistics for the OECD countries are compiled by the OECD secretariat, which supplies them to UNIDO.

Basic source of data:
Annual survey; administrative data.

Major deviations from ISIC (Revision 4):
Data presented in ISIC (Revision 4) were originally classified according to the NACE-BEL classification system.

Reference period:
Calendar year.

Scope:
All registered enterprises.

Method of data collection:
Electronic questionnaire.

Type of enumeration:
Combination of survey and administrative data.

Adjusted for non-response:
Not reported.

Concepts and definitions of variables:
No deviations from the standard UN concepts and definitions are reported.

Related national publications:
None reported.

Belgium

ISIC	Industry	Number of enterprises (number) Note	2013	2014	2015	2016	Number of employees (number) Note	2013	2014	2015	2016	Wages and salaries paid to employees (millions of Euros) Note	2013	2014	2015	2016
1010	Processing/preserving of meat		845	823	754	773		13726	12838	13824	14035		423.4	401.1	433.8	436.5
1020	Processing/preserving of fish, etc.		38	33	32	51		1132	1100	1082	1254		39.3	39.3	40.4	45.0
1030	Processing/preserving of fruit,vegetables		175	181	152	170		8575	8746	9358	9356		305.9	311.2	339.5	347.6
1040	Vegetable and animal oils and fats		33	39	34	22		1553	1580	1313	1603		84.6	89.5	65.1	93.8
1050	Dairy products		433	401	474	415		6869	6865	6590	6414		293.3	286.6	280.7	270.8
106	Grain mill products,starches and starch products		60	72	77	77		2113	2207	2783	3221		102.0	108.1	156.3	184.8
1061	Grain mill products		54	66	70	69		1243	1315	1617	2029		56.7	60.6	92.6	118.3
1062	Starches and starch products		6	6	7	8		870	892	1166	1192		45.4	47.5	63.7	66.4
107	Other food products		4962	5289	4999	4852		41208	40790	39770	40376		1293.5	1314.3	1258.0	1290.6
1071	Bakery products		4183	4472	4026	...		23922	22248	22434	...		548.3	509.8	516.1	...
1072	Sugar		11	11	8	10		1079	1070	755	775		63.7	58.4	42.7	44.9
1073	Cocoa, chocolate and sugar confectionery		396	391	435	377		8164	8598	8401	8602		343.5	357.5	359.3	378.3
1074	Macaroni, noodles, couscous, etc.		21	21	23	...		512	555	509	...		17.4	17.9	17.1	...
1075	Prepared meals and dishes		72	80	113	91		2299	2256	2065	2261		80.3	72.4	67.0	69.8
1079	Other food products n.e.c.		279	314	394	303		5232	6063	5606	5623		240.3	298.3	255.8	251.0
1080	Prepared animal feeds		159	133	143	140		3236	3310	3128	3158		136.6	142.2	137.0	134.4
110	Beverages		279	352	294	420		9899	9432	9524	9682		476.7	477.7	452.6	510.9
1101	Distilling, rectifying and blending of spirits		...	60	60	68		...	442	190	182		...	15.8	7.2	7.0
1102	Wines		...	...	...	...		...	...	...	...		...	...	...	...
1103	Malt liquors and malt		183	211	161	258		5500	5568	5760	5988		259.9	294.3	275.7	329.1
1104	Soft drinks,mineral waters,other bottled waters		23	26	31	35		3856	3285	3457	3396		197.5	162.5	165.7	170.2
1200	Tobacco products		16	18	26	24		1424	1315	1336	1306		48.7	46.9	45.6	44.8
131	Spinning, weaving and finishing of textiles		337	392	489	482		4519	4459	4163	4074		131.7	131.2	123.2	118.3
1311	Preparation and spinning of textile fibres		119	136	166	156		678	697	662	555		16.8	19.3	17.3	14.5
1312	Weaving of textiles		97	116	114	95		2947	2826	2818	2839		89.3	84.7	87.4	85.3
1313	Finishing of textiles		121	140	209	231		894	936	683	680		25.6	27.2	18.5	18.5
139	Other textiles		679	631	670	688		13267	12530	12077	11451		427.4	405.3	392.7	371.3
1391	Knitted and crocheted fabrics		9	7	15	15		378	364	332	327		9.5	9.4	8.9	8.8
1392	Made-up textile articles, except apparel		454	404	469	458		3023	2627	2578	2397		90.5	67.0	66.7	62.4
1393	Carpets and rugs		112	80	76	79		6774	6558	6379	6141		212.8	213.7	214.0	208.2
1394	Cordage, rope, twine and netting		14	...	...	...		120	...	...	...		4.0	...	...	...
1399	Other textiles n.e.c.		90	...	...	...		2972	...	...	...		110.6	...	...	...
1410	Wearing apparel, except fur apparel		740	796	730	667		2942	2558	2659	2563		73.6	64.9	72.1	70.6
1420	Articles of fur		12	10	14	14		30	27	26	23		0.6	0.5	0.5	0.5
1430	Knitted and crocheted apparel		18	24	20	12		171	156	101	103		2.9	3.3	1.8	1.9
151	Leather;luggage,handbags,saddlery,harness;fur		116a/	90	135	110		1038a/	858	259	249		38.7a/	35.0	6.5	6.2
1511	Tanning/dressing of leather; dressing of fur		17	90b/	14	11		175	858b/	155	157		4.7	35.0b/	3.9	4.1
1512	Luggage,handbags,etc.;saddlery/harness		...	...b/	121	99		...	...b/	104	92		...	...b/	2.5	2.1
1520	Footwear		...a/	44	33	17		...a/	218	167	143		...a/	6.1	4.9	3.9
1610	Sawmilling and planing of wood		290	266	251	200		1561	1512	1490	1370		42.1	42.4	41.0	36.4

ISIC Revision 4

Code	Description												
162	Wood products, cork, straw, plaiting materials	284.7	276.4	287.1	270.0	8137	8081	8553	8262	1454	1495	1772	1613
1621	Veneer sheets and wood-based panels	137.9	131.6	123.4	119.1	2979	2893	2761	2785	53	46	67	48
1622	Builders' carpentry and joinery	105.7	98.8	111.8	106.8	3714	3586	3970	3860	1121	1095	1308	1188
1623	Wooden containers	28.7	32.0	33.7	29.4	1005	1115	1223	1099	76	87	114	103
1629	Other wood products;articles of cork,straw	12.4	14.1	18.1	14.5	439	487	599	518	204	267	283	274
170	Paper and paper products	457.7	456.2	500.0	484.9	10770	10886	11656	11546	224	239	256	263
1701	Pulp, paper and paperboard	…	…	150.5	…	…	…	2951	…	…	…	41	…
1702	Corrugated paper and paperboard	184.4	181.5	182.4	176.1	4906	4892	4873	4797	97	126	125	144
1709	Other articles of paper and paperboard	129.8	123.2	167.2	157.3	3099	3026	3832	3713	61	73	90	90
181	Printing and service activities related to printing	…	465.8	499.5	507.9	…	12254	13088	13180	…	4032	4158	3480
1811	Printing	379.1	402.5	413.8	428.4	9825	10225	10544	10746	1860	1736	1811	1627
1812	Service activities related to printing	…	63.2	85.7	79.5	…	2029	2544	2434	…	2296	2347	1853
1820	Reproduction of recorded media	…	0.6	1.1	0.3	…	15	16	8	…	43	76	140
1910	Coke oven products	-	-	-	-	-	-	-	-	-	-	-	-
1920	Refined petroleum products	578.4	…	505.3	544.1	4647	…	4392	4444	11	…	15	17
201	Basic chemicals,fertilizers, etc.	1983.9	2120.3	2049.6	2102.6	26179	26346	26793	27923	215	219	255	233
2011	Basic chemicals	…	1459.2	1369.6	1433.2	…	18108	17509	18669	…	111	131	122
2012	Fertilizers and nitrogen compounds	119.5	71.9	70.8	66.6	1921	1164	1168	1134	40	30	40	28
2013	Plastics and synthetic rubber in primary forms	…	589.1	609.2	602.9	…	7074	8116	8120	…	78	84	83
202	Other chemical products	857.4	929.5	859.9	890.7	15662	16579	15229	15650	329	344	360	303
2021	Pesticides and other agrochemical products	90.6	88.1	91.0	89.8	1269	1236	1225	1250	15	18	14	14
2022	Paints,varnishes;printing ink and mastics	228.4	248.6	181.6	193.8	4131	4480	3259	3497	89	92	99	80
2023	Soap,cleaning and cosmetic preparations	188.5	191.2	191.6	190.3	4521	4602	4634	4608	142	153	157	126
2029	Other chemical products n.e.c.	…	401.5	395.7	416.8	…	6261	6111	6295	…	81	90	83
2030	Man-made fibres	25.6	31.8	51.5	43.8	677	836	1073	1044	18	25	28	21
2100	Pharmaceuticals,medicinal chemicals, etc.	1792.3	1649.5	1662.8	1600.5	24506	23880	23928	22779	99	100	110	115
221	Rubber products	88.6	84.0	93.8	91.8	2161	2055	2187	2292	63	59	94	90
2211	Rubber tyres and tubes	20.7	22.4	23.9	23.8	546	558	598	616	16	14	20	18
2219	Other rubber products	67.9	61.6	69.8	68.0	1615	1497	1589	1676	47	45	74	72
2220	Plastics products	920.6	846.7	836.4	848.2	21262	19930	20067	20092	695	667	719	648
2310	Glass and glass products	374.8	353.5	368.7	380.9	7431	6948	7105	7294	145	165	167	122
239	Non-metallic mineral products n.e.c.	828.2	818.3	807.1	805.3	19717	19279	19733	20422	1472	1348	1442	1415
2391	Refractory products	18.5	13.4	22.6	19.9	415	336	502	525	16	20	22	26
2392	Clay building materials	81.3	79.6	78.8	67.9	1855	1866	1823	1715	43	62	92	53
2393	Other porcelain and ceramic products	…	…	…	…	…	…	…	…	19	…	16	16
2394	Cement, lime and plaster	219.5	212.2	179.5	179.2	3650	3381	2951	3065	19	19	16	19
2395	Articles of concrete, cement and plaster	377.1	393.9	405.5	416.6	10076	10210	10957	11621	525	430	522	517
2396	Cutting, shaping and finishing of stone	53.6	47.1	58.3	60.1	2038	1820	2073	2109	772	731	695	710
2399	Other non-metallic mineral products n.e.c.	59.0	53.9	44.7	44.7	1223	1208	1006	1006	45	35	39	31
2410	Basic iron and steel	891.5	914.7	978.9	969.5	14849	14779	15321	16636	154	137	195	186
2420	Basic precious and other non-ferrous metals	433.2	436.6	421.6	416.8	7812	7716	7687	7773	65	68	86	86
243	Casting of metals	85.5	78.6	88.0	90.4	2296	2130	2405	2429	87	73	61	65
2431	Casting of iron and steel	75.1	63.8	75.0	77.7	1930	1666	1989	2051	36	27	21	24
2432	Casting of non-ferrous metals	10.4	14.8	12.9	12.7	366	464	416	378	51	46	40	41
251	Struct.metal products, tanks, reservoirs	940.4	935.4	…	1868.5c/	25047	25751	…	52012c/	2810	2739	…	6886c/

continued

Belgium

ISIC	Industry	Number of enterprises (number)					Number of employees (number)					Wages and salaries paid to employees (millions of Euros)				
		Note	2013	2014	2015	2016	Note	2013	2014	2015	2016	Note	2013	2014	2015	2016
2511	Structural metal products		2673	2776	2547	2649		21986	21793	22260	21547		764.2	782.5	788.8	781.0
2512	Tanks, reservoirs and containers of metal		...	...	110	99		...	...	1926	1983		...	...	68.5	76.3
2513	Steam generators, excl. hot water boilers		...	96	82	62		...	2297	1565	1517		105.7	...	78.1	83.1
2520	Weapons and ammunition		...c/	...	...	19		...c/	...	...	2156		...c/	...	...	119.5
259	Other metal products;metal working services		...c/	3830	...	4513		...c/	21922	...	20848		...c/	756.8	...	718.3
2591	Forging,pressing,stamping,roll-forming of metal		609	624	...	818		1471	1255	...	1554		48.0	41.1	...	54.1
2592	Treatment and coating of metals machining		2783	2544	2793	2997		14361	13516	12563	12390		477.2	451.8	411.0	404.3
2593	Cutlery, hand tools and general hardware		272	280	370	283		2395	2200	2356	1999		92.7	81.2	85.3	83.6
2599	Other fabricated metal products n.e.c.		...	382	318	415		...	4951	4280	4905		182.7	151.4	176.2
2610	Electronic components and boards		176	120	101	91		2293	2239	2353	2332		118.7	108.9	117.9	120.6
2620	Computers and peripheral equipment		...	84	98	...		...	1075	981	...		...	58.5	55.3	...
2630	Communication equipment		45	66	62	42		1507	1377	1405	1346		82.1	76.6	78.9	79.2
2640	Consumer electronics		...	...	...	...		...	...	...	...		...	...	...	...
265	Measuring,testing equipment; watches, etc.		109	122	111	101		2404	2582	2760	3048		136.6	135.2	153.9	162.2
2651	Measuring/testing/navigating equipment,etc.		98	111	88	77		2352	2536	2706	2997		134.5	133.3	151.8	160.2
2652	Watches and clocks		11	11	23	24		52	46	54	51		2.1	1.9	2.1	2.0
2660	Irradiation/electromedical equipment,etc.		...	...	...	23		...	...	...	841		...	...	...	62.2
2670	Optical instruments and photographic equipment		...	...	...	...		...	...	...	...		...	...	...	...
2680	Magnetic and optical media		...	...	...	...		...	...	...	...		...	...	...	...
2710	Electric motors,generators,transformers,etc.		163	163	189	212		3783	3529	2568	2941		187.8	165.1	121.5	138.1
2720	Batteries and accumulators		...	...	...	...		...	...	...	...		...	...	...	...
273	Wiring and wiring devices		41	41	35	32		2874	2929	3684	3644		137.3	133.1	174.1	178.6
2731	Fibre optic cables		...	...	...	...		...	...	...	...		...	...	...	...
2732	Other electronic and electric wires and cables		16	19	21	16		1548	1605	2105	2100		69.9	71.7	95.4	93.7
2733	Wiring devices		...	...	...	...		...	...	...	...		...	...	...	...
2740	Electric lighting equipment		74	125	180	194		3328	3027	3788	2979		134.9	124.1	149.0	107.2
2750	Domestic appliances		...	...	...	...		...	...	...	...		...	...	...	...
2790	Other electrical equipment		57	66	88	99		2575	2350	2119	2241		153.3	148.5	144.9	152.0
281	General-purpose machinery		801	766	723	761		17198	16720	15153	15773		756.7	750.2	684.6	717.5
2811	Engines/turbines,excl.aircraft,vehicle engines		14	13	15	10		293	310	332	341		12.8	13.6	15.5	17.6
2812	Fluid power equipment		42	40	49	68		474	536	454	419		16.6	19.4	15.9	15.5
2813	Other pumps, compressors, taps and valves		28	30	32	38		3973	3939	3874	3735		195.6	187.1	197.7	189.9
2814	Bearings, gears, gearing and driving elements		31	29	37	30		2322	2228	2353	2709		118.9	119.1	118.5	141.5
2815	Ovens, furnaces and furnace burners		22	26	16	16		129	171	397	254		5.1	7.3	15.4	10.1
2816	Lifting and handling equipment		139	116	99	98		2521	2243	1871	1955		104.2	95.9	72.9	74.9
2817	Office machinery, excl.computers,etc.		...	...	...	...		...	...	...	...		...	...	...	...
2818	Power-driven hand tools		...	...	...	...		...	...	...	...		...	...	...	...
2819	Other general-purpose machinery		514	489	456	484		7336	6995	5863	6348		298.8	298.0	248.2	267.7
282	Special-purpose machinery		483	585	553	567		16098	15543	14524	14572		673.0	709.8	642.3	625.7
2821	Agricultural and forestry machinery		121	146	180	187		4980	5316	5251	5241		219.1	249.4	224.9	231.7
2822	Metal-forming machinery and machine tools		86	102	61	69		1203	1458	1363	1224		50.1	62.0	56.1	52.6

ISIC	Industry	(1)	(2)	(3)	(4)	(1)	(2)	(3)	(4)	(1)	(2)	(3)	(4)
2823	Machinery for metallurgy	...	...	...	4	...	...	...	170	...	...	...	8.1
2824	Mining, quarrying and construction machinery	28	30	31	43	4210	3290	2566	2443	159.8	167.4	128.9	97.8
2825	Food/beverage/tobacco processing machinery	83	98	66	64	1651	1673	1523	1407	69.5	72.2	69.6	60.0
2826	Textile/apparel/leather production machinery	32	38	33	30	2051	1964	1935	2014	83.8	82.4	82.3	85.8
2829	Other special-purpose machinery	...	...	...	...	...	...	...	...	...	...	...	...
2910	Motor vehicles	41	47	31	38	20093	19727	15852	15368	831.4	1009.4	686.8	689.1
2920	Automobile bodies, trailers and semi-trailers	163	224	234	198	4606	4393	4542	4321	185.7	174.3	177.7	177.1
2930	Parts and accessories for motor vehicles	216	153	118	129	11932	10688	8827	8184	493.8	448.4	403.3	366.0
301	Building of ships and boats	27	...	19	...	105	...	103	...	3.8	...	3.7	...
3011	Building of ships and floating structures	11	18	7	4	105	110	100	110	3.8	4.2	3.6	4.0
3012	Building of pleasure and sporting boats	16	...	12	...	-	...	3	...	-	...	0.1	...
3020	Railway locomotives and rolling stock	...	9	9	...	...	761	685	...	...	35.5	32.9	...
3030	Air and spacecraft and related machinery	40	36	28	24	5338	5522	5562	5570	269.0	279.9	284.3	291.0
3040	Military fighting vehicles	-	...	...	...	-	...	...	...	-	...	...	...
309	Transport equipment n.e.c.	...	71	55	48	...	326	388	366	...	10.9	13.9	14.2
3091	Motorcycles	7	...	55d/	...	1	...	388d/	...	...	...	13.9d/	...
3092	Bicycles and invalid carriages	46	64	...d/	41	397	324	...d/	326	14.7	10.8	...d/	13.0
3099	Other transport equipment n.e.c.	...	...	...d/	...	...	...	...d/	...	...d/	...	...d/	...
3100	Furniture	1963	2296	1670	2001	11056	10738	10945	10220	309.2	311.5	309.8	289.9
321	Jewellery, bijouterie and related articles	604	666	796	686	832	750	764	742	24.7	23.0	21.5	20.8
3211	Jewellery and related articles	545	579	731	610	826	739	752	731	24.6	22.8	21.3	20.6
3212	Imitation jewellery and related articles	59	87	65	76	6	11	12	11	0.1	0.1	0.1	0.1
3220	Musical instruments	94	125	98	...	84	76	49	...	1.5	1.3	1.0	...
3230	Sports goods	32	46	49	32	27	14	13	7	0.7	0.3	0.4	0.2
3240	Games and toys	48	75	88	42	701	540	545	563	24.5	19.2	20.1	21.4
3250	Medical and dental instruments and supplies	1054	1161	930	...	3783	3555	4314	...	149.8	135.9	169.2	...
3290	Other manufacturing n.e.c.	201	177	155	124	994	846	892	902	32.8	31.3	32.6	30.3
331	Repair of fabricated metal products/machinery	1562	1778	1637	1728	8661	8915	9694	9576	399.8	408.3	442.2	442.6
3311	Repair of fabricated metal products	140	231	204	155	1637	1624	1664	1845	58.3	56.8	53.2	65.5
3312	Repair of machinery	1024	1127	957	1064	3696	4150	4730	4376	186.7	205.7	231.0	208.7
3313	Repair of electronic and optical equipment	37	28	50	33	421	402	403	440	19.9	20.4	22.4	24.9
3314	Repair of electrical equipment	71	85	120	141	479	498	633	662	29.6	28.5	36.0	36.0
3315	Repair of transport equip., excl. motor vehicles	245	252	276	297	2419	2227	2252	2185	105.0	96.5	99.2	105.7
3319	Repair of other equipment	45	55	30	38	9	14	12	68	0.3	0.4	0.3	1.9
3320	Installation of industrial machinery/equipment	331	351	292	330	6995	6068	7746	8458	368.8	315.0	378.5	403.3
C	Total manufacturing	33468	35747	33788	34132	481964	469717	459424	460512	21707.5	21627.5	21124.1	21376.8

a/ 151 includes 1520.
b/ 1511 includes 1512.
c/ 251 includes 2520 and 259.
d/ 3091 includes 3092 and 3099.

Belgium

ISIC Revision 4		Output (valuation not defined) (millions of Euros)					Value added at factor values (millions of Euros)					Gross fixed capital formation (millions of Euros)		
ISIC	Industry	Note	2013	2014	2015	2016	Note	2013	2014	2015	2016	Note	2015	2016
1010	Processing/preserving of meat		6644.6	6551.1	7317.3	7305.6		841.2	854.8	942.8	949.0		171.1	233.1
1020	Processing/preserving of fish, etc.		483.1	494.1	533.3	591.8		86.1	82.7	89.6	105.5		6.7	11.0
1030	Processing/preserving of fruit,vegetables		4170.4	4261.8	4424.2	4550.3		783.3	902.4	971.1	931.8		318.7	418.7
1040	Vegetable and animal oils and fats		4328.2	3943.8	3578.9	4548.1		229.3	232.3	174.0	209.3		43.3	54.3
1050	Dairy products		4787.3	5006.8	4198.6	3758.3		539.3	587.8	562.8	559.9		168.9	100.6
106	Grain mill products,starches and starch products		2238.0	2217.7	2510.3	2837.0		232.0	281.2	388.7	481.6		78.9	98.4
1061	Grain mill products		1594.4	1599.0	1586.4	1942.3		116.9	152.1	232.6	271.0		37.9	66.3
1062	Starches and starch products		643.5	618.6	923.9	894.7		115.1	129.1	156.1	210.6		41.0	32.0
107	Other food products		12077.4	11702.6	11710.5	12785.8		2944.0	2984.5	2927.1	3153.1		676.5	696.6
1071	Bakery products		3516.2	3646.5	3769.7	...		1201.7	1172.1	1181.1	...		286.0	...
1072	Sugar		1049.4	775.6	537.0	570.9		253.2	182.6	127.9	135.1		33.5	22.8
1073	Cocoa, chocolate and sugar confectionery		4480.6	4209.3	4276.1	4684.1		755.0	798.5	809.2	895.0		162.3	166.5
1074	Macaroni, noodles, couscous, etc.		143.6	138.7	150.5	...		33.1	36.5	36.8	...		2.2	...
1075	Prepared meals and dishes		624.9	560.7	604.4	551.0		133.6	139.2	143.5	144.2		33.8	33.8
1079	Other food products n.e.c.		2262.7	2371.8	2373.0	2610.8		567.4	655.6	628.7	668.1		158.5	154.2
1080	Prepared animal feeds		3875.0	3644.9	4341.8	3278.0		281.6	330.0	315.7	327.5		74.8	63.0
110	Beverages		4628.6	4489.1	4389.8	5070.9		1478.7	1507.3	1465.8	1624.7		401.5	452.8
1101	Distilling, rectifying and blending of spirits		...	194.2	89.4	93.3		...	46.3	17.1	14.3		8.3	1.6
1102	Wines		...	...	...	...		...	...	...	...		...	...
1103	Malt liquors and malt		2630.0	2682.2	2699.6	3423.5		937.1	1006.6	1007.8	1160.4		315.4	344.2
1104	Soft drinks,mineral waters,other bottled waters		1779.6	1546.8	1549.6	1502.7		498.9	435.9	430.6	438.5		75.9	105.5
1200	Tobacco products		518.3	437.7	511.5	478.2		163.0	150.1	157.9	139.4		17.4	16.4
131	Spinning, weaving and finishing of textiles		896.5	976.4	1093.9	1034.7		247.2	276.2	269.8	273.4		38.0	67.2
1311	Preparation and spinning of textile fibres		185.3	224.9	304.8	296.9		40.8	55.5	57.2	52.8		17.4	26.2
1312	Weaving of textiles		551.1	568.3	643.7	588.9		152.3	161.0	170.1	175.4		13.8	28.4
1313	Finishing of textiles		160.1	183.2	145.4	148.9		54.1	59.7	42.5	45.2		6.8	12.6
139	Other textiles		2850.7	2983.6	3077.6	2822.6		756.2	802.4	799.4	762.2		174.0	124.4
1391	Knitted and crocheted fabrics		62.8	56.5	58.6	62.6		23.5	20.9	20.1	23.4		2.7	6.7
1392	Made-up textile articles, except apparel		466.5	471.9	542.0	556.4		145.3	137.9	138.1	142.7		16.2	18.8
1393	Carpets and rugs		1572.7	1680.7	1703.5	1556.7		385.2	415.9	446.0	421.9		132.3	77.8
1394	Cordage, rope, twine and netting		29.2	...	...	...		7.2	...	...	...		...	...
1399	Other textiles n.e.c.		719.4	...	...	...		195.0	...	...	...		...	...
1410	Wearing apparel, except fur apparel		625.5	615.0	729.7	640.9		173.9	174.9	202.4	184.3		16.9	27.0
1420	Articles of fur		4.0	2.5	2.7	2.3		1.8	1.4	0.9	0.8		-	0.1
1430	Knitted and crocheted apparel		14.4	36.1	8.3	7.7		4.4	1.7	2.2	1.9		1.1	1.5
151	Leather;luggage,handbags,saddlery,harness;fur		257.4a/	410.7	56.3	44.3		89.9a/	90.9	19.1	14.9		0.9	11.6
1511	Tanning/dressing of leather; dressing of fur		42.8	410.7b/	31.1	30.4		7.7	90.9b/	7.5	10.8		0.3	9.9
1512	Luggage,handbags,etc.;saddlery/harness		...	...b/	25.2	13.9		...	...b/	11.6	4.1		0.6	1.7
1520	Footwear		...a/	41.8	32.8	25.0		...a/	14.9	11.5	8.3		2.0	0.6
1610	Sawmilling and planing of wood		524.9	534.1	567.9	517.6		113.3	106.0	107.9	92.5		43.2	31.5

162	Wood products, cork, straw, plaiting materials	2416.7	2566.6	2597.2	2673.1	601.1	630.5	631.9	696.8	161.1	267.9
1621	Veneer sheets and wood-based panels	1148.3	1241.9	1384.2	1478.2	255.7	277.1	309.0	368.8	100.4	215.8
1622	Builders' carpentry and joinery	823.3	831.1	745.5	762.1	240.9	251.0	213.2	228.8	40.0	39.5
1623	Wooden containers	314.5	368.7	334.3	336.8	63.4	70.7	68.3	64.5	9.0	8.7
1629	Other wood products;articles of cork,straw	130.5	124.9	133.2	96.0	41.1	31.6	41.3	34.8	11.7	3.9
170	Paper and paper products	4822.3	4501.1	5225.0	4292.9	1035.9	1145.4	1090.9	1066.6	167.7	159.3
1701	Pulp, paper and paperboard	...	1609.7	...	...	...	377.8	...	...	...	...
1702	Corrugated paper and paperboard	1208.7	1266.7	1360.9	1368.2	299.7	332.8	339.7	345.3	75.8	62.4
1709	Other articles of paper and paperboard	1985.0	1624.6	2211.1	1369.5	373.0	434.7	361.6	359.1	51.4	42.1
181	Printing and service activities related to printing	3112.8	3151.2	2938.7	...	1023.9	1056.4	1043.4	...	227.3	...
1811	Printing	2625.5	2650.9	2471.7	2367.6	843.8	852.7	860.0	785.4	192.6	191.2
1812	Service activities related to printing	487.4	500.3	467.0	...	180.2	203.7	183.5	...	34.7	...
1820	Reproduction of recorded media	6.5	6.9	12.8	...	2.1	2.3	0.9	...	0.1	...
1910	Coke oven products	-	-	-	-	-	-	-	-	-	-
1920	Refined petroleum products	53409.2	50233.9	31053.2	...	1258.4	1280.5	...	2181.5	...	861.4
201	Basic chemicals,fertilizers, etc.	27460.2	25608.5	27541.8	21831.6	4999.4	5377.3	6366.2	5923.7	2296.2	1297.4
2011	Basic chemicals	18659.7	18246.3	19860.1	...	3420.0	3717.3	4603.6	...	1757.0	...
2012	Fertilizers and nitrogen compounds	1344.7	1243.0	1338.0	1476.3	237.3	251.9	255.3	260.8	71.6	89.0
2013	Plastics and synthetic rubber in primary forms	7455.9	6119.4	6343.8	8137.7	1342.1	1408.2	1507.2	2057.2	467.4	257.1
202	Other chemical products	7397.4	7097.2	7963.4	...	1997.0	1950.4	2249.6	2057.2	258.1	...
2021	Pesticides and other agrochemical products	327.0	327.0	367.0	451.9	154.9	153.7	163.5	200.0	17.5	18.3
2022	Paints,varnishes;printing ink and mastics	1834.1	1532.4	1877.7	1894.2	432.3	371.6	520.6	483.9	55.6	56.4
2023	Soap,cleaning and cosmetic preparations	1954.4	2059.1	2018.8	2229.6	384.8	379.7	413.7	459.6	67.7	101.8
2029	Other chemical products n.e.c.	3281.9	3178.7	3699.8	...	1024.9	1045.5	1151.8	...	117.2	...
2030	Man-made fibres	864.0	881.2	842.0	734.5	108.8	141.2	83.1	71.3	10.8	11.7
2100	Pharmaceuticals,medicinal chemicals, etc.	15141.0	15310.2	17868.2	21282.5	6497.7	6296.3	6225.5	8663.9	1050.0	810.6
221	Rubber products	676.1	682.4	684.6	698.7	219.8	228.5	214.3	222.0	22.6	30.9
2211	Rubber tyres and tubes	140.0	142.2	163.0	161.5	52.0	51.6	49.9	48.4	4.7	7.7
2219	Other rubber products	536.0	540.2	521.6	537.2	167.8	176.8	164.4	173.6	17.9	23.2
2220	Plastics products	6264.1	6040.2	6021.6	7339.0	1641.3	1727.9	1734.7	2164.8	290.6	573.6
2310	Glass and glass products	1734.4	1708.1	2323.7	1887.9	446.4	487.6	540.2	673.1	137.4	173.4
239	Non-metallic mineral products n.e.c.	5729.4	5773.1	6086.0	5835.9	1785.4	1810.1	1850.5	1867.4	644.0	331.1
2391	Refractory products	122.6	151.0	100.5	87.4	34.2	37.3	26.5	37.0	2.8	3.3
2392	Clay building materials	384.9	459.3	469.4	455.8	168.5	200.5	218.0	210.2	58.4	31.8
2393	Other porcelain and ceramic products	...	...	...	...	...	...	...	...	...	...
2394	Cement, lime and plaster	1408.6	1310.8	1598.5	1594.3	408.6	392.5	453.2	485.7	375.8	95.3
2395	Articles of concrete, cement and plaster	2772.1	2832.2	2944.6	2608.1	896.5	892.8	860.0	821.8	165.9	152.9
2396	Cutting, shaping and finishing of stone	488.2	483.4	398.9	481.6	140.8	146.4	118.0	131.0	16.9	24.1
2399	Other non-metallic mineral products n.e.c.	464.0	448.1	480.9	517.2	94.5	100.3	131.9	136.7	17.9	20.6
2410	Basic iron and steel	9843.5	9033.6	10121.7	9985.7	1416.0	1591.5	1671.7	1934.1	341.6	245.0
2420	Basic precious and other non-ferrous metals	8573.9	8114.1	8247.4	7436.7	957.9	912.0	937.5	892.3	248.4	158.8
243	Casting of metals	409.9	414.3	376.7	377.7	141.5	143.7	133.9	135.4	17.1	20.3
2431	Casting of iron and steel	356.1	338.0	307.6	330.0	123.8	122.0	108.8	117.8	14.6	18.1
2432	Casting of non-ferrous metals	53.8	76.2	69.1	47.6	17.7	21.7	25.1	17.6	2.5	2.2
251	Struct.metal products, tanks, reservoirs	11812.8c/	...	6181.5	6594.5	3718.3c/	...	1794.5	1859.2	226.8	267.4

continued

Belgium

ISIC	Industry	Note	Output (valuation not defined) (millions of Euros)				Note	Value added at factor values (millions of Euros)				Note	Gross fixed capital formation (millions of Euros)	
			2013	2014	2015	2016		2013	2014	2015	2016		2015	2016
2511	Structural metal products		5110.8	5186.9	5157.3	5530.3		1488.1	1512.4	1542.5	1609.9		206.2	238.0
2512	Tanks, reservoirs and containers of metal		...	...	497.3	552.7		...	...	137.8	123.9		10.5	18.8
2513	Steam generators, excl. hot water boilers		...	626.0	526.9	511.4		...	165.4	114.3	125.4		10.1	10.7
2520	Weapons and ammunition		..c/	...	...	782.0		..c/	...	...	329.8		...	33.5
259	Other metal products;metal working services		...c/	4693.0	...	5286.3		..c/	1612.7	...	1743.4		...	391.4
2591	Forging,pressing,stamping,roll-forming of metal		379.9	381.6	...	541.6		99.1	87.0	...	149.4		...	32.5
2592	Treatment and coating of metals;machining		2793.9	2559.9	2598.4	2723.7		1031.0	978.6	931.4	1006.5		164.9	189.0
2593	Cutlery, hand tools and general hardware		451.4	441.1	527.1	466.5		175.8	161.0	186.2	181.7		32.5	22.9
2599	Other fabricated metal products n.e.c.		...	1310.4	1099.9	1554.3		...	386.1	327.2	405.8		42.3	147.1
2610	Electronic components and boards		758.6	908.3	925.0	1056.1		247.3	384.3	297.6	365.2		37.1	18.7
2620	Computers and peripheral equipment		...	283.5	231.4	...		...	104.8	89.8	...		6.7	...
2630	Communication equipment		346.5	335.9	378.5	380.8		158.4	154.8	173.3	189.4		12.8	5.2
2640	Consumer electronics													
265	Measuring,testing equipment; watches, etc.		599.2	623.7	738.5	972.2		246.2	245.6	260.3	327.2		21.5	25.2
2651	Measuring/testing/navigating equipment,etc.		592.8	616.2	726.0	963.2		242.8	242.5	256.3	322.7		21.3	25.0
2652	Watches and clocks		6.4	7.4	12.5	9.0		3.3	3.1	4.1	4.5		0.2	0.3
2660	Irradiation/electromedical equipment,etc.		...	...	...	380.9		...	...	...	151.2		...	12.0
2670	Optical instruments and photographic equipment													
2680	Magnetic and optical media													
2710	Electric motors,generators,transformers,etc.		1031.5	1014.4	705.1	804.5		270.2	283.1	203.7	244.4		21.2	17.0
2720	Batteries and accumulators													
273	Wiring and wiring devices		978.1	1014.2	1037.9	1144.1		253.8	304.8	279.4	332.5		22.7	38.7
2731	Fibre optic cables													
2732	Other electronic and electric wires and cables		643.4	612.4	712.4	711.0		125.4	127.0	157.9	158.0		11.8	15.1
2733	Wiring devices													
2740	Electric lighting equipment		688.4	630.9	777.3	570.3		357.5	299.0	333.8	212.2		30.8	20.1
2750	Domestic appliances													
2790	Other electrical equipment		666.5	732.9	564.8	741.7		278.6	361.6	230.6	294.6		8.0	10.2
281	General-purpose machinery		6162.8	5996.2	5897.3	6656.9		1808.2	1895.5	1900.5	2056.9		175.8	112.1
2811	Engines/turbines,excl.aircraft,vehicle engines		114.8	104.4	110.3	152.4		25.7	35.1	35.5	56.2		85.5	4.6
2812	Fluid power equipment		112.9	149.6	147.2	136.7		31.3	38.2	34.5	35.4		3.7	2.9
2813	Other pumps, compressors, taps and valves		1977.4	1716.7	1864.8	1878.4		759.5	795.4	914.9	870.9		16.9	14.0
2814	Bearings, gears, gearing and driving elements		509.8	546.3	605.3	758.7		158.1	178.4	199.6	256.3		16.0	19.4
2815	Ovens, furnaces and furnace burners		24.1	25.2	73.3	60.2		9.0	11.1	29.1	19.7		2.9	1.6
2816	Lifting and handling equipment		934.4	966.7	528.2	601.3		230.1	220.7	161.7	202.0		15.5	17.3
2817	Office machinery, excl.computers,etc.		...											
2818	Power-driven hand tools													
2819	Other general-purpose machinery		2468.4	2449.1	2561.8	3063.8		584.3	596.7	522.8	614.4		35.3	52.3
282	Special-purpose machinery		4225.3	4542.6	4259.4	4488.1		1349.0	1544.7	1318.7	1415.5		130.9	114.5
2821	Agricultural and forestry machinery		1403.4	1785.9	1600.6	1637.2		399.0	499.0	458.0	484.2		50.1	48.2
2822	Metal-forming machinery and machine tools		358.5	385.5	378.3	375.5		110.3	117.9	111.2	117.8		7.9	10.2

Code	Description	1	2	3	4	5	6	7	8	9	10
2823	Machinery for metallurgy	...	...	...	50.4	...	...	...	23.3	...	0.6
2824	Mining, quarrying and construction machinery	735.7	791.6	609.7	500.0	292.7	400.4	261.8	208.7	19.2	10.9
2825	Food/beverage/tobacco processing machinery	380.6	405.3	416.5	357.0	127.7	138.5	149.9	129.2	11.8	11.0
2826	Textile/apparel/leather production machinery	924.5	783.2	852.1	950.4	264.2	256.1	215.8	261.3	31.3	18.3
2829	Other special-purpose machinery	...	...	...	...	...	...	...	...	...	...
2910	Motor vehicles	12018.6	11531.0	9524.0	9482.5	2291.5	1618.8	1154.1	1101.6	91.3	171.2
2920	Automobile bodies, trailers and semi-trailers	1313.3	1262.5	1483.4	1597.8	311.6	304.5	334.6	324.8	61.8	73.0
2930	Parts and accessories for motor vehicles	4059.3	3843.3	3423.3	3199.7	859.5	760.4	752.7	743.4	88.5	109.4
301	Building of ships and boats	25.3	...	12.4	...	7.2	...	-57.3	...	817.7	...
3011	Building of ships and floating structures	25.0	32.9	11.7	26.3	7.1	-7.5	-57.4	7.0	817.7	0.7
3012	Building of pleasure and sporting boats	0.3	...	0.7	...	0.2	...	0.1	...	-	...
3020	Railway locomotives and rolling stock	...	279.6	226.0	...	...	78.3	58.3	...	6.0	...
3030	Air and spacecraft and related machinery	1446.7	1575.8	1754.1	1800.7	603.1	699.2	775.3	805.1	77.6	81.2
3040	Military fighting vehicles	-	...	...	...	-	...	...	...	...	...
309	Transport equipment n.e.c.	...	109.4	182.3	155.8	...	22.2	33.4	25.4	4.1	3.4
3091	Motorcycles	1.2	...	182.3d/	...	1.0	...	33.4d/	...	4.1d/	...
3092	Bicycles and invalid carriages	139.1	109.0	...d/	132.8	26.5	22.0	...d/	21.1	...d/	2.6
3099	Other transport equipment n.e.c.	...	...	...d/	...	...	...	...d/	...	...d/	...d/
3100	Furniture	2172.8	2190.4	2189.3	2105.6	641.2	666.5	653.9	644.1	76.0	151.0
321	Jewellery, bijouterie and related articles	997.1	1046.2	756.2	927.1	100.6	86.1	82.9	115.3	11.3	19.4
3211	Jewellery and related articles	993.4	1038.7	747.4	921.7	99.4	84.6	81.5	114.4	11.0	19.1
3212	Imitation jewellery and related articles	3.7	7.4	8.8	5.4	1.2	1.5	1.4	0.9	0.2	0.3
3220	Musical instruments	8.2	8.7	10.2	...	3.7	2.9	3.4	...	1.0	...
3230	Sports goods	13.0	10.8	3.0	1.6	4.1	2.1	0.6	0.8	0.1	0.1
3240	Games and toys	120.7	103.8	115.7	127.5	48.7	35.5	46.1	48.7	2.6	4.6
3250	Medical and dental instruments and supplies	783.7	744.4	1094.5	...	321.5	320.2	409.4	...	44.7	...
3290	Other manufacturing n.e.c.	250.0	230.0	260.1	243.4	62.0	57.7	68.6	66.1	7.2	10.0
331	Repair of fabricated metal products/machinery	1989.0	2139.1	2221.5	2531.9	737.1	737.9	793.7	849.5	58.1	77.0
3311	Repair of fabricated metal products	286.4	277.0	242.8	338.9	100.3	92.8	89.0	118.0	4.1	4.6
3312	Repair of machinery	990.9	1150.6	1176.8	1282.1	379.7	393.7	433.8	430.8	38.1	33.2
3313	Repair of electronic and optical equipment	73.3	108.6	85.4	90.8	33.5	34.9	37.1	39.4	2.1	2.7
3314	Repair of electrical equipment	123.4	129.8	157.8	183.3	48.8	48.6	60.8	74.7	2.8	4.8
3315	Repair of transport equip., excl. motor vehicles	510.6	467.3	551.8	611.5	172.9	163.8	170.4	181.7	10.3	31.4
3319	Repair of other equipment	4.4	5.8	6.9	25.4	2.0	4.1	2.5	4.8	0.7	0.2
3320	Installation of industrial machinery/equipment	1954.6	1415.8	2159.7	2068.8	645.9	601.9	690.0	676.0	29.8	23.6
C	Total manufacturing	253620.1	245052.8	223653.4	233503.3	49191.2	49919.1	50931.8	55191.8	11249.3	9788.4

a/ 151 includes 1520.
b/ 1511 includes 1512.
c/ 251 includes 2520 and 259.
d/ 3091 includes 3092 and 3099.

Belgium

Index numbers of industrial production

ISIC Revision 4

(2010=100)

ISIC	Industry	Note	2005	2006	2007	2008	2009	2010	2011	2012	2013	2014	2015	2016
10	Food products		80	84	91	100	97	100	104	107	105	105	109	111
11	Beverages		95	97	101	101	102	100	108	112	112	114	112	124
12	Tobacco products		76	72	73	88	90	100	114	113	99	107	104	100
13	Textiles		112	119	123	110	90	100	97	87	86	93	96	92
14	Wearing apparel		147	142	134	123	104	100	96	87	80	76	76	70
15	Leather and related products		115	118	119	123	101	100	95	100	114	125	120	119
16	Wood products, excluding furniture		91	100	122	112	92	100	99	97	92	98	104	105
17	Paper and paper products		96	100	106	107	95	100	99	100	95	96	97	97
18	Printing and reproduction of recorded media		86	90	93	110	101	100	94	90	84	84	86	87
19	Coke and refined petroleum products		97	98	100	100	95	100	89	96	102	109	100	110
20	Chemicals and chemical products		89	96	98	105	82	100	103	100	97	94	92	90
21	Pharmaceuticals,medicinal chemicals, etc.		70	75	72	80	80	100	111	108	132	152	145	163
22	Rubber and plastics products		91	97	103	103	91	100	101	100	100	102	105	107
23	Other non-metallic mineral products		97	106	113	116	100	100	107	100	95	94	92	94
24	Basic metals		86	101	104	111	77	100	99	96	96	96	105	101
25	Fabricated metal products, except machinery		83	92	113	114	94	100	110	113	113	116	123	122
26	Computer, electronic and optical products		92	74	104	105	89	100	100	98	91	92	90	94
27	Electrical equipment		92	101	107	108	92	100	102	105	91	84	79	82
28	Machinery and equipment n.e.c.		79	92	108	124	92	100	118	115	111	111	110	111
29	Motor vehicles, trailers and semi-trailers		120	126	125	116	83	100	120	110	106	112	114	116
30	Other transport equipment		50	48	61	57	95	100	110	128	150	176	186	184
31	Furniture		90	94	101	103	98	100	100	97	88	86	89	90
32	Other manufacturing		101	104	105	97	92	100	120	124	121	128	128	129
33	Repair and installation of machinery/equipment		82	86	92	108	98	100	106	105	109	114	125	124
C	Total manufacturing		85	90	97	102	89	100	106	105	105	108	109	112

Bermuda

Supplier of information:
Department of Statistics, Government of Bermuda, Hamilton.

Basic source of data:
Annual surveys.

Major deviations from ISIC (Revision 3):
None reported.

Reference period:
Fiscal year referring to the last week of August.

Scope:
All economically active establishments.

Method of data collection:
Mail questionnaires; online survey.

Type of enumeration:
Complete enumeration.

Adjusted for non-response:
Yes.

Concepts and definitions of variables:
Wages and salaries paid to employees is compensation of employees.
Value added is defined as total value added.

Related national publications:
Annual Employment Briefs; Annual Gross Domestic Product Publication, both published by the Department of Statistics, Government of Bermuda, Hamilton.

Bermuda

Wages and salaries paid to employees

ISIC	Industry	Number of establishments (number)					Number of persons engaged (number)					Wages and salaries paid to employees (thousands of Bermuda Dollars)				
		Note	2013	2014	2015	2016	Note	2013	2014	2015	2016	Note	2013	2014	2015	2016
151	Processed meat,fish,fruit,vegetables,fats															
1511	Processing/preserving of meat															
1512	Processing/preserving of fish															
1513	Processing/preserving of fruit & vegetables															
1514	Vegetable and animal oils and fats															
1520	Dairy products		2	2	2	2		6	6	8	8					
153	Grain mill products; starches; animal feeds															
1531	Grain mill products															
1532	Starches and starch products															
1533	Prepared animal feeds															
154	Other food products		8	8	9	12		66	59	61	77					
1541	Bakery products		8	8	9	12		66	59	61	77					
1542	Sugar															
1543	Cocoa, chocolate and sugar confectionery															
1544	Macaroni, noodles & similar products															
1549	Other food products n.e.c.															
155	Beverages															
1551	Distilling, rectifying & blending of spirits															
1552	Wines															
1553	Malt liquors and malt															
1554	Soft drinks; mineral waters															
1600	Tobacco products															
171	Spinning, weaving and finishing of textiles															
1711	Textile fibre preparation; textile weaving															
1712	Finishing of textiles															
172	Other textiles		4		2	2		14								
1721	Made-up textile articles, except apparel		3	2	2	3		10	9	8	8					
1722	Carpets and rugs															
1723	Cordage, rope, twine and netting															
1729	Other textiles n.e.c.		1					4								
1730	Knitted and crocheted fabrics and articles															
1810	Wearing apparel, except fur apparel		4	5	5	4		6	7	7	7					
1820	Dressing & dyeing of fur; processing of fur															
191	Tanning, dressing and processing of leather															
1911	Tanning and dressing of leather															
1912	Luggage, handbags, etc.; saddlery & harness															
1920	Footwear															
2010	Sawmilling and planing of wood		1	1	1	1		4	3	3	2					
202	Products of wood, cork, straw, etc.		7	7	6	6		12	12	10	13					
2021	Veneer sheets, plywood, particle board, etc.															
2022	Builders' carpentry and joinery		1	1	1	1		1	1	1	1					
2023	Wooden containers															
2029	Other wood products; articles of cork/straw		6	6	5	5		11	11	9	12					
210	Paper and paper products															
2101	Pulp, paper and paperboard															
2102	Corrugated paper and paperboard															
2109	Other articles of paper and paperboard															
221	Publishing		10	8	9	6		173	150	147	129					
2211	Publishing of books and other publications		2	2	3	2		16	19	23	19					
2212	Publishing of newspapers, journals, etc.		3	2	2	1		147	121	115	101					
2213	Publishing of recorded media															
2219	Other publishing		5	4	4	3		10	10	9	9					

ISIC Revision 3

Code	Description	1	2	3	4	5	6	7	8
222	Printing and related service activities	8	8	8	9	36	42	45	50
2221	Printing								
2222	Service activities related to printing								
2230	Reproduction of recorded media								
2310	Coke oven products								
2320	Refined petroleum products								
2330	Processing of nuclear fuel								
241	Basic chemicals								
2411	Basic chemicals, except fertilizers								
2412	Fertilizers and nitrogen compounds								
2413	Plastics in primary forms; synthetic rubber								
242	Other chemicals	2	2	2	2	14	15	15	13
2421	Pesticides and other agro-chemical products								
2422	Paints, varnishes, printing ink and mastics	1	1	1	1	6	7	7	8
2423	Pharmaceuticals, medicinal chemicals, etc.								
2424	Soap, cleaning & cosmetic preparations	1	1	1	1	8	6	8	7
2429	Other chemical products n.e.c.	1	1	1	1	7	8		8
2430	Man-made fibres								
251	Rubber products								
2511	Rubber tyres and tubes								
2519	Other rubber products								
2520	Plastic products	3	3	3	3	8	8	8	8
2610	Glass and glass products	1	1	1	1	13	13	12	9
269	Non-metallic mineral products n.e.c.					76			
2691	Pottery, china and earthenware								
2692	Refractory ceramic products								
2693	Struct.non-refractory clay; ceramic products	1	1	1	1	4	5	5	4
2694	Cement, lime and plaster								
2695	Articles of concrete, cement and plaster	3	3	3	3	70	64	64	68
2696	Cutting, shaping & finishing of stone					2			
2699	Other non-metallic mineral products n.e.c.								
2710	Basic iron and steel								
2720	Basic precious and non-ferrous metals								
273	Casting of metals								
2731	Casting of iron and steel								
2732	Casting of non-ferrous metals								
281	Struct.metal products;tanks;steam generators	3	3	3	3	7	7	7	8
2811	Structural metal products								
2812	Tanks, reservoirs and containers of metal								
2813	Steam generators								
289	Other metal products; metal working services	19	20	19	18	35	40	39	37
2891	Metal forging/pressing/stamping/roll-forming								
2892	Treatment & coating of metals								
2893	Cutlery, hand tools and general hardware								
2899	Other fabricated metal products n.e.c.								
291	General purpose machinery								
2911	Engines & turbines (not for transport equipment)								
2912	Pumps, compressors, taps and valves								
2913	Bearings, gears, gearing & driving elements								
2914	Ovens, furnaces and furnace burners								
2915	Lifting and handling equipment								
2919	Other general purpose machinery								
292	Special purpose machinery								
2921	Agricultural and forestry machinery								
2922	Machine tools								
2923	Machinery for metallurgy								
2924	Machinery for mining & construction								
2925	Food/beverage/tobacco processing machinery								
2926	Machinery for textile, apparel and leather								
2927	Weapons and ammunition								
2929	Other special purpose machinery								

continued

Bermuda

ISIC	Industry	\[Establishments\] Note	2013	2014	2015	2016	\[Persons\] Note	2013	2014	2015	2016	\[Wages\] Note	2013	2014	2015	2016
		Number of establishments (number)					**Number of persons engaged** (number)					**Wages and salaries paid to employees** (thousands of Bermuda Dollars)				
2930	Domestic appliances n.e.c.		...	...	...	...		...	...	...	...		...	...	...	...
3000	Office, accounting and computing machinery		...	...	...	...		...	...	...	...		...	...	...	...
3110	Electric motors, generators and transformers		...	...	...	...		...	...	...	...		...	...	...	...
3120	Electricity distribution & control apparatus		...	...	...	...		...	...	...	...		...	...	...	...
3130	Insulated wire and cable		...	...	...	...		...	...	...	...		...	...	...	...
3140	Accumulators, primary cells and batteries		...	...	...	...		...	...	...	...		...	...	...	...
3150	Lighting equipment and electric lamps		...	...	...	...		...	...	...	...		...	...	...	...
3190	Other electrical equipment n.e.c.		2	2	2	2		9	10	4	5		...	...	...	...
3210	Electronic valves, tubes, etc.		...	...	...	...		...	...	...	...		...	...	...	...
3220	TV/radio transmitters; line comm. apparatus		...	...	...	...		...	...	...	...		...	...	...	...
3230	TV and radio receivers and associated goods		...	...	...	...		...	...	...	...		...	...	...	...
331	Medical, measuring, testing appliances, etc.		...	...	...	...		...	...	...	...		...	...	...	...
3311	Medical, surgical and orthopaedic equipment		...	...	...	...		...	...	...	...		...	...	...	...
3312	Measuring/testing/navigating appliances,etc.		...	...	...	...		...	...	...	...		...	...	...	...
3313	Industrial process control equipment		...	...	...	...		...	...	...	...		...	...	...	...
3320	Optical instruments & photographic equipment		...	...	...	...		...	...	...	...		...	...	...	...
3330	Watches and clocks		...	...	...	...		...	...	...	...		...	...	...	...
3410	Motor vehicles		...	...	...	...		...	...	...	...		...	...	...	...
3420	Automobile bodies, trailers & semi-trailers		...	...	...	...		...	...	...	...		...	...	...	...
3430	Parts/accessories for automobiles		...	...	...	...		...	...	...	...		...	...	...	...
351	Building and repairing of ships and boats		25	25	24	25		60	64	61	61		...	...	...	...
3511	Building and repairing of ships		...	...	...	...		...	...	...	...		...	...	...	...
3512	Building/repairing of pleasure/sport. boats		...	...	...	...		...	...	...	...		...	...	...	...
3520	Railway/tramway locomotives & rolling stock		...	...	...	...		...	...	...	...		...	...	...	...
3530	Aircraft and spacecraft		...	...	...	...		...	...	...	...		...	...	...	...
359	Transport equipment n.e.c.		...	...	...	...		...	...	...	...		...	...	...	...
3591	Motorcycles		...	...	...	...		...	...	...	...		...	...	...	...
3592	Bicycles and invalid carriages		...	...	...	...		...	...	...	...		...	...	...	...
3599	Other transport equipment n.e.c.		...	...	...	...		...	...	...	...		...	...	...	...
3610	Furniture		28	28	27	26		65	65	67	70		...	...	...	...
369	Manufacturing n.e.c.		2	2	2	4		4	4	4	6		...	...	...	...
3691	Jewellery and related articles		...	...	...	...		...	...	...	...		...	...	...	...
3692	Musical instruments		...	...	...	...		...	...	...	...		...	...	...	...
3693	Sports goods		...	...	...	...		...	...	...	...		...	...	...	...
3694	Games and toys		...	...	...	...		...	...	...	...		...	...	...	...
3699	Other manufacturing n.e.c.		...	...	...	...		...	...	...	...		...	...	...	...
3710	Recycling of metal waste and scrap		...	1	1	1		1	1	1	1		...	...	...	...
3720	Recycling of non-metal waste and scrap		...	...	...	...		...	...	...	...		...	...	...	...
D	Total manufacturing		136	132	130	157		624	585	573	809		39085	34719	35573	33580

ISIC Revision 3

Bermuda

ISIC Revision 3		Note	Output at basic prices (thousands of Bermuda Dollars)				Note	Value added at basic prices (thousands of Bermuda Dollars)				Note	Gross fixed capital formation (thousands of Bermuda Dollars)	
ISIC	Industry		2013	2014	2015	2016		2013	2014	2015	2016a/		2015	2016
151	Processed meat,fish,fruit,vegetables,fats		...	...	...	...		...	...	...	...		...	...
1511	Processing/preserving of meat		...	...	...	...		...	...	...	...		...	...
1512	Processing/preserving of fish		...	...	...	...		...	...	...	...		...	...
1513	Processing/preserving of fruit & vegetables		...	...	...	...		...	...	...	...		...	...
1514	Vegetable and animal oils and fats		...	...	...	...		...	...	...	...		-1	2
1520	Dairy products		444	518	551	624		...	...	...	...		...	...
153	Grain mill products; starches; animal feeds		...	...	...	...		...	...	...	...		...	...
1531	Grain mill products		...	...	...	...		...	...	...	...		...	...
1532	Starches and starch products		...	...	...	...		...	...	...	...		...	...
1533	Prepared animal feeds		...	...	...	...		...	...	...	...		...	...
154	Other food products		8875	8839	10208	8493		...	...	...	...		-60	62
1541	Bakery products		8875	8839	10208	8493		...	...	...	...		-60	62
1542	Sugar		...	...	...	...		...	...	...	...		...	...
1543	Cocoa, chocolate and sugar confectionery		...	...	...	...		...	...	...	...		...	...
1544	Macaroni, noodles & similar products		...	...	...	...		...	...	...	...		...	...
1549	Other food products n.e.c.		...	...	...	...		...	...	...	...		...	...
155	Beverages		...	...	128	117		...	...	...	...		...	-1
1551	Distilling, rectifying & blending of spirits		...	...	...	...		...	...	...	...		...	...
1552	Wines		...	...	...	...		...	...	...	...		...	...
1553	Malt liquors and malt		...	...	...	...		...	...	...	...		...	...
1554	Soft drinks; mineral waters		...	...	128	117		...	...	...	...		...	-1
1600	Tobacco products		...	...	...	...		...	...	...	...		...	...
171	Spinning, weaving and finishing of textiles		...	...	...	...		...	...	...	...		...	...
1711	Textile fibre preparation; textile weaving		...	...	...	...		...	...	...	...		...	...
1712	Finishing of textiles		...	...	...	...		...	...	...	...		...	...
172	Other textiles		1877	...	...	...		...	...	...	...		...	...
1721	Made-up textile articles, except apparel		906	969	937	637		...	...	...	...		26	...
1722	Carpets and rugs		...	...	...	...		...	...	...	...		...	...
1723	Cordage, rope, twine and netting		971	...	...	...		...	...	...	...		...	...
1729	Other textiles n.e.c.		...	...	...	...		...	...	...	...		...	...
1730	Knitted and crocheted fabrics and articles		...	...	...	...		...	...	...	...		...	...
1810	Wearing apparel, except fur apparel		315	468	531	605		...	...	...	...		-33	-37
1820	Dressing & dyeing of fur; processing of fur		...	...	...	...		...	...	...	...		...	...
191	Tanning, dressing and processing of leather		...	...	...	...		...	...	...	...		...	...
1911	Tanning and dressing of leather		...	...	...	...		...	...	...	...		...	...
1912	Luggage, handbags, etc.; saddlery & harness		...	...	...	...		...	...	...	...		...	...
1920	Footwear		...	...	...	...		...	...	...	...		...	...
2010	Sawmilling and planing of wood		795	896	896	1084		...	...	...	...		-31	21
202	Products of wood, cork, straw, etc.		1036	550	1106	1175		...	...	...	...		16	20
2021	Veneer sheets, plywood, particle board, etc.		...	...	...	...		...	...	...	...		...	...
2022	Builders' carpentry and joinery		31	61	44	25		...	...	...	...		3	-
2023	Wooden containers		...	...	...	...		...	...	...	...		...	...
2029	Other wood products; articles of cork/straw		1005	489	1062	1150		...	...	...	...		13	20
210	Paper and paper products		...	...	...	...		...	...	...	...		...	...
2101	Pulp, paper and paperboard		...	...	...	...		...	...	...	...		...	...
2102	Corrugated paper and paperboard		...	...	...	...		...	...	...	...		...	...
2109	Other articles of paper and paperboard		...	...	...	...		...	...	...	...		...	...
221	Publishing		26636	22917	23967	22462		...	...	...	...		722	-46
2211	Publishing of books and other publications		2969	2857	3481	3102		...	...	...	...		15	686
2212	Publishing of newspapers, journals, etc.		22206	18856	18541	17736		...	...	...	...		...	...
2213	Publishing of recorded media		...	...	...	...		...	...	...	...		...	...
2219	Other publishing		1460	1203	1945	1623		...	...	...	...		...	...

continued

Bermuda

ISIC	Industry	Output at basic prices (thousands of Bermuda Dollars)					Value added at basic prices (thousands of Bermuda Dollars)					Gross fixed capital formation (thousands of Bermuda Dollars)	
		Note	2013	2014	2015	2016	Note	2013	2014	2015	2016a/	Note	2015	2016
222	Printing and related service activities		9153	9482	6872	7872		...	...	...	...		357	-18
2221	Printing		...	...	...	...		...	...	...	...		...	...
2222	Service activities related to printing		...	...	...	...		...	...	...	...		...	...
2230	Reproduction of recorded media		...	...	...	...		...	...	...	...		...	...
2310	Coke oven products		...	...	...	...		...	...	...	...		...	...
2320	Refined petroleum products		...	...	...	...		...	...	...	...		...	...
2330	Processing of nuclear fuel		...	...	...	...		...	...	...	...		...	...
241	Basic chemicals		...	...	...	...		...	...	...	...		...	...
2411	Basic chemicals, except fertilizers		...	...	...	...		...	...	...	...		...	...
2412	Fertilizers and nitrogen compounds		...	...	...	...		...	...	...	...		...	...
2413	Plastics in primary forms; synthetic rubber		...	...	...	...		...	...	...	...		...	...
242	Other chemicals		3699	4059	3956	4082		...	...	...	...		85	112
2421	Pesticides and other agro-chemical products		...	...	...	...		...	...	...	...		...	...
2422	Paints, varnishes, printing ink and mastics		2232	2473	2413	2523		...	...	...	...		-56	83
2423	Pharmaceuticals, medicinal chemicals, etc.		...	...	-	-		...	...	...	...		-	-
2424	Soap, cleaning & cosmetic preparations		1467	1586	1543	1559		...	...	...	...		141	29
2429	Other chemical products n.e.c.		...	...	...	...		...	...	...	...		...	...
2430	Man-made fibres		...	...	...	...		...	...	...	...		...	...
251	Rubber products		...	...	...	...		...	...	...	...		...	...
2511	Rubber tyres and tubes		...	...	...	...		...	...	...	...		...	...
2519	Other rubber products		...	...	...	...		...	...	...	...		...	...
2520	Plastic products		678	659	965	1281		...	...	...	...		8	123
2610	Glass and glass products		1423	1217	1226	870		...	...	...	...		-67	-92
269	Non-metallic mineral products n.e.c.		27799	...	20097	...		...	...	...	...		...	...
2691	Pottery, china and earthenware		...	...	...	...		...	...	...	...		...	...
2692	Refractory ceramic products		...	...	...	...		...	...	...	...		...	...
2693	Struct.non-refractory clay; ceramic products		496	232	251	...		...	...	...	...		-9	...
2694	Cement, lime and plaster		...	...	...	...		...	...	...	...		...	...
2695	Articles of concrete, cement and plaster		27172	17275	19747	24471		...	...	...	...		-241	750
2696	Cutting, shaping & finishing of stone		130	...	100			...	...	...	...		...	...
2699	Other non-metallic mineral products n.e.c.		...	...	...	...		...	...	...	...		...	...
2710	Basic iron and steel		...	...	...	...		...	...	...	...		...	...
2720	Basic precious and non-ferrous metals		...	...	...	...		...	...	...	...		...	...
273	Casting of metals		...	...	...	...		...	...	...	...		...	...
2731	Casting of iron and steel		...	...	...	...		...	...	...	...		...	...
2732	Casting of non-ferrous metals		...	...	...	...		...	...	...	...		...	...
281	Struct.metal products;tanks;steam generators		908	764	837	420		...	...	...	...		...	26
2811	Structural metal products		...	...	...	...		...	...	...	...		...	...
2812	Tanks, reservoirs and containers of metal		...	...	...	...		...	...	...	...		...	...
2813	Steam generators		...	...	...	...		...	...	...	...		...	...
289	Other metal products; metal working services		3799	3012	4880	3065		...	...	...	...		1	1346
2891	Metal forging/pressing/stamping/roll-forming		...	...	...	...		...	...	...	...		...	...
2892	Treatment & coating of metals		...	...	...	...		...	...	...	...		...	...
2893	Cutlery, hand tools and general hardware		...	...	...	...		...	...	...	...		...	...
2899	Other fabricated metal products n.e.c.		...	...	...	...		...	...	...	...		...	...
291	General purpose machinery		...	...	...	...		...	...	...	...		...	...
2911	Engines & turbines (not for transport equipment)		...	...	...	...		...	...	...	...		...	...
2912	Pumps, compressors, taps and valves		...	...	...	...		...	...	...	...		...	...
2913	Bearings, gears, gearing & driving elements		...	...	...	...		...	...	...	...		...	...
2914	Ovens, furnaces and furnace burners		...	...	...	...		...	...	...	...		...	...
2915	Lifting and handling equipment		...	...	...	...		...	...	...	...		...	...
2919	Other general purpose machinery		...	...	...	...		...	...	...	...		...	...

Code	Description									
292	Special purpose machinery	...	...	...	...	...	...	...	...	...	...
2921	Agricultural and forestry machinery	...	...	...	...	...	...	...	...	...	...
2922	Machine tools	...	...	...	...	...	...	...	...	...	...
2923	Machinery for metallurgy	...	...	...	...	...	...	...	...	...	...
2924	Machinery for mining & construction	...	...	...	...	...	...	...	...	...	...
2925	Food/beverage/tobacco processing machinery	...	...	...	...	...	...	...	...	...	...
2926	Machinery for textile, apparel and leather	...	...	...	...	...	...	...	...	...	...
2927	Weapons and ammunition	...	...	...	...	...	...	...	...	...	...
2929	Other special purpose machinery	...	...	...	...	...	...	...	...	...	...
2930	Domestic appliances n.e.c.	...	...	...	...	...	...	...	...	...	...
3000	Office, accounting and computing machinery	...	...	...	...	...	...	...	...	...	...
3110	Electric motors, generators and transformers	...	...	...	...	...	...	...	...	...	...
3120	Electricity distribution & control apparatus	...	...	...	...	...	...	...	...	...	...
3130	Insulated wire and cable	...	...	...	...	...	...	...	...	...	...
3140	Accumulators, primary cells and batteries	...	...	...	...	...	...	...	...	...	...
3150	Lighting equipment and electric lamps	...	...	...	...	...	...	...	...	...	...
3190	Other electrical equipment n.e.c.	2317	2160	2135	2450	...	...	...	...	...	...
3210	Electronic valves, tubes, etc.	...	...	...	...	...	...	...	...	...	...
3220	TV/radio transmitters; line comm. apparatus	...	...	...	...	...	...	...	...	...	...
3230	TV and radio receivers and associated goods	...	...	...	...	...	...	...	...	...	...
331	Medical, measuring, testing appliances, etc.	...	...	...	...	...	...	...	...	...	...
3311	Medical, surgical and orthopaedic equipment	...	...	...	...	...	...	...	...	...	...
3312	Measuring/testing/navigating appliances,etc.	...	...	...	...	...	...	...	...	...	...
3313	Industrial process control equipment	...	...	...	...	...	...	...	...	...	...
3320	Optical instruments & photographic equipment	...	...	...	...	...	...	...	...	...	...
3330	Watches and clocks	...	...	...	...	...	...	...	...	...	...
3410	Motor vehicles	...	...	...	...	...	...	...	...	...	...
3420	Automobile bodies, trailers & semi-trailers	...	...	...	...	...	...	...	...	...	...
3430	Parts/accessories for automobiles	8167	9000	12453	10033	...	...	...	...	...	...
351	Building and repairing of ships and boats	...	...	...	...	...	...	...	...	969	1204
3511	Building and repairing of ships	...	...	...	...	...	...	...	...	...	...
3512	Building/repairing of pleasure/sport. boats	...	...	...	...	...	...	...	...	...	...
3520	Railway/tramway locomotives & rolling stock	...	...	...	...	...	...	...	...	...	...
3530	Aircraft and spacecraft	...	...	...	...	...	...	...	...	...	...
359	Transport equipment n.e.c.	...	...	...	...	...	...	...	...	...	...
3591	Motorcycles	...	...	...	...	...	...	...	...	...	...
3592	Bicycles and invalid carriages	...	...	...	...	...	...	...	...	...	...
3599	Other transport equipment n.e.c.	...	...	...	...	...	...	...	...	...	...
3610	Furniture	5629	5895	5997	8057	...	...	...	...	...	...
369	Manufacturing n.e.c.	498	473	526	447	...	...	...	...	...	...
3691	Jewellery and related articles	...	...	...	...	...	...	...	...	83	-94
3692	Musical instruments	...	...	...	...	...	...	...	...	...	...
3693	Sports goods	...	...	...	...	...	...	...	...	...	...
3694	Games and toys	...	...	...	...	...	...	...	...	...	...
3699	Other manufacturing n.e.c.	...	...	...	...	...	...	...	...	...	...
3710	Recycling of metal waste and scrap	72	65	134	60	...	...	...	...	...	...
3720	Recycling of non-metal waste and scrap	...	...	...	...	...	...	...	...	-4	-30
D	Total manufacturing	104122	89451	98401	98307	49078	44388	49114	46471	1834	4126

a/ Provisional data.

Bolivia (Plurinational State of)

Supplier of information:
Instituto Nacional de Estadística, La Paz.

Basic source of data:
Annual survey.

Major deviations from ISIC (Revision 4):
None reported.

Reference period:
Fiscal year.

Scope:
Enterprises with 20 or more employees or with a revenue of more than 3 million bolivianos.

Method of data collection:
Mail questionnaires.

Type of enumeration:
Complete enumeration.

Adjusted for non-response:
Yes.

Concepts and definitions of variables:
Wages and salaries refers to direct wages and salaries only. Output refers to value of sale of all products only.

Related national publications:
Estadísticas Estructurales de la Industria Manufacturera, Comercio y Servicios 2010 y 2012, published by the Instituto Nacional de Estadística, La Paz.

Bolivia (Plurinational State of)

ISIC	Industry	Number of enterprises (number) Note	2010	2011	2012	2013	Number of employees (number) Note	2010	2011	2012	2013	Wages and salaries paid to employees (thousands of Bolivian Bolivianos) Note	2010	2011	2012	2013
1010	Processing/preserving of meat		21	...	22	...		4002	...	5571	...		96809	...	191651	...
1020	Processing/preserving of fish, etc.		...	...	...	...		...	...	707	...		...	...	22559	...
1030	Processing/preserving of fruit,vegetables		8	...	8	...		896	...	2540	...		14217	...	154944	...
1040	Vegetable and animal oils and fats		9	...	9	...		2361	...	3395	...		126292	...	143110	...
1050	Dairy products		14	...	14	...		3198	...	...	...		92495	...	...	...
106	Grain mill products,starches and starch products		21	...	...	...		3742	...	...	...		53825	...	...	...
1061	Grain mill products		21	...	24	...		3742	...	3645	...		53825	...	82745	...
1062	Starches and starch products		...	...	...	...		...	...	...	...		...	...	...	...
107	Other food products		54	...	...	...		7167	...	...	...		206706	...	...	...
1071	Bakery products		20	...	19	...		2286	...	2850	...		63370	...	81544	...
1072	Sugar		5	...	5	...		2564	...	2910	...		92534	...	147841	...
1073	Cocoa, chocolate and sugar confectionery		6	...	6	...		475	...	487	...		7268	...	14135	...
1074	Macaroni, noodles, couscous, etc.		10	...	10	...		818	...	1046	...		21947	...	31881	...
1075	Prepared meals and dishes		1	...	...	...		26	...	...	...		251	...	...	...
1079	Other food products n.e.c.		12	...	11	...		998	...	1133	...		21337	...	31026	...
1080	Prepared animal feeds		3	...	4	...		94	...	112	...		1898	...	3239	...
110	Beverages		32	...	...	...		4589	...	...	...		314318	...	...	...
1101	Distilling, rectifying and blending of spirits		2	...	3	...		141	...	167	...		6541	...	8572	...
1102	Wines		4	...	4	...		206	...	169	...		5448	...	8980	...
1103	Malt liquors and malt		4	...	5	...		1712	...	2287	...		227489	...	...	...
1104	Soft drinks,mineral waters,other bottled waters		22	...	23a/	...		2530	...	4396a/	...		74841	...	...	...
1200	Tobacco products		1	...	..a/	...		311	...	..a/	...		14458	...	...	...
131	Spinning, weaving and finishing of textiles		8	...	...	...		755	...	...	...		18265	...	...	...
1311	Preparation and spinning of textile fibres		6	...	6	...		683	...	667	...		15663	...	25884	...
1312	Weaving of textiles		2	...	2	...		72	...	79	...		2602	...	2849	...
1313	Finishing of textiles		...	...	...	...		...	...	...	...		...	...	...	...
139	Other textiles		7	...	...	...		595	...	...	...		10703	...	...	...
1391	Knitted and crocheted fabrics		...	...	...	...		...	...	...	...		...	...	...	...
1392	Made-up textile articles, except apparel		3	...	3	...		445	...	396	...		8927	...	12603	...
1393	Carpets and rugs		...	...	...	...		...	...	...	...		...	...	...	...
1394	Cordage, rope, twine and netting		...	...	...	...		...	...	...	...		...	...	...	...
1399	Other textiles n.e.c.		4	...	3	...		150	...	118	...		1776	...	3233	...
1410	Wearing apparel, except fur apparel		24	...	25	...		3997	...	3264	...		77517	...	53448	...
1420	Articles of fur		...	...	...	...		...	...	...	...		...	...	...	...
1430	Knitted and crocheted apparel		12	...	10	...		808	...	597	...		15290	...	16167	...
151	Leather;luggage,handbags,saddlery,harness;fur		19	...	...	...		1068	...	...	...		19698	...	...	...
1511	Tanning/dressing of leather; dressing of fur		16	...	17	...		969	...	1101	...		18048	...	28525	...
1512	Luggage,handbags,etc.;saddlery/harness		3	...	3	...		99	...	109	...		1649	...	2310	...
1520	Footwear		3	...	3	...		837	...	871	...		27677	...	38043	...
1610	Sawmilling and planing of wood		16	...	16	...		671	...	1007	...		11073	...	17456	...

Code	Description						
162	Wood products, cork, straw, plaiting materials	16	…	2947	…	59177	39465
1621	Veneer sheets and wood-based panels	4	5	1676	1619	34904	24050
1622	Builders' carpentry and joinery	11	9	1011	847	19396	…
1623	Wooden containers	1	…	260	…	4877	…
1629	Other wood products;articles of cork,straw	…	…	…	…	…	…
170	Paper and paper products	19	…	2509	…	81719	22244
1701	Pulp, paper and paperboard	4	4	567	634	8831	21396
1702	Corrugated paper and paperboard	5	5	357	459	16434	76885
1709	Other articles of paper and paperboard	10	11	1585	1798	56453	…
181	Printing and service activities related to printing	45	…	2749	…	85910	135423
1811	Printing	10	48	243	2839	5293	…
1812	Service activities related to printing	35	…	2506	…	80618	…
1820	Reproduction of recorded media	…	…	…	…	…	…
1910	Coke oven products	…	…	…	…	…	…
1920	Refined petroleum products	4	3	591	782	82176	125805
201	Basic chemicals,fertilizers, etc.	11	…	617	656	29029	39591
2011	Basic chemicals	10	10	590	…	28361	…
2012	Fertilizers and nitrogen compounds	1	2b/	27	75b/	668	6908b/
2013	Plastics and synthetic rubber in primary forms	…	…	…	…	…	…
202	Other chemical products	14	…	2095	…	97828	…b/
2021	Pesticides and other agrochemical products	1	…b/	26	…b/	1120	…b/
2022	Paints,varnishes;printing ink and mastics	5	5	721	731	33095	44219
2023	Soap,cleaning and cosmetic preparations	6	6	951	1117	40814	42480
2029	Other chemical products n.e.c.	2	2	397	437	22798	15437
2030	Man-made fibres	…	…	…	…	…	…
2100	Pharmaceuticals,medicinal chemicals, etc.	21	21	3640	4409	130460	205780
221	Rubber products	3	…	325	…	4641	…
2211	Rubber tyres and tubes	1	4c/	33	368c/	762	9877c/
2219	Other rubber products	2	…c/	292	…c/	3879	…c/
2220	Plastics products	45	47	4459	5951	108981	166174
2310	Glass and glass products	5	5	629	513	18460	28139
239	Non-metallic mineral products n.e.c.	42	…	9679	…	338065	…
2391	Refractory products	29	…	6570	4143	157730	117043
2392	Clay building materials	…	26	…	…	…	…
2393	Other porcelain and ceramic products	7	…	2205	2712	151881	208244
2394	Cement, lime and plaster	5	8	869	1507d/	27677	68344d/
2395	Articles of concrete, cement and plaster	1	7d/	35	…d/	776	…d/
2396	Cutting, shaping and finishing of stone	…	…d/	…	…d/	…	…
2399	Other non-metallic mineral products n.e.c.	…	…	70	89	2659	3245
2410	Basic iron and steel	2	2	742	1105	48909	68870
2420	Basic precious and other non-ferrous metals	6	8	…	…	…	…
243	Casting of metals	…	…	…	…	…	…
2431	Casting of iron and steel	…	…	…	…	…	…
2432	Casting of non-ferrous metals	…	…	…	…	…	…
251	Struct.metal products, tanks, reservoirs	12	…	776	…	19270	…

continued

Bolivia (Plurinational State of)

ISIC	Industry	Number of enterprises (number) Note	2010	2011	2012	2013	Number of employees (number) Note	2010	2011	2012	2013	Wages and salaries paid to employees (thousands of Bolivian Bolivianos) Note	2010	2011	2012	2013
2511	Structural metal products		10	...	10	...		595	...	728	...		13301	...	15437	...
2512	Tanks, reservoirs and containers of metal		1	...	3e/	...		154	...	203e/	...		5060	...	7938e/	...
2513	Steam generators, excl. hot water boilers		1	...	...e/	...		27	...	...e/	...		909	...	...e/	...
2520	Weapons and ammunition		...	...	...	...		...	...	...	...		...	...	...	...
259	Other metal products;metal working services		12	...	...	...		772	...	...	...		18360	...	...	...
2591	Forging,pressing,stamping,roll-forming of metal		...	...	...	...		...	...	...	...		...	...	...	...
2592	Treatment and coating of metals; machining		...	...	...	...		...	...	...	...		...	...	...	...
2593	Cutlery, hand tools and general hardware		...	...	...e/	...		...	...	...e/	...		...	...	...e/	...
2599	Other fabricated metal products n.e.c.		12	...	13	...		772	...	946	...		18360	...	31265	...
2610	Electronic components and boards		...	...	...	...		...	...	...	...		...	...	...	...
2620	Computers and peripheral equipment		...	...	...	...		...	...	...	...		...	...	...	...
2630	Communication equipment		...	...	...	...		...	...	...	...		...	...	...	...
2640	Consumer electronics		...	...	...	...		...	...	...	...		...	...	...	...
265	Measuring,testing equipment; watches, etc.		...	...	...	...		...	...	...	...		...	...	...	...
2651	Measuring/testing/navigating equipment,etc.		...	...	...	...		...	...	...	...		...	...	...	...
2652	Watches and clocks		...	...	...	...		...	...	...	...		...	...	...	...
2660	Irradiation/electromedical equipment,etc.		...	...	...	...		...	...	...	...		...	...	...	...
2670	Optical instruments and photographic equipment		...	...	...	...		...	...	...	...		...	...	...	...
2680	Magnetic and optical media		...	...	...	...		...	...	...	...		...	...	...	...
2710	Electric motors,generators,transformers,etc.		...	...	...	...		...	...	...	...		...	...	...	...
2720	Batteries and accumulators		2	...	3f/	...		223	...	308f/	...		2762	...	5015f/	...
273	Wiring and wiring devices		1	...	...	...		20	...	...	...		228	...	...	...
2731	Fibre optic cables		...	...	...	...		...	...	...	...		...	...	...	...
2732	Other electronic and electric wires and cables		1	...	...f/	...		20	...	...f/	...		228	...	...f/	...
2733	Wiring devices		...	...	...	...		...	...	...	...		...	...	...	...
2740	Electric lighting equipment		2	...	3	...		72	...	94	...		1545	...	2683	...
2750	Domestic appliances		...	...	...	...		...	...	...	...		...	...	...	...
2790	Other electrical equipment		...	...	...	...		...	...	...	...		...	...	...	...
281	General-purpose machinery		2	...	...	...		23	...	...	...		1106	...	...	...
2811	Engines/turbines,excl.aircraft,vehicle engines		...	...	...	...		...	...	...	...		...	...	...	...
2812	Fluid power equipment		...	...	...	...		...	...	...	...		...	...	...	...
2813	Other pumps, compressors, taps and valves		...	...	...	...		...	...	...	...		...	...	...	...
2814	Bearings, gears, gearing and driving elements		...	...	...	...		...	...	...	...		...	...	...	...
2815	Ovens, furnaces and furnace burners		...	...	...	...		...	...	...	...		...	...	...	...
2816	Lifting and handling equipment		...	...	...	...		...	...	...	...		...	...	...	...
2817	Office machinery, excl.computers,etc.		1	...	...	...		11	...	...	...		529	...	...	...
2818	Power-driven hand tools		...	...	...	...		...	...	...	...		...	...	...	...
2819	Other general-purpose machinery		1	...	...	...		12	...	...	...		577	...	...	...
282	Special-purpose machinery		7	...	...	...		422	...	...	...		6533	...	...	...
2821	Agricultural and forestry machinery		...	...	...	...		...	...	...	...		...	...	...	...
2822	Metal-forming machinery and machine tools		...	...	...	...		...	...	...	...		...	...	...	...

Code	Description						
2823	Machinery for metallurgy	...	...	219	...	3663	...
2824	Mining, quarrying and construction machinery	4	...	60	...	2387	...
2825	Food/beverage/tobacco processing machinery	1	...	13	...	334	...
2826	Textile/apparel/leather production machinery	1	...	130	...	128	...
2829	Other special-purpose machinery	1	...	...	...	...	...
2910	Motor vehicles	...	...	...	...	...	...
2920	Automobile bodies, trailers and semi-trailers	2	...	59	...	994	...
2930	Parts and accessories for motor vehicles	3	...	409	...	11149	...
301	Building of ships and boats	...	...	...	...	...	...
3011	Building of ships and floating structures	...	...	...	...	...	...
3012	Building of pleasure and sporting boats	...	...	...	...	...	...
3020	Railway locomotives and rolling stock	...	...	...	...	...	...
3030	Air and spacecraft and related machinery	...	...	...	...	...	...
3040	Military fighting vehicles	...	...	...	...	...	...
309	Transport equipment n.e.c.	...	...	...	...	...	...
3091	Motorcycles	...	...	...	...	...	...
3092	Bicycles and invalid carriages	...	...	...	...	...	...
3099	Other transport equipment n.e.c.	...	...	...	...	...	...
3100	Furniture	21	24	865	902	15376	20986
321	Jewellery, bijouterie and related articles	3	...	844	...	19170	...
3211	Jewellery and related articles	3	2	844	724	19170	17052
3212	Imitation jewellery and related articles	...	...	...	...	...	...
3220	Musical instruments	...	...	...	...	...	...
3230	Sports goods	...	...	...	...	...	...
3240	Games and toys	1	...	15	...	191	...
3250	Medical and dental instruments and supplies	2g/	...	20	33g/	408	860g/
3290	Other manufacturing n.e.c.	...g/	...g/	...g/	...g/	...g/	...g/
331	Repair of fabricated metal products/machinery	3	...	150	...	3681	3681
3311	Repair of fabricated metal products	...	...	...	...	...	...
3312	Repair of machinery	3	...	150	232	3681	4736
3313	Repair of electronic and optical equipment	...	...	...	...	...	...
3314	Repair of electrical equipment	...	...	...	...	...	...
3315	Repair of transport equip., excl. motor vehicles	...	...	...	...	...	...
3319	Repair of other equipment	...	...	...	...	...	...
3320	Installation of industrial machinery/equipment	...	...	...	...	...	...
C	Total manufacturing	557h/	571	70813h/	77523	2290029h/	3064036

a/ 1104 includes 1200.
b/ 2012 includes 2021.
c/ 2211 includes 2219.
d/ 2395 includes 2396.
e/ 2512 includes 2513 and 2593.
f/ 2720 includes 2732.
g/ 3250 includes 3290.
h/ Sum of available data.

Bolivia (Plurinational State of)

ISIC Revision 4			Output at producers' prices (thousands of Bolivian Bolivianos)					Value added at producers' prices (thousands of Bolivian Bolivianos)					Gross fixed capital formation (thousands of Bolivian Bolivianos)	
ISIC	Industry	Note	2010	2011	2012	2013	Note	2010	2011	2012	2013	Note	2012	2013
1010	Processing/preserving of meat		2933122	...	3197984	...		1159611	...	1454814	...		...	...
1020	Processing/preserving of fish, etc.		...	...	...	...		...	...	...	...		...	...
1030	Processing/preserving of fruit,vegetables		138330	...	159457	...		42523	...	50582	...		...	...
1040	Vegetable and animal oils and fats		5209536	...	8451446	...		1321120	...	2290016	...		...	...
1050	Dairy products		1788155	...	2790699	...		688073	...	1179600	...		...	...
106	Grain mill products,starches and starch products		1099770	...	...	...		251550	...	...	...		...	...
1061	Grain mill products		1099770	...	1317084	...		251550	...	308049	...		...	...
1062	Starches and starch products		...	...	...	...		...	...	...	...		...	...
107	Other food products		3222706	...	...	...		1159122	...	...	...		...	...
1071	Bakery products		678490	...	823776	...		205655	...	308027	...		...	...
1072	Sugar		1667635	...	2754524	...		664722	...	1155491	...		...	...
1073	Cocoa, chocolate and sugar confectionery		57942	...	89036	...		21022	...	37387	...		...	...
1074	Macaroni, noodles, couscous, etc.		374530	...	502161	...		142682	...	163801	...		...	...
1075	Prepared meals and dishes		1732	...	...	...		772	...	...	...		...	...
1079	Other food products n.e.c.		442378	...	487974	...		124268	...	159208	...		...	...
1080	Prepared animal feeds		9160	...	21280	...		3700	...	11338	...		...	...
110	Beverages		3993813	...	...	...		2194730	...	...	...		...	...
1101	Distilling, rectifying and blending of spirits		95439	...	102365	...		21438	...	37381	...		...	...
1102	Wines		85271	...	95403	...		30265	...	40892	...		...	...
1103	Malt liquors and malt		2887785	...	3556135	...		1790599	...	2811028	...		...	...
1104	Soft drinks,mineral waters,other bottled waters		925318	...	2576089a/	...		352428	...	842854a/	...		...	...
1200	Tobacco products		230764	...	...a/	...		95261	...	...a/	...		...	...
131	Spinning, weaving and finishing of textiles		124846	...	...	...		40330	...	...	...		...	...
1311	Preparation and spinning of textile fibres		114734	...	164429	...		34743	...	62051	...		...	...
1312	Weaving of textiles		10112	...	11338	...		5587	...	5217	...		...	...
1313	Finishing of textiles		...	...	...	...		...	...	...	...		...	...
139	Other textiles		38983	...	...	...		17769	...	...	...		...	...
1391	Knitted and crocheted fabrics		...	...	...	...		...	...	...	...		...	...
1392	Made-up textile articles, except apparel		29832	...	63597	...		14194	...	29114	...		...	...
1393	Carpets and rugs		...	...	...	...		...	...	...	...		...	...
1394	Cordage, rope, twine and netting		...	...	...	...		...	...	...	...		...	...
1399	Other textiles n.e.c.		9151	...	9748	...		3575	...	4692	...		...	...
1410	Wearing apparel, except fur apparel		615746	...	311730	...		324940	...	110362	...		...	...
1420	Articles of fur		...	...	...	...		...	...	...	...		...	...
1430	Knitted and crocheted apparel		77012	...	84488	...		35935	...	44960	...		...	...
151	Leather;luggage,handbags,saddlery,harness;fur		389971	...	...	...		106767	...	...	...		...	...
1511	Tanning/dressing of leather; dressing of fur		384689	...	448209	...		105167	...	168721	...		...	...
1512	Luggage,handbags,etc.;saddlery/harness		5283	...	12239	...		1600	...	4450	...		...	...
1520	Footwear		280141	...	481590	...		210277	...	350347	...		...	...
1610	Sawmilling and planing of wood		108120	...	101975	...		26607	...	40561	...		...	...

Code	Description				
162	Wood products, cork, straw, plaiting materials	408024	...	149997	100604
1621	Veneer sheets and wood-based panels	195329	247971	68741	52671
1622	Builders' carpentry and joinery	157786	114380	68270	...
1623	Wooden containers	54909	...	12986	...
1629	Other wood products;articles of cork, straw	...	...	...	...
170	Paper and paper products	920550	429221	361378	223422
1701	Pulp, paper and paperboard	358368	...	110023	142288
1702	Corrugated paper and paperboard	175434	293903	83377	420894
1709	Other articles of paper and paperboard	386747	949438	167978	...
181	Printing and service activities related to printing	431864	...	287494	...
1811	Printing	66456	546368	20289	360522
1812	Service activities related to printing	365409	...	267205	...
1820	Reproduction of recorded media	...	...	...	...
1910	Coke oven products	...	...	...	...
1920	Refined petroleum products	4250469	4772549	1097338	1369437
201	Basic chemicals,fertilizers, etc.	283327	337260	145913	166495
2011	Basic chemicals	265804	254127b/	139726	116342b/
2012	Fertilizers and nitrogen compounds	17523	...	6187	...
2013	Plastics and synthetic rubber in primary forms	...	...	...	...
202	Other chemical products	1473638	...b/	707181	...b/
2021	Pesticides and other agrochemical products	1298	...	...	...b/
2022	Paints,varnishes;printing ink and mastics	394469	483829	116155	132265
2023	Soap,cleaning and cosmetic preparations	845027	933171	536478	631946
2029	Other chemical products n.e.c.	232844	322010	50153	161375
2030	Man-made fibres	...	...	...	...
2100	Pharmaceuticals,medicinal chemicals, etc.	1165720	1217757	619631	641249
221	Rubber products	18617	...	9222	...
2211	Rubber tyres and tubes	5294	47427c/	1601	25303c/
2219	Other rubber products	13323	...c/	7621	...c/
2220	Plastics products	1528418	2066450	419430	622721
2310	Glass and glass products	142262	155909	71609	101242
239	Non-metallic mineral products n.e.c.	3318421	...	1572906	...
2391	Refractory products	1061181	743148	486572	401766
2392	Clay building materials	...	...	...	...
2393	Other porcelain and ceramic products	...	...	...	...
2394	Cement, lime and plaster	1882726	2961915	969660	1494969
2395	Articles of concrete, cement and plaster	371981	619026d/	115521	379281d/
2396	Cutting, shaping and finishing of stone	2533	...d/	1152	...d/
2399	Other non-metallic mineral products n.e.c.	...	...	...	...
2410	Basic iron and steel	12563	62971	...	26519
2420	Basic precious and other non-ferrous metals	2255859	5556749	375112	2009214
243	Casting of metals	...	...	...	...
2431	Casting of iron and steel	...	...	...	...
2432	Casting of non-ferrous metals	...	...	...	...
251	Struct.metal products, tanks, reservoirs	293143	...	72318	...

continued

Bolivia (Plurinational State of)

ISIC	Industry	Note	Output at producers' prices (thousands of Bolivian Bolivianos)				Note	Value added at producers' prices (thousands of Bolivian Bolivianos)				Note	Gross fixed capital formation (thousands of Bolivian Bolivianos)	
			2010	2011	2012	2013		2010	2011	2012	2013		2012	2013
2511	Structural metal products		212199	...	239659	...		50114	...	105177	...		...	...
2512	Tanks, reservoirs and containers of metal		77280	...	90074e/	...		19765	...	27306e/	...		...	...
2513	Steam generators, excl. hot water boilers		3664	...	..e/	...		2439	...	..e/	...		...	...
2520	Weapons and ammunition		...	...	...	...		...	...	...	...		...	...
259	Other metal products;metal working services		243927	...	...	...		64512	...	...	...		...	...
2591	Forging,pressing,stamping,roll-forming of metal		...	...	...	...		...	...	...	...		...	...
2592	Treatment and coating of metals;machining		...	...	...	...		...	...	...	...		...	...
2593	Cutlery, hand tools and general hardware		...	...	..e/	...		...	...	..e/	...		...	...
2599	Other fabricated metal products n.e.c.		243927	...	254789	...		64512	...	99931	...		...	...
2610	Electronic components and boards		...	...	...	...		...	...	...	...		...	...
2620	Computers and peripheral equipment		...	...	...	...		...	...	...	...		...	...
2630	Communication equipment		...	...	...	...		...	...	...	...		...	...
2640	Consumer electronics		...	...	...	...		...	...	...	...		...	...
265	Measuring,testing equipment; watches, etc.		...	...	...	...		...	...	...	...		...	...
2651	Measuring/testing/navigating equipment,etc.		...	...	...	...		...	...	...	...		...	...
2652	Watches and clocks		...	...	...	...		...	...	...	...		...	...
2660	Irradiation/electromedical equipment,etc.		...	...	...	...		...	...	...	...		...	...
2670	Optical instruments and photographic equipment		...	...	...	...		...	...	...	...		...	...
2680	Magnetic and optical media		...	...	...	...		...	...	...	...		...	...
2710	Electric motors,generators,transformers,etc.		118239	...	255836f/	...		53631	...	...	...		...	...
2720	Batteries and accumulators		12252	...	...	...		1248	...	62244f/	...		...	...
273	Wiring and wiring devices		12252	...	...	...		1248	...	...	...		...	...
2731	Fibre optic cables		...	...	..f/	...		...	...	..f/	...		...	...
2732	Other electronic and electric wires and cables		...	...	...	...		...	...	...	...		...	...
2733	Wiring devices		...	...	...	...		...	...	...	...		...	...
2740	Electric lighting equipment		19595	...	30944	...		5691	...	9383	...		...	...
2750	Domestic appliances		...	...	...	...		...	...	...	...		...	...
2790	Other electrical equipment		...	...	...	...		...	...	...	...		...	...
281	General-purpose machinery		17738	...	...	...		5951	...	...	...		...	...
2811	Engines/turbines,excl.aircraft,vehicle engines		...	...	...	...		...	...	...	...		...	...
2812	Fluid power equipment		...	...	...	...		...	...	...	...		...	...
2813	Other pumps, compressors, taps and valves		...	...	...	...		...	...	...	...		...	...
2814	Bearings, gears, gearing and driving elements		...	...	...	...		...	...	...	...		...	...
2815	Ovens, furnaces and furnace burners		...	...	...	...		...	...	...	...		...	...
2816	Lifting and handling equipment		...	...	...	...		...	...	...	...		...	...
2817	Office machinery, excl.computers,etc.		8483	...	...	...		2846	...	...	...		...	...
2818	Power-driven hand tools		...	...	...	...		...	...	...	...		...	...
2819	Other general-purpose machinery		9254	...	...	...		3105	...	...	...		...	...
282	Special-purpose machinery		97506	...	...	...		45612	...	...	...		...	...
2821	Agricultural and forestry machinery		...	...	...	...		...	...	...	...		...	...
2822	Metal-forming machinery and machine tools		...	...	...	...		...	...	...	...		...	...

ISIC Revision 4

Code	Description				
2823	Machinery for metallurgy	60031	…	21940	…
2824	Mining, quarrying and construction machinery	12872	…	7700	…
2825	Food/beverage/tobacco processing machinery	5136	…	3283	…
2826	Textile/apparel/leather production machinery	19468	…	12689	…
2829	Other special-purpose machinery	…	…	…	…
2910	Motor vehicles	11574	…	4377	…
2920	Automobile bodies, trailers and semi-trailers	83929	…	38532	…
2930	Parts and accessories for motor vehicles	…	…	…	…
301	Building of ships and boats	…	…	…	…
3011	Building of ships and floating structures	…	…	…	…
3012	Building of pleasure and sporting boats	…	…	…	…
3020	Railway locomotives and rolling stock	…	…	…	…
3030	Air and spacecraft and related machinery	…	…	…	…
3040	Military fighting vehicles	…	…	…	…
309	Transport equipment n.e.c.	…	…	…	…
3091	Motorcycles	…	…	…	…
3092	Bicycles and invalid carriages	…	…	…	…
3099	Other transport equipment n.e.c.	137122	…	51818	…
3100	Furniture	210047	…	110351	…
321	Jewellery, bijouterie and related articles	396953	…	273071	…
3211	Jewellery and related articles	396953	516398	273071	104502
3212	Imitation jewellery and related articles	…	…	…	…
3220	Musical instruments	…	…	…	…
3230	Sports goods	…	…	…	…
3240	Games and toys	11521g/	…	…	5492g/
3250	Medical and dental instruments and supplies	5041	…	1992	…
3290	Other manufacturing n.e.c.	1610	…g/	869	…g/
331	Repair of fabricated metal products/machinery	28117	…	9257	…
3311	Repair of fabricated metal products	…	…	…	…
3312	Repair of machinery	28117	…	9257	17063
3313	Repair of electronic and optical equipment	…	…	…	…
3314	Repair of electrical equipment	…	…	…	…
3315	Repair of transport equip., excl. motor vehicles	…	…	…	…
3319	Repair of other equipment	…	…	…	…
3320	Installation of industrial machinery/equipment	…	…	…	…
C	Total manufacturing	37936656h/	53649243	14124404h/	21968424

a/ 1104 includes 1200.
b/ 2012 includes 2021.
c/ 2211 includes 2219.
d/ 2395 includes 2396.
e/ 2512 includes 2513 and 2593.
f/ 2720 includes 2732.
g/ 3250 includes 3290.
h/ Sum of available data.

Bolivia (Plurinational State of)

ISIC Revision 3			Index numbers of industrial production (2010=100)											
ISIC	Industry	Note	2005	2006	2007	2008	2009	2010	2011	2012	2013	2014	2015	2016
15	Food and beverages		80	89	92	91	97	100	106	115	...	...	...	...
16	Tobacco products		75	78	83	87	96	100	96	93	...	...	...	...
17	Textiles		105	105	91	99	94	100	97	100	...	...	...	...
18	Wearing apparel, fur		91	96	92	91	93	100	75	77	...	...	...	...
19	Leather, leather products and footwear		105	125	108	113	100	100	116	112	...	...	...	...
20	Wood products (excl. furniture)		112	137	130	148	85	100	99	102	...	...	...	...
21	Paper and paper products		...	...	...	...	...	...	...	...	...	...	...	...
22	Printing and publishing		81	87	88	90	97	100	109	107	...	...	...	...
23	Coke,refined petroleum products,nuclear fuel		86	89	97	105	99	100	103	108	...	...	...	...
24	Chemicals and chemical products		63	73	76	91	96	100	106	106	...	...	...	...
25	Rubber and plastics products		85	74	87	83	93	100	124	132	...	...	...	...
26	Non-metallic mineral products		61	69	74	86	96	100	109	114	...	...	...	...
27	Basic metals		75	75	63	84	100	100	97	97	...	...	...	...
28	Fabricated metal products		63	76	80	80	75	100	85	79	...	...	...	...
29	Machinery and equipment n.e.c.		...	...	...	...	...	...	...	...	...	...	...	...
30	Office, accounting and computing machinery		...	...	...	...	...	...	...	...	...	...	...	...
31	Electrical machinery and apparatus		...	...	...	...	...	...	...	...	...	...	...	...
32	Radio,television and communication equipment		...	...	...	...	...	...	...	...	...	...	...	...
33	Medical, precision and optical instruments		...	...	...	...	...	...	...	...	...	...	...	...
34	Motor vehicles, trailers, semi-trailers		...	...	...	...	...	...	...	...	...	...	...	...
35	Other transport equipment		...	...	...	...	...	...	...	...	...	...	...	...
36	Furniture; manufacturing n.e.c.		113	128	123	109	102	100	76	69	...	...	...	...
37	Recycling		...	...	...	...	...	...	...	...	...	...	...	...
D	Total manufacturing		81	89	92	94	97	100	104	109	...	...	...	...

Bosnia and Herzegovina

Supplier of information:
Agency for Statistics, Sarajevo.

Basic source of data:
Annual survey.

Major deviations from ISIC (Revision 4):
Data presented in ISIC (Revision 4) were originally classified according to NACE (Revision 2).

Reference period:
Calendar year.

Scope:
All enterprises.

Method of data collection:
Mail questionnaires.

Type of enumeration:
Sample survey.

Adjusted for non-response:
Yes.

Concepts and definitions of variables:
Wages and salaries includes employers' contributions (in respect of their employees) paid to social security, pension and insurance schemes as well as the benefits received by employees under these schemes and severance and termination pay; excludes housing and family allowances paid directly by the employer.
Output includes revenue from non-industrial activities.

Related national publications:
Thematic Bulletin Structural Business Statistics 2016, published by the Agency for Statistics, Sarajevo.

Bosnia and Herzegovina

ISIC	Industry	Note	Number of enterprises (number)				Note	Number of employees (number)				Note	Wages and salaries paid to employees (thousands of Bosnian Convertible Marka)			
			2013	2014	2015	2016		2013	2014	2015	2016		2013	2014	2015	2016
1010	Processing/preserving of meat		100	92	94	88		2988	3306	3726	3948		35393	39403	44427	45087
1020	Processing/preserving of fish, etc.		3	3	3	4		156	179	288	383		1513	1636	2355	3278
1030	Processing/preserving of fruit,vegetables		52	55	58	71		1206	861	971	1400		20452	16350	15847	20677
1040	Vegetable and animal oils and fats		4	2	4	6		377	216	297	392		7729	4148	4965	5989
1050	Dairy products		58	46	49	51		1682	1153	1233	1606		28845	20659	22259	25679
106	Grain mill products,starches and starch products		...	...	...	...		...	...	...	...		...	...	...	...
1061	Grain mill products		56	57	53	50		1157	1216	1158	1313		13696	14602	13897	15299
1062	Starches and starch products		1	2	2	1		182	165	188	182		2786	2853	2963	2803
107	Other food products		...	...	...	...		...	...	...	...		...	...	...	...
1071	Bakery products		227	227	235	254		5678	5496	5379	5414		57585	57030	58932	59340
1072	Sugar		5	3	4	4		187	422	155	133		3713	3258	3182	2862
1073	Cocoa, chocolate and sugar confectionery		7	10	10	11		130	519	526	573		1075	7251	7291	7660
1074	Macaroni, noodles, couscous, etc.		14	12	12	9		124	60	136	60		1183	570	1220	589
1075	Prepared meals and dishes		...	...	...	...		...	...	...	...		...	...	...	...
1079	Other food products n.e.c.		85	82	86	84		1400	1586	1404	1587		21756	23421	23663	26128
1080	Prepared animal feeds		45	44	46	46		980	1048	1244	1123		11177	11406	14386	12704
110	Beverages		...	...	...	...		...	...	...	...		...	...	...	...
1101	Distilling, rectifying and blending of spirits		11	8	9	8		106	96	105	121		1085	947	1047	1217
1102	Wines		23	26	27	28		406	359	269	310		4867	5222	3933	4304
1103	Malt liquors and malt		6	7	7	7		1072	962	945	920		24055	22408	18547	18054
1104	Soft drinks,mineral waters,other bottled waters		44	37	43	39		999	981	1062	1070		27250	24253	25225	26526
1200	Tobacco products		6	7	6	6		714	679	736	706		15641	15366	15856	14434
131	Spinning, weaving and finishing of textiles		...	...	...	...		...	...	...	...		...	...	...	...
1311	Preparation and spinning of textile fibres		3	3	3	2		635	510	458	311		6322	5128	3954	3169
1312	Weaving of textiles		5	5	5	5		425	476	424	457		3622	4834	3230	5416
1313	Finishing of textiles		6	6	5	3		36	113	57	85		287	892	457	506
139	Other textiles		...	...	...	...		...	...	...	...		...	...	...	...
1391	Knitted and crocheted fabrics		2	...	1	1		47	...	12	12		426	...	171	101
1392	Made-up textile articles, except apparel		69	67	59	60		4977	5041	4645	4853		54500	54022	47424	44781
1393	Carpets and rugs		3	2	4	3		98	69	42	38		603	444	293	271
1394	Cordage, rope, twine and netting		4	2	4	4		136	45	54	58		1388	506	628	710
1399	Other textiles n.e.c.		15	15	15	17		27	32	78	166		483	476	593	1217
1410	Wearing apparel, except fur apparel		178	173	187	174		8693	9497	10355	10886		70424	80425	92374	102528
1420	Articles of fur		2	...	...	...		18	...	...	...		138	...	...	...
1430	Knitted and crocheted apparel		11	14	14	13		400	650	353	396		4185	5236	3926	4011
151	Leather;luggage,handbags,saddlery,harness;fur		...	...	...	...		...	...	...	...		...	...	...	...
1511	Tanning/dressing of leather; dressing of fur		7	9	9	8		771	658	614	510		11009	9480	14948	5452
1512	Luggage,handbags,etc.;saddlery/harness		9	8	9	9		133	144	151	158		1440	1522	1168	1553
1520	Footwear		83	86	84	85		12615	13525	13692	13683		110251	119588	124205	127680
1610	Sawmilling and planing of wood		535	510	512	522		7160	6360	6797	7661		71318	61883	67134	74051

Code	Description	1	2	3	4	5	6	7	8	9	10	11	12
162	Wood products, cork, straw, plaiting materials	...	...	...	...	...	...	...	...	...	...	...	...
1621	Veneer sheets and wood-based panels	22970	21463	14786	10461	2107	2054	1491	1053	26	25	...	...
1622	Builders' carpentry and joinery	21286	17283	19148	18172	2065	1764	1965	1889	168	165	157	176
1623	Wooden containers	6790	4027	5284	3396	634	369	506	319	40	32	30	29
1629	Other wood products;articles of cork,straw	8782	8423	10111	9076	911	802	884	813	94	88	76	72
170	Paper and paper products	...	...	...	...	...	...	...	...	...	...	...	...
1701	Pulp, paper and paperboard	25984	26032	7658	972	1267	1248	380	68	7	7	8	4
1702	Corrugated paper and paperboard	6421	6099	23988	22868	559	509	1373	1314	50	51	47	49
1709	Other articles of paper and paperboard	14701	15844	13338	9672	793	981	891	566	39	46	46	52
181	Printing and service activities related to printing	...	...	...	...	...	...	...	...	...	...	...	...
1811	Printing	17949	21457	22987	20606	1297	1457	1581	1433	141	144	136	143
1812	Service activities related to printing	2221	1725	1477	4128	182	127	126	446	57	56	53	56
1820	Reproduction of recorded media	212	2746	...	103	22	74	...	13	5	6	...	4
1910	Coke oven products	22135	22629	21758	20962	942	989	961	984	1	1	1	1
1920	Refined petroleum products	36744	45761	49102	45788	1591	1841	1985	2118	7	7	7	5
201	Basic chemicals,fertilizers, etc.	...	...	...	...	...	...	...	...	...	...	...	...
2011	Basic chemicals	24629	22177	21937	22670	1101	1035	1055	1092	18	17	15	16
2012	Fertilizers and nitrogen compounds	294	182	190	189	23	12	11	8	2	2	2	1
2013	Plastics and synthetic rubber in primary forms	5052	4282	3773	4515	332	276	261	282	10	11	11	15
202	Other chemical products	...	...	...	...	...	...	...	...	...	...	...	...
2021	Pesticides and other agrochemical products	46	...	...	50	6	...	...	6	2	...	...	1
2022	Paints,varnishes;printing ink and mastics	1880	1897	2071	2361	160	146	158	183	12	15	15	18
2023	Soap,cleaning and cosmetic preparations	3139	2448	3736	3236	247	282	338	270	26	25	21	20
2029	Other chemical products n.e.c.	30417	23975	18780	17752	1610	1344	1080	1147	31	27	24	24
2030	Man-made fibres	...	...	...	...	...	...	...	...	...	...	...	...
2100	Pharmaceuticals,medicinal chemicals, etc.	41830	39447	40077	30887	966	938	994	1021	7	8	8	11
221	Rubber products	...	...	...	...	...	...	...	...	...	...	...	...
2211	Rubber tyres and tubes	1091	1059	1555	1278	80	68	127	111	17	19	17	18
2219	Other rubber products	3104	1980	3316	1177	247	146	238	107	21	22	20	19
2220	Plastics products	60931	57846	56013	45528	5000	4585	4481	3905	313	296	285	281
2310	Glass and glass products	7962	6307	6606	6467	517	428	450	448	21	22	19	22
239	Non-metallic mineral products n.e.c.	...	...	921	172	...	...	...	...	...	...	4	3
2391	Refractory products	7310	6146	6347	7141	554	464	480	516	10	10	9	11
2392	Clay building materials	261	113	88	88	20	7	6	8	1	1	3	...
2393	Other porcelain and ceramic products	18635	19510	20060	20039	585	597	616	641	11	9	8	9
2394	Cement, lime and plaster	23644	18699	17910	21473	1991	1422	1367	1744	132	128	127	138
2395	Articles of concrete, cement and plaster	8211	10287	7211	6564	820	1117	822	811	96	100	89	90
2396	Cutting, shaping and finishing of stone	1600	3097	2245	2042	97	227	141	148	10	13	12	11
2399	Other non-metallic mineral products n.e.c.	...	...	...	...	...	...	...	...	...	...	...	...
2410	Basic iron and steel	70263	67566	72324	76947	3203	2971	3285	3213	20	26	27	23
2420	Basic precious and other non-ferrous metals	74452	81593	82873	75452	2622	2923	3035	2266	9	8	9	8
243	Casting of metals	...	...	...	...	...	...	...	...	...	...	...	...
2431	Casting of iron and steel	8497	11587	11825	18035	502	554	738	1136	7	7	10	10
2432	Casting of non-ferrous metals	4930	4564	11567	9479	296	315	603	550	12	12	15	14
251	Struct.metal products, tanks, reservoirs	...	...	...	...	...	...	...	...	...	...	...	...

continued

Bosnia and Herzegovina

ISIC	Industry	Number of enterprises (number)					Number of employees (number)					Wages and salaries paid to employees (thousands of Bosnian Convertible Marka)				
		Note	2013	2014	2015	2016	Note	2013	2014	2015	2016	Note	2013	2014	2015	2016
2511	Structural metal products		309	272	281	293		5948	5792	5582	5588		80252	77544	77834	81408
2512	Tanks, reservoirs and containers of metal		18	17	18	18		762	546	849	1049		8713	6820	10533	13141
2513	Steam generators, excl. hot water boilers		1	...	...	...		57	...	...	...		674	...	...	...
2520	Weapons and ammunition		3	5	5	5		406	1313	1367	1595		6288	22081	27853	35058
259	Other metal products;metal working services		...	...	...	...		...	...	...	...		...	...	...	...
2591	Forging,pressing,stamping,roll-forming of metal		21	17	19	21		638	772	803	945		8829	12137	14090	15431
2592	Treatment and coating of metals;machining		137	137	149	173		1834	2302	2474	3068		28872	32208	37159	41531
2593	Cutlery, hand tools and general hardware		40	40	43	45		2517	1786	1905	2112		38045	29652	30424	30948
2599	Other fabricated metal products n.e.c.		119	113	114	119		3406	2082	2451	2441		46777	28280	34085	34553
2610	Electronic components and boards		7	7	6	7		14	4	234	198		162	66	3576	3161
2620	Computers and peripheral equipment		28	23	26	27		440	256	216	320		6154	2838	2626	3931
2630	Communication equipment		4	4	3	3		71	89	68	28		2634	1209	802	369
2640	Consumer electronics		...	1	...	...		...	...	...	...		...	...	...	...
265	Measuring,testing equipment; watches, etc.		...	...	...	...		...	...	...	...		...	...	...	...
2651	Measuring/testing/navigating equipment,etc.		14	14	12	10		224	186	168	164		4222	3945	3599	3245
2652	Watches and clocks		1	...	1	1		...	...	1	2		...	...	15	19
2660	Irradiation/electromedical equipment,etc.		...	...	...	1		...	...	...	3		...	...	...	30
2670	Optical instruments and photographic equipment		3	3	4	1		7	11	110	120		47	192	2008	1992
2680	Magnetic and optical media		...	...	...	...		...	...	...	...		...	...	...	...
2710	Electric motors,generators,transformers,etc.		37	31	31	34		1053	1193	1052	1192		18225	19331	19869	22335
2720	Batteries and accumulators		4	4	5	3		98	84	54	29		810	679	498	294
273	Wiring and wiring devices		...	...	...	...		...	...	...	...		...	...	...	...
2731	Fibre optic cables		...	...	...	1		...	...	...	16		...	...	...	185
2732	Other electronic and electric wires and cables		8	7	8	6		551	689	829	900		8733	8893	9667	10489
2733	Wiring devices		7	8	5	5		208	137	121	122		2724	1728	1353	1484
2740	Electric lighting equipment		10	11	14	13		127	142	152	199		2169	2425	3164	3541
2750	Domestic appliances		7	7	7	9		565	564	414	452		5728	5830	4489	4734
2790	Other electrical equipment		21	19	17	17		472	367	355	443		5706	4452	3731	4103
281	General-purpose machinery		...	...	...	...		...	...	...	...		...	...	...	...
2811	Engines/turbines,excl.aircraft,vehicle engines		...	1	1	3		...	17	17	23		...	266	246	320
2812	Fluid power equipment		6	...	5	5		29	...	60	60		432	...	1050	1101
2813	Other pumps, compressors, taps and valves		8	9	7	4		314	544	309	346		4866	7392	4806	5686
2814	Bearings, gears, gearing and driving elements		10	12	12	11		303	310	374	329		4708	5533	6532	6163
2815	Ovens, furnaces and furnace burners		4	4	2	3		176	192	32	16		2306	3030	666	799
2816	Lifting and handling equipment		26	23	20	19		400	391	342	411		4559	5325	4916	5846
2817	Office machinery, excl.computers,etc.		2	...	3	3		6	...	12	23		72	...	110	316
2818	Power-driven hand tools		2	...	2	2		31	...	25	20		280	...	227	76
2819	Other general-purpose machinery		35	38	37	38		1006	815	1091	1220		18673	16090	20758	20711
282	Special-purpose machinery		...	...	...	...		...	...	...	...		...	...	...	...
2821	Agricultural and forestry machinery		3	3	2	2		117	54	94	41		1107	533	913	437
2822	Metal-forming machinery and machine tools		10	13	12	14		340	400	242	260		4375	5956	3210	4151

ISIC Revision 4

2823	Machinery for metallurgy	..	..	..	..	999	648	417	361	13127	8615	5472	3597
2824	Mining, quarrying and construction machinery	8	9	7	8	20	41	131	168	476	808	2055	2299
2825	Food/beverage/tobacco processing machinery	2	4	7	4	..	..	..	..	..	..	..	..
2826	Textile/apparel/leather production machinery	..	..	..	..	47	7	16	24	679	71	286	243
2829	Other special-purpose machinery	8	4	4	6	367	381	293	128	4169	4254	3381	1878
2910	Motor vehicles	6	6	7	6	415	480	403	472	7293	7406	6299	7218
2920	Automobile bodies, trailers and semi-trailers	8	9	9	12	..	..	..	..	..	..	..	..
2930	Parts and accessories for motor vehicles	35	38	38	37	2014	2350	2472	2665	30750	37864	43138	45637
301	Building of ships and boats	..	..	..	..	..	..	..	..	..	..	..	..
3011	Building of ships and floating structures	2	..	..	..	17	..	..	..	161	613	689	1131
3012	Building of pleasure and sporting boats	4	6	5	5	50	50	48	94	709	..	..	113
3020	Railway locomotives and rolling stock	1	..	1	1	432	..	..	15	7381	..	7014	7180
3030	Air and spacecraft and related machinery	..	..	..	..	..	405	405	402	..	..	..	..
3040	Military fighting vehicles	..	..	..	..	..	..	..	..	..	..	..	..
309	Transport equipment n.e.c.	..	..	..	..	..	..	..	..	..	..	..	..
3091	Motorcycles	..	..	..	..	..	..	..	..	..	..	..	..
3092	Bicycles and invalid carriages	3	2	3	2	81	35	44	33	941	358	408	338
3099	Other transport equipment n.e.c.	..	..	..	..	..	..	..	..	..	..	..	..
3100	Furniture	199	201	211	222	6658	9162	7923	9373	72538	90978	91836	107558
321	Jewellery, bijouterie and related articles	7	6	6	6	46	24	13	45	376	233	109	374
3211	Jewellery and related articles	7	..	2	3	..	..	19	24	..	..	181	206
3212	Imitation jewellery and related articles	..	..	..	..	..	..	..	..	..	..	..	..
3220	Musical instruments	1	..	..	1	44	26	55	98	466	292	710	1082
3230	Sports goods	3	2	3	2	192	263	324	344	2052	3081	3471	4232
3240	Games and toys	10	9	9	12	434	429	403	508	4913	4868	4644	6051
3250	Medical and dental instruments and supplies	26	26	28	31	191	200	225	249	2312	2173	2530	2940
3290	Other manufacturing n.e.c.	23	16	18	18	..	..	..	..	..	..	..	..
331	Repair of fabricated metal products/machinery	4	6	5	6	291	285	266	268	4378	2027	4352	4595
3311	Repair of fabricated metal products	48	50	61	57	360	522	647	497	3836	7515	8194	6466
3312	Repair of machinery	6	8	9	8	9	3	5	24	108	20	39	334
3313	Repair of electronic and optical equipment	17	16	16	20	154	251	161	226	2295	3984	2052	2972
3314	Repair of electrical equipment	8	9	6	4	221	460	61	127	4497	7897	756	1693
3315	Repair of transport equip., excl. motor vehicles	..	1	..	1	..	2	..	1	..	11	..	10
3319	Repair of other equipment	..	..	..	..	..	..	..	..	..	..	..	..
3320	Installation of industrial machinery/equipment	31	33	37	36	363	438	591	665	6698	6366	10822	7921
C	Total manufacturing	4398a/	4235a/	4428	4518a/	121869a/	125976a/	126353	134410a/	1647261a/	1686038a/	1747994	1822111a/

a/ Sum of available data.

Bosnia and Herzegovina

ISIC Revision 4			Output at factor values (thousands of Bosnian Convertible Marka)					Value added at factor values (thousands of Bosnian Convertible Marka)					Gross fixed capital formation (thousands of Bosnian Convertible Marka)		
ISIC	Industry	Note	2013	2014	2015	2016	Note	2013	2014	2015	2016	Note	2015	2016
1010	Processing/preserving of meat		585639	591646	746668	735957		93839	121562	128129	128470		49582	34124
1020	Processing/preserving of fish, etc.		17557	19294	20618	30608		3666	3693	4509	6568		577	972
1030	Processing/preserving of fruit,vegetables		122186	98305	113129	165342		40013	25193	31264	51422		3809	42142
1040	Vegetable and animal oils and fats		137969	113604	180110	222389		13918	13548	22150	30324		2668	17360
1050	Dairy products		349652	301092	288021	313594		71204	44192	52129	55607		13412	13021
106	Grain mill products,starches and starch products													
1061	Grain mill products		180027	181501	168628	195407		24249	30862	30367	40085		6654	5266
1062	Starches and starch products		12845	14306	20064	30066		...	2552	6385	3357		583	470
107	Other food products		...					...					...	
1071	Bakery products		226487	227252	232761	244549		80793	85546	86927	91031		17333	19431
1072	Sugar		154093	69597	81668	116841		17246	5942	9894	7918		1359	...
1073	Cocoa, chocolate and sugar confectionery		6488	72489	100704	80298		2336	26772	48389	24684		5524	10118
1074	Macaroni, noodles, couscous, etc.		5286	3201	6089	2549		1550	1389	2001	1028		222	80
1075	Prepared meals and dishes													
1079	Other food products n.e.c.		207095	189852	194425	258725		57535	50757	51787	102243		14988	13484
1080	Prepared animal feeds		154426	190936	233575	229715		18839	23143	30498	28096		9304	8742
110	Beverages													
1101	Distilling, rectifying and blending of spirits		12026	10051	12107	18874		3379	3129	5690	7692		385	625
1102	Wines		33939	27966	25376	33755		9139	9895	10234	16461		2008	1806
1103	Malt liquors and malt		107851	101746	110477	115433		42879	37326	53028	51310		10084	15563
1104	Soft drinks,mineral waters,other bottled waters		226547	195852	209467	235705		82857	68371	74997	112411		7722	11327
1200	Tobacco products		70845	59904	63293	60555		23339	17203	16965	17728		2012	7921
131	Spinning, weaving and finishing of textiles													
1311	Preparation and spinning of textile fibres		25523	21842	15344	15592		12803	8617	5272	5245		2528	2243
1312	Weaving of textiles		10072	35981	44681	49309		2944	9174	9666	14171		105	2161
1313	Finishing of textiles		899	1378	1213	1618		388	1008	709	1053		106	64
139	Other textiles													
1391	Knitted and crocheted fabrics		651	...	729	1402		306	...	376	297		...	17
1392	Made-up textile articles, except apparel		510044	534530	434078	461198		99044	111782	90334	93138		11062	13011
1393	Carpets and rugs		1655	1463	1027	935		580	574	429	259		-	259
1394	Cordage, rope, twine and netting		7685	2803	3546	4105		2696	1029	1090	1148		139	62
1399	Other textiles n.e.c.		923	1489	2901	5801		494	438	727	2139		36	155
1410	Wearing apparel, except fur apparel		174559	205015	200030	221315		96845	112345	121274	133687		10068	24172
1420	Articles of fur		130					-43						
1430	Knitted and crocheted apparel		17984	21242	16694	20849		8005	8035	5995	6125		3144	391
151	Leather;luggage,handbags,saddlery,harness;fur													
1511	Tanning/dressing of leather; dressing of fur		92858	128845	122940	82244		...	-5161	10926	24298		1145	1199
1512	Luggage,handbags,etc.;saddlery/harness		4394	5218	5567	5055		2128	2424	2863	3202		290	556
1520	Footwear		231769	239098	275094	296989		141863	157828	157662	172313		16703	16793
1610	Sawmilling and planing of wood		501211	468759	538312	594301		140279	120320	140030	149469		36284	38094

162	Wood products, cork, straw, plaiting materials	:	:	:	:	:	:	:	:	:	:
1621	Veneer sheets and wood-based panels	15595	15347	50337	41664	30349	19354	153834	126671	95110	63578
1622	Builders' carpentry and joinery	12092	6862	40719	33762	34987	39282	133751	116065	116921	111845
1623	Wooden containers	2813	769	9167	9492	16618	6825	37385	33523	35495	25603
1629	Other wood products;articles of cork,straw	7427	15059	23439	10408	17266	20835	81900	44600	64986	63343
170	Paper and paper products	:	:	:	:	:	:	:	:	:	:
1701	Pulp, paper and paperboard	15656	15060	27907	48743	12707	1629	164924	208400	79732	9799
1702	Corrugated paper and paperboard	4972	6799	19007	18246	58354	50668	67282	65051	181758	158753
1709	Other articles of paper and paperboard	7227	21727	49758	42255	49008	17306	129793	126362	116850	91153
181	Printing and service activities related to printing	:	:	:	:	:	:	:	:	:	:
1811	Printing	8606	37363	66047	60659	67584	50767	144349	146507	152023	118262
1812	Service activities related to printing	1490	148	4373	3588	2174	6521	11322	7568	4799	12220
1820	Reproduction of recorded media	:	110	223	3321	:	:	294	4062	:	:
1910	Coke oven products	1042	1288	24380	29952	17708	:	181088	235630	228669	164902
1920	Refined petroleum products	24195	22191	42452	-3072	:	:	732828	845316	1188101	1368249
201	Basic chemicals,fertilizers, etc.	:	:	:	:	:	:	:	:	:	:
2011	Basic chemicals	14022	41007	115530	93527	76494	68183	270399	224552	196369	183884
2012	Fertilizers and nitrogen compounds	146	28	533	291	424	264	2651	1683	1821	1900
2013	Plastics and synthetic rubber in primary forms	4718	3825	10065	10927	7588	9621	61765	58404	52829	68893
202	Other chemical products	:	:	:	:	:	:	:	:	:	:
2021	Pesticides and other agrochemical products	970	1188	61	:	:	114	168	:	:	210
2022	Paints,varnishes;printing ink and mastics	2089	2244	7466	4100	5188	4530	23630	17261	17389	14747
2023	Soap,cleaning and cosmetic preparations	10919	24573	6886	7620	4820	5456	22824	20411	16644	14167
2029	Other chemical products n.e.c.	3840	7547	61038	39284	30759	30154	138096	79607	59977	66636
2030	Man-made fibres	:	:	:	:	:	:	:	:	:	:
2100	Pharmaceuticals,medicinal chemicals, etc.	:	:	80663	77204	83136	59597	189041	163325	155978	137834
221	Rubber products	:	:	:	:	:	:	:	:	:	:
2211	Rubber tyres and tubes	496	475	2841	2308	3027	1647	6694	6616	10866	7010
2219	Other rubber products	867	1576	5924	3641	6246	2679	15616	9753	12295	4920
2220	Plastics products	31354	39289	147357	131632	119308	109009	524885	493974	481404	430409
2310	Glass and glass products	5404	3949	14778	10907	15340	14721	41273	31841	38564	40381
239	Non-metallic mineral products n.e.c.	:	:	:	:	:	:	:	:	:	:
2391	Refractory products	1546	420	12101	7711	7392	67	31283	22933	20781	347
2392	Clay building materials	119	9564	-566	531	292	8422	678	569	474	22163
2393	Other porcelain and ceramic products	12660	11339	66548	68558	61374	67325	136586	145559	141285	144379
2394	Cement, lime and plaster	22414	2174	61527	49211	41259	49402	173943	137267	137256	159002
2395	Articles of concrete, cement and plaster	5292	938	13644	15531	13547	13374	44245	46309	41885	38580
2396	Cutting, shaping and finishing of stone	724	:	3538	5889	4339	2915	16411	36836	35085	19228
2399	Other non-metallic mineral products n.e.c.	:	:	:	:	:	:	:	:	:	:
2410	Basic iron and steel	19905	75313	121892	116910	158344	126314	710623	741681	842084	792505
2420	Basic precious and other non-ferrous metals	12634	38875	113135	137117	99749	70840	683690	870948	880103	911408
243	Casting of metals	:	:	:	:	:	:	:	:	:	:
2431	Casting of iron and steel	18547	3597	9142	6516	19511	18369	27925	28945	48831	67339
2432	Casting of non-ferrous metals	4402	1622	10615	10870	61078	35311	29542	32971	155017	129553
251	Struct.metal products, tanks, reservoirs	:	:	:	:	:	:	:	:	:	:

continued

Bosnia and Herzegovina

ISIC	Industry	Note	Output at factor values (thousands of Bosnian Convertible Marka)				Note	Value added at factor values (thousands of Bosnian Convertible Marka)				Note	Gross fixed capital formation (thousands of Bosnian Convertible Marka)	
	ISIC Revision 4		2013	2014	2015	2016		2013	2014	2015	2016		2015	2016
2511	Structural metal products		366403	384731	421531	486372		124667	128306	143428	154326		28599	32223
2512	Tanks, reservoirs and containers of metal		36915	35306	60011	81394		13523	13768	23690	33002		7168	4234
2513	Steam generators, excl. hot water boilers		3238	...	...	...		1458	...	...	...		...	...
2520	Weapons and ammunition		13234	82514	122405	160768		1790	27121	44829	61352		2118	5068
259	Other metal products;metal working services		...	...	...	...		...	...	...	...		...	...
2591	Forging,pressing,stamping,roll-forming of metal		62751	44615	78659	104540		18598	18458	24450	38319		9731	6177
2592	Treatment and coating of metals;machining		109925	159459	207805	231197		47356	66382	101300	100825		17288	27925
2593	Cutlery, hand tools and general hardware		122108	98213	120400	152914		55229	46895	60808	81698		17992	17747
2599	Other fabricated metal products n.e.c.		309805	222704	268391	298079		97468	68214	77040	84026		19799	25123
2610	Electronic components and boards		1080	221	29707	21629		218	124	7863	5831		1220	660
2620	Computers and peripheral equipment		27704	13079	12720	15592		16458	5909	6108	8366		249	1147
2630	Communication equipment		20249	5960	4558	4162		4797	1937	1187	1715		40	111
2640	Consumer electronics		...	12	...	...		...	9	...	...		...	...
265	Measuring,testing equipment; watches, etc.		...	...	...	...		...	...	...	...		...	...
2651	Measuring/testing/navigating equipment,etc.		18868	16107	17156	17718		7111	6460	4965	4525		1213	873
2652	Watches and clocks		29	...	56	239		4	...	11	41		...	29
2660	Irradiation/electromedical equipment,etc.		...	...	...	216		...	...	...	91		...	...
2670	Optical instruments and photographic equipment		70	145	1737	3401		51	...	900	2385		-	160
2680	Magnetic and optical media		...	...	...	...		...	...	...	...		...	...
2710	Electric motors,generators,transformers,etc.		97474	101963	104983	96131		31497	33002	35103	36273		2560	2979
2720	Batteries and accumulators		2073	1225	742	2146		...	...	264	1650		1906	996
273	Wiring and wiring devices		...	...	...	...		...	...	...	...		...	...
2731	Fibre optic cables		...	...	...	589		...	...	...	170		...	...
2732	Other electronic and electric wires and cables		113903	142767	151292	159970		14231	21201	25076	20220		6449	13684
2733	Wiring devices		12513	12675	10941	13888		5555	4880	3803	5448		670	3509
2740	Electric lighting equipment		10152	9776	11532	13019		4152	3465	3940	5765		1591	915
2750	Domestic appliances		26108	21356	21372	23305		7347	4896	6615	8079		1024	1244
2790	Other electrical equipment		23969	20323	18969	21028		9061	6068	5293	7077		3388	205
281	General-purpose machinery		...	...	...	...		...	...	...	...		...	...
2811	Engines/turbines,excl.aircraft,vehicle engines		...	1200	1310	2560		...	879	477	1051		575	201
2812	Fluid power equipment		1878	...	7508	9362		719	...	1557	1150		1616	3032
2813	Other pumps, compressors, taps and valves		20003	19744	17470	18125		7896	7993	7326	7313		4048	2762
2814	Bearings, gears, gearing and driving elements		18842	19784	28140	31790		8349	6282	12360	7731		3941	7786
2815	Ovens, furnaces and furnace burners		10041	7344	3151	1935		4563	3830	1080	1245		-	...
2816	Lifting and handling equipment		30597	33888	31551	33643		12469	12270	10798	14557		3039	3167
2817	Office machinery, excl.computers,etc.		172	...	172	2353		103	...	106	1599		...	856
2818	Power-driven hand tools		272	...	224	12		173	...	134	3		...	...
2819	Other general-purpose machinery		92345	69482	96168	99787		33357	24456	38533	40728		6643	7650
282	Special-purpose machinery		...	...	...	...		...	...	...	...		...	...
2821	Agricultural and forestry machinery		4548	1834	3518	1137		1742	697	1537	535		4	...
2822	Metal-forming machinery and machine tools		23633	30709	12053	14583		9445	12440	5921	6087		7632	3997

ISIC	Industry	(1)	(2)	(3)	(4)	(5)	(6)	(7)	(8)	(9)	(10)
2823	Machinery for metallurgy	32063	15772	13097	10915	10464	...	...	...	...	...
2824	Mining, quarrying and construction machinery	1419	5139	8249	8198	618	6530	5110	4644	5070	260
2825	Food/beverage/tobacco processing machinery	...	912	1345	4931	...	3986	3467	3624	1862	842
2826	Textile/apparel/leather production machinery	...	...	...	...	...	...	...	...	...	...
2829	Other special-purpose machinery	2197	4331	...	...	1639	362	297	1116	78	...
2910	Motor vehicles	5757	7092	...	2194	1673	957	3912	859	-	...
2920	Automobile bodies, trailers and semi-trailers	37349	41749	36192	41657	10416	12951	11316	14025	5241	3643
2930	Parts and accessories for motor vehicles	302407	338516	406360	399521	61334	108401	126979	96479	29680	53712
301	Building of ships and boats	...	...	...	...	...	...	...	...	...	...
3011	Building of ships and floating structures	...	...	...	...	...	...	...	...	...	...
3012	Building of pleasure and sporting boats	2387	2145	2708	9370	939	894	695	895	8	625
3020	Railway locomotives and rolling stock	12546	...	...	576	8808	...	...	264	...	65
3030	Air and spacecraft and related machinery	...	...	9853	11121	...	...	5617	7826	1623	...
3040	Military fighting vehicles	...	...	...	...	...	...	...	...	...	...
309	Transport equipment n.e.c.	...	...	...	...	...	...	...	...	...	...
3091	Motorcycles	...	...	...	...	...	...	...	...	...	...
3092	Bicycles and invalid carriages	3431	2173	2291	1443	1012	986	698	402	6	49
3099	Other transport equipment n.e.c.	...	...	...	...	...	...	...	...	...	...
3100	Furniture	365433	429230	487299	562139	109194	117729	147046	150601	29436	82415
321	Jewellery, bijouterie and related articles	...	...	...	...	...	...	...	...	...	...
3211	Jewellery and related articles	993	354	191	...	673	229	139	1325	...	52
3212	Imitation jewellery and related articles	...	...	1420	2830	...	1389	732	732	...	...
3220	Musical instruments	...	...	...	849	-175	...	...	...	...	...
3230	Sports goods	2943	1779	2875	5523	908	662	1598	1782	105	185
3240	Games and toys	8231	12562	11701	16692	4668	7521	7177	9333	604	1339
3250	Medical and dental instruments and supplies	9815	8751	10147	15322	6354	6161	7011	9909	1146	1420
3290	Other manufacturing n.e.c.	14035	12111	15272	16293	6961	4887	6669	5069	1107	214
331	Repair of fabricated metal products/machinery	...	...	...	...	...	...	...	...	...	...
3311	Repair of fabricated metal products	6820	8841	11486	8366	5298	2698	6563	5164	2	7
3312	Repair of machinery	18304	15789	16549	14372	10457	9829	9485	7811	1036	243
3313	Repair of electronic and optical equipment	146	143	200	370	79	136	73	288	124	...
3314	Repair of electrical equipment	5276	10704	6710	9770	2955	6079	3695	4497	189	520
3315	Repair of transport equip., excl. motor vehicles	8788	13184	3080	5084	5992	7847	1307	3331	16	...
3319	Repair of other equipment	...	165	...	55	...	122	...	50	...	...
3320	Installation of industrial machinery/equipment	20164	35268	36379	33757	11227	13652	22081	15670	2006	1033
C	Total manufacturing	12075926a/	12267513a/	12557266	13151730a/	3065002a/	3340827	3694388a/		872112	896468a/

a/ Sum of available data.

Bosnia and Herzegovina

Index numbers of industrial production

ISIC Revision 4

ISIC	Industry	Note	2005	2006	2007	2008	2009	2010	2011	2012	2013	2014	2015	2016
								(2010=100)						
10	Food products		...	93	98	105	100	100	96	95	101	104	112	121
11	Beverages		...	98	104	110	103	100	99	100	106	105	109	105
12	Tobacco products		...	106	101	107	122	100	88	75	79	68	85	82
13	Textiles		...	100	90	96	89	100	105	80	79	77	73	76
14	Wearing apparel		...	105	107	116	101	100	106	88	111	112	128	123
15	Leather and related products		...	101	93	93	85	100	111	102	113	119	116	112
16	Wood products, excluding furniture		...	142	138	131	94	100	107	99	111	116	116	122
17	Paper and paper products		...	100	96	104	106	100	101	101	104	94	120	102
18	Printing and reproduction of recorded media		...	97	120	121	118	100	100	99	98	121	125	135
19	Coke and refined petroleum products		...	35	45	44	75	100	104	84	90	88	87	81
20	Chemicals and chemical products		...	43	58	74	95	100	114	117	138	155	168	189
21	Pharmaceuticals, medicinal chemicals, etc.		...	32	51	91	97	100	121	144	134	142	134	130
22	Rubber and plastics products		...	96	107	108	83	100	112	111	106	139	149	171
23	Other non-metallic mineral products		...	113	116	129	97	100	100	83	83	82	83	85
24	Basic metals		...	98	100	105	82	100	109	107	103	99	100	94
25	Fabricated metal products, except machinery		...	120	155	148	96	100	106	95	116	124	136	152
26	Computer, electronic and optical products		...	224	304	283	133	100	73	64	60	48	31	28
27	Electrical equipment		...	87	77	110	83	100	120	108	113	111	118	133
28	Machinery and equipment n.e.c.		...	173	209	225	147	100	110	108	130	142	141	143
29	Motor vehicles, trailers and semi-trailers		...	89	127	122	82	100	98	96	117	131	116	114
30	Other transport equipment		...	139	109	211	133	100	68	108	73	65	46	35
31	Furniture		...	88	111	117	87	100	97	115	121	125	147	161
32	Other manufacturing		...	55	85	87	84	100	94	95	154	165	185	219
33	Repair and installation of machinery/equipment		...	128	108	110	77	100	81	81	67	66	60	53
C	Total manufacturing		...	85	94	104	94	100	102	99	104	108	114	117

Botswana

Supplier of information:
Statistics Botswana, Gaborone.

Basic source of data:
Surveys; administrative data.

Major deviations from ISIC (Revision 3):
Data presented in ISIC (Revision 3) were originally classified according to the national classification system (Botswana Standard Industrial Classifications Revision 3).

Reference period:
Calendar year.

Scope:
All units with five or more employees.

Method of data collection:
Mail questionnaires.

Type of enumeration:
Sample survey.

Adjusted for non-response:
Yes.

Concepts and definitions of variables:
No deviations from the standard UN concepts and definitions are reported.

Related national publications:
Labour Statistics (annual); National Accounts of Botswana (annual), both published by the Central Statistics Office, Gaborone.

Botswana

		Establishments (number)					Number of employees (number)					Wages and salaries paid to employees (thousands of Botswana Pula)				
ISIC	Industry	Note	2013	2014	2015	2016	Note	2013	2014	2015	2016	Note	2013	2014	2015	2016
151	Processed meat,fish,fruit,vegetables,fats		…	…	…	…		…	…	…	…		…	…	…	…
1511	Processing/preserving of meat		…	…	…	…		1576	1854	1570	1596		13282	10020	14613	14776
1512	Processing/preserving of fish		…	…	…	…		…	…	…	…		…	…	…	…
1513	Processing/preserving of fruit & vegetables		…	…	…	…		…	…	…	…		…	…	…	…
1514	Vegetable and animal oils and fats		…	…	…	…		…	…	…	…		…	…	…	…
1520	Dairy products		…	…	…	…		411	411	411	505		1772	1772	1772	1814
153	Grain mill products; starches; animal feeds		…	…	…	…		943	1003	942	953		3337	3039	3853	4115
1531	Grain mill products		…	…	…	…		…	…	…	…		…	…	…	…
1532	Starches and starch products		…	…	…	…		…	…	…	…		…	…	…	…
1533	Prepared animal feeds		…	…	…	…		…	…	…	…		…	…	…	…
154	Other food products		…	…	…	…		…	…	…	…		…	…	…	…
1541	Bakery products		…	…	…	…		979	1045	657	742		1745	2476	1342	1487
1542	Sugar		…	…	…	…	a/	…	…	…	…	a/	…	…	…	…
1543	Cocoa, chocolate and sugar confectionery		…	…	…	…	a/	…	…	…	…	a/	…	…	…	…
1544	Macaroni, noodles & similar products		…	…	…	…		…	…	…	…		…	…	…	…
1549	Other food products n.e.c.		…	…	…	…	a/	682	777	692	688	a/	3702	3825	4251	4715
155	Beverages		…	…	…	…		1016	1155	1297	1386		6304	7096	11920	12179
1551	Distilling, rectifying & blending of spirits		…	…	…	…		…	…	…	…		…	…	…	…
1552	Wines		…	…	…	…		…	…	…	…		…	…	…	…
1553	Malt liquors and malt		…	…	…	…		…	…	…	…		…	…	…	…
1554	Soft drinks; mineral waters		…	…	…	…		…	…	…	…		…	…	…	…
1600	Tobacco products		…	…	…	…		…	…	…	…		…	…	…	…
171	Spinning, weaving and finishing of textiles		…	…	…	…	b/	6089	2056	1606	1734	b/	3907	4559	3430	5048
1711	Textile fibre preparation; textile weaving		…	…	…	…		…	…	…	…		…	…	…	…
1712	Finishing of textiles		…	…	…	…		…	…	…	…		…	…	…	…
172	Other textiles		…	…	…	…	b/	…	…	…	…	b/	…	…	…	…
1721	Made-up textile articles, except apparel		…	…	…	…		…	…	…	…		…	…	…	…
1722	Carpets and rugs		…	…	…	…		…	…	…	…		…	…	…	…
1723	Cordage, rope, twine and netting		…	…	…	…		…	…	…	…		…	…	…	…
1729	Other textiles n.e.c.		…	…	…	…		…	…	…	…		…	…	…	…
1730	Knitted and crocheted fabrics and articles		…	…	…	…	b/	…	…	…	…	b/	…	…	…	…
1810	Wearing apparel, except fur apparel		…	…	…	…	c/	2876	3672	3749	3398	c/	2651	4345	5033	6007
1820	Dressing & dyeing of fur; processing of fur		…	…	…	…	c/	…	…	…	…	c/	…	…	…	…
191	Tanning, dressing and processing of leather		…	…	…	…		…	…	…	…		…	…	…	…
1911	Tanning and dressing of leather		…	…	…	…		591	1078	550	…		1154	2634	1073	…
1912	Luggage, handbags, etc.; saddlery & harness		…	…	…	…		…	…	…	…		…	…	…	…
1920	Footwear		…	…	…	…		…	…	…	…		…	…	…	…
2010	Sawmilling and planing of wood		…	…	…	…	d/	2035	2460	1532	1575	d/	6514	9010	5010	6069
202	Products of wood, cork, straw, etc.		…	…	…	…	d/	…	…	…	…	d/	…	…	…	…
2021	Veneer sheets, plywood, particle board, etc.		…	…	…	…		…	…	…	…		…	…	…	…
2022	Builders' carpentry and joinery		…	…	…	…		…	…	…	…		…	…	…	…
2023	Wooden containers		…	…	…	…		…	…	…	…		…	…	…	…
2029	Other wood products; articles of cork/straw		…	…	…	…		…	…	…	…		…	…	…	…
210	Paper and paper products		…	…	…	…		215	201	200	304		1429	585	1435	2413
2101	Pulp, paper and paperboard		…	…	…	…		…	…	…	…		…	…	…	…
2102	Corrugated paper and paperboard		…	…	…	…		…	…	…	…		…	…	…	…
2109	Other articles of paper and paperboard		…	…	…	…		…	…	…	…		…	…	…	…
221	Publishing		…	…	…	…	e/	1380	1445	1504	1585	e/	6921	6861	7326	8298
2211	Publishing of books and other publications		…	…	…	…		…	…	…	…		…	…	…	…
2212	Publishing of newspapers, journals, etc.		…	…	…	…		…	…	…	…		…	…	…	…
2213	Publishing of recorded media		…	…	…	…		…	…	…	…		…	…	…	…
2219	Other publishing		…	…	…	…		…	…	…	…		…	…	…	…

Code	Description										
222	Printing and related service activities					e/					e/
2221	Printing										
2222	Service activities related to printing										
2230	Reproduction of recorded media										
2310	Coke oven products										
2320	Refined petroleum products										
2330	Processing of nuclear fuel										
241	Basic chemicals	8008	7472	7211	8156	f/	1932	1897	1751	2331	f/
2411	Basic chemicals, except fertilizers										
2412	Fertilizers and nitrogen compounds										
2413	Plastics in primary forms; synthetic rubber					f/					f/
242	Other chemicals										
2421	Pesticides and other agro-chemical products										
2422	Paints, varnishes, printing ink and mastics										
2423	Pharmaceuticals, medicinal chemicals, etc.										
2424	Soap, cleaning & cosmetic preparations										
2429	Other chemical products n.e.c.										
2430	Man-made fibres					f/					f/
251	Rubber products	2095	1373	1374	1409	g/	532	506	488	515	g/
2511	Rubber tyres and tubes										
2519	Other rubber products										
2520	Plastic products	14513	14336	10592	13928	g/	6143	6101	4221	5564	g/
2610	Glass and glass products					h/					h/
269	Non-metallic mineral products n.e.c.					h/					h/
2691	Pottery, china and earthenware										
2692	Refractory ceramic products										
2693	Struct.non-refractory clay; ceramic products										
2694	Cement, lime and plaster	1995	1533	1007	900		56		57	58	
2695	Articles of concrete, cement and plaster										
2696	Cutting, shaping & finishing of stone										
2699	Other non-metallic mineral products n.e.c.										
2710	Basic iron and steel										
2720	Basic precious and non-ferrous metals		43					21			
273	Casting of metals										
2731	Casting of iron and steel										
2732	Casting of non-ferrous metals										
281	Struct.metal products;tanks;steam generators	24880	24654	14331	9394	i/	6082	6054	3528	2887	i/
2811	Structural metal products										
2812	Tanks, reservoirs and containers of metal										
2813	Steam generators					i/					i/
289	Other metal products; metal working services										
2891	Metal forging/pressing/stamping/roll-forming										
2892	Treatment & coating of metals										
2893	Cutlery, hand tools and general hardware										
2899	Other fabricated metal products n.e.c.										
291	General purpose machinery	6610	5126	10647	5248	j/	875	740	1281	833	j/
2911	Engines & turbines (not for transport equipment)										
2912	Pumps, compressors, taps and valves										
2913	Bearings, gears, gearing & driving elements										
2914	Ovens, furnaces and furnace burners										
2915	Lifting and handling equipment										
2919	Other general purpose machinery										
292	Special purpose machinery										
2921	Agricultural and forestry machinery					j/					j/
2922	Machine tools										
2923	Machinery for metallurgy										
2924	Machinery for mining & construction										
2925	Food/beverage/tobacco processing machinery										
2926	Machinery for textile, apparel and leather										
2927	Weapons and ammunition										
2929	Other special purpose machinery										

continued

Botswana

ISIC Revision 3		Establishments (number)					Number of employees (number)					Wages and salaries paid to employees (thousands of Botswana Pula)				
ISIC	Industry	Note	2013	2014	2015	2016	Note	2013	2014	2015	2016	Note	2013	2014	2015	2016
2930	Domestic appliances n.e.c.	j/	...	...	...	...	j/	...	...	...	...	j/	...	...	...	...
3000	Office, accounting and computing machinery	k/	...	...	...	...	k/	...	...	...	...	k/	...	...	...	...
3110	Electric motors, generators and transformers	k/	...	...	...	...	k/	1047	1248	1397	1060	k/	4303	5165	5372	5619
3120	Electricity distribution & control apparatus		...	...	...	...		...	...	...	...		...	...	...	...
3130	Insulated wire and cable		...	...	...	...		...	...	...	...		...	...	...	...
3140	Accumulators, primary cells and batteries		...	...	...	...		...	...	...	...		...	...	...	...
3150	Lighting equipment and electric lamps		...	...	...	...		...	...	...	...		...	...	...	...
3190	Other electrical equipment n.e.c.		...	...	...	...		...	...	...	...		...	...	...	...
3210	Electronic valves, tubes, etc.		...	...	...	...		...	...	...	...		...	...	...	...
3220	TV/radio transmitters; line comm. apparatus		...	...	...	...		23	23	23	27		264	278	278	351
3230	TV and radio receivers and associated goods		...	...	...	...		9	12	3	10		35	52	8	44
331	Medical, measuring, testing appliances, etc.		...	...	...	...		...	...	...	...	m/	...	...	...	...
3311	Medical, surgical and orthopaedic equipment		...	...	...	...		...	...	...	...		...	...	...	...
3312	Measuring/testing/navigating appliances,etc.		...	...	...	...		...	...	...	...		...	...	...	...
3313	Industrial process control equipment		...	...	...	...		...	...	...	...		...	...	...	...
3320	Optical instruments & photographic equipment		...	...	...	...		...	...	...	...	m/	...	...	...	...
3330	Watches and clocks		...	...	...	...		...	...	...	...	m/	...	...	...	...
3410	Motor vehicles	n/	...	...	...	...	n/	2429	3517	2263	2657	n/	18477	26063	17074	17448
3420	Automobile bodies, trailers & semi-trailers	n/	...	...	...	...	n/	...	...	...	...	n/	...	...	...	...
3430	Parts/accessories for automobiles	n/	...	...	...	...	n/	...	...	...	...	n/	...	...	...	...
351	Building and repairing of ships and boats		...	...	...	...		...	...	...	...		...	...	...	...
3511	Building and repairing of ships		...	...	...	...		...	...	...	...		...	...	...	...
3512	Building/repairing of pleasure/sport. boats		...	...	...	...		...	...	...	...		...	...	...	...
3520	Railway/tramway locomotives & rolling stock		...	...	...	...		...	...	...	...		...	...	...	...
3530	Aircraft and spacecraft		...	...	...	...		...	...	...	...		...	...	...	...
359	Transport equipment n.e.c.		...	...	...	...		...	...	...	...		...	...	...	...
3591	Motorcycles		...	...	...	...		...	...	...	...		...	...	...	...
3592	Bicycles and invalid carriages		...	...	...	...		...	...	...	...		...	...	...	...
3599	Other transport equipment n.e.c.		...	...	...	...		...	...	...	...		...	...	...	...
3610	Furniture		...	...	...	...		1117	2216	1860	1846		2771	6481	4506	5016
369	Manufacturing n.e.c.		...	...	...	...		834	792	720	808		7714	8002	4657	4961
3691	Jewellery and related articles		...	...	...	...		...	...	...	...		2891	2805	2375	2934
3692	Musical instruments		...	...	...	...		...	...	...	...		...	...	...	...
3693	Sports goods		...	...	...	...		...	...	...	...		...	...	...	...
3694	Games and toys		...	...	...	...		...	...	...	...		...	...	...	...
3699	Other manufacturing n.e.c.		...	...	...	...		2006	2220	1464	2629		4823	5197	2282	2629
3710	Recycling of metal waste and scrap		...	...	...	...		41	41	41	48		85	85	85	95
3720	Recycling of non-metal waste and scrap		...	...	...	...		...	...	...	...		...	...	...	...
D	Total manufacturing		...	...	...	...		40485	40271	37800	39115		136131	154473	147575	161490

a/ 1549 includes 1543 and 1544.
b/ 171 includes 172 and 1730.
c/ 1810 includes 1820.
d/ 2010 includes 202.
e/ 221 includes 222.
f/ 241 includes 242 and 2430.
g/ 251 includes 2520.
h/ 2610 includes 269.
i/ 2811 includes 289.
j/ 291 includes 292 and 2930.
k/ 3110 includes 3000.
m/ 331 includes 3320 and 3330.
n/ 3410 includes 3420 and 3430.

Botswana

ISIC	Industry	Note	Output at basic prices (millions of Botswana Pula)				Note	Value added at basic prices (millions of Botswana Pula)				Note	Gross fixed capital formation (millions of Botswana Pula)	
	ISIC Revision 3		2013	2014	2015	2016		2013	2014	2015	2016		2015	2016
15	Food and beverages	a/	5551.8	5575.0	6219.9	6489.3	a/	1923.6	1915.0	2042.4	2154.5		...	...
16	Tobacco products		...	...	...	...		...	...	...	...		...	...
17	Textiles		517.5	556.4	569.8	574.1		164.8	174.6	178.8	180.2		...	...
18	Wearing apparel, fur		...	...	...	...		...	...	...	...		...	...
19	Leather, leather products and footwear	a/	57.5	58.5	63.2	64.5	a/	15.8	15.7	17.1	17.4		...	...
20	Wood products (excl. furniture)		...	...	...	...		...	...	...	...		...	...
21	Paper and paper products		...	...	...	...		...	...	...	...		...	...
22	Printing and publishing		...	...	...	...		...	...	...	...		...	...
23	Coke,refined petroleum products,nuclear fuel		...	...	...	...		...	...	...	...		...	...
24	Chemicals and chemical products		...	...	...	...		...	...	...	...		...	...
25	Rubber and plastics products		...	...	...	...		...	...	...	...		...	...
26	Non-metallic mineral products		...	...	...	...		...	...	...	...		...	...
27	Basic metals		...	...	...	...		...	...	...	...		...	...
28	Fabricated metal products		...	...	...	...		...	...	...	...		...	...
29	Machinery and equipment n.e.c.		...	...	...	...		...	...	...	...		...	...
30	Office, accounting and computing machinery		...	...	...	...		...	...	...	...		...	...
31	Electrical machinery and apparatus		...	...	...	...		...	...	...	...		...	...
32	Radio,television and communication equipment		...	...	...	...		...	...	...	...		...	...
33	Medical, precision and optical instruments		...	...	...	...		...	...	...	...		...	...
34	Motor vehicles, trailers, semi-trailers		...	...	...	...		...	...	...	...		...	...
35	Other transport equipment		...	...	...	...		...	...	...	...		...	...
36	Furniture; manufacturing n.e.c.	a/	19560.4	22307.4	24261.7	25948.9	a/	3716.5	4238.4	4609.7	4936.9		...	...
37	Recycling		...	...	...	...		...	...	...	...		...	...
D	Total manufacturing	b/	27603.9	30532.8	33310.8	35372.4	b/	7285.1	7740.3	8441.7	8860.2		...	...

a/ Data are aggregated from incomplete 3- and/or 4-digit level of ISICs.
b/ Includes informal sector's contribution.

Bulgaria

Supplier of information:
National Statistical Institute of the Republic of Bulgaria, Sofia.

Basic source of data:
Census/exhaustive survey.

Major deviations from ISIC (Revision 4):
None reported.

Reference period:
Calendar year.

Scope:
All enterprises.

Method of data collection:
Mail questionnaires; online survey.

Type of enumeration:
Complete enumeration.

Adjusted for non-response:
No.

Concepts and definitions of variables:
Output includes revenue from non-industrial activities.
Value added includes cost of non-industrial activities.

Related national publications:
Statistical Yearbook of the Republic of Bulgaria, published by the National Statistical Institute of the Republic of Bulgaria, Sofia.

Bulgaria

ISIC	Industry	Number of enterprises (number) 2013	2014	2015	2016	Number of employees (number) 2013	2014	2015	2016	Wages and salaries paid to employees (millions of Bulgarian Leva) 2013	2014	2015	2016
1010	Processing/preserving of meat	468	484	491	497	15428	15442	15352	15636	101	108	117	140
1020	Processing/preserving of fish, etc.	40	42	43	49	1463	1430	1482	1576	8	9	10	11
1030	Processing/preserving of fruit,vegetables	344	348	366	386	6577	6770	6514	7084	42	45	49	61
1040	Vegetable and animal oils and fats	80	79	81	68	2219	2691	3045	2399	15	20	27	23
1050	Dairy products	300	299	313	313	8646	8351	8076	7983	62	64	62	65
106	Grain mill products,starches and starch products	140	124	130	124	3423	3236	2921	3430	32	34	34	37
1061	Grain mill products	134	119	125	121	3137	2950	…	…	23	24	…	…
1062	Starches and starch products	6	5	5	3	286	286	…	…	9	10	…	…
107	Other food products	3468	3614	3751	3841	34539	35622	36975	35391	236	246	271	281
1071	Bakery products	2822	2929	2991	3069	25151	25646	25875	25337	145	153	164	175
1072	Sugar	3	3	…	2	197	124	76	79	2	1	1	1
1073	Cocoa, chocolate and sugar confectionery	123	141	151	156	3474	3580	3605	3470	48	45	46	45
1074	Macaroni, noodles, couscous, etc.	31	29	30	30	270	230	241	315	1	1	1	2
1075	Prepared meals and dishes	66	60	71	73	1621	1826	2293	1188	10	12	14	9
1079	Other food products n.e.c.	423	452	…	…	3826	4216	4885	5002	30	35	44	50
1080	Prepared animal feeds	118	104	110	105	1600	1465	1827	2016	13	12	16	20
110	Beverages	876	876	897	911	12626	12603	12548	12180	133	140	152	160
1101	Distilling, rectifying and blending of spirits	408	388	401	423	1861	1907	2001	2047	12	12	14	16
1102	Wines	…	…	…	…	3535	3431	3376	3274	26	26	28	30
1103	Malt liquors and malt	…	…	…	…	2377	2428	2351	2233	41	42	45	47
1104	Soft drinks,mineral waters,other bottled waters	214	220	213	211	4853	4837	4820	4626	55	59	64	66
1200	Tobacco products	18	18	17	14	3197	3143	2973	2368	59	58	50	40
131	Spinning, weaving and finishing of textiles	104	92	94	96	6147	5755	5654	5447	48	50	53	55
1311	Preparation and spinning of textile fibres	27	28	33	34	3988	3978	4145	4176	35	38	42	45
1312	Weaving of textiles	44	37	31	30	1703	1311	1044	876	10	8	8	7
1313	Finishing of textiles	33	27	30	32	456	466	465	395	4	4	4	3
139	Other textiles	485	497	508	557	5004	5591	5928	6726	29	37	41	51
1391	Knitted and crocheted fabrics	9	8	6	5	87	118	141	155	…	1	1	1
1392	Made-up textile articles, except apparel	157	155	172	172	2691	2997	3565	3731	15	20	25	29
1393	Carpets and rugs	14	14	11	12	308	295	307	337	2	2	3	3
1394	Cordage, rope, twine and netting	23	26	27	30	114	159	172	176	…	1	1	1
1399	Other textiles n.e.c.	282	294	292	338	1804	2022	1743	2327	11	14	12	17
1410	Wearing apparel, except fur apparel	4125	4119	4129	4176	90098	89235	87368	83747	460	481	511	541
1420	Articles of fur	20	26	26	29	89	97	98	133	…	-	1	1
1430	Knitted and crocheted apparel	260	236	218	223	9638	9112	7953	6823	60	60	57	55
151	Leather;luggage;handbags,saddlery,harness;fur	123	117	131	142	2459	2410	2567	2376	14	15	17	18
1511	Tanning/dressing of leather; dressing of fur	22	22	28	35	172	121	131	115	1	1	1	1
1512	Luggage,handbags,etc.;saddlery/harness	101	95	103	107	2287	2289	2436	2261	13	15	16	17
1520	Footwear	362	368	370	373	12687	12530	11608	10929	59	61	62	66
1610	Sawmilling and planing of wood	700	669	681	675	5885	5587	5801	5747	24	24	27	30

162	Wood products, cork, straw, plaiting materials	1278	1265	1277	1238	9224	9428	9481	8874	58	62	67	69
1621	Veneer sheets and wood-based panels	36	35	35	36	2545	2530	2391	2344	26	27	27	30
1622	Builders' carpentry and joinery	257	236	239	231	1805	1659	1449	1270	8	8	8	8
1623	Wooden containers	179	162	168	175	1750	1659	1822	2023	7	8	9	11
1629	Other wood products;articles of cork,straw	806	832	835	796	3124	3580	3819	3237	16	20	23	20
170	Paper and paper products	506	506	511	512	8545	8743	9808	9744	64	73	91	97
1701	Pulp, paper and paperboard	11	16	15	13	1620	1647	1713	1725	16	18	20	21
1702	Corrugated paper and paperboard	192	185	184	183	3769	4002	4050	4234	30	34	37	41
1709	Other articles of paper and paperboard	303	287	312	316	3156	3094	4045	3785	19	20	34	36
181	Printing and service activities related to printing	1023	1026	1013	1013	8115	8356	8080	8520	67	74	75	85
1811	Printing	728	740	728	730	7420	7681	7369	7782	62	69	69	78
1812	Service activities related to printing	295	286	285	283	695	675	711	738	4	5	6	6
1820	Reproduction of recorded media	12	16	16	19	52	49	46	47	-	-	-	-
1910	Coke oven products	-	-	-	-	-	-	-	-	-	-	-	-
1920	Refined petroleum products	10	13	11	10	2155	2070	2028	1942	63	61	64	65
201	Basic chemicals,fertilizers, etc.	108	114	115	114	3854	3950	4449	4309	58	59	69	75
2011	Basic chemicals	83	85	83	76	1469	1535	2064	1872	27	28	34	33
2012	Fertilizers and nitrogen compounds	19	21	24	26	2002	1987	1945	1832	29	28	32	37
2013	Plastics and synthetic rubber in primary forms	6	8	8	12	383	428	440	605	2	3	3	5
202	Other chemical products	453	467	472	486	8152	8498	8461	8653	81	88	92	101
2021	Pesticides and other agrochemical products	18	18	18	18	279	299	299	331	3	4	4	5
2022	Paints,varnishes;printing ink and mastics	76	72	74	71	1576	1418	1570	1525	16	15	18	19
2023	Soap,cleaning and cosmetic preparations	179	194	195	207	4768	5056	4996	5075	47	51	54	58
2029	Other chemical products n.e.c.	180	183	185	190	1529	1725	1596	1722	15	19	16	19
2030	Man-made fibres	4	5	4	6	510	485	394	558	4	4	3	6
2100	Pharmaceuticals,medicinal chemicals, etc.	56	48	50	52	7955	8238	8253	8419	90	97	103	108
221	Rubber products	183	184	176	171	3633	4200	5056	5385	29	38	49	61
2211	Rubber tyres and tubes	22	17	14	14	52	40	28	95	-	-	49	1
2219	Other rubber products	161	167	162	157	3581	4160	5028	5290	29	38	49	60
2220	Plastics products	1609	1604	1586	1598	19853	20650	21882	22690	128	143	176	201
2310	Glass and glass products	127	121	129	119	4160	4491	4719	5009	45	52	57	68
239	Non-metallic mineral products n.e.c.	1155	1193	1201	1179	15323	16227	15608	15695	139	152	159	167
2391	Refractory products	13	11	10	12	426	446	434	428	4	4	4	5
2392	Clay building materials	44	41	39	37	2318	2237	2124	2165	19	20	21	23
2393	Other porcelain and ceramic products	158	153	151	166	1508	1649	1699	1678	12	14	15	16
2394	Cement, lime and plaster	54	56	55	49	1467	1436	1586	1539	21	22	24	25
2395	Articles of concrete, cement and plaster	465	470	467	447	5665	5716	5904	6036	49	51	58	60
2396	Cutting, shaping and finishing of stone	258	264	282	284	1530	1548	1650	1682	8	9	11	12
2399	Other non-metallic mineral products n.e.c.	163	198	197	184	2409	3195	2211	2167	25	32	26	26
2410	Basic iron and steel	39	42	48	50	2754	2911	3329	4160	33	35	40	58
2420	Basic precious and other non-ferrous metals	41	45	42	40	4552	4863	4813	4797	88	95	95	101
243	Casting of metals	116	102	101	103	3623	3545	3464	3556	27	29	31	35
2431	Casting of iron and steel	60	54	55	56	3142	3106	2956	3028	24	27	27	31
2432	Casting of non-ferrous metals	56	48	46	47	481	439	508	528	3	3	3	4
251	Struct.metal products, tanks, reservoirs	1155	1139	1124	1091	12186	13172	13313	13035	88	101	115	125

continued

Bulgaria

ISIC Revision 4

ISIC	Industry	Number of enterprises (number) Note	2013	2014	2015	2016	Number of employees (number) Note	2013	2014	2015	2016	Wages and salaries paid to employees (millions of Bulgarian Leva) Note	2013	2014	2015	2016
2511	Structural metal products		1080	1063	1054	1025		10157	10797	10987	10748		71	78	91	99
2512	Tanks, reservoirs and containers of metal		65	67	58	56		1908	2241	2194	2165		16	22	22	24
2513	Steam generators, excl. hot water boilers		10	9	12	10		121	134	132	122		1	1	2	1
2520	Weapons and ammunition		19	20	23	23		10739	11799	13965	17413		77	103	132	200
259	Other metal products;metal working services		2432	2424	2443	2452		25825	26115	26345	24757		197	212	232	243
2591	Forging,pressing,stamping,roll-forming of metal		32	28	26	25		531	523	360	316		4	4	3	3
2592	Treatment and coating of metals; machining		1220	1234	1206	1219		11953	11769	11809	10774		92	97	101	105
2593	Cutlery, hand tools and general hardware		102	104	110	98		2735	3161	3238	2794		25	31	35	32
2599	Other fabricated metal products n.e.c.		1078	1058	1101	1110		10606	10662	10938	10873		76	81	94	101
2610	Electronic components and boards		104	105	116	113		2987	3069	3149	3172		35	38	43	47
2620	Computers and peripheral equipment		33	30	35	34		321	322	305	250		3	3	5	3
2630	Communication equipment		56	56	58	50		1034	1132	1292	1120		14	18	20	21
2640	Consumer electronics		...	18	20	...		370	354	583	575		5	5	12	12
265	Measuring;testing equipment; watches, etc.		127	112	122	120		1814	1732	1992	1865		17	18	23	23
2651	Measuring/testing/navigating equipment,etc.		120	106	117	115		1779	1694	1966	1845		16	18	23	22
2652	Watches and clocks		7	6	5	5		35	38	26	20		-	-	-	-
2660	Irradiation/electromedical equipment,etc.		8	10	12	8		...	312	327	...		-	6	6	-
2670	Optical instruments and photographic equipment		30	31	30	28		1320	1411	1502	1641		15	16	19	23
2680	Magnetic and optical media		...	4	3	...		...	57	61	...		...	1	-	...
2710	Electric motors,generators,transformers,etc.		153	158	156	155		7943	8068	8539	8749		87	86	102	108
2720	Batteries and accumulators		10	11	12	12		1281	1002	930	1045		16	12	13	16
273	Wiring and wiring devices		57	62	60	62		3387	3463	3605	3677		27	29	32	36
2731	Fibre optic cables		-	-	-	-		-	-	-	-		-	-	-	-
2732	Other electronic and electric wires and cables		20	20	22	25		1260	1250	1408	1250		12	12	14	13
2733	Wiring devices		37	42	38	37		2127	2213	2197	2427		16	17	18	22
2740	Electric lighting equipment		81	77	81	88		966	1063	1068	1103		7	8	9	10
2750	Domestic appliances		56	55	61	64		3924	3761	3893	4383		46	48	55	67
2790	Other electrical equipment		127	131	118	121		1581	2961	3038	3807		19	41	48	60
281	General-purpose machinery		419	439	452	471		21048	21698	21834	22700		224	245	262	293
2811	Engines/turbines,excl.aircraft,vehicle engines		8	6	6	7		614	501	538	683		6	5	6	8
2812	Fluid power equipment		23	25	29	29		3383	3834	3888	3851		38	46	49	52
2813	Other pumps, compressors, taps and valves		34	37	34	35		4375	4208	4533	4583		63	64	70	74
2814	Bearings, gears, gearing and driving elements		13	16	17	19		1764	1858	1910	2272		15	17	18	25
2815	Ovens, furnaces and furnace burners		13	13	17	19		...	...	...	169		...	...	...	2
2816	Lifting and handling equipment		109	117	107	115		4861	5228	4781	4790		45	50	50	55
2817	Office machinery, excl.computers,etc.		19	20	16	18		1109	1089	956	1028		17	19	17	19
2818	Power-driven hand tools		5	5	3	3		...	...	...	813		...	...	...	7
2819	Other general-purpose machinery		195	200	223	226		3876	3984	4239	4511		34	37	45	50
282	Special-purpose machinery		453	467	484	483		8516	8508	8602	8332		78	87	95	97
2821	Agricultural and forestry machinery		57	54	61	54		1083	1112	1066	970		8	9	9	9
2822	Metal-forming machinery and machine tools		78	74	75	80		2099	1831	1764	1764		17	15	17	18

Code		C1	C2	C3	C4	C5	C6	C7	C8	C9	C10	C11	C12
2823	Machinery for metallurgy	5	4	4	4	505	359	348	472	17	18	16	15
2824	Mining, quarrying and construction machinery	8	9	7	6	688	800	727	625	25	26	23	21
2825	Food/beverage/tobacco processing machinery	34	34	33	26	2517	2635	2596	2568	108	106	103	102
2826	Textile/apparel/leather production machinery	-	-	-	...	5	9	12	9	3	4	5	3
2829	Other special-purpose machinery	22	22	19	16	1883	1969	1882	1660	196	194	192	177
2910	Motor vehicles	...	...	...	...	...	...	...	...	...	...	...	3
2920	Automobile bodies, trailers and semi-trailers	...	...	...	...	...	...	...	...	21	...	...	21
2930	Parts and accessories for motor vehicles	203	176	133	110	21686	20389	17081	13429	99	94	95	91
301	Building of ships and boats	4	6	5	6	495	633	579	645	26	22	20	27
3011	Building of ships and floating structures	...	6	5	5	...	606	550	622	17	15	15	18
3012	Building of pleasure and sporting boats	...	-	-	-	...	27	29	23	9	7	5	9
3020	Railway locomotives and rolling stock	26	24	25	24	1997	1933	...	2133	12	13	12	12
3030	Air and spacecraft and related machinery	-	-	...	-	40	4	...	19	13	8	5	6
3040	Military fighting vehicles	-	-	-	-	-	-	-	-	-	-	-	-
309	Transport equipment n.e.c.	27	23	19	12	2312	2264	2127	1706	28	25	23	23
3091	Motorcycles	-	-	-	-	-	-	-	-	-	-	-	-
3092	Bicycles and invalid carriages	...	...	...	...	...	...	...	...	24	21	20	19
3099	Other transport equipment n.e.c.	...	...	...	...	...	...	...	...	4	4	3	4
3100	Furniture	146	128	111	102	20561	19866	19845	19234	2225	2169	2132	2091
321	Jewellery, bijouterie and related articles	5	4	5	4	688	717	730	670	290	272	268	246
3211	Jewellery and related articles	5	4	4	4	626	646	676	626	237	233	235	222
3212	Imitation jewellery and related articles	-	-	-	-	62	71	54	44	53	39	33	24
3220	Musical instruments	1	1	1	1	142	149	147	149	21	17	20	19
3230	Sports goods	23	21	15	14	1721	1755	1580	1563	54	53	48	39
3240	Games and toys	40	30	24	20	2627	2283	2107	1867	45	37	33	33
3250	Medical and dental instruments and supplies	14	17	11	10	1703	2031	1624	1590	645	622	638	619
3290	Other manufacturing n.e.c.	13	12	13	10	1880	1836	1917	1747	601	561	524	511
331	Repair of fabricated metal products/machinery	193	172	158	148	14060	13477	13409	13720	2263	2170	2084	2014
3311	Repair of fabricated metal products	8	7	7	7	805	875	932	895	142	121	131	115
3312	Repair of machinery	67	62	63	63	5743	5549	5746	6375	1094	1050	1009	987
3313	Repair of electronic and optical equipment	9	7	6	7	441	395	335	353	193	203	195	195
3314	Repair of electrical equipment	9	9	6	7	754	835	646	767	234	228	245	235
3315	Repair of transport equip., excl. motor vehicles	100	86	73	64	6214	5709	5596	5182	457	443	394	367
3319	Repair of other equipment	1	1	1	1	103	114	154	148	143	125	110	115
3320	Installation of industrial machinery/equipment	26	22	18	17	1706	1568	1310	1312	291	274	261	241
C	Total manufacturing	5070	4597	4149	3812	514260	512315	502723	489948	31323	30879	30374	30091

Bulgaria

ISIC	Industry	Output at producers' prices (millions of Bulgarian Leva)					Value added at factor values (millions of Bulgarian Leva)					Gross fixed capital formation (millions of Bulgarian Leva)		
		Note	2013	2014	2015	2016	Note	2013	2014	2015	2016	Note	2015	2016
1010	Processing/preserving of meat		1918	1892	1879	2076		237	254	273	341		...	...
1020	Processing/preserving of fish, etc.		80	78	106	121		25	18	26	31		...	...
1030	Processing/preserving of fruit,vegetables		591	584	604	730		122	123	152	179		...	...
1040	Vegetable and animal oils and fats		546	752	890	871		63	109	128	77		...	...
1050	Dairy products		872	916	833	774		127	144	142	152		...	...
106	Grain mill products,starches and starch products		749	662	682	904		152	141	126	160		...	...
1061	Grain mill products		...	662a/	682a/	904		...	...	...	...		...	...
1062	Starches and starch products			...a/	...a/	...		...	...	...	...		...	...
107	Other food products		1967	1916	2144	2140		515	542	617	636		...	...
1071	Bakery products		1082	1084	1139	1148		296	331	347	358		...	...
1072	Sugar		132	21	...	...		-2	-9	...	...		...	...
1073	Cocoa, chocolate and sugar confectionery		335	345	364	343		108	85	116	113		...	...
1074	Macaroni, noodles, couscous, etc.		15	12	10	12		3	3	3	3		...	...
1075	Prepared meals and dishes		75	85	107	63		21	25	31	15		...	...
1079	Other food products n.e.c.		328	369	...	...		89	107	...	...		...	...
1080	Prepared animal feeds		341	317	366	423		40	47	61	59		...	...
110	Beverages		1758	1637	1669	1788		398	383	380	490		...	...
1101	Distilling, rectifying and blending of spirits		320	308	293	377		25	18	42	43		...	...
1102	Wines		...	...	...	...		...	...	...	...		...	...
1103	Malt liquors and malt		...	...	...	...		...	...	...	...		...	...
1104	Soft drinks,mineral waters,other bottled waters		578	560	584	573		172	183	217	223		...	...
1200	Tobacco products		1621	1613	1680	1336		153	140	167	96		...	...
131	Spinning, weaving and finishing of textiles		513	532	561	557		113	109	117	131		...	...
1311	Preparation and spinning of textile fibres		429	467	495	486		90	96	100	109		...	...
1312	Weaving of textiles		66	47	45	50		16	6	9	14		...	...
1313	Finishing of textiles		18	18	21	21		7	7	7	8		...	...
139	Other textiles		262	309	338	391		77	98	115	128		...	...
1391	Knitted and crocheted fabrics		10	10	...	...		2	2	...	...		...	...
1392	Made-up textile articles, except apparel		149	177	210	230		39	49	65	73		...	...
1393	Carpets and rugs		26	...	...	32		...	...	...	...		...	...
1394	Cordage, rope, twine and netting		2	...	4	...		...	...	2	2		...	...
1399	Other textiles n.e.c.		75	88	81	115		29	33	29	40		...	...
1410	Wearing apparel, except fur apparel		2101	2269	2254	2392		823	886	904	956		...	...
1420	Articles of fur		1	1	3	2		1	1	2	1		...	...
1430	Knitted and crocheted apparel		278	279	264	238		109	112	109	101		...	...
151	Leather;luggage,handbags,saddlery,harness;fur		56	54	63	61		25	26	32	33		...	...
1511	Tanning/dressing of leather; dressing of fur		11	6	10	13		...	...	1	2		...	...
1512	Luggage,handbags,etc.;saddlery/harness		45	48	54	48		25	26	31	31		...	...
1520	Footwear		243	269	260	251		104	112	111	117		...	...
1610	Sawmilling and planing of wood		250	257	282	270		55	61	70	70		...	...

Code		H	G	F	E	D	C	B	A
162	Wood products, cork, straw, plaiting materials	564	604	658	659	135	147	145	170
1621	Veneer sheets and wood-based panels	312	320	327	323	64	62	60	68
1622	Builders' carpentry and joinery	51	51	53	50	14	15	5	13
1623	Wooden containers	76	85	104	126	22	25	30	38
1629	Other wood products;articles of cork,straw	125	148	174	160	35	45	49	51
170	Paper and paper products	930	983	1208	1233	215	242	313	290
1701	Pulp, paper and paperboard	345	350	412	395	72	79	106	72
1702	Corrugated paper and paperboard	374	402	421	430	96	107	110	117
1709	Other articles of paper and paperboard	211	231	375	408	47	56	96	101
181	Printing and service activities related to printing	621b/	681b/	637	659	193b/	213b/	219	238
1811	Printing	578	635	597	617	177	196	203	221
1812	Service activities related to printing	..	..	40	41	..	14	16	17
1820	Reproduction of recorded media	..b/	..b/	8	9	..b/	..b/	2	2
1910	Coke oven products	-	-	-	-	-	-	-	-
1920	Refined petroleum products	..	..	..	..	-6	..	..	..
201	Basic chemicals,fertilizers, etc.	1257	1342	1574	1476	277	327	413	469
2011	Basic chemicals	..	625	736	719	182	209	245	273
2012	Fertilizers and nitrogen compounds	614	641	738	634	84	106	153	178
2013	Plastics and synthetic rubber in primary forms	..	76	100	123	11	12	15	18
202	Other chemical products	..	..	..	..	249	262	..	304
2021	Pesticides and other agrochemical products	..	..	..	..	9	13	..	17
2022	Paints,varnishes;printing ink and mastics	181	146	163	157	34	33	41	42
2023	Soap,cleaning and cosmetic preparations	538	563	576	619	147	155	159	168
2029	Other chemical products n.e.c.	271	345	365	227	59	61	76	77
2030	Man-made fibres	..	..	..	..	5	7	..	13
2100	Pharmaceuticals,medicinal chemicals, etc.	..	..	..	..	290	..	..	..
221	Rubber products	319	397	471	550	84	111	148	176
2211	Rubber tyres and tubes	4	..	2	1	1	..	1	1
2219	Other rubber products	315	469	469	548	83	..	147	175
2220	Plastics products	1811	1946	2161	2307	365	421	515	577
2310	Glass and glass products	614	715	826	897	148	187	208	300
239	Non-metallic mineral products n.e.c.	1481	1679	1775	1628	406	516	571	541
2391	Refractory products	17	22	24	27	7	9	12	14
2392	Clay building materials	212	222	222	244	80	96	88	108
2393	Other porcelain and ceramic products	86	105	105	107	26	35	33	36
2394	Cement, lime and plaster	322	346	411	374	84	110	144	130
2395	Articles of concrete, cement and plaster	533	569	643	613	116	131	151	155
2396	Cutting, shaping and finishing of stone	59	62	79	77	22	22	30	30
2399	Other non-metallic mineral products n.e.c.	252	353	291	186	71	113	113	68
2410	Basic iron and steel	1069	1093	959	1237	68	72	28	164
2420	Basic precious and other non-ferrous metals	6189	6055	6261	5328	313	463	586	601
243	Casting of metals	178	194	186	214	50	60	60	79
2431	Casting of iron and steel	152	167	155	176	42	51	50	66
2432	Casting of non-ferrous metals	26	27	31	37	8	9	10	13
251	Struct.metal products, tanks, reservoirs	715	911	915	937	198	233	264	285

continued

Bulgaria

		Output at producers' prices (millions of Bulgarian Leva)					Value added at factor values (millions of Bulgarian Leva)					Gross fixed capital formation (millions of Bulgarian Leva)		
ISIC	ISIC Revision 4 — Industry	Note	2013	2014	2015	2016	Note	2013	2014	2015	2016	Note	2015	2016
2511	Structural metal products		582	744	753	774		154	181	212	230		...	...
2512	Tanks, reservoirs and containers of metal		128	161	155	159		42	50	48	53		...	...
2513	Steam generators, excl. hot water boilers		5	6	7	4		2	2	3	2		...	...
2520	Weapons and ammunition		304	482	738	1388		138	238	338	665		...	...
259	Other metal products;metal working services		1583	1645	1842	1766		516	548	632	641		...	...
2591	Forging,pressing,stamping,roll-forming of metal		41	40	18	17		10	12	4	6		...	...
2592	Treatment and coating of metals; machining		694	719	754	731		230	238	264	278		...	...
2593	Cutlery, hand tools and general hardware		131	182	212	212		67	84	95	92		...	...
2599	Other fabricated metal products n.e.c.		717	704	858	806		209	214	269	265		...	...
2610	Electronic components and boards		188	233	257	297		76	92	97	115		...	...
2620	Computers and peripheral equipment		29	34	40	...		...	12	12	...		...	...
2630	Communication equipment		96	93	113	141		43	48	59	64		...	...
2640	Consumer electronics		...	23	44	49		11	10	22	21		...	...
265	Measuring,testing equipment; watches, etc.		140	154	221	223		51	60	83	83		...	...
2651	Measuring/testing/navigating equipment,etc.		138	151	219	221		50	59	82	82		...	...
2652	Watches and clocks		2	3	2	2		1	1	1	1		...	...
2660	Irradiation/electromedical equipment,etc.		87	94	94	109		47	45	40	35		...	...
2670	Optical instruments and photographic equipment		73	93	111	123		38	38	48	50		...	...
2680	Magnetic and optical media		...	5	5	...		...	2	2	...		...	...
2710	Electric motors,generators,transformers,etc.		704	734	863	981		183	193	214	257		...	...
2720	Batteries and accumulators		408	345	369	397		70	74	52	55		...	...
273	Wiring and wiring devices		300	301	366	353		56	60	68	74		...	...
2731	Fibre optic cables		-	-	-	-		-	-	-	-		...	...
2732	Other electronic and electric wires and cables		213	206	253	209		30	30	34	31		...	...
2733	Wiring devices		87	95	113	144		26	30	33	43		...	...
2740	Electric lighting equipment		60	67	68	70		15	18	23	23		...	...
2750	Domestic appliances		491	521	583	639		94	106	138	152		...	...
2790	Other electrical equipment		312	367	408	447		80	89	111	132		...	...
281	General-purpose machinery		1809	1875	1984	2127		488	554	594	656		...	...
2811	Engines/turbines,excl.aircraft,vehicle engines		38	30	32	...		11	...	12	15		...	...
2812	Fluid power equipment		233	254	258	284		93	105	108	121		...	...
2813	Other pumps, compressors, taps and valves		516	536	...	...		...	...	154	164		...	...
2814	Bearings, gears, gearing and driving elements		...	...	...	192		...	45	46	57		...	...
2815	Ovens, furnaces and furnace burners		...	...	...	15		1	2	2	5		...	...
2816	Lifting and handling equipment		355	380	361	367		103	112	111	118		...	...
2817	Office machinery, excl.computers,etc.		159	163	185	206		49	46	57	66		...	...
2818	Power-driven hand tools		...	...	...	16		7	7	5	-6		...	...
2819	Other general-purpose machinery		318	313	368	389		86	88	99	116		...	...
282	Special-purpose machinery		561	675	688	663		194	239	239	234		...	...
2821	Agricultural and forestry machinery		49	56	69	49		21	24	27	15		...	...
2822	Metal-forming machinery and machine tools		122	164	165	157		38	48	45	51		...	...

Code	Description								
2823	Machinery for metallurgy	19	26	24	30	6	12	9	12
2824	Mining, quarrying and construction machinery	88	105	108	103	23	30	30	24
2825	Food/beverage/tobacco processing machinery	177	186	171	169	58	68	67	67
2826	Textile/apparel/leather production machinery	...	1	1	-	...	...	-	-
2829	Other special-purpose machinery	106	137	150	156	48	57	61	65
2910	Motor vehicles	...	...	...	...	...	...	...	...
2920	Automobile bodies, trailers and semi-trailers	...	...	...	...	...	...	...	...
2930	Parts and accessories for motor vehicles	1125	1490	1761	1923	271	361	425	459
301	Building of ships and boats	...	...	...	...	...	...	...	...
3011	Building of ships and floating structures	36	48	57	46	16	13	16	15
3012	Building of pleasure and sporting boats	...	...	...	...	...	...	...	...
3020	Railway locomotives and rolling stock	191	198	178	165	47	48	45	44
3030	Air and spacecraft and related machinery	...	...	...	...	...	...	...	...
3040	Military fighting vehicles	-	-	-	-	-	-	-	-
309	Transport equipment n.e.c.	222	294	342	355	43	59	54	66
3091	Motorcycles	-	-	-	-	-	-	-	-
3092	Bicycles and invalid carriages	...	...	...	...	...	...	...	...
3099	Other transport equipment n.e.c.	...	...	...	...	...	...	...	...
3100	Furniture	837	896	944	1001	233	257	289	326
321	Jewellery, bijouterie and related articles	29	28	25	30	10	9	10	11
3211	Jewellery and related articles	27	26	23	28	9	8	9	10
3212	Imitation jewellery and related articles	2	2	2	2	1	1	1	1
3220	Musical instruments	...	...	5	5	...	2	2	...
3230	Sports goods	137	142	158	154	40	47	52	48
3240	Games and toys	157	207	294	429	69	105	159	...
3250	Medical and dental instruments and supplies	...	...	91	89	...	32	32	34
3290	Other manufacturing n.e.c.	80	85	92	99	25	26	27	30
331	Repair of fabricated metal products/machinery	647	763	738	822	283	334	315	394
3311	Repair of fabricated metal products	24	27	29	28	13	13	12	12
3312	Repair of machinery	252	276	250	300	96	128	130	149
3313	Repair of electronic and optical equipment	18	17	28	34	12	11	17	18
3314	Repair of electrical equipment	32	82	55	41	15	18	24	20
3315	Repair of transport equip., excl. motor vehicles	...	353	...	412	...	160	...	192
3319	Repair of other equipment	...	8	...	7	...	4	...	3
3320	Installation of industrial machinery/equipment	98	112	158	145	34	35	55	53
C	Total manufacturing	51076	52383	54235	55236	9345	10395	12152	13955

a/ 1061 includes 1062.
b/ 181 includes 1820.

Bulgaria

Index numbers of industrial production

ISIC Revision 4

(2010=100)

ISIC	Industry	Note	2005	2006	2007	2008	2009	2010	2011	2012	2013	2014	2015	2016
10	Food products		86	92	100	106	96	100	95	94	91	90	90	92
11	Beverages		114	120	139	144	111	100	99	98	101	96	100	105
12	Tobacco products		104	77	89	105	110	100	107	122	117	110	98	77
13	Textiles		151	170	188	156	106	100	105	88	99	110	108	112
14	Wearing apparel		146	160	165	145	108	100	101	95	99	98	96	98
15	Leather and related products		128	141	153	144	101	100	99	85	76	79	77	73
16	Wood products, excluding furniture		122	139	144	135	85	100	104	99	98	99	100	90
17	Paper and paper products		81	78	88	87	61	100	109	104	118	119	124	129
18	Printing and reproduction of recorded media		90	93	102	106	104	100	95	91	101	106	115	119
19	Coke and refined petroleum products		⋮	⋮	⋮	⋮	⋮	⋮	⋮	⋮	⋮	⋮	⋮	⋮
20	Chemicals and chemical products		106	106	111	122	82	100	114	103	97	106	109	113
21	Pharmaceuticals,medicinal chemicals, etc.		116	117	127	117	89	100	113	124	132	136	147	145
22	Rubber and plastics products		90	91	103	120	96	100	103	104	112	127	132	145
23	Other non-metallic mineral products		125	154	180	187	110	100	109	106	111	115	128	124
24	Basic metals		103	114	114	115	98	100	107	98	102	104	99	95
25	Fabricated metal products, except machinery		103	116	130	138	88	100	111	100	107	116	129	162
26	Computer, electronic and optical products		95	82	94	93	94	100	118	124	123	133	146	156
27	Electrical equipment		70	85	103	112	91	100	107	126	120	127	144	148
28	Machinery and equipment n.e.c.		93	106	123	129	94	100	113	125	134	142	142	145
29	Motor vehicles, trailers and semi-trailers		65	80	98	83	69	100	93	86	103	138	156	173
30	Other transport equipment		122	159	164	199	127	100	94	102	76	80	95	88
31	Furniture		102	124	155	149	94	100	112	112	119	123	126	133
32	Other manufacturing		74	89	110	104	108	100	111	127	147	150	175	212
33	Repair and installation of machinery/equipment		89	102	107	118	81	100	91	91	78	85	90	86
C	Total manufacturing		103	112	123	124	96	100	105	105	106	110	114	119

Cabo Verde

Supplier of information:
Instituto Nacional de Estadística, Praia.

Basic source of data:
Annual survey.

Major deviations from ISIC (Revision 3):
None reported.

Reference period:
Calendar year.

Scope:
All enterprises.

Method of data collection:
Direct interview in the field.

Type of enumeration:
Complete enumeration.

Adjusted for non-response:
Yes.

Concepts and definitions of variables:
No deviations from the standard UN concepts and definitions are reported.

Related national publications:
None reported.

Cabo Verde

ISIC	Industry	Number of enterprises (number) Note	2013	2014	2015	2016	Number of employees (number) Note	2013	2014	2015	2016	Wages and salaries (thousands of Cape Verde Escudos) Note	2013	2014	2015	2016
151	Processed meat,fish,fruit,vegetables,fats		1	1	1	1		20	10	20	21		…	…	…	…
1511	Processing/preserving of meat		…	…	…	…		…	…	…	…		…	…	…	…
1512	Processing/preserving of fish		1	1	1	1		20	10	20	21		…	…	…	…
1513	Processing/preserving of fruit & vegetables		…	…	…	…		…	…	…	-		…	…	…	…
1514	Vegetable and animal oils and fats		-	-	-	-		-	-	-	-		…	…	…	…
1520	Dairy products		2	2	2	2		140	140	150	177		…	…	…	…
153	Grain mill products; starches; animal feeds		4	3	4	4		87	80	82	94		…	…	…	…
1531	Grain mill products		1	1	1	1		20	18	19	25		…	…	…	…
1532	Starches and starch products		…	…	…	…		26	24	21	28		…	…	…	…
1533	Prepared animal feeds		2	2	2	2		41	38	42	41		…	…	…	…
154	Other food products		99	95	101	96		1421	1175	1278	1256		…	…	…	…
1541	Bakery products		94	91	96	90		1400	1150	1258	1230		…	…	…	…
1542	Sugar		-	-	-	-		-	-	-	-		…	…	…	…
1543	Cocoa, chocolate and sugar confectionery		-	-	-	-		-	-	-	-		…	…	…	…
1544	Macaroni, noodles & similar products		1	1	1	1		21	25	20	26		…	…	…	…
1549	Other food products n.e.c.		4	3	4	5		…	…	…	…		…	…	…	…
155	Beverages		88	89	93	99		912	811	856	905		…	…	…	…
1551	Distilling, rectifying & blending of spirits		75	79	81	84		160	149	139	169		…	…	…	…
1552	Wines		8	6	7	9		389	341	382	394		…	…	…	…
1553	Malt liquors and malt		1	1	1	1		152	109	122	132		…	…	…	…
1554	Soft drinks; mineral waters		4	3	4	5		211	212	213	210		…	…	…	…
1600	Tobacco products		4	4	4	4		35	38	41	44		…	…	…	…
171	Spinning, weaving and finishing of textiles		4	4	4	5		43	41	45	49		…	…	…	…
1711	Textile fibre preparation; textile weaving		2	2	2	2		18	21	24	24		…	…	…	…
1712	Finishing of textiles		2	2	2	3		25	20	21	25		…	…	…	…
172	Other textiles		6	5	6	7		46	57	67	82		…	…	…	…
1721	Made-up textile articles, except apparel		2	2	2	2		15	14	14	18		…	…	…	…
1722	Carpets and rugs		1	1	1	1		10	11	18	15		…	…	…	…
1723	Cordage, rope, twine and netting		-	-	-	-		-	-	-	-		…	…	…	…
1729	Other textiles n.e.c.		3	2	3	4		21	32	35	49		…	…	…	…
1730	Knitted and crocheted fabrics and articles		-	-	-	-		-	-	-	-		…	…	…	…
1810	Wearing apparel, except fur apparel		13	15	12	14		49	47	45	69		…	…	…	…
1820	Dressing & dyeing of fur; processing of fur		23	23	25	26		78	56	35	89		…	…	…	…
191	Tanning, dressing and processing of leather		-	-	-	-		-	-	-	-		…	…	…	…
1911	Tanning and dressing of leather		-	-	-	-		-	-	-	-		…	…	…	…
1912	Luggage, handbags, etc.; saddlery & harness		…	…	…	…		…	…	…	…		…	…	…	…
1920	Footwear		-	-	-	-		-	-	-	-		…	…	…	…
2010	Sawmilling and planing of wood		10	9	10	10		64	70	70	68		…	…	…	…
202	Products of wood, cork, straw, etc.		9	7	10	11		105	124	113	125		…	…	…	…
2021	Veneer sheets, plywood, particle board, etc.		2	2	2	2		25	26	18	21		…	…	…	…
2022	Builders' carpentry and joinery		3	2	3	4		35	34	30	39		…	…	…	…
2023	Wooden containers		3	2	4	4		40	60	58	51		…	…	…	…
2029	Other wood products; articles of cork/straw		1	1	1	1		5	4	7	14		…	…	…	…
210	Paper and paper products		4	3	4	4		11	10	15	13		…	…	…	…
2101	Pulp, paper and paperboard		1	1	2	2		5	4	7	8		…	…	…	…
2102	Corrugated paper and paperboard		1	1	1	1		3	3	4	2		…	…	…	…
2109	Other articles of paper and paperboard		2	1	1	1		3	3	4	3		…	…	…	…
221	Publishing		2	2	2	2		69	74	69	89		…	…	…	…
2211	Publishing of books and other publications		1	1	1	1		54	56	51	68		…	…	…	…
2212	Publishing of newspapers, journals, etc.		…	…	…	…		…	…	…	…		…	…	…	…
2213	Publishing of recorded media		1	1	1	1		15	18	18	21		…	…	…	…
2219	Other publishing		…	…	…	…		…	…	…	…		…	…	…	…

Code	Description								
222	Printing and related service activities	33	28	35	35	269	275	266	274
2221	Printing	28	24	29	31	243	251	241	250
2222	Service activities related to printing	5	4	6	4	26	24	25	24
2230	Reproduction of recorded media	1	1	1	1	12	14	9	12
2310	Coke oven products	-	-	-	-	-	-	-	-
2320	Refined petroleum products	-	-	-	-	-	-	-	-
2330	Processing of nuclear fuel	-	-	-	-	5	6	7	8
241	Basic chemicals	1	1	1	1	5	6	7	8
2411	Basic chemicals, except fertilizers	1	1	1	1	5	6	7	8
2412	Fertilizers and nitrogen compounds	-	-	-	-	-	-	-	-
2413	Plastics in primary forms; synthetic rubber	-	-	-	-	-	-	-	-
242	Other chemicals	3	3	3	4	40	43	46	52
2421	Pesticides and other agro-chemical products	..	..	..	..	..	..	..	..
2422	Paints, varnishes, printing ink and mastics	2	2	2	3	26	31	32	35
2423	Pharmaceuticals, medicinal chemicals, etc.	1	1	1	1	14	12	14	17
2424	Soap, cleaning & cosmetic preparations	..	..	..	..	..	..	..	..
2429	Other chemical products n.e.c.	..	..	..	..	..	..	..	..
2430	Man-made fibres	1	1	1	1	36	30	28	41
251	Rubber products	-	-	-	-	-	-	-	-
2511	Rubber tyres and tubes	-	-	-	-	-	-	-	-
2519	Other rubber products	-	-	-	-	-	-	-	-
2520	Plastic products	2	2	2	3	49	47	47	48
2610	Glass and glass products	9	8	11	12	103	98	103	110
269	Non-metallic mineral products n.e.c.	2	2	4	4	16	17	18	19
2691	Pottery, china and earthenware	2	1	2	2	8	7	9	14
2692	Refractory ceramic products	1	1	2	2	15	15	15	15
2693	Struct.non-refractory clay; ceramic products	1	1	1	2	19	14	16	17
2694	Cement, lime and plaster	1	1	1	1	18	18	18	18
2695	Articles of concrete, cement and plaster	1	1	1	1	14	14	14	14
2696	Cutting, shaping & finishing of stone	1	1	1	1	13	13	13	13
2699	Other non-metallic mineral products n.e.c.	-	-	-	-	-	-	-	-
2710	Basic iron and steel	-	-	-	-	-	-	-	-
2720	Basic precious and non-ferrous metals	-	-	-	-	-	-	-	-
273	Casting of metals	-	-	-	-	-	-	-	-
2731	Casting of iron and steel	-	-	-	-	-	-	-	-
2732	Casting of non-ferrous metals	-	-	-	-	-	-	-	-
281	Struct.metal products;tanks;steam generators	62	57	59	61	510	511	527	518
2811	Structural metal products	58	52	52	54	440	439	450	446
2812	Tanks, reservoirs and containers of metal	3	4	5	5	28	24	26	28
2813	Steam generators	1	1	2	2	42	48	51	44
289	Other metal products; metal working services	2	2	3	3	10	7	9	13
2891	Metal forging/pressing/stamping/roll-forming	1	1	1	1	2	2	3	4
2892	Treatment & coating of metals	-	-	-	-	-	-	-	-
2893	Cutlery, hand tools and general hardware	-	-	-	-	-	-	-	-
2899	Other fabricated metal products n.e.c.	1	1	2	2	8	5	6	9
291	General purpose machinery	-	-	-	-	-	-	-	-
2911	Engines & turbines (not for transport equipment)	-	-	-	-	-	-	-	-
2912	Pumps, compressors, taps and valves	-	-	-	-	-	-	-	-
2913	Bearings, gears, gearing & driving elements	-	-	-	-	-	-	-	-
2914	Ovens, furnaces and furnace burners	-	-	-	-	-	-	-	-
2915	Lifting and handling equipment	-	-	-	-	-	-	-	-
2919	Other general purpose machinery	-	-	-	-	-	-	-	-
292	Special purpose machinery	-	-	-	-	-	-	-	-
2921	Agricultural and forestry machinery	-	-	-	-	-	-	-	-
2922	Machine tools	-	-	-	-	-	-	-	-
2923	Machinery for metallurgy	-	-	-	-	-	-	-	-
2924	Machinery for mining & construction	-	-	-	-	-	-	-	-
2925	Food/beverage/tobacco processing machinery	-	-	-	-	-	-	-	-
2926	Machinery for textile, apparel and leather	-	-	-	-	-	-	-	-
2927	Weapons and ammunition	-	-	-	-	-	-	-	-
2929	Other special purpose machinery	-	-	-	-	-	-	-	-

continued

Cabo Verde

ISIC	Industry	Number of enterprises (number) Note	2013	2014	2015	2016	Number of employees (number) Note	2013	2014	2015	2016	Wages and salaries (thousands of Cape Verde Escudos) Note	2013	2014	2015	2016
2930	Domestic appliances n.e.c.		-	-	-	-		-	-	-	-		...	...	...	...
3000	Office, accounting and computing machinery		-	-	-	-		-	-	-	-		...	...	...	...
3110	Electric motors, generators and transformers		-	-	-	-		-	-	-	-		...	...	...	...
3120	Electricity distribution & control apparatus		-	-	-	-		-	-	-	-		...	...	...	...
3130	Insulated wire and cable		-	-	-	-		-	-	-	-		...	...	...	...
3140	Accumulators, primary cells and batteries		-	-	-	-		-	-	-	-		...	...	...	...
3150	Lighting equipment and electric lamps		-	-	-	-		-	-	-	-		...	...	...	...
3190	Other electrical equipment n.e.c.		-	-	-	-		-	-	-	-		...	...	...	...
3210	Electronic valves, tubes, etc.		-	-	-	-		-	-	-	-		...	...	...	...
3220	TV/radio transmitters; line comm. apparatus		-	-	-	-		-	-	-	-		...	...	...	...
3230	TV and radio receivers and associated goods		-	-	-	-		-	-	-	-		...	...	...	...
331	Medical, measuring, testing appliances, etc.		-	-	-	-		-	-	-	-		...	...	...	...
3311	Medical, surgical and orthopaedic equipment		-	-	-	-		-	-	-	-		...	...	...	...
3312	Measuring/testing/navigating appliances,etc.		-	-	-	-		-	-	-	-		...	...	...	...
3313	Industrial process control equipment		-	-	-	-		-	-	-	-		...	...	...	...
3320	Optical instruments & photographic equipment		-	-	-	-		-	-	-	-		...	...	...	...
3330	Watches and clocks		-	-	-	-		-	-	-	-		...	...	...	...
3410	Motor vehicles		-	-	-	-		-	-	-	-		...	...	...	...
3420	Automobile bodies, trailers & semi-trailers		-	-	-	-		-	-	-	-		...	...	...	...
3430	Parts/accessories for automobiles		-	-	-	-		-	-	-	-		...	...	...	...
351	Building and repairing of ships and boats		2	2	2	2		150	160	174	210		...	...	...	...
3511	Building and repairing of ships		1	1	1	1		105	115	125	135		...	...	...	...
3512	Building/repairing of pleasure/sport. boats		1	1	1	1		45	45	49	75		...	...	...	...
3520	Railway/tramway locomotives & rolling stock		-	-	-	-		-	-	-	-		...	...	...	...
3530	Aircraft and spacecraft		-	-	-	-		-	-	-	-		...	...	...	...
359	Transport equipment n.e.c.		-	-	-	-		-	-	-	-		...	...	...	...
3591	Motorcycles		-	-	-	-		-	-	-	-		...	...	...	...
3592	Bicycles and invalid carriages		-	-	-	-		-	-	-	-		...	...	...	...
3599	Other transport equipment n.e.c.		-	-	-	-		-	-	-	-		...	...	...	...
3610	Furniture		167	167	167	167		364	385	394	348		...	...	...	...
369	Manufacturing n.e.c.		47	38	38	38		101	102	108	127		...	...	...	...
3691	Jewellery and related articles		1	2	3	3		12	13	14	19		...	...	...	...
3692	Musical instruments		2	1	2	2		8	7	5	14		...	...	...	...
3693	Sports goods		1	2	1	2		6	4	7	8		...	...	...	...
3694	Games and toys		1	1	1	1		4	6	4	7		...	...	...	...
3699	Other manufacturing n.e.c.		42	32	31	30		71	72	78	79		...	...	...	...
3710	Recycling of metal waste and scrap		1	1	2	2		12	21	25	24		...	...	...	...
3720	Recycling of non-metal waste and scrap		1	1	2	2		9	12	14	18		...	...	...	...
D	Total manufacturing		601	573	603	617		4771	4477	4682	4926		...	...	...	...

ISIC Revision 3

Canada

Concepts and definitions of variables:
Wages and salaries includes taxes and social insurance contributions, payable by employees and deducted by employers; it excludes payments in kind such as tips and commissions.

Related national publications:
None reported.

Supplier of information:
Statistics Canada, Ottawa.

Basic source of data:
Annual survey; business register.

Major deviations from ISIC (Revision 4):
Data presented in ISIC (Revision 4) were originally classified according to the North American Industry Classification System (NAICS) Canada 2012.

Reference period:
Fiscal period from 1 April of the reference year to 31 March of the following year.

Scope:
All establishments primarily engaged in manufacturing activities.

Method of data collection:
Mail questionnaires.

Type of enumeration:
Sample survey.

Adjusted for non-response:
Yes.

Canada

ISIC Revision 4

ISIC	Industry	Establishments (number) Note	2013	2014	2015	2016	Number of employees (thousands) Note	2013	2014	2015	2016	Wages and salaries paid to employees (millions of Canadian Dollars) Note	2013	2014	2015	2016
10	Food products		...	...	...	...		...	...	220	231		9080	9325	9672	10024
11	Beverages		...	...	...	...		...	...	32	35		1567	1593	1844a/	1749
12	Tobacco products		...	...	...	...		...	...	2	2		191	209	...a/	185
13	Textiles		...	...	...	...		...	...	17	17		705	737	737	734
14	Wearing apparel		...	...	...	...		...	...	18	19		605	649	627	690
15	Leather and related products		...	...	...	...		...	...	5	...		...	146	160	115
16	Wood products, excluding furniture		...	...	...	...		...	...	96	96		4176	4406	4671	4946
17	Paper and paper products		...	...	...	...		...	...	51	48		3235	3641	3459	3375
18	Printing and reproduction of recorded media		...	...	...	...		...	...	54	56		2523	2510	2521	2577
19	Coke and refined petroleum products		...	...	...	...		...	...	13	13		1150	1252	1238	1204
20	Chemicals and chemical products		...	...	...	...		...	...	54	55		3343	3424	3746	3791
21	Pharmaceuticals,medicinal chemicals, etc.		...	...	...	...		...	...	30	29		1740	1995	1997	2055
22	Rubber and plastics products		...	...	...	...		...	...	101	102		4520	4824	5059	5176
23	Other non-metallic mineral products		...	...	...	...		...	...	51	50		2568	2636	2830	2728
24	Basic metals		...	...	...	...		...	...	58	56		4359	4309	4212	4026
25	Fabricated metal products, except machinery		...	...	...	...		...	...	166	161		8767	9100	9255	9007
26	Computer, electronic and optical products		...	...	...	...		...	...	188b/	...	b/	11054	11522	11786	11336
27	Electrical equipment		...	...	...	...		...	...	33	32		1759	1786	1947	1977
28	Machinery and equipment n.e.c.		...	...	...	...		...	...	...b/	...	b/	...	...	...	...
29	Motor vehicles, trailers and semi-trailers		...	...	...	...		...	...	124	118		6959	6897	7795	7770
30	Other transport equipment		...	...	...	...		...	...	73	70		4257	4810	4860	4627
31	Furniture		...	...	...	...		...	...	76	75		2842	2912	3216	3300
32	Other manufacturing		...	...	...	...		...	...	62	64		2476	2468	2829	2978
33	Repair and installation of machinery/equipment		...	...	...	...		...	...	...	...		...	...	...	...
C	Total manufacturing		...	...	...	...		...	...	1523	1553		77996	81151	84463	84370

a/ 11 includes 12.
b/ 26 includes 28.

Canada

ISIC	Industry	Output Note	Output 2013	Output 2014	Output 2015	Output 2016	VA Note	VA 2013	VA 2014	VA 2015	VA 2016	GFCF Note	GFCF 2015	GFCF 2016
10	Food products		85261	88452	89484	94777		28786	29024	29181	31745		…	…
11	Beverages		10924	11339	11812	12234		6639	6901	7222	7321		…	…
12	Tobacco products		1489	1529	1731	1935		1146	1258	1327	1584		…	…
13	Textiles		3051	3305	3297	3253		1369	1470	1464	1452		…	…
14	Wearing apparel		2047	2266	2147	2499		1019	1105	1156	1263		…	…
15	Leather and related products		498	567	569	389		207	255	261	186		…	…
16	Wood products, excluding furniture		25208	26410	27416	29935		9661	9565	10468	11248		…	…
17	Paper and paper products		23165	25353	25861	25474		8410	9644	10281	10022		…	…
18	Printing and reproduction of recorded media		8869	8551	9037	9322		5178	4851	5253	5278		…	…
19	Coke and refined petroleum products		84977	84584	59444	50574		15924	14682	12100	9366		…	…
20	Chemicals and chemical products		41119	42183	41795	40084		14259	15433	17520	17000		…	…
21	Pharmaceuticals,medicinal chemicals, etc.		8549	10055	9834	10158		4866	6152	5993	6051		…	…
22	Rubber and plastics products		24748	25855	27395	28328		10358	10985	11750	11795		…	…
23	Other non-metallic mineral products		13621	14475	14391	14404		6105	6396	6506	6596		…	…
24	Basic metals		44595	47917	45305	44823		12300	15225	13572	14098		…	…
25	Fabricated metal products, except machinery		33844	34836	34671	34680		16575	17787	17634	17636		…	…
26	Computer, electronic and optical products	a/	47792	47348	46213	46346	a/	22814	23535	23605	23508		…	…
27	Electrical equipment		9012	8901	9750	9829		3692	3717	4281	4397		…	…
28	Machinery and equipment n.e.c.	a/	…	…	…	…	a/	…	…	…	…		…	…
29	Motor vehicles, trailers and semi-trailers		82035	87897	98559	105274		20085	23186	22789	22693		…	…
30	Other transport equipment		23044	28972	32453	31558		10728	11277	14767	13042		…	…
31	Furniture		10256	10446	11506	11961		5116	5254	6088	6256		…	…
32	Other manufacturing		12025	11395	12468	12561		4987	4991	5493	5600		…	…
33	Repair and installation of machinery/equipment		…	…	…	…		…	…	…	…		…	…
C	Total manufacturing		596127	622636	615139	620397		210225	222692	228712	228136		…	…

a/ 26 includes 28.

Canada

Index numbers of industrial production

(2010=100)

ISIC	ISIC Revision 4 — Industry	Note	2005	2006	2007	2008	2009	2010	2011	2012	2013	2014	2015	2016
10	Food products		93	95	95	99	98	100	99	98	99	105	106	112
11	Beverages		106	110	106	105	101	100	98	102	96	99	102	105
12	Tobacco products		198	166	107	84	88	100	96	97	85	85	82	85
13	Textiles		180	158	138	120	97	100	98	98	88	89	91	86
14	Wearing apparel	a/	...	...	157	133	118	100	102	95	90	95	87	81
15	Leather and related products	a/	...	...	...	...	...	...	...	...	...	...	...	...
16	Wood products, excluding furniture		141	140	128	115	95	100	103	107	115	118	124	132
17	Paper and paper products		135	122	121	112	91	100	96	91	87	92	95	94
18	Printing and reproduction of recorded media		135	132	129	127	109	100	96	95	90	90	89	88
19	Coke and refined petroleum products		106	103	105	102	106	100	95	95	95	97	95	94
20	Chemicals and chemical products		123	119	115	107	91	100	107	106	111	105	108	110
21	Pharmaceuticals,medicinal chemicals, etc.		112	122	100	98	103	100	90	96	89	103	119	129
22	Rubber and plastics products		131	123	121	112	92	100	106	109	112	116	119	124
23	Other non-metallic mineral products		116	117	119	115	97	100	102	105	103	105	102	102
24	Basic metals		125	124	122	118	87	100	107	107	103	112	107	110
25	Fabricated metal products, except machinery		120	122	123	112	96	100	108	116	120	119	113	105
26	Computer, electronic and optical products		115	114	108	106	96	100	99	87	79	80	80	79
27	Electrical equipment		113	108	108	112	102	100	110	109	106	96	93	92
28	Machinery and equipment n.e.c.		121	122	122	119	99	100	120	126	125	128	122	115
29	Motor vehicles, trailers and semi-trailers		...	...	140	109	76	100	106	120	115	125	128	132
30	Other transport equipment		97	102	111	120	105	100	107	109	113	123	119	112
31	Furniture		148	138	131	121	99	100	96	97	100	99	102	104
32	Other manufacturing		115	118	113	104	97	100	105	99	102	96	103	102
33	Repair and installation of machinery/equipment		...	...	...	...	...	...	...	...	...	...	...	...
C	Total manufacturing		122	120	117	111	95	100	103	105	105	108	108	109

a/ 14 includes 15.

Chile

Supplier of information:
Instituto Nacional de Estadísticas, Santiago.
Industrial statistics for the OECD countries are compiled by the OECD secretariat, which supplies them to UNIDO.

Basic source of data:
Annual industrial survey.

Major deviations from ISIC (Revision 4):
None reported.

Reference period:
Calendar year.

Scope:
Single-unit establishments with 10 or more employees; all establishments belonging to multi-unit companies.

Method of data collection:
Mail questionnaires; online survey.

Type of enumeration:
Not reported.

Adjusted for non-response:
Not reported.

Concepts and definitions of variables:
No deviations from the standard UN concepts and definitions are reported.

Related national publications:
None reported.

Chile

ISIC	Industry	Number of enterprises (number)					Number of employees (number)					Wages and salaries paid to employees (billions of Chilean Pesos)				
		Note	2013	2014	2015a/	2016a/	Note	2013	2014	2015	2016	Note	2013	2014	2015	2016
10	Food products		790	839	953	1035		120242	125811	118578	135312		...	1780.8	...	...
11	Beverages		118	116	144	157		15525	18002	14637	19152		...	171.0	...	...
12	Tobacco products		...	...	...	...		...	...	...	...		...	...	...	...
13	Textiles		99	111	123	121		3828	5098	5945	5890		...	31.9	...	...
14	Wearing apparel		155	165	167	163		7079	6411	6480	7338		...	39.3	...	...
15	Leather and related products		44	46	44	40		6079	6987	6402	5744		...	47.0	...	...
16	Wood products, excluding furniture		146	162	209	224		19069	18865	22347	22575		...	128.6	...	...
17	Paper and paper products		150	125	151	160		22061	22847	19521	17399		...	201.4	...	...
18	Printing and reproduction of recorded media		117	139	145	132		43100	9238	10568	8931		...	86.1	...	...
19	Coke and refined petroleum products		...	...	...	...		...	...	...	...		...	...	...	...
20	Chemicals and chemical products		174	178	203	208		23450	23826	22814	21939		...	295.4	...	...
21	Pharmaceuticals,medicinal chemicals, etc.		32	46	39	36		8663	13799	9837	9373		...	208.1	...	...
22	Rubber and plastics products		243	263	305	332		18084	16839	24816	26723		...	153.4	...	...
23	Other non-metallic mineral products		232	192	225	210		17546	15743	18492	15156		...	150.2	...	...
24	Basic metals		55	58	45	64		5991	12001	5559	5324		...	256.5	...	...
25	Fabricated metal products, except machinery		316	313	379	397		22402	24083	27640	25302		...	259.6	...	...
26	Computer, electronic and optical products		20	21	23	19		2702	1221	6225	2587		...	9.1	...	...
27	Electrical equipment		85	83	86	89		7767	9348	8506	8374		...	80.1	...	...
28	Machinery and equipment n.e.c.		125	128	141	149		9054	10067	10999	10595		...	109.7	...	...
29	Motor vehicles, trailers and semi-trailers		38	35	32	29		2584	1362	1274	1123		...	10.2	...	...
30	Other transport equipment		6	7	3	10		888	1111	369	785		...	9.7	...	...
31	Furniture		96	101	136	128		9364	10178	9248	9748		...	52.2	...	...
32	Other manufacturing		39	34	39	35		1570	1381	1846	1688		...	8.0	...	...
33	Repair and installation of machinery/equipment		153	159	199	244		17641	15019	22579	22998		...	192.4	...	...
C	Total manufacturing		...	...	3924	4106		...	...	384085	392122		...	...	...	...

a/ Number of establishments.

Chile

ISIC	Industry	Output (valuation not defined)					Value added (valuation not defined)					Gross fixed capital formation		
		Note	(billions of Chilean Pesos)				Note	(billions of Chilean Pesos)				Note	(billions of Chilean Pesos)	
			2013	2014	2015	2016		2013	2014	2015	2016		2015	2016
10	Food products		11730.1	11087.3	...	13957.8		3263.7	3275.1	...	3812.8		...	...
11	Beverages		5959.3	2700.4	...	3301.6		1635.5	1156.8	...	710.0		...	...
12	Tobacco products		...	...	...	...		...	...	...	...		...	...
13	Textiles		126.3	182.4	...	215.4		43.0	69.4	...	85.4		...	...
14	Wearing apparel		158.4	151.9	...	236.3		69.2	72.9	...	83.6		...	...
15	Leather and related products		276.7	223.9	...	198.4		124.0	106.9	...	100.5		...	...
16	Wood products, excluding furniture		1187.4	1246.1	...	2253.6		410.0	366.7	...	616.1		...	...
17	Paper and paper products		2467.5	3585.6	...	2999.5		794.7	1035.3	...	858.9		...	...
18	Printing and reproduction of recorded media		384.9	537.0	...	356.9		165.1	203.8	...	135.5		...	...
19	Coke and refined petroleum products		...	...	...	...		...	...	...	...		...	...
20	Chemicals and chemical products		3498.5	3745.8	...	6239.9		1220.5	1226.2	...	2058.4		...	...
21	Pharmaceuticals,medicinal chemicals, etc.		563.8	838.8	...	720.8		228.5	383.7	...	271.7		...	...
22	Rubber and plastics products		2064.7	1101.8	...	1809.6		925.2	329.1	...	503.9		...	...
23	Other non-metallic mineral products		1622.3	1169.5	...	1500.6		565.1	317.3	...	495.1		...	...
24	Basic metals		788.1	1451.2	...	952.6		115.5	322.1	...	180.6		...	...
25	Fabricated metal products, except machinery		3774.4	1593.9	...	1529.7		1568.5	828.5	...	463.8		...	...
26	Computer, electronic and optical products		24.5	44.5	...	36.4		8.8	24.0	...	14.9		...	...
27	Electrical equipment		405.4	443.9	...	556.1		106.4	147.5	...	160.9		...	...
28	Machinery and equipment n.e.c.		767.9	1026.4	...	821.2		-74.9	593.5	...	252.2		...	...
29	Motor vehicles, trailers and semi-trailers		135.7	43.1	...	63.4		68.4	13.7	...	11.9		...	...
30	Other transport equipment		69.9	60.3	...	52.6		53.9	24.1	...	27.4		...	...
31	Furniture		313.4	224.5	...	288.2		117.2	84.5	...	113.6		...	...
32	Other manufacturing		686.9	29.8	...	68.3		408.7	11.2	...	27.6		...	...
33	Repair and installation of machinery/equipment		689.8	1725.6	...	781.2		326.7	737.4	...	363.4		...	...
C	Total manufacturing		...	...	...	40112.5		...	...	...	11614.8		...	...

Chile

ISIC Revision 4 — Index numbers of industrial production (2010=100)

ISIC	Industry	Note	2005	2006	2007	2008	2009	2010	2011	2012	2013	2014	2015	2016
10	Food products	a/	...	...	...	...	99	100	105	111	116	119	118	119
11	Beverages	a/	...	...	...	...	...	...	...	...	...	...	...	...
12	Tobacco products		...	...	...	...	86	100	98	106	95	100	101	95
13	Textiles		...	...	...	...	...	...	...	...	...	...	...	...
14	Wearing apparel		...	...	...	...	...	...	...	...	...	...	...	...
15	Leather and related products		...	...	...	...	...	...	...	...	...	...	...	...
16	Wood products, excluding furniture		...	...	...	...	94	100	103	94	96	95	99	99
17	Paper and paper products		...	...	...	...	111	100	113	118	120	120	117	117
18	Printing and reproduction of recorded media		...	...	...	...	113	100	107	102	101	89	76	63
19	Coke and refined petroleum products		...	...	...	...	118	100	108	104	108	112	113	110
20	Chemicals and chemical products	b/	...	...	...	...	85	100	100	95	92	90	96	93
21	Pharmaceuticals,medicinal chemicals, etc.	b/	...	...	...	...	...	...	...	...	...	...	...	...
22	Rubber and plastics products		...	...	...	...	89	100	102	107	109	110	113	106
23	Other non-metallic mineral products		...	...	...	...	102	100	113	117	114	110	113	114
24	Basic metals		...	...	...	...	104	100	145	136	119	113	105	118
25	Fabricated metal products, except machinery		...	...	...	...	93	100	110	125	119	106	110	108
26	Computer, electronic and optical products		...	...	...	...	...	...	...	...	...	...	...	...
27	Electrical equipment		...	...	...	...	...	...	...	...	...	...	...	...
28	Machinery and equipment n.e.c.		...	...	...	...	89	100	109	103	98	93	86	82
29	Motor vehicles, trailers and semi-trailers		...	...	...	...	...	...	...	...	...	...	...	...
30	Other transport equipment		...	...	...	...	...	...	...	...	...	...	...	...
31	Furniture		...	...	...	...	78	100	115	121	130	134	130	127
32	Other manufacturing		...	...	...	...	...	...	...	...	...	...	...	...
33	Repair and installation of machinery/equipment		...	...	...	...	...	...	...	...	...	...	...	...
C	Total manufacturing		...	...	...	...	97	100	108	110	111	109	110	110

a/ 10 includes 11.
b/ 20 includes 21.

China

Supplier of information:
National Bureau of Statistics, Beijing.

Basic source of data:
Annual surveys.

Major deviations from ISIC (Revision 4):
Data presented in accordance with ISIC (Revision 4) were originally classified according to the Industrial Classification of The National Economy (GB/T 4754-2011).

Reference period:
Calendar year.

Scope:
For survey on financial status of industrial enterprises: industrial enterprises above designated size (annual revenue above 20 million Chinese Yuan); for survey on employees and wages: all non-private enterprises and sample private enterprises in urban areas.

Method of data collection:
Online survey.

Type of enumeration:
Complete enumeration for survey on financial status of industrial enterprises; sampling method for survey on employees and wages.

Adjusted for non-response:
Not reported.

Concepts and definitions of variables:
No deviations from the standard UN concepts and definitions are reported.

Related national publications:
China Statistical Yearbook (annual), published by the National Bureau of Statistics, Beijing.

China

ISIC Revision 4

ISIC	Industry	Note	Number of enterprises (number)				Note	Number of employees (thousands)				Note	Wages and salaries paid to employees (billions of Chinese Yuan)			
			2013	2014	2015	2016		2013	2014	2015	2016		2013	2014	2015	2016
1010	Processing/preserving of meat		4045	4192	4310	...		1099	1104	1084	1063		38.5	42.0	44.0	46.1
1020	Processing/preserving of fish, etc.		2127	2137	2180	...		556	526	508	479		20.9	21.5	22.2	22.4
1030	Processing/preserving of fruit,vegetables		4117	4340	4604	...		670	689	692	690		22.6	25.1	26.7	28.7
1040	Vegetable and animal oils and fats		2246	2206	2170	...		340	329	320	305		13.0	14.1	14.6	14.7
1050	Dairy products		1074	1091	1110	...		376	369	381	374		15.5	17.1	18.7	19.5
106	Grain mill products,starches and starch products		6951	7232	7506	...		832	841	836	809		26.8	29.4	31.6	32.6
1061	Grain mill products		6088	6363	6641	...		634	650	657	635		20.2	22.5	24.7	25.4
1062	Starches and starch products		863	869	865	...		198	190	180	173		6.6	6.9	6.9	7.2
107	Other food products		9163	9721	10506	...		2168	2208	2252	2264		81.0	87.6	95.3	102.4
1071	Bakery products		1275	1399	1539	...		348	356	385	397		12.3	13.9	16.2	18.1
1072	Sugar		312	301	297	...		159	144	132	124		5.1	4.8	4.7	4.8
1073	Cocoa, chocolate and sugar confectionery		763	771	812	...		207	214	200	196		9.0	10.0	9.5	10.0
1074	Macaroni, noodles, couscous, etc.		1340	1444	1582	...		393	400	401	397		14.4	15.7	17.3	18.3
1075	Prepared meals and dishes		809	834	834	...		221	222	211	204		7.3	8.0	8.2	8.3
1079	Other food products n.e.c.		4664	4972	5442	...		840	873	922	945		33.0	35.3	39.2	42.8
1080	Prepared animal feeds		3804	4061	4208	...		561	586	577	558		22.6	25.6	27.6	28.5
110	Beverages		3425	3561	3726	...		1107	1097	1097	1035		46.7	50.9	53.2	53.8
1101	Distilling, rectifying and blending of spirits		1518	1569	1592	...		520	504	502	488		20.3	20.8	21.6	23.1
1102	Wines		480	505	557	...		77	80	86	87		2.8	3.2	3.7	4.0
1103	Malt liquors and malt		488	476	466	...		239	228	215	182		10.2	11.2	11.3	10.4
1104	Soft drinks,mineral waters,other bottled waters		939	1011	1111	...		272	286	294	278		13.4	15.7	16.6	16.3
1200	Tobacco products		130	128	133	...		202	202	200	186		24.0	25.7	27.0	26.4
131	Spinning, weaving and finishing of textiles		15587	15227	14933	...		3828	3657	3518	3349		136.3	143.7	148.8	149.5
1311	Preparation and spinning of textile fibres		7135	6943	6759	...		2010	1912	1813	1738		66.9	70.4	71.9	73.0
1312	Weaving of textiles		6119	6043	5994	...		1168	1104	1061	994		42.4	44.1	45.5	45.2
1313	Finishing of textiles		2333	2241	2180	...		651	641	643	617		27.0	29.1	31.3	31.4
139	Other textiles		6571	6581	6627	...		1234	1213	1162	1150		47.3	50.5	51.6	54.4
1391	Knitted and crocheted fabrics		2607	2567	2518	...		515	488	459	440		19.4	20.1	20.0	20.5
1392	Made-up textile articles, except apparel		1586	1578	1595	...		284	278	263	255		10.9	11.6	11.8	12.3
1393	Carpets and rugs		345	343	360	...		83	80	77	82		3.0	3.2	3.2	3.8
1394	Cordage, rope, twine and netting		229	238	243	...		31	33	32	32		1.1	1.3	1.4	1.5
1399	Other textiles n.e.c.		1804	1855	1911	...		321	334	331	341		13.0	14.2	15.2	16.4
1410	Wearing apparel, except fur apparel		13245	13278	13278	...		3834	3777	3655	3499		142.9	154.5	160.1	161.5
1420	Articles of fur		404	461	483	...		58	60	62	62		1.8	2.1	2.3	2.4
1430	Knitted and crocheted apparel		3310	3404	3519	...		900	891	894	868		33.2	36.1	39.1	40.3
151	Leather;luggage,handbags,saddlery,harness;fur		2562	2601	2639	...		663	656	640	605		23.2	25.2	26.6	26.6
1511	Tanning/dressing of leather; dressing of fur		801	765	748	...		171	171	167	163		5.8	6.4	6.8	6.8
1512	Luggage,handbags,etc.;saddlery/harness		1761	1836	1891	...		491	485	473	442		17.4	18.8	19.8	19.8
1520	Footwear		4422	4550	4625	...		2024	1959	1886	1759		70.1	74.0	77.1	76.7
1610	Sawmilling and planing of wood		1444	1514	1624	...		194	197	198	191		6.3	6.9	7.5	7.8

Code	Description												
162	Wood products, cork, straw, plaiting materials	54.4	52.7	49.7	43.8	⋮	1276	1318	1337	1322	8053	8157	8303
1621	Veneer sheets and wood-based panels	31.5	30.9	29.3	26.0	⋮	734	766	782	785	4777	4749	4781
1622	Builders' carpentry and joinery	7.8	7.6	7.2	6.2	⋮	178	187	188	178	1169	1261	1296
1623	Wooden containers	1.3	1.3	1.2	1.1	⋮	29	29	30	29	262	264	279
1629	Other wood products;articles of cork,straw	13.7	12.9	12.0	10.6	⋮	336	337	337	330	1845	1883	1947
170	Paper and paper products	65.4	63.3	60.1	56.9	⋮	1336	1390	1432	1497	7413	7178	7156
1701	Pulp, paper and paperboard	31.3	30.1	29.6	28.3	⋮	656	674	713	761	3106	2870	2808
1702	Corrugated paper and paperboard	17.3	17.3	16.4	15.7	⋮	356	384	394	408	2463	2451	2440
1709	Other articles of paper and paperboard	16.9	15.9	14.2	12.9	⋮	324	332	325	328	1844	1857	1908
181	Printing and service activities related to printing	48.9	45.5	42.3	37.1	⋮	953	941	935	905	5021	5248	5409
1811	Printing	47.4	44.4	41.2	36.1	⋮	925	916	910	881	4885	5109	5267
1812	Service activities related to printing	1.5	1.2	1.1	1.0	⋮	28	25	25	25	136	139	142
1820	Reproduction of recorded media	0.4	0.4	0.4	0.3	⋮	6	7	8	8	49	45	42
1910	Coke oven products	14.8	15.4	14.8	14.2	⋮	342	370	379	399	689	617	573
1920	Refined petroleum products	40.7	⋮	⋮	36.7	⋮	524	⋮	⋮	551	1501	1535	1551
201	Basic chemicals,fertilizers, etc.	132.0	129.4	125.6	117.2	⋮	2386	2494	2591	2639	11441	11475	11426
2011	Basic chemicals	66.8	65.2	62.9	59.4	⋮	1195	1250	1298	1341	6223	6144	6046
2012	Fertilizers and nitrogen compounds	30.6	31.4	30.3	28.0	⋮	648	694	713	722	2418	2480	2522
2013	Plastics and synthetic rubber in primary forms	34.6	32.8	32.4	29.9	⋮	544	550	580	575	2800	2851	2858
202	Other chemical products	140.0	134.7	123.9	110.6	⋮	2447	2505	2504	2466	14621	14817	14895
2021	Pesticides and other agrochemical products	10.3	9.8	8.9	8.2	⋮	188	189	194	197	857	838	836
2022	Paints,varnishes;printing ink and mastics	28.8	28.4	26.9	23.2	⋮	452	465	466	446	3306	3357	3359
2023	Soap,cleaning and cosmetic preparations	16.1	14.5	13.2	11.9	⋮	242	236	237	230	784	801	836
2029	Other chemical products n.e.c.	84.8	82.0	74.9	67.2	⋮	1565	1615	1608	1592	9674	9821	9864
2030	Man-made fibres	24.9	22.8	22.2	20.9	⋮	457	456	466	485	2002	1948	1924
2100	Pharmaceuticals,medicinal chemicals, etc.	134.1	123.2	112.1	98.7	⋮	2280	2238	2182	2111	6839	7108	7392
221	Rubber products	42.4	40.6	40.1	35.7	⋮	821	850	878	855	3210	3240	3221
2211	Rubber tyres and tubes	20.0	19.0	18.6	17.0	⋮	363	374	385	379	574	555	533
2219	Other rubber products	22.3	21.7	21.5	18.7	⋮	459	476	493	477	2636	2685	2688
2220	Plastics products	129.6	122.9	114.8	101.9	⋮	2605	2654	2662	2610	15124	15698	16158
2310	Glass and glass products	43.4	42.0	40.3	36.0	⋮	894	925	970	953	3904	4079	4120
239	Non-metallic mineral products n.e.c.	215.9	206.9	197.7	174.1	⋮	4699	4776	4850	4735	28270	29914	31002
2391	Refractory products	12.5	13.0	13.1	12.2	⋮	301	332	356	362	2180	2185	2109
2392	Clay building materials	35.6	34.6	34.5	30.8	⋮	869	894	936	915	4713	4885	4937
2393	Other porcelain and ceramic products	36.8	34.0	29.8	24.7	⋮	751	722	695	661	2062	2100	2209
2394	Cement, lime and plaster	35.4	36.4	37.3	34.8	⋮	761	827	884	929	4312	4138	3995
2395	Articles of concrete, cement and plaster	49.0	45.7	43.2	36.8	⋮	1019	1009	1010	946	8058	9099	9716
2396	Cutting, shaping and finishing of stone	14.6	13.8	12.6	11.5	⋮	311	314	304	292	2219	2464	2718
2399	Other non-metallic mineral products n.e.c.	32.1	29.4	27.3	23.4	⋮	686	676	665	630	4726	5043	5318
2410	Basic iron and steel	150.2	155.0	169.4	170.1	⋮	2734	3000	3319	3505	7038	6616	6082
2420	Basic precious and other non-ferrous metals	101.1	97.1	94.0	86.5	⋮	1904	1945	1998	2013	7181	7195	7050
243	Casting of metals	23.9	24.9	26.5	24.3	⋮	509	562	624	639	4134	3937	3665
2431	Casting of iron and steel	22.3	23.4	25.1	23.1	⋮	480	533	595	613	3972	3747	3458
2432	Casting of non-ferrous metals	1.7	1.5	1.4	1.2	⋮	29	28	28	26	162	190	207
251	Struct.metal products, tanks, reservoirs	66.6	65.4	63.1	56.5	⋮	1283	1334	1357	1316	7532	8002	8257

continued

China

ISIC	Industry	Number of enterprises (number) Note	2013	2014	2015	2016	Number of employees (thousands) Note	2013	2014	2015	2016	Wages and salaries paid to employees (billions of Chinese Yuan) Note	2013	2014	2015	2016
2511	Structural metal products		6189	6637	6910	…		1048	1097	1087	1050		44.2	50.1	52.3	53.5
2512	Tanks, reservoirs and containers of metal		505	520	513	…		100	93	87	84		4.4	4.5	4.4	4.4
2513	Steam generators, excl. hot water boilers		838	845	834	…		169	167	159	148		7.8	8.5	8.7	8.7
2520	Weapons and ammunition		…	…	…	…		…	…	…	…		…	…	…	…
259	Other metal products;metal working services		13402	13644	13761	…		2687	2674	2634	2636		109.1	119.3	126.1	134.8
2591	Forging,pressing,stamping,roll-forming of metal		1741	1765	1757	…		276	275	264	255		10.8	12.0	12.1	12.5
2592	Treatment and coating of metals;machining		1398	1400	1420	…		249	240	248	246		10.6	11.2	12.3	13.1
2593	Cutlery, hand tools and general hardware		3457	3458	3431	…		685	689	664	664		26.9	29.7	30.5	32.7
2599	Other fabricated metal products n.e.c.		6806	7021	7153	…		1476	1469	1458	1470		60.7	66.3	71.2	76.6
2610	Electronic components and boards		9195	9574	9906	…		4452	4552	4441	4501		208.9	234.7	246.9	270.4
2620	Computers and peripheral equipment		1325	1388	1452	…		1762	1736	1528	1181		89.8	93.7	90.2	74.0
2630	Communication equipment		2073	2133	2363	…		1569	1857	1952	2288		84.0	124.7	143.1	179.3
2640	Consumer electronics		1039	1036	1022	…		706	681	641	611		32.6	34.3	34.7	37.0
265	Measuring,testing equipment; watches, etc.		3622	3700	3745	…		845	858	856	824		43.8	48.1	52.0	54.3
2651	Measuring/testing/navigating equipment,etc.		3385	3462	3490	…		735	749	746	717		39.7	43.4	46.9	48.9
2652	Watches and clocks		237	238	255	…		110	110	110	107		4.1	4.7	5.2	5.4
2660	Irradiation/electromedical equipment,etc.		…	…	…	…		…	…	…	…		…	…	…	…
2670	Optical instruments and photographic equipment		477	467	490	…		203	200	191	177		9.3	10.0	10.3	10.2
2680	Magnetic and optical media		…	…	…	…		…	…	…	…		…	…	…	…
2710	Electric motors,generators,transformers,etc.		9016	9299	9441	…		2213	2255	2225	2181		104.1	116.8	124.3	128.9
2720	Batteries and accumulators		1239	1251	1301	…		520	529	544	592		22.4	24.6	27.6	32.8
273	Wiring and wiring devices		4068	4100	4107	…		834	851	821	804		37.0	41.4	41.8	44.2
2731	Fibre optic cables		227	237	271	…		81	83	80	85		5.0	5.4	5.2	5.9
2732	Other electronic and electric wires and cables		3841	3863	3836	…		753	768	740	719		32.0	35.9	36.7	38.3
2733	Wiring devices		…	…	…	…		…	…	…	…		…	…	…	…
2740	Electric lighting equipment		2580	2686	2762	…		636	643	630	623		25.3	28.7	30.6	32.2
2750	Domestic appliances		3360	3398	3433	…		1495	1499	1398	1381		68.1	75.9	77.4	83.3
2790	Other electrical equipment		2182	2318	2429	…		623	643	666	691		29.7	32.7	37.8	40.5
281	General-purpose machinery		18815	19310	19229	…		3743	3804	3682	3530		171.7	193.4	199.0	205.7
2811	Engines/turbines,excl.aircraft,vehicle engines		875	925	909	…		307	295	296	275		15.9	16.1	16.9	17.4
2812	Fluid power equipment		1324	1330	1270	…		219	215	194	180		9.7	10.4	10.2	10.3
2813	Other pumps, compressors, taps and valves		3623	3714	3656	…		703	712	681	647		31.6	35.3	35.7	36.6
2814	Bearings, gears, gearing and driving elements		2905	2938	2892	…		553	562	528	497		22.5	26.3	26.1	26.8
2815	Ovens, furnaces and furnace burners		847	843	833	…		134	130	132	126		5.9	6.4	6.8	7.0
2816	Lifting and handling equipment		2157	2258	2278	…		526	558	541	528		28.3	32.2	33.3	34.8
2817	Office machinery, excl.computers,etc.		249	249	251	…		132	131	122	124		6.7	7.6	7.5	8.3
2818	Power-driven hand tools		412	395	373	…		98	102	95	91		4.4	5.1	5.2	5.3
2819	Other general-purpose machinery		6423	6658	6767	…		1070	1099	1092	1060		46.9	54.0	57.2	59.1
282	Special-purpose machinery		18492	19161	19524	…		3734	3761	3636	3520		175.9	191.3	195.3	203.1
2821	Agricultural and forestry machinery		1473	1539	1585	…		277	279	272	262		11.0	12.0	12.4	12.6
2822	Metal-forming machinery and machine tools		3586	3663	3701	…		647	641	602	563		28.1	30.7	31.1	31.9

2823	Machinery for metallurgy	...	1212	1202	1183	211	218	249	263	10.8	10.7	11.7	11.7
2824	Mining, quarrying and construction machinery	...	3694	3855	3798	833	912	964	975	47.6	49.7	51.6	49.9
2825	Food/beverage/tobacco processing machinery	...	729	790	823	125	123	120	115	6.7	6.2	5.7	4.9
2826	Textile/apparel/leather production machinery	...	1408	1383	1310	205	223	241	255	11.5	11.6	11.8	11.4
2829	Other special-purpose machinery	...	6390	6729	7124	1322	1287	1267	1201	82.1	73.6	67.9	58.9
2910	Motor vehicles	...	1011	1064	1080	1464	1425	1445	1358	128.3	113.8	106.6	89.9
2920	Automobile bodies, trailers and semi-trailers	...	384	378	375	118	130	139	134	7.4	7.9	8.2	7.0
2930	Parts and accessories for motor vehicles	...	11219	12104	12780	3252	3101	2996	2831	197.5	173.7	155.5	132.4
301	Building of ships and boats	...	1329	1244	1246	409	445	458	515	25.7	27.0	25.5	26.3
3011	Building of ships and floating structures	...	1271	1195	1187	401	438	451	507	25.2	26.6	25.1	26.0
3012	Building of pleasure and sporting boats	...	58	49	59	8	8	7	8	0.5	0.4	0.3	0.4
3020	Railway locomotives and rolling stock	...	802	866	894	355	368	363	346	26.6	26.4	23.9	20.1
3030	Air and spacecraft and related machinery	...	181	189	209	62	63	49	56	5.5	5.3	3.9	4.2
3040	Military fighting vehicles	...	...	...	...	...	...	...	...	...	...	...	...
309	Transport equipment n.e.c.	...	2435	2492	2499	579	598	625	611	29.1	28.0	27.7	24.3
3091	Motorcycles	...	1796	1846	1831	435	447	465	458	21.8	20.8	20.5	18.1
3092	Bicycles and invalid carriages	...	532	542	561	127	134	143	136	6.4	6.4	6.5	5.5
3099	Other transport equipment n.e.c.	...	107	104	107	17	17	17	16	0.8	0.8	0.7	0.7
3100	Furniture	...	5078	5288	5546	1214	1196	1196	1169	59.9	55.1	51.5	45.8
321	Jewellery, bijouterie and related articles	...	1579	1739	1902	456	456	451	442	23.0	20.5	19.0	16.3
3211	Jewellery and related articles	...	431	477	536	180	179	174	176	10.7	9.1	8.3	7.4
3212	Imitation jewellery and related articles	...	1148	1262	1366	276	277	276	267	12.3	11.4	10.8	8.9
3220	Musical instruments	...	227	227	232	60	62	61	63	2.9	2.8	2.5	2.3
3230	Sports goods	...	977	1009	1037	259	268	268	268	12.2	11.8	11.0	10.0
3240	Games and toys	...	1636	1720	1797	679	678	674	668	30.7	28.6	26.0	23.4
3250	Medical and dental instruments and supplies	...	1315	1441	1564	425	409	397	381	27.8	24.7	22.0	18.9
3290	Other manufacturing n.e.c.	...	1744	1779	1785	474	479	486	480	23.8	22.5	20.8	18.6
331	Repair of fabricated metal products/machinery	...	429	395	397	156	150	140	159	13.9	11.6	9.1	9.0
3311	Repair of fabricated metal products	...	48	42	47	8	8	8	7	0.4	0.4	0.4	0.3
3312	Repair of machinery	...	94	80	66	18	17	23	26	1.1	1.0	1.1	1.2
3313	Repair of electronic and optical equipment	...	3	6	5	1	1	1	-	0.1	-	-	-
3314	Repair of electrical equipment	...	22	26	31	8	8	8	6	0.5	0.5	0.5	0.3
3315	Repair of transport equip., excl. motor vehicles	...	217	196	204	114	108	92	108	11.3	9.3	6.5	6.7
3319	Repair of other equipment	...	45	45	44	8	8	9	11	0.4	0.4	0.5	0.5
3320	Installation of industrial machinery/equipment	...	...	...	...	...	...	...	...	...	...	...	...
C	Total manufacturing	...	339880	348494	354715	82202	83403	85146	85160	4468.0	4213.6	4011.8	3654.3

China

ISIC	Industry	Output (valuation not defined) (billions of Chinese Yuan)				Value added (valuation not defined) (billions of Chinese Yuan)				Gross fixed capital formation a/ (billions of Chinese Yuan)	
		2013	2014	2015	2016	2013	2014	2015	2016	2015	2016
1010	Processing/preserving of meat	1244.3	1349.4	1366.3	…	…	…	…	…	6.7	…
1020	Processing/preserving of fish, etc.	495.6	508.5	516.7	…	…	…	…	…	1.8	…
1030	Processing/preserving of fruit,vegetables	615.3	680.3	732.5	…	…	…	…	…	15.7	…
1040	Vegetable and animal oils and fats	1052.0	1035.1	1027.4	…	…	…	…	…	3.5	…
1050	Dairy products	440.5	479.8	487.5	…	…	…	…	…	10.3	…
106	Grain mill products,starches and starch products	1478.9	1580.1	1639.1	…	…	…	…	…	22.0	…
1061	Grain mill products	1152.1	1265.0	1353.9	…	…	…	…	…	21.4	…
1062	Starches and starch products	326.9	315.1	285.2	…	…	…	…	…	0.6	…
107	Other food products	1786.4	1976.5	2172.0	…	…	…	…	…	50.5	…
1071	Bakery products	221.8	250.2	288.7	…	…	…	…	…	8.8	…
1072	Sugar	118.6	111.4	120.5	…	…	…	…	…	-1.3	…
1073	Cocoa, chocolate and sugar confectionery	156.7	171.1	185.9	…	…	…	…	…	3.9	…
1074	Macaroni, noodles, couscous, etc.	325.3	364.6	373.5	…	…	…	…	…	6.3	…
1075	Prepared meals and dishes	141.7	154.3	154.7	…	…	…	…	…	4.4	…
1079	Other food products n.e.c.	822.3	924.9	1048.6	…	…	…	…	…	28.3	…
1080	Prepared animal feeds	1004.8	1094.5	1119.5	…	…	…	…	…	15.6	…
110	Beverages	1051.5	1110.7	1171.0	…	…	…	…	…	33.3	…
1101	Distilling, rectifying and blending of spirits	511.0	528.9	559.6	…	…	…	…	…	14.4	…
1102	Wines	79.8	86.5	98.5	…	…	…	…	…	3.8	…
1103	Malt liquors and malt	179.6	188.8	186.1	…	…	…	…	…	1.9	…
1104	Soft drinks,mineral waters,other bottled waters	281.2	306.6	326.8	…	…	…	…	…	13.1	…
1200	Tobacco products	830.8	896.3	934.1	…	…	…	…	…	18.6	…
131	Spinning, weaving and finishing of textiles	2907.0	3089.0	3238.9	…	…	…	…	…	1.8	…
1311	Preparation and spinning of textile fibres	1598.8	1704.2	1803.2	…	…	…	…	…	-5.2	…
1312	Weaving of textiles	885.0	949.5	983.3	…	…	…	…	…	1.0	…
1313	Finishing of textiles	423.2	435.3	452.4	…	…	…	…	…	6.0	…
139	Other textiles	846.5	898.8	929.6	…	…	…	…	…	8.2	…
1391	Knitted and crocheted fabrics	344.7	352.0	350.6	…	…	…	…	…	-1.1	…
1392	Made-up textile articles, except apparel	186.6	193.9	199.7	…	…	…	…	…	1.3	…
1393	Carpets and rugs	59.3	64.6	67.1	…	…	…	…	…	0.5	…
1394	Cordage, rope, twine and netting	21.8	25.2	27.9	…	…	…	…	…	0.8	…
1399	Other textiles n.e.c.	234.2	263.1	284.2	…	…	…	…	…	6.7	…
1410	Wearing apparel, except fur apparel	1742.1	1875.4	1974.9	…	…	…	…	…	27.2	…
1420	Articles of fur	55.0	60.2	64.2	…	…	…	…	…	0.3	…
1430	Knitted and crocheted apparel	341.0	383.8	410.5	…	…	…	…	…	7.5	…
151	Leather;luggage,handbags,saddlery,harness;fur	390.1	428.6	444.8	…	…	…	…	…	2.1	…
1511	Tanning/dressing of leather; dressing of fur	187.2	196.7	208.4	…	…	…	…	…	0.5	…
1512	Luggage,handbags,etc.;saddlery/harness	202.9	231.9	236.4	…	…	…	…	…	1.6	…
1520	Footwear	644.2	703.5	749.8	…	…	…	…	…	5.5	…
1610	Sawmilling and planing of wood	164.0	183.5	191.4	…	…	…	…	…	3.4	…

Code	Description						
162	Wood products, cork, straw, plaiting materials	10.9			1289.2	1222.5	1106.2
1621	Veneer sheets and wood-based panels	6.6			824.2	779.4	709.3
1622	Builders' carpentry and joinery	1.2			193.5	192.4	174.1
1623	Wooden containers	0.5			26.0	27.0	26.2
1629	Other wood products;articles of cork,straw	2.5			245.5	223.6	196.6
170	Paper and paper products	13.9			1442.5	1397.8	1327.7
1701	Pulp, paper and paperboard	5.5			819.3	797.0	766.1
1702	Corrugated paper and paperboard	2.1			339.9	333.5	321.1
1709	Other articles of paper and paperboard	6.3			283.3	267.3	240.5
181	Printing and service activities related to printing	12.6			734.2	670.2	595.4
1811	Printing	12.4			718.7	656.6	582.7
1812	Service activities related to printing	0.2			15.5	13.7	12.7
1820	Reproduction of recorded media	-0.3			6.0	6.3	6.0
1910	Coke oven products	2.5			510.2	563.2	578.2
1920	Refined petroleum products	21.6			2960.3	3559.8	3533.1
201	Basic chemicals,fertilizers, etc.	183.3			4792.0	4881.1	4615.2
2011	Basic chemicals	39.0			2493.1	2581.7	2396.1
2012	Fertilizers and nitrogen compounds	70.6			950.6	911.1	865.5
2013	Plastics and synthetic rubber in primary forms	73.7			1348.3	1388.4	1353.6
202	Other chemical products	88.2			3850.2	3703.0	3318.0
2021	Pesticides and other agrochemical products	7.8			313.6	296.7	283.4
2022	Paints,varnishes;printing ink and mastics	11.7			653.4	621.2	562.0
2023	Soap,cleaning and cosmetic preparations	7.9			345.1	318.0	281.7
2029	Other chemical products n.e.c.	60.7			2538.1	2467.1	2190.9
2030	Man-made fibres	11.3			720.6	715.9	705.5
2100	Pharmaceuticals,medicinal chemicals, etc.	92.3			2573.0	2335.0	2048.4
221	Rubber products	15.3			935.0	917.2	868.5
2211	Rubber tyres and tubes	9.3			545.9	538.1	511.6
2219	Other rubber products	6.0			389.1	379.1	356.9
2220	Plastics products	27.8			2283.6	2174.2	1998.6
2310	Glass and glass products	10.5			802.3	774.8	700.9
239	Non-metallic mineral products n.e.c.	119.2			5085.4	4968.9	4495.8
2391	Refractory products	15.1			436.4	449.5	438.7
2392	Clay building materials	20.2			827.3	789.8	702.1
2393	Other porcelain and ceramic products	20.6			402.7	361.5	316.0
2394	Cement, lime and plaster	15.7			952.5	1064.8	1048.4
2395	Articles of concrete, cement and plaster	11.0			1215.1	1160.0	991.1
2396	Cutting, shaping and finishing of stone	15.0			373.7	328.6	281.7
2399	Other non-metallic mineral products n.e.c.	21.7			877.7	814.5	717.7
2410	Basic iron and steel	64.3			5675.6	6761.5	6971.8
2420	Basic precious and other non-ferrous metals	67.0			5098.3	5100.0	4695.2
243	Casting of metals	-0.1			663.0	703.1	661.8
2431	Casting of iron and steel	-0.6			624.5	671.8	637.8
2432	Casting of non-ferrous metals	0.5			38.4	31.3	24.0
251	Struct.metal products, tanks, reservoirs	13.0			1522.5	1486.0	1328.7

continued

China

ISIC	Industry	Output (valuation not defined) (billions of Chinese Yuan)				Value added (valuation not defined) (billions of Chinese Yuan)				Gross fixed capital formation a/ (billions of Chinese Yuan)	
		2013	2014	2015	2016	2013	2014	2015	2016	2015	2016
2511	Structural metal products	1064.6	1204.7	1232.7	...	...	...	...	...	12.5	...
2512	Tanks, reservoirs and containers of metal	82.3	83.0	84.3	...	...	...	...	...	-4.8	...
2513	Steam generators, excl. hot water boilers	181.8	198.3	205.6	...	...	...	...	...	5.2	...
2520	Weapons and ammunition	...	...	...	...	...	...	...	...	...	...
259	Other metal products;metal working services	2005.8	2175.2	2239.4	...	...	...	...	...	-100.1	...
2591	Forging,pressing,stamping,roll-forming of metal	348.0	389.2	392.8						2.9	
2592	Treatment and coating of metals; machining	234.3	241.8	236.3						1.5	
2593	Cutlery, hand tools and general hardware	415.9	455.6	473.1						10.9	
2599	Other fabricated metal products n.e.c.	1007.6	1088.7	1137.2						-115.3	
2610	Electronic components and boards	2894.4	3158.6	3400.2						81.8	
2620	Computers and peripheral equipment	2202.2	2226.0	2882.6						-59.0	
2630	Communication equipment	1857.3	2157.9	2882.7						30.7	
2640	Consumer electronics	756.1	735.9	774.0						7.3	
265	Measuring,testing equipment; watches, etc.	724.2	796.0	824.2	...	...	...	...	...	14.9	...
2651	Measuring/testing/navigating equipment,etc.	693.6	762.0	785.2						13.6	
2652	Watches and clocks	30.6	34.1	39.1						1.3	
2660	Irradiation/electromedical equipment,etc.	...	...	...							
2670	Optical instruments and photographic equipment	127.4	115.6	111.1						-5.7	
2680	Magnetic and optical media	...	...	...							
2710	Electric motors,generators,transformers,etc.	2329.9	2562.9	2708.2						21.7	
2720	Batteries and accumulators	401.4	424.5	462.9						11.6	
273	Wiring and wiring devices	1335.9	1397.2	1410.4						8.8	
2731	Fibre optic cables	138.4	155.4	164.5						3.4	
2732	Other electronic and electric wires and cables	1197.6	1241.8	1245.9						5.4	
2733	Wiring devices	...	...	...						...	
2740	Electric lighting equipment	366.5	405.3	435.6						4.2	
2750	Domestic appliances	1400.3	1548.2	1512.0						12.7	
2790	Other electrical equipment	448.8	585.6	620.1						0.8	
281	General-purpose machinery	3555.2	3827.7	3824.5						36.7	
2811	Engines/turbines,excl.aircraft,vehicle engines	318.7	337.2	347.5						6.2	
2812	Fluid power equipment	185.1	202.6	191.3						-1.5	
2813	Other pumps, compressors, taps and valves	633.6	675.6	665.8	...	...	...	...	...	9.5	...
2814	Bearings, gears, gearing and driving elements	433.4	480.7	471.3						5.5	
2815	Ovens, furnaces and furnace burners	145.2	148.8	152.4						4.6	
2816	Lifting and handling equipment	639.4	695.2	691.7						8.2	
2817	Office machinery, excl.computers.etc.	120.4	125.1	113.3						0.2	
2818	Power-driven hand tools	94.9	92.7	94.0						-0.4	
2819	Other general-purpose machinery	984.5	1069.9	1097.2						4.4	
282	Special-purpose machinery	3504.2	3747.6	3841.7						82.2	
2821	Agricultural and forestry machinery	258.5	284.4	302.6						7.3	
2822	Metal-forming machinery and machine tools	542.6	591.3	592.9	...	...	...	...	...	15.9	...

Code	Description										
2823	Machinery for metallurgy	214.3	214.2	223.7	:	:	:	:	:	:	7.0
2824	Mining, quarrying and construction machinery	1221.3	1249.8	1189.5	:	:	:	:	:	:	23.9
2825	Food/beverage/tobacco processing machinery	97.3	108.0	122.7	:	:	:	:	:	:	1.8
2826	Textile/apparel/leather production machinery	202.3	203.3	201.5	:	:	:	:	:	:	1.8
2829	Other special-purpose machinery	967.8	1096.6	1208.8	:	:	:	:	:	:	24.5
2910	Motor vehicles	3288.1	3692.5	3709.9	:	:	:	:	:	:	32.0
2920	Automobile bodies, trailers and semi-trailers	145.4	162.9	157.5	:	:	:	:	:	:	-0.3
2930	Parts and accessories for motor vehicles	2601.7	2997.8	3304.2	:	:	:	:	:	:	122.1
301	Building of ships and boats	541.1	576.8	599.3	:	:	:	:	:	:	-4.4
3011	Building of ships and floating structures	536.2	571.8	593.9	:	:	:	:	:	:	-4.4
3012	Building of pleasure and sporting boats	4.9	4.9	5.5	:	:	:	:	:	:	-
3020	Railway locomotives and rolling stock	345.1	425.1	452.0	:	:	:	:	:	:	2.6
3030	Air and spacecraft and related machinery	232.8	242.6	258.5	:	:	:	:	:	:	-6.9
3040	Military fighting vehicles	...	...	...	:	:	:	:	:	:	7.9
309	Transport equipment n.e.c.	464.3	505.0	524.9	:	:	:	:	:	:	7.9
3091	Motorcycles	368.4	404.4	416.5	:	:	:	:	:	:	10.7
3092	Bicycles and invalid carriages	75.2	78.4	84.2	:	:	:	:	:	:	-2.0
3099	Other transport equipment n.e.c.	20.8	22.3	24.2	:	:	:	:	:	:	-0.8
3100	Furniture	664.2	727.3	788.1	:	:	:	:	:	:	14.1
321	Jewellery, bijouterie and related articles	475.6	571.1	571.6	:	:	:	:	:	:	7.4
3211	Jewellery and related articles	335.8	403.2	373.2	:	:	:	:	:	:	2.8
3212	Imitation jewellery and related articles	139.8	167.9	198.3	:	:	:	:	:	:	4.6
3220	Musical instruments	30.0	33.1	36.7	:	:	:	:	:	:	1.0
3230	Sports goods	114.7	130.5	138.9	:	:	:	:	:	:	2.8
3240	Games and toys	210.9	237.3	267.0	:	:	:	:	:	:	7.1
3250	Medical and dental instruments and supplies	210.6	246.6	274.2	:	:	:	:	:	:	-21.4
3290	Other manufacturing n.e.c.	204.5	227.4	238.0	:	:	:	:	:	:	2.5
331	Repair of fabricated metal products/machinery	91.8	84.2	96.4	:	:	:	:	:	:	4.4
3311	Repair of fabricated metal products	6.8	6.2	7.2	:	:	:	:	:	:	0.3
3312	Repair of machinery	13.3	11.3	8.0	:	:	:	:	:	:	-0.8
3313	Repair of electronic and optical equipment	0.1	0.2	0.2	:	:	:	:	:	:	-
3314	Repair of electrical equipment	2.5	2.8	2.3	:	:	:	:	:	:	-
3315	Repair of transport equip., excl. motor vehicles	63.3	57.5	72.1	:	:	:	:	:	:	4.8
3319	Repair of other equipment	5.8	6.2	6.5	:	:	:	:	:	:	-
3320	Installation of industrial machinery/equipment	...	...	...	:	:	:	:	:	:	...
C	Total manufacturing	90175.5	96998.9	98406.6	:	:	18186.8	19562.0	20242.0	:	1306.8

a/ Refers to net increase of fixed assets.

China, Hong Kong SAR

Supplier of information:
Census and Statistics Department, Hong Kong SAR.

Basic source of data:
Annual survey.

Major deviations from ISIC (Revision 4):
Data presented in accordance with ISIC (Revision 4) were originally classified according to Hong Kong Standard Industrial Classification (HSIC) system.

Reference period:
Calendar year.

Scope:
All privately owned establishments.

Method of data collection:
Mail questionnaires; direct interview in the field.

Type of enumeration:
Sample survey.

Adjusted for non-response:
Yes.

Concepts and definitions of variables:
Wages and salaries is compensation of employees.
Output refers to gross output.
Value added refers to total value added.

Related national publications:
Key Statistics on Business Performance and Operating Characteristics of the Industrial Sector, published by the Census and Statistics Department, Hong Kong SAR.

China, Hong Kong SAR

ISIC Revision 4

ISIC	Industry	Number of establishments (number)					Number of employees (number)					Wages and salaries paid to employees (millions of Hong Kong Dollars)				
		Note	2013	2014	2015	2016	Note	2013	2014	2015	2016	Note	2013	2014	2015	2016
10	Food products	a/	788	822	871	872	a/	26200	28000	28800	29100	a/	4826	5132	5467	5682
11	Beverages		...	...	...	...		...	...	...	...		...	...	...	...
12	Tobacco products	a/	12	13	16	19	a/	3200	3100	3200	3300	a/	942	976	1036	1109
13	Textiles	b/	...	...	...	...	b/	...	...	...	...	b/	...	...	...	...
14	Wearing apparel	b/	1350	1140	989	834	b/	11600	8500	6800	6100	b/	2107	1486	1340	1199
15	Leather and related products	c/	...	...	...	...	c/	...	...	...	...	c/	...	...	...	...
16	Wood products, excluding furniture	c/	...	...	...	...	c/	...	...	...	...	c/	...	...	...	...
17	Paper and paper products	d/	...	...	...	...	d/	...	...	...	...	d/	...	...	...	...
18	Printing and reproduction of recorded media	d/	2638	2401	2221	2109	d/	16700	15000	13100	12600	d/	3519	3135	2760	2667
19	Coke and refined petroleum products	e/	...	...	...	...	e/	...	...	...	...	e/	...	...	...	...
20	Chemicals and chemical products	f/	...	...	...	...	f/	...	...	...	...	f/	...	...	...	...
21	Pharmaceuticals,medicinal chemicals, etc.	f/	293	317	308	308	f/	6000	6600	6200	6000	f/	1312	1525	1556	1589
22	Rubber and plastics products	e/	...	...	...	...	e/	...	...	...	...	e/	...	...	...	...
23	Other non-metallic mineral products	e/	435	418	417	404	e/	3600	3600	3500	3500	e/	1007	1044	1165	1207
24	Basic metals	g/	...	...	...	...	g/	...	...	...	...	g/	...	...	...	...
25	Fabricated metal products, except machinery	g/	686	634	605	607	g/	3100	2800	2700	2800	g/	743	695	693	752
26	Computer, electronic and optical products	h/	264	264	251	227	h/	5000	4900	4700	4100	h/	1115	1118	1000	927
27	Electrical equipment	h/	...	...	...	...	h/	...	...	...	...	h/	...	...	...	...
28	Machinery and equipment n.e.c.	i/	319	291	266	258	i/	2000	1800	1700	1500	i/	427	371	348	359
29	Motor vehicles, trailers and semi-trailers	i/	...	...	...	...	i/	...	...	...	...	i/	...	...	...	...
30	Other transport equipment	i/	...	...	...	...	i/	...	...	...	...	i/	...	...	...	...
31	Furniture	c/	...	...	...	...	c/	...	...	...	...	c/	...	...	...	...
32	Other manufacturing	c/	1652	1610	1505	1423	c/	5700	6000	5500	4700	c/	1178	1226	1177	1138
33	Repair and installation of machinery/equipment		921	998	995	976		12200	13200	12900	13900		4123	4552	4564	5011
C	Total manufacturing		9358	8908	8444	8037		95300	93600	89000	87600		21300	21260	21106	21640

a/ 12 includes 11.
b/ 14 includes 13.
c/ 32 includes 15, 16 and 31.
d/ 18 includes 17.
e/ 23 includes 19 and 22.
f/ 21 includes 20.
g/ 25 includes 24.
h/ 26 includes 27.
i/ 28 includes 29 and 30.

China, Hong Kong SAR

ISIC Revision 4			Output at producers' prices					Value added at producers' prices					Gross fixed capital formation	
			(millions of Hong Kong Dollars)					(millions of Hong Kong Dollars)					(millions of Hong Kong Dollars)	
ISIC	Industry	Note	2013	2014	2015	2016	Note	2013	2014	2015	2016	Note	2015	2016
10	Food products		27506	26292	28445	28134		7658	7921	7608	7982		1595	1256
11	Beverages	a/	...	...	...	...	a/	...	...	...	...	a/	...	...
12	Tobacco products	a/	7162	7590	7653	7616	a/	2295	2497	2582	2550	a/	195	321
13	Textiles	b/	...	...	...	...	b/	...	...	...	...	b/	...	...
14	Wearing apparel	b/	10010	5267	4431	4946	b/	2735	1864	1660	1573	b/	30	27
15	Leather and related products	c/	...	...	...	...	c/	...	...	...	...	c/	...	...
16	Wood products, excluding furniture	c/	...	...	...	...	c/	...	...	...	...	c/	...	...
17	Paper and paper products	d/	...	...	...	...	d/	...	...	...	...	d/	...	...
18	Printing and reproduction of recorded media	d/	15116	12341	11265	9606	d/	5243	4405	3960	3611	d/	164	254
19	Coke and refined petroleum products	e/	...	...	...	...	e/	...	...	...	...	e/	...	...
20	Chemicals and chemical products	f/	...	...	...	...	f/	...	...	...	...	f/	...	...
21	Pharmaceuticals, medicinal chemicals, etc.	f/	11432	13141	10657	10154	f/	3044	3481	3227	3792	f/	268	207
22	Rubber and plastics products	e/	...	...	...	...	e/	...	...	...	...	e/	...	...
23	Other non-metallic mineral products	e/	8386	7815	9085	8492	e/	1824	1782	1780	1938	e/	259	274
24	Basic metals	g/	...	...	...	...	g/	...	...	...	...	g/	...	...
25	Fabricated metal products, except machinery	g/	52695	51011	66031	93647	g/	1167	1162	1176	1133	g/	35	150
26	Computer, electronic and optical products	h/	6815	6257	5668	5178	h/	1752	1646	1520	1501	h/	372	83
27	Electrical equipment	h/	...	...	...	...	h/	...	...	...	...	h/	...	...
28	Machinery and equipment n.e.c.	i/	2180	2217	1709	1995	i/	780	722	769	789	i/	-246	5
29	Motor vehicles, trailers and semi-trailers	i/	...	...	...	...	i/	...	...	...	...	i/	...	...
30	Other transport equipment	i/	...	...	...	...	i/	...	...	...	...	i/	...	...
31	Furniture	c/	...	...	...	...	c/	...	...	...	...	c/	...	...
32	Other manufacturing	c/	14811	14527	12749	12770	c/	2484	2358	2225	2161	c/	62	78
33	Repair and installation of machinery/equipment		19310	17022	17560	18232		6444	6550	6607	6420		416	443
C	Total manufacturing		175423	163480	175254	200768		35426	34389	33114	33450		3149	3100

a/ 12 includes 11.
b/ 14 includes 13.
c/ 32 includes 15, 16 and 31.
d/ 18 includes 17.
e/ 23 includes 19 and 22.
f/ 21 includes 20.
g/ 25 includes 24.
h/ 26 includes 27.
i/ 28 includes 29 and 30.

China, Hong Kong SAR

			Index numbers of industrial production

ISIC Revision 4		Note	2005	2006	2007	2008	2009	2010	2011	2012	2013	2014	2015	2016
ISIC	Industry							(2010=100)						
10	Food products	a/	74	81	93	95	94	100	107	112	117	124	130	135
11	Beverages	a/	...	...	...	...	...	...	...	...	...	...	...	...
12	Tobacco products	a/	...	...	...	...	...	...	...	...	...	...	...	...
13	Textiles	b/	223	220	192	155	113	100	89	75	67	62	55	52
14	Wearing apparel	b/	...	...	...	...	...	...	...	...	...	...	...	...
15	Leather and related products	c/	86	91	98	98	94	100	106	111	117	115	113	109
16	Wood products, excluding furniture	c/	...	...	...	...	...	...	...	...	...	...	...	...
17	Paper and paper products	d/	102	105	107	107	99	100	101	98	94	93	93	93
18	Printing and reproduction of recorded media	d/	...	...	...	...	...	...	...	...	...	...	...	...
19	Coke and refined petroleum products	c/	...	...	...	...	...	...	...	...	...	...	...	...
20	Chemicals and chemical products	c/	...	...	...	...	...	...	...	...	...	...	...	...
21	Pharmaceuticals, medicinal chemicals, etc.	c/	...	...	...	...	...	...	...	...	...	...	...	...
22	Rubber and plastics products	c/	...	...	...	...	...	...	...	...	...	...	...	...
23	Other non-metallic mineral products	c/	...	...	...	...	...	...	...	...	...	...	...	...
24	Basic metals	e/	132	128	113	102	91	100	91	82	76	72	64	63
25	Fabricated metal products, except machinery	e/	...	...	...	...	...	...	...	...	...	...	...	...
26	Computer, electronic and optical products	e/	...	...	...	...	...	...	...	...	...	...	...	...
27	Electrical equipment	e/	...	...	...	...	...	...	...	...	...	...	...	...
28	Machinery and equipment n.e.c.	e/	...	...	...	...	...	...	...	...	...	...	...	...
29	Motor vehicles, trailers and semi-trailers	e/	...	...	...	...	...	...	...	...	...	...	...	...
30	Other transport equipment	e/	...	...	...	...	...	...	...	...	...	...	...	...
31	Furniture	c/	...	...	...	...	...	...	...	...	...	...	...	...
32	Other manufacturing	c/	...	...	...	...	...	...	...	...	...	...	...	...
33	Repair and installation of machinery/equipment	c/	...	...	...	...	...	...	...	...	...	...	...	...
C	Total manufacturing		112	114	113	105	97	100	101	100	100	100	98	98

a/ 10 includes 11 and 12.
b/ 13 includes 14.
c/ 15 includes 16, 19, 20, 21, 22, 23, 31, 32 and 33.
d/ 17 includes 18.
e/ 24 includes 25, 26, 27, 28, 29 and 30.

China, Macao SAR

Supplier of information:
Statistics and Census Service, Macao SAR.

Basic source of data:
Industrial survey.

Major deviations from ISIC (Revision 3):
Data presented in accordance with ISIC (Revision 3) were originally classified according to the national classification system - Classification of Economic Activities of Macao (CAM).

Reference period:
Calendar year.

Scope:
All establishments.

Method of data collection:
Questionnaires; direct interview in the field.

Type of enumeration:
Sample survey.

Adjusted for non-response:
Yes.

Concepts and definitions of variables:
Output refers to gross output.
Value added refers to total value added.

Related national publications:
Brief report on Industrial Survey, published by the Statistics and Census Service, Macao SAR.

China, Macao SAR

ISIC Revision 3			Number of establishments (number)					Number of persons engaged (number)					Wages and salaries paid to employees (millions of Macao Patacas)				
ISIC	Industry	Note	2013	2014	2015	2016	Note	2013	2014	2015	2016	Note	2013	2014	2015	2016
15	Food and beverages		283	283	317	345		4074	4461	4655	4707		396.1	468.6	517.5	543.1
16	Tobacco products		...	...	...	...		...	...	...	...		...	...	...	...
17	Textiles		21	21	18	10		498	506	406	315		55.8	61.1	55.0	49.1
18	Wearing apparel, fur		171	139	135	129		2873	1716	1356	1237		210.7	143.3	108.1	113.5
19	Leather, leather products and footwear		...	...	...	...		...	...	...	...		...	...	...	...
20	Wood products (excl. furniture)		...	...				...	...				...	...		
21	Paper and paper products		...	...				...	...				...	...		
22	Printing and publishing		156	153	177	164		1519	1690	1857	1818		183.2	227.0	268.6	256.3
23	Coke,refined petroleum products,nuclear fuel		...	...				...	...				...	...		
24	Chemicals and chemical products		...	...				...	...				...	...		
25	Rubber and plastics products		...	...	...	...		...	...	...	...		...	...	...	...
26	Non-metallic mineral products		18	16	13	13		486	502	493	469		94.4	108.5	114.1	102.7
27	Basic metals		...	...				...	...				...	...		
28	Fabricated metal products		...	...				...	...				...	...		
29	Machinery and equipment n.e.c.		...	...	...	...		...	...	...	...		...	...	...	...
30	Office, accounting and computing machinery		...	...				...	...				...	...		
31	Electrical machinery and apparatus		...	...				...	...				...	...		
32	Radio,television and communication equipment		...	...				...	...				...	...		
33	Medical, precision and optical instruments		...	...				...	...				...	...		
34	Motor vehicles, trailers, semi-trailers		...	...	...	...		...	...	...	...		...	...	...	...
35	Other transport equipment	a/	...	...			a/	...	...			a/	...	...		
36	Furniture; manufacturing n.e.c.		259	245	234	216		2551	2336	2068	2394		317.5	314.0	292.8	349.1
37	Recycling		...	...				...	...				...	...		
D	Total manufacturing		908	857	894	877		11999	11211	10835	10940		1257.6	1322.5	1356.1	1413.7

a/ 36 includes 16,19,20,21,24,25,28,29,30,31,32,33,34,35 and 37.

China, Macao SAR

ISIC Revision 3		Note	Output at producers' prices (millions of Macao Patacas)				Note	Value added at producers' prices (millions of Macao Patacas)				Note	Gross fixed capital formation (millions of Macao Patacas)	
ISIC	Industry		2013	2014	2015	2016		2013	2014	2015	2016		2015	2016
15	Food and beverages		1328.0	1797.0	1740.8	1887.0		554.8	573.9	689.8	774.1		40.3	168.9
16	Tobacco products		...	...	...	...		...	...	...	...		...	...
17	Textiles		478.6	530.6	381.4	381.1		68.9	76.1	62.9	65.4		23.0	25.4
18	Wearing apparel, fur		1111.5	621.8	524.6	434.3		228.1	149.6	131.2	169.4		5.4	8.4
19	Leather, leather products and footwear		...	...	...	...		...	...	...	...		...	...
20	Wood products (excl. furniture)		...	...	...	...		...	...	...	...		...	...
21	Paper and paper products		...	...	...	...		...	...	...	...		...	...
22	Printing and publishing		462.8	635.2	762.4	797.9		182.0	248.4	308.3	286.9		44.6	37.6
23	Coke,refined petroleum products,nuclear fuel		...	...	...	...		...	...	...	...		...	...
24	Chemicals and chemical products		...	...	...	...		...	...	...	...		...	...
25	Rubber and plastics products		...	...	...	...		...	...	...	...		...	...
26	Non-metallic mineral products		1732.2	2238.0	2057.7	1624.9		255.5	390.0	514.9	410.4		49.1	9.4
27	Basic metals		...	...	...	...		...	...	...	...		...	...
28	Fabricated metal products		...	...	...	...		...	...	...	...		...	...
29	Machinery and equipment n.e.c.		...	...	...	...		...	...	...	...		...	...
30	Office, accounting and computing machinery		...	...	...	...		...	...	...	...		...	...
31	Electrical machinery and apparatus		...	...	...	...		...	...	...	...		...	...
32	Radio,television and communication equipment		...	...	...	...		...	...	...	...		...	...
33	Medical, precision and optical instruments		...	...	...	...		...	...	...	...		...	...
34	Motor vehicles, trailers, semi-trailers		...	...	...	...		...	...	...	...		...	...
35	Other transport equipment		...	...	...	...		...	...	...	...		...	...
36	Furniture; manufacturing n.e.c.	a/	1643.0	1752.8	1680.3	1757.8	a/	444.4	474.3	458.3	601.0	a/	-16.7	7.7
37	Recycling		...	...	...	...		...	...	...	...		...	...
D	Total manufacturing		6756.1	7575.4	7147.2	6882.9		1733.7	1912.4	2165.5	2307.2		145.7	257.3

a/ 36 includes 16,19,20,21,24,25,28,29,30,31,32,33,34,35 and 37.

China, Macao SAR

ISIC Revision 3

Index numbers of industrial production

(2010=100)

ISIC	Industry	Note	2005	2006	2007	2008	2009	2010	2011	2012	2013	2014	2015	2016
15	Food and beverages		...	...	...	...	...	...	...	...	...	...	...	...
16	Tobacco products		...	...	...	...	...	...	...	...	...	...	...	...
17	Textiles		...	...	...	...	...	...	...	...	...	...	...	...
18	Wearing apparel, fur		...	...	...	...	...	...	...	...	...	...	...	...
19	Leather, leather products and footwear		...	...	...	...	...	...	...	...	...	...	...	...
20	Wood products (excl. furniture)		...	...	...	...	...	...	...	...	...	...	...	...
21	Paper and paper products		...	...	...	...	...	...	...	...	...	...	...	...
22	Printing and publishing		...	...	...	...	...	...	...	...	...	...	...	...
23	Coke,refined petroleum products,nuclear fuel		...	...	...	...	...	...	...	...	...	...	...	...
24	Chemicals and chemical products		...	...	...	...	...	...	...	...	...	...	...	...
25	Rubber and plastics products		...	...	...	...	...	...	...	...	...	...	...	...
26	Non-metallic mineral products		...	...	...	...	...	...	...	...	...	...	...	...
27	Basic metals		...	...	...	...	...	...	...	...	...	...	...	...
28	Fabricated metal products		...	...	...	...	...	...	...	...	...	...	...	...
29	Machinery and equipment n.e.c.		...	...	...	...	...	...	...	...	...	...	...	...
30	Office, accounting and computing machinery		...	...	...	...	...	...	...	...	...	...	...	...
31	Electrical machinery and apparatus		...	...	...	...	...	...	...	...	...	...	...	...
32	Radio,television and communication equipment		...	...	...	...	...	...	...	...	...	...	...	...
33	Medical, precision and optical instruments		...	...	...	...	...	...	...	...	...	...	...	...
34	Motor vehicles, trailers, semi-trailers		...	...	...	...	...	...	...	...	...	...	...	...
35	Other transport equipment		...	...	...	...	...	...	...	...	...	...	...	...
36	Furniture; manufacturing n.e.c.		...	...	...	...	...	...	...	...	...	...	...	...
37	Recycling		...	...	...	...	...	...	...	...	...	...	...	...
D	Total manufacturing		326	323	306	207	95	100	126	161	188	214	205	229

Colombia

Concepts and definitions of variables:
Wages and salaries excludes housing and family allowances paid directly by the employer. Output excludes value of goods shipped in the same condition as received less the amount paid for these goods and value of fixed assets produced by the unit for its own use.

Supplier of information:
Departamento Administrativo Nacional de Estadística, Bogotá.

Basic source of data:
Annual census/exhaustive survey.

Major deviations from ISIC (Revision 4):
Data presented in accordance with ISIC (Revision 4) were originally classified according to the national classification system.

Reference period:
Calendar year.

Scope:
Establishments with 10 or more employees.

Method of data collection:
Online survey (self entry).

Type of enumeration:
Complete enumeration.

Adjusted for non-response:
Yes.

Related national publications:
Encuesta Mensual Manufacturera (EMM); Muestra Trimestral Manufacturera Regional (MTMR); Encuesta de Desarrollo e Innovación Tecnológica (EDIT) Industria, all published by Departamento Administrativo Nacional de Estadística, Bogotá.

Colombia

- 222 -

ISIC Revision 4		Number of establishments (number)					Number of employees (number)					Wages and salaries paid to employees (millions of Colombian Pesos)				
ISIC	Industry	Note	2013	2014	2015	2016	Note	2013	2014	2015	2016	Note	2013	2014	2015	2016
1010	Processing/preserving of meat		201	201	198	195		24174	25742	29682	31680		279341	316287	354984	401273
1020	Processing/preserving of fish, etc.		7	6	6	7		3812	3432	3367	3316		10497	11941	14125	13680
1030	Processing/preserving of fruit, vegetables		64	65	63	61		3054	3257	3669	3772		30327	32903	39622	45805
1040	Vegetable and animal oils and fats		78	79	77	76		8069	8434	9321	9374		144053	145811	163247	167891
1050	Dairy products		182	182	178	168		19319	19615	21969	22430		304464	314820	325009	314471
106	Grain mill products,starches and starch products		158	154	150	150		9721	8948	10217	11056		125037	133642	159821	179181
1061	Grain mill products		149	145	142	141		9244	8424	9469	10294		110821	119392	139129	156001
1062	Starches and starch products		9	9	8	9		477	524	748	762		14216	14250	20692	23180
107	Other food products		787	779	774	707		58149	60925	66095	67333		829638	902061	1007109	1075956
1071	Bakery products		542	538	535	481		25637	26592	27969	29370		277826	307583	322648	355293
1072	Sugar		18	17	18	17		6729	6793	7893	7967		172520	184175	219983	230211
1073	Cocoa, chocolate and sugar confectionery		60	59	57	51		9128	9509	9940	9130		121527	122094	132925	115738
1074	Macaroni, noodles, couscous, etc.		18	18	18	16		1522	1549	1651	1657		28345	30241	33341	36440
1075	Prepared meals and dishes		7	7	7	8		155	175	192	251		1335	1811	1985	2477
1079	Other food products n.e.c.		142	140	139	134		14978	16307	18450	18958		228086	256159	296227	335798
1080	Prepared animal feeds		84	78	77	79		6387	6529	7719	8125		122594	136855	148027	168341
110	Beverages		136	136	138	131		13899	14076	16352	19047		316077	320994	343957	419678
1101	Distilling, rectifying and blending of spirits		20	20	19	18		1437	1458	1516	1483		30087	36878	37039	39497
1102	Wines		20	20	21	17		456	421	420	395		5982	5469	5561	5646
1103	Malt liquors and malt		13	13	13	13		2222	2159	2848	3059		78857	78992	112361	128524
1104	Soft drinks,mineral waters,other bottled waters		83	83	85	83		9784	10038	11568	14110		201151	199656	188996	246012
1200	Tobacco products		…	…	…	…		…	…	…	…		…	…	…	…
131	Spinning, weaving and finishing of textiles		133	127	120	113		18188	16476	17787	17382		229793	220279	227590	243724
1311	Preparation and spinning of textile fibres		21	19	17	18		3427	2799	2706	2816		33168	27689	30823	36769
1312	Weaving of textiles		44	42	38	36		10386	8848	9766	9084		156923	145461	146402	151382
1313	Finishing of textiles		68	66	65	59		4375	4829	5315	5482		39703	47130	50365	55574
139	Other textiles		203	199	193	178		17601	17872	20219	20560		219853	234052	251107	267001
1391	Knitted and crocheted fabrics		35	34	29	30		7558	7862	8518	8982		125996	131642	127352	135797
1392	Made-up textile articles, except apparel		83	84	79	74		5846	5820	6439	6661		41405	44360	49555	53814
1393	Carpets and rugs		13	12	12	13		508	488	573	538		6226	6786	7060	7572
1394	Cordage, rope, twine and netting		24	22	23	16		1025	976	1007	871		10466	11276	11560	10974
1399	Other textiles n.e.c.		48	47	50	45		2664	2726	3682	3508		35760	39988	55580	58843
1410	Wearing apparel, except fur apparel		990	958	930	864		61027	63322	72251	74724		598420	663457	733671	820146
1420	Articles of fur		…	…	…	…		…	…	…	…		…	…	…	…
1430	Knitted and crocheted apparel		47	44	42	34		3741	4361	2615	2666		49136	57856	25886	27589
151	Leather;luggage,handbags,saddlery,harness;fur		122	114	106	89		6213	5637	5840	5659		65445	68790	65819	74908
1511	Tanning/dressing of leather; dressing of fur		47	46	45	40		2188	2226	2481	2253		21426	25626	26665	27372
1512	Luggage,handbags,etc.;saddlery/harness		49	43	40	32		2141	1916	1958	2010		23120	20245	19041	20620
1520	Footwear		249	236	225	277		13611	14268	15013	16735		134877	150224	144468	173335
1610	Sawmilling and planing of wood		66	63	61	55		1485	1526	1567	1614		16502	17711	19663	21410

Code	Description												
162	Wood products, cork, straw, plaiting materials	122	117	141	...	4604	4406	...	...	46688	45615	...	...	22652
1621	Veneer sheets and wood-based panels	21	17	19	18	1821	1522	1505	1706	20967	17551	19313	20721
1622	Builders' carpentry and joinery	39	40	60	56	1306	1491	2150	1998	11486	13840	20081	9162
1623	Wooden containers	38	39	37	34	1014	942	998	909	9632	9471	9770	6327
1629	Other wood products;articles of cork,straw	24	21	25	23	463	451	633	587	4603	4754	6526	6526
170	Paper and paper products	161	158	144	146	14912	15534	17243	18309	284356	299974	361086	401430
1701	Pulp, paper and paperboard	35	37	34	32	3659	3648	4070	3920	101742	102467	119627	124945
1702	Corrugated paper and paperboard	64	62	55	60	4632	4890	5052	5865	73802	82533	92674	113838
1709	Other articles of paper and paperboard	62	59	55	54	6621	6996	8121	8524	108813	114973	148786	162647
181	Printing and service activities related to printing	496	478	525	453	19521	18635	23330	21932	249865	257937	320840	331227
1811	Printing	455	442	490	424	18614	17773	22361	21121	239430	247317	307833	320127
1812	Service activities related to printing	41	36	35	29	907	862	969	811	10435	10620	13008	11100
1820	Reproduction of recorded media	...	...	...	...	...	...	...	...	...	...	...	...
1910	Coke oven products	11	11	11	11	724	709	639	563	7987	9620	6765	6660
1920	Refined petroleum products	112	111	110	112	3823	3817	4520	4761	130135	144473	182009	197470
201	Basic chemicals,fertilizers, etc.	175	168	165	157	8829	8402	10569	10804	201792	195666	262545	279420
2011	Basic chemicals	97	91	91	87	4708	4339	5494	5602	91856	88873	120820	129701
2012	Fertilizers and nitrogen compounds	50	50	48	44	2578	2414	3036	3089	70725	60899	78693	84194
2013	Plastics and synthetic rubber in primary forms	27	26	26	26	1500	1613	2039	2113	38979	45685	63031	65526
202	Other chemical products	449	440	433	406	36939	37306	41249	42642	659711	678818	774085	815155
2021	Pesticides and other agrochemical products	36	35	36	33	2032	1977	2339	2385	45841	50100	51475	59311
2022	Paints,varnishes;printing ink and mastics	88	85	81	77	3609	3529	4104	4042	61809	57715	72829	75589
2023	Soap,cleaning and cosmetic preparations	196	197	188	178	26178	26523	28125	29186	435316	450993	495616	511887
2029	Other chemical products n.e.c.	129	123	128	118	5120	5277	6681	7029	116744	120009	154165	168367
2030	Man-made fibres	7	6	6	...	1102	1160	1324	...	19801	20305	23821	...
2100	Pharmaceuticals,medicinal chemicals, etc.	219	216	214	207	21602	21877	26373	26399	483265	516273	557148	609150
221	Rubber products	110	105	103	92	4526	4356	4814	4334	68099	61895	67146	61007
2211	Rubber tyres and tubes	33	34	4	...	1123	1203	514	...	15596	16084	10932	...
2219	Other rubber products	71	67	65	59	2568	2719	3005	3034	32054	34369	38122	41620
2220	Plastics products	675	662	638	606	45893	46992	53867	55155	537121	580167	698935	762165
2310	Glass and glass products	78	75	73	72	6778	7110	8021	8608	114054	125562	133721	146060
239	Non-metallic mineral products n.e.c.	419	412	441	429	30252	30720	35275	36095	429695	477684	572826	631672
2391	Refractory products	27	26	24	26	1311	1232	1339	1344	13290	14815	15871	19834
2392	Clay building materials	130	128	130	129	12824	12587	14032	14276	155469	160500	186631	203155
2393	Other porcelain and ceramic products	8	7	7	5	1226	1274	1546	1608	18891	20128	23572	24905
2394	Cement, lime and plaster	38	39	38	40	4152	4515	5566	6081	96238	125117	150086	169658
2395	Articles of concrete, cement and plaster	140	139	171	165	6976	7545	8662	8843	90210	100134	128170	142912
2396	Cutting, shaping and finishing of stone	41	40	39	38	1379	1324	1520	1496	17660	17830	21019	22545
2399	Other non-metallic mineral products n.e.c.	35	33	32	26	2384	2243	2610	2447	37936	39160	47477	48664
2410	Basic iron and steel	124	120	128	122	9611	9534	12301	11920	205781	179618	258878	263370
2420	Basic precious and other non-ferrous metals	46	46	49	44	2505	2429	2735	2683	28865	30991	38188	40316
243	Casting of metals	18	16	15	13	508	505	446	376	5278	5643	5227	4721
2431	Casting of iron and steel	18	16	15	13	508	505	446	376	5278	5643	5227	4721
2432	Casting of non-ferrous metals	...	...	...	...	...	...	...	...	...	...	...	...
251	Struct.metal products, tanks, reservoirs	287	272	269	253	14663	14780	17060	16482	172721	194166	218239	221598

continued

Colombia

ISIC Revision 4

ISIC	Industry	Note	Number of establishments (number)				Note	Number of employees (number)				Note	Wages and salaries paid to employees (millions of Colombian Pesos)			
			2013	2014	2015	2016		2013	2014	2015	2016		2013	2014	2015	2016
2511	Structural metal products		244	229	233	218		12473	12815	15324	15096		143100	166093	188370	196335
2512	Tanks, reservoirs and containers of metal		33	33	26	25		1653	1451	1196	906		23749	21919	21616	17139
2513	Steam generators, excl. hot water boilers		10	10	10	10		537	514	540	480		5872	6153	8253	8124
2520	Weapons and ammunition		3	3	3	…		762	703	852	…		8068	5494	6260	…
259	Other metal products;metal working services		443	440	416	379		19200	19936	21655	21404		238628	268546	285841	306799
2591	Forging,pressing,stamping,roll-forming of metal		92	92	81	80		1851	2177	2448	2230		22253	31098	32996	32365
2592	Treatment and coating of metals machining		52	52	50	44		4386	4529	4842	4582		48393	52810	51373	54023
2593	Cutlery, hand tools and general hardware		299	296	285	255		12963	13230	14365	14592		167981	184639	201472	220411
2599	Other fabricated metal products n.e.c.		…	…	…	…		…	…	…	…		…	…	…	…
2610	Electronic components and boards		…	…	…	…		…	…	…	…		…	…	…	…
2620	Computers and peripheral equipment		…	…	…	…		…	…	…	…		…	…	…	…
2630	Communication equipment		…	…	…	…		…	…	…	…		…	…	…	…
2640	Consumer electronics		…	…	…	…		…	…	…	…		…	…	…	…
265	Measuring,testing equipment; watches, etc.		…	…	…	…		…	…	…	…		…	…	…	…
2651	Measuring/testing/navigating equipment,etc.		…	…	…	…		…	…	…	…		…	…	…	…
2652	Watches and clocks		…	…	…	…		…	…	…	…		…	…	…	…
2660	Irradiation/electromedical equipment,etc.		…	…	…	…		…	…	…	…		…	…	…	…
2670	Optical instruments and photographic equipment		…	…	…	…		…	…	…	…		…	…	…	…
2680	Magnetic and optical media		…	…	…	…		…	…	…	…		…	…	…	…
2710	Electric motors,generators,transformers,etc.		92	91	88	80		7274	7554	8945	8464		161981	185033	218394	211158
2720	Batteries and accumulators		11	11	11	10		1531	1477	1804	2017		25124	24572	34118	40564
273	Wiring and wiring devices		9	9	9	7		1374	1413	1690	1737		25465	27307	39131	46050
2731	Fibre optic cables		…	…	…	…		…	…	…	…		…	…	…	…
2732	Other electronic and electric wires and cables		…	…	…	…		…	…	…	…		…	…	…	…
2733	Wiring devices		9	9	…	…		1374	1413	1690	1737		25465	27307	39131	46050
2740	Electric lighting equipment		36	35	33	30		1986	1858	1955	1896		30745	28908	29550	28243
2750	Domestic appliances		27	26	26	25		6004	6065	6903	7271		71741	79900	86868	103956
2790	Other electrical equipment		44	41	43	36		1425	1306	1660	1604		16801	15890	19745	20913
281	General-purpose machinery		259	248	254	221		11698	11319	13736	13457		140083	148309	188049	189761
2811	Engines/turbines,excl.aircraft,vehicle engines		6	7	6	5		238	270	335	317		3782	4254	5794	5621
2812	Fluid power equipment		…	…	…	…		…	…	…	…		…	…	…	…
2813	Other pumps, compressors, taps and valves		37	34	38	32		2476	2442	2795	2585		34317	36154	45034	41958
2814	Bearings, gears, gearing and driving elements		22	20	20	16		661	599	736	684		8436	8793	11247	11816
2815	Ovens, furnaces and furnace burners		9	8	11	9		408	390	569	512		5610	5393	7712	7181
2816	Lifting and handling equipment		35	35	32	33		1514	1479	1682	1732		21923	23834	26482	25911
2817	Office machinery, excl.computers,etc.		…	…	…	…		…	…	…	…		…	…	…	…
2818	Power-driven hand tools		…	…	…	…		…	…	…	…		…	…	…	…
2819	Other general-purpose machinery		150	144	147	126		6401	6139	7619	7627		66015	69882	91779	97273
282	Special-purpose machinery		290	278	245	198		8429	8378	8863	7967		118992	125687	133229	131776
2821	Agricultural and forestry machinery		28	27	29	30		1280	1242	1708	1835		17113	17396	22096	26907
2822	Metal-forming machinery and machine tools		16	16	17	13		305	305	371	338		2830	3114	4232	4578

2823 Machinery for metallurgy	..	..	..	..	1295	1254	1571	1422	16177	18670	24268	24538
2824 Mining, quarrying and construction machinery	29	27	23	22	1965	1784	1634	1534	28998	26862	25703	27693
2825 Food/beverage/tobacco processing machinery	50	46	41	37	77	73	..	40	826	772	..	525
2826 Textile/apparel/leather production machinery	159	155	135	92	3507	3720	3579	2798	53049	58872	56931	47536
2829 Other special-purpose machinery	16	16	15	15	2837	3503	3695	3243	95230	113621	107338	113692
2910 Motor vehicles	79	76	74	69	4930	5453	5613	5056	44924	53716	62093	67434
2920 Automobile bodies, trailers and semi-trailers	..	..	..	..	..	..	..	..	..	..	..	..
2930 Parts and accessories for motor vehicles	118	113	104	99	7568	7774	8085	7976	93646	90090	92676	105237
301 Building of ships and boats	4	5	..	..	208	225	..	..	1773	2221	..	..
3011 Building of ships and floating structures	..	..	..	..	..	..	..	..	..	..	..	..
3012 Building of pleasure and sporting boats	..	..	..	..	..	..	..	..	..	..	..	..
3020 Railway locomotives and rolling stock	..	..	..	..	..	..	..	..	..	..	..	..
3030 Air and spacecraft and related machinery	..	..	..	..	..	..	..	..	..	..	..	..
3040 Military fighting vehicles	..	..	..	..	..	..	..	..	..	..	..	..
309 Transport equipment n.e.c.	35	34	36	33	5991	6454	7289	7296	82190	91652	103382	113134
3091 Motorcycles	23	23	24	23	5711	6207	7056	7082	78678	88597	100633	110499
3092 Bicycles and invalid carriages	7	6	6	6	100	83	96	115	819	755	829	1140
3099 Other transport equipment n.e.c.	5	5	6	4	180	164	137	99	2692	2301	1920	1495
3100 Furniture	495	469	376	335	22921	22602	18266	18152	232400	250740	194590	205319
321 Jewellery, bijouterie and related articles	26	24	23	21	1994	1701	1787	1651	17700	16025	19966	19382
3211 Jewellery and related articles	26	24	23	21	1994	1701	1787	1651	17700	16025	19966	19382
3212 Imitation jewellery and related articles	..	..	..	..	..	..	..	..	..	..	..	..
3220 Musical instruments	..	..	..	..	..	..	..	..	..	..	..	..
3230 Sports goods	13	13	11	12	531	546	608	638	6068	6821	6873	8315
3240 Games and toys	31	30	28	24	2109	2333	2351	2309	25544	29631	27376	29281
3250 Medical and dental instruments and supplies	74	68	71	67	3017	2821	3551	4105	42782	39696	48111	59443
3290 Other manufacturing n.e.c.	185	183	197	222	8664	8257	10876	15037	136965	146434	151230	239300
331 Repair of fabricated metal products/machinery	..	..	..	..	..	..	..	..	..	..	..	..
3311 Repair of fabricated metal products	..	..	..	..	..	..	..	..	..	..	..	..
3312 Repair of machinery	..	..	..	..	..	..	..	..	..	..	..	..
3313 Repair of electronic and optical equipment	..	..	..	..	..	..	..	..	..	..	..	..
3314 Repair of electrical equipment	..	..	..	..	..	..	..	..	..	..	..	..
3315 Repair of transport equip., excl. motor vehicles	..	..	..	..	..	..	..	..	..	..	..	..
3319 Repair of other equipment	..	..	..	..	..	..	..	..	..	..	..	..
3320 Installation of industrial machinery/equipment	..	..	..	..	..	..	..	..	..	..	..	..
C Total manufacturing	9420	9157	9015	8466	620070	628993	708730	723459	8805666	9377467	10565659	11451587

Colombia

ISIC Revision 4		Note	Output at basic prices (billions of Colombian Pesos)				Note	Value added at basic prices (billions of Colombian Pesos)				Note	Gross fixed capital formation (billions of Colombian Pesos)	
ISIC	Industry		2013	2014	2015	2016		2013	2014	2015	2016		2015	2016
1010	Processing/preserving of meat		7244.5	7866.5	8731.0	9941.7		2472.6	2666.5	2808.9	3184.7		…	…
1020	Processing/preserving of fish, etc.		630.6	617.5	549.8	645.3		136.7	122.0	103.2	134.4		…	…
1030	Processing/preserving of fruit, vegetables		435.5	537.7	534.4	599.2		185.6	239.3	248.8	272.0		…	…
1040	Vegetable and animal oils and fats		3543.4	4060.2	4544.5	5064.0		968.6	1121.0	1149.4	1400.8		…	…
1050	Dairy products		6642.1	7041.3	7668.2	8251.2		2775.5	2882.5	3097.2	3308.4		…	…
106	Grain mill products, starches and starch products		5218.4	5323.0	6295.5	7133.5		1436.1	1462.5	1710.7	2030.7		…	…
1061	Grain mill products		4789.6	4860.9	5799.1	6578.3		1304.4	1319.3	1529.3	1814.6		…	…
1062	Starches and starch products		428.7	462.1	496.4	555.2		131.6	143.2	181.3	216.0		…	…
107	Other food products		13188.3	14115.3	16177.2	18349.5		5948.4	6458.5	7625.9	8449.9		…	…
1071	Bakery products		3070.3	3314.1	3573.0	3959.2		1605.1	1725.4	1819.4	1998.4		…	…
1072	Sugar		3621.2	4048.6	5078.2	5716.4		1426.3	1679.2	2441.0	2823.4		…	…
1073	Cocoa, chocolate and sugar confectionery		2128.0	2318.2	2326.8	2501.3		918.1	983.0	941.3	859.8		…	…
1074	Macaroni, noodles, couscous, etc.		358.8	370.7	453.1	564.5		179.0	184.1	224.0	285.3		…	…
1075	Prepared meals and dishes		14.4	18.2	17.4	20.0		6.4	8.5	8.1	8.7		…	…
1079	Other food products n.e.c.		3995.6	4045.5	4728.7	5588.2		1813.4	1878.3	2192.2	2474.3		…	…
1080	Prepared animal feeds		4873.9	5314.4	6572.5	7521.8		877.7	878.5	1093.2	1645.5		…	…
110	Beverages		11922.8	12616.1	12235.0	13660.3		8224.8	8759.5	8277.9	8943.7		…	…
1101	Distilling, rectifying and blending of spirits		941.2	916.0	913.7	973.6		667.0	637.7	643.0	664.3		…	…
1102	Wines		53.5	51.5	59.6	61.1		29.9	29.6	34.9	34.6		…	…
1103	Malt liquors and malt		5308.0	5558.9	5937.3	6439.8		4293.2	4585.2	4690.6	4926.4		…	…
1104	Soft drinks,mineral waters,other bottled waters		5620.2	6089.7	5324.4	6185.8		3234.8	3506.9	2909.4	3318.4		…	…
1200	Tobacco products		…	…	…	…		…	…	…	…		…	…
131	Spinning, weaving and finishing of textiles		1955.7	1940.9	2105.6	2282.1		760.5	796.2	926.9	897.8		…	…
1311	Preparation and spinning of textile fibres		404.0	343.5	357.9	384.7		136.4	116.7	96.4	117.0		…	…
1312	Weaving of textiles		1261.4	1276.7	1407.6	1508.1		474.9	514.9	659.4	576.6		…	…
1313	Finishing of textiles		290.2	320.6	340.1	389.3		149.2	164.5	171.1	204.1		…	…
139	Other textiles		2312.7	2412.3	2726.0	2958.5		828.5	920.0	980.7	1133.3		…	…
1391	Knitted and crocheted fabrics		1079.2	1089.6	1161.8	1278.0		382.5	412.1	374.1	446.1		…	…
1392	Made-up textile articles, except apparel		542.6	590.1	693.1	771.6		191.9	218.1	227.8	265.5		…	…
1393	Carpets and rugs		43.9	40.7	40.4	44.5		26.9	25.3	25.0	24.0		…	…
1394	Cordage, rope, twine and netting		92.4	91.4	95.1	84.4		40.6	38.1	41.3	37.8		…	…
1399	Other textiles n.e.c.		554.6	600.6	735.5	779.9		186.6	226.3	312.4	359.9		…	…
1410	Wearing apparel, except fur apparel		5947.3	6373.3	7164.8	8282.5		2604.6	2871.0	3401.6	4132.7		…	…
1420	Articles of fur		…	…	…	…		…	…	…	…		…	…
1430	Knitted and crocheted apparel		286.8	264.6	182.3	182.6		148.2	132.2	97.2	96.9		…	…
151	Leather;luggage,handbags,saddlery,harness;fur		583.5	666.7	656.2	611.7		224.0	251.7	243.2	230.0		…	…
1511	Tanning/dressing of leather; dressing of fur		325.4	416.2	389.7	335.9		104.0	139.7	116.0	99.2		…	…
1512	Luggage,handbags,etc.:saddlery/harness		166.5	171.6	187.8	187.4		82.0	81.5	97.0	93.5		…	…
1520	Footwear		1055.8	1164.2	1161.7	1395.1		499.5	558.1	546.8	660.8		…	…
1610	Sawmilling and planing of wood		207.2	227.2	253.1	260.0		73.9	90.2	108.2	117.5		…	…

Code	Description								
162	Wood products, cork, straw, plaiting materials	647.1	653.1	..	..	312.0	284.9	..	..
1621	Veneer sheets and wood-based panels	426.9	408.6	523.4	602.8	212.9	175.5	253.0	287.7
1622	Builders' carpentry and joinery	95.9	115.8	152.8	153.9	46.4	57.3	66.6	70.6
1623	Wooden containers	88.6	91.7	92.3	89.6	35.7	35.3	33.7	32.4
1629	Other wood products;articles of cork,straw	35.7	37.0	48.3	44.8	17.1	16.8	27.1	25.0
170	Paper and paper products	6514.1	6915.9	7781.6	8402.1	2339.4	2520.9	2987.3	3144.9
1701	Pulp, paper and paperboard	1930.5	2055.5	2299.6	2343.9	640.0	698.5	808.7	790.1
1702	Corrugated paper and paperboard	1456.7	1592.6	1642.3	2020.5	456.8	517.7	531.2	696.1
1709	Other articles of paper and paperboard	3126.9	3267.9	3839.7	4037.8	1242.6	1304.7	1647.5	1658.7
181	Printing and service activities related to printing	2454.5	2476.2	3028.6	3090.5	1105.5	1116.7	1378.6	1326.6
1811	Printing	2380.5	2403.3	2955.5	3024.5	1067.9	1081.3	1344.1	1296.6
1812	Service activities related to printing	74.0	72.9	73.1	66.0	37.6	35.5	34.4	30.0
1820	Reproduction of recorded media	..	..	..	..	..	..	..	..
1910	Coke oven products	245.8	293.7	292.0	252.7	104.4	109.3	118.8	83.6
1920	Refined petroleum products	46580.1	44940.8	39182.4	40591.6	12942.9	11577.5	9332.9	5774.6
201	Basic chemicals,fertilizers, etc.	7010.6	7316.5	8229.8	8713.7	1944.0	1931.6	2321.8	2814.3
2011	Basic chemicals	1845.6	1898.1	2170.8	2485.5	835.2	875.2	1011.0	1201.0
2012	Fertilizers and nitrogen compounds	1817.0	1688.2	2136.4	1956.1	526.4	478.4	596.3	489.5
2013	Plastics and synthetic rubber in primary forms	3332.6	3714.4	3922.5	4272.2	579.0	574.5	714.5	1123.9
202	Other chemical products	13261.5	13590.6	15955.0	17289.9	5980.0	6174.2	7470.5	7869.3
2021	Pesticides and other agrochemical products	1880.6	1817.2	2388.2	2669.3	651.7	678.3	934.6	834.2
2022	Paints, varnishes;printing ink and mastics	1290.4	1370.1	1354.2	1487.1	518.4	534.8	504.8	620.0
2023	Soap,cleaning and cosmetic preparations	6910.5	7110.3	8282.1	9054.8	3670.8	3801.7	4696.6	4967.4
2029	Other chemical products n.e.c.	3180.1	3293.0	3930.5	4078.7	1139.1	1159.4	1334.4	1447.7
2030	Man-made fibres	290.5	351.2	367.4	..	143.7	162.5	170.7	..
2100	Pharmaceuticals,medicinal chemicals, etc.	4930.7	5059.2	6064.1	6425.8	3140.1	3198.6	3855.5	4168.5
221	Rubber products	632.4	535.6	515.9	376.8	247.0	214.2	215.0	188.8
2211	Rubber tyres and tubes	131.2	126.7	168.3	..	55.9	53.4	50.1	..
2219	Other rubber products	202.3	206.5	211.6	242.4	102.5	107.4	112.0	131.6
2220	Plastics products	7674.5	8337.3	9609.9	10092.8	2986.5	3131.3	3661.5	3897.6
2310	Glass and glass products	1380.5	1592.5	1775.3	2050.4	658.9	756.1	876.0	1007.8
239	Non-metallic mineral products n.e.c.	9482.6	9996.1	11509.8	11487.1	5551.2	5710.6	6634.1	6369.2
2391	Refractory products	187.1	198.5	172.7	173.7	96.5	112.7	97.3	97.1
2392	Clay building materials	1781.8	1840.1	2078.7	2190.6	1039.3	1109.2	1300.4	1347.0
2393	Other porcelain and ceramic products	162.0	155.4	181.8	199.3	99.7	93.2	113.5	120.2
2394	Cement, lime and plaster	4485.2	4754.4	5360.3	5303.9	3250.1	3385.9	3879.8	3563.1
2395	Articles of concrete, cement and plaster	2322.3	2512.0	3076.7	2963.9	825.9	778.4	984.8	929.3
2396	Cutting, shaping and finishing of stone	174.9	167.1	240.6	244.6	79.6	72.0	101.4	112.0
2399	Other non-metallic mineral products n.e.c.	369.5	368.6	399.0	411.1	160.1	159.2	156.9	200.5
2410	Basic iron and steel	5251.8	6050.8	6209.1	6102.1	2174.5	2604.9	2198.3	2082.6
2420	Basic precious and other non-ferrous metals	3934.8	4399.1	5490.2	6215.0	252.5	325.8	338.1	354.2
243	Casting of metals	33.4	29.6	25.5	26.1	18.7	17.1	15.5	15.6
2431	Casting of iron and steel	33.4	29.6	25.5	26.1	18.7	17.1	15.5	15.6
2432	Casting of non-ferrous metals	..	..	..	..	..	..	..	..
251	Struct.metal products, tanks, reservoirs	1832.1	1870.2	2213.1	2416.1	736.6	742.0	884.9	848.8

continued

Colombia

ISIC	Industry	Note	Output at basic prices (billions of Colombian Pesos) 2013	2014	2015	2016	Note	Value added at basic prices (billions of Colombian Pesos) 2013	2014	2015	2016	Note	Gross fixed capital formation (billions of Colombian Pesos) 2015	2016
2511	Structural metal products		1547.1	1583.9	2011.0	2258.0		606.9	604.6	783.3	769.0		...	
2512	Tanks, reservoirs and containers of metal		220.3	214.4	152.5	109.0		93.3	95.0	74.8	51.4		...	
2513	Steam generators, excl. hot water boilers		64.7	71.8	49.6	49.0		36.4	42.5	26.8	28.4		...	
2520	Weapons and ammunition		128.5	113.9	70.5	...		57.0	50.9	21.1	...		...	
259	Other metal products;metal working services		2417.9	2640.8	2707.9	2885.3		1096.2	1220.7	1242.7	1332.0		...	
2591	Forging,pressing,stamping,roll-forming of metal		142.0	225.4	207.1	198.3		77.1	158.0	151.8	147.0		...	
2592	Treatment and coating of metals machining		410.9	427.1	468.4	486.4		203.4	213.3	237.7	246.8		...	
2593	Cutlery, hand tools and general hardware		...	...	...	...		...	...	...	...		...	
2599	Other fabricated metal products n.e.c.		1864.9	1988.3	2032.5	2200.6		815.7	849.3	853.2	938.2		...	
2610	Electronic components and boards		...	...	...	...		...	...	...	...		...	
2620	Computers and peripheral equipment		...	...	...	...		...	...	...	...		...	
2630	Communication equipment		...	...	...	...		...	...	...	...		...	
2640	Consumer electronics		...	...	...	...		...	...	...	...		...	
265	Measuring,testing equipment; watches, etc.		...	...	...	...		...	...	...	...		...	
2651	Measuring/testing/navigating equipment,etc.		...	...	...	...		...	...	...	...		...	
2652	Watches and clocks		...	...	...	...		...	...	...	...		...	
2660	Irradiation/electromedical equipment,etc.		...	...	...	...		...	...	...	...		...	
2670	Optical instruments and photographic equipment		...	...	...	...		...	...	...	...		...	
2680	Magnetic and optical media		...	...	...	...		...	...	...	...		...	
2710	Electric motors,generators,transformers,etc.		1372.6	1263.5	1438.8	1336.1		564.5	514.8	595.2	538.6		...	
2720	Batteries and accumulators		365.9	449.6	522.5	602.6		165.4	181.5	235.9	240.5		...	
273	Wiring and wiring devices		949.2	986.3	1169.5	1251.5		230.3	209.2	253.9	263.2		...	
2731	Fibre optic cables		...	...	...	...		...	...	...	...		...	
2732	Other electronic and electric wires and cables		949.2	986.3	1169.5	1251.5		230.3	209.2	253.9	263.2		...	
2733	Wiring devices		213.9	199.1	234.1	222.6		90.1	82.7	107.8	103.2		...	
2740	Electric lighting equipment		...	...	...	...		...	...	...	...		...	
2750	Domestic appliances		1142.0	1259.0	1463.8	1777.6		440.8	475.2	538.6	668.8		...	
2790	Other electrical equipment		129.0	126.9	165.5	177.8		60.8	59.2	77.2	83.4		...	
281	General-purpose machinery		1732.7	1768.7	1828.6	1923.5		800.6	837.9	859.9	1016.4		...	
2811	Engines/turbines,excl.aircraft,vehicle engines		28.7	30.4	35.4	30.2		20.6	21.1	23.0	19.8		...	
2812	Fluid power equipment		...	...	...	...		...	...	...	...		...	
2813	Other pumps, compressors, taps and valves		489.0	561.5	601.6	587.3		223.2	270.7	285.6	370.6		...	
2814	Bearings, gears, gearing and driving elements		90.9	92.8	80.9	77.7		38.1	46.1	40.4	45.8		...	
2815	Ovens, furnaces and furnace burners		28.6	30.5	37.5	32.1		15.5	16.9	18.5	17.3		...	
2816	Lifting and handling equipment		259.4	255.5	194.0	206.5		123.2	122.6	107.8	122.2		...	
2817	Office machinery, excl.computers,etc.		...	...	...	...		...	...	...	...		...	
2818	Power-driven hand tools		...	...	...	...		...	...	...	...		...	
2819	Other general-purpose machinery		836.1	798.1	879.2	989.7		375.9	355.6	384.7	440.7		...	
282	Special-purpose machinery		877.6	911.9	843.1	764.7		455.5	461.1	448.6	421.5		...	
2821	Agricultural and forestry machinery		120.2	118.3	151.4	184.2		70.5	65.8	83.8	106.7		...	
2822	Metal-forming machinery and machine tools		21.0	19.2	22.0	22.1		10.9	9.9	11.0	11.9		...	

2823	Machinery for metallurgy	189.6	203.4	176.7	156.5	77.8	88.9	77.8	77.9
2824	Mining, quarrying and construction machinery	195.5	167.9	176.1	153.5	100.4	86.4	96.6	81.5
2825	Food/beverage/tobacco processing machinery	6.5	6.2	..	3.9	2.6	2.2	..	1.6
2826	Textile/apparel/leather production machinery	344.8	396.8	316.9	244.6	193.3	207.9	179.3	141.8
2829	Other special-purpose machinery	..	..	..	..	..	..	..	..
2910	Motor vehicles	3853.1	4297.8	4472.2	4481.8	904.4	1033.7	1176.7	1223.3
2920	Automobile bodies, trailers and semi-trailers	922.0	1022.5	990.6	784.9	259.1	297.0	359.3	292.8
2930	Parts and accessories for motor vehicles	1032.2	1060.4	963.1	1215.7	402.7	392.1	385.1	485.4
301	Building of ships and boats	16.8	19.9	..	..	5.7	7.6	..	..
3011	Building of ships and floating structures	..	..	..	..	..	..	..	..
3012	Building of pleasure and sporting boats	..	..	..	..	..	..	..	..
3020	Railway locomotives and rolling stock	..	..	..	..	..	..	..	..
3030	Air and spacecraft and related machinery	..	..	..	..	..	..	..	..
3040	Military fighting vehicles	..	..	..	..	..	..	..	..
309	Transport equipment n.e.c.	2090.6	2232.5	2300.1	2261.7	629.1	641.9	472.2	428.3
3091	Motorcycles	2078.4	2222.4	2287.1	2244.6	624.6	638.6	467.9	422.8
3092	Bicycles and invalid carriages	4.6	3.7	5.6	7.2	1.5	1.0	2.0	2.5
3099	Other transport equipment n.e.c.	7.7	6.4	7.4	9.9	3.0	2.3	2.3	3.1
3100	Furniture	2343.1	2359.0	1710.8	1743.8	1077.4	1074.8	778.8	808.7
321	Jewellery, bijouterie and related articles	199.1	221.9	243.4	216.2	107.0	122.2	129.1	117.2
3211	Jewellery and related articles	199.1	221.9	243.4	216.2	107.0	122.2	129.1	117.2
3212	Imitation jewellery and related articles	..	..	..	..	..	..	..	..
3220	Musical instruments	..	..	..	..	..	..	..	..
3230	Sports goods	40.9	56.6	50.1	40.1	18.5	28.2	22.9	19.2
3240	Games and toys	127.2	149.5	171.9	169.2	61.6	71.5	105.2	94.7
3250	Medical and dental instruments and supplies	314.6	327.5	358.9	429.7	182.5	198.2	226.4	275.3
3290	Other manufacturing n.e.c.	1756.8	1676.7	1771.6	2679.1	277.9	279.8	887.1	1341.0
331	Repair of fabricated metal products/machinery	..	..	..	..	..	..	..	..
3311	Repair of fabricated metal products	..	..	..	..	..	..	..	..
3312	Repair of machinery	..	..	..	..	..	..	..	..
3313	Repair of electronic and optical equipment	..	..	..	..	..	..	..	..
3314	Repair of electrical equipment	..	..	..	..	..	..	..	..
3315	Repair of transport equip., excl. motor vehicles	..	..	..	..	..	..	..	..
3319	Repair of other equipment	..	..	..	..	..	..	..	..
3320	Installation of industrial machinery/equipment	..	..	..	..	..	..	..	..
C	Total manufacturing	203722.3	212448.0	226246.0	243468.8	78133.0	80397.5	85744.9	88355.5

Colombia

Index numbers of industrial production

(2010=100)

ISIC	ISIC Revision 4 — Industry	Note	2005	2006	2007	2008	2009	2010	2011	2012	2013	2014	2015	2016
10	Food products		87	96	102	102	100	100	105	107	111	115	118	119
11	Beverages		80	87	94	95	102	100	107	113	115	120	130	140
12	Tobacco products		...	...	...	...	...	...	...	...	...	...	...	...
13	Textiles	a/	95	104	114	103	89	100	104	106	100	98	103	103
14	Wearing apparel	a/	...	...	...	...	...	...	...	...	...	...	...	...
15	Leather and related products		90	92	103	96	84	100	111	113	106	111	107	108
16	Wood products, excluding furniture		108	120	145	124	105	100	102	101	94	74	86	86
17	Paper and paper products		85	91	98	102	97	100	93	92	86	86	91	91
18	Printing and reproduction of recorded media		90	96	98	104	101	100	108	95	82	75	81	82
19	Coke and refined petroleum products		118	105	109	101	98	100	101	96	99	86	84	104
20	Chemicals and chemical products		73	79	87	90	91	100	106	102	101	102	104	99
21	Pharmaceuticals, medicinal chemicals, etc.		84	91	93	97	94	100	105	102	102	103	106	107
22	Rubber and plastics products		78	87	96	98	95	100	106	99	93	91	95	96
23	Other non-metallic mineral products		69	91	111	108	100	100	111	110	108	111	115	111
24	Basic metals		100	103	109	100	96	100	92	101	94	93	97	89
25	Fabricated metal products, except machinery		91	96	106	99	95	100	100	104	104	105	104	114
26	Computer, electronic and optical products		...	...	...	...	...	...	...	...	...	...	...	...
27	Electrical equipment		76	90	107	107	92	100	105	101	99	105	105	101
28	Machinery and equipment n.e.c.		79	91	107	108	90	100	101	97	96	91	87	89
29	Motor vehicles, trailers and semi-trailers		93	112	144	100	77	100	115	111	90	95	89	86
30	Other transport equipment		64	89	92	87	88	100	127	135	152	163	153	129
31	Furniture		81	93	101	91	87	100	100	99	98	98	99	99
32	Other manufacturing		111	124	131	126	104	100	100	92	100	98	92	93
33	Repair and installation of machinery/equipment		...	...	...	...	...	...	...	...	...	...	...	...
C	Total manufacturing		86	95	104	101	96	100	105	105	103	105	107	111

a/ 13 includes 14.

Costa Rica

Supplier of information:
Banco Central de Costa Rica, San José.

Basic source of data:
Annual census/exhaustive survey; administrative source.

Major deviations from ISIC (Revision 4):
None reported.

Reference period:
Calendar year.

Scope:
All enterprises.

Method of data collection:
Online survey.

Type of enumeration:
Sample survey.

Adjusted for non-response:
Yes.

Concepts and definitions of variables:
No deviations from the standard UN concepts and definitions are reported.

Related national publications:
None reported.

Costa Rica

| ISIC Revision 4 | | | Number of enterprises | | | | | Employees | | | | | Wages and salaries | | | | |
| ISIC | Industry | Note | (number) | | | | Note | (number) | | | | Note | (Costa Rican Colones) | | | |
			2013	2014	2015	2016		2013	2014	2015	2016		2013	2014	2015	2016
10	Food products		1873	...	...	...		...	...	...	...		...	...	...	...
11	Beverages		63	...	...	...		...	...	...	...		...	...	...	...
12	Tobacco products		8	...	...	...		...	...	...	...		...	...	...	...
13	Textiles		134	...	...	...		...	...	...	...		...	...	...	...
14	Wearing apparel		258	...	...	...		...	...	...	...		...	...	...	...
15	Leather and related products		42	...	...	...		...	...	...	...		...	...	...	...
16	Wood products, excluding furniture		296	...	...	...		...	...	...	...		...	...	...	...
17	Paper and paper products		53	...	...	...		...	...	...	...		...	...	...	...
18	Printing and reproduction of recorded media		639	...	...	...		...	...	...	...		...	...	...	...
19	Coke and refined petroleum products		3	...	...	...		...	...	...	...		...	...	...	...
20	Chemicals and chemical products		195	...	...	...		...	...	...	...		...	...	...	...
21	Pharmaceuticals,medicinal chemicals, etc.		41	...	...	...		...	...	...	...		...	...	...	...
22	Rubber and plastics products		180	...	...	...		...	...	...	...		...	...	...	...
23	Other non-metallic mineral products		231	...	...	...		...	...	...	...		...	...	...	...
24	Basic metals		55	...	...	...		...	...	...	...		...	...	...	...
25	Fabricated metal products, except machinery		415	...	...	...		...	...	...	...		...	...	...	...
26	Computer, electronic and optical products		33	...	...	...		...	...	...	...		...	...	...	...
27	Electrical equipment		33	...	...	...		...	...	...	...		...	...	...	...
28	Machinery and equipment n.e.c.		68	...	...	...		...	...	...	...		...	...	...	...
29	Motor vehicles, trailers and semi-trailers		64	...	...	...		...	...	...	...		...	...	...	...
30	Other transport equipment		6	...	...	...		...	...	...	...		...	...	...	...
31	Furniture		438	...	...	...		...	...	...	...		...	...	...	...
32	Other manufacturing		215	...	...	...		...	...	...	...		...	...	...	...
33	Repair and installation of machinery/equipment		353	...	...	...		...	...	...	...		...	...	...	...
C	Total manufacturing		5696	...	...	...		...	...	...	...		...	...	...	...

Costa Rica

ISIC	Industry	Note	Output at basic prices (billions of Costa Rican Colones) 2013	2014	2015	2016	Note	Value added at basic prices (billions of Costa Rican Colones) 2013	2014	2015	2016	Note	Gross fixed capital formation (billions of Costa Rican Colones) 2015	2016
1010	Processing/preserving of meat		752.6	826.4	865.7	859.1		196.9	215.3	229.4	223.7		...	...
1020	Processing/preserving of fish, etc.		144.2	146.8	152.7	142.4		38.0	37.6	46.3	39.7		...	...
1030	Processing/preserving of fruit,vegetables		296.7	310.8	368.8	426.8		105.0	105.3	121.0	133.8		...	...
1040	Vegetable and animal oils and fats		365.0	360.0	346.0	343.7		97.9	98.6	91.8	68.2		...	...
1050	Dairy products		406.7	429.6	460.2	472.1		130.8	140.8	151.4	153.2		...	...
106	Grain mill products,starches and starch products		358.3	379.4	391.7	388.9		116.1	126.2	138.6	142.2		...	...
1061	Grain mill products		358.3	379.4	391.7	388.9		116.1	126.2	138.6	142.2		...	...
1062	Starches and starch products		...	...	...	...		...	...	...	...		...	...
107	Other food products		1222.4	1323.5	1392.7	1433.8		377.0	413.4	447.3	482.5		...	...
1071	Bakery products		322.1	363.5	375.9	380.8		102.8	111.6	124.2	131.4		...	...
1072	Sugar		199.8	209.0	220.0	209.4		60.7	64.8	73.4	71.9		...	...
1073	Cocoa, chocolate and sugar confectionery		29.1	48.9	57.9	35.1		10.8	17.7	20.6	14.1		...	...
1074	Macaroni, noodles, couscous, etc.		39.7	43.1	47.2	50.1		13.1	14.9	15.8	17.2		...	...
1075	Prepared meals and dishes		340.5	361.5	395.1	422.0		113.1	122.7	132.1	154.5		...	...
1079	Other food products n.e.c.		291.1	297.5	296.5	336.4		76.5	81.7	81.2	93.4		...	...
1080	Prepared animal feeds		140.2	148.3	143.5	153.7		43.5	47.7	51.7	57.4		...	...
110	Beverages		352.7	375.0	375.8	383.5		114.2	113.8	119.2	121.9		...	...
1101	Distilling, rectifying and blending of spirits		19.9	18.1	18.8	18.1		8.4	8.5	8.5	8.2		...	...
1102	Wines		...	...	...	...		...	...	...	...		...	...
1103	Malt liquors and malt		332.8	356.9	356.9	365.4		105.8	105.3	110.7	113.7		...	...
1104	Soft drinks,mineral waters,other bottled waters		...	...	...	...		...	...	...	...		...	...
1200	Tobacco products		...	...	...	...		...	...	...	...		...	...
131	Spinning, weaving and finishing of textiles		63.7	65.0	84.2	86.2		22.9	23.2	28.8	30.7		...	...
1311	Preparation and spinning of textile fibres		...	...	...	...		...	...	...	...		...	...
1312	Weaving of textiles		...	...	...	...		...	...	...	...		...	...
1313	Finishing of textiles		...	...	...	...		...	...	...	...		...	...
139	Other textiles		...	...	...	...		...	...	...	...		...	...
1391	Knitted and crocheted fabrics		...	...	...	...		...	...	...	...		...	...
1392	Made-up textile articles, except apparel		...	...	...	...		...	...	...	...		...	...
1393	Carpets and rugs		...	...	...	...		...	...	...	...		...	...
1394	Cordage, rope, twine and netting		...	...	...	...		...	...	...	...		...	...
1399	Other textiles n.e.c.		...	...	...	...		...	...	...	...		...	...
1410	Wearing apparel, except fur apparel	a/	165.4	171.4	119.5	124.6	a/	86.1	87.3	69.6	73.9		...	...
1420	Articles of fur	a/	...	...	...	...	a/	...	...	...	...		...	...
1430	Knitted and crocheted apparel	a/	...	...	...	...	a/	...	...	...	...		...	...
151	Leather;luggage,handbags,saddlery,harness;fur		18.9	18.6	18.4	15.7		7.0	6.7	6.2	5.2		...	...
1511	Tanning/dressing of leather; dressing of fur		...	...	...	...		...	...	...	...		...	...
1512	Luggage,handbags,etc.;saddlery/harness		...	...	...	...		...	...	...	...		...	...
1520	Footwear		10.0	10.6	10.2	10.0		3.4	3.8	3.9	4.1		...	...
1610	Sawmilling and planing of wood	b/	94.6	101.0	106.7	103.7	b/	40.0	43.6	49.5	44.3		...	...

continued

Costa Rica

| ISIC Revision 4 | | Output at basic prices | | | | | Value added at basic prices | | | | | Gross fixed capital formation | | |
| | | Note | (billions of Costa Rican Colones) | | | | Note | (billions of Costa Rican Colones) | | | | Note | (billions of Costa Rican Colones) | |
ISIC	Industry		2013	2014	2015	2016		2013	2014	2015	2016		2015	2016
162	Wood products, cork, straw, plaiting materials	b/	...	...	...	...	b/	...	...	...	...		...	...
1621	Veneer sheets and wood-based panels		...	...	...	...		...	...	...	...		...	...
1622	Builders' carpentry and joinery		...	...	...	...		...	...	...	...		...	...
1623	Wooden containers		...	...	...	...		...	...	...	...		...	...
1629	Other wood products;articles of cork,straw		...	...	...	...		...	...	...	...		...	...
170	Paper and paper products		314.0	335.0	336.6	325.3		91.0	98.3	95.8	93.6		...	...
1701	Pulp, paper and paperboard		...	...	...	...	c/	91.0	98.3	95.8	93.6		...	...
1702	Corrugated paper and paperboard		...	...	...	...	c/	...	...	...	...		...	...
1709	Other articles of paper and paperboard		...	...	...	...	c/	...	...	...	...		...	...
181	Printing and service activities related to printing	d/	196.3	209.6	203.9	218.7	d/	106.8	112.9	116.5	126.4		...	...
1811	Printing		...	...	...	...		...	...	...	...		...	...
1812	Service activities related to printing		...	...	...	...		...	...	...	...		...	...
1820	Reproduction of recorded media	d/	...	...	...	...	d/	...	...	...	...		...	...
1910	Coke oven products		...	...	...	...		...	...	...	...		...	...
1920	Refined petroleum products		...	...	...	...		...	...	...	...		...	...
201	Basic chemicals,fertilizers, etc.		197.9	190.2	192.7	189.5		52.1	54.6	56.5	50.9		...	...
2011	Basic chemicals		189.7	181.3	184.1	181.6		49.5	51.8	54.2	48.7		...	...
2012	Fertilizers and nitrogen compounds		...	...	...	...		...	...	...	...		...	...
2013	Plastics and synthetic rubber in primary forms		8.2	8.9	8.5	7.8		2.5	2.8	2.3	2.2		...	...
202	Other chemical products		382.9	398.4	422.7	439.9		139.0	143.0	153.2	162.7		...	...
2021	Pesticides and other agrochemical products		88.1	79.2	85.4	98.6		38.3	34.2	36.1	40.7		...	...
2022	Paints,varnishes;printing ink and mastics		106.4	120.5	135.7	138.0		32.1	36.2	43.6	44.5		...	...
2023	Soap,cleaning and cosmetic preparations		174.7	184.2	188.1	186.4		64.4	68.0	69.0	71.4		...	...
2029	Other chemical products n.e.c.		13.8	14.6	13.5	16.9		4.3	4.6	4.5	6.1		...	...
2030	Man-made fibres		...	...	...	...		...	...	...	...		...	...
2100	Pharmaceuticals,medicinal chemicals, etc.		130.8	131.3	158.6	155.8		55.4	57.4	74.3	75.4		...	...
221	Rubber products		145.9	154.7	147.7	138.2		48.3	57.0	56.7	52.7		...	...
2211	Rubber tyres and tubes		...	...	...	...		...	...	...	...		...	...
2219	Other rubber products		...	...	...	...		...	...	...	...		...	...
2220	Plastics products		338.7	377.2	380.0	395.1		105.0	105.2	107.3	119.7		...	...
2310	Glass and glass products		63.4	64.5	55.9	53.5		19.0	20.4	17.5	17.8		...	...
239	Non-metallic mineral products n.e.c.		313.4	354.9	370.8	347.8		122.5	140.8	156.5	136.2		...	...
2391	Refractory products		42.7	43.6	45.0	47.1		18.5	18.1	21.3	22.3		...	...
2392	Clay building materials		...	...	...	...		...	...	...	...		...	...
2393	Other porcelain and ceramic products		...	...	...	...		...	...	...	...		...	...
2394	Cement, lime and plaster		270.8	311.3	325.8	300.7		103.9	122.7	135.2	113.9		...	...
2395	Articles of concrete, cement and plaster		...	...	...	...		...	...	...	...		...	...
2396	Cutting, shaping and finishing of stone		...	...	...	...		...	...	...	...		...	...
2399	Other non-metallic mineral products n.e.c.		...	...	...	...		...	...	...	...		...	...
2410	Basic iron and steel	e/	229.4	235.4	200.4	190.9	e/	59.3	60.8	49.4	40.6		...	...

Code	Description											
2420	Basic precious and other non-ferrous metals	e/	…	…	…	…	e/	…	…	…	…
243	Casting of metals	e/	…	…	…	…	e/	…	…	…	…
2431	Casting of iron and steel		…	…	…	…		…	…	…	…
2432	Casting of non-ferrous metals		…	…	…	…		…	…	…	…
251	Struct.metal products, tanks, reservoirs	f/	69.0	77.0	67.3		f/	178.6	194.3	179.8	161.7
2511	Structural metal products		…	…	…	…		…	…	…	…
2512	Tanks, reservoirs and containers of metal		…	…	…	…		…	…	…	…
2513	Steam generators, excl. hot water boilers		…	…	…	…		…	…	…	…
2520	Weapons and ammunition	f/	…	…	…	…	f/	…	…	…	…
259	Other metal products;metal working services	f/	…	…	…	…	f/	…	…	…	…
2591	Forging,pressing,stamping,roll-forming of metal		…	…	…	…		…	…	…	…
2592	Treatment and coating of metals; machining		…	…	…	…		…	…	…	…
2593	Cutlery, hand tools and general hardware		…	…	…	…		…	…	…	…
2599	Other fabricated metal products n.e.c.		…	…	…	…		…	…	…	…
2610	Electronic components and boards		1.3	3.4	191.8	156.4		19.0	11.4	180.2	247.4
2620	Computers and peripheral equipment		…	…	…	…		…	…	…	…
2630	Communication equipment		…	…	…	…		…	…	…	…
2640	Consumer electronics		…	…	…	…		…	…	…	…
265	Measuring,testing equipment; watches, etc.		…	…	…	…		…	…	…	…
2651	Measuring/testing/navigating equipment,etc.		…	…	…	…		…	…	…	…
2652	Watches and clocks		…	…	…	…		…	…	…	…
2660	Irradiation/electromedical equipment,etc.		…	…	…	…		…	…	…	…
2670	Optical instruments and photographic equipment		28.2	28.8	25.8			60.2	60.3	64.9	52.8
2680	Magnetic and optical media		…	…	…	…		…	…	…	…
2710	Electric motors,generators,transformers,etc.	g/	129.7	128.2	142.9		g/	345.3	337.2	404.0	406.4
2720	Batteries and accumulators	g/	…	…	…	…	g/	…	…	…	…
273	Wiring and wiring devices	g/	…	…	…	…	g/	…	…	…	…
2731	Fibre optic cables		…	…	…	…		…	…	…	…
2732	Other electronic and electric wires and cables		…	…	…	…		…	…	…	…
2733	Wiring devices		…	…	…	…		…	…	…	…
2740	Electric lighting equipment	g/	…	…	…	…	g/	…	…	…	…
2750	Domestic appliances	g/	…	…	…	…	g/	…	…	…	…
2790	Other electrical equipment	g/	…	…	…	…	g/	…	…	…	…
281	General-purpose machinery		…	…	…	…		…	…	…	…
2811	Engines/turbines,excl.aircraft,vehicle engines		…	…	…	…		…	…	…	…
2812	Fluid power equipment		…	…	…	…		…	…	…	…
2813	Other pumps, compressors, taps and valves		…	…	…	…		…	…	…	…
2814	Bearings, gears, gearing and driving elements		…	…	…	…		…	…	…	…
2815	Ovens, furnaces and furnace burners		…	…	…	…		…	…	…	…
2816	Lifting and handling equipment		…	…	…	…		…	…	…	…
2817	Office machinery, excl.computers,etc.		…	…	…	…		…	…	…	…
2818	Power-driven hand tools		…	…	…	…		…	…	…	…
2819	Other general-purpose machinery		…	…	…	…		…	…	…	…
282	Special-purpose machinery		…	…	…	…		…	…	…	…
2821	Agricultural and forestry machinery		…	…	…	…		…	…	…	…
2822	Metal-forming machinery and machine tools		…	…	…	…		…	…	…	…
2823	Machinery for metallurgy		…	…	…	…		…	…	…	…

continued

Costa Rica

ISIC	Industry	Output at basic prices (billions of Costa Rican Colones)					Value added at basic prices (billions of Costa Rican Colones)					Gross fixed capital formation (billions of Costa Rican Colones)		
		Note	2013	2014	2015	2016	Note	2013	2014	2015	2016	Note	2015	2016
2824	Mining, quarrying and construction machinery		...	...	...	...		...	...	...	...		...	...
2825	Food/beverage/tobacco processing machinery		...	...	...	...		...	...	...	...		...	...
2826	Textile/apparel/leather production machinery		...	...	...	...		...	...	...	...		...	...
2829	Other special-purpose machinery		...	...	...	...		...	...	...	...		...	...
2910	Motor vehicles	h/	31.8	29.1	30.6	27.5	h/	14.4	14.1	15.6	13.9		...	...
2920	Automobile bodies, trailers and semi-trailers	h/	...	...	...	...	h/	...	...	...	...		...	...
2930	Parts and accessories for motor vehicles	h/	...	...	...	...	h/	...	...	...	...		...	...
301	Building of ships and boats	i/	3.8	4.0	4.0	3.4	i/	1.3	1.3	1.5	1.4		...	...
3011	Building of ships and floating structures		...	...	...	...		...	...	...	...		...	...
3012	Building of pleasure and sporting boats		...	...	...	...		...	...	...	...		...	...
3020	Railway locomotives and rolling stock	i/	...	...	...	...	i/	...	...	...	...		...	...
3030	Air and spacecraft and related machinery	i/	...	...	...	...	i/	...	...	...	...		...	...
3040	Military fighting vehicles	i/	...	...	...	...	i/	...	...	...	...		...	...
309	Transport equipment n.e.c.	i/	...	...	...	...	i/	...	...	...	...		...	...
3091	Motorcycles		...	...	...	...		...	...	...	...		...	...
3092	Bicycles and invalid carriages		...	...	...	...		...	...	...	...		...	...
3099	Other transport equipment n.e.c.		...	...	...	...		...	...	...	...		...	...
3100	Furniture		144.4	144.4	147.1	146.3		64.8	66.9	70.0	71.1		...	...
321	Jewellery, bijouterie and related articles		...	...	...	...		...	...	...	...		...	...
3211	Jewellery and related articles		...	...	...	...		...	...	...	...		...	...
3212	Imitation jewellery and related articles		...	...	...	...		...	...	...	...		...	...
3220	Musical instruments		...	...	...	...		...	...	...	...		...	...
3230	Sports goods		...	...	...	...		...	...	...	...		...	...
3240	Games and toys		...	...	...	...		...	...	...	...		...	...
3250	Medical and dental instruments and supplies		762.4	960.0	1121.0	1388.5		284.6	343.0	387.2	540.5		...	...
3290	Other manufacturing n.e.c.		128.9	136.9	140.6	139.3		57.3	61.0	66.6	68.0		...	...
331	Repair of fabricated metal products/machinery	j/	216.3	234.3	261.0	285.5	j/	100.5	106.6	115.5	134.1		...	...
3311	Repair of fabricated metal products		...	...	...	...		...	...	...	...		...	...
3312	Repair of machinery		...	...	...	...		...	...	...	...		...	...
3313	Repair of electronic and optical equipment		...	...	...	...		...	...	...	...		...	...
3314	Repair of electrical equipment		...	...	...	...		...	...	...	...		...	...
3315	Repair of transport equip., excl. motor vehicles		...	...	...	...		...	...	...	...		...	...
3319	Repair of other equipment		...	...	...	...		...	...	...	...		...	...
3320	Installation of industrial machinery/equipment	j/	...	...	...	...	j/	...	...	...	...		...	...
C	Total manufacturing	i/	8860.2	9455.0	9613.0	9992.6	j/	3127.8	3309.4	3331.9	3513.8		...	...

a/ 1410 includes 1420 and 1430.
b/ 1610 includes 162.
c/ 1701 includes 1702 and 1709.
d/ 181 includes 1820.
e/ 2410 includes 2420 and 243.
f/ 251 includes 2520 and 259.
g/ 2710 includes 2720, 273, 2740, 2750 and 2790.

h/ 2910 includes 2920 and 2930.
i/ 301 includes 3020, 3030, 3040 and 309.
j/ 331 includes 3320.

Croatia

Supplier of information:
Croatian Bureau of Statistics, Zagreb.

Basic source of data:
Survey on registered establishments; administrative data.

Major deviations from ISIC (Revision 4):
Data presented in ISIC (Revision 4) were originally classified according to NACE (Revision 2).

Reference period:
Calendar year.

Scope:
Before 2014, all establishments; as of 2014, proxy enterprise equal legal units.

Method of data collection:
Data were derived from mail questionnaires and administrative sources.

Type of enumeration:
Complete enumeration.

Adjusted for non-response:
No.

Concepts and definitions of variables:
Figures for wages and salaries (for year 2013) were computed by UNIDO from the reported monthly average wages and salaries per employee. Output and Value added refer to administrative data on proxy enterprise equal legal units.

Related national publications:
None reported.

Croatia

ISIC	Industry	Note	Number of establishments (number)				Note	Number of employees (number)				Note	Wages and salaries paid to employees (millions of Croatian Kunas)			
			2013	2014a/	2015a/	2016a/		2013	2014b/	2015	2016		2013	2014b/	2015	2016
1010	Processing/preserving of meat		479	330	332	324		7607	10849	11091	10754		2822.9c/	753.2	760.1	764.4
1020	Processing/preserving of fish, etc.		92	50	43	50		1082	1732	1476	1346		...c/	120.5	105.7	109.2
1030	Processing/preserving of fruit,vegetables		233	159	160	160		1019	1408	1552	1590		...c/	78.3	91.2	105.3
1040	Vegetable and animal oils and fats		142	105	108	111		1086	921	805	786		...c/	103.8	84.2	80.5
1050	Dairy products		216	104	106	112		3944	4753	4864	4927		...c/	452.2	466.5	481.5
106	Grain mill products,starches and starch products		136	92	78	81		891	1022	927	846		...c/	79.0	80.6	73.4
1061	Grain mill products		130	91	77	79		886	...	927	821		...	...	...	...
1062	Starches and starch products		6	1	1	2		...	...	-	25		...	...	...	...
107	Other food products		1726	1852	1876	1848		19306	31020	30984	32000		...c/	2000.6	2022.6	2193.4
1071	Bakery products		1303	1540	1548	1520		11142	21727	21902	22219		...	1092.4	1105.7	1177.1
1072	Sugar		11	5	5	3		807	734	679	692		...	78.3	69.8	72.5
1073	Cocoa, chocolate and sugar confectionery		40	25	26	26		2331	2363	2375	2426		...	215.2	219.2	223.1
1074	Macaroni, noodles, couscous, etc.		87	57	55	57		218	407	467	471		...	20.1	24.3	27.2
1075	Prepared meals and dishes		13	16	19	18		70	164	150	178		...	11.1	10.5	11.8
1079	Other food products n.e.c.		272	209	176	224		4738	...	2170	6014		...	...	...	...
1080	Prepared animal feeds		91	51	56	54		740	778	779	782		...c/	49.4	58.0	59.7
110	Beverages		629	507	497	500		4910	7019	6677	6240		556.6	761.4	768.1	753.1
1101	Distilling, rectifying and blending of spirits		87	80	73	65		599	...	792	750		556.6d/	...d/	...d/	...d/
1102	Wines		311	335	330	336		1659	2598	2482	2204		...d/	173.9	178.1	...
1103	Malt liquors and malt		57	29	34	47		1239	...	1488	1475		...d/	279.0	279.0	286.8
1104	Soft drinks,mineral waters,other bottled waters		174	63	59	51		1413	1998	1877	1769		...d/	252.6	239.6	244.3
1200	Tobacco products		13	7	6	6		837	789	755	806		103.7	110.1	...	177.7
131	Spinning, weaving and finishing of textiles		140	...	...	...		1743	...	...	...		209.7e/	...	...	...
1311	Preparation and spinning of textile fibres		36	12	14	13		423	513	691	531		...	34.0	36.1	35.1
1312	Weaving of textiles		60	20	21	20		523	514	597	475		...	30.1	45.7	30.4
1313	Finishing of textiles		44	61	56	53		797	614	418	413		...	27.1	24.5	26.1
139	Other textiles		410	385	376	369		2080	2590	2709	2427		...e/	144.9	156.4	150.6
1391	Knitted and crocheted fabrics		30	18	17	16		51	...	424	410		...	...	...	...
1392	Made-up textile articles, except apparel		256	268	274	266		1211	1481	1667	1376		...	78.3	92.4	78.2
1393	Carpets and rugs		7	2	2	2		24	...	2	2		...	...	...	...
1394	Cordage, rope, twine and netting		15	18	16	18		124	82	82	86		...	4.6	...	...
1399	Other textiles n.e.c.		102	79	67	67		670	...	534	553		...	...	...	...
1410	Wearing apparel, except fur apparel		1396	831	829	788		12950	12888	12079	11708		658.9f/	609.3	598.6	603.4
1420	Articles of fur		5	6	6	6		33	11	11	15		...f/	0.2	0.2	0.5
1430	Knitted and crocheted apparel		156	103	95	90		1436	3241	3110	2994		...f/	172.7	171.8	171.1
151	Leather;luggage,handbags,saddlery,harness;fur		165	87	87	94	g/	3326	11208g/	5002	5043	g/	399.7	570.8	611.9	598.5
1511	Tanning/dressing of leather; dressing of fur		29	10	13	15		132	145	153	167		...	8.3	8.0	9.6
1512	Luggage,handbags,etc.;saddlery/harness		136	77	74	79		3194	...	4849	4876		...	...	...	...
1520	Footwear		230	104	102	99		4893	...g/	5769	5984	g/	...	...	...	...
1610	Sawmilling and planing of wood		764	506	493	481		4205	7125	7220	7042		585.6h/	386.4	399.0	410.2

Code	Industry	(1)	(2)	(3)	(4)	(5)	(6)	(7)	(8)	(9)	(10)	(11)	(12)
162	Wood products, cork, straw, plaiting materials	1302	1212	1187	1150	6702	8304	8556	9006	...h/	420.1	461.5	518.6
1621	Veneer sheets and wood-based panels	61	39	30	32	1832	1532	1554	1682	...	95.6	103.1	112.7
1622	Builders' carpentry and joinery	668	683	652	628	3272	4352	4325	4593	...	202.5	219.2	249.3
1623	Wooden containers	125	126	126	121	461	878	923	1058	...	46.6	49.0	61.7
1629	Other wood products;articles of cork,straw	448	364	379	369	1137	1542	1754	1673	...	75.5	90.3	94.8
170	Paper and paper products	348	298	301	295	3285	4209	4280	4336	252.4	329.0	352.0	358.3
1701	Pulp, paper and paperboard	31	16	21	18	568	550	716	723	252.4i/	55.1	66.9	65.2
1702	Corrugated paper and paperboard	165	95	96	100	1695	2106	1926	1954	...i/	151.9	152.8	158.2
1709	Other articles of paper and paperboard	152	187	183	177	1022	1553	1637	1659	...i/	122.0	...	...
181	Printing and service activities related to printing	1790	1399	1300	1248	6067	7515	7402	7466	537.4j/	613.8	613.0	639.0
1811	Printing	1207	927	876	858	4773	...	6554	6661	...	...	...	578.3
1812	Service activities related to printing	583	472	424	390	1294	...	848	805	...	...	...	60.8
1820	Reproduction of recorded media	63	55	46	43	104	67	61	47	...j/	3.4	2.9	2.6
1910	Coke oven products	-	...	-	...	...	-	...	...	411.5k/	-	-	...
1920	Refined petroleum products	34	14	14	15	2833	...	...	4904	...k/	278.0	268.7	265.3
201	Basic chemicals,fertilizers, etc.	153	85	85	101	3460	2678	2523	2410	573.8m/	...	...	...
2011	Basic chemicals	94	45	49	54	537	...	564	566	...	...	65.8	...
2012	Fertilizers and nitrogen compounds	27	21	19	30	2360	...	1696	1703	...	...	...	...
2013	Plastics and synthetic rubber in primary forms	32	19	17	17	563	123	263	141	...m/	13.5	...	15.9
202	Other chemical products	469	...	...	...	3008	...	...	...	...	...	...	...
2021	Pesticides and other agrochemical products	10	6	7	6	202	...	114	100	...	...	...	...
2022	Paints,varnishes;printing ink and mastics	101	46	45	49	719	...	598	626	...	...	56.1	62.6
2023	Soap,cleaning and cosmetic preparations	227	108	121	125	1563	1898	2003	1934	...	156.6	161.9	158.1
2029	Other chemical products n.e.c.	131	78	83	77	524	680	700	658	...m/	54.6	...	...
2030	Man-made fibres	2	-	-	...	...	-	-	...	-	-	-	...
2100	Pharmaceuticals,medicinal chemicals, etc.	79	46	49	50	3953	4850	4847	4864	625.6	757.3	765.5	829.8
221	Rubber products	162	145	140	133	878	842	919	987	495.7n/	65.1	69.6	80.9
2211	Rubber tyres and tubes	26	27	24	25	83	103	104	80	...	7.0	6.1	5.7
2219	Other rubber products	136	118	116	108	795	739	815	907	...	58.1	63.5	75.2
2220	Plastics products	1208	1017	986	967	6167	8862	9600	9893	...n/	581.6	632.2	680.6
2310	Glass and glass products	154	145	145	142	1591	1979	2100	2250	912.3p/	195.5	207.5	224.5
239	Non-metallic mineral products n.e.c.	1140	...	...	...	7870	...	...	...	...p/	...	...	...
2391	Refractory products	11	8	9	8	35	10	11	8	...	0.6	0.6	0.7
2392	Clay building materials	97	31	30	28	1376	968	880	874	...	81.4	80.5	81.7
2393	Other porcelain and ceramic products	119	81	71	65	369	893	784	818	...	53.5	48.8	54.3
2394	Cement, lime and plaster	25	9	8	8	1455	1353	1297	1290	...	199.9	196.3	210.9
2395	Articles of concrete, cement and plaster	409	319	302	302	2660	2950	3022	3212	...	223.9	240.3	268.3
2396	Cutting, shaping and finishing of stone	415	540	523	505	1423	2491	2477	2410	...	144.1	150.8	158.6
2399	Other non-metallic mineral products n.e.c.	64	41	37	37	552	556	537	520	...	56.9	60.1	63.9
2410	Basic iron and steel	49	56	50	45	682	965	692	499	321.5q/	76.9	87.4	60.8
2420	Basic precious and other non-ferrous metals	63	25	28	30	874	781	1118	986	...q/	74.7	...	...
243	Casting of metals	109	73	73	65	2573	2405	2487	2478	...q/	183.3	189.0	200.0
2431	Casting of iron and steel	58	26	27	22	1929	...	1708	1602	...	...	...	127.7
2432	Casting of non-ferrous metals	51	47	46	42	644	...	779	827	...	...	...	...
251	Struct.metal products, tanks, reservoirs	1630	...	...	...	12951	28898r/	...	...	1853.5	2261.8	2408.3	2732.3

continued

Croatia

ISIC	Industry	Number of establishments (number)					Number of employees (number)					Wages and salaries paid to employees (millions of Croatian Kunas)				
		Note	2013	2014a/	2015a/	2016a/	Note	2013	2014b/	2015	2016	Note	2013	2014b/	2015	2016
2511	Structural metal products		1512	1406	1367	1347		10177	12612	12900	13944		...	936.4	931.9	1118.5
2512	Tanks, reservoirs and containers of metal		74	56	48	48		1521	769	700	597		...	61.7	61.7	63.4
2513	Steam generators, excl. hot water boilers		44	14	13	15		1253	1258	1246	1299		...	152.6	133.1	197.8
2520	Weapons and ammunition		9	6	5	7	r/	1436	...r/	1709	1682	r/	...	...	...	...
259	Other metal products;metal working services		2106	...	...	...	r/	9321	...r/	...	...	r/	...	...	...	...
2591	Forging,pressing,stamping,roll-forming of metal		147	100	100	93		792	...	553	543		...	...	...	...
2592	Treatment and coating of metals machining		693	777	765	729		3349	5005	5443	5945		...	415.4	552.2	563.4
2593	Cutlery, hand tools and general hardware		306	228	218	215		1549	1902	1990	2109		...	158.4	176.5	194.4
2599	Other fabricated metal products n.e.c.		960	685	684	652		3631	5089	5297	5294		...	353.3	375.8	394.8
2610	Electronic components and boards		168	61	65	67		1201	315	361	387		491.8s/	17.9	23.0	27.4
2620	Computers and peripheral equipment		548	230	220	219		1313	964	1030	1106		...s/	98.3	109.6	119.0
2630	Communication equipment		121	48	46	47		937	...	2561	2413		...s/	...	571.4	...
2640	Consumer electronics		16	19	22	31		20	...	47	79		...s/	...	1.8	...
265	Measuring,testing equipment; watches, etc.		153	92	90	89		516	1276	1244	1186		...s/	136.7	129.0	128.8
2651	Measuring/testing/navigating equipment,etc.		140	84	83	84		415	1195	1161	1101		...	126.9	121.8	122.1
2652	Watches and clocks		13	8	7	5		101	81	83	85		...	9.8	7.2	6.7
2660	Irradiation/electromedical equipment,etc.		10	10	8	7		146	...	105	115		...s/	...	10.6	...
2670	Optical instruments and photographic equipment		198	38	39	45		355	...	115	127		...s/	...	8.0	...
2680	Magnetic and optical media		3	-	-	...		...	-	...	...		...s/	-	-	...
2710	Electric motors,generators,transformers,etc.		244	157	144	144		5186	5586	5897	5895		913.0t/	682.8	773.5	794.8
2720	Batteries and accumulators		24	7	7	6		47	52	48	44		...t/	2.1	2.1	2.1
273	Wiring and wiring devices		21	25	25	24		1064	1427	1425	1462		...t/	113.1	105.5	108.7
2731	Fibre optic cables		-	-	-	...		-	-	-	...		...	-	-	...
2732	Other electronic and electric wires and cables		20	11	12	12		984	906	846	789		...	80.6	68.2	66.8
2733	Wiring devices		1	14	13	12		80	521	579	673		...	32.5	37.2	42.0
2740	Electric lighting equipment		96	91	93	88		548	727	725	760		...t/	44.3	45.1	51.1
2750	Domestic appliances		72	66	64	57		527	509	454	429		...t/	31.0	28.3	31.2
2790	Other electrical equipment		81	89	90	94		888	2020	2006	2031		...t/	221.9	210.8	222.5
281	General-purpose machinery		631	743u/	729u/	734u/	u/	6687	10798u/	11150u/	11976u/	u/	996.9	956.7	1026.5	1121.7
2811	Engines/turbines,excl.aircraft,vehicle engines		57	41	38	38		2292	1612	1583	2116		...	188.5	198.7	215.7
2812	Fluid power equipment		10	18	19	22		78	103	110	155		...	7.7	8.8	12.1
2813	Other pumps, compressors, taps and valves		83	50	52	53		711	887	935	932		...	71.9	76.9	84.8
2814	Bearings, gears, gearing and driving elements		33	25	22	26		461	333	335	396		...	26.4	27.6	31.5
2815	Ovens, furnaces and furnace burners		24	17	19	20		63	86	242	244		...	6.0	18.2	18.2
2816	Lifting and handling equipment		107	75	74	71		733	753	742	702		...	67.4	70.6	68.9
2817	Office machinery, excl.computers,etc.		25	22	19	18		61	...	83	92		...	...	...	...
2818	Power-driven hand tools		1	7	5	6		2	...	30	34		...	...	...	...
2819	Other general-purpose machinery		291	...	...	210		2286	...	...	2479		...	...	...	240.2
282	Special-purpose machinery		420	...u/	...u/	...u/	u/	4144	...u/	...u/	...u/	u/	...	...	...	...
2821	Agricultural and forestry machinery		88	58	58	59		1016	1139	1208	1239		...	81.9	86.4	106.2
2822	Metal-forming machinery and machine tools		129	68	69	64		781	607	625	608		...	49.9	53.4	56.5

ISIC Revision 4

Code	Description												
2823	Machinery for metallurgy	1	3	3	3	1	8	6	3	...	0.4	0.5	...
2824	Mining, quarrying and construction machinery	31	18	16	18	948	1155	1118	1099	...	94.9	92.2	93.2
2825	Food/beverage/tobacco processing machinery	56	45	45	45	283	...	442	445	...	...	...	38.3
2826	Textile/apparel/leather production machinery	21	6	6	6	...	161	156	157	...	11.9	12.1	...
2829	Other special-purpose machinery	94	77	73	75	1106	...	1300	1275	...	...	...	...
2910	Motor vehicles	28	13	13	16	136	234	349	415	176.0 v/	20.3	32.7	46.2
2920	Automobile bodies, trailers and semi-trailers	32	33	31	35	103	274	271	334	... v/	23.0	23.6	27.7
2930	Parts and accessories for motor vehicles	126	77	76	72	1777	2046	2155	1679	... v/	163.7	165.2	132.2
301	Building of ships and boats	492	247	260	263	9445	6035	6054	5863	963.2 w/	570.1	575.2	573.9
3011	Building of ships and floating structures	311	173	184	190	9021	5701	5744	5568	...	547.0	556.8	554.2
3012	Building of pleasure and sporting boats	181	74	76	73	424	334	310	295	...	23.1	18.4	19.6
3020	Railway locomotives and rolling stock	13	12	12	13	788	566	646	1083	... w/	53.8	66.5	106.0
3030	Air and spacecraft and related machinery	12	12	12	17	302	716	751	907	... w/	103.5	107.6	135.8
3040	Military fighting vehicles	-	1	1	...	-	...	425	...	... w/	...	...	...
309	Transport equipment n.e.c.	34	18	21	22	63	...	131	95	... w/	...	...	6.1
3091	Motorcycles	6	5	6	7	...	21	25	29	...	0.8	1.2	1.5
3092	Bicycles and invalid carriages	26	10	12	12	61	103	102	63	...	5.9	6.4	4.5
3099	Other transport equipment n.e.c.	2	3	3	3	1	...	4	3	...	...	...	0.1
3100	Furniture	1172	949	937	948	8447	9273	9459	10378	471.7	535.7	548.6	650.5
321	Jewellery, bijouterie and related articles	136	428	378	368	251	778	577	613	134.6 x/	30.4	25.6	28.8
3211	Jewellery and related articles	103	288	264	252	228	...	473	464	...	...	...	17.2
3212	Imitation jewellery and related articles	33	140	114	115	23	...	104	110	...	...	...	...
3220	Musical instruments	27	32	34	32	23	153	44	35	... x/	8.1	2.2	1.8
3230	Sports goods	40	35	33	38	43	116	147	162	... x/	5.9	8.5	9.4
3240	Games and toys	61	51	45	47	144	...	97	100	... x/	...	5.4	...
3250	Medical and dental instruments and supplies	229	198	201	207	681	1224	1203	1300	... x/	85.8	86.5	96.4
3290	Other manufacturing n.e.c.	296	475	459	449	876	1246	1059	1032	... x/	53.7	51.1	55.0
331	Repair of fabricated metal products/machinery	872	1123	1144	1197	7188	9229	9113	9316	1092.8 y/	851.2	879.0	893.2
3311	Repair of fabricated metal products	19	58	60	55	1402	1430	1524	1395	...	206.7	230.5	212.2
3312	Repair of machinery	181	501	510	544	650	1827	1780	1998	...	143.7	145.1	152.2
3313	Repair of electronic and optical equipment	96	95	101	99	...	384	448	455	...	34.7	44.1	45.3
3314	Repair of electrical equipment	188	142	135	143	245	402	414	446	...	38.0	37.9	40.9
3315	Repair of transport equip., excl. motor vehicles	385	303	313	332	4783	5147	4905	4998	...	424.7	418.4	441.6
3319	Repair of other equipment	3	24	25	24	15	39	42	24	...	3.5	2.9	...
3320	Installation of industrial machinery/equipment	303	226	236	240	2284	1344	1619	1738	... y/	136.4	168.8	207.4
C	Total manufacturing	24572	20087	19716	19475	201973	244216	245887	253758	16827.6	18928.9	19654.4	21672.0

a/ Number of enterprises.
b/ Methodological break in 2014.
c/ 1010 includes 1020, 1030, 1040, 1050, 106, 107 and 1080.
d/ 1101 includes 1102, 1103 and 1104.
e/ 131 includes 139.
f/ 1410 includes 1420 and 1430.
g/ 151 includes 1520.
h/ 1610 includes 162.
i/ 1701 includes 1702 and 1709.
j/ 181 includes 1820.

k/ 1910 includes 1920.
m/ 201 includes 202 and 2030.
n/ 221 includes 2220.
p/ 2310 includes 239.
q/ 2410 includes 2420 and 243.
r/ 251 includes 2520 and 259.
s/ 2610 includes 2620, 2630, 2640, 265, 2660, 2670 and 2680.
t/ 2710 includes 2720, 273, 2740, 2750 and 2790.
u/ 281 includes 282.
v/ 2910 includes 2920 and 2930.

w/ 301 includes 3020, 3030, 3040 and 309.
x/ 321 includes 3220, 3230, 3240, 3250 and 3290.
y/ 331 includes 3320.

Croatia

	ISIC Revision 4		Output (valuation not defined)					Value added at factor values					Gross fixed capital formation	
			(millions of Croatian Kunas)					(millions of Croatian Kunas)					(millions of Croatian Kunas)	
ISIC	Industry	Note	2013	2014	2015	2016	Note	2013	2014	2015	2016	Note	2015	2016
1010	Processing/preserving of meat		7632.3	8116.2	8097.7	7307.7		1491.3	1505.3	1484.9	1400.8		209.0	417.1
1020	Processing/preserving of fish, etc.		538.0	565.8	563.4	507.5		224.9	213.1	237.2	202.1		29.7	43.7
1030	Processing/preserving of fruit,vegetables		721.3	718.1	791.1	929.2		66.0	177.3	206.7	206.6		66.8	23.8
1040	Vegetable and animal oils and fats		991.9	938.9	930.6	912.3		230.8	212.4	193.2	183.1		113.0	104.3
1050	Dairy products		4856.3	4586.9	4605.1	4475.5		956.1	876.0	962.3	980.6		87.4	96.8
106	Grain mill products,starches and starch products		742.4	746.9	762.9	759.5		188.0	153.5	116.8	194.1		23.3	72.2
1061	Grain mill products		...	...	...	...		...	...	...	...		...	...
1062	Starches and starch products		...	...	...	...		...	...	...	...		...	...
107	Other food products		10638.9	10606.3	10812.0	11556.4		3601.7	3398.2	3589.3	3871.7		515.2	581.2
1071	Bakery products		4016.5	4053.8	4107.2	4360.7		1770.3	1811.6	1859.1	1936.0		167.2	164.3
1072	Sugar		1595.9	1610.1	1360.2	1842.9		355.2	69.1	193.0	293.4		36.6	123.9
1073	Cocoa, chocolate and sugar confectionery		1038.9	1085.4	1149.2	1123.4		334.3	321.1	336.9	330.2		58.6	30.5
1074	Macaroni, noodles, couscous, etc.		178.9	198.4	206.6	236.3		51.2	53.8	62.7	80.8		17.3	24.5
1075	Prepared meals and dishes		69.4	69.0	78.6	86.3		17.3	18.4	17.4	22.5		4.5	4.8
1079	Other food products n.e.c.		...	...	...	...		...	...	...	...		...	...
1080	Prepared animal feeds		744.9	764.7	747.4	805.0		102.6	152.4	161.7	162.1		33.0	44.0
110	Beverages		5731.1	5428.6	5507.8	5468.1		2151.6	1928.7	1958.9	1993.3		249.4	253.0
1101	Distilling, rectifying and blending of spirits		...	...	...	...		...	...	...	...		...	...
1102	Wines		853.9	891.1	859.3	...		312.8	406.4	311.4	...		28.2	...
1103	Malt liquors and malt		2055.9	...	2094.4	2117.5		874.9	...	874.3	861.9		166.0	135.2
1104	Soft drinks,mineral waters,other bottled waters		2113.0	1884.4	1864.1	1788.3		838.8	565.4	571.6	646.2		38.9	30.3
1200	Tobacco products		...	1152.2	...	1160.5		...	411.1	...	270.3		...	112.2
131	Spinning, weaving and finishing of textiles		...	...	...	...		...	...	...	...		...	48.2a/
1311	Preparation and spinning of textile fibres		296.4	465.7	403.7	395.7		61.8	82.4	78.9	70.7		13.6	36.4
1312	Weaving of textiles		147.7	215.6	364.0	241.4		40.1	62.9	139.6	74.5		28.1	4.2
1313	Finishing of textiles		123.3	94.9	108.9	107.8		52.2	35.1	39.6	41.9		0.1	3.4
139	Other textiles		1320.3	1239.8	1158.4	1140.6		312.2	324.4	314.7	268.1		-43.0	...a/
1391	Knitted and crocheted fabrics		...	...	...	...		...	...	...	...		...	...
1392	Made-up textile articles, except apparel		400.0	405.6	485.0	384.6		137.1	147.7	176.0	123.1		3.5	12.3
1393	Carpets and rugs		...	...	...	...		...	...	...	...		...	...
1394	Cordage, rope, twine and netting		...	15.4	...	...		...	6.4	...	...		...	...
1399	Other textiles n.e.c.		29.4	...	...	...		11.8	...	...	...		...	...
1410	Wearing apparel, except fur apparel		1538.1	1615.2	2033.1	2439.5		741.9	790.9	823.1	849.8		42.0	12.8
1420	Articles of fur		0.4	0.6	0.7	1.2		0.2	0.3	0.4	0.7		-	-
1430	Knitted and crocheted apparel		942.0	1148.2	1112.5	1097.9		341.0	379.8	317.5	316.4		42.9	35.0
151	Leather;luggage,handbags,saddlery,harness;fur	b/	2271.0	3266.2	3300.5	3366.7	b/	700.3	862.9	508.4	695.4		168.1b/	65.7b/
1511	Tanning/dressing of leather; dressing of fur		102.0	121.4	130.8	151.0		13.9	19.3	19.8	28.7		1.9	6.1
1512	Luggage,handbags,etc.;saddlery/harness		...	...	...	...		...	...	...	...		...	...
1520	Footwear	b/	...	...	...	...	b/	...	...	...	...		...b/	...b/
1610	Sawmilling and planing of wood		2249.7	2600.7	2793.1	2876.8		681.8	753.8	844.7	793.1		247.5	251.5

Code	Description										
162	Wood products, cork, straw, plaiting materials	93.9	654.6	958.4	941.9	825.1	660.0	3104.2	2642.4	2565.1	2246.9
1621	Veneer sheets and wood-based panels	32.6	50.9	243.3	199.6	191.3	169.9	763.0	682.7	737.2	688.8
1622	Builders' carpentry and joinery	35.7	577.6	440.4	472.8	386.2	284.3	1513.3	1228.4	1150.6	986.5
1623	Wooden containers	3.7	3.9	122.6	109.3	95.3	73.6	335.1	263.5	234.2	207.9
1629	Other wood products;articles of cork,straw	21.9	22.1	152.1	160.1	152.3	132.2	492.8	467.9	443.1	363.7
170	Paper and paper products	220.3	208.6	888.5	747.4	717.5	629.1	3381.9	2927.2	2726.9	2511.2
1701	Pulp, paper and paperboard	60.8	35.0	236.6	156.8	169.0	122.0	990.2	663.3	675.1	647.0
1702	Corrugated paper and paperboard	88.4	75.9	346.6	306.2	292.6	268.4	1295.6	1210.6	1160.3	1048.4
1709	Other articles of paper and paperboard	...	...	...	...	255.8	238.7	...	...	891.4	815.8
181	Printing and service activities related to printing	243.4	230.2	1230.0	1217.0	1171.2	1282.1	3627.5	3527.8	3386.4	3408.7
1811	Printing	128.3	...	1082.9	...	...	...	3318.9	...	...	...
1812	Service activities related to printing	115.1	...	147.0	...	...	...	308.6	233.8	...	...
1820	Reproduction of recorded media	-	-	6.6	6.1	7.8	7.5	19.8	21.8	30.5	28.9
1910	Coke oven products	...	-	...	...	-	...	...	-	-	...
1920	Refined petroleum products	...	...	...	...	...	...	...	...	...	...
201	Basic chemicals,fertilizers, etc.	181.5	97.5	473.6	482.1	316.5	345.8	2655.8	3414.2	3087.9	3179.5
2011	Basic chemicals	...	29.3	...	163.9	...	...	378.7	...	...	...
2012	Fertilizers and nitrogen compounds	...	...	...	...	...	...	...	...	...	...
2013	Plastics and synthetic rubber in primary forms	10.3	...	40.2	...	0.6	...	214.8	205.9	...	...
202	Other chemical products	...	...	...	...	...	31.8	...	...	...	125.0
2021	Pesticides and other agrochemical products	...	40.9	181.0	149.9	...	146.8	608.8	553.9	...	536.8
2022	Paints,varnishes;printing ink and mastics	16.1	40.9	181.0	149.9	...	146.8	608.8	553.9	...	536.8
2023	Soap,cleaning and cosmetic preparations	13.9	43.0	341.1	328.7	248.6	271.7	1353.9	1327.5	1237.7	1202.7
2029	Other chemical products n.e.c.	...	...	...	...	141.2	120.8	...	...	568.4	522.9
2030	Man-made fibres	...	-	...	-	-	...	...	-	-	...
2100	Pharmaceuticals,medicinal chemicals, etc.	774.1	638.7	2322.8	1847.3	2096.3	1962.2	5781.9	5530.3	5241.8	4824.8
221	Rubber products	27.0	63.1	198.2	184.2	171.0	163.3	387.0	329.7	319.2	308.6
2211	Rubber tyres and tubes	-0.2	-	6.3	11.2	14.0	16.2	25.0	20.2	21.4	23.3
2219	Other rubber products	27.2	63.1	192.0	173.1	157.0	147.1	362.0	309.5	297.8	285.3
2220	Plastics products	241.1	225.2	1472.0	1356.9	1133.0	1007.2	5286.1	4862.6	4344.1	4103.5
2310	Glass and glass products	134.4	569.1	612.2	533.4	549.2	505.8	1530.2	1337.0	1308.1	1236.6
239	Non-metallic mineral products n.e.c.	-	-	1.3	0.8	1.5	2.8	2.9	2.4	2.7	8.1
2391	Refractory products	...	-	...	...	...	...	...	...	...	...
2392	Clay building materials	11.8	9.8	163.6	150.9	149.1	163.9	417.9	424.5	401.1	424.9
2393	Other porcelain and ceramic products	67.4	5.8	72.3	74.0	85.8	82.6	191.3	168.0	176.1	202.0
2394	Cement, lime and plaster	69.5	82.2	640.6	716.4	621.2	548.4	1721.0	1897.5	1770.6	1727.2
2395	Articles of concrete, cement and plaster	66.5	11.4	659.3	639.6	506.9	459.2	2057.4	1892.1	1671.5	1638.1
2396	Cutting, shaping and finishing of stone	22.8	6.5	273.5	257.5	247.7	255.0	699.3	623.8	650.0	633.6
2399	Other non-metallic mineral products n.e.c.	29.0	27.4	212.6	179.9	175.0	145.6	750.2	734.0	713.9	660.9
2410	Basic iron and steel	...	...	...	...	79.8	...	...	20.0	883.8	...
2420	Basic precious and other non-ferrous metals	7.6	17.7	43.7	43.8	88.7	305.5	377.2	339.0	1007.1	1369.0
243	Casting of metals	102.1	159.9	410.6	370.0	374.0	326.9	1048.6	1005.1	965.4	891.3
2431	Casting of iron and steel	44.7	...	225.0	...	...	...	575.7	370.8	...	...
2432	Casting of non-ferrous metals	...	...	...	...	...	...	...	...	...	...
251	Struct.metal products, tanks, reservoirs	616.8c/	498.8c/	5506.0	4690.3	4394.2	4127.4	12716.9	11041.5	10419.7	10324.5

continued

Croatia

ISIC	Industry	Output (valuation not defined) Note	Output 2013	Output 2014	Output 2015	Output 2016	Value added at factor values Note	VA 2013	VA 2014	VA 2015	VA 2016	GFCF Note	GFCF 2015	GFCF 2016
			(millions of Croatian Kunas)					(millions of Croatian Kunas)					(millions of Croatian Kunas)	
2511	Structural metal products		4034.8	3926.0	4191.7	5311.4		1460.3	1543.1	1615.3	2004.0		121.8	224.6
2512	Tanks, reservoirs and containers of metal		555.9	326.2	329.0	344.7		223.7	135.0	144.4	121.1		4.9	41.7
2513	Steam generators, excl. hot water boilers		729.7	725.7	750.0	716.3		256.1	259.6	234.8	318.0		8.0	8.5
2520	Weapons and ammunition	c/	...	...	...	...	c/	...	...	...	...		...c/	...c/
259	Other metal products;metal working services	c/	...	...	...	...	c/	...	...	...	...		...c/	...c/
2591	Forging,pressing,stamping,roll-forming of metal		...	...	...	...		...	...	...	...			
2592	Treatment and coating of metals; machining		1542.6	1766.1	1985.9	2101.1		620.2	791.8	980.2	1056.3		102.2	77.5
2593	Cutlery, hand tools and general hardware		789.5	843.4	922.6	1024.6		380.4	395.9	465.6	484.8		177.9	125.3
2599	Other fabricated metal products n.e.c.		1877.9	1975.8	2009.1	2147.9		697.2	735.1	708.5	763.1		56.5	98.9
2610	Electronic components and boards		183.6	163.2	281.4	465.7		60.5	57.4	70.2	75.0		7.7	45.6
2620	Computers and peripheral equipment		434.0	525.5	723.4	957.8		186.6	222.1	246.3	260.1		2.6	15.0
2630	Communication equipment		...	...	1613.1	...		...	...	842.8	...		48.8	...
2640	Consumer electronics		...	...	16.8	...		...	...	7.3	...		-	...
265	Measuring,testing equipment, watches, etc.		681.0	631.2	602.7	594.1		277.2	276.5	274.7	282.3		13.8	13.4
2651	Measuring/testing/navigating equipment,etc.		660.8	605.7	582.8	580.8		269.7	265.6	266.8	276.1		13.7	13.3
2652	Watches and clocks		20.1	25.4	19.9	13.3		7.6	10.9	7.9	6.2		0.1	0.1
2660	Irradiation/electromedical equipment,etc.		29.4	...	32.7	...		17.5	...	19.8	...		0.3	...
2670	Optical instruments and photographic equipment		12.7	...	23.8	...		7.4	...	14.2	...		-	...
2680	Magnetic and optical media		...	-	...	...		...	-	...	...		-	...
2710	Electric motors,generators,transformers,etc.		3203.0	3920.2	4270.1	4272.0		1077.8	1322.8	1446.0	1512.5		105.7	124.4
2720	Batteries and accumulators		17.1	15.9	9.6	6.7		1.7	5.6	-	0.1		0.4	0.2
273	Wiring and wiring devices		1396.4	945.0	1005.8	880.4		201.5	110.2	220.6	163.6		53.6	44.3
2731	Fibre optic cables		...	-	-	...		...	-	-	...		-	...
2732	Other electronic and electric wires and cables		1277.6	795.2	817.4	685.6		152.1	42.1	148.0	89.1		0.2	3.8
2733	Wiring devices		118.8	149.8	188.4	194.9		49.4	68.0	72.5	74.5		53.4	40.5
2740	Electric lighting equipment		201.4	213.4	224.1	281.2		72.3	76.2	84.4	103.2		1.9	-4.8
2750	Domestic appliances		145.6	128.5	129.0	144.9		40.2	54.0	38.5	53.3		-0.2	2.7
2790	Other electrical equipment		710.7	748.6	780.7	831.5		371.7	343.7	328.8	337.9		12.9	18.3
281	General-purpose machinery		2407.2	4997.6d/	5507.7d/	6439.4d/		935.5	1787.0d/	2003.5d/	2123.3d/		197.3d/	240.2d/
2811	Engines/turbines,excl.aircraft,vehicle engines		699.9	620.7	745.8	924.9		274.3	285.1	414.4	352.4		14.8	54.0
2812	Fluid power equipment		21.4	28.1	25.8	43.4		11.4	15.4	14.3	22.6		-	
2813	Other pumps, compressors, taps and valves		279.7	303.7	348.0	413.5		109.7	120.3	146.6	162.6		4.5	25.0
2814	Bearings, gears, gearing and driving elements		79.1	103.5	94.9	111.6		38.8	54.9	49.0	53.0		0.7	1.4
2815	Ovens, furnaces and furnace burners		...	92.0	134.2	81.6		...	22.0	42.0	28.0		-	-
2816	Lifting and handling equipment		336.5	322.2	336.9	382.6		136.0	144.3	139.3	106.4		21.4	11.8
2817	Office machinery, excl.computers,etc.		40.7	...	...	...		10.6	...	...	...		...	...
2818	Power-driven hand tools		925.4	...	...	...		339.1	...	...	...		...	...
2819	Other general-purpose machinery		...	...	...d/	1654.7		...	...	...	521.7		...	59.9
282	Special-purpose machinery		...	...d/	...d/	...d/		...	...	...d/	...d/		...d/	...d/
2821	Agricultural and forestry machinery		682.5	658.1	730.5	797.3		137.1	180.0	205.7	193.6		21.2	26.6
2822	Metal-forming machinery and machine tools		121.3	150.7	162.9	196.7		62.3	75.7	77.3	76.5		3.6	5.3

Code	Description										
2823	Machinery for metallurgy	1.7	1.5	...	...	0.6	0.7	0.9	...	...	14.9
2824	Mining, quarrying and construction machinery	294.4	480.1	497.8	481.3	111.9	178.4	195.1	199.8	11.3	1.8
2825	Food/beverage/tobacco processing machinery	...	...	35.8	165.0	24.9	24.6	23.3	76.3	...	...
2826	Textile/apparel/leather production machinery	37.8	37.3	238.7	...	...	...	...	...	2.3	...
2829	Other special-purpose machinery	...	...	...	...	...	...	...	...	...	...
2910	Motor vehicles	...	99.0	184.8	271.4	...	33.2	52.9	73.4	12.5	11.0
2920	Automobile bodies, trailers and semi-trailers	...	138.4	131.1	157.2	...	45.0	50.7	56.0	26.0	2.5
2930	Parts and accessories for motor vehicles	751.8	867.8	939.2	842.4	141.4	249.4	282.5	278.6	18.8	95.1
301	Building of ships and boats	1999.2	2532.2	2754.1	2273.1	440.3	347.9	502.3	175.2	16.1	64.9
3011	Building of ships and floating structures	1852.0	2418.7	2642.7	2173.3	407.6	298.9	489.8	164.9	15.4	61.0
3012	Building of pleasure and sporting boats	147.3	113.9	111.4	99.8	32.7	49.1	12.5	10.3	0.7	3.8
3020	Railway locomotives and rolling stock	...	258.7	741.5	494.3	...	104.3	168.6	189.5	11.3	26.2
3030	Air and spacecraft and related machinery	240.6	286.4	340.9	354.7	126.4	152.2	142.2	159.4	0.9	3.1
3040	Military fighting vehicles	15.3	...	...	...	...	...	...	7.8	...	...
309	Transport equipment n.e.c.	...	...	...	17.0	8.1	...	...	2.7	...	...
3091	Motorcycles	...	2.4	4.7	5.2	...	1.2	2.3	...	-	-
3092	Bicycles and invalid carriages	12.7	18.1	23.5	11.2	7.0	10.3	12.8	4.9	-0.1	...
3099	Other transport equipment n.e.c.	...	...	...	0.6	...	...	...	0.3	...	...
3100	Furniture	2577.1	2551.2	2835.8	3398.6	877.6	907.0	1003.5	1139.3	134.6	126.6
321	Jewellery, bijouterie and related articles	162.2	128.2	143.0	170.2	66.5	56.6	65.6	68.8	0.2	0.5
3211	Jewellery and related articles	86.5	...	...	91.7	43.1	...	...	39.9	...	...
3212	Imitation jewellery and related articles	...	...	...	...	...	...	...	...	...	...
3220	Musical instruments	4.7	...	6.8	7.6	1.5	...	3.1	3.1	-	-
3230	Sports goods	43.9	45.0	48.7	63.4	20.3	23.4	23.4	25.7	-	-
3240	Games and toys	30.4	35.6	30.6	...	11.2	13.5	13.7	...	-	...
3250	Medical and dental instruments and supplies	268.1	260.2	272.8	348.4	158.1	155.9	161.3	188.8	5.9	2.1
3290	Other manufacturing n.e.c.	338.8	329.0	313.7	354.8	113.9	118.2	114.4	105.1	6.2	2.5
331	Repair of fabricated metal products/machinery	2280.1	2891.0	3396.3	3328.2	1045.7	1269.9	1424.3	1479.3	108.0	79.5
3311	Repair of fabricated metal products	104.8	520.7	643.1	506.8	37.7	232.4	232.5	281.3	1.1	1.9
3312	Repair of machinery	442.0	480.0	502.1	667.0	226.2	246.4	247.2	308.7	15.0	12.1
3313	Repair of electronic and optical equipment	128.3	178.8	272.8	262.2	58.7	74.5	105.2	92.9	0.4	1.1
3314	Repair of electrical equipment	148.6	153.4	163.3	224.3	60.9	80.2	90.2	87.6	-	-
3315	Repair of transport equip., excl. motor vehicles	1449.9	1548.9	1807.7	1659.0	658.4	631.1	744.1	706.5	91.5	64.5
3319	Repair of other equipment	6.5	9.3	7.1	8.9	3.8	5.3	5.1	2.3	-	-
3320	Installation of industrial machinery/equipment	1092.2	619.1	770.6	1003.0	541.3	263.8	327.5	381.2	25.9	6.0
C	Total manufacturing	109675.4	113549.4	119531.6	137445.6	34418.9	35473.5	37492.2	43449.1	6356.7	7161.0

a/ 131 includes 139.
b/ 151 includes 1520.
c/ 251 includes 2520 and 259.
d/ 281 includes 282.

Croatia

ISIC Revision 4

Index numbers of industrial production

(2010=100)

ISIC	Industry	Note	2005	2006	2007	2008	2009	2010	2011	2012	2013	2014	2015	2016
10	Food products		92	98	102	105	99	100	102	100	98	100	105	108
11	Beverages		104	104	113	113	110	100	106	102	100	97	100	100
12	Tobacco products		110	102	108	116	86	100	87	86	75	64	62	63
13	Textiles		105	109	103	93	90	100	89	81	85	81	81	88
14	Wearing apparel		154	134	136	133	106	100	105	91	82	94	87	78
15	Leather and related products		60	78	94	98	77	100	103	89	90	105	132	136
16	Wood products, excluding furniture		104	111	118	120	116	100	101	86	83	85	98	101
17	Paper and paper products		67	73	78	77	87	100	99	95	92	96	100	107
18	Printing and reproduction of recorded media		83	89	102	110	105	100	96	85	83	92	90	92
19	Coke and refined petroleum products		136	118	129	105	114	100	83	88	81	71	79	86
20	Chemicals and chemical products		88	95	101	104	94	100	99	92	92	95	106	119
21	Pharmaceuticals,medicinal chemicals, etc.		152	121	113	133	76	100	94	116	113	127	128	142
22	Rubber and plastics products		111	109	107	104	102	100	104	105	97	120	134	148
23	Other non-metallic mineral products		127	140	144	141	125	100	97	91	89	90	89	91
24	Basic metals		112	116	116	126	95	100	98	77	89	96	84	72
25	Fabricated metal products, except machinery		116	125	144	152	115	100	102	100	104	98	103	119
26	Computer, electronic and optical products		127	114	126	111	100	100	46	35	35	37	36	39
27	Electrical equipment		128	117	124	114	108	100	89	76	71	78	72	88
28	Machinery and equipment n.e.c.		96	123	128	138	99	100	130	92	92	98	97	105
29	Motor vehicles, trailers and semi-trailers		121	145	161	147	131	100	102	103	104	111	131	143
30	Other transport equipment		145	147	144	154	128	100	103	100	55	56	78	69
31	Furniture		97	103	122	116	98	100	105	99	98	105	105	110
32	Other manufacturing		257	269	188	157	106	100	71	51	61	54	52	45
33	Repair and installation of machinery/equipment		60	76	87	82	89	100	113	109	110	110	119	119
C	Total manufacturing		103	107	113	114	102	100	100	95	91	94	97	103

Curaçao

Supplier of information:
Central Bureau of Statistics, Willemstad.

Basic source of data:
Annual survey; administrative data.

Major deviations from ISIC (Revision 4):
None reported.

Reference period:
Calendar year.

Scope:
All enterprises.

Method of data collection:
Questionnaires; direct interview in the field.

Type of enumeration:
Complete enumeration of enterprises with 10 or more persons engaged and a sample of smaller enterprises, which remain in the sample for four consecutive years.

Adjusted for non-response:
Yes.

Concepts and definitions of variables:
Output excludes value of goods shipped in the same condition as received less the amount paid for these goods and net change between the beginning and end of the year in the value of work in process and stocks of goods to be shipped in the same condition as received. It is valued at market prices.
Value added is valued at market prices.

Related national publications:
National Accounts Curaçao, published by the Central Bureau of Statistics, Willemstad.

Curaçao

Number of enterprises a/

ISIC	Industry	Note	(number)			
			2013	2014	2015	2016
C	Total manufacturing		...	425	305	324

Number of persons engaged

ISIC	Industry	Note	(number)			
			2013	2014	2015	2016
C	Total manufacturing		3960	4020	3917	...

Wages and salaries paid to employees

ISIC	Industry	Note	(thousands of Netherlands Antillean Guilders)			
			2013	2014	2015	2016
C	Total manufacturing		248728	256970	...	...

a/ Break between 2014 and 2015

Output (valuation not defined)

ISIC	Industry	Note	(thousands of Netherlands Antillean Guilders)			
			2013	2014	2015	2016
C	Total manufacturing		1039914	1009538	...	...

Value added (valuation not defined)

ISIC	Industry	Note	(thousands of Netherlands Antillean Guilders)			
			2013	2014	2015	2016
C	Total manufacturing		483574	478936	...	...

Gross fixed capital formation

ISIC	Industry	Note	(thousands of Netherlands Antillean Guilders)	
			2015	2016
C	Total manufacturing		...	...

Index numbers of industrial production

ISIC	Industry	Note	(2010=100)											
			2005	2006	2007	2008	2009	2010	2011	2012	2013	2014	2015	2016
C	Total manufacturing		...	...	...	...	...	...	...	...	...	...	...	...

Cyprus

Supplier of information:
Statistical Service, Ministry of Finance, Nicosia.

Basic source of data:
Industrial survey.

Major deviations from ISIC (Revision 4):
None reported.

Reference period:
Calendar year.

Scope:
All privately owned enterprises.

Method of data collection:
Direct interview in the field.

Type of enumeration:
Sample survey.

Adjusted for non-response:
Yes.

Concepts and definitions of variables:
Wages and salaries excludes remuneration for time not worked.
Output includes revenue from non-industrial activities.

Related national publications:
Industrial Statistics (annual), published by the Statistical Service, Ministry of Finance, Nicosia.

Cyprus

ISIC	Industry	Note	Number of enterprises (number) 2013	2014	2015	2016	Note	Number of employees (number) 2013	2014	2015	2016	Note	Wages and salaries paid to employees (thousands of Euros) 2013	2014	2015	2016
1010	Processing/preserving of meat	a/	63	61	57	60	a/	1275	1253	1346	1449	a/	19325	17318	18926	21381
1020	Processing/preserving of fish, etc.	a/	31	33	32	35	a/	173	162	168	173	a/	3260	3087	2868	2905
1030	Processing/preserving of fruit,vegetables		39	41	38	39		716	723	720	739		15214	14351	14338	15026
1040	Vegetable and animal oils and fats	a/	...	...	...	...	a/	...	...	...	...	a/	...	...	...	...
1050	Dairy products		91	101	97	100		1422	1846	1920	2004		29385	39898	40117	43842
106	Grain mill products,starches and starch products		9	9	9	9		268	273	278	287		6589	6218	6368	6538
1061	Grain mill products		9	9	9	9		268	273	278	287		6589	6218	6368	6538
1062	Starches and starch products		-	-	-	-		-	-	-	-		-	-	-	-
107	Other food products		542	548	538	538		6010	5784	5868	6031		78274	73316	74257	79169
1071	Bakery products	b/	437	437	427	422	b/	5370	5166	5269	5394	b/	68174	64092	65510	69671
1072	Sugar		27	35	30	33		212	312	304	334		3611	5360	5163	5902
1073	Cocoa, chocolate and sugar confectionery		27	26	26	30		130	95	99	109		2008	1174	1114	1162
1074	Macaroni, noodles, couscous, etc.		23	23	21	20		89	83	81	67		1409	1167	1059	852
1075	Prepared meals and dishes		19	27	34	33		86	128	115	127		1154	1523	1411	1582
1079	Other food products n.e.c.	b/	...	...	...	...	b/	...	...	...	...	b/	...	...	...	...
1080	Prepared animal feeds		33	34	34	33		311	301	325	348		5440	5488	6068	6686
110	Beverages		78	81	81	83		1338	824	834	886		36577	18060	18093	19141
1101	Distilling, rectifying and blending of spirits		12	12	11	11		63	59	57	59		1100	1042	933	1132
1102	Wines		45	49	50	52		180	194	199	224		3233	3191	3166	3623
1103	Malt liquors and malt		4	4	4	5		459	459	460	477		12431	12368	12314	12601
1104	Soft drinks,mineral waters,other bottled waters		17	16	16	15		636	112	118	126		19813	1459	1680	1785
1200	Tobacco products	c/	3	3	4	4	c/	64	42	53	43	c/	1320	899	1186	876
131	Spinning, weaving and finishing of textiles		19	17	21	21		41	39	39	39		337	298	402	467
1311	Preparation and spinning of textile fibres		-	-	-	-		-	-	-	-		-	-	-	-
1312	Weaving of textiles		-	-	-	-		-	-	-	-		-	-	-	-
1313	Finishing of textiles		19	17	21	21		41	39	39	39		337	298	402	467
139	Other textiles		84	76	82	75		362	344	382	382		4915	4513	4920	5187
1391	Knitted and crocheted fabrics		-	-	4d/	3d/		-	-	2d/	1d/		-	-	19d/	4d/
1392	Made-up textile articles, except apparel		66	59	61	56		338	304	341	342		4664	4162	4623	4827
1393	Carpets and rugs		4	4	...	...										
1394	Cordage, rope, twine and netting		18e/	17e/	...d/	...d/		24e/	40e/	...d/	...d/		251e/	351e/	...d/	...d/
1399	Other textiles n.e.c.		...e/	...e/	17	16		...e/	...e/	39	39		...e/	...e/	278	356
1410	Wearing apparel, except fur apparel		180	171	166	169		319	275	255	243		3692	3474	2428	2516
1420	Articles of fur		-	-	-	-		-	-	-	-		-	-	-	-
1430	Knitted and crocheted apparel		7	7	6	8		21	17	16	20		201	190	148	191
151	Leather;luggage,handbags,saddlery,harness;fur	f/	13	12	11	10	f/	11	9	10	9	f/	141	99	67	63
1511	Tanning/dressing of leather; dressing of fur	f/	13	12	11	10	f/	11	9	10	9	f/	141	99	67	63
1512	Luggage,handbags,etc.;saddlery/harness	f/	...	...	...	...	f/	...	...	...	...	f/	...	...	...	...
1520	Footwear		16	17	15	14		44	39	37	39		456	378	456	414
1610	Sawmilling and planing of wood		5	5	4	5		13	10	8	10		161	132	90	114

Code	Product	fn	A1	A2	A3	A4	B1	B2	B3	B4	C1	C2	C3	C4
162	Wood products, cork, straw, plaiting materials		920	877	851	823	1549	1365	1407	1412	23992	20737	18619	19204
1621	Veneer sheets and wood-based panels		1	1	4g/	4g/	52	49	63g/	61g/	1900	1543	1878g/	1953g/
1622	Builders' carpentry and joinery		892	847	822	789	1455	1278	1324	1317	21636	18846	16543	16898
1623	Wooden containers		27h/	29h/	...g/	...g/	42h/	38h/	...g/	...g/	456h/	348h/	...g/	...g/
1629	Other wood products;articles of cork,straw		...h/	...h/	25	30	...h/	...h/	20	34	...h/	...h/	206	353
170	Paper and paper products		42	43	41	38	548	557	577	594	10112	9639	10453	10311
1701	Pulp, paper and paperboard		-	-	-	27i/	-	-	-	382i/	-	-	-	5990i/
1702	Corrugated paper and paperboard		15	15	12	11	182	165	205	212	4190	3823	4405	4321
1709	Other articles of paper and paperboard		27	28	29	...i/	366	392	372	...i/	5922	5816	6048	...i/
181	Printing and service activities related to printing	i/	261	262	251	254	987	911	863	914	16067	15100	13533	14876
1811	Printing		229	230	221k/	223k/	933	867	821k/	858k/	15315	14388	12925k/	14038k/
1812	Service activities related to printing		32	31	...k/	...k/	51	43	...k/	...k/	752	692	...k/	...k/
1820	Reproduction of recorded media	j/	...	...	...	...	...	...	...	...	...	...	...	...
1910	Coke oven products	c/	...	...	...	...	...	...	...	...	...	...	...	...
1920	Refined petroleum products		...	...	...	...	...	...	...	...	...	...	...	...
201	Basic chemicals,fertilizers, etc.	m/	57	55	49	57	674	642	606	624	12601	11755	11052	11308
2011	Basic chemicals	n/	12	10	11	14	124	123	127	129	2913	2765	2750	2975
2012	Fertilizers and nitrogen compounds		-	-	-	-	-	-	-	-	-	-	-	-
2013	Plastics and synthetic rubber in primary forms		-	-	-	-	-	-	-	-	-	-	-	-
202	Other chemical products	m/	...	...	...	...	...	...	...	...	...	...	...	...
2021	Pesticides and other agrochemical products		3	3	3	3	80	87	89	78	1907	2006	1959	1766
2022	Paints,varnishes;printing ink and mastics		14	14	13	13	207	183	176	192	3756	3297	2797	3219
2023	Soap,cleaning and cosmetic preparations		28	28	22	27	263	249	214	225	4025	3687	3546	3348
2029	Other chemical products n.e.c.	n/	...	...	...	...	...	...	...	...	...	...	...	...
2030	Man-made fibres		-	-	-	-	-	-	-	-	-	-	-	-
2100	Pharmaceuticals,medicinal chemicals, etc.	n/	8	9	7	7	1341	1451	1487	1573	35363	36887	37054	40521
221	Rubber products	p/	9	9	9	8	13	11	12	10	168	161	130	111
2211	Rubber tyres and tubes	p/	9	9	9	8	13	11	12	10	168	161	130	111
2219	Other rubber products		...	...	...	...	...	...	...	...	...	...	...	...
2220	Plastics products	p/	67	67	70	71	863	829	849	885	15278	14603	14904	15540
2310	Glass and glass products		55	53	53	53	208	185	176	206	2710	2183	2001	2559
239	Non-metallic mineral products n.e.c.		276	261	251	250	1872	1633	1562	1619	39258	34099	31435	33962
2391	Refractory products	q/	5	5	5	6	219	230	233	245	9245	8546	8710	9766
2392	Clay building materials		21	22	19	16	136	129	111	103	2804	2715	2183	2070
2393	Other porcelain and ceramic products		34	35	33	33	32	37	16	21	349	500	90	122
2394	Cement, lime and plaster	q/	...	...	...	...	...	...	...	...	...	...	...	...
2395	Articles of concrete, cement and plaster		123	110	104	105	946	798	771	805	17549	14689	13441	14573
2396	Cutting, shaping and finishing of stone		89	85	86	87	495	422	413	430	8391	7169	6572	7035
2399	Other non-metallic mineral products n.e.c.		4	4	4	3	44	17	18	15	920	481	439	396
2410	Basic iron and steel		6r/	4	3	3	316r/	48	38	36	7715r/	1029	760	732
2420	Basic precious and other non-ferrous metals	r/	...r/	3	4	5	...r/	267	248	303	...r/	6027	5819	6166
243	Casting of metals		...	...	...	...	...	...	...	...	...	...	...	...
2431	Casting of iron and steel		-	-	-	-	-	-	-	-	-	-	-	-
2432	Casting of non-ferrous metals		-	-	-	-	-	-	-	-	-	-	-	-
251	Struct.metal products, tanks, reservoirs		901	851	849	818	2294	1992	2020	2102	33535	29615	25942	27681

continued

Cyprus

ISIC Revision 4		Number of enterprises (number)					Number of employees (number)					Wages and salaries paid to employees (thousands of Euros)				
ISIC	Industry	Note	2013	2014	2015	2016	Note	2013	2014	2015	2016	Note	2013	2014	2015	2016
2511	Structural metal products		890	841	839	809		2260	1941	1995	2065		32901	28705	25581	27086
2512	Tanks, reservoirs and containers of metal		11	10	10	9		34	51	25	37		634	910	361	595
2513	Steam generators, excl. hot water boilers		-	-	-	-		-	-	-	-		-	-	-	-
2520	Weapons and ammunition		3	3	3	3		21	22	21	21		397	384	378	329
259	Other metal products;metal working services		303	276	290	284		699	666	671	716		11896	10725	9789	10799
2591	Forging,pressing,stamping,roll-forming of metal		-	-	-	-		-	-	-	-		-	-	-	-
2592	Treatment and coating of metals; machining		143	131	131	127		157	156	145	148		3085	2582	1996	2137
2593	Cutlery, hand tools and general hardware		24	24	23	21		83	91	92	52		1426	1619	1469	828
2599	Other fabricated metal products n.e.c.		136	121	136	136		459	419	434	516		7385	6524	6324	7834
2610	Electronic components and boards		28s/	...	...	...		183s/	...	...	...		4548s/	...	...	...
2620	Computers and peripheral equipment		-	-	-	-		-	-	-	-		-	-	-	-
2630	Communication equipment		...s/	25t/	28t/	30t/		...s/	223t/	255t/	229t/		...s/	6437t/	7523t/	7839t/
2640	Consumer electronics		-	-	-	-		-	-	-	-		-	-	-	-
265	Measuring;testing equipment; watches, etc.		-	-	-	-		-	-	-	-		-	-	-	-
2651	Measuring/testing/navigating equipment,etc.		-	-	-	-		-	-	-	-		-	-	-	-
2652	Watches and clocks		-	-	-	-		-	-	-	-		-	-	-	-
2660	Irradiation/electromedical equipment,etc.		-	-	-	-		-	-	-	-		-	-	-	-
2670	Optical instruments and photographic equipment		-	-	-	-		-	-	-	-		-	-	-	-
2680	Magnetic and optical media		-	-	-	-		-	-	-	-		-	-	-	-
2710	Electric motors,generators,transformers,etc.		26	25	22	22		190	178	165	173		3904	3281	3193	3027
2720	Batteries and accumulators		-	-	-	-		-	-	-	-		-	-	-	-
273	Wiring and wiring devices		...s/	...t/	...t/	...t/		...s/	...t/	...t/	...t/		...s/	...t/	...t/	...t/
2731	Fibre optic cables		-	-	-	-		-	-	-	-		-	-	-	-
2732	Other electronic and electric wires and cables		-	-	-	-		-	-	-	-		-	-	-	-
2733	Wiring devices		...s/	...t/	...t/	...t/		...s/	...t/	...t/	...t/		...s/	...t/	...t/	...t/
2740	Electric lighting equipment		39	36	33	34		163	144	139	135		2187	1976	1844	1892
2750	Domestic appliances	u/	59	52	49	48	u/	519	467	485	497	u/	10110	8793	9147	9102
2790	Other electrical equipment		-	-	-	-		-	-	-	-		-	-	-	-
281	General-purpose machinery		-	-	-	-		-	-	-	-		-	-	-	-
2811	Engines/turbines,excl.aircraft,vehicle engines		-	-	-	-		-	-	-	-		-	-	-	-
2812	Fluid power equipment	v/	4	3	4	3	v/	21	14	18	19	v/	423	281	335	425
2813	Other pumps, compressors, taps and valves		-	-	-	-		-	-	-	-		-	-	-	-
2815	Bearings, gears, gearing and driving elements		-	-	-	-		-	-	-	-		-	-	-	-
2816	Ovens, furnaces and furnace burners	w/	34	32	29	31	w/	363	327	339	353	w/	6885	5994	6406	6614
2817	Office machinery, excl.computers,etc.		-	-	-	-		-	-	-	-		-	-	-	-
2818	Power-driven hand tools	w/	-	-	-	-	w/	-	-	-	-	w/	-	-	-	-
2819	Other general-purpose machinery	u/	...	...	...	...	u/	...	...	...	...	u/	...	...	...	...
282	Special-purpose machinery		...	...	...	...		...	...	...	...		...	...	...	...
2821	Agricultural and forestry machinery		11	9	8	8		55	57	56	63		1036	1013	1050	1085
2822	Metal-forming machinery and machine tools	v/	...	...	...	...	v/	...	...	...	...	v/	...	...	...	...

2823	Machinery for metallurgy	4x/	...	...	...	41x/	...	-	...	752x/	...	...	...
2824	Mining, quarrying and construction machinery	...x/	8y/	8y/	6y/	...x/	69y/	72y/	62y/	...x/	1505y/	1356y/	978y/
2825	Food/beverage/tobacco processing machinery	...x/	...y/	...y/	...y/	...x/	...y/	...y/	...y/	...x/	...y/	...y/	...y/
2826	Textile/apparel/leather production machinery	-	-	-	-	-	-	-	-	1014	-	-	-
2829	Other special-purpose machinery	6	...y/	...y/	...y/	39	...y/	...y/	...y/	...	...y/	...y/	...y/
2910	Motor vehicles	...	22z/	22z/	22z/	...	48z/	58z/	70z/	...	867z/	1147z/	1250z/
2920	Automobile bodies, trailers and semi-trailers	21	...z/	...z/	...z/	39	...z/	...z/	...z/	769	...z/	...z/	...z/
2930	Parts and accessories for motor vehicles	53	50	49	48	59	52	56	60	1038	837	597	660
301	Building of ships and boats	7	5	4	7	26	26	28	37	428	331	363	452
3011	Building of ships and floating structures	7	5	-	-	26	26	-	-	428	331	-	-
3012	Building of pleasure and sporting boats	-	-	4A/	7A/	-	-	28A/	37A/	-	-	363A/	452A/
3020	Railway locomotives and rolling stock	-	-	-	-	-	-	-	-	-	-	-	-
3030	Air and spacecraft and related machinery	-	-	...A/	...A/	-	-	...A/	...A/	-	-	...A/	...A/
3040	Military fighting vehicles	-	-	-	-	-	-	-	-	-	-	-	-
309	Transport equipment n.e.c.	-	-	-	-	-	-	-	-	-	-	-	-
3091	Motorcycles	-	-	-	-	-	-	-	-	-	-	-	-
3092	Bicycles and invalid carriages	-	-	-	-	-	-	-	-	-	-	-	-
3099	Other transport equipment n.e.c.	-	-	-	-	-	-	-	-	-	-	-	-
3100	Furniture	352	340	332	319	854	777	661	721	12819	11076	8617	9718
321	Jewellery, bijouterie and related articles	174	168	164	158	342	310	272	290	5064	4353	3676	3896
3211	Jewellery and related articles	154	148	142	137	336	296	272	290	4904	4173	3676	3896
3212	Imitation jewellery and related articles	20	20	22	21	6	14	-	-	160	180	-	-
3220	Musical instruments	7	6	8B/	8B/	...	...	19B/	42B/	39	40	201B/	529B/
3230	Sports goods	-	-	-	-	-	-	-	-	-	-	-	-
3240	Games and toys	5	3	...B/	...B/	14	19	...B/	...B/	211	200	...B/	...B/
3250	Medical and dental instruments and supplies	82	79	83	85	116	123	123	124	2759	2487	1870	1930
3290	Other manufacturing n.e.c.	43	40	42	42	133	130	114	109	1800	1537	1395	1477
331	Repair of fabricated metal products/machinery	208	219	235	243	854	1051	1363	1741	17901	22029	30676	44947
3311	Repair of fabricated metal products	13	12	9	9	53	58	52	62	1742	1622	1639	1708
3312	Repair of machinery	98	104	110	111	230	273	286	282	4514	5528	4882	4830
3313	Repair of electronic and optical equipment	8	10	9	10	21	15	29	74	437	478	1306	2604
3314	Repair of electrical equipment	21	22	25	25	53	49	45	45	964	944	739	623
3315	Repair of transport equip., excl. motor vehicles	57	66	76	82	441	653	947	1275	9050	13406	22072	35146
3319	Repair of other equipment	11	5	6	6	56	3	4	3	1194	51	38	36
3320	Installation of industrial machinery/equipment	18	17	22	23	61	46	44	80	1174	834	728	1300
C	Total manufacturing	5243	5076	5019	4966	27323	26114	26578	28025	479130	445742	443578	486634

a/ 1020 includes 1040.
b/ 1072 includes 1079.
c/ 1200 includes 1920.
d/ 1391 includes 1394.
e/ 1394 includes 1399.
f/ 1511 includes 1512.
g/ 1621 includes 1623.
h/ 1623 includes 1629.
i/ 1701 includes 1709.
j/ 181 includes 1820.

k/ 1811 includes 1812.
m/ 201 includes 202.
n/ 2011 includes 2029.
p/ 2211 includes 2219.
q/ 2391 includes 2394.
r/ 2410 includes 2420.
s/ 2610 includes 2630, 273 and 2740.
t/ 2630 includes 273 and 2740.
u/ 281 includes 282.
v/ 2812 includes 2822.

w/ 2816 includes 2819.
x/ 2823 includes 2824 and 2825.
y/ 2824 includes 2825 and 2829.
z/ 2910 includes 2920.
A/ 3012 includes 3030.
B/ 3220 includes 3240.

Cyprus

ISIC	Industry	Note	Output at producers' prices (thousands of Euros)				Note	Value added at producers' prices (thousands of Euros)				Note	Gross fixed capital formation (thousands of Euros)		Note
			2013	2014	2015	2016		2013	2014	2015	2016		2015	2016	
1010	Processing/preserving of meat	a/	275373	265726	255221	263596	a/	41453	38531	39719	43750	a/	4056	4750	
1020	Processing/preserving of fish, etc.	a/	30717	31832	28992	27005		6145	5604	5770	5153		121	611	a/
1030	Processing/preserving of fruit,vegetables		86190	89705	95023	101803		27420	28152	30119	32605		1597	4222	a/
1040	Vegetable and animal oils and fats	a/	...	...	...	...	a/	...	...	...	...	a/	...	...	
1050	Dairy products		214162	292677	298100	330854		48718	69509	70166	83017		9366	8953	
106	Grain mill products,starches and starch products		48098	46660	49127	46966		12682	13160	12145	13639		932	826	
1061	Grain mill products		48098	46660	49127	46966		12682	13160	12145	13639		932	826	
1062	Starches and starch products		-					-					-		
107	Other food products		299721	295088	304863	320325		123767	120492	129930	139083		15373	12056	
1071	Bakery products	b/	247110	245182	259394	269903	b/	101693	101213	111613	118033	b/	13925	10060	b/
1072	Sugar		18801	29740	14954	31955		7319	12288	12311	13722		1161	1538	
1073	Cocoa, chocolate and sugar confectionery		9318	5869	5169	6002		3827	2213	2053	2482		155	90	
1074	Macaroni, noodles, couscous, etc.		5331	4493	2922	2710		2290	1498	1265	1398		84	81	
1075	Prepared meals and dishes		5960	9804	8166	9755		2145	3280	2688	3448		48	287	
1079	Other food products n.e.c.		...					...					...		
1080	Prepared animal feeds	b/	98255	100355	93639	94898	b/	14348	14949	15467	16038	b/	1069	853	b/
110	Beverages		184545	103583	100091	108013		76623	51414	50173	55328		1153	3826	
1101	Distilling, rectifying and blending of spirits		10072	9988	8879	9410		4462	4307	3806	3942		110	161	
1102	Wines		19863	19677	17988	20069		9641	9304	8477	9063		1296	2310	
1103	Malt liquors and malt		55921	57616	59310	64988		32646	32897	32629	36723		1021	852	
1104	Soft drinks,mineral waters,other bottled waters		98689	16302	13914	13546		29874	4906	5261	5600		-1274	503	
1200	Tobacco products	c/	14481	5916	7270	5862	c/	5043	1884	2271	2548	c/	-3727	-4675	c/
131	Spinning, weaving and finishing of textiles		1192	1929	1640	3141		443	478	632	1127		-74	-2	
1311	Preparation and spinning of textile fibres		-					-					...	-	
1312	Weaving of textiles		-					-					-	-	
1313	Finishing of textiles		1192	1929	1640	3141		443	478	632	1127		-74	-2	
139	Other textiles		15440	15766	18701	18435		5747	6491	7182	7477		154	338	
1391	Knitted and crocheted fabrics		-		70d/	38d/		-		52d/	29d/		-d/	-8d/	
1392	Made-up textile articles, except apparel		14615	14628	17629	17315		5339	5959	6753	6891		142	220	
1393	Carpets and rugs		-					-					...	...	
1394	Cordage, rope, twine and netting		825e/	1138e/	...d/	...d/		408e/	532e/	...d/	557		...d/	..d/	
1399	Other textiles n.e.c.		...e/	...e/	1002	1082		...e/	...e/	377	557		12	126	
1410	Wearing apparel, except fur apparel		10625	9631	10607	11386		3653	3580	4294	4447		1069	73	
1420	Articles of fur		602	774	538	659		281	335	191	246		...	...	
1430	Knitted and crocheted apparel		-					-					-	-	
151	Leather;luggage,handbags,saddlery,harness;fur		243	214	352	303		77	83	145	145		4	4	
1511	Tanning/dressing of leather; dressing of fur	f/	243	214	352	303	f/	77	83	145	145	f/	4	4	f/
1512	Luggage,handbags,etc.;saddlery/harness	f/	...	...	...	...	f/	...	...	...	...	f/	...	...	f/
1520	Footwear		1283	1213	1365	1277		539	514	579	541		3	17	
1610	Sawmilling and planing of wood		730	715	417	399		220	201	144	111		-	1	

ISIC	Industry	Note										
162	Wood products, cork, straw, plaiting materials		87869	84838	87906	94591	32784	31111	35719	38195	1022	1045
1621	Veneer sheets and wood-based panels		4679	4768	5832g/	6692g/	689	1392	1046g/	2012g/	39g/	-126g/
1622	Builders' carpentry and joinery		82081	79087	81394	86861	31628	29349	34259	35767	972	1057
1623	Wooden containers		1109h/	983h/	...g/	...g/	467h/	370h/	...g/	...g/	...g/	...g/
1629	Other wood products;articles of cork,straw		...h/	...h/	680	1038	...h/	...h/	414	416	11	114
170	Paper and paper products		46757	47620	50261	53552	17493	17304	17122	18907	1188	1220
1701	Pulp, paper and paperboard		-	-	-	30010i/	-	-	-	10022i/	604	815i/
1702	Corrugated paper and paperboard		16555	16535	20134	23542	6249	6230	6995	8885	584	405
1709	Other articles of paper and paperboard		30202	31085	30127	...i/	11244	11074	10127	...i/	...	...i/
181	Printing and service activities related to printing	j/	66200	63476	60217	65380	26628	24893	24244	26272	1660	1991
1811	Printing		63321	60867	58080k/	61956k/	24984	23370	23068k/	24462k/	1619k/	1962k/
1812	Service activities related to printing	j/	2879	2449	...k/	...k/	1644	1479	...k/	...k/	...k/	...k/
1820	Reproduction of recorded media		:	:	:	:	:	:	:	:	:	:
1910	Coke oven products		-	-	-	-	-	-	-	-	-	-
1920	Refined petroleum products	c/	:	:	:	:	:	:	:	:	:	:
201	Basic chemicals,fertilizers, etc.	m/	57802	54185	58176	62008	22916	21641	24014	26402	1811	1554
2011	Basic chemicals	n/	15666	14972	15584	18356	8067	7515	7834	9996	246	362
2012	Fertilizers and nitrogen compounds		-	-	-	-	-	-	-	-	-	-
2013	Plastics and synthetic rubber in primary forms		-	-	-	-	-	-	-	-	-	-
202	Other chemical products	m/	:	:	:	:	:	:	:	:	:	:
2021	Pesticides and other agrochemical products		5521	5815	6915	5699	2900	2410	2825	3126	196	108
2022	Paints,varnishes;printing ink and mastics		18360	16264	17739	18416	4971	5486	5638	6214	148	272
2023	Soap,cleaning and cosmetic preparations		18255	17134	17938	19537	6978	6230	7717	7066	1221	812
2029	Other chemical products n.e.c.	n/	:	:	:	:	:	:	:	:	:	:
2030	Man-made fibres		:	:	:	:	:	:	:	:	:	:
2100	Pharmaceuticals,medicinal chemicals, etc.		188312	189950	205134	205747	74328	78471	88940	94535	4842	10848
221	Rubber products	p/	564	525	710	511	233	195	278	213	-	12
2211	Rubber tyres and tubes	p/	564	525	710	511	233	195	278	213	-	12
2219	Other rubber products		:	:	:	:	:	:	:	:	:	:
2220	Plastics products		68901	75032	70376	80150	24171	24800	24719	29283	5467	5317
2310	Glass and glass products		12534	10515	11040	16473	4808	3444	4110	6336	387	654
239	Non-metallic mineral products n.e.c.	q/	244404	235150	229483	248032	65843	77003	85950	100498	1578	13797
2391	Refractory products		70890	86763	89661	93079	20777	36524	44525	52989	4141	10207
2392	Clay building materials		9074	9762	7851	9423	2974	3667	3340	4766	76	669
2393	Other porcelain and ceramic products		1161	1645	726	691	589	743	455	456	268	-9
2394	Cement, lime and plaster	q/	:	:	:	:	:	:	:	:	:	:
2395	Articles of concrete, cement and plaster		116841	103260	97152	109481	28278	24834	25265	28799	-2385	3733
2396	Cutting, shaping and finishing of stone		26748	24235	26417	28234	11482	9947	10670	11991	356	-834
2399	Other non-metallic mineral products n.e.c.		19690	9485	7676	7124	1743	1288	1695	1497	-878	31
2410	Basic iron and steel		66213r/	38970	32140	36879	24419r/	15062	12755	2892	-	1361
2420	Basic precious and other non-ferrous metals		...r/	12212	11607	11346	...r/	:	:	14083	844	:
243	Casting of metals		-	-	-	-	-	-	-	-	-	-
2431	Casting of iron and steel		-	-	-	-	-	-	-	-	-	-
2432	Casting of non-ferrous metals		-	-	-	-	-	-	-	-	-	-
251	Struct.metal products, tanks, reservoirs		166839	150845	147219	157031	54948	52361	51949	55130	3714	2545

continued

Cyprus

ISIC	Industry	Note	Output 2013	Output 2014	Output 2015	Output 2016	Note	VA 2013	VA 2014	VA 2015	VA 2016	Note	GFCF 2015	GFCF 2016
			(thousands of Euros)					(thousands of Euros)					(thousands of Euros)	
2511	Structural metal products		164253	145202	144796	153988		54072	49939	51280	53943		3672	2473
2512	Tanks, reservoirs and containers of metal		2586	5643	2423	3043		876	2422	669	1187		42	72
2513	Steam generators, excl. hot water boilers		-	-	-	-		920	1220	1272	1028		...	5
2520	Weapons and ammunition		5250	6115	6983	5651							21	
259	Other metal products;metal working services		37857	36694	37018	41896		17235	16383	17177	18766		676	867
2591	Forging,pressing,stamping,roll-forming of metal		-	-	-	-		-	-	-	-			
2592	Treatment and coating of metals;machining		8726	7829	7264	8510		4184	3797	3971	4169		67	79
2593	Cutlery, hand tools and general hardware		5278	6031	6474	2316		2575	2705	2978	1290		269	38
2599	Other fabricated metal products n.e.c.		23853	22834	23280	31070		10476	9881	10228	13307		340	750
2610	Electronic components and boards		23856s/	-	-	-		14720s/	-	-	-			
2620	Computers and peripheral equipment		...	...	...	...		...	...	...	...			
2630	Communication equipment		...s/	32581t/	47789t/	22967t/		...s/	22822t/	30861t/	11162t/		3218t/	3553t/
2640	Consumer electronics		-	-	-	-		-	-	-	-			
265	Measuring,testing equipment; watches, etc.		-	-	-	-		-	-	-	-			
2651	Measuring/testing/navigating equipment,etc.		-	-	-	-		-	-	-	-			
2652	Watches and clocks		-	-	-	-		-	-	-	-			
2660	Irradiation/electromedical equipment,etc.		-	-	-	-		-	-	-	-			
2670	Optical instruments and photographic equipment		-	-	-	-		-	-	-	-			
2680	Magnetic and optical media		-	-	-	-		-	-	-	-			
2710	Electric motors,generators,transformers,etc.		13537	13315	11597	12615		5003	4847	4734	4611		111	40
2720	Batteries and accumulators		-	-	-	-		-	-	-	-			
273	Wiring and wiring devices		...s/	...t/	...t/	...t/		...s/	...t/	...t/	...t/		...t/	...t/
2731	Fibre optic cables		-	-	-	-		-	-	-	-			
2732	Other electronic and electric wires and cables		-	-	-	-		-	-	-	-			
2733	Wiring devices		-	-	-	-		-	-	-	-			
2740	Electric lighting equipment		...s/	...t/	...t/	...t/		...s/	...t/	...t/	...t/			
2750	Domestic appliances		9307	8470	9558	10323		3413	2969	2917	3651		279	111
2790	Other electrical equipment		-	-	-	-		-	-	-	-			
281	General-purpose machinery	u/	42641	40965	49656	54277	u/	20000	18724	20832	21287	u/	2555	3150
2811	Engines/turbines,excl.aircraft,vehicle engines		-	-	-	-		-	-	-	-			
2812	Fluid power equipment	v/	1303	1396	2235	2102	v/	567	575	754	838	v/	127	31
2813	Other pumps, compressors, taps and valves		-	-	-	-		-	-	-	-			
2814	Bearings, gears, gearing and driving elements		-	-	-	-		-	-	-	-			
2815	Ovens, furnaces and furnace burners		-	-	-	-		-	-	-	-			
2816	Lifting and handling equipment	w/	26846	24598	28088	37779	w/	11404	10865	12442	14952	w/	576	586
2817	Office machinery, excl.computers,etc.		-	-	-	-		-	-	-	-			
2818	Power-driven hand tools		-	-	-	-		-	-	-	-			
2819	Other general-purpose machinery	w/	...	...	...	...	w/	...	...	...	...	w/	...	...
282	Special-purpose machinery	u/	...	...	...	...	u/	...	...	...	...	u/	...	...
2821	Agricultural and forestry machinery		6527	4816	8809	9902		3154	1928	3306	3627		163	2047
2822	Metal-forming machinery and machine tools	v/	...	...	...	...	v/	...	...	...	...	v/	...	...

Code	Description										
2823	Machinery for metallurgy	1888x/	...	...	...	781x/	...	...	...	...	...
2824	Mining, quarrying and construction machinery	...x/	10155y/	...	...	...x/	5356y/	4330y/	1870y/	1689y/	486y/
2825	Food/beverage/tobacco processing machinery	...x/	...y/	10524z/	4494z/	...x/	...y/	...y/	...y/	...y/	...y/
2826	Textile/apparel/leather production machinery	-	-	-	-	-	-	-	-	-	-
2829	Other special-purpose machinery	6077	...y/	...z/	...z/	4094	...y/	...y/	...y/	...y/	...y/
2910	Motor vehicles	-	5059A/	7410A/	6797A/	...	1383A/	2486A/	3214A/	104A/	44A/
2920	Automobile bodies, trailers and semi-trailers	3018	...A/	...A/	...A/	942	...A/	...A/	...A/	...A/	...A/
2930	Parts and accessories for motor vehicles	3062	2175	3127	2360	1566	1088	1495	1564	2	10
301	Building of ships and boats	1748	2060	2641	1989	611	840	892	1067	117	217
3011	Building of ships and floating structures	1748	2060	2641B/	1989B/	611	840	892B/	1067B/	117B/	217B/
3012	Building of pleasure and sporting boats	-	-	...B/	...B/	-	-	...B/	...B/	...B/	...B/
3020	Railway locomotives and rolling stock	-	-	-	-	-	-	-	-	-	-
3030	Air and spacecraft and related machinery	-	-	-	-	-	-	-	-	-	-
3040	Military fighting vehicles	-	-	-	-	-	-	-	-	-	-
309	Transport equipment n.e.c.	-	-	-	-	-	-	-	-	-	-
3091	Motorcycles	-	-	-	-	-	-	-	-	-	-
3092	Bicycles and invalid carriages	-	-	-	-	-	-	-	-	-	-
3099	Other transport equipment n.e.c.	-	-	-	-	-	-	-	-	-	-
3100	Furniture	45071	42934	44268	39937	19135	18765	17893	19210	412	603
321	Jewellery, bijouterie and related articles	16386	16654	15730	15558	7185	7215	7520	7560	330	481
3211	Jewellery and related articles	15860	16132	15361	15198	6927	7002	7326	7346	330	478
3212	Imitation jewellery and related articles	526	522	369	360	258	213	194	214	-	3
3220	Musical instruments	109	84	3407C/	1807C/	52	46	718C/	1403C/	298C/	1079C/
3230	Sports goods	881	1192	...C/	...C/	316	448	...C/	...C/	...C/	...C/
3240	Games and toys	5962	5765	7412	7115	3836	3558	4010	4339	60	340
3250	Medical and dental instruments and supplies	6647	6175	6411	5423	2563	2426	2206	2523	132	436
3290	Other manufacturing n.e.c.	...	...	...	...	...	...	...	...	...	...
331	Repair of fabricated metal products/machinery	51144	70716	137152	92149	29217	38247	52264	63929	1316	2291
3311	Repair of fabricated metal products	5339	5359	6491	6023	3080	3281	3216	2943	69	115
3312	Repair of machinery	12242	16805	14629	13967	7447	8917	8053	7880	328	653
3313	Repair of electronic and optical equipment	1889	2645	9404	7721	1144	1563	5279	4459	70	201
3314	Repair of electrical equipment	2859	2527	2134	2216	1837	1525	1223	1291	-10	34
3315	Repair of transport equip., excl. motor vehicles	26532	43272	104289	61994	14469	22909	34352	47230	855	1263
3319	Repair of other equipment	2283	108	205	228	1240	52	141	126	4	25
3320	Installation of industrial machinery/equipment	3995	2475	3902	3023	1837	1142	1456	1885	44	71
C	Total manufacturing	2558523	2518531	2745811	2568974	844281	846272	909514	985200	63284	85495

a/ 1020 includes 1040.
b/ 1072 includes 1079.
c/ 1200 includes 1920.
d/ 1391 includes 1399.
e/ 1394 includes 1399.
f/ 1511 includes 1512.
g/ 1621 includes 1623.
h/ 1623 includes 1629.
i/ 1701 includes 1709.
j/ 181 includes 1820.
k/ 1811 includes 1812.
m/ 201 includes 202.
n/ 2011 includes 2029.
p/ 2211 includes 2219.
q/ 2391 includes 2394.
r/ 2410 includes 2420.
s/ 2610 includes 2630, 273 and 2740.
t/ 2630 includes 273 and 2740.
u/ 281 includes 282.
v/ 2812 includes 2822.

w/ 2816 includes 2819.
x/ 2823 includes 2824 and 2825.
y/ 2824 includes 2825 and 2829.
z/ 2825 includes 2829.
A/ 2910 includes 2920.
B/ 3011 includes 3012.
C/ 3220 includes 3230.

Cyprus

- 258 -

Index numbers of industrial production

ISIC Revision 4

(2010=100)

ISIC	Industry	Note	2005	2006	2007	2008	2009	2010	2011	2012	2013	2014	2015	2016
10	Food products	a/	107	99	103	105	101	100	93	89	84	83	87	96
11	Beverages	a/	...	...	...	...	...	...	...	...	...	...	...	...
12	Tobacco products	a/	...	...	...	...	...	...	...	...	...	...	...	...
13	Textiles	b/	187	180	164	142	111	100	90	75	57	55	56	60
14	Wearing apparel	b/	...	...	...	...	...	...	...	...	...	...	...	...
15	Leather and related products	b/	...	...	...	...	...	...	...	...	...	...	...	...
16	Wood products, excluding furniture	c/	114	115	132	141	131	100	87	73	49	45	50	53
17	Paper and paper products	c/	83	84	86	93	83	100	96	88	72	77	78	82
18	Printing and reproduction of recorded media	c/	...	...	...	...	...	...	...	...	...	...	...	...
19	Coke and refined petroleum products	d/	71	74	85	91	87	100	99	103	109	113	122	118
20	Chemicals and chemical products	d/	...	...	...	...	...	...	...	...	...	...	...	...
21	Pharmaceuticals,medicinal chemicals, etc.	d/	...	...	...	...	...	...	...	...	...	...	...	...
22	Rubber and plastics products		105	108	109	126	107	100	86	70	60	61	57	68
23	Other non-metallic mineral products		133	131	137	144	111	100	85	62	48	43	45	52
24	Basic metals	e/	108	118	126	130	110	100	94	80	60	56	57	61
25	Fabricated metal products, except machinery	e/	...	...	...	...	...	...	...	...	...	...	...	...
26	Computer, electronic and optical products	f/	43	56	67	83	78	100	84	61	40	42	36	42
27	Electrical equipment	f/	...	...	...	...	...	...	...	...	...	...	...	...
28	Machinery and equipment n.e.c.	g/	125	136	132	130	124	100	122	124	79	81	106	107
29	Motor vehicles, trailers and semi-trailers	g/	...	...	...	...	...	...	...	...	...	...	...	...
30	Other transport equipment	g/	...	...	...	...	...	...	...	...	...	...	...	...
31	Furniture	h/	134	137	135	143	113	100	87	75	58	65	74	90
32	Other manufacturing	h/	...	...	...	...	...	...	...	...	...	...	...	...
33	Repair and installation of machinery/equipment	h/	...	...	...	...	...	...	...	...	...	...	...	...
C	Total manufacturing		107	107	112	117	103	100	92	83	71	70	74	81

a/ 10 includes 11 and 12.
b/ 13 includes 14 and 15.
c/ 17 includes 18.
d/ 19 includes 20 and 21.
e/ 24 includes 25.
f/ 26 includes 27.
g/ 28 includes 29 and 30.
h/ 31 includes 32 and 33.

- 259 -

Czechia

Supplier of information:
Czech Statistical Office (CSO), Prague.
Industrial statistics for the OECD countries are compiled by the OECD secretariat, which supplies them to UNIDO.

Basic source of data:
Annual survey; administrative data; business register.

Major deviations from ISIC (Revision 4):
Data presented in ISIC (Revision 4) were originally classified according to the national NACE-related classification system.

Reference period:
Calendar year.

Scope:
All enterprises.

Method of data collection:
Electronic questionnaire and administrative data.

Type of enumeration:
Sample survey.

Adjusted for non-response:
Yes.

Concepts and definitions of variables:
No deviations from the standard UN concepts and definitions are reported.

Related national publications:
Statistical Yearbook of the Czech Republic, published by the Czech Statistical Office (CSO), Prague.

Czechia

		Number of enterprises (number)					Number of employees (thousands)					Wages and salaries paid to employees (millions of Czech Korunas)				
ISIC	Industry	Note	2013	2014	2015	2016	Note	2013	2014	2015	2016	Note	2013	2014	2015	2016
1010	Processing/preserving of meat		1709	1799	1816	1918		21.6	21.0	22.2	21.9		4585	4640	5047	5439
1020	Processing/preserving of fish, etc.		22	20	20	21		0.7	0.7	0.8	0.7		171	182	188	200
1030	Processing/preserving of fruit,vegetables		137	148	137	141		2.7	2.8	3.3	3.3		600	644	772	827
1040	Vegetable and animal oils and fats		15	16	16	15		0.8	0.9	0.9	0.9		278	308	349	346
1050	Dairy products		178	181	172	172		8.6	8.3	8.4	8.6		2411	2250	2439	2655
106	Grain mill products,starches and starch products		190	201	195	198		2.7	2.7	2.8	3.0		769	821	837	919
1061	Grain mill products		190a/	201a/	97	102		2.7a/	2.7a/	2.3	2.5		769a/	821a/	715	784
1062	Starches and starch products		...a/	...a/	98	96		...a/	...a/	0.5	0.5		...a/	...a/	123	135
107	Other food products		4546	4570	4716	4896		47.2	47.3	47.6	46.9		10363	10747	11321	11908
1071	Bakery products		4546b/	4570b/	3139	3259		47.2b/	47.3b/	31.4	30.7		10363b/	10747b/	6408	6729
1072	Sugar		...b/	...b/	11	9		...b/	...b/	1.3	1.3		...b/	...b/	516	533
1073	Cocoa, chocolate and sugar confectionery		...b/	...b/	80	78		...b/	...b/	4.1	4.1		...b/	...b/	1432	1533
1074	Macaroni, noodles, couscous, etc.		...b/	...b/	45	43		...b/	...b/	0.4	0.4		...b/	...b/	115	119
1075	Prepared meals and dishes		...b/	...b/	73	72		...b/	...b/	1.5	1.6		...b/	...b/	344	395
1079	Other food products n.e.c.		...b/	...b/	1368	1435		...b/	...b/	8.8	8.8		...b/	...b/	2504	2606
1080	Prepared animal feeds		369	378	364	383		4.7	4.8	4.7	4.8		1785	1872	1880	1809
110	Beverages		1266	1613	1815	2077		13.4	13.5	13.6	13.9		5079	5182	5341	5658
1101	Distilling, rectifying and blending of spirits	c/	1266	1613	1815	2077	c/	13.4	13.5	13.6	13.9	c/	5079	5182	5341	5658
1102	Wines	c/	...	...	...	...	c/	...	...	...	...	c/	...	...	...	...
1103	Malt liquors and malt	c/	...	...	...	...	c/	...	...	...	...	c/	...	...	...	...
1104	Soft drinks,mineral waters,other bottled waters	c/	...	...	...	...	c/	...	...	...	...	c/	...	...	...	...
1200	Tobacco products		8	7	7	6		...	...	...	...		...	...	...	...
131	Spinning, weaving and finishing of textiles		156	159	154	149		8.8	8.7	8.7	8.1		2247	2346	2321	2244
1311	Preparation and spinning of textile fibres		156d/	47	47	46		8.8d/	1.9	2.0	1.9		2247d/	509	507	527
1312	Weaving of textiles		...d/	58	55	54		...d/	5.8	5.7	5.6		...d/	1625	1558	1592
1313	Finishing of textiles		...d/	54	52	49		...d/	0.9	1.0	0.6		...d/	212	256	124
139	Other textiles		2559	2361	2270	2270		14.8	14.8	15.4	16.1		3388	3566	3920	4290
1391	Knitted and crocheted fabrics		2559e/	2361e/	55	45		14.8e/	14.8e/	0.5	0.5		3388e/	3566e/	120	122
1392	Made-up textile articles, except apparel		...e/	...e/	1523	1556		...e/	...e/	5.7	6.1		...e/	...e/	1189	1346
1393	Carpets and rugs		...e/	...e/	23	23		...e/	...e/	0.4	0.5		...e/	...e/	87	108
1394	Cordage, rope, twine and netting		...e/	...e/	26	27		...e/	...e/	0.8	0.9		...e/	...e/	199	251
1399	Other textiles n.e.c.		...e/	...e/	643	619		...e/	...e/	8.0	8.2		...e/	...e/	2324	2463
1410	Wearing apparel, except fur apparel		9632	10230	10760	11608		14.7	14.6	14.9	14.9		2356	2456	2619	2882
1420	Articles of fur		166	154	141	142		0.1	0.1	0.1	0.1		13	14	14	14
1430	Knitted and crocheted apparel		991	896	838	813		1.5	1.4	1.4	1.4		288	284	278	305
151	Leather;luggage,handbags,saddlery,harness;fur	f/	582	566	533	519	f/	3.3	3.0	3.0	3.3	f/	660	642	696	806
1511	Tanning/dressing of leather; dressing of fur	f/	582	566	533	519	f/	3.3	3.0	3.0	3.3	f/	660	642	696	806
1512	Luggage,handbags,etc.;saddlery/harness	f/	...	...	...	...	f/	...	...	...	...	f/	...	...	...	...
1520	Footwear		208	194	186	175		2.2	2.1	2.0	2.0		374	372	371	384
1610	Sawmilling and planing of wood		1901	1765	1691	1608		6.7	6.5	6.4	6.6		1504	1520	1563	1698

ISIC Revision 4

Note on table: the data are printed as a landscape (rotated) table. Columns are grouped in three blocks of four, each block read left-to-right. Blanks shown in the source as "…"; letter suffixes (g/, h/, i/, j/, k/, m/, n/, p/, q/) are footnote markers reproduced with the values they accompany.

Code	Description	Note	III‑1	III‑2	III‑3	III‑4	II‑1	II‑2	II‑3	II‑4	I‑1	I‑2	I‑3	I‑4
162	Wood products, cork, straw, plaiting materials		25948	25788	25981	26442	25.7	24.8	25.0	24.8	5443	5502	5813	5969
1621	Veneer sheets and wood-based panels		25948g/	25788g/	161	151	25.7g/	24.8g/	3.2	3.3	5443g/	5502g/	949	1049
1622	Builders' carpentry and joinery		…g/	…g/	23370	23936	…g/	…g/	14.1	13.8	…g/	…g/	3069	3076
1623	Wooden containers		…g/	…g/	501	476	…g/	…g/	4.0	4.0	…g/	…g/	960	989
1629	Other wood products;articles of cork,straw		…g/	…g/	1949	1879	…g/	…g/	3.7	3.7	…g/	…g/	835	852
170	Paper and paper products		895	928	950	975	17.8	17.8	18.8	19.4	5316	5383	5900	6172
1701	Pulp, paper and paperboard		895h/	928h/	…	…	17.8h/	17.8h/	…	…	5318h/	5383h/	…	…
1702	Corrugated paper and paperboard		…h/	317	317	317	…h/	…h/	8.1	8.3	…h/	…h/	2406	2593
1709	Other articles of paper and paperboard		…h/	…h/	…	…	…h/	…h/	…	…	…h/	…h/	…	…
181	Printing and service activities related to printing	j/	7598	7546	7528	7571	15.1	16.3i/	16.3i/	17.0i/	4248	4665i/	4793i/	5136i/
1811	Printing	j/	7598	7546	7528	7571	15.1j/	…i/	…i/	…i/	4248j/	…i/	…i/	…i/
1812	Service activities related to printing		…	…	…	…	…j/	…	…	…	…j/	…	…	…
1820	Reproduction of recorded media		959	1127	1245	1521	1.8	…	…	…	473	…	…	…
1910	Coke oven products		9	8	7	8	2.1k/	2.0k/	…k/	…k/	959k/	906k/	…k/	…k/
1920	Refined petroleum products		24	25	18	21	…k/	…k/	…	…	5217	5477	5690	6231
201	Basic chemicals,fertilizers, etc.		1118	1132	1144	1196	14.0	14.4	14.8	15.1	5217	5477	5690	6231
2011	Basic chemicals		1118	1132	1144	1196	14.0	14.4	14.8	15.1	5217	5477	5690	6231
2012	Fertilizers and nitrogen compounds	m/	…	…	…	…	…	…	…	…	…	…	…	…
2013	Plastics and synthetic rubber in primary forms	m/	…	…	…	…	…	…	…	…	…	…	…	…
202	Other chemical products		636	618	608	610	12.2	12.1	12.3	12.5	3845	3929	4095	4371
2021	Pesticides and other agrochemical products		636n/	42	47	48	12.2n/	0.8	0.7	0.6	3845n/	253	232	227
2022	Paints,varnishes;printing ink and mastics		…n/	87	78	80	…n/	2.3	2.3	2.3	…n/	799	783	830
2023	Soap,cleaning and cosmetic preparations		…n/	191	191	187	…n/	…	4.4	4.5	…n/	…	1383	1468
2029	Other chemical products n.e.c.		…n/	…	…	…	…n/	…	…	…	…n/	…	…	…
2030	Man-made fibres		11	11	10	9	1.0	1.1	1.1	0.9	346	311	352	308
2100	Pharmaceuticals,medicinal chemicals, etc.		86	80	78	87	9.7	9.3	9.1	9.6	3596	3649	3617	3831
221	Rubber products		738	716	721	734	19.0	19.8	20.3	21.2	5986	6391	6798	7391
2211	Rubber tyres and tubes		738p/	716p/	328	352	19.0p/	19.8p/	7.5	7.7	5986p/	6391p/	3025	3204
2219	Other rubber products		…p/	393	393	382	…p/	…p/	12.8	13.6	…p/	…p/	3773	4188
2220	Plastics products		2925	2901	2851	2858	57.3	58.1	62.0	65.4	16045	16695	18356	20500
2310	Glass and glass products		2036	2061	2075	2137	21.2	21.5	22.0	22.6	6259	6457	6825	7315
239	Non-metallic mineral products n.e.c.		4168	4096	4032	3984	29.7	29.9	31.3	30.8	9771	10147	10980	11257
2391	Refractory products		…	45	44	45	…	3.1	3.3	3.1	1060	1060	1099	1149
2392	Clay building materials		…	…	…	…	…	…	…	…	…	…	…	…
2393	Other porcelain and ceramic products		…	…	…	…	…	…	…	…	…	…	…	…
2394	Cement, lime and plaster		…	…	…	…	…	…	…	…	…	…	…	…
2395	Articles of concrete, cement and plaster		…	918	918	871	…	…	14.0	13.5	…	…	5145	5134
2396	Cutting, shaping and finishing of stone		1411	1411	1429	1453	…	1.3	1.2	1.2	270	270	273	265
2399	Other non-metallic mineral products n.e.c.		146	142	142	144	…	…	3.1	3.2	1198	1198	1178	1198
2410	Basic iron and steel		146	138	134	142	25.3	26.4	26.2	25.7	8896	9687	9695	9719
2420	Basic precious and other non-ferrous metals		102	102	110	109	3.6	3.3	3.8	4.0	1195	1212	1429	1549
243	Casting of metals		612	651	683	719	14.7	14.2	14.2	14.4	4224	4155	4228	4504
2431	Casting of iron and steel		612q/	651q/	551	592	14.7q/	14.2q/	7.8	8.1	4224q/	4155q/	2330	2517
2432	Casting of non-ferrous metals		…q/	…q/	132	127	…q/	…q/	6.3	6.3	…q/	…q/	1896	1990
251	Struct.metal products, tanks, reservoirs		3498	3503	3533	3679	39.4	39.8	40.2	40.2	11707	12306	12911	13379

Czechia

ISIC Revision 4

		Number of enterprises (number)				Number of employees (thousands)				Wages and salaries paid to employees (millions of Czech Korunas)			
ISIC	Industry	2013	2014	2015	2016	2013	2014	2015	2016	2013	2014	2015	2016
2511	Structural metal products	3498r/	...	2927	3104	39.4r/	...	28.5	28.9	11707r/	...	8879	9346
2512	Tanks, reservoirs and containers of metal	...r/	...	466	444	...r/	...	9.5	9.3	...r/	...	3140	3166
2513	Steam generators, excl. hot water boilers	...r/	147	140	131	...r/	2.3	2.1	2.0	...r/	925	892	868
2520	Weapons and ammunition	97	90	94	89	3.6	3.9	4.0	4.2	1081	1195	1293	1381
259	Other metal products;metal working services	39122	40688	41304	41423	97.7	100.0	105.8	108.0	27175	28896	31698	33863
2591	Forging,pressing,stamping,roll-forming of metal	39122s/	2163	2240	2297	97.7s/	7.3	7.5	7.6	27175s/	2437	2545	2671
2592	Treatment and coating of metals; machining	...s/	...	12542	13018	...s/	...	38.1	39.5	...s/	...	11018	11957
2593	Cutlery, hand tools and general hardware	...s/	...	...	...	...s/	...	...	...	...s/	...	...	...
2599	Other fabricated metal products n.e.c.	...s/	...	1809	1759	...s/	...	30.4	31.1	...s/	...	9278	9840
2610	Electronic components and boards	797	815	829	887	7.7	7.2	7.1	7.3	2149	2247	2100	2303
2620	Computers and peripheral equipment	328	304	289	269	5.8	5.7	5.8	5.9	1548	1517	1626	1892
2630	Communication equipment	860	820	806	773	4.7	4.8	5.1	5.9	1722	1812	1901	2225
2640	Consumer electronics	331	309	297	279	4.1	3.5	3.7	3.8	1354	1195	1208	1233
265	Measuring,testing equipment; watches, etc.	677	687	722	758	14.0	14.5	15.5	17.0	4908	5320	5808	6521
2651	Measuring/testing/navigating equipment,etc.	677t/	687t/	708	744	14.0t/	14.5t/	15.4	16.9	4908t/	5320t/	5780	6491
2652	Watches and clocks	...t/	...t/	14	14	...t/	...t/	0.1	0.1	...t/	...t/	27	30
2660	Irradiation/electromedical equipment,etc.	48	53	50	58	0.4	0.4	0.4	0.3	132	138	123	132
2670	Optical instruments and photographic equipment	137	131	124	122	2.9	3.0	2.9	2.8	735	752	747	838
2680	Magnetic and optical media	141	140	127	118	0.1	0.1	0.1	0.1	18	17	16	16
2710	Electric motors,generators,transformers,etc.	9897	9504	9012	8557	42.0	43.0	43.5	43.5	14297	14688	15290	15664
2720	Batteries and accumulators	44	42	39	40	1.2	1.2	1.2	1.3	559	540	570	603
273	Wiring and wiring devices	347	328	318	281	13.5	14.2	14.9	9.9	3666	4004	4348	3031
2731	Fibre optic cables	347u/	328u/	10	9	13.5u/	14.2u/	0.4	0.3	3666u/	4004u/	68	59
2732	Other electronic and electric wires and cables	...u/	...u/	199	173	...u/	...u/	10.6	5.3	...u/	...u/	3153	1684
2733	Wiring devices	...u/	...u/	109	99	...u/	...u/	3.9	4.3	...u/	...u/	1127	1284
2740	Electric lighting equipment	333	315	299	287	10.1	11.8	13.0	14.0	3180	3720	4708	5250
2750	Domestic appliances	609	597	592	605	5.9	5.8	5.8	6.0	1598	1594	1620	1782
2790	Other electrical equipment	2543	2502	2429	2415	12.8	12.8	12.3	18.6	3377	3494	3385	5680
281	General-purpose machinery	3934	3847	3744	3671	69.9	70.7	72.2	72.3	22959	24301	25080	26196
2811	Engines/turbines,excl.aircraft,vehicle engines	3934v/	3847v/	117	106	69.9v/	70.7v/	3.9	4.0	22959v/	24301v/	1713	1806
2812	Fluid power equipment	...v/	...v/	52	50	...v/	...v/	4.1	4.1	...v/	...v/	1424	1479
2813	Other pumps, compressors, taps and valves	...v/	...v/	287	288	...v/	...v/	15.8	14.9	...v/	...v/	5352	5264
2814	Bearings, gears, gearing and driving elements	...v/	...v/	105	106	...v/	...v/	6.3	6.2	...v/	...v/	2087	2079
2815	Ovens, furnaces and furnace burners	...v/	...v/	59	52	...v/	...v/	1.2	1.3	...v/	...v/	420	481
2816	Lifting and handling equipment	...v/	...v/	1333	1320	...v/	...v/	12.8	13.0	...v/	...v/	4498	4799
2817	Office machinery, excl.computers,etc.	...v/	...v/	76	73	...v/	...v/	0.3	0.3	...v/	...v/	85	87
2818	Power-driven hand tools	...v/	...v/	27	25	...v/	...v/	2.2	2.4	...v/	...v/	687	770
2819	Other general-purpose machinery	...v/	...v/	1688	1651	...v/	...v/	25.7	26.2	...v/	...v/	8817	9429
282	Special-purpose machinery	1640	1524	1450	1384	47.9	48.4	49.8	50.1	15341	15905	16891	17642
2821	Agricultural and forestry machinery	1640w/	291	276	266	47.9w/	7.6	7.6	8.0	15341w/	2294	2433	2630
2822	Metal-forming machinery and machine tools	...w/	...	251	236	...w/	...	11.9	11.7	...w/	...	4220	4293

Code	Description	1	2	3	4	5	6	7	8	9	10	11	12
2823	Machinery for metallurgy	...w/	...	16	14	...w/	...w/	2.2	2.1	...w/	...w/	633	622
2824	Mining, quarrying and construction machinery	...w/	...	101	95	...w/	...w/	8.4	7.9	...w/	...w/	2785	2722
2825	Food/beverage/tobacco processing machinery	...w/	...	109	105	...w/	...w/	2.5	2.6	...w/	...w/	840	900
2826	Textile/apparel/leather production machinery	...w/	...	85	78	...w/	...w/	5.9	6.0	...w/	...w/	1978	2068
2829	Other special-purpose machinery	...w/	...	612	590	...w/	...w/	11.2	11.8	...w/	...w/	3996	4409
2910	Motor vehicles	105	101	91	91	33.6	33.9	34.6	35.9	15785	16288	17393	18562
2920	Automobile bodies, trailers and semi-trailers	208	199	194	185	3.3	3.2	3.3	3.4	943	994	1058	1098
2930	Parts and accessories for motor vehicles	813	825	820	843	103.9	109.5	118.9	126.9	33610	36843	41254	45790
301	Building of ships and boats	134	142	133	136	0.3	0.2	0.2	0.2	44	44	44	49
3011	Building of ships and floating structures	134x/	142x/	99	106	0.3x/	0.2x/	0.2	0.2	44x/	44x/	30	32
3012	Building of pleasure and sporting boats	...x/	...x/	34	30	...x/	...x/	0.1	0.1	...x/	...x/	14	16
3020	Railway locomotives and rolling stock	47	49	52	57	10.4	10.3	10.3	10.2	3538	3660	3726	3882
3030	Air and spacecraft and related machinery	60	63	71	74	7.4	8.2	8.6	8.9	2647	3068	3257	3468
3040	Military fighting vehicles	-	2	3	5	-	-	...	...	-	-	-	-
309	Transport equipment n.e.c.	351	394	412	469	2.5	2.5	...	...	587	587	...	...
3091	Motorcycles	351	394	412	469	2.5y/	2.5y/	...	...	587y/	587y/	...	...
3092	Bicycles and invalid carriages	...	...	...	...	...y/	...y/	...	...	...y/	...y/	...	...
3099	Other transport equipment n.e.c.	...	...	...	...	...y/	...y/	...	...	...y/	...y/	...	...
3100	Furniture	7254	6783	6419	6208	20.2	20.2	20.7	20.9	4466	4654	4888	5247
321	Jewellery, bijouterie and related articles	2317	2511	2710	2950	2.4	2.3	2.1	2.0	455	454	439	443
3211	Jewellery and related articles	2317	2511	2710	2950	2.4	2.3	2.1	2.0	455	454	439	443
3212	Imitation jewellery and related articles	z/	z/	z/	z/								
3220	Musical instruments	335	331	319	314	1.0	1.0	0.9	0.9	249	251	254	268
3230	Sports goods	487	494	499	494	2.6	2.6	2.8	2.8	621	661	690	770
3240	Games and toys	583	579	572	554	5.7	6.0	6.2	6.9	1621	1713	1828	2328
3250	Medical and dental instruments and supplies	2374	2446	2437	2461	12.4	12.7	12.6	13.0	3650	3739	3904	4161
3290	Other manufacturing n.e.c.	2505	2417	2415	2387	7.4	7.3	7.3	7.3	1619	1660	1757	1844
331	Repair of fabricated metal products/machinery	10090	11179	12568	13802	...	...	27.0	27.5	...	...	10041	10435
3311	Repair of fabricated metal products	10090A/	11179A/	4387	5167	...	...	1.4	1.4	...	...	409	430
3312	Repair of machinery	...A/	...A/	4100	4424	...	...	14.7	15.0	...	...	5401	5628
3313	Repair of electronic and optical equipment	...A/	...A/	1677	1613	...	...	1.5	1.7	...	...	679	779
3314	Repair of electrical equipment	...A/	...A/	1836	1979	...	...	5.5	4.9	...	...	2144	1987
3315	Repair of transport equip., excl. motor vehicles	...A/	...A/	317	357	...	...	3.8	4.3	...	...	1383	1573
3319	Repair of other equipment	...A/	...A/	251	262	...	...	0.1	0.2	...	...	25	38
3320	Installation of industrial machinery/equipment	1996	2141	2275	2466	...	...	11.6	12.0	...	...	4627	4955
C	Total manufacturing	167688	170041	172054	175425	1063.9	1077.5	1110.0	1136.3	321861	337211	357478	382112

a/ 1061 includes 1062.
b/ 1071 includes 1072, 1073, 1074, 1075 and 1079.
c/ 1101 includes 1102, 1103 and 1104.
d/ 1311 includes 1312 and 1313.
e/ 1391 includes 1392, 1393, 1394 and 1399.
f/ 1511 includes 1512.
g/ 1621 includes 1622, 1623 and 1629.
h/ 1701 includes 1702 and 1709.
i/ 181 includes 1820.
j/ 1811 includes 1812.

k/ 1910 includes 1920.
l/ 2011 includes 2012 and 2013.
m/ 2021 includes 2022, 2023 and 2029.
n/ 2211 includes 2219.
o/ 2431 includes 2432.
p/ 2511 includes 2512 and 2513.
q/ 2591 includes 2592, 2593 and 2599.
r/ 2651 includes 2652.
s/ 2731 includes 2732 and 2733.
t/ 2811 includes 2812, 2813, 2814, 2815, 2816, 2817, 2818 and 2819.

w/ 2821 includes 2822, 2823, 2824, 2825, 2826 and 2829.
x/ 3011 includes 3012.
y/ 3091 includes 3092 and 3099.
z/ 3211 includes 3212.
A/ 3311 includes 3312, 3313, 3314, 3315 and 3319.

Czechia

ISIC	Industry	Note	Output 2013	Output 2014	Output 2015	Output 2016	Note	VA 2013	VA 2014	VA 2015	VA 2016	Note	GFCF 2015	GFCF 2016
			(millions of Czech Korunas)					(millions of Czech Korunas)					(millions of Czech Korunas)	
1010	Processing/preserving of meat		57130	57611	59064	60432		8269	9269	10328	10373		2360	2284
1020	Processing/preserving of fish, etc.		1871	1994	2021	2074		353	377	404	397		57	100
1030	Processing/preserving of fruit,vegetables		6035	6518	7764	8062		1333	1413	1618	1730		385	308
1040	Vegetable and animal oils and fats		15157	14941	13852	14282		935	1338	919	981		483	330
1050	Dairy products		42464	44033	40940	39340		5960	5334	5674	6823		1525	1627
106	Grain mill products,starches and starch products		10761	10340	10652	10760		1543	1724	1841	2195		559	930
1061	Grain mill products		10761a/	10340a/	9133	9348		1543a/	1724a/	1574	1944		510	776
1062	Starches and starch products		...a/	...a/	1517	1411		...a/	...a/	267	249		49	154
107	Other food products		80343	81765	82544	86414		22735	22904	23610	26136		6607	6772
1071	Bakery products		80343b/	81765b/	31608	32830		22735b/	22904b/	11577	12495		4406	3379
1072	Sugar		...b/	...b/	8574	10660		...b/	...b/	1607	2714		300	465
1073	Cocoa, chocolate and sugar confectionery		...b/	...b/	14403	14577		...b/	...b/	3664	3623		409	719
1074	Macaroni, noodles, couscous, etc.		...b/	...b/	1427	1352		...b/	...b/	246	270		33	27
1075	Prepared meals and dishes		...b/	...b/	2998	3252		...b/	...b/	873	933		213	324
1079	Other food products n.e.c.		...b/	...b/	23531	23747		...b/	...b/	5641	6102		1249	1855
1080	Prepared animal feeds		37084	39082	38412	29451		7490	8426	8249	8537		1206	1438
110	Beverages		63685	62129	63838	64336		19093	19328	19881	21898		4073	4598
1101	Distilling, rectifying and blending of spirits	c/	63685	62129	63838	64336	c/	19093	19328	19881	21898	c/	4073	4598
1102	Wines	c/	:	:	:	:	c/	:	:	:	:	c/		
1103	Malt liquors and malt	c/	:	:	:	:	c/	:	:	:	:	c/		
1104	Soft drinks,mineral waters,other bottled waters	c/	:	:	:	:	c/	:	:	:	:	c/		
1200	Tobacco products		:	:	:	:		:	:	:	:			
131	Spinning, weaving and finishing of textiles		16973	18422	17824	16964		5152	5397	4935	4623		1075	876
1311	Preparation and spinning of textile fibres		16973d/	3235	3609	3531		5152d/	1165	1222	1400		330	251
1312	Weaving of textiles		...d/	14032	12761	12628		...d/	3993	3344	2993		622	608
1313	Finishing of textiles		...d/	1154	1454	806		...d/	240	368	230		123	16
139	Other textiles		29118	32168	32991	34825		8010	9222	9370	10016		2223	2371
1391	Knitted and crocheted fabrics		29118e/	32168e/	878	987		8010e/	9222e/	270	265		44	41
1392	Made-up textile articles, except apparel		...e/	...e/	7289	8318		...e/	...e/	2226	2449		818	892
1393	Carpets and rugs		...e/	...e/	344	416		...e/	...e/	158	192		25	27
1394	Cordage, rope, twine and netting		...e/	...e/	1298	1503		...e/	...e/	453	530		90	273
1399	Other textiles n.e.c.		...e/	...e/	23179	23601		...e/	...e/	6263	6577		1247	1141
1410	Wearing apparel, except fur apparel		12608	13964	14772	15180		4962	5502	5860	6158		584	789
1420	Articles of fur		135	105	93	103		57	47	44	49		5	3
1430	Knitted and crocheted apparel		1380	1407	1459	1538		582	606	627	657		74	73
151	Leather;luggage,handbags,saddlery,harness;fur	f/	3983	3869	4070	4142	f/	1393	1341	1544	1692	f/	166	357
1511	Tanning/dressing of leather; dressing of fur	f/	3983	3869	4070	4142	f/	1393	1341	1544	1692	f/	166	357
1512	Luggage,handbags,etc.;saddlery/harness	f/	:	:	:	:	f/	:	:	:	:	f/		
1520	Footwear		1489	1616	1555	1665		608	633	627	673		44	70
1610	Sawmilling and planing of wood		22805	25259	25408	25658		3975	4587	4474	4901		1833	906

Code	Description									
162	Wood products, cork, straw, plaiting materials	56293	58528	62005	63908	15923	16728	18329	19208	4837	3433
1621	Veneer sheets and wood-based panels	56293g/	58528g/	13841	14923	15923g/	16728g/	3183	3896	1375	427
1622	Builders' carpentry and joinery	..g/	..g/	32069	33195	..g/	..g/	10887	11062	2098	2030
1623	Wooden containers	..g/	..g/	9258	9132	..g/	..g/	2021	2106	518	530
1629	Other wood products;articles of cork,straw	..g/	..g/	6833	6658	..g/	..g/	2240	2144	846	446
170	Paper and paper products	60858	66968	72688	73349	13564	15886	17420	19427	5505	4120
1701	Pulp, paper and paperboard	60858h/	66968h/	...	...	13562h/	15888h/	5857	6667	1645	...
1702	Corrugated paper and paperboard	..h/	..h/	24513	25444	..h/	..h/	...	...	...	1479
1709	Other articles of paper and paperboard	..h/	..h/	...	...	..h/	..h/	...	...	...	...
181	Printing and service activities related to printing	32114	39597i/	40725i/	40278i/	10135	12265i/	12739i/	13147i/	2747i/	2190i/
1811	Printing	32114i/	..i/	..i/	..i/	10135i/	..i/	..i/	..i/	..i/	..i/
1812	Service activities related to printing	..i/	..i/	..i/	..i/	..i/	..i/	..i/	..i/	..i/	..i/
1820	Reproduction of recorded media	3996	..i/	..i/	..i/	1528	..i/	..i/	..i/	..i/	..i/
1910	Coke oven products	123823k/	135232k/	...	...	2097k/	3191k/	...	...	...	...
1920	Refined petroleum products	..k/	..k/	...	...	..k/	..k/	...	...	...	...
201	Basic chemicals,fertilizers, etc.	121610	133142	119018	101986	17620	23753	29115	20730	8257	10822
2011	Basic chemicals	121610	133142	119018	101986	17620	23753	29115	20730	8257	10822
2012	Fertilizers and nitrogen compounds	...	...	...	...	...	...	m/	...	m/	...
2013	Plastics and synthetic rubber in primary forms	...	...	...	...	...	...	m/	...	m/	...
202	Other chemical products	30888	33109	33302	34295	9696	10453	11416	11849	2684	2701
2021	Pesticides and other agrochemical products	30888n/	1743	1659	1441	9696n/	576	518	479	172	54
2022	Paints,varnishes;printing ink and mastics	..n/	7523	7955	8213	..n/	2098	2196	2414	434	408
2023	Soap,cleaning and cosmetic preparations	..n/	...	10672	11079	..n/	...	3702	3801	1151	1327
2029	Other chemical products n.e.c.	..n/	...	...	...	..n/	...	...	...	...	...
2030	Man-made fibres	2925	3070	3374	2809	777	906	865	743	166	162
2100	Pharmaceuticals,medicinal chemicals, etc.	31961	33842	35081	34893	10740	11637	11885	12081	2062	1644
221	Rubber products	96542	101660	103731	102110	26866	31677	33406	33647	4215	3720
2211	Rubber tyres and tubes	96542p/	101660p/	71403	67626	26866p/	31677p/	22639	22200	2403	1749
2219	Other rubber products	..p/	..p/	32328	34485	..p/	..p/	10770	11443	1809	1971
2220	Plastics products	135280	152282	163936	172707	36988	41954	47414	50875	10423	11219
2310	Glass and glass products	42732	46093	48047	47802	15281	16789	18244	17615	3484	4031
239	Non-metallic mineral products n.e.c.	76441	83899	88411	86909	24286	27478	29699	30013	6492	4969
2391	Refractory products	6383	6457	...	6088	2426	2417	2416	2379	415	257
2392	Clay building materials	...	...	...	...	...	...	...	...	...	...
2393	Other porcelain and ceramic products	...	...	...	...	...	...	...	...	...	...
2394	Cement, lime and plaster	...	...	...	...	...	...	...	...	...	...
2395	Articles of concrete, cement and plaster	...	...	42239	41321	...	...	12840	12236	2851	2265
2396	Cutting, shaping and finishing of stone	...	1980	2054	2117	807	824	806	...	175	105
2399	Other non-metallic mineral products n.e.c.	...	...	14229	12944	...	4179	4179	4106	1247	960
2410	Basic iron and steel	136808	144820	129341	121210	20675	27299	24772	23190	5008	3763
2420	Basic precious and other non-ferrous metals	24684	25939	28801	28210	3502	3932	4286	4342	1061	1168
243	Casting of metals	24938	25650	26136	26309	7397	8231	8336	9121	2695	2055
2431	Casting of iron and steel	24938q/	25650q/	13146	13487	7397q/	8231q/	4179	4585	960	925
2432	Casting of non-ferrous metals	..q/	..q/	12990	12822	..q/	..q/	4160	4536	1735	1130
251	Struct.metal products, tanks, reservoirs	86241	91378	91712	91970	22468	25642	26054	27372	5254	4836

continued

Czechia

ISIC	Industry	Output Note	Output (valuation not defined) (millions of Czech Korunas)				Value added Note	Value added at factor values (millions of Czech Korunas)				GFCF Note	Gross fixed capital formation (millions of Czech Korunas)	
			2013	2014	2015	2016		2013	2014	2015	2016		2015	2016
2511	Structural metal products		86241r/	...	65202	64911		22468r/	...	17870	19010		3800	3217
2512	Tanks, reservoirs and containers of metal		...r/	...	21204	21089		...r/	...	6683	6634		1320	1503
2513	Steam generators, excl. hot water boilers		...r/	5298	5306	5969		...r/	1688	1503	1727		131	116
2520	Weapons and ammunition		6622	8074	9081	10219		2588	3431	4089	4634		906	903
259	Other metal products;metal working services		203743	224424	242505	243757		66605	75906	83242	86612		19204	18499
2591	Forging,pressing,stamping,roll-forming of metal		203743s/	19765	20582	20651		66605s/	6190	6503	6799		2120	2138
2592	Treatment and coating of metals; machining		...s/	...	76141	74881		...s/	...	28059	28951		6784	6339
2593	Cutlery, hand tools and general hardware		...s/	...	...	...		...s/	...	...	...		...	...
2599	Other fabricated metal products n.e.c.		...s/	...	73678	76298		...s/	...	23288	24866		5298	5766
2610	Electronic components and boards		15736	14134	12764	14433		4775	5317	5047	5396		1039	1138
2620	Computers and peripheral equipment		117333	142636	155458	155421		3531	3470	4174	3979		237	316
2630	Communication equipment		11403	13647	14466	15553		3902	4238	4256	4728		775	889
2640	Consumer electronics		42423	41681	37236	35855		4357	4188	2158	2820		518	443
265	Measuring,testing equipment; watches, etc.		70434	72392	100168	83897		19340	17218	17625	18572		3789	4850
2651	Measuring/testing/navigating equipment,etc.		70434t/	72392t/	100013	83746		19340t/	17218t/	17546	18507		3781	4844
2652	Watches and clocks		...t/	...t/	155	151		...t/	...t/	79	65		8	5
2660	Irradiation/electromedical equipment,etc.		717	697	737	900		255	270	297	319		60	68
2670	Optical instruments and photographic equipment		2897	2803	2878	3352		1364	1374	1498	1711		183	276
2680	Magnetic and optical media		247	207	259	238		70	52	68	46		8	14
2710	Electric motors,generators,transformers,etc.		110436	118653	118445	115703		34857	38462	38357	36953		3524	3950
2720	Batteries and accumulators		10706	10527	11523	12273		1665	1660	1599	1633		177	257
273	Wiring and wiring devices		35203	39495	42686	26964		7313	8456	9179	6472		2251	1479
2731	Fibre optic cables		35203u/	39495u/	180	160		7313u/	8456u/	101	70		3	65
2732	Other electronic and electric wires and cables		...u/	...u/	34423	17878		...u/	...u/	6427	3585		1547	687
2733	Wiring devices		...u/	...u/	8083	8927		...u/	...u/	2654	2817		701	730
2740	Electric lighting equipment		36827	53183	64681	63798		8789	11370	13609	13652		2556	2176
2750	Domestic appliances		14858	15574	17551	16280		3557	3742	3795	3733		537	846
2790	Other electrical equipment		23808	24628	24933	42146		7965	8354	8525	12230		1028	2284
281	General-purpose machinery		184817	200815	204066	205285		53119	58360	59397	57439		10303	9348
2811	Engines/turbines,excl.aircraft,vehicle engines		184817v/	200815v/	13716	13125		53119v/	58360v/	5336	3801		652	435
2812	Fluid power equipment		...v/	...	8279	8224		...v/	...	2941	3025		442	414
2813	Other pumps, compressors, taps and valves		...v/	...v/	43049	41300		...v/	...v/	11978	11049		2357	1738
2814	Bearings, gears, gearing and driving elements		...v/	...v/	14256	12014		...v/	...v/	4373	3390		1473	849
2815	Ovens, furnaces and furnace burners		...v/	...v/	2662	3739		...v/	...v/	949	1238		82	105
2816	Lifting and handling equipment		...v/	...v/	30569	29794		...v/	...v/	9439	9857		1277	1541
2817	Office machinery, excl.computers,etc.		...v/	...v/	696	706		...v/	...v/	188	176		3	27
2818	Power-driven hand tools		...v/	...v/	4223	4536		...v/	...v/	1432	1511		256	270
2819	Other general-purpose machinery		...v/	...v/	86616	91848		...v/	...v/	22759	23393		3762	3966
282	Special-purpose machinery		110215	117369	122150	120061		32140	35224	35771	35014		8440	7207
2821	Agricultural and forestry machinery		110215w/	18353	18997	19340		32140w/	5130	5224	5504		1637	2187
2822	Metal-forming machinery and machine tools		...w/	...	30362	26534		...w/	...	9201	8467		2341	1176

ISIC Revision 4

ISIC / Description										
2823 Machinery for metallurgy	…	…w/	3197	2882	…	…w/	1192	1144	128	119
2824 Mining, quarrying and construction machinery	…	…w/	20855	19362	…	…w/	5235	4461	1298	1138
2825 Food/beverage/tobacco processing machinery	…	…w/	5412	5285	…	…w/	1656	1676	428	160
2826 Textile/apparel/leather production machinery	…	…w/	11866	12884	…	…w/	4520	4580	862	925
2829 Other special-purpose machinery	…	…w/	31455	33768	…	…w/	8743	9183	1749	1500
2910 Motor vehicles	380467	458967	499792	545725	82872	65342	88992	102973	19330	19686
2920 Automobile bodies, trailers and semi-trailers	6604	8894	9095	8510	1985	1684	2152	2117	360	441
2930 Parts and accessories for motor vehicles	428337	506401	581605	634234	93826	77345	102070	111626	29690	28405
301 Building of ships and boats	462	468	456	378	69	75	87	103	71	27
3011 Building of ships and floating structures	462x/	468x/	360	289	69x/	75x/	57	70	63	24
3012 Building of pleasure and sporting boats	…x/	…x/	95	89	…x/	…x/	30	32	8	3
3020 Railway locomotives and rolling stock	29581	32985	36333	32954	10238	9340	13260	9908	1353	1111
3030 Air and spacecraft and related machinery	16843	19812	19720	21706	6609	5903	6732	7975	1331	757
3040 Military fighting vehicles	-	…	…	…	…	1465	…	…	…	…
309 Transport equipment n.e.c.	5061	…	…	…	…	…	…	…	…	…
3091 Motorcycles	5061y/	…	…	…	…	1465y/	…	…	…	…
3092 Bicycles and invalid carriages	…y/	…	…	…	…	…y/	…	…	…	…
3099 Other transport equipment n.e.c.	…y/	…	…	…	…	…y/	…	…	…	…
3100 Furniture	32000	34417	36382	39013	10164	9579	11280	12279	2177	2376
321 Jewellery, bijouterie and related articles	3312	3574	3364	3650	1168	1146	1195	1308	183	200
3211 Jewellery and related articles	3312	3574	3364	3650	1168	1146	1195	1308	183	200
3212 Imitation jewellery and related articles	…z/	…z/	…	…	…	…	…	…	…z/	…z/
3220 Musical instruments	1182	1242	1217	1330	559	525	524	487	60	111
3230 Sports goods	3783	3987	4239	4588	1426	1294	1528	1660	262	330
3240 Games and toys	16988	19256	22669	23617	4472	4593	4973	5758	3167	2133
3250 Medical and dental instruments and supplies	17362	18383	18951	20549	8016	7726	7927	9005	1405	1746
3290 Other manufacturing n.e.c.	9872	10444	10903	11360	3905	3629	4073	4304	674	619
331 Repair of fabricated metal products/machinery	…	…	63587	69023	…	…	24297	25801	2526	2841
3311 Repair of fabricated metal products	…	…	3333	3633	…	…	1361	1606	79	68
3312 Repair of machinery	…	…	36202	39040	…	…	12371	12541	1462	1665
3313 Repair of electronic and optical equipment	…	…	4777	5291	…	…	2313	2322	175	333
3314 Repair of electrical equipment	…	…	10595	10773	…	…	5063	4734	202	365
3315 Repair of transport equip., excl. motor vehicles	…	…	8317	9813	…	…	3063	4442	592	389
3319 Repair of other equipment	…	…	360	479	…	…	125	157	16	22
3320 Installation of industrial machinery/equipment	…	…	33610	32976	…	…	10333	9989	862	898
C Total manufacturing	3547431	3929530	4094559	4134229	924945	817253	977237	1012945	209050	203607

a/ 1061 includes 1062.
b/ 1071 includes 1072, 1073, 1074, 1075 and 1079.
c/ 1101 includes 1102, 1103 and 1104.
d/ 1311 includes 1312 and 1313.
e/ 1391 includes 1392, 1393, 1394 and 1399.
f/ 1511 includes 1512.
g/ 1621 includes 1622, 1623 and 1629.
h/ 1701 includes 1702 and 1709.
i/ 181 includes 1820.
j/ 1811 includes 1812.

k/ 1910 includes 1920.
m/ 2011 includes 2012 and 2013.
n/ 2021 includes 2022, 2023 and 2029.
p/ 2211 includes 2219.
q/ 2431 includes 2432.
r/ 2511 includes 2512 and 2513.
s/ 2591 includes 2592, 2593 and 2599.
t/ 2651 includes 2652.
u/ 2731 includes 2732 and 2733.
v/ 2811 includes 2812, 2813, 2814, 2815, 2816, 2817, 2818 and 2819.

w/ 2821 includes 2822, 2823, 2824, 2825, 2826 and 2829.
x/ 3011 includes 3012.
y/ 3091 includes 3092 and 3099.
z/ 3211 includes 3212.

Czechia

ISIC Revision 4 — Index numbers of industrial production (2010=100)

ISIC	Industry	Note	2005	2006	2007	2008	2009	2010	2011	2012	2013	2014	2015	2016
10	Food products		106	106	110	97	100	100	97	96	95	98	103	104
11	Beverages		121	132	140	140	111	100	103	98	100	102	105	104
12	Tobacco products		...	...	...	...	...	...	...	...	...	...	...	...
13	Textiles		114	120	130	111	97	100	103	102	102	107	110	116
14	Wearing apparel		167	137	127	120	106	100	97	91	86	81	95	98
15	Leather and related products		126	130	138	123	91	100	110	102	95	102	98	103
16	Wood products, excluding furniture		90	97	105	102	99	100	98	90	97	94	91	94
17	Paper and paper products		99	101	108	103	95	100	101	100	103	110	117	121
18	Printing and reproduction of recorded media		98	90	115	119	99	100	106	103	95	96	92	104
19	Coke and refined petroleum products		94	97	93	106	95	100	93	94	88	98	...	...
20	Chemicals and chemical products		105	104	103	108	94	100	95	100	97	106	101	94
21	Pharmaceuticals,medicinal chemicals, etc.		87	93	97	98	88	100	99	94	100	101	109	112
22	Rubber and plastics products		80	92	109	107	95	100	107	105	106	111	119	124
23	Other non-metallic mineral products		115	112	132	129	102	100	102	98	97	101	107	106
24	Basic metals		111	120	108	113	82	100	106	97	95	99	97	96
25	Fabricated metal products, except machinery		97	104	128	114	86	100	106	105	108	113	123	129
26	Computer, electronic and optical products		59	73	86	93	77	100	97	79	92	109	112	116
27	Electrical equipment		75	87	99	101	85	100	111	122	122	131	141	145
28	Machinery and equipment n.e.c.		82	98	114	121	87	100	111	113	116	120	123	126
29	Motor vehicles, trailers and semi-trailers		67	79	92	92	82	100	121	123	118	135	151	169
30	Other transport equipment		50	62	90	92	90	100	122	121	133	139	146	152
31	Furniture		109	118	131	126	107	100	102	98	102	106	112	119
32	Other manufacturing		102	110	115	118	95	100	104	106	114	120	136	135
33	Repair and installation of machinery/equipment		80	86	89	92	104	100	109	103	105	113	106	109
C	Total manufacturing		89	97	109	107	91	100	108	107	108	115	122	127

Denmark

Supplier of information:
Statistics Denmark, Copenhagen.
Industrial statistics for the OECD countries are compiled by the OECD secretariat, which
supplies them to UNIDO.

Basic source of data:
Annual survey; administrative data; business register.

Major deviations from ISIC (Revision 4):
Data presented in ISIC (Revision 4) were originally classified according to the national
NACE-related classification system.

Reference period:
Calendar year (most enterprises have a fiscal year following the calendar year, some
enterprises have other accounting periods).

Scope:
All enterprises.

Method of data collection:
Electronic questionnaire; collection of annual accounts plus detailed specifications.

Type of enumeration:
Combination of survey and administrative data.

Adjusted for non-response:
Not reported.

Concepts and definitions of variables:
No deviations from the standard UN concepts and definitions are reported.

Related national publications:
Statistical Yearbook of Denmark, published by Statistics Denmark, Copenhagen.

Denmark

ISIC Revision 4

		Number of enterprises (number)					Number of employees (number)					Wages and salaries paid to employees (millions of Danish Kroner)				
ISIC	Industry	Note	2013	2014	2015	2016	Note	2013	2014	2015	2016a/	Note	2013	2014	2015	2016
1010	Processing/preserving of meat		149	143	138	142		17461	17206	16676	13461		5540	5539	5506	5488
1020	Processing/preserving of fish, etc.		98	96	103	92		4077	4070	4136	3669		1207	1237	1302	1306
1030	Processing/preserving of fruit,vegetables		59	60	73	80		744	...	1824	1600		315	...	592	570
1040	Vegetable and animal oils and fats		20	21	19	17		...	554	...	...		...	228	...	...
1050	Dairy products		74	76	64	63		...	...	...	...		...	...	...	...
106	Grain mill products,starches and starch products		23	24	26	28		1181	1241	1297	1083		382	388	435	458
1061	Grain mill products		15	16	18	20		800	834	866	701		257	261	275	299
1062	Starches and starch products		8	8	8	8		381	407	431	382		125	127	160	159
107	Other food products		971	990	973	994		16691	16591	16929	20373		4725	4766	4950	5067
1071	Bakery products		704	676	648	628		...	...	...	...		...	...	...	...
1072	Sugar		5	4	4	4		...	...	...	...		...	...	...	...
1073	Cocoa, chocolate and sugar confectionery		55	55	57	63		2275	2357	2422	2281		701	740	770	732
1074	Macaroni, noodles, couscous, etc.		1	2	1	2		1	...	...	...		...	...	...	...
1075	Prepared meals and dishes		27	52	65	81		127	132	150	316		47	42	46	74
1079	Other food products n.e.c.		179	201	198	216		...	...	...	...		...	...	...	...
1080	Prepared animal feeds		59	57	62	63		3691	3636	3647	2700		1244	1254	1267	1280
110	Beverages		122	122	129	149		4368	4517	3729	2580		1438	1482	1231	1371
1101	Distilling, rectifying and blending of spirits		13	15	15	27		92	99	70	83		51	40	25	34
1102	Wines		22	19	24	24		...	...	...	...		...	...	...	...
1103	Malt liquors and malt		73	75	75	83		...	...	...	...		...	...	...	...
1104	Soft drinks,mineral waters,other bottled waters		14	13	15	15		484	509	505	435		166	174	178	193
1200	Tobacco products		10	10	8	8		697	660	610	425		196	185	180	178
131	Spinning, weaving and finishing of textiles		61	58	53	53		...	330	333	303		...	107	112	115
1311	Preparation and spinning of textile fibres		4	6	7	5		...	31	31	30		...	7	8	9
1312	Weaving of textiles		16	15	14	13		136	126	127	117		53	49	53	57
1313	Finishing of textiles		41	37	32	35		...	173	175	156		...	50	51	49
139	Other textiles		262	259	247	246		3247	3216	3266	2822		993	1006	1040	1065
1391	Knitted and crocheted fabrics		10	9	9	8		...	...	...	...		...	...	...	...
1392	Made-up textile articles, except apparel		165	164	156	151		1639	1578	1555	1341		463	451	456	444
1393	Carpets and rugs		15	16	14	17		665	690	729	620		225	244	255	261
1394	Cordage, rope, twine and netting		25	23	20	20		199	158	173	179		62	52	56	63
1399	Other textiles n.e.c.		47	47	48	50		...	...	...	...		...	...	...	...
1410	Wearing apparel, except fur apparel		304	277	269	313		...	...	...	1223		...	...	...	438
1420	Articles of fur		25	24	24	25		31	57	70	66		10	20	22	19
1430	Knitted and crocheted apparel		19	17	18	17		167	170	158	163		48	50	48	48
151	Leather;luggage,handbags,saddlery,harness;fur		43	41	44	46		97	113	134	...		28	33	39	...
1511	Tanning/dressing of leather; dressing of fur		7	7	8	9		60	77	87	...		17	22	26	...
1512	Luggage,handbags,etc.;saddlery/harness		36	34	36	37		37	36	47	60		11	11	13	17
1520	Footwear		19	18	17	19		52	55	30	40		16	17	8	10
1610	Sawmilling and planing of wood		97	100	90	95		760	747	1127	984		209	210	325	372

Code	Product								b/				
162	Wood products, cork, straw, plaiting materials	425	418	397	414	8338	8395	7969	6992	2424	2462	2334	2359
1621	Veneer sheets and wood-based panels	27	23	21	20	802	824	636	525	223	232	183	185
1622	Builders' carpentry and joinery	241	236	219	240	...	816	806	706	...	227	233	242
1623	Wooden containers	54	54	58	53	...	...	...	...	...	...	...	...
1629	Other wood products;articles of cork,straw	103	105	99	101	347	...	...	...	96	...	...	...
170	Paper and paper products	148	144	138	132	5995	6045	5973	4705	1953	1945	1982	1952
1701	Pulp, paper and paperboard	12	10	11	9	349	254	...	...	145	95	...	...
1702	Corrugated paper and paperboard	58	60	56	54	3217	3325	3291	2553	1023	1047	1045	1088
1709	Other articles of paper and paperboard	78	74	71	69	...	...	...	...	...	...	...	...
181	Printing and service activities related to printing	806	771	715	685	6673	6859	6571	5629	2072	2140	2085	1997
1811	Printing	551	536	510	491	5541	5803	5555	4725	1726	1800	1756	1684
1812	Service activities related to printing	255	235	205	194	...	...	...	... b/	...	...	...	... b/
1820	Reproduction of recorded media	21	21	17	21	...	...	...	... b/	...	...	...	... b/
1910	Coke oven products	-	-	-	-	-	-	-	-	-	-	-	-
1920	Refined petroleum products	4	3	3	5	5109	5245	5496	4021	2128	2281	2425	2458
201	Basic chemicals,fertilizers, etc.	43	44	42	48	...	...	...	...	...	...	...	...
2011	Basic chemicals	22	23	25	26	...	...	...	...	...	...	...	...
2012	Fertilizers and nitrogen compounds	7	6	4	7	284	281	287	250	100	98	103	109
2013	Plastics and synthetic rubber in primary forms	14	15	13	15	...	...	...	...	...	...	...	...
202	Other chemical products	178	185	201	213	...	...	...	...	...	...	...	...
2021	Pesticides and other agrochemical products	6	5	5	5	740	738	1157	1057	239	243	387	446
2022	Paints,varnishes;printing ink and mastics	42	44	46	47	1573	1643	1779	1585	486	515	560	619
2023	Soap,cleaning and cosmetic preparations	79	81	94	107	...	...	...	...	...	...	...	...
2029	Other chemical products n.e.c.	51	55	56	54	...	...	...	...	...	...	...	...
2030	Man-made fibres	2	2	2	2	...	...	...	...	...	...	...	...
2100	Pharmaceuticals,medicinal chemicals, etc.	91	95	102	110	27066	31082	32529	25865	13011	15019	16153	17336
221	Rubber products	58	50	55	54	805	826	824	731	240	243	250	264
2211	Rubber tyres and tubes	20	16	17	17	84	75	68	58	25	22	20	19
2219	Other rubber products	38	34	38	37	721	751	756	673	215	221	230	244
2220	Plastics products	471	471	463	443	15700	14302	14645	12111	5107	4486	4718	4750
2310	Glass and glass products	112	115	105	101	1952	2089	1748	1478	577	620	547	560
239	Non-metallic mineral products n.e.c.	390	372	368	373	...	...	...	...	...	...	...	...
2391	Refractory products	7	6	4	5	...	...	...	...	...	...	...	...
2392	Clay building materials	21	22	20	19	...	...	...	...	...	...	...	...
2393	Other porcelain and ceramic products	69	63	60	76	...	...	...	...	...	...	...	...
2394	Cement, lime and plaster	4	4	5	5	...	...	...	...	...	...	...	...
2395	Articles of concrete, cement and plaster	167	155	154	152	396	410	348	334	122	133	110	109
2396	Cutting, shaping and finishing of stone	88	91	95	86	...	4005	4159	3216	...	1341	1372	1446
2399	Other non-metallic mineral products n.e.c.	34	31	30	30	...	...	...	...	...	...	...	...
2410	Basic iron and steel	92	94	91	90	1134	1204	1253	1041	362	371	405	409
2420	Basic precious and other non-ferrous metals	12	16	16	18	...	...	...	...	...	...	...	...
243	Casting of metals	43	45	51	46	1573	1839	1907	1465	468	527	577	538
2431	Casting of iron and steel	18	19	24	20	1148	1137	1171	929	342	325	354	336
2432	Casting of non-ferrous metals	25	26	27	26	425	702	736	536	125	202	222	203
251	Struct.metal products, tanks, reservoirs	597	597	597	630	...	...	...	...	...	...	...	...

continued

Denmark

ISIC	Industry	Note	Number of enterprises (number) 2013	2014	2015	2016	Note	Number of employees (number) 2013	2014	2015	2016a/	Note	Wages and salaries paid to employees (millions of Danish Kroner) 2013	2014	2015	2016
2511	Structural metal products		544	543	543	574		11459	11454	11499	10074		3636	3850	3764	3982
2512	Tanks, reservoirs and containers of metal		48	49	47	48		1259	1208	1150	932		442	406	411	410
2513	Steam generators, excl. hot water boilers		5	5	7	8		:	:	:	:		:	:	:	:
2520	Weapons and ammunition		18	16	15	19		:	:	:	:		:	:	:	:
259	Other metal products;metal working services		2239	2227	2161	2174		23766	25062	24884	22124		7363	7843	7855	8306
2591	Forging,pressing,stamping,roll-forming of metal		251	256	262	290		948	1009	1090	1001		282	298	325	369
2592	Treatment and coating of metals; machining		1310	1301	1251	1236		10919	11887	11891	11001		3413	3749	3805	4137
2593	Cutlery, hand tools and general hardware		196	194	186	193		2764	2820	2782	2303		883	901	895	879
2599	Other fabricated metal products n.e.c.		482	476	462	455		:	:	:	:		:	:	:	:
2610	Electronic components and boards		87	78	75	71		2047	1547	1483	1192		591	448	450	466
2620	Computers and peripheral equipment		33	34	33	39		782	754	741	487		274	269	301	238
2630	Communication equipment		100	92	92	93		:	:	:	:		:	:	:	:
2640	Consumer electronics		64	66	66	68		1709	1874	1626	1160		538	580	541	452
265	Measuring,testing equipment; watches, etc.		202	205	206	219		8643	8639	9072	7254		3222	3362	3607	3896
2651	Measuring/testing/navigating equipment,etc.		196	199	201	212		8603	8603	9058	7244		3211	3352	3603	3892
2652	Watches and clocks		6	6	5	7		40	36	14	10		11	10	4	4
2660	Irradiation/electromedical equipment,etc.		47	50	45	49		4725	4532	4359	3505		1903	1989	2007	2073
2670	Optical instruments and photographic equipment		29	27	30	32		597	612	652	559		249	256	273	302
2680	Magnetic and optical media		1	1	2	2		:	:	:	:		:	:	:	:
2710	Electric motors,generators,transformers,etc.		138	139	140	140		6021	6387	6377	4874		1985	2070	2253	2257
2720	Batteries and accumulators		-	1	2	3		-	:	:	:		-	:	:	:
273	Wiring and wiring devices		43	38	39	44		2889	2892	2837	2224		1028	1018	1073	1136
2731	Fibre optic cables		6	6	5	5		:	:	:	:		:	:	:	:
2732	Other electronic and electric wires and cables		20	17	18	21		:	:	:	:		:	:	:	:
2733	Wiring devices		17	15	16	18		1684	1690	1697	1287		621	617	695	697
2740	Electric lighting equipment		99	98	101	101		1766	:	:	:		576	:	:	:
2750	Domestic appliances		21	23	19	18		551	552	541	454		167	165	162	179
2790	Other electrical equipment		159	164	152	168		1668	1596	1641	1507		541	526	626	639
281	General-purpose machinery		867	895	906	936		48471	48051	49638	40687		15956	16803	17831	19633
2811	Engines/turbines,excl.aircraft,vehicle engines		114	128	125	131		:	:	16511	14422		:	:	6465	7420
2812	Fluid power equipment		52	49	50	53		:	:	:	:		:	:	:	:
2813	Other pumps, compressors, taps and valves		67	61	66	66		13268	11200	:	:		3844	3904	:	:
2814	Bearings, gears, gearing and driving elements		25	22	23	23		859	868	941	760		265	278	311	308
2815	Ovens, furnaces and furnace burners		55	57	55	52		939	939	980	825		309	296	327	337
2816	Lifting and handling equipment		164	163	157	161		5277	5340	5549	4770		1648	1689	1827	1998
2817	Office machinery, excl.computers,etc.		2	3	2	2		:	:	:	:		:	:	:	:
2818	Power-driven hand tools		2	2	3	4		:	:	:	:		:	:	:	:
2819	Other general-purpose machinery		386	410	425	444		11088	11457	11888	9846		3846	3879	4152	4637
282	Special-purpose machinery		764	773	757	782		16782	17266	18044	14016		5678	5929	6419	6277
2821	Agricultural and forestry machinery		153	160	155	156		3561	3770	3722	2765		1008	1155	1163	1013
2822	Metal-forming machinery and machine tools		100	106	100	98		1060	1112	1169	1053		369	321	419	474

ISIC Revision 4

2823	Machinery for metallurgy	6	6	5	5	...	4	...	2	...	1	...	1
2824	Mining, quarrying and construction machinery	65	68	63	64	1219	1274	1143	933	398	414	377	372
2825	Food/beverage/tobacco processing machinery	139	130	127	129	5976	6080	6632	4710	2233	2295	2562	2451
2826	Textile/apparel/leather production machinery	4	4	4	5	...	...	...	...	...	...	...	...
2829	Other special-purpose machinery	297	299	303	325	4450	...	4780	...	1513	...	1713	...
2910	Motor vehicles	19	19	18	18	...	...	...	...	...	...	...	...
2920	Automobile bodies, trailers and semi-trailers	69	66	65	64	1424	1467	1576	1365	410	433	457	522
2930	Parts and accessories for motor vehicles	67	69	70	71	...	...	...	...	...	...	...	...
301	Building of ships and boats	46	51	55	58	1242	1283	1409	1148	397	404	445	478
3011	Building of ships and floating structures	22	25	28	30	999	1057	1159	909	315	331	365	389
3012	Building of pleasure and sporting boats	24	26	27	28	243	226	250	239	81	73	79	89
3020	Railway locomotives and rolling stock	4	5	5	6	...	...	...	...	...	...	...	...
3030	Air and spacecraft and related machinery	17	17	19	20	457	520	578	442	153	166	190	184
3040	Military fighting vehicles	3	3	3	3	...	...	...	...	...	...	...	...
309	Transport equipment n.e.c.	51	53	54	52	560	703	680	632	175	214	209	231
3091	Motorcycles	1	5	4	5	...	...	...	...	...	...	...	...
3092	Bicycles and invalid carriages	41	41	42	40	...	...	...	460	...	...	...	169
3099	Other transport equipment n.e.c.	9	7	8	7	59	60	57	...	16	16	18	...
3100	Furniture	458	473	489	537	10266	10444	10629	9141	3064	3108	3257	3362
321	Jewellery, bijouterie and related articles	320	308	323	356	784	824	733	758	263	264	248	225
3211	Jewellery and related articles	282	272	291	315	711	756	669	658	242	245	229	207
3212	Imitation jewellery and related articles	38	36	32	41	73	68	64	100	21	19	19	18
3220	Musical instruments	39	39	38	42	168	167	171	165	51	51	51	51
3230	Sports goods	51	54	62	64	...	...	...	...	...	...	...	...
3240	Games and toys	84	81	87	95	...	...	...	...	...	...	...	...
3250	Medical and dental instruments and supplies	409	418	420	417	4413	4384	4403	4029	1432	1445	1493	1633
3290	Other manufacturing n.e.c.	272	265	258	270	906	941	952	922	275	299	319	313
331	Repair of fabricated metal products/machinery	2049	2054	2028	2083	9276	9669	9991	8546	3175	3406	3512	3510
3311	Repair of fabricated metal products	606	597	591	596	1312	1521	1521	1387	415	521	521	517
3312	Repair of machinery	819	838	827	890	2805	2964	3066	2717	916	972	1055	1053
3313	Repair of electronic and optical equipment	45	43	47	40	98	95	99	73	33	32	33	31
3314	Repair of electrical equipment	242	234	226	220	1079	1116	1065	959	375	398	380	392
3315	Repair of transport equip., excl. motor vehicles	290	291	286	285	70	83	83	82	19	24	24	23
3319	Repair of other equipment	47	51	51	52	...	...	...	...	...	...	...	...
3320	Installation of industrial machinery/equipment	285	269	277	295	1331	1484	1503	1355	482	561	609	537
C	Total manufacturing	15062	15007	14832	15244	344458	351232	354525	299553	116780	121589	126683	131471

a/ Methodological break in 2016.
b/ 181 includes 1820.

Denmark

ISIC	Industry	Output (valuation not defined) (millions of Danish Kroner)					Value added at factor values (millions of Danish Kroner)					Gross fixed capital formation (millions of Danish Kroner)	
		Note	2013	2014	2015	2016	Note	2013	2014	2015	2016	2015	2016
1010	Processing/preserving of meat		46450	42017	41373	41039		7750	7580	7986	7986	921	815
1020	Processing/preserving of fish, etc.		13225	13729	15405	15835		1665	1981	2114	1910	366	531
1030	Processing/preserving of fruit,vegetables		...	...	3990	3806		...	...	1038	1045	139	136
1040	Vegetable and animal oils and fats		4531	4190	...	...		813	589	...	...	...	...
1050	Dairy products		...	...	...	...		...	...	...	...	...	...
106	Grain mill products,starches and starch products		3358	3988	3979	4317		961	1076	1081	1236	454	275
1061	Grain mill products		1903	2198	2166	2158		407	486	484	526	114	91
1062	Starches and starch products		1455	1791	1813	2160		553	590	596	710	340	183
107	Other food products		23225	21894	22468	22969		7773	7435	7673	8082	1072	1310
1071	Bakery products		...	...	...	...		...	...	...	...	...	...
1072	Sugar		...	...	...	...		...	...	...	...	...	...
1073	Cocoa, chocolate and sugar confectionery		3564	3659	4004	3842		1058	1103	1241	1134	146	176
1074	Macaroni, noodles, couscous, etc.		...	...	...	...		...	...	...	...	...	...
1075	Prepared meals and dishes		293	264	330	606		72	66	75	113	8	15
1079	Other food products n.e.c.		...	...	...	...		...	...	...	...	...	...
1080	Prepared animal feeds		16843	15749	15830	16394		2292	2424	2482	2553	300	333
110	Beverages		10516	10467	7612	7476		3335	3657	2681	2838	328	540
1101	Distilling, rectifying and blending of spirits		823	501	270	308		315	157	103	113	10	13
1102	Wines		...	...	...	...		...	...	...	...	...	...
1103	Malt liquors and malt		...	...	...	...		...	...	...	...	...	...
1104	Soft drinks,mineral waters,other bottled waters		1068	1032	1070	1054		254	275	313	281	62	100
1200	Tobacco products		4788	10079	9587	8812		480	575	578	594	92	124
131	Spinning, weaving and finishing of textiles		...	620	653	750		...	183	196	217	13	20
1311	Preparation and spinning of textile fibres		...	36	40	51		...	12	13	15	1	1
1312	Weaving of textiles		315	328	357	433		98	97	106	124	7	11
1313	Finishing of textiles		256	256	256	266		74	74	78	78	5	8
139	Other textiles		5276	5391	5298	5432		1561	1643	1741	1730	220	240
1391	Knitted and crocheted fabrics		1941	1978	2056	2126		636	688	715	700	60	49
1392	Made-up textile articles, except apparel		1339	1274	1339	1243		382	381	415	384	56	57
1393	Carpets and rugs		323	253	239	307		98	81	84	102	22	14
1394	Cordage, rope, twine and netting												
1399	Other textiles n.e.c.		...	...	...	...		...	...	...	...	...	...
1410	Wearing apparel, except fur apparel		...	...	...	3040		...	...	...	821	...	68
1420	Articles of fur		72	93	112	138		16	15	13	32	1	1
1430	Knitted and crocheted apparel		256	252	221	283		69	74	63	82	1	9
151	Leather;luggage,handbags,saddlery,harness;fur		193	249	274	...		50	66	69	...	3	...
1511	Tanning/dressing of leather; dressing of fur		92	138	154	...		27	35	38	...	1	1
1512	Luggage,handbags,etc.;saddlery/harness		100	111	119	96		23	31	30	33	1	1
1520	Footwear		96	101	57	70		31	35	17	28	1	4
1610	Sawmilling and planing of wood		1008	1068	1380	1324		307	321	474	544	72	75

ISIC Revision 4

Code	Description											
162	Wood products, cork, straw, plaiting materials		9717	9896	9680	9758	3472	3595	3382	3429	310	296
1621	Veneer sheets and wood-based panels		1119	1199	993	965	349	386	266	290	36	8
1622	Builders' carpentry and joinery		..	..	..	..	..	..	..	..	..	..
1623	Wooden containers		..	1032	1032	1002	..	346	359	364	45	98
1629	Other wood products;articles of cork,straw		366	..	..	..	157	..	..	..	..	..
170	Paper and paper products		9543	9463	9634	9632	3003	2954	2908	3134	401	459
1701	Pulp, paper and paperboard		821	663	..	..	237	165	..	..	..	..
1702	Corrugated paper and paperboard		4717	4622	4759	4945	1535	1466	1528	1673	189	252
1709	Other articles of paper and paperboard		..	..	..	..	..	..	..	..	..	..
181	Printing and service activities related to printing a/	a/	7861	8068	7443	7212	2998	3066	2935	2754	335	274
1811	Printing		6517	6846	6250	6020	2498	2583	2503	2330	289	245
1812	Service activities related to printing		..	..	..	..	..	..	..	..	..	..
1820	Reproduction of recorded media a/	a/	..	..	..	..	..	..	..	..	..	..
1910	Coke oven products		..	..	..	..	..	..	..	..	..	..
1920	Refined petroleum products		..	..	..	..	..	..	..	..	..	..
201	Basic chemicals,fertilizers, etc.		10845	11990	12185	12806	5230	5801	6353	6559	553	887
2011	Basic chemicals		..	..	..	..	..	..	..	..	..	..
2012	Fertilizers and nitrogen compounds		..	312	..	..	..	69	..	..	..	..
2013	Plastics and synthetic rubber in primary forms		308	339	356	401	148	167	172	188	13	19
202	Other chemical products		..	..	..	..	..	..	..	..	..	..
2021	Pesticides and other agrochemical products		..	..	..	..	..	..	..	..	..	..
2022	Paints,varnishes;printing ink and mastics		1504	1413	2077	2419	446	437	643	791	93	59
2023	Soap,cleaning and cosmetic preparations		2267	2446	2593	3021	747	856	844	1039	98	136
2029	Other chemical products n.e.c.		..	..	..	..	..	..	..	..	..	..
2030	Man-made fibres		..	..	..	..	..	..	..	..	..	..
2100	Pharmaceuticals,medicinal chemicals, etc.		73806	87986	98833	102284	35298	42510	48770	50840	4941	5671
221	Rubber products		802	912	940	980	380	415	413	418	48	22
2211	Rubber tyres and tubes		109	107	101	89	43	40	38	36	8	1
2219	Other rubber products		694	806	838	891	336	375	375	383	40	21
2220	Plastics products		28233	19792	20048	20244	11508	7939	8195	8204	895	959
2310	Glass and glass products		2198	2265	2209	1939	871	945	819	859	64	49
239	Non-metallic mineral products n.e.c.		..	..	..	..	..	..	..	..	..	..
2391	Refractory products		..	..	..	..	..	..	..	..	..	..
2392	Clay building materials		..	..	..	..	..	..	..	..	..	..
2393	Other porcelain and ceramic products		..	..	..	..	..	..	..	..	..	..
2394	Cement, lime and plaster		..	..	..	..	..	..	..	..	..	..
2395	Articles of concrete, cement and plaster		..	..	..	..	..	..	..	..	..	..
2396	Cutting, shaping and finishing of stone		455	491	412	431	196	212	186	198	25	25
2399	Other non-metallic mineral products n.e.c.		..	5982	5573	5594	..	2083	2094	2285	569	291
2410	Basic iron and steel		1981	2122	2417	2315	527	545	607	672	..	..
2420	Basic precious and other non-ferrous metals		..	..	..	..	..	..	..	..	57	92
243	Casting of metals		1521	1920	1984	1765	624	737	796	770	88	106
2431	Casting of iron and steel		1123	1182	1261	1160	475	457	498	486	56	85
2432	Casting of non-ferrous metals		398	738	724	604	148	280	298	284	31	22
251	Struct.metal products, tanks, reservoirs		..	..	..	..	..	..	..	..	..	..

continued

Denmark

ISIC	Industry	Output (valuation not defined) (millions of Danish Kroner)					Value added at factor values (millions of Danish Kroner)					Gross fixed capital formation (millions of Danish Kroner)		
		Note	2013	2014	2015	2016	Note	2013	2014	2015	2016	Note	2015	2016
2511	Structural metal products		14864	16228	15469	16762		5158	5391	5202	5583		320	317
2512	Tanks, reservoirs and containers of metal		1492	1456	1467	1417		532	496	471	439		21	10
2513	Steam generators, excl. hot water boilers		...	...	...	...		...	...	...	...		...	...
2520	Weapons and ammunition		...	...	...	...		...	...	...	...		...	...
259	Other metal products;metal working services		25548	26973	26434	28324		11076	11823	11702	12355		1316	1482
2591	Forging,pressing,stamping,roll-forming of metal		1099	1124	1175	1270		482	504	513	583		49	41
2592	Treatment and coating of metals; machining		10821	12203	12234	13302		4975	5489	5574	6025		564	622
2593	Cutlery, hand tools and general hardware		2850	2834	2813	2589		1377	1478	1401	1326		108	143
2599	Other fabricated metal products n.e.c.		...	...	...	...		...	...	...	...		...	...
2610	Electronic components and boards		1870	1571	1605	1689		817	646	667	695		41	52
2620	Computers and peripheral equipment		814	918	929	877		359	340	383	340		18	13
2630	Communication equipment		...	...	...	...		...	...	...	...		...	...
2640	Consumer electronics		3572	4276	3007	3008		942	979	604	779		73	79
265	Measuring,testing equipment; watches, etc.		11105	10946	12829	13784		5559	5947	6667	6984		387	485
2651	Measuring/testing/navigating equipment,etc.		11040	10888	12813	13768		5535	5924	6660	6978		387	485
2652	Watches and clocks		64	58	16	16		25	23	7	7		1	-
2660	Irradiation/electromedical equipment,etc.		8066	7902	8889	9384		3929	4304	4584	4664		302	170
2670	Optical instruments and photographic equipment		989	1006	1089	1304		424	423	493	590		13	14
2680	Magnetic and optical media		...	...	...	...		...	...	...	...		...	...
2710	Electric motors,generators,transformers,etc.		8512	9935	10068	10108		2969	3476	3863	3809		251	334
2720	Batteries and accumulators		-	...	...	...		-	...	...	...		...	...
273	Wiring and wiring devices		3946	3865	4373	4013		1501	1487	1698	1832		106	110
2731	Fibre optic cables		...	...	...	...		...	...	...	...		...	...
2732	Other electronic and electric wires and cables		1938	1912	2237	2137		1012	921	1078	1136		86	63
2733	Wiring devices		2146	...	...	...		855	...	...	...		...	...
2740	Electric lighting equipment		789	897	826	885		307	341	338	379		25	16
2750	Domestic appliances		1894	1870	1880	2254		761	758	876	966		36	89
2790	Other electrical equipment		...	...	...	...		...	...	...	...		...	...
281	General-purpose machinery		101348	99674	114551	121259		31353	24095	24605	29618		2963	3668
2811	Engines/turbines,excl.aircraft,vehicle engines		...	...	59752	64768		...	...	6770	10953		1466	2156
2812	Fluid power equipment		...	...	...	...		...	...	...	...		...	...
2813	Other pumps, compressors, taps and valves		17479	17298	...	...		6392	6586	...	...		...	...
2814	Bearings, gears, gearing and driving elements		1003	1050	1161	1304		403	443	450	482		50	54
2815	Ovens, furnaces and furnace burners		1201	1034	1363	1563		450	432	492	520		45	30
2816	Lifting and handling equipment		5945	6284	6838	7364		2295	2391	2702	2943		146	179
2817	Office machinery, excl.computers,etc.		...	...	...	...		...	...	...	...		...	...
2818	Power-driven hand tools		...	...	...	...		...	...	...	...		...	...
2819	Other general-purpose machinery		16389	14079	18066	16350		5520	5565	5983	6328		387	289
282	Special-purpose machinery		21802	22806	22371	23262		8185	8604	9406	9135		477	439
2821	Agricultural and forestry machinery		4124	4371	4017	4087		1512	1643	1565	1375		151	114
2822	Metal-forming machinery and machine tools		1500	1628	1880	1983		724	705	882	944		17	25

Code	Description										
2823	Machinery for metallurgy	..	7	..	4	..	2	..	1	..	-
2824	Mining, quarrying and construction machinery	1451	1429	1299	1167	609	583	522	454	25	40
2825	Food/beverage/tobacco processing machinery	8310	8816	8055	8616	2926	3100	3573	3408	138	120
2826	Textile/apparel/leather production machinery	..	..	..	..	..	..	..	..	116	..
2829	Other special-purpose machinery	5936	..	6500	..	2171	..	2553	..	..	..
2910	Motor vehicles	..	..	..	..	..	..	..	..	..	..
2920	Automobile bodies, trailers and semi-trailers	1662	1756	1787	2216	535	582	618	721	19	18
2930	Parts and accessories for motor vehicles	..	..	..	..	..	..	..	..	..	..
301	Building of ships and boats	2076	2393	2864	3056	527	582	677	787	116	110
3011	Building of ships and floating structures	1736	2110	2496	2671	456	503	583	660	109	99
3012	Building of pleasure and sporting boats	340	283	368	385	71	79	95	127	7	11
3020	Railway locomotives and rolling stock	..	..	..	..	..	..	..	..	..	..
3030	Air and spacecraft and related machinery	453	289	650	612	187	210	240	243	13	82
3040	Military fighting vehicles	..	..	..	..	..	..	..	..	..	..
309	Transport equipment n.e.c.	764	821	894	1004	284	363	374	408	12	25
3091	Motorcycles	..	..	..	..	..	..	..	..	..	..
3092	Bicycles and invalid carriages	..	..	..	726	..	..	..	295	..	14
3099	Other transport equipment n.e.c.	63	66	89	..	25	27	27	..	3	..
3100	Furniture	13084	12997	13732	14517	4768	4831	5318	5597	336	388
321	Jewellery, bijouterie and related articles	1013	1099	972	911	377	400	396	240	23	31
3211	Jewellery and related articles	924	1016	876	801	350	365	363	200	21	29
3212	Imitation jewellery and related articles	89	83	96	109	28	35	33	39	2	3
3220	Musical instruments	159	148	182	170	78	84	86	85	4	4
3230	Sports goods	..	..	..	..	..	..	..	..	..	..
3240	Games and toys	..	..	..	..	..	..	..	..	..	..
3250	Medical and dental instruments and supplies	6235	6142	6622	7181	2679	2666	3073	3448	161	183
3290	Other manufacturing n.e.c.	1654	1438	1552	1484	511	554	565	531	89	51
331	Repair of fabricated metal products/machinery	11606	11521	12139	12902	4482	4996	5406	5359	271	262
3311	Repair of fabricated metal products	1563	..	1614	1733	694	..	869	844	49	48
3312	Repair of machinery	3760	3316	3137	4018	1421	1541	1651	1668	109	89
3313	Repair of electronic and optical equipment	128	86	131	97	54	51	50	43	1	1
3314	Repair of electrical equipment	1173	872	877	1086	550	538	557	529	11	18
3315	Repair of transport equip., excl. motor vehicles	..	..	..	..	..	..	..	..	..	..
3319	Repair of other equipment	64	93	94	84	31	37	40	36	3	3
3320	Installation of industrial machinery/equipment	1847	1867	2186	2073	726	792	844	865	26	25
C	Total manufacturing	705037	714878	740251	755372	219000	222128	242544	251070	24485	27616

a/ 181 includes 1820.

Denmark

Index numbers of industrial production

ISIC Revision 4

(2010=100)

ISIC	Industry	Note	2005	2006	2007	2008	2009	2010	2011	2012	2013	2014	2015	2016
10	Food products		104	105	105	104	97	100	101	98	100	98	101	105
11	Beverages		119	126	125	128	115	100	101	99	99	106	91	79
12	Tobacco products		130	134	121	111	100	100	38	34	41	46	47	49
13	Textiles		164	155	153	137	106	100	103	92	91	91	90	92
14	Wearing apparel		202	216	161	134	95	100	115	90	93	87	81	89
15	Leather and related products		...	...	...	...	...	...	...	...	...	-	-	-
16	Wood products, excluding furniture		141	163	154	133	96	100	96	92	83	96	97	92
17	Paper and paper products		138	149	143	133	116	100	98	97	96	100	107	105
18	Printing and reproduction of recorded media		165	165	170	164	97	100	98	84	76	72	68	70
19	Coke and refined petroleum products		...	...	...	...	...	...	...	...	...	...	...	...
20	Chemicals and chemical products		104	106	106	107	93	100	100	104	109	121	126	133
21	Pharmaceuticals, medicinal chemicals, etc.		109	110	103	95	95	100	112	131	136	141	129	138
22	Rubber and plastics products		134	137	140	144	99	100	97	91	91	96	92	86
23	Other non-metallic mineral products		136	147	144	145	101	100	104	98	100	107	102	101
24	Basic metals		126	130	142	142	89	100	107	96	102	109	121	118
25	Fabricated metal products, except machinery		125	132	140	141	107	100	105	104	101	110	111	112
26	Computer, electronic and optical products		94	105	111	103	84	100	109	115	97	103	107	113
27	Electrical equipment		117	128	129	131	90	100	103	101	88	92	109	117
28	Machinery and equipment n.e.c.		96	106	118	126	99	100	112	114	123	122	134	140
29	Motor vehicles, trailers and semi-trailers		171	184	167	153	88	100	107	102	97	94	99	122
30	Other transport equipment		174	162	131	131	131	100	65	49	48	52	59	61
31	Furniture		160	162	157	134	103	100	94	86	86	88	89	94
32	Other manufacturing		64	68	68	79	86	100	113	130	147	160	170	176
33	Repair and installation of machinery/equipment		90	106	99	103	100	100	85	70	123	105	128	160
C	Total manufacturing		112	118	118	117	97	100	105	107	110	113	116	121

Dominican Republic

Supplier of information:
Oficina Nacional de Estadística, Santo Domingo.

Basic source of data:
Annual survey; administrative data.

Major deviations from ISIC (Revision 3):
None reported.

Reference period:
Calendar year

Scope:
All economic units registered in the social security and taxed in the reference year.

Method of data collection:
Mail questionnaires; online survey.

Type of enumeration:
Complete enumeration.

Adjusted for non-response:
No.

Concepts and definitions of variables:
No deviations from the standard UN concepts and definitions are reported.

Related national publications:
Resultados generales del Directorio de Empresas y Establecimientos, published by Oficina Nacional de Estadística, Santo Domingo.

Dominican Republic

ISIC Revision 3		Number of establishments (number)					Number of persons engaged (number)					Wages and salaries (Dominican Pesos)				
ISIC	Industry	Note	2013	2014	2015	2016	Note	2013	2014	2015	2016	Note	2013	2014	2015	2016
15	Food and beverages		63	...	...	77		11683	...	...	15161		...	...	...	...
16	Tobacco products		...	...	...	...		...	...	...	...		...	...	...	...
17	Textiles		...	...	...	...		...	...	...	...		...	...	...	...
18	Wearing apparel, fur		3	...	...	1		17	...	...	...		...	...	...	...
19	Leather, leather products and footwear		18	...	...	6		494	...	...	614		...	...	...	...
20	Wood products (excl. furniture)		167	...	...	291		8480	...	...	10883		...	...	...	...
21	Paper and paper products		121	...	...	134		4360	...	...	9344		...	...	...	...
22	Printing and publishing		130	...	...	142		6567	...	...	10761		...	...	...	...
23	Coke,refined petroleum products,nuclear fuel		63	...	...	47		578	...	...	...		...	...	...	...
24	Chemicals and chemical products		66	...	...	38		3131	...	...	925		...	...	...	...
25	Rubber and plastics products		285	...	...	439		5583	...	...	8926		...	...	...	...
26	Non-metallic mineral products		22	...	...	1		3078	...	...	117		...	...	...	...
27	Basic metals		108	...	...	139		1683	...	...	5624		...	...	...	...
28	Fabricated metal products		76	...	...	66		133	...	...	938		...	...	...	...
29	Machinery and equipment n.e.c.		16	...	...	33		541	...	...	1516		...	...	...	...
30	Office, accounting and computing machinery		...	...	...	...		...	...	...	...		...	...	...	...
31	Electrical machinery and apparatus		...	...	...	...		...	...	...	...		...	...	...	...
32	Radio,television and communication equipment		3	...	...	...		830	...	...	...		...	...	...	...
33	Medical, precision and optical instruments		148	...	...	492		1322	...	...	6096		...	...	...	...
34	Motor vehicles, trailers, semi-trailers		...	...	...	...		...	...	...	...		...	...	...	...
35	Other transport equipment		294	...	...	465		16586	...	...	20656		...	...	...	...
36	Furniture; manufacturing n.e.c.		...	...	...	...		...	...	...	...		...	...	...	...
37	Recycling		...	...	...	...		...	...	...	...		...	...	...	...
D	Total manufacturing		5512	...	...	5957		65066	...	...	91561		...	...	...	...

Ecuador

Supplier of information:
Instituto Nacional de Estadística y Censos (INEC), Quito.

Basic source of data:
Annual survey of registered enterprises.

Major deviations from ISIC (Revision 4):
None reported.

Reference period:
Calendar year.

Scope:
Enterprises with 50 or more employees or with an annual turnover of more than one million USD.

Method of data collection:
Online survey.

Type of enumeration:
Complete enumeration.

Adjusted for non-response:
No.

Concepts and definitions of variables:
Wages and salaries refers to direct wages and salaries only. Output includes revenue from non-industrial activities.

Related national publications:
Encuesta Anual de Manufacturera y Minería (annual), published by Instituto Nacional de Estadística y Censos (INEC), Quito.

Ecuador

		Number of enterprises					Number of employees					Wages and salaries paid to employees				
			(number)					(number)					(thousands of US Dollars)			
ISIC	Industry	Note	2013	2014	2015	2016a/	Note	2013	2014	2015	2016a/	Note	2013	2014	2015	2016a/
1010	Processing/preserving of meat		32	29	29	18		11928	12629	13914	12521		113933	133677	149339	137687
1020	Processing/preserving of fish, etc.		67	69	72	74		29735	32687	38939	38748		179322	194521	267611	275939
1030	Processing/preserving of fruit,vegetables		34	31	32	24		8263	7359	7990	7229		55153	53913	61506	59373
1040	Vegetable and animal oils and fats		31	30	32	26		7490	7294	7408	7953		57805	62017	73905	80608
1050	Dairy products		39	37	32	24		6475	4741	4367	5951		60279	44039	47914	76815
106	Grain mill products,starches and starch products		47	49	44	36		2823	3708	3337	3836		25715	34064	36226	41808
1061	Grain mill products		46	48	43	36		2779	3674	3311	3836		25341	33723	35941	41808
1062	Starches and starch products		...	...	...	...		44	34	26	...		374	341	284	...
107	Other food products		99	100	88	50		21140	21840	25242	22850		166665	193701	228129	201119
1071	Bakery products		44	41	31	13		4661	4939	4790	4176		30800	35737	39820	36280
1072	Sugar		7	7	7	6		9452	7126	10965	10386		80014	65422	79536	83582
1073	Cocoa, chocolate and sugar confectionery		14	14	14	10		2270	2490	2717	2972		16176	18842	27251	26706
1074	Macaroni, noodles, couscous, etc.		11	11	11	7		1474	2425	2126	2329		12962	15013	18951	21126
1075	Prepared meals and dishes		...	...	...	...		355	402	399	303		2662	3118	3051	2559
1079	Other food products n.e.c.		21	24	22	12		2928	4458	4245	2684		26053	55569	59520	30867
1080	Prepared animal feeds		24	22	19	18		3298	3604	3388	4502		28227	33016	35829	45953
110	Beverages		28	28	25	14		10246	8020	8591	8224		92884	80442	84516	106696
1101	Distilling, rectifying and blending of spirits		7	7	8	4		1023	566	701	583		11212	6003	6651	6747
1102	Wines		...	...	...	...		91	89	92	41		669	833	867	471
1103	Malt liquors and malt		...	...	...	...		2082	2201	2127	2031		22249	23891	25063	36520
1104	Soft drinks,mineral waters,other bottled waters		18	18	14	7		7050	5164	5671	5569		58753	49715	51935	62958
1200	Tobacco products		...	...	...	...		313	297	194	132		2880	2719	2744	1632
131	Spinning, weaving and finishing of textiles		40	41	39	29		6176	6254	5794	4856		45825	48423	46907	40456
1311	Preparation and spinning of textile fibres		14	12	11	8		1860	1687	1514	1156		12433	12102	11193	8602
1312	Weaving of textiles		26	29	28	21		4316	4567	4280	3700		33392	36321	35714	31854
1313	Finishing of textiles		...	...	...	...		...	...	...	...		...	...	...	...
139	Other textiles		34	36	32	9		2641	2456	1963	1266		18384	18334	15945	9617
1391	Knitted and crocheted fabrics		...	...	...	...		192	106	95	105		1141	691	666	674
1392	Made-up textile articles, except apparel		25	27	23	8		2127	1918	1483	1161		15315	14601	12161	8942
1393	Carpets and rugs		...	...	...	...		44	38	36	...		351	343	335	...
1394	Cordage, rope, twine and netting		...	4	4	...		108	263	260	...		666	1977	2129	...
1399	Other textiles n.e.c.		4	...	...	...		170	131	89	...		911	721	655	...
1410	Wearing apparel, except fur apparel		100	94	62	18		8740	8089	7015	4801		52110	50424	46078	33863
1420	Articles of fur		...	...	...	...		...	...	...	...		...	...	...	...
1430	Knitted and crocheted apparel		7	9	10	...		1084	1029	1274	710		4943	7009	8848	4972
151	Leather;luggage,handbags,saddlery,harness;fur		14	13	13	...		415	363	570	161		2319	2664	4142	1117
1511	Tanning/dressing of leather; dressing of fur		8	8	9	...		295	276	501	161		1692	2050	3681	1117
1512	Luggage,handbags,etc.;saddlery/harness		6	5	4	...		120	87	69	...		627	613	461	...
1520	Footwear		31	29	21	5		3740	3509	3277	2212		23089	22981	22585	17643
1610	Sawmilling and planing of wood		12	14	13	7		1126	1407	1312	1268		8227	9735	12049	11624

Code	Description													
162	Wood products, cork, straw, plaiting materials	21	22	13	9	3134	3096	2811	2415	24118	24747	26828	24533
1621	Veneer sheets and wood-based panels	8	8	7	8	2752	2679	2499	2373	22063	22443	25098	24267
1622	Builders' carpentry and joinery	8	9	4	:	230	265	173	42	1203	1343	798	266
1623	Wooden containers	:	:	:	:	40	37	41	:	195	230	208	:
1629	Other wood products;articles of cork,straw	:	:	:	:	112	115	98	:	657	732	724	:
170	Paper and paper products	55	51	49	32	8899	9046	9418	8816	82621	92115	98312	96030
1701	Pulp, paper and paperboard	:	:	:	:	238	153	140	:	2169	1153	1635	:
1702	Corrugated paper and paperboard	21	20	22	18	4570	4753	4996	5021	43564	47722	53125	55060
1709	Other articles of paper and paperboard	32	30	26	14	4091	4140	4282	3795	36888	43240	43552	40969
181	Printing and service activities related to printing	60	63	50	18	6340	5777	4672	4668	62060	66883	56393	54284
1811	Printing	58	62	49	18	6236	5751	4648	4668	61145	66754	56034	54284
1812	Service activities related to printing	:	:	:	:	104	26	24	:	915	128	359	:
1820	Reproduction of recorded media	:	:	:	:	:	:	:	:	:	:	:	:
1910	Coke oven products	:	:	:	:	:	:	:	:	:	:	:	:
1920	Refined petroleum products	10	10	11	8	6192	5789	5733	5049	148875	156786	133801	127164
201	Basic chemicals,fertilizers, etc.	30	22	23	15	2188	2106	2226	1869	22668	23718	26907	22529
2011	Basic chemicals	13	13	15	10	928	1056	1172	1022	11386	13239	16224	13946
2012	Fertilizers and nitrogen compounds	8	6	5	:	886	768	747	558	7510	7445	7590	5455
2013	Plastics and synthetic rubber in primary forms	9	:	4	4	374	282	307	289	3772	3034	3092	3127
202	Other chemical products	52	53	54	34	7328	7144	7388	6379	78010	85735	95066	90302
2021	Pesticides and other agrochemical products	4	4	5	4	656	788	828	794	9210	12808	13333	13166
2022	Paints,varnishes;printing ink and mastics	15	15	15	12	2183	2194	2185	2181	23158	24363	27062	29347
2023	Soap,cleaning and cosmetic preparations	24	24	23	10	3810	3516	3608	2774	38644	40655	43266	38358
2029	Other chemical products n.e.c.	9	10	11	8	679	646	767	630	6998	7909	11405	9431
2030	Man-made fibres	:	:	:	:	61	94	76	:	542	617	464	:
2100	Pharmaceuticals,medicinal chemicals, etc.	30	31	32	25	3442	3785	4187	4257	35169	41341	48919	47363
221	Rubber products	9	8	11	6	1919	1900	1993	1735	:	20865	24773	22767
2211	Rubber tyres and tubes	6	5	6	5	1580	1529	1534	1424	18590	18415	21375	20249
2219	Other rubber products	:	:	5	:	339	371	459	311	:	2450	3398	2519
2220	Plastics products	102	100	101	58	11621	11465	11497	9478	92607	99118	108183	89899
2310	Glass and glass products	9	8	9	9	887	877	966	664	8789	8639	9893	7540
239	Non-metallic mineral products n.e.c.	71	69	64	30	9726	8590	8445	7037	84834	80932	88479	82643
2391	Refractory products	4	4	4	:	765	719	743	532	4853	4535	6098	4199
2392	Clay building materials	8	9	8	4	3063	2884	2716	2412	23911	24776	25731	22538
2393	Other porcelain and ceramic products	6	5	4	:	399	425	358	257	1904	2340	1867	1779
2394	Cement, lime and plaster	6	5	4	:	2125	1796	1928	1806	27827	23047	29716	33357
2395	Articles of concrete, cement and plaster	44	44	42	20	3139	2601	2590	1948	24582	24506	23930	19594
2396	Cutting, shaping and finishing of stone	:	:	:	:	71	6	5	:	354	29	25	:
2399	Other non-metallic mineral products n.e.c.	16	13	14	12	164	159	105	82	1403	1699	1111	1176
2410	Basic iron and steel	:	:	:	:	4618	5092	5227	4842	49933	56368	59255	54257
2420	Basic precious and other non-ferrous metals	6	5	9	7	785	751	1018	1300	5457	6774	9610	11414
243	Casting of metals	6	:	:	:	363	344	111	116	3085	3311	1559	1588
2431	Casting of iron and steel	6	:	:	:	363	321	111	68	3085	3201	1559	1145
2432	Casting of non-ferrous metals	:	:	:	:	:	23	:	48	:	109	:	443
251	Struct.metal products, tanks, reservoirs	54	49	40	17	3355	2565	3089	3213	26703	23357	29734	27012

continued

Ecuador

ISIC	Industry	Number of enterprises (number) 2013	2014	2015	2016a/	Number of employees (number) 2013	2014	2015	2016a/	Wages and salaries paid to employees (thousands of US Dollars) 2013	2014	2015	2016a/
2511	Structural metal products	45	37	29	11	2556	1583	2262	2554	18759	13776	19985	21303
2512	Tanks, reservoirs and containers of metal	8	11	10	6	792	974	817	659	7909	9516	9693	5709
2513	Steam generators, excl. hot water boilers	...	...	...	...	7	8	10	...	35	66	55	...
2520	Weapons and ammunition	...	...	...	...	...	120	...	...	...	1101	...	...
259	Other metal products;metal working services	19	19	17	8	2653	2635	2504	2501	26535	25131	27964	29361
2591	Forging,pressing,stamping,roll-forming of metal	...	...	...	...	51	...	...	...	516	...	...	...
2592	Treatment and coating of metals; machining	...	...	...	...	...	...	...	...	...	...	...	...
2593	Cutlery, hand tools and general hardware	5	5	...	...	231	209	37	69	1493	1389	338	892
2599	Other fabricated metal products n.e.c.	13	14	15	7	2371	2426	2467	2432	24526	23742	27625	28469
2610	Electronic components and boards	...	...	7 b/	6 b/	118	118	85	80	926	1010	852	842
2620	Computers and peripheral equipment	...	...	.. b/	.. b/	12	11	94	171	89	96	713	1012
2630	Communication equipment	...	...	.. b/	.. b/	38	207	84	64	270	1540	1142	877
2640	Consumer electronics	...	...	.. b/	.. b/	185	306	242	285	1119	1686	2435	3042
265	Measuring,testing equipment; watches, etc.	...	...	.. b/	.. b/	...	...	...	...	...	...	...	...
2651	Measuring/testing/navigating equipment,etc.	...	...	...	...	...	...	...	...	...	...	...	...
2652	Watches and clocks	...	...	...	...	...	...	...	...	...	...	...	...
2660	Irradiation/electromedical equipment,etc.	...	...	.. b/	.. b/	...	...	...	...	...	...	...	...
2670	Optical instruments and photographic equipment	...	...	.. b/	.. b/	...	...	...	...	...	...	...	...
2680	Magnetic and optical media	...	...	.. b/	.. b/	...	...	...	...	...	...	...	...
2710	Electric motors,generators,transformers,etc.	6	6	7	6	667	652	703	654	5322	4376	6195	6252
2720	Batteries and accumulators	...	...	7	...	926	983	987	978	6796	7766	9729	9456
273	Wiring and wiring devices	5	6	6	5	699	836	783	717	5095	6742	7749	7282
2731	Fibre optic cables	...	...	...	...	...	...	...	...	...	...	...	...
2732	Other electronic and electric wires and cables	4	5	5	5	621	760	718	717	4492	6295	7138	7282
2733	Wiring devices	...	...	...	...	78	76	65	...	603	446	612	...
2740	Electric lighting equipment	...	4	...	...	77	70	51	...	959	1001	745	...
2750	Domestic appliances	7	6	5	4	3889	3492	3360	3328	27756	27959	29161	28664
2790	Other electrical equipment	...	...	...	...	...	...	...	...	...	...	...	...
281	General-purpose machinery	16	17	16	6	1791	1763	1728	1402	15978	18660	19049	17001
2811	Engines/turbines,excl.aircraft,vehicle engines	...	...	...	...	...	...	...	...	...	...	...	...
2812	Fluid power equipment	...	...	...	...	209	57	63	62	2197	2313	2247	2081
2813	Other pumps, compressors, taps and valves	...	6	5	...	1150	1261	1256	1152	10641	12542	13540	12921
2814	Bearings, gears, gearing and driving elements	...	...	...	...	59	68	68	...	342	424	460	...
2815	Ovens, furnaces and furnace burners	...	...	...	...	...	...	...	...	...	...	...	...
2816	Lifting and handling equipment	...	...	...	...	...	...	...	...	...	...	...	...
2817	Office machinery, excl.computers,etc.	...	...	...	...	21	24	25	...	148	164	157	...
2818	Power-driven hand tools	...	...	...	...	...	...	...	...	...	...	...	...
2819	Other general-purpose machinery	7	7	7	...	352	353	316	188	2651	3218	2645	1999
282	Special-purpose machinery	9	7	7	...	159	155	397	197	996	1003	4987	2656
2821	Agricultural and forestry machinery	...	...	...	...	9	4	2	...	46	17	9	...
2822	Metal-forming machinery and machine tools	...	...	...	...	...	...	...	...	...	...	...	...

2823	Machinery for metallurgy	…	…	…	…	17	12	…	…	78	68	…	…
2824	Mining, quarrying and construction machinery	…	…	…	4	25	26	281	197	97	107	4232	2656
2825	Food/beverage/tobacco processing machinery	…	…	…	…	101	113	114	…	755	811	747	…
2826	Textile/apparel/leather production machinery	…	…	…	…	…	…	…	…	…	…	…	…
2829	Other special-purpose machinery	…	…	…	…	7	…	…	…	21	…	…	…
2910	Motor vehicles	16	17	7	7	1645	1506	1253	712	18842	17675	17545	10131
2920	Automobile bodies, trailers and semi-trailers	6	8	14	7	1108	1109	1077	577	6307	7954	7896	4584
2930	Parts and accessories for motor vehicles	…	…	6	4	351	966	707	338	2698	7690	6603	3247
301	Building of ships and boats	4	4	4	…	696	743	777	590	7459	7079	7535	7044
3011	Building of ships and floating structures	…	…	…	…	696	740	774	590	7459	7066	7521	7044
3012	Building of pleasure and sporting boats	…	…	…	…	…	3	3	…	…	14	14	…
3020	Railway locomotives and rolling stock	…	…	…	…	…	…	…	…	…	…	…	…
3030	Air and spacecraft and related machinery	…	…	…	…	…	…	…	…	…	…	…	…
3040	Military fighting vehicles	…	…	…	…	…	…	…	…	…	…	…	…
309	Transport equipment n.e.c.	8	5	5	8	1166	478	446	609	8976	3527	3802	5231
3091	Motorcycles	8	5	5	8	1166	478	446	609	8976	3527	3802	5231
3092	Bicycles and invalid carriages	…	…	…	…	…	…	…	…	…	…	…	…
3099	Other transport equipment n.e.c.	41	41	25	11	…	…	…	…	…	…	…	…
3100	Furniture	41	41	25	11	5476	5924	5464	4151	40073	45428	45142	37261
321	Jewellery, bijouterie and related articles	…	4	7c/	…	90	119	107	…	652	1097	1101	…
3211	Jewellery and related articles	…	…	…	…	90	96	85	…	652	962	960	…
3212	Imitation jewellery and related articles	…	…	…c/	…	…	23	22	…	…	135	141	…
3220	Musical instruments	…	…	…c/	…	…	…	…	…	…	…	…	…
3230	Sports goods	…	…	…c/	…	…	…	…	…	…	…	…	…
3240	Games and toys	…	…	…c/	…	212	216	255	…	1029	1077	1301	1481
3250	Medical and dental instruments and supplies	4	4	…c/	…	250	254	211	…	1943	2157	1998	1727
3290	Other manufacturing n.e.c.	8	8	6	…c/	419	421	270	…	3244	3650	3826	3076
331	Repair of fabricated metal products/machinery	…	…	5	8	…	835	669	…	…	…	10655	10064
3311	Repair of fabricated metal products	…	…	…	…	…	292	144	…	…	…	2272	2106
3312	Repair of machinery	…	…	…	…	…	540	440	…	…	…	8337	6363
3313	Repair of electronic and optical equipment	…	…	…	…	…	…	43	…	…	…	…	1003
3314	Repair of electrical equipment	…	…	…	…	…	3	42	…	…	…	46	592
3315	Repair of transport equip., excl. motor vehicles	…	…	…	…	…	…	…	…	…	…	…	…
3319	Repair of other equipment	…	…	…	…	…	…	…	…	…	…	…	…
3320	Installation of industrial machinery/equipment	…	…	8	8	…	189	1200	…	…	…	2699	15671
C	Total manufacturing	d/ 1336	1345	1194	730	d/ 219118	216784	226196	209017	d/ 1866883	1978392	2183275	2112209

a/ Methodological break in 2016.
b/ 2610 includes 2620, 2630, 2640, 265, 2660, 2670 and 2680.
c/ 321 includes 3220, 3230, 3240, 3250 and 3290.
d/ Sum of available data.

Ecuador

ISIC	Industry	Note	Output at basic prices (thousands of US Dollars)				Note	Value added at basic prices (thousands of US Dollars)				Note	Gross fixed capital formation (thousands of US Dollars)	
			2013	2014	2015	2016a/		2013	2014	2015	2016a/		2015	2016a/
1010	Processing/preserving of meat		1268480	1435467	1608907	1410389		333039	264429	371190	349694		85241	34657
1020	Processing/preserving of fish, etc.		3061464	3402866	3416588	3725059		458888	495653	590217	554721		138417	46447
1030	Processing/preserving of fruit,vegetables		446865	467811	502056	443962		126825	137780	155649	107692		39278	35137
1040	Vegetable and animal oils and fats		1188011	1158123	1231786	1226884		167901	177869	204682	176450		22552	33160
1050	Dairy products		1225980	827534	787962	1048073		220435	153572	149976	233555		58926	80500
106	Grain mill products,starches and starch products		500912	555657	513124	563322		74797	103288	108890	111756		9112	14156
1061	Grain mill products		498921	553789	511187	563322		74023	102620	108307	111756		9030	14156
1062	Starches and starch products		1992	1867	1938	...		774	668	583	...		82	...
107	Other food products		1378925	1717557	1981625	1470832		452290	516903	605463	467478		113838	-23358
1071	Bakery products		229379	249784	279699	244309		80166	90616	89832	82971		27234	12472
1072	Sugar		452294	401408	458896	452837		190594	165899	203431	174314		28321	-71653
1073	Cocoa, chocolate and sugar confectionery		193500	263642	329622	288974		45906	49213	69339	60265		30623	11168
1074	Macaroni, noodles, couscous, etc.		101379	113823	149224	151906		30751	34592	46946	51961		6253	19481
1075	Prepared meals and dishes		18941	24586	22067	13254		9985	6068	5313	4524		529	483
1079	Other food products n.e.c.		383432	664312	742117	319553		94887	170515	190602	93442		20878	4691
1080	Prepared animal feeds		706727	869317	1025761	1080715		114192	131530	182984	222896		32454	30885
110	Beverages		1238222	1251146	1342150	1235484		476043	468617	462743	458324		67661	38515
1101	Distilling, rectifying and blending of spirits		69492	56328	58221	59906		24730	17986	16668	18491		-367	2323
1102	Wines		4373	4739	5046	4700		1798	1796	1858	1020		910	41
1103	Malt liquors and malt		466917	503828	523725	476888		248699	283926	275690	277508		19924	20119
1104	Soft drinks,mineral waters,other bottled waters		697440	686251	755158	693990		200815	164910	168527	161305		47195	16032
1200	Tobacco products		39969	43537	35784	32119		9873	8841	10150	2825		1863	-3060
131	Spinning, weaving and finishing of textiles		387615	404587	338677	266490		133107	131858	117024	89486		2821	-8461
1311	Preparation and spinning of textile fibres		115191	104042	80365	56684		38521	32671	29554	19871		-120	1467
1312	Weaving of textiles		272423	300545	258312	209806		94586	99187	87471	69616		2941	-9928
1313	Finishing of textiles		...	...	...	...		...	...	...	...		...	...
139	Other textiles		158138	131014	103204	64938		48191	41736	33932	22410		953	3755
1391	Knitted and crocheted fabrics		14136	7182	6513	5805		4689	2188	2253	2025		249	709
1392	Made-up textile articles, except apparel		127872	101737	77465	59134		38372	31651	24500	20386		726	3046
1393	Carpets and rugs		3248	3209	3227	...		1289	1323	1394	...		12	...
1394	Cordage, rope, twine and netting		4227	12062	11407	...		1530	4128	4382	...		-72	...
1399	Other textiles n.e.c.		8656	6824	4592	...		2310	2447	1404	...		38	...
1410	Wearing apparel, except fur apparel		271957	243742	212522	150018		95540	96519	77829	47762		6427	1887
1420	Articles of fur		...	...	...	...		...	...	...	...		...	...
1430	Knitted and crocheted apparel		25909	30135	48999	33879		11086	13091	18656	11910		1861	1455
151	Leather;luggage,handbags,saddlery,harness;fur		27781	29265	41194	12267		5417	5772	8502	2410		2103	48
1511	Tanning/dressing of leather; dressing of fur		24074	25829	38631	12267		4279	4530	7543	2410		1883	48
1512	Luggage,handbags,etc.;saddlery/harness		3707	3436	2562	...		1138	1243	959	...		220	...
1520	Footwear		181348	172718	160572	119867		50980	58095	57655	42489		7016	2210
1610	Sawmilling and planing of wood		68321	89953	111362	102720		15703	24576	30647	27676		2643	748

Code	Product	(1)	(2)	(3)	(4)	(5)	(6)	(7)	(8)	(9)	(10)
162	Wood products, cork, straw, plaiting materials	232887	291090	290394	284874	83419	93506	87262	82914	13367	21953
1621	Veneer sheets and wood-based panels	220606	276804	277490	283321	79884	89088	83989	82476	12935	21953
1622	Builders' carpentry and joinery	6197	7474	6262	1553	1958	2494	1486	439	438	...
1623	Wooden containers	3084	3634	3366	...	410	592	562	...	-51	...
1629	Other wood products;articles of cork,straw	3000	3178	3276	...	1167	1331	1224	...	44	...
170	Paper and paper products	1232595	1344798	1418396	1273967	267533	297218	330361	272955	10047	65364
1701	Pulp, paper and paperboard	16180	10321	6713	...	4250	2158	2032	...	-21297	...
1702	Corrugated paper and paperboard	764239	805330	891093	795597	129529	154344	175709	142821	3890	56879
1709	Other articles of paper and paperboard	452176	529147	520590	478369	133754	140716	152620	130134	27454	8486
181	Printing and service activities related to printing	346773	359072	286691	273217	149607	146891	123928	106690	2535	54282
1811	Printing	338214	357681	283055	273217	147018	146607	123268	106690	2535	54282
1812	Service activities related to printing	8558	1391	3636	...	2588	284	660	...	...	...
1820	Reproduction of recorded media	...	...	...	...	...	...	...	...	...	...
1910	Coke oven products	...	...	...	...	...	...	...	...	...	...
1920	Refined petroleum products	4628999	4155845	4259947	3697722	3880439	3215593	1577961	239167	162670	28631
201	Basic chemicals,fertilizers, etc.	325226	333405	353000	297557	90187	102232	111526	81088	19556	25374
2011	Basic chemicals	166704	180665	218610	186845	60766	72766	82006	59736	13409	20910
2012	Fertilizers and nitrogen compounds	116864	116115	103372	80611	15204	17611	20079	13088	2078	2944
2013	Plastics and synthetic rubber in primary forms	41658	36625	31017	30102	14216	11855	9442	8264	4069	1520
202	Other chemical products	1002719	1267006	1012923	932766	318431	346620	323460	266814	36699	24841
2021	Pesticides and other agrochemical products	100175	100251	101613	103908	39346	34186	27791	18054	3406	1488
2022	Paints,varnishes;printing ink and mastics	290990	329691	299709	270662	89597	97610	93592	83632	5867	4962
2023	Soap,cleaning and cosmetic preparations	510462	549244	527637	496383	160872	186022	170337	140231	34470	15150
2029	Other chemical products n.e.c.	101093	287821	83965	61813	28616	28801	31739	24897	-7044	3241
2030	Man-made fibres	11253	4246	2661	...	2674	1361	728	...	-125	...
2100	Pharmaceuticals,medicinal chemicals, etc.	408970	337029	383383	407688	183137	105315	123370	120651	10809	24609
221	Rubber products	...	225079	217304	177935	...	79572	80293	63003	21320	9461
2211	Rubber tyres and tubes	216996	213143	198237	167366	67587	73966	71268	57243	17564	8949
2219	Other rubber products	...	11936	19067	10570	...	5606	9026	5759	3756	512
2220	Plastics products	1085005	1167720	1112267	950981	299787	330903	333695	300464	8904	30707
2310	Glass and glass products	87467	99019	101746	80717	36955	42335	45235	28622	3095	4335
239	Non-metallic mineral products n.e.c.	1371081	1378061	1669341	1106521	490847	513240	877000	470907	453182	135194
2391	Refractory products	42778	45999	47757	38323	20622	14912	15595	10961	8828	228
2392	Clay building materials	186720	202073	204308	150280	65807	75518	77488	41516	17574	9198
2393	Other porcelain and ceramic products	5263	7313	7243	5280	2068	3808	4139	2868	-2347	132
2394	Cement, lime and plaster	830696	842811	1152095	723419	323091	341972	708961	362052	423244	103189
2395	Articles of concrete, cement and plaster	280461	250054	243811	175706	72208	69524	67249	49027	5853	22556
2396	Cutting, shaping and finishing of stone	1576	306	296	...	852	160	177	...	274	...
2399	Other non-metallic mineral products n.e.c.	23587	29506	13831	13513	6199	7346	3392	4483	-244	-109
2410	Basic iron and steel	1057369	1169238	1014338	761485	219155	233408	219274	184909	60720	67745
2420	Basic precious and other non-ferrous metals	111361	96208	173322	184951	31140	19608	25404	31494	3091	3438
243	Casting of metals	37343	31759	31759	23590	11692	6712	4138	4067	55	136
2431	Casting of iron and steel	37343	31457	31457	3171	11692	6624	4138	4138	55	165
2432	Casting of non-ferrous metals	...	...	301	20419	...	89	...	1780	...	-29
251	Struct.metal products, tanks, reservoirs	240416	173405	204493	245664	66023	52548	68150	65166	2497	3806

continued

Ecuador

ISIC	Industry	Output at basic prices (thousands of US Dollars)					Value added at basic prices (thousands of US Dollars)					Gross fixed capital formation (thousands of US Dollars)		
		Note	2013	2014	2015	2016a/	Note	2013	2014	2015	2016a/	Note	2015	2016a/
2511	Structural metal products		189274	113162	145512	211458		48840	31534	47057	51104		1959	4086
2512	Tanks, reservoirs and containers of metal		50851	59935	58657	34206		17110	20883	20965	14062		574	-280
2513	Steam generators, excl. hot water boilers		291	309	324	…		74	131	127	…		-36	…
2520	Weapons and ammunition		…	2532	…	…		…	1304	…	…		…	…
259	Other metal products;metal working services		329483	307015	342681	309574		97723	72726	82314	96574		2604	31939
2591	Forging,pressing,stamping,roll-forming of metal		2986	…	…	…		823	…	…	…		…	…
2592	Treatment and coating of metals; machining													
2593	Cutlery, hand tools and general hardware		8337	5365	1750	2606		3184	2561	731	1772		56	115
2599	Other fabricated metal products n.e.c.		318160	301650	340932	306968		93717	70166	81583	94802		2547	31823
2610	Electronic components and boards		13786	8365	5070	5301		3918	2891	3542	2627		416	501
2620	Computers and peripheral equipment		215	364	25150	50663		132	118	2207	2698		4892	180
2630	Communication equipment		1447	32809	24136	20793		422	4919	3571	2345		-2228	10
2640	Consumer electronics		49126	113737	92228	128090		8266	8206	12597	8619		6672	311
265	Measuring,testing equipment; watches, etc.		…	…	…	…		…	…	…	…			
2651	Measuring/testing/navigating equipment,etc.		…	…	…	…		…	…	…	…			
2652	Watches and clocks		…	…	…	…		…	…	…	…			
2660	Irradiation/electromedical equipment,etc.		…	…	…	…		…	…	…	…			
2670	Optical instruments and photographic equipment		…	…	…	…		…	…	…	…			
2680	Magnetic and optical media		…	…	…	…		…	…	…	…			
2710	Electric motors,generators,transformers,etc.		60211	51717	67300	67563		15772	13759	17483	16092		6444	1344
2720	Batteries and accumulators		82880	85809	84215	92822		24017	23689	27983	29795		6801	5727
273	Wiring and wiring devices		133009	159166	176704	138017		20588	31410	34460	29892		2358	5650
2731	Fibre optic cables		…	…	…	…		…	…	…	…			
2732	Other electronic and electric wires and cables		130999	157178	174903	138017		19605	30209	33530	29892		2236	5650
2733	Wiring devices		2010	1989	1801	…		983	1202	930	…		122	…
2740	Electric lighting equipment		11319	7408	7952	…		2361	1534	1324	…		541	…
2750	Domestic appliances		324856	295862	321544	232929		75519	67326	83503	52049		26598	3837
2790	Other electrical equipment		…	…	…	…		…	…	…	…			
281	General-purpose machinery		118397	134269	113525	88700		37316	45035	42480	31727		8989	3480
2811	Engines/turbines, excl.aircraft,vehicle engines		21259	27321	18262	13891		2722	5492	4639	-646			
2812	Fluid power equipment												2021	58
2813	Other pumps, compressors, taps and valves		64767	75780	69173	55202		24635	28416	28207	25031		6793	2751
2814	Bearings, gears, gearing and driving elements		2700	2553	2804	…		636	765	827	…		13	…
2815	Ovens, furnaces and furnace burners		…	…	…	…		…	…	…	…			
2816	Lifting and handling equipment		…	…	…	…		…	…	…	…			
2817	Office machinery, excl.computers,etc.		544	629	659	…		287	323	291	…		18	…
2818	Power-driven hand tools		…	…	…	…		…	…	…	…			
2819	Other general-purpose machinery		29127	27987	22627	19606		9036	10039	8517	7342		143	670
282	Special-purpose machinery		4295	4936	30003	10993		1179	1917	10100	5229		1385	714
2821	Agricultural and forestry machinery		258	172	105	…		83	39	22	…		-4	…
2822	Metal-forming machinery and machine tools		…	…	…	…		…	…	…	…			

2823	Machinery for metallurgy	402	333	...	...	173	140	8523	5229	1265	714
2824	Mining, quarrying and construction machinery	471	574	26591	10993	180	221	1554	...	124	...
2825	Food/beverage/tobacco processing machinery	2819	3857	3307	...	707	1517	...	...	...	...
2826	Textile/apparel/leather production machinery	...	...	...	...	...	...	...	...	...	...
2829	Other special-purpose machinery	345	...	...	...	36	...	...	...	-3844	8931
2910	Motor vehicles	819610	891397	754897	397383	136873	119203	100430	58197	1251	489
2920	Automobile bodies, trailers and semi-trailers	50783	59418	63234	42078	12919	17499	18289	10965	-1013	351
2930	Parts and accessories for motor vehicles	48675	114661	79260	46695	8541	22492	15795	6862	...	...
301	Building of ships and boats	61433	47517	41335	28643	5114	-651	12087	12012	1254	143
3011	Building of ships and floating structures	61331	47391	41210	28643	5109	-695	12040	12012	1254	143
3012	Building of pleasure and sporting boats	102	126	125	...	5	45	46	...	...	...
3020	Railway locomotives and rolling stock	...	...	...	...	...	...	...	...	...	...
3030	Air and spacecraft and related machinery	...	...	...	...	...	...	...	...	...	...
3040	Military fighting vehicles	...	...	...	...	...	...	...	...	...	...
309	Transport equipment n.e.c.	130086	62980	57771	81355	29233	10413	9541	9877	-2128	629
3091	Motorcycles	130086	62980	57771	81355	29233	10413	9541	9877	-2128	629
3092	Bicycles and invalid carriages	...	...	...	...	...	...	...	...	...	...
3099	Other transport equipment n.e.c.	...	...	...	...	...	...	...	...	...	...
3100	Furniture	314093	382693	337931	272874	100244	120418	112791	91893	12931	10653
321	Jewellery, bijouterie and related articles	4779	5442	4034	...	2070	2488	1670	...	-501	...
3211	Jewellery and related articles	4779	5037	3688	...	2070	2229	1432	...	-505	...
3212	Imitation jewellery and related articles	...	405	346	...	...	259	238	...	4	...
3220	Musical instruments	...	...	...	...	...	...	...	...	...	...
3230	Sports goods	...	...	5659	8192	1308	1684	2279	3118	80	3540
3240	Games and toys	4474	4898	15181	12176	4954	5832	5655	4739	1341	1424
3250	Medical and dental instruments and supplies	14895	15563	34776	27211	16612	16942	11823	10865	2221	247
3290	Other manufacturing n.e.c.	37232	41154	...	...	...	...	...	...	...	...
331	Repair of fabricated metal products/machinery	...	...	88332	72244	...	24096	17588	...	950	2081
3311	Repair of fabricated metal products	...	...	23274	7883	...	7045	95	...	421	-255
3312	Repair of machinery	...	...	64530	54677	...	16957	13503	...	478	1201
3313	Repair of electronic and optical equipment	...	...	...	6839	...	...	2935	...	...	1135
3314	Repair of electrical equipment	...	...	529	2845	...	94	1055	...	50	...
3315	Repair of transport equip., excl. motor vehicles	...	...	...	...	...	...	...	...	...	...
3319	Repair of other equipment	...	...	...	...	...	...	...	...	...	...
3320	Installation of industrial machinery/equipment	49757	...	49757	94303	...	5988	18001	18001	-245	68
C	Total manufacturing	27188169	28093123	28792720 b/	25915253 b/	9599002	9008348	8159978 b/	5770209	1479359 b/	870805

a/ Methodological break in 2016.
b/ Sum of available data.

Ecuador

Index numbers of industrial production

ISIC Revision 4

(2010=100)

ISIC	Industry	Note	2005	2006	2007	2008	2009	2010	2011	2012	2013	2014	2015	2016
10	Food products		76	85	94	95	94	100	107	115	118	127	125	115
11	Beverages		76	85	94	95	94	100	107	115	118	127	125	121
12	Tobacco products		154	140	185	122	127	100	103	87	83	83	66	40
13	Textiles		87	88	89	95	88	100	98	100	101	96	78	101
14	Wearing apparel		87	82	101	88	93	100	148	149	115	91	75	50
15	Leather and related products		80	87	90	93	88	100	106	99	116	131	121	111
16	Wood products, excluding furniture		103	113	114	106	98	100	94	94	93	89	88	102
17	Paper and paper products		72	80	83	91	97	100	100	110	128	136	131	101
18	Printing and reproduction of recorded media		87	92	99	102	96	100	103	106	96	96	85	73
19	Coke and refined petroleum products		118	111	136	108	114	100	100	106	134	117	133	130
20	Chemicals and chemical products		75	79	83	104	87	100	105	118	127	127	119	112
21	Pharmaceuticals, medicinal chemicals, etc.		75	79	83	104	87	100	105	118	127	127	119	126
22	Rubber and plastics products		83	91	94	105	96	100	132	140	141	148	136	129
23	Other non-metallic mineral products		72	78	82	89	93	100	105	111	124	117	112	128
24	Basic metals		85	101	97	98	85	100	105	113	126	132	110	120
25	Fabricated metal products, except machinery		94	100	109	124	98	100	108	105	107	105	107	109
26	Computer, electronic and optical products		...	...	...	...	...	...	...	...	...	...	...	...
27	Electrical equipment		86	99	106	119	112	100	118	132	155	155	179	161
28	Machinery and equipment n.e.c.		65	80	91	103	88	100	99	105	103	90	97	...
29	Motor vehicles, trailers and semi-trailers		27	33	48	65	68	100	100	92	77	70	62	52
30	Other transport equipment		...	...	...	...	...	...	...	...	...	...	...	...
31	Furniture		93	82	93	96	94	100	100	103	96	96	87	79
32	Other manufacturing		93	82	93	96	94	100	100	103	96	96	87	76
33	Repair and installation of machinery/equipment		...	...	...	...	...	...	...	...	...	...	...	...
C	Total manufacturing		75	82	90	94	93	100	105	111	116	118	114	113

Egypt

Supplier of information:
Central Agency for Public Mobilisation and Statistics (CAPMAS), Cairo.

Basic source of data:
Annual survey on registered establishments.

Major deviations from ISIC (Revision 4):
None reported.

Reference period:
Calendar year for private sector; fiscal year for public sector.

Scope:
All public establishments; private establishments with 10 or more employees.

Method of data collection:
Direct interview in the field.

Type of enumeration:
Complete enumeration.

Adjusted for non-response:
Yes.

Concepts and definitions of variables:
Number of employees includes home workers.
Wages and salaries includes employers' contributions (in respect of their employees) paid to social security, pension and insurance schemes as well as the benefits received by employees under these schemes and severance and termination pay.

Related national publications:
Annual Bulletin on Industrial Production; Annual Bulletin on Industrial Statistics; Quarterly Bulletin on Industrial Statistics, all published by Central Agency for Public Mobilisation and Statistics, Cairo.

Egypt

			Number of establishments					Number of employees					Wages and salaries paid to employees			
			(number)					(number)					(millions of Egyptian Pounds)			
ISIC	Industry	Note	2012	2013	2014	2015	Note	2012	2013	2014	2015	Note	2012	2013	2014	2015
1010	Processing/preserving of meat		31	31	32	27		8474	9286	11263	10866		258.2	358.5	407.2	338.5
1020	Processing/preserving of fish, etc.		15	13	13	12		936	994	900	911		11.6	13.6	15.2	17.7
1030	Processing/preserving of fruit,vegetables		80	85	89	73		24489	35616	34729	26335		606.9	1249.5	1024.8	822.0
1040	Vegetable and animal oils and fats		34	33	33	31		15132	13737	13273	14701		397.8	393.5	496.3	662.1
1050	Dairy products		51	45	38	35		15199	14053	12616	11494		707.0	803.1	778.1	255.9
106	Grain mill products,starches and starch products		222	224	218	202		23490	24222	21526	24544		663.9	758.8	831.0	1097.4
1061	Grain mill products		219	221	217	199		21760	22562	21490	22915		559.7	656.0	830.0	977.1
1062	Starches and starch products		3	3	1	3		1730	1660	36	1629		104.2	102.8	1.1	120.3
107	Other food products		4270	4268	4134	4188		110978	113533	108692	117527		2518.6	3004.0	3603.9	4931.0
1071	Bakery products		3973	3978	3845	3915		71254	67561	65749	60855		973.2	1104.7	1293.6	1951.7
1072	Sugar		12	12	12	13		18191	18380	18684	19263		986.2	1233.1	1364.6	1467.1
1073	Cocoa, chocolate and sugar confectionery		62	59	51	50		6877	7534	6579	7925		237.5	265.6	418.8	403.7
1074	Macaroni, noodles, couscous, etc.		71	66	61	46		3973	4075	3748	5397		83.7	86.9	129.6	186.1
1075	Prepared meals and dishes		4	-	1	1		872	-	16	89		15.8	-	0.2	2.9
1079	Other food products n.e.c.		148	153	164	163		9811	15983	13916	23998		222.3	313.7	397.1	919.6
1080	Prepared animal feeds		69	72	68	59		9201	8679	7303	6235		215.7	227.2	202.6	236.1
110	Beverages		18	15	14	15		16301	16133	15631	17011		859.0	1027.5	1242.0	2869.4
1101	Distilling, rectifying and blending of spirits		2	3	2	2		604	928	615	814		33.1	47.5	43.4	47.9
1102	Wines		...	1	1	1		...	64	64	64		...	0.9	1.5	1.3
1103	Malt liquors and malt		1	...	1	1		330	...	274	29		14.5	...	10.5	0.7
1104	Soft drinks,mineral waters,other bottled waters		15	11	10	11		15367	15141	14678	16104		811.4	979.0	1186.6	2819.5
1200	Tobacco products		20	19	19	25		16351	16337	16545	13449		737.1	1072.3	1214.6	1535.1
131	Spinning, weaving and finishing of textiles		307	313	313	269		97106	98181	90529	80722		2211.5	2679.7	2742.9	2654.3
1311	Preparation and spinning of textile fibres		82	86	87	86		57184	54302	46979	44621		1362.7	1525.1	1508.3	1623.7
1312	Weaving of textiles		175	177	191	142		35509	35915	40668	31870		782.5	986.6	1183.4	942.6
1313	Finishing of textiles		50	50	35	41		4413	7964	2882	4231		66.3	167.9	51.2	88.0
139	Other textiles		168	143	121	119		29269	27713	27984	30430		834.3	589.3	887.3	888.7
1391	Knitted and crocheted fabrics		28	13	16	18		1510	1240	1040	1051		14.2	12.4	17.6	9.7
1392	Made-up textile articles, except apparel		97	94	82	77		9553	8604	9606	10405		125.0	110.0	143.5	178.0
1393	Carpets and rugs		17	17	20	16		16638	16769	16090	18723		659.2	431.0	670.6	647.0
1394	Cordage, rope, twine and netting		3	3	3	2		866	850	823	184		28.2	33.6	43.4	...
1399	Other textiles n.e.c.		23	16	...	6		702	250	425	67		7.6	2.3	12.1	0.8
1410	Wearing apparel, except fur apparel		342	329	306	255		75182	75832	76414	71486		1046.0	1398.2	1342.9	1504.5
1420	Articles of fur		...	...	...	...		...	...	...	...		...	...	...	...
1430	Knitted and crocheted apparel		38	27	27	22		2866	1395	2874	980		29.4	9.6	37.3	11.5
151	Leather;luggage,handbags,saddlery,harness;fur		35	37	32	29		658	775	1042	710		5.7	9.9	16.8	11.8
1511	Tanning/dressing of leather; dressing of fur		11	17	20	14		214	352	846	378		1.8	5.8	14.9	5.3
1512	Luggage,handbags,etc.;saddlery/harness		24	20	12	14		444	423	196	332		3.9	4.1	1.9	6.5
1520	Footwear		69	60	64	44		2789	2458	2226	1617		27.6	30.3	33.0	25.1
1610	Sawmilling and planing of wood		21	18	25	18		427	353	571	289		4.2	4.7	8.5	3.4

Code		C1	C2	C3	C4	C5	C6	C7	C8	C9	C10	C11	C12
162	Wood products, cork, straw, plaiting materials	42	44	53	31	2490	2297	2481	1854	53.0	61.3	69.5	55.4
1621	Veneer sheets and wood-based panels	11	11	10	9	740	716	944	895	18.9	23.8	30.9	30.6
1622	Builders' carpentry and joinery	22	23	33	18	1169	907	859	622	19.7	18.4	18.3	11.9
1623	Wooden containers	:	:	:	:	:	:	:	:	:	:	:	:
1629	Other wood products;articles of cork,straw	9	10	10	4	581	674	678	337	14.4	19.1	20.4	12.8
170	Paper and paper products	139	136	139	127	22776	24803	26006	22868	664.0	865.6	925.3	826.9
1701	Pulp, paper and paperboard	39	36	41	36	8898	10262	12276	9800	260.7	334.2	421.8	337.5
1702	Corrugated paper and paperboard	61	61	58	53	8532	9772	8402	7823	230.9	312.7	265.4	241.2
1709	Other articles of paper and paperboard	39	39	40	38	5346	4769	5328	5245	172.3	218.7	238.1	248.3
181	Printing and service activities related to printing	128	140	129	119	12733	17685	16510	17544	424.6	598.0	587.9	607.8
1811	Printing	127	138	128	119	12723	17642	16480	17544	424.5	597.3	587.5	607.8
1812	Service activities related to printing	1	2	1	:	10	43	30	:	0.1	0.6	0.5	:
1820	Reproduction of recorded media	1	1	:	:	10	10	:	:	0.1	0.1	:	:
1910	Coke oven products	2	2	2	1	3109	2752	2539	1992	207.3	213.3	189.3	156.8
1920	Refined petroleum products	32	32	:	18	39196	42287	44272	34873	4812.5	6263.0	6969.1	6782.0
201	Basic chemicals,fertilizers, etc.	82	80	81	88	24862	24743	25456	25080	2217.6	2426.2	2619.5	2912.9
2011	Basic chemicals	47	47	49	55	7929	10167	9256	8433	747.6	1076.6	1078.0	1289.7
2012	Fertilizers and nitrogen compounds	17	15	16	15	15698	13509	15354	14518	1443.5	1322.1	1509.9	1561.5
2013	Plastics and synthetic rubber in primary forms	18	18	16	18	1235	1067	846	2129	26.5	27.5	31.6	61.7
202	Other chemical products	199	189	183	154	26702	26744	27309	27602	814.5	922.8	1007.8	1285.6
2021	Pesticides and other agrochemical products	10	9	8	7	1306	1250	1185	1201	78.6	23.3	58.5	26.2
2022	Paints,varnishes;printing ink and mastics	73	64	65	52	11478	10970	10685	10278	342.7	336.2	369.4	693.1
2023	Soap,cleaning and cosmetic preparations	88	87	84	77	11004	11127	12480	13185	266.3	388.4	407.7	451.3
2029	Other chemical products n.e.c.	28	29	26	18	2914	3397	2959	2938	126.8	175.0	172.2	115.0
2030	Man-made fibres	17	:	:	3	676	1197	914	458	8.2	17.6	13.7	33.6
2100	Pharmaceuticals,medicinal chemicals, etc.	50	52	53	57	47710	49506	48670	48194	1962.7	2584.5	2721.3	2685.5
221	Rubber products	105	88	86	64	11731	10548	9546	8659	377.7	405.8	401.5	428.4
2211	Rubber tyres and tubes	15	12	13	7	3527	3249	3012	3699	152.5	169.5	183.7	274.6
2219	Other rubber products	90	76	73	57	8204	7299	6534	4960	225.2	236.3	217.8	153.9
2220	Plastics products	217	232	216	197	19055	19276	21839	20730	386.1	440.3	511.4	556.9
2310	Glass and glass products	45	43	40	32	27453	21672	15054	9382	639.9	728.2	627.6	481.9
239	Non-metallic mineral products n.e.c.	721	707	679	583	68761	68332	69774	73747	1953.9	2605.4	3134.6	3934.3
2391	Refractory products	10	9	7	7	1228	843	843	801	31.7	26.7	28.6	30.4
2392	Clay building materials	508	492	457	404	43400	40415	40600	41837	896.9	1065.9	1169.6	1224.2
2393	Other porcelain and ceramic products	8	7	10	10	3229	3405	3880	6531	164.2	82.2	100.1	293.0
2394	Cement, lime and plaster	16	20	22	18	11254	12604	13580	14672	661.0	1119.7	1522.1	2025.7
2395	Articles of concrete, cement and plaster	61	59	67	45	5856	6321	6554	6335	144.5	199.9	228.0	255.6
2396	Cutting, shaping and finishing of stone	109	110	101	82	2631	3837	3415	2511	32.8	96.7	72.2	68.4
2399	Other non-metallic mineral products n.e.c.	9	10	15	17	1163	907	902	1060	22.9	14.3	13.9	36.9
2410	Basic iron and steel	58	63	62	53	42641	40366	41504	39063	2236.7	2898.0	3067.9	3005.9
2420	Basic precious and other non-ferrous metals	27	17	27	19	18624	17761	16740	15178	841.6	958.6	914.5	1016.9
243	Casting of metals	7	12	3	9	1383	1704	1236	1623	56.6	67.4	59.2	87.3
2431	Casting of iron and steel	5	5	3	8	1354	1555	1236	1571	56.3	65.0	59.2	87.0
2432	Casting of non-ferrous metals	2	7	:	1	29	149	:	52	0.3	2.4	:	0.3
251	Struct.metal products, tanks, reservoirs	60	62	59	50	8540	8283	9583	8349	311.8	323.8	395.9	424.0

continued

Egypt

ISIC	Industry	Note	Number of establishments (number)				Note	Number of employees (number)				Note	Wages and salaries paid to employees (millions of Egyptian Pounds)			
			2012	2013	2014	2015		2012	2013	2014	2015		2012	2013	2014	2015
2511	Structural metal products		46	48	41	36		6936	6594	7253	6577		230.1	218.7	285.6	329.6
2512	Tanks, reservoirs and containers of metal		14	13	18	14		1604	1653	2330	1772		81.7	104.2	110.3	94.4
2513	Steam generators, excl. hot water boilers		...	1	2	...		...	36	...	...		...	0.9	...	...
2520	Weapons and ammunition		1	1	2	1		2522	2436	3280	2466		88.9	101.0	190.8	162.2
259	Other metal products;metal working services		311	299	293	261		20845	23346	19601	19442		415.9	604.8	499.6	644.3
2591	Forging,pressing,stamping,roll-forming of metal		66	46	50	48		2436	2034	1880	2374		32.8	35.0	28.6	57.6
2592	Treatment and coating of metals;machining		13	15	11	8		312	269	249	148		5.5	4.3	4.7	3.2
2593	Cutlery, hand tools and general hardware		30	22	27	21		4970	4834	3830	2574		95.2	120.0	109.8	95.8
2599	Other fabricated metal products n.e.c.		202	216	205	184		13127	16209	13642	14346		282.5	445.5	356.5	487.6
2610	Electronic components and boards		5	5	3	3		639	1077	443	592		14.1	24.5	13.2	17.9
2620	Computers and peripheral equipment		5	6	8	6		1231	1321	549	487		41.5	48.8	27.2	36.0
2630	Communication equipment		7	5	5	2		239	672	654	82		3.7	16.5	5.7	1.1
2640	Consumer electronics		6	6	2	6		8357	7981	95	1540		296.5	351.5	1.4	74.7
265	Measuring,testing equipment; watches, etc.		6	6	4	4		2887	2898	2863	2727		95.7	144.3	165.1	177.0
2651	Measuring/testing/navigating equipment,etc.		5	5	3	3		2870	2884	2811	2675		95.4	144.0	164.9	176.8
2652	Watches and clocks		1	1	1	1		17	14	52	52		0.2	0.3	0.2	0.2
2660	Irradiation/electromedical equipment,etc.		...	2	6	8		...	80	1368	619		...	1.1	25.4	7.5
2670	Optical instruments and photographic equipment		2	1	2	3		33	20	50	113		0.5	0.5	0.6	2.3
2680	Magnetic and optical media		...	...	1	...		...	...	127	...		...	...	2.4	...
2710	Electric motors,generators,transformers,etc.		48	46	47	42		6798	7735	12677	10160		19.7	240.7	579.4	634.1
2720	Batteries and accumulators		4	4	4	3		2972	2915	2914	967		43.7	49.9	45.3	23.0
273	Wiring and wiring devices		20	17	18	19		5924	3429	4841	4666		142.6	118.0	148.3	187.9
2731	Fibre optic cables		...	...	...	1		...	...	...	1431		...	...	...	100.3
2732	Other electronic and electric wires and cables		19	17	15	16		5578	3429	4480	3018		135.2	118.0	140.6	80.1
2733	Wiring devices		1	...	3	2		346	...	361	217		7.4	...	7.6	7.5
2740	Electric lighting equipment		27	30	22	18		3844	4045	5487	3678		99.1	88.2	87.9	123.3
2750	Domestic appliances		51	55	55	44		22653	25500	31170	29697		587.7	787.7	1099.7	988.0
2790	Other electrical equipment		10	7	11	12		662	397	582	454		9.4	7.8	18.2	14.8
281	General-purpose machinery		75	72	66	61		23273	24954	21153	18507		384.9	972.9	892.2	700.0
2811	Engines/turbines,excl.aircraft,vehicle engines		3	3	3	2		4738	4733	2216	1914		179.2	223.6	134.1	137.2
2812	Fluid power equipment		1	1	1	...		120	72	57	...		1.8	1.2	1.4	...
2813	Other pumps, compressors, taps and valves		22	22	21	20		3063	4453	4154	1322		87.6	231.3	234.1	29.8
2814	Bearings, gears, gearing and driving elements		2	...	3	2		30	...	...	108		0.4	...	...	3.0
2815	Ovens, furnaces and furnace burners		6	2	3	3		2056	1398	1404	1323		48.1	57.7	66.6	72.1
2816	Lifting and handling equipment		9	9	7	6		609	424	609	921		16.5	5.6	21.9	29.3
2817	Office machinery, excl.computers,etc.		1	2	1	...		1221	1333	159	...		51.1	54.3	13.4	...
2818	Power-driven hand tools		...	3	...	1		...	133	...	14		...	1.7	...	0.2
2819	Other general-purpose machinery		31	30	30	27		11436	12408	12554	12905		...	397.5	420.8	428.4
282	Special-purpose machinery		28	27	24	27		3695	4005	4490	5982		122.5	180.8	181.8	307.0
2821	Agricultural and forestry machinery		9	11	9	13		813	807	779	1464		12.0	13.3	22.9	51.9
2822	Metal-forming machinery and machine tools		1	2	1	2		22	182	958	216		0.1	2.9	8.3	0.9

ISIC Revision 4

2823	Machinery for metallurgy	...	...	...	...	1100	1510	1447	3061	36.6	77.4	57.9	166.6
2824	Mining, quarrying and construction machinery	5	3	5	3	...	142	10	23	...	2.4	-	0.1
2825	Food/beverage/tobacco processing machinery	...	3	1	1	...	21	20	14	0.9	0.2	0.2	0.2
2826	Textile/apparel/leather production machinery	4	1	1	1	72	...	...	...	...	...	...	...
2829	Other special-purpose machinery	9	7	7	7	1688	1343	1276	1204	72.9	84.6	92.5	87.3
2910	Motor vehicles	47	49	55	47	17703	20303	21424	16030	806.0	838.4	687.7	578.4
2920	Automobile bodies, trailers and semi-trailers	8	7	6	5	864	847	1336	1011	19.3	29.5	30.1	19.8
2930	Parts and accessories for motor vehicles	10	11	6	5	1150	1268	1002	1107	21.7	28.6	19.1	27.3
301	Building of ships and boats	19	21	18	16	6928	6874	7160	4818	287.3	320.9	395.7	351.2
3011	Building of ships and floating structures	18	19	18	15	6889	6829	7160	4771	286.7	320.5	395.7	352.9
3012	Building of pleasure and sporting boats	1	2	...	1	39	45	...	47	0.6	0.4	...	0.7
3020	Railway locomotives and rolling stock	3	3	2	3	1240	1250	1359	5076	50.1	58.6	...	245.4
3030	Air and spacecraft and related machinery	...	...	...	...	...	...	...	...	...	...	...	...
3040	Military fighting vehicles	...	...	...	...	...	...	...	...	...	...	...	...
309	Transport equipment n.e.c.	2	2	...	1	895	280	119	50	9.2	2.4	1.2	0.3
3091	Motorcycles	2	2	...	1	895	280	119	50	9.2	2.4	1.2	0.3
3092	Bicycles and invalid carriages	...	...	...	...	...	...	...	...	...	...	...	...
3099	Other transport equipment n.e.c.	...	...	...	...	...	...	...	...	...	...	...	...
3100	Furniture	141	141	136	122	13308	13796	11507	10011	221.8	235.8	200.6	177.4
321	Jewellery, bijouterie and related articles	13	11	13	15	1167	346	464	1419	14.9	10.1	12.4	34.3
3211	Jewellery and related articles	11	9	11	13	1130	315	433	1392	14.7	9.8	12.1	34.1
3212	Imitation jewellery and related articles	2	2	2	2	37	31	31	27	0.3	0.3	0.3	0.3
3220	Musical instruments	55	56	54	...	...	...	...	...	...	...	...	...
3230	Sports goods	3	4	5	...	...	145	...	...	...	...	...	...
3240	Games and toys	26	21	20	6	50	530	250	250	0.3	1.4	4.4	4.5
3250	Medical and dental instruments and supplies	26	31	29	16	2257	1358	1533	1533	31.1	42.5	44.1	28.5
3290	Other manufacturing n.e.c.	26	29	...	25	3996	2005	2057	2057	69.6	50.9	45.1	45.6
331	Repair of fabricated metal products/machinery	10	6	4	8	1239	1092	533	316	25.7	26.6	10.1	1.2
3311	Repair of fabricated metal products	...	...	1	2	...	10	10	65	...	...	0.1	...
3312	Repair of machinery	8	5	1	4	1028	905	323	220	19.9	20.1	...	0.2
3313	Repair of electronic and optical equipment	...	...	1	1	...	...	14	21	...	...	...	...
3314	Repair of electrical equipment	...	...	...	...	...	...	...	...	...	...	...	...
3315	Repair of transport equip., excl. motor vehicles	2	1	1	-	211	187	186	10	5.8	6.6	10.0	0.2
3319	Repair of other equipment	...	...	...	1	...	...	...	...	...	...	...	...
3320	Installation of industrial machinery/equipment	1	2	2	1	16	37	33	12	0.2	0.7	0.6	0.3
C	Total manufacturing	8692a/	8603a/	8445a/	7894	984687a/	1002486a/	984725a/	932372	33475.6a/	41394.5	44724.9	48762.8a/

a/ Sum of available data.

Egypt

ISIC	Industry	Note	Output at factor values (millions of Egyptian Pounds)				Note	Value added at factor values (millions of Egyptian Pounds)				Note	Gross fixed capital formation (millions of Egyptian Pounds)	
			2012	2013	2014	2015		2012	2013	2014	2015		2014	2015
1010	Processing/preserving of meat		3360.4	4221.9	5852.2	5234.4		418.7	783.4	1448.7	957.5		4073.5 a/	...
1020	Processing/preserving of fish, etc.		115.2	135.8	94.5	81.1		32.2	57.5	35.3	71.5		... a/	...
1030	Processing/preserving of fruit,vegetables		7170.7	10211.1	11070.6	13146.0		1840.0	2957.7	2968.7	3889.9		... a/	...
1040	Vegetable and animal oils and fats		7714.2	7530.6	9358.4	15931.7		991.8	1183.5	1566.5	2734.5		... a/	...
1050	Dairy products		8454.8	8928.1	9855.1	6422.4		1122.5	1560.5	1981.9	1342.3		... a/	...
106	Grain mill products,starches and starch products		13313.6	18734.9	...	22009.9		2335.3	3254.2	4323.1	4090.2		... a/	446.4
1061	Grain mill products		12071.7	17267.5	23667.3	20685.1		2074.9	3010.0	4315.2	3681.5			
1062	Starches and starch products		1241.9	1467.4	...	1324.8		260.4	244.2	8.0	408.7			
107	Other food products		23960.5	23269.3	31613.7	33376.5		6499.5	5980.5	11033.3	11336.5		... a/	836.5
1071	Bakery products		6908.1	6403.8	11020.5	6368.6		2392.7	2340.4	6124.4	3662.9			
1072	Sugar		10367.8	8962.8	10486.9	11132.0		2678.2	2062.3	2782.5	1538.5			
1073	Cocoa, chocolate and sugar confectionery		2087.0	2569.0	2564.8	2884.3		478.8	447.4	598.4	804.6			
1074	Macaroni, noodles, couscous, etc.		1402.0	1254.4	1315.5	2806.5		165.8	121.0	201.5	637.8			
1075	Prepared meals and dishes		250.5	-	1.7	11.0		47.4	-	0.3	3.2			
1079	Other food products n.e.c.		2945.1	4079.2	6224.4	10174.1		736.5	1009.4	1326.3	4689.5			
1080	Prepared animal feeds		3560.3	3516.3	2860.8	3444.0		1003.4	945.7	665.8	1288.4		... a/	105.8
110	Beverages		8885.9	10178.6	10876.7	13339.0		2633.1	2438.9	2963.2	5850.8		709.3	1132.3
1101	Distilling, rectifying and blending of spirits		308.2	601.0	316.5	510.0		201.2	251.4	196.0	279.5			
1102	Wines		...	11.0	36.1	30.8		...	3.0	6.4	...			
1103	Malt liquors and malt		407.9	...	304.5	1.6		38.6	...	125.2	...			
1104	Soft drinks,mineral waters,other bottled waters		8169.8	9566.6	10219.5	12796.4		2393.4	2184.5	2635.6	5568.8		535.8	-371.6
1200	Tobacco products		5744.2	6336.5	6945.4	6532.4		2152.5	1997.1	3033.3	4116.0		1463.5 b/	-40.0
131	Spinning, weaving and finishing of textiles		7332.4	7705.1	8243.6	6141.2		2250.2	2101.5	2964.1	1289.4			
1311	Preparation and spinning of textile fibres		4137.1	4412.2	4597.4	2819.9		1228.3	1306.7	1851.6	454.8			
1312	Weaving of textiles		2818.6	2782.5	3368.7	3031.5		856.7	683.3	998.2	570.9			
1313	Finishing of textiles		376.7	510.4	277.6	289.7		165.2	111.5	114.3	263.7			
139	Other textiles		6393.6	7319.7	8205.1	8053.8		1436.3	2637.5	2233.0	2102.5		... b/	137.6
1391	Knitted and crocheted fabrics		158.5	107.0	139.9	62.0		46.2	19.5	32.1	20.4			
1392	Made-up textile articles, except apparel		1301.2	1392.4	1688.1	1668.8		299.4	291.8	391.5	604.2			
1393	Carpets and rugs		4847.3	5772.4	6062.7	6274.6		1055.1	2310.3	1701.1	1465.7			
1394	Cordage, rope, twine and netting		33.0	34.3	43.2	43.7		21.7	4.7	99.0	10.3			
1399	Other textiles n.e.c.		53.5	13.5	271.2	4.7					1.8			
1410	Wearing apparel, except fur apparel		7421.1	8383.1	10343.4	8861.3		2392.0	2848.9	4754.6	3159.3		233.1 c/	319.9
1420	Articles of fur		...	...	...	...							... c/	
1430	Knitted and crocheted apparel		225.8	60.6	121.2	93.8		59.8	13.4	42.1	49.3		... c/	18.5
151	Leather;luggage,handbags,saddlery,harness;fur		44.9	64.4	113.3	80.1	d/	14.3	23.5	36.7	26.3	d/	24.8	22.1
1511	Tanning/dressing of leather; dressing of fur		24.6	43.3	102.7	57.1		5.9	13.5	33.1	13.6			
1512	Luggage,handbags,etc.;saddlery/harness		20.3	21.1	10.6	23.1		8.4	10.0	3.5	12.7			
1520	Footwear		142.6	155.0	173.9	116.7	d/	50.8	52.1	60.7	53.5			
1610	Sawmilling and planing of wood		50.2	37.0	59.6	32.0		17.1	5.8	12.3	9.8		51.9 e/	...

162	Wood products, cork, straw, plaiting materials	395.7	465.6	529.3	399.8	134.9	164.4	192.6	137.5	...	...e/
1621	Veneer sheets and wood-based panels	119.3	188.3	291.8	275.6	28.1	40.9	78.6	102.2	...	...
1622	Builders' carpentry and joinery	233.1	221.1	135.2	105.3	90.2	103.8	79.4	25.3	...	...
1623	Wooden containers	...	...	...	...	...	...	...	...	...	...
1629	Other wood products;articles of cork, straw	43.3	56.2	102.3	18.9	16.7	19.7	34.6	10.0	554.1	563.6
170	Paper and paper products	9513.8	11113.4	11057.1	10786.2	2354.8	2819.9	2603.3	2942.6	...	...
1701	Pulp, paper and paperboard	3705.4	4404.9	4920.3	4480.7	927.0	1226.9	1231.6	1388.3	...	...
1702	Corrugated paper and paperboard	3315.3	4359.4	3503.1	3532.4	747.8	1044.4	732.4	985.2	...	...
1709	Other articles of paper and paperboard	2493.1	2349.2	2633.7	2773.1	680.0	548.5	639.2	569.0	...	...
181	Printing and service activities related to printing	1923.8	2363.4	2230.7	7054.7	682.8	838.1	1059.2	5938.1	87.9 f/	151.9
1811	Printing	1923.3	2360.9	2228.5	7054.7	682.7	837.9	1059.2	5938.1	...	...
1812	Service activities related to printing	0.5	2.5	2.2	...	0.1	...	...	...	...	...
1820	Reproduction of recorded media	0.4	0.4	...	...	0.2	0.2	...	...	f/	...
1910	Coke oven products	1355.7	868.9	956.2	642.1	358.1	198.8	277.2	-45.4	1189.5 g/	...
1920	Refined petroleum products	127468.3	138608.1	167742.7	108867.7	74951.6	101669.5	125473.9	82214.8	...g/	1675.7
201	Basic chemicals,fertilizers, etc.	19463.3	18711.0	17482.0	15876.9	11395.2	9779.7	7573.8	7218.9	2522.3 h/	741.5
2011	Basic chemicals	4871.1	6326.2	6914.9	5231.0	2264.7	3439.2	3357.3	2938.3	...	...
2012	Fertilizers and nitrogen compounds	14156.9	11869.8	10011.9	9668.7	9036.5	6242.7	4110.5	3881.8	...	...
2013	Plastics and synthetic rubber in primary forms	435.3	514.9	555.3	977.2	94.0	97.8	106.0	398.9	...h/	...
202	Other chemical products	15943.4	18071.4	39804.5	21169.4	6444.2	5757.4	4745.4	6287.1	...h/	46.0
2021	Pesticides and other agrochemical products	800.2	906.0	1395.4	928.1	368.7	282.5	...	430.4	...	...
2022	Paints,varnishes;printing ink and mastics	4611.7	5639.5	6335.5	6711.7	1664.1	1988.7	1794.0	1916.7	...	...
2023	Soap,cleaning and cosmetic preparations	9285.2	9712.8	11559.4	13169.0	4109.3	2993.4	2605.3	3802.2	...	...
2029	Other chemical products n.e.c.	1246.2	1813.2	20514.3	360.5	302.0	492.8	339.9	137.8	...	...
2030	Man-made fibres	194.6	300.5	347.2	463.9	25.9	41.3	59.9	102.7	...	-70.3
2100	Pharmaceuticals,medicinal chemicals, etc.	15342.5	18243.8	19577.9	20286.0	5599.1	6764.7	6076.2	7601.5	2567.4	1195.5
221	Rubber products	4517.3	4779.6	3889.2	4095.6	1158.5	972.2	980.2	1281.0	463.3 i/	50.4
2211	Rubber tyres and tubes	1747.2	2016.1	1814.0	1948.5	393.9	441.0	427.3	501.7	...	...
2219	Other rubber products	2770.1	2763.4	2075.2	2147.1	764.6	531.2	552.9	779.3	...	...
2220	Plastics products	4478.8	4592.9	6619.8	6483.1	905.6	939.0	1184.1	1709.4	...i/	273.2
2310	Glass and glass products	2473.1	...	2115.4	1716.3	954.9	766.5	693.8	539.4	3000.7 l/	-379.3
239	Non-metallic mineral products n.e.c.	24435.5	31618.9	37399.9	38573.8	9056.3	9846.0	12453.5	12420.4	...j/	3745.6
2391	Refractory products	152.1	80.9	128.8	100.9	40.7	...	27.1	36.2	...	...
2392	Clay building materials	5420.9	6432.5	6961.4	7259.1	1721.9	2097.3	2487.4	2341.2	...	...
2393	Other porcelain and ceramic products	1080.2	515.5	793.6	1732.8	439.7	219.0	195.8	520.5	...	...
2394	Cement, lime and plaster	16651.5	21058.9	28071.4	27764.8	5727.9	6602.3	9231.5	8874.5	...	...
2395	Articles of concrete, cement and plaster	654.7	2977.4	885.6	1405.3	303.7	744.7	317.8	438.1	...	...
2396	Cutting, shaping and finishing of stone	232.6	423.3	424.6	...	...	136.0	157.1	137.4	...	...
2399	Other non-metallic mineral products n.e.c.	243.4	130.3	134.4	188.6	57.7	40.2	36.8	72.4	...	...
2410	Basic iron and steel	46812.1	41936.2	42493.2	38482.7	15275.3	9240.0	4485.0	7760.4	3294.4 k/	-2422.5
2420	Basic precious and other non-ferrous metals	19054.6	8862.7	14585.0	13270.8	...	1694.1	3229.8	6345.1	...k/	368.0
243	Casting of metals	441.3	439.2	539.7	509.4	92.7	47.6	128.1	72.4	...k/	108.9
2431	Casting of iron and steel	440.5	409.1	539.7	505.8	92.1	42.6	128.1	72.0	...	...
2432	Casting of non-ferrous metals	0.8	30.0	...	3.6	0.6	5.0	...	0.4	...	...
251	Struct.metal products, tanks, reservoirs	2008.8	2079.6	2326.9	2715.2	584.9	655.9	937.9	924.1	903.7 m/	287.0

continued

Egypt

ISIC Revision 4		Note	Output at factor values (millions of Egyptian Pounds)				Note	Value added at factor values (millions of Egyptian Pounds)				Note	Gross fixed capital formation (millions of Egyptian Pounds)	
ISIC	Industry		2012	2013	2014	2015		2012	2013	2014	2015		2014	2015
2511	Structural metal products		1505.5	1591.9	1886.0	2355.9		424.9	544.8	805.8	846.9		...	...
2512	Tanks, reservoirs and containers of metal		503.3	482.7	440.9	359.3		159.9	110.0	132.1	77.2		...	...
2513	Steam generators, excl. hot water boilers		...	4.9	...	...		...	1.1	...	...		...	...
2520	Weapons and ammunition		208.2	170.3	311.5	206.6		70.3	51.9	...	39.8		...m/	40.4
259	Other metal products;metal working services		4339.4	8418.1	8360.8	7737.4		1433.2	2185.5	1853.7	2091.3		...m/	133.7
2591	Forging,pressing,stamping,roll-forming of metal		695.9	970.4	1141.2	2703.6		108.9	191.7	501.9	265.8		...	...
2592	Treatment and coating of metals; machining		27.7	21.2	37.4	...		9.1	7.5	25.7	12.8		...	...
2593	Cutlery, hand tools and general hardware		668.4	755.5	783.1	703.0		303.2	311.8	359.0	257.5		...	...
2599	Other fabricated metal products n.e.c.		2947.4	6671.1	6399.2	4328.7		1012.0	1674.6	967.1	1555.2		...	...
2610	Electronic components and boards		105.5	388.1	79.1	204.5		31.2	112.4	12.0	145.9		89.9n/	3.5
2620	Computers and peripheral equipment		1334.7	1742.4	947.6	1053.5		774.1	117.7	106.8	143.3		...n/	113.0
2630	Communication equipment		31.9	267.0	349.6	15.8		9.2	87.2	119.2	10.2		...n/	8.3
2640	Consumer electronics		3349.1	1491.4	31.1	1546.9		1963.8	380.8	14.8	483.0		...n/	-10.9
265	Measuring,testing equipment; watches, etc.		...	...	...	...		176.0	248.8	247.1	281.3		...n/	115.6
2651	Measuring/testing/navigating equipment,etc.		...	...	...	...		175.6	248.4	246.6	280.8		...	...
2652	Watches and clocks		1.1	1.3	1.7	1.7		0.3	0.4	0.5	0.5		...	...
2660	Irradiation/electromedical equipment,etc.		...	6.5	226.1	321.0		...	4.7	48.9	57.5		...n/	4.9
2670	Optical instruments and photographic equipment		4.2	3.1	3.1	30.5		1.1	1.4	1.2	14.6		...n/	5.1
2680	Magnetic and optical media		...	...	26.8	...		...	...	9.1	...		...n/	...
2710	Electric motors,generators,transformers,etc.		2530.9	2180.8	3766.9	5381.7		1204.5	663.4	1141.2	2114.3		632.8p/	325.2
2720	Batteries and accumulators		731.0	537.5	283.7	712.5		564.1	202.9	176.3	265.4		...p/	50.8
273	Wiring and wiring devices		2477.8	1766.7	2474.7	2801.1		662.5	311.4	635.7	1171.3		...p/	117.6
2731	Fibre optic cables		...	...	...	622.4		...	...	...	201.3		...	...
2732	Other electronic and electric wires and cables		2419.4	1766.7	2381.3	2143.7		640.7	311.4	624.5	959.6		...	...
2733	Wiring devices		58.4	...	93.3	35.0		21.8	...	11.2	10.4		...	...
2740	Electric lighting equipment		543.0	1288.9	2545.1	631.5		198.3	329.8	169.7	196.2		...p/	10.3
2750	Domestic appliances		7029.5	9921.4	11634.2	10275.9		2217.7	5183.9	3557.0	3030.6		...p/	673.1
2790	Other electrical equipment		179.4	90.7	148.5	113.9		56.3	33.5	40.4	26.6		...p/	14.1
281	General-purpose machinery		5363.3	5731.1	6559.4	5200.0		...	1602.2	2533.2	2274.5		388.9q/	-126.4
2811	Engines/turbines,excl.aircraft,vehicle engines		369.3	368.8	129.3	125.2		72.5	93.7	119.6	...		...	...
2812	Fluid power equipment		8.7	19.3	29.4	...		3.4	8.2	20.5	...		...	...
2813	Other pumps, compressors, taps and valves		282.4	1192.6	1174.0	223.3		70.5	452.0	258.7	109.0		...	...
2814	Bearings, gears, gearing and driving elements		1.8	...	...	10.6		1.1	...	...	5.3		...	...
2815	Ovens, furnaces and furnace burners		354.6	60.6	52.5	127.2		274.8	...	...	28.7		...	...
2816	Lifting and handling equipment		116.1	28.3	132.5	128.0		36.3	10.1	42.7	65.3		...	...
2817	Office machinery, excl.computers,etc.		286.6	307.9	365.0	...		92.3	96.6	150.0	...		...	...
2818	Power-driven hand tools		...	8.0	...	2.8		...	2.8	...	1.3		...	...
2819	Other general-purpose machinery		3943.9	3745.7	4676.6	4582.9		202.2	870.8	1863.2	2037.0		...	...
282	Special-purpose machinery		450.9	680.4	976.2	1037.7		...	421.2	403.4	460.1		...q/	-10.3
2821	Agricultural and forestry machinery		110.5	119.4	143.0	362.6		31.6	32.3	67.4	105.0		...	...
2822	Metal-forming machinery and machine tools		0.6	66.9	91.3	100.8		0.3	16.6	13.9	7.2		...	...

Code	Industry	(1)	(2)	(3)	(4)	(5)	(6)	(7)	(8)		(9)	(10)
2823	Machinery for metallurgy	122.6	75.0	...	407.2	72.4	...	45.0	86.1		...	...
2824	Mining, quarrying and construction machinery	...	9.0	68.9	4.9	...	4.5	0.1	1.5		...	...
2825	Food/beverage/tobacco processing machinery	4.7	0.8	0.2	...	1.2	0.3	0.2	0.2		...	...
2826	Textile/apparel/leather production machinery	...	...	...	...	...	...	...	...		...	...
2829	Other special-purpose machinery	212.6	409.3	671.5	...	96.6	265.1	276.9	196.0		...	...
2910	Motor vehicles	10071.7	11600.7	14829.4	15229.0	1739.6	2634.7	3788.3	5684.6		360.3r/	671.4
2920	Automobile bodies, trailers and semi-trailers	288.4	249.4	369.4	376.8	25.8	25.5	70.0	53.2		..r/	-24.7
2930	Parts and accessories for motor vehicles	215.7	340.4	366.0	357.1	73.8	102.7	51.9	80.8		..r/	9.0
301	Building of ships and boats	504.3	590.0	590.1	...	189.9	284.7	204.2	288.6		290.6s/	74.8
3011	Building of ships and floating structures	501.5	588.8	590.1	...	189.1	284.3	204.2	287.9		...	...
3012	Building of pleasure and sporting boats	2.7	1.2	...	6.8	0.8	0.4	...	0.7		...	...
3020	Railway locomotives and rolling stock	156.9	231.6	189.4	2353.3	71.1	196.2	82.5	562.8		..s/	-179.8
3030	Air and spacecraft and related machinery	...	...	...	...	...	...	...	...		..s/	...
3040	Military fighting vehicles	...	...	...	...	...	...	...	...		..s/	...
309	Transport equipment n.e.c.	446.5	151.1	72.5	173.8	97.4	16.9	12.2	44.1		..s/	98.0
3091	Motorcycles	446.5	151.1	72.5	173.8	97.4	16.9	12.2	44.1		...	...
3092	Bicycles and invalid carriages	...	...	...	...	...	...	...	...		...	...
3099	Other transport equipment n.e.c.	...	...	...	...	...	...	...	...		...	...
3100	Furniture	1428.4	1426.5	1099.5	1185.6	483.7	522.7	376.0	381.2		67.2	72.7
321	Jewellery, bijouterie and related articles	325.3	41.1	49.6	4978.1	108.4	21.9	28.3	4051.8		71.8t/	-11.5
3211	Jewellery and related articles	324.1	39.9	49.6	4976.0	108.0	21.3	27.9	4051.0		...	...
3212	Imitation jewellery and related articles	1.2	1.3	...	2.0	0.5	0.6	0.5	0.9		...	...
3220	Musical instruments	...	...	...	...	...	...	...	...		..t/	...
3230	Sports goods	...	...	...	...	...	...	...	...		..t/	...
3240	Games and toys	2.1	13.4	23.6	30.1	0.5	3.6	7.6	8.0		..t/	2.9
3250	Medical and dental instruments and supplies	336.3	364.8	223.2	234.9	88.5	98.2	88.8	126.9		..t/	56.9
3290	Other manufacturing n.e.c.	525.6	312.6	370.6	419.0	115.3	71.9	72.8	99.0		..t/	2.3
331	Repair of fabricated metal products/machinery	57.1	43.1	14.1	...	37.9	33.4	6.8	...	u/	1.3	5.6
3311	Repair of fabricated metal products	...	...	0.3	...	...	0.2	0.2	2.3		...	...
3312	Repair of machinery	48.7	35.1	5.4	...	32.9	26.8	1.8	1.2		...	...
3313	Repair of electronic and optical equipment	...	...	0.3	...	...	...	0.1	...		...	...
3314	Repair of electrical equipment	...	...	...	...	...	...	...	...		...	...
3315	Repair of transport equip., excl. motor vehicles	8.4	8.1	8.1	...	5.0	6.6	4.6	...		...	...
3319	Repair of other equipment	...	...	...	...	...	...	...	0.2		...	...
3320	Installation of industrial machinery/equipment	0.4	1.1	1.1	...	0.3	0.9	0.7	0.3	u/	...	...
C	Total manufacturing	442904.7	472314.1	566256.2v/	497258.3	169493.0v/	196988.5	228812.2	210364.5		23578.0	12894.3v/

a/ 1010 includes 1020, 1030, 1040, 1050, 106, 107 and 1080.
b/ 131 includes 139.
c/ 1410 includes 1420 and 1430.
d/ 151 includes 1520.
e/ 1610 includes 1620.
f/ 181 includes 1820.
g/ 1910 includes 1920.
h/ 201 includes 202 and 2030.
i/ 221 includes 2220.
j/ 2310 includes 239.

k/ 2410 includes 2420 and 243.
m/ 251 includes 2520 and 259.
n/ 2610 includes 2620, 2630, 2640, 265, 2660, 2670 and 2680.
p/ 2710 includes 2720, 273, 2740, 2750 and 2790.
q/ 281 includes 282.
r/ 2910 includes 2920 and 2930.
s/ 301 includes 3020, 3030, 3040 and 309.
t/ 321 includes 3220, 3230, 3240, 3250 and 3290.
u/ 331 includes 3320.
v/ Sum of available data.

Egypt

ISIC Revision 4 — **Index numbers of industrial production (2010=100)**

ISIC	Industry	Note	2005	2006	2007	2008	2009	2010	2011	2012	2013	2014	2015	2016
10	Food products	a/	...	...	...	...	88	100	109	118	116	137	116	114
11	Beverages	a/	...	...	...	...	...	...	...	...	...	...	...	60
12	Tobacco products		...	...	...	...	103	100	105	112	110	126	134	60
13	Textiles		...	...	...	...	77	100	138	75	75	76	74	83
14	Wearing apparel		...	...	...	...	97	100	114	93	90	74	122	129
15	Leather and related products		...	...	...	...	165	100	70	67	67	47	38	60
16	Wood products, excluding furniture		...	...	...	...	...	...	...	...	...	...	87	149
17	Paper and paper products		...	...	...	...	92	100	114	124	133	133	125	119
18	Printing and reproduction of recorded media		...	...	...	...	92	100	149	132	121	220	165	152
19	Coke and refined petroleum products		...	...	...	...	...	...	...	...	...	...	...	...
20	Chemicals and chemical products	b/	...	...	...	...	92	100	104	105	107	117	123	130
21	Pharmaceuticals,medicinal chemicals, etc.	b/	...	...	...	...	...	...	...	...	...	...	...	...
22	Rubber and plastics products		...	...	...	...	95	100	104	119	103	96	110	101
23	Other non-metallic mineral products		...	...	...	...	104	100	77	79	74	73	66	72
24	Basic metals		...	...	...	...	117	100	84	95	92	94	84	77
25	Fabricated metal products, except machinery		...	...	...	...	93	100	93	100	92	102	105	127
26	Computer, electronic and optical products		...	...	...	...	58	100	95	83	118	...	...	...
27	Electrical equipment		...	...	...	...	127	100	77	64	60	55	54	73
28	Machinery and equipment n.e.c.		...	...	...	...	98	100	86	84	83	76	88	98
29	Motor vehicles, trailers and semi-trailers		...	...	...	...	81	100	80	117	122	155	160	132
30	Other transport equipment		...	...	...	...	...	...	...	...	...	...	...	...
31	Furniture	c/	...	...	...	...	103	100	96	121	127	129	144	143
32	Other manufacturing	c/	...	...	...	...	...	...	...	...	...	...	...	...
33	Repair and installation of machinery/equipment		...	...	...	...	...	...	...	...	...	...	...	...
C	Total manufacturing		...	...	...	...	101	100	94	97	96	100	101	104

a/ 10 includes 11.
b/ 20 includes 21.
c/ 31 includes 32.

Eritrea

Supplier of information:
Ministry of Trade and Industry, Planning and Statistics Division, Asmara.

Basic source of data:
Census of the manufacturing industries.

Major deviations from ISIC (Revision 3):
None reported.

Reference period:
Calendar year.

Scope:
Establishments with 10 or more employees.

Method of data collection:
Questionnaires; direct interview in the field.

Type of enumeration:
Complete enumeration.

Adjusted for non-response:
No.

Concepts and definitions of variables:
Number of employees includes temporary and contract workers.
Wages and salaries includes employers' contributions paid to social security, pension and insurance schemes as well as the benefits received by employees under these schemes and severance and termination pay.
Output includes revenue from non-industrial activities.
Value added refers to total value added.

Related national publications:
Industrial Statistics Bulletin, published by the Ministry of Trade and Industry, Planning and Statistics Division, Asmara.

Eritrea

ISIC Revision 3

ISIC	Industry	Note	Number of establishments (number) 2013	2014	2015	2016	Note	Number of employees (number) 2013	2014	2015	2016	Note	Wages and salaries paid to employees (millions of Eritrean Nakfa) 2013	2014	2015	2016
151	Processed meat,fish,fruit,vegetables,fats		1	1	1	1		6	6	3	4		0.1	0.1	-	0.1
1511	Processing/preserving of meat		...	...	...	...		...	...	...	...		...	...	...	...
1512	Processing/preserving of fish		...	...	...	...		...	...	...	...		...	...	...	...
1513	Processing/preserving of fruit & vegetables		...	...	...	...		...	...	...	...		...	...	...	...
1514	Vegetable and animal oils and fats		1	1	1	1		6	6	3	4		0.1	0.1	-	0.1
1520	Dairy products		5	5	4	5		329	329	292	371		5.4	5.6	7.4	9.9
153	Grain mill products; starches; animal feeds		5	5	4	5		435	472	391	447		10.1	8.6	7.6	8.6
1531	Grain mill products		2	2	2	2		379	412	361	387		8.9	6.5	6.9	7.3
1532	Starches and starch products															
1533	Prepared animal feeds		3	3	2	3		56	60	30	60		1.2	2.1	0.8	1.4
154	Other food products		51	27	36	38		785	561	532	596		11.5	8.9	15.5	10.3
1541	Bakery products		47	24	32	35		645	464	410	509		9.7	6.8	13.3	8.4
1542	Sugar															
1543	Cocoa, chocolate and sugar confectionery		1	1	1	1		39	37	37	37		0.8	1.0	1.0	0.6
1544	Macaroni, noodles & similar products		3	2	3	2		101	60	85	50		1.1	1.1	1.2	1.2
1549	Other food products n.e.c.															
155	Beverages		20	20	24	28		1376	1342	1486	1376		49.2	57.0	56.3	61.5
1551	Distilling, rectifying & blending of spirits		2	2	2	2		150	151	145	38		2.3	2.8	1.9	0.5
1552	Wines		1	1	1	1		24	27	25	27		1.5	1.3	1.4	1.5
1553	Malt liquors and malt		1	1	1	1		392	416	464	471		15.9	21.5	26.1	27.2
1554	Soft drinks; mineral waters		16	16	20	24		810	748	852	840		23.4	27.9	26.9	32.2
1600	Tobacco products		1	1	1	1		40	38	35	32		13.6	12.4	12.3	10.5
171	Spinning, weaving and finishing of textiles		5	5	5	5		2300	2115	2142	1421		77.8	81.7	73.9	69.3
1711	Textile fibre preparation; textile weaving		5	5	5	5		2300	2115	2142	1421		77.8	81.7	73.9	69.3
1712	Finishing of textiles															
172	Other textiles															
1721	Made-up textile articles, except apparel															
1722	Carpets and rugs															
1723	Cordage, rope, twine and netting															
1729	Other textiles n.e.c.															
1730	Knitted and crocheted fabrics and articles		3	3	3	3		183	185	123	88		4.2	4.6	4.6	2.1
1810	Wearing apparel, except fur apparel		5	4	4	4		270	274	247	213		4.2	4.5	4.5	10.1
1820	Dressing & dyeing of fur; processing of fur															
191	Tanning, dressing and processing of leather		6	6	6	6		452	358	234	227		10.8	9.8	8.1	5.9
1911	Tanning and dressing of leather		5	5	5	5		433	339	215	224		10.5	9.4	7.7	5.8
1912	Luggage, handbags, etc.; saddlery & harness		1	1	1	1		19	19	19	3		0.3	0.4	0.3	-
1920	Footwear		14	14	14	13		851	759	733	650		16.7	18.1	19.0	15.5
2010	Sawmilling and planing of wood															
202	Products of wood, cork, straw, etc.															
2021	Veneer sheets, plywood, particle board, etc.															
2022	Builders' carpentry and joinery															
2023	Wooden containers															
2029	Other wood products; articles of cork/straw															
210	Paper and paper products		4	4	4	2		111	98	78	31		1.4	1.5	1.4	0.7
2101	Pulp, paper and paperboard		2	2	2	1		36	43	36	17		0.5	0.6	0.6	0.4
2102	Corrugated paper and paperboard															
2109	Other articles of paper and paperboard		2	2	2	1		75	55	42	14		0.9	0.8	0.8	0.3
221	Publishing															
2211	Publishing of books and other publications															
2212	Publishing of newspapers, journals, etc.															
2213	Publishing of recorded media															
2219	Other publishing		...	...	...	...		...	...	...	...		...	...	...	...

Code	Description													
222	Printing and related service activities	13.2	12.3	10.0	10.0	10.0	585	535	518	549	11	11	11	13
2221	Printing	13.2	12.3	10.0	10.0	10.0	585	535	518	549	11	11	11	13
2222	Service activities related to printing													
2230	Reproduction of recorded media													
2310	Coke oven products													
2320	Refined petroleum products													
2330	Processing of nuclear fuel													
241	Basic chemicals	0.9	0.9	1.0	1.0	1.0	25	23	21	18	2	2	2	2
2411	Basic chemicals, except fertilizers	0.9	0.9	1.0	1.0	1.0	25	23	21	18	2	2	2	2
2412	Fertilizers and nitrogen compounds													
2413	Plastics in primary forms; synthetic rubber	31.4	22.1	19.3	16.3		681	710	719	768	18	20	20	21
242	Other chemicals													
2421	Pesticides and other agro-chemical products	0.5	1.5	2.0	2.4		26	61	60	95	2	3	3	5
2422	Paints, varnishes, printing ink and mastics	11.4	10.6	9.0	6.0		330	278	307	320	2	3	2	3
2423	Pharmaceuticals, medicinal chemicals, etc.	5.6	5.9	5.1	4.6		180	223	216	231	11	11	11	10
2424	Soap, cleaning & cosmetic preparations	13.8	4.1	3.4	3.1		145	148	136	122	4	4	4	4
2429	Other chemical products n.e.c.													
2430	Man-made fibres													
251	Rubber products													
2511	Rubber tyres and tubes													
2519	Other rubber products													
2520	Plastic products	5.3	5.4	6.2	9.5		250	324	294	524	12	12	12	11
2610	Glass and glass products	1.2	1.2	1.0	1.0		56	55	58	55	2	2	2	2
269	Non-metallic mineral products n.e.c.	36.3	37.4	25.6	41.6		847	1214	972	952	22	31	30	30
2691	Pottery, china and earthenware													
2692	Refractory ceramic products													
2693	Struct.non-refractory clay; ceramic products	1.1	6.2	5.8	3.5		56	322	308	139	8	13	13	12
2694	Cement, lime and plaster	19.8	15.8	4.7	24.1		359	453	166	334	4	4	3	4
2695	Articles of concrete, cement and plaster	5.4	6.1	5.4	4.9		156	161	191	178	4	7	8	8
2696	Cutting, shaping & finishing of stone	7.6	6.7	6.8	6.7		228	229	234	242	3	3	3	3
2699	Other non-metallic mineral products n.e.c.	2.4	2.5	2.8	2.4		48	49	73	59	3	3	3	3
2710	Basic iron and steel													
2720	Basic precious and non-ferrous metals													
273	Casting of metals													
2731	Casting of iron and steel													
2732	Casting of non-ferrous metals													
281	Struct.metal products;tanks;steam generators	1.9	1.3	1.4	1.3		66	44	49	45	5	5	5	5
2811	Structural metal products	1.9	1.3	1.4	1.3		66	44	49	45	5	5	5	5
2812	Tanks, reservoirs and containers of metal													
2813	Steam generators													
289	Other metal products; metal working services	8.0	7.2	8.5	7.1		251	257	318	381	7	6	7	7
2891	Metal forging/pressing/stamping/roll-forming													
2892	Treatment & coating of metals	0.7	0.8	0.8	0.8		35	35	35	42	1	1	1	1
2893	Cutlery, hand tools and general hardware	7.3	6.4	6.5	6.3		216	222	283	339	6	5	6	6
2899	Other fabricated metal products n.e.c.	1.0	1.1	1.3	1.1		65	65	69	80	1	1	1	1
291	General purpose machinery													
2911	Engines & turbines (not for transport equipment)													
2912	Pumps, compressors, taps and valves													
2913	Bearings, gears, gearing & driving elements	1.0	1.1	1.1	1.1		65	65	69	80	1	1	1	1
2914	Ovens, furnaces and furnace burners													
2915	Lifting and handling equipment													
2919	Other general purpose machinery													
292	Special purpose machinery													
2921	Agricultural and forestry machinery													
2922	Machine tools													
2923	Machinery for metallurgy													
2924	Machinery for mining & construction													
2925	Food/beverage/tobacco processing machinery													
2926	Machinery for textile, apparel and leather													
2927	Weapons and ammunition													
2929	Other special purpose machinery													

continued

Eritrea

ISIC	Industry	Number of establishments (number) Note	2013	2014	2015	2016	Number of employees (number) Note	2013	2014	2015	2016	Wages and salaries paid to employees (millions of Eritrean Nakfa) Note	2013	2014	2015	2016
2930	Domestic appliances n.e.c.		...	...	...	...		...	...	...	...		...	...	...	...
3000	Office, accounting and computing machinery		...	...	...	...		...	...	...	...		...	...	...	...
3110	Electric motors, generators and transformers		...	...	...	...		...	...	...	...		...	...	...	...
3120	Electricity distribution & control apparatus		...	...	...	...		...	...	...	...		...	...	...	...
3130	Insulated wire and cable		...	...	...	...		...	...	...	...		...	...	...	...
3140	Accumulators, primary cells and batteries		...	...	...	...		...	...	...	...		...	...	...	...
3150	Lighting equipment and electric lamps		...	...	...	...		...	...	...	...		...	...	...	...
3190	Other electrical equipment n.e.c.		...	...	...	...		...	...	...	...		...	...	...	...
3210	Electronic valves, tubes, etc.		...	...	...	...		...	...	...	...		...	...	...	...
3220	TV/radio transmitters; line comm. apparatus		...	...	...	...		...	...	...	...		...	...	...	...
3230	TV and radio receivers and associated goods		...	...	...	...		...	...	...	...		...	...	...	...
331	Medical, measuring, testing appliances, etc.		...	...	...	...		...	...	...	...		...	...	...	...
3311	Medical, surgical and orthopaedic equipment		...	...	...	...		...	...	...	...		...	...	...	...
3312	Measuring/testing/navigating appliances,etc.		...	...	...	...		...	...	...	...		...	...	...	...
3313	Industrial process control equipment		...	...	...	...		...	...	...	...		...	...	...	...
3320	Optical instruments & photographic equipment		...	...	...	...		...	...	...	...		...	...	...	...
3330	Watches and clocks		...	...	...	...		...	...	...	...		...	...	...	...
3410	Motor vehicles		...	...	...	...		...	...	...	...		...	...	...	...
3420	Automobile bodies, trailers & semi-trailers		1	1	1	1		28	28	21	17		0.5	0.6	0.4	0.6
3430	Parts/accessories for automobiles		3	4	4	4		48	53	52	51		1.6	1.7	1.8	1.8
351	Building and repairing of ships and boats		...	...	...	...		...	...	...	...		...	...	...	...
3511	Building and repairing of ships		...	...	...	...		...	...	...	...		...	...	...	...
3512	Building/repairing of pleasure/sport. boats		...	...	...	...		...	...	...	...		...	...	...	...
3520	Railway/tramway locomotives & rolling stock		...	...	...	...		...	...	...	...		...	...	...	...
3530	Aircraft and spacecraft		...	...	...	...		...	...	...	...		...	...	...	...
359	Transport equipment n.e.c.		...	...	...	...		...	...	...	...		...	...	...	...
3591	Motorcycles		...	...	...	...		...	...	...	...		...	...	...	...
3592	Bicycles and invalid carriages		...	...	...	...		...	...	...	...		...	...	...	...
3599	Other transport equipment n.e.c.		...	...	...	...		...	...	...	...		...	...	...	...
3610	Furniture		32	32	31	30		2343	2358	1965	1901		47.8	42.6	44.0	49.3
369	Manufacturing n.e.c.		...	...	...	...		...	...	...	...		...	...	...	...
3691	Jewellery and related articles		...	...	...	...		...	...	...	...		...	...	...	...
3692	Musical instruments		...	...	...	...		...	...	...	...		...	...	...	...
3693	Sports goods		...	...	...	...		...	...	...	...		...	...	...	...
3694	Games and toys		...	...	...	...		...	...	...	...		...	...	...	...
3699	Other manufacturing n.e.c.		...	...	...	...		...	...	...	...		...	...	...	...
3710	Recycling of metal waste and scrap		...	...	...	...		...	...	...	...		...	...	...	...
3720	Recycling of non-metal waste and scrap		...	...	...	...		...	...	...	...		...	...	...	...
D	Total manufacturing	a/	246	223	231	228	a/	12929	11994	11561	10251	a/	343.7	346.7	347.1	355.1

a/ Sum of available data.

Eritrea

ISIC	Industry	Note	Output at producers' prices (millions of Eritrean Nakfa)				Note	Value added at producers' prices (millions of Eritrean Nakfa)				Note	Gross fixed capital formation (millions of Eritrean Nakfa)	
			2013	2014	2015	2016		2013	2014	2015	2016		2015	2016
151	Processed meat,fish,fruit,vegetables,fats		0.4	0.3	0.1	-		0.2	-	-0.1	-		...	...
1511	Processing/preserving of meat		...	...	...	...		...	...	...	...		...	...
1512	Processing/preserving of fish													
1513	Processing/preserving of fruit & vegetables		...		...			...		...			...	
1514	Vegetable and animal oils and fats		0.4	0.3	0.1	-		0.2	-	-0.1	-			
1520	Dairy products		93.3	82.6	83.1	119.8		19.0	18.8	13.9	8.1		-	0.2
153	Grain mill products; starches; animal feeds		268.8	220.6	583.2	268.9		-82.2	46.2	43.9	56.6		7.9	3.7
1531	Grain mill products		231.8	183.7	559.7	233.0		-90.5	35.7	39.5	48.9		7.7	3.7
1532	Starches and starch products		37.0	36.9	23.5	35.9		8.3	10.5	4.4	7.7		0.2	
1533	Prepared animal feeds		58.6	66.5	112.4	111.9		16.2	18.6	19.0	18.5		2.3	
154	Other food products		46.1	53.1	102.9	107.0		13.3	13.9	16.1	18.0		-	
1541	Bakery products		...	...	...	...		...	...	...	...			
1542	Sugar													
1543	Cocoa, chocolate and sugar confectionery		4.7	7.3	2.4	0.8		1.5	2.3	1.2	0.4		2.2	
1544	Macaroni, noodles & similar products		7.8	6.1	7.1	4.1		1.4	2.4	1.7	0.1			
1549	Other food products n.e.c.		...	...	...	...		...	...	...	...			
155	Beverages		1199.8	1077.4	1025.3	1219.4		784.3	720.2	717.1	837.4		16.2	
1551	Distilling, rectifying & blending of spirits		65.4	60.2	15.2	0.4		55.9	50.5	7.6	-1.2		-	
1552	Wines		3.2	7.3	5.2	2.5		2.1	5.8	4.2	1.9		13.6	11.5
1553	Malt liquors and malt		698.5	800.9	682.8	832.5		521.9	571.6	515.3	582.3		2.5	15.2
1554	Soft drinks; mineral waters		432.7	209.0	322.1	383.9		204.3	92.3	190.0	254.4		-0.1	
1600	Tobacco products		209.3	76.9	-	6.6		181.8	58.6	-	-0.4			
171	Spinning, weaving and finishing of textiles		380.2	415.3	354.0	272.6		128.6	167.4	141.2	140.3		14.0	7.6
1711	Textile fibre preparation; textile weaving		380.2	415.3	354.0	272.6		128.6	167.4	141.2	140.3		14.0	7.6
1712	Finishing of textiles													
172	Other textiles													
1721	Made-up textile articles, except apparel													
1722	Carpets and rugs													
1723	Cordage, rope, twine and netting													
1729	Other textiles n.e.c.		10.0	13.3	29.9	3.8		7.1	8.9	14.1	2.0			
1730	Knitted and crocheted fabrics and articles		42.0	48.8	60.4	48.3		19.4	27.8	30.2	32.8			
1810	Wearing apparel, except fur apparel												0.6	0.1
1820	Dressing & dyeing of fur; processing of fur													
191	Tanning, dressing and processing of leather		105.3	70.6	39.5	14.3		16.7	20.4	18.4	8.1		0.5	
1911	Tanning and dressing of leather		104.4	70.1	38.8	14.2		16.3	20.1	18.1	8.0		0.5	
1912	Luggage, handbags, etc.; saddlery & harness		0.9	0.5	0.6	0.1		0.4	0.3	0.3	-			
1920	Footwear		115.6	114.1	99.9	81.7		50.1	63.0	56.8	53.1		0.1	3.1
2010	Sawmilling and planing of wood													
202	Products of wood, cork, straw, etc.													
2021	Veneer sheets, plywood, particle board, etc.													
2022	Builders' carpentry and joinery													
2023	Wooden containers													
2029	Other wood products; articles of cork/straw													
210	Paper and paper products		6.4	6.7	4.0	0.6		2.5	2.5	1.9	0.1			
2101	Pulp, paper and paperboard		0.9	1.7	1.5	0.6		0.2	1.0	0.8	0.2			
2102	Corrugated paper and paperboard													
2109	Other articles of paper and paperboard		5.5	5.0	2.5	0.1		2.3	1.5	1.1	-0.1		0.1	
221	Publishing													
2211	Publishing of books and other publications		...	...	...	...		...	...	...	...		...	...
2212	Publishing of newspapers, journals, etc.		...	...	...	...		...	...	...	...		...	...
2213	Publishing of recorded media		...	...	...	...		...	...	...	...		...	...
2219	Other publishing		...	...	...	...		...	...	...	...		...	...

continued

Eritrea

ISIC	Industry	Output Note	Output 2013	Output 2014	Output 2015	Output 2016	VA Note	VA 2013	VA 2014	VA 2015	VA 2016	GFCF Note	GFCF 2015	GFCF 2016
			Output at producers' prices (millions of Eritrean Nakfa)					**Value added at producers' prices** (millions of Eritrean Nakfa)					**Gross fixed capital formation** (millions of Eritrean Nakfa)	
222	Printing and related service activities		94.0	108.0	107.7	119.9		45.0	54.0	54.9	64.3		1.4	3.9
2221	Printing		94.0	108.0	107.7	119.9		45.0	54.0	54.9	64.3		1.4	3.9
2222	Service activities related to printing		...	...	...	...		...	...	...	...		...	...
2230	Reproduction of recorded media		...	...	...	...		...	...	...	...		...	...
2310	Coke oven products		...	...	...	...		...	...	...	...		...	...
2320	Refined petroleum products		...	...	...	...		...	...	...	...		...	...
2330	Processing of nuclear fuel		...	...	...	...		...	...	...	...		...	...
241	Basic chemicals		14.4	13.8	11.8	14.5		4.2	7.4	8.7	10.8		-	-
2411	Basic chemicals, except fertilizers		14.4	13.8	11.8	14.5		4.2	7.4	8.7	10.8		-	-
2412	Fertilizers and nitrogen compounds		...	...	...	...		...	...	...	...		...	...
2413	Plastics in primary forms; synthetic rubber		...	...	...	...		...	...	...	...		...	...
242	Other chemicals		223.6	241.3	155.5	105.8		104.1	99.5	59.1	43.5			
2421	Pesticides and other agro-chemical products		14.0	11.9	8.9	3.6		4.4	4.2	3.7	2.6			
2422	Paints, varnishes, printing ink and mastics		119.5	101.6	60.2	50.9		66.2	49.0	18.0	14.5			
2423	Pharmaceuticals, medicinal chemicals, etc.		71.0	105.8	60.7	28.7		23.9	32.7	25.0	12.5		2.2	0.4
2424	Soap, cleaning & cosmetic preparations		19.1	22.1	25.7	22.7		9.6	13.6	12.4	13.8		0.7	0.1
2429	Other chemical products n.e.c.												0.2	0.5
2430	Man-made fibres		...	...	...	...		...	...	...	...		...	...
251	Rubber products		...	...	...	...		...	...	...	...		...	...
2511	Rubber tyres and tubes		...	...	...	...		...	...	...	...		...	...
2519	Other rubber products		...	...	...	...		...	...	...	...		...	...
2520	Plastic products		54.2	46.4	40.9	38.8		34.7	25.3	20.4	20.6		0.8	0.6
2610	Glass and glass products		9.5	14.4	14.7	8.0		4.9	7.9	9.4	4.3		-	
269	Non-metallic mineral products n.e.c.		139.6	143.0	219.5	423.7		28.3	37.9	57.7	131.3			
2691	Pottery, china and earthenware		...	...	...	...		...	...	...	...		...	...
2692	Refractory ceramic products		...	...	...	...		...	...	...	...		...	...
2693	Struct.non-refractory clay; ceramic products		14.1	19.0	21.1	3.7		5.9	5.9	5.8	0.9			0.9
2694	Cement, lime and plaster		47.1	47.5	131.5	371.5		-14.0	0.3	20.6	110.1		31.6	74.1
2695	Articles of concrete, cement and plaster		38.0	39.9	34.0	19.8		23.2	21.0	21.9	11.6		0.5	0.5
2696	Cutting, shaping & finishing of stone		26.5	22.6	22.2	21.6		7.3	3.5	4.4	4.7		-1.5	4.7
2699	Other non-metallic mineral products n.e.c.		14.0	14.0	10.8	7.1		6.0	7.2	5.0	4.0		3.2	4.0
2710	Basic iron and steel		...	...	...	...		...	...	...	...		...	...
2720	Basic precious and non-ferrous metals		...	...	...	...		...	...	...	...		...	...
273	Casting of metals		...	...	...	...		...	...	...	...		...	...
2731	Casting of iron and steel		...	...	...	...		...	...	...	...		...	...
2732	Casting of non-ferrous metals		...	...	...	...		...	...	...	...		...	...
281	Struct.metal products;tanks;steam generators		6.7	9.0	7.7	11.7		2.2	3.2	2.7	5.8			
2811	Structural metal products		6.7	9.0	7.7	11.7		2.2	3.2	2.7	5.8			
2812	Tanks, reservoirs and containers of metal		...	...	...	...		...	...	...	...		...	...
2813	Steam generators		...	...	...	...		...	...	...	...		...	...
289	Other metal products; metal working services		39.5	40.1	29.5	23.7		16.4	18.9	14.4	12.2			
2891	Metal forging/pressing/stamping/roll-forming		...	...	...	...		...	...	...	...		...	...
2892	Treatment & coating of metals		...	...	...	...		...	...	...	...		...	...
2893	Cutlery, hand tools and general hardware		4.4	7.0	2.3	2.0		1.1	2.4	1.1	1.1			
2899	Other fabricated metal products n.e.c.		35.1	33.2	27.2	21.7		15.4	16.5	13.3	11.1			
291	General purpose machinery		7.9	9.7	6.3	6.3		1.9	5.3	0.6	4.0		0.1	
2911	Engines & turbines (not for transport equipment)		...	...	...	...		...	...	...	...		...	...
2912	Pumps, compressors, taps and valves		...	...	...	...		...	...	...	...		...	...
2913	Bearings, gears, gearing & driving elements		7.9	9.7	6.3	6.3		1.9	5.3	0.6	4.0		0.1	
2914	Ovens, furnaces and furnace burners		...	...	...	...		...	...	...	...		...	...
2915	Lifting and handling equipment		...	...	...	...		...	...	...	...		...	...
2919	Other general purpose machinery		...	...	...	...		...	...	...	...		...	...

ISIC Revision 3

Code	Industry	(1)	(2)	(3)	(4)	(5)	(6)	(7)	(8)	(9)	(10)
292	Special purpose machinery	…	…	…	…	…	…	…	…	…	…
2921	Agricultural and forestry machinery	…	…	…	…	…	…	…	…	…	…
2922	Machine tools	…	…	…	…	…	…	…	…	…	…
2923	Machinery for metallurgy	…	…	…	…	…	…	…	…	…	…
2924	Machinery for mining & construction	…	…	…	…	…	…	…	…	…	…
2925	Food/beverage/tobacco processing machinery	…	…	…	…	…	…	…	…	…	…
2926	Machinery for textile, apparel and leather	…	…	…	…	…	…	…	…	…	…
2927	Weapons and ammunition	…	…	…	…	…	…	…	…	…	…
2929	Other special purpose machinery	…	…	…	…	…	…	…	…	…	…
2930	Domestic appliances n.e.c.	…	…	…	…	…	…	…	…	…	…
3000	Office, accounting and computing machinery	…	…	…	…	…	…	…	…	…	…
3110	Electric motors, generators and transformers	…	…	…	…	…	…	…	…	…	…
3120	Electricity distribution & control apparatus	…	…	…	…	…	…	…	…	…	…
3130	Insulated wire and cable	…	…	…	…	…	…	…	…	…	…
3140	Accumulators, primary cells and batteries	…	…	…	…	…	…	…	…	…	…
3150	Lighting equipment and electric lamps	…	…	…	…	…	…	…	…	…	…
3190	Other electrical equipment n.e.c.	…	…	…	…	…	…	…	…	…	…
3210	Electronic valves, tubes, etc.	…	…	…	…	…	…	…	…	…	…
3220	TV/radio transmitters; line comm. apparatus	…	…	…	…	…	…	…	…	…	…
3230	TV and radio receivers and associated goods	…	…	…	…	…	…	…	…	…	…
331	Medical, measuring, testing appliances, etc.	…	…	…	…	…	…	…	…	…	…
3311	Medical, surgical and orthopaedic equipment	…	…	…	…	…	…	…	…	…	…
3312	Measuring/testing/navigating appliances, etc.	…	…	…	…	…	…	…	…	…	…
3313	Industrial process control equipment	…	…	…	…	…	…	…	…	…	…
3320	Optical instruments & photographic equipment	…	…	…	…	…	…	…	…	…	…
3330	Watches and clocks	…	…	…	…	…	…	…	…	…	…
3410	Motor vehicles	…	…	…	…	…	…	…	…	…	…
3420	Automobile bodies, trailers & semi-trailers	1.7	3.0	0.9	0.8	1.5	0.9	0.4	0.6	…	…
3430	Parts/accessories for automobiles	7.6	9.5	7.2	11.1	6.5	4.7	4.8	8.1	…	…
351	Building and repairing of ships and boats	…	…	…	…	…	…	…	…	…	…
3511	Building and repairing of ships	…	…	…	…	…	…	…	…	…	…
3512	Building/repairing of pleasure/sport. boats	…	…	…	…	…	…	…	…	…	…
3520	Railway/tramway locomotives & rolling stock	…	…	…	…	…	…	…	…	…	…
3530	Aircraft and spacecraft	…	…	…	…	…	…	…	…	…	…
359	Transport equipment n.e.c.	…	…	…	…	…	…	…	…	…	…
3591	Motorcycles	…	…	…	…	…	…	…	…	…	…
3592	Bicycles and invalid carriages	…	…	…	…	…	…	…	…	…	…
3599	Other transport equipment n.e.c.	…	…	…	…	…	…	…	…	…	…
3610	Furniture	372.0	367.0	295.5	189.7	165.5	159.6	96.3	93.4	6.0	1.3
369	Manufacturing n.e.c.	…	…	…	…	…	…	…	…	…	…
3691	Jewellery and related articles	…	…	…	…	…	…	…	…	…	…
3692	Musical instruments	…	…	…	…	…	…	…	…	…	…
3693	Sports goods	…	…	…	…	…	…	…	…	…	…
3694	Games and toys	…	…	…	…	…	…	…	…	…	…
3699	Other manufacturing n.e.c.	…	…	…	…	…	…	…	…	…	…
3710	Recycling of metal waste and scrap	…	…	…	…	…	…	…	…	…	…
3720	Recycling of non-metal waste and scrap	…	…	…	…	…	…	…	…	…	…
D	Total manufacturing	3460.2 a/	3198.4	3288.9 a/	3101.8 a/	1585.4	1550.7 a/	1385.8	1555.4	86.6	120.9 a/

a/ Sum of available data.

Estonia

Supplier of information:
Statistics Estonia, Tallinn.

Basic source of data:
Annual survey; administrative source.

Major deviations from ISIC (Revision 4):
None reported.

Reference period:
Calendar year.

Scope:
All enterprises.

Method of data collection:
Online survey.

Type of enumeration:
Sample survey.

Adjusted for non-response:
Yes.

Concepts and definitions of variables:
Number of employees includes home workers, paid working proprietors, seasonal workers, apprentices on the pay-roll, persons on strike or on short-term leave. Wages and salaries is compensation of employees.

Related national publications:
Statistical Yearbook of Estonia; Quarterly Bulletin of Statistics, both published by Statistics Estonia, Tallinn.

Estonia

ISIC	Industry	Note	2013	2014	2015	2016	Note	2013	2014	2015	2016	Note	2013	2014	2015	2016
			Number of enterprises (number)					**Number of employees (thousands)**					**Wages and salaries paid to employees (thousands of Euros)**			
1010	Processing/preserving of meat		55	55	62	70		2.7	3.1	3.0	2.9		25010	31854	33615	34620
1020	Processing/preserving of fish, etc.		55	57	70	68		1.9	1.8	1.9	1.6		16018	16775	17316	15429
1030	Processing/preserving of fruit,vegetables		46	52	59	66		0.7	0.7	0.8	0.8		6350	6758	7323	8950
1040	Vegetable and animal oils and fats		6	8	9	11		...	...	0.1	...		...	...	1000	...
1050	Dairy products		28	27	29	34		2.1	2.0	2.1	2.1		22656	23068	25189	27115
106	Grain mill products,starches and starch products		16	15	15	13		...	...	...	...		...	...	1842	...
1061	Grain mill products		16	15	15	13		...	...	...	...		...	...	1842	...
1062	Starches and starch products		-	-	-	-		-	-	-	-		-	-	-	-
107	Other food products		229	242	289	316		5.2	5.4	5.6	5.5		47268	53148	58620	58924
1071	Bakery products		130	127	149	161		...	...	...	...		...	...	...	...
1072	Sugar		-	-	1	1		-	-	...	...		-	-	...	...
1073	Cocoa, chocolate and sugar confectionery		19	25	29	31		...	0.5	...	0.5		...	6280	...	6672
1074	Macaroni, noodles, couscous, etc.		1	1	1	1		...	...	...	...		...	...	...	...
1075	Prepared meals and dishes		42	41	46	50		1.2	1.2	1.3	1.3		9889	11100	12343	13431
1079	Other food products n.e.c.		37	48	63	72		0.7	0.7	0.2	0.7		8594	9502	...	9720
1080	Prepared animal feeds		16	20	19	19		0.2	0.2	0.2	...		2443	2761	2869	...
110	Beverages		39	48	62	86		1.5	1.6	1.5	1.5		22135	24816	24959	24353
1101	Distilling, rectifying and blending of spirits		6	7	8	8		0.4	0.4	0.4	0.4		6381	6921	6751	6157
1102	Wines		4	5	8	13		...	0.1	...	0.1		...	682	...	719
1103	Malt liquors and malt		13	19	31	44		...	0.8	...	...		...	14278	...	...
1104	Soft drinks,mineral waters,other bottled waters		16	17	15	21		0.3	0.2	...	0.2		2902	2935	...	3224
1200	Tobacco products		-	-	-	-		-	-	-	-		-	-	-	-
131	Spinning, weaving and finishing of textiles		41	37	37	41		0.5	0.5	0.4	0.4		3610	3855	3673	4211
1311	Preparation and spinning of textile fibres		10	10	8	9		0.2	...	0.2	0.2		1850	...	2267	2756
1312	Weaving of textiles		14	14	14	13		0.1	...	...	...		313	...	...	...
1313	Finishing of textiles		17	13	15	19		0.2	0.2	...	...		1447	1430	...	...
139	Other textiles		197	197	230	236		3.6	3.7	4.0	4.0		28807	32118	38683	40799
1391	Knitted and crocheted fabrics		1	2	3	3		...	-	-	...		...	...	76	...
1392	Made-up textile articles, except apparel		144	141	165	171		2.8	2.9	3.2	3.1		22196	25251	30189	31900
1393	Carpets and rugs		8	7	7	7		...	0.3	0.4	0.4		...	3651	4540	5508
1394	Cordage, rope, twine and netting		7	7	7	8		0.2	0.2	...	0.2		1229	1204	...	1258
1399	Other textiles n.e.c.		37	40	48	47		...	...	...	...		...	...	...	...
1410	Wearing apparel, except fur apparel		401	434	458	452		5.8	5.7	5.6	5.3		36846	38979	38890	41076
1420	Articles of fur		11	15	17	14		...	-	-	-		...	125	125	85
1430	Knitted and crocheted apparel		50	50	54	58		...	0.5	0.4	0.4		...	3402	2890	2990
151	Leather;luggage,handbags,saddlery,harness;fur		45	48	46	57		0.5	0.5	0.5	0.4		3016	3408	3458	3380
1511	Tanning/dressing of leather; dressing of fur		12	13	13	12		0.1	0.1	0.1	0.1		1012	986	990	597
1512	Luggage,handbags,etc.;saddlery/harness		33	35	33	45		0.3	0.3	0.3	0.4		2003	2422	2468	2784
1520	Footwear		24	22	24	25		0.8	0.7	0.7	0.6		6019	6479	5576	5720
1610	Sawmilling and planing of wood		394	402	401	393		4.7	4.9	5.2	5.1		50139	55511	61423	66721

162	Wood products, cork, straw, plaiting materials	152217	137251	126742	109437	11.9	11.8	11.4	10.7	693	701	682	667
1621	Veneer sheets and wood-based panels	26606	24817	23882	...	2.1	2.1	2.1	...	25	22	28	20
1622	Builders' carpentry and joinery	105060	91362	83231	...	7.7	7.4	7.1	...	414	416	406	405
1623	Wooden containers	12746	11811	10322	10063	1.3	1.3	1.3	1.2	83	85	84	84
1629	Other wood products;articles of cork,straw	7806	9261	9306	7413	0.8	0.9	1.0	0.9	171	178	164	158
170	Paper and paper products	20161	19580	18459	17355	1.4	1.4	1.4	1.4	61	61	59	58
1701	Pulp, paper and paperboard	8099	8368	8223	7859	0.5	0.5	0.5	0.5	4	5	5	3
1702	Corrugated paper and paperboard	6520	6448	6133	5746	0.5	0.5	0.5	0.5	27	29	31	31
1709	Other articles of paper and paperboard	...	4764	4103	3751	...	0.4	0.4	0.4	30	27	23	24
181	Printing and service activities related to printing a/	38119	35389	33576	31274	2.9	2.9	2.8	2.7	377	383	357	362
1811	Printing	36973	...	...	...	2.8	...	...	...	327	327	308	310
1812	Service activities related to printing	...	...	1225	...	...	...	...	0.1	50	56	49	52
1820	Reproduction of recorded media a/	...	...	...	...	...	...	...	...	1	3	4	6
1910	Coke oven products	-	-	-	-	-	-	-	-	-	-	-	-
1920	Refined petroleum products	21536	22182	24609	22045	1.5	1.7	1.7	1.6	6	5	5	7
201	Basic chemicals,fertilizers, etc.	13160	17734	16913	16507	1.0	1.3	1.5	1.5	17	21	20	15
2011	Basic chemicals	12040	17734b/	12373	11225	0.9	1.3b/	0.9	0.9	10	9	11	6
2012	Fertilizers and nitrogen compounds	...b/	...b/	...	...	...b/	...b/	...	...	5	9	6	7
2013	Plastics and synthetic rubber in primary forms	...	...	...	...	...	...	...	...	2	3	3	2
202	Other chemical products	23030	20055	17588	16849	1.3	1.2	1.1	1.0	93	90	77	77
2021	Pesticides and other agrochemical products	...	...	...	...	...	...	...	...	-	1	-	1
2022	Paints,varnishes;printing ink and mastics	13904	12933	11906	12032	0.7	0.7	0.7	0.7	20	19	18	19
2023	Soap,cleaning and cosmetic preparations	...	4224	2850	2080	...	0.3	0.2	0.2	52	45	38	36
2029	Other chemical products n.e.c.	2752	...	2832	...	0.2	...	0.2	...	21	25	21	21
2030	Man-made fibres	-	-	-	-	-	-	-	-	-	-	-	-
2100	Pharmaceuticals,medicinal chemicals, etc.	6166	6166	6414	5941	0.3	0.3	0.3	0.3	15	14	12	11
221	Rubber products	8278	8195	8349	7532	0.7	0.7	0.7	0.7	29	25	24	25
2211	Rubber tyres and tubes	1434	1399	1474	1353	0.1	0.1	0.1	0.1	11	11	10	11
2219	Other rubber products	6844	6796	6875	6179	0.6	0.6	0.6	0.6	18	14	14	14
2220	Plastics products	43008	38556	38349	34885	3.3	3.2	3.2	3.1	194	188	170	177
2310	Glass and glass products	18941	17658	16862	15597	1.2	1.2	1.2	1.1	40	46	43	42
239	Non-metallic mineral products n.e.c.	53071	50010	46257	42221	3.2	3.2	3.1	3.0	212	209	184	198
2391	Refractory products	...	...	...	...	...	...	...	...	1	1	1	1
2392	Clay building materials	1599	...	...	...	0.1	...	...	...	9	9	6	9
2393	Other porcelain and ceramic products	965	674	622	551	0.1	0.1	0.1	0.1	29	29	20	23
2394	Cement, lime and plaster	4779	...	...	...	0.2	...	...	...	2	2	2	2
2395	Articles of concrete, cement and plaster	38580	35375	32538	29146	2.3	2.2	2.2	2.1	80	72	69	77
2396	Cutting, shaping and finishing of stone	6693	6997	6098	5762	0.5	0.5	0.4	0.4	84	87	77	78
2399	Other non-metallic mineral products n.e.c.	436	457	392	397	-	-	-	-	7	9	9	8
2410	Basic iron and steel	...	5669	...	...	...	0.3	...	...	14	15	12	8
2420	Basic precious and other non-ferrous metals	1083	2102	1605	1637	0.1	0.1	0.1	...	2	5	5	4
243	Casting of metals	1249	1450	...	...	0.1	0.2	0.2	0.2	11	9	11	10
2431	Casting of iron and steel	...	1450c/	1605c/	1637c/	...	0.1c/	0.2c/	0.2c/	3	2	3	2
2432	Casting of non-ferrous metals	890	...c/	...c/	...c/	0.1	...c/	...c/	...c/	8	7	8	8
251	Struct.metal products, tanks, reservoirs	102785	98395	91653	85907	7.3	7.1	7.0	6.8	547	532	526	519

continued

Estonia

ISIC Revision 4

ISIC	Industry	Number of enterprises (number)				Number of employees (thousands)				Wages and salaries paid to employees (thousands of Euros)			
		2013	2014	2015	2016	2013	2014	2015	2016	2013	2014	2015	2016
2511	Structural metal products	497	500	507	526	6.3	6.5	6.6	6.8	80547	86424	93260	97688
2512	Tanks, reservoirs and containers of metal	18	22	22	18	...	...	...	...	...	...	...	...
2513	Steam generators, excl. hot water boilers	4	4	3	3	...	...	...	...	...	...	...	...
2520	Weapons and ammunition	2	2	-	1	...	...	-	...	...	...	-	...
259	Other metal products;metal working services	630	674	691	732	5.4	5.7	5.7	6.0	59626	67185	71380	82244
2591	Forging,pressing,stamping,roll-forming of metal	67	66	70	73	0.4	0.3	0.3	0.3	4247	3129	3603	4132
2592	Treatment and coating of metals; machining	320	340	350	388	2.3	2.4	2.5	2.9	23795	27109	29032	37881
2593	Cutlery, hand tools and general hardware	26	29	26	29	0.3	0.4	0.4	0.4	3155	4418	4696	5091
2599	Other fabricated metal products n.e.c.	217	239	245	242	2.3	2.6	2.6	2.4	28429	32529	34049	35140
2610	Electronic components and boards	29	29	29	31	2.6	2.5	2.5	2.4	25891	25904	25601	26108
2620	Computers and peripheral equipment	14	16	9	10	...	0.1	...	0.1	...	1648	...	1928
2630	Communication equipment	11	10	11	13	...	...	...	...	...	...	...	...
2640	Consumer electronics	10	13	14	13	0.1	...	0.1	...	801	...	1058	...
265	Measuring,testing equipment; watches, etc.	33	39	39	37	...	0.5	0.5	0.4	...	6833	6843	6883
2651	Measuring/testing/navigating equipment,etc.	31	35	35	33	...	0.5	0.5	0.4	...	6828	6808	6825
2652	Watches and clocks	2	4	4	4	...	-	-	-	...	5	35	57
2660	Irradiation/electromedical equipment,etc.	5	4	4	5	...	-	...	0.4	...	...	...	5065
2670	Optical instruments and photographic equipment	5	5	7	6	-	-	...	-	234	186	...	264
2680	Magnetic and optical media	1	-	1	1	-	-	-	...	-	-	...	...
2710	Electric motors,generators,transformers,etc.	45	45	46	49	3.5	3.6	3.5	3.7	51416	54825	54908	60608
2720	Batteries and accumulators	3	3	3	2	-	...	...	...	104	...	...	...
273	Wiring and wiring devices	12	12	13	14	0.6	0.7	0.7	0.8	6921	7626	8496	10700
2731	Fibre optic cables	-	-	-	-	-	-	-	-	-	-	-	-
2732	Other electronic and electric wires and cables	10	10	11	12	...	...	...	...	...	...	...	...
2733	Wiring devices	2	2	2	2	...	...	...	...	...	...	...	...
2740	Electric lighting equipment	20	26	27	25	0.3	0.4	0.4	0.4	3967	4622	5450	6105
2750	Domestic appliances	3	3	5	4	-	...	...	-	316	...	...	271
2790	Other electrical equipment	31	31	37	36	0.9	0.9	0.8	0.9	5976	6029	6899	7674
281	General-purpose machinery	64	66	75	84	...	...	2.1	...	...	...	30741	...
2811	Engines/turbines,excl.aircraft,vehicle engines	-	-	1	1	...	...	...	...	...	-	...	...
2812	Fluid power equipment	7	7	7	5	0.1	0.1	0.1	0.1	1315	1607	1809	1617
2813	Other pumps, compressors, taps and valves	3	4	5	5	-	...	...	-	375	...	...	79
2814	Bearings, gears, gearing and driving elements	-	-	-	3	-	-	-	-	-	-	-	-
2815	Ovens, furnaces and furnace burners	3	3	3	5	...	0.1	...	...	...	1131	...	...
2816	Lifting and handling equipment	19	21	21	23	1.2	1.3	1.3	1.3	16667	18047	19474	20887
2817	Office machinery, excl.computers,etc.	-	-	1	1	-	-	-	-	-	-	-	-
2818	Power-driven hand tools	-	-	-	1	-	-	-	-	-	-	-	-
2819	Other general-purpose machinery	32	31	37	41	...	0.5	...	0.6	...	7330	...	9047
282	Special-purpose machinery	84	81	100	100	1.8	1.7	1.8	1.7	26392	28251	30107	30395
2821	Agricultural and forestry machinery	26	27	27	29	0.6	0.6	0.6	0.6	9043	9791	10005	10212
2822	Metal-forming machinery and machine tools	9	6	11	9	0.1	...	0.2	0.2	2771	...	4592	3748

2823	Machinery for metallurgy	2	2	1	1	..	..	..	0.1	2070	..	..	2092
2824	Mining, quarrying and construction machinery	7	8	12	11	0.2	..	..	..	2858	2671	..	..
2825	Food/beverage/tobacco processing machinery	6	4	3	4	0.2	0.2	0.2	..	..	..	..	..
2826	Textile/apparel/leather production machinery	1	2	2	1	..	..	..	..	..	..	..	..
2829	Other special-purpose machinery	33	32	44	45	..	..	..	..	..	..	..	..
2910	Motor vehicles	4	4	5	7	..	..	..	..	..	..	..	..
2920	Automobile bodies, trailers and semi-trailers	32	32	39	37	0.7	0.7	..	..	7624	7540	..	..
2930	Parts and accessories for motor vehicles	23	22	24	24	..	..	2.6	2.3	..	..	33970	31746
301	Building of ships and boats	66	64	72	79	..	..	..	0.8	..	..	..	10463
3011	Building of ships and floating structures	31	33	38	46	0.3	0.3	..	0.4	3493	4960	..	6166
3012	Building of pleasure and sporting boats	35	31	34	33	0.3	..	..	0.3	..	..	..	4298
3020	Railway locomotives and rolling stock	-	-	-	1	-	-	-	..	-	-	-	..
3030	Air and spacecraft and related machinery	-	-	-	1	-	-	-	..	-	-	-	..
3040	Military fighting vehicles	-	-	-	-	-	-	-	..	-	-	-	..
309	Transport equipment n.e.c.	4	7	9	8	..	..	..	..	..	..	..	..
3091	Motorcycles	1	1	1	1	..	..	..	..	..	..	..	..
3092	Bicycles and invalid carriages	1	2	4	4	..	..	..	..	..	..	..	..
3099	Other transport equipment n.e.c.	2	4	4	3	-	-	-	..	..	-	..	..
3100	Furniture	610	641	704	719	7.4	7.5	7.8	7.9	69733	75270	81222	89082
321	Jewellery, bijouterie and related articles	48	57	50	53	..	..	..	..	..	..	..	..
3211	Jewellery and related articles	34	39	36	35	..	..	..	..	..	..	..	..
3212	Imitation jewellery and related articles	14	18	14	18	-	-	-	-	92	74	104	172
3220	Musical instruments	7	7	8	10	..	..	..	..	..	..	..	..
3230	Sports goods	20	21	24	28	0.4	0.3	0.3	0.3	2765	2854	2872	2573
3240	Games and toys	22	21	24	29	-	-	-	-	14	78	89	137
3250	Medical and dental instruments and supplies	76	82	84	89	1.0	1.0	..	1.0	11464	12017	..	13572
3290	Other manufacturing n.e.c.	87	107	108	107	0.7	0.6	0.6	0.7	5323	5679	6068	7309
331	Repair of fabricated metal products/machinery	454	472	509	509	4.0	4.2	4.2	3.6	53049	58637	61395	53960
3311	Repair of fabricated metal products	29	30	29	28	0.1	0.2	0.1	..	1046	1820	1358	..
3312	Repair of machinery	199	205	223	220	1.5	1.4	1.4	0.8	20193	20942	20243	11148
3313	Repair of electronic and optical equipment	26	24	29	26	0.2	0.1	0.1	0.1	2116	2187	1910	1310
3314	Repair of electrical equipment	33	33	35	36	0.2	0.3	0.3	0.2	3407	4104	3850	4413
3315	Repair of transport equip., excl. motor vehicles	138	143	158	155	..	..	2.3	..	..	..	33160	..
3319	Repair of other equipment	29	37	35	44	..	..	0.1	0.1	..	..	875	844
3320	Installation of industrial machinery/equipment	87	95	94	124	0.4	0.5	0.4	0.4	5413	5855	5996	5613
C	Total manufacturing	6381	6611	7053	7259	103.4	106.7	108.3	107.1	1131731	1241424	1313863	1385372

a/ 181 includes 1820.
b/ 2011 includes 2012 and 2013.
c/ 2431 includes 2432.

Estonia

ISIC	Industry	Note	Output at producers' prices (thousands of Euros)				Note	Value added at factor values (thousands of Euros)				Note	Gross fixed capital formation a/ (thousands of Euros)	
			2013	2014	2015	2016		2013	2014	2015	2016		2015	2016
1010	Processing/preserving of meat		243609	293261	293165	299440		53243	66672	70082	69885		19600	22100
1020	Processing/preserving of fish, etc.		149019	160589	157718	117022		29632	27489	25325	22005		8000	5600
1030	Processing/preserving of fruit,vegetables		60816	69622	70691	90560		12702	17773	18017	20082		2800	6100
1040	Vegetable and animal oils and fats		...	...	61468	...		...	...	4609	...		2700	-
1050	Dairy products		337007	346651	293738	296403		57273	65908	66571	61207		15600	11700
106	Grain mill products,starches and starch products		...	...	30989	...		...	...	8135	...		1300	...
1061	Grain mill products		...	...	30989	...		...	...	8135	...		1300	...
1062	Starches and starch products		-	-	-	-		-	-	...	...		-	...
107	Other food products		335660	361752	364969	377334		94221	112667	112258	119623		16700	15600
1071	Bakery products		...	...	...	...		-	...	...	...		...	...
1072	Sugar		-	-	...	...		-	-	...	...		...	...
1073	Cocoa, chocolate and sugar confectionery		...	45763	...	47398		...	15650	...	18017		...	2400
1074	Macaroni, noodles, couscous, etc.													...
1075	Prepared meals and dishes		58602	66005	68833	76978		18117	23111	24020	28018		1800	1600
1079	Other food products n.e.c.		105130	104222	...	108090		18224	21469	...	19915		...	...
1080	Prepared animal feeds		40807	45123	38723	...		5869	8787	9056	...		3400	...
110	Beverages		195990	208868	189517	194764		66724	72990	64000	70435		15100	15600
1101	Distilling, rectifying and blending of spirits		36348	41156	37298	39169		14701	17333	12695	16503		1900	1000
1102	Wines		...	7577	...	6349		...	2222	...	2187		...	...
1103	Malt liquors and malt		...	147478	...	...		...	46704	...	...		...	...
1104	Soft drinks,mineral waters,other bottled waters		14322	12657	...	15435		6277	6732	...	7570		...	2600
1200	Tobacco products		-	-	-	-		-	-	-	-		-	-
131	Spinning, weaving and finishing of textiles		18380	30896	36317	45975		5821	6060	7764	8740		...	...
1311	Preparation and spinning of textile fibres		9596	...	25180	34543		4135	...	4888	6039		2500	2400
1312	Weaving of textiles		1627	...	...	...		515	...	...	...			
1313	Finishing of textiles		7157	7866	...	...		1171	728	...	...			
139	Other textiles		217021	226909	269239	269210		60607	66198	75782	77601		10800	8100
1391	Knitted and crocheted fabrics		...	...	285	...		...	...	138	...		-	...
1392	Made-up textile articles, except apparel		184040	193400	227188	225138		47637	52734	58287	59135		4900	5300
1393	Carpets and rugs		...	18015	24218	28078		...	6525	9918	12920		5000	2300
1394	Cordage, rope, twine and netting		5239	5234	...	4781		3384	3197	...	1702		...	200
1399	Other textiles n.e.c.		...	...	...	...		...	...	...	...			
1410	Wearing apparel, except fur apparel		141671	136630	125261	155913		61134	62719	63737	67393		3300	3700
1420	Articles of fur		...	281	390	244		...	162	181	126		-	-
1430	Knitted and crocheted apparel		...	10829	8585	11193		...	5213	3712	4638		200	600
151	Leather;luggage,handbags,saddlery,harness;fur		11608	11230	12939	15317		5034	5628	5918	6663		600b/	1100
1511	Tanning/dressing of leather; dressing of fur		5626	4752	4380	4682		1662	1512	1611	865		100	300
1512	Luggage,handbags,etc.;saddlery/harness		5982	6478	8559	10634		3371	4116	4308	5798		100	800
1520	Footwear		20523	20677	17489	23922		9911	9250	8305	9592		...b/	400
1610	Sawmilling and planing of wood		618158	685837	708405	759800		140774	153459	171972	179485		59900	69000

Code	Description										
162	Wood products, cork, straw, plaiting materials	822869	949476	1035038	1070820	232229	275686	300470	303052	108000	121600
1621	Veneer sheets and wood-based panels	…	204706	203070	202325	…	55911	61592	64943	42500	82200
1622	Builders' carpentry and joinery	…	572387	633680	691516	…	162895	169540	187693	20900	30800
1623	Wooden containers	76483	80352	80466	80249	24683	25814	27081	28069	1500	3900
1629	Other wood products;articles of cork,straw	76131	92032	117821	96730	27360	31066	42258	22347	43100	4700
170	Paper and paper products	197256	203119	209635	210949	47151	50015	54599	55649	13000	6500
1701	Pulp, paper and paperboard	115880	117777	121144	117258	25195	29412	34476	32699	…	…
1702	Corrugated paper and paperboard	46774	47686	48206	46817	14049	13640	12727	14534	4100	2700
1709	Other articles of paper and paperboard	34602	37656	40284	…	7906	6962	7395	…	…	…
181	Printing and service activities related to printing c/	211558	214687	217254	229065	72437	74429	73310	79380	10800	17400
1811	Printing	…	…	…	218771	…	…	…	76284	…	17100
1812	Service activities related to printing c/	…	9010	…	…	…	2811	…	…	…	…
1820	Reproduction of recorded media c/	…	…	…	…	…	…	…	…	…	…
1910	Coke oven products	-	-	-	-	-	-	-	-	-	-
1920	Refined petroleum products	280043	274708	239287	217031	103889	97680	69019	77426	106000	…
201	Basic chemicals,fertilizers, etc.	233373	217505	180064	156066	15269	56937	36178	43102	8300	8700
2011	Basic chemicals	178429	215097	180064d/	153967	26044	30992	36178d/	42197	8300	8700
2012	Fertilizers and nitrogen compounds	…	…	…d/	…	…	…	…d/	…	…	…d/
2013	Plastics and synthetic rubber in primary forms	…	…	…d/	…	…	…	…d/	…	…	…d/
202	Other chemical products	269615	249273	212267	196549	63629	56655	59527	65214	…	…
2021	Pesticides and other agrochemical products	…	…	…	-	…	…	…	-	…	…
2022	Paints, varnishes;printing ink and mastics	219151	196613	147822	120352	44865	36277	33893	36408	2000	2200
2023	Soap,cleaning and cosmetic preparations	15125	16675	24766	…	4630	4947	7880	…	900	…
2029	Other chemical products n.e.c.	…	…	…	36557	…	15432	…	15537	…	…
2030	Man-made fibres	…	…	…	-	-	-	-	-	-	-
2100	Pharmaceuticals,medicinal chemicals, etc.	38362	38243	42209	43782	8638	8607	8435	14587	4500	…
221	Rubber products	40465	40357	38657	37872	13665	14920	14799	14014	700	1800
2211	Rubber tyres and tubes	9084	8214	7336	6396	2476	2519	2316	1722	100	800
2219	Other rubber products	31382	32143	31321	31476	11189	12401	12482	12292	600	1000
2220	Plastics products	268893	276932	268067	297944	75856	79163	77463	89513	20200	22200
2310	Glass and glass products	106971	109863	115961	119505	35277	34898	40117	42609	9100	3900
239	Non-metallic mineral products n.e.c.	243218	262839	252250	294450	83458	85976	89746	109521	…	…
2391	Refractory products	…	…	…	…	…	…	…	2547	…	…
2392	Clay building materials	2272	2217	2385	4661	974	554	1122	1829	…	…
2393	Other porcelain and ceramic products	…	…	…	4572	…	…	…	15262	…	…
2394	Cement, lime and plaster	…	…	…	31297	…	…	…	…	…	…
2395	Articles of concrete, cement and plaster	152837	171833	178246	213219	49129	56535	62760	76287	5000	2100
2396	Cutting, shaping and finishing of stone	26947	26521	30998	33594	12616	10351	10073	11778	…	…
2399	Other non-metallic mineral products n.e.c.	7931	8561	7146	7054	1354	1553	1546	1783	…	…
2410	Basic iron and steel	…	…	24060	…	…	…	10096	…	4900	…
2420	Basic precious and other non-ferrous metals	…	…	46864	22019	…	…	4916	3764	700	…
243	Casting of metals	10282e/	8054e/	6147	6522	2833e/	2523e/	2120	1954	1300	…
2431	Casting of iron and steel	10282e/	8054e/	6147e/	…	2833e/	2523e/	2120e/	…	1300e/	…
2432	Casting of non-ferrous metals	…e/	…e/	…e/	5424	…e/	…e/	…e/	1436	…e/	…
251	Struct.metal products, tanks, reservoirs	528602	570484	553428	562644	141327	150742	161376	170852	…	…

continued

Estonia

ISIC	Industry	Note	Output at producers' prices (thousands of Euros)				Note	Value added at factor values (thousands of Euros)				Note	Gross fixed capital formation a/ (thousands of Euros)	
			2013	2014	2015	2016		2013	2014	2015	2016		2015	2016
2511	Structural metal products		501989	539139	529877	542407		132843	142703	153609	163528		30000	23900
2512	Tanks, reservoirs and containers of metal		...	...	...	...		...	...	...	...		...	...
2513	Steam generators, excl. hot water boilers		...	...	...	...		...	...	...	...		...	...
2520	Weapons and ammunition		-	...	-	...		...	...	-	...		-	-
259	Other metal products;metal working services		367368	400758	438227	480935		172437	147361	147668	172541		24000	42400
2591	Forging,pressing,stamping,roll-forming of metal		35970	25856	26028	28356		8363	5987	7251	7638		600	1300
2592	Treatment and coating of metals; machining		124216	132513	148389	189279		97878	55690	59818	73343		12800	18700
2593	Cutlery, hand tools and general hardware		13266	19798	22010	23728		6018	9497	9925	10934		...	...
2599	Other fabricated metal products n.e.c.		193916	222592	241801	239573		60178	76187	70675	80626		...	...
2610	Electronic components and boards		240230	246290	252233	262016		43870	51977	52145	50783		4400	3000
2620	Computers and peripheral equipment		...	12044	...	9473		...	-21	...	3154		...	800
2630	Communication equipment		...	...	...	...		...	...	...	...		...	...
2640	Consumer electronics		3780	...	4257	...		1283	...	1318	...		100	...
265	Measuring;testing equipment; watches, etc.		...	63198	72216	66657		...	13303	15492	14917		2100	2600
2651	Measuring/testing/navigating equipment,etc.		...	63099	72007	66355		...	13246	15397	14815		2100	2600
2652	Watches and clocks		...	98	209	302		...	57	95	101		-	100
2660	Irradiation/electromedical equipment,etc.		...	...	...	8994		...	...	...	7287		...	100
2670	Optical instruments and photographic equipment		1027	1109	...	840		216	344	...	264		...	100
2680	Magnetic and optical media		...	-	...	...		...	-	...	...		...	...
2710	Electric motors,generators,transformers,etc.		399002	365672	388274	418867		113687	105012	96621	118899		11800	13600
2720	Batteries and accumulators		229	-	...	...		-102	...	...	...		2400	800
273	Wiring and wiring devices		62268	70308	79559	100927		17618	18982	20635	25988		-	...
2731	Fibre optic cables		-	-	-	-		-	-	-	-		-	-
2732	Other electronic and electric wires and cables		...	...	...	...		...	...	...	...		...	...
2733	Wiring devices		...	...	...	...		...	...	...	...		...	...
2740	Electric lighting equipment		36258	45852	57222	61457		12285	16443	21484	22132		1100	700
2750	Domestic appliances		3079	...	...	2457		533	...	...	275		...	...
2790	Other electrical equipment		27075	31188	30469	31776		11713	10812	11396	12613		1100	800
281	General-purpose machinery		...	...	142577	...		...	...	53292	...		8400	21600f/
2811	Engines/turbines,excl.aircraft,vehicle engines		-	-	...	...		...	...	...	...		...	...
2812	Fluid power equipment		6171	6944	8414	6220		2695	3105	3180	2672		700	600
2813	Other pumps, compressors, taps and valves		615	...	...	432		-288	...	...	8		...	100
2814	Bearings, gears, gearing and driving elements		-	-	-	...		-	-	-	...		-	...
2815	Ovens, furnaces and furnace burners		...	4150	...	...		...	2090	...	...		...	...
2816	Lifting and handling equipment		82704	88330	88795	88655		29271	32656	34866	35760		6000	5900
2817	Office machinery, excl.computers,etc.		-	-	-	-		-	-	-	-		-	-
2818	Power-driven hand tools		-	-	...	...		-	...	...	...		...	...
2819	Other general-purpose machinery		...	38860	...	46766		...	12559	...	15593		...	...
282	Special-purpose machinery		174478	180768	212196	200662		53399	58945	64886	60126		5100	...f/
2821	Agricultural and forestry machinery		71557	75385	73777	78288		20642	23103	21529	21569		2600	5600
2822	Metal-forming machinery and machine tools		33186	...	57227	44538		8306	...	14645	10325		...	...

ISIC Revision 4

2823	Machinery for metallurgy	11213	...	...	5000	...	...	4663	...	...
2824	Mining, quarrying and construction machinery	11438	12131	10867	3244	5395	...	...	...	...
2825	Food/beverage/tobacco processing machinery	...	...	...	...	...	...	...	...	...
2826	Textile/apparel/leather production machinery	...	...	...	...	...	...	...	...	...
2829	Other special-purpose machinery	...	...	...	...	...	...	...	...	...
2910	Motor vehicles	...	...	...	...	...	...	...	...	...
2920	Automobile bodies, trailers and semi-trailers	50992	54537	261684	15335	15940	75900	75508	...	...
2930	Parts and accessories for motor vehicles	...	...	255497	...	...	...	...	6500	5100
301	Building of ships and boats	...	...	73368	...	...	...	24275	...	5700
3011	Building of ships and floating structures	24299	35569	50737	9168	11030	...	15151	...	3700
3012	Building of pleasure and sporting boats	...	...	22631	...	...	...	9124	...	2000
3020	Railway locomotives and rolling stock	-	-	...	-	-	-	-	...	...
3030	Air and spacecraft and related machinery	-	-	...	-	-	-	-	...	...
3040	Military fighting vehicles	-	-	...	-	-	-	-	...	...
309	Transport equipment n.e.c.	...	...	...	...	...	...	...	...	...
3091	Motorcycles	...	...	...	...	...	...	...	...	...
3092	Bicycles and invalid carriages	...	...	...	...	...	...	...	...	...
3099	Other transport equipment n.e.c.	...	23	...	...	9	...	...	...	...
3100	Furniture	407319	414397	502858	117274	126887	137638	158332	16800	24400
321	Jewellery, bijouterie and related articles	...	...	...	...	...	...	...	...	...
3211	Jewellery and related articles	...	...	-	-	-	-	-	...	...
3212	Imitation jewellery and related articles	400	382	952	130	174	202	447	...	-
3220	Musical instruments	...	...	...	...	...	...	...	...	...
3230	Sports goods	11279	10865	10726	5798	5325	5192	4827	200	300
3240	Games and toys	168	693	1351	89	164	322	392	...	-
3250	Medical and dental instruments and supplies	62753	62975	68486	24810	23964	...	23095	6400	...
3290	Other manufacturing n.e.c.	42312	42837	49820	11805	12103	11291	14023	1600	2900
331	Repair of fabricated metal products/machinery	239061	306287	300398	91675	103035	107888	90888	15500	7900
3311	Repair of fabricated metal products	3844	6600	5732	2217	3725	2807	...	400	...
3312	Repair of machinery	75617	70115	73510	34449	34106	34647	20722	3400	1900
3313	Repair of electronic and optical equipment	5399	7131	6595	3434	3396	3095	2491	100	100
3314	Repair of electrical equipment	15980	19720	16855	7140	7891	8589	9534	800	300
3315	Repair of transport equip., excl. motor vehicles	...	...	194091	...	...	56416	...	...	...
3319	Repair of other equipment	...	4294	4019	...	...	2334	1928	200	600
3320	Installation of industrial machinery/equipment	30540	29187	31570	10473	11520	12711	11409	1800	1200
C	Total manufacturing	9892610	10407793	10735737	2476971	2659556	2693631	2862691	634500	592000

a/ Derived from OECD's databases.
b/ 151 includes 1520.
c/ 181 includes 1820.
d/ 2011 includes 2012 and 2013.
e/ 2431 includes 2432.
f/ 281 includes 282.

Estonia

ISIC Revision 4 — Index numbers of industrial production (2010=100)

ISIC	Industry	Note	2005	2006	2007	2008	2009	2010	2011	2012	2013	2014	2015	2016
10	Food products		104	109	109	107	98	100	104	103	109	116	116	116
11	Beverages		127	143	152	129	116	100	101	114	112	118	106	101
12	Tobacco products		:	:	:	:	:	:	:	:	:	:	:	:
13	Textiles		117	121	120	111	93	100	109	114	109	119	135	152
14	Wearing apparel		158	164	153	136	94	100	117	122	121	118	106	114
15	Leather and related products		140	142	130	120	88	100	133	124	128	125	120	137
16	Wood products, excluding furniture		121	129	124	101	75	100	115	117	124	137	151	159
17	Paper and paper products		82	103	118	104	81	100	108	111	110	112	111	114
18	Printing and reproduction of recorded media		73	81	90	96	84	100	107	115	115	115	116	122
19	Coke and refined petroleum products		84	91	120	116	93	100	100	108	116	129	140	114
20	Chemicals and chemical products		120	128	134	154	86	100	128	127	133	124	110	104
21	Pharmaceuticals,medicinal chemicals, etc.		73	79	79	90	80	100	118	117	128	109	102	96
22	Rubber and plastics products		104	139	142	120	81	100	109	108	108	113	109	117
23	Other non-metallic mineral products		141	167	184	140	89	100	111	114	118	123	122	131
24	Basic metals		89	91	146	127	67	100	96	85	88	97	95	100
25	Fabricated metal products, except machinery		100	121	131	135	93	100	118	111	116	121	123	121
26	Computer, electronic and optical products		31	35	40	44	41	100	191	200	208	221	208	201
27	Electrical equipment		77	95	113	131	91	100	125	133	136	134	141	161
28	Machinery and equipment n.e.c.		100	115	132	132	75	100	145	153	153	154	164	165
29	Motor vehicles, trailers and semi-trailers		54	60	72	77	49	100	118	111	111	114	124	131
30	Other transport equipment		102	89	121	112	90	100	120	119	121	118	110	113
31	Furniture		123	129	130	118	87	100	112	114	115	114	126	131
32	Other manufacturing		96	105	129	128	90	100	102	108	122	127	133	136
33	Repair and installation of machinery/equipment		117	122	138	146	102	100	115	124	140	166	168	157
C	Total manufacturing		97	108	114	109	81	100	123	125	129	136	138	141

Finland

Supplier of information:
Statistics Finland, Helsinki.
Industrial statistics for the OECD countries are compiled by the OECD secretariat, which supplies them to UNIDO.

Basic source of data:
Annual survey; administrative data; business register.

Major deviations from ISIC (Revision 4):
Data presented in ISIC (Revision 4) were originally classified according to the national NACE-related classification system.

Reference period:
Calendar year.

Scope:
All enterprises.

Method of data collection:
Mainly electronic questionnaire and administrative data.

Type of enumeration:
Combination of survey and administrative data.

Adjusted for non-response:
Not reported.

Concepts and definitions of variables:
No deviations from the standard UN concepts and definitions are reported.

Related national publications:
Structural business and financial statement statistics, Statistics Finland, Helsinki.

Finland

ISIC Revision 4

ISIC	Industry	Note	Number of enterprises (number)				Note	Number of employees (number)				Note	Wages and salaries paid to employees (millions of Euros)			
			2013	2014	2015	2016		2013	2014	2015	2016		2013	2014	2015	2016
1010	Processing/preserving of meat		202	207	210	213		8146	8883	9052	8994		273.9	300.8	304.1	315.1
1020	Processing/preserving of fish, etc.		149	140	147	140		...	1163	905	889		...	32.9	24.2	23.8
1030	Processing/preserving of fruit,vegetables		149	154	155	143		1522	1545	1949	1574		46.3	47.1	64.8	47.8
1040	Vegetable and animal oils and fats		21	20	20	19		...	188	171	152		...	7.3	6.4	6.5
1050	Dairy products		61	61	71	67		6095	6264	6174	5678		237.9	245.0	232.9	217.1
106	Grain mill products,starches and starch products		70	66	71	60		690	778	802	865		28.7	37.9	40.2	42.5
1061	Grain mill products		64	60	65	54		560	645	665	726		23.4	31.9	34.1	36.5
1062	Starches and starch products		6	6	6	6		130	133	138	139		5.3	6.0	6.1	6.0
107	Other food products		926	920	992	902		15991	15462	15482	15466		503.7	489.4	499.3	507.4
1071	Bakery products		695	681	747	662		...	...	8978	8948		...	...	270.2	271.0
1072	Sugar		3	3	3	4		306	318	305	295		13.1	14.2	14.5	13.5
1073	Cocoa, chocolate and sugar confectionery		37	36	40	41		2023	1997	2001	1911		69.9	68.4	70.4	70.2
1074	Macaroni, noodles, couscous, etc.		2	2	4	4		...	...	16	18		...	...	0.2	0.2
1075	Prepared meals and dishes		64	65	67	65		2858	2451	2388	2324		91.0	76.7	77.6	76.8
1079	Other food products n.e.c.		125	133	131	126		1507	1636	1793	1969		55.6	60.0	66.6	75.6
1080	Prepared animal feeds		72	76	76	74		911	1008	930	930		35.2	38.0	39.0	36.9
110	Beverages		87	90	104	126		3634	3348	3259	3211		159.5	141.3	138.6	144.9
1101	Distilling, rectifying and blending of spirits		12	13	18	23		763	762	764	744		34.6	34.8	34.5	34.9
1102	Wines		24	24	24	25		119	...	...	...		4.1	...	...	...
1103	Malt liquors and malt		27	32	39	56		2545	2428	2292	2250		113.3	101.4	97.8	103.1
1104	Soft drinks,mineral waters,other bottled waters		24	21	23	22		206	...	90	103		7.5	...	2.7	3.3
1200	Tobacco products		1	-	-	-		-	-	-	-		-	-	-	-
131	Spinning, weaving and finishing of textiles		186	170	170	160		3222a/	...	-	354		102.5a/	...	...	10.0
1311	Preparation and spinning of textile fibres		20	19	18	18		...	...	...	126		...	...	...	4.6
1312	Weaving of textiles		19	18	16	14		26	36	...	37		0.6	0.7	...	0.8
1313	Finishing of textiles		147	133	136	128		199	...	...	191		5.1	...	...	4.6
139	Other textiles		587	565	544	504		...a/	2637	1830	1878		...a/	86.7	59.1	60.0
1391	Knitted and crocheted fabrics		13	11	12	9		...	49	50	38		...	1.2	1.1	1.1
1392	Made-up textile articles, except apparel		307	294	285	261		1066	1025	1030	1099		29.0	27.8	28.5	31.1
1393	Carpets and rugs		68	66	62	64		57	59	51	49		1.5	1.5	1.3	1.5
1394	Cordage, rope, twine and netting		17	17	17	17		103	109	121	120		3.4	3.5	4.1	4.5
1399	Other textiles n.e.c.		182	177	168	153		1567	1394	579	571		56.2	52.7	24.1	21.8
1410	Wearing apparel, except fur apparel		916	870	829	820		3287	3148	2898	2568		95.9	90.2	84.6	77.3
1420	Articles of fur		38	32	30	25		72	66	40	46		1.8	1.7	1.2	1.3
1430	Knitted and crocheted apparel		69	61	57	57		168	163	153	...		4.5	3.9	3.7	...
151	Leather;luggage,handbags,saddlery,harness;fur		133	133	135	123		...	287	299	265		...	6.2	6.2	5.7
1511	Tanning/dressing of leather; dressing of fur		28	28	27	25		192	176	193	175		4.6	3.9	3.9	3.7
1512	Luggage,handbags,etc.;saddlery/harness		105	105	108	98		...	111	106	91		...	2.4	2.3	2.0
1520	Footwear		53	49	48	46		1108	1115	1044	932		31.8	31.7	28.6	27.0
1610	Sawmilling and planing of wood		804	778	734	692		8165	8219	8056	7988		277.5	281.2	278.0	286.4

Code	Description												
162	Wood products, cork, straw, plaiting materials	1262	1190	1119	1070	12690	11904	11598	11809	389.5	365.0	366.6	375.5
1621	Veneer sheets and wood-based panels	27	26	24	25	2715	2669	2716	2781	97.0	99.9	103.5	106.3
1622	Builders' carpentry and joinery	745	706	670	647	8572	7898	7588	7749	252.7	228.4	226.0	231.9
1623	Wooden containers	125	122	112	107	978	923	892	891	29.6	26.4	26.8	27.2
1629	Other wood products;articles of cork,straw	365	336	313	291	425	415	401	389	10.3	10.3	10.3	10.1
170	Paper and paper products	189	187	178	180	23001	22243	21584	21913	1140.9	1109.9	1135.2	1116.2
1701	Pulp, paper and paperboard	53	53	50	51	19448	18808	18328	18661	1001.6	975.7	995.4	980.3
1702	Corrugated paper and paperboard	64	64	63	63	1895	1850	1692	1711	71.1	68.5	64.9	67.9
1709	Other articles of paper and paperboard	72	70	65	66	...	...	...	...	...	...	...	...
181	Printing and service activities related to printing	918	887	863	814	9185	8487	7867	7047	318.2	289.8	272.2	250.2
1811	Printing	704	681	664	629	8404	7889	7328	6492	291.8	271.0	252.0	231.6
1812	Service activities related to printing	214	206	199	185	782	599	539	555	26.5	18.8	20.2	18.5
1820	Reproduction of recorded media	146	128	123	135	69	69	90	82	2.0	2.0	2.5	3.0
1910	Coke oven products	-	1	-	-	-	...	-	-	-	:	-	-
1920	Refined petroleum products	17	17	17	16	...	...	...	...	407.8	400.6	409.8	400.0
201	Basic chemicals,fertilizers, etc.	104	108	100	96	7643	7741	7662	7546	238.9	237.4	242.5	237.8
2011	Basic chemicals	55	59	53	52	4638	4712	4585	4499	51.6	50.0	51.9	51.5
2012	Fertilizers and nitrogen compounds	15	14	14	13	1069	1098	1079	1078	117.3	113.2	115.4	110.7
2013	Plastics and synthetic rubber in primary forms	34	35	33	31	1935	1931	1998	1970	...	...	...	...
202	Other chemical products	186	187	191	191	...	...	...	...	0.5	...	...	...
2021	Pesticides and other agrochemical products	3	3	5	3	...	...	...	...	...	...	...	...
2022	Paints,varnishes;printing ink and mastics	35	35	33	33	...	1691	1729	1690	...	68.8	72.4	70.1
2023	Soap,cleaning and cosmetic preparations	65	68	71	70	793	911	881	837	19.5	33.5	33.6	32.3
2029	Other chemical products n.e.c.	83	81	82	85	...	2516	2566	...	...	109.3	115.3	...
2030	Man-made fibres	4	2	1	1	25	...	...	...	1.3	...	...	...
2100	Pharmaceuticals,medicinal chemicals, etc.	32	34	31	28	...	4541	...	4484	...	221.0	...	233.4
221	Rubber products	61	58	55	55	12934b/	2256	2204	2116	477.6b/	97.9	93.9	91.4
2211	Rubber tyres and tubes	16	14	14	14	1240	1223	1220	1116	56.7	61.1	58.9	54.8
2219	Other rubber products	45	44	41	41	...	1033	984	999	...	36.8	35.0	36.6
2220	Plastics products	518	500	486	485	...b/	10726	10462	10288	...b/	392.6	389.7	399.4
2310	Glass and glass products	126	124	120	123	3746	3569	3683	2694	147.4	134.8	147.8	121.4
239	Non-metallic mineral products n.e.c.	634	620	598	585	...	...	...	9997	...	...	...	386.7
2391	Refractory products	6	6	6	5	...	...	...	51	...	...	...	1.9
2392	Clay building materials	8	7	5	5	...	...	...	134	...	...	...	4.9
2393	Other porcelain and ceramic products	120	119	110	103	...	...	...	...	...	...	...	...
2394	Cement, lime and plaster	5	5	5	5	...	...	...	...	...	...	...	...
2395	Articles of concrete, cement and plaster	229	223	222	219	1314	1244	1170	1136	39.9	37.1	35.0	33.9
2396	Cutting, shaping and finishing of stone	235	228	218	217	1695	1749	1750	1695	...	71.8	75.5	73.2
2399	Other non-metallic mineral products n.e.c.	31	32	32	31	...	...	...	...	...	...	...	...
2410	Basic iron and steel	78	75	76	73	...	3132	3219	3372	...	136.5	140.0	148.1
2420	Basic precious and other non-ferrous metals	28	25	25	25	2089	1747	1626	1671	64.9	62.3	58.0	59.5
243	Casting of metals	43	43	43	41	1605	1281	1158	1226	47.4	45.2	41.3	43.2
2431	Casting of iron and steel	19	21	20	19	484	466	469	445	17.5	17.1	16.7	16.3
2432	Casting of non-ferrous metals	24	22	23	22	...	...	...	...	...	...	...	...
251	Struct.metal products, tanks, reservoirs	1448	1410	1380	1368	14204	13269	13257	...	496.9	460.4	...	465.5

continued

Finland

ISIC	Industry	Note	Number of enterprises (number) 2013	2014	2015	2016	Note	Number of employees (number) 2013	2014	2015	2016	Note	Wages and salaries paid to employees (millions of Euros) 2013	2014	2015	2016
2511	Structural metal products		1358	1324	1296	1281		11151	11170	11130	11390		355.9	365.6	375.7	385.7
2512	Tanks, reservoirs and containers of metal		62	58	57	62		1120	1086	1060	1018		41.4	38.5	35.5	39.4
2513	Steam generators, excl. hot water boilers		28	28	27	25		1933	...	1079	849		99.5	...	49.3	40.2
2520	Weapons and ammunition		27	24	26	30		...	...	519	528		...	...	22.0	22.1
259	Other metal products;metal working services		3259	3170	3064	3013		...	25013	24893	25650		...	822.9	831.1	880.5
2591	Forging,pressing,stamping,roll-forming of metal		104	103	96	99		155	195	183	184		4.7	5.0	5.7	5.1
2592	Treatment and coating of metals;machining		2125	2070	1983	1938		17547	17194	17152	16798		558.2	552.2	564.4	560.1
2593	Cutlery, hand tools and general hardware		247	236	232	216		...	2659	2670	3533		...	100.8	96.4	137.4
2599	Other fabricated metal products n.e.c.		783	761	753	760		...	...	4888	5134		...	...	164.8	178.0
2610	Electronic components and boards		150	148	155	155		...	1904	1926	2023		...	71.0	81.4	87.4
2620	Computers and peripheral equipment		50	50	48	51		333	363	352	379		12.8	13.2	12.7	13.5
2630	Communication equipment		59	54	60	63		15759	16068	13454	12000		1094.8	1054.2	1157.3	802.1
2640	Consumer electronics		27	27	29	31		...	...	...	182		...	...	...	6.3
265	Measuring,testing equipment; watches, etc.		231	237	230	221		5573	6114	6097	6191		255.3	278.8	279.6	294.5
2651	Measuring/testing/navigating equipment,etc.		228	234	226	218		5571	6113	6095	6188		255.2	278.8	279.5	294.4
2652	Watches and clocks		3	3	4	3		2	2	2	3		0.1	-	-	0.1
2660	Irradiation/electromedical equipment,etc.		29	31	30	32		2138	2169	2223	2355		97.3	97.1	102.6	110.2
2670	Optical instruments and photographic equipment		16	16	16	15		61	...	...	...		2.6	...	...	...
2680	Magnetic and optical media		3	3	2	3		1	1	...	...		-	-	...	...
2710	Electric motors,generators,transformers,etc.		125	123	119	120		11803	11795	11567	11201		520.1	537.7	525.5	511.6
2720	Batteries and accumulators		8	6	7	7		53	24	27	32		1.6	0.8	0.9	0.9
273	Wiring and wiring devices		20	23	24	24		1555	1595	1556	1404		60.6	64.0	61.2	59.8
2731	Fibre optic cables		4	4	4	4		143	147	160	150		5.7	6.6	6.5	6.7
2732	Other electronic and electric wires and cables		11	14	14	13		1090	1111	1133	1131		43.5	44.2	47.0	49.2
2733	Wiring devices		5	5	6	7		322	338	263	123		11.5	13.2	7.7	4.0
2740	Electric lighting equipment		80	83	81	75		1353	1417	1442	1399		47.5	48.8	51.5	50.6
2750	Domestic appliances		32	32	31	31		827	...	753	764		25.7	...	24.2	25.4
2790	Other electrical equipment		155	148	152	145		2290	2074	2129	2041		78.3	71.3	74.0	70.1
281	General-purpose machinery		745	723	686	657		26229	25994	24708	24015		1122.1	1132.7	1065.8	1056.3
2811	Engines/turbines,excl.aircraft,vehicle engines		27	26	28	26		4539	4481	4599	4517		243.4	244.8	246.7	223.3
2812	Fluid power equipment		34	36	34	32		1246	1215	1138	1018		41.3	39.7	36.8	37.8
2813	Other pumps, compressors, taps and valves		45	41	37	36		3821	3867	2820	2813		168.3	162.7	110.1	116.2
2814	Bearings, gears, gearing and driving elements		39	36	38	38		1847	1826	1818	1792		70.4	74.0	70.1	71.8
2815	Ovens, furnaces and furnace burners		37	37	35	33		720	717	679	596		26.2	25.9	24.4	20.7
2816	Lifting and handling equipment		151	142	133	133		7227	7200	7150	7454		311.8	324.1	324.4	350.7
2817	Office machinery, excl.computers,etc.		5	4	4	4		16	17	16	14		0.8	0.8	0.8	0.8
2818	Power-driven hand tools		10	10	10	9		59	55	49	56		1.8	1.7	1.6	2.1
2819	Other general-purpose machinery		397	391	367	346		6753	6616	6439	5755		258.1	259.0	250.8	233.0
282	Special-purpose machinery		726	701	683	657		23115	23010	23265	23197		1005.4	973.2	1060.2	1061.9
2821	Agricultural and forestry machinery		144	144	144	139		4346	4455	4278	4196		162.8	169.8	170.7	172.3
2822	Metal-forming machinery and machine tools		82	74	73	69		1998	2123	1742	1798		81.7	84.4	73.5	78.3

Code		A	B	C	D	E	F	G	H	I	J	K	L
2823	Machinery for metallurgy	16	12	11	12	48	49	51	51	2.6	2.6	2.6	2.7
2824	Mining, quarrying and construction machinery	97	94	88	86	6561	6848	6588	6323	291.9	297.1	300.3	283.2
2825	Food/beverage/tobacco processing machinery	67	67	65	63	621	635	648	622	21.4	22.5	24.1	22.3
2826	Textile/apparel/leather production machinery	19	17	16	13	31	30	27	21	0.9	0.9	0.9	0.7
2829	Other special-purpose machinery	301	293	286	275	9510	8870	9932	10187	444.1	395.9	488.2	502.5
2910	Motor vehicles	29	30	29	32	2161	2749	3085	3111	90.2	103.5	119.6	116.3
2920	Automobile bodies, trailers and semi-trailers	138	129	115	107	3416	3229	3113	3015	109.1	105.2	104.7	108.7
2930	Parts and accessories for motor vehicles	92	86	91	88	990	855	927	826	35.6	28.7	31.8	30.2
301	Building of ships and boats	324	309	313	292	...	5820	5297	5366	...	183.9	202.1	213.8
3011	Building of ships and floating structures	96	97	100	96	4166	4108	3506	3594	168.8	125.8	139.9	151.7
3012	Building of pleasure and sporting boats	228	212	213	196	...	1713	1791	1772	...	58.0	62.2	62.2
3020	Railway locomotives and rolling stock	2	2	2	1	...	...	...	...	...	...	...	...
3030	Air and spacecraft and related machinery	7	7	9	11	...	1384	1335	1341	...	63.6	60.3	62.9
3040	Military fighting vehicles	2	2	3	3	...	...	466	395	...	...	24.9	23.8
309	Transport equipment n.e.c.	31	30	34	34	229	245	...	...	7.5	7.6	...	...
3091	Motorcycles	3	3	3	4	1	1	1	...	-	-	...	...
3092	Bicycles and invalid carriages	12	12	13	13	94	108	103	100	3.1	3.2	3.5	3.1
3099	Other transport equipment n.e.c.	16	15	18	17	134	137	...	127	4.4	4.3	4.3	4.3
3100	Furniture	992	943	908	866	7201	6724	6481	6337	213.3	204.4	200.5	201.9
321	Jewellery, bijouterie and related articles	355	341	342	338	614	546	524	504	18.3	18.1	17.8	17.1
3211	Jewellery and related articles	302	290	289	282	578	508	483	477	17.3	17.0	16.8	16.4
3212	Imitation jewellery and related articles	53	51	53	56	37	38	40	27	1.1	1.1	1.1	0.7
3220	Musical instruments	85	81	88	87	65	62	57	57	1.9	1.7	1.6	1.6
3230	Sports goods	138	137	143	151	898	886	864	865	30.8	29.8	28.9	28.4
3240	Games and toys	42	37	36	31	93	104	196	174	2.4	3.0	6.6	6.0
3250	Medical and dental instruments and supplies	456	455	452	445	1718	1653	1647	1644	63.2	60.0	62.2	61.7
3290	Other manufacturing n.e.c.	217	228	234	240	955	1000	1012	979	32.3	30.8	30.5	31.4
331	Repair of fabricated metal products/machinery	2143	2155	2230	2250	11550	12230	12826	12182	436.3	451.1	509.1	475.8
3311	Repair of fabricated metal products	151	155	149	157	1187	1190	1581	1661	41.1	43.0	61.8	62.9
3312	Repair of machinery	1506	1502	1552	1548	8062	8895	9228	7881	297.2	328.0	366.9	306.1
3313	Repair of electronic and optical equipment	74	77	83	79	169	233	245	241	6.4	9.1	9.8	10.0
3314	Repair of electrical equipment	61	62	66	71	237	233	252	287	7.7	8.1	8.7	10.0
3315	Repair of transport equip., excl. motor vehicles	316	315	328	336	1878	1656	1489	2068	83.4	62.2	61.2	85.7
3319	Repair of other equipment	35	44	52	59	19	24	31	44	0.5	0.6	0.8	1.3
3320	Installation of industrial machinery/equipment	469	483	497	501	5260	3494	4581	4688	202.4	124.6	180.6	199.6
C	Total manufacturing	21582	21042	20768	20264	339165	334814	327409	320467	13657.9	13440.3	13688.5	13293.5

a/ 131 includes 139.
b/ 221 includes 2220.

Finland

ISIC Revision 4		Note	Output (valuation not defined) (millions of Euros)				Note	Value added at factor values (millions of Euros)				Note	Gross fixed capital formation (millions of Euros)	
ISIC	Industry		2013	2014	2015	2016		2013	2014	2015	2016		2015	2016
1010	Processing/preserving of meat		2314.2	2431.0	2425.3	2397.9		442.8	486.5	489.4	497.3		66.1	52.7
1020	Processing/preserving of fish, etc.		...	335.3	289.3	286.5		...	63.3	44.4	44.2		7.2	16.9
1030	Processing/preserving of fruit, vegetables		349.5	347.1	427.7	334.6		92.5	87.1	117.3	86.2		16.8	18.4
1040	Vegetable and animal oils and fats		...	52.2	47.3	48.8		...	10.9	11.6	11.4		0.9	2.4
1050	Dairy products		2600.4	2549.2	2271.2	2187.6		458.1	442.5	407.3	349.8		118.0	170.6
106	Grain mill products, starches and starch products		311.1	450.8	428.9	469.5		58.9	96.0	91.6	89.4		17.3	26.0
1061	Grain mill products		232.5	365.3	345.9	382.3		49.3	82.9	79.8	76.1		14.4	21.2
1062	Starches and starch products		78.6	85.6	83.0	87.0		9.6	13.1	11.8	13.3		2.9	4.9
107	Other food products		2973.0	2837.1	2830.4	2884.7		941.6	896.1	878.0	920.7		93.1	95.9
1071	Bakery products		...	...	1043.3	1074.8		...	...	419.1	444.6		43.7	43.9
1072	Sugar		266.4	275.7	227.4	205.5		47.8	51.2	31.9	17.4		5.4	3.1
1073	Cocoa, chocolate and sugar confectionery		574.6	474.6	479.3	473.6		150.4	144.3	149.6	153.4		18.3	16.4
1074	Macaroni, noodles, couscous, etc.		...	...	0.7	0.3		...	...	0.3	-0.1		-	0.1
1075	Prepared meals and dishes		482.8	436.2	416.9	424.7		157.1	128.3	126.5	135.0		12.4	17.4
1079	Other food products n.e.c.		565.3	627.4	662.8	705.7		159.3	153.2	150.7	170.2		13.3	15.0
1080	Prepared animal feeds		623.1	629.5	600.7	536.9		77.2	90.1	87.8	77.7		18.2	14.9
110	Beverages		1221.0	1032.1	952.9	1034.9		368.8	336.3	319.9	356.8		73.4	45.9
1101	Distilling, rectifying and blending of spirits		261.9	246.4	258.4	258.3		62.9	69.7	68.1	74.1		20.6	8.7
1102	Wines		30.4					8.8					-	-
1103	Malt liquors and malt		836.6	729.2	642.3	713.2		268.9	247.1	231.4	261.3		49.6	34.0
1104	Soft drinks, mineral waters, other bottled waters		92.1	...	28.9	38.6		28.3	...	13.4	14.3		1.5	2.3
1200	Tobacco products		...	-	-	-		...	-	-	-		-	-
131	Spinning, weaving and finishing of textiles		473.0a/	...	...	46.1		174.7a/	...	...	18.1		...	0.6
1311	Preparation and spinning of textile fibres		...	...	...	21.8		...	...	...	8.0		...	0.2
1312	Weaving of textiles		2.4	2.6	...	2.4		1.0	1.1	...	1.1		...	-
1313	Finishing of textiles		22.5	...	...	21.9		9.4	...	...	9.0		...	0.4
139	Other textiles		...a/	410.8	320.2	332.8		...a/	148.7	107.3	113.9		10.8	7.3
1391	Knitted and crocheted fabrics		...	7.2	6.6	7.0		...	2.0	2.0	1.9		-	-
1392	Made-up textile articles, except apparel		136.6	128.8	129.5	141.5		50.5	46.1	50.2	55.2		3.4	3.6
1393	Carpets and rugs		12.5	11.4	10.3	11.8		3.5	3.5	3.0	3.6		0.1	0.3
1394	Cordage, rope, twine and netting		18.7	20.8	22.5	21.2		5.4	6.0	6.4	6.3		0.4	0.4
1399	Other textiles n.e.c.		250.2	242.6	151.2	151.2		94.1	91.2	45.8	46.8		6.9	3.0
1410	Wearing apparel, except fur apparel		449.0	419.6	397.9	389.4		148.1	147.7	141.1	132.0		5.3	7.5
1420	Articles of fur		6.4	6.2	4.6	4.5		2.8	1.6	2.0	1.7		-	-
1430	Knitted and crocheted apparel		14.5	16.4	13.5	...		6.5	6.0	5.7	...		0.1	-
151	Leather; luggage, handbags, saddlery, harness; fur		...	34.5	35.6	31.6		...	10.9	11.0	9.9		1.5	0.8
1511	Tanning/dressing of leather; dressing of fur		20.7	20.3	22.2	18.4		6.8	6.1	6.4	5.7		1.1	0.5
1512	Luggage, handbags, etc.; saddlery/harness		...	14.2	13.4	13.1		...	4.9	4.6	4.2		0.4	0.3
1520	Footwear		179.8	181.7	165.5	179.7		70.2	69.6	59.1	60.8		2.0	2.6
1610	Sawmilling and planing of wood		3153.6	3357.8	3208.9	3325.7		540.4	575.4	568.4	564.4		114.5	128.5

162	Wood products, cork, straw, plaiting materials	2312.3	2028.1	2049.0	2194.3	583.6	593.4	613.1	623.7	64.8	77.0
1621	Veneer sheets and wood-based panels	638.3	589.4	613.8	615.1	146.0	176.3	186.3	184.7	12.4	13.1
1622	Builders' carpentry and joinery	1452.8	1246.9	1237.7	1370.2	369.2	353.1	361.7	373.1	42.7	56.9
1623	Wooden containers	165.6	142.3	146.8	154.6	48.2	44.8	45.2	46.7	5.7	5.4
1629	Other wood products;articles of cork,straw	55.5	49.5	50.7	54.5	20.3	19.3	19.8	19.3	4.0	1.7
170	Paper and paper products	13779.8	13511.0	13705.7	13938.2	2807.3	3018.0	3283.1	3189.3	763.9	651.7
1701	Pulp, paper and paperboard	12956.9	12747.7	12916.5	13164.1	2531.9	2750.4	3012.3	2901.0	746.9	636.8
1702	Corrugated paper and paperboard	406.2	350.1	322.3	327.5	112.5	115.5	100.9	102.2	8.0	6.2
1709	Other articles of paper and paperboard	...	...	...	...	...	...	...	...	...	...
181	Printing and service activities related to printing	1360.4	1217.8	1144.1	1072.1	513.7	454.8	432.1	394.5	40.9	38.3
1811	Printing	1279.6	1163.1	1086.0	1020.8	471.0	424.2	401.4	367.2	39.3	37.6
1812	Service activities related to printing	80.8	54.7	58.1	51.2	42.6	30.6	30.8	27.4	1.6	0.7
1820	Reproduction of recorded media	13.0	12.4	13.8	19.3	4.8	4.5	5.3	8.4	0.5	0.9
1910	Coke oven products	-	...	-	-	-	...	-	-	-	-
1920	Refined petroleum products	...	...	...	...	...	...	...	...	...	...
201	Basic chemicals,fertilizers, etc.	4234.8	4096.0	4375.6	4134.0	1073.9	1089.8	1242.7	1172.5	373.8	321.8
2011	Basic chemicals	2418.4	2397.2	2701.0	2615.4	647.4	692.3	789.4	739.2	116.0	209.0
2012	Fertilizers and nitrogen compounds	780.0	753.5	782.1	648.8	148.8	153.8	198.3	158.3	104.2	81.4
2013	Plastics and synthetic rubber in primary forms	1036.4	945.3	892.4	869.8	277.7	243.6	254.9	275.1	153.7	31.5
202	Other chemical products	...	...	...	...	...	...	...	...	...	...
2021	Pesticides and other agrochemical products	4.6	...	...	...	1.5	...	...	...	...	...
2022	Paints,varnishes;printing ink and mastics	...	467.0	466.4	420.5	...	139.8	134.1	133.3	6.1	10.6
2023	Soap,cleaning and cosmetic preparations	93.5	172.0	176.5	169.0	37.4	58.2	62.8	50.9	1.8	3.8
2029	Other chemical products n.e.c.	5.5	1166.1	1200.3	...	-0.2	346.6	358.6	358.8	31.0	...
2030	Man-made fibres	...	1678.1	...	2033.5	...	1063.9	...	...	...	...
2100	Pharmaceuticals,medicinal chemicals, etc.	2749.5b/	652.6	663.8	630.2	859.3b/	210.8	...	1276.9	...	41.6
221	Rubber products	360.2	481.9	507.2	477.1	117.9	146.2	247.0	256.6	58.9	45.1
2211	Rubber tyres and tubes	...	170.7	156.6	153.1	...	...	183.5	191.9	54.1	37.2
2219	Other rubber products	...	...	...	...	...	64.6	63.5	64.7	4.8	7.9
2220	Plastics products	...b/	2308.6	2250.4	2296.8	...b/	694.8	673.0	745.5	77.5	90.1
2310	Glass and glass products	625.1	592.9	720.3	569.8	234.5	227.1	262.8	219.7	13.0	15.3
239	Non-metallic mineral products n.e.c.	...	2274.3	2203.2	2330.3	...	...	...	766.2	...	93.3
2391	Refractory products	...	...	14.0	18.0	...	...	...	6.0	...	0.2
2392	Clay building materials	...	...	...	...	...	...	...	5.4	...	0.2
2393	Other porcelain and ceramic products	...	...	...	...	...	...	...	...	...	...
2394	Cement, lime and plaster	...	...	...	...	...	...	...	...	...	...
2395	Articles of concrete, cement and plaster	165.4	153.9	141.6	139.0	60.6	56.7	54.7	54.7	7.0	6.5
2396	Cutting, shaping and finishing of stone	...	...	...	...	...	...	...	...	...	...
2399	Other non-metallic mineral products n.e.c.	...	422.3	429.3	445.0	...	139.5	157.7	163.9	26.9	36.1
2410	Basic iron and steel	...	...	...	...	...	...	...	...	...	...
2420	Basic precious and other non-ferrous metals	...	2274.3	2203.2	2142.5	...	428.2	485.4	459.8	101.6	84.3
243	Casting of metals	266.8	260.5	235.2	239.9	84.4	97.1	79.3	72.1	4.1	9.0
2431	Casting of iron and steel	197.6	185.8	169.1	174.4	58.3	68.2	58.6	50.2	2.5	7.2
2432	Casting of non-ferrous metals	69.2	74.6	66.1	65.5	26.1	29.0	20.7	21.9	1.6	1.8
251	Struct.metal products, tanks, reservoirs	2724.4	2276.6	...	2416.0	793.0	...	713.1	760.5	58.9	75.0

continued

Finland

ISIC Revision 4

ISIC	Industry	Note	Output (valuation not defined) (millions of Euros) 2013	2014	2015	2016	Note	Value added at factor values (millions of Euros) 2013	2014	2015	2016	Note	Gross fixed capital formation (millions of Euros) 2015	2016
2511	Structural metal products		1885.4	1804.7	1897.1	2009.9		583.0	555.9	594.6	640.5		55.1	70.2
2512	Tanks, reservoirs and containers of metal		203.0	172.7	183.8	217.6		65.3	51.7	48.4	58.4		2.0	2.4
2513	Steam generators, excl. hot water boilers		636.0	...	195.8	188.5		144.7	...	70.1	61.5		1.8	2.4
2520	Weapons and ammunition		...	...	126.4	119.8		...	55.4	52.7			4.1	9.0
259	Other metal products;metal working services		...	3700.4	4086.9	4061.7		...	1372.7	1453.5	1553.3		185.6	160.7
2591	Forging,pressing,stamping,roll-forming of metal		23.0	25.5	28.8	27.7		9.6	10.6	11.9	11.1		1.3	0.9
2592	Treatment and coating of metals;machining		2358.6	2368.6	2427.5	2457.0		901.8	914.4	917.6	947.9		129.3	102.9
2593	Cutlery, hand tools and general hardware		...	440.0	788.9	650.0		...	162.0	237.0	285.5		14.3	15.6
2599	Other fabricated metal products n.e.c.		...	...	841.7	927.0		...	...	287.0	308.6		40.6	41.2
2610	Electronic components and boards		...	425.0	348.3	390.0		...	100.1	116.4	132.8		9.0	8.0
2620	Computers and peripheral equipment		58.2	63.6	58.1	55.6		17.1	18.5	18.3	19.4		0.3	0.7
2630	Communication equipment		8300.9	6964.3	5967.6	6066.8		820.0	807.6	304.5	1279.1		177.0	118.6
2640	Consumer electronics		...	...	...	27.9		...	...	...	11.3		...	1.1
265	Measuring,testing equipment; watches, etc.		1063.9	1120.9	1173.8	1195.5		418.6	477.5	487.2	497.4		38.2	40.6
2651	Measuring/testing/navigating equipment,etc.		1063.8	1120.7	1173.6	1195.3		418.7	477.4	487.1	497.3		38.2	40.6
2652	Watches and clocks		0.1	0.1	0.2	0.2		-0.1	0.1	0.1	0.1		-	-
2660	Irradiation/electromedical equipment,etc.		659.2	718.5	745.8	786.5		220.3	254.6	270.5	267.4		7.9	9.5
2670	Optical instruments and photographic equipment		11.6	0.2	...	...		4.8	0.1	...	...		...	...
2680	Magnetic and optical media		0.2	0.2	...	...		0.1	0.1	...	...		...	...
2710	Electric motors,generators,transformers,etc.		3068.9	3095.0	3238.7	3214.7		1076.1	1078.1	1063.3	1044.9		64.6	60.2
2720	Batteries and accumulators		3.6	2.7	2.7	4.8		-	0.5	0.8	2.4		-	0.1
273	Wiring and wiring devices		482.3	538.0	498.1	505.8		117.0	117.0	116.5	142.9		32.1	39.3
2731	Fibre optic cables		33.2	42.6	40.9	41.3		11.8	15.8	16.8	17.2		0.6	0.6
2732	Other electronic and electric wires and cables		393.0	448.4	432.3	447.4		78.3	91.2	94.8	118.2		30.6	38.3
2733	Wiring devices		56.0	47.1	24.9	17.1		26.8	10.0	4.9	7.6		0.9	0.4
2740	Electric lighting equipment		267.1	295.2	313.4	327.1		110.6	124.0	123.1	106.7		11.7	13.5
2750	Domestic appliances		123.6	...	122.0	110.9		44.4	...	46.0	47.1		1.4	2.4
2790	Other electrical equipment		392.1	355.8	402.7	381.4		116.9	113.0	124.2	108.0		5.6	4.9
281	General-purpose machinery		7244.6	6656.6	6353.1	5945.2		1862.3	1909.6	1707.6	1737.9		97.1	94.6
2811	Engines/turbines,excl.aircraft,vehicle engines		2035.5	1629.9	1625.8	1168.0		439.3	411.1	384.8	341.9		16.1	19.7
2812	Fluid power equipment		175.7	174.4	156.4	165.5		58.1	60.9	57.2	59.8		4.6	4.6
2813	Other pumps, compressors, taps and valves		870.1	852.6	625.9	652.0		300.6	288.2	207.7	220.5		9.3	14.4
2814	Bearings, gears, gearing and driving elements		299.1	348.1	332.9	330.4		88.7	100.3	94.4	93.5		14.9	7.2
2815	Ovens, furnaces and furnace burners		150.1	127.7	115.3	108.0		41.1	36.5	29.8	24.2		1.3	3.8
2816	Lifting and handling equipment		2297.7	2299.0	2314.7	2393.2		477.9	553.8	520.4	615.9		23.6	21.8
2817	Office machinery, excl.computers,etc.		4.3	3.6	2.4	2.3		1.6	1.4	1.2	1.1		0.1	-
2818	Power-driven hand tools		12.5	7.3	7.1	11.9		3.2	2.5	2.5	3.8		0.2	0.5
2819	Other general-purpose machinery		1399.6	1214.1	1172.8	1113.9		451.7	454.8	409.6	377.2		27.0	22.5
282	Special-purpose machinery		6393.0	6377.9	7289.0	6915.7		1571.3	1705.4	1907.2	1871.6		110.6	132.2
2821	Agricultural and forestry machinery		930.6	1067.2	1123.5	1138.9		258.8	315.2	334.0	352.4		52.8	33.0
2822	Metal-forming machinery and machine tools		400.9	419.3	376.8	398.6		139.0	137.6	129.3	138.8		4.8	8.5

Code	Description										
2823	Machinery for metallurgy	15.5	15.9	13.4	17.5	5.2	5.6	4.7	5.6	-	-
2824	Mining, quarrying and construction machinery	2301.3	2054.5	2197.6	2067.8	554.7	488.1	555.5	499.6	24.8	16.2
2825	Food/beverage/tobacco processing machinery	104.3	109.8	98.0	96.1	34.8	37.6	34.0	33.1	3.9	1.7
2826	Textile/apparel/leather production machinery	4.8	3.6	3.5	2.5	2.2	1.6	1.7	1.2	-	0.3
2829	Other special-purpose machinery	2635.5	2707.7	3476.4	3194.6	576.7	719.7	848.0	840.8	24.3	72.5
2910	Motor vehicles	648.2	718.4	785.1	759.8	146.2	193.9	227.3	201.5	13.1	35.6
2920	Automobile bodies, trailers and semi-trailers	549.0	550.4	536.4	575.2	164.5	156.1	162.0	171.2	7.7	9.5
2930	Parts and accessories for motor vehicles	187.8	131.3	185.3	174.1	63.9	39.8	52.7	58.0	4.6	7.1
301	Building of ships and boats	...	1113.2	1325.0	1672.3	...	246.7	246.9	305.8	12.9	16.3
3011	Building of ships and floating structures	821.1	863.5	1032.2	1373.0	146.8	168.4	152.1	211.0	6.8	9.5
3012	Building of pleasure and sporting boats	...	249.8	292.7	299.3	...	78.3	94.7	94.9	6.1	6.8
3020	Railway locomotives and rolling stock	...	...	...	...	...	...	...	...	...	...
3030	Air and spacecraft and related machinery	...	175.0	172.1	202.3	...	91.3	84.4	80.8	1.8	3.3
3040	Military fighting vehicles	...	...	130.9	188.2	...	52.2	52.2	73.8	1.7	1.2
309	Transport equipment n.e.c.	34.1	32.0	...	...	10.5	10.8	-	...	...	...
3091	Motorcycles	0.1	0.1	0.2	...	-	-	-	...	-	...
3092	Bicycles and invalid carriages	18.5	17.7	11.5	18.3	4.1	4.6	4.3	5.3	-	-
3099	Other transport equipment n.e.c.	15.5	14.2	...	14.1	6.3	6.1	...	5.9	...	0.9
3100	Furniture	1036.3	1006.0	999.9	1034.1	311.7	300.4	306.7	328.6	21.5	49.9
321	Jewellery, bijouterie and related articles	99.9	91.3	104.0	103.5	26.6	28.3	29.2	28.8	0.5	1.3
3211	Jewellery and related articles	91.3	83.2	95.7	100.2	24.7	26.3	27.6	27.5	0.5	1.3
3212	Imitation jewellery and related articles	8.5	8.0	8.3	3.2	1.9	1.9	1.6	1.3	-	-
3220	Musical instruments	7.4	7.1	7.1	6.3	3.3	3.1	3.2	3.0	0.1	0.1
3230	Sports goods	142.1	119.8	113.2	119.4	47.3	50.9	49.6	41.8	2.1	1.3
3240	Games and toys	10.6	10.5	25.4	30.1	3.7	4.0	11.0	8.4	1.1	4.1
3250	Medical and dental instruments and supplies	251.7	218.2	222.3	213.2	108.5	97.7	99.1	101.8	5.0	9.2
3290	Other manufacturing n.e.c.	163.0	153.7	140.7	138.7	60.8	52.4	50.7	57.5	2.9	5.1
331	Repair of fabricated metal products/machinery	1597.6	1621.3	1849.8	1839.3	629.2	694.9	783.7	762.9	54.0	51.2
3311	Repair of fabricated metal products	165.5	175.5	237.0	241.0	66.3	69.3	97.4	101.9	14.7	6.2
3312	Repair of machinery	1108.8	1112.9	1279.7	1104.1	463.5	498.3	547.0	475.2	21.6	26.3
3313	Repair of electronic and optical equipment	32.8	37.3	35.4	35.0	10.4	16.5	17.7	17.6	0.5	0.8
3314	Repair of electrical equipment	25.8	25.8	29.0	33.8	11.8	12.1	13.6	15.6	0.8	0.4
3315	Repair of transport equip., excl. motor vehicles	261.4	265.7	263.4	417.0	75.7	97.1	106.1	149.8	16.3	17.0
3319	Repair of other equipment	3.4	3.9	5.3	8.4	1.5	1.6	2.0	2.7	0.3	0.5
3320	Installation of industrial machinery/equipment	569.9	412.4	678.1	774.5	273.8	183.5	291.5	327.1	8.9	11.0
C	Total manufacturing	105717.7	102620.7	100602.9	101034.5	24507.5	24610.7	25154.4	26983.5	3689.1	3251.8

a/ 131 includes 139.
b/ 221 includes 2220.

Finland

ISIC Revision 4 — Index numbers of industrial production (2010=100)

ISIC	Industry	Note	2005	2006	2007	2008	2009	2010	2011	2012	2013	2014	2015	2016
10	Food products		97	96	97	98	96	100	100	100	99	98	95	96
11	Beverages		112	115	116	113	102	100	102	98	99	96	93	98
12	Tobacco products		:	:	:	:	:	:	:	:	:	:	:	:
13	Textiles		127	134	132	111	91	100	102	94	87	87	91	92
14	Wearing apparel		131	124	115	117	95	100	100	92	85	75	67	61
15	Leather and related products		80	85	90	91	81	100	102	100	96	90	72	70
16	Wood products, excluding furniture		129	135	134	112	88	100	101	97	98	97	96	99
17	Paper and paper products		102	117	118	110	90	100	95	93	93	92	92	91
18	Printing and reproduction of recorded media		122	129	129	122	103	100	102	99	89	86	80	79
19	Coke and refined petroleum products		:	:	:	:	:	:	:	:	:	:	:	:
20	Chemicals and chemical products		:	:	:	:	:	:	:	:	:	:	:	:
21	Pharmaceuticals, medicinal chemicals, etc.		:	:	:	:	:	:	:	:	:	:	:	:
22	Rubber and plastics products		:	:	:	:	:	:	:	:	:	:	:	:
23	Other non-metallic mineral products		117	123	129	122	91	100	106	101	97	95	94	100
24	Basic metals		110	113	104	100	77	100	104	99	97	103	105	110
25	Fabricated metal products, except machinery		113	123	133	139	97	100	106	102	95	95	93	94
26	Computer, electronic and optical products		:	:	:	:	:	:	:	:	:	:	:	:
27	Electrical equipment		:	:	:	:	:	:	:	:	:	:	:	:
28	Machinery and equipment n.e.c.		104	112	125	128	96	100	114	117	109	106	109	117
29	Motor vehicles, trailers and semi-trailers		:	:	:	:	:	:	:	:	:	:	:	:
30	Other transport equipment		:	:	:	:	:	:	:	:	:	:	:	:
31	Furniture		120	130	136	132	96	100	102	99	87	82	79	82
32	Other manufacturing		94	115	133	117	101	100	104	103	96	86	91	93
33	Repair and installation of machinery/equipment		103	116	120	122	99	100	104	105	94	90	94	92
C	Total manufacturing		102	111	117	120	95	100	103	101	97	96	95	97

France

Supplier of information:
Institut National de la Statistique et des Études Économiques, Paris.
Industrial statistics for the OECD countries are compiled by the OECD secretariat, which supplies them to UNIDO.

Basic source of data:
Annual survey; administrative data; business register.

Major deviations from ISIC (Revision 4):
Data presented in ISIC (Revision 4) were originally classified according to the national NACE-related classification system (Nomenclature d'Activités Française - NAF Revision 2).

Reference period:
Calendar year.

Scope:
All enterprises.

Method of data collection:
Not reported.

Type of enumeration:
Combination of survey and administrative data.

Adjusted for non-response:
Not reported.

Concepts and definitions of variables:
No deviations from the standard UN concepts and definitions are reported.

Related national publications:
None reported.

France

ISIC	Industry	Number of enterprises (number) 2013	2014a/	2015a/	2016	Number of employees (thousands) 2013	2014a/	2015a/	2016	Wages and salaries paid to employees (millions of Euros) 2013	2014a/	2015a/	2016
1010	Processing/preserving of meat	7970	8425	8399	6392	123.1	121.2	118.3	120.5	3349	3407	3390	3413
1020	Processing/preserving of fish, etc.	351	327	380	495	13.3	12.5	12.1	13.6	356	339	344	397
1030	Processing/preserving of fruit,vegetables	1360	1397	1282	1388	24.2	22.4	24.6	25.0	741	706	777	790
1040	Vegetable and animal oils and fats	235	277	320	244	3.5	3.5	4.1	3.9	153	154	169	167
1050	Dairy products	1273	1268	1316	1222	56.2	59.8	60.8	60.1	1855	2007	2045	2063
106	Grain mill products,starches and starch products	462	425	427	471	14.5	14.4	14.8	14.6	566	573	573	588
1061	Grain mill products	453	416	415	460	9.5	9.4	9.9	9.5	328	333	333	337
1062	Starches and starch products	9	9	11	11	5.0	4.9	4.9	5.1	237	240	241	251
107	Other food products	45399	46617	44280	45126	275.0	291.0	233.2	299.7	7174	7465	7549	7829
1071	Bakery products	40247	41108	38984	40354	191.0	206.6	148.4	216.5	4390	4610	4681	4951
1072	Sugar	23	38	45	33	4.5	7.3	7.0	6.2	181	281	284	294
1073	Cocoa, chocolate and sugar confectionery	1380	1430	1422	1340	24.0	21.2	20.3	19.3	762	694	674	645
1074	Macaroni, noodles, couscous, etc.	287	261	246	260	3.1	3.2	3.1	3.5	110	113	115	122
1075	Prepared meals and dishes	1581	1510	1307	1161	20.9	20.1	20.5	20.1	584	567	576	570
1079	Other food products n.e.c.	1881	2271	2277	1976	31.5	32.5	33.9	34.2	1147	1200	1220	1246
1080	Prepared animal feeds	428	436	455	474	18.9	18.7	20.9	17.8	733	729	726	726
110	Beverages	3125	3051	4113	3946	69.6	49.7	56.6	46.5	1915	1884	1983	1975
1101	Distilling, rectifying and blending of spirits	860	816	1027	941	8.2	8.4	8.7	8.8	373	360	376	389
1102	Wines	1630	1441	1947	1766	44.7	...	28.6	18.7	719	684	729	704
1103	Malt liquors and malt	440	578	863	973	4.1	...	4.1	4.4	213	223	205	188
1104	Soft drinks,mineral waters,other bottled waters	194	216	276	265	12.6	14.2	15.3	14.6	609	617	673	695
1200	Tobacco products	6	8	8	9	...	...	...	...	...	90	129	99
131	Spinning, weaving and finishing of textiles	1062	1168	913	1110	11.4	11.3	11.1	11.0	344	343	340	340
1311	Preparation and spinning of textile fibres	176	93	208	265	2.6	3.2	3.1	3.2	72	88	89	89
1312	Weaving of textiles	332	357	328	272	6.4	5.8	5.8	5.8	202	189	186	194
1313	Finishing of textiles	554	718	377	573	2.4	2.4	2.2	2.0	70	66	65	58
139	Other textiles	4261	5771	4809	5542	27.3	26.3	24.6	25.2	819	810	791	787
1391	Knitted and crocheted fabrics	146	181	143	155	0.8	0.9	0.9	0.9	22	26	27	28
1392	Made-up textile articles, except apparel	2586	3451	2965	3520	12.2	11.0	10.8	11.1	342	316	326	318
1393	Carpets and rugs	43	69	55	58	1.6	1.8	1.5	1.7	58	69	58	60
1394	Cordage, rope, twine and netting	109	140	123	128	0.8	0.6	0.6	0.6	22	18	18	19
1399	Other textiles n.e.c.	1378	1929	1523	1681	12.0	11.9	10.8	11.0	376	380	362	362
1410	Wearing apparel, except fur apparel	10761	10432	9259	10086	33.2	33.4	32.4	30.6	962	953	926	850
1420	Articles of fur	97	86	88	75	0.2	0.2	0.1	0.2	9	9	9	8
1430	Knitted and crocheted apparel	439	478	419	472	6.6	6.2	7.4	6.7	192	208	239	229
151	Leather;luggage,handbags,saddlery,harness;fur	1934	1900	1966	2373	20.5	21.0	...	21.5	587	618	682	680
1511	Tanning/dressing of leather; dressing of fur	131	91	114	117	2.0	1.9	2.0	2.0	61	58	62	61
1512	Luggage,handbags,etc.;saddlery/harness	1804	1809	1852	2257	18.5	19.1	...	19.6	527	560	620	619
1520	Footwear	359	384	352	292	5.7	5.3	...	5.0	...	152	156	139
1610	Sawmilling and planing of wood	3000	3247	2931	3033	16.9	17.8	16.7	16.8	492	516	522	534

Code	Description												
162	Wood products, cork, straw, plaiting materials	8822	7706	7097	6291	45.2	43.6	40.4	37.6	1314	1283	1210	1156
1621	Veneer sheets and wood-based panels	113	124	104	81	5.8	5.5	5.3	5.1	175	181	171	166
1622	Builders' carpentry and joinery	4805	3155	2927	2443	21.9	21.0	18.9	17.2	642	610	568	532
1623	Wooden containers	874	845	902	754	13.4	13.2	12.6	11.9	372	372	358	349
1629	Other wood products;articles of cork,straw	3030	3581	3164	3013	4.1	4.0	3.6	3.4	125	120	113	110
170	Paper and paper products	1724	1889	1425	1638	65.5	64.6	64.4	64.1	2306	2280	2327	2306
1701	Pulp, paper and paperboard	140	130	147	113	16.0	15.6	16.3	15.2	654	631	693	658
1702	Corrugated paper and paperboard	684	679	494	593	30.4	29.7	29.0	29.6	987	977	965	974
1709	Other articles of paper and paperboard	900	1080	784	933	19.2	19.3	19.2	19.4	665	672	668	674
181	Printing and service activities related to printing	19065	21320	17920	17256	59.1	57.1	54.7	53.8	1997	1945	1970b/	1831
1811	Printing	5556	5775	5341	5231	44.1	42.6	41.2	40.1	1473	1436	...	1349
1812	Service activities related to printing	13509	15546	12578	12025	15.0	14.5	13.5	13.8	523	509	498	482
1820	Reproduction of recorded media	333	455	313	325	1.2	1.0	1.1	0.4	38	28	...b/	11
1910	Coke oven products	-	-	1	1	-	-	-	-	-	-	-	-
1920	Refined petroleum products	56	50	42	36	...	...	...	...	720	548	1040	1049
201	Basic chemicals,fertilizers, etc.	760	802	654	588	66.2	54.6	52.1	52.4	3330	2683	2552	2677
2011	Basic chemicals	437	459	370	339	49.3	38.2	35.0	35.4	2538	1909	1746	1829
2012	Fertilizers and nitrogen compounds	124	133	106	93	4.7	4.6	4.5	4.5	194	198	194	195
2013	Plastics and synthetic rubber in primary forms	199	210	178	157	12.2	11.8	12.6	12.6	598	575	613	653
202	Other chemical products	2134	2023	2501	2441	79.1	89.8	95.1	92.0	3227	4066	4225	4248
2021	Pesticides and other agrochemical products	79	43	65	89	5.8	5.8	9.8	6.4	317	331	333	336
2022	Paints,varnishes;printing ink and mastics	300	203	271	274	13.9	11.8	11.1	12.3	555	472	452	497
2023	Soap,cleaning and cosmetic preparations	1146	1228	1534	1523	38.2	50.7	52.5	52.2	1476	2344	2515	2451
2029	Other chemical products n.e.c.	609	548	631	556	21.2	21.5	21.7	21.0	878	919	926	964
2030	Man-made fibres	23	15	14	13	0.7	0.7	0.7	0.7	23	24	23	22
2100	Pharmaceuticals,medicinal chemicals, etc.	390	347	335	644	79.0	88.8	...	...	3887	4828	4547	4761
221	Rubber products	355	638	665	482	48.9	46.0	37.8	37.4	1883	1795	1545	1559
2211	Rubber tyres and tubes	54	78	79	57	26.4	24.7	24.3	23.8	1101	1060	1071	1082
2219	Other rubber products	302	560	586	424	22.5	21.3	13.6	13.5	782	735	474	477
2220	Plastics products	3589	3517	3462	3565	112.0	109.1	108.3	108.2	3642	3590	3663	3731
2310	Glass and glass products	1489	1633	1449	1503	39.9	38.0	38.1	36.9	1391	1329	1367	1353
239	Non-metallic mineral products n.e.c.	7826	8250	6773	7980	75.5	74.9	71.2	70.3	2715	2743	2640	2641
2391	Refractory products	64	67	55	53	2.4	3.8	3.7	3.4	99	162	158	155
2392	Clay building materials	147	168	201	232	7.3	6.5	6.3	6.4	229	223	217	220
2393	Other porcelain and ceramic products	2588	3008	2529	2910	6.8	6.0	5.5	5.3	199	190	174	171
2394	Cement, lime and plaster	56	38	47	49	5.9	6.1	6.6	5.7	290	299	298	304
2395	Articles of concrete, cement and plaster	1441	1423	1093	1280	35.2	38.7	37.0	35.4	1220	1397	1359	1321
2396	Cutting, shaping and finishing of stone	3054	3273	2483	2694	7.6	8.3	6.5	8.8	229	266	214	256
2399	Other non-metallic mineral products n.e.c.	475	271	365	763	10.4	5.4	5.6	5.3	450	205	221	214
2410	Basic iron and steel	415	474	373	413	40.0	38.4	38.8	37.1	1592	1675	1618	1575
2420	Basic precious and other non-ferrous metals	198	176	190	176	14.7	19.1	18.1	20.2	591	931	931	923
243	Casting of metals	438	436	358	320	23.3	19.7	19.3	18.7	734	620	600	585
2431	Casting of iron and steel	135	115	92	83	13.9	9.8	9.9	9.4	446	307	307	299
2432	Casting of non-ferrous metals	303	322	267	237	9.4	9.9	9.4	9.4	288	313	293	286
251	Struct.metal products, tanks, reservoirs	5679	5944	6280	6240	...	...	...	...	...	...	...	...

continued

France

ISIC	Industry	Number of enterprises (number)				Number of employees (thousands)				Wages and salaries paid to employees (millions of Euros)			
		2013	2014a/	2015a/	2016	2013	2014a/	2015a/	2016	2013	2014a/	2015a/	2016
2511	Structural metal products	5485	5767	6086	6067	75.6	76.4	75.0	73.5	2350	2402	2458	2420
2512	Tanks, reservoirs and containers of metal	142	124	156	137	8.8	8.0	8.8	8.9	...	273	303	...
2513	Steam generators, excl. hot water boilers	52	53	38	36	...	...	...	...	...	...	...	...
2520	Weapons and ammunition	173	45	108	132	...	...	...	...	379	...	...	413
259	Other metal products;metal working services	15435	15486	13103	14726	216.6	211.4	210.5	203.5	7120	7119	7169	6983
2591	Forging,pressing,stamping,roll-forming of metal	1637	1718	1724	1874	41.0	40.8	40.8	39.7	1301	1347	1325	1314
2592	Treatment and coating of metals;machining	9853	9474	8326	8545	104.6	101.8	101.1	97.4	3444	3410	3460	3308
2593	Cutlery, hand tools and general hardware	1815	1960	1333	2473	24.4	23.9	23.6	22.3	813	821	823	805
2599	Other fabricated metal products n.e.c.	2131	2334	1721	1833	46.6	44.8	45.0	44.2	1562	1541	1561	1556
2610	Electronic components and boards	840	806	899	805	45.6	42.6	46.0	43.7	1866	1743	1770	...
2620	Computers and peripheral equipment	273	283	226	227	5.4	5.7	5.1	...	255	261	...	237
2630	Communication equipment	345	366	283	272	16.3	15.7	16.1	16.3	1348	873	912	...
2640	Consumer electronics	230	184	277	317	...	...	1.6	...	58	57	62	53
265	Measuring,testing equipment; watches, etc.	965	938	1074	814	53.3	52.4	55.8	51.7	2583	2617	2696	2623
2651	Measuring/testing/navigating equipment,etc.	804	759	881	655	51.7	50.7	54.2	49.8	2527	2559	2639	2556
2652	Watches and clocks	161	180	194	159	1.7	1.7	1.6	1.9	56	58	56	67
2660	Irradiation/electromedical equipment,etc.	...	99	117	268	4.8	5.0	5.0	4.9	285	310	318	314
2670	Optical instruments and photographic equipment	147	147	135	103	2.0	1.9	2.1	2.2	...	77	...	93
2680	Magnetic and optical media	...	11	10	11	...	...	0.1	...	...	2	...	...
2710	Electric motors,generators,transformers,etc.	621	621	697	712	44.8	45.8	46.7	45.4	1772	1865	1923	1913
2720	Batteries and accumulators	36	31	24	30	4.0	3.7	3.7	2.3	162	153	156	97
273	Wiring and wiring devices	261	308	145	187	23.1	25.0	25.5	24.3	895	1009	1047	1023
2731	Fibre optic cables	7	16	7	10	1.4	1.5	1.4	1.3	70	76	81	85
2732	Other electronic and electric wires and cables	91	126	61	76	9.4	10.0	10.1	9.8	349	390	399	390
2733	Wiring devices	163	167	77	101	12.3	13.5	13.9	13.2	475	543	567	548
2740	Electric lighting equipment	843	1116	843	933	15.9	10.4	10.6	10.4	634	371	378	390
2750	Domestic appliances	150	159	167	115	15.5	13.7	13.3	14.1	563	557	513	568
2790	Other electrical equipment	466	381	188	323	11.0	9.1	9.2	9.8	389	327	326	356
281	General-purpose machinery	2862	2561	2193	2310	121.6	119.3	120.4	116.2	4762	4703	4957	4963
2811	Engines/turbines,excl.aircraft,vehicle engines	109	98	78	87	11.5	9.3	7.9	8.7	559	423	375	389
2812	Fluid power equipment	252	279	227	267	8.9	8.9	8.1	8.0	337	355	340	338
2813	Other pumps, compressors, taps and valves	278	292	244	278	25.0	26.4	30.1	28.0	982	1053	1333	1341
2814	Bearings, gears, gearing and driving elements	88	111	96	108	11.5	12.0	12.1	11.7	428	453	455	463
2815	Ovens, furnaces and furnace burners	94	76	61	60	3.5	3.4	3.0	2.6	159	157	143	139
2816	Lifting and handling equipment	642	454	403	410	21.9	20.6	20.5	20.4	808	769	806	810
2817	Office machinery, excl.computers,etc.	44	19	13	15	1.5	1.4	1.3	1.2	51	51	50	47
2818	Power-driven hand tools	12	10	8	7	0.7	0.5	0.5	0.4	29	17	17	17
2819	Other general-purpose machinery	1343	1223	1062	1077	37.0	36.7	36.9	35.1	1409	1424	1438	1419
282	Special-purpose machinery	2136	2167	2025	1929	57.4	56.2	58.2	56.3	2172	2141	2255	2165
2821	Agricultural and forestry machinery	512	514	385	546	16.8	16.9	16.9	17.3	553	566	575	577
2822	Metal-forming machinery and machine tools	393	382	387	301	6.7	6.5	6.6	6.3	259	258	254	248

Code	Description												
2823	Machinery for metallurgy	32	61	56	63	0.9	1.4	1.4	1.4	19	25	33	24
2824	Mining, quarrying and construction machinery	293	326	320	321	7.2	7.7	7.8	8.0	106	125	118	127
2825	Food/beverage/tobacco processing machinery	347	351	343	313	9.5	9.8	9.5	8.9	342	409	430	387
2826	Textile/apparel/leather production machinery	153	152	144	141	3.3	3.3	3.2	3.2	57	72	84	87
2829	Other special-purpose machinery	515	536	453	523	11.9	12.5	10.9	12.2	559	624	607	607
2910	Motor vehicles	5097	5186	5355	5668	111.3	119.0	122.6	129.6	171	114	171	208
2920	Automobile bodies, trailers and semi-trailers	737	707	701	706	23.6	22.9	23.2	24.0	1072	991	1106	1110
2930	Parts and accessories for motor vehicles	3227	3186	3249	2954	78.2	81.3	84.3	80.4	681	612	764	629
301	Building of ships and boats	...	895	857	823	21.9	21.5	21.5	21.1	449	500	539	513
3011	Building of ships and floating structures	689	689	660	625	14.8	14.6	14.5	14.2	145	160	163	132
3012	Building of pleasure and sporting boats	210	206	197	198	7.1	6.9	6.9	6.9	304	340	376	382
3020	Railway locomotives and rolling stock	...	719	713	720	13.0	14.1	14.8	15.0	39	42	39	28
3030	Air and spacecraft and related machinery	6787	...	5575	4906	119.7	...	110.9	99.2	172	224	203	225
3040	Military fighting vehicles	...	...	118	115	0.5	...	2.2	2.3	4	5	5	5
309	Transport equipment n.e.c.	120	129	122	121	3.3	...	3.6	3.3	232	302	240	263
3091	Motorcycles	47	54	54	48	1.2	...	1.5	1.2	88	111	86	84
3092	Bicycles and invalid carriages	65	69	64	67	1.8	2.0	1.9	1.9	116	157	118	120
3099	Other transport equipment n.e.c.	8	6	4	7	0.2	0.2	0.1	0.2	27	34	35	59
3100	Furniture	1251	1351	1415	1399	39.5	41.6	44.8	45.9	8513	9252	9223	12423
321	Jewellery, bijouterie and related articles	308	299	319	282	8.3	7.9	9.2	8.0	9282	8348	11303	9125
3211	Jewellery and related articles	...	...	245	282c/	8.3c/	7.9c/	6.9	5.9	9282c/	...	3021	2792
3212	Imitation jewellery and related articles	75	76	74	...c/	...c/	...c/	2.3	2.1	...c/	5855	8282	6333
3220	Musical instruments	55	64	49	57	1.5	1.6	1.5	1.7	1024	1436	969	1044
3230	Sports goods	149	152	152	153	3.9	4.2	4.2	4.3	367	656	615	553
3240	Games and toys	59	56	57	51	1.8	1.8	1.9	1.7	787	672	960	758
3250	Medical and dental instruments and supplies	1930	1878	1832	1773	48.3	46.4	48.0	47.1	7057	7482	7665	7491
3290	Other manufacturing n.e.c.	285	287	293	318	8.1	8.3	8.9	9.2	3367	3324	4030	4053
331	Repair of fabricated metal products/machinery	3885	4521	5119	4630	98.5	116.4	136.8	110.9	17278	16539	19931	16686
3311	Repair of fabricated metal products	980	862	797	720	23.3	22.8	22.3	19.5	1307	1292	1616	1343
3312	Repair of machinery	1757	1666	1588	2235	45.3	42.2	41.0	50.7	9892	9407	11135	8800
3313	Repair of electronic and optical equipment	264	259	278	310	5.8	6.5	...	7.0	654	619	717	641
3314	Repair of electrical equipment	315	354	383	580	8.7	8.6	10.0	13.8	1419	1362	1653	1661
3315	Repair of transport equip., excl. motor vehicles	525	1336	2025	729	14.0	...	...	18.2	3364	3256	4043	3648
3319	Repair of other equipment	44	44	48	56	1.4	1.3	1.5	1.7	641	603	769	593
3320	Installation of industrial machinery/equipment	2754	2899	3157	2982	68.9	69.2	79.2	78.2	8681	8721	10246	9540
C	Total manufacturing	108526	108421	108176	105985	2812.8	2815.4	2905.6	2903.7	216049	213303	235092	226372

a/ Methodological break.
b/ 181 includes 1820.
c/ 3211 includes 3212.

France

ISIC	Industry	Output (valuation not defined) (millions of Euros)				Value added at factor values (millions of Euros)				Gross fixed capital formation (millions of Euros)	
		2013	2014a/	2015a/	2016	2013	2014a/	2015a/	2016	2015a/	2016
1010	Processing/preserving of meat	32740	34227	33436	32481	5557	6009	5934	5739	906	867
1020	Processing/preserving of fish, etc.	3172	3195	3303	3775	604	599	625	652	97	92
1030	Processing/preserving of fruit,vegetables	6939	6598	7188	7400	1459	1454	1619	1567	368	294
1040	Vegetable and animal oils and fats	5020	4854	5457	5602	367	427	356	270	87	99
1050	Dairy products	28333	30614	28518	27421	3914	4512	4711	4612	1076	1122
106	Grain mill products,starches and starch products	7196	6974	6734	6818	1147	1226	1237	1381	226	233
1061	Grain mill products	4024	3923	3768	3820	628	645	634	682	151	137
1062	Starches and starch products	3172	3051	2966	2999	519	581	603	699	76	97
107	Other food products	42697	46503	46508	46050	13974	14260	14115	14593	2239	2505
1071	Bakery products	18551	20886	21228	21601	7639	8080	8146	8479	1168	1326
1072	Sugar	2517	3694	3201	3502	727	826	561	726	256	266
1073	Cocoa, chocolate and sugar confectionery	6766	5594	5677	4509	1717	1446	1460	1348	186	201
1074	Macaroni, noodles, couscous, etc.	887	1046	1079	1001	256	229	229	206	76	82
1075	Prepared meals and dishes	4366	4448	4629	4622	980	982	1024	1026	140	155
1079	Other food products n.e.c.	9610	10836	10695	10816	2656	2696	2695	2808	413	474
1080	Prepared animal feeds	11460	11885	11349	10583	1531	1660	1644	1621	319	350
110	Beverages	25196	26123	27723	28334	6321	6028	6371	6556	1312	1016
1101	Distilling, rectifying and blending of spirits	4732	5036	5289	5626	1680	1521	1747	1795	222	247
1102	Wines	10413	10020	10741	10782	2539	2161	2192	2216	591	267
1103	Malt liquors and malt	3056	3514	3327	2675	698	745	658	601	176	150
1104	Soft drinks,mineral waters,other bottled waters	6995	7553	8367	9250	1405	1601	1775	1945	323	352
1200	Tobacco products	...	1198	1103	1142	...	537	417	575	...	...
131	Spinning, weaving and finishing of textiles	2105	2199	2240	2240	581	439	587	565	72	84
1311	Preparation and spinning of textile fibres	476	613	674	703	153	149	162	146	28	34
1312	Weaving of textiles	1357	1300	1313	1312	334	331	334	330	30	34
1313	Finishing of textiles	272	285	253	225	95	-42	91	88	14	16
139	Other textiles	4337	4597	4633	4589	1373	1371	1396	1406	153	185
1391	Knitted and crocheted fabrics	145	156	149	146	29	36	38	39	4	6
1392	Made-up textile articles, except apparel	1538	1568	1653	1586	526	486	520	509	36	42
1393	Carpets and rugs	335	383	439	423	82	90	107	108	20	23
1394	Cordage, rope, twine and netting	120	126	92	92	35	36	30	30	2	4
1399	Other textiles n.e.c.	2199	2363	2301	2342	701	724	700	721	92	110
1410	Wearing apparel, except fur apparel	4828	6730	5716	4913	1615	1826	1588	1307	110	107
1420	Articles of fur	57	58	65	70	17	20	20	22	1	1
1430	Knitted and crocheted apparel	816	1038	1194	1126	337	360	427	400	21	24
151	Leather;luggage,handbags,saddlery,harness;fur	3180	3907	4216	4876	1588	1732	1850	1994	101	163
1511	Tanning/dressing of leather; dressing of fur	548	509	492	532	116	95	93	108	18	36
1512	Luggage,handbags,etc.;saddlery/harness	2633	3398	3724	4344	1473	1637	1757	1886	83	127
1520	Footwear	...	865	738	669	...	254	227	189	14	21
1610	Sawmilling and planing of wood	3145	3596	3622	3919	829	899	842	930	187	207

Code	Description										
162	Wood products, cork, straw, plaiting materials	385	308	2002	2031	2114	2095	7343	7437	7866	7434
1621	Veneer sheets and wood-based panels	164	108	331	334	290	270	1604	1645	1647	1509
1622	Builders' carpentry and joinery	119	105	833	845	928	975	2772	2848	3202	3092
1623	Wooden containers	67	61	637	653	684	623	2227	2224	2281	2163
1629	Other wood products;articles of cork,straw	35	34	201	199	212	226	740	720	738	670
170	Paper and paper products	…	968	4266	4101	4037	3939	16836	17147	16756	16578
1701	Pulp, paper and paperboard	…	274	1231	1219	1120	1086	6160	6493	6167	6254
1702	Corrugated paper and paperboard	…	340	1678	1599	1610	1604	6190	6146	6063	5990
1709	Other articles of paper and paperboard	…	354	1357	1284	1307	1250	4486	4508	4527	4334
181	Printing and service activities related to printing	…	335	3088	3098b/	3135	3164	8626	8727b/	8715	8713
1811	Printing	274	270	2214	…	2274	2268	6644	…	6751	6735
1812	Service activities related to printing	…	65	874	839	860	896	1982	1944	1964	1978
1820	Reproduction of recorded media	…	-	15	…b/	32	48	52	…b/	119	177
1910	Coke oven products	-	…	-1	-2	-	-	-	-	-	-
1920	Refined petroleum products	…	…	3026	2106	-264	535	32094	36728	44645	52430
201	Basic chemicals,fertilizers, etc.	1658	1442	6735	6626	6007	6922	27379	28105	36029	39636
2011	Basic chemicals	932	949	4488	4482	4704	5605	16389	16789	25044	28154
2012	Fertilizers and nitrogen compounds	186	126	353	371	329	349	1880	2356	2288	2297
2013	Plastics and synthetic rubber in primary forms	540	367	1894	1773	974	968	9106	8960	8698	9185
202	Other chemical products	1180	1435	10467	10150	9504	7360	35654	35206	33269	28879
2021	Pesticides and other agrochemical products	122	87	777	750	750	728	3505	3587	3594	3226
2022	Paints,varnishes;printing ink and mastics	100	83	1046	881	913	1035	3498	3122	3259	3525
2023	Soap,cleaning and cosmetic preparations	669	939	6069	6063	5560	3406	19913	19961	18187	12319
2029	Other chemical products n.e.c.	288	326	2575	2456	2280	2191	8738	8536	8229	9809
2030	Man-made fibres	99	46	28	27	39	37	108	124	144	138
2100	Pharmaceuticals,medicinal chemicals, etc.	1457	1234	11260	10107	9439	9518	35756	35238	31525	27666
221	Rubber products	705	756	2888	2858	3310	3515	6553	6624	8092	8634
2211	Rubber tyres and tubes	705c/	756c/	2063	2050	2015	2118	4303	4378	4561	4942
2219	Other rubber products	…c/	…c/	826	808	1294	1396	2251	2246	3531	3693
2220	Plastics products	983	1079	6921	6761	6441	6433	22833	22467	21860	21339
2310	Glass and glass products	567	593	2322	2326	2359	2493	6753	6781	6638	6476
239	Non-metallic mineral products n.e.c.	900	871	5174	5100	5584	5397	18763	18847	20742	19926
2391	Refractory products	25	23	260	257	250	152	854	860	840	479
2392	Clay building materials	110	87	512	500	504	532	1162	1159	1220	1180
2393	Other porcelain and ceramic products	41	25	250	254	420	262	686	718	1392	719
2394	Cement, lime and plaster	153	139	968	938	985	970	2788	2828	3011	2874
2395	Articles of concrete, cement and plaster	…	…	2311	2306	2545	2284	10169	10160	10902	9611
2396	Cutting, shaping and finishing of stone	45	29	431	327	403	393	1006	766	934	852
2399	Other non-metallic mineral products n.e.c.	85	127	442	519	476	804	2098	2357	2444	4209
2410	Basic iron and steel	…	…	2558	2664	2702	2366	14001	15285	16560	16168
2420	Basic precious and other non-ferrous metals	773	363	1998	1948	1853	1447	8054	8403	7829	7234
243	Casting of metals	146	132	914	897	971	1133	2716	2826	3005	3625
2431	Casting of iron and steel	74	75	463	454	468	686	1341	1412	1523	2265
2432	Casting of non-ferrous metals	72	57	451	443	503	447	1375	1414	1482	1361
251	Struct.metal products, tanks, reservoirs	…	…	…	…	…	…	…	…	…	…

continued

France

ISIC	Industry	Note	Output (valuation not defined) (millions of Euros)				Note	Value added at factor values (millions of Euros)				Note	Gross fixed capital formation (millions of Euros)	
			2013	2014a/	2015a/	2016		2013	2014a/	2015a/	2016		2015a/	2016
2511	Structural metal products		12557	12463	12726	13011		4048	3962	4075	4131		342	404
2512	Tanks, reservoirs and containers of metal		...	1821	2024	...		...	586	639	...		102	82
2513	Steam generators, excl. hot water boilers												...	...
2520	Weapons and ammunition		2315	...	...	2480		849	...	...	853		...	...
259	Other metal products;metal working services		32944	34000	34092	33753		12154	12132	12375	12304		1646	1777
2591	Forging,pressing,stamping,roll-forming of metal		7325	7884	7708	7574		2183	2257	2249	2257		316	367
2592	Treatment and coating of metals;machining		13891	13944	14146	13975		5783	5772	5794	5643		821	764
2593	Cutlery, hand tools and general hardware		2986	3140	3176	3214		1330	1338	1362	1386		124	148
2599	Other fabricated metal products n.e.c.		8743	9033	9062	8991		2857	2766	2970	3016		385	498
2610	Electronic components and boards		9098	8675	9142	...		3002	2805	2896	...		276	336
2620	Computers and peripheral equipment		1695	1766	...	1311		418	425	...	334		108	19
2630	Communication equipment		7540	4144	4572	...		900	1401	1497	...		68	54
2640	Consumer electronics		400	434	415	338		128	106	133	121		7	8
265	Measuring,testing equipment; watches, etc.		11050	11814	11992	12308		4638	4768	4853	4984		366	344
2651	Measuring/testing/navigating equipment,etc.		10844	11607	11801	12073		4553	4687	4776	4887		360	337
2652	Watches and clocks		206	206	192	236		85	81	77	96		6	6
2660	Irradiation/electromedical equipment,etc.		1589	1943	2277	2389		526	534	589	606		36	30
2670	Optical instruments and photographic equipment		...	356	...	431		...	135	...	162		16	13
2680	Magnetic and optical media		...	12	...	...		...	3	...	...		1	-
2710	Electric motors,generators,transformers,etc.		9150	10248	10323	10106		2951	3033	3017	2977		353	541
2720	Batteries and accumulators		766	890	956	721		231	273	305	206		45	59
273	Wiring and wiring devices		6548	6950	6778	6777		1678	1958	1993	2058		157	169
2731	Fibre optic cables		472	520	706	892		109	110	140	181		14	20
2732	Other electronic and electric wires and cables		3820	3693	3435	3378		608	644	638	701		61	70
2733	Wiring devices		2256	2738	2637	2508		961	1204	1215	1175		82	79
2740	Electric lighting equipment		2689	1927	1929	2048		1105	711	727	725		64	63
2750	Domestic appliances		3122	3371	3130	3604		1019	990	960	1066		123	177
2790	Other electrical equipment		2074	1558	1549	1744		682	557	538	593		52	54
281	General-purpose machinery		26506	29359	29482	29377		8619	9196	9188	8979		882	802
2811	Engines/turbines,excl.aircraft,vehicle engines		2922	3606	2168	2307		641	880	536	680		58	82
2812	Fluid power equipment		1759	1932	1820	1724		643	674	633	620		52	36
2813	Other pumps, compressors, taps and valves		5810	6758	8756	8287		2100	2352	2745	2474		371	283
2814	Bearings, gears, gearing and driving elements		1992	2483	2473	2640		790	820	791	839		111	103
2815	Ovens, furnaces and furnace burners		993	1092	817	740		282	318	233	233		8	10
2816	Lifting and handling equipment		4921	5061	5017	5117		1428	1425	1487	1381		88	92
2817	Office machinery, excl.computers,etc.		333	347	337	320		115	113	119	118		7	15
2818	Power-driven hand tools		113	85	81	85		58	32	31	37		3	1
2819	Other general-purpose machinery		7663	7995	8013	8157		2561	2583	2615	2596		184	179
282	Special-purpose machinery		12767	12940	13493	13472		3948	3715	3856	3879		303	360
2821	Agricultural and forestry machinery		4620	4569	4239	4421		1103	1031	948	1030		102	120
2822	Metal-forming machinery and machine tools		1210	1164	1258	1268		441	376	418	426		33	55

Code	Description										
2823	Machinery for metallurgy	404	321	305	137	91	92	70	41	5	5
2824	Mining, quarrying and construction machinery	1705	1763	1771	1585	604	548	554	479	46	41
2825	Food/beverage/tobacco processing machinery	1469	1733	1782	1785	552	614	610	645	40	48
2826	Textile/apparel/leather production machinery	861	865	964	1079	291	305	343	391	25	34
2829	Other special-purpose machinery	2497	2525	3175	3198	867	749	912	867	51	58
2910	Motor vehicles	34034	47725	52447	57057	7455	8886	10551	11012	1959	2182
2920	Automobile bodies, trailers and semi-trailers	3807	3874	3998	4415	1086	1072	1129	1259	125	123
2930	Parts and accessories for motor vehicles	17698	20072	21358	22414	4473	5017	5361	5757	856	811
301	Building of ships and boats	5233	5289	5718	...	1533	1366	1500	...	295	...
3011	Building of ships and floating structures	4340	4307	4599	...	1232	1049	1110	...	155	...
3012	Building of pleasure and sporting boats	893	982	1120	1246	301	317	390	424	139	130
3020	Railway locomotives and rolling stock	3933	4605	3920	...	987	1232	1157	...	129	...
3030	Air and spacecraft and related machinery	37461	41308	...	100416	10223	12193	...	15109	...	1813
3040	Military fighting vehicles	745	802	...	...	270	290	...	...	...	9
309	Transport equipment n.e.c.	731	819	885	880	159	181	199	183	20	31
3091	Motorcycles	271	364	382	410	27	46	60	62	10	15
3092	Bicycles and invalid carriages	418	432	458	423	120	130	129	109	10	15
3099	Other transport equipment n.e.c.	42	22	44	47	12	5	10	12	1	1
3100	Furniture	6685	7094	7003	6557	2174	2133	2201	2054	209	243
321	Jewellery, bijouterie and related articles	1546	2223	1813	1941	527	771	634	669	72	90
3211	Jewellery and related articles	1546d/	1688	...	...	527d/	557	...	...	...	...
3212	Imitation jewellery and related articles	...d/	536	408	447	...d/	214	153	177	27	35
3220	Musical instruments	188	207	237	218	102	102	125	113	16	19
3230	Sports goods	754	804	798	898	274	259	279	350	29	35
3240	Games and toys	289	366	518	389	97	113	162	81	17	25
3250	Medical and dental instruments and supplies	6531	7895	8107	8724	3490	3542	3531	3924	346	391
3290	Other manufacturing n.e.c.	1338	1450	1411	1652	563	552	546	534	97	157
331	Repair of fabricated metal products/machinery	15173	17283	17430	15221	7752	8628	8161	6649	1001	570
3311	Repair of fabricated metal products	2598	2997	3223	3838	1112	1189	1331	1654	81	84
3312	Repair of machinery	5929	5993	6091	6298	3671	2631	2827	2922	202	250
3313	Repair of electronic and optical equipment	1124	1191	891	954	642	540	448	487	13	24
3314	Repair of electrical equipment	1900	1440	1254	1200	958	694	607	609	19	20
3315	Repair of transport equip., excl. motor vehicles	3455	5488	5788	2760	1286	3496	2873	902	...	185
3319	Repair of other equipment	167	173	185	172	84	78	76	75	6	6
3320	Installation of industrial machinery/equipment	12537	14208	12954	12702	4882	4948	4628	4650	210	209
C	Total manufacturing	743808	783988	781094	833139	192889	201020	208142	213732	30032	31057

a/ Methodological break.
b/ 181 includes 1820.
c/ 2211 includes 2219.
d/ 3211 includes 3212.

France

Index numbers of industrial production
(2010=100)

ISIC Revision 4

ISIC	Industry	Note	2005	2006	2007	2008	2009	2010	2011	2012	2013	2014	2015	2016
10	Food products		99	98	100	100	99	100	103	103	100	100	101	100
11	Beverages		96	100	100	96	94	100	104	104	100	106	110	110
12	Tobacco products		105	100	105	108	98	100	97	101	83	46	32	28
13	Textiles		164	147	141	125	95	100	99	99	99	100	103	100
14	Wearing apparel		287	254	227	168	114	100	100	98	86	89	82	82
15	Leather and related products		156	141	108	100	91	100	106	110	98	100	98	95
16	Wood products, excluding furniture		127	131	131	123	104	100	103	95	92	87	86	85
17	Paper and paper products		116	114	114	108	98	100	96	89	87	83	82	80
18	Printing and reproduction of recorded media		127	122	120	111	102	100	98	92	89	93	90	90
19	Coke and refined petroleum products		130	127	126	129	111	100	100	87	86	84	88	87
20	Chemicals and chemical products		104	104	110	107	93	100	106	104	107	111	115	117
21	Pharmaceuticals, medicinal chemicals, etc.		99	101	102	101	102	100	96	101	101	97	114	112
22	Rubber and plastics products		122	120	121	112	94	100	104	98	96	95	100	103
23	Other non-metallic mineral products		120	121	125	119	96	100	110	98	96	93	89	90
24	Basic metals		130	134	132	125	88	100	103	94	92	94	89	85
25	Fabricated metal products, except machinery		122	126	129	121	94	100	106	101	97	95	97	98
26	Computer, electronic and optical products		119	123	119	115	99	100	101	96	100	97	104	103
27	Electrical equipment		108	116	121	120	95	100	103	98	97	91	88	89
28	Machinery and equipment n.e.c.		128	135	142	143	96	100	107	106	101	104	103	103
29	Motor vehicles, trailers and semi-trailers		145	132	132	116	88	100	105	93	87	90	97	101
30	Other transport equipment		84	93	97	100	96	100	105	108	119	118	117	122
31	Furniture		134	132	132	123	102	100	102	96	93	88	89	91
32	Other manufacturing		98	103	97	102	96	100	98	94	95	101	100	104
33	Repair and installation of machinery/equipment		95	99	104	105	94	100	105	106	104	105	104	102
C	Total manufacturing		114	115	116	112	96	100	103	101	100	99	101	102

Georgia

Supplier of information:
National Statistics Office of Georgia (GEOSTAT), Tbilisi.

Basic source of data:
Survey.

Major deviations from ISIC (Revision 4):
Data presented in ISIC (Revision 4) were originally classified according to NACE Rev. 2.

Reference period:
Calendar year.

Scope:
All enterprises.

Method of data collection:
Mail questionnaires, direct interviews in the field and on-line survey (self entry).

Type of enumeration:
Sample survey.

Adjusted for non-response:
Yes.

Concepts and definitions of variables:
None reported.

Related national publications:
Entrepreneurship in Georgia; Statistical Yearbook, both published by National Statistics Office of Georgia, Tbilisi.

Georgia

ISIC Revision 4 — Number of enterprises (number), Number of employees (number), Wages and salaries paid to employees (thousands of Georgian Lari)

ISIC	Industry	Ent. Note	Ent. 2013	Ent. 2014	Ent. 2015	Ent. 2016	Emp. Note	Emp. 2013	Emp. 2014	Emp. 2015	Emp. 2016	Wage Note	Wage 2013	Wage 2014	Wage 2015	Wage 2016
1010	Processing/preserving of meat		164	222	203	240		2824	2936	2620	3457		23430	26665	23606	31529
1020	Processing/preserving of fish, etc.		28	38	44	40		231	266	260	298		1955	2036	2695	2875
1030	Processing/preserving of fruit,vegetables		167	182	182	245		2227	2565	3252	3525		8627	9811	12881	15016
1040	Vegetable and animal oils and fats		14	10	12	18		163	147	172	149		959	903	1178	943
1050	Dairy products		85	103	113	139		2104	2251	2357	2657		21098	24913	30600	31508
106	Grain mill products,starches and starch products		94	100	97	117		2190	2286	2149	2199		17078	18394	19719	19420
1061	Grain mill products		91	98	95	115		...	...	...	...		...	...	...	...
1062	Starches and starch products		3	2	2	2		...	...	...	...		...	...	...	...
107	Other food products		1531	2021	2115	2279		9124	10494	9681	11235		45485	56248	55604	65249
1071	Bakery products		1332	1792	1887	2036		7135	7817	7018	8892		30742	36446	36246	48197
1072	Sugar		4	4	4	5		...	...	...	...		...	...	...	...
1073	Cocoa, chocolate and sugar confectionery		17	27	15	22		446	465	495	523		5322	5534	5546	5414
1074	Macaroni, noodles, couscous, etc.		57	65	72	71		439	398	542	412		1874	1608	2253	1704
1075	Prepared meals and dishes		3	3	4	5		...	...	...	...		...	...	...	...
1079	Other food products n.e.c.		118	130	133	140		545	710	810	749		308	5841	3982	4117
1080	Prepared animal feeds		11	12	15	16		147	130	163	190		1202	1312	1914	2320
110	Beverages		344	410	414	460		9499	10259	9882	10426		95684	113293	125554	132121
1101	Distilling, rectifying and blending of spirits		39	52	53	54		727	819	1026	883		6216	9398	11034	8870
1102	Wines		175	217	214	258		4644	4972	4587	5221		32383	38423	41741	49471
1103	Malt liquors and malt		18	25	23	23		1602	1540	1547	1661		23723	24391	28188	28309
1104	Soft drinks,mineral waters,other bottled waters		112	116	124	125		2526	2928	2722	2661		33362	41081	44591	45471
1200	Tobacco products		12	12	9	10		431	425	430	346		4794	5798	6604	4807
131	Spinning, weaving and finishing of textiles		14	29	27	32		...	...	...	...		...	...	...	...
1311	Preparation and spinning of textile fibres		7	18	15	16		...	...	...	...		...	...	...	...
1312	Weaving of textiles		4	5	6	8		...	...	...	...		...	...	...	...
1313	Finishing of textiles		3	6	6	8		...	...	...	...		...	...	...	...
139	Other textiles		40	47	50	70		...	...	...	...		...	...	...	...
1391	Knitted and crocheted fabrics		...	...	...	...		...	...	...	...		...	...	...	...
1392	Made-up textile articles, except apparel		32	38	40	59		...	...	...	...		...	...	...	...
1393	Carpets and rugs		...	1	...	...		...	...	...	...		...	...	...	...
1394	Cordage, rope, twine and netting		2	2	3	2		...	...	...	...		...	...	...	...
1399	Other textiles n.e.c.		6	6	7	9		...	...	...	...		...	...	...	...
1410	Wearing apparel, except fur apparel		196	243	279	303		...	...	...	...		...	...	...	...
1420	Articles of fur		...	6	6	8		...	...	...	...		...	...	...	...
1430	Knitted and crocheted apparel		4	...	...	...		...	...	...	...		...	...	...	...
151	Leather;luggage,handbags,saddlery,harness;fur		16	20	18	23		153	153	207	155		1529	1616	1794	1568
1511	Tanning/dressing of leather; dressing of fur		11	13	13	15		...	...	...	...		...	...	...	...
1512	Luggage,handbags,etc.;saddlery/harness		5	7	5	8		...	...	...	...		...	...	...	...
1520	Footwear		71	98	74	78		402	297	239	343		868	944	634	776
1610	Sawmilling and planing of wood		113	112	130	148		770	788	671	829		4375	4007	3723	4620

Code	Description												
162	Wood products, cork, straw, plaiting materials	112	133	155	175	445	729	652	872	4077	5531	5871	8463
1621	Veneer sheets and wood-based panels	2	2	11	13	...	...	...	...	...	...	...	...
1622	Builders' carpentry and joinery	87	101	110	112	...	...	...	...	...	...	...	...
1623	Wooden containers	2	2	11	13	...	...	...	...	...	...	...	...
1629	Other wood products;articles of cork,straw	21	28	23	37	...	...	...	...	...	...	...	...
170	Paper and paper products	78	87	84	102	869	965	1035	1150	7150	7738	9418	10958
1701	Pulp, paper and paperboard	8	7	7	9	...	...	...	...	...	...	...	...
1702	Corrugated paper and paperboard	15	21	24	28	...	...	...	...	...	...	...	...
1709	Other articles of paper and paperboard	55	59	53	65	...	...	...	...	...	...	...	...
181	Printing and service activities related to printing	260	285	298	310	...	...	...	...	...	...	...	...
1811	Printing	228	240	234	246	...	...	...	...	...	...	...	...
1812	Service activities related to printing	32	45	64	64	...	...	...	...	...	...	...	...
1820	Reproduction of recorded media	4	9	10	9	...	...	...	...	...	...	...	...
1910	Coke oven products	-	-	-	-	...	...	...	...	...	...	...	...
1920	Refined petroleum products	7	10	7	15	...	...	...	...	...	...	...	...
201	Basic chemicals,fertilizers, etc.	37	47	42	52	2812	2975	2907	2990	34092	37753	47154	41848
2011	Basic chemicals	30	38	35	42	...	...	...	...	...	...	...	...
2012	Fertilizers and nitrogen compounds	4	5	6	7	...	...	...	...	...	...	...	...
2013	Plastics and synthetic rubber in primary forms	3	4	1	3	...	...	...	...	...	...	...	...
202	Other chemical products	49	59	46	62	227	309	337	434	3314	3692	4753	5329
2021	Pesticides and other agrochemical products	3	3	2	3	...	...	...	...	...	...	...	...
2022	Paints,varnishes;printing ink and mastics	12	18	16	20	90	141	160	140	1835	2228	2635	2962
2023	Soap,cleaning and cosmetic preparations	21	30	23	32	102	110	133	267	756	607	1017	1428
2029	Other chemical products n.e.c.	13	8	5	7	17	37	22	13	644	757	955	840
2030	Man-made fibres	1	1	1	1	...	...	...	...	...	...	...	...
2100	Pharmaceuticals,medicinal chemicals, etc.	67	83	75	83	2328	2245	2696	2595	24876	26018	33147	36769
221	Rubber products	8	6	6	6	65	54	65	53	501	512	571	548
2211	Rubber tyres and tubes	...	...	...	...	65	54	65	53	...	...	...	...
2219	Other rubber products	8	6	6	6	...	...	...	...	...	...	...	...
2220	Plastics products	525	744	854	912	2573	3202	3197	3091	15670	18868	22986	23472
2310	Glass and glass products	28	40	54	54	...	...	...	...	...	...	...	...
239	Non-metallic mineral products n.e.c.	721	846	837	987	8043	7464	7972	7733	64405	67668	74741	81904
2391	Refractory products	...	8	5	9	6	18	11	149	37	52	52	270
2392	Clay building materials	16	27	20	31	213	254	232	192	1029	1057	1306	1318
2393	Other porcelain and ceramic products	15	13	23	34	33	64	82	94	256	432	634	936
2394	Cement, lime and plaster	78	88	82	93	2416	1898	1844	1896	21842	20164	18788	21511
2395	Articles of concrete, cement and plaster	436	493	483	537	4452	4435	4837	4572	37322	42298	46819	53569
2396	Cutting, shaping and finishing of stone	170	214	218	278	797	754	931	798	3378	3505	6990	4151
2399	Other non-metallic mineral products n.e.c.	6	3	6	5	126	41	35	32	541	160	154	148
2410	Basic iron and steel	30	26	32	42	10472	10359	9490	9050	96874	103980	104386	93933
2420	Basic precious and other non-ferrous metals	10	9	4	6	794	724	28	...	15847	14483	386	5358
243	Casting of metals	12	14	15	22	426	417	439	552	4098	3983	4244	...
2431	Casting of iron and steel	8	9	8	10	426	417	439	552	...	...	...	...
2432	Casting of non-ferrous metals	4	5	7	12	...	...	...	...	...	...	...	...
251	Struct.metal products, tanks, reservoirs	145	184	228	252	1647	2037	2028	2366	13833	20120	23415	29737

continued

Georgia

| ISIC | Industry | Note | Number of enterprises (number) 2013 | 2014 | 2015 | 2016 | Note | Number of employees (number) 2013 | 2014 | 2015 | 2016 | Note | Wages and salaries paid to employees (thousands of Georgian Lari) 2013 | 2014 | 2015 | 2016 |

ISIC	Industry	Note	\multicolumn{4}{Number of enterprises (number)}	Note	\multicolumn{4}{Number of employees (number)}	Note	\multicolumn{4}{Wages and salaries paid to employees (thousands of Georgian Lari)}
			2013	2014	2015	2016		2013	2014	2015	2016		2013	2014	2015	2016
2511	Structural metal products		142	181	224	246		1645	1955	1988	2304		13833	19569	22886	29736
2512	Tanks, reservoirs and containers of metal		3	2	4	6		...	...	...	...		...	...	...	...
2513	Steam generators, excl. hot water boilers		...	...	...	...		...	...	...	...		...	...	...	...
2520	Weapons and ammunition		...	...	...	...		...	...	...	...		...	...	...	...
259	Other metal products;metal working services		195	232	222	238		1257	877	873	629		9381	5229	7141	6170
2591	Forging,pressing,stamping,roll-forming of metal		20	20	22	20		...	...	...	...		...	...	...	...
2592	Treatment and coating of metals; machining		32	43	44	50		...	...	...	...		...	...	...	...
2593	Cutlery, hand tools and general hardware		4	4	5	6		...	...	...	...		...	...	...	...
2599	Other fabricated metal products n.e.c.		139	165	151	162		1235	865	863	603		9317	5210	7119	5794
2610	Electronic components and boards		2	2	3	4		...	...	...	...		...	...	...	...
2620	Computers and peripheral equipment		3	3	4	5		...	...	...	...		...	...	...	...
2630	Communication equipment		1	1	2	2		...	...	...	...		...	...	...	...
2640	Consumer electronics		...	...	...	...		...	...	...	...		...	...	...	...
265	Measuring,testing equipment; watches, etc.		...	...	1	1		...	...	...	...		...	...	...	...
2651	Measuring/testing/navigating equipment,etc.		...	...	1	1		...	...	...	...		...	...	...	...
2652	Watches and clocks		...	...	...	...		...	...	...	...		...	...	...	...
2660	Irradiation/electromedical equipment,etc.		...	...	1	1		...	...	...	...		...	...	...	...
2670	Optical instruments and photographic equipment		...	1	1	1		...	...	...	...		...	...	...	...
2680	Magnetic and optical media		...	...	...	...		...	...	...	...		...	...	...	...
2710	Electric motors,generators,transformers,etc.		6	8	9	11		...	...	...	...		...	...	...	...
2720	Batteries and accumulators		2	3	3	3		...	...	...	...		...	...	...	...
273	Wiring and wiring devices		5	5	6	8		...	...	...	...		...	...	...	...
2731	Fibre optic cables		...	...	...	...		...	...	...	...		...	...	...	...
2732	Other electronic and electric wires and cables		4	4	5	6		...	...	...	...		...	...	...	...
2733	Wiring devices		1	1	1	2		...	...	...	...		...	...	...	...
2740	Electric lighting equipment		5	5	6	8		...	...	...	...		...	...	...	...
2750	Domestic appliances		6	8	7	13		...	...	...	...		...	...	...	...
2790	Other electrical equipment		5	6	6	8		...	...	...	...		...	...	...	...
281	General-purpose machinery		16	22	25	32		16	47	38	26		171	288	284	261
2811	Engines/turbines,excl.aircraft,vehicle engines		...	1	1	...		...	...	...	...		...	...	...	...
2812	Fluid power equipment		1	1	1	1		...	...	...	...		...	...	...	...
2813	Other pumps, compressors, taps and valves		1	1	1	1		...	...	...	...		...	...	...	...
2814	Bearings, gears, gearing and driving elements		...	1	1	1		...	...	...	...		...	...	...	...
2815	Ovens, furnaces and furnace burners		5	6	6	9		...	...	...	...		...	...	...	...
2816	Lifting and handling equipment		3	3	3	4		...	...	...	...		...	...	...	...
2817	Office machinery, excl.computers,etc.		3	3	3	3		...	...	...	...		...	...	...	...
2818	Power-driven hand tools		1	1	1	1		...	...	...	...		...	...	...	...
2819	Other general-purpose machinery		2	6	9	12		...	...	...	...		...	...	...	...
282	Special-purpose machinery		11	11	15	20		138	197	113	263		730	852	747	1553
2821	Agricultural and forestry machinery		...	...	1	2		...	...	...	...		...	...	...	...
2822	Metal-forming machinery and machine tools		4	4	4	6		...	...	...	...		...	...	...	...

Code	Description												
2823	Machinery for metallurgy	1	1	1	1	…	…	…	…	…	…	…	…
2824	Mining, quarrying and construction machinery	1	1	2	2	…	…	…	…	…	…	…	…
2825	Food/beverage/tobacco processing machinery	5	5	6	7	…	…	…	…	…	…	…	…
2826	Textile/apparel/leather production machinery	…	…	…	…	…	…	…	…	…	…	…	…
2829	Other special-purpose machinery	…	…	1	2	…	…	…	…	…	…	…	…
2910	Motor vehicles	…	…	…	…	…	…	…	…	…	…	…	…
2920	Automobile bodies, trailers and semi-trailers	…	2	…	…	…	…	…	…	…	…	…	…
2930	Parts and accessories for motor vehicles	1	2	2	2	…	…	…	…	…	…	…	…
301	Building of ships and boats	…	…	…	…	…	…	…	…	…	…	…	…
3011	Building of ships and floating structures	…	…	…	…	…	…	…	…	…	…	…	…
3012	Building of pleasure and sporting boats	…	…	…	…	…	…	…	…	…	…	…	…
3020	Railway locomotives and rolling stock	1	1	1	1	…	…	…	…	…	…	…	…
3030	Air and spacecraft and related machinery	1	2	2	2	…	…	…	…	…	…	…	…
3040	Military fighting vehicles	…	…	…	…	…	…	…	…	…	…	…	…
309	Transport equipment n.e.c.	…	…	…	…	…	…	…	…	…	…	…	…
3091	Motorcycles	…	1	…	1	…	…	…	…	…	…	…	…
3092	Bicycles and invalid carriages	…	…	1	1	…	…	…	…	…	…	…	…
3099	Other transport equipment n.e.c.	…	…	…	…	…	…	…	…	…	…	…	…
3100	Furniture	473	615	754	894	2600	2990	3078	2845	17556	24270	21502	21006
321	Jewellery, bijouterie and related articles	22	27	33	42	…	…	…	…	…	…	…	…
3211	Jewellery and related articles	15	19	25	33	…	…	…	…	…	…	…	…
3212	Imitation jewellery and related articles	7	8	8	9	…	…	…	…	…	…	…	…
3220	Musical instruments	…	…	…	…	…	…	…	…	…	…	…	…
3230	Sports goods	3	7	7	10	…	…	…	…	…	…	…	…
3240	Games and toys	4	5	5	6	…	…	…	…	…	…	…	…
3250	Medical and dental instruments and supplies	11	13	18	24	…	…	…	…	…	…	…	…
3290	Other manufacturing n.e.c.	…	…	…	…	…	…	…	…	…	…	…	…
331	Repair of fabricated metal products/machinery	207	223	253	300	…	…	…	…	…	…	…	…
3311	Repair of fabricated metal products	1	1	2	2	…	…	…	…	…	…	…	…
3312	Repair of machinery	82	87	98	128	…	…	…	…	…	…	…	…
3313	Repair of electronic and optical equipment	8	8	10	13	…	…	…	…	…	…	…	…
3314	Repair of electrical equipment	103	112	127	136	…	…	…	…	…	…	…	…
3315	Repair of transport equip., excl. motor vehicles	5	5	6	10	…	…	…	…	…	…	…	…
3319	Repair of other equipment	8	10	10	11	…	…	…	…	…	…	…	…
3320	Installation of industrial machinery/equipment	46	57	60	65	…	…	…	…	…	…	…	…
C	Total manufacturing	6020	7502	7982	9027	80068	82277	82631	85842	662720	710402	769543	804923

Georgia

ISIC	Industry	Note	Output (valuation not defined) (millions of Georgian Lari)				Note	Value added (valuation not defined) (millions of Georgian Lari)				Note	Gross fixed capital formation (millions of Georgian Lari)	
			2013	2014	2015	2016		2013	2014	2015	2016		2015	2016
1010	Processing/preserving of meat		193.3	216.4	213.3	262.7		46.9	58.5	43.2	69.2		22.7	66.5
1020	Processing/preserving of fish, etc.		43.0	53.4	73.3	29.1		21.3	27.8	38.3	7.9		31.0	38.2
1030	Processing/preserving of fruit,vegetables		307.8	379.5	454.6	592.3		22.4	43.4	32.5	91.4		59.7	69.3
1040	Vegetable and animal oils and fats		20.0	8.8	9.7	14.0		1.3	2.7	1.4	1.4		4.0	6.1
1050	Dairy products		171.7	209.1	223.2	259.9		50.6	61.9	51.8	61.0		68.7	69.1
106	Grain mill products,starches and starch products		355.6	385.9	395.8	357.7		46.3	65.9	79.0	42.1		87.5	80.8
1061	Grain mill products		…	…	…	…		…	…	…	…		…	…
1062	Starches and starch products		…	…	…	…		…	…	…	…		…	…
107	Other food products		446.3	491.4	496.9	558.0		124.5	132.3	117.8	140.4		139.0	163.6
1071	Bakery products		249.3	272.8	282.6	357.8		77.5	83.1	83.2	107.5		35.4	59.8
1072	Sugar		…	…	…	…		…	…	…	…		…	…
1073	Cocoa, chocolate and sugar confectionery		43.9	44.0	44.2	69.8		20.2	15.6	5.9	10.1		67.1	70.6
1074	Macaroni, noodles, couscous, etc.		17.0	16.8	21.7	16.0		4.6	4.2	5.4	4.5		3.9	2.7
1075	Prepared meals and dishes		…	…	…	…		…	…	…	…		…	…
1079	Other food products n.e.c.		29.2	26.2	36.9	38.7		6.9	5.5	8.8	9.7		9.8	13.4
1080	Prepared animal feeds		10.5	18.0	21.7	25.2		4.2	2.3	3.9	2.7		4.1	9.1
110	Beverages		1064.0	1338.8	1157.7	1293.6		423.7	515.2	432.5	524.7		646.9	720.5
1101	Distilling, rectifying and blending of spirits		152.9	130.7	104.3	153.9		64.7	44.9	30.1	50.0		50.3	63.9
1102	Wines		320.0	482.0	370.1	441.5		120.3	179.0	133.9	205.0		202.1	242.6
1103	Malt liquors and malt		192.8	225.8	197.5	193.4		40.4	56.3	64.7	73.1		161.3	189.3
1104	Soft drinks,mineral waters,other bottled waters		398.2	500.4	485.8	504.8		198.3	234.9	203.8	196.7		233.2	224.7
1200	Tobacco products		57.9	52.8	40.1	29.3		8.4	11.3	12.8	8.7		30.1	28.7
131	Spinning, weaving and finishing of textiles		…	…	…	…		…	…	…	…		…	…
1311	Preparation and spinning of textile fibres		…	…	…	…		…	…	…	…		…	…
1312	Weaving of textiles		…	…	…	…		…	…	…	…		…	…
1313	Finishing of textiles		…	…	…	…		…	…	…	…		…	…
139	Other textiles		…	…	…	…		…	…	…	…		…	…
1391	Knitted and crocheted fabrics		…	…	…	…		…	…	…	…		…	…
1392	Made-up textile articles, except apparel		…	…	…	…		…	…	…	…		…	…
1393	Carpets and rugs		…	…	…	…		…	…	…	…		…	…
1394	Cordage, rope, twine and netting		…	…	…	…		…	…	…	…		…	…
1399	Other textiles n.e.c.		…	…	…	…		…	…	…	…		…	…
1410	Wearing apparel, except fur apparel		…	…	…	…		…	…	…	…		…	…
1420	Articles of fur		…	…	…	…		…	…	…	…		…	…
1430	Knitted and crocheted apparel		…	…	…	…		…	…	…	…		…	…
151	Leather;luggage,handbags,saddlery,harness;fur		8.4	11.2	16.7	12.0		1.4	2.8	9.7	3.4		3.4	3.4
1511	Tanning/dressing of leather; dressing of fur		…	…	…	…		…	…	…	…		…	…
1512	Luggage,handbags,etc.;saddlery/harness		…	…	…	…		…	…	…	…		…	…
1520	Footwear		6.5	5.6	6.1	6.7		2.3	1.9	1.6	2.7		0.6	1.5
1610	Sawmilling and planing of wood		27.3	31.2	27.4	30.0		11.0	14.1	15.4	11.7		28.0	7.9

Code	Description										
162	Wood products, cork, straw, plaiting materials	16.7	18.0	16.1	23.3	13.6	16.2	63.9	53.2	40.7	41.5
1621	Veneer sheets and wood-based panels	…	…	…	…	…	…	…	…	…	…
1622	Builders' carpentry and joinery	…	…	…	…	…	…	…	…	…	…
1623	Wooden containers	…	…	…	…	…	…	…	…	…	…
1629	Other wood products;articles of cork,straw	…	…	…	…	…	…	…	…	…	…
170	Paper and paper products	20.5	0.6	28.5	27.8	22.0	19.0	76.8	64.9	60.1	51.0
1701	Pulp, paper and paperboard	…	…	…	…	…	…	…	…	…	…
1702	Corrugated paper and paperboard	…	…	…	…	…	…	…	…	…	…
1709	Other articles of paper and paperboard	…	…	…	…	…	…	…	…	…	…
181	Printing and service activities related to printing	…	…	…	…	…	…	…	…	…	…
1811	Printing	…	…	…	…	…	…	…	…	…	…
1812	Service activities related to printing	…	…	…	…	…	…	…	…	…	…
1820	Reproduction of recorded media	…	…	…	…	…	…	…	…	…	…
1910	Coke oven products	…	…	…	…	…	…	…	…	…	…
1920	Refined petroleum products	…	…	…	…	…	…	…	…	…	…
201	Basic chemicals,fertilizers, etc.	90.3	89.4	74.0	144.4	131.4	134.1	274.7	349.6	312.9	323.2
2011	Basic chemicals	…	…	…	…	…	…	…	…	…	…
2012	Fertilizers and nitrogen compounds	…	…	…	…	…	…	…	…	…	…
2013	Plastics and synthetic rubber in primary forms	…	…	…	…	…	…	…	…	…	…
202	Other chemical products	8.8	6.9	12.0	12.4	9.3	7.3	31.6	27.4	22.3	19.5
2021	Pesticides and other agrochemical products	5.0	4.8	7.6	7.3	5.9	3.8	18.7	16.7	14.2	9.8
2022	Paints,varnishes;printing ink and mastics	2.9	1.7	2.9	2.6	1.7	1.4	9.6	6.1	3.9	4.3
2023	Soap,cleaning and cosmetic preparations	0.1	0.2	1.2	2.2	1.1	1.5	2.4	3.4	2.4	3.5
2029	Other chemical products n.e.c.	…	…	…	…	…	…	…	…	…	…
2030	Man-made fibres	…	…	…	…	…	…	…	…	…	…
2100	Pharmaceuticals,medicinal chemicals, etc.	48.5	53.4	70.1	54.0	56.8	41.4	145.6	147.5	137.9	107.2
221	Rubber products	0.4	0.8	1.0	0.9	1.6	1.1	3.2	3.8	4.6	3.5
2211	Rubber tyres and tubes	…	…	…	…	…	…	…	…	…	…
2219	Other rubber products	…	…	…	…	…	…	…	…	…	…
2220	Plastics products	58.8	45.7	75.3	61.5	51.7	31.9	300.9	229.0	218.4	143.0
2310	Glass and glass products	…	…	…	…	…	…	…	…	…	…
239	Non-metallic mineral products n.e.c.	407.7	368.6	298.4	210.2	192.1	170.2	913.4	826.3	730.7	651.7
2391	Refractory products	…	…	0.4	0.1	0.1	0.1	0.8	0.1	0.2	0.1
2392	Clay building materials	3.9	3.6	2.8	2.4	1.8	1.8	6.2	5.8	4.5	4.7
2393	Other porcelain and ceramic products	0.4	0.3	2.0	1.6	0.7	0.4	4.0	3.2	1.9	1.1
2394	Cement, lime and plaster	243.3	206.5	68.2	72.3	74.7	66.7	355.5	340.9	313.2	293.6
2395	Articles of concrete, cement and plaster	149.2	153.9	212.5	117.6	104.7	93.7	519.4	446.3	388.3	326.0
2396	Cutting, shaping and finishing of stone	8.7	2.9	11.8	15.7	9.9	5.5	26.0	29.1	21.7	17.6
2399	Other non-metallic mineral products n.e.c.	1.7	1.2	0.7	0.5	0.4	2.0	1.6	1.0	0.9	8.6
2410	Basic iron and steel	382.2	300.3	156.0	278.4	112.5	159.4	677.4	747.6	816.5	768.5
2420	Basic precious and other non-ferrous metals	…	1.3	…	0.1	26.2	30.8	…	5.8	110.9	128.9
243	Casting of metals	24.8	25.4	8.6	16.5	7.4	5.6	63.1	45.7	57.0	56.4
2431	Casting of iron and steel	…	…	…	…	…	…	…	…	…	…
2432	Casting of non-ferrous metals	…	…	…	…	…	…	…	…	…	…
251	Struct.metal products, tanks, reservoirs	55.8	42.6	60.0	86.5	26.2	17.5	186.2	147.8	95.9	50.5

continued

Georgia

ISIC	Industry	Output (valuation not defined) (millions of Georgian Lari)					Value added (valuation not defined) (millions of Georgian Lari)					Gross fixed capital formation (millions of Georgian Lari)		
	ISIC Revision 4	Note	2013	2014	2015	2016	Note	2013	2014	2015	2016	Note	2015	2016
2511	Structural metal products		50.5	84.4	142.8	178.8		17.4	25.2	84.7	57.0		42.1	52.8
2512	Tanks, reservoirs and containers of metal		...	...	...	...		...	...	...	...		...	...
2513	Steam generators, excl. hot water boilers		...	...	...	...		...	...	...	...		...	...
2520	Weapons and ammunition		...	...	...	...		...	...	...	...		...	...
259	Other metal products;metal working services		39.9	34.9	42.8	40.9		18.5	14.7	14.5	15.7		10.2	4.9
2591	Forging,pressing,stamping,roll-forming of metal		...	...	...	...		...	...	...	...		...	...
2592	Treatment and coating of metals; machining		...	...	...	...		...	...	...	...		...	...
2593	Cutlery, hand tools and general hardware		...	...	...	...		...	...	...	...		...	...
2599	Other fabricated metal products n.e.c.		39.5	34.6	42.0	38.9		18.5	14.7	14.4	15.0		10.2	4.8
2610	Electronic components and boards		...	...	...	...		...	...	...	...		...	...
2620	Computers and peripheral equipment		...	...	...	...		...	...	...	...		...	...
2630	Communication equipment		...	...	...	...		...	...	...	...		...	...
2640	Consumer electronics		...	...	...	...		...	...	...	...		...	...
265	Measuring;testing equipment, watches, etc.		...	...	...	...		...	...	...	...		...	...
2651	Measuring/testing/navigating equipment,etc.		...	...	...	...		...	...	...	...		...	...
2652	Watches and clocks		...	...	...	...		...	...	...	...		...	...
2660	Irradiation/electromedical equipment,etc.		...	...	...	...		...	...	...	...		...	...
2670	Optical instruments and photographic equipment		...	...	...	...		...	...	...	...		...	...
2680	Magnetic and optical media		...	...	...	...		...	...	...	...		...	...
2710	Electric motors,generators,transformers,etc.		...	...	...	...		...	...	...	...		...	...
2720	Batteries and accumulators		...	...	...	...		...	...	...	...		...	...
273	Wiring and wiring devices		...	...	...	...		...	...	...	...		...	...
2731	Fibre optic cables		...	...	...	...		...	...	...	...		...	...
2732	Other electronic and electric wires and cables		...	...	...	...		...	...	...	...		...	...
2733	Wiring devices		...	...	...	...		...	...	...	...		...	...
2740	Electric lighting equipment		...	...	...	...		...	...	...	...		...	...
2750	Domestic appliances		...	...	...	...		...	...	...	...		...	...
2790	Other electrical equipment		...	...	...	...		...	...	...	...		...	...
281	General-purpose machinery		1.2	1.5	0.5	0.5		0.4	0.4	0.3	0.3		0.1	1.4
2811	Engines/turbines,excl.aircraft,vehicle engines		...	...	...	...		...	...	...	...		...	...
2812	Fluid power equipment		...	...	...	...		...	...	...	...		...	...
2813	Other pumps, compressors, taps and valves		...	...	...	...		...	...	...	...		...	...
2814	Bearings, gears, gearing and driving elements		...	...	...	...		...	...	...	...		...	...
2815	Ovens, furnaces and furnace burners		...	...	...	...		...	...	...	...		...	...
2816	Lifting and handling equipment		...	...	...	...		...	...	...	...		...	...
2817	Office machinery, excl.computers,etc.		...	...	...	...		...	...	...	...		...	...
2818	Power-driven hand tools		...	...	...	...		...	...	...	...		...	...
2819	Other general-purpose machinery		...	...	...	...		...	...	...	...		...	...
282	Special-purpose machinery		3.1	4.0	2.3	5.4		0.8	1.7	1.0	2.3		1.5	8.0
2821	Agricultural and forestry machinery		...	...	...	...		...	...	...	...		...	...
2822	Metal-forming machinery and machine tools		...	...	...	...		...	...	...	...		...	...

Code	Description										
2823	Machinery for metallurgy	:	:	:	:	:	:	:	:	:	:
2824	Mining, quarrying and construction machinery	:	:	:	:	:	:	:	:	:	:
2825	Food/beverage/tobacco processing machinery	:	:	:	:	:	:	:	:	:	:
2826	Textile/apparel/lleather production machinery	:	:	:	:	:	:	:	:	:	:
2829	Other special-purpose machinery	:	:	:	:	:	:	:	:	:	:
2910	Motor vehicles	:	:	:	:	:	:	:	:	:	:
2920	Automobile bodies, trailers and semi-trailers	:	:	:	:	:	:	:	:	:	:
2930	Parts and accessories for motor vehicles	:	:	:	:	:	:	:	:	:	:
301	Building of ships and boats	:	:	:	:	:	:	:	:	:	:
3011	Building of ships and floating structures	:	:	:	:	:	:	:	:	:	:
3012	Building of pleasure and sporting boats	:	:	:	:	:	:	:	:	:	:
3020	Railway locomotives and rolling stock	:	:	:	:	:	:	:	:	:	:
3030	Air and spacecraft and related machinery	:	:	:	:	:	:	:	:	:	:
3040	Military fighting vehicles	:	:	:	:	:	:	:	:	:	:
309	Transport equipment n.e.c.	:	:	:	:	:	:	:	:	:	:
3091	Motorcycles	:	:	:	:	:	:	:	:	:	:
3092	Bicycles and invalid carriages	:	:	:	:	:	:	:	:	:	:
3099	Other transport equipment n.e.c.	:	:	:	:	:	:	:	:	:	:
3100	Furniture	32.1	33.5	27.8	47.0	35.8	47.9	105.4	138.2	145.9	158.0
321	Jewellery, bijouterie and related articles	:	:	:	:	:	:	:	:	:	:
3211	Jewellery and related articles	:	:	:	:	:	:	:	:	:	:
3212	Imitation jewellery and related articles	:	:	:	:	:	:	:	:	:	:
3220	Musical instruments	:	:	:	:	:	:	:	:	:	:
3230	Sports goods	:	:	:	:	:	:	:	:	:	:
3240	Games and toys	:	:	:	:	:	:	:	:	:	:
3250	Medical and dental instruments and supplies	:	:	:	:	:	:	:	:	:	:
3290	Other manufacturing n.e.c.	:	:	:	:	:	:	:	:	:	:
331	Repair of fabricated metal products/machinery	:	:	:	:	:	:	:	:	:	:
3311	Repair of fabricated metal products	:	:	:	:	:	:	:	:	:	:
3312	Repair of machinery	:	:	:	:	:	:	:	:	:	:
3313	Repair of electronic and optical equipment	:	:	:	:	:	:	:	:	:	:
3314	Repair of electrical equipment	:	:	:	:	:	:	:	:	:	:
3315	Repair of transport equip., excl. motor vehicles	:	:	:	:	:	:	:	:	:	:
3319	Repair of other equipment	:	:	:	:	:	:	:	:	:	:
3320	Installation of industrial machinery/equipment	:	:	:	:	:	:	:	:	:	:
C	Total manufacturing	2438.9	2760.5	1676.8	1838.3	2048.7	2068.3	5801.1	6551.6	6536.7	7049.2

Georgia

Index numbers of industrial production

(2010=100)

ISIC	Industry	Note	2005	2006	2007	2008	2009	2010	2011	2012	2013	2014	2015	2016
10	Food products		:	:	:	:	:	:	:	:	:	:	:	:
11	Beverages		:	:	:	:	:	:	:	:	:	:	:	:
12	Tobacco products		:	:	:	:	:	:	:	:	:	:	:	:
13	Textiles		:	:	:	:	:	:	:	:	:	:	:	:
14	Wearing apparel		:	:	:	:	:	:	:	:	:	:	:	:
15	Leather and related products		:	:	:	:	:	:	:	:	:	:	:	:
16	Wood products, excluding furniture		:	:	:	:	:	:	:	:	:	:	:	:
17	Paper and paper products		:	:	:	:	:	:	:	:	:	:	:	:
18	Printing and reproduction of recorded media		:	:	:	:	:	:	:	:	:	:	:	:
19	Coke and refined petroleum products		:	:	:	:	:	:	:	:	:	:	:	:
20	Chemicals and chemical products		:	:	:	:	:	:	:	:	:	:	:	:
21	Pharmaceuticals, medicinal chemicals, etc.		:	:	:	:	:	:	:	:	:	:	:	:
22	Rubber and plastics products		:	:	:	:	:	:	:	:	:	:	:	:
23	Other non-metallic mineral products		:	:	:	:	:	:	:	:	:	:	:	:
24	Basic metals		:	:	:	:	:	:	:	:	:	:	:	:
25	Fabricated metal products, except machinery		:	:	:	:	:	:	:	:	:	:	:	:
26	Computer, electronic and optical products		:	:	:	:	:	:	:	:	:	:	:	:
27	Electrical equipment		:	:	:	:	:	:	:	:	:	:	:	:
28	Machinery and equipment n.e.c.		:	:	:	:	:	:	:	:	:	:	:	:
29	Motor vehicles, trailers and semi-trailers		:	:	:	:	:	:	:	:	:	:	:	:
30	Other transport equipment		:	:	:	:	:	:	:	:	:	:	:	:
31	Furniture		:	:	:	:	:	:	:	:	:	:	:	:
32	Other manufacturing		:	:	:	:	:	:	:	:	:	:	:	:
33	Repair and installation of machinery/equipment		:	:	:	:	:	:	:	:	:	:	:	:
C	Total manufacturing		71	96	103	97	84	100	126	134	133	141	150	155

Germany

Supplier of information:
Federal Statistical Office, Wiesbaden.
Industrial statistics for the OECD countries are compiled by the OECD secretariat, which supplies them to UNIDO.

Basic source of data:
Annual surveys.

Major deviations from ISIC (Revision 4):
Data presented in ISIC (Revision 4) were originally classified according to the national NACE-related classification system.

Reference period:
Calendar year.

Scope:
All enterprises.

Method of data collection:
Not reported.

Type of enumeration:
Enterprises with 20 employees or more are surveyed, while a sampling method is used for smaller enterprises.

Adjusted for non-response:
Not reported.

Concepts and definitions of variables:
No deviations from the standard UN concepts and definitions are reported.

Related national publications:
None reported.

Germany

ISIC Revision 4			Number of enterprises (number)					Number of employees (thousands)					Wages and salaries paid to employees (millions of Euros)				
ISIC	Industry	Note	2013	2014	2015	2016	Note	2013	2014	2015	2016	Note	2013	2014	2015	2016
1010	Processing/preserving of meat		10224	9440	10206	8925		175.0	167.6	175.9	179.4		3505	3453	3600	3772
1020	Processing/preserving of fish, etc.		204	252	201	151		7.6	7.7	7.6	6.8		206	216	214	202
1030	Processing/preserving of fruit,vegetables		646	699	658	751		32.5	32.7	32.7	34.2		959	1021	1055	1164
1040	Vegetable and animal oils and fats		142	161	149	161		5.2	5.4	5.8	5.3		224	240	258	266
1050	Dairy products		519	536	589	645		42.1	44.8	44.7	43.9		1687	1798	1898	1866
106	Grain mill products,starches and starch products		548	624	510	489		14.4	14.8	15.2	15.9		493	513	534	561
1061	Grain mill products		525	601	493	470		11.6	12.0	12.5	12.9		351	368	388	407
1062	Starches and starch products		23	23	17	19		2.8	2.8	2.7	3.0		142	146	146	153
107	Other food products		14876	15417	12867	12723		474.7	460.8	453.9	491.7		9836	9909	10137	10857
1071	Bakery products		13211	13690	11165	11243		368.5	353.0	347.0	379.1		6049	5927	6086	6503
1072	Sugar		7	9	9	8		5.1	5.3	5.4	5.5		292	298	300	309
1073	Cocoa, chocolate and sugar confectionery		310	312	341	355		35.5	35.5	35.4	35.9		1097	1149	1154	1189
1074	Macaroni, noodles, couscous, etc.		121	132	181	127		2.1	2.5	2.2	1.9		49	51	53	53
1075	Prepared meals and dishes		326	327	284	277		13.0	14.7	14.5	15.8		365	437	469	484
1079	Other food products n.e.c.		902	946	887	712		50.5	49.8	49.4	53.5		1985	2047	2075	2319
1080	Prepared animal feeds		545	624	588	581		17.1	18.5	18.4	18.9		656	689	715	738
110	Beverages		1932	1977	2142	2166		68.3	66.9	66.7	67.4		2721	2761	2963	3193
1101	Distilling, rectifying and blending of spirits		563	657	663	741		4.7	5.0	4.0	4.6		136	161	128	147
1102	Wines		...	...	...	...		...	...	...	...		...	...	...	...
1103	Malt liquors and malt		757	678	783	769		31.9	30.1	31.2	31.6		1273	1261	1356	1372
1104	Soft drinks,mineral waters,other bottled waters		260	265	277	262		26.6	26.4	26.4	26.1		1147	1175	1325	1499
1200	Tobacco products		36	21	26	38		10.5	10.5	10.3	10.0		608	631	656	660
131	Spinning, weaving and finishing of textiles		1460	1539	1699	1362		26.6	26.7	24.9	23.3		782	786	738	731
1311	Preparation and spinning of textile fibres		75	90	123	88		4.0	3.8	3.4	3.4		117	114	102	108
1312	Weaving of textiles		235	226	193	219		10.8	10.0	9.8	10.1		367	343	338	346
1313	Finishing of textiles		1150	1223	1383	1055		11.8	12.9	11.7	9.8		297	329	298	277
139	Other textiles		2291	2510	2356	2442		50.1	49.0	49.9	50.2		1596	1614	1683	1680
1391	Knitted and crocheted fabrics		126	154	134	135		3.6	3.5	3.1	3.2		115	118	111	111
1392	Made-up textile articles, except apparel		980	1035	1027	1001		17.3	17.0	16.9	16.1		471	489	478	446
1393	Carpets and rugs		118	98	110	109		3.3	3.0	3.0	3.1		117	105	110	105
1394	Cordage, rope, twine and netting		...	...	...	88		...	...	...	1.6		...	...	...	45
1399	Other textiles n.e.c.		...	...	...	1109		...	...	...	26.2		...	...	...	972
1410	Wearing apparel, except fur apparel		2432	2489	2663	2695		34.5	35.8	33.3	33.2		1071	1128	1080	1159
1420	Articles of fur		...	...	...	...		...	...	...	...		...	...	...	...
1430	Knitted and crocheted apparel		...	...	...	...		...	...	...	...		...	...	...	...
151	Leather;luggage,handbags,saddlery,harness;fur		730	778	915	960		6.9	6.2	6.0	7.1		178	159	168	183
1511	Tanning/dressing of leather; dressing of fur		83	61	75	109		2.4	2.2	2.4	2.6		82	72	83	90
1512	Luggage,handbags,etc.;saddlery/harness		647	717	840	851		4.5	4.0	3.6	4.5		96	86	85	93
1520	Footwear		292	513	378	388		9.1	9.1	8.6	8.9		262	274	264	276
1610	Sawmilling and planing of wood		1962	2307	2087	2158		23.8	22.8	22.5	23.2		629	619	669	658

Note: This page presents a single wide statistical table rotated 90° on the printed page. No column headers appear on this page. The twelve numeric columns are arranged in three groups of four; they are reproduced below as group I (columns 1–4), group II (columns 5–8) and group III (columns 9–12). A colon (:) denotes data not available. Footnote marker a/ is printed against the rows so marked.

Code	Description	I-1	I-2	I-3	I-4	II-1	II-2	II-3	II-4	III-1	III-2	III-3	III-4
162	Wood products, cork, straw, plaiting materials	9594	10312	10952	9957	100.7	97.3	105.6	97.7	2946	2985	3118	3019
1621	Veneer sheets and wood-based panels	212	274	174	217	14.3	14.6	14.7	15.0	533	567	588	566
1622	Builders' carpentry and joinery	6783	7247	7839	6974	64.8	61.9	68.7	61.4	1879	1871	1979	1907
1623	Wooden containers	820	838	858	779	12.2	11.8	12.4	12.1	314	318	318	319
1629 a/	Other wood products;articles of cork,straw	1779	1953	2081	1986	9.4	9.0	9.8	9.3	220	229	234	228
170	Paper and paper products	1836	1698	1640	1706	142.1	144.3	144.3	143.1	5671	5907	5977	6040
1701	Pulp, paper and paperboard	355	313	295	354	39.7	39.2	40.0	39.8	1875	1886	1915	1948
1702	Corrugated paper and paperboard	755	706	727	764	56.6	55.5	56.3	56.5	2052	2054	2108	2171
1709	Other articles of paper and paperboard	727	680	618	588	45.7	49.6	48.1	46.8	1744	1968	1953	1922
181	Printing and service activities related to printing	11536	11002	10065	10046	144.2	138.7	134.5	137.3	4483	4259	4287	4209
1811	Printing	7728	7837	6507	6700	108.8	107.6	104.7	108.3	3383	3308	3335	3387
1812	Service activities related to printing	3809	3164	3558	3347	35.3	31.2	29.7	29.1	1101	951	953	822
1820	Reproduction of recorded media	317	438	277	268	5.1	4.7	4.4	2.4	184	173	160	78
1910 a/	Coke oven products	80	85	54	73	19.3	22.6	22.3	22.2	1307	1673	1725	1864
1920 a/	Refined petroleum products	:	:	:	:	:	:	:	:	:	:	:	:
201	Basic chemicals,fertilizers, etc.	989	922	1049	1072	182.9	180.7	177.0	173.2	11297	11556	11996	11887
2011	Basic chemicals	524	481	551	522	125.5	123.7	118.1	110.6	8086	8215	8375	8010
2012	Fertilizers and nitrogen compounds	98	88	90	98	11.2	10.9	11.3	11.2	535	566	596	554
2013	Plastics and synthetic rubber in primary forms	368	353	408	453	46.2	46.1	47.5	51.5	2676	2775	3025	3324
202	Other chemical products	2220	2214	1957	2004	145.6	146.1	146.0	156.4	6730	6996	7238	8010
2021	Pesticides and other agrochemical products	92	58	64	71	3.9	4.1	4.4	4.1	164	180	195	196
2022	Paints,varnishes;printing ink and mastics	432	443	415	364	42.1	42.5	42.7	43.0	1984	2079	2143	2189
2023	Soap,cleaning and cosmetic preparations	837	813	671	772	46.2	46.7	45.7	50.3	1982	2069	2134	2404
2029	Other chemical products n.e.c.	859	900	807	798	53.3	52.9	53.2	59.0	2600	2669	2766	3221
2030	Man-made fibres	59	47	50	46	7.8	8.3	8.0	8.8	313	350	349	392
2100	Pharmaceuticals,medicinal chemicals, etc.	643	669	554	580	125.7	127.5	128.4	130.7	7270	7543	7922	8228
221	Rubber products	799	914	743	765	75.0	78.6	78.9	79.5	3092	3406	3512	3668
2211	Rubber tyres and tubes	225	240	231	213	23.7	24.5	24.6	24.8	1124	1225	1266	1296
2219	Other rubber products	574	673	512	552	51.3	54.0	54.3	54.8	1968	2181	2246	2372
2220	Plastics products	6344	6565	6116	6194	334.4	335.3	341.4	346.3	11689	11977	12495	12852
2310	Glass and glass products	1213	1505	1391	1409	58.5	59.4	58.9	59.0	2090	2145	2170	2232
239	Non-metallic mineral products n.e.c.	8732	8883	9216	8510	175.4	178.7	170.4	175.7	6456	6760	6762	7069
2391	Refractory products	104	109	108	79	6.9	6.4	6.6	6.3	284	280	285	285
2392	Clay building materials	229	240	241	221	15.2	14.6	14.5	14.5	592	584	603	603
2393	Other porcelain and ceramic products	:	69	66	62	12.0	12.0	11.8	13.9	612	621	669	789
2394	Cement, lime and plaster	2169	2191	2224	1969	70.2	71.5	70.1	68.2	2561	2686	2713	2670
2395	Articles of concrete, cement and plaster	4945	4843	5260	4989	23.9	25.4	20.7	25.6	542	623	532	682
2396	Cutting, shaping and finishing of stone	460	472	434	467	26.6	27.5	26.2	27.1	1164	1206	1212	1281
2399	Other non-metallic mineral products n.e.c.	1196	1152	1167	1134	125.8	128.3	127.8	124.6	6012	6158	6232	6249
2410	Basic iron and steel	763	769	773	699	56.4	55.8	58.4	61.0	2760	2823	3038	3227
2420	Basic precious and other non-ferrous metals	813	786	757	761	77.1	77.8	78.0	77.4	3104	3229	3331	3369
243	Casting of metals	813	786	757	761	42.5	42.7	43.3	43.3	1744	1783	1860	1917
2431	Casting of iron and steel	358	345	328	309	34.6	35.1	34.7	34.1	1360	1446	1472	1451
2432	Casting of non-ferrous metals	455	440	429	452	34.6	35.1	34.7	34.1	1360	1446	1472	1451
251	Struct.metal products, tanks, reservoirs	11580	11972	11455	12378	206.0	198.3	195.0	210.2	6716	6661	6745	7252

continued

Germany

ISIC Revision 4

ISIC	Industry	Number of enterprises (number) 2013	2014	2015	2016	Number of employees (thousands) 2013	2014	2015	2016	Wages and salaries paid to employees (millions of Euros) 2013	2014	2015	2016
2511	Structural metal products	11023	11420	10892	11844	177.4	170.2	167.2	184.1	5452	5383	5425	6009
2512	Tanks, reservoirs and containers of metal	471	466	487	467	23.4	23.3	23.3	21.9	1005	1028	1063	1013
2513	Steam generators, excl. hot water boilers	87	87	76	67	5.3	4.8	4.5	4.2	259	250	257	230
2520	Weapons and ammunition	211	235	202	201	12.0	12.4	12.1	12.6	619	669	689	718
259	Other metal products;metal working services	30660	31938	31632	30243	626.9	634.2	634.6	640.6	22074	22833	22925	23709
2591	Forging,pressing,stamping,roll-forming of metal	1476	1449	1499	1601	115.1	114.4	114.5	117.4	4570	4625	4734	4894
2592	Treatment and coating of metals;machining	20749	21446	21540	20174	244.3	250.6	254.6	254.3	7255	7600	7648	7901
2593	Cutlery, hand tools and general hardware	4139	4743	4003	4057	137.6	139.1	136.9	139.9	5396	5634	5635	5856
2599	Other fabricated metal products n.e.c.	4296	4300	4590	4411	129.8	130.0	128.6	129.1	4853	4974	4909	5057
2610	Electronic components and boards	2047	1921	1794	1767	73.6	71.8	75.0	76.7	3598	3592	3959	4099
2620	Computers and peripheral equipment	1053	1225	812	830	20.6	21.7	20.7	19.8	1066	1111	1058	1086
2630	Communication equipment	895	801	790	769	24.0	23.6	23.4	23.2	1092	1089	1098	1097
2640	Consumer electronics	261	273	277		13.3	11.9	11.5		611	570	543	
265	Measuring,testing equipment; watches, etc.	2726	2837	2606	2400	149.1	152.4	154.4	167.3	7106	7475	7840	8772
2651	Measuring/testing/navigating equipment,etc.	2577	2708	2441	2251	145.1	148.5	150.3	163.2	6976	7337	7700	8624
2652	Watches and clocks	149	129	165	149	4.0	3.9	4.0	4.2	130	138	139	148
2660	Irradiation/electromedical equipment,etc.	325	324	269	241	10.1	10.3	22.6	23.4	468	482	1353	1439
2670	Optical instruments and photographic equipment	652	666	570	608	26.6	26.6	27.0	26.9	1336	1324	1457	1431
2680	Magnetic and optical media	111	111	89		0.5	0.5	0.4		17	13	10	
2710	Electric motors,generators,transformers,etc.	2292	2406	2377	2254	276.3	276.5	260.1	257.0	15227	15148	14820	14770
2720	Batteries and accumulators	75	101	93	88	8.2	8.9	9.4	8.4	386	409	451	383
273	Wiring and wiring devices	1191	1239	1117	1066	79.1	78.8	78.1	81.3	3465	3526	3640	3833
2731	Fibre optic cables	29	31	25	27	1.6	1.6	1.5	1.5	55	52	55	58
2732	Other electronic and electric wires and cables	349	311	337	348	20.9	20.9	20.2	22.1	805	802	813	891
2733	Wiring devices	813	897	755	692	56.7	56.4	56.3	57.7	2606	2672	2772	2885
2740	Electric lighting equipment	847	834	884	905	36.8	37.7	33.7	37.7	1645	1780	1644	1835
2750	Domestic appliances	273	284	290	285	49.1	49.3	47.4	48.1	2427	2534	2489	2583
2790	Other electrical equipment	1502	1569	1189	1357	54.0	51.7	52.5	52.9	2391	2386	2466	2558
281	General-purpose machinery	8301	8218	7796	8131	649.9	661.9	670.9	679.5	32487	34046	35727	37046
2811	Engines/turbines,excl.aircraft,vehicle engines	225	184	199	209	115.8	116.6	123.3	124.9	7145	7465	8151	8801
2812	Fluid power equipment	369	412	385	370	51.6	52.0	51.2	49.3	2691	2808	2865	2717
2813	Other pumps, compressors, taps and valves	915	868	898	904	93.5	95.0	94.6	95.3	4365	4618	4713	4871
2814	Bearings, gears, gearing and driving elements	711	825	731	647	89.0	94.0	95.7	93.7	4273	4612	4805	4816
2815	Ovens, furnaces and furnace burners	434	425	430	524	13.9	14.1	14.1	15.0	650	674	689	727
2816	Lifting and handling equipment	1091	882	1162	1114	73.4	72.4	73.8	77.4	3328	3404	3582	3794
2817	Office machinery, excl.computers,etc.	93	131	95	53	3.8	3.3	4.1	3.9	169	148	168	222
2818	Power-driven hand tools	250	223	192	208	10.6	10.9	11.7	11.8	520	551	609	628
2819	Other general-purpose machinery	4213	4267	3704	4102	198.3	203.4	202.4	208.1	9347	9765	10147	10471
282	Special-purpose machinery	8092	8286	7921	7732	429.3	430.8	432.4	430.9	20138	20756	21228	21546
2821	Agricultural and forestry machinery	638	532	588	577	40.2	38.8	39.1	39.8	1829	1815	1878	1883
2822	Metal-forming machinery and machine tools	2317	2424	2280	2089	112.5	113.6	114.3	114.1	5187	5346	5525	5796

Code	Description												
2823	Machinery for metallurgy	171	171	191	193	11.1	10.7	10.1	9.9	671	658	641	550
2824	Mining, quarrying and construction machinery	311	378	378	422	44.4	44.4	44.9	44.2	2176	2332	2387	2461
2825	Food/beverage/tobacco processing machinery	514	493	558	488	27.3	27.3	27.3	27.5	1279	1334	1350	1329
2826	Textile/apparel/leather production machinery	254	246	239	234	21.0	20.8	21.2	22.2	1010	1021	1031	1124
2829	Other special-purpose machinery	3818	3765	3771	3993	172.8	175.1	175.6	173.2	7985	8251	8417	8403
2910	Motor vehicles	184	199	193	262	503.4	518.4	532.4	536.5	33597	35952	37945	38836
2920	Automobile bodies, trailers and semi-trailers	1154	1257	1210	1308	40.1	42.5	43.1	43.0	1458	1569	1623	1648
2930	Parts and accessories for motor vehicles	1230	1127	1232	1264	269.9	275.5	273.6	273.1	12916	13469	13813	14224
301	Building of ships and boats	500	509	456	470	18.9	19.0	20.4	19.8	900	908	984	1008
3011	Building of ships and floating structures	130	134	100	121	12.6	12.9	12.9	12.5	636	657	663	686
3012	Building of pleasure and sporting boats	369	375	356	350	6.3	6.1	7.5	7.3	264	251	322	322
3020	Railway locomotives and rolling stock	102	100	81	68	21.0	21.8	22.1	20.6	1118	1209	1275	1235
3030	Air and spacecraft and related machinery	202	133	206	160	74.8	75.0	75.1	70.3	5007	5182	5393	4947
3040	Military fighting vehicles	...	...	...	...	...	...	...	...	...	...	...	...
309	Transport equipment n.e.c.	...	...	...	...	...	...	...	...	...	...	...	...
3091	Motorcycles	119	186	193	184	5.2	4.6	6.4	6.0	171	148	210	207
3092	Bicycles and invalid carriages	...	...	...	...	...	...	...	...	...	...	...	...
3099	Other transport equipment n.e.c.	...	...	...	...	...	...	...	...	...	...	...	...
3100	Furniture	10276	10475	8904	11053	135.1	132.2	132.4	137.9	4231	4269	4307	4524
321	Jewellery, bijouterie and related articles	3446	3273	2905	3374	10.8	7.5	10.3	11.6	232	183	224	246
3211	Jewellery and related articles	3202	3048	2720	3197	9.7	6.7	9.6	10.4	212	166	207	218
3212	Imitation jewellery and related articles	244	225	185	177	1.2	0.8	0.7	1.2	20	17	17	28
3220	Musical instruments	1281	1337	1052	1351	6.3	5.6	6.1	6.0	171	162	162	171
3230	Sports goods	382	355	343	358	6.7	7.1	6.7	7.1	199	217	212	217
3240	Games and toys	579	561	384	553	13.1	13.3	13.3	13.7	420	424	447	456
3250	Medical and dental instruments and supplies	11322	12208	11976	12220	174.0	177.5	175.4	164.1	5772	6187	6071	6069
3290	Other manufacturing n.e.c.	2216	2063	1789	2067	28.0	30.1	31.1	27.7	888	953	967	901
331	Repair of fabricated metal products/machinery	10384	9298	8495	9887	132.5	136.5	128.2	132.0	5252	5385	5165	5511
3311	Repair of fabricated metal products	988	760	888	1047	13.1	14.1	12.1	13.9	515	531	455	498
3312	Repair of machinery	6420	5712	5314	5941	60.7	60.0	58.9	59.4	2261	2208	2170	2331
3313	Repair of electronic and optical equipment	427	400	363	387	5.0	6.3	4.6	5.9	179	214	172	270
3314	Repair of electrical equipment	602	549	529	990	11.8	13.2	10.9	10.8	435	482	400	414
3315	Repair of transport equip., excl. motor vehicles	1534	1421	1045	1052	39.6	39.7	39.5	39.5	1804	1879	1911	1920
3319	Repair of other equipment	415	456	354	470	2.3	3.1	2.2	2.5	58	70	58	79
3320	Installation of industrial machinery/equipment	4534	4471	3852	4331	90.7	90.4	91.7	90.8	3850	4051	4097	4146
C	Total manufacturing	201826	205028	202824	212602	7061.2	7093.7	7104.1	7198.2	300306	311009	320591	330050

a/ 1910 includes 1920.

Germany

ISIC	Industry	Output (valuation not defined) (millions of Euros)					Value added at factor values (millions of Euros)					Gross fixed capital formation (millions of Euros)		
		Note	2013	2014	2015	2016	Note	2013	2014	2015	2016	Note	2015	2016
1010	Processing/preserving of meat		43778	42924	42578	43032		5989	6388	6569	6964		808	1061
1020	Processing/preserving of fish, etc.		2008	1962	2019	2035		352	333	372	364		34	46
1030	Processing/preserving of fruit,vegetables		9260	9279	9367	9805		1884	1879	1960	2016		298	344
1040	Vegetable and animal oils and fats		5620	5249	5078	5063		362	444	447	476		128	144
1050	Dairy products		28583	27892	25391	25295		3163	3226	3378	3483		860	911
106	Grain mill products,starches and starch products		6342	6001	5839	6530		1172	1151	1060	1173		249	226
1061	Grain mill products		4576	4326	4225	4853		825	822	781	820		158	172
1062	Starches and starch products		1766	1674	1614	1677		347	330	280	352		91	54
107	Other food products		52298	52697	53078	55199		16289	16343	17623	19422		2338	2366
1071	Bakery products		21655	21323	21526	22399		9567	9583	10173	10872		1050	1153
1072	Sugar		3388	2895	2482	2545		772	539	579	665		163	170
1073	Cocoa, chocolate and sugar confectionery		9655	10156	9722	9915		2020	2030	2108	2479		348	348
1074	Macaroni, noodles, couscous, etc.		397	391	427	460		93	108	125	130		16	11
1075	Prepared meals and dishes		2545	2906	3666	2984		576	738	965	832		108	100
1079	Other food products n.e.c.		14658	15026	15254	16896		3261	3346	3673	4443		652	584
1080	Prepared animal feeds		9432	9446	9659	9621		1492	1585	1606	1644		176	247
110	Beverages		19506	20029	19410	20379		5054	5127	5391	5767		1476	1232
1101	Distilling, rectifying and blending of spirits		2652	3252	2466	2627		355	418	370	389		87	39
1102	Wines		...	...	...	...		...	...	...	...		36	...
1103	Malt liquors and malt		8435	8342	8539	8768		2604	2576	2762	2784		707	659
1104	Soft drinks,mineral waters,other bottled waters		6140	6211	6352	6813		1725	1785	1928	2179		646	488
1200	Tobacco products		13693	14104	15054	14140		1493	1546	1667	1786		169	110
131	Spinning, weaving and finishing of textiles		3559	3610	3492	3494		1171	1218	1142	1129		147	160
1311	Preparation and spinning of textile fibres		621	599	548	565		190	184	163	160		13	14
1312	Weaving of textiles		1750	1735	1713	1775		510	527	508	547		73	85
1313	Finishing of textiles		1189	1276	1231	1154		471	507	472	421		60	61
139	Other textiles		8085	8422	8659	8711		2529	2655	2738	2936		270	319
1391	Knitted and crocheted fabrics		655	695	681	702		169	180	162	197		14	17
1392	Made-up textile articles, except apparel		2180	2279	2267	2233		779	814	817	831		45	52
1393	Carpets and rugs		587	642	612	597		144	151	148	161		11	18
1394	Cordage, rope, twine and netting		...	...	...	221		...	...	...	78		11	12
1399	Other textiles n.e.c.		...	...	...	4958		...	...	...	1670		189	221
1410	Wearing apparel, except fur apparel		6870	7542	6606	6939		1968	2258	1867	1882		183	108
1420	Articles of fur		...	...	...	...		...	...	...	...		...	...
1430	Knitted and crocheted apparel		...	...	...	...		...	...	...	...		...	...
151	Leather;luggage,handbags,saddlery,harness;fur		1041	995	962	952		272	253	258	309		17	25
1511	Tanning/dressing of leather; dressing of fur		697	670	652	620		134	118	118	136		9	16
1512	Luggage,handbags,etc.;saddlery/harness		344	325	310	333		137	135	139	172		9	9
1520	Footwear		1420	1720	1624	1650		433	489	431	463		120	155
1610	Sawmilling and planing of wood		6190	6387	6279	6236		1094	1120	1239	1330		230	223

162	Wood products, cork, straw, plaiting materials	17216	17771	18837	17829	4795	4966	5341	5260	599	635
1621	Veneer sheets and wood-based panels	5433	5290	5755	5253	826	829	966	1060	306	211
1622	Builders' carpentry and joinery	8932	9215	9553	9339	3013	3174	3242	3217	218	...
1623	Wooden containers	1705	1794	1902	1889	544	527	597	582	35	...
1629	Other wood products;articles of cork,straw	1147	1472	1627	1348	411	436	536	402	40	91
170	Paper and paper products	37259	37044	37455	37858	9608	10110	10344	10599	1339	1598
1701	Pulp, paper and paperboard	15684	15723	16074	16511	3143	3594	3837	3843	423	561
1702	Corrugated paper and paperboard	11808	11632	11798	12042	3415	3419	3500	3523	496	538
1709	Other articles of paper and paperboard	9767	9689	9582	9304	3051	3096	3007	3233	420	499
181	Printing and service activities related to printing	18968	18091	17363	18587	7077	6721	6628	6927	770	873
1811	Printing	15749	15379	14715	16052	5370	5293	5185	5576	691	776
1812	Service activities related to printing	3219	2711	2648	2535	1707	1427	1443	1351	78	97
1820	Reproduction of recorded media	765	688	668	406	258	268	215	144	25	14
1910 a/	Coke oven products	109216	100699	81261	75813 a/	3559	2275	4073	4820	6	839a/
1920 a/	Refined petroleum products				a/					751	...a/
201	Basic chemicals,fertilizers, etc.	89604	86413	87720	80395	22695	22760	25201	24953	3835	3402
2011	Basic chemicals	59657	59345	59285	50076	15533	15679	17206	16330	2723	2130
2012	Fertilizers and nitrogen compounds	4030	3820	4011	3168	1486	1505	1655	1115	374	295
2013	Plastics and synthetic rubber in primary forms	25917	23248	24424	27151	5677	5576	6340	7508	737	978
202	Other chemical products	41244	44004	44260	46843	12180	13433	13711	16182	1294	1620
2021	Pesticides and other agrochemical products	986	1121	1211	1133	307	348	395	349	62	50
2022	Paints,varnishes;printing ink and mastics	10290	10920	10684	11048	3337	3674	3704	4148	255	280
2023	Soap,cleaning and cosmetic preparations	12764	14510	13903	14673	3162	3790	3984	5158	378	629
2029	Other chemical products n.e.c.	17204	17453	18462	19989	5374	5621	5628	6526	598	662
2030	Man-made fibres	2288	2401	2236	2325	587	664	615	721	55	64
2100	Pharmaceuticals,medicinal chemicals, etc.	42828	43841	44220	46993	15754	17101	16020	17763	2001	2435
221	Rubber products	14030	14999	14831	15203	5196	5700	5733	6142	751	595
2211	Rubber tyres and tubes	5126	5412	5135	5453	2031	2195	2187	2416	364	278
2219	Other rubber products	8903	9587	9696	9750	3165	3505	3546	3726	387	317
2220	Plastics products	58808	59775	62009	64013	18583	18978	20000	21580	2803	2698
2310	Glass and glass products	9554	9807	9824	10198	3397	3662	3613	4005	469	564
239	Non-metallic mineral products n.e.c.	33941	35229	33729	35108	11271	12102	11649	12680	1475	1526
2391	Refractory products	1520	1523	1482	1498	475	483	456	452	58	39
2392	Clay building materials	2386	2351	2329	2394	915	923	947	986	114	111
2393	Other porcelain and ceramic products									103	99
2394	Cement, lime and plaster	3743	3815	3730	4411	1227	1326	1286	1742	270	339
2395	Articles of concrete, cement and plaster	14705	14903	15272	14717	4397	4641	4695	4546	578	545
2396	Cutting, shaping and finishing of stone	2326	3054	1791	2578	1064	1195	959	1295	92	132
2399	Other non-metallic mineral products n.e.c.	6937	6995	6615	7028	2050	2220	2169	2432	260	261
2410	Basic iron and steel	50714	49449	47874	43455	9442	9842	9529	9427	1352	1324
2420	Basic precious and other non-ferrous metals	32131	31722	33885	33375	4438	4318	4874	5252	793	711
243	Casting of metals	14547	14682	14975	13800	4598	4868	4894	4853	623	632
2431	Casting of iron and steel	7477	7472	7607	7345	2498	2621	2690	2644	276	288
2432	Casting of non-ferrous metals	7069	7211	7368	6455	2101	2247	2204	2208	346	344
251	Struct.metal products, tanks, reservoirs	29591	28664	29693	30114	10713	10688	11069	11314	802	835

continued

Germany

ISIC	Industry	Note	Output (valuation not defined) (millions of Euros)				Note	Value added at factor values (millions of Euros)				Note	Gross fixed capital formation (millions of Euros)	
			2013	2014	2015	2016		2013	2014	2015	2016		2015	2016
2511	Structural metal products		24311	23738	24561	25288		8879	9009	9214	9614		705	721
2512	Tanks, reservoirs and containers of metal		4147	3771	4057	3865		1472	1306	1462	1390		84	103
2513	Steam generators, excl. hot water boilers		1133	1155	1076	962		362	373	393	310		12	12
2520	Weapons and ammunition		2539	2375	2423	2931		1066	997	1006	1202		83	86
259	Other metal products;metal working services		90361	93580	91532	95801		36101	37825	37496	40486		4125	4353
2591	Forging,pressing,stamping,roll-forming of metal		20958	21134	20839	22217		6800	7041	6949	8120		841	913
2592	Treatment and coating of metals; machining		27576	28799	28554	30744		12538	12947	13125	14302		1505	1578
2593	Cutlery, hand tools and general hardware		19096	20434	20503	21082		8569	9187	9182	9606		966	1039
2599	Other fabricated metal products n.e.c.		22731	23213	21636	21758		8194	8649	8239	8459		813	823
2610	Electronic components and boards		17329	17232	19869	19832		5013	5563	6974	7659		1114	1095
2620	Computers and peripheral equipment		5111	5193	5386	4901		1549	1765	1739	1585		70	...
2630	Communication equipment		4786	5195	5360	5265		1757	2015	2030	2061		150	120
2640	Consumer electronics		2944	2850	3007	...		677	776	843	...		61	67
265	Measuring,testing equipment; watches, etc.		27075	27916	29026	33633		11756	12207	12583	13798		855	1039
2651	Measuring/testing/navigating equipment,etc.		26564	27391	28498	33086		11515	11953	12328	13543		836	1016
2652	Watches and clocks		511	525	528	547		241	254	255	256		19	24
2660	Irradiation/electromedical equipment,etc.		2494	2402	7376	7918		954	953	2844	3244		94	107
2670	Optical instruments and photographic equipment		5650	5813	6382	6483		2380	2498	2557	2754		196	201
2680	Magnetic and optical media		132	85	77	...		37	27	21	...		3	...
2710	Electric motors,generators,transformers,etc.		56899	57475	54666	54674		21792	23329	20719	21141		1198	1283
2720	Batteries and accumulators		2541	2448	3870	2420		488	506	436	466		88	81
273	Wiring and wiring devices		15722	15989	15725	16243		5553	5948	6026	6310		614	638
2731	Fibre optic cables		248	247	242	248		78	72	72	79		8	8
2732	Other electronic and electric wires and cables		5711	5511	5351	5227		1198	1286	1301	1359		80	100
2733	Wiring devices		9763	10231	10133	10768		4278	4590	4653	4871		526	531
2740	Electric lighting equipment		6158	7779	6445	7785		2448	2794	2316	2557		207	195
2750	Domestic appliances		9315	9520	10082	10740		3198	3301	3543	3922		386	392
2790	Other electrical equipment		9069	9296	9266	9769		3694	3785	4062	3985		287	255
281	General-purpose machinery		135425	140294	145812	150392		48771	51856	53091	55444		4908	5199
2811	Engines/turbines,excl.aircraft,vehicle engines		29340	30108	32853	35814		9635	10250	10634	11388		1511	1735
2812	Fluid power equipment		8581	8955	9019	8607		3732	3882	3754	3895		396	292
2813	Other pumps, compressors, taps and valves		20124	20764	20738	20627		7489	7809	7935	7901		720	681
2814	Bearings, gears, gearing and driving elements		15723	17423	18006	17665		6399	7064	7335	7452		721	786
2815	Ovens, furnaces and furnace burners		2838	2774	2648	3077		993	984	986	1075		55	97
2816	Lifting and handling equipment		15562	15836	16524	17356		5142	5461	5441	6050		350	369
2817	Office machinery, excl.computers,etc.		971	930	1007	1086		260	241	248	238		12	12
2818	Power-driven hand tools		2128	2289	2518	2561		949	1026	1096	1129		121	87
2819	Other general-purpose machinery		40158	41215	42499	43600		14172	15139	15662	16315		1023	1140
282	Special-purpose machinery		92499	94565	92975	95071		31223	32302	32226	33251		2150	2297
2821	Agricultural and forestry machinery		12811	11628	11108	11184		3727	3483	3264	3118		282	294
2822	Metal-forming machinery and machine tools		21252	21865	21999	22483		7649	8039	8317	8739		532	600

2823	Machinery for metallurgy	2891	2796	2554	2605	995	911	673	829	22	29
2824	Mining, quarrying and construction machinery	12941	13948	13389	13193	3630	3731	3611	3690	310	278
2825	Food/beverage/tobacco processing machinery	5363	5819	5423	5911	1997	2079	1955	2284	120	150
2826	Textile/apparel/leather production machinery	4743	4658	4587	4764	1685	1647	1566	1743	134	98
2829	Other special-purpose machinery	32499	33852	33915	34932	11542	12412	12843	12847	751	848
2910	Motor vehicles	237680	259630	284313	292785	56385	65476	70381	79163	11719	12788
2920	Automobile bodies, trailers and semi-trailers	9026	9527	10244	10904	2235	2327	2582	2759	205	171
2930	Parts and accessories for motor vehicles	70474	75164	76235	80326	19720	21576	21848	23716	2405	2469
301	Building of ships and boats	6270	6467	5976	6406	1262	1244	929	1516	86	95
3011	Building of ships and floating structures	4129	4807	4030	4560	743	879	467	1037	43	53
3012	Building of pleasure and sporting boats	2142	1660	1947	1845	519	365	462	479	43	42
3020	Railway locomotives and rolling stock	5325	5964	5834	5191	1259	1545	1682	1441	126	106
3030	Air and spacecraft and related machinery	24189	25397	27559	28642	7479	8196	8490	8728	915	896
3040	Military fighting vehicles	⋮	⋮	⋮	⋮	⋮	⋮	⋮	⋮	⋮	⋮
309	Transport equipment n.e.c.	⋮	⋮	⋮	⋮	⋮	⋮	⋮	⋮	12	10
3091	Motorcycles	⋮	⋮	⋮	⋮	⋮	⋮	⋮	⋮	24	23
3092	Bicycles and invalid carriages	1067	928	1156	1758	232	246	299	393	⋮	⋮
3099	Other transport equipment n.e.c.	⋮	⋮	⋮	⋮	⋮	⋮	⋮	⋮	⋮	⋮
3100	Furniture	19237	19666	20662	22556	6650	6832	7087	7476	578	560
321	Jewellery, bijouterie and related articles	1203	939	1185	1685	449	374	485	636	47	41
3211	Jewellery and related articles	1129	868	1113	1578	415	340	454	588	42	39
3212	Imitation jewellery and related articles	74	70	73	107	35	34	31	47	5	2
3220	Musical instruments	487	603	605	691	286	319	328	330	20	31
3230	Sports goods	813	824	854	842	312	317	335	335	17	25
3240	Games and toys	2681	2700	2834	2725	1105	1119	1273	1221	376	255
3250	Medical and dental instruments and supplies	20603	20593	21469	21416	10021	10368	10408	10424	899	835
3290	Other manufacturing n.e.c.	3561	3753	3865	3871	1527	1673	1751	1792	127	125
331	Repair of fabricated metal products/machinery	22154	22269	21581	23157	8184	8569	8293	8429	408	389
3311	Repair of fabricated metal products	1555	1712	1390	1730	760	839	701	744	25	28
3312	Repair of machinery	8835	8405	7539	8294	3406	3504	3398	3670	175	160
3313	Repair of electronic and optical equipment	538	707	591	796	255	351	291	400	24	13
3314	Repair of electrical equipment	1478	1681	1306	1199	685	821	656	588	18	17
3315	Repair of transport equip., excl. motor vehicles	9559	9560	10521	10852	2985	2940	3129	2889	159	166
3319	Repair of other equipment	189	204	234	287	93	114	119	138	8	6
3320	Installation of industrial machinery/equipment	15251	16695	15969	16494	5532	5773	5910	6049	207	209
C	Total manufacturing	1748344	1787370	1808881	1841942	490617	519793	534932	569864	62042	64563

a/ 1910 includes 1920.

Germany

ISIC Revision 4

Index numbers of industrial production (2010=100)

ISIC	Industry	Note	2005	2006	2007	2008	2009	2010	2011	2012	2013	2014	2015	2016
10	Food products		94	96	99	99	98	100	101	101	100	101	101	102
11	Beverages		108	110	105	103	99	100	104	103	104	105	98	99
12	Tobacco products		182	171	166	121	117	100	96	82	77	73	74	75
13	Textiles		116	115	116	111	89	100	102	94	93	96	98	99
14	Wearing apparel		169	149	137	117	100	100	99	90	87	91	87	87
15	Leather and related products		92	88	99	91	93	100	106	97	96	110	118	116
16	Wood products, excluding furniture		103	110	109	107	94	100	116	116	114	112	111	112
17	Paper and paper products		91	95	100	100	93	100	101	99	97	96	97	96
18	Printing and reproduction of recorded media		101	104	106	107	99	100	101	98	94	94	92	90
19	Coke and refined petroleum products		113	112	111	111	102	100	100	102	99	98	101	102
20	Chemicals and chemical products		98	101	103	99	85	100	101	98	99	97	97	97
21	Pharmaceuticals, medicinal chemicals, etc.		84	88	98	102	99	100	105	102	108	113	118	122
22	Rubber and plastics products		93	97	103	101	88	100	106	104	105	106	108	111
23	Other non-metallic mineral products		102	108	109	106	93	100	108	103	103	105	105	108
24	Basic metals		103	111	115	113	83	100	105	101	100	103	103	103
25	Fabricated metal products, except machinery		95	102	109	112	87	100	112	110	111	114	115	118
26	Computer, electronic and optical products		76	90	103	110	86	100	114	112	112	116	120	124
27	Electrical equipment		93	101	107	108	85	100	109	105	102	104	103	104
28	Machinery and equipment n.e.c.		98	105	116	122	90	100	114	115	113	115	115	115
29	Motor vehicles, trailers and semi-trailers		97	100	106	102	80	100	113	113	114	119	120	122
30	Other transport equipment		87	95	99	108	106	100	113	120	124	126	135	144
31	Furniture		107	115	117	115	98	100	103	102	97	97	101	101
32	Other manufacturing		89	95	99	101	93	100	105	108	111	116	120	124
33	Repair and installation of machinery/equipment		88	93	101	114	97	100	108	108	109	111	117	115
C	Total manufacturing		95	101	107	108	89	100	109	107	107	109	111	112

Greece

Supplier of information:
National Statistical Service of Greece, Athens.
Industrial statistics for the OECD countries are compiled by the OECD secretariat, which supplies them to UNIDO.

Basic source of data:
Annual survey; administrative data; business register.

Major deviations from ISIC (Revision 4):
Data presented in ISIC (Revision 4) were originally classified according to the national NACE-related classification system.

Reference period:
Calendar year.

Scope:
All enterprises.

Method of data collection:
Not reported.

Type of enumeration:
Administrative data as main source beginning with reference year 2015; survey conducted on large enterprises of each sector.

Adjusted for non-response:
Not reported.

Concepts and definitions of variables:
No deviations from the standard UN concepts and definitions are reported.

Related national publications:
None reported.

Greece

ISIC	Industry	Number of enterprises (number)				Number of employees (number)				Wages and salaries paid to employees (millions of Euros)			
		2013	2014	2015a/	2016	2013	2014	2015a/	2016	2013	2014	2015a/	2016
1010	Processing/preserving of meat	477	444	441	439	7058	7089	8711	9125	109.2	110.1	138.5	144.0
1020	Processing/preserving of fish, etc.	92	83	92	87	1832	1027	1267	1317	34.6	16.4	18.7	17.7
1030	Processing/preserving of fruit,vegetables	632	588	726	749	10352	10176	12808	13103	173.0	170.7	197.0	205.9
1040	Vegetable and animal oils and fats	1507	1406	1824	1956	3638	3525	3704	4118	59.9	60.2	53.3	58.5
1050	Dairy products	882	824	884	905	9508	8938	9273	9673	185.0	174.5	182.7	184.6
106	Grain mill products,starches and starch products	315	291	272	276	2900	2880	2990	2866	55.5	53.5	59.0	57.8
1061	Grain mill products	305	281	262	266	2888	2868	2976	2854	55.4	53.4	58.8	57.7
1062	Starches and starch products	10	10	10	10	12	12	14	12	0.2	0.1	0.2	0.2
107	Other food products	10541	9834	11239	11205	32601	32574	43200	48218	516.5	499.9	600.6	634.3
1071	Bakery products	9295	8675	9799	9757	23437	22855	32344	37354	331.0	310.2	385.4	418.5
1072	Sugar	...	...	...	4	...	...	...	418	...	...	...	11.1
1073	Cocoa, chocolate and sugar confectionery	461	433	487	476	3011	3001	3392	3278	52.3	52.2	60.2	61.3
1074	Macaroni, noodles, couscous, etc.	191	178	295	301	856	840	716	822	18.2	18.4	17.6	19.3
1075	Prepared meals and dishes	54	49	99	104	183	202	603	683	2.6	2.7	6.8	7.9
1079	Other food products n.e.c.	...	...	...	563	...	...	...	5663	...	...	...	116.2
1080	Prepared animal feeds	228	215	212	219	1429	1454	1639	1634	26.7	27.1	29.8	28.1
110	Beverages	755	757	1013	1097	8562	8463	8191	7856	210.8	217.5	225.4	223.2
1101	Distilling, rectifying and blending of spirits	197	197	300	306	614	615	548	633	11.1	10.7	11.1	13.2
1102	Wines	441	441	570	642	2827	2772	2610	2463	53.5	52.7	50.7	51.7
1103	Malt liquors and malt	16	16	35	40	1736	1718	1672	1425	56.5	62.9	63.8	55.1
1104	Soft drinks,mineral waters,other bottled waters	101	103	108	109	3385	3358	3361	3335	89.6	91.2	99.7	103.2
1200	Tobacco products	6	6	18	20	1748	1790	1926	1838	67.1	68.0	67.4	79.3
131	Spinning, weaving and finishing of textiles	405	426	397	388	2563	2363	2013	2041	38.6	35.1	31.8	30.1
1311	Preparation and spinning of textile fibres	66	69	63	61	1110	1138	1102	1112	19.2	18.4	18.5	17.6
1312	Weaving of textiles	96	98	85	82	459	261	194	196	4.8	3.4	2.7	2.8
1313	Finishing of textiles	243	259	249	245	994	964	717	733	14.6	13.3	10.6	9.7
139	Other textiles	1225	1295	1269	1257	4643	4608	3895	4232	69.8	68.5	62.1	68.2
1391	Knitted and crocheted fabrics	103	105	73	69	565	459	332	325	8.2	6.3	4.8	4.8
1392	Made-up textile articles, except apparel	795	848	876	877	2010	2079	1355	1555	27.8	28.0	19.9	23.5
1393	Carpets and rugs	24	23	26	26	208	191	185	196	2.9	2.9	2.9	2.9
1394	Cordage, rope, twine and netting	46	48	48	47	753	761	932	985	12.8	12.8	15.4	16.3
1399	Other textiles n.e.c.	257	271	246	238	1108	1118	1091	1171	18.1	18.6	19.2	20.8
1410	Wearing apparel, except fur apparel	4875	5558	3708	3735	8912	9475	8155	9027	121.8	122.2	101.4	109.6
1420	Articles of fur	1161	1328	828	829	1827	2105	1568	1862	21.4	22.9	13.7	14.9
1430	Knitted and crocheted apparel	246	282	174	165	394	415	408	389	5.1	5.1	5.6	4.5
151	Leather;luggage,handbags,saddlery,harness;fur	384	421	284	279	580	604	871	949	6.3	7.1	10.9	11.9
1511	Tanning/dressing of leather; dressing of fur	175	193	102	99	321	346	551	586	3.5	4.2	7.0	7.5
1512	Luggage,handbags,etc.;saddlery/harness	209	228	182	180	259	258	320	363	2.8	2.9	3.8	4.5
1520	Footwear	665	723	509	508	1227	1273	1120	1237	15.0	15.2	13.4	14.4
1610	Sawmilling and planing of wood	296	309	278	270	557	603	731	855	7.6	8.0	8.7	9.8

Code	Description													
162	Wood products, cork, straw, plaiting materials	2876	2982	2703	2845	3590	3494	2583	3515	49.1	48.6	32.4	42.2
1621	Veneer sheets and wood-based panels	58	61	56	54	723	685	679	651	13.6	12.0	11.7	10.9
1622	Builders' carpentry and joinery	2054	2127	1734	1730	2014	1957	1126	1792	25.4	27.0	12.4	20.1
1623	Wooden containers	201	209	178	192	329	317	417	530	4.1	3.6	4.4	5.3
1629	Other wood products;articles of cork, straw	563	585	735	869	524	535	361	542	6.1	6.1	3.9	5.9
170	Paper and paper products	633	641	673	639	6492	6938	6676	6797	126.5	130.9	138.3	144.3
1701	Pulp, paper and paperboard	:	90	87	89	:	785	755	715	:	16.8	18.3	17.8
1702	Corrugated paper and paperboard	222	225	230	216	2613	2702	2884	2881	50.5	49.7	56.0	58.2
1709	Other articles of paper and paperboard	:	:	:	:	:	:	:	:	:	:	:	:
181	Printing and service activities related to printing	2336	2217	2756	2651	7409	6702	6011	6602	131.0	117.4	101.5	109.7
1811	Printing	1402	1330	1645	1592	5250	4763	4483	4812	99.2	88.4	78.6	83.2
1812	Service activities related to printing	934	887	1111	1059	2160	1939	1528	1790	31.8	29.1	22.9	26.5
1820	Reproduction of recorded media	81	78	73	64	438	412	410	424	8.7	8.0	7.6	7.7
1910	Coke oven products	11	11	7	7	32	32	8	8	0.7	0.5	0.1	0.1
1920	Refined petroleum products	37	36	33	34	3908	3882	3557	3370	220.1	206.8	218.7	234.0
201	Basic chemicals,fertilizers, etc.	176	171	191	188	2600	2412	2380	1849	68.4	62.7	64.8	50.7
2011	Basic chemicals	:	:	:	78	:	:	:	838	:	:	:	23.4
2012	Fertilizers and nitrogen compounds	41	40	46	49	821	846	815	477	26.1	25.4	24.1	13.9
2013	Plastics and synthetic rubber in primary forms	:	:	:	:	:	:	:	:	:	:	:	:
202	Other chemical products	498	492	790	784	8894	8500	7786	7811	195.7	189.9	188.0	193.1
2021	Pesticides and other agrochemical products	21	21	24	25	547	526	598	609	13.5	12.9	17.5	18.5
2022	Paints,varnishes;printing ink and mastics	135	133	128	124	2443	2346	1840	1784	49.5	48.4	41.3	39.9
2023	Soap,cleaning and cosmetic preparations	236	234	439	440	4615	4391	3978	4135	107.1	102.4	95.9	101.5
2029	Other chemical products n.e.c.	106	104	199	195	1290	1237	1370	1283	25.5	26.2	33.4	33.2
2030	Man-made fibres	3	3	8	7	7	7	23	20	0.1	0.1	0.3	0.3
2100	Pharmaceuticals,medicinal chemicals, etc.	93	80	90	92	10077	7051	9030	8969	242.4	174.6	260.3	268.4
221	Rubber products	129	130	109	99	1027	966	607	431	21.0	18.5	14.6	19.6
2211	Rubber tyres and tubes	31	32	26	25	134	140	36	46	2.0	1.9	0.5	0.7
2219	Other rubber products	98	98	83	74	893	826	571	385	19.0	16.6	14.0	18.8
2220	Plastics products	1085	1096	926	926	12416	12352	9807	9721	225.1	214.4	185.7	187.5
2310	Glass and glass products	279	278	283	279	1123	1067	965	1020	21.2	19.5	18.5	19.0
239	Non-metallic mineral products n.e.c.	2915	2881	3030	3032	13070	12656	11167	11983	268.0	247.3	239.0	252.6
2391	Refractory products	27	27	29	26	220	214	207	185	3.8	3.6	3.1	3.4
2392	Clay building materials	91	85	82	87	787	524	520	456	14.2	8.5	8.0	7.3
2393	Other porcelain and ceramic products	:	357	:	:	:	595	:	:	:	7.2	:	:
2394	Cement, lime and plaster	175	177	125	121	2341	2120	1759	1607	91.5	85.5	85.5	81.3
2395	Articles of concrete, cement and plaster	1120	1111	1122	1128	5036	5131	4083	4397	86.0	81.6	72.0	77.6
2396	Cutting, shaping and finishing of stone	1020	1006	1045	1049	3301	3327	2982	3518	50.7	48.4	45.9	56.5
2399	Other non-metallic mineral products n.e.c.	119	118	110	105	753	746	1347	1403	13.1	12.6	21.9	23.0
2410	Basic iron and steel	582	549	210	209	7307	6599	3007	2949	161.8	135.4	93.1	90.4
2420	Basic precious and other non-ferrous metals	206	200	88	77	5889	5937	4404	1860	143.1	145.2	114.9	38.3
243	Casting of metals	297	281	99	94	2713	2527	638	675	45.4	39.6	13.4	15.0
2431	Casting of iron and steel	200	188	61	61	1890	1755	485	510	32.7	28.6	11.4	12.4
2432	Casting of non-ferrous metals	97	93	38	33	823	772	153	165	12.7	11.0	2.1	2.5
251	Struct.metal products, tanks, reservoirs	5241	5445	6364	6396	12227	12093	9878	12216	172.0	162.8	138.8	174.5

continued

Greece

ISIC Revision 4

ISIC	Industry	Number of enterprises (number)				Number of employees (number)					Wages and salaries paid to employees (millions of Euros)				
		2013	2014	2015a/	2016	Note	2013	2014	2015a/	2016	Note	2013	2014	2015a/	2016
2511	Structural metal products	5096	5301	6211	6232		11584	11529	9236	11558		162.7	154.2	128.8	163.9
2512	Tanks, reservoirs and containers of metal	134	132	138	149		596	512	552	564		8.8	8.1	8.7	9.2
2513	Steam generators, excl. hot water boilers	11	12	15	15		47	52	90	94		0.5	0.6	1.3	1.4
2520	Weapons and ammunition	22	24	31	26		898	825	558	567		18.6	21.3	11.5	11.0
259	Other metal products;metal working services	2113	2203	2657	2574		8706	8845	8001	8196		177.0	169.0	160.8	166.9
2591	Forging,pressing,stamping,roll-forming of metal	196	206	245	230		311	320	259	328		3.9	3.9	2.9	3.8
2592	Treatment and coating of metals;machining	632	664	908	885		1814	1795	1668	1789		30.0	26.5	25.0	25.0
2593	Cutlery, hand tools and general hardware	261	267	298	279		2009	2059	2048	2147		42.2	43.5	48.1	54.4
2599	Other fabricated metal products n.e.c.	1024	1066	1206	1180		4573	4671	4026	3932		100.9	95.0	84.9	83.7
2610	Electronic components and boards	78	62	128	132		591	556	444	779		9.9	10.1	14.7	23.4
2620	Computers and peripheral equipment	46	32	77	83		204	137	160	166		2.6	2.2	2.6	2.8
2630	Communication equipment	47	36	75	77		490	419	398	423		9.1	8.2	7.9	8.7
2640	Consumer electronics	24	17	39	38		67	45	27	30		0.9	0.8	0.4	0.4
265	Measuring,testing equipment; watches, etc.	61	49	86	82		1111	1227	1244	897		23.6	25.5	28.8	16.8
2651	Measuring/testing/navigating equipment,etc.	55	44	76	71		1099	1219	1244	895		23.4	25.3	28.8	16.7
2652	Watches and clocks	6	5	10	11		12	8	-	2		0.2	0.2	-	-
2660	Irradiation/electromedical equipment,etc.	7	5	18	15		80	92	84	11		2.1	2.6	2.6	0.2
2670	Optical instruments and photographic equipment	13	11	15	15		106	101	104	113		1.8	1.8	1.9	2.1
2680	Magnetic and optical media	4	3	7	8		6	3	20	9		0.2	0.1	0.7	0.3
2710	Electric motors,generators,transformers,etc.	208	192	219	201		1452	1317	1283	1263		27.2	24.2	27.2	28.6
2720	Batteries and accumulators	13	13	15	15		459	557	588	626		12.1	11.4	12.9	14.0
273	Wiring and wiring devices	35	34	40	41		1117	1064	1070	1128		28.3	26.2	27.4	23.4
2731	Fibre optic cables	...	...	...	...		...	...	...	...		...	...	...	...
2732	Other electronic and electric wires and cables	26	25	30	...		1065	1012	1009	...		27.6	25.6	26.2	...
2733	Wiring devices	...	...	...	11		...	...	...	63		...	...	...	1.2
2740	Electric lighting equipment	281	263	376	376		944	811	956	1006		12.6	10.7	13.0	13.8
2750	Domestic appliances	212	202	218	210		1785	1465	1425	1357		35.3	29.8	33.7	32.7
2790	Other electrical equipment	85	81	78	72		428	523	522	186		8.9	10.2	11.3	3.5
281	General-purpose machinery	695	675	754	740		5794	5712	4328	4306		93.8	99.6	80.6	81.7
2811	Engines/turbines,excl.aircraft,vehicle engines	33	32	35	36		157	144	107	121		2.8	2.7	1.6	1.8
2812	Fluid power equipment	17	17	32	36		76	74	86	92		1.2	1.2	1.4	1.5
2813	Other pumps, compressors, taps and valves	72	71	70	67		496	503	387	392		8.0	8.4	7.0	6.7
2814	Bearings, gears, gearing and driving elements	32	31	36	38		169	165	67	77		2.5	2.6	1.1	1.2
2815	Ovens, furnaces and furnace burners	29	29	29	30		258	244	119	93		3.7	3.4	1.8	1.6
2816	Lifting and handling equipment	149	140	149	143		2132	1962	1695	1782		33.8	32.1	29.4	32.2
2817	Office machinery, excl.computers,etc.	9	9	10	10		35	35	62	57		0.6	0.6	1.2	1.0
2818	Power-driven hand tools	4	4	5	5		17	16	-	-		0.3	0.3	-	-
2819	Other general-purpose machinery	350	342	388	375		2454	2569	1805	1692		41.0	48.5	37.1	35.6
282	Special-purpose machinery	1056	1026	1231	1213		5898	6089	3541	3899		91.8	93.3	58.2	64.0
2821	Agricultural and forestry machinery	353	345	443	450		1661	1619	718	908		24.4	23.9	10.0	12.0
2822	Metal-forming machinery and machine tools	363	351	416	400		1840	1803	896	1028		27.4	27.1	12.7	14.5

Code	Description												
2823	Machinery for metallurgy	61	59	65	64	343	354	206	247	5.2	5.8	3.5	4.2
2824	Mining, quarrying and construction machinery	42	40	41	37	258	225	130	123	4.5	3.5	2.1	2.1
2825	Food/beverage/tobacco processing machinery	103	100	117	117	819	764	724	753	11.8	11.9	12.1	13.4
2826	Textile/apparel/leather production machinery	32	31	34	34	237	250	184	197	5.0	4.6	3.4	3.8
2829	Other special-purpose machinery	102	100	115	111	740	1074	683	643	13.6	16.5	14.4	14.0
2910	Motor vehicles	11	11	21	18	443	155	423	409	7.7	2.3	7.6	7.3
2920	Automobile bodies, trailers and semi-trailers	86	84	143	136	747	757	428	443	13.9	13.4	8.5	9.4
2930	Parts and accessories for motor vehicles	104	105	256	259	888	898	560	569	12.5	12.0	6.9	7.6
301	Building of ships and boats	175	...	274	267	1570	...	1378	1511	35.1	...	33.9	33.3
3011	Building of ships and floating structures	115	...	191	190	1373	...	1229	1348	32.9	...	31.3	30.4
3012	Building of pleasure and sporting boats	60	...	83	77	197	...	149	163	2.3	...	2.5	2.9
3020	Railway locomotives and rolling stock	...	...	4	5	...	...	9	9	...	...	0.3	0.4
3030	Air and spacecraft and related machinery	...	16	20	21	...	1443	1448	1406	...	33.1	35.0	32.3
3040	Military fighting vehicles	-	-	-	-	-	-	-	-	-	-	-	-
309	Transport equipment n.e.c.	21	21	30	31	231	219	202	221	4.1	3.9	3.5	3.8
3091	Motorcycles	...	...	10	12	...	...	6	10	...	...	0.1	0.1
3092	Bicycles and invalid carriages	13	13	17	16	209	197	184	195	3.7	3.6	3.2	3.4
3099	Other transport equipment n.e.c.	...	...	3	3	...	...	12	16	...	...	0.2	0.2
3100	Furniture	2934	3152	4056	4040	5837	6017	6031	7405	69.4	69.7	68.6	83.9
321	Jewellery, bijouterie and related articles	2199	2032	1842	1860	2624	2531	1525	2093	31.5	31.4	17.4	23.6
3211	Jewellery and related articles	1968	1818	1842 b/	1860 b/	2251	2125	1525 b/	2093 b/	27.3	26.9	17.4 b/	23.6 b/
3212	Imitation jewellery and related articles	231	214	... b/	... b/	373	406	... b/	... b/	4.2	4.5	... b/	... b/
3220	Musical instruments	97	87	75	76	114	108	46	80	1.3	1.2	0.3	0.5
3230	Sports goods	72	66	41	42	317	271	278	375	4.1	3.3	3.2	3.8
3240	Games and toys	150	140	77	74	169	157	120	141	2.0	2.0	1.4	1.5
3250	Medical and dental instruments and supplies	393	360	1570	1526	865	866	1826	2238	11.1	10.8	21.7	28.0
3290	Other manufacturing n.e.c.	675	624	520	524	898	809	695	797	10.6	10.0	7.7	8.6
331	Repair of fabricated metal products/machinery	3060	3418	3634	3689	7296	7542	8481	9671	121.2	122.5	132.6	145.3
3311	Repair of fabricated metal products	114	130	146	155	227	238	201	237	3.8	4.2	3.9	4.1
3312	Repair of machinery	1562	1744	1909	1922	2853	2956	1842	2365	43.2	42.6	29.1	37.4
3313	Repair of electronic and optical equipment	194	220	257	257	283	318	163	236	3.8	4.5	2.6	4.0
3314	Repair of electrical equipment	350	393	432	435	481	540	523	630	6.2	7.3	12.5	12.3
3315	Repair of transport equip., excl. motor vehicles	825	914	870	898	3434	3471	5746	6188	63.8	63.6	84.3	87.4
3319	Repair of other equipment	15	17	20	22	18	20	6	15	0.3	0.3	-	0.1
3320	Installation of industrial machinery/equipment	570	637	612	569	995	1033	1001	1163	13.4	14.5	13.4	15.1
C	Total manufacturing	57736	58211	61840	61862	254199	247159	240611	254053	4753.4	4518.5	4508.4	4643.0

a/ Methodological break in 2015.
b/ 3211 includes 3212.

Greece

ISIC	Industry	Note	Output (valuation not defined) (millions of Euros)				Note	Value added at factor values (millions of Euros)				Note	Gross fixed capital formation (millions of Euros)	
			2013	2014	2015a/	2016		2013	2014	2015a/	2016		2015	2016
1010	Processing/preserving of meat		1147.8	1218.5	1375.7	1444.2		219.2	229.4	286.1	272.1		38.8	32.3
1020	Processing/preserving of fish, etc.		429.6	131.1	188.6	169.6		43.7	36.7	44.8	40.4		5.5	6.7
1030	Processing/preserving of fruit,vegetables		1296.0	1317.3	1672.7	1621.1		392.7	398.2	464.0	479.2		60.6	53.2
1040	Vegetable and animal oils and fats		846.5	794.8	825.3	847.3		177.3	157.4	185.1	181.4		40.4	30.5
1050	Dairy products		1844.3	1926.8	2167.1	2095.3		358.0	405.5	444.1	408.8		86.4	97.5
106	Grain mill products,starches and starch products		587.4	560.3	630.0	574.2		125.6	112.3	116.6	120.7		16.1	11.1
1061	Grain mill products		586.0	558.8	628.9	573.2		125.2	111.8	116.3	120.4		14.6	11.1
1062	Starches and starch products		1.4	1.5	1.0	1.0		0.4	0.5	0.3	0.2		1.5	-
107	Other food products		3674.4	3672.9	3470.3	3416.4		1215.3	1185.1	1046.5	933.0		140.3	144.6
1071	Bakery products		2215.0	2198.4	1930.4	1876.2		759.9	747.6	616.4	558.2		83.7	93.0
1072	Sugar		...	...	...	34.2		...	...	...	1.5		...	-
1073	Cocoa, chocolate and sugar confectionery		370.5	391.4	411.9	414.6		118.0	119.0	129.7	123.6		16.7	16.8
1074	Macaroni, noodles, couscous, etc.		183.2	177.1	169.8	165.7		47.8	44.8	40.0	48.7		10.0	7.1
1075	Prepared meals and dishes		15.3	16.8	30.1	34.0		5.4	6.1	11.4	11.5		1.2	0.6
1079	Other food products n.e.c.		...	...	...	891.7		...	...	...	189.5		...	27.0
1080	Prepared animal feeds		493.7	540.1	520.3	504.9		82.8	99.2	95.0	95.7		8.6	9.8
110	Beverages		1694.8	1647.8	1747.2	1781.0		435.1	435.8	473.5	481.8		93.6	97.8
1101	Distilling, rectifying and blending of spirits		110.2	109.3	121.2	132.8		28.2	31.0	31.6	37.8		4.5	4.1
1102	Wines		320.7	311.5	369.2	373.7		102.0	103.7	109.6	109.2		26.1	20.2
1103	Malt liquors and malt		474.2	475.7	467.0	484.9		138.6	141.4	138.1	137.3		26.1	28.4
1104	Soft drinks,mineral waters,other bottled waters		789.7	751.2	789.8	789.7		166.3	159.7	194.2	197.5		36.9	45.1
1200	Tobacco products		456.8	496.7	560.7	616.4		165.7	214.2	226.0	257.6		36.9	31.2
131	Spinning, weaving and finishing of textiles		200.0	176.7	195.7	178.7		48.6	53.8	46.9	48.1		6.2	15.4
1311	Preparation and spinning of textile fibres		93.5	90.9	99.6	93.7		23.3	26.7	18.1	19.2		2.1	2.1
1312	Weaving of textiles		32.6	24.2	29.9	30.7		4.1	6.8	4.8	6.7		1.4	9.9
1313	Finishing of textiles		73.9	61.6	66.2	54.3		21.2	20.3	24.0	22.2		2.7	3.4
139	Other textiles		399.4	393.7	428.2	441.0		98.4	124.6	139.1	139.5		19.3	31.2
1391	Knitted and crocheted fabrics		45.2	40.1	42.2	40.4		5.6	10.1	8.7	8.7		0.3	0.4
1392	Made-up textile articles, except apparel		130.5	126.2	109.5	116.1		29.5	42.6	32.7	34.5		3.1	1.9
1393	Carpets and rugs		10.9	11.5	12.3	12.5		3.1	4.1	4.3	4.4		0.5	0.4
1394	Cordage, rope, twine and netting		95.4	99.9	135.3	133.4		38.6	35.5	54.3	52.8		4.4	8.4
1399	Other textiles n.e.c.		117.4	116.0	128.9	138.6		21.7	32.2	39.1	39.2		11.0	20.0
1410	Wearing apparel, except fur apparel		686.3	635.3	669.8	660.1		206.0	208.0	167.6	173.0		10.2	12.0
1420	Articles of fur		184.1	151.2	132.0	113.8		46.9	40.6	20.8	14.6		3.7	2.5
1430	Knitted and crocheted apparel		31.0	27.2	49.6	22.0		8.3	7.7	-16.2	-1.7		0.8	0.4
151	Leather;luggage,handbags,saddlery,harness;fur		29.7	28.6	66.8	69.0		10.8	10.3	20.9	20.4		2.3	1.5
1511	Tanning/dressing of leather; dressing of fur		17.1	18.9	50.0	51.1		6.8	7.1	14.6	13.2		2.0	1.3
1512	Luggage,handbags,etc.;saddlery/harness		12.6	9.7	16.7	17.9		4.0	3.2	6.3	7.2		0.3	0.2
1520	Footwear		72.5	60.7	82.5	87.6		24.0	20.6	23.7	21.9		1.1	1.8
1610	Sawmilling and planing of wood		47.7	52.3	73.8	71.8		11.6	12.5	14.0	16.7		4.0	1.4

Code	Description										
162	Wood products, cork, straw, plaiting materials	261.3	237.3	249.4	236.8	53.5	29.1	47.8	53.3	6.6	7.2
1621	Veneer sheets and wood-based panels	78.8	76.4	86.2	79.9	10.0	-11.8	10.3	15.8	1.7	2.2
1622	Builders' carpentry and joinery	125.0	107.7	90.5	87.3	29.9	27.5	18.9	20.4	2.5	2.1
1623	Wooden containers	27.2	26.5	48.4	46.5	6.2	6.8	11.1	10.6	1.5	2.0
1629	Other wood products;articles of cork,straw	30.2	26.8	24.2	23.0	7.4	6.5	7.4	6.4	1.0	0.9
170	Paper and paper products	1063.1	1154.9	1234.5	1240.1	253.6	275.7	302.8	304.8	53.0	74.2
1701	Pulp, paper and paperboard		162.6	157.5	174.4		36.6	40.5	36.4	10.0	20.9
1702	Corrugated paper and paperboard	350.8	372.3	432.9	422.2	94.3	103.4	114.6	118.7	18.9	17.2
1709	Other articles of paper and paperboard	...	...	...	...	...	...	...	...	...	...
181	Printing and service activities related to printing	516.9	479.5	554.0	574.5	184.5	214.1	199.2	189.4	21.4	29.6
1811	Printing	394.5	367.7	424.9	440.1	134.1	167.2	146.0	139.8	16.7	22.8
1812	Service activities related to printing	122.4	111.8	129.1	134.4	50.4	47.0	53.3	49.6	4.7	6.8
1820	Reproduction of recorded media	26.0	19.9	18.3	21.3	13.9	12.0	11.6	11.0	1.6	1.7
1910	Coke oven products	6.4	4.7	0.5	0.4	3.4	0.9	0.2	0.2	0.1	-
1920	Refined petroleum products	17162.4	17584.0	10338.5	12304.0	742.0	543.8	1681.1	1822.8	208.3	112.3
201	Basic chemicals,fertilizers, etc.	804.7	745.7	579.7	854.2	162.2	175.0	157.3	176.5	14.3	21.4
2011	Basic chemicals	254.6	290.3	206.3	330.6				56.8		12.1
2012	Fertilizers and nitrogen compounds			115.5		50.6	63.0	44.5	24.6	2.2	4.0
2013	Plastics and synthetic rubber in primary forms	...	...	...	...	...	...	...	...	...	...
202	Other chemical products	1234.2	1232.3	1302.9	1229.2	461.6	515.5	411.4	411.2	38.1	34.5
2021	Pesticides and other agrochemical products	101.1	115.9	130.8	132.6	29.4	33.6	37.8	38.2	1.6	1.0
2022	Paints, varnishes;printing ink and mastics	350.5	338.7	278.4	275.6	118.9	116.7	93.7	92.2	4.6	4.1
2023	Soap,cleaning and cosmetic preparations	620.9	595.8	592.6	525.4	259.9	309.5	201.8	203.4	20.8	20.8
2029	Other chemical products n.e.c.	161.7	181.8	301.1	295.6	53.4	55.7	78.1	77.4	11.2	8.6
2030	Man-made fibres	1.7	1.7	4.0	4.3	0.5	0.5	0.7	0.9	-	-
2100	Pharmaceuticals,medicinal chemicals, etc.	1478.9	1000.0	1425.6	1447.0	618.6	408.2	554.7	539.3	78.9	86.5
221	Rubber products	129.7	96.5	43.5	83.3	39.8	29.7	29.2	5.1	1.7	1.0
2211	Rubber tyres and tubes	11.5	11.9	3.5	3.2	2.1	3.4	0.9	0.8	0.4	0.1
2219	Other rubber products	118.2	84.6	40.0	80.1	37.7	26.3	28.3	4.3	1.3	0.9
2220	Plastics products	1600.8	1612.0	1567.6	1562.9	412.6	484.5	443.9	436.1	58.5	75.7
2310	Glass and glass products	107.5	96.6	105.6	96.6	52.5	68.1	38.7	39.3	8.0	8.4
239	Non-metallic mineral products n.e.c.	1550.2	1626.1	1686.3	1619.9	443.7	592.7	559.0	473.9	63.5	51.5
2391	Refractory products	17.5	16.9	14.1	13.6	6.7	6.3	4.4	5.7	0.6	0.3
2392	Clay building materials	55.5	44.8	39.2	41.4	17.5	16.6	14.9	15.8	4.5	2.6
2393	Other porcelain and ceramic products		46.4		46.4	12.8	12.8	12.8			
2394	Cement, lime and plaster	508.8	523.1	541.0	527.2	139.9	279.0	232.8	142.9	25.2	12.9
2395	Articles of concrete, cement and plaster	534.1	601.5	591.6	567.1	123.1	142.2	143.9	144.7	15.6	15.5
2396	Cutting, shaping and finishing of stone	298.1	302.8	312.9	277.6	114.8	106.8	107.3	102.5	11.6	15.7
2399	Other non-metallic mineral products n.e.c.	88.1	90.7	169.0	175.0	28.5	29.0	56.6	59.3	5.5	3.9
2410	Basic iron and steel	1194.4	1179.1	654.4	855.1	123.6	172.6	97.1	94.9	17.9	5.6
2420	Basic precious and other non-ferrous metals	2358.0	2505.9	562.2	2501.1	635.4	451.9	412.5	86.7	76.3	14.8
243	Casting of metals	455.5	482.9	293.0	230.9	58.1	75.8	30.5	49.4	3.8	6.1
2431	Casting of iron and steel	374.6	397.6	270.7	210.3	37.5	52.8	23.2	39.8	3.1	5.5
2432	Casting of non-ferrous metals	80.8	85.3	22.3	20.5	20.6	23.1	7.4	9.6	0.8	0.5
251	Struct.metal products, tanks, reservoirs	1470.2	1426.1	1303.5	1352.4	475.1	475.3	306.9	302.3	35.6	32.0

continued

Greece

ISIC Revision 4

ISIC	Industry	Output Note	Output 2013	Output 2014	Output 2015a/	Output 2016	VA Note	VA 2013	VA 2014	VA 2015a/	VA 2016	GFCF Note	GFCF 2015	GFCF 2016
			(millions of Euros)					(millions of Euros)					(millions of Euros)	
2511	Structural metal products		1404.0	1368.4	1292.0	1244.4		455.6	454.2	285.4	283.1		34.3	30.9
2512	Tanks, reservoirs and containers of metal		61.8	52.9	54.1	54.8		17.6	19.2	18.2	17.4		1.3	1.2
2513	Steam generators, excl. hot water boilers		4.4	4.8	6.4	4.3		1.9	1.9	3.3	1.8		0.1	-
2520	Weapons and ammunition		61.1	71.6	43.4	48.3		-5.2	17.9	18.0	169.1		0.3	0.2
259	Other metal products;metal working services		1443.8	1372.9	1219.5	1070.7		424.2	419.3	437.1	352.6		64.6	61.1
2591	Forging,pressing,stamping,roll-forming of metal		40.7	40.1	20.5	19.6		13.1	13.9	8.0	6.8		0.6	0.8
2592	Treatment and coating of metals;machining		247.5	218.4	190.4	119.7		79.1	71.7	56.3	46.0		4.3	2.6
2593	Cutlery, hand tools and general hardware		234.4	233.3	264.2	274.3		114.0	113.2	152.8	136.1		24.3	40.5
2599	Other fabricated metal products n.e.c.		921.3	881.2	744.3	657.0		218.2	220.4	220.0	163.6		35.3	17.1
2610	Electronic components and boards		54.4	53.7	52.9	117.3		23.2	26.6	25.1	41.5		1.4	1.7
2620	Computers and peripheral equipment		21.6	21.6	14.5	16.0		11.7	10.6	5.8	9.5		0.3	0.9
2630	Communication equipment		50.9	48.1	37.1	37.3		23.4	23.1	16.5	17.5		1.2	1.0
2640	Consumer electronics		10.5	10.0	2.7	2.3		5.1	4.9	1.0	0.7		0.1	0.3
265	Measuring,testing equipment; watches, etc.		180.1	198.1	208.4	187.0		52.4	59.8	59.4	37.1		5.9	3.0
2651	Measuring/testing/navigating equipment,etc.		177.4	195.2	208.3	186.9		51.1	58.4	59.4	37.1		5.9	3.0
2652	Watches and clocks		2.6	2.9	0.2	0.1		1.3	1.5	-	-		-	-
2660	Irradiation/electromedical equipment,etc.		9.8	11.7	12.7	0.8		5.3	7.2	9.0	0.4		0.7	-
2670	Optical instruments and photographic equipment		40.8	33.2	40.3	26.2		11.2	10.8	9.9	7.6		1.5	1.7
2680	Magnetic and optical media		1.8	1.8	3.4	1.1		0.8	0.9	-	0.4		-	0.1
2710	Electric motors,generators,transformers,etc.		177.1	120.6	129.7	135.6		58.2	40.6	43.3	42.9		2.7	2.3
2720	Batteries and accumulators		89.8	109.2	123.2	160.1		20.6	11.2	29.5	38.2		3.1	5.5
273	Wiring and wiring devices		435.0	434.2	486.0	334.2		40.6	35.4	73.8	23.9		10.7	6.4
2731	Fibre optic cables		...	...	...	...		...	...	...	...		...	...
2732	Other electronic and electric wires and cables		431.2	430.3	477.0	...		39.1	34.2	71.4	...		10.7	...
2733	Wiring devices		...	...	...	8.6		...	...	...	1.9		...	0.2
2740	Electric lighting equipment		93.6	79.0	73.7	78.6		34.9	27.7	25.7	26.1		3.1	2.0
2750	Domestic appliances		207.4	174.5	198.2	182.5		70.2	53.8	60.5	62.0		3.8	3.8
2790	Other electrical equipment		105.9	97.8	75.9	14.7		30.9	27.1	29.3	6.6		4.7	0.2
281	General-purpose machinery		434.3	762.8	390.5	382.7		177.2	121.1	168.1	147.5		13.4	11.1
2811	Engines/turbines,excl.aircraft,vehicle engines		11.5	27.1	8.4	6.2		5.3	1.4	4.4	2.1		0.3	0.4
2812	Fluid power equipment		5.3	14.1	6.2	6.5		2.3	0.5	2.7	3.3		0.1	0.1
2813	Other pumps, compressors, taps and valves		38.8	74.9	38.8	36.6		14.9	7.2	13.5	12.8		0.7	1.0
2814	Bearings, gears, gearing and driving elements		11.6	27.6	5.4	5.7		5.1	1.8	2.7	2.9		0.5	0.1
2815	Ovens, furnaces and furnace burners		20.2	32.6	9.4	6.2		7.1	3.6	3.9	2.2		0.7	0.2
2816	Lifting and handling equipment		158.3	228.9	151.3	158.0		66.9	48.3	54.7	55.8		5.8	4.0
2817	Office machinery, excl.computers,etc.		2.7	7.6	5.1	4.2		1.1	0.1	2.2	1.7		0.1	0.1
2818	Power-driven hand tools		1.2	3.4	-	-		0.5	-	-	-		-	-
2819	Other general-purpose machinery		184.6	346.7	165.8	159.4		73.9	58.3	83.9	66.6		5.2	5.1
282	Special-purpose machinery		445.8	985.3	364.4	314.7		182.6	81.5	140.4	107.8		9.3	7.3
2821	Agricultural and forestry machinery		112.8	291.9	78.7	70.7		46.3	7.0	28.6	23.1		2.6	1.5
2822	Metal-forming machinery and machine tools		127.3	310.4	75.1	70.8		52.6	12.7	29.5	28.8		2.2	1.7

2823	Machinery for metallurgy	26.9	60.0	22.5	20.7	11.3	5.3	9.1	8.2	0.7	0.9
2824	Mining, quarrying and construction machinery	17.5	33.8	8.8	10.5	8.7	2.8	3.6	3.6	0.2	0.1
2825	Food/beverage/tobacco processing machinery	56.2	99.3	65.3	60.4	22.6	14.4	25.9	23.6	1.7	0.8
2826	Textile/apparel/leather production machinery	28.7	40.5	23.6	11.2	10.1	6.0	7.3	-6.7	0.2	0.7
2829	Other special-purpose machinery	76.5	149.4	90.4	70.5	31.0	33.4	36.4	27.0	1.7	1.6
2910	Motor vehicles	10.2	18.6	17.4	17.1	-10.9	-	4.9	2.3	0.7	0.6
2920	Automobile bodies, trailers and semi-trailers	71.3	60.5	38.4	31.1	34.4	23.6	14.6	11.9	3.6	1.9
2930	Parts and accessories for motor vehicles	70.2	66.0	37.1	35.7	24.2	19.6	14.7	12.6	0.9	0.7
301	Building of ships and boats	102.1	...	160.9	76.7	47.6	...	71.7	37.5	1.8	4.0
3011	Building of ships and floating structures	90.0	...	146.1	63.2	41.5	...	67.2	33.7	1.2	3.5
3012	Building of pleasure and sporting boats	12.1	...	14.8	13.5	6.2	...	4.5	3.8	0.6	0.4
3020	Railway locomotives and rolling stock	...	...	2.6	5.8	...	...	-0.1	1.1	-	-
3030	Air and spacecraft and related machinery	...	144.9	144.0	84.2	...	66.5	51.3	41.5	1.4	1.0
3040	Military fighting vehicles	-	-	-	-	-	-	-0.1	-	-	-
309	Transport equipment n.e.c.	17.7	14.9	22.7	32.1	7.9	7.3	6.6	7.7	0.3	1.9
3091	Motorcycles	...	...	0.7	1.0	...	...	0.2	0.5	-	0.1
3092	Bicycles and invalid carriages	16.4	13.9	14.3	17.6	7.1	6.7	6.1	6.5	0.2	0.3
3099	Other transport equipment n.e.c.	...	...	7.6	13.5	...	...	0.2	0.7	0.1	1.5
3100	Furniture	390.0	412.7	405.8	437.0	111.7	120.4	115.8	138.5	17.1	12.9
321	Jewellery, bijouterie and related articles	158.6	174.8	95.3	95.0	78.6	76.1	30.2	29.8	2.5	2.7
3211	Jewellery and related articles	137.9	152.2	95.3b/	95.0b/	68.2	65.4	30.2b/	29.8b/	2.5b/	2.7b/
3212	Imitation jewellery and related articles	20.8	22.6	...b/	...b/	10.4	10.7	...b/	...b/	...b/	...b/
3220	Musical instruments	6.4	7.0	1.7	1.5	3.3	3.2	0.5	0.2	0.1	0.1
3230	Sports goods	22.6	18.9	15.5	17.5	8.8	7.5	6.8	7.0	0.9	0.4
3240	Games and toys	10.2	11.6	9.2	10.6	5.1	5.1	3.4	3.3	0.2	0.3
3250	Medical and dental instruments and supplies	46.1	47.4	91.5	107.1	24.9	23.4	41.7	48.5	6.0	3.6
3290	Other manufacturing n.e.c.	52.8	56.1	47.0	48.5	25.3	24.3	15.3	16.0	2.1	0.8
331	Repair of fabricated metal products/machinery	417.8	392.9	533.8	509.9	251.4	253.0	268.7	244.9	14.4	10.1
3311	Repair of fabricated metal products	13.0	18.9	27.6	18.4	7.6	8.1	11.6	9.3	0.3	0.2
3312	Repair of machinery	162.9	152.5	158.1	154.2	97.5	97.0	71.4	66.8	5.2	4.8
3313	Repair of electronic and optical equipment	15.1	16.1	14.8	13.5	9.4	10.6	7.9	7.5	0.4	0.4
3314	Repair of electrical equipment	25.6	26.2	64.5	52.5	16.0	17.6	23.1	18.5	1.5	0.9
3315	Repair of transport equip., excl. motor vehicles	200.1	178.2	268.4	270.8	120.3	118.8	154.5	142.6	7.1	3.8
3319	Repair of other equipment	1.1	1.1	0.4	0.5	0.7	0.8	0.2	0.2	-	-
3320	Installation of industrial machinery/equipment	62.8	56.6	113.3	84.6	34.5	36.8	29.4	32.0	2.0	2.6
C	Total manufacturing	51014.1	51449.6	46281.7	41341.9	10288.3	9959.6	10911.4	10425.7	1443.5	1295.7

a/ Methodological break in 2015.
b/ 3211 includes 3212.

Greece

ISIC Revision 4 — Index numbers of industrial production (2010=100)

ISIC	Industry	Note	2005	2006	2007	2008	2009	2010	2011	2012	2013	2014	2015	2016
10	Food products		103	104	107	107	104	100	97	95	91	94	92	94
11	Beverages		103	105	114	113	108	100	94	88	86	86	88	87
12	Tobacco products		134	124	129	124	121	100	111	101	103	99	117	120
13	Textiles		240	219	224	175	127	100	85	75	68	61	64	65
14	Wearing apparel		208	190	205	171	130	100	81	72	67	63	54	50
15	Leather and related products		202	190	196	187	159	100	87	62	61	53	46	51
16	Wood products, excluding furniture		166	157	139	126	92	100	84	61	47	42	40	43
17	Paper and paper products		106	109	112	107	104	100	95	87	89	97	99	97
18	Printing and reproduction of recorded media		132	143	138	131	117	100	77	63	59	58	53	53
19	Coke and refined petroleum products		90	96	99	95	95	100	85	106	110	118	120	129
20	Chemicals and chemical products		118	116	121	115	99	100	98	89	91	92	95	102
21	Pharmaceuticals,medicinal chemicals, etc.		65	72	80	82	98	100	99	94	103	98	106	110
22	Rubber and plastics products		117	123	128	125	108	100	94	89	87	89	93	91
23	Other non-metallic mineral products		168	176	165	154	117	100	66	56	55	56	56	64
24	Basic metals		108	114	116	109	89	100	107	102	97	102	106	112
25	Fabricated metal products, except machinery		125	138	134	121	100	100	93	86	79	78	76	83
26	Computer, electronic and optical products		326	295	242	235	136	100	75	78	90	99	127	101
27	Electrical equipment		127	131	133	131	104	100	87	82	71	64	70	72
28	Machinery and equipment n.e.c.		154	174	173	172	127	100	95	83	84	84	87	96
29	Motor vehicles, trailers and semi-trailers		138	115	137	115	100	100	60	62	63	66	58	76
30	Other transport equipment		182	168	192	188	153	100	78	47	59	29	79	79
31	Furniture		159	167	173	169	124	100	78	56	47	48	48	52
32	Other manufacturing		155	156	153	128	112	100	90	77	78	82	88	90
33	Repair and installation of machinery/equipment		172	160	168	152	129	100	94	73	71	73	60	56
C	Total manufacturing		119	122	124	119	105	100	91	88	87	88	90	94

Hungary

Supplier of information:
Hungarian Central Statistical Office, Budapest.
Industrial statistics for the OECD countries are compiled by the OECD secretariat, which supplies them to UNIDO.

Basic source of data:
Annual surveys; administrative data; business register.

Major deviations from ISIC (Revision 4):
Data presented in ISIC (Revision 4) were originally classified according to the national NACE-related classification system.

Reference period:
Calendar year.

Scope:
Enterprises with one or more employees.

Method of data collection:
Not reported.

Type of enumeration:
Not reported.

Adjusted for non-response:
Not reported.

Concepts and definitions of variables:
No deviations from the standard UN concepts and definitions are reported.

Related national publications:
None reported.

Hungary

ISIC Revision 4			Number of enterprises (number)					Number of employees (number)					Wages and salaries paid to employees (billions of Hungarian Forints)				
ISIC	Industry	Note	2013	2014	2015	2016	Note	2013	2014	2015	2016	Note	2013	2014	2015	2016
1010	Processing/preserving of meat		603	613	613	614		26490	25744	25439	25899		61.6	59.6	64.0	69.4
1020	Processing/preserving of fish, etc.		10	9	9	8		12	49	7	8		-	-	-	-
1030	Processing/preserving of fruit, vegetables		515	536	544	559		7508	7861	7933	8183		17.1	19.1	20.1	23.0
1040	Vegetable and animal oils and fats		72	75	68	62		940	944	1045	1075		5.3	5.6	6.3	6.2
1050	Dairy products		106	115	128	127		6492	6516	6576	6532		18.4	19.4	21.3	21.0
106	Grain mill products,starches and starch products		141	138	135	128		2130	2206	2206	2289		7.3	7.6	7.9	8.3
1061	Grain mill products		130	127	126	119		1823	1887	1897	1958		5.0	5.1	5.5	5.8
1062	Starches and starch products		11	11	9	9		307	319	309	331		2.3	2.4	2.3	2.6
107	Other food products		2740	2803	2853	2917		39005	40064	43262	39376		79.0	86.1	93.8	87.7
1071	Bakery products		1903	1918	1967	1993		26910	27040	27686	27467		44.1	46.6	50.2	53.6
1072	Sugar		7	7	7	8		292	289	248	248		1.5	1.4	1.2	1.2
1073	Cocoa, chocolate and sugar confectionery		252	266	287	308		3107	3027	3076	3317		6.6	6.8	7.2	8.2
1074	Macaroni, noodles, couscous, etc.		204	204	192	203		1593	1675	1619	1685		3.1	3.7	3.8	4.2
1075	Prepared meals and dishes		35	41	40	40		770	799	787	991		2.1	2.2	1.8	2.7
1079	Other food products n.e.c.		339	367	360	365		6333	7234	9846	5668		21.6	25.5	29.5	18.0
1080	Prepared animal feeds		187	173	175	178		4455	4568	4606	6646		15.7	16.9	17.8	29.5
110	Beverages		2251	2238	2287	2245		11795	11865	11978	11663		39.4	40.6	43.1	42.8
1101	Distilling, rectifying and blending of spirits		542	562	587	578		1818	1910	1733	1726		4.6	4.8	4.8	5.2
1102	Wines		913	912	...	...		3857	3957	...	...		8.6	9.1	...	...
1103	Malt liquors and malt		53	57	...	...		1918	1908	...	...		9.5	9.4	...	...
1104	Soft drinks,mineral waters,other bottled waters		743	707	735	702		4202	4090	4158	3766		16.7	17.4	18.4	16.8
1200	Tobacco products		6	6	8	7		1253	1313	1352	1308		6.1	5.9	6.1	5.5
131	Spinning, weaving and finishing of textiles		179	170	178	186		2510	2453	2321	2288		6.2	6.5	6.3	6.4
1311	Preparation and spinning of textile fibres		34	36	35	34		1523	1483	1279	1197		3.9	3.9	3.4	3.3
1312	Weaving of textiles		34	29	30	34		750	719	725	745		2.0	2.1	2.2	2.4
1313	Finishing of textiles		111	105	113	118		237	251	317	346		0.4	0.5	0.7	0.7
139	Other textiles		886	866	967	988		6219	6375	11318	10709		11.3	12.3	17.9	17.3
1391	Knitted and crocheted fabrics		72	71	67	63		293	296	270	228		0.4	0.5	0.4	0.4
1392	Made-up textile articles, except apparel		351	339	378	401		3903	3662	8621	8408		6.8	6.8	12.1	12.1
1393	Carpets and rugs		31	28	28	28		214	244	251	166		0.3	0.4	0.4	0.3
1394	Cordage, rope, twine and netting		33	30	29	27		177	188	191	190		0.4	0.4	0.4	0.5
1399	Other textiles n.e.c.		399	398	465	469		1632	1985	1985	1717		3.3	4.3	4.5	4.0
1410	Wearing apparel, except fur apparel		2542	2513	2680	2752		19334	18385	17414	18742		29.3	29.0	28.5	31.5
1420	Articles of fur		57	55	62	58		60	65	57	67		0.1	0.1	0.1	0.1
1430	Knitted and crocheted apparel		172	165	170	155		2086	2064	1984	2219		2.8	2.9	2.8	3.6
151	Leather;luggage,handbags,saddlery,harness;fur		237	245	261	273		3177	3977	4814	5426		7.5	9.7	13.0	15.6
1511	Tanning/dressing of leather; dressing of fur		30	25	26	25		47	45	41	42		0.1	0.1	0.1	0.1
1512	Luggage,handbags,etc.;saddlery/harness		207	220	235	248		3130	3932	4773	5384		7.5	9.6	12.9	15.5
1520	Footwear		263	246	240	248		7313	7085	7002	6699		12.0	12.0	12.2	12.5
1610	Sawmilling and planing of wood		710	695	677	655		4400	4415	4782	4647		6.2	6.5	7.9	8.2

162	Wood products, cork, straw, plaiting materials	2528	2488	2622	2649	10994	11376	11507	11947	20.0	21.1	22.0	24.5
1621	Veneer sheets and wood-based panels	41	41	40	39	1222	1221	936	1175	3.2	3.4	3.0	3.8
1622	Builders' carpentry and joinery	1664	1613	1708	1718	6091	6056	6312	6543	11.0	11.5	12.3	13.7
1623	Wooden containers	298	310	312	309	2454	2959	3055	2981	4.0	4.6	4.9	5.0
1629	Other wood products;articles of cork,straw	525	524	562	583	1227	1140	1204	1248	1.8	1.6	1.8	2.0
170	Paper and paper products	530	523	522	527	11083	11314	13996	14706	37.1	39.7	43.9	49.8
1701	Pulp, paper and paperboard	...	...	...	...	...	...	...	...	...	...	...	...
1702	Corrugated paper and paperboard	241	243	244	246	5176	5514	8062	8490	17.1	18.3	21.6	24.5
1709	Other articles of paper and paperboard	260	252	252	253	5011	4935	5015	5228	15.5	16.8	17.1	19.7
181	Printing and service activities related to printing	3198	3198	3153	3098	13263	13302	14928	14755	31.3	32.9	35.9	36.7
1811	Printing	1449	1424	1407	1382	10047	10476	12181	12085	25.3	27.6	30.7	31.5
1812	Service activities related to printing	1749	1774	1746	1716	3216	2826	2747	2670	5.9	5.2	5.2	5.2
1820	Reproduction of recorded media	133	135	123	114	184	182	167	128	0.3	0.4	0.3	0.2
1910	Coke oven products	4	3	3	3	744	663	658	647	3.3	3.2	3.2	3.4
1920	Refined petroleum products	10	7	5	5	5349	5252	5024	4988	48.2	51.5	48.7	52.8
201	Basic chemicals,fertilizers, etc.	185	175	182	175	7995	8128	8367	8242	41.5	42.6	46.7	48.1
2011	Basic chemicals	...	...	...	...	...	...	...	...	...	...	...	...
2012	Fertilizers and nitrogen compounds	20	18	17	20	816	979	984	989	3.6	4.4	5.2	5.2
2013	Plastics and synthetic rubber in primary forms	...	...	...	...	...	...	...	...	...	...	...	...
202	Other chemical products	386	430	472	...	5306	6008	6374	...	18.8	21.4	22.9	22.9
2021	Pesticides and other agrochemical products	39	33	35	...	802	809	748	...	2.9	3.3	3.3	3.3
2022	Paints,varnishes;printing ink and mastics	60	56	53	53	1213	1230	1219	1255	4.2	4.4	4.9	5.3
2023	Soap,cleaning and cosmetic preparations	189	241	281	293	2434	2896	3403	3610	8.8	9.7	11.2	12.3
2029	Other chemical products n.e.c.	98	100	103	104	857	1073	1004	901	2.9	3.9	3.6	3.3
2030	Man-made fibres	3	3	3	...	19	18	19	...	-	-	-	-
2100	Pharmaceuticals,medicinal chemicals, etc.	80	85	83	88	17055	17551	17432	18067	95.4	115.6	117.5	124.4
221	Rubber products	237	227	220	222	11386	12135	12809	13684	45.4	50.6	57.6	62.4
2211	Rubber tyres and tubes	39	40	37	37	4469	5099	5263	5461	21.9	25.1	29.1	29.8
2219	Other rubber products	198	187	183	185	6917	7036	7546	8223	23.5	25.5	28.5	32.6
2220	Plastics products	1690	1686	1667	1651	30628	32951	34973	36608	81.2	88.8	100.3	112.5
2310	Glass and glass products	320	322	321	321	4546	4607	5188	5387	13.8	14.8	16.9	19.0
239	Non-metallic mineral products n.e.c.	1618	1618	1660	1661	17117	17666	18625	18439	54.9	57.8	63.5	68.5
2391	Refractory products	27	28	23	23	861	904	873	849	3.0	3.2	3.3	3.3
2392	Clay building materials	58	52	52	52	1728	1627	1669	1689	5.0	5.2	5.8	6.3
2393	Other porcelain and ceramic products	322	334	370	373	5006	5339	5683	5230	15.0	16.9	19.0	19.2
2394	Cement, lime and plaster	53	46	45	45	816	760	766	783	6.0	4.6	4.6	4.7
2395	Articles of concrete, cement and plaster	527	522	524	521	5544	5619	5912	6138	18.1	19.0	20.5	22.8
2396	Cutting, shaping and finishing of stone	551	558	568	567	1215	1217	1190	1208	1.5	1.5	1.6	1.7
2399	Other non-metallic mineral products n.e.c.	80	78	78	80	1947	2200	2532	2542	6.4	7.3	8.8	10.4
2410	Basic iron and steel	101	105	97	91	6510	7242	6686	6589	30.8	32.5	31.8	33.0
2420	Basic precious and other non-ferrous metals	33	32	33	33	4459	4350	4581	4725	20.8	21.7	23.4	25.6
243	Casting of metals	150	155	156	153	4834	5493	5971	6578	14.9	18.4	21.5	24.9
2431	Casting of iron and steel	40	44	44	43	1380	1670	1662	1704	4.1	5.3	5.5	5.8
2432	Casting of non-ferrous metals	110	111	112	110	3454	3823	4309	4874	10.9	13.1	16.0	19.1
251	Struct.metal products, tanks, reservoirs	2893	2870	2855	2861	27350	27694	28459	28751	69.2	75.0	79.9	79.5

continued

Hungary

ISIC	Industry	Number of enterprises (number) 2013	2014	2015	2016	Number of employees (number) 2013	2014	2015	2016	Wages and salaries paid to employees (billions of Hungarian Forints) 2013	2014	2015	2016
2511	Structural metal products	2666	2653	2641	2648	23592	24127	24476	24901	59.5	64.3	68.1	68.2
2512	Tanks, reservoirs and containers of metal	196	189	189	187	3522	3311	3711	3584	9.2	10.1	11.2	10.7
2513	Steam generators, excl. hot water boilers	31	28	25	26	236	256	272	266	0.5	0.6	0.6	0.7
2520	Weapons and ammunition	7	13	12	13	310	326	339	363	0.9	1.0	1.1	1.3
259	Other metal products;metal working services	4958	4962	5176	5272	39215	41034	44445	47099	102.7	112.7	129.3	141.5
2591	Forging,pressing,stamping,roll-forming of metal	142	135	134	133	2811	2290	3023	3292	8.8	7.3	10.9	11.9
2592	Treatment and coating of metals; machining	3647	3646	3865	3970	24340	25905	27719	29290	58.2	65.1	75.0	81.4
2593	Cutlery, hand tools and general hardware	582	584	586	585	5478	5542	5889	6248	17.6	19.1	20.3	22.5
2599	Other fabricated metal products n.e.c.	587	597	591	584	6586	7297	7814	8269	18.0	21.1	23.1	25.7
2610	Electronic components and boards	276	276	292	279	11707	11049	11845	14135	40.0	40.4	45.4	59.3
2620	Computers and peripheral equipment	169	170	155	150	7093	7064	7500	7282	26.5	31.6	33.0	33.4
2630	Communication equipment	360	341	319	305	18447	12689	11742	12937	67.5	50.0	42.6	47.0
2640	Consumer electronics	..	..	..	..	..	..	..	..	..	..	..	..
265	Measuring,testing equipment; watches, etc.	412	394	399	403	4011	4074	4431	4228	12.6	13.6	15.7	15.6
2651	Measuring/testing/navigating equipment,etc.	396	379	379	384	3987	4051	4403	4195	12.6	13.6	15.6	15.5
2652	Watches and clocks	16	15	20	19	24	23	28	33	-	..	0.1	0.1
2660	Irradiation/electromedical equipment,etc.	87	91	89	87	739	693	827	948	2.6	2.5	3.3	3.8
2670	Optical instruments and photographic equipment	108	108	111	115	983	981	643	764	2.6	2.8	1.9	2.6
2680	Magnetic and optical media	..	..	..	..	..	..	..	..	..	..	..	..
2710	Electric motors,generators,transformers,etc.	309	298	293	287	12190	13611	13553	13780	34.8	49.7	51.2	55.3
2720	Batteries and accumulators	12	11	11	10	89	155	152	135	0.2	0.3	0.4	0.3
273	Wiring and wiring devices	68	73	75	86	8836	9487	9739	10530	26.9	30.8	33.5	39.6
2731	Fibre optic cables	..	3	..	..	..	364	..	..	..	0.9	..	..
2732	Other electronic and electric wires and cables	46	49	50	58	4017	4060	4039	4242	10.0	10.7	11.7	13.1
2733	Wiring devices	..	21	..	..	..	5063	..	..	..	19.3	..	..
2740	Electric lighting equipment	141	136	134	141	3010	3031	3114	3352	8.3	9.0	9.9	11.5
2750	Domestic appliances	71	69	75	79	8995	8375	8334	8920	23.9	23.2	24.3	28.6
2790	Other electrical equipment	252	248	247	260	4399	4779	5000	4967	12.6	15.1	16.6	17.1
281	General-purpose machinery	1512	1493	1425	1383	42432	42731	44844	45603	151.8	161.7	174.8	186.2
2811	Engines/turbines,excl.aircraft,vehicle engines	59	63	65	57	16093	16438	17272	15864	65.1	70.2	74.4	72.1
2812	Fluid power equipment	60	62	65	62	2088	1718	2174	2283	8.3	6.8	9.3	10.5
2813	Other pumps, compressors, taps and valves	119	114	108	113	5078	4928	5147	7173	19.5	20.1	20.7	30.1
2814	Bearings, gears, gearing and driving elements	54	55	54	55	2114	2235	2373	2335	6.7	7.6	8.2	8.6
2815	Ovens, furnaces and furnace burners	58	61	55	51	278	364	341	256	0.7	0.8	0.8	0.7
2816	Lifting and handling equipment	266	265	255	249	4460	4276	4179	3941	12.7	12.9	13.3	13.5
2817	Office machinery, excl.computers,etc.	26	24	24	22	445	345	362	369	1.4	0.9	0.9	1.1
2818	Power-driven hand tools	18	19	19	18	1633	1683	1924	2326	5.7	6.5	7.8	9.8
2819	Other general-purpose machinery	852	830	780	756	10243	10744	11072	11056	31.6	36.0	39.4	39.9
282	Special-purpose machinery	1004	988	961	982	16078	16320	15944	15432	53.0	55.8	56.8	57.2
2821	Agricultural and forestry machinery	152	144	149	145	5196	5398	5345	4999	14.7	16.3	17.4	16.9
2822	Metal-forming machinery and machine tools	173	168	166	171	1564	1336	1453	1506	5.3	4.6	5.4	5.8

Code	Description												
2823	Machinery for metallurgy	8	6	4	4	65	53	15	18	0.1	0.2	-	-
2824	Mining, quarrying and construction machinery	63	61	60	60	2045	2026	1763	1459	6.7	7.2	5.9	4.9
2825	Food/beverage/tobacco processing machinery	205	211	201	199	3178	3339	3351	3125	11.0	11.7	11.9	11.7
2826	Textile/apparel/leather production machinery	30	30	32	28	345	343	362	398	1.1	1.0	1.2	1.3
2829	Other special-purpose machinery	373	368	349	375	3685	3825	3655	3927	14.0	14.9	14.9	16.6
2910	Motor vehicles	46	47	52	50	16675	18751	20037	20066	96.7	110.6	122.1	127.5
2920	Automobile bodies, trailers and semi-trailers	108	104	107	114	2727	4195	3192	3312	9.2	13.7	11.0	12.9
2930	Parts and accessories for motor vehicles	329	333	335	323	54802	59538	65163	69412	193.6	215.4	254.4	286.2
301	Building of ships and boats	92	90	97	93	298	284	290	273	0.4	0.5	0.5	0.4
3011	Building of ships and floating structures	31	29	29	29	121	128	136	110	0.2	0.3	0.3	0.2
3012	Building of pleasure and sporting boats	61	61	68	64	177	156	154	163	0.2	0.2	0.2	0.2
3020	Railway locomotives and rolling stock	38	37	...	...	2945	3360	...	...	13.4	15.1	...	...
3030	Air and spacecraft and related machinery	...	...	37	36	...	...	502	648	...	...	1.6	2.1
3040	Military fighting vehicles	...	...	...	...	...	...	...	...	...	...	...	...
309	Transport equipment n.e.c.	56	64	69	62	999	920	1068	1103	2.0	1.9	2.4	2.6
3091	Motorcycles	8	8	11	8	93	101	620	663	0.2	0.2	1.5	1.7
3092	Bicycles and invalid carriages	31	37	42	37	861	764	413	401	1.8	1.7	0.9	0.8
3099	Other transport equipment n.e.c.	17	19	16	17	45	55	35	39	-	0.1	0.1	0.1
3100	Furniture	2400	2456	2618	2735	15281	15444	16567	16945	28.8	30.6	33.7	36.3
321	Jewellery, bijouterie and related articles	580	631	785	874	654	623	645	658	1.0	1.1	1.2	1.3
3211	Jewellery and related articles	370	351	411	427	585	536	577	584	1.0	1.0	1.1	1.2
3212	Imitation jewellery and related articles	210	280	374	447	69	87	68	74	0.1	0.1	0.1	0.1
3220	Musical instruments	82	82	100	104	146	137	135	125	0.3	0.3	0.2	0.3
3230	Sports goods	135	149	161	173	1031	1210	1339	1379	2.5	3.0	3.3	3.8
3240	Games and toys	177	187	192	198	2365	2565	3004	3984	7.6	9.1	11.1	13.2
3250	Medical and dental instruments and supplies	1512	1486	1617	1684	11358	11807	12789	13860	32.4	35.0	38.9	44.9
3290	Other manufacturing n.e.c.	976	948	1016	1126	2488	3015	6574	6528	4.4	4.9	9.2	9.4
331	Repair of fabricated metal products/machinery	4166	4311	4756	4836	15169	12069	12730	13942	47.1	38.7	43.1	50.9
3311	Repair of fabricated metal products	286	302	348	363	547	348	355	426	1.7	0.7	0.6	0.8
3312	Repair of machinery	2398	2513	2791	2865	6079	7436	8134	8375	17.1	21.7	25.7	28.4
3313	Repair of electronic and optical equipment	860	816	860	839	841	776	783	787	2.3	2.3	2.4	2.6
3314	Repair of electrical equipment	376	383	410	413	961	1119	1068	1202	2.0	2.4	2.4	3.5
3315	Repair of transport equip., excl. motor vehicles	150	166	191	206	6620	2210	2154	2589	23.8	11.0	11.3	13.9
3319	Repair of other equipment	96	131	156	150	121	180	236	563	0.2	0.6	0.7	1.6
3320	Installation of industrial machinery/equipment	1167	1201	1255	1294	4623	4721	4568	4522	15.9	17.2	14.2	16.0
C	Total manufacturing	47475	47614	49310	49951	640670	653729	691324	712180	2001.2	2150.3	2334.4	2533.3

Hungary

ISIC	Industry	Output (valuation not defined) (billions of Hungarian Forints)				Value added at factor values (billions of Hungarian Forints)				Gross fixed capital formation (billions of Hungarian Forints)	
		2013	2014	2015	2016	2013	2014	2015	2016	2015	2016
1010	Processing/preserving of meat	726.5	720.2	740.6	792.3	97.8	110.6	127.5	128.6	25.9	43.6
1020	Processing/preserving of fish, etc.	0.1	0.1	0.2	0.1	...	-	...	-	-	-
1030	Processing/preserving of fruit,vegetables	218.1	244.4	232.4	264.8	46.1	54.5	51.2	57.4	14.8	12.7
1040	Vegetable and animal oils and fats	167.8	163.0	188.1	185.7	18.4	23.5	25.1	22.5	3.6	8.5
1050	Dairy products	254.6	279.3	266.1	260.4	38.4	42.8	47.4	49.3	10.0	7.5
106	Grain mill products,starches and starch products	215.8	191.6	194.6	194.8	42.9	40.5	35.7	43.6	9.4	7.6
1061	Grain mill products	100.9	93.7	97.6	92.0	14.6	13.3	11.6	16.0	4.1	4.1
1062	Starches and starch products	114.9	97.9	97.0	102.8	28.4	27.2	24.1	27.6	5.3	3.5
107	Other food products	621.2	653.4	703.8	614.1	162.0	175.2	196.4	183.3	37.8	50.9
1071	Bakery products	241.8	244.1	255.5	263.6	78.6	83.9	91.5	97.3	14.4	19.1
1072	Sugar	38.1	23.3	26.0	30.4	4.7	0.3	3.5	4.1	3.3	1.8
1073	Cocoa, chocolate and sugar confectionery	52.7	56.8	63.4	71.7	13.0	14.6	17.5	18.0	4.5	7.8
1074	Macaroni, noodles, couscous, etc.	34.0	38.0	38.6	39.6	8.0	8.4	9.2	10.8	2.2	5.5
1075	Prepared meals and dishes	18.1	18.3	17.9	24.2	5.1	4.3	4.3	6.9	2.0	6.3
1079	Other food products n.e.c.	236.5	273.0	302.3	184.6	52.6	63.6	70.3	46.2	11.3	10.4
1080	Prepared animal feeds	289.6	305.4	314.2	422.7	42.7	49.0	43.2	71.8	8.0	16.5
110	Beverages	492.7	501.2	534.7	538.4	102.1	98.2	108.3	106.0	34.2	29.9
1101	Distilling, rectifying and blending of spirits	57.8	66.0	54.8	68.5	16.5	20.1	12.2	14.9	1.9	2.4
1102	Wines	103.3	95.4	...	...	22.7	21.2	...	...	...	...
1103	Malt liquors and malt	140.6	137.6	...	...	22.9	17.6	...	...	...	...
1104	Soft drinks,mineral waters,other bottled waters	191.0	202.2	227.3	212.9	39.9	39.3	48.7	46.2	14.7	12.9
1200	Tobacco products	150.0	137.7	143.6	144.9	7.3	15.7	12.0	13.1	1.9	2.7
131	Spinning, weaving and finishing of textiles	39.1	43.9	42.6	51.4	11.7	13.2	12.8	12.1	1.5	2.1
1311	Preparation and spinning of textile fibres	21.3	23.4	20.3	20.0	6.9	7.7	6.6	6.3	0.6	0.4
1312	Weaving of textiles	15.6	16.9	17.3	16.7	4.2	4.4	4.8	4.2	0.7	1.1
1313	Finishing of textiles	2.1	3.6	5.0	14.7	0.5	1.0	1.4	1.6	0.2	0.6
139	Other textiles	68.8	78.9	87.7	87.9	20.8	25.1	26.4	24.9	5.6	4.9
1391	Knitted and crocheted fabrics	2.0	2.3	2.1	2.2	1.0	1.2	1.1	1.1	0.4	0.2
1392	Made-up textile articles, except apparel	39.0	44.1	50.6	55.2	13.0	14.1	14.8	14.0	4.1	2.7
1393	Carpets and rugs	1.4	1.6	1.7	1.5	0.7	0.7	0.8	0.7	-	-
1394	Cordage, rope, twine and netting	2.7	3.1	3.1	3.1	0.8	1.0	1.0	1.0	0.3	0.1
1399	Other textiles n.e.c.	23.7	27.8	30.2	25.8	5.3	8.1	8.8	8.2	0.9	2.0
1410	Wearing apparel, except fur apparel	87.8	86.2	84.9	87.9	47.5	46.5	44.7	45.4	3.9	2.8
1420	Articles of fur	0.4	0.5	0.4	0.4	0.2	0.2	0.2	0.2	-	0.1
1430	Knitted and crocheted apparel	7.0	7.0	6.8	9.6	8.6	6.9	6.7	8.7	0.8	0.8
151	Leather;luggage,handbags,saddlery,harness;fur	81.5	109.5	133.9	147.1	21.3	23.0	26.6	34.9	8.1	7.8
1511	Tanning/dressing of leather; dressing of fur	0.6	0.4	0.6	0.6	0.1	0.1	0.1	0.1	...	-
1512	Luggage,handbags,etc.;saddlery/harness	80.9	109.1	133.3	146.4	21.2	22.9	26.5	34.8	8.1	7.8
1520	Footwear	55.7	58.9	52.0	51.7	17.5	19.5	19.2	19.4	1.4	1.5
1610	Sawmilling and planing of wood	47.1	54.0	67.1	67.4	11.4	13.4	15.7	16.2	4.7	5.8

Code	Description										
162	Wood products, cork, straw, plaiting materials	50.4	16.6	56.1	51.8	47.1	42.5	204.3	189.1	178.1	155.3
1621	Veneer sheets and wood-based panels	40.9	6.8	15.2	11.8	12.0	8.9	60.0	52.0	55.4	44.0
1622	Builders' carpentry and joinery	6.4	6.8	27.0	26.0	23.0	21.6	95.8	88.4	77.3	72.7
1623	Wooden containers	2.3	1.6	10.2	10.3	9.1	8.9	37.9	37.9	35.4	29.9
1629	Other wood products;articles of cork,straw	0.8	1.5	3.6	3.7	3.1	3.1	10.7	10.8	10.0	8.8
170	Paper and paper products	73.0	53.6	135.4	119.8	113.9	101.0	493.9	458.8	424.6	387.0
1701	Pulp, paper and paperboard	...	...	...	...	...	...	...	...	...	...
1702	Corrugated paper and paperboard	15.1	14.5	53.5	44.0	40.1	39.8	214.2	193.8	172.8	161.8
1709	Other articles of paper and paperboard	45.0	28.8	48.3	44.7	43.0	37.2	139.9	130.6	127.4	111.1
181	Printing and service activities related to printing	19.6	22.6	74.9	77.5	68.4	68.8	225.2	224.1	215.3	198.5
1811	Printing	17.9	20.3	63.3	65.6	56.5	55.6	199.3	198.3	188.2	169.3
1812	Service activities related to printing	1.6	2.3	11.6	11.9	11.9	13.1	25.8	25.8	27.2	29.1
1820	Reproduction of recorded media	0.1	-	0.5	0.7	0.8	0.7	1.3	1.6	1.7	1.6
1910	Coke oven products	0.1	0.3	5.1	8.1	6.9	4.7	86.4	108.0	99.3	96.2
1920	Refined petroleum products	65.5	45.1	237.8	197.3	208.5	264.6	1543.0	1646.8	2182.0	2198.3
201	Basic chemicals,fertilizers, etc.	113.4	88.0	336.4	326.2	209.0	157.3	1209.4	1278.1	1163.3	1162.5
2011	Basic chemicals	...	...	...	...	...	...	...	...	...	...
2012	Fertilizers and nitrogen compounds	33.4	36.3	19.4	27.5	31.9	12.9	69.0	84.9	92.4	57.3
2013	Plastics and synthetic rubber in primary forms	...	...	...	...	...	...	...	...	...	...
202	Other chemical products	...	15.2	...	68.6	79.4	57.9	...	306.9	394.7	248.9
2021	Pesticides and other agrochemical products	...	2.3	...	9.2	8.8	8.0	...	24.9	25.9	24.0
2022	Paints,varnishes;printing ink and mastics	1.9	1.9	14.2	13.1	11.9	10.0	43.7	42.5	40.0	35.8
2023	Soap,cleaning and cosmetic preparations	9.4	10.4	36.3	32.5	36.1	30.8	173.1	165.3	150.2	120.7
2029	Other chemical products n.e.c.	2.2	0.5	13.8	13.8	22.7	9.2	74.5	74.2	178.6	68.3
2030	Man-made fibres	...	-	...	0.1	0.1	0.1	...	0.2	0.2	0.2
2100	Pharmaceuticals,medicinal chemicals, etc.	72.4	61.8	386.2	402.0	370.2	335.6	905.3	904.8	839.6	790.9
221	Rubber products	109.9	66.1	214.7	209.2	184.7	173.7	582.4	574.0	506.0	481.3
2211	Rubber tyres and tubes	88.5	53.4	143.0	134.8	116.9	113.0	348.7	341.5	302.8	302.1
2219	Other rubber products	21.3	12.7	71.8	74.4	67.9	60.7	233.7	232.5	203.2	179.3
2220	Plastics products	81.2	79.6	254.0	235.0	213.0	182.5	980.4	933.5	840.4	737.5
2310	Glass and glass products	10.3	10.3	44.3	38.7	37.4	34.9	150.6	145.9	121.3	114.4
239	Non-metallic mineral products n.e.c.	43.7	54.6	184.7	180.6	157.1	137.5	529.8	522.9	460.6	400.5
2391	Refractory products	1.2	1.0	6.5	6.6	5.6	5.8	19.9	20.7	18.0	18.2
2392	Clay building materials	5.8	1.5	16.2	13.8	11.5	9.6	40.3	36.2	30.3	28.8
2393	Other porcelain and ceramic products	10.9	26.4	49.9	57.0	53.5	48.4	129.1	136.9	123.2	107.7
2394	Cement, lime and plaster	2.6	2.1	16.1	16.2	13.5	11.4	46.4	46.4	41.3	39.1
2395	Articles of concrete, cement and plaster	15.3	14.8	60.5	53.6	47.9	41.2	187.8	173.3	156.6	139.2
2396	Cutting, shaping and finishing of stone	1.0	0.7	4.5	3.3	3.8	3.3	12.3	10.6	10.8	8.7
2399	Other non-metallic mineral products n.e.c.	7.0	8.0	31.1	30.0	21.3	17.6	94.0	98.8	80.4	58.9
2410	Basic iron and steel	17.8	11.4	61.3	46.7	45.7	35.6	317.9	331.8	354.4	338.8
2420	Basic precious and other non-ferrous metals	20.4	14.6	89.9	76.8	68.0	55.4	330.7	334.7	299.8	286.2
243	Casting of metals	23.5	11.3	48.8	47.1	40.3	31.4	148.0	143.8	121.4	102.6
2431	Casting of iron and steel	2.0	1.9	7.6	10.2	10.2	7.4	27.5	31.4	30.3	24.4
2432	Casting of non-ferrous metals	21.5	9.4	41.2	36.8	30.1	24.0	120.5	112.4	91.1	78.2
251	Struct.metal products, tanks, reservoirs	33.5	25.3	147.3	147.8	139.8	129.8	448.7	428.4	410.6	386.5

continued

Hungary

ISIC	Industry	Note	Output (valuation not defined) (billions of Hungarian Forints)				Note	Value added at factor values (billions of Hungarian Forints)				Note	Gross fixed capital formation (billions of Hungarian Forints)	
			2013	2014	2015	2016		2013	2014	2015	2016		2015	2016
2511	Structural metal products		325.8	345.8	364.1	384.6		108.9	117.1	125.0	125.2		21.7	29.0
2512	Tanks, reservoirs and containers of metal		58.0	61.0	61.8	61.4		19.4	21.1	21.5	20.7		3.3	4.2
2513	Steam generators, excl. hot water boilers		2.7	3.7	2.4	2.6		1.5	1.7	1.3	1.4		0.3	0.2
2520	Weapons and ammunition		5.9	6.6	7.9	8.8		1.7	1.8	2.3	2.7		0.7	0.5
259	Other metal products;metal working services		662.2	747.7	836.1	883.6		229.5	257.9	286.5	309.2		77.8	101.0
2591	Forging,pressing,stamping,roll-forming of metal		75.6	67.9	94.7	100.6		19.6	16.2	22.7	24.6		6.1	5.0
2592	Treatment and coating of metals; machining		351.8	399.0	422.4	456.6		134.3	155.8	169.2	182.7		48.0	67.5
2593	Cutlery, hand tools and general hardware		98.8	107.3	116.9	123.2		38.9	41.7	45.5	49.1		12.7	14.8
2599	Other fabricated metal products n.e.c.		136.1	173.5	202.0	203.2		36.7	44.1	49.2	52.7		11.1	13.8
2610	Electronic components and boards		491.3	514.9	588.4	779.8		85.5	84.5	90.2	128.2		43.5	49.6
2620	Computers and peripheral equipment		465.1	523.3	544.8	453.4		66.6	83.1	84.2	61.0		9.2	11.1
2630	Communication equipment		1049.0	860.3	749.7	823.2		183.2	170.0	146.4	119.9		7.5	10.6
2640	Consumer electronics		...	...	...	...		...	...	...	...		...	...
265	Measuring,testing equipment; watches, etc.		72.8	75.2	92.8	94.0		26.3	26.2	33.4	32.7		4.4	6.3
2651	Measuring/testing/navigating equipment,etc.		72.5	75.0	92.4	93.5		26.2	26.1	33.2	32.5		4.4	6.2
2652	Watches and clocks		0.2	0.3	0.4	0.5		0.1	0.2	0.2	0.2		-	0.1
2660	Irradiation/electromedical equipment,etc.		12.5	12.5	22.4	23.4		4.8	4.5	8.1	8.6		1.6	0.5
2670	Optical instruments and photographic equipment		14.8	16.4	7.1	10.6		5.6	5.6	3.6	4.9		0.5	1.0
2680	Magnetic and optical media		...	...	...	...		...	...	...	...		...	...
2710	Electric motors,generators,transformers,etc.		252.2	333.8	354.2	377.5		64.2	98.7	88.9	90.9		18.1	14.0
2720	Batteries and accumulators		1.0	1.4	2.0	2.7		0.4	0.7	0.8	0.8		0.1	-
273	Wiring and wiring devices		299.6	318.7	341.3	358.4		79.1	79.7	82.7	93.6		21.4	27.7
2731	Fibre optic cables		...	1.3	...	...		...	1.1	...	...		...	...
2732	Other electronic and electric wires and cables		164.3	165.7	170.7	155.6		22.4	24.8	27.0	24.6		6.0	6.9
2733	Wiring devices		...	151.7	...	...		...	53.9	...	...		...	...
2740	Electric lighting equipment		66.6	80.9	95.4	110.2		17.2	21.1	24.5	26.7		3.0	6.1
2750	Domestic appliances		254.4	240.1	258.8	269.6		51.3	54.0	57.7	63.5		9.9	10.5
2790	Other electrical equipment		104.7	118.1	124.5	117.4		31.3	38.2	37.3	33.9		9.1	7.6
281	General-purpose machinery		1723.0	1851.6	1945.8	1623.0		639.6	710.8	845.0	511.8		69.3	75.9
2811	Engines/turbines,excl.aircraft,vehicle engines		958.1	1060.8	1203.2	790.1		443.1	513.1	646.6	274.9		25.6	30.3
2812	Fluid power equipment		53.1	40.7	58.6	66.0		19.6	15.3	19.3	22.3		7.5	3.5
2813	Other pumps, compressors, taps and valves		200.4	224.0	135.9	176.0		49.6	51.9	46.0	68.4		6.4	11.6
2814	Bearings, gears, gearing and driving elements		43.6	51.0	50.2	49.6		14.5	15.8	17.0	17.8		8.1	6.2
2815	Ovens, furnaces and furnace burners		5.0	6.2	5.9	3.9		1.5	2.1	2.0	1.4		0.4	0.2
2816	Lifting and handling equipment		82.4	81.2	81.4	77.3		23.2	23.7	25.4	25.2		4.7	4.7
2817	Office machinery, excl.computers,etc.		33.3	6.3	5.6	6.2		4.2	2.1	1.4	1.9		-	0.4
2818	Power-driven hand tools		72.7	87.4	100.7	126.8		12.6	13.4	16.6	19.9		6.1	6.7
2819	Other general-purpose machinery		274.4	294.0	304.4	327.2		71.3	73.5	70.7	80.0		10.4	12.3
282	Special-purpose machinery		358.6	375.3	359.7	356.6		112.2	121.8	109.6	114.6		18.9	19.7
2821	Agricultural and forestry machinery		135.4	142.3	144.9	133.2		31.5	36.8	31.4	33.6		6.6	6.4
2822	Metal-forming machinery and machine tools		26.2	24.5	31.7	34.3		12.3	9.9	12.9	13.8		2.4	1.7

Code	Description									
2823	Machinery for metallurgy	0.9	1.1	0.1	0.1	0.4	0.4	0.1	-	-	-
2824	Mining, quarrying and construction machinery	38.1	40.3	27.3	20.5	12.0	12.9	10.2	8.4	1.5	1.4
2825	Food/beverage/tobacco processing machinery	69.6	68.5	60.5	61.4	24.3	25.5	21.8	22.5	2.2	2.6
2826	Textile/apparel/leather production machinery	4.5	4.3	5.5	6.9	2.0	2.1	2.4	2.7	0.7	0.3
2829	Other special-purpose machinery	83.9	94.3	89.7	100.3	29.6	34.2	30.8	33.5	5.5	7.4
2910	Motor vehicles	2822.5	3698.6	4315.8	4158.7	475.9	579.2	680.0	695.7	201.1	165.5
2920	Automobile bodies, trailers and semi-trailers	79.4	113.5	106.0	115.7	18.5	27.5	23.0	27.5	7.2	10.9
2930	Parts and accessories for motor vehicles	2442.9	2863.0	3330.6	3538.4	474.2	547.9	609.8	664.0	192.2	217.9
301	Building of ships and boats	3.1	3.1	3.4	2.7	1.1	0.9	1.3	1.0	0.7	0.1
3011	Building of ships and floating structures	1.3	1.4	1.6	1.1	0.4	0.5	0.6	0.5	0.6	-
3012	Building of pleasure and sporting boats	1.8	1.8	1.8	1.7	0.7	0.4	0.7	0.6	0.2	0.1
3020	Railway locomotives and rolling stock	85.3	132.0	..	..	33.0	49.6	..	..	..	..
3030	Air and spacecraft and related machinery	..	..	9.8	13.4	..	3.6	3.6	5.0	2.9	1.7
3040	Military fighting vehicles	..	..	..	..	..	..	..	..	..	..
309	Transport equipment n.e.c.	34.5	29.7	46.5	59.1	4.9	3.7	4.6	5.4	0.5	0.7
3091	Motorcycles	0.7	0.9	39.8	53.3	0.3	0.4	2.9	3.7	0.3	0.4
3092	Bicycles and invalid carriages	33.6	28.6	6.4	5.6	4.5	3.2	1.5	1.5	0.2	0.3
3099	Other transport equipment n.e.c.	0.2	0.3	0.2	0.2	0.1	0.1	0.1	0.1	-	-
3100	Furniture	161.1	177.4	201.0	210.9	50.1	54.5	61.6	67.4	10.7	10.3
321	Jewellery, bijouterie and related articles	4.0	5.5	7.0	6.2	1.7	2.0	2.8	2.4	0.2	0.2
3211	Jewellery and related articles	3.7	5.0	6.5	5.5	1.6	1.8	2.6	2.1	0.2	0.2
3212	Imitation jewellery and related articles	0.3	0.5	0.6	0.7	0.1	0.2	0.2	0.3	-	-
3220	Musical instruments	1.0	1.1	0.9	1.2	0.4	0.5	0.4	0.3	-	0.1
3230	Sports goods	25.9	32.2	35.1	37.5	6.4	9.5	11.2	12.0	2.0	0.4
3240	Games and toys	33.9	46.9	48.0	51.1	16.4	23.2	25.3	29.2	10.9	18.0
3250	Medical and dental instruments and supplies	200.1	216.4	260.4	296.9	82.1	80.4	99.3	116.9	30.8	35.6
3290	Other manufacturing n.e.c.	33.2	30.4	33.7	37.4	12.4	10.3	11.2	12.7	2.5	3.0
331	Repair of fabricated metal products/machinery	186.8	187.8	219.5	244.6	81.5	89.1	83.3	95.1	8.5	18.1
3311	Repair of fabricated metal products	4.7	3.7	4.2	4.9	2.8	1.9	1.7	2.3	0.3	0.2
3312	Repair of machinery	69.2	118.5	139.1	152.0	32.7	59.8	51.6	55.9	5.6	11.1
3313	Repair of electronic and optical equipment	10.8	10.2	12.7	12.3	4.6	4.7	5.1	5.6	0.2	0.3
3314	Repair of electrical equipment	8.5	11.2	12.6	16.0	4.2	5.2	6.3	7.9	0.6	0.9
3315	Repair of transport equip., excl. motor vehicles	93.0	41.8	47.8	51.9	36.8	16.4	17.2	19.1	1.6	4.5
3319	Repair of other equipment	0.7	2.5	3.0	7.6	0.4	1.1	1.4	4.3	0.2	1.0
3320	Installation of industrial machinery/equipment	69.9	79.1	79.2	82.7	31.8	33.4	35.0	35.8	3.0	4.7
C	Total manufacturing	24448.3	26824.3	28534.6	28673.2	5517.3	6137.5	6794.8	6784.8	1542.9	1818.3

Hungary

| ISIC Revision 4 | | | Index numbers of industrial production (2010=100) | | | | | | | | | | | |
ISIC	Industry	Note	2005	2006	2007	2008	2009	2010	2011	2012	2013	2014	2015	2016
10	Food products		113	113	107	101	101	100	103	108	107	111	116	118
11	Beverages		107	115	120	103	102	100	104	103	105	111	118	113
12	Tobacco products		167	181	211	210	84	100	90	122	127	140	128	123
13	Textiles		156	146	117	111	85	100	121	136	120	141	154	137
14	Wearing apparel		209	203	183	137	114	100	100	98	92	100	88	93
15	Leather and related products		71	96	145	150	106	100	155	133	142	168	177	185
16	Wood products, excluding furniture		100	98	95	110	85	100	88	90	84	94	92	107
17	Paper and paper products		78	83	88	81	79	100	100	100	100	105	115	121
18	Printing and reproduction of recorded media		101	103	104	103	93	100	101	94	101	116	106	104
19	Coke and refined petroleum products		111	109	114	110	98	100	98	88	87	87	85	84
20	Chemicals and chemical products		106	105	112	105	88	100	108	107	113	123	126	124
21	Pharmaceuticals,medicinal chemicals, etc.		82	92	88	94	94	100	109	114	100	101	105	102
22	Rubber and plastics products		80	95	106	107	84	100	111	115	112	117	136	139
23	Other non-metallic mineral products		107	114	141	146	110	100	107	100	98	104	117	122
24	Basic metals		154	177	165	159	83	100	108	102	105	109	113	118
25	Fabricated metal products, except machinery		104	112	127	135	94	100	118	123	122	131	135	141
26	Computer, electronic and optical products		73	86	98	96	82	100	95	78	69	70	75	82
27	Electrical equipment		139	148	152	145	114	100	89	89	91	97	103	109
28	Machinery and equipment n.e.c.		54	59	69	78	71	100	144	145	141	147	146	131
29	Motor vehicles, trailers and semi-trailers		84	103	119	119	84	100	112	122	144	174	202	203
30	Other transport equipment		94	91	115	157	94	100	118	110	125	144	138	142
31	Furniture		99	113	124	151	111	100	99	100	100	105	123	118
32	Other manufacturing		41	52	56	68	81	100	106	116	126	141	163	181
33	Repair and installation of machinery/equipment		70	74	81	104	124	100	105	125	119	129	145	141
C	Total manufacturing		92	102	110	110	89	100	106	104	106	115	124	126

Iceland

Supplier of information:
Statistics Iceland, Reykjavik.
Industrial statistics for the OECD countries are compiled by the OECD secretariat, which supplies them to UNIDO.

Basic source of data:
Not reported.

Major deviations from ISIC (Revision 4):
Data presented in ISIC (Revision 4) were originally classified according to the national NACE-related classification system.

Reference period:
Calendar year.

Scope:
All enterprises.

Method of data collection:
Not reported.

Type of enumeration:
Not reported.

Adjusted for non-response:
Not reported

Concepts and definitions of variables:
No deviations from the standard UN concepts and definitions are reported.

Related national publications:
Statistical Yearbook of Iceland, published by Statistics Iceland, Reykjavik.

			Number of enterprises (number)					Number of employees (number)					Wages and salaries paid to employees (millions of Icelandic Kronur)			
ISIC	Industry	Note	2013	2014	2015	2016a/	Note	2013	2014	2015	2016a/b/	Note	2013	2014	2015	2016a/
1010	Processing/preserving of meat		...	...	33	34		...	...	1574	1623		...	...	7169	7935
1020	Processing/preserving of fish, etc.		...	...	219	213		...	...	5819	5613		...	...	42017	40705
1030	Processing/preserving of fruit,vegetables		...	...	6	7		...	...	80	87		...	...	366	427
1040	Vegetable and animal oils and fats		...	...	4	3		...	...	171	176		...	...	1141	1256
1050	Dairy products		...	...	13	10		...	...	628	636		...	...	3555	3994
106	Grain mill products,starches and starch products		...	...	2	2		...	...	-	-		...	...	-	-
1061	Grain mill products		...	...	2	...		...	...	-	...		...	...	-	...
1062	Starches and starch products		...	...	-	...		...	...	-	...		...	...	-	...
107	Other food products		...	...	135	144		...	...	2039	2166		...	...	7242	8336
1071	Bakery products		...	...	62	...		...	...	1153	...		...	...	3540	...
1072	Sugar		...	...	-	...		...	...	-	...		...	...	-	...
1073	Cocoa, chocolate and sugar confectionery		...	...	7	...		...	...	302	...		...	...	1404	...
1074	Macaroni, noodles, couscous, etc.		...	...	1	...		...	...	10	...		...	...	29	...
1075	Prepared meals and dishes		...	...	7	...		...	...	57	...		...	...	234	...
1079	Other food products n.e.c.		...	...	58	...		...	...	517	...		...	...	2019	...
1080	Prepared animal feeds		...	...	18	17		...	...	202	220		...	...	1214	1349
110	Beverages		...	...	21	24		...	...	717	748		...	...	3950	4555
1101	Distilling, rectifying and blending of spirits		...	...	7	24c/		...	...	18	748c/		...	...	102	4555c/
1102	Wines		...	...	2	..c/		...	...	3	..c/		...	...	15	..c/
1103	Malt liquors and malt		...	...	3	..c/		...	...	15	..c/		...	...	73	..c/
1104	Soft drinks,mineral waters,other bottled waters		...	...	9	..c/		...	...	681	..c/		...	...	3760	..c/
1200	Tobacco products		...	...	-	-		...	...	-	-		...	...	-	-
131	Spinning, weaving and finishing of textiles		...	...	11	11		...	...	50	48		...	...	234	254
1311	Preparation and spinning of textile fibres		...	...	4	...		...	...	46	...		...	...	234	...
1312	Weaving of textiles		...	...	6	...		...	...	2	...		...	...	-	...
1313	Finishing of textiles		...	...	1	...		...	...	2	...		...	...	...	...
139	Other textiles		...	...	48	45		...	...	216	208		...	...	1112	1162
1391	Knitted and crocheted fabrics		...	...	4	...		...	...	4	...		...	...	-	...
1392	Made-up textile articles, except apparel		...	...	28	...		...	...	83	...		...	...	307	...
1393	Carpets and rugs		...	...	-	...		...	...	-	...		...	...	-	...
1394	Cordage, rope, twine and netting		...	...	9	...		...	...	124	...		...	...	790	...
1399	Other textiles n.e.c.		...	...	7	...		...	...	5	...		...	...	15	...
1410	Wearing apparel, except fur apparel		...	...	40	36		...	...	51	37		...	...	146	147
1420	Articles of fur		...	...	1	1		...	...	5	5		...	...	15	27
1430	Knitted and crocheted apparel		...	...	7	7		...	...	56	50		...	...	190	187
151	Leather;luggage,handbags,saddlery,harness;fur		...	...	7	6		...	...	34	6		...	...	132	27
1511	Tanning/dressing of leather; dressing of fur		...	...	2	...		...	...	28	...		...	...	102	...
1512	Luggage,handbags,etc.;saddlery/harness		...	...	5	...		...	...	6	...		...	...	29	...
1520	Footwear		...	...	2	2		...	...	-	1		...	...	-	-
1610	Sawmilling and planing of wood		...	...	6	4		...	...	6	5		...	...	15	27

Code	Description												
162	Wood products, cork, straw, plaiting materials	…	84	76	…	…	191	191	…	…	863	1002	…
1621	Veneer sheets and wood-based panels	…	54	…	…	…	147	-	…	…	702	-	…
1622	Builders' carpentry and joinery	…	7	…	…	…	24	…	…	…	88	…	…
1623	Wooden containers	…	23	…	…	…	20	…	…	…	59	…	…
1629	Other wood products;articles of cork,straw	…	…	…	…	…	…	…	…	…	…	…	…
170	Paper and paper products	…	6	6	…	…	47	52	…	…	263	334	…
1701	Pulp, paper and paperboard	…	-	6d/	…	…	-	52d/	…	…	-	334d/	…
1702	Corrugated paper and paperboard	…	2	…d/	…	…	2	…d/	…	…	15	…d/	…
1709	Other articles of paper and paperboard	…	4	…d/	…	…	45	…d/	…	…	249	…d/	…
181	Printing and service activities related to printing	…	126	117	…	…	741	789	…	…	4404	4609	…
1811	Printing	…	89	…	…	…	693	…	…	…	4199	…	…
1812	Service activities related to printing	…	37	…	…	…	49	…	…	…	205	…	…
1820	Reproduction of recorded media	…	6	4	…	…	2	4	…	…	-	-	…
1910	Coke oven products	…	…	…	…	…	…	…	…	…	…	…	…
1920	Refined petroleum products	…	2	2	…	…	4	4	…	…	29	40	…
201	Basic chemicals,fertilizers, etc.	…	11	12	…	…	127	155	…	…	878	948	…
2011	Basic chemicals	…	8	…	…	…	105	…	…	…	746	…	…
2012	Fertilizers and nitrogen compounds	…	3	…	…	…	21	…	…	…	132	…	…
2013	Plastics and synthetic rubber in primary forms	…	-	…	…	…	-	…	…	…	-	…	…
202	Other chemical products	…	32	33	…	…	96	103	…	…	468	548	…
2021	Pesticides and other agrochemical products	…	1	…	…	…	-	…	…	…	-	…	…
2022	Paints,varnishes;printing ink and mastics	…	-	…	…	…	42	…	…	…	219	…	…
2023	Soap,cleaning and cosmetic preparations	…	22	…	…	…	43	…	…	…	176	…	…
2029	Other chemical products n.e.c.	…	9	…	…	…	12	…	…	…	73	-	…
2030	Man-made fibres	…	-	-	…	…	-	-	…	…	-	-	…
2100	Pharmaceuticals,medicinal chemicals, etc.	…	13	11	…	…	719	476	…	…	5998	4449	…
221	Rubber products	…	4	3	…	…	22	8	…	…	102	53	…
2211	Rubber tyres and tubes	…	1	…	…	…	14	…	…	…	59	…	…
2219	Other rubber products	…	3	…	…	…	8	…	…	…	44	…	…
2220	Plastics products	…	31	33	…	…	294	305	…	…	1770	1830	…
2310	Glass and glass products	…	17	16	…	…	86	94	…	…	439	508	…
239	Non-metallic mineral products n.e.c.	…	64	72	…	…	654	681	…	…	3818	4449	…
2391	Refractory products	…	-	…	…	…	-	…	…	…	-	…	…
2392	Clay building materials	…	-	…	…	…	-	…	…	…	-	…	…
2393	Other porcelain and ceramic products	…	20	…	…	…	21	…	…	…	59	…	…
2394	Cement, lime and plaster	…	1	…	…	…	9	…	…	…	44	…	…
2395	Articles of concrete, cement and plaster	…	27	…	…	…	421	…	…	…	2399	…	…
2396	Cutting, shaping and finishing of stone	…	12	…	…	…	65	…	…	…	336	…	…
2399	Other non-metallic mineral products n.e.c.	…	4	…	…	…	138	…	…	…	995	…	…
2410	Basic iron and steel	…	7	6	…	…	227	225	…	…	1697	1630	…
2420	Basic precious and other non-ferrous metals	…	5	5	…	…	1697	1694	…	…	12509	13680	…
243	Casting of metals	…	2	2	…	…	15	15	…	…	117	120	…
2431	Casting of iron and steel	…	1	…	…	…	7	…	…	…	73	…	…
2432	Casting of non-ferrous metals	…	1	…	…	…	8	…	…	…	44	…	…
251	Struct.metal products, tanks, reservoirs	…	16	15	…	…	177	180	…	…	951	1095	…

continued

Iceland

ISIC Revision 4			Number of enterprises (number)					Number of employees (number)					Wages and salaries paid to employees (millions of Icelandic Kronur)			
ISIC	Industry	Note	2013	2014	2015	2016a/	Note	2013	2014	2015	2016a/b/	Note	2013	2014	2015	2016a/
2511	Structural metal products		...	...	16	...		...	...	178	...		...	...	951	...
2512	Tanks, reservoirs and containers of metal		...	...	-	...		...	...	-	...		...	...	-	...
2513	Steam generators, excl. hot water boilers		...	...	-	...		...	...	-	...		...	...	-	-
2520	Weapons and ammunition		...	...	2	2		...	...	5	5		...	...	29	27
259	Other metal products;metal working services		...	...	335	342		...	...	1406	1450		...	...	7973	9097
2591	Forging,pressing,stamping,roll-forming of metal		...	...	23	...		...	...	42	...		...	...	176	...
2592	Treatment and coating of metals; machining		...	...	295	...		...	...	1340	...		...	...	7695	...
2593	Cutlery, hand tools and general hardware		...	...	4	...		...	...	8	...		...	...	29	...
2599	Other fabricated metal products n.e.c.		...	...	13	...		...	...	16	...		...	...	73	...
2610	Electronic components and boards		...	...	1	-		...	...	1	-		...	...	15	...
2620	Computers and peripheral equipment		...	...	1	1		...	...	7	-		...	...	29	...
2630	Communication equipment		...	...	1	1		...	...	-	1		...	...	...	...
2640	Consumer electronics		...	...	-	-		...	...	-	-		...	...	...	...
265	Measuring,testing equipment; watches, etc.		...	...	11	8		...	...	77	51		...	...	571	361
2651	Measuring/testing/navigating equipment,etc.		...	...	8	...		...	...	72	...		...	...	541	...
2652	Watches and clocks		...	...	3	...		...	...	5	...		...	...	29	...
2660	Irradiation/electromedical equipment,etc.		...	...	1	1		...	...	1	4		...	...	15	27
2670	Optical instruments and photographic equipment		...	...	-	-		...	...	-	-		...	...	-	-
2680	Magnetic and optical media		...	...	-	-		...	...	-	-		...	...	...	...
2710	Electric motors,generators,transformers,etc.		...	...	1	2		...	...	26	27		...	...	234	240
2720	Batteries and accumulators		...	...	1	1		...	...	1	1		...	...	...	...
273	Wiring and wiring devices		...	...	1	-		...	...	1	-		...	...	...	-
2731	Fibre optic cables		...	...	1	...		...	...	1	...		...	...	-	...
2732	Other electronic and electric wires and cables		...	...	...	...		...	...	...	...		...	...	...	...
2733	Wiring devices		...	...	-	...		...	...	-	...		...	...	-	...
2740	Electric lighting equipment		...	...	7	8		...	...	39	40		...	...	190	200
2750	Domestic appliances		...	...	1	1		...	...	-	1		...	...	-	...
2790	Other electrical equipment		...	...	8	6		...	...	139	143		...	...	966	1015
281	General-purpose machinery		...	...	43	42		...	...	162	175		...	...	1083	1256
2811	Engines/turbines,excl.aircraft,vehicle engines		...	...	9	...		...	...	11	...		...	...	44	...
2812	Fluid power equipment		...	...	-	...		...	...	-	...		...	...	-	...
2813	Other pumps, compressors, taps and valves		...	...	-	...		...	...	-	...		...	...	-	...
2814	Bearings, gears, gearing and driving elements		...	...	-	...		...	...	-	...		...	...	-	...
2815	Ovens, furnaces and furnace burners		...	...	-	...		...	...	-	...		...	...	-	...
2816	Lifting and handling equipment		...	...	6	...		...	...	26	...		...	...	117	...
2817	Office machinery, excl.computers,etc.		...	...	-	...		...	...	-	...		...	...	-	...
2818	Power-driven hand tools		...	...	-	...		...	...	-	...		...	...	-	...
2819	Other general-purpose machinery		...	...	28	...		...	...	125	...		...	...	922	...
282	Special-purpose machinery		...	...	33	33		...	...	823	892		...	...	7300	8430
2821	Agricultural and forestry machinery		...	...	1	...		...	...	-	...		...	...	-	...
2822	Metal-forming machinery and machine tools		...	...	-	...		...	...	...	...		...	...	...	...

Code	Description	(1)	(2)	(3)	(4)	(5)	(6)
2823	Machinery for metallurgy	2	...	1	...	15	...
2824	Mining, quarrying and construction machinery	-	...	799	...	-	...
2825	Food/beverage/tobacco processing machinery	25	...	2	...	7139	...
2826	Textile/apparel/leather production machinery	1	...	20	...	146	...
2829	Other special-purpose machinery	4	...	-	...	-	...
2910	Motor vehicles	-	...	-	...	-	...
2920	Automobile bodies, trailers and semi-trailers	14	...	64	60	336	347
2930	Parts and accessories for motor vehicles	5	...	13	14	59	67
301	Building of ships and boats	13	12	73	67	351	334
3011	Building of ships and floating structures	11	...	71	...	351	...
3012	Building of pleasure and sporting boats	2	...	2	...	...	...
3020	Railway locomotives and rolling stock	-	...	-	...	-	...
3030	Air and spacecraft and related machinery	1	1	1	...	-	...
3040	Military fighting vehicles	-	...	-	...	-	...
309	Transport equipment n.e.c.	1	1	1	1	-	...
3091	Motorcycles	-	...	-	...	-	...
3092	Bicycles and invalid carriages	1	...	1	...	-	...
3099	Other transport equipment n.e.c.	-	...	-	...	-	...
3100	Furniture	63	63	341	353	1712	1924
321	Jewellery, bijouterie and related articles	68	65	91	66	410	281
3211	Jewellery and related articles	64	...	90	...	395	...
3212	Imitation jewellery and related articles	4	...	1	...	15	27
3220	Musical instruments	11	11	8	4	...	...
3230	Sports goods	2	2	-	1	...	...
3240	Games and toys	12	12	21	4	88	13
3250	Medical and dental instruments and supplies	52	52	582	611	4418	4996
3290	Other manufacturing n.e.c.	52	55	77	83	219	267
331	Repair of fabricated metal products/machinery	188	188	1281	1210	7725	8002
3311	Repair of fabricated metal products	4	...	43	...	336	...
3312	Repair of machinery	76	...	520	...	3497	...
3313	Repair of electronic and optical equipment	17	...	58	...	366	...
3314	Repair of electrical equipment	21	...	67	...	380	...
3315	Repair of transport equip., excl. motor vehicles	62	...	585	...	3116	...
3319	Repair of other equipment	8	...	9	...	29	...
3320	Installation of industrial machinery/equipment	6	7	38	42	322	361
C	Total manufacturing	1934	1915	22028	21911	136908	143048

a/ Preliminary data.
b/ Number of persons engaged.
c/ 1101 includes 1102, 1103 and 1104.
d/ 1701 includes 1702 and 1709.

Iceland

ISIC	Industry	Output (valuation not defined) (millions of Icelandic Kronur)					Value added at factor values (millions of Icelandic Kronur)					Gross fixed capital formation (millions of Icelandic Kronur)		
		Note	2013	2014	2015	2016a/	Note	2013	2014	2015	2016	Note	2015	2016
1010	Processing/preserving of meat		...	...	34132	35441		...	...	10709	...		...	...
1020	Processing/preserving of fish, etc.		...	...	224541	183165		...	...	89989	...		...	...
1030	Processing/preserving of fruit,vegetables		...	...	1580	1563		...	...	688	...		...	...
1040	Vegetable and animal oils and fats		...	...	11514	8330		...	...	2750	...		...	...
1050	Dairy products		...	...	11953	7575		...	...	5281	...		...	...
106	Grain mill products,starches and starch products		...	...	15	13		...	...	15	...		...	...
1061	Grain mill products		...	...	15	...		...	...	15	...		...	...
1062	Starches and starch products		...	...	-	...		...	...	-	...		...	...
107	Other food products		...	...	19165	16538		...	...	10709	...		...	...
1071	Bakery products		...	...	8354	...		...	...	4974	...		...	...
1072	Sugar		...	...	-	...		...	...	-	...		...	...
1073	Cocoa, chocolate and sugar confectionery		...	...	3614	...		...	...	2107	...		...	...
1074	Macaroni, noodles, couscous, etc.		...	...	73	...		...	...	44	...		...	...
1075	Prepared meals and dishes		...	...	556	...		...	...	278	...		...	...
1079	Other food products n.e.c.		...	...	6584	...		...	...	3306	...		...	...
1080	Prepared animal feeds		...	...	7110	7054		...	...	2472	...		...	...
110	Beverages		...	...	27256	26852		...	...	6803	...		...	...
1101	Distilling, rectifying and blending of spirits		...	...	293	26852b/		...	...	176	...		...	...
1102	Wines		...	...	29	...b/		...	...	-	...		...	...
1103	Malt liquors and malt		...	...	249	...b/		...	...	146	...		...	...
1104	Soft drinks,mineral waters,other bottled waters		...	...	26700	...b/		...	...	6481	...		...	...
1200	Tobacco products		...	...	-	-		...	...	-	...		...	...
131	Spinning, weaving and finishing of textiles		...	...	600	655		...	...	395	...		...	...
1311	Preparation and spinning of textile fibres		...	...	556	...		...	...	380	...		...	...
1312	Weaving of textiles		...	...	29	...		...	...	15	...		...	...
1313	Finishing of textiles		...	...	15	...		...	...	-	...		...	...
139	Other textiles		...	...	2941	2672		...	...	2077	...		...	...
1391	Knitted and crocheted fabrics		...	...	29	...		...	...	15	...		...	...
1392	Made-up textile articles, except apparel		...	...	644	...		...	...	424	...		...	...
1393	Carpets and rugs		...	...	-	...		...	...	-	...		...	...
1394	Cordage, rope, twine and netting		...	...	2209	...		...	...	1609	...		...	...
1399	Other textiles n.e.c.		...	...	59	...		...	...	29	...		...	...
1410	Wearing apparel, except fur apparel		...	...	322	307		...	...	219	...		...	...
1420	Articles of fur		...	...	73	53		...	...	59	...		...	...
1430	Knitted and crocheted apparel		...	...	424	454		...	...	249	...		...	...
151	Leather;luggage,handbags,saddlery,harness;fur		...	...	527	94		...	...	190	...		...	...
1511	Tanning/dressing of leather; dressing of fur		...	...	454	...		...	...	146	...		...	...
1512	Luggage,handbags,etc.;saddlery/harness		...	...	73	...		...	...	44	...		...	...
1520	Footwear		...	...	15	13		...	...	-	...		...	...
1610	Sawmilling and planing of wood		...	...	59	40		...	...	15	...		...	...

Code	Description	1	2	3	4	5	6	7	8
162	Wood products, cork, straw, plaiting materials	1287	...	...	...	2165	2792	...	...
1621	Veneer sheets and wood-based panels	-	...	...	...	1609	...	...	...
1622	Builders' carpentry and joinery	1039	...	...	...	424	...	...	...
1623	Wooden containers	161	...	...	...	146	...	...	...
1629	Other wood products;articles of cork,straw	73	...	...	...	...	...	...	...
170	Paper and paper products	410	...	...	...	702	1029	...	...
1701	Pulp, paper and paperboard	-	...	...	...	-	1029c/	...	...
1702	Corrugated paper and paperboard	15	...	...	...	44	..c/	...	...
1709	Other articles of paper and paperboard	380	...	...	...	658	..c/	...	...
181	Printing and service activities related to printing	6306	...	...	...	12553	12945	...	...
1811	Printing	5984	...	...	...	12128	...	...	...
1812	Service activities related to printing	322	...	...	...	439	...	...	...
1820	Reproduction of recorded media	15	...	...	...	15	13	...	...
1910	Coke oven products	-	...	...	...	...	...	...	...
1920	Refined petroleum products	-15	...	...	...	-	53	...	...
201	Basic chemicals,fertilizers, etc.	424	...	...	...	3570	5103	...	...
2011	Basic chemicals	161	...	...	...	3028	...	...	...
2012	Fertilizers and nitrogen compounds	263	...	...	...	541	...	...	...
2013	Plastics and synthetic rubber in primary forms	-	...	...	...	-	...	...	...
202	Other chemical products	936	...	...	...	3014	3286	...	...
2021	Pesticides and other agrochemical products	-	...	...	...	-	...	...	...
2022	Paints,varnishes;printing ink and mastics	380	...	...	...	1317	...	...	...
2023	Soap,cleaning and cosmetic preparations	293	...	...	...	1200	...	...	...
2029	Other chemical products n.e.c.	263	...	...	...	497	...	...	...
2030	Man-made fibres	-	...	...	...	-	...	...	...
2100	Pharmaceuticals,medicinal chemicals, etc.	5954	...	...	...	45368	8964	...	...
221	Rubber products	161	...	...	...	249	94	...	...
2211	Rubber tyres and tubes	102	...	...	...	161	...	...	...
2219	Other rubber products	59	...	...	...	88	...	...	...
2220	Plastics products	3365	...	...	...	6964	6372	...	...
2310	Glass and glass products	629	...	...	...	1112	1109	...	...
239	Non-metallic mineral products n.e.c.	7066	...	...	...	14337	18355	...	...
2391	Refractory products	-	...	...	...	-	...	...	...
2392	Clay building materials	73	...	...	...	117	...	...	...
2393	Other porcelain and ceramic products	176	...	...	...	395	...	...	...
2394	Cement, lime and plaster	4287	...	...	...	7008	...	...	...
2395	Articles of concrete, cement and plaster	512	...	...	...	717	...	...	...
2396	Cutting, shaping and finishing of stone	2034	...	...	...	6115	...	...	...
2399	Other non-metallic mineral products n.e.c.	6115	...	...	...	19297	14080	...	...
2410	Basic iron and steel	46597	...	...	...	225258	180654	...	...
2420	Basic precious and other non-ferrous metals	219	...	...	...	410	508	...	...
243	Casting of metals	161	...	...	...	307	...	...	...
2431	Casting of iron and steel	59	...	...	...	102	...	...	...
2432	Casting of non-ferrous metals	1448	...	...	...	2926	3660	...	...
251	Struct.metal products, tanks, reservoirs	...	...	...	...	...	...	...	...

continued

Iceland

ISIC Revision 4		Output (valuation not defined) (millions of Icelandic Kronur)					Value added at factor values (millions of Icelandic Kronur)					Gross fixed capital formation (millions of Icelandic Kronur)		
ISIC	Industry	Note	2013	2014	2015	2016a/	Note	2013	2014	2015	2016	Note	2015	2016
2511	Structural metal products		...	...	2926	...		...	...	1448	...		...	...
2512	Tanks, reservoirs and containers of metal		...	...	-	...		...	...	-	...		...	...
2513	Steam generators, excl. hot water boilers		...	...	-	...		...	...	-	...		...	...
2520	Weapons and ammunition		...	...	73	80		...	...	59	...		...	...
259	Other metal products;metal working services		...	...	17702	19624		...	...	12245	...		...	...
2591	Forging,pressing,stamping,roll-forming of metal		...	...	380	...		...	...	293	...		...	...
2592	Treatment and coating of metals; machining		...	...	17073	...		...	...	11792	...		...	...
2593	Cutlery, hand tools and general hardware		...	...	44	...		...	...	29	...		...	...
2599	Other fabricated metal products n.e.c.		...	...	205	...		...	...	132	...		...	...
2610	Electronic components and boards		...	...	44	-		...	...	44	...		...	...
2620	Computers and peripheral equipment		...	...	44	-		...	...	29	...		...	...
2630	Communication equipment		...	...	-	-		...	...	-	...		...	...
2640	Consumer electronics		...	...	-	-		...	...	-	...		...	...
265	Measuring,testing equipment; watches, etc.		...	...	1068	427		...	...	761	...		...	...
2651	Measuring/testing/navigating equipment,etc.		...	...	966	...		...	...	702	...		...	...
2652	Watches and clocks		...	...	102	40		...	...	59	...		...	...
2660	Irradiation/electromedical equipment,etc.		...	...	15	-		...	...	-	...		...	...
2670	Optical instruments and photographic equipment		...	...	-	-		...	...	-	...		...	...
2680	Magnetic and optical media		...	...	-	-		...	...	-	...		...	...
2710	Electric motors,generators,transformers,etc.		...	...	439	387		...	...	351	...		...	...
2720	Batteries and accumulators		...	...	-	-		...	...	-	...		...	...
273	Wiring and wiring devices		...	...	15	-		...	...	-	...		...	...
2731	Fibre optic cables		...	...	15	...		...	...	-	...		...	...
2732	Other electronic and electric wires and cables		...	...	-	...		...	...	-	...		...	...
2733	Wiring devices		...	...	-	...		...	...	-	...		...	...
2740	Electric lighting equipment		...	...	336	387		...	...	278	...		...	...
2750	Domestic appliances		...	...	-	-		...	...	-	...		...	...
2790	Other electrical equipment		...	...	5252	4302		...	...	1551	...		...	...
281	General-purpose machinery		...	...	2604	2899		...	...	2107	...		...	...
2811	Engines/turbines,excl.aircraft,vehicle engines		...	...	102	...		...	...	73	...		...	...
2812	Fluid power equipment		...	...	-	...		...	...	-	...		...	...
2813	Other pumps, compressors, taps and valves		...	...	-	...		...	...	-	...		...	...
2814	Bearings, gears, gearing and driving elements		...	...	-	...		...	...	-	...		...	...
2815	Ovens, furnaces and furnace burners		...	...	-	...		...	...	-	...		...	...
2816	Lifting and handling equipment		...	...	263	...		...	...	176	...		...	...
2817	Office machinery, excl.computers,etc.		...	...	-	...		...	...	-	...		...	...
2818	Power-driven hand tools		...	...	-	...		...	...	-	...		...	...
2819	Other general-purpose machinery		...	...	2238	...		...	...	1843	...		...	...
282	Special-purpose machinery		...	...	24183	25729		...	...	10168	...		...	...
2821	Agricultural and forestry machinery		...	...	-	...		...	...	-	...		...	...
2822	Metal-forming machinery and machine tools		...	...	-	...		...	...	-	...		...	...

Code	Description			
2823	Machinery for metallurgy	29	:	15
2824	Mining, quarrying and construction machinery	-	:	-
2825	Food/beverage/tobacco processing machinery	24008	:	10007
2826	Textile/apparel/leather production machinery	-	:	-
2829	Other special-purpose machinery	161	:	132
2910	Motor vehicles	-	-	-
2920	Automobile bodies, trailers and semi-trailers	805	855	468
2930	Parts and accessories for motor vehicles	176	187	132
301	Building of ships and boats	644	628	512
3011	Building of ships and floating structures	644	:	527
3012	Building of pleasure and sporting boats	-	:	-15
3020	Railway locomotives and rolling stock	-	-	-
3030	Air and spacecraft and related machinery	-	-	-
3040	Military fighting vehicles	-	-	-
309	Transport equipment n.e.c.	-	-	-
3091	Motorcycles	-	-	-
3092	Bicycles and invalid carriages	-	-	-
3099	Other transport equipment n.e.c.	-	-	-
3100	Furniture	3892	4609	2458
321	Jewellery, bijouterie and related articles	1170	828	629
3211	Jewellery and related articles	1170	:	614
3212	Imitation jewellery and related articles	15	53	-
3220	Musical instruments	44	:	29
3230	Sports goods	-	-	-
3240	Games and toys	132	27	59
3250	Medical and dental instruments and supplies	25676	22069	12055
3290	Other manufacturing n.e.c.	512	601	322
331	Repair of fabricated metal products/machinery	15215	15777	11294
3311	Repair of fabricated metal products	556	:	497
3312	Repair of machinery	6554	:	4930
3313	Repair of electronic and optical equipment	878	:	600
3314	Repair of electrical equipment	863	:	614
3315	Repair of transport equip., excl. motor vehicles	6262	:	4579
3319	Repair of other equipment	102	:	44
3320	Installation of industrial machinery/equipment	614	574	468
C	Total manufacturing	780847	650396	269514

a/ Preliminary data.
b/ 1101 includes 1102, 1103 and 1104.
c/ 1701 includes 1702 and 1709.

Iceland

Index numbers of industrial production

ISIC Revision 4

(2010=100)

ISIC	Industry	Note	2005	2006	2007	2008	2009	2010	2011	2012	2013	2014	2015	2016
10	Food products	a/	91	87	90	97	98	100	112	117	129	126	129	122
11	Beverages	a/	...	...	...	...	...	...	...	...	...	...	...	...
12	Tobacco products	a/	...	...	...	...	...	...	...	...	...	...	...	...
13	Textiles	b/	127	129	125	86	93	100	99	106	100	96	91	81
14	Wearing apparel	b/	...	...	...	...	...	...	...	...	...	...	...	...
15	Leather and related products	b/	...	...	...	...	...	...	...	...	...	...	...	...
16	Wood products, excluding furniture	c/	214	224	209	159	112	100	93	88	96	97	95	106
17	Paper and paper products	c/	...	...	...	...	...	...	...	...	...	...	...	...
18	Printing and reproduction of recorded media		73	81	82	90	90	100	113	116	135	138	98	95
19	Coke and refined petroleum products		...	...	...	...	...	...	...	...	...	...	...	...
20	Chemicals and chemical products	d/	89	86	84	95	99	100	109	110	114	126	127	150
21	Pharmaceuticals, medicinal chemicals, etc.	d/	...	...	...	...	...	...	...	...	...	...	...	...
22	Rubber and plastics products		164	166	177	146	105	100	105	121	112	116	127	115
23	Other non-metallic mineral products		271	328	362	294	141	100	97	94	105	127	144	172
24	Basic metals		40	47	62	89	98	100	100	99	103	103	106	106
25	Fabricated metal products, except machinery		147	162	176	134	98	100	103	102	102	111	116	130
26	Computer, electronic and optical products		182	202	109	105	108	100	192	159	104	99	96	87
27	Electrical equipment		40	39	34	48	64	100	125	127	131	123	126	117
28	Machinery and equipment n.e.c.		74	77	79	94	84	100	114	138	131	149	148	163
29	Motor vehicles, trailers and semi-trailers		194	182	183	158	123	100	120	102	99	107	120	124
30	Other transport equipment		287	300	155	142	93	100	95	111	128	142	135	105
31	Furniture	e/	112	114	90	92	86	100	112	122	138	153	242	227
32	Other manufacturing	e/	...	...	...	...	...	...	...	...	...	...	...	...
33	Repair and installation of machinery/equipment		138	142	85	122	102	100	131	130	136	153	154	169
C	Total manufacturing		87	90	94	101	98	100	108	111	119	121	128	128

a/ 10 includes 11 and 12.
b/ 13 includes 14 and 15.
c/ 16 includes 17.
d/ 20 includes 21.
e/ 31 includes 32.

India

Supplier of information:
Central Statistics Office, Industrial Statistics Wing, Kolkata.

Basic source of data:
Annual survey of registered establishments.

Major deviations from ISIC (Revision 4):
Data were originally classified according to the National Industrial Classification 2008, which was based on ISIC Revision 4.

Reference period:
From 1 April of the year indicated to 31 March of the following year. However, individual factory returns for an accounting year ending on any day during the reference period are accepted.

Scope:
All manufacturing units registered under sections 2m(i) & 2m(ii) of Factories Act,1948; Bidi & Cigar units employing 10 or more workers with aid of power or 20 or more workers without aid of power and registered under Bidi & Cigar (Conditions of Employment) Act, 1966 and electricity undertakings engaged in generation, transmission and distribution of electricity and not registered with Central Electricity Authority.

Method of data collection:
Online survey.

Type of enumeration:
Sample survey.

Adjusted for non-response:
Yes.

Concepts and definitions of variables:
Wages and salaries refers to compensation of employees and it excludes payments in kind.
Output refers to gross output.
Value added refers to total value added.

Related national publications:
Annual Survey of Industries, published by the Central Statistics Office, Industrial Statistics Wing, Kolkata.

India

ISIC	Industry	Note	Number of establishments (number) 2012	2013	2014	2015	Note	Number of employees (thousands) 2012	2013	2014	2015	Note	Wages and salaries paid to employees (billions of Indian Rupees) 2012	2013	2014	2015
1010	Processing/preserving of meat		140	148	170	148		22.1	25.6	30.0	28.8		3.2	4.7	5.1	5.5
1020	Processing/preserving of fish, etc.		462	466	427	534		36.7	44.1	53.1	65.8		4.1	5.7	7.3	9.4
1030	Processing/preserving of fruit, vegetables		1110	1101	1133	1192		54.8	58.0	60.4	60.4		6.1	8.2	8.5	10.0
1040	Vegetable and animal oils and fats		3312	3300	3240	3147		110.0	106.4	105.3	94.6		13.3	14.1	15.4	16.3
1050	Dairy products		1695	1753	1783	1943		134.9	145.4	143.7	163.6		25.7	38.4	33.3	40.2
106	Grain mill products, starches and starch products		18854	19016	19652	19811		314.4	309.8	317.3	317.9		27.7	30.3	33.3	36.7
1061	Grain mill products		18131	18272	18953	19141		294.9	287.1	296.1	294.5		25.0	26.7	29.7	33.1
1062	Starches and starch products		723	744	699	670		19.5	22.7	21.3	23.3		2.7	3.6	3.6	3.6
107	Other food products		8649	8743	9103	9405		822.4	833.5	824.3	799.4		99.2	109.8	121.0	128.5
1071	Bakery products		1519	1498	1613	1626		96.4	96.1	99.5	101.7		14.4	13.1	15.4	16.1
1072	Sugar		859	791	763	780		259.8	247.8	239.8	232.4		41.4	43.0	46.5	47.6
1073	Cocoa, chocolate and sugar confectionery		539	505	594	564		30.6	37.2	43.9	42.3		6.1	8.1	11.1	11.0
1074	Macaroni, noodles, couscous, etc.		129	105	91	89		8.4	9.9	7.8	7.9		1.1	1.3	1.4	1.6
1075	Prepared meals and dishes		352	298	277	364		16.2	18.1	19.9	30.9		3.0	3.5	4.2	6.5
1079	Other food products n.e.c.		5251	5546	5765	5983		410.9	424.3	413.3	384.2		33.1	40.8	42.4	45.6
1080	Prepared animal feeds		873	820	881	918		38.5	44.6	64.5	54.7		5.7	8.1	15.7	11.2
110	Beverages		2080	2103	2219	2220		141.4	157.8	159.8	164.4		23.9	32.0	33.5	37.5
1101	Distilling, rectifying and blending of spirits		365	369	395	376		47.8	54.2	53.5	57.9		7.3	10.1	10.2	13.2
1102	Wines		78	71	74	70		8.5	7.9	7.2	7.1		1.2	2.1	1.5	1.7
1103	Malt liquors and malt		154	143	153	150		29.1	28.3	29.7	31.1		5.2	5.2	6.3	7.7
1104	Soft drinks; mineral waters, other bottled waters		1483	1520	1597	1624		55.9	67.4	69.4	68.3		10.2	14.6	15.5	15.0
1200	Tobacco products		3417	3294	3315	3825		425.7	443.3	437.1	507.5		19.4	20.2	23.6	28.0
131	Spinning, weaving and finishing of textiles		13120	13353	13106	12634		1149.9	1232.2	1228.7	1246.9		132.6	159.3	172.8	193.0
1311	Preparation and spinning of textile fibres		6286	6360	6345	5864		678.1	712.6	745.4	704.5		75.3	89.4	99.3	102.7
1312	Weaving of textiles		3030	2948	2785	2940		232.0	233.1	210.5	232.0		29.0	33.2	33.8	40.8
1313	Finishing of textiles		3804	4045	3976	3831		239.8	286.4	272.8	310.3		28.3	36.8	39.7	49.4
139	Other textiles		5348	5293	5637	5035		254.0	258.0	304.0	313.9		29.9	34.5	46.0	50.7
1391	Knitted and crocheted fabrics		1641	1658	1713	1197		42.7	33.0	42.4	37.6		4.9	5.2	6.8	6.1
1392	Made-up textile articles, except apparel		1150	1116	1232	1265		86.0	91.7	116.0	109.5		10.0	12.3	17.3	18.3
1393	Carpets and rugs		543	466	529	490		24.0	35.8	34.4	61.2		2.7	4.2	4.4	7.5
1394	Cordage, rope, twine and netting		790	740	829	783		47.9	51.8	45.5	44.9		5.2	5.8	5.6	7.0
1399	Other textiles n.e.c.		1224	1313	1334	1300		53.3	45.7	65.7	60.7		7.1	7.0	11.8	11.7
1410	Wearing apparel, except fur apparel		6143	6284	6405	6436		660.7	712.5	712.3	754.3		75.0	90.1	95.5	114.4
1420	Articles of fur		10	13	11	7		0.9	0.6	1.2	0.8		0.1	0.1	0.2	0.1
1430	Knitted and crocheted apparel		3122	3228	3440	3754		258.8	263.0	273.1	325.7		24.1	29.4	33.0	43.3
151	Leather; luggage, handbags, saddlery, harness; fur		1993	1946	1972	2085		90.8	103.9	97.1	124.1		9.3	11.9	13.2	17.9
1511	Tanning/dressing of leather; dressing of fur		1350	1289	1248	1234		42.4	46.7	43.1	49.6		4.1	5.2	5.3	6.4
1512	Luggage, handbags, etc.; saddlery/harness		643	657	724	850		48.4	57.2	54.0	74.5		5.2	6.7	7.9	11.5
1520	Footwear		2062	2279	2369	2424		193.6	206.5	228.7	254.5		19.4	25.5	29.2	36.5
1610	Sawmilling and planing of wood		1432	1377	1341	1283		8.2	7.7	6.8	6.6		0.7	0.6	0.7	0.6

Code	Description												
162	Wood products, cork, straw, plaiting materials	12.9	10.7	8.4	8.4	80.1	76.9	68.9	66.5	2846	2893	3051	3131
1621	Veneer sheets and wood-based panels	8.7	7.0	6.3	5.2	53.7	51.5	51.1	46.7	1937	1941	2161	2118
1622	Builders' carpentry and joinery	0.8	0.8	0.6	0.4	5.1	4.6	3.8	3.2	127	117	119	138
1623	Wooden containers	1.4	1.2	0.7	0.7	8.6	7.6	5.5	6.3	338	315	275	395
1629	Other wood products;articles of cork,straw	2.0	1.8	0.9	2.0	12.7	13.2	8.5	10.3	444	520	496	480
170	Paper and paper products	50.8	44.9	41.9	37.5	246.3	239.5	246.3	233.8	6488	6810	6765	6911
1701	Pulp, paper and paperboard	21.2	19.9	18.4	17.3	87.3	93.6	93.6	95.3	1342	1221	1181	1128
1702	Corrugated paper and paperboard	17.6	13.4	13.0	10.9	104.4	88.4	98.8	88.8	3984	4362	4252	4493
1709	Other articles of paper and paperboard	12.0	11.6	10.5	9.3	54.6	57.5	53.9	49.6	1162	1227	1332	1290
181	Printing and service activities related to printing	41.2	42.4	34.2	36.2	153.9	168.7	155.1	165.4	4518	4526	4604	4626
1811	Printing	39.0	38.6	32.3	34.4	141.1	150.0	142.6	153.0	3950	4063	4011	4031
1812	Service activities related to printing	2.2	3.9	1.9	1.8	12.8	18.7	12.5	12.5	568	463	593	595
1820	Reproduction of recorded media	0.4	0.5	0.1	0.1	1.2	2.2	0.6	0.6	21	21	22	16
1910	Coke oven products	8.7	8.5	8.4	7.9	26.4	28.5	28.7	29.9	708	719	724	738
1920	Refined petroleum products	68.6	59.4	48.5	40.4	116.6	93.9	80.9	69.7	828	859	898	907
201	Basic chemicals,fertilizers, etc.	110.5	101.0	91.3	80.4	298.9	283.5	279.0	272.9	4400	4425	4536	4584
2011	Basic chemicals	56.0	50.9	42.8	38.1	183.0	174.0	163.2	156.4	3272	3310	3295	3272
2012	Fertilizers and nitrogen compounds	37.4	35.1	33.1	30.2	74.6	73.1	76.8	82.2	703	716	769	772
2013	Plastics and synthetic rubber in primary forms	17.2	15.0	15.4	12.1	41.3	36.5	38.9	34.3	425	399	472	540
202	Other chemical products	111.1	96.6	73.5	61.3	414.7	401.0	397.6	332.8	6906	6882	7036	7295
2021	Pesticides and other agrochemical products	19.9	16.5	15.5	11.7	72.3	61.9	59.9	51.2	594	571	625	597
2022	Paints,varnishes;printing ink and mastics	18.6	19.3	14.5	10.3	54.4	59.8	88.6	44.9	1259	1251	1281	1428
2023	Soap,cleaning and cosmetic preparations	31.5	32.2	20.1	16.3	134.4	138.5	112.2	105.0	1787	1792	1862	1909
2029	Other chemical products n.e.c.	41.1	28.6	23.4	22.9	153.6	140.8	136.9	131.7	3266	3268	3268	3361
2030	Man-made fibres	7.6	6.6	8.0	6.5	27.2	25.2	28.7	25.9	122	159	143	136
2100	Pharmaceuticals,medicinal chemicals, etc.	234.3	195.7	171.8	142.2	650.1	609.8	618.0	531.6	4907	4961	4908	5036
221	Rubber products	54.8	44.0	47.7	32.9	208.9	185.3	218.1	180.6	2878	2727	2767	2864
2211	Rubber tyres and tubes	33.2	29.1	27.0	20.9	109.2	106.6	106.7	95.2	778	666	610	604
2219	Other rubber products	21.6	14.8	20.7	12.1	99.7	78.7	111.4	85.4	2100	2061	2157	2260
2220	Plastics products	85.3	77.6	56.7	52.5	432.2	408.2	369.5	355.4	9799	10420	10781	10926
2310	Glass and glass products	14.6	13.3	11.3	10.4	66.6	67.8	61.9	64.9	847	781	808	871
239	Non-metallic mineral products n.e.c.	140.3	152.6	113.2	101.2	923.8	915.5	894.7	811.0	24406	24816	26397	26758
2391	Refractory products	11.2	11.1	9.6	9.0	53.6	52.1	51.1	51.9	1224	1137	1275	1230
2392	Clay building materials	23.4	22.6	19.4	16.0	383.5	388.4	381.2	329.5	8634	8924	9786	9938
2393	Other porcelain and ceramic products	11.5	11.8	7.9	8.0	63.8	70.4	52.1	53.0	951	950	1024	1089
2394	Cement, lime and plaster	53.5	51.4	44.9	39.8	179.9	175.0	164.1	154.8	1367	1450	1487	1378
2395	Articles of concrete, cement and plaster	17.1	35.2	10.8	10.0	80.6	89.2	78.6	81.4	2648	2651	2793	2817
2396	Cutting, shaping and finishing of stone	16.3	14.4	13.2	12.4	120.4	110.2	120.3	105.4	8344	8584	8962	9095
2399	Other non-metallic mineral products n.e.c.	7.4	6.2	7.4	6.0	42.0	30.1	47.4	35.0	1238	1120	1070	1210
2410	Basic iron and steel	210.0	210.5	193.4	177.3	608.3	666.5	649.8	679.0	6033	5924	5899	5839
2420	Basic precious and other non-ferrous metals	41.6	38.0	34.9	31.5	117.2	107.4	106.9	106.7	1808	1738	1699	1891
243	Casting of metals	47.4	43.5	38.0	37.3	219.8	227.8	216.8	228.9	4037	4121	4025	4052
2431	Casting of iron and steel	41.0	38.0	32.7	31.8	192.6	199.4	185.6	198.2	3484	3613	3482	3553
2432	Casting of non-ferrous metals	6.4	5.5	5.3	5.5	27.2	28.5	31.2	30.8	553	508	543	499
251	Struct.metal products, tanks, reservoirs	63.3	54.4	51.8	51.3	242.9	223.1	228.8	242.0	4901	4742	4750	4921

continued

India

ISIC	Industry	Number of establishments (number)					Number of employees (thousands)					Wages and salaries paid to employees (billions of Indian Rupees)				
		Note	2012	2013	2014	2015	Note	2012	2013	2014	2015	Note	2012	2013	2014	2015
2511	Structural metal products		3089	3006	3083	3131		151.2	150.2	147.8	165.9		26.1	27.4	28.8	37.3
2512	Tanks, reservoirs and containers of metal		1399	1322	1356	1419		58.7	48.2	47.6	47.2		9.9	8.6	8.9	9.4
2513	Steam generators, excl. hot water boilers		413	414	311	370		32.2	30.3	27.7	29.8		15.4	15.8	16.7	16.6
2520	Weapons and ammunition		45	101	66	69		1.8	2.1	2.4	3.8		0.3	0.5	0.6	1.0
259	Other metal products;metal working services		11260	11805	11847	12117		383.5	442.5	396.6	408.5		56.0	73.3	73.1	82.0
2591	Forging,pressing,stamping,roll-forming of metal		1289	1491	1421	1452		63.3	71.2	59.5	64.5		10.0	13.1	11.9	14.7
2592	Treatment and coating of metals;machining		2016	2044	2110	2104		38.2	42.9	48.3	43.4		5.4	7.5	8.9	8.9
2593	Cutlery, hand tools and general hardware		1989	1836	1746	1587		71.9	79.0	66.6	66.7		10.7	14.0	13.7	14.1
2599	Other fabricated metal products n.e.c.		5966	6434	6570	6974		210.2	249.4	222.2	233.9		29.9	38.7	38.6	44.3
2610	Electronic components and boards		1122	1077	1023	1034		71.4	76.5	79.9	78.1		17.8	21.2	23.3	23.2
2620	Computers and peripheral equipment		147	162	86	125		29.8	24.6	15.8	17.2		10.0	24.6	25.4	26.8
2630	Communication equipment		265	280	224	249		40.0	41.5	30.5	40.6		14.1	13.5	13.7	19.3
2640	Consumer electronics		271	270	198	218		22.3	26.3	26.3	17.9		9.7	11.9	13.4	5.9
265	Measuring,testing equipment; watches, etc.		549	534	676	590		43.8	45.8	49.9	51.9		13.5	15.1	19.2	22.7
2651	Measuring/testing/navigating equipment,etc.		425	426	562	464		30.7	36.4	39.7	40.6		9.9	11.5	15.8	17.5
2652	Watches and clocks		124	108	114	126		13.1	9.4	10.2	11.3		3.6	3.6	3.4	5.2
2660	Irradiation/electromedical equipment,etc.		142	105	85	76		8.4	6.0	6.5	4.7		5.6	...	2.1	1.7
2670	Optical instruments and photographic equipment		80	72	56	78		2.6	1.9	3.3	2.5		0.5	0.4	1.0	0.6
2680	Magnetic and optical media		6	4	4	5		0.2	-	0.1	0.6		-	-	-	0.3
2710	Electric motors,generators,transformers,etc.		2956	2797	3002	3035		218.9	198.2	207.7	202.3		65.5	63.8	66.8	72.8
2720	Batteries and accumulators		515	436	491	507		48.0	43.8	51.3	48.5		10.4	10.5	12.5	13.7
273	Wiring and wiring devices		1440	1360	1469	1346		85.4	95.1	92.7	94.4		14.9	17.5	19.7	20.4
2731	Fibre optic cables		271	169	145	131		12.8	10.6	11.3	9.6		2.8	2.9	3.1	2.8
2732	Other electronic and electric wires and cables		692	759	837	887		42.6	51.8	53.0	57.0		7.5	10.0	11.6	12.5
2733	Wiring devices		477	432	487	328		30.0	32.7	28.3	27.8		4.6	4.6	5.0	5.1
2740	Electric lighting equipment		551	519	587	595		45.4	52.5	47.9	51.8		7.2	9.5	10.6	11.1
2750	Domestic appliances		1107	999	963	1039		49.0	53.4	43.9	51.3		11.3	14.0	9.8	11.5
2790	Other electrical equipment		1132	1223	1128	1005		52.3	69.4	60.5	51.3		9.3	16.1	13.6	12.8
281	General-purpose machinery		5945	5711	6172	6161		339.0	337.8	399.2	404.7		91.7	96.9	132.7	137.6
2811	Engines/turbines,excl.aircraft,vehicle engines		638	556	565	549		55.2	55.7	64.6	68.9		21.0	21.8	33.0	27.9
2812	Fluid power equipment		758	700	683	824		25.9	26.5	32.6	43.8		6.8	6.5	8.1	18.4
2813	Other pumps, compressors, taps and valves		1001	1070	1212	1202		83.6	78.7	101.4	87.2		20.0	22.1	33.6	28.0
2814	Bearings, gears, gearing and driving elements		683	700	711	685		50.6	52.3	54.2	56.1		13.0	14.3	17.2	17.7
2815	Ovens, furnaces and furnace burners		93	115	132	140		8.5	10.3	10.4	10.1		2.1	2.5	3.0	2.6
2816	Lifting and handling equipment		438	455	449	526		32.4	34.5	35.4	37.1		9.1	10.0	10.7	12.7
2817	Office machinery, excl.computers,etc.		39	60	41	38		1.5	2.5	1.5	1.5		0.3	0.4	0.3	0.4
2818	Power-driven hand tools		118	127	169	145		6.4	3.6	3.2	3.2		1.5	0.8	1.4	1.1
2819	Other general-purpose machinery		2177	1928	2210	2051		74.9	73.7	95.9	96.7		17.9	18.5	25.6	28.8
282	Special-purpose machinery		5934	6021	6106	5963		329.6	305.7	309.2	318.7		93.6	92.9	100.6	112.1
2821	Agricultural and forestry machinery		917	843	865	845		60.2	60.0	64.9	60.6		19.1	20.9	22.2	23.9
2822	Metal-forming machinery and machine tools		1177	1122	1272	1173		60.3	43.7	54.2	49.7		20.8	13.8	18.6	17.6

ISIC Revision 4

2823	Machinery for metallurgy	1.5	2.6	1.2	1.6	7.0	4.2	6.9	3.4	143	102	135	86
2824	Mining, quarrying and construction machinery	16.8	12.7	11.9	11.1	42.7	45.7	44.0	41.8	464	570	636	565
2825	Food/beverage/tobacco processing machinery	9.6	7.5	6.7	6.9	27.9	22.6	21.6	28.3	622	641	557	525
2826	Textile/apparel/leather production machinery	10.4	8.4	7.8	8.5	38.4	36.7	33.7	40.2	840	866	816	910
2829	Other special-purpose machinery	32.4	28.6	30.6	25.6	93.1	92.8	83.8	94.8	1771	1877	1825	1860
2910	Motor vehicles	89.3	80.4	75.2	68.3	148.5	176.5	187.3	185.8	255	188	182	182
2920	Automobile bodies, trailers and semi-trailers	17.3	14.1	12.4	13.7	54.5	50.0	58.2	58.4	643	568	701	699
2930	Parts and accessories for motor vehicles	177.3	152.3	125.8	109.9	560.8	565.3	646.5	687.8	4660	4842	4974	5006
301	Building of ships and boats	6.9	7.2	8.2	9.0	41.2	28.0	24.7	17.1	133	124	119	105
3011	Building of ships and floating structures	6.7	7.2	8.2	8.9	40.9	27.7	24.4	16.5	125	117	112	98
3012	Building of pleasure and sporting boats	0.2	-	-	0.1	0.3	0.3	0.2	0.6	8	7	7	7
3020	Railway locomotives and rolling stock	7.2	7.8	6.7	6.4	30.4	27.2	34.0	27.2	353	302	392	316
3030	Air and spacecraft and related machinery	5.7	5.0	4.4	4.2	16.0	10.8	13.7	13.1	114	90	80	79
3040	Military fighting vehicles	0.2	0.2	0.1	0.1	1.1	0.6	1.4	1.1	55	36	53	52
309	Transport equipment n.e.c.	65.3	59.1	48.4	41.2	204.7	215.9	227.9	249.4	1744	1745	1676	1649
3091	Motorcycles	59.3	53.5	43.2	36.8	169.6	179.5	189.5	212.3	967	945	875	897
3092	Bicycles and invalid carriages	5.4	4.7	4.6	4.0	32.7	33.0	34.1	34.5	650	721	730	699
3099	Other transport equipment n.e.c.	0.6	0.9	0.7	0.4	2.4	3.4	4.3	2.6	127	79	71	53
3100	Furniture	10.5	13.9	12.8	12.5	63.9	59.8	56.6	52.9	1384	1456	1552	1532
321	Jewellery, bijouterie and related articles	39.1	35.7	32.4	27.1	155.0	157.2	160.9	172.3	1480	1447	1435	1409
3211	Jewellery and related articles	38.3	35.3	31.9	26.9	152.9	153.8	158.3	168.5	1366	1323	1319	1272
3212	Imitation jewellery and related articles	0.8	0.4	0.5	0.3	2.2	3.3	2.7	3.8	114	124	116	137
3220	Musical instruments	0.2	0.2	0.2	-	0.4	0.3	0.5	0.6	14	11	21	25
3230	Sports goods	2.0	1.9	1.1	1.0	9.0	8.4	13.1	12.2	178	165	192	191
3240	Games and toys	1.4	0.9	0.3	0.4	2.6	2.1	5.7	8.2	145	90	121	151
3250	Medical and dental instruments and supplies	9.7	9.2	7.8	7.6	38.2	41.4	44.3	46.5	387	462	510	465
3290	Other manufacturing n.e.c.	15.8	10.5	9.5	7.8	61.0	63.7	65.4	76.4	996	1037	1041	1015
331	Repair of fabricated metal products/machinery	14.3	10.6	9.0	9.1	27.2	29.6	29.1	31.4	690	680	637	712
3311	Repair of fabricated metal products	1.0	1.0	0.8	0.9	5.4	4.5	3.6	4.3	139	137	106	155
3312	Repair of machinery	5.5	4.2	4.1	4.2	10.4	10.1	10.9	12.0	202	215	180	271
3313	Repair of electronic and optical equipment	0.1	0.2	0.4	0.4	1.5	1.9	1.0	0.2	71	68	75	32
3314	Repair of electrical equipment	0.8	0.8	0.5	0.5	2.8	3.7	3.7	3.7	119	94	105	93
3315	Repair of transport equip., excl. motor vehicles	2.8	3.0	2.5	2.9	5.9	5.2	7.3	6.4	123	106	127	107
3319	Repair of other equipment	4.2	1.5	0.7	0.2	1.1	4.2	2.6	5.0	36	60	44	54
3320	Installation of industrial machinery/equipment	2.0	3.7	1.5	1.5	5.7	5.1	15.3	6.6	78	89	87	71
C	Total manufacturing	3123.0	2838.1	2499.7	2186.1	12307.0	12868.2	13186.5	13614.5	207051	208849	213973	216174

India

ISIC	Industry	Output Note	Output at basic prices (billions of Indian Rupees) 2012	2013	2014	2015	VA Note	Value added at basic prices (billions of Indian Rupees) 2012	2013	2014	2015	GFCF Note	Gross fixed capital formation (billions of Indian Rupees) 2014	2015
1010	Processing/preserving of meat		168.9	275.2	253.9	237.1		14.1	29.1	20.1	20.2		5.5	6.0
1020	Processing/preserving of fish, etc.		168.0	270.6	274.7	293.0		15.4	19.3	24.5	31.6		5.2	9.1
1030	Processing/preserving of fruit,vegetables		109.1	138.9	149.3	181.7		24.7	30.1	23.0	45.8		7.6	8.2
1040	Vegetable and animal oils and fats		1654.7	1570.0	1644.6	1530.5		86.1	70.1	67.3	91.5		12.2	16.4
1050	Dairy products		824.6	1106.6	1346.6	1401.0		67.8	100.7	96.4	109.4		47.9	48.3
106	Grain mill products,starches and starch products		1823.3	1860.8	2107.3	2174.5		175.3	152.7	132.1	138.7		39.3	41.7
1061	Grain mill products		1739.5	1757.5	2007.7	2067.7		160.6	139.4	114.9	124.8		30.6	29.2
1062	Starches and starch products		83.8	103.4	99.6	106.8		14.7	13.3	17.2	13.9		8.7	12.6
107	Other food products		1992.7	2141.3	2392.4	2439.2		259.5	278.0	340.3	380.3		122.9	113.1
1071	Bakery products		221.1	204.8	220.7	225.0		35.0	45.2	46.9	49.2		11.5	7.7
1072	Sugar		1001.7	858.8	974.0	992.2		108.5	88.8	106.9	115.5		65.8	52.8
1073	Cocoa, chocolate and sugar confectionery		121.9	147.5	160.1	164.5		30.2	27.7	20.9	32.5		13.5	12.9
1074	Macaroni, noodles, couscous, etc.		26.3	39.7	30.4	25.1		9.5	8.2	8.9	7.3		2.0	0.5
1075	Prepared meals and dishes		19.4	27.6	43.5	37.5		5.2	6.7	9.0	8.5		0.4	1.8
1079	Other food products n.e.c.		602.4	862.7	963.7	994.9		71.1	101.4	147.7	167.4		29.8	37.5
1080	Prepared animal feeds		240.8	371.7	454.0	417.1		20.4	35.3	56.3	41.0		10.2	13.6
110	Beverages		522.6	610.9	720.0	709.7		144.1	144.1	156.6	180.3		52.4	44.5
1101	Distilling, rectifying and blending of spirits		191.7	248.5	280.3	283.1		44.0	54.7	51.9	65.4		12.6	11.5
1102	Wines		27.8	29.5	24.9	31.6		6.5	5.9	5.5	6.3		1.2	1.4
1103	Malt liquors and malt		145.5	117.4	151.6	141.9		57.3	31.2	38.0	35.2		10.4	8.3
1104	Soft drinks,mineral waters,other bottled waters		157.7	215.5	263.1	253.2		36.4	52.3	61.2	73.4		28.1	23.3
1200	Tobacco products		328.8	348.5	406.5	473.8		128.5	126.2	155.2	191.8		7.2	4.1
131	Spinning, weaving and finishing of textiles		2642.2	3171.8	3181.4	3068.0		486.7	485.8	467.6	482.3		102.5	163.5
1311	Preparation and spinning of textile fibres		1684.1	2085.3	1857.0	1804.5		260.3	308.3	266.1	262.0		62.8	96.2
1312	Weaving of textiles		556.5	598.5	805.4	688.7		158.0	95.4	110.2	108.8		17.1	35.9
1313	Finishing of textiles		401.6	488.0	519.0	574.9		68.4	82.1	91.4	111.5		22.5	31.5
139	Other textiles		459.9	554.2	639.1	680.0		93.4	99.7	127.1	139.3		39.9	44.2
1391	Knitted and crocheted fabrics		69.1	69.1	102.2	91.1		13.9	14.7	27.2	13.9		7.4	4.4
1392	Made-up textile articles, except apparel		187.2	240.7	253.7	266.5		40.2	43.6	48.6	50.7		11.7	22.1
1393	Carpets and rugs		42.3	73.4	65.0	76.4		8.0	12.5	12.8	16.4		2.2	2.8
1394	Cordage, rope, twine and netting		61.5	67.6	69.9	72.6		10.6	11.3	11.9	15.5		2.6	1.4
1399	Other textiles n.e.c.		99.8	103.4	148.3	173.4		20.6	17.5	26.7	42.7		16.1	13.5
1410	Wearing apparel, except fur apparel		575.6	884.5	684.2	818.8		138.0	173.1	178.9	222.9		21.8	22.2
1420	Articles of fur		0.9	1.0	1.4	0.8		0.1	0.1	0.4	0.2		0.1	-
1430	Knitted and crocheted apparel		327.8	364.0	332.8	414.4		53.3	71.7	64.9	88.4		11.8	15.1
151	Leather;luggage,handbags,saddlery,harness;fur		131.1	170.0	183.8	241.1		18.0	24.2	27.7	37.5		-142.1	7.0
1511	Tanning/dressing of leather; dressing of fur		80.4	111.1	115.9	147.5		8.5	12.1	14.8	16.7		-143.9	4.4
1512	Luggage,handbags,etc.;saddlery/harness		50.7	58.9	68.0	93.5		9.4	12.1	12.9	20.8		1.8	2.6
1520	Footwear		281.7	306.4	325.7	360.8		46.5	61.4	63.3	71.0		12.7	14.4
1610	Sawmilling and planing of wood		35.9	33.4	16.0	21.0		1.9	2.1	1.8	1.4		0.1	0.2

Code	Description										
162	Wood products, cork, straw, plaiting materials	150.5	179.0	188.3	188.1	24.3	27.1	34.9	41.2	6.5	10.6
1621	Veneer sheets and wood-based panels	106.9	144.3	132.1	135.8	16.0	18.8	26.0	30.9	3.6	6.1
1622	Builders' carpentry and joinery	6.6	5.5	9.8	10.0	1.3	1.3	0.2	0.9	0.6	0.6
1623	Wooden containers	12.0	11.1	19.7	18.2	2.5	3.2	4.0	4.4	1.0	0.5
1629	Other wood products;articles of cork,straw	25.0	18.0	26.8	24.1	4.5	3.8	4.7	5.0	1.3	3.4
170	Paper and paper products	686.0	842.2	924.2	948.9	107.0	144.7	147.4	160.4	57.6	53.3
1701	Pulp, paper and paperboard	331.6	416.5	436.8	412.8	39.8	64.5	58.5	61.6	23.6	21.3
1702	Corrugated paper and paperboard	183.0	220.1	236.7	301.1	34.7	41.2	38.0	54.9	13.0	13.1
1709	Other articles of paper and paperboard	171.4	205.6	250.7	235.0	32.5	39.0	51.0	43.8	20.9	18.9
181	Printing and service activities related to printing	338.3	305.9	430.9	379.6	94.1	69.8	115.0	121.6	24.8	17.2
1811	Printing	318.0	286.2	380.7	355.0	88.1	64.2	106.7	116.3	22.9	15.5
1812	Service activities related to printing	20.4	19.7	50.2	24.6	6.0	5.6	8.3	5.3	1.9	1.7
1820	Reproduction of recorded media	1.6	2.7	3.5	1.2	0.8	1.9	1.2	0.2	0.3	0.1
1910	Coke oven products	250.9	200.3	198.9	215.3	84.6	27.1	28.8	25.4	2.1	5.2
1920	Refined petroleum products	10292.5	10944.4	10128.9	8199.9	1178.4	1118.4	1469.7	1603.8	507.7	605.5
201	Basic chemicals,fertilizers, etc.	2773.0	3047.2	3100.7	3526.2	472.6	482.0	432.2	670.1	135.3	280.5
2011	Basic chemicals	1001.6	1082.2	1293.9	1267.8	216.2	172.7	193.0	235.8	104.9	130.0
2012	Fertilizers and nitrogen compounds	1041.2	1068.1	1104.4	1243.5	159.4	174.1	160.2	206.6	20.5	24.1
2013	Plastics and synthetic rubber in primary forms	730.2	897.0	702.3	1014.8	97.0	135.1	79.0	227.7	9.9	126.4
202	Other chemical products	1745.9	1817.5	2295.9	2405.8	380.8	392.6	486.0	664.3	70.7	75.2
2021	Pesticides and other agrochemical products	280.2	367.9	398.7	449.7	60.9	69.3	84.4	120.0	13.7	14.1
2022	Paints,varnishes;printing ink and mastics	313.2	342.7	410.2	423.4	71.4	75.1	82.4	100.2	11.3	21.9
2023	Soap,cleaning and cosmetic preparations	535.9	604.4	983.2	859.1	134.4	152.5	221.8	294.1	26.7	20.2
2029	Other chemical products n.e.c.	616.5	502.6	503.8	673.6	114.2	95.6	97.5	150.1	19.0	19.0
2030	Man-made fibres	210.8	274.2	175.9	160.2	40.1	57.6	34.7	20.1	5.7	5.3
2100	Pharmaceuticals,medicinal chemicals, etc.	1902.8	2145.6	2318.3	2657.4	613.8	723.3	811.2	915.8	184.1	161.7
221	Rubber products	703.0	779.1	739.8	758.9	130.1	184.9	161.3	195.1	26.8	52.5
2211	Rubber tyres and tubes	500.2	517.0	537.0	513.3	94.0	125.2	123.1	137.7	17.4	42.0
2219	Other rubber products	202.8	262.0	202.8	245.6	36.1	59.7	38.2	57.3	9.4	10.5
2220	Plastics products	1238.9	1376.0	1649.7	1663.6	180.2	246.2	291.3	300.6	74.6	83.9
2310	Glass and glass products	164.9	154.9	188.1	208.4	34.4	35.9	40.4	52.1	14.0	14.2
239	Non-metallic mineral products n.e.c.	1788.0	1775.4	2123.7	2009.5	502.3	472.7	547.1	510.7	202.9	180.4
2391	Refractory products	112.7	118.0	156.3	142.8	23.9	26.8	33.9	31.5	7.7	11.1
2392	Clay building materials	64.4	84.2	96.7	89.3	25.0	31.9	37.6	35.5	2.2	3.9
2393	Other porcelain and ceramic products	130.5	120.6	199.4	169.2	18.1	22.0	33.9	34.8	6.1	11.6
2394	Cement, lime and plaster	1023.1	1017.1	1140.8	1098.7	329.7	292.9	301.9	294.7	127.4	125.4
2395	Articles of concrete, cement and plaster	198.5	154.7	242.0	221.8	47.0	32.1	73.1	45.6	45.7	13.5
2396	Cutting, shaping and finishing of stone	155.7	178.6	197.3	185.9	37.2	42.5	43.8	44.1	11.0	10.4
2399	Other non-metallic mineral products n.e.c.	103.0	102.3	91.3	101.9	21.4	24.6	22.9	24.4	2.8	4.6
2410	Basic iron and steel	5537.5	6418.1	6049.0	5180.0	584.8	1091.4	823.4	521.1	536.5	477.8
2420	Basic precious and other non-ferrous metals	1371.2	1391.6	1678.3	2263.5	311.9	205.5	316.5	302.1	60.5	82.2
243	Casting of metals	775.2	770.1	791.8	904.0	130.2	113.7	116.1	125.8	31.4	28.2
2431	Casting of iron and steel	697.6	679.9	715.1	818.2	117.7	101.5	104.2	111.2	28.0	24.4
2432	Casting of non-ferrous metals	77.6	90.2	76.8	85.8	12.6	12.2	11.9	14.6	3.4	3.8
251	Struct.metal products, tanks, reservoirs	775.4	723.4	725.9	794.0	164.6	147.9	134.3	174.3	18.2	24.0

continued

India

ISIC Revision 4			Output at basic prices (billions of Indian Rupees)					Value added at basic prices (billions of Indian Rupees)					Gross fixed capital formation (billions of Indian Rupees)		
ISIC	Industry	Note	Note	2012	2013	2014	2015	Note	2012	2013	2014	2015	Note	2014	2015
2511	Structural metal products			431.9	462.8	458.1	555.6		75.7	81.8	81.2	128.7		12.3	16.7
2512	Tanks, reservoirs and containers of metal			151.6	126.6	141.9	124.7		24.5	25.1	21.2	22.1		3.8	1.6
2513	Steam generators, excl. hot water boilers			192.0	134.1	125.9	113.6		64.4	41.0	31.8	23.4		2.1	5.8
2520	Weapons and ammunition			4.7	5.7	7.2	9.8		2.1	2.5	2.4	2.7		0.3	0.8
259	Other metal products;metal working services			844.8	994.9	1005.0	1106.3		199.2	196.7	225.1	219.8		46.7	56.9
2591	Forging,pressing,stamping,roll-forming of metal			214.6	189.4	186.3	209.7		32.5	35.5	39.9	44.0		8.6	11.8
2592	Treatment and coating of metals; machining			80.3	99.3	101.8	119.9		17.6	20.1	26.7	22.6		5.4	6.1
2593	Cutlery, hand tools and general hardware			133.4	132.8	140.2	144.0		49.4	33.0	36.0	36.1		6.4	6.3
2599	Other fabricated metal products n.e.c.			416.6	573.4	576.7	632.8		99.7	108.1	122.5	117.2		26.3	32.7
2610	Electronic components and boards			200.0	240.9	231.1	219.6		39.1	52.3	49.2	50.7		10.2	9.0
2620	Computers and peripheral equipment			183.2	249.8	228.0	238.0		26.6	48.5	42.1	47.1		3.9	2.4
2630	Communication equipment			146.2	218.7	175.9	519.3		34.3	37.7	32.9	81.7		1.2	8.1
2640	Consumer electronics			355.6	351.4	350.7	178.3		56.9	55.1	49.6	29.1		6.2	3.4
265	Measuring,testing equipment; watches, etc.			124.7	140.8	172.0	188.5		39.2	39.5	53.2	64.7		6.1	5.8
2651	Measuring/testing/navigating equipment,etc.			88.6	97.2	123.7	137.1		25.2	25.3	33.7	37.5		4.8	5.0
2652	Watches and clocks			36.1	43.6	48.2	51.5		13.9	14.2	19.5	27.2		1.2	0.8
2660	Irradiation/electromedical equipment,etc.			54.4	47.5	49.2	48.2		13.7	11.8	6.1	11.6		1.5	0.9
2670	Optical instruments and photographic equipment			3.7	2.9	8.7	5.5		1.4	1.2	3.0	1.8		0.4	0.2
2680	Magnetic and optical media			0.3	0.1	0.1	3.1		0.1	-	-	0.8		-	0.2
2710	Electric motors,generators,transformers,etc.			906.7	826.3	804.3	894.6		207.9	182.3	164.7	207.5		20.7	25.7
2720	Batteries and accumulators			190.3	216.9	268.4	253.7		34.2	38.4	51.8	52.1		13.2	11.4
273	Wiring and wiring devices			489.1	569.0	668.4	631.2		69.8	65.9	74.5	80.8		8.9	18.2
2731	Fibre optic cables			63.9	66.4	73.7	84.4		7.4	9.3	10.8	15.3		-1.9	2.6
2732	Other electronic and electric wires and cables			342.8	437.1	527.2	476.8		41.8	38.9	46.4	46.7		9.0	13.7
2733	Wiring devices			82.4	65.4	67.6	70.0		20.6	17.7	17.3	18.8		1.8	1.8
2740	Electric lighting equipment			111.0	135.3	112.9	146.1		19.5	23.9	20.2	26.6		5.3	5.2
2750	Domestic appliances			297.5	291.5	286.2	368.6		47.0	50.5	58.4	84.2		7.9	8.9
2790	Other electrical equipment			140.3	234.9	182.2	181.0		25.3	40.7	34.5	36.5		5.5	7.5
281	General-purpose machinery			1346.8	1203.8	1437.8	1620.2		370.5	281.4	369.4	434.4		62.1	61.2
2811	Engines/turbines,excl.aircraft,vehicle engines			339.4	284.3	360.7	360.8		82.1	73.7	101.0	119.8		13.3	18.4
2812	Fluid power equipment			73.9	70.2	91.1	150.7		19.3	17.3	25.3	47.9		5.0	4.5
2813	Other pumps, compressors, taps and valves			303.9	250.1	337.4	397.0		119.4	64.0	93.0	94.0		14.6	11.1
2814	Bearings, gears, gearing and driving elements			160.3	187.1	192.9	213.0		39.0	42.7	50.2	58.4		9.9	12.2
2815	Ovens, furnaces and furnace burners			25.1	35.0	28.8	20.1		5.1	7.0	6.0	5.4		1.3	1.9
2816	Lifting and handling equipment			155.5	122.6	117.6	134.5		51.8	26.2	27.6	30.5		3.4	2.9
2817	Office machinery, excl.computers,etc.			2.6	6.9	1.7	2.5		0.8	1.3	0.7	0.8		0.1	0.1
2818	Power-driven hand tools			11.9	6.5	11.2	10.1		2.6	1.5	1.4	2.0		0.7	0.2
2819	Other general-purpose machinery			274.1	241.1	296.4	331.5		50.3	47.6	64.2	75.6		13.8	9.8
282	Special-purpose machinery			1199.2	1153.2	1292.3	1245.2		292.9	268.2	291.2	287.9		57.9	42.7
2821	Agricultural and forestry machinery			388.3	448.2	423.2	389.5		94.3	103.0	94.9	86.6		11.5	9.6
2822	Metal-forming machinery and machine tools			176.1	100.6	194.1	133.4		43.5	21.3	46.2	36.3		8.7	7.5

2823	Machinery for metallurgy	26.8	18.7	28.6	16.8	7.2	5.1	4.6	3.3	3.0	0.9
2824	Mining, quarrying and construction machinery	203.6	172.2	197.8	192.9	55.9	33.3	24.8	30.5	6.0	3.2
2825	Food/beverage/tobacco processing machinery	73.6	73.2	73.9	95.9	16.7	17.6	15.3	22.7	2.1	3.3
2826	Textile/apparel/leather production machinery	98.0	91.5	97.7	133.2	20.6	20.0	21.4	35.1	5.1	5.1
2829	Other special-purpose machinery	232.8	248.8	277.0	283.6	54.7	67.9	84.0	73.4	21.3	13.1
2910	Motor vehicles	2140.5	2158.6	2509.0	2759.5	308.8	271.1	437.3	496.1	124.7	143.8
2920	Automobile bodies, trailers and semi-trailers	133.9	124.1	151.8	160.8	22.8	21.9	30.4	36.4	3.2	5.0
2930	Parts and accessories for motor vehicles	1706.5	1680.9	2012.4	2293.3	376.3	338.2	392.2	499.8	126.2	119.3
301	Building of ships and boats	86.7	81.6	50.9	42.1	24.1	21.5	3.7	-2.4	10.0	0.9
3011	Building of ships and floating structures	86.5	81.3	50.7	41.7	24.1	21.5	3.6	-2.6	10.0	0.8
3012	Building of pleasure and sporting boats	0.3	0.3	0.3	0.4	0.1	-	0.1	0.2	-	0.1
3020	Railway locomotives and rolling stock	89.3	69.8	122.1	101.3	20.0	13.7	23.4	19.0	3.0	2.9
3030	Air and spacecraft and related machinery	25.0	26.5	38.6	39.1	8.2	9.7	15.5	13.0	2.4	2.8
3040	Military fighting vehicles	0.7	0.5	0.6	1.0	0.2	0.1	0.3	0.2	0.1	0.1
309	Transport equipment n.e.c.	1125.0	1186.2	1288.4	1436.0	196.8	208.6	241.1	279.9	46.5	41.2
3091	Motorcycles	1017.7	1057.4	1185.9	1281.5	181.2	190.4	230.2	259.8	43.6	36.1
3092	Bicycles and invalid carriages	93.9	118.8	89.2	143.6	10.5	16.3	9.2	17.9	1.8	4.8
3099	Other transport equipment n.e.c.	13.5	10.0	13.3	10.9	5.1	1.9	1.7	2.2	1.1	0.3
3100	Furniture	147.4	152.8	157.8	130.1	29.3	26.9	33.3	33.1	2.8	6.7
321	Jewellery, bijouterie and related articles	1365.7	1458.3	1910.0	1437.4	89.3	92.7	136.6	98.7	11.0	8.9
3211	Jewellery and related articles	1363.1	1454.1	1907.0	1431.7	88.7	91.4	135.9	97.2	10.6	8.7
3212	Imitation jewellery and related articles	2.6	4.1	2.9	5.7	0.6	1.3	0.7	1.5	0.4	0.2
3220	Musical instruments	0.8	0.8	1.9	2.1	0.1	0.1	-0.1	0.1	0.5	0.4
3230	Sports goods	12.0	12.9	20.0	22.6	2.3	2.8	4.9	4.9	0.7	1.6
3240	Games and toys	6.9	3.6	12.0	13.4	0.7	0.6	2.7	3.0	0.7	1.1
3250	Medical and dental instruments and supplies	70.3	79.1	85.9	75.1	23.1	24.7	30.7	27.1	4.7	4.4
3290	Other manufacturing n.e.c.	121.1	214.2	161.0	242.3	23.5	26.5	25.9	42.2	17.6	9.1
331	Repair of fabricated metal products/machinery	76.1	60.9	66.3	63.6	18.7	22.3	21.4	19.2	3.0	2.8
3311	Repair of fabricated metal products	10.2	4.2	7.1	10.6	1.9	1.5	1.8	2.8	-0.1	0.1
3312	Repair of machinery	31.5	27.4	23.7	23.3	9.0	9.6	8.2	5.0	1.6	1.3
3313	Repair of electronic and optical equipment	1.7	2.8	1.7	0.4	0.6	0.7	0.5	0.1	-	-
3314	Repair of electrical equipment	3.8	4.1	5.5	4.3	1.0	1.3	1.4	0.3	0.1	0.1
3315	Repair of transport equip., excl. motor vehicles	26.9	17.5	23.9	11.1	5.7	8.2	7.1	3.6	1.2	0.7
3319	Repair of other equipment	1.9	4.9	4.4	14.1	0.5	1.0	2.4	7.4	0.1	0.5
3320	Installation of industrial machinery/equipment	14.3	14.6	21.5	16.7	3.1	3.7	6.6	4.0	0.4	0.7
C	Total manufacturing	56715.9	61536.7	64716.0	64620.9	9436.0	9928.3	10929.5	11972.2	2932.4	3349.8

ISIC Revision 4

Index numbers of industrial production

(2010=100)

ISIC	Industry	Note	2005	2006	2007	2008	2009	2010	2011	2012	2013	2014	2015	2016
10	Food products	a/	79	92	103	95	93	100	115	119	117	123	115	107
11	Beverages	a/	…	…	…	…	…	…	…	…	…	…	…	…
12	Tobacco products		97	99	95	99	98	100	105	105	106	107	107	100
13	Textiles		80	86	92	88	94	100	99	105	109	112	115	116
14	Wearing apparel		80	96	105	95	96	100	92	101	121	127	135	134
15	Leather and related products		80	91	96	91	93	100	104	111	117	129	127	117
16	Wood products, excluding furniture		68	81	95	99	102	100	102	94	92	96	99	96
17	Paper and paper products		81	84	86	90	92	100	105	106	105	109	112	112
18	Printing and reproduction of recorded media		76	83	94	96	90	100	130	123	123	118	108	106
19	Coke and refined petroleum products		83	93	98	102	100	100	103	112	118	119	126	133
20	Chemicals and chemical products	b/	82	90	96	93	98	100	100	103	113	112	117	120
21	Pharmaceuticals,medicinal chemicals, etc.	b/	…	…	…	…	…	…	…	…	…	…	…	…
22	Rubber and plastics products		61	65	73	77	90	100	100	100	98	102	103	105
23	Other non-metallic mineral products		71	79	86	89	96	100	105	107	108	111	112	110
24	Basic metals		65	75	88	90	92	100	109	111	111	125	127	136
25	Fabricated metal products, except machinery		61	73	79	79	87	100	111	106	99	98	99	99
26	Computer, electronic and optical products		50	65	85	93	93	100	106	106	86	58	58	59
27	Electrical equipment		25	28	79	112	97	100	78	78	90	108	96	63
28	Machinery and equipment n.e.c.		49	59	72	67	77	100	94	90	86	89	91	95
29	Motor vehicles, trailers and semi-trailers		47	59	65	59	77	100	111	105	95	97	105	111
30	Other transport equipment		55	63	61	64	81	100	112	112	118	126	128	129
31	Furniture	c/	82	79	94	101	108	100	98	93	80	86	124	121
32	Other manufacturing	c/	…	…	…	…	…	…	…	…	…	…	…	…
33	Repair and installation of machinery/equipment		…	…	…	…	…	…	…	…	…	…	…	…
C	Total manufacturing		63	72	85	88	92	100	103	104	104	106	108	108

a/ 10 includes 11.
b/ 20 includes 21.
c/ 31 includes 32.

Indonesia

Supplier of information:
Central Bureau of Statistics (BPS), Jakarta.

Basic source of data:
Survey on registered establishments.

Major deviations from ISIC (Revision 4):
None reported.

Reference period:
Calendar year.

Scope:
Establishments with 20 or more employees.

Method of data collection:
Mail questionnaires.

Type of enumeration:
Complete enumeration.

Adjusted for non-response:
Yes.

Concepts and definitions of variables:
No deviations from the standard UN concepts and definitions are reported.

Related national publications:
Annual Manufacturing Survey, published by the Central Bureau of Statistics (BPS), Jakarta.

Indonesia

ISIC Revision 4		Number of establishments (number)					Number of employees (thousands)					Wages and salaries paid to employees (billions of Indonesian Rupiahs)				
ISIC	Industry	Note	2012	2013	2014a/	2015a/	Note	2012	2013	2014a/	2015a/	Note	2012	2013a/	2014a/	2015a/
10	Food products		5662	5795	5975	6453		885	902	878	858		24167	17118	24227	25894
11	Beverages		345	367	374	422		47	52	53	60		1279	948	1675	2109
12	Tobacco products		945	866	862	940		325	363	356	346		6961	6612	4859	6391
13	Textiles		2246	2287	2555	2612		482	478	547	514		10179	8688	12374	13439
14	Wearing apparel		2248	2075	2141	2360		600	571	637	684		12122	10727	13830	16776
15	Leather and related products		684	671	694	738		257	267	279	314		6737	7047	6537	6277
16	Wood products, excluding furniture		1112	1067	1106	1220		225	230	228	243		5246	4491	5231	6922
17	Paper and paper products		463	477	485	508		129	136	181	133		4369	3984	5563	6180
18	Printing and reproduction of recorded media		529	533	528	616		52	51	51	55		1440	1461	2410	2921
19	Coke and refined petroleum products		70	72	80	81		7	6	6	7		168	191	206	336
20	Chemicals and chemical products		911	978	1002	1075		185	203	193	194		9357	7660	10326	11413
21	Pharmaceuticals,medicinal chemicals, etc.		246	236	239	256		64	61	58	58		3528	1202	2037	2404
22	Rubber and plastics products		1603	1729	1794	1875		354	366	391	443		13396	8322	13372	16707
23	Other non-metallic mineral products		1624	1581	1618	1714		193	182	177	186		8367	5110	7767	8195
24	Basic metals		274	306	323	330		60	73	73	69		4006	3295	4038	4472
25	Fabricated metal products, except machinery		938	958	951	1022		162	173	161	156		5245	4921	6374	5741
26	Computer, electronic and optical products		308	351	342	365		159	151	145	154		4661	5177	5915	7690
27	Electrical equipment		306	333	336	345		115	119	125	104		9376	4531	6533	5540
28	Machinery and equipment n.e.c.		341	364	379	407		57	59	62	71		1997	1547	2847	3917
29	Motor vehicles, trailers and semi-trailers		307	366	380	412		119	138	140	148		6595	6336	10329	12825
30	Other transport equipment		277	315	331	380		85	86	90	103		2912	2693	3501	5586
31	Furniture		1419	1284	1327	1400		190	165	172	167		5046	2873	3437	4455
32	Other manufacturing		649	602	602	654		160	154	160	166		3682	3270	3942	4811
33	Repair and installation of machinery/equipment		85	85	105	137		18	18	19	13		801	706	882	701
C	Total manufacturing	b/	23592	23698	24529	26322	b/	4929	5005	5181	5247	b/	151635	118910	158212	181702

a/ Data were derived from the official website
b/ Sum of available data.

Indonesia

ISIC Revision 4		Note	Output at producers' prices (billions of Indonesian Rupiahs)				Note	Value added at producers' prices (billions of Indonesian Rupiahs)				Note	Gross fixed capital formation (billions of Indonesian Rupiahs)	
ISIC	Industry		2012	2013	2014a/	2015a/		2012	2013	2014a/	2015a/		2014	2015
10	Food products		718677	901892	923855	1021526		222838	294518	325026	344965		...	...
11	Beverages		18229	27339	34790	40693		10796	16285	20851	25855		...	...
12	Tobacco products		161073	198783	192101	206158		91946	125587	134140	128906		...	...
13	Textiles		140638	171971	214966	286614		47838	80000	84794	85319		...	...
14	Wearing apparel		71988	94865	102045	147736		44002	54995	53369	59947		...	...
15	Leather and related products		68463	58094	52545	83665		26024	28170	34025	59456		...	...
16	Wood products, excluding furniture		50879	50770	55181	70281		19979	22445	22201	39245		...	...
17	Paper and paper products		136400	149427	148066	148490		55640	59337	58876	53605		...	...
18	Printing and reproduction of recorded media		17302	17190	24239	31965		6894	9282	11919	12857		...	...
19	Coke and refined petroleum products		6067	16139	6814	7018		1699	3518	2567	3836		...	...
20	Chemicals and chemical products		337839	453209	419321	483822		126470	182879	211005	216359		...	...
21	Pharmaceuticals,medicinal chemicals, etc.		29598	23611	28584	33530		13781	11932	15427	14604		...	...
22	Rubber and plastics products		234355	205744	313202	335464		59355	88844	137064	132143		...	...
23	Other non-metallic mineral products		94864	82158	122361	151440		45425	47317	78895	105610		...	...
24	Basic metals		119280	132219	169430	169849		38820	62695	67217	77771		...	...
25	Fabricated metal products, except machinery		117095	98228	99913	76846		42102	40661	41434	34454		...	...
26	Computer, electronic and optical products		49781	95285	96973	157520		28477	40434	38912	62659		...	...
27	Electrical equipment		112072	128762	181196	136205		49115	75753	70888	69460		...	...
28	Machinery and equipment n.e.c.		38126	41648	60624	70924		19606	23728	33605	48408		...	...
29	Motor vehicles, trailers and semi-trailers		196221	186980	207261	359728		126238	130564	148575	194688		...	...
30	Other transport equipment		106835	100764	102796	87741		56463	51207	58092	48600		...	...
31	Furniture		22569	21364	34160	42762		8423	11243	21823	21186		...	...
32	Other manufacturing		16643	28338	28219	35727		9054	11312	15583	21825		...	...
33	Repair and installation of machinery/equipment		4628	4423	4967	6874		2414	2630	3166	5057		...	...
C	Total manufacturing	b/	2869622	3289204	3623609	4192579	b/	1153398	1475338	1689456	1866814		...	...

a/ Data were derived from the official website
b/ Sum of available data.

Indonesia

ISIC Revision 4 — Index numbers of industrial production (2010=100)

ISIC	Industry	Note	2005	2006	2007	2008	2009	2010	2011	2012	2013	2014	2015	2016
10	Food products		71	79	83	86	94	100	107	120	133	147	157	167
11	Beverages		71	79	83	86	94	100	110	109	110	113	113	112
12	Tobacco products		58	57	66	76	96	100	99	105	104	112	118	114
13	Textiles		87	92	102	106	100	100	92	85	77	73	72	69
14	Wearing apparel		119	199	153	109	99	100	113	119	129	134	119	111
15	Leather and related products		82	79	79	90	91	100	128	120	125	132	137	148
16	Wood products, excluding furniture		237	139	117	110	106	100	68	65	71	77	78	79
17	Paper and paper products		101	84	97	100	102	100	102	98	96	98	95	92
18	Printing and reproduction of recorded media		...	...	...	...	...	100	117	116	127	126	132	131
19	Coke and refined petroleum products		...	...	...	...	...	...	...	...	...	...	...	...
20	Chemicals and chemical products		58	73	99	92	95	100	105	113	122	130	131	131
21	Pharmaceuticals, medicinal chemicals, etc.		58	73	99	92	95	100	123	141	135	149	168	182
22	Rubber and plastics products		109	100	87	95	98	100	102	114	110	110	116	106
23	Other non-metallic mineral products		98	109	110	99	97	100	114	126	129	134	143	152
24	Basic metals		70	86	96	102	97	100	109	99	109	116	123	123
25	Fabricated metal products, except machinery		146	160	122	104	96	100	119	122	136	140	153	153
26	Computer, electronic and optical products		30	55	83	94	92	100	97	107	117	112	116	117
27	Electrical equipment		132	130	101	103	104	100	118	132	142	156	156	144
28	Machinery and equipment n.e.c.		75	73	104	95	94	100	133	122	116	126	129	133
29	Motor vehicles, trailers and semi-trailers		103	55	72	88	84	100	121	125	139	145	153	153
30	Other transport equipment		106	67	61	83	87	100	78	81	79	76	71	72
31	Furniture		86	85	73	97	97	100	110	103	107	109	113	114
32	Other manufacturing		86	85	73	97	97	100	83	80	78	82	87	81
33	Repair and installation of machinery/equipment		...	...	...	...	...	100	91	98	93	88	92	88
C	Total manufacturing		88	87	92	94	96	100	104	108	115	120	126	131

Iran (Islamic Republic of)

Supplier of information:
Statistical Centre of Iran, Teheran.

Basic source of data:
Census; survey.

Major deviations from ISIC (Revision 3):
None reported.

Reference period:
Fiscal year.

Scope:
Establishments with 10 or more employees.

Method of data collection:
Questionnaires; direct interview in the field.

Type of enumeration:
Complete enumeration for large and medium establishments; sample survey for small establishments with less than 50 employees.

Adjusted for non-response:
Yes.

Concepts and definitions of variables:
Wages and salaries includes employers' contributions paid to social security, pension and insurance schemes as well as the benefits received by employees under these schemes and severance and termination pay.
Output includes revenues from non-industrial activities.

Related national publications:
Iran Statistical Yearbook, published by the Statistical Centre of Iran, Teheran.

Iran (Islamic Republic of)

ISIC	Industry	Number of establishments (number)					Number of employees (number)					Wages and salaries paid to employees (billions of Iranian Rials)				
		Note	2012	2013	2014	2015	Note	2012	2013	2014	2015	Note	2012	2013	2014	2015
151	Processed meat,fish,fruit,vegetables,fats		844	852	880	792		54803	61333	61728	60111		4916	6868	9176	10720
1511	Processing/preserving of meat		349	359	354	332		23087	26289	27127	26374		2003	2721	3506	3941
1512	Processing/preserving of fish		80	82	78	72		4496	4749	4735	4219		382	496	594	632
1513	Processing/preserving of fruit & vegetables		342	341	373	315		17488	20580	20215	19490		1457	2042	2976	3343
1514	Vegetable and animal oils and fats		73	71	75	73		9731	9716	9652	10028		1074	1609	2099	2804
1520	Dairy products		308	311	302	277		36481	39424	44357	47959		3490	5275	8026	10483
153	Grain mill products; starches; animal feeds		476	476	499	492		17235	18275	18141	18559		1744	2130	2525	3016
1531	Grain mill products		317	317	323	317		10507	11208	11289	11771		1038	1230	1546	1892
1532	Starches and starch products		20	20	22	21		1253	1362	1426	1319		107	153	178	208
1533	Prepared animal feeds		138	139	154	154		5475	5705	5426	5469		599	747	801	916
154	Other food products		988	1004	979	875		67821	80666	76583	74413		6774	9391	11518	14094
1541	Bakery products		348	364	379	336		20547	22918	23285	23475		1932	2570	3152	3998
1542	Sugar		83	91	87	77		17141	20282	21062	19520		2183	2805	3713	4459
1543	Cocoa, chocolate and sugar confectionery		96	101	99	87		7988	13758	9649	9098		611	1258	1295	1414
1544	Macaroni, noodles & similar products		77	65	54	44		2809	3047	2759	2682		262	394	492	479
1549	Other food products n.e.c.		384	383	361	331		19336	20662	19829	19638		1786	2364	2866	3744
155	Beverages		122	116	119	106		12921	13727	14059	13855		1545	1890	2842	3011
1551	Distilling, rectifying & blending of spirits		11	11	10	9		509	506	462	465		44	46	67	73
1552	Wines															
1553	Malt liquors and malt		17	16	13	13		1890	2355	2926	3226		191	476	900	1110
1554	Soft drinks; mineral waters		94	89	96	84		10522	10866	10671	10164		1310	1369	1875	1827
1600	Tobacco products		3	5	5	6		7266	7192	7110	6581		1992	2380	2116	2312
171	Spinning, weaving and finishing of textiles		563	558	540	524		53031	56759	53744	50621		4829	6656	7361	7945
1711	Textile fibre preparation; textile weaving		486	475	464	452		49730	53060	49928	47206		4549	6271	6870	7416
1712	Finishing of textiles		76	84	76	72		3300	3699	3816	3415		280	385	491	530
172	Other textiles		462	451	434	395		25625	27891	28410	26818		2318	2994	3859	4359
1721	Made-up textile articles, except apparel		58	55	61	56		3703	4027	5119	4945		341	438	676	750
1722	Carpets and rugs		378	369	348	317		21037	22215	21498	20368		1905	2374	2929	3340
1723	Cordage, rope, twine and netting		6	6	9	9		187	181	391	325		13	14	54	45
1729	Other textiles n.e.c.		20	21	17	13		698	1468	1402	1180		59	168	200	224
1730	Knitted and crocheted fabrics and articles		46	47	43	33		1260	1206	1437	1042		108	123	194	145
1810	Wearing apparel, except fur apparel		132	130	119	101		6817	7654	7491	6998		608	809	947	1096
1820	Dressing & dyeing of fur; processing of fur															
191	Tanning, dressing and processing of leather		78	68	66	60		2307	2525	2687	2171		195	280	363	354
1911	Tanning and dressing of leather		72	62	62	58		2185	2284	2601	2130		187	259	353	348
1912	Luggage, handbags, etc.; saddlery & harness		6	6	4	2		122	241	86	41		8	21	10	6
1920	Footwear		110	97	75	63		4227	4833	4447	4390		329	463	542	610
2010	Sawmilling and planing of wood		21	20	15	13		659	677	629	591		66	92	93	100
202	Products of wood, cork, straw, etc.		103	101	96	94		6028	8067	8432	7908		740	1209	1498	1627
2021	Veneer sheets, plywood, particle board, etc.		50	52	52	48		4851	6616	6828	6256		655	1066	1297	1410
2022	Builders' carpentry and joinery		37	30	27	25		809	799	902	770		57	82	124	107
2023	Wooden containers		6	6	7	7		169	255	255	248		12	23	31	34
2029	Other wood products; articles of cork/straw		10	13	10	14		199	397	447	634		15	39	46	76
210	Paper and paper products		334	330	328	321		19560	22822	23362	23770		2074	3135	3768	4259
2101	Pulp, paper and paperboard		78	82	87	86		6832	7501	7795	7909		925	1270	1625	1497
2102	Corrugated paper and paperboard		168	161	161	146		7220	8323	8316	7956		662	973	1150	1349
2109	Other articles of paper and paperboard		88	87	80	89		5508	6998	7250	7905		488	891	993	1414
221	Publishing		27	28	25	22		2728	2336	1780	1740		369	452	389	518
2211	Publishing of books and other publications		12	12	11	10		983	1040	515	471		98	131	95	97
2212	Publishing of newspapers, journals, etc.		13	13	12	11		1517	1267	1243	1258		215	318	292	419
2213	Publishing of recorded media			3	2	1			30	22	11			3	2	
2219	Other publishing				2											

Code	Description												
222	Printing and related service activities	1118	994	780	480	5674	5490	5335	5121	125	122	133	160
2221	Printing	959	900	677	388	5048	5037	4849	4415	107	109	121	134
2222	Service activities related to printing	159	159	103	92	626	453	486	706	18	3	12	26
2230	Reproduction of recorded media	42	90	41	54	57	208	243	405	2	3	3	4
2310	Coke oven products	…	…	…	…	…	…	…	…	…	…	…	7
2320	Refined petroleum products	73	42	36	21	282	320	215	233	5	6	7	133
2330	Processing of nuclear fuel	14302	15308	11283	6204	24553	25929	30713	23263	133	142	145	133
241	Basic chemicals	3240	23820	15622	12260	69021	67703	64806	56629	365	381	349	337
2411	Basic chemicals, except fertilizers	12937	7902	5440	3509	25827	26353	26176	20640	205	211	197	191
2412	Fertilizers and nitrogen compounds	5214	4884	3297	2598	12040	11361	10033	9482	49	53	49	45
2413	Plastics in primary forms; synthetic rubber	13889	11034	6886	6153	31154	29989	28597	26507	111	118	103	101
242	Other chemicals	16259	13607	10405	7095	62586	63917	61285	53971	584	623	604	571
2421	Pesticides and other agro-chemical products	320	232	198	120	1508	1484	1486	1237	28	30	29	27
2422	Paints, varnishes, printing ink and mastics	1594	1427	1102	843	8013	8615	7947	7211	156	171	169	156
2423	Pharmaceuticals, medicinal chemicals, etc.	9395	7276	5181	3270	28332	26819	25927	22328	178	177	175	159
2424	Soap, cleaning & cosmetic preparations	3441	3376	2893	2179	16819	18950	19359	16967	128	137	137	135
2429	Other chemical products n.e.c.	1539	1295	1032	683	7914	8019	6567	6228	94	108	93	94
2430	Man-made fibres	1003	770	549	381	4610	4501	4268	3668	38	35	33	32
251	Rubber products	4163	4007	2935	2317	17168	17310	16741	18166	94	106	113	113
2511	Rubber tyres and tubes	3438	3293	2491	1866	12702	12678	12731	13379	20	22	26	25
2519	Other rubber products	725	714	444	451	4466	4632	4010	4787	74	84	87	88
2520	Plastic products	7244	6720	5117	4010	41873	45609	45272	43320	820	900	925	893
2610	Glass and glass products	3825	3169	2253	1674	18137	19138	17234	15627	108	127	126	133
269	Non-metallic mineral products n.e.c.	28183	27332	21366	18131	131918	148869	154671	156567	2428	2851	3040	3059
2691	Pottery, china and earthenware	1805	1686	1221	974	10395	11133	10346	10357	55	58	54	58
2692	Refractory ceramic products	917	1054	485	318	3748	3746	3294	2824	37	36	33	28
2693	Struct.non-refractory clay; ceramic products	7857	8510	8357	7649	49935	60061	67649	68753	928	1170	1353	1367
2694	Cement, lime and plaster	11186	10157	6314	4675	30209	32192	32014	32247	174	187	180	180
2695	Articles of concrete, cement and plaster	2656	2556	2109	2287	14863	17438	16600	18502	453	537	438	416
2696	Cutting, shaping & finishing of stone	1116	909	1004	824	6866	7290	9135	9252	354	409	520	542
2699	Other non-metallic mineral products n.e.c.	2647	2461	1877	1403	15902	17010	15633	14632	427	455	461	468
2710	Basic iron and steel	41433	31537	26105	16542	94677	91262	90004	80942	252	257	280	269
2720	Basic precious and non-ferrous metals	5885	8800	7103	3706	23444	25904	25108	23077	199	207	198	191
273	Casting of metals	3587	3467	2185	1513	15638	17466	15334	14298	190	209	198	195
2731	Casting of iron and steel	3216	3022	1976	1372	13623	15146	13477	12699	157	176	160	157
2732	Casting of non-ferrous metals	371	446	210	141	2015	2319	1857	1599	33	34	38	38
281	Struct.metal products;tanks;steam generators	8139	7938	4910	4091	37466	39500	37930	37362	385	431	429	467
2811	Structural metal products	4574	4033	3001	2392	23697	25512	24587	24633	272	300	308	342
2812	Tanks, reservoirs and containers of metal	3417	3775	1825	1627	13028	13283	12671	12074	111	129	119	123
2813	Steam generators	148	130	84	72	741	705	672	655	2	2	2	2
289	Other metal products; metal working services	6946	6026	4840	3439	34935	36865	37428	34522	587	641	666	677
2891	Metal forging/pressing/stamping/roll-forming	298	296	307	176	1664	1623	2294	1585	28	37	39	39
2892	Treatment & coating of metals	1163	1038	780	556	5581	6178	6314	5486	136	151	157	162
2893	Cutlery, hand tools and general hardware	519	509	348	274	3028	3444	3312	3188	50	64	58	57
2899	Other fabricated metal products n.e.c.	4966	4183	3405	2433	24662	25621	25509	24263	373	390	411	419
291	General purpose machinery	8318	6888	4603	3380	36845	37039	35511	33709	406	414	412	420
2911	Engines & turbines (not for transport equipment)	2368	2169	903	634	5534	5567	5864	4340	25	28	27	16
2912	Pumps, compressors, taps and valves	1979	1628	1152	959	9976	10294	9563	10286	121	127	122	134
2913	Bearings, gears, gearing & driving elements	352	263	188	106	1605	1681	1401	1148	33	32	32	33
2914	Ovens, furnaces and furnace burners	276	285	218	184	1682	1793	1849	1906	26	25	27	26
2915	Lifting and handling equipment	708	609	457	353	3511	3674	3300	3587	52	51	54	66
2919	Other general purpose machinery	2635	1933	1686	1145	14537	14030	13534	12442	149	151	150	145
292	Special purpose machinery	4264	4296	2782	2301	19837	22112	19943	21180	328	369	344	340
2921	Agricultural and forestry machinery	1098	1007	694	704	4611	5151	5002	5477	91	102	78	74
2922	Machine tools	711	754	643	413	3399	4121	4187	3710	60	71	71	67
2923	Machinery for metallurgy	91	54	14	17	546	397	128	210	5	4	3	4
2924	Machinery for mining & construction	1226	1374	563	468	4610	5108	3250	3971	40	47	45	51
2925	Food/beverage/tobacco processing machinery	505	456	355	313	2897	3238	3195	3788	70	77	75	75
2926	Machinery for textile, apparel and leather	227	212	204	86	1043	1072	1212	719	11	11	12	12
2927	Weapons and ammunition	…	…	…	…	…	…	…	…	…	…	…	…
2929	Other special purpose machinery	405	439	310	301	2731	3026	2969	3305	51	57	60	57

continued

Iran (Islamic Republic of)

ISIC Revision 3		Number of establishments (number)					Number of employees (number)					Wages and salaries paid to employees (billions of Iranian Rials)				
ISIC	Industry	Note	2012	2013	2014	2015	Note	2012	2013	2014	2015	Note	2012	2013	2014	2015
2930	Domestic appliances n.e.c.		212	205	190	165		20175	21095	21800	18861		2167	2770	3733	3734
3000	Office, accounting and computing machinery		38	31	34	25		5574	5565	6434	5860		893	1115	1848	2487
3110	Electric motors, generators and transformers		73	80	77	67		11272	11469	13024	12212		1526	2099	3140	3679
3120	Electricity distribution & control apparatus		162	164	166	158		10647	11508	12705	12763		1199	1440	2074	2303
3130	Insulated wire and cable		127	125	119	113		9022	9888	9842	8985		925	1431	1753	1785
3140	Accumulators, primary cells and batteries		13	10	11	12		4289	2176	2188	2152		709	230	512	402
3150	Lighting equipment and electric lamps		68	60	67	59		4365	3875	4655	4202		387	421	655	684
3190	Other electrical equipment n.e.c.		38	38	35	31		9941	5609	6126	5409		941	736	1160	1182
3210	Electronic valves, tubes, etc.		26	24	26	23		954	922	1219	1171		85	116	188	191
3220	TV/radio transmitters; line comm. apparatus		20	15	18	17		3154	3196	2818	2408		343	345	529	546
3230	TV and radio receivers and associated goods		27	24	26	23		2515	3520	3594	3753		277	459	568	817
331	Medical, measuring, testing appliances, etc.		140	129	124	118		12208	12708	12550	11766		1208	1579	1980	2333
3311	Medical, surgical and orthopaedic equipment		100	93	90	84		6885	6869	7524	6968		679	962	1165	1379
3312	Measuring/testing/navigating appliances,etc.		36	33	31	31		5241	5778	4965	4744		523	608	806	953
3313	Industrial process control equipment		4	3	3	3		82	61	61	54		6	9	8	1
3320	Optical instruments & photographic equipment		11	8	9	7		579	763	952	896		46	186	234	239
3330	Watches and clocks		4	3	4	3		281	267	285	282		36	27	36	51
3410	Motor vehicles		43	44	42	39		66616	66970	70435	73620		15599	18684	29370	36584
3420	Automobile bodies, trailers & semi-trailers		44	47	52	44		3099	3149	3581	3588		270	342	504	563
3430	Parts/accessories for automobiles		573	574	583	522		60573	61263	74951	70234		6904	8545	13878	15099
351	Building and repairing of ships and boats		32	30	29	28		5304	4871	4328	3364		548	699	1046	1122
3511	Building and repairing of ships		14	14	16	16		4735	4295	3855	3028		483	641	986	1064
3512	Building/repairing of pleasure/sport. boats		18	16	13	12		569	576	473	336		65	58	60	59
3520	Railway/tramway locomotives & rolling stock		16	16	15	10		2850	3760	3753	3300		264	654	548	1085
3530	Aircraft and spacecraft		2	4	3	4		2183	2282	2265	2301		633	1867	987	1776
359	Transport equipment n.e.c.		88	73	73	61		3653	3256	3888	3653		297	313	650	747
3591	Motorcycles		76	62	62	52		3281	2925	3447	3318		262	277	586	690
3592	Bicycles and invalid carriages		7	5	5	4		290	240	274	196		30	29	46	35
3599	Other transport equipment n.e.c.		5	6	6	5		82	91	167	139		6	8	18	22
3610	Furniture		242	224	227	217		11853	10977	11766	10281		1189	1327	1993	2178
369	Manufacturing n.e.c.		165	163	163	141		5920	6276	6217	5475		485	663	788	871
3691	Jewellery and related articles		12	12	9	8		485	470	437	455		33	46	54	75
3692	Musical instruments		1	1	2	2		20	20	31	61		1	2	4	8
3693	Sports goods		5	4	5	6		244	255	257	320		20	27	35	47
3694	Games and toys		7	5	8	9		653	554	576	401		50	56	78	61
3699	Other manufacturing n.e.c.		140	142	139	116		4518	4977	4916	4238		381	532	618	679
3710	Recycling of metal waste and scrap		3	3	7	9		46	46	218	306		3	4	30	44
3720	Recycling of non-metal waste and scrap		8	9	5	10		290	302	73	380		26	33	8	67
D	Total manufacturing		14793	14702	14460	13129		1198192	1273146	1303206	1253470		156657	215958	288238	332043

Iran (Islamic Republic of)

ISIC Revision 3		Output at producers' prices (billions of Iranian Rials)					Value added at producers' prices (billions of Iranian Rials)					Gross fixed capital formation (billions of Iranian Rials)		
ISIC	Industry	Note	2012	2013	2014	2015	Note	2012	2013	2014	2015	Note	2014	2015
151	Processed meat,fish,fruit,vegetables,fats		114683	155622	176583	207073		27678	33078	48566	48456		5501	4467
1511	Processing/preserving of meat		31139	39620	42470	43729		6245	7775	9937	10602		2438	1852
1512	Processing/preserving of fish		5045	6497	7788	7393		1739	2332	2739	3091		95	183
1513	Processing/preserving of fruit & vegetables		30367	48112	60548	52466		9727	12278	17688	14276		1106	1291
1514	Vegetable and animal oils and fats		48131	61393	65777	103486		9967	10694	18202	20487		1862	1141
1520	Dairy products		71508	93045	112091	113355		20006	28923	32474	29537		3675	4264
153	Grain mill products; starches; animal feeds		60432	76375	87961	96981		8772	12812	14460	15533		2103	3044
1531	Grain mill products		42686	50903	60160	68335		4911	8078	8964	9141		1504	2120
1532	Starches and starch products		1507	2599	4035	4038		449	865	1095	1292		142	153
1533	Prepared animal feeds		16239	22874	23766	24607		3412	3870	4401	5100		456	770
154	Other food products		71840	97662	109022	113423		25138	32514	36686	41042		5110	4177
1541	Bakery products		13883	20191	22200	23920		6310	7846	8727	9933		1152	1084
1542	Sugar		25642	28685	37139	38518		8118	8906	11160	11177		1354	1630
1543	Cocoa, chocolate and sugar confectionery		4995	9757	8301	8519		1833	4261	2730	2845		491	195
1544	Macaroni, noodles & similar products		2698	4927	6205	6359		780	1242	1819	2540		108	141
1549	Other food products n.e.c.		24622	34101	35178	36108		8097	10259	12251	14547		2006	1126
155	Beverages		19238	25884	31796	30280		7090	8421	11348	9705		2183	1641
1551	Distilling, rectifying & blending of spirits		570	1136	1249	1331		300	356	409	464		33	205
1552	Wines		4125	5204	6251	6939		1472	1393	2129	2537		314	-68
1553	Malt liquors and malt		14542	19544	24297	22011		5318	6672	8811	6704		1836	1504
1554	Soft drinks; mineral waters		6527	12484	7817	7673		3933	5961	3407	4629		212	303
1600	Tobacco products		41607	57705	57641	52418		12997	16573	17132	17287		2256	3094
171	Spinning, weaving and finishing of textiles		39490	55115	55188	50307		12044	15529	15892	16156		2073	3025
1711	Textile fibre preparation; textile weaving		2116	2590	2453	2112		953	1044	1240	1131		182	69
1712	Finishing of textiles		22012	28444	29955	29929		6541	9400	11479	12034		4693	3985
172	Other textiles		3228	4364	4982	4745		1012	1245	1967	1775		134	203
1721	Made-up textile articles, except apparel		18224	22948	23040	23514		5374	7815	8884	9681		4512	3741
1722	Carpets and rugs		133	175	366	244		37	44	124	74		3	2
1723	Cordage, rope, twine and netting		428	956	1567	1425		118	296	505	504		45	39
1729	Other textiles n.e.c.		620	569	685	569		230	213	311	259		4	27
1730	Knitted and crocheted fabrics and articles		3315	4281	5589	5443		1516	2131	2543	2263		110	88
1810	Wearing apparel, except fur apparel		3661	4586	5158	3293		908	1188	1796	946		53	94
1820	Dressing & dyeing of fur; processing of fur													
191	Tanning, dressing and processing of leather		3596	4518	5113	3278		889	1165	1771	941		53	94
1911	Tanning and dressing of leather													
1912	Luggage, handbags, etc.; saddlery & harness		65	68	44	14		20	23	25	5		-	
1920	Footwear		2752	2965	3113	3632		973	900	1062	1150		157	59
2010	Sawmilling and planing of wood		470	385	314	275		254	153	166	174		21	11
202	Products of wood, cork, straw, etc.		10368	16408	18302	19506		2645	4575	4723	8586		1050	976
2021	Veneer sheets, plywood, particle board, etc.		9627	15572	16937	18423		2417	4260	4128	8178		909	879
2022	Builders' carpentry and joinery		588	600	901	558		167	219	429	256		88	12
2023	Wooden containers		74	137	291	329		35	50	74	59		50	49
2029	Other wood products; articles of cork/straw		79	99	173	196		35	47	93	93		3	36
210	Paper and paper products		17497	41447	45899	48615		5009	11157	14794	16696		2185	1824
2101	Pulp, paper and paperboard		6125	10467	12358	11117		1628	3150	4101	3672		654	465
2102	Corrugated paper and paperboard		6416	13008	11170	9916		2138	3311	3397	3461		969	431
2109	Other articles of paper and paperboard		4956	17973	22371	27582		1243	4695	7296	9563		561	928
221	Publishing		1938	1912	1832	2013		1085	728	796	754		104	16
2211	Publishing of books and other publications		891	702	231	276		546	300	153	131		85	3
2212	Publishing of newspapers, journals, etc.		813	1197	1597	1736		509	421	641	622		19	12
2213	Publishing of recorded media			14	4	1			7	2	-			
2219	Other publishing													

continued

Iran (Islamic Republic of)

ISIC Revision 3			Output at producers' prices (billions of Iranian Rials)					Value added at producers' prices (billions of Iranian Rials)					Gross fixed capital formation (billions of Iranian Rials)	
ISIC	Industry	Note	2012	2013	2014	2015	Note	2012	2013	2014	2015	Note	2014	2015
222	Printing and related service activities		4836	6161	8507	7992		1466	1715	3268	3296		-12	15
2221	Printing		4144	5249	7870	7274		1255	1426	2945	2919		235	258
2222	Service activities related to printing		692	912	637	717		211	289	323	377		-246	-243
2230	Reproduction of recorded media		347	124	97	37		165	58	43	22		23	22
2310	Coke oven products		49	209	474	517		16	87	181	310		11	12
2320	Refined petroleum products		1031987	2039540	1620130	986473		76445	153936	93376	72619		10113	6573
2330	Processing of nuclear fuel													
241	Basic chemicals		511810	683367	773579	641279		200332	248941	290782	245823		21759	15827
2411	Basic chemicals, except fertilizers		210237	288479	315770	245766		76973	96706	115807	82986		13536	8534
2412	Fertilizers and nitrogen compounds		50404	44906	70228	52504		40892	36013	48877	30937		352	1020
2413	Plastics in primary forms; synthetic rubber		251169	349983	387581	343008		82467	116222	126098	131899		7872	6272
242	Other chemicals		90819	147910	162597	174428		34883	56382	63730	78272		5127	7643
2421	Pesticides and other agro-chemical products		2298	3350	3544	3532		784	1096	1251	1543		12	60
2422	Paints, varnishes, printing ink and mastics		11743	16596	19069	16157		3181	4486	5575	5090		563	550
2423	Pharmaceuticals, medicinal chemicals, etc.		36756	67269	77981	93963		16424	29546	33628	46687		2421	4182
2424	Soap, cleaning & cosmetic preparations		28365	46163	45752	43950		10269	17276	18711	19142		864	1290
2429	Other chemical products n.e.c.		11657	14532	16251	16827		4224	3977	4565	5809		1268	1562
2430	Man-made fibres		6330	8293	7035	6125		719	990	1399	1011		178	105
251	Rubber products		23066	30619	35067	27700		8373	7602	13507	11117		1007	2817
2511	Rubber tyres and tubes		19661	26311	30400	23939		6717	6154	11649	9649		723	2285
2519	Other rubber products		3405	4308	4667	3761		1656	1447	1858	1469		284	532
2520	Plastic products		50622	63784	71580	69510		15664	18247	21976	22510		4433	4805
2610	Glass and glass products		11396	21182	20624	21344		4870	9551	9459	10543		1775	3236
269	Non-metallic mineral products n.e.c.		149086	187290	197894	164022		74106	94739	104542	81501		11266	13523
2691	Pottery, china and earthenware		4347	5545	5741	5892		2308	3008	2954	3386		631	397
2692	Refractory ceramic products		4081	6675	6960	5894		1448	2560	3141	3161		101	413
2693	Struct.non-refractory clay; ceramic products		38774	49650	52265	44949		18594	25683	27940	22292		2589	2996
2694	Cement, lime and plaster		55850	75513	82796	61237		33603	42715	48523	32727		4736	7056
2695	Articles of concrete, cement and plaster		24119	19550	19419	19275		9680	9252	8701	8479		1290	916
2696	Cutting, shaping & finishing of stone		5693	7412	5508	5507		2683	3432	2618	2751		383	721
2699	Other non-metallic mineral products n.e.c.		16221	22945	25206	21269		5791	8090	10665	8705		1536	1023
2710	Basic iron and steel		348692	529904	510621	388201		114317	161564	163123	115650		13869	13776
2720	Basic precious and non-ferrous metals		124750	139047	139565	105464		45006	34916	69042	51376		9654	9146
273	Casting of metals		12890	17833	29016	24400		4021	5444	8648	8368		1350	3186
2731	Casting of iron and steel		11720	15397	25631	21005		3646	4901	7439	7127		1267	3130
2732	Casting of non-ferrous metals		1170	2435	3385	3395		375	543	1209	1241		83	55
281	Struct.metal products;tanks;steam generators		30960	42387	50623	58596		12602	16494	20284	23959		2577	1696
2811	Structural metal products		18028	24371	28996	34477		6035	8097	10183	13476		1810	1043
2812	Tanks, reservoirs and containers of metal		11888	16725	19986	21343		5742	7409	8744	9007		696	546
2813	Steam generators		1044	1291	1641	2776		826	988	1357	1476		71	107
289	Other metal products; metal working services		37366	57673	53723	55740		13303	16135	15668	18519		2795	2009
2891	Metal forging/pressing/stamping/roll-forming		4804	10921	5219	6646		1096	2077	897	934		196	-80
2892	Treatment & coating of metals		4609	9690	10217	9807		1923	2710	2460	3171		179	687
2893	Cutlery, hand tools and general hardware		1891	2301	3110	2277		673	826	1222	908		78	96
2899	Other fabricated metal products n.e.c.		26063	34761	35178	37011		9611	10523	11090	13506		2342	1306
291	General purpose machinery		31027	44380	57728	58608		12061	16894	22059	23465		1965	2067
2911	Engines & turbines (not for transport equipment)		7332	13963	15242	20824		3808	5648	5881	7363		366	457
2912	Pumps, compressors, taps and valves		7176	9335	12111	11755		2605	3662	5527	5320		1075	800
2913	Bearings, gears, gearing & driving elements		462	901	1560	1859		210	433	696	600		92	22
2914	Ovens, furnaces and furnace burners		1600	1402	2187	1784		385	421	1083	508		41	7
2915	Lifting and handling equipment		2280	2792	3566	4073		718	1047	1480	1625		156	160
2919	Other general purpose machinery		12177	15987	23062	18313		4336	5682	7391	8048		235	623

Code	Description										
292	Special purpose machinery	18939	25684	31634	28991	6279	8278	11576	12585	1064	1088
2921	Agricultural and forestry machinery	8657	12209	14721	9671	2335	3789	4085	3250	520	150
2922	Machine tools	2405	3451	3525	2952	958	1366	1440	1180	108	191
2923	Machinery for metallurgy	52	119	453	453	26	39	151	116	12	11
2924	Machinery for mining & construction	2801	3061	7374	8260	903	719	3278	4044	114	513
2925	Food/beverage/tobacco processing machinery	2539	2222	2266	2095	650	800	1066	979	179	101
2926	Machinery for textile, apparel and leather	477	2096	853	749	189	517	380	341	6	10
2927	Weapons and ammunition										
2929	Other special purpose machinery	2008	2526	2442	4811	1218	1047	1175	2675	124	112
2930	Domestic appliances n.e.c.	23689	39139	39984	33317	6381	11481	12516	9137	2001	1200
3000	Office, accounting and computing machinery	6522	8633	8976	8275	2173	3047	3813	3396	39	218
3110	Electric motors, generators and transformers	17355	21793	23103	27215	5684	7128	8355	9461	2734	580
3120	Electricity distribution & control apparatus	6790	10978	12037	13537	2833	4264	5526	6137	623	528
3130	Insulated wire and cable	21523	27704	33102	27564	5066	5925	9056	5297	1108	400
3140	Accumulators, primary cells and batteries	5779	5832	4248	3528	1625	1190	1020	1367	135	177
3150	Lighting equipment and electric lamps	3357	6262	6049	5652	1169	2432	1952	2024	292	121
3190	Other electrical equipment n.e.c.	13322	6233	8751	7097	3870	2016	2580	2347	407	168
3210	Electronic valves, tubes, etc.	680	637	685	800	265	317	305	240	75	36
3220	TV/radio transmitters; line comm. apparatus	2927	3354	4088	3960	772	1534	1279	1946	13	60
3230	TV and radio receivers and associated goods	2184	19637	23788	19930	901	4754	5660	4585	146	307
331	Medical, measuring, testing appliances, etc.	10958	12765	14637	21366	4644	4885	5764	13117	669	813
3311	Medical, surgical and orthopaedic equipment	5530	5659	7635	8395	2283	2341	3368	3861	362	411
3312	Measuring/testing/navigating appliances, etc.	5404	7054	6894	12964	2350	2525	2355	9254	300	400
3313	Industrial process control equipment	24	52	108	7	11	19	41	2	6	1
3320	Optical instruments & photographic equipment	1318	1338	1781	1704	434	677	1072	1236	28	31
3330	Watches and clocks	176	101	164	130	80	68	66	72		
3410	Motor vehicles	183774	218088	352983	310985	27115	46528	96281	70502	4651	16100
3420	Automobile bodies, trailers & semi-trailers	2300	3877	7395	5002	697	1208	2524	1947	5025	329
3430	Parts/accessories for automobiles	59564	71648	139076	138494	16656	22377	44599	38980	3786	5338
351	Building and repairing of ships and boats	13500	9722	7221	4877	2891	2475	4041	2878	25	143
3511	Building and repairing of ships	12984	9297	6967	4694	2738	2324	3944	2802	20	140
3512	Building/repairing of pleasure/sport. boats	516	425	254	183	153	151	98	76	5	3
3520	Railway/tramway locomotives & rolling stock	768	3271	3830	2629	406	1179	1605	1442	35	21
3530	Aircraft and spacecraft	1962	3345	1440	1798	1174	2398	1164	1430	31	31
359	Transport equipment n.e.c.	4314	5884	13442	12043	1008	1275	3078	2619	246	320
3591	Motorcycles	3813	5504	12790	11651	911	1210	2955	2551	233	293
3592	Bicycles and invalid carriages	401	322	565	313	63	47	88	47	12	25
3599	Other transport equipment n.e.c.	101	58	87	79	35	19	36	21	1	1
3610	Furniture	6545	8328	10238	10166	2465	3050	3605	4155	445	172
369	Manufacturing n.e.c.	4619	4611	4999	4604	1628	1661	2004	1842	247	315
3691	Jewellery and related articles	301	245	311	291	55	78	97	95	6	19
3692	Musical instruments	15	13	18	33	2	3	6	12	-	2
3693	Sports goods	99	104	106	148	48	40	50	75	-	-
3694	Games and toys	85	80	172	314	37	28	70	164	152	188
3699	Other manufacturing n.e.c.	4119	4168	4391	3817	1486	1512	1780	1496	89	106
3710	Recycling of metal waste and scrap	15	22	941	434	12	18	79	97	16	3
3720	Recycling of non-metal waste and scrap	129	189	34	258	36	58	15	80	-	8
D	Total manufacturing	3327512	5158555	5187244	4219268	839389	1157131	1332365	1176331	141147	143037

Iran (Islamic Republic of)

Index numbers of industrial production

(2010=100)

ISIC Revision 3

ISIC	Industry	Note	2005	2006	2007	2008	2009	2010	2011	2012	2013	2014	2015	2016
15	Food and beverages	a/	66	69	87	86	85	100	...	...	...	...	...	...
16	Tobacco products		...	...	...	...	...	...	...	...	...	...	...	...
17	Textiles		91	88	102	115	100	100	...	...	...	...	...	...
18	Wearing apparel, fur		...	...	...	...	...	...	...	...	...	...	...	...
19	Leather, leather products and footwear		...	...	...	...	...	...	...	...	...	...	...	...
20	Wood products (excl. furniture)		...	...	...	...	...	...	...	...	...	...	...	...
21	Paper and paper products		...	...	...	...	...	...	...	...	...	...	...	...
22	Printing and publishing		...	...	...	...	...	...	...	...	...	...	...	...
23	Coke,refined petroleum products,nuclear fuel		...	...	...	...	...	...	...	...	...	...	...	...
24	Chemicals and chemical products		48	59	81	88	106	100	...	...	...	...	...	...
25	Rubber and plastics products		...	...	...	...	...	...	...	...	...	...	...	...
26	Non-metallic mineral products		49	53	63	77	80	100	...	...	...	...	...	...
27	Basic metals		...	...	...	...	...	...	...	...	...	...	...	...
28	Fabricated metal products		65	61	83	100	99	100	...	...	...	...	...	...
29	Machinery and equipment n.e.c.	b/	49	54	70	81	77	100	...	...	...	...	...	...
30	Office, accounting and computing machinery	b/	...	...	...	...	...	...	...	...	...	...	...	...
31	Electrical machinery and apparatus	c/	71	69	83	93	101	100	...	...	...	...	...	...
32	Radio,television and communication equipment	c/	...	...	...	...	...	...	...	...	...	...	...	...
33	Medical, precision and optical instruments		...	...	...	...	...	...	...	...	...	...	...	...
34	Motor vehicles, trailers, semi-trailers	d/	65	71	73	79	88	100	...	...	...	...	...	...
35	Other transport equipment	d/	...	...	...	...	...	...	...	...	...	...	...	...
36	Furniture; manufacturing n.e.c.		...	...	...	...	...	...	...	...	...	...	...	...
37	Recycling		...	...	...	...	...	...	...	...	...	...	...	...
D	Total manufacturing		59	64	80	86	91	100	103	93	88	91	91	97

a/ 15 excludes beverages.
b/ 29 includes 30.
c/ 31 includes 32.
d/ 34 includes 35.

Iraq

Supplier of information:
Central Statistical Organization, Ministry of Planning, Baghdad.

Basic source of data:
Annual industrial survey.

Major deviations from ISIC (Revision 4):
None reported.

Reference period:
Calendar year.

Scope:
Establishments with 30 or more employees.

Method of data collection:
Not reported.

Type of enumeration:
Sample survey.

Adjusted for non-response:
Not reported.

Concepts and definitions of variables:
Wages and salaries includes employers' contributions (in respect of their employees) paid to social security, pension and insurance schemes as well as the benefits received by employees under these schemes and severance and termination pay.

Related national publications:
Statistic of Large Industrial Establishments, published by the Central Statistical Organization; Baghdad.

Iraq

ISIC Revision 4		Number of establishments (number)					Number of employees (number)					Wages and salaries paid to employees (millions of Iraqi Dinars)				
ISIC	Industry	Note	2014a/	2015a/	2016a/	2017	Note	2014a/	2015a/	2016a/	2017	Note	2014a/	2015a/	2016a/	2017
10	Food products		137	143	148	...		12230	12497	12106	...		99508	93253	78834	...
11	Beverages		18	19	19	...		3293	3462	2977	...		32471	35476	39698	...
12	Tobacco products		1	1	1	...		2122	1956	1811	...		22415	20724	17282	...
13	Textiles		5	5	6	...		15624	13452	9734	...		144935	133105	91737	...
14	Wearing apparel		...	...	1	...		...	...	1294	...		...	...	10045	...
15	Leather and related products		1	1	1	...		3714	3436	3172	...		27317	27343	23119	...
16	Wood products, excluding furniture		...	...	1	...		...	...	9	...		...	...	66	...
17	Paper and paper products		...	...	...	...		...	...	...	...		...	...	...	...
18	Printing and reproduction of recorded media		8	8	8	...		1235	1421	1190	...		8935	10684	9450	...
19	Coke and refined petroleum products		29	19	23	...		16644	17729	18739	...		390568	380557	360094	...
20	Chemicals and chemical products		13	13	9	...		13752	12791	9734	...		170302	152203	125151	...
21	Pharmaceuticals, medicinal chemicals, etc.		2	3	2	...		94	120	65	...		601	722	340	...
22	Rubber and plastics products		7	8	10	...		1109	1100	3964	...		9327	9350	35471	...
23	Other non-metallic mineral products		370	352	334	...		37093	34170	25969	...		359760	278673	173277	...
24	Basic metals		3	3	3	...		1661	1582	3911	...		19377	17484	32185	...
25	Fabricated metal products, except machinery		2	4	3	...		5284	6126	3350	...		65325	76181	39011	...
26	Computer, electronic and optical products		1	1	1	...		400	400	309	...		3805	3745	1843	...
27	Electrical equipment		9	9	7	...		12620	11324	10978	...		131803	123311	111979	...
28	Machinery and equipment n.e.c.		2	2	1	...		4244	3989	1712	...		48997	47057	15652	...
29	Motor vehicles, trailers and semi-trailers		2	2	2	...		2612	2523	5178	...		32355	32039	52304	...
30	Other transport equipment		1	1	1	...		212	169	144	...		1703	1259	845	...
31	Furniture		3	4	2	...		243	225	83	...		1726	964	632	...
32	Other manufacturing		...	...	...	...		...	...	...	...		...	...	...	...
33	Repair and installation of machinery/equipment		...	...	...	...		...	...	...	...		...	...	...	...
C	Total manufacturing	b/	614	598	583	...	b/	134186	128472	116429	...	b/	1571230	1444129	1219014	...

a/ Data were derived from the official website
b/ Sum of available data.

Iraq

ISIC Revision 4			Output at factor values (millions of Iraqi Dinars)					Value added (millions of Iraqi Dinars)						Gross fixed capital formation (millions of Iraqi Dinars)		
ISIC	Industry	Note	2014a/	2015a/	2016a/	2017	Note	2014	2015	2016	2017	Note	2016	2017
10	Food products		213507	600955	978329	...		...	...	...	...		...	...
11	Beverages		508150	468257	450175	...		...	...	...	...		...	...
12	Tobacco products		3078	1925	1119	...		...	...	...	...		...	...
13	Textiles		22062	14423	8897	...		...	...	...	...		...	...
14	Wearing apparel		...	...	5634	...		...	...	...	...		...	...
15	Leather and related products		4983	7892	2993	...		...	...	...	...		...	...
16	Wood products, excluding furniture		...	...	4248	...		...	...	...	...		...	...
17	Paper and paper products		...	...	...	...		...	...	...	...		...	...
18	Printing and reproduction of recorded media		48538	44656	19846	...		...	...	...	...		...	...
19	Coke and refined petroleum products		1994464	3043683	2398057	...		...	...	...	...		...	...
20	Chemicals and chemical products		169120	68759	175992	...		...	...	...	...		...	...
21	Pharmaceuticals,medicinal chemicals, etc.		2350	1371	945	...		...	...	...	...		...	...
22	Rubber and plastics products		37253	26609	32834	...		...	...	...	...		...	...
23	Other non-metallic mineral products		822160	965296	597486	...		...	...	...	...		...	...
24	Basic metals		98137	25007	24875	...		...	...	...	...		...	...
25	Fabricated metal products, except machinery		52713	22255	23170	...		...	...	...	...		...	...
26	Computer, electronic and optical products		...	3474	337	...		...	...	...	...		...	...
27	Electrical equipment		240388	62248	33404	...		...	...	...	...		...	...
28	Machinery and equipment n.e.c.		19984	14809	1854	...		...	...	...	...		...	...
29	Motor vehicles, trailers and semi-trailers		94904	90048	101141	...		...	...	...	...		...	...
30	Other transport equipment		2232	325	602	...		...	...	...	...		...	...
31	Furniture		...	840	327	...		...	...	...	...		...	...
32	Other manufacturing		...	...	...	...		...	...	...	...		...	...
33	Repair and installation of machinery/equipment		...	...	...	...		...	...	...	...		...	...
C	Total manufacturing	b/	4334023	5462831	4862263	...		...	...	...	...		...	...

a/ Data were derived from the official website
b/ Sum of available data.

Ireland

Supplier of information:
Irish Central Statistics Office, Dublin.
Industrial statistics for the OECD countries are compiled by the OECD secretariat, which supplies them to UNIDO.

Basic source of data:
Annual surveys; administrative data; business registers.

Major deviations from ISIC (Revision 4):
Data presented in ISIC (Revision 4) were originally classified according to NACE Rev. 2.

Reference period:
Calendar year.

Scope:
All units wholly or primarily engaged in industrial production.

Method of data collection:
Not reported.

Type of enumeration:
Census covers principally all enterprises; detail of questionnaire depends on size; administrative data is used to estimate enterprises with less than 3 persons engaged.

Adjusted for non-response:
Not reported.

Concepts and definitions of variables:
No deviations from the standard UN concepts and definitions are reported.

Related national publications:
Statistical Yearbook of Ireland, published by Irish Central Statistics Office, Dublin.

Ireland

ISIC Revision 4		Number of enterprises (number)					Number of employees (number)					Wages and salaries paid to employees (millions of Euros)				
ISIC	Industry	Note	2013	2014	2015a/	2016a/	Note	2013	2014	2015a/	2016a/	Note	2013	2014	2015a/	2016a/
1010	Processing/preserving of meat		251	230	247	241		14803	14971	16491	17438		446.0	460.4	499.0	535.1
1020	Processing/preserving of fish, etc.		105	101	108	115		2226	2360	2284	2429		71.5	82.6	73.3	76.2
1030	Processing/preserving of fruit,vegetables		88	87	110	102		1362	1383	1340	1476		46.4	49.5	50.8	57.7
1040	Vegetable and animal oils and fats		12	12	13	15		94	106	202	272		3.6	4.1	7.5	11.1
1050	Dairy products		160	149	161	156		6820	6594	7286	8133		305.7	304.6	314.3	372.5
106	Grain mill products,starches and starch products		38	38	40	47		220	232	235	299		10.0	10.6	10.9	14.5
1061	Grain mill products		38	38	40	47	b/	220	232	235	299	b/	10.0	10.6	10.9	14.5
1062	Starches and starch products		...	...	...	...	b/	...	...	...	...	b/	...	...	...	...
107	Other food products		710	762	823	902		12077	12967	14369	14250		501.6	565.2	586.2	596.7
1071	Bakery products		...	...	...	...		...	...	...	...		...	...	...	...
1072	Sugar		–	–	...	...		–	–	...	...		–	–	...	...
1073	Cocoa, chocolate and sugar confectionery		...	...	57	...		...	...	1969	...		...	...	86.5	...
1074	Macaroni, noodles, couscous, etc.		...	...	...	...		...	...	...	...		...	...	...	...
1075	Prepared meals and dishes		...	...	...	53		...	...	...	2098		...	...	...	63.2
1079	Other food products n.e.c.		...	...	...	...		...	...	...	...		...	...	...	...
1080	Prepared animal feeds		129	132	135	137		2040	2177	2390	2514		82.3	84.4	92.2	102.0
110	Beverages		102	123	...	...		4079	3956	...	...		208.7	211.9	...	...
1101	Distilling, rectifying and blending of spirits		...	...	...	...		...	...	...	...		...	...	...	...
1102	Wines		...	...	...	...		...	...	...	...		...	...	...	...
1103	Malt liquors and malt		...	...	...	...		...	...	...	...		...	...	...	...
1104	Soft drinks,mineral waters,other bottled waters		26	27	...	...		1066	911	...	...		44.5	38.0	...	...
1200	Tobacco products		...	...	...	...		...	...	...	...		...	...	...	...
131	Spinning, weaving and finishing of textiles		108	...	126	129		577	...	615	615		19.3	...	22.5	22.0
1311	Preparation and spinning of textile fibres		24	...	30	32		64	...	77	44		1.7	...	1.9	1.0
1312	Weaving of textiles		31	...	43	38		385	...	404	371		14.2	...	16.2	15.0
1313	Finishing of textiles		53	49	53	59		128	137	134	200		3.4	4.5	4.4	6.0
139	Other textiles		295	289	295	292		1000	1028	1101	1205		34.5	36.0	36.3	37.9
1391	Knitted and crocheted fabrics		...	...	3	...		...	...	–	...		...	...	...	...
1392	Made-up textile articles, except apparel		212	207	210	206		597	633	707	750		19.1	21.4	22.3	23.4
1393	Carpets and rugs		8	10	12	...		52	47	57	...		2.0	1.4	1.9	...
1394	Cordage, rope, twine and netting		...	...	...	18		...	...	...	134		...	...	...	5.0
1399	Other textiles n.e.c.		...	...	...	...		...	...	...	...		...	...	...	...
1410	Wearing apparel, except fur apparel		281	289	292	301		647	579	421	476		18.6	17.6	11.9	14.2
1420	Articles of fur		...	...	...	...		...	...	...	...		...	...	...	...
1430	Knitted and crocheted apparel		...	...	...	...		...	...	...	...		...	...	...	...
151	Leather;luggage,handbags,saddlery,harness;fur	c/	55	60	65	60	c/	131	143	165	170	c/	4.2	4.7	5.6	5.6
1511	Tanning/dressing of leather; dressing of fur		37	42	45	44		40	43	65	71		1.3	1.4	2.0	2.1
1512	Luggage,handbags,etc.;saddlery/harness		...	...	...	...		...	...	...	...		...	...	...	...
1520	Footwear	c/	...	...	...	...	c/	...	...	...	...	c/	...	...	...	...
1610	Sawmilling and planing of wood		125	122	118	116		879	924	997	1051		31.4	34.0	41.3	41.1

162	Wood products, cork, straw, plaiting materials		730	770	829	875	2703	2841	3066	3467	99.1	106.0	135.4	138.1
1621	Veneer sheets and wood-based panels		...	...	...	21	...	...	...	608	...	...	...	34.5
1622	Builders' carpentry and joinery		63	58	60	58	351	352	336	334	12.2	11.8	11.9	12.2
1623	Wooden containers		144	146	157	...	287	315	355	...	8.3	9.5	13.3	...
1629	Other wood products;articles of cork,straw		...	...	...	...	...	...	...	...	...	...	...	...
170	Paper and paper products		197	201	203	206	2881	2974	3106	3091	103.3	112.5	136.6	124.6
1701	Pulp, paper and paperboard		50	48	48	47	1652	1686	1794	1776	54.3	60.9	79.4	67.0
1702	Corrugated paper and paperboard		...	...	...	...	...	...	...	...	...	...	...	...
1709	Other articles of paper and paperboard		...	...	...	...	...	...	...	...	...	...	...	...
181	Printing and service activities related to printing	d/	1005	1014	1007	1032	4511	4593	4569	5142	177.1	168.3	199.3	210.9
1811	Printing	d/	1005	1014	1007	1032	4511	4593	4569	5142	177.1	168.3	199.3	210.9
1812	Service activities related to printing	d/	...	...	...	...	...	...	...	...	...	...	...	...
1820	Reproduction of recorded media		155	159	170	159	646	601	514	481	28.3	28.0	29.1	27.7
1910	Coke oven products		...	...	...	...	...	...	...	...	...	...	...	...
1920	Refined petroleum products		91	88	...	...	4929	5067	...	...	307.7	345.7	...	...
201	Basic chemicals,fertilizers, etc.		...	...	...	...	...	...	...	...	...	...	...	...
2011	Basic chemicals		20	20	...	...	861	893	...	...	38.0	41.8	...	...
2012	Fertilizers and nitrogen compounds		...	...	...	...	...	...	...	...	...	...	...	...
2013	Plastics and synthetic rubber in primary forms		26	27	...	...	424	470	...	...	19.8	30.0	...	...
202	Other chemical products		...	...	...	...	...	...	...	...	...	...	...	...
2021	Pesticides and other agrochemical products		...	...	...	...	...	...	...	...	...	...	...	...
2022	Paints,varnishes;printing ink and mastics		31	28	...	...	336	333	...	...	15.7	17.3	...	...
2023	Soap,cleaning and cosmetic preparations		...	...	...	...	...	...	...	...	...	...	...	...
2029	Other chemical products n.e.c.		...	...	...	...	...	...	...	...	...	...	...	...
2030	Man-made fibres		...	...	...	...	...	...	...	...	...	...	...	...
2100	Pharmaceuticals,medicinal chemicals, etc.		153	155	...	...	13039	16125	...	...	761.5	1066.6	...	...
221	Rubber products		73	69	75	72	677	679	751	532	21.4	23.0	27.0	19.9
2211	Rubber tyres and tubes		40	36	38	36	62	67	79	89	2.3	2.8	3.1	3.8
2219	Other rubber products		33	33	37	36	615	612	672	443	19.1	20.1	23.9	16.0
2220	Plastics products		423	409	400	410	7316	7421	6964	9318	255.0	274.1	276.7	366.9
2310	Glass and glass products		155	153	153	146	905	1091	1078	1156	32.6	42.4	38.8	44.6
239	Non-metallic mineral products n.e.c.		...	...	...	903	...	...	...	7143	...	...	...	330.0
2391	Refractory products		57	64	67	8	82	95	114	60	3.4	4.5	5.1	7.2
2392	Clay building materials		...	...	...	75	...	...	...	156	...	...	...	...
2393	Other porcelain and ceramic products		...	...	...	...	...	...	...	...	...	...	...	...
2394	Cement, lime and plaster		...	...	...	...	...	...	...	...	...	...	...	...
2395	Articles of concrete, cement and plaster		308	295	295	311	776	799	859	868	27.7	31.9	33.4	37.3
2396	Cutting, shaping and finishing of stone		...	...	...	...	...	...	...	...	...	...	...	...
2399	Other non-metallic mineral products n.e.c.		...	...	...	...	...	...	...	...	...	...	...	...
2410	Basic iron and steel		259	246	255	271	1432	1592	1593	1710	60.2	72.7	68.8	76.6
2420	Basic precious and other non-ferrous metals		45	45	50	47	847	898	915	972	47.1	48.5	53.2	58.2
243	Casting of metals		54	50	51	53	122	119	134	133	4.3	3.8	4.8	5.3
2431	Casting of iron and steel		40	36	38	37	112	108	117	117	4.0	3.4	4.1	4.6
2432	Casting of non-ferrous metals		...	...	13	...	...	...	17	...	...	...	0.7	...
251	Struct.metal products, tanks, reservoirs		...	...	...	...	...	...	...	...	...	...	...	...

continued

Ireland

ISIC Revision 4

ISIC	Industry	Note	Number of enterprises (number) 2013	2014	2015a/	2016a/	Note	Number of employees (number) 2013	2014	2015a/	2016a/	Note	Wages and salaries paid to employees (millions of Euros) 2013	2014	2015a/	2016a/
2511	Structural metal products		609	583	618	618		3179	3578	4010	4614		121.8	139.9	160.6	195.9
2512	Tanks, reservoirs and containers of metal		111	129	...	...		1592	1830	...	...		59.7	73.6	...	...
2513	Steam generators, excl. hot water boilers		...	...	...	...		...	...	...	...		...	...	...	...
2520	Weapons and ammunition		...	...	...	...		...	...	...	...		...	...	...	...
259	Other metal products;metal working services		2364	2247	2271	2206		5995	6356	6742	7429		240.2	257.1	282.1	326.5
2591	Forging,pressing,stamping,roll-forming of metal		23	22	23	22		299	303	399	419		12.3	9.8	16.0	20.8
2592	Treatment and coating of metals;machining		1997	1896	...	1838		2428	2611	...	3086		95.1	104.0	...	135.4
2593	Cutlery, hand tools and general hardware		...	...	...	...		...	...	...	...		...	...	...	...
2599	Other fabricated metal products n.e.c.		...	...	...	...		...	...	...	...		...	...	...	...
2610	Electronic components and boards		92	94	...	...		5771	6056	...	...		329.7	452.7	...	...
2620	Computers and peripheral equipment		62	63	...	...		4308	4248	...	...		210.5	221.9	...	...
2630	Communication equipment		...	...	...	...		...	...	...	...		...	...	...	...
2640	Consumer electronics		...	...	...	...		...	...	...	...		...	...	...	...
265	Measuring,testing equipment; watches, etc.		95	97	...	...		1729	1901	...	...		77.0	88.4	...	...
2651	Measuring/testing/navigating equipment,etc.		82	83	...	...		1713	1884	...	...		76.3	87.7	...	...
2652	Watches and clocks		13	14	...	...		16	17	...	...		0.7	0.8	...	...
2660	Irradiation/electromedical equipment,etc.		14	14	...	...		1541	1803	...	...		63.6	75.6	...	...
2670	Optical instruments and photographic equipment		...	...	...	...		...	...	...	...		...	...	...	...
2680	Magnetic and optical media		...	...	...	...		...	...	...	...		...	...	...	...
2710	Electric motors,generators,transformers,etc.		94	92	89	89		1786	1850	1895	2068		58.4	65.0	68.6	67.5
2720	Batteries and accumulators		28	25	...	...		...	...	...	...		...	...	...	...
273	Wiring and wiring devices		...	...	...	...		773	706	...	...		31.1	33.1	...	...
2731	Fibre optic cables		28e/	25e/	...	...		773e/	706e/	...	...		31.1e/	33.1e/	...	...
2732	Other electronic and electric wires and cables		..e/	..e/	...	...		..e/	..e/	...	...		..e/	..e/	...	...
2733	Wiring devices		..e/	..e/	...	...		..e/	..e/	...	...		..e/	..e/	...	...
2740	Electric lighting equipment		67	67	63	73		90	94	100	145		3.2	3.7	4.0	5.4
2750	Domestic appliances		...	...	...	...		...	...	...	...		...	...	...	...
2790	Other electrical equipment		58	54	52	49		689	671	476	456		26.8	28.0	20.7	20.8
281	General-purpose machinery		318	322	...	...		7640	8019	...	...		316.5	351.6	...	...
2811	Engines/turbines,excl.aircraft,vehicle engines		16	16	...	...		193	198	...	...		9.5	7.2	...	...
2812	Fluid power equipment		14	12	...	...		524	600	...	...		15.9	21.4	...	...
2813	Other pumps, compressors, taps and valves		36	35	...	...		1778	1752	...	...		76.6	81.2	...	...
2814	Bearings, gears, gearing and driving elements		15	17	...	...		129	138	...	...		4.7	5.3	...	...
2815	Ovens, furnaces and furnace burners		9	8	...	...		119	127	...	...		3.3	3.8	...	...
2816	Lifting and handling equipment		48	48	...	...		1539	1664	...	...		67.3	72.3	...	...
2817	Office machinery, excl.computers,etc.		...	...	...	...		...	...	...	...		...	...	...	...
2818	Power-driven hand tools		...	...	...	...		...	...	...	...		...	...	...	...
2819	Other general-purpose machinery		150	158	...	...		2187	2409	...	...		85.0	110.8	...	...
282	Special-purpose machinery		256	261	...	...		2917	3122	...	...		110.2	125.5	...	...
2821	Agricultural and forestry machinery		72	79	...	...		1065	1144	...	...		38.1	45.3	...	...
2822	Metal-forming machinery and machine tools		64	68	...	...		632	667	...	...		22.7	25.0	...	...

2823	Machinery for metallurgy	-	-	-	…	-	…	-	…	-	-	…	…
2824	Mining, quarrying and construction machinery	15	13	…	…	…	…	…	…	9.2	10.7	…	…
2825	Food/beverage/tobacco processing machinery	40	39	…	…	…	…	…	…	16.6	16.8	…	…
2826	Textile/apparel/leather production machinery	…	…	…	…	…	…	…	…	…	…	…	…
2829	Other special-purpose machinery	…	…	…	…	…	…	…	…	…	…	…	…
2910	Motor vehicles	125f/	…	24	23	2668f/	…	160	172	96.3f/	…	5.7	6.4
2920	Automobile bodies, trailers and semi-trailers	..f/	56	56	58	..f/	…	483	455	..f/	…	17.4	17.3
2930	Parts and accessories for motor vehicles	..f/	46	53	56	..f/	2151	2268	2350	..f/	83.0	88.7	97.2
301	Building of ships and boats	…	41	47	45	…	105	107	87	…	3.4	4.0	3.8
3011	Building of ships and floating structures	…	41g/	47g/	17	…	105g/	107g/	60	…	3.4g/	4.0g/	2.5
3012	Building of pleasure and sporting boats	31	..g/	..g/	28	17	..g/	..g/	27	0.6	..g/	..g/	1.2
3020	Railway locomotives and rolling stock	…	…	…	…	…	…	…	…	…	…	…	…
3030	Air and spacecraft and related machinery	…	…	…	12	…	…	…	55	…	…	…	3.3
3040	Military fighting vehicles	-	-	-	-	-	-	-	-	-	-	-	-
309	Transport equipment n.e.c.	…	16	17	…	…	13	18	…	…	0.6	0.8	…
3091	Motorcycles	…	4	5	6	…	-	-	…	…	-	-	…
3092	Bicycles and invalid carriages	…	…	…	7	…	…	…	15	…	…	…	0.7
3099	Other transport equipment n.e.c.	…	…	…	…	…	…	…	…	…	…	…	…
3100	Furniture	1149	1110	…	…	3465	3712	…	…	141.9	160.6	…	…
321	Jewellery, bijouterie and related articles	…	…	…	…	…	…	…	…	…	…	…	…
3211	Jewellery and related articles	…	…	…	…	…	…	…	…	…	…	…	…
3212	Imitation jewellery and related articles	…	…	…	…	…	…	…	…	…	…	…	…
3220	Musical instruments	52	55	…	…	20	22	…	…	1.0	1.2	…	…
3230	Sports goods	94	97	…	…	90	90	…	…	3.5	3.4	…	…
3240	Games and toys	…	…	…	…	…	…	…	…	…	…	…	…
3250	Medical and dental instruments and supplies	261	268	…	…	23931	24497	…	…	1110.4	1235.8	…	…
3290	Other manufacturing n.e.c.	204	203	…	…	1540	1638	…	…	56.5	67.8	…	…
331	Repair of fabricated metal products/machinery	1025	1081	…	…	4283	4711	…	…	208.9	219.8	…	…
3311	Repair of fabricated metal products	110	115	…	…	177	189	…	…	7.8	8.7	…	…
3312	Repair of machinery	588	610	…	…	1553	1693	…	…	82.1	87.9	…	…
3313	Repair of electronic and optical equipment	41	49	…	…	121	132	…	…	4.8	5.3	…	…
3314	Repair of electrical equipment	89	96	…	…	571	663	…	…	23.7	30.6	…	…
3315	Repair of transport equip., excl. motor vehicles	…	…	…	…	…	…	…	…	…	…	…	…
3319	Repair of other equipment	…	…	…	…	…	…	…	…	…	…	…	…
3320	Installation of industrial machinery/equipment	139	164	…	…	621	691	…	…	25.0	29.3	…	…
C	Total manufacturing	14649	14628	15242	15583	174302	183190	192978	206095	7539.7	8519.9	8868.5	9579.5

a/ See Explanatory notes for more details for data from 2015 onwards.
b/ 1061 includes 1062.
c/ 151 includes 1520.
d/ 1811 includes 1812.
e/ 2731 includes 2732 and 2733.
f/ 2910 includes 2920 and 2930.
g/ 3011 includes 3012.

Ireland

ISIC	Industry	Note	Output (valuation not defined) (millions of Euros) 2013	2014	2015a/	2016a/	Note	Value added at factor values (millions of Euros) 2013	2014	2015a/	2016a/	Note	Gross fixed capital formation (millions of Euros) 2015a/	2016a/
1010	Processing/preserving of meat		5118.9	5290.4	5461.8	5488.7		725.1	860.9	794.7	776.3		34.5	46.0
1020	Processing/preserving of fish, etc.		543.1	498.1	535.6	580.8		125.6	127.9	130.1	163.2		9.6	7.0
1030	Processing/preserving of fruit,vegetables		297.8	284.2	231.6	252.5		82.4	94.2	78.0	96.4		7.6	4.2
1040	Vegetable and animal oils and fats		23.6	38.6	67.9	71.2		5.5	9.0	16.8	21.1		7.4	0.6
1050	Dairy products		3457.5	4025.3	3733.9	3826.7		568.3	572.8	567.3	537.3		40.2	59.1
106	Grain mill products,starches and starch products		91.2	46.1	49.0	50.1		24.9	16.9	18.5	16.5		1.0	1.8
1061	Grain mill products	b/	91.2	46.1	49.0	50.1	b/	24.9	16.9	18.5	16.5	b/	1.0	1.8
1062	Starches and starch products	b/	...	...	...	...	b/	...	...	...	...	b/	...	...
107	Other food products		10366.3	11186.7	12607.5	11347.8		5516.8	5789.9	6243.2	5865.6		60.9	56.6
1071	Bakery products		...	...	...	...		...	...	...	...		...	...
1072	Sugar		-	-	...	...		-	-	...	...		...	...
1073	Cocoa, chocolate and sugar confectionery		...	...	286.5	...		...	...	131.3	...		3.1	...
1074	Macaroni, noodles, couscous, etc.		...	...	...	...		...	...	...	...		...	...
1075	Prepared meals and dishes		...	...	...	260.8		...	...	...	71.4		...	1.5
1079	Other food products n.e.c.		...	...	...	...		...	...	...	...		...	...
1080	Prepared animal feeds		1001.4	993.7	1082.8	1058.7		177.6	148.2	164.6	211.9		21.6	14.1
110	Beverages		3195.0	3271.1	...	...		1112.5	1124.4	...	...		...	...
1101	Distilling, rectifying and blending of spirits		...	...	...	...		...	...	...	...		...	...
1102	Wines		...	...	...	...		...	...	...	...		...	...
1103	Malt liquors and malt		...	...	...	...		...	...	...	...		...	...
1104	Soft drinks,mineral waters,other bottled waters		448.5	306.9	...	...		158.5	92.2	...	...		...	...
1200	Tobacco products		...	...	...	...		...	...	...	...		...	...
131	Spinning, weaving and finishing of textiles		92.7	...	98.0	112.0		36.8	...	33.0	26.2		1.0	1.7
1311	Preparation and spinning of textile fibres		8.9	...	13.9	5.9		2.6	...	4.4	2.6		0.2	0.4
1312	Weaving of textiles		71.3	...	67.6	85.2		28.4	...	23.2	12.5		0.4	0.4
1313	Finishing of textiles		12.5	17.0	16.5	20.9		5.8	6.9	5.4	11.1		0.4	0.9
139	Other textiles		162.9	156.6	161.8	141.0		55.6	66.1	49.9	54.8		3.0	4.7
1391	Knitted and crocheted fabrics		...	...	0.3	...		...	...	0.1	...		-	...
1392	Made-up textile articles, except apparel		68.9	70.8	76.8	85.0		25.3	33.9	28.7	34.7		2.0	2.9
1393	Carpets and rugs		8.3	5.5	7.0	...		2.8	2.5	2.8	...		0.1	0.7
1394	Cordage, rope, twine and netting		...	...	...	16.2		...	...	...	7.3		...	...
1399	Other textiles n.e.c.		...	...	...	...		...	...	...	...		...	...
1410	Wearing apparel, except fur apparel		68.1	66.9	46.5	47.7		25.4	28.9	16.6	22.9		1.5	3.0
1420	Articles of fur		...	...	...	...		...	...	...	...		...	...
1430	Knitted and crocheted apparel		...	...	...	...		...	...	...	...		...	...
151	Leather;luggage,handbags,saddlery,harness;fur	c/	35.5	32.2	35.7	38.9	c/	3.2	11.1	12.1	14.3	c/	0.7	0.6
1511	Tanning/dressing of leather; dressing of fur		...	...	...	...		...	...	...	...		...	...
1512	Luggage,handbags,etc.;saddlery/harness		9.9	10.2	12.9	11.6		3.0	3.6	3.8	5.4		0.2	0.4
1520	Footwear	c/	...	...	...	...	c/	...	...	...	...	c/	...	...
1610	Sawmilling and planing of wood		217.9	300.6	278.3	255.2		56.0	77.9	71.5	67.3		3.1	3.3

ISIC	Industry										
162	Wood products, cork, straw, plaiting materials	520.4	551.6	624.4	631.4	143.4	186.9	196.3	239.2	12.5	20.9
1621	Veneer sheets and wood-based panels	...	...	...	230.8	...	...	...	66.2	...	3.8
1622	Builders' carpentry and joinery	54.6	54.4	56.6	53.6	18.7	18.6	18.7	20.2	1.3	2.0
1623	Wooden containers	41.3	42.6	52.5	...	18.8	18.0	19.2	...	1.5	...
1629	Other wood products;articles of cork,straw	436.4	466.6	513.6	482.4	143.0	160.9	202.7	174.6	7.9	5.7
170	Paper and paper products	226.4	248.9	292.2	280.0	69.5	76.2	113.0	94.9	2.6	2.7
1701	Pulp, paper and paperboard	...	...	...	...	...	...	...	...	...	...
1702	Corrugated paper and paperboard	...	...	...	...	...	...	...	...	...	...
1709	Other articles of paper and paperboard	...	...	...	...	...	...	...	...	...	...
181	Printing and service activities related to printing d/	671.6	629.3	653.8	671.2	248.1	249.8	287.1	331.1	14.7	20.4
1811	Printing d/	671.6	629.3	653.8	671.2	248.1	249.8	287.1	331.1	14.7	20.4
1812	Service activities related to printing	...	...	...	...	...	...	...	...	...	...
1820	Reproduction of recorded media	464.7	482.4	364.9	237.7	189.7	166.0	204.5	126.3	7.1	9.8
1910	Coke oven products	-	...	...	...	-	...	...	...	-	...
1920	Refined petroleum products	...	...	...	...	...	...	...	...	...	...
201	Basic chemicals,fertilizers, etc.	10132.5	7327.4	...	...	4054.8	2881.6	...	...	...	...
2011	Basic chemicals	...	...	...	...	...	...	...	...	...	...
2012	Fertilizers and nitrogen compounds	454.6	435.8	...	...	65.8	115.2	...	...	...	...
2013	Plastics and synthetic rubber in primary forms	304.6	265.2	...	...	109.3	89.1	...	...	...	...
202	Other chemical products	...	...	...	...	...	...	...	...	...	...
2021	Pesticides and other agrochemical products	...	...	...	...	...	...	...	...	...	...
2022	Paints,varnishes;printing ink and mastics	77.6	96.3	...	...	24.5	31.9	...	...	...	...
2023	Soap,cleaning and cosmetic preparations	...	...	...	...	...	...	...	...	...	...
2029	Other chemical products n.e.c.	...	...	...	...	...	...	...	...	...	...
2030	Man-made fibres	...	...	...	...	...	...	...	...	...	...
2100	Pharmaceuticals,medicinal chemicals, etc.	31913.8	43685.6	...	...	10992.7	12657.6	...	...	...	...
221	Rubber products	89.5	91.3	107.6	88.9	42.0	44.7	45.7	34.2	1.2	2.4
2211	Rubber tyres and tubes	10.4	10.8	11.0	10.3	3.7	4.7	3.9	5.3	0.4	0.8
2219	Other rubber products	79.2	80.5	96.6	78.6	38.3	40.1	41.8	28.9	0.9	1.6
2220	Plastics products	1228.1	1401.9	1457.3	1706.7	429.8	509.0	513.4	644.8	23.3	16.5
2310	Glass and glass products	113.1	156.1	130.6	139.7	43.0	65.9	55.0	63.4	1.6	3.2
239	Non-metallic mineral products n.e.c.	...	...	...	1807.9	...	...	...	641.6	...	39.6
2391	Refractory products	14.9	16.7	22.3	32.3	4.7	7.4	8.3	9.2	1.1	1.5
2392	Clay building materials	...	...	...	24.2	...	...	...	10.6	...	1.4
2393	Other porcelain and ceramic products	...	...	...	...	...	...	...	...	...	...
2394	Cement, lime and plaster	...	...	...	...	...	...	...	...	...	...
2395	Articles of concrete, cement and plaster	117.4	114.4	122.9	117.8	44.4	51.8	48.5	55.1	3.7	7.6
2396	Cutting, shaping and finishing of stone	...	...	...	...	...	...	...	...	...	...
2399	Other non-metallic mineral products n.e.c.	...	...	...	...	...	...	...	...	...	...
2410	Basic iron and steel	265.8	303.6	314.9	338.9	103.6	117.5	103.0	128.5	4.2	10.6
2420	Basic precious and other non-ferrous metals	385.8	368.8	503.3	404.4	71.6	94.6	146.8	99.8	7.6	5.6
243	Casting of metals	18.9	17.0	23.4	20.3	8.4	9.1	9.9	10.5	0.6	1.2
2431	Casting of iron and steel	17.1	15.2	21.2	17.8	7.5	8.0	9.1	8.7	0.5	0.8
2432	Casting of non-ferrous metals	...	...	...	2.3	...	...	...	0.9	...	0.2
251	Struct.metal products, tanks, reservoirs	...	...	...	...	...	...	...	...	...	...

continued

Ireland

ISIC	Industry	Note	Output (valuation not defined) (millions of Euros)				Note	Value added at factor values (millions of Euros)				Note	Gross fixed capital formation (millions of Euros)	
			2013	2014	2015a/	2016a/		2013	2014	2015a/	2016a/		2015a/	2016a/
2511	Structural metal products		580.6	656.9	772.8	954.0		205.7	254.5	288.8	366.2		12.9	18.5
2512	Tanks, reservoirs and containers of metal		256.1	281.4	...	...		96.4	118.7	...	...		...	...
2513	Steam generators, excl. hot water boilers		...	...	...	...		...	...	...	...		...	...
2520	Weapons and ammunition		...	...	...	...		...	...	...	...		...	...
259	Other metal products;metal working services		1010.2	1061.0	1134.1	1362.9		446.9	496.5	443.8	641.9		27.0	49.7
2591	Forging,pressing,stamping,roll-forming of metal		40.9	44.1	68.5	87.0		15.5	16.3	26.2	28.3		0.5	0.9
2592	Treatment and coating of metals; machining		470.1	455.3	...	474.2		214.8	232.6	...	255.1		...	32.6
2593	Cutlery, hand tools and general hardware		...	...	...	...		...	...	...	...		...	...
2599	Other fabricated metal products n.e.c.		...	...	...	...		...	...	...	...		...	...
2610	Electronic components and boards		2949.1	2807.0	...	...		1046.9	561.3	...	...		...	...
2620	Computers and peripheral equipment		6307.9	6546.8	...	...		843.7	1245.2	...	...		...	...
2630	Communication equipment		...	...	...	...		...	...	...	...		...	...
2640	Consumer electronics		...	...	...	...		...	...	...	...		...	...
265	Measuring,testing equipment; watches, etc.		829.3	916.0	...	...		391.6	445.5	...	...		...	...
2651	Measuring/testing/navigating equipment,etc.		824.7	911.1	...	...		389.7	443.5	...	...		...	...
2652	Watches and clocks		4.6	4.9	...	...		1.8	2.0	...	...		...	...
2660	Irradiation/electromedical equipment,etc.		584.1	686.9	...	...		152.0	177.6	...	...		...	...
2670	Optical instruments and photographic equipment		...	...	...	...		...	...	...	...		...	...
2680	Magnetic and optical media		...	...	...	...		...	...	...	...		...	...
2710	Electric motors,generators,transformers,etc.		360.5	422.1	470.0	468.6		105.9	151.2	124.3	166.1		6.9	12.1
2720	Batteries and accumulators		...	...	...	...		...	...	...	...		...	...
273	Wiring and wiring devices		267.1	233.3	...	...		68.6	66.0	...	...		...	...
2731	Fibre optic cables		267.1e/	233.3e/	...	...		68.6e/	66.0e/	...	...		...	...
2732	Other electronic and electric wires and cables		..e/	..e/	...	...		..e/	..e/	...	...		...	...
2733	Wiring devices		..e/	..e/	...	...		..e/	..e/	...	...		...	...
2740	Electric lighting equipment		11.8	9.7	13.8	15.9		4.9	5.5	5.2	7.3		0.4	1.0
2750	Domestic appliances		...	...	...	...		...	...	...	...		...	...
2790	Other electrical equipment		101.3	106.1	75.7	75.4		37.0	34.8	33.2	34.6		0.6	0.8
281	General-purpose machinery		2115.7	2121.3	...	...		738.1	810.3	...	...		...	...
2811	Engines/turbines,excl.aircraft,vehicle engines		19.4	25.5	...	...		9.2	7.6	...	...		...	...
2812	Fluid power equipment		79.0	100.9	...	...		27.5	32.1	...	...		...	...
2813	Other pumps, compressors, taps and valves		401.4	407.5	...	...		164.0	139.8	...	...		...	...
2814	Bearings, gears, gearing and driving elements		15.7	16.2	...	...		6.9	8.6	...	...		...	...
2815	Ovens, furnaces and furnace burners		11.9	13.1	...	...		7.2	6.3	...	...		...	...
2816	Lifting and handling equipment		524.9	577.5	...	...		144.7	166.1	...	...		...	...
2817	Office machinery, excl.computers,etc.		...	...	...	...		...	...	...	...		...	...
2818	Power-driven hand tools		...	...	...	...		...	...	...	...		...	...
2819	Other general-purpose machinery		781.8	709.0	...	...		275.8	327.4	...	...		...	...
282	Special-purpose machinery		465.7	503.1	...	...		178.4	204.1	...	...		...	...
2821	Agricultural and forestry machinery		168.1	175.4	...	...		58.0	64.7	...	...		...	...
2822	Metal-forming machinery and machine tools		72.0	68.9	...	...		33.8	36.0	...	...		...	...

2823	Machinery for metallurgy	–	–	–	…	…	…	–	…	–	…
2824	Mining, quarrying and construction machinery	59.9	74.5	…	…	23.0	24.6	…	…	…	…
2825	Food/beverage/tobacco processing machinery	81.7	86.7	…	…	24.7	32.6	…	…	…	…
2826	Textile/apparel/leather production machinery	…	…	…	…	…	…	…	…	…	…
2829	Other special-purpose machinery	…	…	…	…	…	…	…	…	…	…
2910	Motor vehicles	596.1f/	…	29.9	29.2	193.0f/	…	8.2	8.0	1.2	2.3
2920	Automobile bodies, trailers and semi-trailers	…f/	76.5	82.4	…	…f/	…	26.1	25.4	2.0	1.5
2930	Parts and accessories for motor vehicles	…f/	526.6	547.3	451.9	…f/	174.7	162.1	54.1	22.4	19.2
301	Building of ships and boats	13.3	14.3	12.0	…	…	5.7	4.2	6.0	0.4	0.7
3011	Building of ships and floating structures	13.3g/	14.3g/	8.6	…	1.7	5.7g/	4.2g/	3.6	0.4g/	0.2
3012	Building of pleasure and sporting boats	…g/	…g/	3.3	…	…g/	…g/	…g/	2.4	…g/	0.5
3020	Railway locomotives and rolling stock	…	…	…	…	…	…	…	…	…	…
3030	Air and spacecraft and related machinery	…	…	18.5	…	…	…	…	3.8	…	0.3
3040	Military fighting vehicles	–	–	–	…	–	…	–	…	–	…
309	Transport equipment n.e.c.	2.2	2.9	…	…	1.4	1.4	1.1	…	0.2	0.2
3091	Motorcycles	0.3	0.5	…	…	0.2	0.2	0.2	0.3	–	0.1
3092	Bicycles and invalid carriages	…	…	1.5	…	…	…	…	0.9	…	0.2
3099	Other transport equipment n.e.c.	…	…	…	…	…	…	…	…	…	…
3100	Furniture	571.3	612.0	…	…	210.8	255.2	…	…	…	…
321	Jewellery, bijouterie and related articles	…	…	…	…	…	…	…	…	…	…
3211	Jewellery and related articles	…	…	…	…	…	…	…	…	…	…
3212	Imitation jewellery and related articles	…	…	…	…	…	…	…	…	…	…
3220	Musical instruments	8.1	7.3	…	…	3.7	4.4	…	…	…	…
3230	Sports goods	15.2	14.3	…	…	7.1	8.5	…	…	…	…
3240	Games and toys	…	…	…	…	…	…	…	…	…	…
3250	Medical and dental instruments and supplies	9934.8	10411.5	…	…	4082.3	4065.8	…	…	…	…
3290	Other manufacturing n.e.c.	255.9	221.4	…	…	119.1	102.1	…	…	…	…
331	Repair of fabricated metal products/machinery	774.1	823.5	…	…	344.3	392.5	…	…	…	…
3311	Repair of fabricated metal products	34.1	32.9	…	…	15.1	18.5	…	…	…	…
3312	Repair of machinery	267.0	276.1	…	…	133.4	146.0	…	…	…	…
3313	Repair of electronic and optical equipment	14.3	18.5	…	…	7.8	9.9	…	…	…	…
3314	Repair of electrical equipment	156.4	172.7	…	…	41.7	56.5	…	…	…	…
3315	Repair of transport equip., excl. motor vehicles	…	…	…	…	…	…	…	…	…	…
3319	Repair of other equipment	…	…	…	…	…	…	…	…	…	…
3320	Installation of industrial machinery/equipment	113.7	121.6	…	…	44.6	47.3	…	…	…	…
C	Total manufacturing	105621.6	116927.0	192126.2	192183.8	35596.6	36881.1	89205.1	86628.5	1169.0	1550.2

a/ See Explanatory notes for more details for data from 2015 onwards.
b/ 1061 includes 1062.
c/ 151 includes 1520.
d/ 1811 includes 1812.
e/ 2731 includes 2732 and 2733.
f/ 2910 includes 2920 and 2930.
g/ 3011 includes 3012.

Ireland

Index numbers of industrial production

ISIC Revision 4

(2010=100)

ISIC	Industry	Note	2005	2006	2007	2008	2009	2010	2011	2012	2013	2014	2015	2016
10	Food products		103	101	104	102	98	100	118	123	123	127	144	141
11	Beverages		86	105	104	96	93	100	90	86	91	95	102	105
12	Tobacco products		...	...	...	...	...	100	...	...	...	...	...	...
13	Textiles		153	140	136	134	105	100	...	...	...	...	...	...
14	Wearing apparel		349	223	141	116	111	100	...	...	...	...	...	...
15	Leather and related products		89	84	102	109	109	100	...	...	...	...	...	...
16	Wood products, excluding furniture		210	228	215	156	103	100	92	83	91	86	86	87
17	Paper and paper products		150	147	149	138	106	100	...	...	...	...	...	...
18	Printing and reproduction of recorded media		121	119	129	123	106	100	...	...	...	...	...	...
19	Coke and refined petroleum products		...	...	...	...	...	100	...	...	...	...	...	...
20	Chemicals and chemical products		82	90	100	96	86	100	119	135	138	117	122	97
21	Pharmaceuticals, medicinal chemicals, etc.		66	68	73	71	84	100	...	...	...	...	...	...
22	Rubber and plastics products		128	131	135	122	96	100	99	94	97	90	97	101
23	Other non-metallic mineral products		226	228	237	197	118	100	100	86	86	92	103	116
24	Basic metals		115	121	138	141	85	100	...	...	...	...	...	...
25	Fabricated metal products, except machinery		146	148	161	154	96	100	...	...	...	...	...	...
26	Computer, electronic and optical products		164	181	191	192	136	100	...	...	...	...	...	...
27	Electrical equipment		195	210	200	185	117	100	117	118	121	113	113	130
28	Machinery and equipment n.e.c.		106	120	126	116	88	100	...	...	...	...	...	...
29	Motor vehicles, trailers and semi-trailers		156	160	167	152	82	100	...	...	...	...	...	...
30	Other transport equipment		106	104	114	142	104	100	...	...	...	...	...	...
31	Furniture		200	196	217	183	117	100	...	...	...	...	...	...
32	Other manufacturing		74	71	77	84	83	100	...	...	...	...	...	...
33	Repair and installation of machinery/equipment		90	99	100	116	109	100	...	...	...	...	...	...
C	Total manufacturing		91	94	99	97	93	100	100	99	96	118	166	167

Israel

Supplier of information:
Central Bureau of Statistics, Jerusalem.

Basic source of data:
Annual survey; administrative source.

Major deviations from ISIC (Revision 4):
None reported.

Reference period:
Calendar year.

Scope:
All establishments.

Method of data collection:
Collection of balance sheets and profit-and-loss statements from income tax authorities.

Type of enumeration:
Sample survey.

Adjusted for non-response:
Yes.

Concepts and definitions of variables:
No deviations from the standard UN concepts and definitions are reported.

Related national publications:
Manufacturing, Mining and Quarrying Survey, published by the Central Bureau of Statistics, Jerusalem.

Israel

ISIC	Industry	Note	Number of establishments (number)				Note	Number of persons engaged (thousands)				Note	Wages and salaries paid to employees (millions of Israeli New Sheqalim)			
			2012	2013	2014	2015		2012	2013	2014	2015		2012	2013	2014	2015
1010	Processing/preserving of meat		174	194	159	176		10.2	10.8	11.3	11.5		1018	1121	1292	1319
1020	Processing/preserving of fish, etc.	a/	181	189	203	268	a/	5.2	5.5	6.4	6.4	a/	586	639	777	782
1030	Processing/preserving of fruit,vegetables	a/	...	...	...	...	a/	...	...	...	...	a/	...	...	...	...
1040	Vegetable and animal oils and fats		112	107	97	91		2.1	1.8	0.7	0.8		351	293	92	106
1050	Dairy products		156	142	143	148		8.0	8.0	7.7	7.6		1166	1177	1178	1262
106	Grain mill products,starches and starch products		41	36	39	41		1.0	1.0	1.0	1.0		162	165	173	176
1061	Grain mill products		...	...	...	...		...	...	...	...		...	...	...	...
1062	Starches and starch products		...	...	...	...		...	...	...	...		...	...	...	...
107	Other food products		2079	2016	1894	1884		33.7	31.1	29.7	30.5		3558	3484	3616	3551
1071	Bakery products	b/	1683	1616	1570	1519	b/	18.5	18.1	17.9	18.4	b/	1496	1509	1704	1738
1072	Sugar	b/	73	79	84	63	b/	3.4	2.8	3.3	3.5	b/	485	471	604	497
1073	Cocoa, chocolate and sugar confectionery		16	12	20	22		1.5	1.4	1.5	1.4		193	199	199	199
1074	Macaroni, noodles, couscous, etc.	c/	307	310	220	280	c/	10.3	8.8	7.0	7.3	c/	1384	1306	1109	1117
1075	Prepared meals and dishes	c/	...	...	...	...	c/	...	...	...	...	c/	...	...	...	...
1079	Other food products n.e.c.	c/	...	...	...	...	c/	...	...	...	...	c/	...	...	...	...
1080	Prepared animal feeds		...	...	...	...		...	...	...	...		...	...	...	...
110	Beverages		...	...	...	...		...	...	...	...		...	...	...	...
1101	Distilling, rectifying and blending of spirits	d/	157	173	189	183	d/	1.5	1.5	1.7	1.6	d/	193	184	210	185
1102	Wines	d/	...	...	...	...	d/	...	...	...	...	d/	...	...	...	...
1103	Malt liquors and malt	e/	58	59	47	54	e/	3.3	3.5	3.3	3.4	e/	676	656	688	713
1104	Soft drinks,mineral waters,other bottled waters	e/	...	...	...	...	e/	...	...	...	...	e/	...	...	...	...
1200	Tobacco products	e/	...	...	...	...	e/	...	...	...	...	e/	...	...	...	...
131	Spinning, weaving and finishing of textiles		97	92	72	71		1.5	1.4	0.7	0.7		231	209	89	90
1311	Preparation and spinning of textile fibres		...	...	...	...		...	...	...	...		...	...	...	...
1312	Weaving of textiles		...	...	...	...		...	...	...	...		...	...	...	...
1313	Finishing of textiles		...	...	...	...		...	...	...	...		...	...	...	...
139	Other textiles		328	260	318	224		3.1	2.9	4.0	3.2		351	294	495	447
1391	Knitted and crocheted fabrics		...	...	...	...		...	...	...	...		...	...	...	...
1392	Made-up textile articles, except apparel		...	...	...	...		...	...	...	...		...	...	...	...
1393	Carpets and rugs		...	...	...	...		...	...	...	...		...	...	...	...
1394	Cordage, rope, twine and netting		...	...	...	...		...	...	...	...		...	...	...	...
1399	Other textiles n.e.c.		...	...	...	...		...	...	...	...		...	...	...	...
1410	Wearing apparel, except fur apparel	f/	933	965	925	939	f/	7.8	8.8	7.4	8.6	f/	678	748	680	785
1420	Articles of fur	f/	...	...	...	...	f/	...	...	...	...	f/	...	...	...	...
1430	Knitted and crocheted apparel	f/	...	...	...	...	f/	...	...	...	...	f/	...	...	...	...
151	Leather;luggage,handbags,saddlery,harness;fur		118	120	175g/	162g/		0.4	0.5	1.4g/	1.6g/		32	36	129g/	156g/
1511	Tanning/dressing of leather; dressing of fur		...	...	...	...		...	...	...	...		...	...	...	...
1512	Luggage,handbags,etc.;saddlery/harness		...	...	...	...		...	...	...	...		...	...	...	...
1520	Footwear		78	61	...g/	...g/		1.5	1.4	...g/	...g/		133	139	...g/	...g/
1610	Sawmilling and planing of wood	h/	557	523	576	462	h/	3.2	3.2	3.0	3.1	h/	343	343	320	353

ISIC	Industry	Note												
162	Wood products, cork, straw, plaiting materials	h/	…	…	…	…	…	…	…	…	…	…	…	…
1621	Veneer sheets and wood-based panels		…	…	…	…	…	…	…	…	…	…	…	…
1622	Builders' carpentry and joinery		…	…	…	…	…	…	…	…	…	…	…	…
1623	Wooden containers		…	…	…	…	…	…	…	…	…	…	…	…
1629	Other wood products;articles of cork,straw		…	…	…	…	…	…	…	…	…	…	…	…
170	Paper and paper products	i/	267	271	206	235	8.2	8.2	7.6	7.9	1145	1228	1153	1274
1701	Pulp, paper and paperboard		…	…	…	…	…	…	…	…	…	…	…	…
1702	Corrugated paper and paperboard		…	…	…	…	…	…	…	…	…	…	…	…
1709	Other articles of paper and paperboard		…	…	…	…	…	…	…	…	…	…	…	…
181	Printing and service activities related to printing	i/	1600	1607	1614	1551	10.3	9.8	9.7	9.8	1178	1144	1165	1191
1811	Printing		…	…	…	…	…	…	…	…	…	…	…	…
1812	Service activities related to printing		…	…	…	…	…	…	…	…	…	…	…	…
1820	Reproduction of recorded media	i/	…	…	…	…	…	…	…	…	…	…	…	…
1910	Coke oven products	j/	450	462	464	452	20.0	21.0	21.6	20.7	4695	4644	4965	4693
1920	Refined petroleum products	j/	…	…	…	…	…	…	…	…	…	…	…	…
201	Basic chemicals,fertilizers, etc.	j/	…	…	…	…	…	…	…	…	…	…	…	…
2011	Basic chemicals		…	…	…	…	…	…	…	…	…	…	…	…
2012	Fertilizers and nitrogen compounds		…	…	…	…	…	…	…	…	…	…	…	…
2013	Plastics and synthetic rubber in primary forms	i/	…	…	…	…	…	…	…	…	…	…	…	…
202	Other chemical products		…	…	…	…	…	…	…	…	…	…	…	…
2021	Pesticides and other agrochemical products		…	…	…	…	…	…	…	…	…	…	…	…
2022	Paints,varnishes;printing ink and mastics		…	…	…	…	…	…	…	…	…	…	…	…
2023	Soap,cleaning and cosmetic preparations		…	…	…	…	…	…	…	…	…	…	…	…
2029	Other chemical products n.e.c.	i/	…	…	…	…	…	…	…	…	…	…	…	…
2030	Man-made fibres	j/	…	…	…	…	…	…	…	…	…	…	…	…
2100	Pharmaceuticals,medicinal chemicals, etc.		62	55	56	67	13.5	13.1	12.7	12.9	3581	3611	3512	3753
221	Rubber products		64	111	82	57	2.0	2.0	2.0	1.8	285	287	294	271
2211	Rubber tyres and tubes		…	…	…	…	…	…	…	…	…	…	…	…
2219	Other rubber products		…	…	…	…	…	…	…	…	…	…	…	…
2220	Plastics products		642	626	629	604	21.0	19.7	19.7	19.7	2868	2796	2912	2934
2310	Glass and glass products		184	182	118	117	1.9	1.8	1.7	1.9	253	246	253	251
239	Non-metallic mineral products n.e.c.		958	903	1055	901	8.9	9.1	8.2	8.7	1491	1526	1485	1647
2391	Refractory products	k/	206	208	212	217	1.6	1.8	1.2	1.5	363	428	352	396
2392	Clay building materials	k/	…	…	…	…	…	…	…	…	…	…	…	…
2393	Other porcelain and ceramic products	k/	…	…	…	…	…	…	…	…	…	…	…	…
2394	Cement, lime and plaster	k/	…	…	…	…	…	…	…	…	…	…	…	…
2395	Articles of concrete, cement and plaster		252	195	320	290	4.7	4.6	4.4	4.6	731	721	758	834
2396	Cutting, shaping and finishing of stone	m/	500	500	523	394	2.6	2.8	2.6	2.6	396	378	375	417
2399	Other non-metallic mineral products n.e.c.	m/	…	…	…	…	…	…	…	…	…	…	…	…
2410	Basic iron and steel		62	84	85	76	2.3	2.7	3.1	3.0	401	443	538	483
2420	Basic precious and other non-ferrous metals		91	157	154	152	1.7	1.9	1.5	1.7	233	263	248	253
243	Casting of metals		194	155	113	107	2.6	2.2	2.1	1.5	293	288	301	218
2431	Casting of iron and steel		…	…	…	…	…	…	…	…	…	…	…	…
2432	Casting of non-ferrous metals		…	…	…	…	…	…	…	…	…	…	…	…
251	Struct.metal products, tanks, reservoirs		567	494	566	706	9.6	9.9	12.8	12.1	1222	1321	1764	1665

continued

Israel

ISIC	Industry	Number of establishments (number)					Number of persons engaged (thousands)					Wages and salaries paid to employees (millions of Israeli New Sheqalim)				
		Note	2012	2013	2014	2015	Note	2012	2013	2014	2015	Note	2012	2013	2014	2015
2511	Structural metal products		...	...	...	...		...	...	...	...		...	...	...	...
2512	Tanks, reservoirs and containers of metal		...	...	...	...		...	...	...	...		...	...	...	...
2513	Steam generators, excl. hot water boilers		...	...	...	...		...	...	...	...		...	...	...	...
2520	Weapons and ammunition	n/	3611	3465	2971	3118	n/	36.7	36.6	26.2	29.0	n/	5036	5161	5474	4506
259	Other metal products;metal working services	n/	...	...	...	...	n/	...	...	...	...	n/	...	...	...	...
2591	Forging,pressing,stamping,roll-forming of metal		...	...	...	...		...	...	...	...		...	...	...	...
2592	Treatment and coating of metals; machining		...	...	...	...		...	...	...	...		...	...	...	...
2593	Cutlery, hand tools and general hardware		...	...	...	...		...	...	...	...		...	...	...	...
2599	Other fabricated metal products n.e.c.		...	...	...	...		...	...	...	...		...	...	...	...
2610	Electronic components and boards		272	309	172p/	240p/		19.5	19.2	18.9p/	19.3p/		3717	3366	3715p/	3566p/
2620	Computers and peripheral equipment		10	8	..p/	..p/		1.2	0.9	..p/	..p/		365	307	..p/	..p/
2630	Communication equipment		80	78	80	77		14.3	14.0	13.6	13.1		4418	4290	4711	4492
2640	Consumer electronics	q/	31	28	22	35	q/	0.5	0.5	0.9	0.9	q/	115	127	310	309
265	Measuring,testing equipment; watches, etc.		198	188	174	168		26.8	28.4	25.0	25.6		8186	9074	8345	9025
2651	Measuring/testing/navigating equipment,etc.		...	...	...	...		...	...	...	...		...	...	...	...
2652	Watches and clocks		...	...	...	...		...	...	...	...		...	...	...	...
2660	Irradiation/electromedical equipment,etc.		76	79	57	67		4.6	4.4	4.6	5.1		1405	1366	1374	1605
2670	Optical instruments and photographic equipment		43	46	51	44		3.4	2.9	2.7	3.0		925	772	706	804
2680	Magnetic and optical media	q/	...	...	...	...	q/	...	...	...	...	q/	...	...	...	...
2710	Electric motors,generators,transformers,etc.		...	...	...	...		...	...	...	...		...	...	...	...
2720	Batteries and accumulators		...	...	...	...		...	...	...	...		...	...	...	...
273	Wiring and wiring devices		33	36	36	36		1.5	1.7	1.9	1.8		213	229	258	262
2731	Fibre optic cables		...	...	...	...		...	...	...	...		...	...	...	...
2732	Other electronic and electric wires and cables		...	...	...	...		...	...	...	...		...	...	...	...
2733	Wiring devices		...	...	...	...		...	...	...	...		...	...	...	...
2740	Electric lighting equipment		...	...	...	...		...	...	...	...		...	...	...	...
2750	Domestic appliances		...	...	...	19		...	...	...	0.9		...	...	...	209
2790	Other electrical equipment		...	...	...	...		...	...	...	...		...	...	...	...
281	General-purpose machinery		414	442	488	527		12.6	13.6	12.8	13.7		2318	2496	2337	2344
2811	Engines/turbines,excl.aircraft,vehicle engines		...	...	...	...		...	...	...	...		...	...	...	...
2812	Fluid power equipment		...	...	...	...		...	...	...	...		...	...	...	...
2813	Other pumps, compressors, taps and valves		...	...	...	...		...	...	...	...		...	...	...	...
2814	Bearings, gears, gearing and driving elements		...	...	...	...		...	...	...	...		...	...	...	...
2815	Ovens, furnaces and furnace burners		...	...	...	...		...	...	...	...		...	...	...	...
2816	Lifting and handling equipment		...	...	...	...		...	...	...	...		...	...	...	...
2817	Office machinery, excl.computers,etc.		...	...	...	...		...	...	...	...		...	...	...	...
2818	Power-driven hand tools		...	...	...	...		...	...	...	...		...	...	...	...
2819	Other general-purpose machinery		...	...	...	...		...	...	...	...		...	...	...	...
282	Special-purpose machinery		226	248	261	286		4.6	5.6	5.5	6.3		1161	1375	1351	1565
2821	Agricultural and forestry machinery		...	...	...	...		...	...	...	...		...	...	...	...
2822	Metal-forming machinery and machine tools		...	...	...	...		...	...	...	...		...	...	...	...

ISIC Revision 4

2823	Machinery for metallurgy		...	...	...	...	...	...	...	...	...	...	...	...
2824	Mining, quarrying and construction machinery		...	...	...	...	...	...	...	...	...	...	...	...
2825	Food/beverage/tobacco processing machinery		...	...	...	...	...	...	...	...	...	...	...	...
2826	Textile/apparel/leather production machinery		...	...	...	...	...	...	...	...	...	...	...	...
2829	Other special-purpose machinery		...	...	...	...	...	...	...	...	...	...	...	...
2910	Motor vehicles	r/	719	820	913	865	5.0	5.1	5.5	5.4	119	114	118	106
2920	Automobile bodies, trailers and semi-trailers	r/	...	...	...	...	...	...	...	...	...	...	...	...
2930	Parts and accessories for motor vehicles	r/	...	...	...	...	...	...	...	...	...	...	...	...
301	Building of ships and boats	s/	4297	4535	4425	4534	14.7	15.3	15.3	14.7	64	65	46	43
3011	Building of ships and floating structures		...	...	...	...	...	...	...	...	...	...	...	...
3012	Building of pleasure and sporting boats		...	...	...	...	...	...	...	...	...	...	...	...
3020	Railway locomotives and rolling stock	s/	...	...	...	...	...	...	...	...	...	...	...	...
3030	Air and spacecraft and related machinery	s/	...	...	...	...	...	...	...	...	...	...	...	...
3040	Military fighting vehicles	s/	...	...	...	...	...	...	...	...	...	...	...	...
309	Transport equipment n.e.c.	s/	...	...	...	...	...	...	...	...	...	...	...	...
3091	Motorcycles		...	...	...	...	...	...	...	...	...	...	...	...
3092	Bicycles and invalid carriages		...	...	...	...	...	...	...	...	...	...	...	...
3099	Other transport equipment n.e.c.		...	...	...	...	...	...	...	...	...	...	...	...
3100	Furniture		1731	1735	1785	1872	17.4	16.0	17.4	17.1	4047	3837	3795	3509
321	Jewellery, bijouterie and related articles		384	399	394	367	4.5	4.5	4.5	4.2	977	966	989	930
3211	Jewellery and related articles		...	...	...	...	...	...	...	...	...	...	...	...
3212	Imitation jewellery and related articles		...	...	...	...	...	...	...	...	...	...	...	...
3220	Musical instruments	t/	179	206	174	146	1.7	1.8	1.7	1.4	185	187	188	247
3230	Sports goods		...	...	...	...	...	...	...	...	...	...	...	...
3240	Games and toys	t/	...	...	...	...	...	...	...	...	...	...	...	...
3250	Medical and dental instruments and supplies		515	829	1274	1168	4.1	6.2	7.7	7.6	730	846	487	767
3290	Other manufacturing n.e.c.	t/	...	...	...	...	...	...	...	...	...	...	...	...
331	Repair of fabricated metal products/machinery	u/	280	361	416	849	1.9	2.3	2.9	5.9	428	510	700	787
3311	Repair of fabricated metal products	u/	...	...	...	...	...	...	...	...	...	...	...	...
3312	Repair of machinery	u/	...	...	...	...	...	...	...	...	...	...	...	...
3313	Repair of electronic and optical equipment	u/	...	...	...	...	...	...	...	...	...	...	...	...
3314	Repair of electrical equipment	u/	...	...	...	...	...	...	...	...	...	...	...	...
3315	Repair of transport equip., excl. motor vehicles	v/	90	275	209	176	0.6	1.1	1.0	1.3	47	83	69	135
3319	Repair of other equipment	v/	...	...	...	...	...	...	...	...	...	...	...	...
3320	Installation of industrial machinery/equipment	v/	...	...	...	...	...	...	...	...	...	...	...	...
C	Total manufacturing		64372	66230	67692	68146	367.3	370.4	357.4	363.3	22119	21857	20960	21097

a/ 1020 includes 1030.
b/ 1072 includes 1073.
c/ 1075 includes 1079 and 1080.
d/ 1101 includes 1102.
e/ 1103 includes 1104 and 1200.
f/ 1410 includes 1420 and 1430.
g/ 151 includes 1520.
h/ 1610 includes 162.
i/ 181 includes 1820.
j/ 1910 includes 1920, 201, 202 and 2030.

k/ 2391 includes 2392, 2393 and 2394.
m/ 2396 includes 2399.
n/ 2520 includes 259.
p/ 2610 includes 2620.
q/ 2640 includes 2680.
r/ 2910 includes 2920 and 2930.
s/ 301 includes 3020, 3030, 3040 and 309.
t/ 3220 includes 3240 and 3290.
u/ 3311 includes 3312, 3313 and 3314.
v/ 3315 includes 3319 and 3320.

Israel

ISIC	Industry	Note	Output at basic prices (millions of Israeli New Sheqalim)				Note	Value added at basic prices (millions of Israeli New Sheqalim)				Note	Gross fixed capital formation (millions of Israeli New Sheqalim)	
			2012	2013	2014	2015		2012	2013	2014	2015		2014	2015
1010	Processing/preserving of meat		10152	11557	10661	11596		1438	1782	1953	2139		316	280
1020	Processing/preserving of fish, etc.	a/	5655	5849	6539	6336	a/	1024	1063	1373	1400	a/	230	153
1030	Processing/preserving of fruit,vegetables	a/	...	...	...	...	a/	...	...	...	...	a/	...	...
1040	Vegetable and animal oils and fats		2291	2082	948	1091		581	544	193	235		29	41
1050	Dairy products		8671	8987	8599	8412		2069	2001	2083	2149		481	465
106	Grain mill products,starches and starch products		2365	2332	2030	1975		399	407	379	315		76	68
1061	Grain mill products		...	...	...	...		...	...	...	...		...	...
1062	Starches and starch products		...	...	...	...		...	...	...	...		...	...
107	Other food products		21340	20709	19335	19286		5635	5649	5651	5842		796	625
1071	Bakery products	b/	6072	6061	6069	6496	b/	2030	2167	2338	2484	b/	320	267
1072	Sugar	b/	1076	1026	1422	1532	b/	643	631	798	701	b/	167	111
1073	Cocoa, chocolate and sugar confectionery		...	...	...	...		...	...	...	...		...	...
1074	Macaroni, noodles, couscous, etc.		812	772	846	785		391	403	410	408		56	33
1075	Prepared meals and dishes	c/	13380	12850	10998	10473	c/	2571	2449	2105	2249	c/	253	214
1079	Other food products n.e.c.	c/	...	...	...	...	c/	...	...	...	...	c/	...	...
1080	Prepared animal feeds	c/	...	...	...	...	c/	...	...	...	...	c/	...	...
110	Beverages		...	...	...	...		...	...	...	...		...	...
1101	Distilling, rectifying and blending of spirits	d/	986	1067	1162	1008	d/	315	287	406	373	d/	122	73
1102	Wines	d/	...	...	...	...	d/	...	...	...	...	d/	...	...
1103	Malt liquors and malt	e/	3729	3854	3522	3640	e/	1290	1413	1424	1490	e/	234	208
1104	Soft drinks,mineral waters,other bottled waters	e/	...	...	...	...	e/	...	...	...	...	e/	...	...
1200	Tobacco products	e/	...	...	...	...	e/	...	...	...	...	e/	...	...
131	Spinning, weaving and finishing of textiles		2201	2133	501	450		463	407	160	130		7	10
1311	Preparation and spinning of textile fibres		...	...	...	...		...	...	...	...		...	...
1312	Weaving of textiles		...	...	...	...		...	...	...	...		...	...
1313	Finishing of textiles		...	...	...	...		...	...	...	...		...	...
139	Other textiles		1824	1815	2841	3204		540	463	905	917		56	154
1391	Knitted and crocheted fabrics		...	...	...	...		...	...	...	...		...	...
1392	Made-up textile articles, except apparel		...	...	...	...		...	...	...	...		...	...
1393	Carpets and rugs		...	...	...	...		...	...	...	...		...	...
1394	Cordage, rope, twine and netting		...	...	...	...		...	...	...	...		...	...
1399	Other textiles n.e.c.		...	...	...	...		...	...	...	...		...	...
1410	Wearing apparel, except fur apparel	f/	3347	2636	2464	2638	f/	936	1077	1013	1080	f/	83	171
1420	Articles of fur	f/	...	...	...	...	f/	...	...	...	...	f/	...	...
1430	Knitted and crocheted apparel	f/	...	...	...	...	f/	...	...	...	...	f/	...	...
151	Leather;luggage,handbags,saddlery,harness;fur		130	150	532g/	620g/		50	51	223g/	249g/		7g/	6g/
1511	Tanning/dressing of leather; dressing of fur		...	...	...	...		...	...	...	...		...	...
1512	Luggage,handbags,etc.;saddlery/harness		...	...	...	...		...	...	...	...		...	...
1520	Footwear		483	472	...g/	...g/		218	208	...g/	...g/		...g/	...g/
1610	Sawmilling and planing of wood	h/	1877	1958	1624	1899	h/	540	515	499	646	h/	60	34

Code	Description													
162	Wood products, cork, straw, plaiting materials	h/	...	...	...	...	h/	...	...	...	...	h/	...	...
1621	Veneer sheets and wood-based panels		...	...	...	...		...	...	...	...		...	...
1622	Builders' carpentry and joinery		...	...	...	...		...	...	...	...		...	...
1623	Wooden containers		...	...	...	...		...	...	...	...		...	...
1629	Other wood products;articles of cork,straw		...	...	...	...		...	...	...	...		...	...
170	Paper and paper products		6770	6761	6172	6815		1651	1797	1680	1899		343	276
1701	Pulp, paper and paperboard		...	...	...	...		...	...	...	...		...	...
1702	Corrugated paper and paperboard		...	...	...	...		...	...	...	...		...	...
1709	Other articles of paper and paperboard		...	...	...	...		...	...	...	...		...	...
181	Printing and service activities related to printing	i/	4265	4037	3790	3807	i/	1643	1700	1663	1729	i/	230	261
1811	Printing		...	...	...	...		...	...	...	...		...	...
1812	Service activities related to printing		...	...	...	...		...	...	...	...		...	...
1820	Reproduction of recorded media	i/	...	...	...	...	i/	...	...	...	...	i/	...	...
1910	Coke oven products	j/	82843	80334	76337	57292	j/	8460	8621	9923	11275	j/	1819	1830
1920	Refined petroleum products	j/	...	...	...	...	j/	...	...	...	...	j/	...	...
201	Basic chemicals,fertilizers, etc.	j/	...	...	...	...	j/	...	...	...	...	j/	...	...
2011	Basic chemicals		...	...	...	...		...	...	...	...		...	...
2012	Fertilizers and nitrogen compounds		...	...	...	...		...	...	...	...		...	...
2013	Plastics and synthetic rubber in primary forms	j/	...	...	...	...	j/	...	...	...	...	j/	...	...
202	Other chemical products		...	...	...	...		...	...	...	...		...	...
2021	Pesticides and other agrochemical products		...	...	...	...		...	...	...	...		...	...
2022	Paints,varnishes;printing ink and mastics		...	...	...	...		...	...	...	...		...	...
2023	Soap,cleaning and cosmetic preparations		...	...	...	...		...	...	...	...		...	...
2029	Other chemical products n.e.c.	j/	...	...	...	...	j/	...	...	...	...	j/	...	...
2030	Man-made fibres		...	...	...	...		...	...	...	...		...	...
2100	Pharmaceuticals,medicinal chemicals, etc.		30898	28218	24287	30789		13268	11662	10001	15717		1431	1606
221	Rubber products		1263	1152	1018	934		455	471	478	445		38	31
2211	Rubber tyres and tubes		...	...	...	...		...	...	...	...		...	...
2219	Other rubber products		...	...	...	...		...	...	...	...		...	...
2220	Plastics products		16789	15922	15503	15370		4972	4553	4998	5030		734	656
2310	Glass and glass products		1028	936	958	944		263	229	313	340		32	20
239	Non-metallic mineral products n.e.c.		11175	11379	11806	12977		2947	3088	3028	3333		676	926
2391	Refractory products	k/	2391	2765	2502	2849	k/	912	952	842	943	k/	260	176
2392	Clay building materials	k/	...	...	...	...	k/	...	...	...	...	k/	...	...
2393	Other porcelain and ceramic products	k/	...	...	...	...	k/	...	...	...	...	k/	...	...
2394	Cement, lime and plaster	k/	...	...	...	...	k/	...	...	...	...	k/	...	...
2395	Articles of concrete, cement and plaster	m/	6340	5955	7038	7353	m/	1278	1332	1372	1396	m/	254	573
2396	Cutting, shaping and finishing of stone	m/	2444	2660	2266	2776	m/	757	805	814	994	m/	162	177
2399	Other non-metallic mineral products n.e.c.		...	...	...	...		...	...	...	...		...	...
2410	Basic iron and steel		6777	6335	6136	5469		661	806	855	848		152	235
2420	Basic precious and other non-ferrous metals		1555	1601	1579	1522		370	402	434	395		73	36
243	Casting of metals		1630	1595	1072	779		363	359	398	299		50	26
2431	Casting of iron and steel		...	...	...	...		...	...	...	...		...	...
2432	Casting of non-ferrous metals		...	...	...	...		...	...	...	...		...	...
251	Struct.metal products, tanks, reservoirs		6014	5600	7096	6254		1898	1896	2614	2439		366	241

continued

Israel

| ISIC Revision 4 | | Output at basic prices | | | | | | Value added at basic prices | | | | | | Gross fixed capital formation | | |
| | | | (millions of Israeli New Sheqalim) | | | | | (millions of Israeli New Sheqalim) | | | | | (millions of Israeli New Sheqalim) | | |
ISIC	Industry	Note	2012	2013	2014	2015	Note	2012	2013	2014	2015	Note	2014	2015
2511	Structural metal products		...	...	...	...		...	...	...	...		...	...
2512	Tanks, reservoirs and containers of metal		...	...	...	...		...	...	...	...		...	...
2513	Steam generators, excl. hot water boilers		...	...	...	...		...	...	...	...		...	...
2520	Weapons and ammunition	n/	17570	18084	12737	14897	n/	8534	8293	6794	7704	n/	567	390
259	Other metal products;metal working services	n/	...	...	...	...	n/	...	...	...	...	n/	...	...
2591	Forging,pressing,stamping,roll-forming of metal		...	...	...	...		...	...	...	...		...	...
2592	Treatment and coating of metals machining		...	...	...	...		...	...	...	...		...	...
2593	Cutlery, hand tools and general hardware		...	...	...	...		...	...	...	...		...	...
2599	Other fabricated metal products n.e.c.		...	...	...	...		...	...	...	...		...	...
2610	Electronic components and boards		24287	17903	20961p/	20105p/		15633	10864	12180p/	12014p/		629p/	1576p/
2620	Computers and peripheral equipment		1285	912	...p/	...p/		524	445	...p/	...p/		...p/	...p/
2630	Communication equipment		14811	13523	14028	13572		4807	4822	5157	4338		386	275
2640	Consumer electronics	q/	391	443	842	740	q/	142	144	412	374		8	4
265	Measuring,testing equipment; watches. etc.		25179	27081	26102	27206		11056	11417	11362	12071		880	856
2651	Measuring/testing/navigating equipment,etc.		...	...	...	...		...	...	...	...		...	...
2652	Watches and clocks		...	...	...	...		...	...	...	...		...	...
2660	Irradiation/electromedical equipment,etc.		8135	8223	8847	9815		2595	2497	2551	2533		156	178
2670	Optical instruments and photographic equipment		2797	2463	2246	3190		1224	1021	997	1247		44	74
2680	Magnetic and optical media	q/	...	...	...	...	q/	...	...	...	...	q/	...	...
2710	Electric motors,generators,transformers,etc.		...	...	...	...		...	...	...	...		...	...
2720	Batteries and accumulators		...	...	...	...		...	...	...	...		...	...
273	Wiring and wiring devices		1461	1285	1199	1214		320	294	338	333		17	34
2731	Fibre optic cables		...	...	...	...		...	...	...	...		...	...
2732	Other electronic and electric wires and cables		...	...	...	...		...	...	...	...		...	...
2733	Wiring devices		...	...	...	...		...	...	...	...		...	...
2740	Electric lighting equipment		...	...	...	...		...	...	...	...		...	...
2750	Domestic appliances		...	...	...	497		...	...	...	256		...	8
2790	Other electrical equipment		...	...	...	...		...	...	...	...		...	...
281	General-purpose machinery		10049	9132	8726	8840		2643	2731	3807	3550		273	430
2811	Engines/turbines,excl.aircraft,vehicle engines		...	...	...	...		...	...	...	...		...	...
2812	Fluid power equipment		...	...	...	...		...	...	...	...		...	...
2813	Other pumps, compressors, taps and valves		...	...	...	...		...	...	...	...		...	...
2814	Bearings, gears, gearing and driving elements		...	...	...	...		...	...	...	...		...	...
2815	Ovens, furnaces and furnace burners		...	...	...	...		...	...	...	...		...	...
2816	Lifting and handling equipment		...	...	...	...		...	...	...	...		...	...
2817	Office machinery, excl.computers,etc.		...	...	...	...		...	...	...	...		...	...
2818	Power-driven hand tools		...	...	...	...		...	...	...	...		...	...
2819	Other general-purpose machinery		...	...	...	...		...	...	...	...		...	...
282	Special-purpose machinery		5909	6243	7133	7690		1610	1918	2242	2123		291	373
2821	Agricultural and forestry machinery		...	...	...	...		...	...	...	...		...	...
2822	Metal-forming machinery and machine tools		...	...	...	...		...	...	...	...		...	...

Code	Description											
2823	Machinery for metallurgy		:	:	:	:	:	:	:	:	:	:
2824	Mining, quarrying and construction machinery		:	:	:	:	:	:	:	:	:	:
2825	Food/beverage/tobacco processing machinery		:	:	:	:	:	:	:	:	:	:
2826	Textile/apparel/leather production machinery		:	:	:	:	:	:	:	:	:	:
2829	Other special-purpose machinery		:	:	:	:	:	:	:	:	:	:
2910	Motor vehicles	r/	3190	3031	2961	3288	1073	1042	1000	1150	122	82
2920	Automobile bodies, trailers and semi-trailers	r/	:	:	:	:	:	:	:	:	:	:
2930	Parts and accessories for motor vehicles	r/	:	:	:	:	:	:	:	:	:	:
301	Building of ships and boats	s/	10622	11280	11348	11585	4911	4955	5025	5222	423	462
3011	Building of ships and floating structures		:	:	:	:	:	:	:	:	:	:
3012	Building of pleasure and sporting boats		:	:	:	:	:	:	:	:	:	:
3020	Railway locomotives and rolling stock	s/	:	:	:	:	:	:	:	:	:	:
3030	Air and spacecraft and related machinery	s/	:	:	:	:	:	:	:	:	:	:
3040	Military fighting vehicles	s/	:	:	:	:	:	:	:	:	:	:
309	Transport equipment n.e.c.	s/	:	:	:	:	:	:	:	:	:	:
3091	Motorcycles		:	:	:	:	:	:	:	:	:	:
3092	Bicycles and invalid carriages		:	:	:	:	:	:	:	:	:	:
3099	Other transport equipment n.e.c.		:	:	:	:	:	:	:	:	:	:
3100	Furniture		6612	6191	6527	7110	2444	2721	2515	2637	247	322
321	Jewellery, bijouterie and related articles		1868	1618	1582	1587	518	531	603	566	40	27
3211	Jewellery and related articles		:	:	:	:	:	:	:	:	:	:
3212	Imitation jewellery and related articles		:	:	:	:	:	:	:	:	:	:
3220	Musical instruments	t/	737	833	628	590	275	265	219	199	8	8
3230	Sports goods		:	:	:	:	:	:	:	:	:	:
3240	Games and toys	t/	:	:	:	:	:	:	:	:	:	:
3250	Medical and dental instruments and supplies		2062	3234	3815	3711	911	1327	1735	1593	230	177
3290	Other manufacturing n.e.c.	t/	:	:	:	:	:	:	:	:	:	:
331	Repair of fabricated metal products/machinery	u/	954	1077	1213	2321	394	500	544	1078	16	15
3311	Repair of fabricated metal products	u/	:	:	:	:	:	:	:	:	:	:
3312	Repair of machinery	u/	:	:	:	:	:	:	:	:	:	:
3313	Repair of electronic and optical equipment	u/	:	:	:	:	:	:	:	:	:	:
3314	Repair of electrical equipment	u/	:	:	:	:	:	:	:	:	:	:
3315	Repair of transport equip., excl. motor vehicles	v/	205	1314	460	632	128	408	315	270	7	8
3319	Repair of other equipment	v/	:	:	:	:	:	:	:	:	:	:
3320	Installation of industrial machinery/equipment	v/	:	:	:	:	:	:	:	:	:	:
C	Total manufacturing		379323	368733	352642	347107	113671	109267	111998	121247	12972	13798

a/ 1020 includes 1030.
b/ 1072 includes 1073.
c/ 1075 includes 1079 and 1080.
d/ 1101 includes 1102.
e/ 1103 includes 1104 and 1200.
f/ 1410 includes 1420 and 1430.
g/ 151 includes 1520.
h/ 1610 includes 162.
i/ 181 includes 1820.
j/ 1910 includes 1920, 201, 202 and 2030.

k/ 2391 includes 2392, 2393 and 2394.
m/ 2396 includes 2399.
n/ 2520 includes 259.
p/ 2610 includes 2620.
q/ 2640 includes 2680.
r/ 2910 includes 2920 and 2930.
s/ 301 includes 3020, 3030, 3040 and 309.
t/ 3220 includes 3240 and 3290.
u/ 3311 includes 3312, 3313 and 3314.
v/ 3315 includes 3319 and 3320.

Israel

Index numbers of industrial production

ISIC Revision 4

(2010=100)

ISIC	Industry	Note	2005	2006	2007	2008	2009	2010	2011	2012	2013	2014	2015	2016
10	Food products		96	98	101	99	98	100	104	104	105	105	106	110
11	Beverages	a/	90	92	96	97	96	100	98	101	100	101	103	109
12	Tobacco products	a/	...	...	...	...	...	...	...	...	...	...	...	...
13	Textiles		114	119	115	112	95	100	87	80	73	73	74	85
14	Wearing apparel		126	131	121	119	105	100	109	107	105	109	107	104
15	Leather and related products		98	104	111	110	91	100	92	88	84	86	91	91
16	Wood products, excluding furniture		85	83	94	99	91	100	108	121	122	128	136	159
17	Paper and paper products		91	93	97	96	95	100	100	91	87	86	98	115
18	Printing and reproduction of recorded media		106	112	110	111	101	100	96	94	96	95	94	94
19	Coke and refined petroleum products	b/	95	91	100	105	95	100	106	108	110	109	110	110
20	Chemicals and chemical products	b/	...	...	...	...	...	...	...	...	...	...	...	...
21	Pharmaceuticals,medicinal chemicals, etc.		37	58	54	84	78	100	91	103	103	99	118	105
22	Rubber and plastics products		81	84	92	98	86	100	107	106	105	106	106	114
23	Other non-metallic mineral products		100	104	113	111	98	100	104	112	116	124	130	135
24	Basic metals		107	108	114	107	88	100	106	106	105	103	102	101
25	Fabricated metal products, except machinery		91	101	104	105	85	100	111	114	111	115	116	118
26	Computer, electronic and optical products		77	86	94	94	97	100	103	113	108	109	103	100
27	Electrical equipment		92	98	106	108	94	100	101	100	101	98	101	109
28	Machinery and equipment n.e.c.		77	82	91	105	100	100	104	115	113	117	119	117
29	Motor vehicles, trailers and semi-trailers		88	96	104	100	100	100	88	86	82	76	72	73
30	Other transport equipment		82	85	96	111	106	100	108	106	114	121	130	138
31	Furniture		91	97	103	104	95	100	104	100	96	100	105	112
32	Other manufacturing		95	93	103	103	96	100	95	97	101	101	101	112
33	Repair and installation of machinery/equipment		...	...	...	...	...	...	...	...	...	...	...	...
C	Total manufacturing		80	87	92	98	93	100	102	107	106	107	109	109

a/ 11 includes 12.
b/ 19 includes 20.

Italy

Supplier of information:
Istituto Nazionale di Statistica (National Institute of Statistics), Rome.
Industrial statistics for the OECD countries are compiled by the OECD secretariat, which
supplies them to UNIDO.

Basic source of data:
Annual surveys; administrative data; business register.

Major deviations from ISIC (Revision 4):
Data presented in ISIC (Revision 4) were originally classified according to the national
NACE-related classification system.

Reference period:
Calendar year.

Scope:
All enterprises.

Method of data collection:
Not reported.

Type of enumeration:
Enterprises with 100 or more employees are completely enumerated; enterprises below
that threshold are sampled.

Adjusted for non-response:
Not reported.

Concepts and definitions of variables:
No deviations from the standard UN concepts and definitions are reported.

Related national publications:
None reported.

Italy

ISIC Revision 4

ISIC	Industry	Number of enterprises (number) 2013	2014	2015	2016	Number of employees (thousands) 2013	2014	2015	2016	Wages and salaries paid to employees (millions of Euros) 2013	2014	2015	2016
1010	Processing/preserving of meat	3500	3458	3463	3421	52.2	52.9	53.2	55.3	1427	1433	1460	1559
1020	Processing/preserving of fish, etc.	395	402	402	416	5.1	5.0	5.0	5.3	135	132	137	145
1030	Processing/preserving of fruit,vegetables	1778	1753	1726	1775	27.1	27.9	28.1	29.7	701	723	758	802
1040	Vegetable and animal oils and fats	3306	3189	3261	3206	7.0	7.0	7.6	7.9	193	196	219	233
1050	Dairy products	3420	3446	3470	3535	39.2	38.5	38.1	39.1	1176	1170	1178	1193
106	Grain mill products,starches and starch products	983	965	947	961	7.9	8.2	8.1	8.4	259	272	273	288
1061	Grain mill products	965	957	939	953	6.4	6.8	6.6	7.0	194	207	208	221
1062	Starches and starch products	18	8	8	8	1.4	1.4	1.4	1.4	64	66	66	67
107	Other food products	40786	39489	39323	39541	164.2	163.0	165.3	171.0	3979	3987	4117	4305
1071	Bakery products	31261	30269	30257	30613	93.1	92.4	93.9	99.0	1704	1696	1767	1884
1072	Sugar	12	10	10	11	0.9	1.0	0.8	0.7	31	32	26	25
1073	Cocoa, chocolate and sugar confectionery	781	719	691	674	18.5	18.4	18.3	17.2	676	658	682	644
1074	Macaroni, noodles, couscous, etc.	4296	4158	4056	4056	19.1	18.8	19.4	20.4	576	581	614	662
1075	Prepared meals and dishes	1126	1085	1081	1075	6.8	6.9	6.5	7.0	160	161	150	164
1079	Other food products n.e.c.	3310	3248	3228	3112	25.6	25.6	26.4	26.7	833	858	878	927
1080	Prepared animal feeds	523	519	504	505	6.8	6.6	6.7	6.9	227	223	230	242
110	Beverages	2949	3191	3219	3390	31.9	34.2	33.8	36.4	1111	1203	1194	1294
1101	Distilling, rectifying and blending of spirits	515	518	522	532	4.2	4.2	4.2	4.4	166	178	170	182
1102	Wines	...	...	...	...	...	...	...	...	...	...	...	...
1103	Malt liquors and malt	...	...	...	...	...	...	...	...	...	...	...	...
1104	Soft drinks,mineral waters,other bottled waters	232	233	226	234	9.9	9.6	9.5	9.7	370	362	367	382
1200	Tobacco products	6	6	6	7	0.6	0.6	0.5	1.2	19	18	16	52
131	Spinning, weaving and finishing of textiles	6046	6000	5789	5458	69.8	66.9	65.5	59.4	1746	1765	1792	1655
1311	Preparation and spinning of textile fibres	1775	1714	1618	1548	16.6	15.5	15.0	14.7	391	389	391	398
1312	Weaving of textiles	1984	1928	1873	1847	30.0	28.6	27.5	26.4	797	813	825	803
1313	Finishing of textiles	2287	2358	2298	2063	23.2	22.8	23.0	18.3	558	563	576	454
139	Other textiles	8721	8359	8077	8350	40.5	39.3	38.8	40.8	934	956	967	1032
1391	Knitted and crocheted fabrics	830	761	748	751	4.6	4.1	3.9	4.0	114	109	105	110
1392	Made-up textile articles, except apparel	4539	4376	4222	4482	12.7	12.1	12.3	13.5	249	250	253	278
1393	Carpets and rugs	125	120	116	115	1.1	1.0	1.0	0.8	26	26	28	25
1394	Cordage, rope, twine and netting	157	151	147	149	0.9	0.9	0.9	0.9	19	19	20	21
1399	Other textiles n.e.c.	3070	2951	2844	2853	21.3	21.2	20.7	21.5	526	552	562	598
1410	Wearing apparel, except fur apparel	25846	24884	24527	24225	140.1	138.6	139.3	143.7	2781	2769	2856	2947
1420	Articles of fur	846	820	790	770	1.0	1.0	1.0	1.0	18	19	19	20
1430	Knitted and crocheted apparel	3970	3738	3548	3322	26.0	26.1	25.0	23.2	530	540	538	530
151	Leather;luggage,handbags,saddlery,harness;fur	7101	7135	7129	7181	50.7	52.6	54.2	56.0	1265	1299	1367	1508
1511	Tanning/dressing of leather; dressing of fur	1867	1878	1856	1847	20.2	20.3	20.3	20.5	571	570	580	602
1512	Luggage,handbags,etc.;saddlery/harness	5234	5257	5273	5334	30.5	32.4	33.9	35.5	693	730	787	906
1520	Footwear	8532	8301	8106	8027	69.5	69.4	68.1	68.6	1528	1536	1558	1585
1610	Sawmilling and planing of wood	4090	3940	3557	3361	11.3	10.0	9.6	9.0	226	206	207	198

162	Wood products, cork, straw, plaiting materials	27126	26061	24606	23833	68.0	63.8	59.7	58.4	1421	1355	1338	1347
1621	Veneer sheets and wood-based panels	438	309	279	281	7.8	6.8	6.2	6.3	195	182	187	195
1622	Builders' carpentry and joinery	21668	20981	19527	18655	45.3	42.5	39.1	37.1	902	858	825	808
1623	Wooden containers	1098	1082	1079	1103	7.1	7.5	7.4	7.8	155	163	168	178
1629	Other wood products;articles of cork,straw	3922	3689	3721	3794	7.8	6.9	6.9	7.2	169	151	158	166
170	Paper and paper products	3906	3801	3723	3763	66.9	66.5	65.8	66.7	1995	2026	2062	2099
1701	Pulp, paper and paperboard	223	211	205	206	11.5	10.7	10.2	11.7	369	361	364	421
1702	Corrugated paper and paperboard	1149	1131	1154	1162	21.5	22.2	22.1	22.7	617	657	662	684
1709	Other articles of paper and paperboard	2534	2459	2364	2395	33.9	33.6	33.5	32.3	1009	1008	1037	994
181	Printing and service activities related to printing	15851	15206	14869	15057	65.1	62.5	60.5	65.6	1654	1594	1569	1737
1811	Printing	12370	11872	11610	11813	52.3	50.4	48.7	53.8	1335	1287	1263	1437
1812	Service activities related to printing	3481	3334	3259	3244	12.8	12.1	11.9	11.9	319	308	305	300
1820	Reproduction of recorded media	280	263	240	229	0.8	0.5	0.4	0.3	26	12	12	9
1910	Coke oven products	4	294a/	281a/	291a/	0.3	11.1a/	10.9a/	10.9a/	10	531a/	552a/	539a/
1920	Refined petroleum products	293	...a/	...a/	...a/	12.9	...a/	...a/	...a/	610	...a/	...a/	...a/
201	Basic chemicals,fertilizers, etc.	1067	1048	1023	1008	38.0	36.8	36.5	37.2	1534	1488	1558	1615
2011	Basic chemicals	499	492	466	455	22.5	21.6	21.2	21.3	938	888	930	957
2012	Fertilizers and nitrogen compounds	179	184	180	182	2.5	2.7	2.8	2.8	91	100	106	110
2013	Plastics and synthetic rubber in primary forms	389	372	377	371	13.0	12.5	12.6	13.0	506	499	522	548
202	Other chemical products	3287	3252	3262	3281	64.5	63.8	62.9	64.6	2360	2344	2380	2431
2021	Pesticides and other agrochemical products	45	43	40	37	1.9	2.2	1.9	1.9	82	103	88	92
2022	Paints,varnishes;printing ink and mastics	838	836	831	800	18.4	18.2	17.8	18.0	660	671	680	692
2023	Soap,cleaning and cosmetic preparations	1374	1373	1414	1442	24.8	24.7	24.8	25.9	851	828	861	869
2029	Other chemical products n.e.c.	1030	1000	977	1002	19.3	18.7	18.3	18.8	768	742	751	779
2030	Man-made fibres	36	24	23	23	2.5	2.1	2.0	2.1	72	67	69	72
2100	Pharmaceuticals,medicinal chemicals, etc.	464	446	453	456	59.7	56.8	57.4	58.3	2914	2745	2792	2884
221	Rubber products	1408	1395	1375	1351	37.5	37.4	37.2	37.2	1212	1239	1280	1272
2211	Rubber tyres and tubes	138	131	116	119	11.2	10.6	10.1	9.9	442	430	440	415
2219	Other rubber products	1270	1264	1259	1232	26.3	26.7	27.1	27.3	770	809	840	858
2220	Plastics products	8882	8699	8596	8508	125.0	121.9	121.6	124.5	3473	3471	3575	3718
2310	Glass and glass products	3865	3652	3545	3518	31.2	30.3	29.5	29.7	917	907	904	930
239	Non-metallic mineral products n.e.c.	16866	16179	15644	15455	122.1	112.7	105.3	103.1	3226	3087	3061	3115
2391	Refractory products	120	113	105	108	2.4	2.4	2.4	2.3	80	81	81	86
2392	Clay building materials	729	702	675	642	27.6	25.8	24.0	23.7	862	850	856	891
2393	Other porcelain and ceramic products	2416	2284	2242	2226	9.9	8.9	8.4	8.4	211	203	202	212
2394	Cement, lime and plaster	180	172	158	156	8.9	8.0	7.3	6.9	305	293	280	272
2395	Articles of concrete, cement and plaster	3302	3203	3068	3043	34.4	31.7	29.1	28.1	825	776	768	771
2396	Cutting, shaping and finishing of stone	9116	8752	8488	8382	28.4	25.7	24.6	24.0	634	583	578	573
2399	Other non-metallic mineral products n.e.c.	1003	953	908	898	10.6	10.2	9.6	9.8	309	301	298	312
2410	Basic iron and steel	1877	1781	1722	1685	71.8	70.9	69.7	68.4	2330	2326	2279	2484
2420	Basic precious and other non-ferrous metals	665	636	647	688	17.6	17.5	17.2	17.5	541	558	584	598
243	Casting of metals	1111	1055	1038	1044	27.4	26.8	26.7	26.2	804	815	824	814
2431	Casting of iron and steel	187	177	176	185	9.5	9.2	9.0	9.1	287	284	283	282
2432	Casting of non-ferrous metals	924	878	862	859	17.9	17.6	17.7	17.2	517	531	542	531
251	Struct.metal products, tanks, reservoirs	33144	31837	30721	30377	137.5	130.8	126.6	126.1	3352	3221	3252	3276

continued

Italy

ISIC	Industry	Number of enterprises (number)					Number of employees (thousands)					Wages and salaries paid to employees (millions of Euros)				
		Note	2013	2014	2015	2016	Note	2013	2014	2015	2016	Note	2013	2014	2015	2016
2511	Structural metal products		32401	31122	30016	29687		123.5	116.7	112.3	111.7		2930	2798	2802	2810
2512	Tanks, reservoirs and containers of metal		614	592	584	575		11.7	11.6	11.7	11.9		336	334	348	364
2513	Steam generators, excl. hot water boilers		129	123	121	115		2.3	2.4	2.6	2.5		85	90	102	102
2520	Weapons and ammunition		248	224	205	207		6.9	6.8	6.8	5.6		280	275	286	222
259	Other metal products;metal working services		32244	32305	32259	32491		277.4	278.7	280.7	289.4		7773	7903	8194	8507
2591	Forging,pressing,stamping,roll-forming of metal		1432	1397	1422	1396		37.8	36.8	37.0	37.7		1178	1169	1219	1257
2592	Treatment and coating of metals;machining		14265	14891	15077	15437		104.8	110.9	113.2	118.9		2804	2977	3112	3278
2593	Cutlery, hand tools and general hardware		4863	4670	4540	4524		45.8	45.6	46.2	47.5		1360	1379	1449	1497
2599	Other fabricated metal products n.e.c.		11684	11347	11220	11134		89.1	85.4	84.4	85.3		2431	2378	2414	2474
2610	Electronic components and boards		2067	2046	1977	1952		34.4	32.2	32.0	32.2		1101	1029	1073	1094
2620	Computers and peripheral equipment		530	473	463	462		5.4	4.6	4.4	4.3		181	158	164	164
2630	Communication equipment		785	728	743	714		16.9	14.2	12.6	12.8		601	517	435	475
2640	Consumer electronics		209	183	...	...		2.2	2.1	...	...		64	62	...	...
265	Measuring,testing equipment; watches, etc.		852	836	833	861		25.7	26.7	27.1	17.6		1026	1064	1088	669
2651	Measuring/testing/navigating equipment,etc.		781	772	764	796		25.2	26.3	26.5	17.1		1013	1052	1068	651
2652	Watches and clocks		71	64	69	65		0.5	0.4	0.6	0.6		13	12	20	18
2660	Irradiation/electromedical equipment,etc.		621	593	580	556		11.8	11.8	11.4	10.5		408	406	409	373
2670	Optical instruments and photographic equipment		133	130	129	143		2.2	1.8	1.9	1.9		77	58	61	65
2680	Magnetic and optical media		22	18	...	...		0.1	0.1	...	...		1	1	...	...
2710	Electric motors,generators,transformers,etc.		2821	2738	2679	2541		49.5	49.5	49.2	49.5		1598	1649	1699	1766
2720	Batteries and accumulators		63	65	66	70		2.9	2.8	2.8	2.8		102	99	99	99
273	Wiring and wiring devices		942	961	912	924		15.5	15.4	14.6	15.1		441	450	428	453
2731	Fibre optic cables		30	31	29	25		1.1	0.7	0.7	0.7		53	22	23	24
2732	Other electronic and electric wires and cables		496	488	459	462		10.2	10.1	9.3	9.3		279	302	276	282
2733	Wiring devices		416	442	424	437		4.2	4.7	4.6	5.2		109	126	129	147
2740	Electric lighting equipment		1482	1448	1417	1391		14.4	14.2	15.6	16.0		405	409	458	472
2750	Domestic appliances		493	526	527	528		36.0	35.4	31.2	30.3		1034	1074	998	967
2790	Other electrical equipment		2939	2772	2762	2799		30.4	28.5	27.4	27.5		915	873	860	780
281	General-purpose machinery		10439	10644	10588	10430		239.8	242.8	243.1	249.8		8564	8781	8791	9053
2811	Engines/turbines,excl.aircraft,vehicle engines		192	187	183	194		14.4	17.0	14.3	13.8		639	917	641	565
2812	Fluid power equipment		252	260	290	283		14.8	14.7	16.2	16.1		550	545	607	606
2813	Other pumps, compressors, taps and valves		1650	1699	1642	1619		43.0	43.8	44.0	44.9		1448	1486	1524	1569
2814	Bearings, gears, gearing and driving elements		838	819	765	737		24.8	25.1	25.7	25.6		835	858	890	912
2815	Ovens, furnaces and furnace burners		570	562	567	560		11.6	11.3	11.9	11.8		369	357	403	398
2816	Lifting and handling equipment		1697	1578	1527	1514		29.5	29.0	29.0	29.9		961	976	1018	1057
2817	Office machinery, excl.computers,etc.		351	325	319	282		1.3	1.3	1.2	1.1		32	32	30	29
2818	Power-driven hand tools		30	24	28	29		0.3	0.2	0.2	0.2		9	8	7	7
2819	Other general-purpose machinery		4859	5190	5267	5212		100.1	100.4	100.6	106.3		3721	3603	3671	3910
282	Special-purpose machinery		13178	12537	12173	12138		181.2	180.3	181.0	183.9		6011	6140	6330	6580
2821	Agricultural and forestry machinery		1908	1838	1791	1772		29.1	28.7	28.7	28.7		866	873	879	900
2822	Metal-forming machinery and machine tools		1837	1814	1762	1739		33.9	34.0	34.1	34.6		1163	1224	1253	1316

Code		A	B	C	D	E	F	G	H	I	J	K	L
2823	Machinery for metallurgy	2082	1905	1800	1801	20.0	18.8	18.7	18.7	688	646	655	666
2824	Mining, quarrying and construction machinery	1144	1012	951	920	18.5	17.4	16.9	16.6	553	536	538	545
2825	Food/beverage/tobacco processing machinery	2294	2182	2155	2183	28.7	28.5	28.6	29.8	970	988	998	1064
2826	Textile/apparel/leather production machinery	1026	973	921	924	12.0	12.0	11.8	12.1	378	389	396	415
2829	Other special-purpose machinery	2887	2813	2793	2799	39.0	40.9	42.3	43.4	1394	1485	1611	1674
2910	Motor vehicles	154	144	135	124	65.1	65.1	65.9	66.6	1675	1925	2108	2167
2920	Automobile bodies, trailers and semi-trailers	721	704	700	696	10.5	9.5	9.3	9.5	268	248	270	290
2930	Parts and accessories for motor vehicles	1451	1405	1407	1447	83.2	82.1	82.7	83.7	2549	2617	2768	2827
301	Building of ships and boats	1261	1183	1218	1275	21.3	21.2	21.8	22.9	671	681	729	774
3011	Building of ships and floating structures	760	706	671	705	13.7	14.3	15.1	16.1	458	480	521	555
3012	Building of pleasure and sporting boats	501	477	547	570	7.5	6.9	6.6	6.8	213	201	209	219
3020	Railway locomotives and rolling stock	..	132	..	..	..	10.6	..	..	..	384	..	..
3030	Air and spacecraft and related machinery	173	184	188	187	30.3	32.6	31.8	43.9	1178	1384	1338	1969
3040	Military fighting vehicles	..	-	..	..	..	-	..	..	..	-	..	..
309	Transport equipment n.e.c.	910	889	870	857	16.4	15.7	15.3	15.4	462	462	471	485
3091	Motorcycles	375	375	374	375	10.9	10.3	10.1	10.4	319	321	331	347
3092	Bicycles and invalid carriages	502	485	469	455	5.2	5.1	5.0	4.7	133	131	132	131
3099	Other transport equipment n.e.c.	33	29	27	27	0.4	0.3	0.3	0.2	10	10	9	7
3100	Furniture	18773	18130	18108	18615	115.9	110.9	107.0	109.0	2634	2601	2671	2777
321	Jewellery, bijouterie and related articles	8088	7821	7714	7698	20.0	20.6	20.8	21.3	435	462	485	484
3211	Jewellery and related articles	6529	6248	6112	6088	18.3	18.9	19.1	19.5	404	424	446	443
3212	Imitation jewellery and related articles	1559	1573	1602	1610	1.7	1.7	1.7	1.8	31	37	39	41
3220	Musical instruments	659	647	654	690	1.3	1.1	1.1	1.1	28	25	24	26
3230	Sports goods	625	617	614	634	4.0	4.0	4.4	4.6	113	120	140	146
3240	Games and toys	401	380	371	359	2.4	2.6	2.5	2.3	62	65	63	64
3250	Medical and dental instruments and supplies	17288	17028	16753	16760	36.8	36.5	38.2	41.3	946	989	1076	1163
3290	Other manufacturing n.e.c.	3504	3428	3382	3377	14.9	15.0	14.6	15.0	338	352	352	365
331	Repair of fabricated metal products/machinery	31757	31278	31061	30519	75.3	75.2	77.8	79.2	1937	1965	2098	2110
3311	Repair of fabricated metal products	3497	3422	3510	3525	7.9	7.2	7.8	8.7	192	176	194	215
3312	Repair of machinery	19197	19072	18903	18479	42.1	41.6	42.9	43.8	1056	1056	1127	1150
3313	Repair of electronic and optical equipment	4367	3974	3840	3655	9.1	9.0	8.9	7.9	268	272	274	226
3314	Repair of electrical equipment	1914	1960	1912	1872	5.6	5.8	5.8	5.6	148	157	163	158
3315	Repair of transport equip., excl. motor vehicles	2235	2251	2255	2330	9.9	10.8	11.6	12.4	257	290	324	343
3319	Repair of other equipment	547	599	641	658	0.8	0.7	0.7	0.8	17	15	16	18
3320	Installation of industrial machinery/equipment	8439	8001	7897	8060	42.6	37.6	37.6	36.7	1255	1087	1124	1084
C	Total manufacturing	407344	396422	389317	387866	3202.8	3148.1	3122.4	3174.7	92213	92549	94528	97490

a/ 1910 includes 1920.

Italy

ISIC	Industry	Note	Output (valuation not defined) (millions of Euros)				Note	Value added at factor values (millions of Euros)				Note	Gross fixed capital formation (millions of Euros)	
			2013	2014	2015	2016		2013	2014	2015	2016		2015	2016
1010	Processing/preserving of meat		22865	23057	23282	21772		2735	2850	3018	3101		413	481
1020	Processing/preserving of fish, etc.		2065	2071	2199	2366		346	356	366	403		38	41
1030	Processing/preserving of fruit,vegetables		9499	10136	10529	10746		1553	1689	1755	1939		408	473
1040	Vegetable and animal oils and fats		6814	6213	7383	7663		656	613	720	674		159	139
1050	Dairy products		18559	18440	17816	17907		2678	2749	2873	2830		399	427
106	Grain mill products,starches and starch products		6500	7419	6984	6861		760	829	827	963		127	161
1061	Grain mill products		5186	6277	5905	5656		565	621	611	749		98	135
1062	Starches and starch products		1314	1142	1079	1205		195	208	217	214		29	26
107	Other food products		36176	36318	38126	39387		9907	10025	10274	10816		1428	1518
1071	Bakery products		10643	10630	11216	11477		3766	3812	3959	4164		385	474
1072	Sugar		715	575	429	447		66	32	48	62		16	15
1073	Cocoa, chocolate and sugar confectionery		6559	6607	6760	7307		1773	1616	1732	1759		210	140
1074	Macaroni, noodles, couscous, etc.		6741	6791	7302	7256		1555	1536	1598	1787		252	287
1075	Prepared meals and dishes		1263	1334	1316	1387		295	336	326	352		127	92
1079	Other food products n.e.c.		10255	10380	11104	11513		2453	2693	2612	2693		438	511
1080	Prepared animal feeds		5380	4692	5007	5077		599	625	617	681		90	94
110	Beverages		17513	18225	18837	20311		3275	3445	3772	4136		559	982
1101	Distilling, rectifying and blending of spirits		2574	2664	2589	2751		642	621	659	743		58	52
1102	Wines		...	...	...	...		...	...	...	...		...	...
1103	Malt liquors and malt		...	...	...	...		...	...	...	...		...	...
1104	Soft drinks,mineral waters,other bottled waters		4757	4759	5228	5176		976	926	1193	1232		130	343
1200	Tobacco products		135	138	118	532		55	50	52	135		4	6
131	Spinning, weaving and finishing of textiles		12769	12914	12767	11662		3422	3686	3658	3404		334	437
1311	Preparation and spinning of textile fibres		3813	3746	3723	3676		826	885	892	876		92	80
1312	Weaving of textiles		6159	6343	6264	6085		1549	1697	1659	1661		116	207
1313	Finishing of textiles		2798	2825	2780	1902		1048	1104	1107	867		126	151
139	Other textiles		8109	8389	8555	8841		2110	2252	2337	2521		193	289
1391	Knitted and crocheted fabrics		945	903	827	818		282	282	273	270		29	45
1392	Made-up textile articles, except apparel		2228	2186	2267	2402		541	554	568	632		16	44
1393	Carpets and rugs		233	240	274	272		56	61	68	67		9	9
1394	Cordage, rope, twine and netting		181	177	197	212		40	41	45	47		7	10
1399	Other textiles n.e.c.		4522	4883	4990	5137		1191	1315	1383	1505		132	181
1410	Wearing apparel, except fur apparel		23722	23411	23536	23764		5562	5832	5840	6255		389	362
1420	Articles of fur		202	198	179	193		56	58	47	56		-	3
1430	Knitted and crocheted apparel		4261	4279	4046	4085		1147	1214	1137	1171		83	104
151	Leather;luggage,handbags,saddlery,harness;fur		14010	14957	14496	14227		3301	3595	3525	3435		381	372
1511	Tanning/dressing of leather; dressing of fur		7037	7644	7298	7080		1242	1301	1290	1339		147	176
1512	Luggage,handbags,etc.;saddlery/harness		6974	7313	7198	7147		2060	2294	2235	2095		234	195
1520	Footwear		13793	14217	13975	14024		3377	3465	3557	3732		224	199
1610	Sawmilling and planing of wood		2057	2008	2042	2033		549	510	512	502		57	71

Code	Product									
162	Wood products, cork, straw, plaiting materials	11167	10985	10671	10936	3078	3044	3050	3216	578	391
1621	Veneer sheets and wood-based panels	1888	1878	1948	2039	406	431	470	575	124	147
1622	Builders' carpentry and joinery	6550	6211	5881	5882	1993	1914	1884	1888	364	152
1623	Wooden containers	1410	1618	1579	1692	330	372	361	392	41	61
1629	Other wood products;articles of cork,straw	1319	1278	1263	1324	349	326	336	361	48	31
170	Paper and paper products	20992	21684	22361	22328	4594	4998	4952	5321	869	1091
1701	Pulp, paper and paperboard	4889	4681	4959	5482	883	980	990	1226	224	324
1702	Corrugated paper and paperboard	6211	6627	6920	7157	1309	1482	1496	1681	232	290
1709	Other articles of paper and paperboard	9892	10376	10482	9690	2402	2537	2466	2414	413	477
181	Printing and service activities related to printing	10380	9824	10091	10853	3441	3478	3504	3895	244	591
1811	Printing	8691	8209	8479	9346	2805	2831	2894	3302	211	509
1812	Service activities related to printing	1689	1615	1612	1507	636	647	610	593	32	83
1820	Reproduction of recorded media	320	96	89	76	58	24	21	24	1	2
1910	Coke oven products	160	34050a/	32122a/	26947a/	24	-346a/	1351a/	1964a/	449a/	396a/
1920	Refined petroleum products	46115	...a/	...a/	...a/	747	...a/	...a/	...a/	...a/	...a/
201	Basic chemicals,fertilizers, etc.	23934	23262	23341	23138	3572	3532	4200	4904	800	952
2011	Basic chemicals	14185	13172	13347	13368	2007	1838	2282	2712	549	679
2012	Fertilizers and nitrogen compounds	1716	1816	1663	1522	251	336	299	296	25	45
2013	Plastics and synthetic rubber in primary forms	8034	8274	8331	8249	1314	1358	1619	1896	226	228
202	Other chemical products	25607	24878	25219	24990	5869	5952	6213	6545	791	803
2021	Pesticides and other agrochemical products	866	1159	993	953	182	226	218	234	19	24
2022	Paints,varnishes;printing ink and mastics	5844	5870	5920	5994	1494	1539	1576	1623	171	144
2023	Soap,cleaning and cosmetic preparations	8479	8230	8755	8551	2180	2184	2299	2446	375	348
2029	Other chemical products n.e.c.	10417	9619	9551	9493	2013	2002	2121	2242	227	287
2030	Man-made fibres	1082	1262	1194	1161	180	147	174	175	14	19
2100	Pharmaceuticals,medicinal chemicals, etc.	25144	23839	24151	23981	8011	7649	8050	8330	852	998
221	Rubber products	8877	9010	9496	9352	2671	2854	3018	3076	350	343
2211	Rubber tyres and tubes	3628	3389	3581	3519	977	1006	1121	1129	116	143
2219	Other rubber products	5250	5621	5914	5833	1693	1848	1897	1947	234	200
2220	Plastics products	30177	30871	31385	31808	7463	7723	8137	8646	1160	1527
2310	Glass and glass products	6042	5841	5955	5841	1998	1887	1968	2148	430	531
239	Non-metallic mineral products n.e.c.	23442	22520	22647	22852	6378	6420	6531	6844	920	1049
2391	Refractory products	532	550	507	566	163	175	164	166	8	14
2392	Clay building materials	5395	5482	5768	6153	1621	1807	1904	2133	341	471
2393	Other porcelain and ceramic products	987	1067	901	1029	387	389	374	415	18	28
2394	Cement, lime and plaster	2325	2143	1977	1904	609	561	475	483	151	135
2395	Articles of concrete, cement and plaster	6746	6246	6352	6234	1541	1473	1541	1544	163	242
2396	Cutting, shaping and finishing of stone	4756	4354	4523	4294	1390	1330	1366	1357	171	94
2399	Other non-metallic mineral products n.e.c.	2699	2678	2619	2672	668	685	707	747	68	64
2410	Basic iron and steel	34421	34366	31312	30625	4286	4881	4418	5107	945	1009
2420	Basic precious and other non-ferrous metals	13731	13630	14073	13677	1070	1273	1476	1466	273	353
243	Casting of metals	6381	6322	6510	6234	1552	1672	1713	1800	290	361
2431	Casting of iron and steel	2100	2115	2065	2055	579	607	589	638	107	119
2432	Casting of non-ferrous metals	4281	4207	4444	4179	972	1065	1124	1162	183	242
251	Struct.metal products, tanks, reservoirs	22579	21431	22010	21758	6773	6619	6805	6779	447	591

continued

Italy

ISIC Revision 4		Note	Output (valuation not defined) (millions of Euros)				Note	Value added at factor values (millions of Euros)				Note	Gross fixed capital formation (millions of Euros)	
ISIC	Industry		2013	2014	2015	2016		2013	2014	2015	2016		2015	2016
2511	Structural metal products		19641	18600	18752	18523		5955	5823	5947	5973		379	493
2512	Tanks, reservoirs and containers of metal		2351	2255	2379	2401		654	651	697	688		60	92
2513	Steam generators, excl. hot water boilers		586	576	879	835		164	145	160	118		8	6
2520	Weapons and ammunition		1825	1753	1868	1375		562	624	645	502		40	38
259	Other metal products;metal working services		51563	52003	53298	53102		16857	17642	18323	19319		2590	2005
2591	Forging,pressing,stamping,roll-forming of metal		10681	10244	10442	9986		2708	2677	2802	2817		664	438
2592	Treatment and coating of metals; machining		16104	16949	17562	17475		5892	6525	6830	7395		963	558
2593	Cutlery, hand tools and general hardware		7315	7630	7889	8252		2868	3044	3184	3358		282	298
2599	Other fabricated metal products n.e.c.		17464	17180	17406	17390		5389	5396	5507	5751		681	711
2610	Electronic components and boards		5691	5486	5756	5683		2049	1951	2014	1890		199	227
2620	Computers and peripheral equipment		1576	1221	1235	1259		314	250	322	352		11	20
2630	Communication equipment		3640	3209	2753	3088		1110	1014	936	900		58	75
2640	Consumer electronics		584	517	:	:		131	137	:	:		:	:
265	Measuring,testing equipment; watches, etc.		4938	5544	5791	3858		1709	1932	2056	1446		117	93
2651	Measuring/testing/navigating equipment,etc.		4778	5374	5554	3666		1675	1894	2000	1397		110	91
2652	Watches and clocks		160	170	237	192		34	38	56	49		7	2
2660	Irradiation/electromedical equipment,etc.		3012	2596	2680	2367		937	886	905	786		145	105
2670	Optical instruments and photographic equipment		593	458	504	512		172	139	154	156		8	9
2680	Magnetic and optical media		10	14	:	:		3	3	:	:		:	:
2710	Electric motors,generators,transformers,etc.		12360	12009	12660	12785		3957	3567	3803	3775		274	340
2720	Batteries and accumulators		1128	1124	1242	1319		191	173	198	207		33	47
273	Wiring and wiring devices		6631	6478	5690	5626		1009	928	929	1004		114	130
2731	Fibre optic cables		682	120	170	166		64	30	37	40		11	10
2732	Other electronic and electric wires and cables		5294	5578	4695	4451		723	632	621	623		84	91
2733	Wiring devices		655	780	826	1009		222	266	270	341		19	30
2740	Electric lighting equipment		3072	3140	3554	3772		867	842	1028	1115		78	105
2750	Domestic appliances		7807	8893	8389	7862		1952	2090	2054	1949		194	217
2790	Other electrical equipment		6471	6126	6165	6443		1998	1931	1941	2089		85	127
281	General-purpose machinery		64748	66506	64018	66299		18718	19699	19397	19953		1806	1979
2811	Engines/turbines,excl.aircraft,vehicle engines		6250	10288	5996	5730		1609	2325	1621	1344		135	162
2812	Fluid power equipment		3686	3663	3893	3796		1195	1184	1301	1266		152	195
2813	Other pumps, compressors, taps and valves		11568	12224	12194	12600		3579	3796	3802	3885		446	429
2814	Bearings, gears, gearing and driving elements		5297	5595	5809	5903		1697	1856	1888	1918		177	155
2815	Ovens, furnaces and furnace burners		2675	2504	2873	2810		736	697	813	785		85	151
2816	Lifting and handling equipment		7226	7575	8166	8431		1926	2046	2127	2247		195	220
2817	Office machinery, excl.computers,etc.		202	187	195	193		56	55	57	52		5	2
2818	Power-driven hand tools		57	55	60	69		19	17	17	20		1	3
2819	Other general-purpose machinery		27789	24415	24832	26766		7902	7723	7771	8436		611	663
282	Special-purpose machinery		43922	44538	47983	47269		12146	12685	13582	14201		822	1053
2821	Agricultural and forestry machinery		7930	7587	8230	7900		1789	1793	1925	1967		159	151
2822	Metal-forming machinery and machine tools		7297	7555	8301	8584		2201	2393	2630	2788		185	300

2823	Machinery for metallurgy	4953	4511	4663	4200	1416	1323	1337	1366	83	97
2824	Mining, quarrying and construction machinery	4403	4232	4586	4313	980	1005	1087	1036	70	73
2825	Food/beverage/tobacco processing machinery	6823	7212	7237	7391	2107	2206	2277	2498	81	162
2826	Textile/apparel/leather production machinery	2682	2753	2899	2999	843	836	853	943	57	48
2829	Other special-purpose machinery	9833	10689	12067	11882	2811	3129	3474	3604	187	223
2910	Motor vehicles	25163	28277	33575	38208	3547	3664	4404	5427	2105	2171
2920	Automobile bodies, trailers and semi-trailers	1938	1971	2123	2537	424	433	521	578	74	98
2930	Parts and accessories for motor vehicles	18683	19752	21465	21770	4946	5181	5540	5860	849	862
301	Building of ships and boats	5939	6391	6669	7509	1062	1244	1152	1566	180	283
3011	Building of ships and floating structures	4220	4725	4900	5500	779	944	814	1110	95	210
3012	Building of pleasure and sporting boats	1720	1666	1769	2009	282	300	339	456	84	73
3020	Railway locomotives and rolling stock	...	3154	...	...	690	...	...	...	...	...
3030	Air and spacecraft and related machinery	8600	10283	10935	11824	2454	3060	2995	4362	208	258
3040	Military fighting vehicles	...	-	...	...	...	-	...	...	...	...
309	Transport equipment n.e.c.	3818	3677	3990	3992	813	866	853	933	105	108
3091	Motorcycles	2522	2413	2681	2756	518	562	553	637	85	84
3092	Bicycles and invalid carriages	1245	1211	1263	1201	277	284	282	283	20	23
3099	Other transport equipment n.e.c.	51	53	46	35	18	20	18	14	1	1
3100	Furniture	19456	20101	20989	22004	5106	5280	5627	6036	557	790
321	Jewellery, bijouterie and related articles	5187	5502	5474	5677	1032	1133	1144	1163	80	121
3211	Jewellery and related articles	4905	5123	5102	5303	943	1007	1018	1034	74	112
3212	Imitation jewellery and related articles	282	379	372	374	89	126	126	129	6	8
3220	Musical instruments	153	138	139	156	62	56	58	58	6	4
3230	Sports goods	1164	1249	1563	1285	264	290	358	402	34	37
3240	Games and toys	584	608	574	641	110	132	140	178	20	50
3250	Medical and dental instruments and supplies	5684	6022	6709	7223	2286	2406	2622	2818	208	284
3290	Other manufacturing n.e.c.	2436	2598	2571	2772	741	773	776	815	72	102
331	Repair of fabricated metal products/machinery	10054	10363	10712	10839	4390	4502	4774	4822	291	427
3311	Repair of fabricated metal products	903	839	895	977	406	395	431	464	20	39
3312	Repair of machinery	5774	5953	5989	6234	2500	2526	2659	2694	187	242
3313	Repair of electronic and optical equipment	1318	1326	1312	1113	603	624	617	568	38	22
3314	Repair of electrical equipment	758	848	896	903	340	374	393	402	12	24
3315	Repair of transport equip., excl. motor vehicles	1178	1296	1510	1493	505	549	634	652	31	94
3319	Repair of other equipment	123	101	110	120	35	35	39	41	4	6
3320	Installation of industrial machinery/equipment	7163	6447	6683	6437	2461	2204	2309	2295	376	60
C	Total manufacturing	853491	849097	864159	867728	198679	204054	212950	224995	26501	29478

a/ 1910 includes 1920.

Italy

Index numbers of industrial production (2010=100)

ISIC Revision 4

ISIC	Industry	Note	2005	2006	2007	2008	2009	2010	2011	2012	2013	2014	2015	2016
10	Food products		97	98	99	99	98	100	99	98	97	98	98	100
11	Beverages		95	100	102	99	100	100	102	102	98	96	98	97
12	Tobacco products		142	136	126	110	114	100	13	14	14	16	10	9
13	Textiles		132	132	128	112	89	100	95	85	85	87	86	84
14	Wearing apparel		75	85	96	101	96	100	93	85	77	75	77	72
15	Leather and related products		131	130	127	116	99	100	102	98	100	98	92	91
16	Wood products, excluding furniture		151	152	150	130	101	100	96	83	77	73	71	72
17	Paper and paper products		106	109	112	106	95	100	100	96	97	99	100	97
18	Printing and reproduction of recorded media		117	111	108	111	100	100	98	87	76	73	71	66
19	Coke and refined petroleum products		112	111	112	107	97	100	96	90	80	76	84	82
20	Chemicals and chemical products		106	110	115	107	93	100	96	91	90	90	92	93
21	Pharmaceuticals, medicinal chemicals, etc.		96	102	96	99	99	100	101	100	105	103	110	111
22	Rubber and plastics products		116	118	125	118	96	100	102	94	95	98	102	103
23	Other non-metallic mineral products		139	138	137	129	99	100	99	89	81	80	80	81
24	Basic metals		118	126	127	119	83	100	105	98	91	93	92	95
25	Fabricated metal products, except machinery		129	129	138	133	94	100	105	96	97	96	93	95
26	Computer, electronic and optical products		108	112	112	103	93	100	97	88	86	88	91	93
27	Electrical equipment		127	135	133	122	88	100	95	84	84	74	76	73
28	Machinery and equipment n.e.c.		120	127	132	128	86	100	108	105	100	99	100	102
29	Motor vehicles, trailers and semi-trailers		113	122	132	128	84	100	101	85	82	84	108	114
30	Other transport equipment		99	111	119	125	110	100	95	93	87	95	96	99
31	Furniture		114	110	115	119	99	100	99	92	83	82	81	82
32	Other manufacturing		113	121	115	101	85	100	99	94	95	100	100	98
33	Repair and installation of machinery/equipment		85	91	97	104	89	100	108	97	89	85	88	91
C	Total manufacturing		113	116	120	116	93	100	101	94	92	91	93	94

Japan

Supplier of information:
Ministry of Economy, Trade and Industry (METI), Tokyo. Industrial statistics for the OECD countries are compiled by the OECD secretariat, which supplies them to UNIDO.

Basic source of data:
Manufacturing census; survey.

Major deviations from ISIC (Revision 4):
Data presented in ISIC (Revision 4) were originally classified according to the Japanese Standard Industrial Classification (JSIC).

Reference period:
Calendar year.

Scope:
Census covers all establishments in years ending with 0, 3, 5 or 8. For other years, establishments with four or more employees are covered; data on wages and investment refer to establishments with 30 or more employees.

Method of data collection:
Data are collected by mail/online questionnaires and field enumerators.

Type of enumeration:
Not reported.

Adjusted for non-response:
No.

Concepts and definitions of variables:
Wages and salaries relates to total cash payments, including basic wages, bonuses and other premiums, allowances and employees' retirement and termination allowances.

Related national publications:
None reported.

Japan

ISIC Revision 4

ISIC	Industry		Number of establishments (number)					Number of employees (thousands)					Wages and salaries paid to employees (billions of Japanese Yen)			
		Note	2011	2012	2013	2014	Note	2011	2012	2013	2014	Note	2011	2012	2013	2014
10	Food products		…	30952	…	…		…	1103.9	1114.6	1114.0		…	2335.3	2353.8	2366.5
11	Beverages		…	2103	…	…		…	62.6	62.6	61.9		…	190.0	193.3	190.4
12	Tobacco products		…	12	…	…		…	2.9	2.7	2.6		…	21.5	21.1	19.6
13	Textiles		…	7937	…	…		…	134.0	130.1	129.1		…	236.6	233.9	234.9
14	Wearing apparel		…	6979	…	…		…	131.2	126.2	119.7		…	148.0	145.8	138.7
15	Leather and related products		…	1833	…	…		…	25.7	26.2	25.2		…	32.9	33.6	34.0
16	Wood products, excluding furniture		…	8890	…	…		…	118.9	116.5	114.9		…	172.4	176.8	180.1
17	Paper and paper products		…	6382	…	…		…	178.4	174.9	174.3		…	531.3	529.8	526.2
18	Printing and reproduction of recorded media		…	12898	…	…		…	284.6	279.3	269.7		…	721.4	724.2	706.5
19	Coke and refined petroleum products		…	915	…	…		…	23.3	23.1	23.4		…	120.6	116.2	110.4
20	Chemicals and chemical products		…	4104	…	…		…	243.0	243.1	241.4		…	1191.2	1177.8	1207.6
21	Pharmaceuticals, medicinal chemicals, etc.		…	800	…	…		…	88.6	88.5	89.1		…	447.9	446.3	447.6
22	Rubber and plastics products		…	16074	…	…		…	497.3	482.9	477.0		…	1477.4	1481.9	1487.1
23	Other non-metallic mineral products		…	10260	…	…		…	226.3	224.5	223.1		…	578.9	590.8	605.7
24	Basic metals		…	6881	…	…		…	301.8	296.0	294.6		…	1295.6	1276.8	1323.9
25	Fabricated metal products, except machinery		…	28779	…	…		…	586.8	580.2	579.8		…	1506.7	1492.5	1508.3
26	Computer, electronic and optical products		…	9700	…	…		…	649.0	627.7	612.8		…	2937.6	2811.2	2868.8
27	Electrical equipment		…	9871	…	…		…	386.4	385.9	393.3		…	1516.6	1530.8	1621.7
28	Machinery and equipment n.e.c.		…	28080	…	…		…	864.3	863.7	866.5		…	3189.9	3222.5	3284.0
29	Motor vehicles, trailers and semi-trailers		…	8889	…	…		…	814.1	825.2	825.9		…	4093.3	4245.1	4388.1
30	Other transport equipment		…	2331	…	…		…	117.1	119.2	117.2		…	519.9	551.0	537.1
31	Furniture		…	4553	…	…		…	76.0	76.9	76.5		…	163.2	170.4	168.7
32	Other manufacturing		…	6102	…	…		…	147.1	147.7	146.8		…	399.6	417.2	423.0
33	Repair and installation of machinery/equipment		…	-	-	-		…	-	-	-		…	-	-	-
C	Total manufacturing		…	215325	208029	…		…	7063.4	7017.8	6978.7		…	23828.0	23942.9	24378.9

Japan

ISIC Revision 4		Output (valuation not defined) (billions of Japanese Yen)					Value added at basic prices (billions of Japanese Yen)					Gross fixed capital formation (billions of Japanese Yen)		
ISIC	Industry	Note	2011	2012	2013	2014	Note	2011	2012	2013	2014	Note	2013	2014
10	Food products		…	24821.1	25438.5	26403.1		…	8907.1	8973.8	9088.7		741.4	774.8
11	Beverages		…	5506.1	5451.4	5540.5		…	1942.1	1837.3	1836.6		143.2	168.0
12	Tobacco products		…	2257.1	2175.7	2131.8		…	518.4	475.3	467.3		58.6	72.1
13	Textiles		…	2232.8	2128.3	2202.1		…	886.0	845.3	853.4		41.7	60.3
14	Wearing apparel		…	1039.1	978.6	948.3		…	509.4	493.2	463.7		10.9	10.0
15	Leather and related products		…	393.9	394.0	392.2		…	152.6	148.8	142.0		3.1	2.7
16	Wood products, excluding furniture		…	2473.2	2656.7	2727.3		…	889.1	930.3	923.6		50.3	57.3
17	Paper and paper products		…	6464.3	6373.4	6614.0		…	2127.4	2077.1	2061.7		254.3	248.8
18	Printing and reproduction of recorded media		…	5593.2	5550.1	5532.5		…	2534.0	2561.4	2571.4		134.4	141.0
19	Coke and refined petroleum products		…	16817.0	17482.2	18178.1		…	1030.1	1177.3	667.2		114.8	152.2
20	Chemicals and chemical products		…	18237.7	19679.4	20147.1		…	5878.0	6270.1	6228.7		720.3	751.6
21	Pharmaceuticals, medicinal chemicals, etc.		…	7489.8	7472.8	7369.4		…	4196.1	4192.6	3854.0		357.1	318.3
22	Rubber and plastics products		…	13505.9	13567.7	13939.5		…	5321.4	5319.5	5379.7		536.2	531.9
23	Other non-metallic mineral products		…	6298.7	6404.1	6701.8		…	2760.0	2866.7	2937.1		218.2	223.8
24	Basic metals		…	22822.2	22918.1	24689.1		…	4038.3	4421.0	4777.6		827.8	737.9
25	Fabricated metal products, except machinery		…	14158.1	13997.4	14499.0		…	5921.8	5881.5	5908.5		421.7	439.0
26	Computer, electronic and optical products		…	23166.9	22203.4	23689.9		…	7673.6	7823.8	8611.8		1081.7	1066.9
27	Electrical equipment		…	13255.8	13617.1	14926.5		…	4786.8	4779.5	5219.7		396.0	430.2
28	Machinery and equipment n.e.c.		…	27262.6	26578.4	28470.9		…	10440.3	10288.3	10845.6		769.4	807.7
29	Motor vehicles, trailers and semi-trailers		…	44887.8	46292.0	47823.4		…	13899.4	14787.8	15313.4		1235.3	1330.2
30	Other transport equipment		…	4582.0	4635.9	5152.7		…	1621.3	1622.9	1665.8		145.5	167.6
31	Furniture		…	1315.4	1407.9	1479.1		…	542.7	571.1	613.3		34.0	38.6
32	Other manufacturing		…	3462.8	3516.5	3651.8		…	1589.8	1585.6	1617.0		104.2	121.9
33	Repair and installation of machinery/equipment		…	-	-	-		…	-	-	-		-	-
C	Total manufacturing		…	268043.3	270919.7	283209.9		…	88165.5	89930.2	92048.1		8399.7	8652.7

Japan

Index numbers of industrial production

ISIC Revision 4

(2010=100)

ISIC	Industry	Note	2005	2006	2007	2008	2009	2010	2011	2012	2013	2014	2015	2016
10	Food products		...	...	...	101	101	100	100	102	102	101	102	103
11	Beverages		...	...	...	103	99	100	96	98	98	97	97	97
12	Tobacco products		...	...	...	...	...	...	...	...	...	...	...	...
13	Textiles		...	...	...	122	95	100	104	104	102	103	102	100
14	Wearing apparel		...	...	...	121	105	100	98	94	88	81	76	73
15	Leather and related products		...	...	...	127	103	100	96	92	86	83	76	74
16	Wood products, excluding furniture		...	...	...	116	98	100	101	100	104	101	95	101
17	Paper and paper products		...	...	...	109	95	100	98	97	98	99	99	100
18	Printing and reproduction of recorded media		...	...	...	99	98	100	95	96	92	91	89	87
19	Coke and refined petroleum products		...	...	...	106	100	100	94	94	95	91	91	91
20	Chemicals and chemical products		...	...	...	102	93	100	97	93	95	94	96	98
21	Pharmaceuticals,medicinal chemicals, etc.		...	...	...	...	...	...	...	...	...	...	...	...
22	Rubber and plastics products		...	...	...	109	89	100	98	98	98	98	96	97
23	Other non-metallic mineral products		...	...	...	108	84	100	97	97	100	102	99	99
24	Basic metals		...	...	...	111	80	100	97	98	97	99	94	95
25	Fabricated metal products, except machinery		...	...	...	119	99	100	99	101	99	99	96	95
26	Computer, electronic and optical products		...	...	...	106	82	100	91	87	84	86	89	86
27	Electrical equipment		...	...	...	109	86	100	100	100	105	107	101	99
28	Machinery and equipment n.e.c.		...	...	...	125	73	100	114	107	105	118	117	115
29	Motor vehicles, trailers and semi-trailers		...	...	...	118	78	100	89	103	101	102	99	100
30	Other transport equipment		...	...	...	99	96	100	106	98	95	100	96	99
31	Furniture		...	...	...	118	99	100	102	102	106	105	100	103
32	Other manufacturing		...	...	...	109	94	100	98	99	98	97	94	93
33	Repair and installation of machinery/equipment		...	...	...	...	...	...	...	...	...	...	...	...
C	Total manufacturing		...	...	...	111	87	100	97	98	97	99	98	98

Jordan

Supplier of information:
Department of Statistics, Amman.

Basic source of data:
Annual industrial survey.

Major deviations from ISIC (Revision 4):
None reported.

Reference period:
Calendar year.

Scope:
All establishments.

Method of data collection:
Direct interview in the field.

Type of enumeration:
Complete enumeration.

Adjusted for non-response:
Yes.

Concepts and definitions of variables:
Output refers to gross output and includes revenue from non-industrial activities.
Value added refers to total value added.

Related national publications:
Industry Survey (annual); Statistical Yearbook, both published by the Department of Statistics, Amman.

Jordan

ISIC	Industry	Note	Number of establishments (number) 2013	2014	2015	2016	Note	Number of employees (number) 2013	2014	2015	2016	Note	Wages and salaries paid to employees (thousands of Jordanian Dinars) 2013	2014	2015	2016
1010	Processing/preserving of meat		23	22	14	17		6779	6695	6954	7003		33776	33547	37295	40918
1020	Processing/preserving of fish, etc.		...	...	...	...		...	...	...	...		...	...	...	...
1030	Processing/preserving of fruit,vegetables		65	71	125	89		1631	1588	1747	2296		8281	8530	9945	13421
1040	Vegetable and animal oils and fats		35	110	136	137		959	1225	1073	1379		6878	7838	8690	9107
1050	Dairy products		737	736	392	382		3876	4151	4223	6009		12705	13265	20314	30118
106	Grain mill products,starches and starch products		103	103	111	...		1023	1061	1055	...		5848	6708	6164	...
1061	Grain mill products		103	103	111	74		1023	1061	1055	1042		5848	6708	6164	7419
1062	Starches and starch products															
107	Other food products		3175	3167	3985	...		21501	22177	23012	...		79161	85398	98545	...
1071	Bakery products		2179	2173	3098	3012		15483	15984	16307	20004		54463	58824	66458	78345
1072	Sugar															
1073	Cocoa, chocolate and sugar confectionery		127	127	71	57		1778	1765	1775	2283		7140	8683	9920	11479
1074	Macaroni, noodles, couscous, etc.															
1075	Prepared meals and dishes															
1079	Other food products n.e.c.		869	867	816	768		4240	4428	4930	5512		17558	17891	22167	24382
1080	Prepared animal feeds		151	148	164	137		1067	1048	1089	1154		5203	6033	6728	6397
110	Beverages		131	133	91	...		4311	4021	4998	...		34238	35315	40166	...
1101	Distilling, rectifying and blending of spirits		2	2	3	2		182	200	208	353		1344	1636	1761	2121
1102	Wines															
1103	Malt liquors and malt		3	3	3	3		231	234	207	240		2748	2975	1678	1792
1104	Soft drinks,mineral waters,other bottled waters		126	128	85	79		3898	3587	4583	3980		30146	30704	36727	31271
1200	Tobacco products		36	42	36	30		1681	1946	1761	1145		10049	10656	10773	8256
131	Spinning, weaving and finishing of textiles		6	6	11	...		296	231	219	...		2323	2162	1674	...
1311	Preparation and spinning of textile fibres															
1312	Weaving of textiles		6	6	11	9		296	231	219	229		2323	2162	1674	2350
1313	Finishing of textiles															
139	Other textiles		709	709	726	...		2117	2032	2357	...		5308	5491	10408	...
1391	Knitted and crocheted fabrics															
1392	Made-up textile articles, except apparel		650	650	637	633		1324	1285	1364	894		2043	2145	4504	2999
1393	Carpets and rugs		19	19	22	28		490	505	690	1017		2685	2929	5679	11358
1394	Cordage, rope, twine and netting															
1399	Other textiles n.e.c.		40	40	67	55		303	242	303	296		580	417	225	486
1410	Wearing apparel, except fur apparel		2139	2134	3035	3087		28817	30999	33093	47721		85380	97278	111441	144723
1420	Articles of fur		9	9	2	5		28	30	44	47		89	112	237	203
1430	Knitted and crocheted apparel		32	32	20	18		965	780	219	187		2410	2121	983	962
151	Leather;luggage,handbags,saddlery,harness;fur		36	30	33	...		1128	330	230	...		948	1362	735	...
1511	Tanning/dressing of leather; dressing of fur		14	8	9	11		86	90	72	87		278	417	457	313
1512	Luggage,handbags,etc.;saddlery/harness		22	22	24	34		221	240	158	179		670	945	278	584
1520	Footwear		77	75	88	76		821	915	1345	1400		3465	3829	4462	4515
1610	Sawmilling and planing of wood		18	18	21	20		156	156	168	136		1084	1118	252	537

ISIC Revision 4

Code	Industry	A1	A2	A3	A4	B1	B2	B3	B4	C1	C2	C3	C4
162	Wood products, cork, straw, plaiting materials	4818	5728	8681	…	3162	3160	4520	…	1361	1359	1765	…
1621	Veneer sheets and wood-based panels	94	108	16	101	53	61	66	103	34	34	32	43
1622	Builders' carpentry and joinery	3399	3820	6815	10848	2367	2296	3708	4541	1059	1058	1531	1514
1623	Wooden containers	713	1051	921	927	304	344	374	415	66	66	68	79
1629	Other wood products;articles of cork,straw	612	749	929	492	438	459	372	296	202	201	134	133
170	Paper and paper products	31758	26397	29876	…	4199	4089	3563	…	114	117	138	…
1701	Pulp, paper and paperboard	3376	2622	2764	3077	416	380	528	572	17	17	13	14
1702	Corrugated paper and paperboard	6576	6818	10541	17150	1153	1139	1379	2029	65	65	70	70
1709	Other articles of paper and paperboard	21806	16957	16571	22809	2630	2570	1656	2431	32	35	55	45
181	Printing and service activities related to printing	31978	36419	48590	…	5703	5750	5978	…	635	646	753	…
1811	Printing	28991	33310	47866	61602	5123	5166	5786	7126	554	557	716	770
1812	Service activities related to printing	2987	3109	724	1496	580	584	192	284	81	89	37	45
1820	Reproduction of recorded media	…	…	…	…	…	…	…	…	…	…	…	…
1910	Coke oven products	…	…	…	…	…	…	…	…	…	…	…	…
1920	Refined petroleum products	32500	34878	38025	37558	3285	3279	2970	2922	1	1	1	1
201	Basic chemicals,fertilizers, etc.	46545	46885	70552	…	3721	3732	4352	…	55	59	60	…
2011	Basic chemicals	12610	13719	29447	33869	1454	1439	1848	2075	20	20	26	25
2012	Fertilizers and nitrogen compounds	31272	30423	37582	35813	1768	1853	1738	1635	12	16	21	23
2013	Plastics and synthetic rubber in primary forms	2663	2743	3523	2312	499	440	766	427	23	23	13	17
202	Other chemical products	41378	42101	46777	…	6522	7007	6692	…	178	189	242	…
2021	Pesticides and other agrochemical products	5626	4922	4259	4486	616	609	645	610	10	10	7	14
2022	Paints,varnishes;printing ink and mastics	12655	12955	15919	21503	1749	1960	1919	2713	69	69	62	67
2023	Soap,cleaning and cosmetic preparations	20634	21047	21158	23789	3773	4037	3819	3813	86	95	147	100
2029	Other chemical products n.e.c.	2463	3177	5441	7458	384	401	309	578	13	15	26	26
2030	Man-made fibres	…	…	…	…	…	…	…	…	…	…	…	…
2100	Pharmaceuticals,medicinal chemicals, etc.	110229	120932	139266	159357	7897	8796	10247	12389	44	44	49	49
221	Rubber products	474	482	318	…	129	108	112	…	25	25	23	…
2211	Rubber tyres and tubes	209	181	157	591	90	67	70	111	19	19	19	22
2219	Other rubber products	265	301	161	407	39	41	42	80	6	6	4	6
2220	Plastics products	28651	33315	47257	60779	5615	5681	6867	8908	222	226	332	376
2310	Glass and glass products	3360	3532	3946	7058	976	1007	852	1325	65	66	64	68
239	Non-metallic mineral products n.e.c.	66625	74762	94989	…	15088	15500	17148	…	2535	2533	2641	…
2391	Refractory products	…	…	…	…	…	…	…	…	…	…	…	…
2392	Clay building materials	533	527	340	364	214	212	128	150	13	13	18	20
2393	Other porcelain and ceramic products	1734	1593	1872	3096	391	410	407	431	46	46	38	42
2394	Cement, lime and plaster	23118	25161	33285	28583	1709	1733	1687	1670	38	36	17	17
2395	Articles of concrete, cement and plaster	24798	29681	34590	41366	7298	7554	8146	8714	1543	1543	1479	1489
2396	Cutting, shaping and finishing of stone	14773	16048	22425	27815	5316	5426	6552	6997	890	890	1078	1111
2399	Other non-metallic mineral products n.e.c.	1669	1752	2477	2739	160	165	228	276	5	5	11	11
2410	Basic iron and steel	16982	17994	21864	30420	2439	2468	2650	3970	18	19	36	38
2420	Basic precious and other non-ferrous metals	2717	3199	3679	4644	724	784	712	1140	10	7	9	13
243	Casting of metals	2004	1862	944	…	410	357	234	…	41	41	44	…
2431	Casting of iron and steel	1589	1267	890	847	276	260	185	156	20	20	33	33
2432	Casting of non-ferrous metals	415	595	54	423	134	97	49	111	21	21	11	17
251	Struct.metal products, tanks, reservoirs	41550	40951	40734	…	14145	13674	13803	…	2640	3639	4015	…

continued

Jordan

ISIC	Industry	Note	Number of establishments (number) 2013	2014	2015	2016	Note	Number of employees (number) 2013	2014	2015	2016	Note	Wages and salaries paid to employees (thousands of Jordanian Dinars) 2013	2014	2015	2016
2511	Structural metal products		2563	3562	3928	3973		13898	13464	13473	13793		40994	40413	40241	46976
2512	Tanks, reservoirs and containers of metal		77	77	87	89		247	210	330	255		556	538	493	966
2513	Steam generators, excl. hot water boilers		…	…	…	…		…	…	…	…		…	…	…	…
2520	Weapons and ammunition		…	…	…	…		…	…	…	…		…	…	…	…
259	Other metal products;metal working services		944	944	1037	…		4193	3971	4923	…		16654	16977	22788	…
2591	Forging,pressing,stamping,roll-forming of metal		88	88	112	93		304	365	563	637		661	1066	2030	2860
2592	Treatment and coating of metals; machining		602	602	698	700		1931	1684	1820	1746		4070	3285	3658	3423
2593	Cutlery, hand tools and general hardware		29	29	30	30		170	165	175	181		466	622	375	411
2599	Other fabricated metal products n.e.c.		225	225	197	198		1788	1757	2365	3128		11457	12004	16725	27497
2610	Electronic components and boards		25	25	25	27		435	482	565	557		2394	2596	4696	4583
2620	Computers and peripheral equipment		6	6	…	…		42	42	…	…		475	522	124	…
2630	Communication equipment		…	…	…	…		…	…	…	…		…	…	…	…
2640	Consumer electronics		2	2	2	2		559	543	292	292		2177	2207	1340	1340
265	Measuring,testing equipment; watches, etc.		1	1	2	…		10	8	16	…		33	29	127	…
2651	Measuring/testing/navigating equipment,etc.		1	1	2	3		10	8	16	21		33	29	127	135
2652	Watches and clocks		…	…	…	…		…	…	…	…		…	…	…	…
2660	Irradiation/electromedical equipment,etc.		2	2	2	2		36	32	60	60		525	578	552	1100
2670	Optical instruments and photographic equipment		…	…	2	2		…	…	…	…		…	…	…	…
2680	Magnetic and optical media		3	3	2	2		24	18	14	16		69	77	40	59
2710	Electric motors,generators,transformers,etc.		23	23	24	29		238	230	256	343		1598	1436	2820	3079
2720	Batteries and accumulators		…	…	3	3		…	…	90	…		…	…	…	…
273	Wiring and wiring devices		8	8	12	…		1500	1468	1689	…		9550	9463	8131	…
2731	Fibre optic cables		…	…	…	…		…	…	…	…		…	…	…	…
2732	Other electronic and electric wires and cables		8	8	12	9		1500	1468	1689	1842		9550	9463	8131	16498
2733	Wiring devices		…	…	…	…		…	…	…	…		…	…	…	…
2740	Electric lighting equipment		8	8	9	11		80	48	65	102		125	125	296	501
2750	Domestic appliances		61	61	101	100		1382	1258	1209	1119		12198	6919	10186	6782
2790	Other electrical equipment		26	27	12	14		581	530	393	481		3140	4503	5910	7161
281	General-purpose machinery		52	54	118	…		2465	2628	2790	…		12996	14253	16771	…
2811	Engines/turbines,excl.aircraft,vehicle engines		…	…	…	…		…	…	…	…		…	…	…	…
2812	Fluid power equipment		…	…	…	…		…	…	…	…		…	…	…	…
2813	Other pumps, compressors, taps and valves		9	9	13	15		100	105	171	281		383	513	1412	1746
2814	Bearings, gears, gearing and driving elements		…	…	…	…		…	…	…	…		…	…	…	…
2815	Ovens, furnaces and furnace burners		…	…	…	…		…	…	…	…		…	…	…	…
2816	Lifting and handling equipment		11	12	13	12		438	463	469	549		1487	1752	3499	3690
2817	Office machinery, excl.computers,etc.		…	…	…	…		…	…	…	…		…	…	…	…
2818	Power-driven hand tools		…	…	…	…		…	…	…	…		…	…	…	…
2819	Other general-purpose machinery		32	33	92	98		1927	2060	2150	2185		11126	11988	11860	11947
282	Special-purpose machinery		38	39	40	…		304	260	279	…		1373	1352	1367	…
2821	Agricultural and forestry machinery		8	9	6	8		39	33	30	33		85	64	101	198
2822	Metal-forming machinery and machine tools		…	…	…	…		…	…	…	…		…	…	…	…

ISIC Revision 4

Code	Description												
2823	Machinery for metallurgy	⋮	⋮	⋮	⋮	53	65	64	153	167	202	110	294
2824	Mining, quarrying and construction machinery	10	10	8	13	80	78	51	57	660	597	203	227
2825	Food/beverage/tobacco processing machinery	10	10	8	13	⋮	⋮	⋮	⋮	⋮	⋮	⋮	⋮
2826	Textile/apparel/leather production machinery	⋮	10	18	21	132	84	134	197	461	489	953	1308
2829	Other special-purpose machinery	10	10	18	21	712	682	951	1105	2672	2488	3653	4220
2910	Motor vehicles	⋮	⋮	⋮	⋮	⋮	⋮	⋮	⋮	⋮	⋮	⋮	⋮
2920	Automobile bodies, trailers and semi-trailers	111	111	234	252	179	178	213	322	459	361	1224	2105
2930	Parts and accessories for motor vehicles	84	84	57	69	⋮	⋮	⋮	⋮	⋮	⋮	⋮	⋮
301	Building of ships and boats	⋮	⋮	⋮	⋮	⋮	⋮	⋮	⋮	⋮	⋮	⋮	⋮
3011	Building of ships and floating structures	⋮	⋮	⋮	⋮	⋮	⋮	⋮	⋮	⋮	⋮	⋮	⋮
3012	Building of pleasure and sporting boats	⋮	⋮	⋮	⋮	⋮	⋮	⋮	⋮	⋮	⋮	⋮	⋮
3020	Railway locomotives and rolling stock	⋮	⋮	⋮	⋮	⋮	⋮	⋮	⋮	⋮	⋮	⋮	⋮
3030	Air and spacecraft and related machinery	⋮	⋮	⋮	⋮	⋮	⋮	⋮	⋮	⋮	⋮	⋮	⋮
3040	Military fighting vehicles	⋮	⋮	⋮	⋮	⋮	⋮	⋮	⋮	⋮	⋮	⋮	⋮
309	Transport equipment n.e.c.	⋮	⋮	⋮	⋮	⋮	⋮	⋮	⋮	⋮	⋮	⋮	⋮
3091	Motorcycles	⋮	⋮	⋮	⋮	⋮	⋮	⋮	⋮	⋮	⋮	⋮	⋮
3092	Bicycles and invalid carriages	⋮	⋮	⋮	⋮	⋮	⋮	⋮	⋮	⋮	⋮	⋮	⋮
3099	Other transport equipment n.e.c.	⋮	⋮	⋮	⋮	⋮	⋮	⋮	⋮	⋮	⋮	⋮	⋮
3100	Furniture	3147	3141	3983	4074	10433	10570	12898	17123	27093	30340	41278	56194
321	Jewellery, bijouterie and related articles	203	204	209	219	1439	1249	1100	1918	4688	4131	5009	9181
3211	Jewellery and related articles	203	204	209	219	1439	1249	1100	1918	4688	4131	5009	9181
3212	Imitation jewellery and related articles	⋮	⋮	⋮	⋮	⋮	⋮	⋮	⋮	⋮	⋮	⋮	⋮
3220	Musical instruments	⋮	⋮	⋮	⋮	⋮	⋮	⋮	⋮	⋮	⋮	⋮	⋮
3230	Sports goods	5	5	5	5	37	35	28	29	32	42	184	189
3240	Games and toys	158	158	195	196	600	553	783	1009	2985	2888	3807	5264
3250	Medical and dental instruments and supplies	42	42	72	68	287	314	502	519	822	863	1821	2016
3290	Other manufacturing n.e.c.	⋮	⋮	⋮	⋮	⋮	⋮	⋮	⋮	⋮	⋮	⋮	⋮
331	Repair of fabricated metal products/machinery	617	618	711	⋮	2742	2822	4486	⋮	15495	18455	32283	⋮
3311	Repair of fabricated metal products	119	119	176	176	170	155	280	255	46	102	195	165
3312	Repair of machinery	259	260	291	309	947	1104	1472	1479	4081	5249	6297	6905
3313	Repair of electronic and optical equipment	10	10	41	41	15	15	123	133	17	17	179	221
3314	Repair of electrical equipment	219	219	192	190	320	317	375	390	208	177	229	320
3315	Repair of transport equip., excl. motor vehicles	10	10	11	13	1290	1231	2236	2203	11143	12927	25383	24559
3319	Repair of other equipment	⋮	⋮	⋮	⋮	⋮	⋮	⋮	⋮	⋮	⋮	⋮	⋮
3320	Installation of industrial machinery/equipment	⋮	⋮	⋮	⋮	⋮	⋮	⋮	⋮	⋮	⋮	⋮	⋮
C	Total manufacturing a/	21989	22090	26017	26138	179449	182698	197889	238104	910506	930822	1128717	1341955

a/ Sum of available data.

Jordan

ISIC	Industry	Output at producers' prices (thousands of Jordanian Dinars)					Value added at producers' prices (thousands of Jordanian Dinars)					Gross fixed capital formation (thousands of Jordanian Dinars)		
		Note	2013	2014	2015	2016	Note	2013	2014	2015	2016	Note	2015	2016
1010	Processing/preserving of meat		682938	633126	676886	695266		187831	216978	236134	199939		33799	22886
1020	Processing/preserving of fish, etc.		...	...	...	...		...	...	...	...		...	...
1030	Processing/preserving of fruit,vegetables		100841	102979	116358	115766		31015	33021	38529	40646		4788	5401
1040	Vegetable and animal oils and fats		216612	234512	231987	216875		86550	101323	89888	66099		4586	855
1050	Dairy products		175213	159994	226591	372097		53498	56886	77250	140273		6116	28712
106	Grain mill products,starches and starch products		81231	109467	153506	140501		18972	29370	33575	24533		4424	3267
1061	Grain mill products		81231	109467	153506	140501		18972	29370	33575	...		4424	...
1062	Starches and starch products		...	...	...	...		...	...	...	...		...	...
107	Other food products		764767	816832	892842	...		242395	244493	294172	...		21230	...
1071	Bakery products		370556	404183	461872	618474		111927	124018	160842	198697		15625	15508
1072	Sugar		...	...	...	...		...	...	...	...		...	...
1073	Cocoa, chocolate and sugar confectionery		109526	110702	117309	100945		28656	25062	35072	33303		1942	862
1074	Macaroni, noodles, couscous, etc.		...	...	...	...		...	...	...	...		...	...
1075	Prepared meals and dishes		...	...	...	...		...	...	...	...		...	...
1079	Other food products n.e.c.		284685	301947	313661	320539		101812	95413	98258	108484		3663	11962
1080	Prepared animal feeds		75503	90361	107823	164738		14933	26911	32086	33610		2207	273
110	Beverages		512134	527568	613636	...		262914	267479	335624	...		28290	...
1101	Distilling, rectifying and blending of spirits		28776	19285	28357	34696		17546	10622	18919	24872		269	228
1102	Wines		...	...	...	...		...	...	...	...		...	...
1103	Malt liquors and malt		94692	96608	111259	111506		74476	76273	88878	101685		3689	2583
1104	Soft drinks,mineral waters,other bottled waters		388666	411675	474020	341846		170892	180584	227827	171173		24332	16688
1200	Tobacco products		667526	681460	681020	479270		471777	482308	507909	399490		8570	2380
131	Spinning, weaving and finishing of textiles		15607	16877	12458	...		8694	10402	7958	...		222	...
1311	Preparation and spinning of textile fibres		...	...	...	...		...	...	...	...		...	...
1312	Weaving of textiles		15607	16877	12458	14021		8694	10402	7958	7738		222	22
1313	Finishing of textiles		...	...	...	...		...	...	...	...		...	...
139	Other textiles		47582	47731	73872	...		20735	22378	35823	...		10661	...
1391	Knitted and crocheted fabrics		...	...	...	...		...	...	...	...		...	...
1392	Made-up textile articles, except apparel		14220	16549	24104	21911		5885	7715	12513	10428		410	101
1393	Carpets and rugs		31352	30041	48379	97960		13837	14020	22369	33944		10250	5585
1394	Cordage, rope, twine and netting		2010	1141	1389	2493		1013	643	941	1314		1	118
1399	Other textiles n.e.c.		...	...	...	...		...	...	...	...		...	...
1410	Wearing apparel, except fur apparel		386910	466497	489188	811773		192967	199238	213217	362811		2744	3132
1420	Articles of fur		346	514	1153	1084		147	235	639	761		-	-
1430	Knitted and crocheted apparel		9020	7219	5336	6933		4457	3582	1719	2552		25	120
151	Leather;luggage,handbags,saddlery,harness;fur		6437	6463	5205	...		1950	2551	2036	...		...	...
1511	Tanning/dressing of leather; dressing of fur		2027	1527	2185	1951		526	633	849	556		-	556
1512	Luggage,handbags,etc.;saddlery/harness		4410	4936	3020	5048		1424	1918	1187	2508		-	2508
1520	Footwear		30186	42269	36144	56300		9762	10745	8764	17526		34	973
1610	Sawmilling and planing of wood		5834	10526	3863	18595		1421	3903	1131	2816		-	2

Code	Description										
162	Wood products, cork, straw, plaiting materials	39631	35663	48161	…	14025	13429	19565	…	266	…
1621	Veneer sheets and wood-based panels	793	475	450	714	256	262	211	368	-	-
1622	Builders' carpentry and joinery	29568	26969	40687	50615	10343	9835	16456	18845	266	1029
1623	Wooden containers	5437	4766	4437	5661	1581	1788	1511	1960	-	-
1629	Other wood products;articles of cork,straw	3833	3453	2587	2098	1845	1544	1387	1268	-	-
170	Paper and paper products	320067	353328	383931	…	103877	100376	110318	…	12599	…
1701	Pulp, paper and paperboard	46504	52868	48992	63863	7304	9170	7489	6904	4325	-
1702	Corrugated paper and paperboard	71621	73176	92093	106119	26556	25748	33360	39954	1658	9570
1709	Other articles of paper and paperboard	201942	227284	242846	295581	70017	65458	69469	90658	6616	22139
181	Printing and service activities related to printing	167614	226477	228457	…	88924	121737	114735	…	9709	…
1811	Printing	156654	216854	224643	328784	82318	116064	112619	144214	9698	11390
1812	Service activities related to printing	10960	9623	3814	6098	6606	5673	2116	2443	11	15
1820	Reproduction of recorded media	…	…	…	…	…	…	…	…	…	…
1910	Coke oven products	…	…	…	…	…	…	…	…	…	…
1920	Refined petroleum products	4203824	4579982	2864234	1591257	330470	380040	512598	528135	54505	34771
201	Basic chemicals,fertilizers, etc.	648022	715418	812687	…	289373	306551	302190	…	40501	…
2011	Basic chemicals	264825	216538	260072	223353	132818	118315	103168	125899	31424	8581
2012	Fertilizers and nitrogen compounds	352996	461293	496531	435330	147581	176440	187070	159278	8963	40627
2013	Plastics and synthetic rubber in primary forms	30201	37587	56084	20212	8974	11796	11952	4866	114	2272
202	Other chemical products	566810	515373	526867	…	177939	159608	154697	…	15137	…
2021	Pesticides and other agrochemical products	60648	64359	41621	44447	17485	19008	9189	16326	1628	785
2022	Paints,varnishes;printing ink and mastics	192008	162852	175205	240413	52157	44529	48481	76469	7231	15082
2023	Soap,cleaning and cosmetic preparations	247972	240162	263824	248142	77759	75827	82141	99305	5052	10697
2029	Other chemical products n.e.c.	66182	48000	46217	61349	30538	20244	14886	20165	1226	4232
2030	Man-made fibres	…	…	…	…	…	…	…	…	…	…
2100	Pharmaceuticals,medicinal chemicals, etc.	817355	1039442	1040317	1083058	439094	568143	578403	487474	48473	46456
221	Rubber products	2601	1982	1804	…	1170	899	880	…	…	…
2211	Rubber tyres and tubes	1651	938	1171	2442	638	356	548	1237	-	-
2219	Other rubber products	950	1044	633	3366	532	543	332	1705	-	77
2220	Plastics products	399932	458062	524859	582724	109386	129712	150321	178216	10181	16973
2310	Glass and glass products	24409	24937	21906	37873	8845	10165	9151	16493	165	432
239	Non-metallic mineral products n.e.c.	736498	959788	1004652	…	358235	496840	509547	…	18070	…
2391	Refractory products	3726	3719	626	314	1757	1801	510	250	…	…
2392	Clay building materials	16227	16231	17433	23061	7425	7437	5825	7426	-	250
2393	Other porcelain and ceramic products	372163	482451	496248	424585	222109	315938	316692	281735	435	1344
2394	Cement, lime and plaster	233970	331614	334319	440752	84670	124597	127004	137976	9480	3620
2395	Articles of concrete, cement and plaster	95485	108357	128304	184552	40066	43359	53646	76011	7267	17288
2396	Cutting, shaping and finishing of stone	14927	17416	27722	24520	2208	3708	5870	5722	888	820
2399	Other non-metallic mineral products n.e.c.	…	…	…	…	…	…	…	…	-	-
2410	Basic iron and steel	432654	529566	613816	719039	156946	201204	212243	266913	4436	8296
2420	Basic precious and other non-ferrous metals	61178	66633	78285	75042	28039	31201	37348	31821	1014	1632
243	Casting of metals	21146	6212	2665	…	6546	2909	1353	…	14	…
2431	Casting of iron and steel	19808	4454	2433	2127	5760	1952	1259	1043	14	…
2432	Casting of non-ferrous metals	1338	1758	232	2585	786	957	94	1059	-	…
251	Struct.metal products, tanks, reservoirs	265813	295564	237233	…	106877	120653	92697	…	1506	…

continued

Jordan

ISIC Revision 4			Output at producers' prices (thousands of Jordanian Dinars)					Value added at producers' prices (thousands of Jordanian Dinars)					Gross fixed capital formation (thousands of Jordanian Dinars)	
ISIC	Industry	Note	2013	2014	2015	2016	Note	2013	2014	2015	2016	Note	2015	2016
2511	Structural metal products		262354	290702	234483	313974		105780	119158	91469	127677		1506	858
2512	Tanks, reservoirs and containers of metal		3459	4862	2750	4262		1097	1495	1228	1957		-	82
2513	Steam generators, excl. hot water boilers		...	...	...	...		...	...	...	...		...	...
2520	Weapons and ammunition		...	...	...	...		...	...	...	...		...	...
259	Other metal products;metal working services		288795	266807	320932	...		93042	100980	125042	...		24504	...
2591	Forging,pressing,stamping,roll-forming of metal		4430	8677	15663	19134		1741	3913	5580	6428		28	294
2592	Treatment and coating of metals,machining		16816	15989	22567	17891		8956	8799	13694	9991		-	-
2593	Cutlery, hand tools and general hardware		3737	4261	1128	1490		1342	2137	696	837		27	6
2599	Other fabricated metal products n.e.c.		263812	237880	281574	397093		81003	86131	105072	166903		24449	10007
2610	Electronic components and boards		21510	26357	27261	28193		8764	12275	10415	13201		199	2242
2620	Computers and peripheral equipment		449	553	450	...		377	485	227	...		-	-
2630	Communication equipment		...	...	...	...		...	...	...	...		...	...
2640	Consumer electronics		75064	72111	24073	24073		26586	26059	7726	8033		449	449
265	Measuring,testing equipment; watches, etc.		276	154	1394	...		69	50	437	...		41	...
2651	Measuring/testing/navigating equipment,etc.		276	154	1394	1130		69	50	437	379		41	1
2652	Watches and clocks		...	...	...	...		...	...	...	...		...	...
2660	Irradiation/electromedical equipment,etc.		3489	3464	7173	7173		807	1018	2375	2375		218	218
2670	Optical instruments and photographic equipment		...	...	...	...		...	...	...	...		...	...
2680	Magnetic and optical media		214	217	198	78		121	133	138	39		-	-
2710	Electric motors,generators,transformers,etc.		25380	16180	40717	48275		5034	3441	10091	11637		72	799
2720	Batteries and accumulators		...	...	...	...		...	...	...	...		...	106
273	Wiring and wiring devices		211461	201220	224744	...		46576	46958	56566	...		1783	...
2731	Fibre optic cables		...	...	...	...		...	...	...	...		...	...
2732	Other electronic and electric wires and cables		211461	201220	224744	205142		46576	46958	56566	51714		1783	1886
2733	Wiring devices		...	...	...	...		...	...	...	...		...	...
2740	Electric lighting equipment		1624	1687	1862	1287		263	368	799	605		-	...
2750	Domestic appliances		375689	76126	100146	93472		49413	27953	35638	29275		633	875
2790	Other electrical equipment		21352	23894	31661	36985		8296	10327	14792	18473		6158	1810
281	General-purpose machinery		106350	122028	178450	...		36289	48850	70132	...		28308	...
2811	Engines/turbines,excl.aircraft,vehicle engines		...	...	...	...		...	...	...	...		...	...
2812	Fluid power equipment		...	...	...	...		...	...	...	...		...	...
2813	Other pumps, compressors, taps and valves		1874	2710	8237	12380		683	896	2887	8393		481	926
2814	Bearings, gears, gearing and driving elements		...	...	...	...		...	...	...	...		...	...
2815	Ovens, furnaces and furnace burners		...	...	...	...		...	...	...	...		...	...
2816	Lifting and handling equipment		21993	27932	55123	29885		8220	11989	20648	10161		125	45
2817	Office machinery, excl.computers,etc.		...	...	...	...		...	...	...	...		...	...
2818	Power-driven hand tools		...	...	...	...		...	...	...	...		...	...
2819	Other general-purpose machinery		82483	91386	115090	103427		27386	35965	46597	40656		27702	837
282	Special-purpose machinery		7725	3964	5198	...		2843	1411	2675	...		4	3
2821	Agricultural and forestry machinery		350	363	408	336		141	148	197	206		-	...
2822	Metal-forming machinery and machine tools		...	...	...	...		...	...	...	...		...	...

Code	Description										
2823	Machinery for metallurgy	821	798	332	793	402	289	206	370	..	..
2824	Mining, quarrying and construction machinery	2726	1373	863	783	1194	691	462	492	-	243
2825	Food/beverage/tobacco processing machinery	..	..	..	..	..	..	..	..	-	-
2826	Textile/apparel/leather production machinery	..	..	..	..	..	..	..	..	..	..
2829	Other special-purpose machinery	3828	1430	3595	5268	1106	283	1810	1558	4	67
2910	Motor vehicles	..	..	..	..	..	..	..	..	..	..
2920	Automobile bodies, trailers and semi-trailers	50533	15355	35654	33405	19691	7633	20394	13759	539	415
2930	Parts and accessories for motor vehicles	1506	1432	11119	17063	890	857	6777	7752	2	119
301	Building of ships and boats	..	..	..	..	..	..	..	..	..	..
3011	Building of ships and floating structures	..	..	..	..	..	..	..	..	..	..
3012	Building of pleasure and sporting boats	..	..	..	..	..	..	..	..	..	..
3020	Railway locomotives and rolling stock	..	..	..	..	..	..	..	..	..	..
3030	Air and spacecraft and related machinery	..	..	..	..	..	..	..	..	..	..
3040	Military fighting vehicles	..	..	..	..	..	..	..	..	..	..
309	Transport equipment n.e.c.	..	..	..	..	..	..	..	..	..	..
3091	Motorcycles	..	..	..	..	..	..	..	..	..	..
3092	Bicycles and invalid carriages	..	..	..	..	..	..	..	..	..	..
3099	Other transport equipment n.e.c.	..	..	..	..	..	..	..	..	..	..
3100	Furniture	173660	185091	224215	317343	65673	74702	96945	140293	2487	2465
321	Jewellery, bijouterie and related articles	94731	87849	112309	..	19432	15350	21766	32677	1510	975
3211	Jewellery and related articles	94731	87849	112309	107358	19432	15350	21766	32677	1510	975
3212	Imitation jewellery and related articles	..	..	..	..	..	..	..	..	..	..
3220	Musical instruments	..	..	..	..	..	..	..	..	..	..
3230	Sports goods	..	..	..	..	..	..	..	..	..	..
3240	Games and toys	273	321	279	377	116	147	109	151	3	27
3250	Medical and dental instruments and supplies	15045	15662	15947	31915	8666	8562	7921	19042	387	1663
3290	Other manufacturing n.e.c.	9331	7286	11800	11005	4324	4715	4632	4254	21	590
331	Repair of fabricated metal products/machinery	85055	90395	127672	..	55081	55107	76449	..	5452	..
3311	Repair of fabricated metal products	985	1170	1409	1649	678	831	870	982	-	-
3312	Repair of machinery	25363	25886	24757	29567	15444	12125	9222	15811	245	382
3313	Repair of electronic and optical equipment	101	137	615	656	64	93	386	461	-	-
3314	Repair of electrical equipment	1933	1973	1729	2411	1096	1130	1096	1560	-	-
3315	Repair of transport equip., excl. motor vehicles	56673	61229	99162	91399	37799	40928	64875	56900	5207	6541
3319	Repair of other equipment	..	..	..	..	..	..	..	..	..	..
3320	Installation of industrial machinery/equipment	..	..	..	..	..	..	..	..	..	..
C	Total manufacturing	14055753 a/	14980975	14220996	14077336	4282117 a/	4802651	5294546	5622898	421466 a/	414717

a/ Sum of available data.

Jordan

ISIC Revision 4 — Index numbers of industrial production (2010=100)

ISIC	Industry	Note	2005	2006	2007	2008	2009	2010	2011	2012	2013	2014	2015	2016
10	Food products		80	83	74	77	99	100	110	117	121	115	101	85
11	Beverages		70	76	90	103	96	100	94	100	99	108	93	90
12	Tobacco products		77	87	97	97	93	100	121	120	160	155	149	138
13	Textiles		77	89	99	86	96	100	104	106	105	108	91	111
14	Wearing apparel		104	109	98	109	103	100	131	158	165	176	168	328
15	Leather and related products		340	403	49	307	514	100	44	47	101	180	212	283
16	Wood products, excluding furniture		95	90	95	96	97	100	102	103	105	104	108	147
17	Paper and paper products		123	130	141	131	107	100	107	110	110	109	103	98
18	Printing and reproduction of recorded media		101	105	106	87	113	100	100	95	88	78	69	66
19	Coke and refined petroleum products		125	120	116	117	105	100	98	107	95	94	97	84
20	Chemicals and chemical products		93	101	92	91	89	100	101	107	125	116	90	88
21	Pharmaceuticals,medicinal chemicals, etc.		76	81	94	106	114	100	83	96	90	80	70	79
22	Rubber and plastics products		115	105	118	92	110	100	101	116	108	110	99	146
23	Other non-metallic mineral products		121	128	133	133	121	100	99	92	89	99	103	91
24	Basic metals		137	115	122	116	104	100	103	106	102	100	102	78
25	Fabricated metal products, except machinery		64	73	93	97	99	100	100	100	87	96	60	77
26	Computer, electronic and optical products		146	105	68	52	174	100	110	113	100	88	72	48
27	Electrical equipment		105	169	185	188	168	100	121	110	97	98	74	101
28	Machinery and equipment n.e.c.		136	145	187	184	167	100	103	58	85	73	159	64
29	Motor vehicles, trailers and semi-trailers		226	191	195	166	171	100	107	115	146	98	86	66
30	Other transport equipment		...	...	...	...	...	...	...	...	...	...	...	...
31	Furniture		60	64	77	74	75	100	109	196	193	200	208	228
32	Other manufacturing		147	139	145	115	94	100	117	109	105	113	73	83
33	Repair and installation of machinery/equipment		...	...	...	...	...	...	...	...	...	...	...	...
C	Total manufacturing		95	102	104	105	106	100	103	110	109	108	97	96

Kazakhstan

Supplier of information:
Ministry of National Economy of the Republic of Kazakhstan, Committe on Statistics, Almaty.

Basic source of data:
Survey on registered establishments.

Major deviations from ISIC (Revision 4):
Data presented in ISIC Revision 4 were originally classified according to NACE revision 2.

Reference period:
Calendar year.

Scope:
All establishments.

Method of data collection:
Mail questionnaires; online survey.

Type of enumeration:
Complete enumeration.

Adjusted for non-response:
Yes.

Concepts and definitions of variables:
Figures for wages and salaries were computed by UNIDO from reported monthly wages and salaries per employee.

Related national publications:
None reported.

Kazakhstan

ISIC	Industry	Number of enterprises Note	(number) 2013	2014	2015	2016	Number of employees Note	(number) 2013	2014	2015	2016	Wages and salaries Note	(millions of Kazakhstan Tenge) 2013	2014	2015	2016
1010	Processing/preserving of meat		493	475	483	522		5216	5558	4943	4771		4237	5149	4911	3713
1020	Processing/preserving of fish, etc.		134	129	128	132		726	1021	1101	982		511	671	728	666
1030	Processing/preserving of fruit, vegetables		143	153	164	180		836	755	595	575		1092	1068	896	928
1040	Vegetable and animal oils and fats		124	126	137	148		5116	5275	5370	5404		5507	6164	6636	7204
1050	Dairy products		388	408	407	438		8689	8677	7703	8068		7266	8257	7926	8160
106	Grain mill products,starches and starch products		808	795	743	747		10586	10834	8689	8530		7893	9199	7848	8556
1061	Grain mill products		799	785	732	732		10458	10646	8451	8283		7801	9026	7644	8285
1062	Starches and starch products		9	10	11	15		128	188	238	247		92	173	205	270
107	Other food products		1440	1807	1422	1572		30881	30394	27735	19014		20213	32318	30701	23724
1071	Bakery products		853	824	790	975		9662	8975	7139	8225		7706	7725	6672	9619
1072	Sugar		33	29	30	30		1505	1646	1383	1723		1050	1165	986	1482
1073	Cocoa, chocolate and sugar confectionery		73	68	62	66		7520	7042	6938	6370		8794	9059	8861	9789
1074	Macaroni, noodles, couscous, etc.		29	31	35	117		1548	1446	1006	980		1351	1455	1218	1134
1075	Prepared meals and dishes		67	73	87	111		256	710	1019	744		232	644	1020	847
1079	Other food products n.e.c.		385	782	418	273		10390	10575	10250	972		1080	12270	11944	853
1080	Prepared animal feeds		65	76	87	105		153	174	...	8		136	172	16	8
110	Beverages		768	759	736	741		13961	13311	11150	10285		8785	18401	16602	19086
1101	Distilling, rectifying and blending of spirits		174	163	146	143		4513	4090	2977	2288		3237	3288	2770	2625
1102	Wines		73	62	52	62		535	557	359	357		444	468	397	181
1103	Malt liquors and malt		6	6	5	95		92	92	...	3498		186	203	...	10140
1104	Soft drinks,mineral waters,other bottled waters		412	424	435	441		5013	4823	4386	4142		4918	5230	4779	4876
1200	Tobacco products		10	20	11	11		1563	1485	1379	1297		13	7634	7860	8280
131	Spinning, weaving and finishing of textiles		113	122	115	210		3802	4094	4415	4878		1978	2402	2704	3235
1311	Preparation and spinning of textile fibres		...	...	...	119		-	...	...	4354		-	...	...	2778
1312	Weaving of textiles		34	34	36	40		538	555	444	524		317	370	342	457
1313	Finishing of textiles		28	36	48	51		325	...	93	...		1067	...	24	...
139	Other textiles		...	302	274	290		2292	2259	1590	1708		1468	1522	1274	1732
1391	Knitted and crocheted fabrics		6	6	4	5		...	...	...	...		...	...	...	...
1392	Made-up textile articles, except apparel		185	191	169	176		1328	1249	1061	1162		1393	922	927	1316
1393	Carpets and rugs		13	14	14	14		...	118	177	229		...	96	128	185
1394	Cordage, rope, twine and netting		1	1	1	1		...	...	...	...		...	...	...	...
1399	Other textiles n.e.c.		21	52	53	94		390	328	72	317		14	177	40	184
1410	Wearing apparel, except fur apparel		813	808	786	837		4444	4922	4492	4636		3203	3626	3700	2727
1420	Articles of fur		36	33	33	32		-	...	...	133		-	77	78	170
1430	Knitted and crocheted apparel		55	52	58	70		...	148	104	299		433	...	...	254
151	Leather;luggage,handbags,saddlery,harness;fur		110	114	110	115		565	525	427	450		345	368	374	363
1511	Tanning/dressing of leather; dressing of fur		106	110	104	104		565	525	427	450		345	368	374	363
1512	Luggage,handbags,etc.;saddlery/harness		4	4	6	11		...	...	...	...		...	...	...	...
1520	Footwear		71	74	77	80		770	750	671	556		547	607	647	607
1610	Sawmilling and planing of wood		204	210	200	207		125	117	101	92		108	107	101	110

ISIC Revision 4

Code	Description												
162	Wood products, cork, straw, plaiting materials	554	528	481	484	1152	1062	568	399	2742	999	463	277
1621	Veneer sheets and wood-based panels	20	19	22	25	262	202	188	296	147	73	69	158
1622	Builders' carpentry and joinery	411	386	350	353	867	788	380	103	770	823	383	64
1623	Wooden containers	15	16	16	15	23	72	...	...	1825	103	...	...
1629	Other wood products;articles of cork, straw	100	99	86	91	...	...	...	...	...	...	17	...
170	Paper and paper products	308	339	380	422	1892	2155	1872	1805	1749	2619	2265	2150
1701	Pulp, paper and paperboard	35	38	39	57	...	...	...	201	...	...	...	79
1702	Corrugated paper and paperboard	70	71	73	86	1431	1569	1274	1175	1709	2146	1826	1879
1709	Other articles of paper and paperboard	28	46	56	279	53	...	...	421	40	...	...	192
181	Printing and service activities related to printing	1452	1438	1355	1356	3330	2993	2116	1782	4535	4314	3473	3472
1811	Printing	122	120	108	1177	1018	901	331	1781	1087	993	378	2846
1812	Service activities related to printing	1163	1150	1077	179	2265	1741	1785	...	3418	2994	3098	...
1820	Reproduction of recorded media	41	41	31	31	...	...	...	...	...	...	...	...
1910	Coke oven products	16	14	15	19	298	293	...	...	416	455	...	...
1920	Refined petroleum products	225	239	257	269	9309	9232	8723	8027	25916	30325	33554	32752
201	Basic chemicals,fertilizers, etc.	325	325	346	342	16123	15784	15552	15265	20909	22964	23773	26289
2011	Basic chemicals	82	79	79	224	10054	9325	9145	11587	14376	15206	15432	13742
2012	Fertilizers and nitrogen compounds	50	52	55	51	1965	2150	2409	2624	2349	2963	3682	4462
2013	Plastics and synthetic rubber in primary forms	63	62	69	67	622	719	756	1054	875	1142	1329	1002
202	Other chemical products	354	382	434	552	1246	1270	980	1403	2784	1649	1606	2440
2021	Pesticides and other agrochemical products	39	41	43	45	60	58	...	183	48	122	...	463
2022	Paints,varnishes;printing ink and mastics	138	134	139	149	127	239	95	174	191	377	147	393
2023	Soap,cleaning and cosmetic preparations	89	104	121	153	...	...	...	...	2029	...	...	...
2029	Other chemical products n.e.c.	88	103	131	205	569	613	334	1046	516	653	365	1069
2030	Man-made fibres	7	7	7	9	...	...	...	...	...	...	...	-
2100	Pharmaceuticals,medicinal chemicals, etc.	346	353	319	319	2824	2966	2471	2550	2200	5359	5403	4702
221	Rubber products	102	116	133	151	1076	778	285	252	1539	1124	560	565
2211	Rubber tyres and tubes	25	28	30	35	49	...	...	...	289	...	...	...
2219	Other rubber products	77	88	103	116	1027	778	285	...	1250	1124	560	...
2220	Plastics products	1673	1726	1727	1780	5262	5684	4506	4159	5731	6723	5292	5337
2310	Glass and glass products	118	126	134	142	1197	1249	1123	1343	1371	1539	964	587
239	Non-metallic mineral products n.e.c.	2961	3238	3498	2814	43540	43205	36005	29510	34980	56111	48992	42124
2391	Refractory products	39	46	49	50	383	341	275	472	348	339	278	647
2392	Clay building materials	566	563	570	580	2590	3201	2399	1900	2236	3276	2660	2893
2393	Other porcelain and ceramic products	57	57	56	29	131	...	103	...	91	...	149	...
2394	Cement, lime and plaster	1297	1470	1623	120	22625	22206	18448	6702	27920	30139	26611	8864
2395	Articles of concrete, cement and plaster	752	834	908	1703	15500	15500	12663	18775	2396	20386	17186	28906
2396	Cutting, shaping and finishing of stone	157	162	175	192	250	349	200	124	125	220	140	79
2399	Other non-metallic mineral products n.e.c.	93	106	117	140	2061	1608	1917	1537	1864	1751	1968	735
2410	Basic iron and steel	57	65	67	186	33186	31851	32836	33596	50541	55447	59063	41747
2420	Basic precious and other non-ferrous metals	96	97	106	127	48304	42984	40169	42310	93705	96279	97525	110739
243	Casting of metals	62	61	63	67	2967	2797	...	1646	8645	3312	...	2126
2431	Casting of iron and steel	40	39	38	42	2500	2300	1705	1096	2131	2299	1505	988
2432	Casting of non-ferrous metals	13	13	15	25	467	497	530	549	866	1013	1087	532
251	Struct.metal products, tanks, reservoirs	667	698	716	1061	12121	11888	11821	9737	15234	16500	16977	17485

continued

Kazakhstan

ISIC	Industry	Note	Number of enterprises (number)				Note	Number of employees (number)				Note	Wages and salaries paid to employees (millions of Kazakhstan Tenge)			
	ISIC Revision 4		2013	2014	2015	2016		2013	2014	2015	2016		2013	2014	2015	2016
2511	Structural metal products		594	620	637	963		10811	10453	10382	8367		13635	14821	15258	6811
2512	Tanks, reservoirs and containers of metal		18	21	24	78		759	737	764	1201		1108	1006	1082	1338
2513	Steam generators, excl. hot water boilers		55	57	55	20		551	698	675	169		491	673	637	445
2520	Weapons and ammunition		6	7	6	6		1	…	…	…		…	…	…	…
259	Other metal products;metal working services		460	498	527	736		4935	3848	2918	2513		6793	5868	5100	3607
2591	Forging,pressing,stamping,roll-forming of metal		63	65	73	81		153	154	…	30		265	149	…	34
2592	Treatment and coating of metals machining		130	135	141	159		2267	1788	1554	1194		3456	3080	2735	2452
2593	Cutlery, hand tools and general hardware		70	68	65	84		158	130	144	19		159	110	323	7
2599	Other fabricated metal products n.e.c.		197	230	248	412		2357	1776	1220	1270		2913	2529	2042	427
2610	Electronic components and boards		22	24	28	33		557	915	798	622		1605	2880	2874	1275
2620	Computers and peripheral equipment		28	34	37	37		223	214	178	179		441	488	377	569
2630	Communication equipment		35	34	34	34		…	…	…	…		…	…	…	…
2640	Consumer electronics		17	22	20	16		…	…	…	…		320	265	265	…
265	Measuring,testing equipment; watches, etc.		42	44	49	53		423	450	413	381		430	620	601	607
2651	Measuring/testing/navigating equipment,etc.		37	39	45	48		423	450	413	381		430	620	601	607
2652	Watches and clocks		5	5	4	5		…	…	…	…		…	…	…	…
2660	Irradiation/electromedical equipment,etc.		11	11	11	11		198	198	181	285		269	279	221	297
2670	Optical instruments and photographic equipment		9	9	9	8		129	163	167	155		39	179	200	182
2680	Magnetic and optical media		2	2	…	-		89	86	…	-		47	45	…	-
2710	Electric motors,generators,transformers,etc.		82	89	106	119		2850	2961	2466	2462		4182	4864	3859	4458
2720	Batteries and accumulators		29	32	27	28		1039	1008	941	819		872	1044	862	1046
273	Wiring and wiring devices		33	43	51	60		1831	1818	1723	1626		2351	2509	2540	2669
2731	Fibre optic cables		4	7	8	11		…	…	…	…		…	…	…	…
2732	Other electronic and electric wires and cables		24	31	36	39		1830	1818	1723	1626		2350	2509	2540	2669
2733	Wiring devices		5	5	7	10		4	130	…	…		14	72	…	…
2740	Electric lighting equipment		35	43	51	63		…	…	…	…		…	…	…	…
2750	Domestic appliances		29	32	30	33		…	…	…	…		…	…	…	…
2790	Other electrical equipment		69	69	70	82		1601	1580	1173	1091		1795	1854	1547	1502
281	General-purpose machinery		215	231	237	315		4855	4208	3526	5175		7654	6919	8705	7744
2811	Engines/turbines,excl.aircraft,vehicle engines		16	16	18	19		246	101	…	…		238	115	…	…
2812	Fluid power equipment		12	11	11	11		…	…	…	…		…	…	…	…
2813	Other pumps, compressors, taps and valves		19	24	25	47		382	354	329	1247		508	436	329	1938
2814	Bearings, gears, gearing and driving elements		30	31	32	30		2839	2481	2199	2157		2758	2796	2429	2583
2815	Ovens, furnaces and furnace burners		13	13	12	15		…	…	…	…		…	…	…	…
2816	Lifting and handling equipment		36	40	44	45		794	699	467	625		775	753	644	1204
2817	Office machinery, excl.computers,etc.		5	5	7	9		…	…	…	…		…	…	…	…
2818	Power-driven hand tools		…	…	…	-		-	…	…	…		-	…	…	-
2819	Other general-purpose machinery		84	91	88	139		548	580	531	1146		563	…	…	1677
282	Special-purpose machinery		260	290	278	300		11864	11659	9473	9021		17181	15566	12913	10258
2821	Agricultural and forestry machinery		77	83	73	78		1901	1980	1772	1518		1798	2110	2007	1839
2822	Metal-forming machinery and machine tools		14	14	13	25		…	…	…	…		…	…	…	…

Code	Activity												
2823	Machinery for metallurgy	8	10	10	8	803	753	549	526	874	871	577	704
2824	Mining, quarrying and construction machinery	45	60	56	57	4810	4497	4003	3094	6106	6313	6166	5581
2825	Food/beverage/tobacco processing machinery	13	15	13	16	110	59	183	244	2826	29	202	314
2826	Textile/apparel/leather production machinery	2	1	1	3	:	:	:	:	:	:	:	1820
2829	Other special-purpose machinery	101	107	112	113	4240	4370	2966	3639	5577	6243	3961	3322
2910	Motor vehicles	27	31	32	33	1617	2291	1995	1846	2463	3778	3308	:
2920	Automobile bodies, trailers and semi-trailers	12	20	21	26	118	116	:	:	119	141	30	:
2930	Parts and accessories for motor vehicles	26	25	28	26	:	:	:	:	711	:	:	:
301	Building of ships and boats	13	12	14	14	928	923	909	912	1467	1557	1392	1678
3011	Building of ships and floating structures	8	8	9	10	928	923	909	912	1467	1557	1392	1678
3012	Building of pleasure and sporting boats	5	4	5	4	:	:	:	:	:	:	:	:
3020	Railway locomotives and rolling stock	48	52	51	51	3654	3633	3539	3243	4920	5276	5409	5904
3030	Air and spacecraft and related machinery	13	16	17	21	219	269	204	195	3040	515	154	147
3040	Military fighting vehicles	:	1	3	3	-	:	705	669	-	3091	1067	918
309	Transport equipment n.e.c.	12	14	13	16	:	:	:	:	:	:	:	:
3091	Motorcycles	:	:	:	1	-	:	:	:	-	:	:	:
3092	Bicycles and invalid carriages	10	10	9	9	:	:	:	:	:	:	:	:
3099	Other transport equipment n.e.c.	2	4	4	6	:	:	:	:	:	31	:	:
3100	Furniture	1016	1057	1073	1174	1727	2149	1236	1333	1242	1645	865	528
321	Jewellery, bijouterie and related articles	75	78	78	83	336	332	325	354	835	3220	3220	1025
3211	Jewellery and related articles	59	63	62	72	:	1	:	320	:	:	:	801
3212	Imitation jewellery and related articles	11	10	11	11	:	:	:	:	110	3220	3220	:
3220	Musical instruments	3	8	4	4	:	:	:	:	:	:	:	:
3230	Sports goods	3	8	4	11	:	:	:	:	:	:	:	:
3240	Games and toys	4	6	9	12	168	152	135	139	135	119	130	144
3250	Medical and dental instruments and supplies	61	61	61	61	834	768	786	715	808	897	1032	932
3290	Other manufacturing n.e.c.	148	212	258	309	382	474	457	306	541	721	718	335
331	Repair of fabricated metal products/machinery	1958	1946	1987	2079	55219	54620	51673	43583	75190	84330	84200	88901
3311	Repair of fabricated metal products	79	83	89	93	2081	2180	2325	2029	2568	3084	3561	3317
3312	Repair of machinery	1048	1039	1067	1110	18574	18195	17025	16937	26768	30571	31492	34177
3313	Repair of electronic and optical equipment	201	209	216	236	:	:	:	:	2704	:	:	:
3314	Repair of electrical equipment	306	294	290	299	3418	3598	3445	3317	6361	8129	8611	9852
3315	Repair of transport equip., excl. motor vehicles	20	19	19	298	127	67	:	20561	277	129	:	40426
3319	Repair of other equipment	22	20	35	43	:	:	798	739	:	:	1055	1129
3320	Installation of industrial machinery/equipment	115	144	169	191	394	319	300	439	499	537	538	695
C	Total manufacturing	21162	22228	22259	22616	375194	367310	332329	303534	502194	556308	533578	564548

Kazakhstan

ISIC	Industry	Output at basic prices (millions of Kazakhstan Tenge)					Value added at basic prices (millions of Kazakhstan Tenge)					Gross fixed capital formation (millions of Kazakhstan Tenge)	
		Note	2013	2014	2015	2016	Note	2013	2014	2015	2016	Note	2015	2016
1010	Processing/preserving of meat		938323a/	1137628a/	1194770a/	205820		78263	85689	86862	112145		6628	7953
1020	Processing/preserving of fish, etc.		...a/	...a/	...a/	14030		4351	5509	6484	7446		147	468
1030	Processing/preserving of fruit,vegetables		...a/	...a/	...a/	113479		54291	53315	62837	74913		2033	2472
1040	Vegetable and animal oils and fats		...a/	...a/	...a/	136877		52201	59208	55747	70833		5765	16972
1050	Dairy products		...a/	...a/	...a/	233477		97097	121510	114133	132284		11054	12407
106	Grain mill products,starches and starch products		...a/	...a/	...a/	334154		134574	139392	158941	192167		10650	15884
1061	Grain mill products		...	...	...	332427		134317	138613	158284	191107		9312	15677
1062	Starches and starch products		...	...	...	1727		257	780	657	1060		1337	207
107	Other food products		...a/	...a/	...a/	442055		87666	111061	105299	263632		24889	23317
1071	Bakery products		...	...	...	180120		65277	85294	78050	114549		13741	6518
1072	Sugar		...	...	...	87918		13519	15691	16175	51532		460	2745
1073	Cocoa, chocolate and sugar confectionery		...	...	...	73340		8870	10076	11075	40127		8036	7528
1074	Macaroni, noodles, couscous, etc.		...	...	...	21886		...	...	...	12290		133	1191
1075	Prepared meals and dishes		...	...	...	23899		...	...	...	14057		218	1474
1079	Other food products n.e.c.		...	...	...	54892		...	...	...	31078		1077	3861
1080	Prepared animal feeds		...a/	...a/	...a/	43267		70381	87285	84688	20258		910	21001
110	Beverages		378786	461234	497280	544654		243341	292173	297048	327550		18301	13185
1101	Distilling, rectifying and blending of spirits		...	...	...	315830		134228	165399	196660	211189		4174	290
1102	Wines		...	...	...	8047		1932	2837	2806	5236		183	18
1103	Malt liquors and malt		...	...	...	77346		280	345	524	37368		55	7527
1104	Soft drinks,mineral waters,other bottled waters		...	...	...	143433		13	7	12	73756		6372	5350
1200	Tobacco products		109354	103156	94460	105620		61132	57866	54115	59328		4365	10857
131	Spinning, weaving and finishing of textiles		55359b/	42067b/	44822b/	35690		10625	8301	8873	15093		4771	2657
1311	Preparation and spinning of textile fibres		...	...	...	29080		-	...	...	12007		4062	1683
1312	Weaving of textiles		...	...	...	6598		...	...	...	3081		710	973
1313	Finishing of textiles		...	...	...	12		...	...	...	5		-	
139	Other textiles		...b/	...b/	...b/	27526		6238	6264	6457	8478		3514	1514
1391	Knitted and crocheted fabrics		...	...	...	3		2	3	3	1		2	...
1392	Made-up textile articles, except apparel		...	...	...	20751		4904	4278	4520	5363		1342	1475
1393	Carpets and rugs		...	...	...	4267		96	745	1187	2006		2008	1
1394	Cordage, rope, twine and netting		...	...	...	380		133	139	42	171		-	38
1399	Other textiles n.e.c.		...	...	...	2125		...	656	403	938		46	38
1410	Wearing apparel, except fur apparel		26849c/	29823c/	36543c/	35264		13246	14581	16864	17068		1309	990
1420	Articles of fur		...c/	...c/	...c/	174		...	286	130	100		-	185
1430	Knitted and crocheted apparel		...c/	...c/	...c/	1452		255	312	336	548		4672	41
151	Leather;luggage,handbags,saddlery,harness;fur		4440d/	7345d/	6479d/	830		825	1462	987	636		31	540
1511	Tanning/dressing of leather; dressing of fur		...	...	...d/	786		804	1357	950	610		31	540
1512	Luggage,handbags,etc.;saddlery/harness		...	...	...	44		21	105	37	27		-	...
1520	Footwear		...d/	...d/	...d/	7724		2760	3868	4085	5885		149	446
1610	Sawmilling and planing of wood		12849e/	19464e/	20588e/	9288		4117	4868	5954	6043		247	40

Code	Product	(1)	(2)	(3)	(4)	(5)	(6)	(7)	(8)	(9)	(10)
162	Wood products, cork, straw, plaiting materials	316	1536	9508	7178	7744	6585	15460	...e/	...e/	...e/
1621	Veneer sheets and wood-based panels	246	136	3355	1640	1461	1024	6005	...	...	...
1622	Builders' carpentry and joinery	17	-	3979	...	...	...	6205	...	...	...
1623	Wooden containers	-	1394	1358	4176	4718	4432	2074	...	...	...
1629	Other wood products;articles of cork,straw	52	6	816	357	557	661	1177	...	...	...
170	Paper and paper products	10557	5927	35014	26019	2419	1775	56047	34465	38783	38987
1701	Pulp, paper and paperboard	4634	59	4154	...	...	...	8428	...	...	...
1702	Corrugated paper and paperboard	1474	547	16364	...	...	...	25045	...	...	...
1709	Other articles of paper and paperboard	4449	18	14495	...	...	...	22575	...	...	...
181	Printing and service activities related to printing	2383	4164	26534	28906	23824	27155	51293	53643f/	46257f/	55762f/
1811	Printing	2359	133	25294	3337	3516	3507	48676	...	...	...
1812	Service activities related to printing	24	4000	1240	24303	19201	22615	2617	...	...	...
1820	Reproduction of recorded media	23	79	126	76	26	70	194	..f/	..f/	..f/
1910	Coke oven products	5	753	41655	33691	34427	29674	80002	1187013g/	1001398g/	9077118g/
1920	Refined petroleum products	318905	253104	546112	465449	516104	582890	1000690	..g/	..g/	..g/
201	Basic chemicals,fertilizers, etc.	76228	34216	169932	153144	148257	120838	267791	227090h/	268991h/	289469h/
2011	Basic chemicals	20774	93	133856	14962	14871	16721	205193	...	...	...
2012	Fertilizers and nitrogen compounds	289	10108	29863	15931	15464	12956	51491	...	...	...
2013	Plastics and synthetic rubber in primary forms	51963	11978	6212	85583	81233	58629	11107	..h/	..h/	..h/
202	Other chemical products	11592	7272	46810	9220	6654	8575	72823	...	...	...
2021	Pesticides and other agrochemical products	2913	835	11430	...	...	...	18740	...	...	...
2022	Paints,varnishes;printing ink and mastics	59	564	9096	...	...	...	13134	...	...	...
2023	Soap,cleaning and cosmetic preparations	291	358	3452	...	...	...	5238	...	...	...
2029	Other chemical products n.e.c.	2318	5515	22832	...	...	...	35711	..h/	...	...
2030	Man-made fibres	83	-	474	8171	7967	10229	766	..h/	..h/	..h/
2100	Pharmaceuticals,medicinal chemicals, etc.	13181	14951	101363	85554	1073	763	130304	132203	110882	111583
221	Rubber products	377	224	2996	2559	3936	3215	6468	1458154i/	1597116i/	152564i/
2211	Rubber tyres and tubes	-	-	6	12	268	600	12	...	...	...
2219	Other rubber products	377	224	2990	2547	3668	2615	6456	...	...	...
2220	Plastics products	13286	8421	76506	64818	63794	57710	183359	..i/	..i/	..i/
2310	Glass and glass products	19978	2664	9861	7317	5107	5763	14500	466011i/	531165i/	510831i/
239	Non-metallic mineral products n.e.c.	69898	106041	301834	18690	16165	20992	506382	..j/	..j/	..j/
2391	Refractory products	1191	3467	2256	94	123	...	4834	...	...	...
2392	Clay building materials	4035	4451	7383	...	...	...	12911	...	...	...
2393	Other porcelain and ceramic products	3	37	36	...	...	...	56	...	...	...
2394	Cement, lime and plaster	27753	59117	101965	...	...	...	157020	...	...	...
2395	Articles of concrete, cement and plaster	32120	34851	154741	...	...	...	273699	...	...	...
2396	Cutting, shaping and finishing of stone	2357	1466	4942	...	...	...	9180	...	...	...
2399	Other non-metallic mineral products n.e.c.	2438	2653	30512	18597	16042	...	48683	...	...	...
2410	Basic iron and steel	56555	160373	670971	428154	412534	349538	1657411	2496998k/	2670666k/	2990824k/
2420	Basic precious and other non-ferrous metals	295740	305256	1373217	17708	17256	17602	2797461	..k/	..k/	..k/
243	Casting of metals	7050	1032	6124	17617	18971	20996	13362	...	...	...
2431	Casting of iron and steel	6686	212	5824	4734	5467	...	12802	...	...	...
2432	Casting of non-ferrous metals	364	683	299	1	...	...	559	...	...	...
251	Struct.metal products, tanks, reservoirs	7835	15418	91781	61331	71274	65605	141640	184950m/	187197m/	185703m/

continued

Kazakhstan

ISIC Revision 4

Output at basic prices and Value added at basic prices in millions of Kazakhstan Tenge; Gross fixed capital formation in millions of Kazakhstan Tenge.

ISIC	Industry	Note	Output 2013	Output 2014	Output 2015	Output 2016	Note	VA 2013	VA 2014	VA 2015	VA 2016	Note	GFCF 2015	GFCF 2016
2511	Structural metal products		...	...	...	124402		...	63693	53503	79321		14649	4203
2512	Tanks, reservoirs and containers of metal		...	...	...	8377		...	7581	7828	5958		501	583
2513	Steam generators, excl. hot water boilers		...	...	...	8862		...	5481	5042	6502		268	3049
2520	Weapons and ammunition		...m/	...m/	...m/	...m/		4926	...	...	...		4	...
259	Other metal products;metal working services		...m/	...m/	...m/	100691		35844	10086	34050	74748		2453	5150
2591	Forging,pressing,stamping,roll-forming of metal		...	...	...	3701		...	846	1050	2303		90	3145
2592	Treatment and coating of metals; machining		...	...	...	28274		...	2899	2761	19683		1621	414
2593	Cutlery, hand tools and general hardware		...	...	...	2366		...	5430	6975	1198		290	296
2599	Other fabricated metal products n.e.c.		...	...	...	66350		...	911	21814	51564		453	1295
2610	Electronic components and boards		32555n/	34872n/	34056n/	158		737	1148	490	44		2339	2573
2620	Computers and peripheral equipment		...	...	...n/	3171		1043	968	1838	1074		5	18
2630	Communication equipment		...	...	...n/	8876		3884	3595	2166	3537		12	2
2640	Consumer electronics		...	...	...n/	10434		3757	3054	1979	2672		-	...
265	Measuring,testing equipment; watches, etc.		...	...	...n/	6966		465	1041	2307	2750		322	205
2651	Measuring/testing/navigating equipment,etc.		...	...	...	6957		...	1041	2307	2747		322	205
2652	Watches and clocks		...	...	...	8		...	...	...	3		...	...
2660	Irradiation/electromedical equipment,etc.		...	...	...n/	1763		439	428	293	598		152	-
2670	Optical instruments and photographic equipment		...	...	...n/	6548		...	752	1309	1250		-	-
2680	Magnetic and optical media		...	...	...n/	-		...	...	...	-		-	-
2710	Electric motors,generators,transformers,etc.		77957p/	85081p/	78788p/	42826		22870	24082	19247	25410		4823	2266
2720	Batteries and accumulators		...	...	...p/	18245		5844	6881	5175	9813		312	1014
273	Wiring and wiring devices		...	...	...p/	31451		11769	14475	12451	18471		5432	1289
2731	Fibre optic cables		...	...	...	1735		1118	911	432	703		683	46
2732	Other electronic and electric wires and cables		...	...	...p/	28750		10220	13244	11485	17187		4750	1243
2733	Wiring devices		...	...	...	966		431	320	534	581		-	...
2740	Electric lighting equipment		...	...	...p/	4989		572	991	1179	2801		636	566
2750	Domestic appliances		...	...	...p/	670		1479	629	311	324		159	170
2790	Other electrical equipment		...	...	...p/	21602		2196	1797	7258	12891		851	1651
281	General-purpose machinery		96784q/	108910q/	89658q/	49984		25492	24087	14534	36082		2972	2647
2811	Engines/turbines,excl.aircraft,vehicle engines		...	...	...	1497		146	241	148	694		423	262
2812	Fluid power equipment		...	...	...	44		575	235	10	27		-	1
2813	Other pumps, compressors, taps and valves		...	...	...	20829		8750	8744	4639	14935		115	167
2814	Bearings, gears, gearing and driving elements		...	...	...	11783		5215	7746	4941	9088		1061	949
2815	Ovens, furnaces and furnace burners		...	...	...	286		10806	7121	4796	163		-	...
2816	Lifting and handling equipment		...	...	...	7827		...	...	...	5388		320	157
2817	Office machinery, excl.computers,etc.		...	...	...	...		...	...	...	...		-	9
2818	Power-driven hand tools		...	...	...	-		...	...	...	-		-	...
2819	Other general-purpose machinery		...	...	...	7719		...	...	...	5787		97	1102
282	Special-purpose machinery		...q/	...q/	...q/	68176		10232	10096	9731	51662		16069	17240
2821	Agricultural and forestry machinery		...	...	...	33304		1020	466	386	26432		11386	2999
2822	Metal-forming machinery and machine tools		...	...	...	199		3687	3455	4584	139		11	-

2823	Machinery for metallurgy	...	...	...	4174	27	27	32	2474	19	21
2824	Mining, quarrying and construction machinery	...	...	...	15615	80	13	5	12177	344	11349
2825	Food/beverage/tobacco processing machinery	...	...	...	692	3323	3221	2343	504	1334	171
2826	Textile/apparel/leather production machinery	...	...	...	1	...	2913	2380	1	2973	1432
2829	Other special-purpose machinery	...	...	...	14191	2913	...	...	9935	3101	1583
2910	Motor vehicles	162767r/	184974r/	70369r/	47844r/	64976	76869	35945	22412	37	1583
2920	Automobile bodies, trailers and semi-trailers	...r/	...r/	...r/	1732	1148	1521	1245	687	-	29
2930	Parts and accessories for motor vehicles	...r/	...r/	...r/	403	207	233	190	250	...	322
301	Building of ships and boats	184360s/	125749s/	75069s/	4127	...	2447	1232	1710	42	474
3011	Building of ships and floating structures	...	...	...	4087	...	...	...	1690	42	474
3012	Building of pleasure and sporting boats	...	...	...	40	...	...	...	19	-	-
3020	Railway locomotives and rolling stock	...s/	...s/	...s/	73950	38303	26697	14508	23094	21724	2940
3030	Air and spacecraft and related machinery	...s/	...s/	...s/	4295	...	2371	...	1604	5849	3738
3040	Military fighting vehicles	...s/	...s/	...s/	...	-	-	...	...	4	...
309	Transport equipment n.e.c.	...s/	...s/	...s/	1118	106	273	98	697	-	...
3091	Motorcycles	...	...	...	...	-	-	...	...	-	...
3092	Bicycles and invalid carriages	...	...	...	159	...	91	87	92	-	...
3099	Other transport equipment n.e.c.	...	...	...	959	...	183	11	605	-	...
3100	Furniture	26276	33570	30216	35760	19001	21316	19393	23181	1357	1188
321	Jewellery, bijouterie and related articles	12910t/	12689t/	13129t/	3954	2422	2255	1823	2335	73	499
3211	Jewellery and related articles	...t/	...t/	...t/	3922	1865	1961	1608	2319	73	499
3212	Imitation jewellery and related articles	...t/	...t/	...t/	32	490	276	205	16	...	...
3220	Musical instruments	...t/	...t/	...t/	6	2	3	2	2	...	...
3230	Sports goods	...t/	...t/	...t/	580	333	268	145	356	...	...
3240	Games and toys	...t/	...t/	...t/	142	84	77	58	70	8	1
3250	Medical and dental instruments and supplies	...t/	...t/	...t/	5667	3169	3020	3711	3310	427	510
3290	Other manufacturing n.e.c.	...t/	...t/	...t/	1984	1430	1690	1468	816	729	683
331	Repair of fabricated metal products/machinery	343318u/	363592u/	331414u/	389376	138305	145308	130117	161508	8659	13093
3311	Repair of fabricated metal products	...	...	...	10711	9105	9616	7016	7423	212	115
3312	Repair of machinery	...	...	...	211913	58733	63908	62346	84167	5458	4475
3313	Repair of electronic and optical equipment	...	...	...	22071	4284	5212	5631	8545	88	48
3314	Repair of electrical equipment	...	...	...	45410	15239	14295	11301	15440	609	488
3315	Repair of transport equip., excl. motor vehicles	...	...	...	94376	633	548	935	43635	2045	7909
3319	Repair of other equipment	...	...	...	4896	1177	2070	1480	2298	72	58
3320	Installation of industrial machinery/equipment	...u/	...u/	...u/	19526	8473	12619	9726	10516	170	46
C	Total manufacturing	7391112	7765207	7861081	10254354	3828487	4093849	4201012	5321900	1102806	2527977

a/ 1010 includes 1020, 1030, 1040, 1050, 106, 107 and 1080.
b/ 131 includes 139.
c/ 1410 includes 1420 and 1430.
d/ 151 includes 1520.
e/ 1610 includes 162.
f/ 181 includes 1820.
g/ 1910 includes 1920.
h/ 201 includes 202 and 2030.
i/ 221 includes 2220.
j/ 2310 includes 239.

k/ 2410 includes 2420 and 243.
m/ 251 includes 2520 and 259.
n/ 2610 includes 2620, 2630, 2640, 265, 2660, 2670 and 2680.
p/ 2710 includes 2720, 273, 2740, 2750 and 2790.
q/ 281 includes 282.
r/ 2910 includes 2920 and 2930.
s/ 301 includes 3020, 3030, 3040 and 309.
t/ 321 includes 3220, 3230, 3240, 3250 and 3290.
u/ 331 includes 3320.

Kazakhstan

Index numbers of industrial production

ISIC Revision 4

ISIC	Industry	Note	2005	2006	2007	2008	2009	2010	2011	2012	2013	2014	2015	2016
								(2010=100)						
10	Food products		83	87	90	92	95	100	101	103	109	113	114	119
11	Beverages		78	84	91	83	79	100	95	111	120	128	126	127
12	Tobacco products		123	126	129	117	110	100	105	113	109	106	91	91
13	Textiles		133	135	106	119	100	100	83	90	88	89	90	92
14	Wearing apparel		71	70	77	78	81	100	110	121	121	129	137	138
15	Leather and related products		64	71	118	152	146	100	120	145	140	155	160	162
16	Wood products, excluding furniture		71	64	71	69	67	100	124	135	123	126	132	139
17	Paper and paper products		85	104	108	90	97	100	102	102	113	124	106	110
18	Printing and reproduction of recorded media		...	...	...	...	...	...	...	...	...	...	...	...
19	Coke and refined petroleum products		73	76	83	84	88	100	101	102	105	108	105	106
20	Chemicals and chemical products		83	85	101	109	82	100	130	134	138	140	143	140
21	Pharmaceuticals, medicinal chemicals, etc.		33	43	53	54	70	100	99	104	105	107	109	113
22	Rubber and plastics products		43	57	75	80	74	100	120	124	127	128	139	140
23	Other non-metallic mineral products		80	96	123	98	90	100	117	129	147	157	165	156
24	Basic metals		85	90	94	92	89	100	108	106	101	102	117	125
25	Fabricated metal products, except machinery		60	79	107	99	102	100	109	106	116	115	112	116
26	Computer, electronic and optical products		95	105	113	102	77	100	81	100	100	78	82	64
27	Electrical equipment		53	64	74	81	83	100	98	105	118	122	120	124
28	Machinery and equipment n.e.c.		86	81	90	92	73	100	126	137	136	138	101	92
29	Motor vehicles, trailers and semi-trailers		70	185	239	129	47	100	211	418	777	782	353	225
30	Other transport equipment		...	...	...	...	...	...	...	...	...	...	...	...
31	Furniture		...	...	...	...	...	...	...	...	...	...	...	...
32	Other manufacturing		...	...	...	...	...	...	...	...	...	...	...	...
33	Repair and installation of machinery/equipment		...	...	...	...	...	...	...	...	...	...	...	...
C	Total manufacturing		80	85	93	90	88	100	108	109	111	112	113	113

Kuwait

Supplier of information:
Central Statistical Bureau, Kuwait City.

Basic source of data:
Annual survey.

Major deviations from ISIC (Revision 3):
None reported.

Reference period:
Calendar year.

Scope:
All establishments.

Method of data collection:
Direct interview in the field.

Type of enumeration:
Sample survey.

Adjusted for non-response:
Not reported.

Concepts and definitions of variables:
Wages and salaries is compensation of employees.
Output refers to gross output.
Value added refers to total value added.

Related national publications:
Annual Survey of Establishments (Industry), published by the Central Statistical Bureau, Kuwait City.

Kuwait

ISIC	Industry	Number of establishments (number)					Number of employees (number)					Wages and salaries paid to employees (millions of Kuwaiti Dinars)				
		Note	2013	2014	2015	2016	Note	2013	2014	2015	2016	Note	2013	2014	2015	2016
151	Processed meat,fish,fruit,vegetables,fats		17	18	18	18		2336	2417	2442	2554		8.3	8.7	9.6	9.4
1511	Processing/preserving of meat		...	...	...	...		...	...	...	...		...	...	...	...
1512	Processing/preserving of fish		...	...	...	...		...	...	...	...		...	...	...	...
1513	Processing/preserving of fruit & vegetables		...	...	...	...		...	...	...	...		...	...	...	...
1514	Vegetable and animal oils and fats		...	...	...	...		...	...	...	...		...	...	...	...
1520	Dairy products		4	4	4	4		2985	3107	3233	3210		17.2	18.3	19.2	19.2
153	Grain mill products; starches; animal feeds		11	9	10	10		2495	2892	2902	2956		13.1	19.3	18.1	19.2
1531	Grain mill products		...	...	...	...		...	...	...	...		...	...	...	...
1532	Starches and starch products		...	...	...	...		...	...	...	...		...	...	...	...
1533	Prepared animal feeds		...	...	...	...		...	...	...	...		...	...	...	...
154	Other food products		615	617	617	617		12487	12238	12252	12245		32.6	34.4	36.2	37.0
1541	Bakery products		...	...	...	...		...	...	...	...		...	...	...	...
1542	Sugar		...	...	...	...		...	...	...	...		...	...	...	...
1543	Cocoa, chocolate and sugar confectionery		...	...	...	...		...	...	...	...		...	...	...	...
1544	Macaroni, noodles & similar products		...	...	...	...		...	...	...	...		...	...	...	...
1549	Other food products n.e.c.		...	...	...	...		...	...	...	...		...	...	...	...
155	Beverages		6	6	6	6		3505	3788	3976	4007		15.8	14.6	15.1	16.3
1551	Distilling, rectifying & blending of spirits		...	...	...	...		...	...	...	...		...	...	...	...
1552	Wines		...	...	...	...		...	...	...	...		...	...	...	...
1553	Malt liquors and malt		...	...	...	...		...	...	...	...		...	...	...	...
1554	Soft drinks; mineral waters		...	...	...	...		...	...	...	...		...	...	...	...
1600	Tobacco products		...	...	...	...		...	...	...	...		...	...	...	...
171	Spinning, weaving and finishing of textiles		...	...	...	...		...	...	...	...		...	...	...	...
1711	Textile fibre preparation; textile weaving		...	...	...	...		...	...	...	...		...	...	...	...
1712	Finishing of textiles		...	...	...	...		...	...	...	...		...	...	...	...
172	Other textiles		298	293	293	293		2123	2281	2293	2324		5.5	6.1	6.0	6.4
1721	Made-up textile articles, except apparel		...	...	...	...		...	...	...	...		...	...	...	...
1722	Carpets and rugs		...	...	...	...		...	...	...	...		...	...	...	...
1723	Cordage, rope, twine and netting		...	...	...	...		...	...	...	...		...	...	...	...
1729	Other textiles n.e.c		...	...	...	...		...	...	...	...		...	...	...	...
1730	Knitted and crocheted fabrics and articles		...	...	...	...		...	...	...	...		...	...	...	...
1810	Wearing apparel, except fur apparel		2558	2558	2557	2564		15320	14695	14709	14659		30.7	31.3	34.6	35.2
1820	Dressing & dyeing of fur; processing of fur		...	...	...	...		...	...	...	...		...	...	...	...
191	Tanning, dressing and processing of leather		3	3	3	3		118	117	118	118		0.2	0.2	0.2	0.2
1911	Tanning and dressing of leather		...	...	...	...		...	...	...	...		...	...	...	...
1912	Luggage, handbags, etc.; saddlery & harness		...	...	...	...		...	...	...	...		...	...	...	...
1920	Footwear		2	2	2	2		112	107	115	122		0.3	0.3	0.3	0.4
2010	Sawmilling and planing of wood		...	...	...	...		...	...	...	...		...	...	...	...
202	Products of wood, cork, straw, etc.		123	124	125	125		1420	1392	1454	1285		3.1	3.3	3.5	3.5
2021	Veneer sheets, plywood, particle board, etc.		...	...	...	...		...	...	...	...		...	...	...	...
2022	Builders' carpentry and joinery		...	...	...	...		...	...	...	...		...	...	...	...
2023	Wooden containers		...	...	...	...		...	...	...	...		...	...	...	...
2029	Other wood products; articles of cork/straw		...	...	...	...		...	...	...	...		...	...	...	...
210	Paper and paper products		30	28	29	29		2351	2151	2206	2430		11.9	10.8	13.1	13.6
2101	Pulp, paper and paperboard		...	...	...	...		...	...	...	...		...	...	...	...
2102	Corrugated paper and paperboard		...	...	...	...		...	...	...	...		...	...	...	...
2109	Other articles of paper and paperboard		...	...	...	...		...	...	...	...		...	...	...	...
221	Publishing		20	21	20	17		3225	3009	2949	2792		25.8	26.2	26.8	25.6
2211	Publishing of books and other publications		...	...	...	...		...	...	...	...		...	...	...	...
2212	Publishing of newspapers, journals, etc.		...	...	...	...		...	...	...	...		...	...	...	...
2213	Publishing of recorded media		...	...	...	...		...	...	...	...		...	...	...	...
2219	Other publishing		...	...	...	...		...	...	...	...		...	...	...	...

Code	Description	80	80	81	81	81	2502	2600	2621	2761				
222	Printing and related service activities										9.1	9.7	10.6	11.0
2221	Printing													
2222	Service activities related to printing													
2230	Reproduction of recorded media													
2310	Coke oven products	1	1	1	1	1	154	164	167	148	0.8	1.0	2.2	1.9
2320	Refined petroleum products	1	1	1	1	1	6211	6941	7255	7261	372.3	447.9	398.5	399.9
2330	Processing of nuclear fuel													
241	Basic chemicals	17	17	17	17	17	4550	4545	4610	4593	116.1	110.6	106.8	101.7
2411	Basic chemicals, except fertilizers													
2412	Fertilizers and nitrogen compounds													
2413	Plastics in primary forms; synthetic rubber													
242	Other chemicals	21	21	21	21	21	1716	1794	1866	1912	8.6	9.3	9.3	9.8
2421	Pesticides and other agro-chemical products													
2422	Paints, varnishes, printing ink and mastics													
2423	Pharmaceuticals, medicinal chemicals, etc.													
2424	Soap, cleaning & cosmetic preparations													
2429	Other chemical products n.e.c.													
2430	Man-made fibres													
251	Rubber products	3	4	4	4	4	385	589	625	628	1.1	1.4	1.5	2.0
2511	Rubber tyres and tubes													
2519	Other rubber products	41	41	38	38	40					15.7	18.0	18.6	20.6
2520	Plastic products	153	153	154	154	154	4462	4546	4512	4772	3.9	4.2	4.5	4.6
2610	Glass and glass products	43	44	44	46	49	1188	1212	1202	1237	42.9	49.1	47.8	48.3
269	Non-metallic mineral products n.e.c.						10602	11246	11013	11017				
2691	Pottery, china and earthenware													
2692	Refractory ceramic products													
2693	Struct.non-refractory clay; ceramic products													
2694	Cement, lime and plaster													
2695	Articles of concrete, cement and plaster													
2696	Cutting, shaping & finishing of stone													
2699	Other non-metallic mineral products n.e.c.													
2710	Basic iron and steel	4	4	4	4	4	1108	1248	1278	1876	10.8	14.9	14.5	16.0
2720	Basic precious and non-ferrous metals	3	3	3	3	3	298	310	342	332	0.8	0.9	0.9	0.9
273	Casting of metals	1	1	1	1	1	6	7	7	8	-	-	-	-
2731	Casting of iron and steel													
2732	Casting of non-ferrous metals													
281	Struct.metal products;tanks;steam generators	729	745	742	742	737	9612	9516	9663	10011	28.3	30.8	29.1	31.0
2811	Structural metal products													
2812	Tanks, reservoirs and containers of metal													
2813	Steam generators													
289	Other metal products; metal working services	162	149	150	150	150	2343	2219	2298	2353	7.4	7.9	9.5	8.9
2891	Metal forging/pressing/stamping/roll-forming													
2892	Treatment & coating of metals													
2893	Cutlery, hand tools and general hardware													
2899	Other fabricated metal products n.e.c.													
291	General purpose machinery	56	55	55	55	55	1347	1350	2227	2104	4.2	4.2	6.0	6.7
2911	Engines & turbines (not for transport equipment)													
2912	Pumps, compressors, taps and valves													
2913	Bearings, gears, gearing & driving elements													
2914	Ovens, furnaces and furnace burners													
2915	Lifting and handling equipment													
2919	Other general purpose machinery													
292	Special purpose machinery	3	3	3	3	3	94	212	215	209	1.0	1.7	1.7	1.8
2921	Agricultural and forestry machinery													
2922	Machine tools													
2923	Machinery for metallurgy													
2924	Machinery for mining & construction													
2925	Food/beverage/tobacco processing machinery													
2926	Machinery for textile, apparel and leather													
2927	Weapons and ammunition													
2929	Other special purpose machinery													

continued

Kuwait

ISIC	Industry	Number of establishments (number)					Number of employees (number)					Wages and salaries paid to employees (millions of Kuwaiti Dinars)				
		Note	2013	2014	2015	2016	Note	2013	2014	2015	2016	Note	2013	2014	2015	2016
2930	Domestic appliances n.e.c.		3	3	3	3		87	88	96	98		0.3	0.3	0.3	0.3
3000	Office, accounting and computing machinery		...	...	...	...		...	...	...	...		...	...	...	...
3110	Electric motors, generators and transformers															
3120	Electricity distribution & control apparatus		12	12	12	12		3288	3564	3801	3936		13.2	14.9	14.9	18.1
3130	Insulated wire and cable		1	1	1	1		561	553	658	681		6.0	5.6	5.6	6.6
3140	Accumulators, primary cells and batteries															
3150	Lighting equipment and electric lamps							...	...	...	...		...	...	...	...
3190	Other electrical equipment n.e.c.															
3210	Electronic valves, tubes, etc.		...	...	...	...		...	...	...	...					
3220	TV/radio transmitters; line comm. apparatus		...	...	...	...		...	...	...	...					
3230	TV and radio receivers and associated goods		...	...	...	...		...	...	...	...					
331	Medical, measuring, testing appliances, etc.		7	8	8	8		5702	5207	5649	5852		35.4	26.1	33.0	30.1
3311	Medical, surgical and orthopaedic equipment															
3312	Measuring/testing/navigating appliances,etc.															
3313	Industrial process control equipment															
3320	Optical instruments & photographic equipment															
3330	Watches and clocks		...	...	...	...		...	...	...	...		...	...	...	...
3410	Motor vehicles															
3420	Automobile bodies, trailers & semi-trailers		8	8	7	7		292	293	306	308		1.1	1.1	1.3	1.3
3430	Parts/accessories for automobiles		1	1	1	1		50	50	50	50		0.1	0.1	0.1	0.2
351	Building and repairing of ships and boats		18	18	17	17		5194	5423	6406	8901		17.6	18.9	25.6	31.6
3511	Building and repairing of ships															
3512	Building/repairing of pleasure/sport. boats															
3520	Railway/tramway locomotives & rolling stock															
3530	Aircraft and spacecraft															
359	Transport equipment n.e.c.															
3591	Motorcycles															
3592	Bicycles and invalid carriages															
3599	Other transport equipment n.e.c.		...	...	...	...		...	...	...	...					
3610	Furniture		359	365	370	381		5417	5334	5459	5713		14.1	16.1	16.9	17.3
369	Manufacturing n.e.c.		92	87	87	87		684	728	737	706		1.8	2.0	2.2	2.5
3691	Jewellery and related articles		...	...	...	...		...	...	...	...		...	...	...	...
3692	Musical instruments															
3693	Sports goods															
3694	Games and toys															
3699	Other manufacturing n.e.c.							...	...	...	...		...	...	...	...
3710	Recycling of metal waste and scrap		1	1	1	1		1020	1020	1020	1954		1.6	1.6	1.6	3.3
3720	Recycling of non-metal waste and scrap		2	2	2	2		200	199	198	199		0.9	0.6	0.9	1.1
D	Total manufacturing		5509	5508	5514	5529		117550	119152	122930	128322		879.4	972.4	946.6	963.8

Kuwait

| ISIC Revision 3 | | Output at producers' prices | | | | | Value added at producers' prices | | | | | Gross fixed capital formation | | |
| | | Note | (millions of Kuwaiti Dinars) | | | | Note | (millions of Kuwaiti Dinars) | | | | Note | (millions of Kuwaiti Dinars) | |
ISIC	Industry		2013	2014	2015	2016		2013	2014	2015	2016		2015	2016
151	Processed meat,fish,fruit,vegetables,fats		51.1	57.9	63.6	67.7		16.9	18.6	21.5	24.0		1.6	1.7
1511	Processing/preserving of meat													
1512	Processing/preserving of fish													
1513	Processing/preserving of fruit & vegetables													
1514	Vegetable and animal oils and fats													
1520	Dairy products		112.6	120.5	125.6	126.0		35.7	35.0	41.2	41.5		8.3	8.0
153	Grain mill products; starches; animal feeds		83.5	103.9	105.3	103.3		16.2	19.8	22.2	22.3		5.8	1.3
1531	Grain mill products													
1532	Starches and starch products													
1533	Prepared animal feeds													
154	Other food products		171.0	173.0	184.5	187.7		55.5	57.1	62.8	64.1		9.4	4.4
1541	Bakery products													
1542	Sugar													
1543	Cocoa, chocolate and sugar confectionery													
1544	Macaroni, noodles & similar products													
1549	Other food products n.e.c.													
155	Beverages		112.5	122.7	124.5	115.8		29.1	29.4	32.8	31.2		5.0	9.8
1551	Distilling, rectifying & blending of spirits													
1552	Wines													
1553	Malt liquors and malt													
1554	Soft drinks; mineral waters													
1600	Tobacco products													
171	Spinning, weaving and finishing of textiles													
1711	Textile fibre preparation; textile weaving													
1712	Finishing of textiles													
172	Other textiles		27.4	29.8	29.2	29.3		10.9	12.5	12.2	12.7		0.3	0.3
1721	Made-up textile articles, except apparel													
1722	Carpets and rugs													
1723	Cordage, rope, twine and netting													
1729	Other textiles n.e.c.													
1730	Knitted and crocheted fabrics and articles													
1810	Wearing apparel, except fur apparel		96.3	103.8	110.8	121.6		56.4	59.2	65.6	69.6		0.2	0.1
1820	Dressing & dyeing of fur; processing of fur													
191	Tanning, dressing and processing of leather		1.1	1.1	1.1	1.1		-	-	-	-			
1911	Tanning and dressing of leather													
1912	Luggage, handbags, etc.; saddlery & harness													
1920	Footwear		2.1	1.9	2.7	2.5		1.0	0.8	0.9	0.7		0.3	-
2010	Sawmilling and planing of wood													
202	Products of wood, cork, straw, etc.		21.4	21.8	23.1	20.6		6.9	7.0	7.5	7.4		0.4	0.2
2021	Veneer sheets, plywood, particle board, etc.													
2022	Builders' carpentry and joinery													
2023	Wooden containers													
2029	Other wood products; articles of cork/straw													
210	Paper and paper products		91.8	88.8	97.2	103.6		26.3	22.9	25.9	27.6		3.0	5.3
2101	Pulp, paper and paperboard													
2102	Corrugated paper and paperboard													
2109	Other articles of paper and paperboard													
221	Publishing		73.0	73.3	75.3	67.2		34.4	35.6	38.2	34.9		0.9	3.3
2211	Publishing of books and other publications													
2212	Publishing of newspapers, journals, etc.													
2213	Publishing of recorded media													
2219	Other publishing													

continued

Kuwait

ISIC	Industry	Note	Output at producers' prices (millions of Kuwaiti Dinars)				Note	Value added at producers' prices (millions of Kuwaiti Dinars)				Note	Gross fixed capital formation (millions of Kuwaiti Dinars)	
			2013	2014	2015	2016		2013	2014	2015	2016		2015	2016
222	Printing and related service activities		44.5	45.7	44.4	46.3		17.4	18.5	18.7	19.7		3.9	1.9
2221	Printing		…	…	…	…		…	…	…	…		…	…
2222	Service activities related to printing		…	…	…	…		…	…	…	…		…	…
2230	Reproduction of recorded media		…	…	…	…		…	…	…	…		…	…
2310	Coke oven products		46.3	39.9	34.2	26.0		11.4	11.5	13.4	8.9		0.9	0.3
2320	Refined petroleum products		13552.8	11384.3	8312.5	7352.4		1373.4	1153.7	914.4	844.8		1356.8	2063.3
2330	Processing of nuclear fuel		…	…	…	…		…	…	…	…		…	…
241	Basic chemicals		2135.4	1943.7	1589.6	2012.4		691.7	517.8	505.1	579.7		322.9	72.5
2411	Basic chemicals, except fertilizers		…	…	…	…		…	…	…	…		…	…
2412	Fertilizers and nitrogen compounds		…	…	…	…		…	…	…	…		…	…
2413	Plastics in primary forms; synthetic rubber		69.9	71.7	74.2	75.9		22.5	23.3	23.9	26.1		1.6	-1.3
242	Other chemicals		…	…	…	…		…	…	…	…		…	…
2421	Pesticides and other agro-chemical products		…	…	…	…		…	…	…	…		…	…
2422	Paints, varnishes, printing ink and mastics		…	…	…	…		…	…	…	…		…	…
2423	Pharmaceuticals, medicinal chemicals, etc.		…	…	…	…		…	…	…	…		…	…
2424	Soap, cleaning & cosmetic preparations		…	…	…	…		…	…	…	…		…	…
2429	Other chemical products n.e.c.		…	…	…	…		…	…	…	…		…	…
2430	Man-made fibres		…	…	…	…		…	…	…	…		…	…
251	Rubber products		8.4	12.2	12.9	13.1		1.9	3.4	3.3	4.0		0.1	0.4
2511	Rubber tyres and tubes		…	…	…	…		…	…	…	…		…	…
2519	Other rubber products		…	…	…	…		…	…	…	…		…	…
2520	Plastic products		128.4	142.8	153.6	152.5		35.7	38.3	44.7	48.7		5.3	9.1
2610	Glass and glass products		23.7	22.1	24.9	23.0		9.5	9.5	10.9	10.0		1.8	9.0
269	Non-metallic mineral products n.e.c.		431.0	491.1	549.8	497.3		121.9	138.8	140.2	142.7		22.7	39.1
2691	Pottery, china and earthenware		…	…	…	…		…	…	…	…		…	…
2692	Refractory ceramic products		…	…	…	…		…	…	…	…		…	…
2693	Struct.non-refractory clay; ceramic products		…	…	…	…		…	…	…	…		…	…
2694	Cement, lime and plaster		…	…	…	…		…	…	…	…		…	…
2695	Articles of concrete, cement and plaster		…	…	…	…		…	…	…	…		…	…
2696	Cutting, shaping & finishing of stone		…	…	…	…		…	…	…	…		…	…
2699	Other non-metallic mineral products n.e.c.		…	…	…	…		…	…	…	…		…	…
2710	Basic iron and steel		152.8	191.2	185.0	180.9		37.5	43.1	40.9	54.6		4.4	7.6
2720	Basic precious and non-ferrous metals		9.8	9.4	10.2	9.6		2.3	2.3	2.1	2.4		0.6	0.9
273	Casting of metals		0.1	0.1	0.1	0.1		0.1	-	0.1	-		-	-
2731	Casting of iron and steel		…	…	…	…		…	…	…	…		…	…
2732	Casting of non-ferrous metals		…	…	…	…		…	…	…	…		…	…
281	Struct.metal products;tanks;steam generators		165.2	172.4	179.6	185.2		51.1	54.4	56.5	61.2		4.8	3.9
2811	Structural metal products		…	…	…	…		…	…	…	…		…	…
2812	Tanks, reservoirs and containers of metal		…	…	…	…		…	…	…	…		…	…
2813	Steam generators		…	…	…	…		…	…	…	…		…	…
289	Other metal products; metal working services		55.6	64.3	57.5	54.7		13.7	11.5	16.0	16.6		8.5	0.9
2891	Metal forging/pressing/stamping/roll-forming		…	…	…	…		…	…	…	…		…	…
2892	Treatment & coating of metals		…	…	…	…		…	…	…	…		…	…
2893	Cutlery, hand tools and general hardware		…	…	…	…		…	…	…	…		…	…
2899	Other fabricated metal products n.e.c.		…	…	…	…		…	…	…	…		…	…
291	General purpose machinery		43.2	44.6	42.3	46.9		9.7	9.9	13.0	14.5		2.2	5.3
2911	Engines & turbines (not for transport equipment)		…	…	…	…		…	…	…	…		…	…
2912	Pumps, compressors, taps and valves		…	…	…	…		…	…	…	…		…	…
2913	Bearings, gears, gearing & driving elements		…	…	…	…		…	…	…	…		…	…
2914	Ovens, furnaces and furnace burners		…	…	…	…		…	…	…	…		…	…
2915	Lifting and handling equipment		…	…	…	…		…	…	…	…		…	…
2919	Other general purpose machinery		…	…	…	…		…	…	…	…		…	…

Code	Description										
292	Special purpose machinery	10.4	8.7	6.7	8.6	2.5	3.0	2.7	3.1	0.1	0.2
2921	Agricultural and forestry machinery	:	:	:	:	:	:	:	:	:	:
2922	Machine tools	:	:	:	:	:	:	:	:	:	:
2923	Machinery for metallurgy	:	:	:	:	:	:	:	:	:	:
2924	Machinery for mining & construction	:	:	:	:	:	:	:	:	:	:
2925	Food/beverage/tobacco processing machinery	:	:	:	:	:	:	:	:	:	:
2926	Machinery for textile, apparel and leather	:	:	:	:	:	:	:	:	:	:
2927	Weapons and ammunition	:	:	:	:	:	:	:	:	:	:
2929	Other special purpose machinery	:	:	:	:	:	:	:	:	:	:
2930	Domestic appliances n.e.c.	1.2	1.5	1.6	1.5	0.6	0.7	0.7	0.6	-	-
3000	Office, accounting and computing machinery	:	:	:	:	:	:	:	:	:	:
3110	Electric motors, generators and transformers	137.2	136.0	150.2	176.0	33.9	38.5	40.8	53.4	6.7	7.9
3120	Electricity distribution & control apparatus	102.5	114.7	85.8	79.9	10.6	15.8	8.9	14.4	0.7	0.3
3130	Insulated wire and cable	:	:	:	:	:	:	:	:	:	:
3140	Accumulators, primary cells and batteries	:	:	:	:	:	:	:	:	:	:
3150	Lighting equipment and electric lamps	:	:	:	:	:	:	:	:	:	:
3190	Other electrical equipment n.e.c.	:	:	:	:	:	:	:	:	:	:
3210	Electronic valves, tubes, etc.	:	:	:	:	:	:	:	:	:	:
3220	TV/radio transmitters; line comm. apparatus	:	:	:	:	:	:	:	:	:	:
3230	TV and radio receivers and associated goods	:	:	:	:	:	:	:	:	:	:
331	Medical, measuring, testing appliances, etc.	55.6	55.8	80.6	77.5	32.2	35.6	43.0	40.4	11.8	12.3
3311	Medical, surgical and orthopaedic equipment	:	:	:	:	:	:	:	:	:	:
3312	Measuring/testing/navigating appliances,etc.	:	:	:	:	:	:	:	:	:	:
3313	Industrial process control equipment	:	:	:	:	:	:	:	:	:	:
3320	Optical instruments & photographic equipment	:	:	:	:	:	:	:	:	:	:
3330	Watches and clocks	:	:	:	:	:	:	:	:	:	:
3410	Motor vehicles	5.8	5.9	8.2	8.1	2.3	2.3	2.7	2.7	0.2	0.3
3420	Automobile bodies, trailers & semi-trailers	0.6	0.5	0.5	0.6	0.3	0.2	0.2	0.3	-	-
3430	Parts/accessories for automobiles	:	:	:	:	:	:	:	:	:	:
351	Building and repairing of ships and boats	64.4	90.4	102.0	104.7	25.2	28.9	36.6	47.3	11.4	12.2
3511	Building and repairing of ships	:	:	:	:	:	:	:	:	:	:
3512	Building/repairing of pleasure/sport. boats	:	:	:	:	:	:	:	:	:	:
3520	Railway/tramway locomotives & rolling stock	:	:	:	:	:	:	:	:	:	:
3530	Aircraft and spacecraft	:	:	:	:	:	:	:	:	:	:
359	Transport equipment n.e.c.	:	:	:	:	:	:	:	:	:	:
3591	Motorcycles	:	:	:	:	:	:	:	:	:	:
3592	Bicycles and invalid carriages	:	:	:	:	:	:	:	:	:	:
3599	Other transport equipment n.e.c.	:	:	:	:	:	:	:	:	:	:
3610	Furniture	76.4	81.7	86.9	90.7	29.4	31.1	33.6	33.2	2.1	1.2
369	Manufacturing n.e.c.	46.7	42.5	52.2	41.2	3.1	5.7	7.3	7.1	0.3	0.1
3691	Jewellery and related articles	:	:	:	:	:	:	:	:	:	:
3692	Musical instruments	:	:	:	:	:	:	:	:	:	:
3693	Sports goods	:	:	:	:	:	:	:	:	:	:
3694	Games and toys	:	:	:	:	:	:	:	:	:	:
3699	Other manufacturing n.e.c.	:	:	:	:	:	:	:	:	:	:
3710	Recycling of metal waste and scrap	16.1	16.1	16.1	12.6	2.5	2.5	2.5	5.2	0.2	0.3
3720	Recycling of non-metal waste and scrap	3.4	2.6	3.5	3.8	2.3	1.7	2.3	2.7	0.1	0.1
D	Total manufacturing	18231.0	16090.4	12807.9	12227.9	2833.8	2499.9	2315.1	2380.4	1805.5	2282.0

Kuwait

Index numbers of industrial production

ISIC	Industry	Note	2005	2006	2007	2008	2009	2010	2011	2012	2013	2014	2015	2016
	ISIC Revision 3							(2010=100)						
15	Food and beverages		…	…	…	…	…	100	110	95	99	101	105	82
16	Tobacco products		…	…	…	…	…	…	…	…	…	…	…	…
17	Textiles		…	…	…	…	…	100	105	105	117	121	115	113
18	Wearing apparel, fur		…	…	…	…	…	100	94	102	108	115	124	136
19	Leather, leather products and footwear		…	…	…	…	…	100	117	117	100	87	110	103
20	Wood products (excl. furniture)		…	…	…	…	…	100	83	112	119	111	113	89
21	Paper and paper products		…	…	…	…	…	100	102	103	111	107	117	124
22	Printing and publishing		…	…	…	…	…	100	100	95	99	100	101	94
23	Coke,refined petroleum products,nuclear fuel		…	…	…	…	…	100	121	128	122	102	75	109
24	Chemicals and chemical products		…	…	…	…	…	100	140	203	181	156	135	167
25	Rubber and plastics products		…	…	…	…	…	100	106	98	106	119	142	146
26	Non-metallic mineral products		…	…	…	…	…	100	113	116	106	126	145	122
27	Basic metals		…	…	…	…	…	100	119	126	179	223	223	220
28	Fabricated metal products		…	…	…	…	…	100	111	101	87	77	76	76
29	Machinery and equipment n.e.c.		…	…	…	…	…	100	89	108	117	117	107	119
30	Office, accounting and computing machinery		…	…	…	…	…	…	…	…	…	…	…	…
31	Electrical machinery and apparatus		…	…	…	…	…	100	119	115	122	126	116	121
32	Radio,television and communication equipment		…	…	…	…	…	…	…	…	…	…	…	…
33	Medical, precision and optical instruments		…	…	…	…	…	100	81	72	73	68	98	94
34	Motor vehicles, trailers, semi-trailers		…	…	…	…	…	100	107	127	79	77	104	104
35	Other transport equipment		…	…	…	…	…	100	153	125	107	151	167	162
36	Furniture; manufacturing n.e.c.		…	…	…	…	…	100	148	154	122	115	128	113
37	Recycling		…	…	…	…	…	100	114	118	114	96	97	77
D	Total manufacturing		…	…	…	…	…	100	121	130	124	108	86	114

Kyrgyzstan

Supplier of information:
National Statistical Committee of the Kyrgyz Republic, Bishkek.

Basic source of data:
Annual industrial survey.

Major deviations from ISIC (Revision 4):
None reported.

Reference period:
Calendar year.

Scope:
All establishments.

Method of data collection:
Direct interview in the field.

Type of enumeration:
Complete enumeration.

Adjusted for non-response:
Not reported

Concepts and definitions of variables:
No deviations from the standard UN concepts and definitions are reported.

Related national publications:
None reported.

Kyrgyzstan

ISIC	Industry	Number of establishments (number)				Note	Number of employees (number)				Note	Wages and salaries paid to employees (thousands of Kyrgyzstan Soms)				Note
		2013	2014	2015	2016		2013	2014	2015	2016		2013	2014	2015	2016	
1010	Processing/preserving of meat	25	13	13	14		832	735	731	798		126990	113009	108868	136419	
1020	Processing/preserving of fish, etc.	2	2	2	2		40	29	29	36		1449	1331	1368	1747	
1030	Processing/preserving of fruit,vegetables	28	27	27	27		323	355	389	314		15622	14475	18677	17819	
1040	Vegetable and animal oils and fats	5	2	...	...		12	...	...	...		499	...	...	...	
1050	Dairy products	44	42	40	40		1661	1599	1558	1419		218846	246109	255595	254199	
106	Grain mill products,starches and starch products	47	33	29	31		1327	1389	1173	1155		90900	100027	89538	85863	
1061	Grain mill products	47	33	29	30		1327	1389	1173	1135		90900	100027	89538	85143	
1062	Starches and starch products	...	-	-	1		-	-	-	20		-	-	-	720	
107	Other food products	76	62	89	93		2860	2758	2699	2975		205795	245390	308334	383803	
1071	Bakery products	57	44	56	57		1549	1415	1355	1443		62504	74616	121022	131371	
1072	Sugar	6	5	6	6		702	730	657	840		106825	122380	122777	185491	
1073	Cocoa, chocolate and sugar confectionery	3	3	7	7		57	31	50	48		1344	1558	2652	2210	
1074	Macaroni, noodles, couscous, etc.	6	6	5	6		194	275	316	374		10932	14610	19050	22489	
1075	Prepared meals and dishes	...	...	...	...		349	296	...	...		23774	31598	...	...	
1079	Other food products n.e.c.	4	4	15	17		9	11	321	270		417	628	42833	42242	
1080	Prepared animal feeds	9	3	3	32		51	27	84	72		3153	2066	18393	15697	
110	Beverages	80	79	72	74		4487	4255	4715	4479		473244	545533	567404	552387	
1101	Distilling, rectifying and blending of spirits	19	19	19	15		1533	1615	1561	1145		145484	168674	152719	126649	
1102	Wines	14	13	15	17		286	144	305	361		8771	7011	15800	19399	
1103	Malt liquors and malt	14	17	11	12		381	1462	416	403		62875	118669	79328	79870	
1104	Soft drinks,mineral waters,other bottled waters	33	30	27	30		2287	1034	2433	2570		256114	251179	319556	326469	
1200	Tobacco products	3	4	4	3		241	191	87	65		54139	65221	22755	...	
131	Spinning, weaving and finishing of textiles	38	38	33	34		1134	907	696	585		69321	66388	39768	35319	
1311	Preparation and spinning of textile fibres	35	36	32	32		956	836	695	551		56220	58772	37650	32993	
1312	Weaving of textiles	3	2	1	2		178	71	1	34		13101	7616	...	2327	
1313	Finishing of textiles	-	-	-	-		-	-	-	-		-	-	-	-	
139	Other textiles	19	20	16	19		651	637	287	254		69400	33833	25923	22850	
1391	Knitted and crocheted fabrics	...	...	-	-		358	329	-	-		37073	1468	-	-	
1392	Made-up textile articles, except apparel	11	10	7	7		98	104	80	63		6291	7653	8060	7915	
1393	Carpets and rugs	3	3	3	3		29	31	28	9		1888	2044	1930	1344	
1394	Cordage, rope, twine and netting	1	2	2	2		-	...	20	20		-	...	1636	1946	
1399	Other textiles n.e.c.	4	5	4	7		166	173	159	162		24148	22669	14297	11646	
1410	Wearing apparel, except fur apparel	46	41	37	34		786	646	525	487		54032	50819	46494	38254	
1420	Articles of fur	25	...	...	1		25	...	...	23		1540	3723	...	1439	
1430	Knitted and crocheted apparel	13	12	9	10		...	...	341	478		...	...	40234	50695	
151	Leather;luggage,handbags,saddlery,harness;fur	6	7	6	4		86	111	102	60		6460	8682	8890	5884	
1511	Tanning/dressing of leather; dressing of fur	6	7	6	4		86	111	102	60		6460	8682	8890	5884	
1512	Luggage,handbags,etc.;saddlery/harness	-	-	-	-		-	-	-	-		-	-	-	-	
1520	Footwear	8	11	13	15		117	216	111	226		6424	10325	6459	14940	
1610	Sawmilling and planing of wood	37	8	6	5		223	57	20	...		6838	...	665	288	

Code	Description	1	2	3	4	5	6	7	8	9	10	11	12
162	Wood products, cork, straw, plaiting materials	6574	7954	8677	9912	128	151	138	265	15	9	12	17
1621	Veneer sheets and wood-based panels	1432	⋯	-	-	27	10	-	-	-	-	-	-
1622	Builders' carpentry and joinery	4698	7532	6706	8405	93	133	124	176	3	1	-	-
1623	Wooden containers	444	422	435	1507	8	8	14	89	7	5	4	11
1629	Other wood products;articles of cork,straw	-	-	-	-	-	-	-	-	5	3	5	6
170	Paper and paper products	76759	69529	70750	64347	622	620	711	685	23	20	22	21
1701	Pulp, paper and paperboard	2569	2387	2302	2474	35	36	48	43	2	4	4	4
1702	Corrugated paper and paperboard	60453	57498	56307	49817	411	449	460	451	4	6	7	8
1709	Other articles of paper and paperboard	13738	9643	12141	12057	176	135	203	191	17	10	11	9
181	Printing and service activities related to printing	138348	141998	128957	123918	1180	1284	1306	1347	96	95	100	109
1811	Printing	137420	140989	21731	122587	1167	1270	1291	1328	8	90	7	8
1812	Service activities related to printing	-	27	1072	1331	13	⋯	15	19	88	⋯	93	101
1820	Reproduction of recorded media	-	⋯	-	-	⋯	2	-	-	⋯	1	-	-
1910	Coke oven products	-	-	-	-	-	-	-	-	-	-	-	-
1920	Refined petroleum products	375123	332443	317944	70998	1294	1236	1141	331	9	9	7	7
201	Basic chemicals,fertilizers, etc.	120518	187491	219807	103981	935	1029	1101	847	23	18	17	15
2011	Basic chemicals	119946	187113	7345	6594	921	1022	125	121	18	16	12	10
2012	Fertilizers and nitrogen compounds	201	49	212402	97274	8	⋯	931	722	3	1	1	4
2013	Plastics and synthetic rubber in primary forms	26370	23498	16459	24040	6	2	45	4	2	1	4	1
202	Other chemical products	-	-	-	-	240	247	227	302	15	14	12	17
2021	Pesticides and other agrochemical products	-	-	-	-	-	-	-	-	-	-	-	-
2022	Paints,varnishes;printing ink and mastics	8839	9722	8831	14975	99	120	109	173	6	6	7	7
2023	Soap,cleaning and cosmetic preparations	10173	7877	7628	6456	104	90	99	102	5	4	5	6
2029	Other chemical products n.e.c.	7358	5899	⋯	2610	37	37	19	27	4	4	⋯	4
2030	Man-made fibres	-	⋯	⋯	⋯	-	8	5	8	-	⋯	1	1
2100	Pharmaceuticals,medicinal chemicals, etc.	8484	8487	9127	8788	121	134	145	159	17	14	18	21
221	Rubber products	528	425	457	458	8	7	7	8	2	2	2	3
2211	Rubber tyres and tubes	-	-	-	-	-	-	-	-	-	-	-	-
2219	Other rubber products	528	425	457	458	8	7	7	8	2	2	2	3
2220	Plastics products	105277	103196	126411	81400	977	1073	1054	1033	107	108	111	110
2310	Glass and glass products	207250	202545	218727	222272	1305	1341	1387	1362	8	8	8	6
239	Non-metallic mineral products n.e.c.	1196529	1195739	1213779	1132099	6372	6949	7324	7683	213	200	197	214
2391	Refractory products	2124	1753	557	273	23	24	24	15	3	3	3	2
2392	Clay building materials	70487	92319	138227	131310	1320	1525	1917	1831	81	75	76	77
2393	Other porcelain and ceramic products	929	1106	1358	1456	13	16	18	19	3	3	3	3
2394	Cement, lime and plaster	521521	559084	586781	523944	2012	2331	2417	2421	10	11	13	10
2395	Articles of concrete, cement and plaster	467002	449370	391986	412057	2088	2139	2031	2675	66	62	64	71
2396	Cutting, shaping and finishing of stone	37084	42283	48216	39870	396	461	486	484	27	24	19	20
2399	Other non-metallic mineral products n.e.c.	97382	49824	46654	23189	520	453	431	238	23	22	19	31
2410	Basic iron and steel	2156	2050	1789	1789	35	26	26	22	3	2	2	2
2420	Basic precious and other non-ferrous metals	5959062	5549206	5519393	5056751	4261	4334	4560	4865	7	7	6	7
243	Casting of metals	4406	2002	3221	1117	85	37	52	38	10	7	8	9
2431	Casting of iron and steel	4406	2002	3221	1079	85	37	52	37	9	7	8	8
2432	Casting of non-ferrous metals	-	-	-	38	-	-	-	1	-	-	-	1
251	Struct.metal products, tanks, reservoirs	75655	69318	69234	84338	645	674	895	1003	38	35	38	38

continued

Kyrgyzstan

ISIC	Industry	Number of establishments (number)					Number of employees (number)					Wages and salaries paid to employees (thousands of Kyrgyzstan Soms)				
		Note	2013	2014	2015	2016	Note	2013	2014	2015	2016	Note	2013	2014	2015	2016
2511	Structural metal products		24	24	22	25		694	427	389	376		61899	49262	42977	47524
2512	Tanks, reservoirs and containers of metal		14	14	10	13		239	233	207	196		16354	19972	18927	21019
2513	Steam generators, excl. hot water boilers		-	-	3	...		-	-	78	73		-	-	7414	7112
2520	Weapons and ammunition		4	4	3	3		1042	1006	1037	954		217465	...	165855	195748
259	Other metal products;metal working services		47	38	40	40		614	611	793	575		54095	50284	65700	64740
2591	Forging,pressing,stamping,roll-forming of metal		5	6	6	6		51	55	54	54		4707	6281	6831	6959
2592	Treatment and coating of metals machining		5	4	4	4		266	317	395	215		30285	23044	28751	29075
2593	Cutlery, hand tools and general hardware		16	8	8	8		73	...	70	118		4742	...	8072	10452
2599	Other fabricated metal products n.e.c.		21	20	22	22		224	239	274	188		14362	20960	22046	18254
2610	Electronic components and boards		1	1	2	2		...	...	5	3		...	...	74	36
2620	Computers and peripheral equipment		5	7	3	4		18	17	10	12		1333	1362	932	1067
2630	Communication equipment		3	2	2	2		...	...	23	29		...	...	9642	15111
2640	Consumer electronics		2	2	-	1		...	...	-	4		...	...	-	313
265	Measuring,testing equipment; watches, etc.		2	5	2	5		...	...	3	12		...	...	169	6480
2651	Measuring/testing/navigating equipment,etc.		2	5	2	5		...	...	3	12		...	...	169	6480
2652	Watches and clocks		-	-	-	-		-	-	-	-		-	-	-	-
2660	Irradiation/electromedical equipment,etc.		2	3	1	1		-	-	5	5		-	...	624	734
2670	Optical instruments and photographic equipment		-	-	1	2		-	-	3	8		-	-	...	441
2680	Magnetic and optical media		-	-	-	-		-	-	-	-		-	-	-	-
2710	Electric motors,generators,transformers,etc.		5	5	5	5		347	245	257	253		49792	33489	42079	43847
2720	Batteries and accumulators		1	-	-	-		154					8972			
273	Wiring and wiring devices		1	1	1	1		74	64	65	59		3280	3589	3758	3499
2731	Fibre optic cables		-	-	-	-		-	-	-	-		-	-	-	-
2732	Other electronic and electric wires and cables		1	1	1	1		74	64	65	59		3280	3589	3758	3499
2733	Wiring devices		-	-	-	-		-	-	-	-		-	-	-	-
2740	Electric lighting equipment		4	3	3	2		2790	2741	2701	2597		414140	452082	428939	403887
2750	Domestic appliances		6	7	7	6		...	...	109	57		...	...	8889	4290
2790	Other electrical equipment		1	1	2	2		22	10	6	2		1082	658	438	126
281	General-purpose machinery		9	11	11	5		213	157	118	113		20847	15881	12823	12409
2811	Engines/turbines,excl.aircraft,vehicle engines		-	-	1	-		-	-	5	-		-	-	351	-
2812	Fluid power equipment		-	1	-	-		-	-	-	-		-	-	-	-
2813	Other pumps, compressors, taps and valves		2	2	4	4		15	13	51	48		743	...	5457	3711
2814	Bearings, gears, gearing and driving elements		1	1	1	1		...	...	6	5		...	...	236	257
2815	Ovens, furnaces and furnace burners		-	-	-	-		-	-	-	-		-	-	-	-
2816	Lifting and handling equipment		2	3	2	-		13	12	8	8		1635	1890	1740	2455
2817	Office machinery, excl.computers,etc.		1	-	-	-		101	...	-	-		8056	-	-	-
2818	Power-driven hand tools		-	-	-	-		-	-	-	-		-	-	-	-
2819	Other general-purpose machinery		3	4	3	...		2	3	48	52		...	...	5038	5985
282	Special-purpose machinery		15	17	15	13		545	163	52	37		47147	8217	3504	2465
2821	Agricultural and forestry machinery		6	7	7	6		251	61	35	23		15264	4621	2234	1421
2822	Metal-forming machinery and machine tools		1	1	1	-		64	8	-	-		4536	...	...	...

2823	Machinery for metallurgy	-	-	-	-	-	-	-	-	-	-	-	-
2824	Mining, quarrying and construction machinery	3	4	2	2	165	35	...	...	23180	...	...	...
2825	Food/beverage/tobacco processing machinery	2	3	3	3	21	22	10	8	1481	1458	759	675
2826	Textile/apparel/leather production machinery	1	-	-	2	-	-	-	6	-	-	-	368
2829	Other special-purpose machinery	1	2	2	-	44	37	7	-	2685	1364	511	-
2910	Motor vehicles	1	1	-	-	-	-	-	-	-	-	-	-
2920	Automobile bodies, trailers and semi-trailers	1	-	-	-	6	-	-	-	162	-	-	-
2930	Parts and accessories for motor vehicles	1	1	1	1	553	571	563	556	135316	135645	133424	159197
301	Building of ships and boats	...	...	-	...	...	...	-	...	...	...	-	...
3011	Building of ships and floating structures	...	...	-	...	...	...	-	...	...	...	-	...
3012	Building of pleasure and sporting boats	...	...	-	...	...	...	-	...	...	...	-	...
3020	Railway locomotives and rolling stock	...	...	-	...	...	...	-	...	...	...	-	...
3030	Air and spacecraft and related machinery	...	...	-	...	...	...	-	...	...	...	-	...
3040	Military fighting vehicles	...	...	-	...	...	...	-	...	...	...	-	...
309	Transport equipment n.e.c.	...	...	...	...	...	...	...	...	...	...	...	...
3091	Motorcycles	...	...	-	...	...	...	-	...	...	...	-	...
3092	Bicycles and invalid carriages	...	...	-	...	...	...	-	...	...	...	-	...
3099	Other transport equipment n.e.c.	...	...	...	...	...	...	...	...	...	...	...	...
3100	Furniture	46	46	43	46	831	893	781	722	65012	88350	85166	63934
321	Jewellery, bijouterie and related articles	16	21	5	5	178	256	279	272	18430	26211	31721	30772
3211	Jewellery and related articles	6	5	5	5	178	256	279	272	18430	26211	31721	30772
3212	Imitation jewellery and related articles	-	-	-	-	-	-	-	-	-	-	-	-
3220	Musical instruments	-	-	-	1	-	-	-	1	-	-	-	18
3230	Sports goods	-	-	-	-	-	-	-	-	-	-	-	-
3240	Games and toys	-	-	-	-	-	-	-	-	-	-	-	-
3250	Medical and dental instruments and supplies	2	2	3	3	...	...	139	144	...	...	23612	26420
3290	Other manufacturing n.e.c.	8	9	5	7	195	190	165	141	8202	8922	8980	7124
331	Repair of fabricated metal products/machinery	78	42	48	45	...	...	621	546	...	...	99371	97877
3311	Repair of fabricated metal products	-	-	-	-	-	-	-	-	-	-	-	-
3312	Repair of machinery	48	21	22	20	...	...	282	247	...	...	42849	39606
3313	Repair of electronic and optical equipment	8	2	6	5	...	...	44	41	...	...	17228	21009
3314	Repair of electrical equipment	18	16	17	17	...	...	210	181	...	...	26134	25769
3315	Repair of transport equip., excl. motor vehicles	-	-	-	-	-	-	-	-	-	-	-	-
3319	Repair of other equipment	4	3	3	3	...	...	85	65	...	...	13160	11493
3320	Installation of industrial machinery/equipment	2	3	2	3	...	...	8	12	...	...	725	987
C	Total manufacturing	1360	1220	1154	1235	43373	41491	40442	38753	9674754	10308013	10582280	11067273

ISIC Revision 4		Note	Output at producers' prices (millions of Kyrgyzstan Soms)				Note	Value added (valuation not defined) (millions of Kyrgyzstan Soms)				Note	Gross fixed capital formation (millions of Kyrgyzstan Soms)	
ISIC	Industry		2013	2014	2015	2016		2013	2014	2015	2016		2015	2016
1010	Processing/preserving of meat		1727.1	1612.0	1865.2	2246.9		998.5	1256.0	978.0	1613.8		...	...
1020	Processing/preserving of fish, etc.		81.9	89.2	83.1	190.0		20.0	22.3	20.4	46.5		...	...
1030	Processing/preserving of fruit,vegetables		346.6	362.6	331.6	408.2		142.8	130.6	108.4	179.0		...	...
1040	Vegetable and animal oils and fats		71.3	67.8	73.6	66.3		...	...	...	...		...	...
1050	Dairy products		3417.4	4269.7	3780.7	4943.6		865.2	1113.2	1171.2	2137.0		...	...
106	Grain mill products,starches and starch products		3579.6	4664.6	3257.6	3296.8		2009.2	1617.0	1548.0	1135.4		...	...
1061	Grain mill products		3579.6	4664.6	3257.6	3291.4		2009.2	1617.0	1548.0	1133.6		...	...
1062	Starches and starch products		-	-	-	5.3		-	-	-	1.9		...	...
107	Other food products		5505.0	6108.8	7344.7	8257.5		2820.2	2086.1	2492.7	2816.8		...	...
1071	Bakery products		3942.7	4516.9	4941.7	4958.8		2158.4	1421.8	1704.4	1524.9		...	...
1072	Sugar		727.4	723.6	685.5	1651.1		296.4	226.9	277.7	872.9		...	...
1073	Cocoa, chocolate and sugar confectionery		21.2	24.2	27.6	35.3		2.8	7.5	8.8	12.8		...	...
1074	Macaroni, noodles, couscous, etc.		522.0	541.2	703.3	533.1		136.3	148.0	163.6	199.0		...	...
1075	Prepared meals and dishes		...	...	18.8	...		34.0	38.7	16.8	...		...	...
1079	Other food products n.e.c.		51.6	109.4	967.7	1079.2		...	...	321.4	204.5		...	...
1080	Prepared animal feeds		240.0	193.5	316.9	257.0		82.9	69.9	110.2	100.0		...	...
110	Beverages		5977.6	6143.9	6042.5	6233.5		2382.5	2137.0	2189.4	1235.0		...	...
1101	Distilling, rectifying and blending of spirits		2353.4	2002.5	1577.1	1388.8		943.6	725.9	647.3	487.8		...	...
1102	Wines		114.5	64.5	224.2	269.4		44.6	44.6	116.7	104.7		...	...
1103	Malt liquors and malt		506.6	717.6	602.3	600.1		245.3	282.7	231.6	297.0		...	...
1104	Soft drinks,mineral waters,other bottled waters		3003.2	3423.8	3638.9	3975.2		1149.0	1100.6	1193.8	345.5		...	...
1200	Tobacco products		495.7	304.4	33.3	...		129.9	95.7	14.1	...		...	...
131	Spinning, weaving and finishing of textiles		705.4	613.7	691.3	795.1		174.9	94.1	227.7	123.5		...	...
1311	Preparation and spinning of textile fibres		688.0	613.7	691.3	795.1		171.2	94.0	227.7	123.5		...	...
1312	Weaving of textiles		17.4	-	-	-		3.7	-	...	-		...	...
1313	Finishing of textiles		-	-	-	-		-	-	...	-		...	...
139	Other textiles		350.7	339.4	173.0	145.6		158.7	130.9	83.3	68.8		...	...
1391	Knitted and crocheted fabrics		...	...	-	-		-	-	-	-		...	...
1392	Made-up textile articles, except apparel		126.6	106.7	86.8	70.6		73.2	55.1	42.4	37.0		...	...
1393	Carpets and rugs		152.0	156.0	34.4	20.9		40.5	40.3	12.8	8.7		...	...
1394	Cordage, rope, twine and netting		5.1	3.5	5.2	5.8		-	-	1.5	0.9		...	...
1399	Other textiles n.e.c.		67.0	73.2	46.6	48.4		45.0	35.5	26.5	22.2		...	...
1410	Wearing apparel, except fur apparel		6870.0	4516.7	3479.7	4712.3		2225.6	1832.2	1738.5	2338.5		...	...
1420	Articles of fur		5.8	5.4	5.7	15.6		1.7	1.2	1.8	1.9		...	...
1430	Knitted and crocheted apparel		361.0	337.5	303.3	368.7		126.8	127.4	111.4	158.1		...	...
151	Leather;luggage,handbags,saddlery,harness;fur		52.8	45.9	67.7	39.3		18.7	19.7	24.5	18.9		...	...
1511	Tanning/dressing of leather; dressing of fur		52.4	45.5	67.0	38.5		18.6	19.7	24.3	18.4		...	...
1512	Luggage,handbags,etc.;saddlery/harness		-	-	-	-		-	-	-	-		...	...
1520	Footwear		200.2	286.2	684.6	532.1		94.9	80.8	185.9	139.8		...	...
1610	Sawmilling and planing of wood		81.9	71.2	78.0	84.9		52.6	...	62.6	62.2		...	...

Code	Description								
162	Wood products, cork, straw, plaiting materials	125.2	108.9	112.6	128.1	254.7	254.0	225.4	225.0
1621	Veneer sheets and wood-based panels	-	-	-	-	-	1.7	-	-
1622	Builders' carpentry and joinery	1.2	...	-	-	3.5	142.8	133.7	133.7
1623	Wooden containers	52.7		...	...	152.6	142.8	133.7	137.7
1629	Other wood products;articles of cork,straw	71.3	45.5	57.0	33.7	98.6	109.5	85.6	87.2
170	Paper and paper products	574.7	224.6	200.0	317.8	591.3	569.4	687.5	669.7
1701	Pulp, paper and paperboard	3.6	4.5	4.0	14.1	12.5	13.9	13.9	14.1
1702	Corrugated paper and paperboard	98.5	119.5	106.9	231.0	374.6	372.7	448.1	424.6
1709	Other articles of paper and paperboard	...	100.6	89.0	72.7	204.2	182.8	225.4	202.9
181	Printing and service activities related to printing	104.4	405.5	353.5	330.0	1111.2	1163.6	1057.2	933.9
1811	Printing	101.5	402.5	57.8	75.3	1104.8	1156.4	117.2	129.2
1812	Service activities related to printing	-	...	295.6	254.7	...	...	939.9	804.8
1820	Reproduction of recorded media	-	0.3	-	-	-	1.1	-	-
1910	Coke oven products	-	-	-	-	-			-
1920	Refined petroleum products	2519.8	2410.9	1616.7	394.3	7990.5	6528.2	3198.2	865.2
201	Basic chemicals,fertilizers, etc.	72.9	227.3	535.2	390.6	121.2	365.4	771.3	654.2
2011	Basic chemicals	66.6	226.6	534.7	390.1	93.2	362.9	768.8	651.7
2012	Fertilizers and nitrogen compounds	2.0	0.6	...	...	6.7	2.2	...	...
2013	Plastics and synthetic rubber in primary forms	4.3	0.1	0.5	0.5	21.2	0.2	2.6	2.5
202	Other chemical products	170.7	126.3	163.1	211.7	575.9	404.5	317.5	398.9
2021	Pesticides and other agrochemical products	-	-	-	-	-	-	-	-
2022	Paints,varnishes;printing ink and mastics	80.0	72.9	57.0	148.0	228.1	203.5	174.6	252.4
2023	Soap,cleaning and cosmetic preparations	53.3	24.1	47.8	39.0	156.5	110.4	142.9	132.8
2029	Other chemical products n.e.c.	37.4	29.3	58.3	24.8	191.3	90.6	...	...
2030	Man-made fibres				...		...	...	...
2100	Pharmaceuticals,medicinal chemicals, etc.	101.2	64.4	73.6	55.8	241.3	228.1	173.9	155.3
221	Rubber products	15.4	15.3	14.8	6.8	43.7	62.6	41.3	31.1
2211	Rubber tyres and tubes	-	-	...	-	-	-	-	-
2219	Other rubber products	15.4	15.3	14.8	6.8	43.7	62.6	41.3	31.1
2220	Plastics products	830.1	647.9	914.7	600.7	2298.0	2331.2	2214.3	2109.6
2310	Glass and glass products	565.8	693.3	676.9	609.9	1754.5	1472.3	1954.4	1930.1
239	Non-metallic mineral products n.e.c.	3526.1	4635.5	4871.4	5059.5	10301.3	12457.9	13094.7	13182.6
2391	Refractory products	...	0.9	1.2	1.3	16.3	9.2	6.4	4.2
2392	Clay building materials	185.2	204.0	274.9	269.5	484.9	485.8	635.6	618.8
2393	Other porcelain and ceramic products	0.7	0.9	1.5	1.8	2.1	1.7	4.8	3.4
2394	Cement, lime and plaster	2005.2	2841.7	3078.1	3261.7	5137.1	6931.7	7851.1	7532.7
2395	Articles of concrete, cement and plaster	1117.4	1298.5	1307.8	1292.8	3865.6	4013.4	3957.9	4265.0
2396	Cutting, shaping and finishing of stone	72.1	141.8	104.5	118.3	342.8	400.8	272.8	246.8
2399	Other non-metallic mineral products n.e.c.	145.3	147.7	103.2	114.0	452.5	615.3	366.0	511.7
2410	Basic iron and steel	137.1	62.9	157.0	133.8	469.6	310.7		
2420	Basic precious and other non-ferrous metals	50823.8	40311.0	35686.3	38026.2	97809.3	79607.0		
243	Casting of metals	25.1	3.4	99.2	63.0	338.3	31.6	65.0	23.4
2431	Casting of iron and steel	25.1	3.4	99.2	61.7	338.3	31.6	60.8	20.1
2432	Casting of non-ferrous metals	-	-	-	1.2	-	-	-	3.3
251	Struct.metal products, tanks, reservoirs	326.3	267.9	351.4	258.4	1467.3	960.6	1009.3	915.3

continued

Kyrgyzstan

ISIC	Industry	Output at producers' prices (millions of Kyrgyzstan Soms)					Value added (valuation not defined) (millions of Kyrgyzstan Soms)					Gross fixed capital formation (millions of Kyrgyzstan Soms)		
		Note	2013	2014	2015	2016	Note	2013	2014	2015	2016	Note	2015	2016
2511	Structural metal products		545.9	684.1	657.0	1093.4		220.7	325.6	191.0	223.0		...	...
2512	Tanks, reservoirs and containers of metal		369.4	325.2	170.7	300.4		37.7	25.9	40.5	88.7		...	...
2513	Steam generators, excl. hot water boilers		-	-	132.9	73.5		-	-	36.4	14.7		...	...
2520	Weapons and ammunition		494.5	429.0	570.8	763.5		196.6	181.4	316.3	362.0		...	...
259	Other metal products;metal working services		683.5	720.5	731.9	478.9		288.6	198.0	213.6	531.6		...	...
2591	Forging,pressing,stamping,roll-forming of metal		174.4	163.8	144.4	160.8		61.1	48.5	30.7	47.7		...	...
2592	Treatment and coating of metals; machining		200.9	82.8	113.1	115.2		48.9	23.9	52.7	300.3		...	...
2593	Cutlery, hand tools and general hardware		...	-	77.0	82.2		25.1	25.0	24.8	30.3		...	...
2599	Other fabricated metal products n.e.c.		308.1	473.9	397.3	120.7		153.5	100.5	105.5	153.4		...	...
2610	Electronic components and boards		0.4	...	0.5	0.9		0.2	0.1	0.2	0.3		...	...
2620	Computers and peripheral equipment		11.1	2.8	4.1	3.3		2.6	1.5	1.6	1.4		...	...
2630	Communication equipment		38.5	50.2	58.4	50.4		3.6	3.2	23.9	26.7		...	...
2640	Consumer electronics		...	5.5	-	4.8		...	...	-	2.1		...	...
265	Measuring,testing equipment; watches, etc.		3.0	6.8	0.3	33.9		0.9	2.6	0.1	0.2		...	...
2651	Measuring/testing/navigating equipment,etc.		3.0	6.8	0.3	33.9		0.9	2.6	0.1	0.2		...	...
2652	Watches and clocks		-	-	-	-		-	-	-	-		...	...
2660	Irradiation/electromedical equipment,etc.		...	...	2.3	3.6		1.5	2.5	0.8	2.1		...	...
2670	Optical instruments and photographic equipment		-	-	1.7	2.9		-	-	...	2.0		...	...
2680	Magnetic and optical media		-	-	-	-		-	-	-	-		...	...
2710	Electric motors,generators,transformers,etc.		195.0	223.5	268.0	243.8		108.9	103.6	141.8	120.7		...	...
2720	Batteries and accumulators		...	1622.5	...	-		...	-	-	-		...	...
273	Wiring and wiring devices		1328.8	...	...	...		6.1	1.8	4.7	4.0		...	...
2731	Fibre optic cables		-	-	-	-		-	-	-	-		...	...
2732	Other electronic and electric wires and cables		14.1	...	6.8	1.1		6.1	1.8	4.7	4.0		...	...
2733	Wiring devices		...	-	-	-		-	-	-	-		...	...
2740	Electric lighting equipment		1301.3	1589.9	1370.6	1197.3		628.9	921.3	776.2	838.6		...	...
2750	Domestic appliances		27.5	32.5	130.4	108.1		15.7	13.1	68.9	44.2		...	...
2790	Other electrical equipment		...	19.1	6.7	...		1.2	9.1	3.1	...		...	...
281	General-purpose machinery		202.6	246.9	219.3	187.9		63.9	121.7	71.6	68.8		...	...
2811	Engines/turbines,excl.aircraft,vehicle engines		-	-	-	-		-	-	-	-		...	...
2812	Fluid power equipment		-	-	3.3	-		-	-	0.9	-		...	...
2813	Other pumps, compressors, taps and valves		44.2	49.4	39.9	21.4		15.6	16.0	16.0	6.7		...	...
2814	Bearings, gears, gearing and driving elements		0.4	0.3	0.3	0.2		0.3	0.1	...	0.1		...	...
2815	Ovens, furnaces and furnace burners		-	-	-	-		-	-	-	-		...	...
2816	Lifting and handling equipment		9.7	7.5	10.5	12.3		3.8	4.5	1.7	7.3		...	...
2817	Office machinery, excl.computers,etc.		...	-	-	-		...	...	...	-		...	...
2818	Power-driven hand tools		-	-	-	-		-	-	-	-		...	...
2819	Other general-purpose machinery		147.2	188.4	163.8	152.3		43.8	100.7	49.7	54.0		...	...
282	Special-purpose machinery		101.4	136.3	61.1	34.7		56.5	73.4	29.6	15.1		...	...
2821	Agricultural and forestry machinery		93.0	119.9	39.6	18.1		36.1	65.7	14.2	7.6		...	...
2822	Metal-forming machinery and machine tools		...	1.0	...	...		9.9	0.5	...	-		...	...

Code	Description									
2823	Machinery for metallurgy	...	-	...	...	1.5	-	-	...	-
2824	Mining, quarrying and construction machinery	...	1.1	1.5	...	8.2	5.1	8.6	...	-
2825	Food/beverage/tobacco processing machinery	...	4.0	4.0	...	...	5.1	8.6	...	-
2826	Textile/apparel/leather production machinery	...	-	4.5	...	7.1	11.5	12.9	...	-
2829	Other special-purpose machinery	...	-	4.9	3.3	7.1	11.5	12.9	...	3.3
2910	Motor vehicles	...	-	-	-	-	-	-	-	-
2920	Automobile bodies, trailers and semi-trailers	...	-	-	9.2	0.8	-	-	-	-
2930	Parts and accessories for motor vehicles	...	401.2	215.7	250.4	405.3	905.6	607.3	746.4	1017.2
301	Building of ships and boats	...	...	...	...	...	...	...	...	...
3011	Building of ships and floating structures	...	...	...	...	...	...	...	...	...
3012	Building of pleasure and sporting boats	...	...	...	...	...	...	...	...	...
3020	Railway locomotives and rolling stock	...	...	...	...	...	...	...	...	...
3030	Air and spacecraft and related machinery	...	...	...	...	...	...	...	...	...
3040	Military fighting vehicles	...	...	...	...	...	...	...	...	...
309	Transport equipment n.e.c.	...	0.1	0.1	0.1	0.1	0.3	0.4	...	...
3091	Motorcycles	...	...	...	...	...	...	...	...	...
3092	Bicycles and invalid carriages	...	...	...	...	...	...	...	...	...
3099	Other transport equipment n.e.c.	...	0.1	0.1	0.1	0.1	0.3	0.4	...	...
3100	Furniture	...	264.6	263.4	290.6	270.9	821.7	735.2	823.8	684.8
321	Jewellery, bijouterie and related articles	...	16.2	35.5	28.9	25.7	30.1	98.6	56.4	64.9
3211	Jewellery and related articles	...	16.2	35.5	28.9	25.7	30.1	98.6	56.4	63.1
3212	Imitation jewellery and related articles	...	-	-	-	-	0.5	-	-	-
3220	Musical instruments	...	0.4	-	-	0.1	-	-	-	-
3230	Sports goods	...	-	-	-	-	-	-	-	-
3240	Games and toys	...	-	-	-	-	-	-	-	-
3250	Medical and dental instruments and supplies	...	32.4	24.0	27.4	29.8	60.6	52.5	54.0	48.0
3290	Other manufacturing n.e.c.	...	4.7	6.8	6.5	8.6	16.3	14.0	17.7	16.9
331	Repair of fabricated metal products/machinery	...	169.0	130.0	166.4	214.1	368.5	288.2	360.9	490.2
3311	Repair of fabricated metal products	...	-	-	-	-	-	-	-	-
3312	Repair of machinery	...	51.0	46.6	50.9	76.7	128.5	123.9	111.4	171.7
3313	Repair of electronic and optical equipment	...	19.5	19.1	2.9	8.7	6.2	14.5	4.2	18.2
3314	Repair of electrical equipment	...	80.7	51.6	84.2	93.8	210.0	131.4	202.3	244.3
3315	Repair of transport equip., excl. motor vehicles	...	-	-	-	-	-	-	-	-
3319	Repair of other equipment	...	12.8	12.8	...	...	23.9	18.4	43.0	56.0
3320	Installation of industrial machinery/equipment	...	2.0	3.3	1.6	0.4	3.3	3.5	2.5	0.6
C	Total manufacturing	...	75321.7	63910.1	59557.2	61437.9	163296.1	140604.2	141886.5	142664.2

Kyrgyzstan

Index numbers of industrial production

ISIC Revision 4

(2010=100)

ISIC	Industry	Note	2005	2006	2007	2008	2009	2010	2011	2012	2013	2014	2015	2016
10	Food products	a/	..	..	..	..	..	100	100	104	107	112	104	117
11	Beverages	a/	..	..	..	..	..	..	..	..	..	..	..	..
12	Tobacco products	a/	..	..	..	..	..	..	..	..	..	..	..	..
13	Textiles	b/	..	..	..	..	..	100	149	200	170	141	125	97
14	Wearing apparel	b/	..	..	..	..	..	..	..	..	..	..	..	..
15	Leather and related products	b/	..	..	..	..	..	..	..	..	..	..	..	..
16	Wood products, excluding furniture	c/	..	..	..	..	..	100	117	248	272	252	261	268
17	Paper and paper products	c/	..	..	..	..	..	..	..	..	..	..	..	..
18	Printing and reproduction of recorded media	c/	..	..	..	..	..	..	..	..	..	..	..	..
19	Coke and refined petroleum products		..	..	..	..	..	100	83	77	74	171	296	428
20	Chemicals and chemical products		..	..	..	..	..	100	155	181	189	180	115	69
21	Pharmaceuticals, medicinal chemicals, etc.		..	..	..	..	..	100	60	63	94	121	165	163
22	Rubber and plastics products	d/	..	..	..	..	..	100	114	122	157	167	148	137
23	Other non-metallic mineral products	d/	..	..	..	..	..	..	..	..	..	..	..	..
24	Basic metals	e/	..	..	..	..	..	100	105	58	106	99	91	96
25	Fabricated metal products, except machinery	e/	..	..	..	..	..	..	..	..	..	..	..	..
26	Computer, electronic and optical products	f/	..	..	..	..	..	100	88	91	98	95	84	77
27	Electrical equipment	f/	..	..	..	..	..	..	..	..	..	..	..	..
28	Machinery and equipment n.e.c.	f/	..	..	..	..	..	..	..	..	..	..	..	..
29	Motor vehicles, trailers and semi-trailers	g/	..	..	..	..	..	100	163	183	225	186	131	143
30	Other transport equipment	g/	..	..	..	..	..	..	..	..	..	..	..	..
31	Furniture	h/	..	..	..	..	..	100	76	74	78	77	83	79
32	Other manufacturing	h/	..	..	..	..	..	..	..	..	..	..	..	..
33	Repair and installation of machinery/equipment	h/	..	..	..	..	..	..	..	..	..	..	..	..
C	Total manufacturing		..	..	..	..	..	100	107	80	116	112	104	109

a/ 10 includes 11 and 12.
b/ 13 includes 14 and 15.
c/ 16 includes 17 and 18.
d/ 22 includes 23.
e/ 24 includes 25.
f/ 26 includes 27 and 28.
g/ 29 includes 30.
h/ 31 includes 32 and 33.

Lao People's Dem Rep

Supplier of information:
Ministry of Industry and Commerce, Vientiane.

Basic source of data:
Survey of industrial establishments.

Major deviations from ISIC (Revision 4):
None reported.

Reference period:
Calendar year.

Scope:
All registered establishments.

Method of data collection:
Direct interview in the field.

Type of enumeration:
Not reported.

Adjusted for non-response:
Yes.

Concepts and definitions of variables:
Wages and salaries is compensation of employees.
Output refers to gross output.
Value added refers to total value added.

Related national publications:
Enhancement of Industrial Statistics in the Lao People's Dem Rep, published by the
Ministry of Industry and Commerce, Vientiane.

Lao People's Dem Rep

- 488 -

ISIC	Industry	Number of establishments (number)					Number of employees (number)					Wages and salaries paid to employees (millions of Lao Kips)				
		Note	2013	2014	2015	2016	Note	2013	2014	2015	2016	Note	2013	2014	2015	2016
10	Food products		...	...	7761	...		...	...	15239	...		...	...	145967	...
11	Beverages		...	...	854	...		...	...	6848	...		...	...	205307	...
12	Tobacco products		...	...	3	...		...	...	896	...		...	...	10437	...
13	Textiles		...	...	73	...		...	...	3418	...		...	...	62804	...
14	Wearing apparel		...	...	437	...		...	...	26054	...		...	...	301481	...
15	Leather and related products		...	...	59	...		...	...	989	...		...	...	11938	...
16	Wood products, excluding furniture		...	...	391	...		...	...	9582	...		...	...	94265	...
17	Paper and paper products		...	...	25	...		...	...	914	...		...	...	16705	...
18	Printing and reproduction of recorded media		...	...	10	...		...	...	1661	...		...	...	15590	...
19	Coke and refined petroleum products		...	...	162	...		...	...	2186	...		...	...	32226	...
20	Chemicals and chemical products		...	...	118	...		...	...	2401	...		...	...	28622	...
21	Pharmaceuticals,medicinal chemicals, etc.		...	...	17	...		...	...	1468	...		...	...	53546	...
22	Rubber and plastics products		...	...	92	...		...	...	3783	...		...	...	58187	...
23	Other non-metallic mineral products		...	...	1454	...		...	...	20684	...		...	...	412717	...
24	Basic metals		...	...	37	...		...	...	932	...		...	...	26980	...
25	Fabricated metal products, except machinery		...	...	367	...		...	...	2543	...		...	...	39325	...
26	Computer, electronic and optical products		...	...	2	...		...	...	665	...		...	...	8295	...
27	Electrical equipment		...	...	10	...		...	...	663	...		...	...	14033	...
28	Machinery and equipment n.e.c.		...	...	3	...		...	...	25	...		...	...	1065	...
29	Motor vehicles, trailers and semi-trailers		...	...	1	...		...	...	1741	...		...	...	32494	...
30	Other transport equipment		...	...	4	...		...	...	193	...		...	...	7009	...
31	Furniture		...	...	784	...		...	...	11650	...		...	...	202756	...
32	Other manufacturing		...	...	484	...		...	...	4050	...		...	...	86501	...
33	Repair and installation of machinery/equipment		...	...	...	...		...	...	...	...		...	...	...	...
C	Total manufacturing		...	...	13148	...		...	...	118585	...		...	...	1668251	...

ISIC Revision 4

Lao People's Dem Rep

				Output at basic prices (millions of Lao Kips)					Value added at basic prices (millions of Lao Kips)					Gross fixed capital formation (millions of Lao Kips)	
ISIC	**Industry**	**Note**	**2013**	**2014**	**2015**	**2016**	**Note**	**2013**	**2014**	**2015**	**2016**	**Note**	**2015**	**2016**		
10	Food products		...	...	4358302	...		...	...	1658612	...		97176	...		
11	Beverages		...	...	3802060	...		...	...	3281373	...		733432	...		
12	Tobacco products		...	...	36881	...		...	...	19622	...		11	...		
13	Textiles		...	...	751305	...		...	...	599678	...		-	...		
14	Wearing apparel		...	...	2395449	...		...	...	1706600	...		9641	...		
15	Leather and related products		...	...	38166	...		...	...	30843	...		66	...		
16	Wood products, excluding furniture		...	...	1057912	...		...	...	442384	...		196589	...		
17	Paper and paper products		...	...	206514	...		...	...	170036	...		655	...		
18	Printing and reproduction of recorded media		...	...	34564	...		...	...	23897	...		-	...		
19	Coke and refined petroleum products		...	...	200812	...		...	...	138678	...		188609	...		
20	Chemicals and chemical products		...	...	654787	...		...	...	223431	...		3611	...		
21	Pharmaceuticals,medicinal chemicals, etc.		...	...	190987	...		...	...	113608	...		1793	...		
22	Rubber and plastics products		...	...	1630231	...		...	...	811800	...		8540	...		
23	Other non-metallic mineral products		...	...	6482693	...		...	...	3135140	...		158749	...		
24	Basic metals		...	...	350697	...		...	...	268350	...		-	...		
25	Fabricated metal products, except machinery		...	...	999764	...		...	...	629644	...		6408	...		
26	Computer, electronic and optical products		...	...	51721	...		...	...	41127	...		3	...		
27	Electrical equipment		...	...	142403	...		...	...	87769	...		30911	...		
28	Machinery and equipment n.e.c.		...	...	30769	...		...	...	9670	...		-764	...		
29	Motor vehicles, trailers and semi-trailers		...	...	69780	...		...	...	43024	...		-	...		
30	Other transport equipment		...	...	66643	...		...	...	42632	...		-	...		
31	Furniture		...	...	1348212	...		...	...	879691	...		2584	...		
32	Other manufacturing		...	...	897438	...		...	...	511069	...		62201	...		
33	Repair and installation of machinery/equipment		...	...	...	...		...	...	...	...		...	...		
C	Total manufacturing		...	...	25798088	...		...	...	14868675	...		1500216	...		

Latvia

Supplier of information:
Central Statistical Bureau of Latvia, Riga.

Basic source of data:
Annual census, survey, administrative source.

Major deviations from ISIC (Revision 4):
None reported.

Reference period:
Calendar year.

Scope:
All enterprises.

Method of data collection:
Online survey.

Type of enumeration:
Complete enumeration; sample survey.

Adjusted for non-response:
Yes.

Concepts and definitions of variables:
Wages and salaries excludes housing and family allowances paid directly by the employer and payments in kind.

Related national publications:
Statistical Yearbook; Informative Review on Basic Indicators of Structural Business Statistics, both published by the Central Statistical Bureau of Latvia, Riga.

Latvia

ISIC Revision 4

ISIC	Industry	Number of enterprises (number) Note	2013	2014	2015	2016	Number of employees (number) Note	2013	2014	2015	2016	Wages and salaries paid to employees (thousands of Euros) Note	2013	2014	2015	2016
1010	Processing/preserving of meat		157	156	151	168		4609	4739	4518	4544		23256	26890	32290	33339
1020	Processing/preserving of fish, etc.		111	111	112	115		6217	5712	4170	3741		29387	29224	22159	20689
1030	Processing/preserving of fruit,vegetables		63	69	80	90		763	826	910	876		...	...	...	...
1040	Vegetable and animal oils and fats		11	11	11	13		138	139	119	109					
1050	Dairy products		52	50	54	64		3120	3266	3110	3524		27687	30009	31110	33557
106	Grain mill products,starches and starch products		29	26	26	27		436	451	474	511		...	...	...	...
1061	Grain mill products		27	24	24	26		380	389	409	441		...	...	...	...
1062	Starches and starch products		2	2	2	1		56	62	65	70		...	...	...	...
107	Other food products		427	444	526	571		7537	7808	7612	7345		46016	48964	52353	56059
1071	Bakery products		291	290	354	385		5321	5502	5275	4943		29004	30497	31896	33041
1072	Sugar		-	-	-	1		-	-	-	1		-	-	-	1
1073	Cocoa, chocolate and sugar confectionery		31	34	32	41		994	1123	1137	1151		...	...	...	...
1074	Macaroni, noodles, couscous, etc.		1	2	1	1		1	1	1	1					
1075	Prepared meals and dishes		27	31	34	38		474	454	392	417		2309	2575	2125	2317
1079	Other food products n.e.c.		77	87	105	105		747	728	807	832		6167	6275	7464	8343
1080	Prepared animal feeds		30	30	27	27		364	338	272	278		2482	2485	2345	2565
110	Beverages		88	106	116	126		2382	2296	2381	2431		24916	22794	23971	25916
1101	Distilling, rectifying and blending of spirits		17	17	18	16		722	724	733	743		...	...	...	...
1102	Wines		21	30	35	43		33	47	47	52		60	117	144	165
1103	Malt liquors and malt		25	27	31	37		838	617	659	693		8811	5770	6176	6960
1104	Soft drinks,mineral waters,other bottled waters		25	32	32	30		788	908	942	943		...	...	...	...
1200	Tobacco products		2	4	5	4		21	22	21	19		...	...	...	...
131	Spinning, weaving and finishing of textiles		99	98	97	112		314	315	311	280		...	1588	1606	1833
1311	Preparation and spinning of textile fibres		14	13	15	15		46	50	50	46		154	157	179	213
1312	Weaving of textiles		34	33	28	38		195	202	198	192					
1313	Finishing of textiles		51	52	54	59		73	63	63	42		212	201	193	168
139	Other textiles		369	384	410	454		2144	2457	2370	2351		...	...	...	...
1391	Knitted and crocheted fabrics		111	113	101	107		562	542	447	441		...	...	...	...
1392	Made-up textile articles, except apparel		126	129	142	161		917	1213	1203	1183		4397	6010	6576	7238
1393	Carpets and rugs		1	2	2	3		2	1	2	2					
1394	Cordage, rope, twine and netting		12	12	14	14		382	392	450	481		1581	1810	2298	2670
1399	Other textiles n.e.c.		119	128	151	169		281	309	268	244		1401	1566	1411	1391
1410	Wearing apparel, except fur apparel		963	998	1147	1246		8439	8267	7591	7471		34910	34676	33854	36031
1420	Articles of fur		10	12	13	10		13	16	17	14		27	29	37	35
1430	Knitted and crocheted apparel		105	95	94	102		1605	1115	984	1000		7905	6613	6066	6636
151	Leather;luggage,handbags,saddlery,harness;fur		46	49	61	59		197	200	162	151		583	660	637	650
1511	Tanning/dressing of leather; dressing of fur		9	9	12	10		44	42	24	9		...	...	...	...
1512	Luggage,handbags,etc.;saddlery/harness		37	40	49	49		153	158	138	142		...	...	...	...
1520	Footwear		17	18	22	23		224	223	171	168		1250	1322	835	948
1610	Sawmilling and planing of wood		870	859	870	898		12943	13849	13299	12983		72367	82624	87308	95844

Code	Description												
162	Wood products, cork, straw, plaiting materials	1005	1024	1138	1164	11215	11540	11188	11277	76042	81315	88246	97288
1621	Veneer sheets and wood-based panels	34	31	32	29	3024	3070	3232	2730	34733	36625	41547	37655
1622	Builders' carpentry and joinery	502	507	571	580	3887	4122	3575	4500	…	…	…	…
1623	Wooden containers	177	166	179	179	2292	2300	2391	2369	…	…	…	…
1629	Other wood products;articles of cork,straw	291	320	356	376	2012	2048	1989	1678	11634	13056	14203	14086
170	Paper and paper products	106	96	101	109	1502	1378	1344	1408	12096	12142	12623	13516
1701	Pulp, paper and paperboard	3	5	4	5	145	47	3	10	…	…	…	…
1702	Corrugated paper and paperboard	42	39	42	42	774	742	725	749	7159	7251	7420	7551
1709	Other articles of paper and paperboard	61	52	55	62	583	589	616	649	…	…	…	…
181	Printing and service activities related to printing	475	471	463	469	3211	3439	3382	3214	23725	28267	30600	31681
1811	Printing	350	336	332	338	2894	3079	3022	2887	22335	26435	28504	29483
1812	Service activities related to printing	125	135	131	131	316	360	360	327	1391	1832	2096	2198
1820	Reproduction of recorded media	18	19	19	18	16	16	15	16	60	44	56	66
1910	Coke oven products	2	3	3	1	1	4	6	2	…	…	…	…
1920	Refined petroleum products	8	9	13	10	29	37	53	45	409	…	…	…
201	Basic chemicals,fertilizers, etc.	69	77	77	82	697	757	692	910	4457	4945	5168	7879
2011	Basic chemicals	33	38	36	40	475	518	454	622	2823	3060	3055	5225
2012	Fertilizers and nitrogen compounds	31	34	33	34	187	200	193	236	1407	1641	1880	2338
2013	Plastics and synthetic rubber in primary forms	5	5	8	8	35	39	44	52	…	…	…	…
202	Other chemical products	131	133	141	145	1776	1920	1928	1738	14023	15656	16253	15583
2021	Pesticides and other agrochemical products	8	7	9	9	37	34	37	40	…	…	…	…
2022	Paints,varnishes;printing ink and mastics	19	20	21	18	545	548	552	346	4287	4690	5080	3206
2023	Soap,cleaning and cosmetic preparations	71	70	76	78	974	1108	1096	1114	…	…	…	…
2029	Other chemical products n.e.c.	33	36	35	40	220	230	243	238	…	…	…	…
2030	Man-made fibres	1	1	2	4	105	104	109	119	…	…	…	…
2100	Pharmaceuticals,medicinal chemicals, etc.	27	29	28	34	2033	2035	2039	2113	1708	1824	1821	2119
221	Rubber products	22	25	24	26	233	240	253	269	…	…	…	…
2211	Rubber tyres and tubes	3	3	3	3	51	50	49	43	…	…	…	…
2219	Other rubber products	19	22	21	23	182	190	204	226	1225	1336	1379	1681
2220	Plastics products	220	223	219	210	2639	2689	2736	2656	16396	17905	21090	22261
2310	Glass and glass products	50	48	53	60	1583	1683	1745	1906	16044	18543	20525	22880
239	Non-metallic mineral products n.e.c.	365	359	380	404	3251	3450	3526	3553	31589	35805	37236	43023
2391	Refractory products	3	2	2	1	14	3	3	3	…	…	…	…
2392	Clay building materials	10	10	9	6	250	267	200	167	…	…	…	…
2393	Other porcelain and ceramic products	61	57	68	68	136	168	231	215	333	515	1067	1197
2394	Cement, lime and plaster	2	2	2	3	316	312	340	355	…	…	…	…
2395	Articles of concrete, cement and plaster	140	141	152	159	2116	2225	2259	2351	20446	23814	24767	29991
2396	Cutting, shaping and finishing of stone	134	134	138	159	353	411	413	378	881	1222	1457	1479
2399	Other non-metallic mineral products n.e.c.	15	13	9	8	66	64	80	84	…	…	…	…
2410	Basic iron and steel	25	22	20	20	2589	725	975	628	…	…	…	…
2420	Basic precious and other non-ferrous metals	7	9	12	10	377	254	227	187	…	…	…	…
243	Casting of metals	3	3	7	7	15	16	92	72	…	…	…	…
2431	Casting of iron and steel	1	1	2	2	-	-	68	58	…	…	…	…
2432	Casting of non-ferrous metals	2	2	5	5	15	16	24	14	…	…	…	…
251	Struct.metal products, tanks, reservoirs	482	504	498	514	5574	6080	5618	5773	43468	51923	50646	58986

continued

Latvia

ISIC	Industry	Note	Number of enterprises (number)				Note	Number of employees (number)				Note	Wages and salaries paid to employees (thousands of Euros)			
			2013	2014	2015	2016		2013	2014	2015	2016		2013	2014	2015	2016
2511	Structural metal products		453	477	471	489		5108	5601	5165	5347		40658	48558	46592	54966
2512	Tanks, reservoirs and containers of metal		29	27	27	25		466	479	453	426		2810	3364	4054	4020
2513	Steam generators, excl. hot water boilers		-	-	-	-							…	…	…	-
2520	Weapons and ammunition		1	1	1	1		15	14	13	13		…	…	…	-
259	Other metal products;metal working services		504	543	588	598		4778	4887	4727	4604		…	…	…	…
2591	Forging,pressing,stamping,roll-forming of metal		29	28	28	32		122	127	93	100					
2592	Treatment and coating of metals;machining		223	260	288	309		1514	1701	1743	1827		9245	10992	12826	14975
2593	Cutlery, hand tools and general hardware		35	30	33	30		742	699	771	707		4860	4997	5770	5921
2599	Other fabricated metal products n.e.c.		216	225	239	227		2399	2360	2120	1970		18018	19106	15431	16278
2610	Electronic components and boards		32	32	35	38		566	647	668	752		…	…	…	…
2620	Computers and peripheral equipment		26	28	29	31		61	57	72	65		296	…	…	…
2630	Communication equipment		23	26	25	23		376	393	423	433					
2640	Consumer electronics		18	18	23	21		80	103	95	96		523	683	816	893
265	Measuring,testing equipment; watches, etc.		33	33	39	44		371	385	452	434		3405	3598	4476	4350
2651	Measuring/testing/navigating equipment,etc.		30	30	36	39		360	373	446	427		3340	3541	4447	4309
2652	Watches and clocks		3	3	3	5		11	12	6	7		65	…	…	…
2660	Irradiation/electromedical equipment,etc.		-	1	1	2		-	1	3	4		-	…	…	…
2670	Optical instruments and photographic equipment		4	4	3	3		65	77	76	80		-	-	-	-
2680	Magnetic and optical media		-	-	-	-		-	-	-	-					
2710	Electric motors,generators,transformers,etc.		33	37	38	38		1559	1580	1258	1304		15378	…	…	…
2720	Batteries and accumulators		1	2	3	2		2	2	2	2					
273	Wiring and wiring devices		17	18	20	20		984	1043	1097	1185		9037	9045	11004	11964
2731	Fibre optic cables		4	3	4	3		187	216	240	247		2451	2277	…	…
2732	Other electronic and electric wires and cables		6	8	7	8		509	548	544	615					
2733	Wiring devices		7	7	9	9		288	279	313	323					
2740	Electric lighting equipment		21	21	31	31		101	105	121	131		472	600	1070	1042
2750	Domestic appliances		8	8	8	7		28	40	41	38					
2790	Other electrical equipment		23	25	28	33		174	165	133	111		1797	1770	1358	1052
281	General-purpose machinery		102	119	123	130		2228	2330	2434	2344		12564	5205	21294	23125
2811	Engines/turbines,excl.aircraft,vehicle engines		3	6	4	4		8	14	8	8					
2812	Fluid power equipment		8	9	11	10		246	217	300	238					
2813	Other pumps, compressors, taps and valves		6	6	5	5		50	51	43	29					
2814	Bearings, gears, gearing and driving elements		3	4	4	5		363	349	310	282					
2815	Ovens, furnaces and furnace burners		8	7	10	9		38	33	35	33					
2816	Lifting and handling equipment		14	15	15	15		584	624	552	591		5928	6349	5010	5345
2817	Office machinery, excl.computers,etc.		4	7	5	4		87	92	106	131					
2818	Power-driven hand tools		5	4	3	4		13	13	58	51		31	17		
2819	Other general-purpose machinery		51	61	66	74		839	937	1022	981		6605	7733	9205	9736
282	Special-purpose machinery		63	66	75	74		1270	1139	1177	1139		11473	11194	11784	12556
2821	Agricultural and forestry machinery		21	21	20	22		645	560	519	509		5532	5594	4963	5285
2822	Metal-forming machinery and machine tools		17	19	21	20		342	288	311	258		2460	1860	2277	2272

Code	Description												
2823	Machinery for metallurgy	1	-	-	-	2	-	-	-	:	:	-	-
2824	Mining, quarrying and construction machinery	4	6	5	3	5	8	11	9	:	:	:	:
2825	Food/beverage/tobacco processing machinery	4	5	11	10	34	33	33	42	:	:	:	:
2826	Textile/apparel/leather production machinery	-	-	-	-	-	-	-	-	-	-	-	-
2829	Other special-purpose machinery	16	15	18	19	242	250	302	321	:	:	:	:
2910	Motor vehicles	7	8	9	6	200	184	138	76	2458	2256	1552	908
2920	Automobile bodies, trailers and semi-trailers	13	17	21	25	496	507	620	632	3470	4160	5580	5877
2930	Parts and accessories for motor vehicles	28	30	31	32	921	1007	1071	1189	:	12330	13510	15501
301	Building of ships and boats	43	41	47	49	973	898	946	1072	:	:	:	:
3011	Building of ships and floating structures	15	14	14	12	792	727	642	697	:	:	:	:
3012	Building of pleasure and sporting boats	28	27	33	37	181	172	304	375	1562	1771	2812	3449
3020	Railway locomotives and rolling stock	5	7	10	8	1176	1198	1023	747	:	:	:	:
3030	Air and spacecraft and related machinery	5	6	9	13	41	57	69	103	:	:	:	:
3040	Military fighting vehicles	-	-	-	-	-	-	-	-	-	-	-	-
309	Transport equipment n.e.c.	12	9	11	16	15	24	29	32	44	74	170	116
3091	Motorcycles	2	1	1	-	5	5	2	-	:	:	:	-
3092	Bicycles and invalid carriages	6	6	8	12	8	17	25	25	:	:	:	:
3099	Other transport equipment n.e.c.	4	2	2	4	2	2	2	7	3	:	:	:
3100	Furniture	703	727	769	793	6428	6535	6589	6713	32874	38086	40715	45736
321	Jewellery, bijouterie and related articles	149	135	155	171	99	111	98	108	:	:	:	:
3211	Jewellery and related articles	114	96	108	110	83	91	75	84	:	:	:	:
3212	Imitation jewellery and related articles	35	39	47	61	16	20	23	24	45	66	84	111
3220	Musical instruments	4	7	8	8	8	11	13	15	30	51	72	111
3230	Sports goods	26	39	37	41	89	134	113	143	336	563	606	859
3240	Games and toys	54	60	62	71	364	302	258	253	1339	1367	1504	1623
3250	Medical and dental instruments and supplies	73	83	89	90	580	622	654	660	2827	3136	3898	4759
3290	Other manufacturing n.e.c.	200	210	219	231	893	1041	995	997	5488	6555	6837	7308
331	Repair of fabricated metal products/machinery	758	786	859	931	5868	5317	5063	5101	49146	43428	44087	44124
3311	Repair of fabricated metal products	68	71	78	91	348	227	180	177	1347	989	963	1234
3312	Repair of machinery	320	334	375	396	1312	1478	1534	1589	8733	10394	12056	12955
3313	Repair of electronic and optical equipment	41	48	51	59	105	129	130	120	728	784	932	670
3314	Repair of electrical equipment	74	76	90	92	704	312	346	338	8049	1953	2890	2630
3315	Repair of transport equip., excl. motor vehicles	213	215	215	240	3312	3091	2778	2785	29788	28853	26646	26000
3319	Repair of other equipment	41	42	50	53	87	80	96	92	501	454	599	635
3320	Installation of industrial machinery/equipment	81	83	97	113	292	407	465	485	2006	2723	3648	4743
C	Total manufacturing	9537	9805	10523	11090	119411	119725	115356	114744	814336	862812	904281	973778

Latvia

ISIC	Industry	Note	Output at producers' prices (thousands of Euros)				Note	Value added at factor values (thousands of Euros)				Note	Gross fixed capital formation (thousands of Euros)	
			2013	2014	2015	2016		2013	2014	2015	2016		2015	2016
1010	Processing/preserving of meat		331882	317262	319157	338577		65973	56775	67067	68208		11276	16638
1020	Processing/preserving of fish, etc.		224045	209712	155979	148761		59682	52598	44469	39309		8675	4425
1030	Processing/preserving of fruit,vegetables		...	...	...	...		...	...	...	...		...	...
1040	Vegetable and animal oils and fats													
1050	Dairy products		367636	394573	325509	333148		54374	67270	71709	71054		11067	14537
106	Grain mill products,starches and starch products		...	...	...	...		...	...	...	...		...	...
1061	Grain mill products		...	...	...	...		...	...	...	...		...	...
1062	Starches and starch products		...	...	...	...		...	...	...	...		...	...
107	Other food products		325364	333028	325339	334246		89329	99492	96774	103681		28393	18810
1071	Bakery products		165334	172587	165424	171980		48842	56169	55571	57372		13687	9316
1072	Sugar		-	-	-	-		-	-	-	-		-	-
1073	Cocoa, chocolate and sugar confectionery		...	...	...	...		...	...	...	...		...	...
1074	Macaroni, noodles, couscous, etc.		...	...	...	...		...	...	...	...		...	...
1075	Prepared meals and dishes		20094	21684	14964	15978		4212	5362	4531	4998		6024	621
1079	Other food products n.e.c.		60335	55958	60284	67853		14734	15604	16317	21334		2092	2304
1080	Prepared animal feeds		58334	51795	43234	38512		8555	9530	7683	7345		4734	4764
110	Beverages		277607	246966	208988	231525		49984	63834	65192	63789		35472	13988
1101	Distilling, rectifying and blending of spirits		...	...	...	...		...	...	...	...		...	...
1102	Wines		356	747	806	838		72	204	222	256		111	112
1103	Malt liquors and malt		95283	72776	73177	75407		13552	18972	17771	20821		5030	6014
1104	Soft drinks,mineral waters,other bottled waters		...	...	...	...		...	...	...	...		...	-
1200	Tobacco products		...	...	...	...		...	...	...	...		...	-
131	Spinning, weaving and finishing of textiles		...	14080	13122	13561		...	2640	2539	3007		277	191
1311	Preparation and spinning of textile fibres		1678	350	858	1155		317	145	402	449		...	...
1312	Weaving of textiles		...	...	...	...		...	...	...	...		...	...
1313	Finishing of textiles		1405	1090	1031	590		344	249	232	203		71	61
139	Other textiles		...	...	...	...		...	...	...	...		...	...
1391	Knitted and crocheted fabrics		...	...	...	...		...	...	...	...		...	...
1392	Made-up textile articles, except apparel		28628	34579	35239	35894		8395	10518	11379	12718		1098	1169
1393	Carpets and rugs		...	...	...	...		...	...	...	...		...	...
1394	Cordage, rope, twine and netting		11055	12648	14522	14504		3204	3435	4464	5323		386	702
1399	Other textiles n.e.c.		5754	6268	5939	6738		2425	2894	2379	2312		...	283
1410	Wearing apparel, except fur apparel		164275	143669	130386	127432		55034	54988	50198	52885		2299	5016
1420	Articles of fur		86	58	112	47		44	32	4	34		-	...
1430	Knitted and crocheted apparel		24284	16495	15728	16630		12442	9131	9119	9323		296	976
151	Leather;luggage,handbags,saddlery,harness;fur		4100	3352	2130	2036		886	928	914	892		...	25
1511	Tanning/dressing of leather; dressing of fur		...	...	...	...		...	...	...	...		...	...
1512	Luggage,handbags,etc.;saddlery/harness		...	...	...	...		...	...	...	...		...	...
1520	Footwear		3602	3450	2046	2171		2486	2547	1301	1515		18	76
1610	Sawmilling and planing of wood		938386	1036692	981417	1030833		181091	204688	202016	218847		52810	35464

162	Wood products, cork, straw, plaiting materials	890363	927573	975170	1036008	248420	249943	286228	305691	65467	72380
1621	Veneer sheets and wood-based panels	426453	442856	464595	433185	137463	135522	154135	157240	27441	30160
1622	Builders' carpentry and joinery	:	:	:	:	:	:	:	:	:	:
1623	Wooden containers	:	:	:	:	:	:	:	:	:	:
1629	Other wood products;articles of cork,straw	196997	214623	258409	242587	43501	49909	65132	58499	16882	23839
170	Paper and paper products	121913	118105	116755	117727	31687	33148	31031	31241	:	:
1701	Pulp, paper and paperboard	75754	76351	74904	74788	19672	21213	19724	19354	:	:
1702	Corrugated paper and paperboard	:	:	:	:	:	:	:	:	4375	2422
1709	Other articles of paper and paperboard	:	:	:	:	:	:	:	:	:	:
181	Printing and service activities related to printing	223079	207609	205160	205281	59479	63042	62581	62590	29466	17069
1811	Printing	212146	197141	194601	197142	56644	58886	58096	58753	29276	9986
1812	Service activities related to printing	10933	10468	10560	8139	2835	4156	4485	3838	190	7083
1820	Reproduction of recorded media	1071	395	848	339	280	116	142	181	-	6
1910	Coke oven products	:	:	:	:	:	:	:	:	:	:
1920	Refined petroleum products	5677	:	:	:	1263	:	:	:	:	:
201	Basic chemicals,fertilizers, etc.	38883	41523	48268	61013	7616	10516	9075	15375	2842	6543
2011	Basic chemicals	23760	18329	16718	31581	2595	6325	3887	9818	1055	4737
2012	Fertilizers and nitrogen compounds	12633	20310	27632	26682	3945	3622	4572	5043	484	1550
2013	Plastics and synthetic rubber in primary forms	:	:	:	:	:	:	:	:	:	:
202	Other chemical products	165072	166905	166828	138608	24320	31923	32117	29190	4102	2501
2021	Pesticides and other agrochemical products	:	:	:	:	:	:	:	:	:	:
2022	Paints,varnishes;printing ink and mastics	43541	44268	40352	25679	10995	10901	11366	6340	1837	914
2023	Soap,cleaning and cosmetic preparations	:	:	:	:	:	:	:	:	:	:
2029	Other chemical products n.e.c.	:	:	:	:	:	:	:	:	:	:
2030	Man-made fibres	:	:	:	:	:	:	:	:	:	:
2100	Pharmaceuticals,medicinal chemicals, etc.	:	:	:	:	:	:	:	:	:	:
221	Rubber products	14286	12721	12794	13855	4057	3382	3788	3396	664	3695
2211	Rubber tyres and tubes	:	:	:	:	:	:	:	:	:	:
2219	Other rubber products	11253	10269	10612	12099	2918	2477	2794	2565	638	3636
2220	Plastics products	185935	174095	177295	172054	44010	39581	46250	50215	14117	17743
2310	Glass and glass products	130805	144651	145838	164434	40395	50012	61115	62615	15294	33801
239	Non-metallic mineral products n.e.c.	326719	324806	298633	298063	100575	92722	84186	97187	14289	13601
2391	Refractory products	:	:	:	:	:	:	:	:	:	:
2392	Clay building materials	:	:	:	:	:	:	:	:	:	:
2393	Other porcelain and ceramic products	2481	2824	5925	6115	375	863	1731	2084	239	227
2394	Cement, lime and plaster	:	:	:	:	:	:	:	:	:	:
2395	Articles of concrete, cement and plaster	188483	197985	185211	200142	56001	54459	56756	70149	5493	5979
2396	Cutting, shaping and finishing of stone	5882	7446	7439	7024	2022	2172	2336	3052	374	323
2399	Other non-metallic mineral products n.e.c.	:	:	:	:	:	:	:	:	:	:
2410	Basic iron and steel	:	:	:	:	:	:	:	:	:	:
2420	Basic precious and other non-ferrous metals	:	:	:	:	:	:	:	:	:	:
243	Casting of metals	:	:	:	:	:	:	:	:	:	:
2431	Casting of iron and steel	:	:	:	:	:	:	:	:	:	:
2432	Casting of non-ferrous metals	:	:	:	:	:	:	:	:	:	:
251	Struct.metal products, tanks, reservoirs	322237	339579	312276	329632	88752	94986	99167	99560	13418	14014

continued

Latvia

ISIC	Industry	Note	Output at producers' prices (thousands of Euros)				Note	Value added at factor values (thousands of Euros)				Note	Gross fixed capital formation (thousands of Euros)	
			2013	2014	2015	2016		2013	2014	2015	2016		2015	2016
2511	Structural metal products		298788	312745	285661	306092		80254	85805	90153	90546		7997	12338
2512	Tanks, reservoirs and containers of metal		23449	26833	26615	23540		8497	9181	9014	9015		5421	1676
2513	Steam generators, excl. hot water boilers		-	-	-	-		-	-	-	-		-	-
2520	Weapons and ammunition		…	…	…	…		…	…	…	…		…	…
259	Other metal products;metal working services		…	…	…	…		…	…	…	…		…	…
2591	Forging,pressing,stamping,roll-forming of metal		65146	68383	74486	82954		23616	25019	28092	34593		4223	4423
2592	Treatment and coating of metals;machining		28572	28222	30208	29053		11142	9913	11845	12101		5755	4518
2593	Cutlery, hand tools and general hardware		136655	142819	113167	105758		45198	41460	30605	32985		7327	4544
2599	Other fabricated metal products n.e.c.		…	…	…	…		…	…	…	…		…	…
2610	Electronic components and boards		2360	…	…	…		521	…	…	…		…	772
2620	Computers and peripheral equipment		…	…	…	…		…	…	…	…		…	…
2630	Communication equipment		2618	2671	4934	5659		-199	413	…	1947		…	…
2640	Consumer electronics		…	…	…	…		…	…	…	…		…	…
265	Measuring,testing equipment; watches, etc.		20212	20751	28746	22589		6208	7599	9081	7528		850	…
2651	Measuring/testing/navigating equipment,etc.		20102	20556	28662	22446		6189	7463	9059	7488		830	…
2652	Watches and clocks		110	-	…	…		19	-	…	…		…	…
2660	Irradiation/electromedical equipment,etc.		-	-	…	…		…	…	…	…		…	…
2670	Optical instruments and photographic equipment		…	-	-	-		…	-	-	-		…	…
2680	Magnetic and optical media		-	…	…	…		…	…	…	…		…	…
2710	Electric motors,generators,transformers,etc.		89489	…	…	…		30949	…	…	…		…	…
2720	Batteries and accumulators		85042	90934	111099	107505		22720	24883	34823	32468		10160	5681
273	Wiring and wiring devices		18840	24208	32892	32144		7098	9990	15859	16686		1509	559
2731	Fibre optic cables		…	…	…	…		…	…	…	…		…	…
2732	Other electronic and electric wires and cables		…	…	…	…		…	…	…	…		…	…
2733	Wiring devices		3703	5457	9858	6248		690	1559	3077	1799		208	385
2740	Electric lighting equipment		…	…	…	…		…	…	…	…		…	…
2750	Domestic appliances		11739	7454	4418	3016		3538	3261	1654	782		54	37
2790	Other electrical equipment		96010	27433	127911	125127		25686	11055	42031	40936		5258	3894
281	General-purpose machinery		…	…	…	…		…	…	…	…		…	…
2811	Engines/turbines,excl.aircraft,vehicle engines		…	…	…	…		…	…	…	…		…	…
2812	Fluid power equipment		…	…	…	…		…	…	…	…		…	…
2813	Other pumps, compressors, taps and valves		…	…	…	…		…	…	…	…		…	…
2814	Bearings, gears, gearing and driving elements		…	…	…	…		…	…	…	…		…	…
2815	Ovens, furnaces and furnace burners		59332	37737	39136	34996		12995	12236	13207	11373		1529	1194
2816	Lifting and handling equipment		…	…	…	…		…	…	…	…		…	…
2817	Office machinery, excl.computers,etc.		125	94	…	…		47	13	…	-		…	…
2818	Power-driven hand tools		36554	53262	54519	51841		12644	17810	18598	16968		1765	1005
2819	Other general-purpose machinery		61161	56771	66051	75011		24650	18897	22110	22155		1971	2632
282	Special-purpose machinery		26095	25525	28047	26686		12717	10162	9753	9902		333	571
2821	Agricultural and forestry machinery		11030	9412	9173	9963		4003	2937	3942	2937		429	1064
2822	Metal-forming machinery and machine tools													

2823	Machinery for metallurgy	…	…	…	…	…	…	…	…	…	-
2824	Mining, quarrying and construction machinery	…	…	…	…	…	…	…	…	…	…
2825	Food/beverage/tobacco processing machinery	-	-	-	-	-	-	-	-	…	…
2826	Textile/apparel/leather production machinery	-	-	-	-	-	-	-	-	-	-
2829	Other special-purpose machinery	…	…	…	…	…	…	…	…	…	…
2910	Motor vehicles	8064	6617	…	…	3447	3085	…	…	43	22
2920	Automobile bodies, trailers and semi-trailers	28690	37697	40676	45784	7730	11218	10912	11984	2913	528
2930	Parts and accessories for motor vehicles	…	97356	97771	107266	…	32609	32820	39342	8310	8878
301	Building of ships and boats	…	…	…	…	…	…	…	…	…	…
3011	Building of ships and floating structures	8914	8519	…	…	2577	…	…	…	…	…
3012	Building of pleasure and sporting boats	…	…	…	30242	2654	4408	5458	…	482	898
3020	Railway locomotives and rolling stock	…	…	…	…	…	…	…	…	…	…
3030	Air and spacecraft and related machinery	…	…	…	…	…	…	…	…	…	…
3040	Military fighting vehicles	-	-	-	-	-	-	-	-	-	-
309	Transport equipment n.e.c.	356	344	495	424	78	59	99	…	24	103
3091	Motorcycles	…	…	…	…	…	…	…	…	…	…
3092	Bicycles and invalid carriages	…	…	…	-	…	…	…	-	-	-
3099	Other transport equipment n.e.c.	18	…	…	…	8	…	…	…	…	…
3100	Furniture	211800	233263	238935	244293	59708	65658	71665	77692	10857	12272
321	Jewellery, bijouterie and related articles	…	…	…	…	…	…	…	…	…	…
3211	Jewellery and related articles	…	…	…	…	…	…	…	…	…	…
3212	Imitation jewellery and related articles	801	223	355	405	313	94	133	184	…	…
3220	Musical instruments	84	185	395	…	55	70	148	…	…	…
3230	Sports goods	3256	3600	4916	8406	560	932	1092	2380	68	244
3240	Games and toys	3959	5156	5113	5580	1998	2007	2429	2480	58	77
3250	Medical and dental instruments and supplies	18491	17454	18216	20282	8450	7944	9757	11194	495	1092
3290	Other manufacturing n.e.c.	37476	38661	36232	39573	12048	12870	12616	13567	3697	1834
331	Repair of fabricated metal products/machinery	245425	187641	180318	177146	91646	80857	82078	75473	29682	34639
3311	Repair of fabricated metal products	10581	5123	3169	3748	3134	1579	1272	1889	96	116
3312	Repair of machinery	54577	54572	60862	70123	20170	21261	24158	23846	6547	4083
3313	Repair of electronic and optical equipment	10986	11237	14820	10368	1187	1799	2290	1349	315	459
3314	Repair of electrical equipment	47149	8548	12155	9891	13684	3874	5098	3619	263	318
3315	Repair of transport equip., excl. motor vehicles	121120	107085	88010	81738	53259	51583	48607	43987	22442	29442
3319	Repair of other equipment	1012	1076	1303	1277	213	760	653	782	19	220
3320	Installation of industrial machinery/equipment	20318	22273	27039	32630	5722	5464	7029	8372	949	547
C	Total manufacturing	7480550	7332837	7264433	7408891	1883141	1958501	2073535	2156321	482275	426137

Latvia

ISIC Revision 4

Index numbers of industrial production (2010=100)

ISIC	Industry	Note	2005	2006	2007	2008	2009	2010	2011	2012	2013	2014	2015	2016
10	Food products		112	117	116	115	101	100	101	103	109	111	105	107
11	Beverages		103	118	130	124	96	100	94	99	107	95	92	96
12	Tobacco products		...	...	...	...	...	...	...	...	...	...	...	...
13	Textiles		140	163	170	147	80	100	102	109	113	103	98	101
14	Wearing apparel		155	152	150	133	86	100	128	129	131	109	92	89
15	Leather and related products		142	145	134	98	...	100	115	123	116	107	45	79
16	Wood products, excluding furniture		92	90	84	74	75	100	113	119	122	130	140	151
17	Paper and paper products		85	91	102	95	87	100	97	107	115	109	106	109
18	Printing and reproduction of recorded media		106	114	106	104	82	100	101	112	117	119	121	126
19	Coke and refined petroleum products		...	...	...	...	...	...	...	...	...	...	...	...
20	Chemicals and chemical products		69	87	82	93	94	100	97	113	102	114	118	117
21	Pharmaceuticals,medicinal chemicals, etc.		100	126	124	124	103	100	112	113	97	...	...	...
22	Rubber and plastics products		117	131	149	129	90	100	102	104	107	110	111	113
23	Other non-metallic mineral products		182	200	166	142	85	100	124	135	141	143	129	144
24	Basic metals		94	97	99	94	84	100	100	133	59	30	...	...
25	Fabricated metal products, except machinery		85	100	119	128	79	100	134	145	147	150	145	159
26	Computer, electronic and optical products		70	87	85	112	79	100	116	135	171	276	386	448
27	Electrical equipment		108	118	131	118	73	100	148	183	199	209	197	211
28	Machinery and equipment n.e.c.		98	114	119	132	85	100	137	149	151	155	167	181
29	Motor vehicles, trailers and semi-trailers		59	90	120	120	59	100	160	186	197	207	205	218
30	Other transport equipment		113	111	113	128	65	100	119	133	134	...	...	...
31	Furniture		179	191	174	124	102	100	105	111	122	134	152	160
32	Other manufacturing		81	121	122	103	93	100	96	99	103	99	99	106
33	Repair and installation of machinery/equipment		107	79	98	149	111	100	115	160	127	95	93	90
C	Total manufacturing		105	111	111	108	86	100	112	122	122	122	127	134

Liechtenstein

Supplier of information:
Office of Statistics, Vaduz.

Basic source of data:
Annual survey on registered establishments.

Major deviations from ISIC (Revision 4):
None reported.

Reference period:
Calendar year.

Scope:
All establishments.

Method of data collection:
Mail questionnaires.

Type of enumeration:
Complete enumeration.

Adjusted for non-response:
No.

Concepts and definitions of variables:
No deviations from the standard UN concepts and definitions are reported.

Related national publications:
Beschäftigungsstatistik, published by the Office of Statistics, Vaduz.

Liechtenstein

ISIC Revision 4			Number of establishments					Number of employees					Wages and salaries				
ISIC	Industry	Note	(number)				Note	(number)				Note	(Swiss Francs)			
			2013	2014	2015	2016		2013	2014	2015	2016		2013	2014	2015	2016
10	Food products		17	19	18	17		1835	1856	1809	1810		...	...	...	...
11	Beverages		3	2	2	3		23	6	7	10		...	...	...	...
12	Tobacco products		-	-	-	-		-	-	-	-		...	...	...	...
13	Textiles		6	6	6	5		71	62	60	67		...	...	...	...
14	Wearing apparel		10	11	12	13		9	7	10	5		...	...	...	...
15	Leather and related products		1	1	1	2		1	1	1	...		...	...	...	...
16	Wood products, excluding furniture		46	43	38	39		273	271	277	266		...	...	...	...
17	Paper and paper products		-	-	-	-		-	-	-	-		...	...	...	...
18	Printing and reproduction of recorded media		18	18	17	16		176	172	153	153		...	...	...	...
19	Coke and refined petroleum products		-	-	-	-		-	-	-	-		...	...	...	...
20	Chemicals and chemical products		2	2	2	3		65	70	115	132		...	...	...	...
21	Pharmaceuticals,medicinal chemicals, etc.		-	-	-	-		-	-	-	-		...	...	...	...
22	Rubber and plastics products		5	5	5	5		46	50	46	44		...	...	...	...
23	Other non-metallic mineral products		11	11	12	12		594	584	579	516		...	...	...	...
24	Basic metals		3	3	3	3		13	13	14	15		...	...	...	...
25	Fabricated metal products, except machinery		59	57	55	59		1068	1053	1177	1203		...	...	...	...
26	Computer, electronic and optical products		18	18	18	19		500	506	489	502		...	...	...	...
27	Electrical equipment		9	9	7	5		317	316	315	284		...	...	...	...
28	Machinery and equipment n.e.c.		39	37	38	39		2907	2965	2744	2686		...	...	...	...
29	Motor vehicles, trailers and semi-trailers		7	8	8	8		1911	1959	2011	2218		...	...	...	...
30	Other transport equipment		2	2	2	1		26	22	18	13		...	...	...	...
31	Furniture		5	5	5	5		112	113	113	121		...	...	...	...
32	Other manufacturing		44	43	40	41		1177	1163	1138	1166		...	...	...	...
33	Repair and installation of machinery/equipment		15	14	19	19		108	94	117	108		...	...	...	...
C	Total manufacturing		320	314	308	314		11232	11283	11193	11319		...	...	...	...

Lithuania

Supplier of information:
Statistics Lithuania, Vilnius.

Basic source of data:
Annual survey; administrative data.

Major deviations from ISIC (Revision 4):
None reported.

Reference period:
Calendar year.

Scope:
All registered enterprises.

Method of data collection:
Mail questionnaires, online survey and administrative data.

Type of enumeration:
Complete enumeration.

Adjusted for non-response:
Yes.

Concepts and definitions of variables:
Output includes revenue from non-industrial activities.
Value added includes cost of non-industrial activities.

Related national publications:
None reported.

Lithuania

ISIC	Industry	Number of enterprises (number)					Number of employees (number)					Wages and salaries paid to employees (thousands of Euros)				
		Note	2013	2014	2015	2016	Note	2013	2014	2015	2016	Note	2013	2014	2015	2016
1010	Processing/preserving of meat		202	207	218	222		7903	7734	7713	7768		36282	39706	45578	52212
1020	Processing/preserving of fish, etc.		88	89	85	80		4725	4853	5360	5160		32608	33375	37995	40281
1030	Processing/preserving of fruit,vegetables		318	371	398	445		997	1118	1164	1197		5591	6471	7608	8324
1040	Vegetable and animal oils and fats		7	10	17	17		116	108	116	126		1072	1249	1238	1222
1050	Dairy products		46	48	32	32		7607	7508	7407	7286		59941	62786	65005	68631
106	Grain mill products,starches and starch products		67	59	45	36		1229	1248	1336	1188		10386	11228	12936	13123
1061	Grain mill products		65	57	43	35		...	...	...	...		...	...	...	...
1062	Starches and starch products		2	2	2	1		...	...	...	...		...	...	...	...
107	Other food products		641	688	746	792		13803	13875	14285	14012		78504	80539	87370	93918
1071	Bakery products		480	498	539	572		9511	9493	9700	9454		46663	48742	52901	57645
1072	Sugar		2	2	2	2		...	...	...	...		...	...	...	...
1073	Cocoa, chocolate and sugar confectionery		21	27	27	35		1607	1486	1514	1507		14257	12675	13483	14430
1074	Macaroni, noodles, couscous, etc.		8	9	8	6		112	121	114	105		639	915	843	703
1075	Prepared meals and dishes		71	88	99	100		965	1122	1217	1218		5043	5866	6764	7508
1079	Other food products n.e.c.		59	64	71	77		...	...	...	...		...	...	...	...
1080	Prepared animal feeds		31	35	37	33		2092	2101	2122	2160		22529	22883	24385	26905
110	Beverages		89	94	93	85		...	3465	3514	3354		...	37508	39919	41500
1101	Distilling, rectifying and blending of spirits		4	4	4	3		554	401	423	...		5840	4307	4747	...
1102	Wines		5	6	7	8		283	...	...	...		2141	...	...	...
1103	Malt liquors and malt		53	52	49	47		1910	...	...	1850		21057	...	...	23271
1104	Soft drinks,mineral waters,other bottled waters		27	32	33	27		443	687	702	669		3062	6580	7255	8111
1200	Tobacco products		1	1	1	1		...	...	...	...		...	...	...	...
131	Spinning, weaving and finishing of textiles		93	102	110	133		2802	3041	3120	3064		18592	20651	22161	23986
1311	Preparation and spinning of textile fibres		37	41	42	49		1371	1463	1474	1526		9228	10035	10465	11772
1312	Weaving of textiles		35	41	47	49		855	991	1082	1250		6032	6899	7966	9842
1313	Finishing of textiles		21	20	21	35		576	587	564	288		3332	3716	3729	2372
139	Other textiles		658	798	804	840		4872	4910	5435	5878		29744	32015	36141	42944
1391	Knitted and crocheted fabrics		167	195	144	153		208	183	187	186		1208	1227	1280	1334
1392	Made-up textile articles, except apparel		373	470	503	513		3273	3148	3540	3740		19004	19446	22610	25821
1393	Carpets and rugs		2	3	3	5		...	20	24	36		...	133	149	183
1394	Cordage, rope, twine and netting		10	10	10	10		702	785	858	993		5273	6238	6957	8779
1399	Other textiles n.e.c.		106	120	144	159		...	774	826	923		...	4971	5145	6827
1410	Wearing apparel, except fur apparel		2236	2444	2465	2665		17053	17037	16787	16158		82481	87100	90286	96575
1420	Articles of fur		62	61	59	61		160	153	145	121		584	556	573	504
1430	Knitted and crocheted apparel		133	168	228	265		1898	1775	1734	1661		9488	8902	9757	10059
151	Leather;luggage,handbags,saddlery,harness;fur		126	127	128	198		460	575	547	542		1940	2458	2636	2778
1511	Tanning/dressing of leather; dressing of fur		10	11	10	10		221	225	210	213		1088	1117	1234	1275
1512	Luggage,handbags,etc.;saddlery/harness		116	116	118	188		239	350	337	329		852	1341	1402	1503
1520	Footwear		52	49	44	50		516	419	384	342		3106	2154	2170	2273
1610	Sawmilling and planing of wood		578	573	594	596		8108	8265	7911	7655		35582	38150	40625	43133

162	Wood products, cork, straw, plaiting materials	107092	95572	85393	69829	13835	13540	13200	11773	3076	3330	2921	2496
1621	Veneer sheets and wood-based panels	16781	15611	15172	11947	1474	1437	1464	1189	27	24	28	28
1622	Builders' carpentry and joinery	64986	55460	46562	37457	7635	7140	6587	5991	1972	2335	1937	1728
1623	Wooden containers	12295	11731	11818	11128	2354	2448	2695	2635	167	128	129	123
1629	Other wood products;articles of cork,straw	13030	12771	11841	9298	2372	2515	2454	1958	910	843	827	617
170	Paper and paper products	50546	42809	39233	...	4573	4248	4097	...	145	96	94	84
1701	Pulp, paper and paperboard	3398	2994	2850	2628	247	247	243	258	6	6	8	7
1702	Corrugated paper and paperboard	20484	18385	16691	14461	2000	1967	1882	1682	45	41	37	31
1709	Other articles of paper and paperboard	26664	21431	19693	17249	2326	2034	1972	1837	94	49	49	46
181	Printing and service activities related to printing	34569	34144	31413	29100	4137	4239	4162	4009	661	625	605	537
1811	Printing	31331	31318	28619	26466	3756	3863	3787	3631	269	240	235	224
1812	Service activities related to printing	3238	2826	2793	2634	381	376	375	378	392	385	370	313
1820	Reproduction of recorded media	2	8	11	5	2	5	5	4	3	3	3	5
1910	Coke oven products	-	-	-	-	-	-	-	-	-	-	-	-
1920	Refined petroleum products	...	...	...	...	...	...	...	...	5	9	8	7
201	Basic chemicals,fertilizers, etc.	64584	62149	58983	55525	3612	3729	3772	3708	36	37	40	33
2011	Basic chemicals	12564	10639	9333	...	787	714	704	...	16	18	21	17
2012	Fertilizers and nitrogen compounds	46693	45433	42973	39455	2535	2586	2619	2581	14	13	12	9
2013	Plastics and synthetic rubber in primary forms	5326	6078	6677	8368	290	429	449	...	6	6	7	7
202	Other chemical products	...	...	9786	8368	...	...	1198	1051	104	109	97	91
2021	Pesticides and other agrochemical products	...	...	83	70	...	...	15	13	1	1	3	3
2022	Paints,varnishes;printing ink and mastics	3611	3140	2921	2541	432	414	404	380	22	22	22	25
2023	Soap,cleaning and cosmetic preparations	4960	4161	3755	3086	607	559	506	421	69	69	58	48
2029	Other chemical products n.e.c.	2890	3259	3027	2672	238	288	273	237	12	17	14	15
2030	Man-made fibres	...	...	3523	3323	...	...	417	422	4	3	3	3
2100	Pharmaceuticals,medicinal chemicals, etc.	...	8047	8217	7781	...	...	659	695	17	22	24	20
221	Rubber products	2583	2412	2458	2305	373	378	379	382	32	30	25	28
2211	Rubber tyres and tubes	395	332	407	383	56	48	46	52	6	6	6	7
2219	Other rubber products	2188	2080	2051	1922	317	330	333	330	26	24	19	21
2220	Plastics products	84188	72662	66490	57985	8820	8345	8088	7641	372	341	348	333
2310	Glass and glass products	19090	17313	15913	11968	1915	1890	1807	1535	90	90	90	84
239	Non-metallic mineral products n.e.c.	57096	50394	50715	48235	6232	6187	6380	6671	1360	1387	1298	1203
2391	Refractory products	...	...	...	...	...	...	...	...	4	5	5	3
2392	Clay building materials	1989	1954	2300	2706	345	374	448	517	12	11	13	15
2393	Other porcelain and ceramic products	1979	1823	1757	2194	492	506	524	563	331	317	284	272
2394	Cement, lime and plaster	...	...	...	...	...	...	...	...	2	2	2	1
2395	Articles of concrete, cement and plaster	32412	26925	27433	24565	3216	3106	3058	3283	357	394	324	276
2396	Cutting, shaping and finishing of stone	4085	3794	3605	3709	1072	1125	1093	1138	643	648	659	625
2399	Other non-metallic mineral products n.e.c.	9507	8492	8166	8506	467	461	472	564	11	10	12	11
2410	Basic iron and steel	4406	4381	...	7294	444	...	443	777	20	18	19	18
2420	Basic precious and other non-ferrous metals	...	...	...	...	...	...	...	...	-	2	1	-
243	Casting of metals	1431	1452	1572	1087	164	190	204	116	10	12	11	9
2431	Casting of iron and steel	841	...	1037	...	78	...	106	...	3	4	4	3
2432	Casting of non-ferrous metals	590	...	535	...	86	...	98	...	7	8	7	6
251	Struct.metal products, tanks, reservoirs	...	58700	...	...	...	6652	...	...	391	350	344	312

continued

Lithuania

ISIC	Industry	Number of enterprises (number)				Number of employees (number)				Wages and salaries paid to employees (thousands of Euros)			
		2013	2014	2015	2016	2013	2014	2015	2016	2013	2014	2015	2016
2511	Structural metal products	278	311	314	359	4336	4693	5343	5645	27781	34775	44901	53738
2512	Tanks, reservoirs and containers of metal	34	33	36	32	…	-	1309	…	…	-	13799	…
2513	Steam generators, excl. hot water boilers	-	-	-	-	-	-	-	-	-	-	-	-
2520	Weapons and ammunition	2	2	2	1	…	…	…	…	…	…	…	…
259	Other metal products;metal working services	1139	1244	1417	1478	6487	6907	…	7856	44274	49653	…	68945
2591	Forging,pressing,stamping,roll-forming of metal	43	39	38	39	709	643	…	1191	5385	5097	…	11722
2592	Treatment and coating of metals; machining	221	268	316	369	1464	1544	1641	1770	9931	11116	13003	15134
2593	Cutlery, hand tools and general hardware	659	693	785	748	525	531	538	541	2811	3045	3318	3630
2599	Other fabricated metal products n.e.c.	216	244	278	322	3789	4189	4078	4354	26147	30396	31789	38459
2610	Electronic components and boards	16	21	21	23	666	776	864	795	5074	6483	7417	7416
2620	Computers and peripheral equipment	18	13	13	10	127	96	53	131	693	561	278	1429
2630	Communication equipment	17	20	19	16	439	464	461	441	4632	4941	5488	5583
2640	Consumer electronics	12	14	12	9	280	…	…	…	…	…	…	…
265	Measuring;testing equipment; watches, etc.	52	55	53	55	1292	1270	1258	1442	13780	14586	15437	18993
2651	Measuring/testing/navigating equipment,etc.	51	53	50	52	…	…	1234	1420	…	…	15349	18913
2652	Watches and clocks	1	2	3	3	…	…	24	22	…	…	88	80
2660	Irradiation/electromedical equipment,etc.	6	5	5	4	…	…	56	53	…	…	418	477
2670	Optical instruments and photographic equipment	12	14	15	16	334	390	407	466	7024	8048	9307	11467
2680	Magnetic and optical media	2	2	1	1	…	…	…	…	…	…	…	…
2710	Electric motors,generators,transformers,etc.	43	44	44	42	1402	1537	1628	1668	12258	13834	15388	16389
2720	Batteries and accumulators	2	1	1	1	…	…	…	…	…	…	…	…
273	Wiring and wiring devices	16	19	15	13	1070	937	…	…	6330	5397	…	…
2731	Fibre optic cables	-	-	-	-								
2732	Other electronic and electric wires and cables	9	8	8	7	763	589	375	410	4209	3050	2726	3133
2733	Wiring devices	7	11	7	6	307	348	…	…	2121	2347	…	…
2740	Electric lighting equipment	16	17	17	19	445	540	516	664	2751	3396	4263	4855
2750	Domestic appliances	16	15	16	15	1962	…	1929	1892	14611	…	15586	15885
2790	Other electrical equipment	13	17	15	12	…	61	43	42	…	258	241	192
281	General-purpose machinery	101	111	109	110	4599	4488	4480	4487	39688	42635	41998	46202
2811	Engines/turbines,excl.aircraft,vehicle engines	4	5	5	4	16	18	19	10	31	33	58	66
2812	Fluid power equipment	7	9	8	7	35	77	72	69	207	455	491	483
2813	Other pumps, compressors, taps and valves	5	6	6	7	415	458	393	434	3373	3246	2384	4282
2814	Bearings, gears, gearing and driving elements	8	6	4	4	120	103	103	101	546	542	637	705
2815	Ovens, furnaces and furnace burners	8	12	12	11	834	791	747	730	5300	7536	5777	6090
2816	Lifting and handling equipment	17	19	19	23	244	303	293	312	2252	2935	2796	3134
2817	Office machinery, excl.computers,etc.	7	5	7	6	…	…	…	…	…	…	…	…
2818	Power-driven hand tools	1	2	2	2	…	…	…	…	…	…	…	…
2819	Other general-purpose machinery	44	47	46	46	2474	2233	2271	2254	23134	22426	23852	24807
282	Special-purpose machinery	74	79	78	78	1645	1886	1765	1802	12649	16486	16170	17892
2821	Agricultural and forestry machinery	12	12	10	10	486	510	491	491	3749	4254	4546	4824
2822	Metal-forming machinery and machine tools	32	36	33	33	654	687	566	510	5059	5704	4954	4216

Code	Description												
2823	Machinery for metallurgy	1	1	1	1	⋮	⋮	⋮	⋮	⋮	⋮	⋮	⋮
2824	Mining, quarrying and construction machinery	-	1	1	1	177	211	223	242	1326	1685	1743	2313
2825	Food/beverage/tobacco processing machinery	8	10	13	11	⋮	⋮	⋮	⋮	⋮	⋮	⋮	⋮
2826	Textile/apparel/leather production machinery	1	1	1	1	⋮	⋮	⋮	⋮	⋮	⋮	⋮	⋮
2829	Other special-purpose machinery	20	18	19	21	⋮	421	425	498	⋮	4383	4362	5877
2910	Motor vehicles	7	7	4	4	91	131	197	213	610	989	1749	2302
2920	Automobile bodies, trailers and semi-trailers	12	17	18	19	577	736	730	892	5774	7791	8783	11400
2930	Parts and accessories for motor vehicles	22	23	27	29	1368	2855	3480	3845	9246	18118	26802	33417
301	Building of ships and boats	41	47	50	52	828	880	1079	1428	9110	9158	12940	17015
3011	Building of ships and floating structures	19	22	26	27	678	713	893	1176	7747	7642	11053	14235
3012	Building of pleasure and sporting boats	22	25	24	25	150	167	186	252	1363	1516	1887	2780
3020	Railway locomotives and rolling stock	1	1	2	2	⋮	⋮	⋮	⋮	⋮	⋮	⋮	⋮
3030	Air and spacecraft and related machinery	4	3	4	2	107	97	108	⋮	485	492	667	⋮
3040	Military fighting vehicles	-	-	-	-	-	-	-	-	-	-	-	-
309	Transport equipment n.e.c.	7	6	7	7	⋮	⋮	⋮	⋮	⋮	⋮	⋮	⋮
3091	Motorcycles	1	-	-	-	⋮	⋮	⋮	⋮	⋮	⋮	⋮	⋮
3092	Bicycles and invalid carriages	5	5	6	6	⋮	⋮	⋮	495	⋮	⋮	⋮	4162
3099	Other transport equipment n.e.c.	1	1	1	1	⋮	⋮	⋮	⋮	⋮	⋮	⋮	⋮
3100	Furniture	1645	1869	2023	2057	24612	26394	26909	27747	157938	178943	190753	212809
321	Jewellery, bijouterie and related articles	798	920	1129	1154	877	993	971	977	3870	4954	5386	5558
3211	Jewellery and related articles	309	362	379	395	557	615	622	636	2587	3216	3391	3636
3212	Imitation jewellery and related articles	489	558	750	759	320	378	349	341	1282	1738	1995	1923
3220	Musical instruments	⋮	-	1	1	⋮	⋮	⋮	⋮	⋮	⋮	⋮	⋮
3230	Sports goods	39	41	56	51	174	170	174	125	796	815	867	771
3240	Games and toys	26	34	54	60	⋮	⋮	⋮	⋮	⋮	⋮	⋮	125
3250	Medical and dental instruments and supplies	291	313	333	347	⋮	⋮	⋮	⋮	⋮	⋮	⋮	⋮
3290	Other manufacturing n.e.c.	174	225	322	412	1390	1482	1543	1599	10014	12111	12755	13843
331	Repair of fabricated metal products/machinery	764	870	898	940	7978	8251	7996	7765	70625	82561	83210	86885
3311	Repair of fabricated metal products	34	32	34	44	178	185	211	261	892	985	1144	1818
3312	Repair of machinery	343	406	438	440	2370	2476	2524	2364	19857	22475	23992	23696
3313	Repair of electronic and optical equipment	23	25	24	23	97	93	80	73	520	508	372	488
3314	Repair of electrical equipment	200	220	221	240	450	415	442	485	4313	4123	4295	4618
3315	Repair of transport equip., excl. motor vehicles	154	172	168	178	4842	5029	4673	4510	44834	54193	53019	55821
3319	Repair of other equipment	10	15	13	15	41	53	66	72	210	276	387	444
3320	Installation of industrial machinery/equipment	38	49	52	53	397	477	548	575	3610	4465	5466	6525
C	Total manufacturing	16120	17975	19398	19969	191476	199695	203369	205868	1344687	1489737	1613710	1782888

Lithuania

ISIC	Industry	Note	Output at producers' prices (millions of Euros)				Note	Value added at factor values (millions of Euros)				Note	Gross fixed capital formation (millions of Euros)	
			2013	2014	2015	2016		2013	2014	2015	2016		2015	2016
1010	Processing/preserving of meat		673.9	672.8	636.0	563.4		78.2	73.0	84.8	90.6		9.6	14.3
1020	Processing/preserving of fish, etc.		393.3	467.9	510.6	527.0		58.7	83.8	84.6	75.4		10.7	11.3
1030	Processing/preserving of fruit,vegetables		72.0	73.9	81.3	80.7		15.6	18.7	20.9	20.7		4.2	4.4
1040	Vegetable and animal oils and fats		18.7	24.9	37.1	30.7		2.3	3.6	4.2	4.0		1.1	0.5
1050	Dairy products		1068.8	1046.5	855.6	858.1		132.0	135.8	167.2	170.2		35.6	65.6
106	Grain mill products,starches and starch products		181.7	183.6	214.9	223.6		27.5	28.5	29.7	51.5		22.7	9.8
1061	Grain mill products		...	...	...	...		...	...	...	...		...	...
1062	Starches and starch products		...	...	...	...		...	...	...	...		...	...
107	Other food products		592.7	538.6	539.0	565.9		172.2	158.8	179.9	185.8		49.4	35.3
1071	Bakery products		228.6	242.6	252.4	256.2		77.9	86.3	91.3	94.0		34.3	14.9
1072	Sugar		...	...	...	...		...	...	...	...		...	...
1073	Cocoa, chocolate and sugar confectionery		133.0	76.9	74.5	78.7		39.2	26.9	25.7	28.4		9.0	3.7
1074	Macaroni, noodles, couscous, etc.		8.1	11.6	8.5	9.1		2.3	2.0	2.6	2.1		0.2	0.7
1075	Prepared meals and dishes		35.7	44.6	48.8	54.8		9.0	13.4	16.4	17.9		1.8	7.1
1079	Other food products n.e.c.		...	...	...	...		...	...	...	...		...	...
1080	Prepared animal feeds		436.1	445.8	461.2	470.9		82.2	70.6	106.5	95.9		13.0	22.7
110	Beverages		...	530.9	504.1	476.0		...	122.3	139.7	122.3		23.3	21.7
1101	Distilling, rectifying and blending of spirits		73.8	54.8	58.6	...		17.7	15.1	15.2	...		3.8	...
1102	Wines		71.7	...	...	...		10.3	...	...	...		...	...
1103	Malt liquors and malt		278.9	...	...	255.7		53.6	...	...	64.3		...	13.6
1104	Soft drinks,mineral waters,other bottled waters		36.1	83.5	101.2	89.4		8.5	18.8	24.7	26.2		6.2	4.1
1200	Tobacco products		...	...	...	...		...	...	...	...		...	...
131	Spinning, weaving and finishing of textiles		106.8	114.5	119.1	131.0		34.4	39.3	40.4	49.6		11.2	8.3
1311	Preparation and spinning of textile fibres		60.9	64.7	66.7	71.4		18.3	20.2	20.3	24.9		7.2	4.1
1312	Weaving of textiles		30.1	32.5	37.0	47.1		9.7	11.3	13.0	18.9		3.4	3.4
1313	Finishing of textiles		15.8	17.2	15.4	12.5		6.3	7.8	7.1	5.8		0.6	0.8
139	Other textiles		227.3	235.3	261.2	283.0		64.5	69.3	70.6	84.4		10.0	12.5
1391	Knitted and crocheted fabrics		8.5	8.6	7.8	7.5		2.3	2.5	2.6	2.4		0.1	0.1
1392	Made-up textile articles, except apparel		148.4	145.0	163.4	171.9		41.6	40.3	40.5	47.9		4.6	6.7
1393	Carpets and rugs		...	0.6	0.7	0.8		...	0.2	0.2	0.3		-	-
1394	Cordage, rope, twine and netting		34.8	37.7	41.2	48.1		12.2	13.6	16.0	19.0		4.2	3.1
1399	Other textiles n.e.c.		...	43.4	48.1	54.6		...	12.6	11.3	14.8		1.1	2.5
1410	Wearing apparel, except fur apparel		333.6	364.6	367.3	383.9		143.1	151.7	154.3	162.6		18.0	12.4
1420	Articles of fur		2.1	1.6	1.7	1.7		0.9	0.5	0.6	0.7		-	-
1430	Knitted and crocheted apparel		36.6	32.7	33.6	35.1		13.4	13.0	15.4	17.1		1.0	1.5
151	Leather;luggage,handbags,saddlery,harness;fur		11.3	12.5	15.8	14.7		3.2	4.2	4.6	4.6		0.2	0.3
1511	Tanning/dressing of leather; dressing of fur		8.2	7.8	10.4	9.2		1.6	1.8	1.8	1.9		0.1	0.3
1512	Luggage,handbags,etc.;saddlery/harness		3.1	4.7	5.4	5.5		1.7	2.4	2.8	2.6		0.2	0.1
1520	Footwear		13.0	9.7	8.7	9.1		5.2	3.9	3.7	3.8		0.2	0.2
1610	Sawmilling and planing of wood		301.2	362.2	357.7	368.8		71.4	83.7	79.4	81.7		24.3	22.2

Code	Description										
162	Wood products, cork, straw, plaiting materials	39.9	39.6	215.9	194.3	189.5	154.4	783.1	756.0	707.5	600.3
1621	Veneer sheets and wood-based panels	10.2	8.7	35.0	48.1	48.0	37.5	165.1	172.6	164.8	155.0
1622	Builders' carpentry and joinery	20.1	17.8	137.0	99.5	87.5	73.5	436.9	387.5	341.1	274.6
1623	Wooden containers	3.5	3.8	20.5	21.3	25.2	20.2	89.2	94.0	97.2	89.8
1629	Other wood products;articles of cork,straw	6.1	9.3	23.4	25.3	28.9	23.2	91.9	102.0	104.4	80.9
170	Paper and paper products	57.1	38.6	129.8	116.8	110.6	...	446.3	418.5	390.8	...
1701	Pulp, paper and paperboard	14.6	6.9	9.7	11.8	9.4	7.4	41.2	44.3	43.1	42.8
1702	Corrugated paper and paperboard	17.8	15.8	45.0	38.2	37.0	33.5	175.3	167.4	157.1	145.0
1709	Other articles of paper and paperboard	24.7	15.9	75.1	66.8	64.3	56.8	229.7	206.8	190.6	174.8
181	Printing and service activities related to printing	18.7	10.8	71.8	74.8	69.1	63.5	211.9	215.7	210.9	202.1
1811	Printing	17.7	9.0	64.9	68.5	62.9	58.0	193.6	200.3	195.3	188.3
1812	Service activities related to printing	1.0	1.8	6.9	6.3	6.2	5.5	18.3	15.4	15.6	13.8
1820	Reproduction of recorded media	...	...	-	-	-	-	0.1	0.1	0.1	0.1
1910	Coke oven products	-	-	-	-	-	-	-	-	-	-
1920	Refined petroleum products	73.9	...	306.3	314.3	164.7	66.7	1472.1	1757.1	1639.4	1639.4
201	Basic chemicals,fertilizers,etc.	7.9	69.4	130.1	71.4	52.9	...	205.4	142.8	97.9	...
2011	Basic chemicals	58.3	13.7	124.2	215.9	88.4	13.7	749.0	1056.9	954.9	915.8
2012	Fertilizers and nitrogen compounds	7.7	44.5	52.0	27.0	23.4	...	517.7	557.4	586.7	...
2013	Plastics and synthetic rubber in primary forms	...	11.2	...	...	37.3	...	...	...	199.2	214.1
202	Other chemical products	...	...	...	...	0.2	26.7	...	27.4	0.5	0.4
2021	Pesticides and other agrochemical products	7.4	1.9	8.1	7.8	7.7	0.1	27.9	26.7	28.8	26.3
2022	Paints,varnishes;printing ink and mastics	1.1	1.2	11.3	9.0	8.8	7.4	28.9	27.4	24.5	21.6
2023	Soap,cleaning and cosmetic preparations	1.0	2.1	12.0	23.6	20.7	7.3	125.0	148.9	145.4	165.9
2029	Other chemical products n.e.c.	...	...	...	...	8.3	11.8	...	192.9	38.0	34.0
2030	Man-made fibres	3.0	...	...	121.5	62.4	6.3	...	...	38.0	38.0
2100	Pharmaceuticals,medicinal chemicals, etc.	...	3.0	...	121.5	62.4	31.7	...	192.9	149.3	110.7
221	Rubber products	1.5	1.7	5.8	4.9	5.0	4.8	11.5	10.3	11.0	11.0
2211	Rubber tyres and tubes	0.2	-	0.9	0.5	0.5	0.5	2.5	2.0	2.5	2.7
2219	Other rubber products	1.3	1.7	4.9	4.4	4.5	4.3	9.0	8.3	8.5	8.3
2220	Plastics products	50.0	60.7	215.6	181.4	186.7	154.2	886.6	863.6	827.9	757.3
2310	Glass and glass products	8.2	7.8	47.9	40.6	38.8	27.1	153.3	140.5	137.5	108.1
239	Non-metallic mineral products n.e.c.	46.2	28.3	119.3	111.0	120.9	116.8	374.2	356.7	382.5	394.3
2391	Refractory products	0.6	0.3	3.2	2.0	2.4	...	6.8	4.5	6.7	9.3
2392	Clay building materials	0.3	0.2	4.0	3.9	3.2	3.0	6.9	6.6	6.0	15.5
2393	Other porcelain and ceramic products	...	...	...	...	...	4.6	...	...	...	...
2394	Cement, lime and plaster	...	...	...	...	...	...	...	...	...	...
2395	Articles of concrete, cement and plaster	35.3	17.5	69.3	54.8	65.8	57.0	213.5	191.2	216.2	193.6
2396	Cutting, shaping and finishing of stone	0.8	0.9	8.3	8.4	7.9	7.0	19.1	18.9	18.3	16.8
2399	Other non-metallic mineral products n.e.c.	5.8	5.9	22.5	24.8	24.8	29.3	68.5	67.3	64.6	83.6
2410	Basic iron and steel	0.3	0.8	6.7	6.9	6.9	12.9	46.8	55.4	...	82.4
2420	Basic precious and other non-ferrous metals	-	-	-	-	...	-	-	-	...	...
243	Casting of metals	0.1	0.1	2.3	2.7	1.5	...	7.1	9.3	9.3	3.7
2431	Casting of iron and steel	-	...	1.2	...	1.6	1.7	2.3	...	3.5	...
2432	Casting of non-ferrous metals	0.1	0.1	1.1	...	-0.1	...	4.8	...	5.9	...
251	Struct.metal products, tanks, reservoirs	...	16.7	...	114.2	...	...	...	381.2	...	...

continued

Lithuania

ISIC	Industry	Output at producers' prices (millions of Euros) Note	2013	2014	2015	2016	Value added at factor values (millions of Euros) Note	2013	2014	2015	2016	Gross fixed capital formation (millions of Euros) Note	2015	2016
2511	Structural metal products		217.0	245.2	284.7	308.9		60.9	73.8	89.7	101.8		13.8	16.9
2512	Tanks, reservoirs and containers of metal		-	-	96.5	-		..	-	24.5	..		2.9	-
2513	Steam generators, excl. hot water boilers		-	-	-	-		-	-	-	-		-	-
2520	Weapons and ammunition		..	..	..	..		..	..	..	..		..	..
259	Other metal products;metal working services		277.0	302.2	..	409.9		88.1	103.6	..	139.5		..	39.4
2591	Forging,pressing,stamping,roll-forming of metal		42.2	40.6	..	99.8		12.0	12.4	..	25.2		5.4	14.6
2592	Treatment and coating of metals; machining		49.0	64.3	74.0	88.2		16.0	21.0	24.6	30.1		5.4	5.1
2593	Cutlery, hand tools and general hardware		16.3	17.8	19.7	20.6		6.0	8.0	8.3	7.1		0.9	2.0
2599	Other fabricated metal products n.e.c.		169.7	179.5	181.5	201.2		54.1	62.1	63.6	77.1		16.2	17.7
2610	Electronic components and boards		28.6	36.6	47.6	47.5		7.8	9.5	13.2	14.2		4.4	3.0
2620	Computers and peripheral equipment		8.9	8.1	9.2	13.3		1.4	1.4	1.1	2.7		0.1	0.3
2630	Communication equipment		20.0	22.9	25.5	25.9		6.7	6.9	8.0	8.1		1.1	0.7
2640	Consumer electronics		..	..	..	..		..	..	..	..		..	..
265	Measuring,testing equipment; watches, etc.		72.1	64.6	96.7	116.0		32.9	31.1	42.5	46.1		5.6	3.9
2651	Measuring/testing/navigating equipment,etc.		..	..	96.4	115.7		..	..	42.5	46.0		5.6	3.9
2652	Watches and clocks		..	..	0.2	0.2		..	..	0.1	0.1		-	-
2660	Irradiation/electromedical equipment,etc.		..	..	5.0	4.8		..	..	1.8	2.2		0.1	..
2670	Optical instruments and photographic equipment		35.6	42.6	51.9	64.7		21.6	21.7	27.3	35.0		3.0	2.0
2680	Magnetic and optical media		..	..	..	..		..	..	..	..		..	..
2710	Electric motors,generators,transformers,etc.		90.5	100.6	109.4	114.5		22.9	27.8	29.0	33.1		2.2	2.2
2720	Batteries and accumulators		..	..	..	..		..	..	..	..		..	..
273	Wiring and wiring devices		46.0	46.7	..	..		14.3	13.1	..	..		..	..
2731	Fibre optic cables		-	-	-	-		-	-	-	-		-	-
2732	Other electronic and electric wires and cables		27.5	27.0	28.1	28.4		7.0	6.2	5.8	7.6		1.0	0.9
2733	Wiring devices		18.5	19.6	..	..		7.2	6.9	..	..		..	..
2740	Electric lighting equipment		34.3	38.1	38.4	52.2		6.4	7.5	9.3	11.2		3.6	1.8
2750	Domestic appliances		127.9	..	123.2	115.9		33.3	..	35.4	35.5		4.6	6.0
2790	Other electrical equipment		..	1.9	0.9	0.8		..	0.2	0.2	0.4		-	-
281	General-purpose machinery		292.9	291.0	276.7	290.2		101.4	97.7	97.0	98.9		23.1	18.5
2811	Engines/turbines,excl.aircraft,vehicle engines		0.1	0.2	0.1	0.2		-	0.1	0.1	0.1		..	..
2812	Fluid power equipment		3.2	4.4	3.0	3.9		0.6	1.1	1.3	1.8		0.2	0.2
2813	Other pumps, compressors, taps and valves		13.6	13.2	14.5	13.0		6.5	7.0	4.4	4.2		3.1	4.3
2814	Bearings, gears, gearing and driving elements		5.2	1.7	1.7	1.7		1.5	1.1	1.1	1.1		0.1	1.0
2815	Ovens, furnaces and furnace burners		29.7	28.1	26.5	27.3		11.1	12.0	11.4	9.8		2.6	0.6
2816	Lifting and handling equipment		24.0	23.2	20.7	19.6		6.8	5.2	4.7	5.4		0.3	..
2817	Office machinery, excl.computers,etc.		..	..	..	..		..	..	..	..		..	..
2818	Power-driven hand tools		..	..	..	..		..	..	..	..		..	..
2819	Other general-purpose machinery		170.6	165.2	150.8	152.9		65.9	60.1	61.6	61.5		14.9	9.5
282	Special-purpose machinery		62.8	90.3	91.9	93.5		24.2	29.3	31.3	34.5		6.1	5.6
2821	Agricultural and forestry machinery		22.5	32.7	29.4	33.3		7.1	10.2	9.5	11.7		2.6	2.4
2822	Metal-forming machinery and machine tools		19.3	24.0	23.7	15.2		7.9	8.9	8.5	6.2		0.4	0.7

Code	Description										
2823	Machinery for metallurgy	:	:	:	:	:	:	:	:	:	:
2824	Mining, quarrying and construction machinery	8.1	8.8	14.1	16.7	2.6	2.9	3.3	4.4	0.7	0.3
2825	Food/beverage/tobacco processing machinery	:	:	:	:	:	:	:	:	:	:
2826	Textile/apparel/leather production machinery	:	:	:	:	:	:	:	:	:	:
2829	Other special-purpose machinery	:	22.1	21.3	24.9	5.8	5.8	8.5	10.1	2.0	2.0
2910	Motor vehicles	12.3	17.8	20.1	26.1	1.7	2.4	3.6	5.3	0.1	0.2
2920	Automobile bodies, trailers and semi-trailers	117.6	115.1	87.1	121.4	19.4	21.2	19.0	28.8	5.9	9.5
2930	Parts and accessories for motor vehicles	58.5	108.1	140.0	156.0	19.5	35.1	51.0	67.7	5.9	11.0
301	Building of ships and boats	67.6	64.2	62.4	84.7	5.3	12.6	23.1	28.8	1.3	2.4
3011	Building of ships and floating structures	59.3	53.0	51.8	69.9	2.3	8.7	19.2	24.6	0.3	1.6
3012	Building of pleasure and sporting boats	8.3	11.2	10.6	14.8	3.1	4.0	3.9	4.1	1.0	0.8
3020	Railway locomotives and rolling stock	:	:	:	:	:	:	:	:	:	:
3030	Air and spacecraft and related machinery	5.9	1.9	2.6	:	2.0	0.7	1.0	:	:	:
3040	Military fighting vehicles	-	-	-	-	-	-	-	-	-	-
309	Transport equipment n.e.c.	:	:	:	:	:	:	:	:	:	:
3091	Motorcycles	-	-	-	-	-	-	-	-	-	-
3092	Bicycles and invalid carriages	:	:	:	41.2	:	:	:	4.4	:	0.3
3099	Other transport equipment n.e.c.	:	:	:	:	:	:	:	:	:	:
3100	Furniture	1180.6	1376.6	1412.8	1466.5	296.2	363.6	391.0	415.0	61.5	63.1
321	Jewellery, bijouterie and related articles	46.1	48.3	53.5	43.1	15.8	18.5	20.8	17.9	1.9	1.3
3211	Jewellery and related articles	22.9	31.2	31.1	24.5	8.5	10.7	10.9	10.2	1.6	1.2
3212	Imitation jewellery and related articles	23.2	17.2	22.4	18.5	7.3	7.8	9.8	7.7	0.4	0.2
3220	Musical instruments	:	:	:	:	-	:	:	:	:	:
3230	Sports goods	11.1	10.4	9.9	:	2.0	2.2	2.3	:	0.1	:
3240	Games and toys	:	:	:	3.0	:	:	:	1.2	:	-
3250	Medical and dental instruments and supplies	:	:	:	:	:	:	:	:	:	:
3290	Other manufacturing n.e.c.	40.2	50.6	57.3	61.0	17.7	21.3	22.3	23.7	7.7	4.1
331	Repair of fabricated metal products/machinery	406.4	430.3	418.2	441.1	125.7	126.7	143.8	154.2	16.3	11.6
3311	Repair of fabricated metal products	7.0	7.1	8.2	13.2	2.0	2.1	2.2	3.7	0.3	0.3
3312	Repair of machinery	87.6	112.8	109.5	93.5	35.2	39.1	44.3	44.1	6.0	4.5
3313	Repair of electronic and optical equipment	2.0	2.0	1.4	1.8	1.0	1.0	0.6	0.9	0.1	0.2
3314	Repair of electrical equipment	15.5	13.7	20.7	17.4	7.6	6.6	8.9	8.8	0.4	0.6
3315	Repair of transport equip., excl. motor vehicles	292.7	292.6	275.7	312.7	79.3	77.4	86.9	95.8	9.3	6.0
3319	Repair of other equipment	1.5	2.1	2.7	2.4	0.5	0.5	0.9	0.8	0.2	0.1
3320	Installation of industrial machinery/equipment	18.5	23.4	22.0	26.8	6.5	8.9	8.9	11.4	1.0	0.9
C	Total manufacturing	19098.9	18379.5	17995.1	17660.5	2875.3	3280.0	4034.5	4213.0	771.5	816.7

Lithuania

Index numbers of industrial production

ISIC Revision 4

(2010=100)

ISIC	Industry	Note	2005	2006	2007	2008	2009	2010	2011	2012	2013	2014	2015	2016
10	Food products		91	100	113	109	101	100	108	117	120	126	128	131
11	Beverages		93	98	113	113	101	100	99	94	105	111	120	127
12	Tobacco products		...	...	...	...	...	...	...	...	...	...	...	...
13	Textiles		118	131	136	109	86	100	123	138	125	145	142	163
14	Wearing apparel		138	141	131	111	83	100	119	119	135	143	138	145
15	Leather and related products		106	96	118	107	66	100	114	113	106	107	98	81
16	Wood products, excluding furniture		109	115	125	114	90	100	110	109	129	138	157	169
17	Paper and paper products		56	74	78	73	70	100	112	116	150	165	176	188
18	Printing and reproduction of recorded media		101	115	124	132	91	100	132	151	164	165	214	216
19	Coke and refined petroleum products		...	...	...	...	...	...	...	...	...	...	...	...
20	Chemicals and chemical products		50	64	104	92	91	100	105	116	109	119	119	124
21	Pharmaceuticals, medicinal chemicals, etc.		51	65	69	56	63	100	90	109	150	205	288	338
22	Rubber and plastics products		95	113	111	103	80	100	114	122	133	142	149	156
23	Other non-metallic mineral products		148	200	202	167	87	100	124	126	137	150	142	153
24	Basic metals		48	43	62	111	99	100	127	142	157	84	83	87
25	Fabricated metal products, except machinery		126	162	202	141	86	100	138	150	146	168	180	210
26	Computer, electronic and optical products		103	102	93	86	92	100	96	89	80	90	119	145
27	Electrical equipment		112	112	120	126	72	100	120	170	188	204	211	224
28	Machinery and equipment n.e.c.		54	71	77	124	88	100	125	133	159	157	175	185
29	Motor vehicles, trailers and semi-trailers		197	229	261	217	61	100	153	158	189	236	245	308
30	Other transport equipment		100	101	109	126	101	100	59	95	116	82	94	82
31	Furniture		72	92	107	113	91	100	134	162	173	201	229	233
32	Other manufacturing		59	63	94	118	108	100	118	121	131	149	156	168
33	Repair and installation of machinery/equipment		69	86	96	101	91	100	100	132	142	160	147	147
C	Total manufacturing		96	102	103	110	93	100	110	116	121	122	129	133

Luxembourg

Supplier of information:
Service central de la statistique et des études économiques (STATEC), Luxembourg.
Industrial statistics for the OECD countries are compiled by the OECD secretariat, which supplies them to UNIDO.

Basic source of data:
Annual surveys; administrative sources; company accounts.

Major deviations from ISIC (Revision 4):
Data presented in ISIC (Revision 4) were originally classified according to the national NACE-related classification system (NACE-LUX).

Reference period:
Calendar year.

Scope:
All enterprises included in the business register.

Method of data collection:
Not reported.

Type of enumeration:
Complete enumeration for enterprises exceeding employment or turnover threshold; sample survey for enterprises below threshold values.

Adjusted for non-response:
Yes.

Concepts and definitions of variables:
No deviations from the standard UN concepts and definitions are reported.

Related national publications:
None reported.

Luxembourg

ISIC	Industry	Number of enterprises (number)					Number of employees (number)					Wages and salaries paid to employees (millions of Euros)				
		Note	2013	2014	2015	2016	Note	2013	2014	2015	2016	Note	2013	2014	2015	2016
10	Food products		132	130	128	124		4941	4870	5085	5259		144	148	153	159
11	Beverages		30	31	30	31		461	474	476	480		21	21	21	21
12	Tobacco products		1	1	1	1		...	...	...	...		...	...	...	...
13	Textiles		20	20	19	17		...	...	...	...		...	...	...	...
14	Wearing apparel		15	12	15	13		...	...	...	...		...	...	...	...
15	Leather and related products		-	-	-	-		-	-	-	-		-	-	-	-
16	Wood products, excluding furniture		23	23	23	19		697	631	607	588		26	26	25	25
17	Paper and paper products		3	3	3	3		...	...	...	...		...	...	...	...
18	Printing and reproduction of recorded media		96	92	85	80		721	707	696	609		30	29	30	26
19	Coke and refined petroleum products		-	-	-	-		-	-	-	-		-	-	-	-
20	Chemicals and chemical products		17	17	16	16		882	948	1008	1119		35	37	39	44
21	Pharmaceuticals,medicinal chemicals, etc.		1	1	1	1		...	...	...	...		...	...	...	...
22	Rubber and plastics products		28	25	24	25		...	...	...	...		...	...	...	...
23	Other non-metallic mineral products		35	38	33	35		2350	2347	2261	2329		109	116	114	119
24	Basic metals		8	8	8	9		...	...	...	...		...	...	...	...
25	Fabricated metal products, except machinery		194	187	181	181		3696	3591	3619	3547		159	157	157	156
26	Computer, electronic and optical products		9	9	10	9		...	...	...	...		...	...	...	...
27	Electrical equipment		14	12	11	12		691	625	489	488		29	27	21	21
28	Machinery and equipment n.e.c.		26	26	24	24		3859	3906	4012	4122		193	203	220	228
29	Motor vehicles, trailers and semi-trailers		12	12	10	9		...	...	...	...		...	...	...	...
30	Other transport equipment		1	1	1	1		...	...	...	...		...	...	...	...
31	Furniture		30	28	27	26		163	155	160	163		6	6	6	6
32	Other manufacturing		84	81	81	74		549	544	557	577		20	20	21	23
33	Repair and installation of machinery/equipment		60	55	55	57		440	446	464	452		22	25	28	30
C	Total manufacturing		839	812	786	767		33375	33143	33121	33440		1600	1626	1641	1653

ISIC Revision 4

Luxembourg

- 515 -

| ISIC Revision 4 | | Output (valuation not defined) | | | | | Value added at factor values | | | | | Gross fixed capital formation | | |
| | | | (millions of Euros) | | | | | (millions of Euros) | | | | | (millions of Euros) | |
ISIC	Industry	Note	2013	2014	2015	2016	Note	2013	2014	2015	2016	Note	2015	2016
10	Food products		578	611	735	729		203	217	229	238		26	31
11	Beverages		158	162	162	164		53	55	56	52		8	8
12	Tobacco products		...	...	...	...		...	...	...	...		...	...
13	Textiles		...	...	...	...		...	...	...	...		...	...
14	Wearing apparel		...	...	...	...		...	...	...	...		...	...
15	Leather and related products		-	-	-	-		-	-	-	-		-	-
16	Wood products, excluding furniture		192	190	197	200		41	38	39	41		8	11
17	Paper and paper products		...	...	...	...		...	...	...	...		...	...
18	Printing and reproduction of recorded media		103	107	100	94		42	45	41	40		7	12
19	Coke and refined petroleum products		-	-	-	-		-	-	-	-		-	-
20	Chemicals and chemical products		264	302	296	319		66	75	74	84		9	17
21	Pharmaceuticals, medicinal chemicals, etc.		...	...	...	...		...	...	...	...		...	...
22	Rubber and plastics products		...	...	...	...		...	...	...	...		...	...
23	Other non-metallic mineral products		536	601	690	939		171	178	179	261		26	36
24	Basic metals		...	...	...	...		...	...	...	...		...	...
25	Fabricated metal products, except machinery		683	691	690	665		225	229	228	231		18	34
26	Computer, electronic and optical products		...	...	...	...		...	...	...	...		...	...
27	Electrical equipment		105	96	94	93		39	33	31	31		2	3
28	Machinery and equipment n.e.c.		1122	1077	1163	1159		359	350	388	376		79	39
29	Motor vehicles, trailers and semi-trailers		...	...	...	...		...	...	...	...		...	...
30	Other transport equipment		...	...	...	...		...	...	...	...		...	...
31	Furniture		17	18	17	16		7	7	8	8		-	1
32	Other manufacturing		52	53	44	48		26	26	28	29		1	1
33	Repair and installation of machinery/equipment		101	95	107	91		40	35	49	47		10	4
C	Total manufacturing		8775	9128	10776	10886		2375	2524	2601	3118		436	402

Luxembourg

Index numbers of industrial production

ISIC Revision 4

(2010=100)

ISIC	Industry	Note	2005	2006	2007	2008	2009	2010	2011	2012	2013	2014	2015	2016
10	Food products	a/	...	...	...	...	...	100	99	98	97	98	107	106
11	Beverages	a/	...	...	...	...	...	100	105	102	95	96	93	89
12	Tobacco products	a/	...	...	...	...	...	...	...	...	...	...	...	...
13	Textiles	b/	...	...	...	...	...	100	95	97	98	95	108	92
14	Wearing apparel	b/	...	...	...	...	...	...	...	...	...	...	...	...
15	Leather and related products	b/	...	...	...	...	...	...	...	...	...	...	...	...
16	Wood products, excluding furniture	c/	...	...	...	...	...	100	98	91	95	95	99	114
17	Paper and paper products	c/	...	...	...	...	...	100	72	66	64	55	55	49
18	Printing and reproduction of recorded media		...	...	...	...	...	...	...	...	...	...	...	...
19	Coke and refined petroleum products		...	...	...	...	...	...	...	...	...	...	...	...
20	Chemicals and chemical products	d/	...	...	...	...	...	100	101	94	97	99	101	93
21	Pharmaceuticals, medicinal chemicals, etc.	d/	...	...	...	...	...	...	...	...	...	...	...	...
22	Rubber and plastics products		...	...	...	...	...	100	114	103	104	118	117	122
23	Other non-metallic mineral products		...	...	...	...	...	100	94	85	74	85	88	97
24	Basic metals		...	...	...	...	...	100	105	94	93	91	82	88
25	Fabricated metal products, except machinery		...	...	...	...	...	100	97	95	94	101	89	95
26	Computer, electronic and optical products	e/	...	...	...	...	...	100	100	103	110	94	94	94
27	Electrical equipment	e/	...	...	...	...	...	...	...	...	...	...	...	...
28	Machinery and equipment n.e.c.	f/	...	...	...	...	...	100	116	124	116	111	125	120
29	Motor vehicles, trailers and semi-trailers	f/	...	...	...	...	...	100	95	87	85	102	103	94
30	Other transport equipment	f/	...	...	...	...	...	...	...	...	...	...	...	...
31	Furniture	f/	...	...	...	...	...	...	...	...	...	...	...	...
32	Other manufacturing	f/	...	...	...	...	...	...	...	...	...	...	...	...
33	Repair and installation of machinery/equipment	f/	...	...	...	...	...	...	...	...	...	...	...	...
C	Total manufacturing		...	...	...	...	...	100	103	98	96	103	99	101

a/ 11 includes 12.
b/ 13 includes 14 and 15.
c/ 17 includes 18.
d/ 20 includes 21.
e/ 26 includes 27.
f/ 29 includes 30, 31, 32 and 33.

Malta

Supplier of information:
National Statistics Office, Valletta.

Basic source of data:
Annual survey.

Major deviations from ISIC (Revision 4):
Data presented in ISIC (Revision 4) were originally classified according to NACE (Revision 2).

Reference period:
Calendar year.

Scope:
All privately owned enterprises.

Method of data collection:
Questionnaires are distributed by mail.

Type of enumeration:
Sample survey.

Adjusted for non-response:
Yes.

Concepts and definitions of variables:
Number of employees includes home workers.
Wages and salaries includes employers' contributions (in respect of their employees) paid to social security, pension and insurance schemes as well as the benefits received by employees under these schemes and severance and termination pay.
Output includes revenue from non-industrial activities.

Related national publications:
Structural Business Statistics, published by the National Statistics Office, Valletta.

Malta

ISIC Revision 4			Number of enterprises (number)					Number of employees (number)					Wages and salaries paid to employees (thousands of Euros)				
ISIC	Industry	Note	2012	2013	2014	2015	Note	2012	2013	2014	2015	Note	2012	2013	2014	2015
10	Food products		382	376	369	353		...	2430	...	...		...	...	...	...
11	Beverages		20	21	15	15		867	...	...	933		...	...	...	...
12	Tobacco products		...	...	...	...		...	...	...	...		...	...	...	...
13	Textiles		...	...	...	...		...	...	...	...		...	...	...	...
14	Wearing apparel		54	36	39	43		...	...	290	...		...	...	2871	...
15	Leather and related products		...	...	...	...		...	...	...	...		...	...	...	...
16	Wood products, excluding furniture		91	79	81	74		...	...	230	251		...	...	2791	3006
17	Paper and paper products		25	...	...	...		228	...	...	...		...	...	...	...
18	Printing and reproduction of recorded media		133	128	131	127		...	1468	1445	1348		28813	29194	29167	25930
19	Coke and refined petroleum products		...	...	...	...		...	...	...	...		...	...	...	...
20	Chemicals and chemical products		42	38	41	42		271	288	290	278		4135	4481	5206	5087
21	Pharmaceuticals, medicinal chemicals, etc.		...	...	18	17		...	...	...	1165		...	...	...	33668
22	Rubber and plastics products		45	43	41	42		...	...	...	1789		...	...	...	...
23	Other non-metallic mineral products		155	143	145	144		1222	1167	1179	1238		14466	16011	16527	16614
24	Basic metals		13	14	14	15		16	16	5	15		186	198	57	...
25	Fabricated metal products, except machinery		392	349	358	347		1147	1114	1123	1111		15017	17002	18270	21278
26	Computer, electronic and optical products		...	18	18	...		...	...	...	...		...	...	...	...
27	Electrical equipment		...	31	30	30		...	513	...	514		...	8939	9628	9588
28	Machinery and equipment n.e.c.		...	23	24	25		...	...	...	...		...	...	...	...
29	Motor vehicles, trailers and semi-trailers		...	...	...	...		...	...	...	...		...	...	...	...
30	Other transport equipment		11	12	13	...		...	...	16	...		...	...	214	...
31	Furniture		580	535	518	492		600	734	790	814		7138	8953	9476	9886
32	Other manufacturing		85	82	86	87		...	...	...	...		...	...	...	...
33	Repair and installation of machinery/equipment		111	105	121	132		1272	1317	...	1350		31162	...	...	35621
C	Total manufacturing	a/	2139a/	2033a/	2062a/	2076	a/	5623	9047	5877	11195	a/	100917	84778	94207	175513

a/ Sum of available data.

Malta

ISIC Revision 4

ISIC	Industry	Note	Output at factor values (thousands of Euros)				Note	Value added at factor values (thousands of Euros)				Note	Gross fixed capital formation (thousands of Euros)	
			2012	2013	2014	2015		2012	2013	2014	2015		2014	2015
10	Food products		...	...	...	...		...	...	...	...		...	...
11	Beverages		...	...	...	...		...	...	...	...		...	...
12	Tobacco products		...	...	...	...		...	...	...	...		...	...
13	Textiles		...	...	...	...		...	...	...	...		...	...
14	Wearing apparel		11133	11593	11165	11402		4379	4257	4323	4314		176	173
15	Leather and related products		...	...	...	...		...	...	...	...		...	...
16	Wood products, excluding furniture		11050	9494	12492	13133		4532	5061	6280	5627		49	732
17	Paper and paper products		...	...	...	...		...	...	...	...		...	...
18	Printing and reproduction of recorded media		146355	159318	154570	159592		58660	56663	56301	61421		4753	8083
19	Coke and refined petroleum products		...	...	...	...		...	...	...	...		...	...
20	Chemicals and chemical products		27651	27179	31108	28787		8045	8305	11504	10616		1580	1061
21	Pharmaceuticals, medicinal chemicals, etc.		...	...	...	...		...	...	...	...		...	...
22	Rubber and plastics products		...	...	...	...		...	...	...	...		...	...
23	Other non-metallic mineral products		92415	92018	93369	115740		26999	27350	27200	29872		1981	15672
24	Basic metals		941	943	897	547		336	324	261	374		...	131
25	Fabricated metal products, except machinery		92652	87574	90325	105164		29524	25165	36690	33261		2757	6819
26	Computer, electronic and optical products		...	...	...	...		...	...	...	...		...	...
27	Electrical equipment		...	...	52769	51389		...	...	20065	18289		1896	630
28	Machinery and equipment n.e.c.		...	...	...	...		...	...	...	...		...	...
29	Motor vehicles, trailers and semi-trailers		...	...	...	...		...	...	...	...		...	...
30	Other transport equipment		...	...	2118	...		...	...	652	...		67	...
31	Furniture		35599	41713	43890	48350		17476	18602	20116	20222		1010	768
32	Other manufacturing		...	...	...	...		...	...	...	...		...	...
33	Repair and installation of machinery/equipment		...	...	...	177347		...	...	...	66104		...	9834
C	Total manufacturing	a/	417796	429832	492703	711451	a/	149951	145727	183392	250100	a/	14269	43903

a/ Sum of available data.

Malta

Index numbers of industrial production

(2010=100)

ISIC	Industry	Note	2005	2006	2007	2008	2009	2010	2011	2012	2013	2014	2015	2016
10	Food products		...	...	...	...	...	...	...	...	...	...	...	...
11	Beverages		...	...	...	...	...	...	...	...	...	...	...	...
12	Tobacco products		...	...	...	...	...	...	...	...	...	...	...	...
13	Textiles		...	...	...	...	...	...	...	...	...	...	...	...
14	Wearing apparel		...	...	...	...	...	...	...	...	...	...	...	...
15	Leather and related products		...	...	...	...	...	...	...	...	...	...	...	...
16	Wood products, excluding furniture		...	...	...	...	...	...	...	...	...	...	...	...
17	Paper and paper products		...	...	...	...	...	...	...	...	...	...	...	...
18	Printing and reproduction of recorded media		...	...	...	...	...	...	...	...	...	...	...	...
19	Coke and refined petroleum products		...	...	...	...	...	...	...	...	...	...	...	...
20	Chemicals and chemical products		...	...	...	...	...	...	...	...	...	...	...	...
21	Pharmaceuticals,medicinal chemicals, etc.		...	...	...	...	...	...	...	...	...	...	...	...
22	Rubber and plastics products		...	...	...	...	...	...	...	...	...	...	...	...
23	Other non-metallic mineral products		...	...	...	...	...	...	...	...	...	...	...	...
24	Basic metals		...	...	...	...	...	...	...	...	...	...	...	...
25	Fabricated metal products, except machinery		...	...	...	...	...	...	...	...	...	...	...	...
26	Computer, electronic and optical products		...	...	...	...	...	...	...	...	...	...	...	...
27	Electrical equipment		...	...	...	...	...	...	...	...	...	...	...	...
28	Machinery and equipment n.e.c.		...	...	...	...	...	...	...	...	...	...	...	...
29	Motor vehicles, trailers and semi-trailers		...	...	...	...	...	...	...	...	...	...	...	...
30	Other transport equipment		...	...	...	...	...	...	...	...	...	...	...	...
31	Furniture		...	...	...	...	...	...	...	...	...	...	...	...
32	Other manufacturing		...	...	...	...	...	...	...	...	...	...	...	...
33	Repair and installation of machinery/equipment		...	...	...	...	...	...	...	...	...	...	...	...
C	Total manufacturing		97	104	112	108	91	100	100	105	100	93	99	95

ISIC Revision 4

Mauritius

Supplier of information:
Statistics Mauritius, Port-Louis.

Basic source of data:
Annual survey; administrative source.

Major deviations from ISIC (Revision 4):
None reported.

Reference period:
Calendar year.

Scope:
Establishments with 10 or more persons engaged.

Method of data collection:
Mail questionnaires.

Type of enumeration:
Sample survey.

Adjusted for non-response:
Yes.

Concepts and definitions of variables:
Wages and salaries includes employers' contributions (in respect of their employees) paid to social security, pension and insurance schemes as well as the benefits received by employees under these schemes and severance and termination pay.

Related national publications:
Annual Digest of Industrial Statistics, published by Statistics Mauritius, Port-Louis.

Mauritius

ISIC	Industry	Note	Number of establishments (number) 2013	2014	2015	2016	Note	Number of employees (number) 2013	2014	2015	2016	Note	Wages and salaries paid to employees (millions of Mauritian Rupees) 2013	2014	2015	2016
10	Food products		110	109	109	108		11313	11567	11772	11448		2789	2525	2382	2384
11	Beverages		16	16	14	13		2634	2686	2500	2332		1258	1096	1003	1034
12	Tobacco products		...	...	...	...		...	...	...	...		...	...	...	...
13	Textiles		33	31	31	32		5355	5256	5312	5477		1752	1695	1712	1965
14	Wearing apparel		152	143	139	133		36921	37305	36588	35550		7758	7852	8628	8392
15	Leather and related products		13	13	13	13		750	719	762	742		145	155	146	157
16	Wood products, excluding furniture		12	10	10	10		623	563	413	403		37	38	43	35
17	Paper and paper products		13	13	13	13		585	675	647	649		163	209	208	192
18	Printing and reproduction of recorded media		37	40	39	36		1641	1578	1572	1443		387	351	388	446
19	Coke and refined petroleum products	a/	34	35	36	35	a/	2456	2378	2433	2429	a/	829	746	764	700
20	Chemicals and chemical products	a/	...	...	...	...	a/	...	...	...	...	a/	...	...	...	...
21	Pharmaceuticals, medicinal chemicals, etc.	a/	...	...	...	...	a/	...	...	...	...	a/	...	...	...	...
22	Rubber and plastics products		33	33	32	32		1439	1390	1353	1351		347	435	445	326
23	Other non-metallic mineral products		15	15	15	14		1204	1243	914	840		646	722	670	666
24	Basic metals		5	5	5	5		472	450	436	400		80	119	112	82
25	Fabricated metal products, except machinery		50	50	51	47		2010	1834	1957	1749		544	599	621	645
26	Computer, electronic and optical products		15	15	14	14		1329	1247	1268	1194		246	220	208	281
27	Electrical equipment		9	9	9	9		293	340	320	290		70	65	75	74
28	Machinery and equipment n.e.c.		2	3	3	3		252	261	205	193		104	168	190	115
29	Motor vehicles, trailers and semi-trailers	b/	9	7	6	6	b/	437	291	232	187	b/	210	221	242	265
30	Other transport equipment	b/	...	...	...	...	b/	...	...	...	...	b/	...	...	...	...
31	Furniture		32	30	29	29		853	883	844	845		167	204	197	232
32	Other manufacturing		33	32	35	34		2761	2799	2807	2737		595	584	581	668
33	Repair and installation of machinery/equipment		8	8	8	8		679	692	728	758		30	34	34	40
C	Total manufacturing	c/	631	617	611	594	c/	74007	74157	73063	71017	c/	18157	18038	18649	18699

a/ 19 includes 20 and 21.
b/ 29 includes 30.
c/ Sum of available data.

Mauritius

ISIC	Industry	Note	Output at basic prices (millions of Mauritian Rupees) 2013	2014	2015	2016	Note	Value added at basic prices (millions of Mauritian Rupees) 2013	2014	2015	2016	Note	Gross fixed capital formation (millions of Mauritian Rupees) 2015	2016
10	Food products		42334	40822	33828	32721		9581	9430	8861	8903		...	...
11	Beverages		12245	12497	12376	12312		7429	7478	7219	7530		...	...
12	Tobacco products		...	...	...	...		...	...	...	...		...	...
13	Textiles		8377	8103	8026	8125		2572	2590	2640	3183		...	...
14	Wearing apparel		25516	24837	28143	26994		11888	11591	12848	11458		...	...
15	Leather and related products		651	666	614	554		262	277	253	240		...	...
16	Wood products, excluding furniture		112	120	130	154		77	90	97	108		...	...
17	Paper and paper products		1317	1470	1476	1484		511	533	514	513		...	...
18	Printing and reproduction of recorded media		1770	1778	1646	1884		896	792	789	939		...	...
19	Coke and refined petroleum products	a/	5861	5473	5313	5395	a/	2433	2061	2086	2095		...	...
20	Chemicals and chemical products	a/	...	...	...	...	a/	...	...	...	...		...	...
21	Pharmaceuticals, medicinal chemicals, etc.	a/	...	...	...	...	a/	...	...	...	...		...	...
22	Rubber and plastics products		2817	2810	2369	2560		974	1014	954	1116		...	...
23	Other non-metallic mineral products		3661	3410	3055	3212		1212	1279	1176	1070		...	...
24	Basic metals		1172	1092	988	637		333	348	321	212		...	...
25	Fabricated metal products, except machinery		2320	2464	2261	2274		1014	1207	1103	1114		...	...
26	Computer, electronic and optical products		1265	1282	1152	1047		481	402	370	494		...	...
27	Electrical equipment		474	445	490	497		166	188	197	195		...	...
28	Machinery and equipment n.e.c.		672	787	669	422		409	490	615	388		...	...
29	Motor vehicles, trailers and semi-trailers	b/	1404	1531	1625	1846	b/	854	958	871	1041		...	...
30	Other transport equipment	b/	...	...	...	...	b/	...	...	...	...		...	...
31	Furniture		927	1131	882	1020		326	399	357	432		...	...
32	Other manufacturing		2008	2277	2237	2241		1005	1139	1087	932		...	...
33	Repair and installation of machinery/equipment		104	143	133	145		62	68	66	84		...	...
C	Total manufacturing	c/	115007	113138	107413	105524	c/	42485	42334	42424	42047		3738	3731

ISIC Revision 4

a/ 19 includes 20 and 21.
b/ 29 includes 30.
c/ Sum of available data.

Mauritius

Index numbers of industrial production

ISIC Revision 4

ISIC	Industry	Note	2005	2006	2007	2008	2009	2010	2011	2012	2013	2014	2015	2016
								(2010=100)						
10	Food products		...	...	...	90	97	100	95	102	102	104	107	108
11	Beverages		...	...	...	97	97	100	108	113	111	115	117	120
12	Tobacco products		...	...	...	...	...	...	...	...	...	...	...	...
13	Textiles		...	...	...	116	90	100	116	112	110	111	112	111
14	Wearing apparel		...	...	...	98	103	100	101	101	104	106	102	95
15	Leather and related products	d/	...	...	...	...	...	...	...	...	...	...	...	...
16	Wood products, excluding furniture	d/	...	...	...	...	...	...	...	...	...	...	...	...
17	Paper and paper products	d/	...	...	...	...	...	...	...	...	...	...	...	...
18	Printing and reproduction of recorded media	d/	...	...	...	89	96	100	83	91	89	101	98	113
19	Coke and refined petroleum products	d/	...	...	...	...	...	...	...	...	...	...	...	...
20	Chemicals and chemical products	a/	...	...	...	88	89	100	97	89	85	80	76	72
21	Pharmaceuticals, medicinal chemicals, etc.	a/	...	...	...	...	...	...	...	...	...	...	...	...
22	Rubber and plastics products	b/	...	...	...	119	113	100	105	102	115	107	105	91
23	Other non-metallic mineral products	b/	...	...	...	...	...	...	...	...	...	...	...	...
24	Basic metals	c/	...	...	...	100	101	100	99	91	88	84	80	77
25	Fabricated metal products, except machinery	c/	...	...	...	...	...	...	...	...	...	...	...	...
26	Computer, electronic and optical products	d/	...	...	...	...	...	...	...	...	...	...	...	...
27	Electrical equipment	d/	...	...	...	...	...	...	...	...	...	...	...	...
28	Machinery and equipment n.e.c.	d/	...	...	...	...	...	...	...	...	...	...	...	...
29	Motor vehicles, trailers and semi-trailers	d/	...	...	...	...	...	...	...	...	...	...	...	...
30	Other transport equipment	d/	...	...	...	...	...	...	...	...	...	...	...	...
31	Furniture	d/	...	...	...	91	102	100	92	94	98	94	100	140
32	Other manufacturing	d/	...	...	...	83	165	100	89	90	110	120	125	131
33	Repair and installation of machinery/equipment	d/	...	...	...	...	...	...	...	...	...	...	...	...
C	Total manufacturing		...	...	...	96	98	100	101	103	107	110	110	110

a/ 20 includes 21.
b/ 22 includes 23.
c/ 24 includes 25.
d/ 32 includes 15-17, 19, 26-30, 32 and 33.

Mexico

Supplier of information:
Instituto Nacional de Estadística y Geografía (INEGI), Aguascalientes.

Basic source of data:
Annual and monthly industrial surveys; economic census in every five years.

Major deviations from ISIC (Revision 4):
Data presented in ISIC (Revision 4) were originally classified according to the North American Industry Classification System (NAICS).

Reference period:
Calendar year.

Scope:
Not reported.

Method of data collection:
The inquiry is conducted by mail and interviews.

Type of enumeration:
Not reported.

Adjusted for non-response:
No.

Concepts and definitions of variables:
No deviations from the standard UN concepts and definitions are reported.

Related national publications:
Encuesta Anual de la Industria Manufacturera (EAIM), published by the Instituto Nacional de Estadística y Geografía (INEGI), Aguascalientes.

Mexico

ISIC Revision 4			Number of establishments (number)					Number of employees (thousands)					Wages and salaries paid to employees (millions of Mexican Pesos)				
ISIC	Industry	Note	2013	2014	2015	2016	Note	2013	2014	2015	2016	Note	2013	2014	2015	2016
1010	Processing/preserving of meat		128	127	122	119		58.4	61.6	62.5	63.6		5661	6126	6651	7156
1020	Processing/preserving of fish, etc.		53	52	47	42		7.7	8.4	8.2	8.3		250	278	282	274
1030	Processing/preserving of fruit,vegetables		104	101	98	96		41.3	42.0	43.2	45.5		4057	4184	4477	5018
1040	Vegetable and animal oils and fats		30	30	30	30		8.5	9.0	9.5	9.7		1524	1768	1965	2080
1050	Dairy products		109	103	101	100		40.7	40.3	40.2	40.3		4726	4878	5141	5448
106	Grain mill products,starches and starch products		...	...	...	...		...	...	...	...		...	...	...	...
1061	Grain mill products		98	97	93	90		14.2	14.1	13.8	14.3		1676	1797	1726	1849
1062	Starches and starch products		6	6	6	6		2.3	2.3	2.3	2.4		315	271	263	280
107	Other food products		...	...	...	...		...	...	...	...		...	...	...	...
1071	Bakery products		44466	44470	44460	44476		160.4	163.4	162.4	164.2		10317	11140	11628	12517
1072	Sugar		58	58	56	56		31.1	30.6	30.5	30.9		7005	7194	7364	8131
1073	Cocoa, chocolate and sugar confectionery		82	81	79	78		33.5	33.8	34.5	34.9		3441	3701	3795	4127
1074	Macaroni, noodles, couscous, etc.		85182	85185	85168	85173		149.5	151.2	154.7	155.3		6123	6481	7377	7656
1075	Prepared meals and dishes		...	...	...	...		...	...	...	...		...	...	...	...
1079	Other food products n.e.c.		176	172	171	169		34.3	34.8	35.1	36.1		3241	3334	3388	3631
1080	Prepared animal feeds		105	104	99	98		10.6	10.6	11.1	11.5		561	689	787	877
110	Beverages		13324	13347	13339	13350		109.9	110.1	110.1	113.4		11850	12486	12033	12044
1101	Distilling, rectifying and blending of spirits		49	48	46	46		4.8	5.8	5.8	6.1		247	480	507	578
1102	Wines		9	9	9	9		1.8	1.9	1.9	1.9		39	41	43	44
1103	Malt liquors and malt		15	15	15	15		10.9	10.5	11.3	11.7		1775	1735	2029	2079
1104	Soft drinks,mineral waters,other bottled waters		13251	13275	13269	13280		92.4	91.9	91.2	93.7		9788	10230	9454	9343
1200	Tobacco products		7	7	7	7		2.2	2.2	2.2	2.1		324	342	364	355
131	Spinning, weaving and finishing of textiles		...	...	...	...		...	...	...	...		...	...	...	...
1311	Preparation and spinning of textile fibres		56	55	53	50		10.1	9.8	9.4	9.3		708	768	794	790
1312	Weaving of textiles		139	133	131	127		38.8	37.2	38.7	39.8		3799	4017	4246	4508
1313	Finishing of textiles		43	42	41	40		9.6	10.1	9.8	9.9		764	800	797	851
139	Other textiles		135	127	122	121		18.4	19.7	19.9	20.2		1362	1611	1820	1977
1391	Knitted and crocheted fabrics		...	...	...	...		...	...	...	...		...	...	...	...
1392	Made-up textile articles, except apparel		39	37	34	34		8.4	8.7	8.9	9.1		604	890	985	1068
1393	Carpets and rugs		4	3	3	3		0.7	0.6	0.6	0.4		143	19	18	8
1394	Cordage, rope, twine and netting		15	16	16	15		1.0	1.4	1.4	1.4		93	125	134	143
1399	Other textiles n.e.c.		...	...	...	...		...	...	...	...		...	...	...	...
1410	Wearing apparel, except fur apparel		593	559	528	507		133.6	132.5	133.5	131.7		8785	9637	10115	10619
1420	Articles of fur		...	...	...	...		...	...	...	...		...	...	...	...
1430	Knitted and crocheted apparel		106	106	95	86		17.1	15.5	13.0	11.7		1225	1148	1029	970
151	Leather;luggage,handbags,saddlery,harness;fur		...	...	...	...		...	...	...	...		...	...	...	...
1511	Tanning/dressing of leather; dressing of fur		74	72	71	69		14.1	14.1	15.1	15.7		1238	1322	1489	1613
1512	Luggage,handbags,etc.;saddlery/harness		80	78	78	74		3.9	3.8	3.8	3.9		322	347	361	388
1520	Footwear		253	237	229	223		48.2	47.3	46.7	44.9		3910	4257	4506	4589
1610	Sawmilling and planing of wood		73	66	63	62		3.0	2.8	2.7	2.6		220	212	213	215

Code	Description												
162	Wood products, cork, straw, plaiting materials	213	202	193	181	12.1	11.8	11.8	11.9	964	961	1007	1057
1621	Veneer sheets and wood-based panels	21	21	20	20	3.4	3.5	3.4	3.4	250	241	265	263
1622	Builders' carpentry and joinery	61	55	53	48	3.1	2.9	2.9	3.2	288	294	308	364
1623	Wooden containers	105	101	97	92	4.1	3.9	4.0	3.9	336	329	348	337
1629	Other wood products;articles of cork,straw	26	25	23	21	1.4	1.5	1.4	1.3	90	96	87	92
170	Paper and paper products	307	298	292	284	70.2	70.8	71.0	71.9	10509	11207	11695	12143
1701	Pulp, paper and paperboard	60	60	60	57	20.3	20.6	20.8	20.8	3634	3952	4088	3923
1702	Corrugated paper and paperboard	247	238	232	227	49.8	50.2	50.3	51.1	6875	7255	7607	8220
1709	Other articles of paper and paperboard	...	...	...	...	...	...	...	...	...	...	...	...
181	Printing and service activities related to printing	216	207	204	197	30.2	30.1	29.9	30.3	3156	3642	3945	4210
1811	Printing	52	51	50	48	8.9	9.2	8.8	8.5	710	1068	1087	1152
1812	Service activities related to printing	...	...	...	...	...	...	...	...	...	...	...	...
1820	Reproduction of recorded media	...	...	...	...	...	...	...	...	...	...	...	...
1910	Coke oven products	...	...	...	...	...	...	...	...	...	...	...	...
1920	Refined petroleum products a/	55	53	53	51	29.7	30.5	29.1	26.8	13244	14766	14022	13242
201	Basic chemicals,fertilizers, etc.	490	477	469	462	111.3	110.6	108.5	108.9	25483	24918	25055	25291
2011	Basic chemicals	140	137	137	134	35.7	34.3	32.2	31.8	13137	12825	12208	11398
2012	Fertilizers and nitrogen compounds	14	14	14	13	2.9	3.0	3.1	3.1	522	613	619	669
2013	Plastics and synthetic rubber in primary forms	62	62	62	61	11.8	11.6	12.1	12.1	1073	1177	1344	1447
202	Other chemical products a/	...	...	...	...	...	...	...	...	...	...	...	...
2021	Pesticides and other agrochemical products	21	21	21	22	2.6	3.1	3.0	3.1	187	345	429	480
2022	Paints,varnishes;printing ink and mastics	61	59	57	57	9.5	11.3	11.1	11.3	1450	1515	1760	1895
2023	Soap,cleaning and cosmetic preparations	81	79	77	77	32.1	30.4	29.8	30.3	6932	6199	6326	6880
2029	Other chemical products n.e.c.	111	105	101	98	16.6	16.9	17.2	17.1	2182	2245	2369	2523
2030	Man-made fibres a/	...	...	...	...	...	...	...	...	...	...	...	...
2100	Pharmaceuticals,medicinal chemicals, etc.	110	106	107	103	45.0	42.8	42.2	42.4	10078	10166	10241	10834
221	Rubber products	124	124	122	120	30.4	32.2	34.3	36.6	4701	5157	4937	5414
2211	Rubber tyres and tubes	10	10	10	10	6.4	6.3	6.4	6.6	2205	2277	1469	1436
2219	Other rubber products	114	114	112	110	24.1	25.9	27.9	29.9	2495	2880	3467	3978
2220	Plastics products	800	760	732	725	156.0	156.8	158.6	161.2	14081	14870	15883	17929
2310	Glass and glass products	97	89	85	82	31.3	31.9	32.7	32.9	2771	2685	2879	4193
239	Non-metallic mineral products n.e.c.	...	...	...	...	...	...	...	...	...	...	...	...
2391	Refractory products	16	16	16	16	1.8	1.9	1.9	1.9	375	407	429	439
2392	Clay building materials	...	...	...	...	...	...	...	...	...	...	...	...
2393	Other porcelain and ceramic products	...	...	...	...	...	...	...	...	...	...	...	...
2394	Cement, lime and plaster	47	44	44	44	4.2	4.3	4.3	4.4	688	708	720	757
2395	Articles of concrete, cement and plaster b/	389	386	384	403	25.2	25.1	25.4	25.6	4107	3346	2817	2940
2396	Cutting, shaping and finishing of stone b/	104	100	94	89	8.4	8.6	8.3	7.9	995	1004	1064	1110
2399	Other non-metallic mineral products n.e.c.	...	...	...	...	...	...	...	...	...	...	...	...
2410	Basic iron and steel	...	...	...	...	...	...	...	...	...	...	...	...
2420	Basic precious and other non-ferrous metals	66	66	65	64	18.6	19.3	20.2	21.8	2366	2496	2643	2986
243	Casting of metals	122	119	116	112	18.1	18.4	18.7	18.2	1908	2163	2385	2554
2431	Casting of iron and steel	68	67	66	64	11.5	11.5	11.5	10.6	1142	1215	1342	1348
2432	Casting of non-ferrous metals	54	52	50	48	6.6	6.9	7.2	7.6	766	947	1043	1206
251	Struct.metal products, tanks, reservoirs c/	53662	53632	53606	53629	206.6	223.4	229.9	238.0	21079	23346	24975	27362

continued

Mexico

ISIC Revision 4

ISIC	Industry	Number of establishments (number) Note	2013	2014	2015	2016	Number of employees (thousands) Note	2013	2014	2015	2016	Wages and salaries paid to employees (millions of Mexican Pesos) Note	2013	2014	2015	2016
2511	Structural metal products		53039	53021	53012	53042		87.8	97.3	99.7	103.6		6027	6872	7211	8046
2512	Tanks, reservoirs and containers of metal		87	85	84	82		13.9	14.4	15.0	15.7		1890	2018	2243	2461
2513	Steam generators, excl. hot water boilers		...	...	...	...		...	...	...	...		...	...	...	...
2520	Weapons and ammunition	c/	...	...	...	...	c/	...	...	...	...	c/	...	...	...	...
259	Other metal products;metal working services	c/	...	...	...	...	c/	...	...	...	...	c/	...	...	...	...
2591	Forging,pressing,stamping,roll-forming of metal		76	74	72	72		9.7	11.1	12.8	12.7		1100	1300	1447	1612
2592	Treatment and coating of metals; machining		71	72	72	73		14.3	15.6	16.1	16.2		1935	2028	2430	2621
2593	Cutlery, hand tools and general hardware		43	41	39	38		15.0	16.3	17.2	18.6		828	837	836	933
2599	Other fabricated metal products n.e.c.		346	339	327	322		65.9	68.8	69.1	71.3		9299	10291	10808	11689
2610	Electronic components and boards		204	196	191	189		111.4	108.6	115.0	122.8		13581	15807	18054	20819
2620	Computers and peripheral equipment		29	29	27	27		33.8	39.2	40.2	42.6		3206	4107	4794	5535
2630	Communication equipment		51	48	47	47		43.8	38.8	40.2	43.1		5359	5355	5744	6374
2640	Consumer electronics		52	51	48	47		43.9	43.9	45.1	46.5		6089	6245	6754	7487
265	Measuring,testing equipment; watches, etc.		42	40	40	40		12.8	13.5	14.1	15.4		1786	2041	1960	2166
2651	Measuring/testing/navigating equipment,etc.		42	40	40	40		12.8	13.5	14.1	15.4		1786	2041	1960	2166
2652	Watches and clocks		...	...	...	...		...	...	...	...		...	...	...	...
2660	Irradiation/electromedical equipment,etc.		...	...	...	...		...	...	...	...		...	...	...	...
2670	Optical instruments and photographic equipment		...	...	...	...		...	...	...	...		...	...	...	...
2680	Magnetic and optical media		11	10	10	9		4.3	5.0	4.8	4.6		811	1002	961	1017
2710	Electric motors,generators,transformers,etc.		99	102	97	98		44.9	48.8	49.7	52.4		5921	7018	7612	8188
2720	Batteries and accumulators		12	12	12	11		4.7	4.8	4.8	4.9		763	889	925	982
273	Wiring and wiring devices		47	43	45	44		14.9	15.3	15.4	15.8		1481	1593	1677	1741
2731	Fibre optic cables		...	...	...	...		...	...	...	...		...	...	...	...
2732	Other electronic and electric wires and cables		...	...	...	...		...	...	...	...		...	...	...	...
2733	Wiring devices		...	...	...	...		...	...	...	...		...	...	...	...
2740	Electric lighting equipment		42	36	35	32		11.7	12.5	13.4	15.7		1756	1900	2105	2691
2750	Domestic appliances		75	74	72	71		51.4	53.6	54.8	57.9		5030	5208	4553	4584
2790	Other electrical equipment		27	26	25	26		9.7	9.8	10.3	11.3		1279	1354	1432	1681
281	General-purpose machinery	d/	455	445	435	423	d/	97.2	100.3	105.4	109.5	d/	14657	15787	17428	18988
2811	Engines/turbines,excl.aircraft,vehicle engines		19	18	19	19		11.3	11.2	11.9	12.2		2486	2521	2626	2906
2812	Fluid power equipment		...	...	...	...		...	...	...	...		...	...	...	...
2813	Other pumps, compressors, taps and valves		...	...	...	...		...	...	...	...		...	...	...	...
2814	Bearings, gears, gearing and driving elements		...	...	...	...		...	...	...	...		...	...	...	...
2815	Ovens, furnaces and furnace burners		...	...	...	...		...	...	...	...		...	...	...	...
2816	Lifting and handling equipment		44	40	40	40		8.7	9.5	10.6	11.9		1648	1967	2233	2629
2817	Office machinery, excl.computers,etc.		...	...	...	...		...	...	...	...		...	...	...	...
2818	Power-driven hand tools		...	...	...	...		...	...	...	...		...	...	...	...
2819	Other general-purpose machinery	d/	164	164	161	157	d/	41.2	44.9	49.1	53.2	d/	4981	5778	6819	7626
282	Special-purpose machinery		...	...	...	...		...	...	...	...		...	...	...	...
2821	Agricultural and forestry machinery		28	28	28	28		9.2	8.9	9.3	9.1		1138	1224	1343	1418
2822	Metal-forming machinery and machine tools		15	13	12	12		0.4	0.4	0.4	0.4		86	75	77	88

Code	Description	(1)	(2)	(3)	(4)	(5)	(6)	(7)	(8)	(9)	(10)	(11)	(12)
2823	Machinery for metallurgy	52	50	47	44	3.1	3.1	3.1	3.1	526	560	596	586
2824	Mining, quarrying and construction machinery	29	29	29	29	10.5	9.2	8.3	6.9	1606	1307	1260	1086
2825	Food/beverage/tobacco processing machinery	23	21	18	17	3.6	3.1	2.7	2.9	686	646	639	716
2826	Textile/apparel/leather production machinery	5	5	5	4	–	–	–	–	7	7	8	8
2829	Other special-purpose machinery	17	17	17	16	3.1	3.2	3.4	3.5	456	483	519	551
2910	Motor vehicles	23	26	28	30	61.5	72.6	77.2	83.7	17127	19279	21079	22379
2920	Automobile bodies, trailers and semi-trailers	59	59	59	59	11.7	11.9	12.6	13.1	1201	1352	1529	1710
2930	Parts and accessories for motor vehicles	666	683	688	700	545.0	604.3	646.0	677.1	58447	68850	79968	89896
301	Building of ships and boats	15	14	14	14	6.1	5.3	4.1	2.4	645	631	589	328
3011	Building of ships and floating structures	..	..	..	..	..	..	..	..	..	..	..	..
3012	Building of pleasure and sporting boats	..	..	..	..	..	..	..	..	..	..	..	..
3020	Railway locomotives and rolling stock	14	15	15	16	9.8	11.6	13.1	12.5	1189	1587	1859	2001
3030	Air and spacecraft and related machinery	40	42	42	42	19.5	22.6	24.9	24.2	2162	2498	2870	3677
3040	Military fighting vehicles	..	..	..	..	..	..	..	..	..	..	..	..
309	Transport equipment n.e.c.	20	19	20	19	6.5	6.9	7.9	8.3	862	1052	1334	1453
3091	Motorcycles	9	8	9	9	4.9	5.5	6.5	6.6	724	898	1172	1263
3092	Bicycles and invalid carriages	11	11	11	10	1.6	1.4	1.5	1.6	138	154	162	189
3099	Other transport equipment n.e.c.	..	..	..	..	..	..	..	..	..	..	..	..
3100	Furniture	312	306	297	292	46.9	48.2	50.9	51.9	4785	5070	5492	5924
321	Jewellery, bijouterie and related articles	..	..	..	..	..	..	..	..	..	..	..	..
3211	Jewellery and related articles	63	59	56	52	4.2	4.3	4.3	4.4	347	374	389	406
3212	Imitation jewellery and related articles	..	..	..	..	..	..	..	..	..	..	..	..
3220	Musical instruments	14	13	13	12	1.6	1.5	1.5	1.5	180	184	205	217
3230	Sports goods	41	39	36	35	3.1	3.1	2.5	2.4	325	305	266	249
3240	Games and toys	37	32	31	31	10.5	10.1	10.2	10.9	1270	1359	1508	1888
3250	Medical and dental instruments and supplies	190	181	181	175	100.6	105.2	111.8	121.8	13812	14680	16234	19314
3290	Other manufacturing n.e.c.	105	101	98	96	14.3	15.4	14.9	14.7	1549	1680	1758	1879
331	Repair of fabricated metal products/machinery	..	..	..	..	..	..	..	..	..	..	..	..
3311	Repair of fabricated metal products	..	..	..	..	..	..	..	..	..	..	..	..
3312	Repair of machinery	..	..	..	..	..	..	..	..	..	..	..	..
3313	Repair of electronic and optical equipment	..	..	..	..	..	..	..	..	..	..	..	..
3314	Repair of electrical equipment	..	..	..	..	..	..	..	..	..	..	..	..
3315	Repair of transport equip., excl. motor vehicles	..	..	..	..	..	..	..	..	..	..	..	..
3319	Repair of other equipment	..	..	..	..	..	..	..	..	..	..	..	..
3320	Installation of industrial machinery/equipment	..	..	..	..	..	..	..	..	..	..	..	..
C	Total manufacturing	205339	205079	204813	204723	3227.3	3346.9	3442.1	3541.5	382035	416577	445510	483767

a/ 201 includes 202 and 2030.
b/ 2396 includes 2399.
c/ 251 includes 2520 and 259.
d/ 281 includes 282.

Mexico

ISIC Revision 4			Output at producers' prices (billions of Mexican Pesos)					Value added at producers' prices (billions of Mexican Pesos)					Gross fixed capital formation (billions of Mexican Pesos)	
Note	ISIC	Industry	Note	2013	2014	2015	2016	Note	2013	2014	2015	2016	Note	2015	2016
	1010	Processing/preserving of meat		87.9	103.3	113.7	119.9		22.2	29.1	33.6	34.4		2.8	2.1
	1020	Processing/preserving of fish, etc.		11.5	11.1	11.2	12.5		2.3	2.3	2.3	2.7		0.2	0.2
	1030	Processing/preserving of fruit,vegetables		63.1	67.2	72.3	82.2		24.6	26.9	29.0	33.3		1.8	1.7
	1040	Vegetable and animal oils and fats		60.7	61.8	62.1	67.2		9.3	9.6	9.9	10.0		0.9	0.7
	1050	Dairy products		119.7	124.3	125.4	129.6		35.3	37.1	38.0	39.7		4.2	2.4
	106	Grain mill products,starches and starch products		...	...	...	...		...	...	...	...		...	...
	1061	Grain mill products		57.7	56.2	55.2	59.2		12.4	11.9	11.9	13.0		0.8	0.8
	1062	Starches and starch products		19.3	18.9	19.9	24.0		4.2	4.2	4.6	5.9		0.5	0.3
	107	Other food products		...	...	...	...		...	...	...	...		...	...
	1071	Bakery products		109.0	112.1	121.3	127.5		50.9	52.6	58.4	60.9		2.1	2.1
	1072	Sugar		48.8	45.2	49.1	65.9		16.1	14.9	16.7	22.9		1.1	2.4
	1073	Cocoa, chocolate and sugar confectionery		44.5	45.0	48.6	52.6		17.8	18.4	19.6	21.4		3.7	3.4
	1074	Macaroni, noodles, couscous, etc.		38.2	38.3	39.9	41.5		13.1	13.7	13.8	14.2		0.1	-
	1075	Prepared meals and dishes		...	...	...	...		...	...	...	...		...	...
	1079	Other food products n.e.c.		135.9	137.5	145.5	159.9		73.6	72.9	76.6	85.8		3.4	3.4
	1080	Prepared animal feeds		65.3	65.7	71.8	79.7		11.1	11.4	12.4	13.9		1.2	0.9
	110	Beverages		266.8	281.6	314.8	339.4		117.5	128.1	143.4	153.4		8.2	7.5
	1101	Distilling, rectifying and blending of spirits		19.3	27.4	31.8	36.4		9.4	14.8	17.6	20.2		0.4	0.9
	1102	Wines		3.9	3.9	4.1	4.2		1.4	1.4	1.5	1.5		-	-
	1103	Malt liquors and malt		79.6	86.4	102.0	107.5		33.6	36.8	43.5	45.3		5.4	2.8
	1104	Soft drinks,mineral waters,other bottled waters		164.0	163.8	176.9	191.4		73.1	75.0	80.8	86.4		2.3	3.7
	1200	Tobacco products		38.5	41.8	39.4	43.0		31.9	34.8	32.5	35.6		0.7	0.4
	131	Spinning, weaving and finishing of textiles		...	...	...	...		...	...	...	...		...	...
	1311	Preparation and spinning of textile fibres		8.3	8.1	8.5	8.7		2.5	2.5	2.7	2.8		0.3	0.2
	1312	Weaving of textiles		33.7	37.1	40.8	42.9		10.8	12.2	14.0	14.8		1.1	2.1
	1313	Finishing of textiles		7.7	8.4	9.8	10.6		2.7	2.9	3.5	3.9		0.1	0.2
	139	Other textiles		11.4	12.2	12.9	14.5		3.6	4.1	4.6	5.2		0.1	0.3
	1391	Knitted and crocheted fabrics		...	...	...	...		...	...	...	...		...	...
	1392	Made-up textile articles, except apparel		5.2	5.4	5.8	6.8		1.7	2.0	2.3	2.7		-	0.1
	1393	Carpets and rugs		0.8	0.9	1.0	0.9		0.4	0.3	0.4	0.4		-	0.1
	1394	Cordage, rope, twine and netting		0.6	0.8	0.8	0.9		0.2	0.2	0.2	0.3		-	-
	1399	Other textiles n.e.c.		...	...	...	...		...	...	...	...		...	...
	1410	Wearing apparel, except fur apparel		48.7	50.1	53.9	56.9		19.7	21.5	23.4	24.7		0.4	0.5
	1420	Articles of fur		...	...	...	...		...	...	...	...		...	...
	1430	Knitted and crocheted apparel		8.8	8.8	8.7	8.9		2.7	2.7	2.7	2.6		0.3	0.1
	151	Leather;luggage,handbags,saddlery,harness;fur		...	...	...	...		...	...	...	...		...	...
	1511	Tanning/dressing of leather; dressing of fur		11.3	11.9	15.3	16.1		3.5	3.8	5.1	5.5		0.2	0.2
	1512	Luggage,handbags,etc.;saddlery/harness		1.2	1.3	1.5	1.5		0.4	0.5	0.6	0.6		-	-
	1520	Footwear		25.1	26.3	27.7	27.4		8.5	9.4	10.0	9.8		0.2	0.2
	1610	Sawmilling and planing of wood		1.5	1.5	1.6	1.6		0.5	0.5	0.5	0.5		-	-

Code	Product		col1	col2	col3	col4	col5	col6	col7	col8	col9	col10
162	Wood products, cork, straw, plaiting materials		0.1	0.2	3.7	3.0	2.5	2.5	12.8	11.0	9.5	9.6
1621	Veneer sheets and wood-based panels		-	0.1	1.2	1.0	0.8	0.9	4.4	3.8	3.4	3.6
1622	Builders' carpentry and joinery		-	-	1.1	0.9	0.7	0.6	3.5	3.0	2.4	2.3
1623	Wooden containers		-	-	1.2	1.0	0.8	0.8	3.9	3.4	3.0	3.0
1629	Other wood products;articles of cork,straw		-	-	0.3	0.2	0.2	0.2	1.0	0.8	0.7	0.7
170	Paper and paper products		5.6	4.1	48.7	43.7	40.4	39.2	186.5	170.1	156.1	150.7
1701	Pulp, paper and paperboard		1.9	1.4	19.0	17.1	15.2	14.8	69.1	63.7	58.3	56.3
1702	Corrugated paper and paperboard		3.6	2.7	29.7	26.5	25.3	24.5	117.4	106.3	97.8	94.4
1709	Other articles of paper and paperboard			...	...	...	...	...	...	...	...	...
181	Printing and service activities related to printing		0.5	0.7	10.6	10.0	8.8	8.4	29.7	27.1	23.7	24.2
1811	Printing		-	0.2	2.6	2.7	2.4	2.5	9.0	8.4	7.9	8.8
1812	Service activities related to printing			...	...	...	...	...	...	...	...	...
1820	Reproduction of recorded media			...	...	...	...	...	...	...	...	...
1910	Coke oven products			...	...	...	...	...	...	...	...	...
1920	Refined petroleum products	a/	0.5	-2.4	270.6	332.6	207.4	202.7	540.6	674.3	868.1	851.1
201	Basic chemicals,fertilizers, etc.	a/	29.3	14.7	161.7	141.3	148.2	156.9	618.6	575.2	654.6	617.7
2011	Basic chemicals		20.5	6.4	65.4	49.3	59.3	72.4	287.2	265.0	354.7	329.8
2012	Fertilizers and nitrogen compounds		0.6	0.3	3.2	3.3	2.9	2.3	14.2	14.7	13.1	13.0
2013	Plastics and synthetic rubber in primary forms		3.0	3.5	19.1	17.3	16.0	14.4	103.9	95.7	96.1	91.5
202	Other chemical products	a/		0.1	4.5	4.5	4.0	3.8	14.7	14.7	13.3	12.4
2021	Pesticides and other agrochemical products		0.3	0.1	4.5	4.5	4.0	3.8	14.7	14.7	13.3	12.4
2022	Paints,varnishes;printing ink and mastics		1.6	0.6	11.8	10.7	9.3	8.1	43.4	39.5	36.2	31.0
2023	Soap,cleaning and cosmetic preparations		2.5	2.8	42.3	41.5	43.0	44.1	111.5	104.8	102.9	106.1
2029	Other chemical products n.e.c.		0.8	1.0	15.3	14.7	13.6	11.8	43.6	40.9	38.4	33.9
2030	Man-made fibres	a/		...	...	...	...	...	...	...	...	...
2100	Pharmaceuticals,medicinal chemicals, etc.		2.9	5.0	58.4	56.5	52.6	55.2	121.6	117.9	112.1	117.6
221	Rubber products		1.4	1.2	22.7	20.5	17.7	16.5	54.2	50.2	43.1	40.5
2211	Rubber tyres and tubes		0.6	0.5	8.1	7.5	7.4	7.9	19.1	17.8	16.0	16.3
2219	Other rubber products		0.8	0.6	14.5	13.0	10.2	8.7	35.2	32.4	27.2	24.2
2220	Plastics products		7.2	5.6	67.1	59.9	50.0	45.9	216.3	197.0	178.7	165.2
2310	Glass and glass products		1.7	1.1	22.0	18.4	15.8	15.3	59.1	52.5	46.5	44.7
239	Non-metallic mineral products n.e.c.			...	...	...	...	...	...	...	...	...
2391	Refractory products		-	0.1	1.4	1.3	1.2	1.3	3.8	3.5	3.4	3.4
2392	Clay building materials			...	...	...	...	...	...	...	...	...
2393	Other porcelain and ceramic products			...	...	...	...	...	...	...	...	...
2394	Cement, lime and plaster		0.5	1.0	3.4	3.0	2.9	2.6	9.0	7.8	7.4	6.6
2395	Articles of concrete, cement and plaster	b/	2.2	2.2	54.4	46.7	41.9	39.7	113.3	97.8	87.3	80.7
2396	Cutting, shaping and finishing of stone	b/	0.1	0.1	3.8	3.8	3.4	3.1	9.8	9.5	8.6	7.8
2399	Other non-metallic mineral products n.e.c.			...	...	...	...	...	...	...	...	...
2410	Basic iron and steel			...	...	...	...	...	...	...	...	...
2420	Basic precious and other non-ferrous metals		2.1	1.9	30.4	27.8	26.5	27.0	152.6	135.1	128.0	127.8
243	Casting of metals		0.8	0.8	10.0	8.9	8.4	7.7	25.2	23.2	22.2	20.4
2431	Casting of iron and steel		0.4	0.5	5.7	5.1	5.2	4.7	16.6	15.5	15.6	14.2
2432	Casting of non-ferrous metals		0.4	0.3	4.3	3.7	3.2	3.0	8.7	7.7	6.6	6.2
251	Struct.metal products, tanks, reservoirs	c/	4.8	4.4	89.9	80.6	74.7	66.5	258.0	236.3	220.3	197.3

continued

Mexico

ISIC	Industry	Note	Output 2013	2014	2015	2016	Note	VA 2013	2014	2015	2016	Note	GFCF 2015	2016
			(billions of Mexican Pesos)					(billions of Mexican Pesos)					(billions of Mexican Pesos)	
2511	Structural metal products		29.4	35.4	37.8	41.6		11.9	14.4	15.2	17.3		0.3	0.2
2512	Tanks, reservoirs and containers of metal		29.1	31.2	35.7	37.0		8.3	9.2	11.0	11.7		0.5	0.8
2513	Steam generators, excl. hot water boilers		...	...	...	...		...	...	...	...		...	...
2520	Weapons and ammunition	c/	...	...	...	...	c/	...	...	...	...		...	...
259	Other metal products;metal working services	c/	...	...	...	...	c/	...	...	...	...		...	...
2591	Forging,pressing,stamping,roll-forming of metal		13.2	15.0	16.6	17.9		3.8	4.1	4.9	5.4		0.3	0.4
2592	Treatment and coating of metals; machining		31.7	38.7	41.5	46.0		6.9	8.7	9.5	10.8		1.2	1.3
2593	Cutlery, hand tools and general hardware		19.9	21.1	23.2	27.6		8.0	8.6	9.4	11.4		0.5	0.4
2599	Other fabricated metal products n.e.c.		73.9	78.8	81.5	87.9		27.6	29.7	30.8	33.2		1.6	1.8
2610	Electronic components and boards		38.0	39.4	45.4	52.3		23.5	26.0	30.1	34.9		0.9	1.4
2620	Computers and peripheral equipment		20.8	28.8	31.7	34.4		6.6	8.7	10.2	11.5		0.4	0.3
2630	Communication equipment		16.7	16.0	17.4	19.6		11.0	10.3	11.1	12.5		-0.3	-
2640	Consumer electronics		16.0	17.9	18.7	19.8		8.5	9.4	10.0	11.0		0.4	0.4
265	Measuring,testing equipment; watches, etc.		11.0	11.1	13.9	16.8		3.4	3.6	4.4	5.4		0.1	0.1
2651	Measuring/testing/navigating equipment,etc.		11.0	11.1	13.9	16.8		3.4	3.6	4.4	5.4		0.1	0.1
2652	Watches and clocks		...	...	...	...		...	...	...	...		...	...
2660	Irradiation/electromedical equipment,etc.		...	...	...	...		...	...	...	...		...	...
2670	Optical instruments and photographic equipment		...	...	...	...		...	...	...	...		...	...
2680	Magnetic and optical media		4.7	5.1	5.6	5.6		2.0	2.3	2.6	2.6		0.1	0.1
2710	Electric motors,generators,transformers,etc.		36.6	47.8	53.5	57.3		13.7	19.3	22.3	24.5		0.5	0.7
2720	Batteries and accumulators		10.8	10.7	11.0	12.2		4.2	4.1	4.2	4.7		0.2	-
273	Wiring and wiring devices		39.4	39.7	42.1	45.9		10.1	10.2	11.1	12.0		0.3	0.3
2731	Fibre optic cables		...	...	...	...		...	...	...	...		...	...
2732	Other electronic and electric wires and cables		...	...	...	...		...	...	...	...		...	...
2733	Wiring devices		...	...	...	...		...	...	...	...		...	...
2740	Electric lighting equipment		5.8	5.7	6.2	7.1		2.9	3.1	3.5	4.4		-0.1	0.2
2750	Domestic appliances		53.3	56.7	67.2	77.3		16.1	16.3	17.3	19.3		0.8	1.0
2790	Other electrical equipment		3.8	4.0	4.3	5.7		2.0	2.2	2.4	3.1		0.1	0.2
281	General-purpose machinery	d/	129.4	135.5	147.9	161.6	d/	51.1	54.8	59.6	65.7	d/	0.9	0.7
2811	Engines/turbines,excl.aircraft,vehicle engines		33.1	35.1	36.5	39.2		14.5	15.4	15.2	16.3		0.4	-0.1
2812	Fluid power equipment		...	...	...	...		...	...	...	...		...	...
2813	Other pumps, compressors, taps and valves	d/	...	...	...	...	d/	...	...	...	...		...	...
2814	Bearings, gears, gearing and driving elements		...	...	...	...		...	...	...	...		...	...
2815	Ovens, furnaces and furnace burners		...	...	...	...		...	...	...	...		...	...
2816	Lifting and handling equipment		6.7	7.5	8.5	10.7		2.9	3.6	4.1	5.2		0.2	0.2
2817	Office machinery, excl.computers,etc.		...	...	...	...		...	...	...	...		...	...
2818	Power-driven hand tools		...	...	...	...		...	...	...	...		...	...
2819	Other general-purpose machinery		47.0	51.5	58.1	66.6		18.3	20.5	23.4	26.9		1.1	1.1
282	Special-purpose machinery	d/	...	...	...	...	d/	...	...	...	...	d/	...	...
2821	Agricultural and forestry machinery		13.1	12.8	13.6	13.7		4.5	4.5	4.8	5.0		-	-
2822	Metal-forming machinery and machine tools		0.4	0.3	0.3	0.3		0.2	0.1	0.1	0.1		-	-

Code	Description	1	2	3	4	5	6	7	8	9	10
2823	Machinery for metallurgy	2.6	2.7	3.2	3.0	1.1	1.2	1.4	1.4	0.2	0.2
2824	Mining, quarrying and construction machinery	13.3	11.7	10.2	8.8	4.6	4.1	3.7	3.1	-1.3	-0.9
2825	Food/beverage/tobacco processing machinery	2.9	2.7	3.2	3.7	1.4	1.3	1.6	1.9	0.1	0.1
2826	Textile/apparel/leather production machinery	-	-	-	-	-	-	-	-	-	-
2829	Other special-purpose machinery	2.4	2.7	4.2	4.9	1.0	1.1	1.7	2.1	-	-
2910	Motor vehicles	748.4	854.4	1000.5	1084.6	142.6	168.9	206.9	229.1	25.5	26.9
2920	Automobile bodies, trailers and semi-trailers	13.5	15.5	17.2	20.9	4.2	5.1	5.7	6.8	0.2	0.1
2930	Parts and accessories for motor vehicles	629.7	729.5	848.4	941.8	199.7	236.7	282.4	320.0	22.9	25.3
301	Building of ships and boats	6.2	4.4	5.8	2.7	2.0	1.5	2.3	1.0	0.2	-
3011	Building of ships and floating structures	:	:	:	:	:	:	:	:	:	:
3012	Building of pleasure and sporting boats	:	:	:	:	:	:	:	:	:	:
3020	Railway locomotives and rolling stock	18.8	25.4	33.5	31.9	4.0	5.7	7.3	6.9	0.7	0.8
3030	Air and spacecraft and related machinery	15.3	17.7	20.2	22.3	5.8	6.6	7.3	8.4	0.4	0.3
3040	Military fighting vehicles	:	:	:	:	:	:	:	:	:	:
309	Transport equipment n.e.c.	4.5	4.3	5.3	5.9	2.3	2.3	2.8	3.3	0.1	0.1
3091	Motorcycles	2.8	2.8	3.5	4.1	1.6	1.7	2.1	2.6	0.1	0.1
3092	Bicycles and invalid carriages	1.7	1.5	1.8	1.8	0.7	0.6	0.7	0.7	-	-
3099	Other transport equipment n.e.c.	:	:	:	:	:	:	:	:	:	:
3100	Furniture	24.9	25.8	28.6	30.3	9.7	10.5	11.7	12.8	0.5	0.6
321	Jewellery, bijouterie and related articles	:	:	:	:	:	:	:	:	:	:
3211	Jewellery and related articles	1.9	2.1	2.5	2.8	0.7	0.7	0.8	0.8	0.1	0.1
3212	Imitation jewellery and related articles	:	:	:	:	:	:	:	:	-	:
3220	Musical instruments	1.0	1.1	1.2	1.1	0.3	0.4	0.4	0.4	-	-
3230	Sports goods	0.8	0.8	0.8	0.8	0.4	0.4	0.4	0.4	-	-
3240	Games and toys	5.8	5.9	6.7	7.3	2.4	2.2	2.6	2.9	0.2	0.7
3250	Medical and dental instruments and supplies	30.0	32.9	37.1	44.3	19.2	21.3	24.8	30.0	1.1	1.8
3290	Other manufacturing n.e.c.	11.0	11.5	12.2	13.1	4.4	4.5	4.8	5.2	0.3	0.3
331	Repair of fabricated metal products/machinery	:	:	:	:	:	:	:	:	:	:
3311	Repair of fabricated metal products	:	:	:	:	:	:	:	:	:	:
3312	Repair of machinery	:	:	:	:	:	:	:	:	:	:
3313	Repair of electronic and optical equipment	:	:	:	:	:	:	:	:	:	:
3314	Repair of electrical equipment	:	:	:	:	:	:	:	:	:	:
3315	Repair of transport equip., excl. motor vehicles	:	:	:	:	:	:	:	:	:	:
3319	Repair of other equipment	:	:	:	:	:	:	:	:	:	:
3320	Installation of industrial machinery/equipment	:	:	:	:	:	:	:	:	:	:
C	Total manufacturing	6027.8	6457.6	6682.2	7097.9	1858.8	1990.9	2289.2	2437.5	144.1	166.9

a/ 201 includes 202 and 2030.
b/ 2396 includes 2399.
c/ 251 includes 2520 and 259.
d/ 281 includes 282.

Mexico

Index numbers of industrial production

ISIC Revision 4

(2010=100)

ISIC	Industry	Note	2005	2006	2007	2008	2009	2010	2011	2012	2013	2014	2015	2016
10	Food products		94	95	96	98	98	100	102	105	106	107	109	112
11	Beverages	a/	92	98	99	102	101	100	103	106	107	110	116	125
12	Tobacco products	a/	...	...	...	...	...	...	...	...	...	...	...	...
13	Textiles		111	112	112	104	97	100	97	98	97	99	105	107
14	Wearing apparel		100	100	98	102	101	100	97	97	101	100	104	104
15	Leather and related products		108	110	106	99	94	100	96	98	97	97	99	98
16	Wood products, excluding furniture		108	110	112	104	97	100	103	117	114	115	120	114
17	Paper and paper products		89	92	94	96	96	100	100	104	106	109	113	118
18	Printing and reproduction of recorded media		85	93	93	98	91	100	103	98	91	90	94	94
19	Coke and refined petroleum products		110	110	108	108	108	100	96	97	101	96	90	78
20	Chemicals and chemical products	b/	98	102	102	101	99	100	98	97	98	97	94	91
21	Pharmaceuticals, medicinal chemicals, etc.	b/	...	...	...	...	...	...	...	...	...	...	...	...
22	Rubber and plastics products		94	95	97	94	87	100	107	110	104	107	113	112
23	Other non-metallic mineral products		103	107	110	107	95	100	104	105	102	105	112	115
24	Basic metals		119	122	120	112	88	100	99	100	100	108	104	106
25	Fabricated metal products, except machinery		98	105	105	105	91	100	107	108	98	104	109	110
26	Computer, electronic and optical products		120	128	129	121	93	100	100	105	110	124	134	142
27	Electrical equipment		114	120	117	112	101	100	95	98	96	103	108	113
28	Machinery and equipment n.e.c.		91	94	91	91	66	100	114	120	105	115	116	117
29	Motor vehicles, trailers and semi-trailers	c/	84	96	100	98	72	100	113	128	136	149	159	161
30	Other transport equipment	c/	...	...	...	...	...	...	...	...	...	...	...	...
31	Furniture		106	106	105	101	95	100	101	105	99	96	103	99
32	Other manufacturing		94	101	101	105	103	100	105	112	112	115	119	124
33	Repair and installation of machinery/equipment		...	...	...	...	...	...	...	...	...	...	...	...
C	Total manufacturing		99	103	104	102	92	100	103	107	108	112	115	117

a/ 11 includes 12.
b/ 20 includes 21.
c/ 29 includes 30.

Mongolia

Supplier of information:
National Statistical Office of Mongolia, Ulaanbaatar.

Basic source of data:
Annual survey.

Major deviations from ISIC (Revision 4):
None reported.

Reference period:
Calendar year.

Scope:
All registered establishments.

Method of data collection:
Mail questionnaires; direct interview in the field.

Type of enumeration:
Sample survey.

Adjusted for non-response:
Yes.

Concepts and definitions of variables:
Wages and salaries includes employers' contributions (in respect of their employees) paid to social security, pension and insurance schemes as well as the benefits received by employees under these schemes and severance and termination pay; excludes housing and family allowances paid directly by the employer.
Output includes revenue from non-industrial activities.

Related national publications:
Monthly Bulletin of Statistics; Statistical Yearbook, both published by the National Statistical Office of Mongolia, Ulaanbaatar.

Mongolia

ISIC	Industry	Note	Number of establishments (number) 2013	2014	2015	2016	Note	Number of employees (number) 2013	2014	2015	2016	Note	Wages and salaries paid to employees (millions of Mongolian Togrog) 2013	2014	2015	2016
10	Food products		970	1169	1222	1279		9938	11099	14529	12954		51390	60397	71963	76397
11	Beverages		129	123	120	118		4985	4667	5487	5007		32593	43505	46199	44363
12	Tobacco products		2	3	3	3		153	137	137	137		977	726	1976	2219
13	Textiles		307	391	396	398		6380	8170	9300	9215		23475	24639	27082	22244
14	Wearing apparel		360	470	513	553		2952	3579	3689	4346		40986	35059	39014	47841
15	Leather and related products		132	152	143	144		987	1051	1031	1018		3333	4269	6432	3936
16	Wood products, excluding furniture		481	578	575	537		2932	3120	3122	2408		14155	13672	11066	10245
17	Paper and paper products		41	42	42	43		519	591	1135	1030		1934	4082	5353	8653
18	Printing and reproduction of recorded media		304	309	342	346		2184	2204	3431	2881		10231	12479	11703	16050
19	Coke and refined petroleum products		9	16	19	15		60	399	367	314		14146	17144	28554	28704
20	Chemicals and chemical products		39	45	49	49		737	890	3009	962		11041	9058	6659	11994
21	Pharmaceuticals,medicinal chemicals, etc.		65	40	38	30		669	535	868	574		5836	8684	10050	9447
22	Rubber and plastics products		48	110	112	119		401	739	850	1134		3064	4500	3999	5195
23	Other non-metallic mineral products		321	474	519	498		7370	7010	8955	7626		42069	42027	42283	34566
24	Basic metals		56	71	82	85		1185	2560	3247	3175		20226	28375	28880	17996
25	Fabricated metal products, except machinery		123	113	124	119		1373	1563	2325	1351		4654	8151	24963	5703
26	Computer, electronic and optical products		18	16	14	10		46	46	43	37		62	119	120	192
27	Electrical equipment		89	52	38	32		597	538	509	201		4157	5800	4798	1039
28	Machinery and equipment n.e.c.		17	18	16	14		212	102	285	55		661	503	3420	603
29	Motor vehicles, trailers and semi-trailers		8	6	5	6		22	54	16	21		134	129	291	325
30	Other transport equipment		6	3	5	3		45	5	6	6		175	19	51	86
31	Furniture		90	141	152	180		276	497	542	735		2701	3816	5121	5573
32	Other manufacturing		116	94	86	86		606	558	579	633		2355	2774	1898	6229
33	Repair and installation of machinery/equipment		142	144	160	189		683	666	2306	1129		6741	5704	6241	7115
C	Total manufacturing		3873a/	4580a/	4775	4856		45312a/	50780a/	65768	56949		297096a/	335636a/	389361	366715

a/ Sum of available data.

Mongolia

ISIC	Industry	Output at basic prices (millions of Mongolian Togrog)					Value added at basic prices (millions of Mongolian Togrog)					Gross fixed capital formation (millions of Mongolian Togrog)		
		Note	2013	2014	2015	2016	Note	2013	2014	2015	2016	Note	2015	2016
10	Food products		545855	655328	632970	740401		150002	164313	165011	175346		22793	31369
11	Beverages		512811	676556	642532	653838		175918	196907	230644	244120		42816	38213
12	Tobacco products		59507	71373	62917	67486		12604	35203	28536	10911		889	988
13	Textiles		283860	312184	316859	338964		93553	124463	120391	53534		5927	6046
14	Wearing apparel		226326	276879	288721	333961		82855	140077	135276	129169		11748	12488
15	Leather and related products		86378	59118	67027	67249		22737	12997	14046	22106		1210	720
16	Wood products, excluding furniture		95674	94976	109317	112070		32738	18181	33365	53803		1446	935
17	Paper and paper products		17369	33247	47726	38319		5077	6563	15444	7396		1322	1248
18	Printing and reproduction of recorded media		73461	67058	72621	88659		32296	26459	28106	38151		2781	5258
19	Coke and refined petroleum products		563531	676748	138140	345230		300215	343696	28756	138859		96598	55723
20	Chemicals and chemical products		53552	59767	55872	123052		13838	21918	20373	29358		2602	3688
21	Pharmaceuticals,medicinal chemicals, etc.		25993	62726	66211	48051		8708	25675	28163	18387		2132	2777
22	Rubber and plastics products		53163	75344	38916	35782		13816	15257	9900	6973		1949	1584
23	Other non-metallic mineral products		330737	366540	315711	237482		122827	134374	118707	66550		14511	11775
24	Basic metals		126854	311863	305415	243938		46487	148993	146102	164534		16925	4300
25	Fabricated metal products, except machinery		58410	57652	80198	46749		12891	17640	32097	13526		6125	3120
26	Computer, electronic and optical products		312	588	1485	2839		115	162	351	1313		12	5
27	Electrical equipment		47696	65641	56551	8279		16914	29950	23406	657		8820	456
28	Machinery and equipment n.e.c.		9177	8390	11930	9303		3175	4839	5618	2466		267	279
29	Motor vehicles, trailers and semi-trailers		1375	910	5017	1598		580	357	1473	192		122	164
30	Other transport equipment		1106	268	103	37		618	56	18	17		16	24
31	Furniture		23611	33768	45657	81236		8291	15530	20332	29889		395	1011
32	Other manufacturing		16251	18272	20644	18533		5346	6754	8494	7367		156	323
33	Repair and installation of machinery/equipment		45356	53109	54610	52758		14536	15951	14760	13530		558	1202
C	Total manufacturing		3258367a/	4038304a/	3437152	3695815		1176134a/	1506316a/	1229368	1228156		242120	183696

a/ Sum of available data.

Mongolia

Index numbers of industrial production

ISIC	Industry	Note	2005	2006	2007	2008	2009	2010	2011	2012	2013	2014	2015	2016
10	Food products	a/	...	...	...	90	124	100	107	107	153	144	123	125
11	Beverages	a/	...	...	...	...	...	...	...	...	...	...	...	...
12	Tobacco products		...	...	...	...	97	100	124	102	92	94	74	72
13	Textiles		...	...	...	144	128	100	118	96	108	121	123	133
14	Wearing apparel		...	...	...	321	99	100	280	...	...	...	...	380
15	Leather and related products		...	...	...	86	132	100	162	387	338	717	770	494
16	Wood products, excluding furniture		...	...	...	140	94	100	103	111	85	93	82	89
17	Paper and paper products		...	...	...	54	104	100	132	190	177	269	310	206
18	Printing and reproduction of recorded media		...	...	...	120	96	100	90	132	158	119	137	129
19	Coke and refined petroleum products	b/	...	...	...	-	-	100	100	240	261	149	82	127
20	Chemicals and chemical products	b/	...	...	...	77	63	100	174	243	174	135	139	204
21	Pharmaceuticals, medicinal chemicals, etc.		...	...	...	...	...	...	...	...	...	...	...	...
22	Rubber and plastics products		...	...	...	...	...	100	125	357	311	423	375	321
23	Other non-metallic mineral products		...	...	...	101	69	100	141	173	153	183	121	104
24	Basic metals		...	...	...	120	71	100	91	97	105	127	123	81
25	Fabricated metal products, except machinery		...	...	...	32	84	100	89	192	151	250	188	149
26	Computer, electronic and optical products		...	...	...	208	121	100	74	...	...	63	...	138
27	Electrical equipment		...	...	...	...	...	100	...	...	...	155	64	...
28	Machinery and equipment n.e.c.		...	...	...	...	...	...	...	...	...	...	...	...
29	Motor vehicles, trailers and semi-trailers		...	...	...	...	...	...	...	...	...	...	...	...
30	Other transport equipment	c/	...	...	...	103	151	100	84	115	61	57	60	46
31	Furniture	c/	...	...	...	289	102	100	130	419	174	431	390	220
32	Other manufacturing		...	...	...	...	...	...	...	...	...	...	...	...
33	Repair and installation of machinery/equipment		...	...	...	...	...	...	...	...	...	...	...	...
C	Total manufacturing		...	...	...	90	83	100	116	138	136	154	145	131

a/ 10 includes 11.
b/ 20 includes 21.
c/ 31 includes 32.

Netherlands

Supplier of information:
Central Bureau of Statistics, The Hague.
Industrial statistics for the OECD countries are compiled by the OECD secretariat, which supplies them to UNIDO.

Basic source of data:
Annual surveys; administrative data; business register.

Major deviations from ISIC (Revision 4):
Data presented in ISIC (Revision 4) were originally classified according to the national NACE-related classification system.

Reference period:
Calendar year.

Scope:
All enterprises.

Method of data collection:
Mail questionnaires; electronic questionnaires.

Type of enumeration:
Enterprises with 50 or more employees are completely enumerated; businesses with fewer than 50 employees are sampled; data for smaller businesses is mainly derived from administrative sources.

Adjusted for non-response:
Not reported.

Concepts and definitions of variables:
No deviations from the standard UN concepts and definitions are reported.

Related national publications:
None reported.

Netherlands

ISIC	Industry	Note	Number of enterprises (number) 2013	2014	2015	2016	Note	Number of employees (number) 2013	2014	2015	2016	Note	Wages and salaries paid to employees (millions of Euros) 2013	2014	2015	2016
1010	Processing/preserving of meat		616	604	616	621		14178	14990	15082	15119		486	508	519	540
1020	Processing/preserving of fish, etc.		147	141	144	150		3172	3109	3072	3123		83	95	90	86
1030	Processing/preserving of fruit,vegetables		168	169	184	184		9812	9796	9604	9641		411	399	413	437
1040	Vegetable and animal oils and fats		44	40	38	47		2834	2843	2764	2746		130	138	136	133
1050	Dairy products		313	311	320	296		12695	13562	14820	15291		545	725	806	809
106	Grain mill products,starches and starch products		116	112	114	112		3261	3243	3248	3272		159	164	169	172
1061	Grain mill products		104	100	100	101		1240	1204	1213	1229		53	54	53	57
1062	Starches and starch products		12	12	14	11		2021	2039	2034	2043		106	110	116	115
107	Other food products		3709	3743	4012	4174		61888	60814	61290	62130		1956	1991	2007	2060
1071	Bakery products		2963	2933	3106	3188		38765	38422	38375	38457		...	...	...	...
1072	Sugar		3	4	3	3										
1073	Cocoa, chocolate and sugar confectionery		222	229	240	263		6457	6361	6407	6516		301	304	327	339
1074	Macaroni, noodles, couscous, etc.		33	35	36	38		72	206	203	243		...	...	...	...
1075	Prepared meals and dishes		199	200	232	233		3655	3462	3972	4186		...	...	...	...
1079	Other food products n.e.c.		289	342	395	449										
1080	Prepared animal feeds		184	181	187	201		7247	7040	7356	7524		334	316	365	365
110	Beverages		290	338	450	563		6459	6410	6475	6647		345	356	359	369
1101	Distilling, rectifying and blending of spirits		48	44	56	75		600	611	636	603		...	...	...	...
1102	Wines		67	68	81	84										
1103	Malt liquors and malt		147	194	269	353										
1104	Soft drinks,mineral waters,other bottled waters		28	32	44	51		2060	1977	1933	2003		107	106	103	106
1200	Tobacco products		19	18	18	20		2943	2782	1328	1297		154	151	63	64
131	Spinning, weaving and finishing of textiles		428	446	471	522		2890	2828	2852	2589		...	...	...	...
1311	Preparation and spinning of textile fibres		30	33	39	39		197	203	195	133		...	...	...	...
1312	Weaving of textiles		33	36	35	38		992	976	992	879		...	...	...	...
1313	Finishing of textiles		365	377	397	445		1701	1649	1665	1577		...	...	...	...
139	Other textiles		1584	1621	1655	1662	a/	7905	7824	7812	7744	a/	288	284	301	291
1391	Knitted and crocheted fabrics		13	14	16	19	a/	116	113	99	83	a/	288	284	301	291
1392	Made-up textile articles, except apparel		922	937	948	952	a/	3437	3293	3174	3011	a/	...	...	...	...
1393	Carpets and rugs		77	75	71	70	a/	2214	2246	2299	2444	a/	...	...	...	...
1394	Cordage, rope, twine and netting		36	34	35	35		171	165	163	164		...	...	...	...
1399	Other textiles n.e.c.		536	561	585	586	a/	1967	2007	2077	2043	a/	...	...	...	...
1410	Wearing apparel, except fur apparel		2241	2248	2299	2371		2558	1996	1748	1756		55	61b/	51	53
1420	Articles of fur		5	5	6	5		-	-	-	-		...	..b/	...	...
1430	Knitted and crocheted apparel		50	57	63	61		117	109	104	97		...	..b/	4	4
151	Leather;luggage,handbags,saddlery,harness;fur		334	360	406	446		947	865	896	918		34	29	34	33
1511	Tanning/dressing of leather; dressing of fur		39	42	48	46	c/	461	420	438	466	c/	34	29	34	33
1512	Luggage,handbags,etc.;saddlery/harness		295	318	358	400	c/	486	445	458	452	c/	...	...	...	...
1520	Footwear		127	131	134	142		610	621	636	670		...	...	...	...
1610	Sawmilling and planing of wood		273	281	290	305		1144	1148	1175	1253		40	39	40	43

Code	Product												Notes
162	Wood products, cork, straw, plaiting materials	2159	2157	2226	2321	10782	10103	10306	10791	354	349	387	367	d/
1621	Veneer sheets and wood-based panels	27	25	28	28	270	259	270	287	354	349	387	387	d/
1622	Builders' carpentry and joinery	1401	1394	1424	1494	7707	7000	7101	7559	...	...	...	...	d/
1623	Wooden containers	138	129	135	140	1755	1821	1895	1884	...	...	...	...	d/
1629	Other wood products;articles of cork,straw	593	609	639	659	1050	1023	1040	1062	765	804	783	808	
170	Paper and paper products	370	378	378	368	17597	17413	17158	17034	310	331	328	343	
1701	Pulp, paper and paperboard	51	53	56	54	7464	7849	7622	7795	850	793	743	694	
1702	Corrugated paper and paperboard	174	183	181	181	...	...	...	...	...	...	...	...	
1709	Other articles of paper and paperboard	145	142	141	133	...	...	...	...	850	793	743	694	
181	Printing and service activities related to printing	3787	3656	3492	3375	22939	20744	19041	18942	850	793	743	694	e/
1811	Printing	2645	2557	2384	2299	19264	17386	15879	15829	850	793	743	694	e/
1812	Service activities related to printing	1142	1099	1108	1076	3675	3358	3163	3113	...	...	...	...	
1820	Reproduction of recorded media	489	471	473	479	614	541	558	420	26	24	27	19	
1910	Coke oven products	-	-	-	-	-	-	-	-	-	-	-	-	
1920	Refined petroleum products	38	43	45	29	5207	5420	5297	5414	1697	1702	1643	1686	
201	Basic chemicals,fertilizers, etc.	332	332	340	351	24704	23921	24013	24037	114	120	120	122	
2011	Basic chemicals	142	147	150	152	14032	13745	13927	13875	...	...	...	...	
2012	Fertilizers and nitrogen compounds	41	39	41	49	1783	1837	1815	1849	...	...	...	...	
2013	Plastics and synthetic rubber in primary forms	148	146	149	150	8888	8340	8270	8312	...	...	...	...	
202	Other chemical products	486	481	501	508	17785	17843	17729	18033	293	294	271	283	
2021	Pesticides and other agrochemical products	20	17	18	18	393	365	405	381	...	...	...	...	
2022	Paints,varnishes;printing ink and mastics	105	99	98	93	6092	5996	5720	5711	...	...	...	...	
2023	Soap,cleaning and cosmetic preparations	223	224	246	260	3823	3875	3848	3980	...	...	...	...	
2029	Other chemical products n.e.c.	138	141	139	137	2044	1938	1891	1991	118	119	122	132	
2030	Man-made fibres	36	31	32	34	12308	12438	12722	12672	642	666	669	701	
2100	Pharmaceuticals,medicinal chemicals, etc.	205	208	218	223	3286	3445	3452	3543	151	171	174	191	f/
221	Rubber products	103	105	110	107	3286	3445	3452	3543	151	171	174	191	f/
2211	Rubber tyres and tubes	13	11	13	11	...	...	...	...	...	...	...	...	f/
2219	Other rubber products	90	94	97	96	26509	26349	27012	27809	1064	1078	1130	1187	f/
2220	Plastics products	1306	1285	1295	1310	4655	4470	4275	4253	218	218	219	202	
2310	Glass and glass products	731	731	743	742	...	...	...	...	...	...	...	...	
239	Non-metallic mineral products n.e.c.	1298	1301	1286	1289	...	...	...	...	...	...	...	...	
2391	Refractory products	13	17	19	22	...	...	...	...	...	...	...	...	
2392	Clay building materials	44	45	46	45	...	...	...	...	...	...	...	...	
2393	Other porcelain and ceramic products	261	258	255	260	...	...	...	...	...	...	...	...	
2394	Cement, lime and plaster	4	4	7	6	10386	8778	8626	8606	58	61	71	67	
2395	Articles of concrete, cement and plaster	475	480	472	479	1646	1566	1624	1638	...	...	...	...	
2396	Cutting, shaping and finishing of stone	422	422	416	415	2512	2468	2247	2079	...	...	...	...	
2399	Other non-metallic mineral products n.e.c.	79	75	71	62	...	...	...	...	...	...	...	...	
2410	Basic iron and steel	161	177	175	201	4942	4727	4778	4873	224	221	231	234	
2420	Basic precious and other non-ferrous metals	125	122	123	118	3347	3437	3483	3345	...	141	143	146	
243	Casting of metals	124	112	108	108	3347	3437	3483	3345	...g/	141g/	143g/	146g/	g/
2431	Casting of iron and steel	40	35	34	36	...	...	...	...	...	...	...	...g/	g/
2432	Casting of non-ferrous metals	84	77	74	72	...	...	...	...	...	...	...	...g/	g/
251	Struct.metal products, tanks, reservoirs	2533	2532	2529	2549	3132h/				...				

continued

Netherlands

ISIC Revision 4		Number of enterprises (number)					Number of employees (number)					Wages and salaries paid to employees (millions of Euros)				
ISIC	Industry	Note	2013	2014	2015	2016	Note	2013	2014	2015	2016	Note	2013	2014	2015	2016
2511	Structural metal products		2420	2432	2430	2446		33234	32232	32288	32934		...	...	...	...
2512	Tanks, reservoirs and containers of metal		104	94	92	95		4590	4289	4359	4279		...	...	...	...
2513	Steam generators, excl. hot water boilers		9	6	7	8		...	...	...	...		...	...	...	...
2520	Weapons and ammunition		12	13	13	12		...	...	...	...		..h/	...	...	...
259	Other metal products;metal working services		8304	8412	8639	8953		43465	44836	45305	46498		..h/	1667	1728	...
2591	Forging,pressing,stamping,roll-forming of metal		534	522	512	500		7777	8030	8188	8218		293	298	312	314
2592	Treatment and coating of metals; machining		6408	6560	6808	7107		20653	20952	21228	21996		729	720	752	778
2593	Cutlery, hand tools and general hardware		420	413	423	457		...	...	...	...		...	...	...	...
2599	Other fabricated metal products n.e.c.		942	917	896	889		10164	10877	10872	11054		...	...	...	...
2610	Electronic components and boards		313	315	324	326		6911	6331	6388	6427		418	463	470	441
2620	Computers and peripheral equipment		215	215	214	217		640	1286	1267	1301		23	47	...	...
2630	Communication equipment		121	115	112	112		990	1009	945	871		55	...	...	...
2640	Consumer electronics		210	209	224	216		920	1030	958	660		58	48	48	...
265	Measuring,testing equipment; watches, etc.		472	492	481	480		10688	10574	10397	10221	i/	540	549	523	534
2651	Measuring/testing/navigating equipment,etc.		421	436	419	422		10467	10344	10157	10005	i/	540	549	523	534
2652	Watches and clocks		51	56	62	58		221	230	240	216		...	...	...	...
2660	Irradiation/electromedical equipment,etc.		94	87	78	70		4985	4988	4865	4138		...	32	37	43
2670	Optical instruments and photographic equipment		132	128	122	120		746	918	912	858		...	...	...	...
2680	Magnetic and optical media		45	44	45	38		57	57	71	78		...	...	...	...
2710	Electric motors,generators,transformers,etc.		390	372	324	320		6868	6358	6003	6315		224	226	243	249
2720	Batteries and accumulators		18	18	23	26		86	84	94	104		...	...	...	...
273	Wiring and wiring devices		73	76	78	81		2507	2455	2428	2471		132	130	117	126
2731	Fibre optic cables		20	20	21	19		456	902	984	951	j/	132	130	117	126
2732	Other electronic and electric wires and cables		46	49	50	55		1936	1465	1391	1441	j/	...	...	...	...
2733	Wiring devices		7	7	7	7		115	87	53	79	j/	...	...	...	...
2740	Electric lighting equipment		321	333	345	352		5100	4814	4427	5352		282	285	276	374
2750	Domestic appliances		108	108	98	102		3449	3442	3448	3523		163	171	...	...
2790	Other electrical equipment		327	325	325	318		2670	2636	3233	3281		...	...	...	...
281	General-purpose machinery		1726	1696	1644	1650		43682	43839	43526	44052		1966	2035	2085	2123
2811	Engines/turbines,excl.aircraft,vehicle engines		151	139	129	133		1906	1973	2025	1876		...	...	...	...
2812	Fluid power equipment		84	85	87	86		2896	3924	3809	3772		...	...	...	...
2813	Other pumps, compressors, taps and valves		139	131	125	129		6284	5429	5258	5092		...	...	...	...
2814	Bearings, gears, gearing and driving elements		57	53	50	55		1610	1592	1426	1619		...	...	...	...
2815	Ovens, furnaces and furnace burners		43	42	42	44		...	...	...	...		...	...	...	...
2816	Lifting and handling equipment		299	294	288	294		10766	10881	11203	11648		511	568	590	603
2817	Office machinery, excl.computers,etc.		14	14	15	14		63	61	64	79		...	...	...	...
2818	Power-driven hand tools		22	21	21	24		...	...	...	...		...	...	...	...
2819	Other general-purpose machinery		917	917	887	871		16528	16571	16432	16707		...	...	...	...
282	Special-purpose machinery		1394	1395	1403	1452		34804	35922	36254	36905		1767	1881	1979	2070
2821	Agricultural and forestry machinery		345	334	308	307		7400	7603	7317	7376		276	280	305	307
2822	Metal-forming machinery and machine tools		164	160	160	161		1937	1920	1880	1916		...	...	...	...

Code	Description												
2823	Machinery for metallurgy	14	12	14	15	22	50	48	61	..	..	..	..
2824	Mining, quarrying and construction machinery	68	66	67	68	2364	2425	2317	2232	..	..	..	..
2825	Food/beverage/tobacco processing machinery	215	210	207	212	7272	7224	7244	7498	..	..	..	..
2826	Textile/apparel/leather production machinery	50	47	43	40	453	461	496	552	..	..	..	..
2829	Other special-purpose machinery	538	566	604	649	15357	16238	16952	17270	..	..	..	..
2910	Motor vehicles	154	152	149	146	8469	8492	9588	10037	200	438	514	524
2920	Automobile bodies, trailers and semi-trailers	452	427	427	432	5579	5553	6012	6279	..	207	226	240
2930	Parts and accessories for motor vehicles	170	167	170	163	4357	4285	4315	4375	..	182	190	191
301	Building of ships and boats [k]	1160	1132	1105	1095	10824	10945	10794	10579	523	543	491	489
3011	Building of ships and floating structures [k]	262	273	257	273	6542	6621	6330	5845	523	543	491	489
3012	Building of pleasure and sporting boats	898	859	848	822	4282	4324	4464	4734	..	..	..	..
3020	Railway locomotives and rolling stock	16	15	18	15	303	312	251	250	..	..	..	..
3030	Air and spacecraft and related machinery	75	72	63	60	3798	3810	3820	3619	..	..	..	..
3040	Military fighting vehicles	2	2	2	2	201	209	210	175	..	..	..	..
309	Transport equipment n.e.c. [m]	235	235	248	257	2408	2303	2285	2314	88	90	87	85
3091	Motorcycles [m]	59	56	68	76	103	94	93	102	88	90	87	85
3092	Bicycles and invalid carriages	131	135	134	132	2124	2017	2002	1987	..	..	..	..
3099	Other transport equipment n.e.c. [m]	45	44	46	49	181	192	190	225	578	599	633	590
3100	Furniture	7717	7943	8308	8624	17335	16578	16392	17020	..	..	..	..
321	Jewellery, bijouterie and related articles [n]	1717	1827	1935	2000	779	692	707	629	18	29	24	19
3211	Jewellery and related articles [n]	1263	1304	1399	1467	779	692	707	629	18	29	24	19
3212	Imitation jewellery and related articles	454	523	536	533	479	443	449	435	..	..	..	..
3220	Musical instruments	345	354	367	378	829	797	778	842	..	..	..	..
3230	Sports goods	203	211	224	231	479	454	459	489	..	..	..	..
3240	Games and toys	342	363	387	417	..	..	..	..	..	..	..	..
3250	Medical and dental instruments and supplies	1902	1917	1927	1993	10820	10706	10813	10796	366	377	388	381
3290	Other manufacturing n.e.c.	620	691	719	746	1613	1755	1712	1917	58	73	75	68
331	Repair of fabricated metal products/machinery	5066	5377	5879	6251	30197	29567	30184	30852	1333	1323	1438	1449
3311	Repair of fabricated metal products	39	46	60	67	540	497	484	528	23	21	22	37
3312	Repair of machinery	3258	3495	3839	4138	13528	13303	13348	13585	..	..	..	..
3313	Repair of electronic and optical equipment	94	104	97	108	84	96	78	83	..	..	..	..
3314	Repair of electrical equipment	207	218	259	270	..	..	..	..	..	..	..	..
3315	Repair of transport equip., excl. motor vehicles	1433	1479	1578	1609	97	94	92	121	..	..	..	..
3319	Repair of other equipment	35	35	46	59	..	..	..	..	..	..	..	..
3320	Installation of industrial machinery/equipment	1124	1228	1436	1594	10043	10419	10701	10635	430	458	495	506
C	Total manufacturing	60506	61394	63337	65243	642196	634970	635949	643894	27782	28577	29191	29685

a/ 1391 includes 1392, 1393, 1394 and 1399.
b/ 1410 includes 1420 and 1430.
c/ 1511 includes 1512.
d/ 1621 includes 1622, 1623 and 1629.
e/ 1811 includes 1812.
f/ 2211 includes 2219.
g/ 2431 includes 2432.
h/ 251 includes 2520 and 259.
i/ 2651 includes 2652.
j/ 2731 includes 2732 and 2733.

k/ 3011 includes 3012.
m/ 3091 includes 3092 and 3099.
n/ 3211 includes 3212.

Netherlands

ISIC	Industry	Note	Output (valuation not defined) (millions of Euros)				Note	Value added at factor values (millions of Euros)				Note	Gross fixed capital formation (millions of Euros)	
			2013	2014	2015	2016		2013	2014	2015	2016		2015	2016
1010	Processing/preserving of meat		10373	10129	9980	10425		920	1018	1113	1108		135	164
1020	Processing/preserving of fish, etc.		759	840	813	870		151	174	170	167		17	23
1030	Processing/preserving of fruit,vegetables		4481	4354	4547	5226		883	882	928	973		184	305
1040	Vegetable and animal oils and fats		5710	4291	4625	4779		267	361	335	430		50	52
1050	Dairy products		10358	11266	11127	11370		1346	1473	1606	1517		535	470
106	Grain mill products,starches and starch products		2107	2131	2067	2196		379	399	469	478		79	124
1061	Grain mill products		772	742	705	766		138	145	163	164		18	16
1062	Starches and starch products		1335	1390	1362	1430		241	254	306	314		61	108
107	Other food products		16226	17024	18655	19776		4831	4563	4400	5195		576	476
1071	Bakery products		...	...	...	...		...	...	...	...		203	182
1072	Sugar		...	...	...	...		...	...	...	...		38	31
1073	Cocoa, chocolate and sugar confectionery		3419	3656	4057	4079		733	759	809	836		90	69
1074	Macaroni, noodles, couscous, etc.		...	...	...	...		...	...	...	...		1	-
1075	Prepared meals and dishes		...	...	...	...		...	...	...	...		44	29
1079	Other food products n.e.c.		...	...	...	...		...	...	...	...		200	166
1080	Prepared animal feeds		7931	7202	7571	7598		857	740	915	967		126	160
110	Beverages		4643	4651	4827	4796		1302	1290	1398	1466		206	242
1101	Distilling, rectifying and blending of spirits		...	...	...	...		...	...	...	...		6	14
1102	Wines		...	...	...	...		...	...	...	...		1	2
1103	Malt liquors and malt		...	...	...	...		...	...	...	...		149	141
1104	Soft drinks,mineral waters,other bottled waters		1401	1327	1331	1314		311	303	296	327		51	85
1200	Tobacco products		1976	2070	884	873		542	517	259	201		11	41
131	Spinning, weaving and finishing of textiles		...	...	...	...		...	...	...	...		15	14
1311	Preparation and spinning of textile fibres		...	...	...	...		...	...	...	...		2	-
1312	Weaving of textiles		...	...	...	...		...	...	...	...		5	4
1313	Finishing of textiles		...	...	...	...		...	...	...	...		8	10
139	Other textiles	a/	1950	2025	2113	2170		599	622	656	658		54	39
1391	Knitted and crocheted fabrics	a/	1950	2025	2113	2170		599	622	656	658		-	
1392	Made-up textile articles, except apparel	a/	...	...	...	...		...	...	...	...		17	13
1393	Carpets and rugs		...	...	...	...		...	...	...	...		25	17
1394	Cordage, rope, twine and netting	a/	...	...	...	...		...	...	...	...		1	-
1399	Other textiles n.e.c.	a/	...	...	...	...		...	...	...	...		11	9
1410	Wearing apparel, except fur apparel		336	380b/	298	391		107	111b/	80	98		...	...
1420	Articles of fur		...	..b/	...	...		...	..b/	...	...		-	...
1430	Knitted and crocheted apparel		...	..b/	35	40		...	..b/	16	18		...	...
151	Leather;luggage,handbags,saddlery,harness;fur		259	240	260	240		84	63	70	59		8	5
1511	Tanning/dressing of leather; dressing of fur	c/	259	240	260	240		84	63	70	59		6	3
1512	Luggage,handbags,etc.;saddlery/harness	c/	...	...	...	...		...	...	...	...		2	2
1520	Footwear		...	...	...	...		...	...	...	...		5	...
1610	Sawmilling and planing of wood		268	287	302	354		85	90	94	95		9	13

Code	Description	fn										
162	Wood products, cork, straw, plaiting materials	d/	56	73	584	627	696	777	1940	2054	2285	2444
1621	Veneer sheets and wood-based panels	d/	1	2	584	627	696	777	1940	2054	2285	2444
1622	Builders' carpentry and joinery	d/	34	46	…	…	…	…	…	…	…	…
1623	Wooden containers	d/	11	19	…	…	…	…	…	…	…	…
1629	Other wood products;articles of cork,straw	d/	10	6	…	…	…	…	…	…	…	…
170	Paper and paper products		180	323	1465	1628	1542	1535	5644	6727	6648	6764
1701	Pulp, paper and paperboard		41	168	…	…	…	…	…	…	…	…
1702	Corrugated paper and paperboard		80	79	565	599	584	602	2058	2211	2205	2252
1709	Other articles of paper and paperboard		59	76	…	…	…	…	…	…	…	…
181	Printing and service activities related to printing	e/	101	119	1409	1332	1271	1243	3899	3722	3436	3436
1811	Printing	e/	85	105	1409	1332	1271	1243	3899	3722	3436	3436
1812	Service activities related to printing		16	14	…	…	…	…	…	…	…	…
1820	Reproduction of recorded media		1	2	44	41	39	31	121	116	131	61
1910	Coke oven products		-	-	-	-	-	-	-	-	-	-
1920	Refined petroleum products		…	402	4979	4672	5820	6540	37345	36375	33631	30425
201	Basic chemicals,fertilizers, etc.		1512	1122	…	…	…	…	…	…	…	…
2011	Basic chemicals		1150	561	533	639	659	481	2172	2104	2079	1554
2012	Fertilizers and nitrogen compounds		130	141	…	…	…	…	…	…	…	…
2013	Plastics and synthetic rubber in primary forms		232	420	…	…	…	…	…	…	…	…
202	Other chemical products		207	245	…	…	…	…	…	…	…	…
2021	Pesticides and other agrochemical products		10	11	…	…	…	…	…	…	…	…
2022	Paints,varnishes;printing ink and mastics		40	38	676	668	527	702	1942	2143	2486	2678
2023	Soap,cleaning and cosmetic preparations		40	41	…	…	…	…	…	…	…	…
2029	Other chemical products n.e.c.		117	155	283	331	325	337	731	793	821	898
2030	Man-made fibres		32	43	1798	1698	2027	2086	4287	4288	5089	5587
2100	Pharmaceuticals,medicinal chemicals, etc.		…	169	312	371	326	382	803	927	823	991
221	Rubber products	f/	39	28	312	371	326	382	803	927	823	991
2211	Rubber tyres and tubes	f/	23	16	…	…	…	…	…	…	…	…
2219	Other rubber products		16	13	…	…	…	…	…	…	…	…
2220	Plastics products		245	301	2002	2168	2337	2474	6683	6879	7468	7728
2310	Glass and glass products		32	29	384	393	365	365	941	955	903	894
239	Non-metallic mineral products n.e.c.		157	…	…	…	…	…	…	…	…	…
2391	Refractory products		4	2	…	…	…	…	…	…	…	…
2392	Clay building materials		29	21	…	…	…	…	…	…	…	…
2393	Other porcelain and ceramic products		1	2	…	…	…	…	…	…	…	…
2394	Cement, lime and plaster		7	…	…	…	…	…	…	…	…	…
2395	Articles of concrete, cement and plaster		96	89	96	99	117	118	222	231	286	288
2396	Cutting, shaping and finishing of stone		8	6	…	…	…	…	…	…	…	…
2399	Other non-metallic mineral products n.e.c.		13	…	…	…	…	…	…	…	…	…
2410	Basic iron and steel		…	…	396	425	422	479	1790	1887	1898	1866
2420	Basic precious and other non-ferrous metals		56	60	…	…	…	…	…	…	…	…
243	Casting of metals		…	39	…	206	197	213	…	665	675g/	680g/
2431	Casting of iron and steel		…	16	…g/	206g/	197g/	213g/	…g/	665g/	675g/	680g/
2432	Casting of non-ferrous metals		…	23	…g/	…g/	…g/	…g/	…g/	…g/	…g/	…g/
251	Struct.metal products, tanks, reservoirs		…	274	5894h/	…	…	…	17818h/	…	…	…

continued

Netherlands

ISIC Revision 4

ISIC	Industry	Out. Note	Output (valuation not defined) (millions of Euros) 2013	2014	2015	2016	VA Note	Value added at factor values (millions of Euros) 2013	2014	2015	2016	GFCF Note	Gross fixed capital formation (millions of Euros) 2015	2016
2511	Structural metal products		…	…	…	…		…	…	…	…		159	243
2512	Tanks, reservoirs and containers of metal		…	…	…	…		…	…	…	…		32	30
2513	Steam generators, excl. hot water boilers		…	…	…	…		…	…	…	…		…	1
2520	Weapons and ammunition		..h/	…	…	…		..h/	…	…	…		…	-
259	Other metal products;metal working services		..h/	9318	9819	…		..h/	3463	3562	…		373	383
2591	Forging,pressing,stamping,roll-forming of metal		1698	1796	1915	1889		530	544	587	597		68	51
2592	Treatment and coating of metals; machining		3732	3778	4140	4396		1587	1658	1705	1816		156	177
2593	Cutlery, hand tools and general hardware		…	…	…	…		…	…	…	…		39	49
2599	Other fabricated metal products n.e.c.		…	…	…	…		…	…	…	…		111	107
2610	Electronic components and boards		2344	2415	3710	3637		1092	1415	1611	1553		72	78
2620	Computers and peripheral equipment		459	…	…	…		67	73	…	…		1	…
2630	Communication equipment		279	227	…	…		75	77	90	…		6	6
2640	Consumer electronics		384	271	290	…		101	…	…	…		2	2
265	Measuring,testing equipment; watches, etc.	i/	2452	2390	2487	2444	i/	974	971	927	896		39	47
2651	Measuring/testing/navigating equipment,etc.	i/	2452	2390	2487	2444	i/	974	971	927	896		38	44
2652	Watches and clocks		…	…	…	…		…	…	…	…		1	3
2660	Irradiation/electromedical equipment,etc.		…	135	144	146		…	57	59	59		8	…
2670	Optical instruments and photographic equipment		…	…	…	…		…	…	…	…		…	4
2680	Magnetic and optical media		…	…	…	…		…	…	…	…		…	-
2710	Electric motors,generators,transformers,etc.		1178	1281	1283	1441		362	380	397	459		16	18
2720	Batteries and accumulators		…	…	…	…		…	…	…	…		-	…
273	Wiring and wiring devices		871	835	831	811		234	215	222	225		10	31
2731	Fibre optic cables	j/	871	835	831	811	j/	234	215	222	225		3	4
2732	Other electronic and electric wires and cables	j/	…	…	…	…	j/	…	…	…	…		6	27
2733	Wiring devices	j/	…	…	…	…	j/	…	…	…	…		-	1
2740	Electric lighting equipment		1571	1372	1453	1981		528	435	476	606		10	15
2750	Domestic appliances		588	608	…	…		334	344	…	…		54	41
2790	Other electrical equipment		…	…	…	…		…	…	…	…		16	26
281	General-purpose machinery		10526	11349	11261	11552		3488	3712	3736	3808		260	266
2811	Engines/turbines,excl.aircraft,vehicle engines		…	…	…	…		…	…	…	…		17	11
2812	Fluid power equipment		…	…	…	…		…	…	…	…		22	15
2813	Other pumps, compressors, taps and valves		…	…	…	…		…	…	…	…		26	21
2814	Bearings, gears, gearing and driving elements		…	…	…	…		…	…	…	…		13	10
2815	Ovens, furnaces and furnace burners		…	…	…	…		…	…	…	…		5	4
2816	Lifting and handling equipment		3113	3441	3500	3464		992	1026	1083	1103		68	91
2817	Office machinery, excl.computers,etc.		…	…	…	…		…	…	…	…		25	32
2818	Power-driven hand tools		…	…	…	…		…	…	…	…		3	-
2819	Other general-purpose machinery		…	…	…	…		…	…	…	…		82	83
282	Special-purpose machinery		13424	14191	13482	14293		4144	4661	4617	5033		616	454
2821	Agricultural and forestry machinery		2081	2073	2166	2232		537	561	577	629		28	45
2822	Metal-forming machinery and machine tools		…	…	…	…		…	…	…	…		7	13

2823	Machinery for metallurgy	:	:	:	:	:	:	:	:	:	-	35
2824	Mining, quarrying and construction machinery	:	:	:	:	:	:	:	:	:	33	40
2825	Food/beverage/tobacco processing machinery	:	:	:	:	:	:	:	:	:	40	43
2826	Textile/apparel/leather production machinery	:	:	:	:	:	:	:	:	:	2	2
2829	Other special-purpose machinery	:	4413	7286	8054	:	904	1272	1229	122	98
2910	Motor vehicles	1119	:	:	:	332	:	:	:	505	317
2920	Automobile bodies, trailers and semi-trailers	1218	1476	1615	:	368	418	429	:	39	43
2930	Parts and accessories for motor vehicles	1215	1280	1499	:	399	446	:	:	72	37
301	Building of ships and boats	5266	5356	5667	4652	1053	1039	997	731	67	56
3011	Building of ships and floating structures k/	5266	5356	5667	4652	1053	1039	997	731	35	14
3012	Building of pleasure and sporting boats k/	:	:	:	:	:	:	:	:	32	42
3020	Railway locomotives and rolling stock	:	:	:	:	:	:	:	:	:	:
3030	Air and spacecraft and related machinery	:	:	:	:	:	:	:	:	16	16
3040	Military fighting vehicles	:	:	:	:	:	:	:	:	:	:
309	Transport equipment n.e.c. m/	852	972	1035	1029	177	205	203	195	21	14
3091	Motorcycles m/	852	972	1035	1029	177	205	203	195	1	1
3092	Bicycles and invalid carriages m/	:	:	:	:	:	:	:	:	19	13
3099	Other transport equipment n.e.c. m/	:	:	:	:	:	:	:	:	1	:
3100	Furniture	2911	2978	3216	3457	1072	1090	1191	1201	90	103
321	Jewellery, bijouterie and related articles	140	171	173	135	59	45	38	51	7	1
3211	Jewellery and related articles n/	140	171	173	135	59	45	38	51	5	1
3212	Imitation jewellery and related articles n/	:	:	:	:	:	:	:	:	1	:
3220	Musical instruments	:	:	:	:	:	:	:	:	1	2
3230	Sports goods	:	:	:	:	:	:	:	:	:	4
3240	Games and toys	:	:	:	:	:	:	:	:	:	2
3250	Medical and dental instruments and supplies	1474	1467	1510	1532	710	755	702	741	36	35
3290	Other manufacturing n.e.c.	401	494	492	513	107	142	140	99	6	13
331	Repair of fabricated metal products/machinery	6288	6381	6719	6762	2173	2207	1945	2024	345	381
3311	Repair of fabricated metal products	76	85	104	129	30	35	39	62	1	2
3312	Repair of machinery	:	:	:	:	:	:	:	:	44	54
3313	Repair of electronic and optical equipment	:	:	:	:	:	:	:	:	1	1
3314	Repair of electrical equipment	:	:	:	:	:	:	:	:	3	3
3315	Repair of transport equip., excl. motor vehicles	:	:	:	:	:	:	:	:	296	321
3319	Repair of other equipment	:	:	:	:	:	:	:	:	-	1
3320	Installation of industrial machinery/equipment	2123	2408	2549	2457	740	841	863	857	29	19
C	Total manufacturing	273813	294155	295427	294407	57777	58677	63067	67208	8047	7927

a/ 1391 includes 1392, 1393, 1394 and 1399.
b/ 1410 includes 1420 and 1430.
c/ 1511 includes 1512.
d/ 1621 includes 1622, 1623 and 1629.
e/ 1811 includes 1812.
f/ 2211 includes 2219.
g/ 2431 includes 2432.
h/ 251 includes 2520 and 259.
i/ 2651 includes 2652.
j/ 2731 includes 2732 and 2733.

k/ 3011 includes 3012.
m/ 3091 includes 3092 and 3099.
n/ 3211 includes 3212.

Netherlands

Index numbers of industrial production

ISIC Revision 4

ISIC	Industry	Note	2005	2006	2007	2008	2009	2010	2011	2012	2013	2014	2015	2016
								(2010=100)						
10	Food products		93	95	97	97	97	100	102	100	104	106	109	113
11	Beverages		96	103	107	102	97	100	99	99	99	98	99	99
12	Tobacco products		110	109	115	103	104	100	103	96	93	58	21	20
13	Textiles		96	98	105	102	89	100	104	101	103	104	107	105
14	Wearing apparel		96	98	105	102	89	100	99	96	92	91	91	94
15	Leather and related products		95	97	104	101	88	100	102	98	99	106	105	98
16	Wood products, excluding furniture		114	116	122	122	105	100	104	95	90	93	101	105
17	Paper and paper products		105	111	109	105	94	100	100	100	100	100	102	104
18	Printing and reproduction of recorded media		98	96	101	100	97	100	102	99	99	100	98	99
19	Coke and refined petroleum products		105	101	109	118	120	100	102	99	97	98	103	100
20	Chemicals and chemical products		90	95	99	93	90	100	98	104	99	99	96	104
21	Pharmaceuticals, medicinal chemicals, etc.		84	90	103	91	99	100	105	110	112	120	126	119
22	Rubber and plastics products		92	97	105	103	92	100	103	101	101	105	108	113
23	Other non-metallic mineral products		119	128	131	130	108	100	107	100	94	95	99	100
24	Basic metals		91	93	100	100	77	100	98	99	101	107	107	108
25	Fabricated metal products, except machinery		93	96	105	105	92	100	106	103	101	102	104	105
26	Computer, electronic and optical products		88	87	92	92	82	100	109	113	110	112	117	124
27	Electrical equipment		98	108	122	125	101	100	102	96	94	95	98	111
28	Machinery and equipment n.e.c.		90	98	106	101	83	100	107	104	105	110	110	109
29	Motor vehicles, trailers and semi-trailers		122	124	135	139	65	100	133	120	112	117	139	164
30	Other transport equipment		88	89	107	107	102	100	100	102	99	101	103	100
31	Furniture		106	107	119	128	102	100	99	97	90	90	101	103
32	Other manufacturing		94	96	99	102	99	100	99	99	98	99	99	98
33	Repair and installation of machinery/equipment		84	90	97	98	102	100	103	107	106	103	103	104
C	Total manufacturing		95	98	104	102	94	100	103	103	102	103	103	106

New Zealand

Supplier of information:
Statistics New Zealand, Wellington.
Industrial statistics for the OECD countries are compiled by the OECD secretariat, which supplies them to UNIDO.

Basic source of data:
Annual survey; longitudinal business frame.

Major deviations from ISIC (Revision 4):
Data presented in accordance with ISIC (Revision 4) were originally classified according to the Australian and New Zealand Standard Industrial Classification (ANZSIC) system.

Reference period:
Fiscal year beginning 1 April of the year indicated.

Scope:
Enterprises that meet at least one of the following criteria are covered by annual survey: annual goods and services tax (GST) expenses or sales are greater than NZD 30,000; rolling mean employee count is greater than three; is part of a group of enterprises.

Method of data collection:
Not reported.

Type of enumeration:
Not reported.

Adjusted for non-response:
Not reported.

Concepts and definitions of variables:
No deviations from the standard UN concepts and definitions are reported.

Related national publications:
None reported.

New Zealand

ISIC	Industry	Number of enterprises (number)					Number of persons engaged (number)					Wages and salaries paid to employees (millions of New Zealand Dollars)				
		Note	2012	2013	2014	2015	Note	2012	2013	2014	2015	Note	2012	2013	2014	2015
1010	Processing/preserving of meat		192	192	204	201		29500	29200	30500	30700		3872a/	1278	1342	1433
1020	Processing/preserving of fish, etc.		78	78	78	75		7000	5900	6300	6400		...a/	268	277	271
1030	Processing/preserving of fruit,vegetables		63	60	57	63		4350	4100	4150	4200		...a/	208	182	154
1040	Vegetable and animal oils and fats		21	21	18	21		330	340	420	360		...a/	...	...	...
1050	Dairy products		78	84	90	93		10600	11700	15600	16000		...a/	...	1203	1265
106	Grain mill products,starches and starch products		30	30	30	33		880	1250	1400	1400		...a/	...	77	81
1061	Grain mill products		30	30	30	33		880	1250	1400	1400		...	...	77	81
1062	Starches and starch products		-	-	-	-		-	-	-	-		...	...	...	...
107	Other food products		1305	1317	1329	1344		21250	21100	22220	23010		...a/	847	...	...
1071	Bakery products		936	933	948	945		12300	11800	12400	12600		...	471	...	...
1072	Sugar		6	6	3	3		200	200	220	210		...	...	...	...
1073	Cocoa, chocolate and sugar confectionery		57	60	57	60		1950	2100	2300	2400		...	72	...	...
1074	Macaroni, noodles, couscous, etc.		-	-	-	-		-	-	-	-		...	...	...	...
1075	Prepared meals and dishes		-	-	-	-		-	-	-	-		...	...	...	...
1079	Other food products n.e.c.		306	318	321	336		6800	7000	7300	7800		...	...	...	...
1080	Prepared animal feeds		60	66	66	66		860	920	950	970		...a/	16	23	22
110	Beverages		279	291	291	318		8990	9340	9300	9590	b/	492	487	525	553
1101	Distilling, rectifying and blending of spirits		12	12	15	15		490	490	450	440		...	...	...	...
1102	Wines		180	177	171	177		4500	4800	4800	4900		...	...	...	...
1103	Malt liquors and malt		36	48	54	66		1750	1750	1700	1750		...	...	...	...
1104	Soft drinks,mineral waters,other bottled waters		51	54	51	60		2250	2300	2350	2500		...	...	...	...
1200	Tobacco products		3	3	3	3		250	260	250	250	b/	...	...	...	...
131	Spinning, weaving and finishing of textiles		117	117	117	117		2100	1930	2110	1990		226c/	114	105	112
1311	Preparation and spinning of textile fibres		42	42	42	45		1300	1150	1200	1150		...	78	64	65
1312	Weaving of textiles		-	-	-	-		-	-	-	-		...	...	-	...
1313	Finishing of textiles		75	75	75	72		800	780	910	840		...	36	41	47
139	Other textiles		297	300	303	294		3210	3240	3400	3450		...c/	112	123	138
1391	Knitted and crocheted fabrics		36	36	36	33		710	680	680	670		...	...	...	22
1392	Made-up textile articles, except apparel		237	237	237	231		1750	1750	1800	1900		...	53	62	69
1393	Carpets and rugs		12	15	15	15		570	620	730	710		...	...	...	...
1394	Cordage, rope, twine and netting		12	12	15	15		180	190	190	170		...	...	...	...
1399	Other textiles n.e.c.		-	-	-	-		-	-	-	-		...	...	...	...
1410	Wearing apparel, except fur apparel		351	330	306	291		2900	2650	2450	2350		118d/	109	111	99
1420	Articles of fur		-	-	-	-		-	-	-	-		...d/	...	...	...
1430	Knitted and crocheted apparel		-	-	-	-		-	-	-	-		...d/	...	...	...
151	Leather;luggage,handbags,saddlery,harness;fur		36	39	39	36		1250	1250	1450	1350		62e/	46	48	58
1511	Tanning/dressing of leather; dressing of fur		36	39	39	36		1250	1250	1450	1350		...	46	48	58
1512	Luggage,handbags,etc.;saddlery/harness		-	-	-	-		-	-	-	-		...	...	...	...
1520	Footwear		9	9	9	12		140	150	110	110		...e/	16	18	5
1610	Sawmilling and planing of wood		255	237	234	234		7500	6200	6300	6600		758f/	397	380	365

Code		1	2	3	4	5	6	7	8	9	10	11	12
162	Wood products, cork, straw, plaiting materials	508	417	351	…f/	9250	9050	8550	8250	765	765	774	792
1621	Veneer sheets and wood-based panels	…	…	…	…	1700	1650	1700	1700	30	27	24	24
1622	Builders' carpentry and joinery	306	228	187	…	5700	5600	5100	4800	573	573	582	594
1623	Wooden containers	-	-	-	…	-	-	-	-	-	-	-	-
1629	Other wood products;articles of cork,straw	70	64	55	…	1850	1800	1750	1750	162	165	168	174
170	Paper and paper products	386	388	415	415	4900	5200	4950	5150	60	57	60	60
1701	Pulp, paper and paperboard	…	…	…	415g/	2300	2400	1650	1700	12	12	12	12
1702	Corrugated paper and paperboard	…	…	…	…g/	1400	1400	1900	1900	21	21	24	24
1709	Other articles of paper and paperboard	50	62	65	…g/	1200	1400	1400	1550	27	24	24	24
181	Printing and service activities related to printing	426	417	395	402h/	7600	7910	8240	8630	660	660	672	717
1811	Printing	388	386	364	…	6900	7200	7500	7900	555	558	570	603
1812	Service activities related to printing	38	31	31	…	700	710	740	730	105	102	102	114
1820	Reproduction of recorded media	5	7	7	…h/	100	110	120	130	21	18	21	18
1910	Coke oven products	-	-	-	210i/	-	-	-	-	-	-	-	-
1920	Refined petroleum products	220	218	210	…i/	3000	3000	2850	2800	24	27	21	18
201	Basic chemicals,fertilizers, etc.	233	222	221	455j/	3230	3200	3010	3460	87	90	87	84
2011	Basic chemicals	59	61	…	…	1000	870	610	510	21	21	18	15
2012	Fertilizers and nitrogen compounds	134	123	120	…	1650	1750	1800	1850	33	36	36	39
2013	Plastics and synthetic rubber in primary forms	40	38	40	…j/	580	580	600	1100	33	33	33	30
202	Other chemical products	249	242	234	…	4410	4360	4190	4130	171	165	159	165
2021	Pesticides and other agrochemical products	…	…	…	…	180	210	220	210	6	6	6	6
2022	Paints,varnishes;printing ink and mastics	128	126	120	…	2100	2100	2000	2000	39	39	39	42
2023	Soap,cleaning and cosmetic preparations	68	68	62	…	1600	1400	1300	1250	84	75	75	75
2029	Other chemical products n.e.c.	38	35	39	…	530	650	670	670	42	45	39	42
2030	Man-made fibres	-	-	-	…j/	-	-	-	-	-	-	-	-
2100	Pharmaceuticals,medicinal chemicals, etc.	152	153	153	125	2800	2650	2650	2750	72	69	72	72
221	Rubber products	32	41	36	538k/	680	730	730	690	39	42	42	42
2211	Rubber tyres and tubes	…	…	…	…	170	190	180	140	12	15	12	9
2219	Other rubber products	…	26	25	…k/	510	540	550	550	27	27	30	33
2220	Plastics products	530	512	502	…k/	9200	9000	9000	8900	372	366	381	384
2310	Glass and glass products	130	130	112	457m/	2000	1850	1900	1900	69	63	66	66
239	Non-metallic mineral products n.e.c.	367	365	345	…m/	7800	8225	7205	6255	336	330	333	336
2391	Refractory products	-	-	-	…	30	35	25	25	3	3	6	6
2392	Clay building materials	12	10	9	…	440	450	420	420	54	51	51	51
2393	Other porcelain and ceramic products	…	…	…	…	550	690	630	700	12	12	12	12
2394	Cement, lime and plaster	…	…	…	…	-	-	-	-	-	-	-	-
2395	Articles of concrete, cement and plaster	244	237	215	…	6100	6400	5500	4500	180	177	171	177
2396	Cutting, shaping and finishing of stone	-	-	-	…	-	-	-	-	-	-	-	-
2399	Other non-metallic mineral products n.e.c.	27	25	25	…	680	650	630	610	93	90	90	87
2410	Basic iron and steel	…	…	206	421n/	1650	1750	1750	1700	45	45	45	51
2420	Basic precious and other non-ferrous metals	…	…	179	…n/	2650	2600	2650	2700	33	33	36	33
243	Casting of metals	34	39	36	…n/	540	610	650	660	36	36	30	36
2431	Casting of iron and steel	…	…	…	…	330	420	430	460	18	18	15	21
2432	Casting of non-ferrous metals	…	…	…	…	210	190	220	200	18	18	15	15
251	Struct.metal products, tanks, reservoirs	565	501	481	956p/	12350	11890	11150	10460	732	732	732	744

continued

New Zealand

ISIC Revision 4

ISIC	Industry	Number of enterprises (number)					Number of persons engaged (number)					Wages and salaries paid to employees (millions of New Zealand Dollars)				
		Note	2012	2013	2014	2015	Note	2012	2013	2014	2015	Note	2012	2013	2014	2015
2511	Structural metal products		723	711	714	711		9900	10600	11300	11800		...	452	462	528
2512	Tanks, reservoirs and containers of metal		21	21	18	21		560	550	590	550		...	29	39	37
2513	Steam generators, excl. hot water boilers		-	-	-	-		-	-	-	-		-	-	-	-
2520	Weapons and ammunition		-	-	-	-		-	-	-	-		...p/	...	...	...
259	Other metal products;metal working services		1017	984	972	966		11010	11180	11600	11430		...p/	479	487	515
2591	Forging,pressing,stamping,roll-forming of metal		18	15	15	12		160	180	150	130		...	...	...	...
2592	Treatment and coating of metals; machining		180	174	171	183		1350	1300	1350	1300		...	45	46	50
2593	Cutlery, hand tools and general hardware		-	-	-	-		-	-	-	-		-	-	-	-
2599	Other fabricated metal products n.e.c.		819	795	786	771		9500	9700	10100	10000		...	425	434	459
2610	Electronic components and boards		15	15	12	15		-	-	-	-		272 q/	...	...	...
2620	Computers and peripheral equipment		12	12	12	15		100	80	95	110		...q/	1	1	2
2630	Communication equipment		12	12	12	15		800	720	790	760		...q/	...	...	...
2640	Consumer electronics		114	117	117	108		2650	2550	2800	2750		...q/	167	147	144
265	Measuring,testing equipment; watches, etc.		36	36	39	39		620	640	670	720		...q/	25	42	44
2651	Measuring/testing/navigating equipment,etc.		36	36	39	39		620	640	670	720		...	25	42	44
2652	Watches and clocks		-	-	-	-		-	-	-	-		-	-	-	-
2660	Irradiation/electromedical equipment,etc.		-	-	-	-		-	-	-	-		...q/	...	...	...
2670	Optical instruments and photographic equipment		12	12	12	12		160	150	150	160		...q/	...	...	...
2680	Magnetic and optical media		-	-	-	-		-	-	-	-		...q/	...	...	...
2710	Electric motors,generators,transformers,etc.		-	-	-	-		-	-	-	-		247 r/	...	...	...
2720	Batteries and accumulators		-	-	-	-		-	-	-	-		...r/	...	...	...
273	Wiring and wiring devices		12	9	9	15		480	480	430	400		...r/	41	41	40
2731	Fibre optic cables		-	-	-	-		-	-	-	-		-	-	-	-
2732	Other electronic and electric wires and cables		12	9	9	15		480	480	430	400		...	41	41	40
2733	Wiring devices		-	-	-	-		-	-	-	-		-	-	-	-
2740	Electric lighting equipment		45	36	39	39		470	430	410	420		...r/	11	16	5
2750	Domestic appliances		30	30	36	30		1600	1750	1750	1850		...r/	92	90	111
2790	Other electrical equipment		108	105	105	99		2500	2450	2350	2350		...r/	93	90	105
281	General-purpose machinery		1077	1068	1071	1095		11830	11860	12100	12320		798 s/	632	608	688
2811	Engines/turbines,excl.aircraft,vehicle engines		18	15	18	18		210	210	240	270		-	-	-	-
2812	Fluid power equipment		-	-	-	-		-	-	-	-		...	...	...	...
2813	Other pumps, compressors, taps and valves		-	-	-	-		-	-	-	-		...	...	...	...
2814	Bearings, gears, gearing and driving elements		-	-	-	-		-	-	-	-		...	...	...	...
2815	Ovens, furnaces and furnace burners		-	-	-	-		-	-	-	-		...	...	...	...
2816	Lifting and handling equipment		36	42	39	39		620	650	700	730		...	39	25	42
2817	Office machinery, excl.computers,etc.		-	-	-	-		-	-	-	-		...	...	...	...
2818	Power-driven hand tools		96	93	90	87		1000	900	960	920		...	59	48	68
2819	Other general-purpose machinery		927	918	924	951		10000	10100	10200	10400		...	524	524	565
282	Special-purpose machinery		207	207	216	210		3300	3400	3660	3550		...s/	165	190	201
2821	Agricultural and forestry machinery		132	132	135	129		2300	2300	2500	2400		...	104	122	143
2822	Metal-forming machinery and machine tools		-	-	-	-		-	-	-	-		...	...	...	...

Code	Description												
2823	Machinery for metallurgy	15	-	-	-	-	-	-	-	…	…	…	12
2824	Mining, quarrying and construction machinery	-	12	15	15	320	230	230	220	…	…	…	-
2825	Food/beverage/tobacco processing machinery	-	-	-	-	-	-	-	-	…	…	…	-
2826	Textile/apparel/leather production machinery	-	-	-	-	-	-	-	-	…	…	…	-
2829	Other special-purpose machinery	60	63	66	66	680	870	930	930	…	40	54	46
2910	Motor vehicles	24	24	30	30	160	160	210	230	192t/	1	1	1
2920	Automobile bodies, trailers and semi-trailers	156	150	159	165	2050	2250	2300	2400	..t/	103	114	144
2930	Parts and accessories for motor vehicles	138	135	135	126	1300	1300	1250	1200	..t/	87	89	102
301	Building of ships and boats	252	243	246	243	3050	2870	2650	2680	521u/	180	178	140
3011	Building of ships and floating structures	21	18	18	21	900	770	450	480	…	63	57	49
3012	Building of pleasure and sporting boats	231	225	228	222	2150	2100	2200	2200	…	116	122	91
3020	Railway locomotives and rolling stock	3	3	3	-	9	35	60	60	..u/	…	…	…
3030	Air and spacecraft and related machinery	96	96	93	99	1700	1650	1650	1900	..u/	334	311	336
3040	Military fighting vehicles	-	-	-	-	-	-	-	-	..u/	1	1	1
309	Transport equipment n.e.c.	15	18	21	21	85	85	95	110	..u/	1	1	1
3091	Motorcycles	-	-	-	-	-	-	-	-	…	…	…	…
3092	Bicycles and invalid carriages	-	-	-	-	-	-	-	-	…	…	…	…
3099	Other transport equipment n.e.c.	15	18	21	21	85	85	95	110	…	1	1	1
3100	Furniture	645	651	633	627	4950	5500	5500	5700	227	227	228	235
321	Jewellery, bijouterie and related articles	138	138	138	132	650	650	630	610	266v/	22	23	24
3211	Jewellery and related articles	138	138	138	132	650	650	630	610	…	22	23	24
3212	Imitation jewellery and related articles	-	-	-	-	-	-	-	-	…	…	…	…
3220	Musical instruments	-	-	-	-	-	-	-	-	..v/	…	…	…
3230	Sports goods	60	54	57	63	380	370	350	380	..v/	13	13	12
3240	Games and toys	-	-	-	-	-	-	-	-	..v/	…	…	…
3250	Medical and dental instruments and supplies	129	129	132	135	2700	2900	3050	3300	..v/	165	173	202
3290	Other manufacturing n.e.c.	168	183	198	210	1450	1600	1650	1750	..v/	63	69	74
331	Repair of fabricated metal products/machinery	570	585	597	612	3670	3990	4240	4260	172w/	175	184	204
3311	Repair of fabricated metal products	-	-	-	-	-	-	-	-	…	…	…	…
3312	Repair of machinery	432	450	453	468	3250	3550	3750	3750	…	161	166	186
3313	Repair of electronic and optical equipment	-	-	-	-	-	-	-	-	…	…	…	…
3314	Repair of electrical equipment	-	-	-	-	-	-	-	-	…	…	…	…
3315	Repair of transport equip., excl. motor vehicles	-	-	-	-	-	-	-	-	…	…	…	…
3319	Repair of other equipment	138	135	144	144	420	440	490	510	…	13	18	18
3320	Installation of industrial machinery/equipment	-	-	-	-	-	-	-	-	..w/	…	…	…
C	Total manufacturing	11865	11745	11754	11838	227349	228175	239485	242290	12201	12151	12501	13122

a/ 1010 includes 1020, 1030, 1040, 1050, 106, 107 and 1080.
b/ 110 includes 1200.
c/ 131 includes 139.
d/ 1410 includes 1420 and 1430.
e/ 151 includes 1520.
f/ 1610 includes 162.
g/ 1701 includes 1702 and 1709.
h/ 181 includes 1820.
i/ 1910 includes 1920.
j/ 201 includes 202 and 2030.

k/ 221 includes 2220.
m/ 2310 includes 239.
n/ 2410 includes 2420 and 243.
p/ 251 includes 2520 and 259.
q/ 2610 includes 2620, 2630, 2640, 265, 2660, 2670 and 2680.
r/ 2710 includes 2720, 273, 2740, 2750 and 2790.
s/ 281 includes 282.
t/ 2910 includes 2920 and 2930.
u/ 301 includes 3020, 3030, 3040 and 309.
v/ 321 includes 3220, 3230, 3240, 3250 and 3290.

w/ 331 includes 3320.

New Zealand

ISIC Revision 4		Note	Output (valuation not defined) (millions of New Zealand Dollars)				Note	Value added (valuation not defined) (millions of New Zealand Dollars)				Note	Gross fixed capital formation (millions of New Zealand Dollars)	
ISIC	Industry		2012	2013	2014	2015		2012	2013	2014	2015		2014	2015
1010	Processing/preserving of meat		34904a/	9138	9866	11173		6463a/	1685	1715	2034		...	...
1020	Processing/preserving of fish, etc.		...a/	1417	1507	1450		...a/	405	469	479		...	...
1030	Processing/preserving of fruit,vegetables		...a/	1545	1514	1392		...a/	412	381	354		...	...
1040	Vegetable and animal oils and fats		...a/	...	...	...		...a/	...	21	...		...	...
1050	Dairy products		...a/	17247	...	16898		...a/	2307	1726	...		...	...
106	Grain mill products,starches and starch products		...a/	...	631	674		...	...	137	157		...	...
1061	Grain mill products		...	...	631	674		...	...	137	157		...	...
1062	Starches and starch products		...	...	-	-		...	...	-	-		...	...
107	Other food products		...a/	...	4382	...		...a/	...	1393	1453		...	...
1071	Bakery products		...	...	1820	...		...	...	598	619		...	...
1072	Sugar		...	...	...	...		...	...	...	...		...	...
1073	Cocoa, chocolate and sugar confectionery		...	...	372	...		...	...	131	158		...	...
1074	Macaroni, noodles, couscous, etc.		...	...	...	...		...	...	...	...		...	...
1075	Prepared meals and dishes		...	...	...	...		...	...	...	...		...	...
1079	Other food products n.e.c.		...	...	...	...		...	...	...	...		...	...
1080	Prepared animal feeds		...a/	299	418	298		...a/	37	45	32		...	...
110	Beverages	b/	5212	5096	5092	5063	b/	2473	2338	2461	2433		...	...
1101	Distilling, rectifying and blending of spirits		...	...	...	...		...	...	...	...		...	...
1102	Wines		...	...	...	...		...	...	...	...		...	...
1103	Malt liquors and malt		...	...	...	...		...	...	...	...		...	...
1104	Soft drinks,mineral waters,other bottled waters		...	...	...	...		...	...	...	...		...	...
1200	Tobacco products	b/	...	...	...	...	b/	...	...	...	...		...	...
131	Spinning, weaving and finishing of textiles		1498c/	837	786	803		340c/	184	172	175		...	...
1311	Preparation and spinning of textile fibres		...	672	617	615		...	127	113	118		...	...
1312	Weaving of textiles		...	-	-	-		...	-	-	-		...	...
1313	Finishing of textiles		...	165	169	188		...	57	59	57		...	...
139	Other textiles		...c/	662	745	785		...c/	155	206	203		...	...
1391	Knitted and crocheted fabrics		...	...	...	74		...	...	...	32		...	...
1392	Made-up textile articles, except apparel		...	244	262	284		...	76	97	105		...	...
1393	Carpets and rugs		...	...	...	...		...	...	...	...		...	...
1394	Cordage, rope, twine and netting		...	...	...	...		...	...	...	...		...	...
1399	Other textiles n.e.c.		...	...	...	...		...	...	...	...		...	...
1410	Wearing apparel, except fur apparel		384d/	353	360	389		153d/	149	152	166		...	...
1420	Articles of fur		...d/	...	...	...		...d/	...	...	...		...	...
1430	Knitted and crocheted apparel		...d/	...	...	...		...d/	...	...	...		...	...
151	Leather;luggage,handbags,saddlery,harness;fur		306e/	266	319	289		78e/	...	63	85		...	...
1511	Tanning/dressing of leather; dressing of fur		...	266	319	289		...	63	63	85		...	...
1512	Luggage,handbags,etc.;saddlery/harness		...	-	-	-		...	-	-	-		...	...
1520	Footwear		...e/	40	42	18		...e/	15	17	7		...	...
1610	Sawmilling and planing of wood		4336f/	2525	2486	2476		1148f/	593	579	582		...	...

Code	Description								
162	Wood products, cork, straw, plaiting materials	595	597	553	...f/	2180	2029	1802	...f/
1621	Veneer sheets and wood-based panels	339	332	299	...	1130	995	831	...
1622	Builders' carpentry and joinery	...	...	...	...	...	...	...	...
1623	Wooden containers	...	...	...	...	...	...	...	...
1629	Other wood products;articles of cork,straw	86	81	67	...	297	281	214	...
170	Paper and paper products	576	617	541	541	2779	2877	2917	2918
1701	Pulp, paper and paperboard	...	...	...	541g/	...	...	...	2918g/
1702	Corrugated paper and paperboard	95	96	105	...g/	348	390	431	...g/
1709	Other articles of paper and paperboard	...	...	...	...g/	...	...	...	...g/
181	Printing and service activities related to printing	659	638	658	667h/	1626	1536	1553	1576h/
1811	Printing	606	582	600	...	1489	1388	1418	...
1812	Service activities related to printing	54	56	58	...	137	148	135	...
1820	Reproduction of recorded media	10	8	9	...h/	17	19	22	...h/
1910	Coke oven products	-	-	-	3811i/	-	-	-	10021i/
1920	Refined petroleum products	2750	2736	2765	...i/	8212	8990	8923	...i/
201	Basic chemicals,fertilizers, etc.	620	627	460	915j/	2827	2605	2408	3901j/
2011	Basic chemicals	298	253	257	...	...	...	...	...
2012	Fertilizers and nitrogen compounds	248	301	...	...	...	...	...	...
2013	Plastics and synthetic rubber in primary forms	74	73	56	...j/	295	266	285	...j/
202	Other chemical products	455	462	454	...	1473	1530	1494	...
2021	Pesticides and other agrochemical products	...	...	...	...	...	...	...	...
2022	Paints,varnishes;printing ink and mastics	238	245	222	...	753	742	711	711
2023	Soap,cleaning and cosmetic preparations	120	115	120	...	343	348	348	345
2029	Other chemical products n.e.c.	78	78	90	...j/	...	...	...	...
2030	Man-made fibres	-	-	...	...j/	-	-	...	...j/
2100	Pharmaceuticals,medicinal chemicals, etc.	273	251	261	211	781	746	726	630
221	Rubber products	81	70	74	992k/	178	204	156	2640k/
2211	Rubber tyres and tubes	...	...	...	...	...	...	...	...
2219	Other rubber products	...	...	...	...	103	128	116	116
2220	Plastics products	899	903	911	...k/	2434	2451	2483	...k/
2310	Glass and glass products	273	245	218	867m/	576	558	513	2377m/
239	Non-metallic mineral products n.e.c.	778	790	651	...m/	2345	2218	1918	...m/
2391	Refractory products	...	...	...	...	...	...	...	...
2392	Clay building materials	22	25	17	...	57	64	57	...
2393	Other porcelain and ceramic products	...	...	...	...	...	...	...	...
2394	Cement, lime and plaster	...	...	...	...	1635	1491	1203	...
2395	Articles of concrete, cement and plaster	529	535	414	...	...	...	...	...
2396	Cutting, shaping and finishing of stone	...	...	...	...	...	...	...	...
2399	Other non-metallic mineral products n.e.c.	46	38	44	...	108	97	105	...
2410	Basic iron and steel	293	292	268	518n/	...	...	...	3479n/
2420	Basic precious and other non-ferrous metals	305	217	200	...n/	187	211	221	...n/
243	Casting of metals	46	45	50	...n/	...	...	...	...
2431	Casting of iron and steel	...	...	...	...	...	...	...	...
2432	Casting of non-ferrous metals	...	...	...	...	...	...	...	...
251	Struct.metal products, tanks, reservoirs	992	867	817	1671p/	3052	2790	2599	4775p/

continued

New Zealand

ISIC	Industry	Output (valuation not defined) (millions of New Zealand Dollars)					Value added (valuation not defined) (millions of New Zealand Dollars)					Gross fixed capital formation (millions of New Zealand Dollars)		
	ISIC Revision 4	Note	2012	2013	2014	2015	Note	2012	2013	2014	2015	Note	2014	2015
2511	Structural metal products		...	2384	2638	2902		...	761	809	950		...	...
2512	Tanks, reservoirs and containers of metal		...	215	153	150		...	56	58	42		...	...
2513	Steam generators, excl. hot water boilers		...	-	-	-		...	-	-	-		...	...
2520	Weapons and ammunition		...p/					...p/					...	...
259	Other metal products;metal working services		...p/	2252	2256	2221		...p/	862	911	827		...	...
2591	Forging,pressing,stamping,roll-forming of metal								...	...	...			
2592	Treatment and coating of metals; machining		...	214	185	199			87	85	98			
2593	Cutlery, hand tools and general hardware								...	...	...			
2599	Other fabricated metal products n.e.c.		...	2004	2039	1996			761	815	719			
2610	Electronic components and boards		1210q/					376q/	...	...	...			
2620	Computers and peripheral equipment		...q/	9	10	10		...q/	3	5	3			
2630	Communication equipment		...q/					...q/						
2640	Consumer electronics		...q/	764	803	779		...q/	201	222	228			
265	Measuring,testing equipment; watches, etc.		...q/	131	156	160		...q/	38	65	60		...	
2651	Measuring/testing/navigating equipment,etc.			131	156	160			38	65	60			
2652	Watches and clocks		...q/	-	-	-		...q/			-			
2660	Irradiation/electromedical equipment,etc.		...q/					...q/						
2670	Optical instruments and photographic equipment		...q/					...q/						
2680	Magnetic and optical media		...q/					...q/						
2710	Electric motors,generators,transformers,etc.		1340r/					280r/						
2720	Batteries and accumulators		...r/					...r/						
273	Wiring and wiring devices		...r/					...r/	45	76	63			
2731	Fibre optic cables													
2732	Other electronic and electric wires and cables								45	76	63			
2733	Wiring devices													
2740	Electric lighting equipment		...r/	50	69	41		...r/	23	23	19			
2750	Domestic appliances		...r/					...r/	135	71	124			
2790	Other electrical equipment		...r/	448	432	471		...r/	143	155	160			
281	General-purpose machinery		3305s/	2387	2395	2549		1332s/	1030	1022	1141		...	...
2811	Engines/turbines,excl.aircraft,vehicle engines													
2812	Fluid power equipment													
2813	Other pumps, compressors, taps and valves												...	...
2814	Bearings, gears, gearing and driving elements													
2815	Ovens, furnaces and furnace burners													
2816	Lifting and handling equipment		...	149	141	147			50	45	70			
2817	Office machinery, excl.computers,etc.													
2818	Power-driven hand tools		...	194	162	219			89	76	105			
2819	Other general-purpose machinery		...	1992	2040	2127			874	882	945			
282	Special-purpose machinery		...s/	913	904	991		...s/	295	318	324			
2821	Agricultural and forestry machinery		...	597	600	748			172	209	227			
2822	Metal-forming machinery and machine tools		...					...					...	

Code	Activity								
2823	Machinery for metallurgy	...	...	...	...	...	...	...	...
2824	Mining, quarrying and construction machinery	...	...	...	55	...	...	...	25
2825	Food/beverage/tobacco processing machinery	...	...	...	...	...	...	...	...
2826	Textile/apparel/leather production machinery	...	...	...	...	...	...	...	...
2829	Other special-purpose machinery	...	231	250	188	...	93	91	72
2910	Motor vehicles	820 t/	9	10	68	210 t/	3	3	-2
2920	Automobile bodies, trailers and semi-trailers	... t/	499	469	606	... t/	144	172	227
2930	Parts and accessories for motor vehicles	... t/	312	328	394	... t/	64	90	137
301	Building of ships and boats	1726 u/	521	546	437	651 u/	199	223	143
3011	Building of ships and floating structures	...	169	147	113	...	71	69	40
3012	Building of pleasure and sporting boats	...	353	399	324	...	128	155	102
3020	Railway locomotives and rolling stock	... u/	...	...	...	... u/	...	...	...
3030	Air and spacecraft and related machinery	... u/	1133	1109	1257	... u/	407	427	482
3040	Military fighting vehicles	... u/	...	...	...	... u/	...	...	...
309	Transport equipment n.e.c.	... u/	6	6	8	... u/	2	2	2
3091	Motorcycles	...	...	...	...	...	...	...	...
3092	Bicycles and invalid carriages	...	...	...	...	...	...	...	...
3099	Other transport equipment n.e.c.	...	6	6	8	...	2	2	2
3100	Furniture	953	958	1054	1081	...	374	401	415
321	Jewellery, bijouterie and related articles	1014 v/	176	166	165	475 v/	50	47	51
3211	Jewellery and related articles	...	176	166	165	...	50	47	51
3212	Imitation jewellery and related articles	...	-	-	-	...	-	-	-
3220	Musical instruments	... v/	...	...	...	... v/	...	...	...
3230	Sports goods	... v/	65	61	58	... v/	23	25	23
3240	Games and toys	... v/	...	...	...	... v/	...	...	...
3250	Medical and dental instruments and supplies	... v/	531	572	672	... v/	272	295	370
3290	Other manufacturing n.e.c.	... v/	270	276	294	... v/	118	118	133
331	Repair of fabricated metal products/machinery	619 w/	623	666	737	313 w/	316	333	386
3311	Repair of fabricated metal products	...	...	...	...	...	...	...	...
3312	Repair of machinery	...	561	598	664	...	279	295	345
3313	Repair of electronic and optical equipment	...	...	...	...	...	...	...	...
3314	Repair of electrical equipment	...	...	...	...	...	...	...	...
3315	Repair of transport equip., excl. motor vehicles	...	...	...	...	...	...	...	...
3319	Repair of other equipment	...	62	68	72	...	36	38	41
3320	Installation of industrial machinery/equipment	... w/	-	-	-	... w/	-	-	-
C	Total manufacturing	89944	88701	96128	92597	24860	23611	23994	26587

a/ 1010 includes 1020, 1030, 1040, 1050, 106, 107 and 1080.
b/ 110 includes 1200.
c/ 131 includes 139.
d/ 1410 includes 1420 and 1430.
e/ 151 includes 1520.
f/ 1610 includes 162.
g/ 1701 includes 1702 and 1709.
h/ 181 includes 1820.
i/ 1910 includes 1920.
j/ 201 includes 202 and 2030.

k/ 221 includes 2220.
m/ 2310 includes 239.
n/ 2410 includes 2420 and 243.
p/ 251 includes 2520 and 259.
q/ 2610 includes 2620, 2630, 2640, 265, 2660, 2670 and 2680.
r/ 2710 includes 2720, 273, 2740, 2750 and 2790.
s/ 281 includes 282.
t/ 2910 includes 2920 and 2930.
u/ 301 includes 3020, 3030, 3040 and 309.
v/ 321 includes 3220, 3230, 3240, 3250 and 3290.

w/ 331 includes 3320.

New Zealand

Index numbers of industrial production

| ISIC Revision 4 | | | | (2010=100) | | | | | | | | | | |
ISIC	Industry	Note	2005	2006	2007	2008	2009	2010	2011	2012	2013	2014	2015	2016
10	Food products	a/	105	109	105	106	102	100	98	100	105	105	105	108
11	Beverages	a/	...	...	...	...	...	...	...	...	...	...	...	...
12	Tobacco products	a/	...	...	...	...	...	...	...	...	...	...	...	...
13	Textiles	b/	120	118	122	119	109	100	103	90	89	91	93	88
14	Wearing apparel	b/	...	...	...	...	...	...	...	...	...	...	...	...
15	Leather and related products	b/	...	...	...	...	...	...	...	...	...	...	...	...
16	Wood products, excluding furniture	c/	112	112	110	110	97	100	105	102	99	100	101	106
17	Paper and paper products	c/	...	...	...	...	...	...	...	...	...	...	...	...
18	Printing and reproduction of recorded media	d/	129	126	117	117	105	100	98	92	91	90	93	85
19	Coke and refined petroleum products	d/	117	117	113	112	104	100	105	105	109	110	106	110
20	Chemicals and chemical products	d/	...	...	...	...	...	...	...	...	...	...	...	...
21	Pharmaceuticals,medicinal chemicals, etc.	d/	...	...	...	...	...	...	...	...	...	...	...	...
22	Rubber and plastics products	d/	...	...	...	...	...	...	...	...	...	...	...	...
23	Other non-metallic mineral products	e/	118	117	121	128	116	100	99	97	105	118	127	130
24	Basic metals	e/	149	148	141	136	116	100	103	99	99	100	106	109
25	Fabricated metal products, except machinery	e/	...	...	...	...	...	...	...	...	...	...	...	...
26	Computer, electronic and optical products	f/	115	117	111	120	107	100	108	109	105	104	110	112
27	Electrical equipment	f/	...	...	...	...	...	...	...	...	...	...	...	...
28	Machinery and equipment n.e.c.	f/	...	...	...	...	...	...	...	...	...	...	...	...
29	Motor vehicles, trailers and semi-trailers	f/	...	...	...	...	...	...	...	...	...	...	...	...
30	Other transport equipment	f/	...	...	...	...	...	...	...	...	...	...	...	...
31	Furniture	g/	139	136	132	122	105	100	100	98	96	100	101	102
32	Other manufacturing	g/	...	...	...	...	...	...	...	...	...	...	...	...
33	Repair and installation of machinery/equipment		...	...	...	...	...	...	...	...	...	...	...	...
C	Total manufacturing		116	117	114	115	105	100	102	102	103	104	106	108

a/ 10 includes 11 and 12.
b/ 13 includes 14 and 15.
c/ 16 includes 17.
d/ 19 includes 20, 21 and 22.
e/ 24 includes 25.
f/ 26 includes 27, 28, 29 and 30.
g/ 31 includes 32.

Niger

Supplier of information:
Institut national de la statistique, Niamey.

Basic source of data:
Survey; administrative source.

Major deviations from ISIC (Revision 3):
Data presented in accordance with ISIC (Revision 3) were originally classified according to the national classification system.

Reference period:
Calendar year.

Scope:
Not reported.

Method of data collection:
Mail questionnaires and direct interview in the field.

Type of enumeration:
Complete enumeration.

Adjusted for non-response:
Yes.

Concepts and definitions of variables:
No deviations from the standard UN concepts and definitions are reported.

Related national publications:
Comptes économiques de la Nation, published by the Institut national de la statistique, Niamey.

Niger

ISIC	Industry	Number of establishments (number)					Number of employees (number)					Wages and salaries paid to employees (millions of West African CFA Francs)				
		Note	2013a/	2014a/	2015a/	2016a/	Note	2013a/	2014a/	2015a/	2016a/	Note	2013	2014a/	2015a/	2016a/
15	Food and beverages		23692	24402	25134	26338		4758	4899	5044	5246		...	10584	11386	11862
16	Tobacco products		...	...	...	...		...	...	...	...		...	...	...	...
17	Textiles		29947	30845	31771	32102		3907	4023	4143	4328		...	2930	2821	2939
18	Wearing apparel, fur		...	...	...	...		...	...	...	...		...	...	...	...
19	Leather, leather products and footwear		...	...	...	...		...	...	...	...		...	...	...	...
20	Wood products (excl. furniture)		3067	3159	3254	3288		1988	2047	2108	2251		...	...	...	...
21	Paper and paper products		4157	4314	4478	4508		1184	1215	1246	1294		...	...	...	...
22	Printing and publishing		...	...	...	...		...	...	...	...		...	...	...	...
23	Coke,refined petroleum products,nuclear fuel		...	...	...	...		670	689	709	725		...	18888	20392	22285
24	Chemicals and chemical products		4902	5087	5280	5315		...	...	...	...		...	...	...	...
25	Rubber and plastics products		...	...	...	...		...	...	...	...		...	...	...	...
26	Non-metallic mineral products		...	...	...	...		...	...	...	...		...	...	...	...
27	Basic metals		...	...	...	...		...	...	...	...		...	...	...	...
28	Fabricated metal products		...	...	...	...		...	...	...	...		...	...	...	...
29	Machinery and equipment n.e.c.		...	...	...	...		...	...	...	...		...	...	...	...
30	Office, accounting and computing machinery		...	...	...	...		...	...	...	...		...	...	...	...
31	Electrical machinery and apparatus		...	...	...	...		...	...	...	...		...	...	...	...
32	Radio,television and communication equipment		...	...	...	...		...	...	...	...		...	...	...	...
33	Medical, precision and optical instruments		...	...	...	...		...	...	...	...		...	...	...	...
34	Motor vehicles, trailers, semi-trailers		...	...	...	...		...	...	...	...		...	...	...	...
35	Other transport equipment		...	...	...	...		...	...	...	...		...	...	...	...
36	Furniture; manufacturing n.e.c.		15367	15636	15910	16014		4954	5097	5244	5392		...	4297	6496	6768
37	Recycling		...	...	...	...		...	...	...	...		...	...	...	...
D	Total manufacturing		81132	83443	85827	87565		17461	17970	18494	19236		...	36699	41095	43854

a/ Data are aggregated from incomplete 3- and/or 4-digit level of ISICs.

Niger

ISIC	Industry	Note	Output (valuation not defined) (millions of West African CFA Francs) 2013	2014a/	2015a/	2016a/	Note	Value added (valuation not defined) (millions of West African CFA Francs) 2013	2014a/	2015a/	2016a/	Note	Gross fixed capital formation (millions of West African CFA Francs) 2015	2016
15	Food and beverages		...	288346	301560	306296		...	91474	90752	111215		...	...
16	Tobacco products		...	...	...	...		...	...	...	...		...	...
17	Textiles		...	47797	51239	53838		...	21007	23872	28444		...	...
18	Wearing apparel, fur		...	...	...	...		...	...	...	...		...	...
19	Leather, leather products and footwear		...	...	...	...		...	...	...	...		...	...
20	Wood products (excl. furniture)		...	...	...	...		...	...	...	...		...	...
21	Paper and paper products		...	...	...	...		...	...	...	...		...	...
22	Printing and publishing		...	...	...	...		...	...	...	...		...	...
23	Coke, refined petroleum products, nuclear fuel		...	354364	266095	231281		...	49501	26100	49106		...	...
24	Chemicals and chemical products		...	...	...	...		...	...	...	...		...	...
25	Rubber and plastics products		...	...	...	...		...	...	...	...		...	...
26	Non-metallic mineral products		...	...	...	...		...	...	...	...		...	...
27	Basic metals		...	...	...	...		...	...	...	...		...	...
28	Fabricated metal products		...	...	...	...		...	...	...	...		...	...
29	Machinery and equipment n.e.c.		...	...	...	...		...	...	...	...		...	...
30	Office, accounting and computing machinery		...	...	...	...		...	...	...	...		...	...
31	Electrical machinery and apparatus		...	...	...	...		...	...	...	...		...	...
32	Radio, television and communication equipment		...	...	...	...		...	...	...	...		...	...
33	Medical, precision and optical instruments		...	...	...	...		...	...	...	...		...	...
34	Motor vehicles, trailers, semi-trailers		...	...	...	...		...	...	...	...		...	...
35	Other transport equipment		...	...	...	...		...	...	...	...		...	...
36	Furniture; manufacturing n.e.c.		...	115675	114033	116070		...	56623	51438	64533		...	...
37	Recycling		...	...	...	...		...	...	...	...		...	...
D	Total manufacturing		...	806182	732927	707485		...	218605	192162	253298		45500	45720

a/ Data are aggregated from incomplete 3- and/or 4-digit level of ISICs.

Niger

Index numbers of industrial production

ISIC Revision 3

(2010=100)

ISIC	Industry	Note	2005	2006	2007	2008	2009	2010	2011	2012	2013	2014	2015	2016
15	Food and beverages		...	...	...	...	78	100	102	102	150	121	151	130
16	Tobacco products		...	...	...	...	...	...	...	...	...	...	...	...
17	Textiles	a/	...	...	...	...	104	100	57	76	78	56	57	49
18	Wearing apparel, fur	a/	...	...	...	...	...	...	...	...	...	...	...	...
19	Leather, leather products and footwear		...	...	...	...	...	...	...	...	...	...	...	...
20	Wood products (excl. furniture)		...	...	...	...	...	...	...	...	...	...	...	...
21	Paper and paper products		...	...	...	...	...	...	...	...	...	...	...	...
22	Printing and publishing		...	...	...	...	166	100	199	108	76	100	181	712
23	Coke,refined petroleum products,nuclear fuel		...	...	...	...	...	...	...	...	...	...	...	...
24	Chemicals and chemical products	b/	...	...	...	...	106	100	199	94	106	99	92	85
25	Rubber and plastics products	b/	...	...	...	...	...	...	...	...	...	...	...	...
26	Non-metallic mineral products		...	...	...	...	137	100	243	247	97	69	173	20
27	Basic metals	c/	...	...	...	...	91	100	181	105	79	143	151	158
28	Fabricated metal products	c/	...	...	...	...	...	...	...	...	...	...	...	...
29	Machinery and equipment n.e.c.		...	...	...	...	...	...	...	...	...	...	...	...
30	Office, accounting and computing machinery		...	...	...	...	...	...	...	...	...	...	...	...
31	Electrical machinery and apparatus		...	...	...	...	...	...	...	...	...	...	...	...
32	Radio,television and communication equipment		...	...	...	...	...	...	...	...	...	...	...	...
33	Medical, precision and optical instruments		...	...	...	...	...	...	...	...	...	...	...	...
34	Motor vehicles, trailers, semi-trailers		...	...	...	...	...	...	...	...	...	...	...	...
35	Other transport equipment		...	...	...	...	...	...	...	...	...	...	...	...
36	Furniture; manufacturing n.e.c.		...	...	...	...	...	...	...	...	...	...	...	...
37	Recycling		...	...	...	...	...	...	...	...	...	...	...	...
D	Total manufacturing		...	46	46	53	94	100	134	115	156	142	122	130

a/ 17 includes 18.
b/ 24 includes 25.
c/ 27 includes 28.

Norway

Supplier of information:
Statistics Norway, Oslo.
Industrial statistics for the OECD countries are compiled by the OECD secretariat, which supplies them to UNIDO.

Basic source of data:
Annual inquires; registers; annual company accounts.

Major deviations from ISIC (Revision 4):
Data presented in ISIC (Revision 4) were originally classified according to the national NACE-related classification system.

Reference period:
Calendar year.

Scope:
Enterprises with individual proprietorship, where the owner works alone and local kind-of-activity-units with employment of less than half a man-year are excluded.

Method of data collection:
Not reported.

Type of enumeration:
Not reported.

Adjusted for non-response:
Not reported.

Concepts and definitions of variables:
No deviations from the standard UN concepts and definitions are reported.

Related national publications:
Statistical Yearbook of Norway, published by Statistics Norway, Oslo.

Norway

ISIC	Industry	Number of enterprises (number) Note	2013	2014	2015	2016	Number of employees (number) Note	2013	2014	2015	2016	Wages and salaries paid to employees (millions of Norwegian Kroner) Note	2013	2014	2015	2016
1010	Processing/preserving of meat		335	328	368	363		13349	13139	12640	12488		5131	5324	5196	5269
1020	Processing/preserving of fish, etc.		466	441	446	448		9722	9867	10661	10497		3902	4228	4377	4417
1030	Processing/preserving of fruit,vegetables		75	79	83	96		1184	1236	1297	1407		498	536	552	622
1040	Vegetable and animal oils and fats		30	31	32	34		406	415	398	542		226	238	209	319
1050	Dairy products		59	60	65	73		6862	7312	6811	6800		3323	3408	3327	3411
106	Grain mill products,starches and starch products		35	33	35	35		591	564	580	571		274	277	279	295
1061	Grain mill products		35	33	34	34		591	564	580	571		274	277	279a/	295a/
1062	Starches and starch products		-	-	-	1		-	-	-	-		-	-	...a/	...a/
107	Other food products		873	929	995	1053		11475	11660	13405	13714		3859	3952	4237	4525
1071	Bakery products		659	688	733	764		8284	8446	9614	9618		...	...	...	2699
1072	Sugar		1	1	1	1		2	2	1	2		...	...	...	...
1073	Cocoa, chocolate and sugar confectionery		42	43	44	42		1276	1176	1201	1190		554	539	531	528
1074	Macaroni, noodles, couscous, etc.		1	1	2	-		1	2	5	-		...	...	...	-
1075	Prepared meals and dishes		41	44	47	53		369	409	691	1016		123	137	229	390
1079	Other food products n.e.c.		129	152	168	193		1543	1625	1893	1888		...	...	...	...
1080	Prepared animal feeds		85	82	86	85		2193	2276	2393	2308		1160	1252	1289	1257
110	Beverages		113	142	199	244		3913	3682	3638	3616		1832	1759	1734	1779
1101	Distilling, rectifying and blending of spirits		18	17	20	23		176	172	170	171		...	...	...	...
1102	Wines		5	4	5	5		1	-	1	1		...	...	...	...
1103	Malt liquors and malt		49	76	124	166		2373	2320	2199	2192		1137	1115	...	...
1104	Soft drinks,mineral waters,other bottled waters		41	45	50	50		1363	1190	1268	1252		615	572	599	575
1200	Tobacco products		-	-	-	-		-	-	-	-		-	-	-	-
131	Spinning, weaving and finishing of textiles		133	121	119	117		495	478	484	483		184	175	172	170
1311	Preparation and spinning of textile fibres		17	20	20	26		196	192	179	188		72	65	61	65
1312	Weaving of textiles		42	38	36	33		164	158	164	150		62	61	58	55
1313	Finishing of textiles		74	63	63	58		135	128	141	145		51	48	53	50
139	Other textiles		453	446	445	447		2167	2152	2140	2137		846	868	872	914
1391	Knitted and crocheted fabrics		11	8	7	9		9	8	1	1		...	...	...	...
1392	Made-up textile articles, except apparel		297	300	297	293		1064	1108	1070	1091		410	438	438	470
1393	Carpets and rugs		8	7	6	6		40	34	17	19		16	11	4	4
1394	Cordage, rope, twine and netting		49	44	40	42		802	720	795	789		326	312	328	348
1399	Other textiles n.e.c.		88	87	95	97		252	282	257	237		...	...	...	...
1410	Wearing apparel, except fur apparel		743	773	822	866		977	991	1038	1228		322	348	329	404
1420	Articles of fur		24	18	21	20		16	13	13	11		3	3	2	2
1430	Knitted and crocheted apparel		70	69	73	63		181	160	177	182		61	53	54	57
151	Leather;luggage,handbags,saddlery,harness;fur		47	44	52	53		66	71	104	105		20	21	25	27
1511	Tanning/dressing of leather; dressing of fur		13	12	16	15		52	50	81	82		15	16	20	20
1512	Luggage,handbags,etc.;saddlery/harness		34	32	36	38		14	21	23	23		5	5	5	7
1520	Footwear		15	11	7	8		45	24	17	22		17	8	5	7
1610	Sawmilling and planing of wood		748	711	706	667		3458	3449	3542	3429		1261	1287	1360	1381

ISIC Revision 4

162	Wood products, cork, straw, plaiting materials	3979	3764	3724	3743	9465	9285	9191	9349	1093	1059	1051	1033
1621	Veneer sheets and wood-based panels	518	492	465	472	1015	967	978	1010	25	24	21	21
1622	Builders' carpentry and joinery	3236	3055	3033	3055	7785	7634	7520	7665	673	639	630	627
1623	Wooden containers	109	106	114	115	333	327	336	321	78	74	75	71
1629	Other wood products;articles of cork,straw	115	111	111	101	332	357	357	353	317	322	325	314
170	Paper and paper products	1405	1376	1241	1354	3113	2762	2835	2718	70	66	61	65
1701	Pulp, paper and paperboard	1057	839	682	792	1784	1503	1630	1972	17	14	13	15
1702	Corrugated paper and paperboard	273	450	444	434	1012	984	999	572	21	18	18	18
1709	Other articles of paper and paperboard	73	87	...	...	317	275	206	174	32	34	30	32
181	Printing and service activities related to printing	2138	...	2366	2579	5826	5229	5360	5022	1097	1036	968	920
1811	Printing	1842	...	2048	2230	4943	4445	4549	4252	634	612	576	566
1812	Service activities related to printing	295	...	319	351	883	784	811	770	463	424	392	354
1820	Reproduction of recorded media	2	1	5	5	13	13	5	5	54	49	46	46
1910	Coke oven products	-	-	...	6b/	4	3	-	-	1	1	-	-
1920	Refined petroleum products	...	...	3691	..b/	9	7	643	423	8	9	11	13
201	Basic chemicals,fertilizers, etc.	...	...	...	3579	6542	6654	7004	7098	81	73	72	79
2011	Basic chemicals	...	...	...	...	4814	4961	5109	5140	50	44	40	46
2012	Fertilizers and nitrogen compounds	...	...	...	...	1033	1072	1204	1264	21	21	23	23
2013	Plastics and synthetic rubber in primary forms	449	435	361	369	695	621	691	694	10	8	9	10
202	Other chemical products	...	...	...	...	3159	3199	3228	3194	131	129	137	143
2021	Pesticides and other agrochemical products	...	...	...	...	1	-	3	3	3	2	3	3
2022	Paints,varnishes;printing ink and mastics	808	804	...	713	1155	1210	1213	1208	23	23	25	22
2023	Soap,cleaning and cosmetic preparations	469	467	464	474	966	920	947	888	57	59	62	65
2029	Other chemical products n.e.c.	...	...	...	...	1037	1069	1065	1095	48	45	47	53
2030	Man-made fibres	-	-	-	-	-	-	-	-	-	-	-	-
2100	Pharmaceuticals,medicinal chemicals, etc.	...	...	...	1699	2730	2839	2577	2510	33	32	37	34
221	Rubber products	295	303	312	315	659	643	590	554	40	40	42	41
2211	Rubber tyres and tubes	47	48	48	44	113	113	118	124	11	11	11	12
2219	Other rubber products	248	255	264	270	546	530	472	430	29	29	31	29
2220	Plastics products	1843	1720	1762	1683	3881	3919	3988	3963	336	327	324	306
2310	Glass and glass products	635	...	...	708	1699	1478	1506	1459	101	105	104	103
239	Non-metallic mineral products n.e.c.	...	...	...	3	9474	9620	9749	9503	583	556	543	524
2391	Refractory products	5	5	3	3	8	9	14	15	5	5	5	5
2392	Clay building materials	-	-	-	...	35	-	-	-	1	-	-	-
2393	Other porcelain and ceramic products	...	...	...	...	289	313	530	489	145	135	130	125
2394	Cement, lime and plaster	...	...	...	...	511	487	470	479	7	8	8	9
2395	Articles of concrete, cement and plaster	220	226	246	250	5116	5167	4978	4932	243	237	228	218
2396	Cutting, shaping and finishing of stone	...	...	...	...	632	600	567	546	150	139	142	136
2399	Other non-metallic mineral products n.e.c.	2027	1964	...	...	2883	3044	3190	3042	32	32	30	31
2410	Basic iron and steel	1038	1027	1037	995	1940	1930	1938	1906	54	47	44	48
2420	Basic precious and other non-ferrous metals	4072	3989	3554	3746	6509	6846	7399	7589	25	22	24	25
243	Casting of metals	268	273	329	422	971	757	649	599	44	41	47	46
2431	Casting of iron and steel	205	201	329c/	422c/	784	580	472	432	20	19	26	24
2432	Casting of non-ferrous metals	62	71	..c/	..c/	187	177	177	167	24	22	21	22
251	Struct.metal products, tanks, reservoirs	...	...	...	...	7673	8081	7832	7348	464	464	446	430

continued

Norway

ISIC Revision 4

ISIC	Industry	Number of enterprises (number)					Number of employees (number)					Wages and salaries paid to employees (millions of Norwegian Kroner)				
		Note	2013	2014	2015	2016	Note	2013	2014	2015	2016	Note	2013	2014	2015	2016
2511	Structural metal products		438	435	420	405		7146	7519	7308	6803		3182	3441	3319	3094
2512	Tanks, reservoirs and containers of metal		24	27	24	23		426	459	430	449		...	211	...	...
2513	Steam generators, excl. hot water boilers		2	2	2	2		101	103	94	96		...	...	...	...
2520	Weapons and ammunition		32	35	36	38		2876	2874	2910	2956		1800	1876	1911	2001
259	Other metal products;metal working services		1904	1876	1876	1851		12971	12896	12255	11116		...	...	...	4958
2591	Forging,pressing,stamping,roll-forming of metal		52	45	44	44		252	168	163	180		95	...	64	75
2592	Treatment and coating of metals; machining		1433	1416	1416	1402		8073	8223	7507	6694		3604	3702	3314	2911
2593	Cutlery, hand tools and general hardware		83	88	92	98		1143	1058	1141	999		514	492	538	478
2599	Other fabricated metal products n.e.c.		336	327	324	307		3503	3447	3444	3243		...	...	...	...
2610	Electronic components and boards		52	53	51	55		1526	1514	1614	1529		757	814	896	887
2620	Computers and peripheral equipment		13	12	13	15		202	204	208	196		97	104	104	88
2630	Communication equipment		46	42	40	41		896	900	928	920		518	556	571	582
2640	Consumer electronics		15	14	18	19		289	282	278	258		149	154	131	117
265	Measuring,testing equipment; watches, etc.		138	131	127	128		4480	4643	4626	4486		...	...	2991	3058
2651	Measuring/testing/navigating equipment,etc.		133	127	123	123		4474	4638	4618	4478		...d/	...	2991d/	3058d/
2652	Watches and clocks		5	4	4	5		6	5	8	8		...	...	...	..d/
2660	Irradiation/electromedical equipment,etc.		6	4	3	3		205	209	215	221		...	...	...	...
2670	Optical instruments and photographic equipment		15	16	16	16		85	133	239	210		42	63	...	...
2680	Magnetic and optical media		4	5	3	4		1	1	2	15		-	-	-	...
2710	Electric motors,generators,transformers,etc.		124	116	109	106		2383	2341	2465	2101		1255	...	1443	1249
2720	Batteries and accumulators		3	3	2	5		5	5	3	21		...	1	...	...
273	Wiring and wiring devices		16	16	16	21		2053	2159	2152	2071		1356	...	1476	1471
2731	Fibre optic cables		2	1	1	3		48	50	52	57		1356e/	...	1476e/	1471e/
2732	Other electronic and electric wires and cables		10	11	11	12		1870	1974	1964	1875		...e/	...e/	...e/	...e/
2733	Wiring devices		4	4	4	6		135	135	136	139		...	...	...	...
2740	Electric lighting equipment		39	36	34	30		694	684	676	607		343	352	357	334
2750	Domestic appliances		36	36	35	36		912	864	821	783		...	392	378	348
2790	Other electrical equipment		169	160	146	146		723	737	753	664		386	383	...	...
281	General-purpose machinery		629	600	568	545		13141	13100	12988	11856		7724	8105	7845	6933
2811	Engines/turbines,excl.aircraft,vehicle engines		37	34	29	25		1641	1600	1565	1395		1007	1029	987	916
2812	Fluid power equipment		39	37	35	36		1145	1031	983	779		610	647	582	471
2813	Other pumps, compressors, taps and valves		42	47	49	47		2410	2830	2854	2745		1521	1830	1810	1647
2814	Bearings, gears, gearing and driving elements		8	7	7	6		333	358	350	327		169	186	187	187
2815	Ovens, furnaces and furnace burners		9	8	6	6		145	134	133	135		66	62	61	...
2816	Lifting and handling equipment		96	95	91	91		4883	4780	4649	4246		3103	3186	3064	2621
2817	Office machinery, excl.computers,etc.		-	-	-	-		8	-	-	-		-	-	-	-
2818	Power-driven hand tools		4	3	3	3		-	-	-	-		...	...	...	...
2819	Other general-purpose machinery		394	369	348	331		2576	2367	2454	2229		1248	1164	1154	1031
282	Special-purpose machinery		546	523	501	482		9247	9933	10160	8143		5626	6434	7081	4383
2821	Agricultural and forestry machinery		262	248	236	226		1292	1306	1236	1208		515	525	495	497
2822	Metal-forming machinery and machine tools		60	58	59	55		336	304	313	296		159	145	148	141

2823	Machinery for metallurgy		7	5	5	6		38	46	55	53		...	...	...	...
2824	Mining, quarrying and construction machinery		51	51	49	46		5833	6565	6810	4757		4079	4885	5538	2813
2825	Food/beverage/tobacco processing machinery		60	58	55	55		481	499	593	628		250	272	317	332
2826	Textile/apparel/leather production machinery		4	3	3	3		23	25	27	24		...	...	...	...
2829	Other special-purpose machinery		102	100	94	91		1244	1188	1126	1177		...	...	...	...
2910	Motor vehicles		9	9	6	7		43	77	59	60		18	35	...	28
2920	Automobile bodies, trailers and semi-trailers		61	57	60	63		911	978	1036	1155		393	426	...	533
2930	Parts and accessories for motor vehicles		53	52	51	48		2340	1860	1552	1569		1088	867	727	776
301	Building of ships and boats		433	437	422	400		26526	27921	25646	19551		14594	15544	14451	11753
3011	Building of ships and floating structures		267	276	275	259		26121	27564	25256	19170		14437	15396	14301	11602
3012	Building of pleasure and sporting boats		166	161	147	141		405	357	390	381		157	148	149	151
3020	Railway locomotives and rolling stock		1	2	2	2		9	10	11	1		...	...	...	...
3030	Air and spacecraft and related machinery		5	6	6	8		495	498	520	519		...	...	...	...
3040	Military fighting vehicles		-	-	-	-		-	-	-	-		-	-	-	-
309	Transport equipment n.e.c.		23	25	24	23		288	274	239	158		129	125	108	77
3091	Motorcycles		1	2	4	2		1	2	4	4		...	...	...	...
3092	Bicycles and invalid carriages		16	18	15	16		249	230	186	112		111	104	86	57
3099	Other transport equipment n.e.c.		6	5	5	5		38	42	49	42		...	...	...	...
3100	Furniture		929	893	882	867		5242	4983	4940	4919		1942	1892	1889	1984
321	Jewellery, bijouterie and related articles		324	322	330	328		489	483	511	491		159	167	168	164
3211	Jewellery and related articles		289	281	285	277		478	479	504	483		159f/	167f/	168f/	...
3212	Imitation jewellery and related articles		35	41	45	51		11	4	7	8		...f/	...f/	...f/	2
3220	Musical instruments		52	53	50	46		27	24	25	29		9	7	7	9
3230	Sports goods		65	59	62	61		435	404	424	417		194	192	200	209
3240	Games and toys		25	28	30	32		13	17	22	26		4	4	4	6
3250	Medical and dental instruments and supplies		344	333	322	323		1915	1907	1979	1906		909	910	918	943
3290	Other manufacturing n.e.c.		248	246	233	250		397	407	433	431		126	140	142	149
331	Repair of fabricated metal products/machinery		2304	2359	2473	2539		14504	15032	15415	15153		7257	7765	7978	7862
3311	Repair of fabricated metal products		100	95	97	105		679	661	757	797		323	323	391	377
3312	Repair of machinery		1262	1327	1422	1498		6275	6607	6801	6740		3355	3551	3632	3671
3313	Repair of electronic and optical equipment		40	37	45	46		30	33	48	123		10	12	16	47
3314	Repair of electrical equipment		63	69	66	67		409	447	419	347		233	261	223	196
3315	Repair of transport equip., excl. motor vehicles		755	740	748	730		6851	7040	7121	6856		3246	3526	3612	3456
3319	Repair of other equipment		84	91	95	93		260	244	269	290		91	92	104	115
3320	Installation of industrial machinery/equipment		91	83	83	77		3429	3661	3375	3161		2369	2563	2474	2282
C	Total manufacturing		17273	17016	17141	17143		230519	232769	233312	220479		112470	116711	117065	111372

a/ 1061 includes 1062.
b/ 1910 includes 1920.
c/ 2431 includes 2432.
d/ 2651 includes 2652.
e/ 2731 includes 2732 and 2733.
f/ 3211 includes 3212.

Norway

ISIC	Industry	Note	Output (valuation not defined) (millions of Norwegian Kroner)				Note	Value added at factor values (millions of Norwegian Kroner)				Note	Gross fixed capital formation (millions of Norwegian Kroner)	
			2013	2014	2015	2016		2013	2014	2015	2016		2015	2016
1010	Processing/preserving of meat		40825	43328	44153	45794		8447	8629	8837	9327		1263	1372
1020	Processing/preserving of fish, etc.		39427	49386	51989	58864		7154	8501	8471	7652		1358	1553
1030	Processing/preserving of fruit,vegetables		3144	3352	3550	4008		925	980	1014	1133		225	234
1040	Vegetable and animal oils and fats		2874	2700	2765	3748		373	181	164	717		47	140
1050	Dairy products		19266	20233	21065	20883		6248	6720	6953	7089		1116	1118
106	Grain mill products,starches and starch products		2614	2690	2654	2656		547	615	635	669		89	98
1061	Grain mill products		2614	2690	2654a/	2656a/		547	615	635a/	669a/		89a/	98a/
1062	Starches and starch products		..a/	-	..a/	..a/		-	..	..a/	..a/		..a/	..a/
107	Other food products		17304	18165	20117	22067		6288	6677	7161	7937		674	942
1071	Bakery products		..	..	..	9695		..	..	..	4105		..	528
1072	Sugar		..	..	..	..		..	..	..	..		..	..
1073	Cocoa, chocolate and sugar confectionery		2706	2735	3098	3124		1095	1071	1162	1181		100	126
1074	Macaroni, noodles, couscous, etc.		..	..	..	-		..	..	..	-		..	-
1075	Prepared meals and dishes		851	859	1531	2362		210	210	373	634		47	73
1079	Other food products n.e.c.		..	..	..	..		..	..	..	..		..	..
1080	Prepared animal feeds		22598	24783	27100	24485		2433	2531	2881	3022		673	873
110	Beverages		16809	18677	19121	20463		3732	3582	3649	3956		625	753
1101	Distilling, rectifying and blending of spirits		..	..	..	..		..	..	..	..		..	..
1102	Wines		..	..	..	..		..	..	..	..		..	..
1103	Malt liquors and malt		11547	13353	..	..		2468	2332	..	..		..	..
1104	Soft drinks,mineral waters,other bottled waters		4595	4688	4979	4935		1058	1061	1103	1164		204	259
1200	Tobacco products		..	-	..	-		..	-	..	-		-	..
131	Spinning, weaving and finishing of textiles		661	690	652	669		277	270	291	274		15	35
1311	Preparation and spinning of textile fibres		280	281	292	321		119	109	112	118		9	20
1312	Weaving of textiles		206	209	220	198		87	94	106	85		4	11
1313	Finishing of textiles		175	201	140	151		71	66	73	72		2	4
139	Other textiles		3465	3896	3919	4102		1400	1500	1488	1592		121	155
1391	Knitted and crocheted fabrics		..	..	..	..		..	..	..	..		..	..
1392	Made-up textile articles, except apparel		1598	1799	1856	1958		678	722	720	805		30	36
1393	Carpets and rugs		27	51	10	12		15	15	6	6		-	..
1394	Cordage, rope, twine and netting		1465	1627	1694	1819		568	588	631	658		81	80
1399	Other textiles n.e.c.		..	..	..	..		..	..	..	..		..	..
1410	Wearing apparel, except fur apparel		1798	1884	2043	2603		692	756	717	891		35	61
1420	Articles of fur		19	11	10	11		6	4	3	4		1	1
1430	Knitted and crocheted apparel		205	180	189	229		85	75	89	101		4	5
151	Leather;luggage,handbags,saddlery,harness;fur		94	89	97	119		32	30	39	47		9	6
1511	Tanning/dressing of leather; dressing of fur		68	63	72	77		23	21	30	32		7	5
1512	Luggage,handbags,etc.;saddlery/harness		27	27	24	42		9	9	9	16		2	1
1520	Footwear		118	23	18	25		30	11	8	10		-	..
1610	Sawmilling and planing of wood		7848	8749	9260	9873		2105	2335	2489	2636		403	374

162	Wood products, cork, straw, plaiting materials	15422	15812	16919	18020	5187	5181	5583	5916	460	602
1621	Veneer sheets and wood-based panels	2559	2655	2830	2936	703	794	865	852	114	194
1622	Builders' carpentry and joinery	11904	11990	12943	13863	4159	4026	4368	4695	292	337
1623	Wooden containers	539	621	532	594	176	180	162	175	17	31
1629	Other wood products;articles of cork,straw	419	546	616	628	148	182	188	194	38	40
170	Paper and paper products	8288	7930	12006	12638	1694	1938	2105	2285	122	138
1701	Pulp, paper and paperboard	5839	5457	9507	11006	892	1167	1368	1748	86	97
1702	Corrugated paper and paperboard	1856	1973	2055	1323	622	625	625	430	31	34
1709	Other articles of paper and paperboard	...	...	444	309	...	...	112	106	4	7
181	Printing and service activities related to printing	9737	9045	...	8216	4147	3734	...	3438	...	233
1811	Printing	8425	7813	...	7093	3576	3196	...	2935	...	209
1812	Service activities related to printing	1311	1232	...	1122	571	537	...	504	-	23
1820	Reproduction of recorded media	23	24	14	12	12	13	5	5	-	2
1910	Coke oven products	16b/	...	...	...	5b/	...	-	-	-	-
1920	Refined petroleum products	..b/	...	...	...	..b/	9991	...	...	...	...
201	Basic chemicals,fertilizers, etc.	38898	42611	...	...	8327	...	...	...	...	...
2011	Basic chemicals	...	...	...	...	...	...	...	...	...	...
2012	Fertilizers and nitrogen compounds	...	...	...	...	...	...	...	...	...	...
2013	Plastics and synthetic rubber in primary forms	7521	7182	7715	3975	1140	1074	1700	1155	65	85
202	Other chemical products	...	...	...	...	...	...	...	...	...	...
2021	Pesticides and other agrochemical products	...	...	...	...	...	...	...	...	...	...
2022	Paints,varnishes;printing ink and mastics	3437	...	4265	4120	1066	...	1284	1115	52	86
2023	Soap,cleaning and cosmetic preparations	2744	2653	2860	2787	1037	1003	1001	1030	95	119
2029	Other chemical products n.e.c.	...	...	...	...	...	...	...	...	...	...
2030	Man-made fibres	-	-	-	-	-	-	-	-	-	-
2100	Pharmaceuticals,medicinal chemicals, etc.	9547	...	...	...	4646	...	...	...	...	...
221	Rubber products	998	967	959	807	482	498	437	366	15	27
2211	Rubber tyres and tubes	169	188	187	185	57	71	63	62	6	1
2219	Other rubber products	828	779	771	622	424	426	374	304	9	26
2220	Plastics products	9285	9465	9286	10222	2995	3188	3074	3359	401	412
2310	Glass and glass products	2692	...	...	2744	1048	...	...	1182	...	155
239	Non-metallic mineral products n.e.c.	9	11	...	17	4	4	...	7	...	...
2391	Refractory products	...	-	...	...	...	...	7	...	-	1
2392	Clay building materials	-	...	-	-	-	-	-	-	-	-
2393	Other porcelain and ceramic products	...	...	...	...	...	...	...	...	...	...
2394	Cement, lime and plaster	...	...	...	...	...	...	...	...	...	...
2395	Articles of concrete, cement and plaster	...	...	...	...	...	...	...	...	...	...
2396	Cutting, shaping and finishing of stone	831	832	786	792	400	387	369	368	30	39
2399	Other non-metallic mineral products n.e.c.	...	...	11245	10997	...	...	3242	3169	610	613
2410	Basic iron and steel	10823	11116	10859	10421	2235	2449	2443	2652	814	429
2420	Basic precious and other non-ferrous metals	43022	50167	53155	51374	6572	9364	9726	10006	2044	3923
243	Casting of metals	1394	1134	891	886	568	487	411	348	38	20
2431	Casting of iron and steel	1394c/	1134c/	651	668	568c/	487c/	318	264	35	18
2432	Casting of non-ferrous metals	..c/	..c/	240	218	..c/	..c/	92	85	2	2
251	Struct.metal products, tanks, reservoirs	...	...	...	...	...	...	...	...	...	...

continued

Norway

ISIC	Industry	Note	Output 2013	Output 2014	Output 2015	Output 2016	Note	VA 2013	VA 2014	VA 2015	VA 2016	Note	GFCF 2015	GFCF 2016
	ISIC Revision 4		(millions of Norwegian Kroner)					(millions of Norwegian Kroner)					(millions of Norwegian Kroner)	
2511	Structural metal products		12314	13109	12594	11722		4720	4846	4665	4359		254	198
2512	Tanks, reservoirs and containers of metal		...	883	...	...		...	338	...	...		...	...
2513	Steam generators, excl. hot water boilers													
2520	Weapons and ammunition		8050	7109	6908	8233		3212	3016	3096	3071		125	229
259	Other metal products;metal working services		...	...	...	17792		...	...	...	6934		...	595
2591	Forging,pressing,stamping,roll-forming of metal		308	...	194	255		126	...	98	106		7	7
2592	Treatment and coating of metals; machining		12847	13352	11474	10081		5732	5536	4771	4074		366	268
2593	Cutlery, hand tools and general hardware		1823	1943	1946	1767		927	854	890	745		62	51
2599	Other fabricated metal products n.e.c.													
2610	Electronic components and boards		3475	3760	4530	4425		1322	1440	1760	1621		138	102
2620	Computers and peripheral equipment		547	616	583	494		187	194	189	170		3	1
2630	Communication equipment		1824	1972	2175	1884		888	980	1061	923		23	32
2640	Consumer electronics		575	520	523	489		209	287	203	131		9	7
265	Measuring,testing equipment; watches, etc.		...	...	12913	11383		...	...	4528	3660		149	137
2651	Measuring/testing/navigating equipment,etc.		...	...	12913d/	11383d/		...	...	4528d/	3660d/		149d/	137d/
2652	Watches and clocks		...	...	...d/	...d/		...	...	...d/	...d/		...d/	...d/
2660	Irradiation/electromedical equipment,etc.													
2670	Optical instruments and photographic equipment		173	328	...	...		55	119	...	...		...	...
2680	Magnetic and optical media		3	3	2	...		1	1	...	...		-	...
2710	Electric motors,generators,transformers,etc.		5997	...	6420	5554		2048	...	2230	1873		68	74
2720	Batteries and accumulators		...	3	...	...		...	1	...	...			
273	Wiring and wiring devices		7105	...	7746	7634		2362	...	2739	2926		317	281
2731	Fibre optic cables		7105e/	...	7746e/	7634e/		2362e/	...	2739e/	2926e/		317e/	281e/
2732	Other electronic and electric wires and cables		...e/	...	...e/	...e/		...e/	...	...e/	...e/		...e/	...e/
2733	Wiring devices		...e/	...	...e/	...e/		...e/	...	...e/	...e/		...e/	...e/
2740	Electric lighting equipment		1094	1189	1215	1195		545	578	590	519		21	31
2750	Domestic appliances		...	1410	...	...		...	531	...	...		...	...
2790	Other electrical equipment		1385	1445	1443	1179		596	601	561	430		25	17
281	General-purpose machinery		40997	41971	38899	31106		12089	12461	11848	9369		716	520
2811	Engines/turbines,excl.aircraft,vehicle engines		6576	5927	5893	4178		1908	1420	1423	1028		113	109
2812	Fluid power equipment		3153	4229	3585	3047		998	1124	1055	884		55	14
2813	Other pumps, compressors, taps and valves		8302	9899	9111	7245		2652	3522	4068	3330		243	164
2814	Bearings, gears, gearing and driving elements		686	738	748	764		220	279	289	318		18	8
2815	Ovens, furnaces and furnace burners		244	246	227	...		102	104	106	...		4	...
2816	Lifting and handling equipment		17204	16044	14542	11061		4281	4324	3177	2176		140	158
2817	Office machinery, excl.computers.etc.		-	-	-	-		-	-	-	-		-	-
2818	Power-driven hand tools		-	-	-	...		-	-	-	...		-	-
2819	Other general-purpose machinery		4830	4889	4792	4616		1928	1687	1729	1538		144	59
282	Special-purpose machinery		47022	56281	44874	21469		12097	14452	13022	6568		320	292
2821	Agricultural and forestry machinery		2050	2077	1933	2010		768	810	773	771		112	106
2822	Metal-forming machinery and machine tools		627	517	490	411		318	270	255	213		14	17

2823	Machinery for metallurgy	40393	49664	38216	14302	9750	12063	10566	3922	..	..
2824	Mining, quarrying and construction machinery	1034	1084	1316	1508	390	368	444	571	132	45
2825	Food/beverage/tobacco processing machinery	..	..	..	..	..	..	..	..	31	27
2826	Textile/apparel/leather production machinery	..	..	..	..	..	..	..	..	..	..
2829	Other special-purpose machinery	..	..	..	..	..	..	..	..	..	..
2910	Motor vehicles	94	183	..	105	23	44	..	26	..	3
2920	Automobile bodies, trailers and semi-trailers	1953	2120	..	2990	615	645	..	861	..	43
2930	Parts and accessories for motor vehicles	5170	4064	3444	3764	1605	1487	1211	1271	197	187
301	Building of ships and boats	84679	86663	73843	55419	23238	23642	20050	16246	1478	749
3011	Building of ships and floating structures	83998	86116	73187	54504	23054	23430	19816	15986	1453	731
3012	Building of pleasure and sporting boats	681	546	656	915	185	211	234	260	24	18
3020	Railway locomotives and rolling stock	..	..	..	..	..	..	..	..	..	..
3030	Air and spacecraft and related machinery	..	..	..	..	..	..	..	..	..	..
3040	Military fighting vehicles	-	-	-	-	-	-	-	-	-	-
309	Transport equipment n.e.c.	575	454	427	394	188	156	153	133	4	2
3091	Motorcycles	..	..	..	..	..	..	..	..	..	..
3092	Bicycles and invalid carriages	451	346	319	305	142	116	115	101	4	2
3099	Other transport equipment n.e.c.	..	..	..	..	..	..	..	..	..	..
3100	Furniture	7872	7824	7623	8207	3286	3132	3045	3413	196	173
321	Jewellery, bijouterie and related articles	618	593	709	647	255	269	305	291	11	7
3211	Jewellery and related articles	618f/	593f/	709f/	..	255f/	269f/	305f/	..	11f/	..
3212	Imitation jewellery and related articles	..f/	..f/	..f/	16	..f/	..f/	..f/	4	..f/	-
3220	Musical instruments	29	27	26	33	14	11	13	17	1	1
3230	Sports goods	759	831	810	753	343	320	293	318	38	15
3240	Games and toys	14	14	14	23	7	7	9	13	-	-
3250	Medical and dental instruments and supplies	3275	3395	3160	3676	1355	1279	1193	1825	57	41
3290	Other manufacturing n.e.c.	447	617	632	616	206	217	234	240	55	16
331	Repair of fabricated metal products/machinery	26494	26988	28138	27510	10852	11222	11014	11157	1189	953
3311	Repair of fabricated metal products	965	941	1061	1207	508	480	563	551	24	24
3312	Repair of machinery	10818	11527	11052	11524	4799	5288	5023	5290	287	286
3313	Repair of electronic and optical equipment	34	42	50	109	21	26	29	67	2	3
3314	Repair of electrical equipment	482	602	595	561	297	348	289	260	16	5
3315	Repair of transport equip., excl. motor vehicles	13829	13514	15088	13768	5065	4927	4972	4829	834	617
3319	Repair of other equipment	365	361	292	343	162	155	140	160	25	19
3320	Installation of industrial machinery/equipment	12532	12632	10129	9710	4031	4506	3807	3745	58	46
C	Total manufacturing	680759	728613	746861	693736	193287	205512	205716	195803	21918	25292

a/ 1061 includes 1062.
b/ 1910 includes 1920.
c/ 2431 includes 2432.
d/ 2651 includes 2652.
e/ 2731 includes 2732 and 2733.
f/ 3211 includes 3212.

Norway

ISIC Revision 4

Index numbers of industrial production
(2010=100)

ISIC	Industry	Note	2005	2006	2007	2008	2009	2010	2011	2012	2013	2014	2015	2016
10	Food products		94	94	98	99	100	100	98	101	101	104	104	103
11	Beverages		106	109	103	104	103	100	98	97	91	92	90	96
12	Tobacco products		...	...	...	...	...	...	...	...	...	...	...	...
13	Textiles		156	178	169	139	113	100	107	102	102	106	107	117
14	Wearing apparel		140	135	142	127	121	100	97	90	88	87	81	85
15	Leather and related products		286	260	224	160	144	100	106	102	45	19	11	9
16	Wood products, excluding furniture		117	118	121	107	88	100	96	95	91	91	93	95
17	Paper and paper products		126	121	116	108	94	100	89	74	68	65	64	69
18	Printing and reproduction of recorded media		106	109	111	110	103	100	101	95	92	90	83	77
19	Coke and refined petroleum products		...	...	...	...	...	...	...	...	...	...	...	...
20	Chemicals and chemical products		81	81	84	87	82	100	97	82	82	82	83	81
21	Pharmaceuticals,medicinal chemicals, etc.		87	85	92	89	76	100	99	114	95	97	108	168
22	Rubber and plastics products		116	122	123	121	99	100	101	95	92	93	91	98
23	Other non-metallic mineral products		101	111	117	116	98	100	101	100	102	96	94	95
24	Basic metals		107	110	112	109	87	100	92	88	84	87	81	84
25	Fabricated metal products, except machinery		79	90	100	110	103	100	104	109	112	115	109	101
26	Computer, electronic and optical products		79	84	91	101	102	100	104	104	109	117	121	114
27	Electrical equipment		106	116	123	128	105	100	118	116	126	130	120	111
28	Machinery and equipment n.e.c.		69	75	81	95	100	100	106	120	136	150	144	117
29	Motor vehicles, trailers and semi-trailers		120	124	135	134	99	100	108	110	121	131	138	144
30	Other transport equipment		67	81	90	101	104	100	104	117	132	140	117	108
31	Furniture		156	156	162	148	109	100	93	90	82	77	74	72
32	Other manufacturing		101	96	97	95	92	100	106	93	95	96	96	96
33	Repair and installation of machinery/equipment		61	69	84	97	99	100	101	103	109	114	111	93
C	Total manufacturing		91	95	101	104	98	100	101	104	107	111	107	102

Oman

Supplier of information:
Ministry of Commerce and Industry, Muscat.

Basic source of data:
Annual survey.

Major deviations from ISIC (Revision 4):
None reported.

Reference period:
Calendar year.

Scope:
Licensed establishments with 10 or more employees.

Method of data collection:
Data were collected by direct interview in the field and by mail questionnaires.

Type of enumeration:
Complete enumeration.

Adjusted for non-response:
Yes.

Concepts and definitions of variables:
Output refers to gross output.

Related national publications:
Industrial Statistical Book; Features of the Manufacturing Sector of Large and Medium Industries; Annual Industrial Report, all published by the Industrial Information Department, Ministry of Commerce and Industry, Muscat.

Oman

ISIC Revision 4		Number of establishments (number)					Number of employees (number)					Wages and salaries paid to employees (thousands of Omani Rials)				
ISIC	Industry	2013	2014	2015	2016	Note	2013	2014	2015	2016	Note	2013	2014	2015	2016	Note
1010	Processing/preserving of meat	1	2	2	2		655	1078	1082	1108		3414	5146	6397	6828	
1020	Processing/preserving of fish, etc.	17	14	14	17		1011	920	939	858		4666	4006	3101	3365	
1030	Processing/preserving of fruit,vegetables	8	6	7	7		800	836	915	953		3401	4094	4510	4373	
1040	Vegetable and animal oils and fats	1	2	2	3		600	760	861	299		5943	7299	8283	1716	
1050	Dairy products	3	2	2	2		912	726	780	169		4718	3432	4064	949	
106	Grain mill products,starches and starch products	3	4	4	4		452	730	799	808		3108	6104	6836	7075	
1061	Grain mill products	1	2	2	2		240	506	590	582		2679	5747	6350	6714	
1062	Starches and starch products	2	2	2	2		212	224	209	226		429	357	486	361	
107	Other food products	46	47	48	51		4006	5178	4820	6020		17082	21603	24609	30128	
1071	Bakery products	27	30	30	32		2390	3183	2927	3333		8418	10440	12494	13290	
1072	Sugar	...	...	...	...		...	...	...	...		...	...	...	...	
1073	Cocoa, chocolate and sugar confectionery	...	1	1	1		...	349	337	388		...	1940	2095	2372	
1074	Macaroni, noodles, couscous, etc.	1	1	1	1		131	139	134	102		1104	1223	1177	918	
1075	Prepared meals and dishes	1	1	1	1		49	48	51	53		335	358	375	394	
1079	Other food products n.e.c.	17	14	15	16		1436	1459	1371	2144		7225	7642	8468	13153	
1080	Prepared animal feeds	1	3	3	3		22	143	143	129		243	1085	1202	1245	
110	Beverages	29	24	27	31		2248	2542	2645	3039		13296	16773	22816	21841	
1101	Distilling, rectifying and blending of spirits	...	...	...	...		...	...	...	...		...	...	...	...	
1102	Wines	...	...	...	...		...	...	...	...		...	...	...	...	
1103	Malt liquors and malt	...	...	...	...		...	...	...	...		...	...	...	...	
1104	Soft drinks,mineral waters,other bottled waters	29	24	27	31		2248	2542	2645	3039		13296	16773	22816	21841	
1200	Tobacco products	...	...	...	...		...	...	...	...		...	...	...	...	
131	Spinning, weaving and finishing of textiles	2	2	2	2		193	196	197	191		1027	1016	1056	988	
1311	Preparation and spinning of textile fibres	1	1	1	1		167	158	153	147		1008	912	898	831	
1312	Weaving of textiles	...	...	...	...		...	...	...	...		...	...	...	...	
1313	Finishing of textiles	1	1	1	1		26	38	44	44		20	104	158	158	
139	Other textiles	4	7	8	7		212	436	451	395		431	2027	2036	1926	
1391	Knitted and crocheted fabrics	...	...	...	...		...	...	...	...		...	...	...	...	
1392	Made-up textile articles, except apparel	1	4	5	4		18	255	259	225		41	1126	1147	1156	
1393	Carpets and rugs	...	...	...	...		...	...	...	...		...	...	...	...	
1394	Cordage, rope, twine and netting	...	...	...	...		...	...	...	...		...	...	...	...	
1399	Other textiles n.e.c.	3	3	3	3		194	181	192	170		390	901	889	770	
1410	Wearing apparel, except fur apparel	3	3	3	3		260	447	604	580		1032	1464	1424	1442	
1420	Articles of fur	...	...	...	...		...	...	...	...		...	...	...	...	
1430	Knitted and crocheted apparel	...	...	...	...		...	...	...	...		...	...	...	...	
151	Leather;luggage,handbags,saddlery,harness;fur	...	...	...	...		...	...	...	...		...	...	...	...	
1511	Tanning/dressing of leather; dressing of fur	...	...	...	...		...	...	...	...		...	...	...	...	
1512	Luggage,handbags,etc.;saddlery/harness	...	...	...	...		...	...	...	...		...	...	...	...	
1520	Footwear	2	2	3	4		116	106	110	168		438	499	568	849	
1610	Sawmilling and planing of wood	3	2	1	1		...a/	3107	4304	4417		...a/	11431	14196	14196	

Code	Product	(1)	(2)	(3)	(4)	(5)	(6)	(7)	(8)	(9)	(10)	(11)	(12)
162	Wood products, cork, straw, plaiting materials	4776	3932	3121	11774	1202	970	887	3848	20	17	16	15
1621	Veneer sheets and wood-based panels	599	698	391	9352a/	197	205	210	3351a/	1	1	1	1
1622	Builders' carpentry and joinery	3893	3024	2551	2355	915	681	606	467	14	14	13	13
1623	Wooden containers	..	..	..	..	..	..	..	..	..	..	..	..
1629	Other wood products;articles of cork,straw	284	211	178	67	90	84	71	30	5	2	2	1
170	Paper and paper products	3827	3428	3222	2225	711	617	593	396	12	11	11	7
1701	Pulp, paper and paperboard	252	333	212	218	43	44	42	38	2	2	2	2
1702	Corrugated paper and paperboard	1817	1968	1707	1108	218	220	219	174	2	2	2	1
1709	Other articles of paper and paperboard	1758	1127	1302	898	450	353	332	184	8	7	7	4
181	Printing and service activities related to printing	12778	13616	11735	10933	1784	1940	1900	1785	34	35	32	32
1811	Printing	8353	9279	7795	6336	1320	1425	1376	1227	28	28	25	24
1812	Service activities related to printing	4425	4337	3940	4597	464	515	524	558	6	7	7	8
1820	Reproduction of recorded media	54	70	45	50	11	10	11	15	1	1	1	1
1910	Coke oven products	51	45	41	38	11	10	10	10	1	1	1	1
1920	Refined petroleum products	55687	55939	41305	42601	3003	2724	2172	1761	12	12	8	6
201	Basic chemicals,fertilizers, etc.	41086	37377	37962	38748	3039	3048	3045	3131	26	29	28	28
2011	Basic chemicals	16327	14875	13320	13305	1287	1351	1350	1320	18	20	20	18
2012	Fertilizers and nitrogen compounds	21293	19545	21660	22175	1171	1199	1209	1251	5	6	6	7
2013	Plastics and synthetic rubber in primary forms	3466	2957	2982	3268	581	498	486	560	3	3	2	3
202	Other chemical products	20369	17049	14851	13239	2186	2091	1985	1793	30	27	26	25
2021	Pesticides and other agrochemical products	667	599	554	530	110	104	105	92	2	2	2	2
2022	Paints,varnishes;printing ink and mastics	10549	9785	7620	5540	1096	1076	921	795	8	8	7	6
2023	Soap,cleaning and cosmetic preparations	6620	4379	4316	4868	694	630	693	637	14	11	11	11
2029	Other chemical products n.e.c.	2533	2286	2361	2302	286	281	266	269	6	6	6	6
2030	Man-made fibres	..	..	..	..	..	..	..	..	..	..	..	..
2100	Pharmaceuticals,medicinal chemicals, etc.	4967	1821	1774	4667	695	267	269	617	5	1	1	3
221	Rubber products	4118	2114	1905	1291	481	380	409	231	9	8	9	9
2211	Rubber tyres and tubes	1486	1559	1410	778	207	275	300	110	6	6	6	5
2219	Other rubber products	2633	554	495	513	274	105	109	121	3	2	3	4
2220	Plastics products	24224	25939	22319	17998	4288	4475	4438	3770	54	53	51	49
2310	Glass and glass products	4601	4060	3825	4125	1056	964	936	817	16	14	13	11
239	Non-metallic mineral products n.e.c.	86729	82399	74093	66467	16866	16315	15057	13656	236	210	187	190
2391	Refractory products	630	821	508	305	165	176	154	82	..	..	..	..
2392	Clay building materials	6050	6208	6033	5446	667	762	777	768	4	5	4	3
2393	Other porcelain and ceramic products	19125	16603	14757	13732	1435	1326	1321	1219	4	4	4	4
2394	Cement, lime and plaster	24450	24551	20269	17809	5688	5340	4701	4446	11	8	8	8
2395	Articles of concrete, cement and plaster	25860	24277	24400	23871	6171	5960	6560	6053	118	102	91	93
2396	Cutting, shaping and finishing of stone	10613	9939	8124	5303	2740	2751	1544	1088	71	65	57	57
2399	Other non-metallic mineral products n.e.c.	38444	34315	27491	29839	4919	5858	3806	4730	28	26	23	25
2410	Basic iron and steel	..	..	..	..	..	..	..	..	17	17	14	13
2420	Basic precious and other non-ferrous metals	1430	6438	4495	5271	457	799	408	643	3	6	2	3
243	Casting of metals	45433	43567	37807	36684	3066	2795	2535	2246	16	14	11	12
2431	Casting of iron and steel	13890	11235	13451	12290	1537	1278	1480	1174	9	8	7	8
2432	Casting of non-ferrous metals	31542	32331	24356	24395	1529	1517	1055	1072	7	6	4	4
251	Struct.metal products, tanks, reservoirs	67422	58533	50111	46660	13296	12733	10211	9868	73	72	63	60

continued

Oman

ISIC Revision 4

ISIC	Industry	Note	Number of establishments (number) 2013	2014	2015	2016	Note	Number of employees (number) 2013	2014	2015	2016	Note	Wages and salaries paid to employees (thousands of Omani Rials) 2013	2014	2015	2016
2511	Structural metal products		50	54	63	64		6744	6722	8803	9430		32279	36888	43619	52079
2512	Tanks, reservoirs and containers of metal		10	9	9	9		3124	3489	3930	3866		14381	13222	14914	15342
2513	Steam generators, excl. hot water boilers		...	2	2	2		115	130	150	155		...	...	...	...
2520	Weapons and ammunition		2	2	2	2		...	...	...	...		1027	1077	1533	2129
259	Other metal products;metal working services		20	20	20	24		2137	2021	1988	3037		12272	13250	12423	21592
2591	Forging,pressing,stamping,roll-forming of metal		1	2	2	3		176	228	235	297		509	719	824	1170
2592	Treatment and coating of metals; machining		7	6	6	7		839	779	664	746		5875	6195	4121	5318
2593	Cutlery, hand tools and general hardware		...	...	...	...		...	...	...	...		...	...	...	...
2599	Other fabricated metal products n.e.c.		12	12	12	14		1122	1014	1089	1994		5888	6337	7479	15103
2610	Electronic components and boards		2	2	2	2		110	105	123b/	119b/		548	538	650b/	702b/
2620	Computers and peripheral equipment		...	1	1	1		...	20	...b/	...b/		...	45	...b/	...b/
2630	Communication equipment		...	...	...	...		...	...	...	...		...	...	...	...
2640	Consumer electronics		...	...	...	...		...	...	...	...		...	...	...	...
265	Measuring,testing equipment; watches, etc.		...	...	...	...		...	...	...	...		...	...	...	...
2651	Measuring/testing/navigating equipment,etc.		...	...	...	...		...	...	...	...		...	...	...	...
2652	Watches and clocks		...	...	...	...		...	...	...	...		...	...	...	...
2660	Irradiation/electromedical equipment,etc.		...	...	...	...		...	...	...	...		...	...	...	...
2670	Optical instruments and photographic equipment		...	...	...	...		...	...	...	...		...	...	...	...
2680	Magnetic and optical media		1	1	1	1		223	219	189	227		1594	1712	1875	1934
2710	Electric motors,generators,transformers,etc.		10	9	9	9		982	989	990	1053		5870	5675	6740	7342
2720	Batteries and accumulators		2	2	2	2		429	361	359	353		2683	2540	2784	2874
273	Wiring and wiring devices		6	6	5	6		1474	1680	1588	1791		13487	15656	18249	16806
2731	Fibre optic cables		1	1	1	1		191	311	292	315		3315	4406	4476	3899
2732	Other electronic and electric wires and cables		3	3	3	4		1199	1263	1296c/	1476c/		10028	10778	13773c/	12907c/
2733	Wiring devices		2	2	1	1		84	106	...c/	...c/		144	471	...c/	...c/
2740	Electric lighting equipment		4	5	5	5		102	116	118	154		322	531	703	915
2750	Domestic appliances		1	2	2	2		167	208	240	248		1048	1483	1370	1434
2790	Other electrical equipment		1	1	1	1		19	16	17	16		180	180	225	193
281	General-purpose machinery		10	8	6	9		499	416	350	824		3970	3145	1835	8462
2811	Engines/turbines,excl.aircraft,vehicle engines		...	...	...	...		...	...	...	...		...	...	...	...
2812	Fluid power equipment		...	...	...	...		...	...	...	...		...	...	...	...
2813	Other pumps, compressors, taps and valves		2	2	1	1		126	128	72	80		1007	1132	785	786
2814	Bearings, gears, gearing and driving elements		...	...	...	...		...	...	...	...		...	...	...	...
2815	Ovens, furnaces and furnace burners		...	...	...	...		...	...	...	...		...	...	...	...
2816	Lifting and handling equipment		1	1	1	2		13	13	181d/	41		55	61	616d/	186
2817	Office machinery, excl.computers,etc.		1	...	...	1		88	...	...d/	431		583	...	...d/	5301
2818	Power-driven hand tools		2	1	1	2		173	177	...d/	172		2008	1598	...d/	1926
2819	Other general-purpose machinery		4	4	3	3		99	98	97	100		317	355	434	263
282	Special-purpose machinery		2	2	2	2		214	242	283	281		2747	3647	4614	5025
2821	Agricultural and forestry machinery		...	...	...	...		...	...	...	...		...	...	...	...
2822	Metal-forming machinery and machine tools		...	...	...	...		...	...	...	...		...	...	...	...

2823	Machinery for metallurgy	...	1	1	1	164	188	231	232	2062	2964	3861	4393
2824	Mining, quarrying and construction machinery	...	1	1	1	...	...	...	...	...	...	...	...
2825	Food/beverage/tobacco processing machinery	...	...	...	...	...	...	...	...	...	...	...	...
2826	Textile/apparel/leather production machinery	...	1	1	1	50	54	52	49	685	683	753	632
2829	Other special-purpose machinery	1	1	1	1	...	...	...	...	...	...	...	...
2910	Motor vehicles	...	...	...	...	...	...	...	...	...	...	...	...
2920	Automobile bodies, trailers and semi-trailers	1	1	...	...	46	48	...	...	263	285	...	...
2930	Parts and accessories for motor vehicles	1	1	2	2	55	63	132	134	215	235	590	688
301	Building of ships and boats	2	3	5	5	1334	1571	1418	1585	12761	13152	4158	13440
3011	Building of ships and floating structures	2	2	4	4	1334	1549	1403	1585 e/	12761	13102	4082	13440 e/
3012	Building of pleasure and sporting boats	...	1	1	1	...	22	15	... e/	...	49	77	... e/
3020	Railway locomotives and rolling stock	...	...	...	...	...	...	...	...	...	...	...	...
3030	Air and spacecraft and related machinery	...	...	...	...	...	...	...	...	...	...	...	...
3040	Military fighting vehicles	...	...	...	...	...	...	...	...	...	...	...	...
309	Transport equipment n.e.c.	...	...	...	...	...	...	...	...	...	...	...	...
3091	Motorcycles	...	...	...	...	...	...	...	...	...	...	...	...
3092	Bicycles and invalid carriages	...	...	...	...	...	...	...	...	...	...	...	...
3099	Other transport equipment n.e.c.	...	...	...	...	...	...	...	...	...	...	...	...
3100	Furniture	16	17	20	22	2398	2403	2673	3032	8978	9283	10950	11782
321	Jewellery, bijouterie and related articles	...	3	3	3	...	119	124	122	...	318	509	681
3211	Jewellery and related articles	...	3	3	3	...	119	124	122	...	318	509	681
3212	Imitation jewellery and related articles	...	...	...	...	...	...	...	...	...	...	...	...
3220	Musical instruments	...	...	...	...	...	...	...	...	...	...	...	...
3230	Sports goods	...	...	...	...	...	...	...	...	...	...	...	...
3240	Games and toys	...	...	...	...	...	...	...	...	...	...	...	...
3250	Medical and dental instruments and supplies	1	2	2	1	27	63	58	30	97	234	223	95
3290	Other manufacturing n.e.c.	1	1	1	1	24	29	20	24	132	161	137	86
331	Repair of fabricated metal products/machinery	1	1	1	1	24	29	20	24	132	161	137	86
3311	Repair of fabricated metal products	...	...	...	...	...	...	...	...	...	...	...	...
3312	Repair of machinery	...	...	...	...	...	...	...	...	...	...	...	...
3313	Repair of electronic and optical equipment	...	...	...	...	...	...	...	...	...	...	...	...
3314	Repair of electrical equipment	...	...	...	...	...	...	...	...	...	...	...	...
3315	Repair of transport equip., excl. motor vehicles	1	1	1	1	24	29	20	24	132	161	137	86
3319	Repair of other equipment	...	...	...	...	...	...	...	...	...	...	...	...
3320	Installation of industrial machinery/equipment	3	2	2	2	1149	742	1004	1103	6556	4333	5860	4225
C	Total manufacturing	674	685	747	804	72308	77438	86470	90493	466161	499563	567167	613324

a/ 1621 includes 1610.
b/ 2610 includes 2620.
c/ 2732 includes 2733.
d/ 2816 includes 2818.
e/ 3011 includes 3012.

Oman

ISIC Revision 4			Output at basic prices (thousands of Omani Rials)					Value added at basic prices (thousands of Omani Rials)					Gross fixed capital formation (thousands of Omani Rials)	
ISIC	Industry	Note	2013	2014	2015	2016	Note	2013	2014	2015	2016	Note	2015	2016
1010	Processing/preserving of meat		25870	37541	40290	40910		11630	15036	19261	20841		4580	2205
1020	Processing/preserving of fish, etc.		46670	36903	37980	51040		15352	11451	12388	13781		953	-1052
1030	Processing/preserving of fruit,vegetables		30327	31695	34008	36728		12820	9194	12754	13856		3202	4382
1040	Vegetable and animal oils and fats		91815	105687	104964	28793		15179	15173	22500	10413		4874	540
1050	Dairy products		20691	20103	26716	39671		5974	4829	17161	7577		1347	75
106	Grain mill products,starches and starch products		38938	105591	106185	94368		7001	20465	21745	71452		-3010	2829
1061	Grain mill products		35731	102044	102806	91021		5761	19218	20694	70262		-2941	2686
1062	Starches and starch products		3207	3547	3379	3347		1240	1247	1051	1190		-70	143
107	Other food products		147135	183147	197815	191571		57325	68307	79645	87446		4116	3780
1071	Bakery products		35457	57410	64039	73613		18597	24303	30380	37545		2369	1815
1072	Sugar		...	...	...	...		...	...	...	...		...	...
1073	Cocoa, chocolate and sugar confectionery			10054	11016	10599			2918	4087	3624		340	311
1074	Macaroni, noodles, couscous, etc.		19711	20349	17756	9298		4238	4994	6001	1727		125	5
1075	Prepared meals and dishes		2068	1731	1883	1794		843	741	702	924		-	-
1079	Other food products n.e.c.		89899	93603	103122	96268		33648	35351	38475	43626		1282	1650
1080	Prepared animal feeds		29304	45393	170301	42845		1035	3743	105995	9001		1693	647
110	Beverages		78749	92261	90430	115648		24508	27468	36615	70673		17926	10092
1101	Distilling, rectifying and blending of spirits		...	...	...	...		...	...	...	...		...	...
1102	Wines		...	...	...	...		...	...	...	...		...	...
1103	Malt liquors and malt		...	...	...	...		...	...	...	...		...	...
1104	Soft drinks,mineral waters,other bottled waters		78749	92261	90430	115648		24508	27468	36615	70673		17926	10092
1200	Tobacco products		...	...	...	...		...	...	...	...		...	...
131	Spinning, weaving and finishing of textiles		3881	3259	4703	2308		1729	1654	1741	1331		7	34
1311	Preparation and spinning of textile fibres		3064	2448	4042	1587		1224	1290	1427	925		7	34
1312	Weaving of textiles		...	811	661	720		...	365	314	406		...	...
1313	Finishing of textiles		817	811	661	720		505	365	314	406		-	-
139	Other textiles		6357	12703	13711	12946		2031	4381	4599	4705		54	258
1391	Knitted and crocheted fabrics		...	...	...	...		...	...	...	...		...	...
1392	Made-up textile articles, except apparel		332	7240	8319	8885		100	2160	2129	2826		10	-
1393	Carpets and rugs		...	...	...	...		...	...	...	...		...	...
1394	Cordage, rope, twine and netting		...	...	...	...		...	...	...	...		...	...
1399	Other textiles n.e.c.		6025	5464	5392	4061		1931	2221	2470	1879		44	258
1410	Wearing apparel, except fur apparel		2291	4982	4270	3721		1287	3254	2277	1704		-27	4
1420	Articles of fur		...	...	...	...		...	...	...	...		...	...
1430	Knitted and crocheted apparel		...	...	...	...		...	...	...	...		...	...
151	Leather;luggage,handbags,saddlery,harness;fur		...	...	...	...		...	...	...	...		...	...
1511	Tanning/dressing of leather; dressing of fur		...	...	...	...		...	...	...	...		...	...
1512	Luggage,handbags,etc.;saddlery/harness		...	...	...	...		...	...	...	...		...	...
1520	Footwear		2563	2950	3292	6636		782	915	1446	4350		24	40
1610	Sawmilling and planing of wood		...a/	65311	69462	106590		...a/	21298	56891	28152		-	838

Code	Description	(1)	(2)	(3)	(4)	(5)	(6)	(7)	(8)	(9)	(10)
162	Wood products, cork, straw, plaiting materials	75105	44864	18799	29522	23581	16375	8653	19470	140	50
1621	Veneer sheets and wood-based panels	34579a/	1799	2319	1510	10057a/	507	744	935	37	9
1622	Builders' carpentry and joinery	10800	12101	15439	26788	4340	5700	7525	17963	103	40
1623	Wooden containers	:	:	:	:	:	:	:	:	:	:
1629	Other wood products;articles of cork,straw	29726	30963	1041	1223	9184	10167	384	571	-	1
170	Paper and paper products	22022	33176	30827	33211	6460	11056	10327	12055	1890	1213
1701	Pulp, paper and paperboard	2041	1928	1844	1423	892	871	674	711	1465	24
1702	Corrugated paper and paperboard	11683	20425	21144	16583	2825	6449	7195	5789	197	601
1709	Other articles of paper and paperboard	8298	10824	7839	15206	2743	3736	2457	5556	227	589
181	Printing and service activities related to printing	44331	44077	58346	40555	21089	21120	36455	20827	5122	544
1811	Printing	24747	25983	41053	28117	12093	12433	26789	15166	3944	465
1812	Service activities related to printing	19584	18094	17294	12438	8996	8687	9666	5661	1178	79
1820	Reproduction of recorded media	372	389	152	160	168	225	39	88	11	1
1910	Coke oven products	171	186	205	158	62	63	95	71	-	-
1920	Refined petroleum products	4148419	5810476	2914761	2746929	791263	1336391	1028655	578150	588808	791619
201	Basic chemicals,fertilizers, etc.	643981	574675	564808	488114	405373	360159	354460	282817	13778	5383
2011	Basic chemicals	304815	280438	240704	234761	167778	159769	127420	127971	7083	3369
2012	Fertilizers and nitrogen compounds	322461	279522	307977	236507	230581	194003	217807	145955	4560	1113
2013	Plastics and synthetic rubber in primary forms	16705	14715	16127	16846	7014	6386	9234	8891	2135	901
202	Other chemical products	149863	89887	104041	139021	113924	43094	58000	74826	13254	11745
2021	Pesticides and other agrochemical products	6049	6224	5901	6306	2229	2297	1553	3125	119	157
2022	Paints,varnishes;printing ink and mastics	19260	28149	46048	60412	10454	13484	27543	39962	11188	10278
2023	Soap,cleaning and cosmetic preparations	105980	35505	34784	54926	88848	14862	17130	19480	-10	814
2029	Other chemical products n.e.c.	18575	20009	17308	17377	12392	12451	11774	12259	1956	496
2030	Man-made fibres	:	:	:	:	:	:	:	:	:	:
2100	Pharmaceuticals,medicinal chemicals, etc.	24050	11247	7706	27750	11831	4944	2889	14944	697	865
221	Rubber products	17866	18653	21021	29291	7381	9037	10334	14311	530	13464
2211	Rubber tyres and tubes	11918	11780	14540	13826	5679	6821	8676	9260	469	12875
2219	Other rubber products	5948	6873	6481	15465	1702	2216	1659	5051	61	590
2220	Plastics products	138751	161938	192770	147478	36912	44693	85508	58934	1828	8464
2310	Glass and glass products	19497	18518	21116	23890	8851	8904	10683	10823	679	1963
239	Non-metallic mineral products n.e.c.	557273	576656	671761	606938	322363	316242	372923	304527	84709	60194
2391	Refractory products	2044	3499	5629	5669	792	1486	2185	3030	:	58
2392	Clay building materials	36108	35899	33876	28707	25628	29311	21797	14624	1024	1236
2393	Other porcelain and ceramic products	131826	124830	168988	153134	89302	83557	99088	85346	1329	18659
2394	Cement, lime and plaster	149168	164188	192491	213633	58843	56589	84345	92114	18829	11328
2395	Articles of concrete, cement and plaster	165029	169411	199743	129409	104855	101025	139570	73156	9086	19089
2396	Cutting, shaping and finishing of stone	73098	78829	71034	76385	42943	44274	25939	36256	7047	9824
2399	Other non-metallic mineral products n.e.c.									47395	
2410	Basic iron and steel	485545	459532	465424	545930	205335	195178	153031	176731	106431	10695
2420	Basic precious and other non-ferrous metals	40253	42105	45619	11786	12180	8269	18980	5786	914	346
243	Casting of metals	469508	445158	426786	439138	239676	178597	191471	194082	38486	29189
2431	Casting of iron and steel	195139	189963	126818	126567	75422	70167	74586	56644	8260	798
2432	Casting of non-ferrous metals	274369	255194	299968	312570	164254	108430	116885	137438	30226	28391
251	Struct.metal products, tanks, reservoirs	288807	376739	427303	357370	129462	167443	242786	198851	23381	8378

continued

Oman

ISIC	Industry	Output at basic prices (thousands of Omani Rials)				Value added at basic prices (thousands of Omani Rials)				Gross fixed capital formation (thousands of Omani Rials)	
		2013	2014	2015	2016	2013	2014	2015	2016	2015	2016
2511	Structural metal products	200579	295566	332124	247577	81787	119075	159681	119632	22536	5891
2512	Tanks, reservoirs and containers of metal	88229	81173	95179	109793	47676	48368	83105	79219	845	2486
2513	Steam generators, excl. hot water boilers	...	...	...	...	...	...	...	...	...	...
2520	Weapons and ammunition	8961	8851	9181	7514	5124	5287	4353	4647	635	131
259	Other metal products;metal working services	65610	93393	114608	198653	33974	48786	57659	65783	1056	8734
2591	Forging,pressing,stamping,roll-forming of metal	1581	2206	11053	6676	703	1013	3998	1727	51	203
2592	Treatment and coating of metals; machining	34237	52050	50147	32728	18853	28724	27609	20345	710	520
2593	Cutlery, hand tools and general hardware	...	...	...	...	...	...	...	...	...	...
2599	Other fabricated metal products n.e.c.	29792	39137	53408	159249	14418	19049	26052	43712	295	8010
2610	Electronic components and boards	2536	2485	2879b/	2779b/	830	1033	1085b/	1327b/	-830b/	-785b/
2620	Computers and peripheral equipment	...	406	...b/	...b/	...	59	...b/	...b/	...b/	...b/
2630	Communication equipment	...	...	...	...	...	...	...	...	...	...
2640	Consumer electronics	...	...	...	...	...	...	...	...	...	...
265	Measuring,testing equipment; watches, etc.	...	...	...	...	...	...	...	...	...	...
2651	Measuring/testing/navigating equipment,etc.	...	...	...	...	...	...	...	...	...	...
2652	Watches and clocks	...	...	...	...	...	...	...	...	...	...
2660	Irradiation/electromedical equipment,etc.	...	...	...	...	...	...	...	...	...	...
2670	Optical instruments and photographic equipment	...	...	...	...	...	...	...	...	...	...
2680	Magnetic and optical media	43479	42173	31685	34559	16058	9651	7080	7071	264	230
2710	Electric motors,generators,transformers,etc.	52206	57375	67668	77910	16664	18765	27133	29776	-2	580
2720	Batteries and accumulators	16555	14779	17127	15120	3857	3972	5713	4996	139	132
273	Wiring and wiring devices	362440	340536	444013	321694	127546	119261	137767	62257	3695	2925
2731	Fibre optic cables	19682	14612	6838	29060	4893	5840	5146	24122	187	41
2732	Other electronic and electric wires and cables	339219	323061	437176c/	292634c/	120520	112385	132620c/	38136c/	3507c/	2885c/
2733	Wiring devices	3539	2863	...c/	...c/	2132	1036	...c/	...c/	...c/	...c/
2740	Electric lighting equipment	2205	8596	4314	4591	804	2566	1699	1957	398	-
2750	Domestic appliances	5609	8811	8997	9928	2357	3769	3975	2929	307	306
2790	Other electrical equipment	5032	5397	1330	4186	1135	1183	1100	3015	106	3
281	General-purpose machinery	15921	26327	12559	38750	8358	16015	5045	27501	270	1656
2811	Engines/turbines,excl.aircraft,vehicle engines	...	...	...	...	...	...	...	...	...	...
2812	Fluid power equipment	...	...	...	...	...	...	...	...	...	...
2813	Other pumps, compressors, taps and valves	4942	6665	4763	4031	2975	3990	1597	3503	101	34
2814	Bearings, gears, gearing and driving elements	...	...	...	...	...	...	...	...	...	...
2815	Ovens, furnaces and furnace burners	...	...	...	...	...	...	...	...	...	...
2816	Lifting and handling equipment	156	222	4323d/	1025	94	134	1717d/	387	146d/	16
2817	Office machinery, excl.computers,etc.	983	...	...	8413	807	...	...	6970	...	162
2818	Power-driven hand tools	7415	16851	...d/	23468	3777	10762	...d/	16153	...d/	1442
2819	Other general-purpose machinery	2426	2588	3473	1813	705	1129	1730	488	24	1
282	Special-purpose machinery	41013	43603	48102	16014	25652	28326	44617	12823	3643	275
2821	Agricultural and forestry machinery	...	...	...	...	...	...	...	...	...	...
2822	Metal-forming machinery and machine tools	...	...	...	...	...	...	...	...	...	...

Code	Industry	(1)	(2)	(3)	(4)	(5)	(6)	(7)	(8)	(9)	(10)
2823	Machinery for metallurgy	34475	39184	42899	12210	23022	26119	41899	10927	3368	244
2824	Mining, quarrying and construction machinery	…	…	…	…	…	…	…	…	…	…
2825	Food/beverage/tobacco processing machinery	…	…	…	…	…	…	…	…	…	…
2826	Textile/apparel/leather production machinery	6539	4418	5203	3803	2629	2207	2718	1896	275	32
2829	Other special-purpose machinery	…	…	…	…	…	…	…	…	…	…
2910	Motor vehicles	…	…	…	…	…	…	…	…	…	…
2920	Automobile bodies, trailers and semi-trailers	6224	6065	…	…	2309	2186	…	…	…	…
2930	Parts and accessories for motor vehicles	407	555	7432	7292	268	360	3032	5791	49	56
301	Building of ships and boats	1273	30539	17269	31039	-6818	14725	12206	12715	-	870
3011	Building of ships and floating structures	1273	30268	17079	31039e/	-6818	14600	12122	12715e/	-	870e/
3012	Building of pleasure and sporting boats	…	271	190	…e/	…	124	84	…e/	-	…e/
3020	Railway locomotives and rolling stock	…	…	…	…	…	…	…	…	…	…
3030	Air and spacecraft and related machinery	…	…	…	…	…	…	…	…	…	…
3040	Military fighting vehicles	…	…	…	…	…	…	…	…	…	…
309	Transport equipment n.e.c.	…	…	…	…	…	…	…	…	…	…
3091	Motorcycles	…	…	…	…	…	…	…	…	…	…
3092	Bicycles and invalid carriages	…	…	…	…	…	…	…	…	…	…
3099	Other transport equipment n.e.c.	…	…	…	…	…	…	…	…	…	…
3100	Furniture	48095	37648	45472	38665	24221	18779	23377	22800	160	1266
321	Jewellery, bijouterie and related articles	…	14080	18441	16949	…	4259	6031	5880	34	2
3211	Jewellery and related articles	…	14080	18441	16949	…	4259	6031	5880	34	2
3212	Imitation jewellery and related articles	…	…	…	…	…	…	…	…	…	…
3220	Musical instruments	…	…	…	…	…	…	…	…	…	…
3230	Sports goods	…	…	…	…	…	…	…	…	…	…
3240	Games and toys	…	…	…	…	…	…	…	…	…	…
3250	Medical and dental instruments and supplies	…	…	…	…	…	…	…	…	…	…
3290	Other manufacturing n.e.c.	399	763	840	466	181	354	548	246	-	5
331	Repair of fabricated metal products/machinery	326	374	299	332	204	229	170	227	-	-
3311	Repair of fabricated metal products	…	…	…	…	…	…	…	…	…	…
3312	Repair of machinery	…	…	…	…	…	…	…	…	…	…
3313	Repair of electronic and optical equipment	…	…	…	…	…	…	…	…	…	…
3314	Repair of electrical equipment	326	374	299	332	204	229	170	227	-	-
3315	Repair of transport equip., excl. motor vehicles	…	…	…	…	…	…	…	…	-	-
3319	Repair of other equipment	…	…	…	…	…	…	…	…	…	…
3320	Installation of industrial machinery/equipment	55721	28825	38917	37913	50351	25792	35515	28121	9	346
C	Total manufacturing	8384418	10227386	7766708	7305375	2805637	3254316	3358412	2612440	926332	985519

a/ 1621 includes 1610.
b/ 2610 includes 2620.
c/ 2732 includes 2733.
d/ 2816 includes 2818.
e/ 3011 includes 3012.

Panama

Supplier of information:
Instituto Nacional de Estadística y Censo, Contraloría General de la República, Panama.

Basic source of data:
Annual census/exhaustive survey.

Major deviations from ISIC (Revision 4):
None reported.

Reference period:
Calendar year.

Scope:
All privately owned enterprises.

Method of data collection:
Mail questionnaires and direct interviews in the field.

Type of enumeration:
Sample survey.

Adjusted for non-response:
Yes.

Concepts and definitions of variables:
Wages and salaries includes employers' contributions (in respect of their employees) paid to social security, pension and insurance schemes as well as the benefits received by employees under these schemes and severance and termination pay; it excludes remuneration for time not worked.
Output refers to value of sale of all products only.

Related national publications:
Anual Boletín de la Encuesta Entre Empresas No Financieras, published by the Instituto Nacional de Estadística y Censo, Panama.

ISIC Revision 4		Number of enterprises					Number of employees					Wages and salaries paid to employees				
			(number)					(number)					(thousands of Panamanian Balboas)			
ISIC	Industry	Note	2013	2014	2015	2016a/	Note	2013	2014	2015	2016a/	Note	2013	2014	2015	2016a/
1010	Processing/preserving of meat		30	30	30	24		7278	7223	7899	8219		51899	56897	61478	70813
1020	Processing/preserving of fish, etc.		18	19	20	21		1308	1408	1341	1645		9155	10466	11267	13481
1030	Processing/preserving of fruit, vegetables		10	10	11	10		261	259	315	290		757	1463	3043	2908
1040	Vegetable and animal oils and fats		3	3	3	3		1194	1134	946	872		8889	9559	9454	9121
1050	Dairy products		20	17	19	17		3490	3630	4109	4122		40048	39768	38967	41712
106	Grain mill products,starches and starch products		49	48	51	55		1428	1493	1679	1842		11034	12583	14285	18265
1061	Grain mill products		49	48	51	55		1428	1493	1679	1842		11034	12583	14285	18265
1062	Starches and starch products		...	...	...	...		...	...	...	...		...	...	...	...
107	Other food products		186	173	183	185		9758	11850	14069	14189		69782	84977	102193	110268
1071	Bakery products		141	128	137	140		5210	4991	6672	6074		36620	42117	55941	55411
1072	Sugar		4	4	4	4		2412	4650	5285	6096		16923	25453	28728	36675
1073	Cocoa, chocolate and sugar confectionery		...	...	...	...		...	...	...	...		...	...	...	...
1074	Macaroni, noodles, couscous, etc.		6	6	6	6		199	234	261	295		1368	1806	2026	2440
1075	Prepared meals and dishes		...	...	...	...		...	...	...	...		...	...	...	...
1079	Other food products n.e.c.		35	35	36	35		1937	1975	1851	1724		14871	15601	15498	15742
1080	Prepared animal feeds		10	10	10	10		593	605	658	809		4670	4768	5516	6892
110	Beverages		16	18	17	16		2410	2731	2782	2778		33669	38106	38462	43378
1101	Distilling, rectifying and blending of spirits		6	6	5	5		2271	2570	2413	2460		32913	37093	34950	39524
1102	Wines		...	...	...	...		...	...	...	...		...	...	...	...
1103	Malt liquors and malt		...	...	...	...		...	...	...	...		...	...	...	...
1104	Soft drinks,mineral waters,other bottled waters		10	12	12	11		139	161	369	318		756	1012	3512	3854
1200	Tobacco products		...	...	...	...		...	...	...	...		...	...	...	...
131	Spinning, weaving and finishing of textiles		12	17	17	17		620	668	730	687		5654	5678	5867	6223
1311	Preparation and spinning of textile fibres		...	...	...	...		...	...	...	...		...	...	...	...
1312	Weaving of textiles		...	...	...	...		...	...	...	...		...	...	...	...
1313	Finishing of textiles		12	17	17	17		620	668	730	687		5654	5678	5867	6223
139	Other textiles		8	10	7	7		167	247	144	128		1131	1644	1546	1832
1391	Knitted and crocheted fabrics		8	...	...	...		167	...	...	...		1131	...	...	...
1392	Made-up textile articles, except apparel		...	...	...	...		...	...	...	...		...	...	...	...
1393	Carpets and rugs		...	...	...	...		...	...	...	...		...	...	...	...
1394	Cordage, rope, twine and netting		...	...	...	...		...	...	...	...		...	...	...	...
1399	Other textiles n.e.c.		...	10	7	7		...	247	144	128		1131	1644	1546	1832
1410	Wearing apparel, except fur apparel		35	36	27	26		1587	1244	825	989		8849	9113	6856	7394
1420	Articles of fur		...	...	...	...		...	...	...	...		...	...	...	...
1430	Knitted and crocheted apparel		...	...	...	...		...	...	...	...		...	...	...	...
151	Leather;luggage,handbags,saddlery,harness;fur		6	6	6	6		255	243	250	252		1474	1849	1890	1925
1511	Tanning/dressing of leather; dressing of fur		6	6	6	6		255	243	250	252		1474	1849	1890	1925
1512	Luggage,handbags,etc.;saddlery/harness		...	...	...	...		...	...	...	...		...	...	...	...
1520	Footwear		3	3	3	3		34	34	31	30		149	147	156	154
1610	Sawmilling and planing of wood		8	9	7	7		256	270	336	207		1367	1772	2627	1572

Code	Description												
162	Wood products, cork, straw, plaiting materials	16	14	10	9	208	166	157	123	1542	1248	1079	928
1621	Veneer sheets and wood-based panels	5	3	3	…	103	67	71	…	884	551	531	…
1622	Builders' carpentry and joinery	11	11	7	3	105	99	86	66	658	696	548	545
1623	Wooden containers	7	8	9	6	393	390	402	387	…	…	548	383
1629	Other wood products;articles of cork,straw	…	…	…	…	…	…	…	…	…	…	…	…
170	Paper and paper products	15	13	14	13	1169	1022	1025	976	11351	10013	10845	10336
1701	Pulp, paper and paperboard	3	…	…	…	142	…	…	…	1609	…	…	…
1702	Corrugated paper and paperboard	5	5	5	4	634	632	623	589	6217	3594	6846	6291
1709	Other articles of paper and paperboard	7	8	9	9	393	390	402	387	3525	3594	3999	4045
181	Printing and service activities related to printing	96	95	89	86	2447	2309	2015	1978	26016	20065	22800	21302
1811	Printing	93	92	86	86	2231	2098	1827	1978	23601	19068	20454	21302
1812	Service activities related to printing	3	3	3	…	216	211	188	…	2415	997	2346	…
1820	Reproduction of recorded media	…	…	…	…	…	…	…	…	…	…	…	…
1910	Coke oven products	…	…	…	…	…	…	…	…	…	…	…	…
1920	Refined petroleum products	…	…	…	…	…	…	…	…	…	…	…	…
201	Basic chemicals,fertilizers, etc.	9	9	9	9	597	544	623	691	6461	5927	7335	8330
2011	Basic chemicals	9	9	9	9	597	544	623	691	6461	5927	7335	8330
2012	Fertilizers and nitrogen compounds	…	…	…	…	…	…	…	…	…	…	…	…
2013	Plastics and synthetic rubber in primary forms	…	…	…	…	…	…	…	…	…	…	…	…
202	Other chemical products	26	26	30	27	691	682	565	562	6606	7214	6608	6472
2021	Pesticides and other agrochemical products	4	4	4	4	148	145	131	124	1697	1858	1711	1568
2022	Paints,varnishes;printing ink and mastics	4	4	4	4	148	145	131	124	1697	1858	1711	1568
2023	Soap,cleaning and cosmetic preparations	18	21	18	19	461	446	330	339	3773	3880	3198	3282
2029	Other chemical products n.e.c.	4	5	4	4	82	91	104	99	1136	1476	1699	1622
2030	Man-made fibres	…	…	…	…	…	…	…	…	…	…	…	…
2100	Pharmaceuticals,medicinal chemicals, etc.	9	9	9	4	950	994	982	432	11669	13774	14042	7617
221	Rubber products	…	…	…	…	…	…	…	…	…	…	…	…
2211	Rubber tyres and tubes	…	…	…	…	…	…	…	…	…	…	…	…
2219	Other rubber products	…	…	…	…	…	…	…	…	…	…	…	…
2220	Plastics products	33	34	29	31	1711	1510	1139	1304	17077	18497	15186	17603
2310	Glass and glass products	5	5	5	…	278	15	15	…	349	75	75	…
239	Non-metallic mineral products n.e.c.	64	62	60	64	2591	2941	2760	2851	30631	37831	38462	39902
2391	Refractory products	6	4	4	4	176	193	196	177	1163	1581	1647	1756
2392	Clay building materials	…	…	…	…	…	…	…	…	…	…	…	…
2393	Other porcelain and ceramic products	…	…	…	…	…	…	…	…	…	…	…	…
2394	Cement, lime and plaster	3	4	4	4	695	1008	972	1007	14221	18139	19725	20356
2395	Articles of concrete, cement and plaster	52	51	52	56	1685	1710	1592	1667	15093	17892	17090	17790
2396	Cutting, shaping and finishing of stone	3	3	…	…	35	30	…	…	154	219	…	…
2399	Other non-metallic mineral products n.e.c.	…	…	…	…	…	…	…	…	…	…	…	…
2410	Basic iron and steel	6	5	3	3	648	582	527	511	5700	6683	7615	5867
2420	Basic precious and other non-ferrous metals	…	…	…	…	…	…	…	…	…	…	…	…
243	Casting of metals	…	…	…	…	…	…	…	…	…	…	…	…
2431	Casting of iron and steel	…	…	…	…	…	…	…	…	…	…	…	…
2432	Casting of non-ferrous metals	…	…	…	…	…	…	…	…	…	…	…	…
251	Struct.metal products, tanks, reservoirs	77	79	82	77	1282	1333	1425	1279	10623	10497	12185	12886

continued

Panama

ISIC Revision 4		Number of enterprises (number)					Number of employees (number)					Wages and salaries paid to employees (thousands of Panamanian Balboas)				
ISIC	Industry	Note	2013	2014	2015	2016a/	Note	2013	2014	2015	2016a/	Note	2013	2014	2015	2016a/
2511	Structural metal products		73	76	79	74		1194	1256	1349	1194		9974	9902	11537	12190
2512	Tanks, reservoirs and containers of metal		4	3	3	3		88	77	76	85		649	595	648	696
2513	Steam generators, excl. hot water boilers		...	...	...	...		...	...	...	...		...	...	...	...
2520	Weapons and ammunition		...	...	...	...		...	...	...	...		...	...	...	...
259	Other metal products;metal working services		23	24	25	24		427	421	400	395		4403	4638	4772	4918
2591	Forging,pressing,stamping,roll-forming of metal		...	...	...	...		...	...	...	...		...	...	...	...
2592	Treatment and coating of metals; machining		...	...	...	...		...	...	...	...		...	...	...	...
2593	Cutlery, hand tools and general hardware		...	...	...	...		...	...	...	...		...	...	...	...
2599	Other fabricated metal products n.e.c.		23	24	25	24		427	421	400	395		4403	4638	4772	4918
2610	Electronic components and boards		...	...	...	...		...	...	...	...		...	...	...	...
2620	Computers and peripheral equipment		...	...	...	...		...	...	...	...		...	...	...	...
2630	Communication equipment		...	...	...	...		...	...	...	...		...	...	...	...
2640	Consumer electronics		...	...	...	...		...	...	...	...		...	...	...	...
265	Measuring,testing equipment; watches, etc.		...	...	...	...		...	...	...	...		...	...	...	...
2651	Measuring/testing/navigating equipment,etc.		...	...	...	...		...	...	...	...		...	...	...	...
2652	Watches and clocks		...	...	...	...		...	...	...	...		...	...	...	...
2660	Irradiation/electromedical equipment,etc.		...	...	...	...		...	...	...	...		...	...	...	...
2670	Optical instruments and photographic equipment		...	...	...	...		...	...	...	...		...	...	...	...
2680	Magnetic and optical media		...	...	...	...		...	...	...	...		...	...	...	...
2710	Electric motors,generators,transformers,etc.		...	...	...	...		...	...	...	...		...	...	...	...
2720	Batteries and accumulators		...	...	...	...		...	...	...	...		...	...	...	...
273	Wiring and wiring devices		...	...	...	...		...	...	...	...		...	...	...	...
2731	Fibre optic cables		...	...	...	...		...	...	...	...		...	...	...	...
2732	Other electronic and electric wires and cables		...	...	...	...		...	...	...	...		...	...	...	...
2733	Wiring devices		...	...	...	...		...	...	...	...		...	...	...	...
2740	Electric lighting equipment		5	4	5	6		374	344	367	320		3130	2898	2978	3011
2750	Domestic appliances		...	...	...	...		...	...	...	...		...	...	...	...
2790	Other electrical equipment		...	...	...	...		...	...	...	...		...	...	...	...
281	General-purpose machinery		...	...	...	...		...	...	...	...		...	...	...	...
2811	Engines/turbines,excl.aircraft,vehicle engines		...	...	...	...		...	...	...	...		...	...	...	...
2812	Fluid power equipment		...	...	...	...		...	...	...	...		...	...	...	...
2813	Other pumps, compressors, taps and valves		...	...	...	...		...	...	...	...		...	...	...	...
2814	Bearings, gears, gearing and driving elements		...	...	...	...		...	...	...	...		...	...	...	...
2815	Ovens, furnaces and furnace burners		...	...	...	...		...	...	...	...		...	...	...	...
2816	Lifting and handling equipment		...	...	...	...		...	...	...	...		...	...	...	...
2817	Office machinery, excl.computers,etc.		...	...	...	...		...	...	...	...		...	...	...	...
2818	Power-driven hand tools		...	...	...	...		...	...	...	...		...	...	...	...
2819	Other general-purpose machinery		...	...	...	...		...	...	...	...		...	...	...	...
282	Special-purpose machinery		4	3	3	3		88	38	33	32		554	326	301	312
2821	Agricultural and forestry machinery		4	3	3	3		88	38	33	32		554	326	301	312
2822	Metal-forming machinery and machine tools		...	...	...	...		...	...	...	...		...	...	...	...

Code	Description												
2823	Machinery for metallurgy	...	...	...	...	...	...	...	...	...	...	...	...
2824	Mining, quarrying and construction machinery	...	...	...	...	...	...	...	...	...	...	...	...
2825	Food/beverage/tobacco processing machinery	...	...	...	...	...	...	...	...	...	...	...	...
2826	Textile/apparel/leather production machinery	...	...	...	...	...	...	...	...	...	...	...	...
2829	Other special-purpose machinery	...	...	...	...	...	...	...	...	...	...	...	...
2910	Motor vehicles	...	...	...	...	...	...	...	...	...	...	...	...
2920	Automobile bodies, trailers and semi-trailers	...	...	...	...	...	...	...	...	...	...	...	...
2930	Parts and accessories for motor vehicles	...	3	3	3	14	17	24	25	174	180	194	201
301	Building of ships and boats	...	...	...	6	...	...	...	132	...	...	...	1201
3011	Building of ships and floating structures	...	...	...	6	...	...	...	132	...	...	...	1201
3012	Building of pleasure and sporting boats	...	...	...	...	...	...	...	...	...	...	...	...
3020	Railway locomotives and rolling stock	...	...	...	...	...	...	...	...	...	...	...	...
3030	Air and spacecraft and related machinery	...	...	...	...	...	...	...	...	...	...	...	...
3040	Military fighting vehicles	...	...	...	...	...	...	...	...	...	...	...	...
309	Transport equipment n.e.c.	...	...	...	...	...	...	...	...	...	...	...	...
3091	Motorcycles	...	...	...	...	...	...	...	...	...	...	...	...
3092	Bicycles and invalid carriages	...	...	...	...	...	...	...	...	...	...	...	...
3099	Other transport equipment n.e.c.	...	...	...	...	...	...	...	...	...	...	...	...
3100	Furniture	63	67	75	80	1360	1489	1544	1631	11326	11788	12046	10543
321	Jewellery, bijouterie and related articles	...	...	...	...	...	...	...	...	...	...	...	...
3211	Jewellery and related articles	...	...	...	...	...	...	...	...	...	...	...	...
3212	Imitation jewellery and related articles	...	...	...	...	...	...	...	...	...	...	...	...
3220	Musical instruments	...	...	...	...	...	...	...	...	...	...	...	...
3230	Sports goods	...	...	...	...	...	...	...	...	...	...	...	...
3240	Games and toys	3	3	3	4	57	60	61	72	552	566	544	608
3250	Medical and dental instruments and supplies	6	9	9	9	76	84	86	79	746	825	768	704
3290	Other manufacturing n.e.c.	14	18	9	5	344	407	250	139	3292	3883	2276	842
331	Repair of fabricated metal products/machinery	47	44	49	49	1128	1587	1929	2257	18771	17595	23687	29988
3311	Repair of fabricated metal products	4	4	3	3	255	246	234	218	3029	3057	2568	2324
3312	Repair of machinery	10	10	10	11	147	147	148	178	1218	1144	1258	1681
3313	Repair of electronic and optical equipment	10	3	3	3	...	...	36	34	...	...	625	550
3314	Repair of electrical equipment	12	11	11	11	126	189	127	107	1727	1984	1258	1038
3315	Repair of transport equip., excl. motor vehicles	21	19	22	21	600	1005	1384	1720	12797	11410	17978	24395
3319	Repair of other equipment	...	...	...	...	...	...	...	...	...	...	...	...
3320	Installation of industrial machinery/equipment	...	...	...	...	...	...	...	...	...	...	...	...
C	Total manufacturing	900	928	940	958	48435	49830	51789	51491	428726	457990	482722	510283

a/ Provisional data.

Panama

			Output at producers' prices (thousands of Panamanian Balboas)					Value added (thousands of Panamanian Balboas)					Gross fixed capital formation (thousands of Panamanian Balboas)	
ISIC	Industry (ISIC Revision 4)	Note	2013	2014	2015	2016a/	Note	2013	2014	2015	2016	Note	2015	2016
1010	Processing/preserving of meat		525495	562887	604340	598676		...	...	...	...		...	...
1020	Processing/preserving of fish, etc.		133460	160083	148512	175294		...	...	...	...		...	...
1030	Processing/preserving of fruit,vegetables		9711	9416	27025	17597		...	...	...	...		...	...
1040	Vegetable and animal oils and fats		95886	86346	80085	73930		...	...	...	...		...	...
1050	Dairy products		406373	428765	453071	344344		...	...	...	...		...	...
106	Grain mill products,starches and starch products		222732	226807	221228	258634		...	...	...	...		...	...
1061	Grain mill products		222732	226807	221228	258634		...	...	...	...		...	...
1062	Starches and starch products		...	...	...	...		...	...	...	...		...	...
107	Other food products		558594	546361	612407	618700		...	...	...	...		...	...
1071	Bakery products		261813	246276	320695	320438		...	...	...	...		...	...
1072	Sugar		147170	143948	153086	156213		...	...	...	...		...	...
1073	Cocoa, chocolate and sugar confectionery		11881	13971	14061	14356		...	...	...	...		...	...
1074	Macaroni, noodles, couscous, etc.		...	...	...	...		...	...	...	...		...	...
1075	Prepared meals and dishes		...	...	...	...		...	...	...	...		...	...
1079	Other food products n.e.c.		137730	142166	124565	127693		...	...	...	...		...	...
1080	Prepared animal feeds		57144	58954	62921	63751		...	...	...	...		...	...
110	Beverages		360091	337286	341409	381219		...	...	...	...		...	...
1101	Distilling, rectifying and blending of spirits		355353	332137	324374	363276		...	...	...	...		...	...
1102	Wines		...	...	...	...		...	...	...	...		...	...
1103	Malt liquors and malt		...	...	...	...		...	...	...	...		...	...
1104	Soft drinks,mineral waters,other bottled waters		4738	5149	17035	17943		...	...	...	...		...	...
1200	Tobacco products		...	...	...	...		...	...	...	...		...	...
131	Spinning, weaving and finishing of textiles		32039	36396	34128	32697		...	...	...	...		...	...
1311	Preparation and spinning of textile fibres		...	...	...	...		...	...	...	...		...	...
1312	Weaving of textiles		...	...	...	...		...	...	...	...		...	...
1313	Finishing of textiles		32039	36396	34128	32697		...	...	...	...		...	...
139	Other textiles		9607	12921	9693	6689		...	...	...	...		...	...
1391	Knitted and crocheted fabrics		9607	12921	9693	6689		...	...	...	...		...	...
1392	Made-up textile articles, except apparel		...	...	...	...		...	...	...	...		...	...
1393	Carpets and rugs		...	...	...	...		...	...	...	...		...	...
1394	Cordage, rope, twine and netting		...	...	...	...		...	...	...	...		...	...
1399	Other textiles n.e.c.		...	12921	9693	6689		...	...	...	...		...	...
1410	Wearing apparel, except fur apparel		41121	43100	30056	26079		...	...	...	...		...	...
1420	Articles of fur		...	...	...	...		...	...	...	...		...	...
1430	Knitted and crocheted apparel		...	...	...	...		...	...	...	...		...	...
151	Leather;luggage,handbags,saddlery,harness;fur		18320	20668	16013	13353		...	...	...	...		...	...
1511	Tanning/dressing of leather; dressing of fur		18320	20668	16013	13353		...	...	...	...		...	...
1512	Luggage,handbags,etc.;saddlery/harness		...	...	...	...		...	...	...	...		...	...
1520	Footwear		573	380	508	720		...	...	...	...		...	...
1610	Sawmilling and planing of wood		8150	10521	7897	5666		...	...	...	...		...	...

Code	Description								
162	Wood products, cork, straw, plaiting materials	...	...	...	...	11148	7935	7449	7048
1621	Veneer sheets and wood-based panels	...	...	...	...	...	...	...	...
1622	Builders' carpentry and joinery	...	...	...	...	8568	5434	5451	5283
1623	Wooden containers	...	...	...	...	2580	2500	1998	1765
1629	Other wood products;articles of cork,straw	...	...	...	...	...	...	...	...
170	Paper and paper products	...	...	...	...	101764	86479	81184	69824
1701	Pulp, paper and paperboard	...	...	...	...	19101	...	...	...
1702	Corrugated paper and paperboard	...	...	...	...	52558	55028	50614	39858
1709	Other articles of paper and paperboard	...	...	...	...	30105	31451	30570	29966
181	Printing and service activities related to printing	...	...	...	...	140404	142337	122932	123157
1811	Printing	...	...	...	...	126318	129109	112095	123157
1812	Service activities related to printing	...	...	...	...	14086	13229	10837	...
1820	Reproduction of recorded media	...	...	...	...	...	...	...	...
1910	Coke oven products	...	...	...	...	...	...	...	...
1920	Refined petroleum products	...	...	...	...	...	...	...	...
201	Basic chemicals,fertilizers, etc.	...	...	...	...	60947	50932	63448	65326
2011	Basic chemicals	...	...	...	...	60947	50932	63448	65326
2012	Fertilizers and nitrogen compounds	...	...	...	...	...	...	...	...
2013	Plastics and synthetic rubber in primary forms	...	...	...	...	71541	72390	64762	51837
202	Other chemical products	...	...	...	...	...	...	...	...
2021	Pesticides and other agrochemical products	...	...	...	...	24573	27589	24293	17486
2022	Paints,varnishes;printing ink and mastics	...	...	...	...	...	...	...	...
2023	Soap,cleaning and cosmetic preparations	...	...	...	...	28548	28834	31106	27859
2029	Other chemical products n.e.c.	...	...	...	...	18420	15967	9363	6492
2030	Man-made fibres	...	...	...	...	...	...	...	...
2100	Pharmaceuticals,medicinal chemicals, etc.	...	...	...	...	53597	43665	46296	55840
221	Rubber products	...	...	...	...	...	...	...	...
2211	Rubber tyres and tubes	...	...	...	...	...	...	...	...
2219	Other rubber products	...	...	...	...	...	...	...	...
2220	Plastics products	...	...	...	...	154520	177023	244187	127445
2310	Glass and glass products	...	...	...	...	28687	700	672	...
239	Non-metallic mineral products n.e.c.	...	...	...	...	705104	698601	808501	619421
2391	Refractory products	...	...	...	...	7763	9312	9513	7758
2392	Clay building materials	...	...	...	...	...	...	...	...
2393	Other porcelain and ceramic products	...	...	...	...	...	...	...	...
2394	Cement, lime and plaster	...	...	...	...	437055	445783	593116	423505
2395	Articles of concrete, cement and plaster	...	...	...	...	258814	242099	205872	188158
2396	Cutting, shaping and finishing of stone	...	...	...	...	1472	1407	...	...
2399	Other non-metallic mineral products n.e.c.	...	...	...	...	...	...	...	...
2410	Basic iron and steel	...	...	...	...	127027	95250	52090	43603
2420	Basic precious and other non-ferrous metals	...	...	...	...	...	...	...	...
243	Casting of metals	...	...	...	...	...	...	...	...
2431	Casting of iron and steel	...	...	...	...	...	...	...	...
2432	Casting of non-ferrous metals	...	...	...	...	...	...	...	...
251	Struct.metal products, tanks, reservoirs	...	...	...	...	89753	67631	81351	75108

continued

Panama

ISIC	Industry	Note	Output at producers' prices (thousands of Panamanian Balboas) 2013	2014	2015	2016a/	Note	Value added (thousands of Panamanian Balboas) 2013	2014	2015	2016	Note	Gross fixed capital formation (thousands of Panamanian Balboas) 2015	2016
2511	Structural metal products		85575	63556	77597	70964		...	...	...	...		...	...
2512	Tanks, reservoirs and containers of metal		4178	4075	3754	4144		...	...	...	...		...	...
2513	Steam generators, excl. hot water boilers		...	...	...	...		...	...	...	...		...	...
2520	Weapons and ammunition		...	...	...	...		...	...	...	...		...	...
259	Other metal products;metal working services		35159	33041	40805	43497		...	...	...	...		...	...
2591	Forging,pressing,stamping,roll-forming of metal		...	...	...	...		...	...	...	...		...	...
2592	Treatment and coating of metals machining		...	...	...	...		...	...	...	...		...	...
2593	Cutlery, hand tools and general hardware		...	...	...	...		...	...	...	...		...	...
2599	Other fabricated metal products n.e.c.		35159	33041	40805	43497		...	...	...	...		...	...
2610	Electronic components and boards		...	...	...	...		...	...	...	...		...	...
2620	Computers and peripheral equipment		...	...	...	...		...	...	...	...		...	...
2630	Communication equipment		...	...	...	...		...	...	...	...		...	...
2640	Consumer electronics		...	...	...	...		...	...	...	...		...	...
265	Measuring,testing equipment; watches, etc.		...	...	...	...		...	...	...	...		...	...
2651	Measuring/testing/navigating equipment,etc.		...	...	...	...		...	...	...	...		...	...
2652	Watches and clocks		...	...	...	...		...	...	...	...		...	...
2660	Irradiation/electromedical equipment,etc.		...	...	...	...		...	...	...	...		...	...
2670	Optical instruments and photographic equipment		...	...	...	...		...	...	...	...		...	...
2680	Magnetic and optical media		...	...	...	...		...	...	...	...		...	...
2710	Electric motors,generators,transformers,etc.		...	...	...	...		...	...	...	...		...	...
2720	Batteries and accumulators		...	...	...	...		...	...	...	...		...	...
273	Wiring and wiring devices		...	...	...	...		...	...	...	...		...	...
2731	Fibre optic cables		...	...	...	...		...	...	...	...		...	...
2732	Other electronic and electric wires and cables		...	...	...	...		...	...	...	...		...	...
2733	Wiring devices		...	...	...	...		...	...	...	...		...	...
2740	Electric lighting equipment		17030	11457	12045	16359		...	...	...	...		...	...
2750	Domestic appliances		...	...	...	...		...	...	...	...		...	...
2790	Other electrical equipment		...	...	...	...		...	...	...	...		...	...
281	General-purpose machinery		...	...	...	...		...	...	...	...		...	...
2811	Engines/turbines,excl.aircraft,vehicle engines		...	...	...	...		...	...	...	...		...	...
2812	Fluid power equipment		...	...	...	...		...	...	...	...		...	...
2813	Other pumps, compressors, taps and valves		...	...	...	...		...	...	...	...		...	...
2814	Bearings, gears, gearing and driving elements		...	...	...	...		...	...	...	...		...	...
2815	Ovens, furnaces and furnace burners		...	...	...	...		...	...	...	...		...	...
2816	Lifting and handling equipment		...	...	...	...		...	...	...	...		...	...
2817	Office machinery, excl.computers,etc.		...	...	...	...		...	...	...	...		...	...
2818	Power-driven hand tools		...	...	...	...		...	...	...	...		...	...
2819	Other general-purpose machinery		3061	1386	1469	1297		...	...	...	...		...	...
282	Special-purpose machinery		3061	1386	1469	1297		...	...	...	...		...	...
2821	Agricultural and forestry machinery		...	...	...	...		...	...	...	...		...	...
2822	Metal-forming machinery and machine tools		...	...	...	...		...	...	...	...		...	...

Code	Description							
2823	Machinery for metallurgy	...	...	...	...	...	...	...
2824	Mining, quarrying and construction machinery	...	...	...	...	...	...	...
2825	Food/beverage/tobacco processing machinery	...	...	...	...	...	...	...
2826	Textile/apparel/leather production machinery	...	...	...	...	...	...	...
2829	Other special-purpose machinery	...	...	...	...	...	...	...
2910	Motor vehicles	...	...	...	...	...	...	...
2920	Automobile bodies, trailers and semi-trailers	...	...	...	...	...	...	...
2930	Parts and accessories for motor vehicles	...	...	...	1532	1547	1336	1123
301	Building of ships and boats	...	...	...	5644	...	...	...
3011	Building of ships and floating structures	...	...	...	5644	...	...	...
3012	Building of pleasure and sporting boats	...	...	...	...	...	...	...
3020	Railway locomotives and rolling stock	...	...	...	...	...	...	...
3030	Air and spacecraft and related machinery	...	...	...	...	...	...	...
3040	Military fighting vehicles	...	...	...	...	...	...	...
309	Transport equipment n.e.c.	...	...	...	...	...	...	...
3091	Motorcycles	...	...	...	...	...	...	...
3092	Bicycles and invalid carriages	...	...	...	...	...	...	...
3099	Other transport equipment n.e.c.	...	...	...	...	...	...	...
3100	Furniture	...	...	...	67024	69800	66220	60828
321	Jewellery, bijouterie and related articles	...	...	...	...	...	...	...
3211	Jewellery and related articles	...	...	...	...	...	...	...
3212	Imitation jewellery and related articles	...	...	...	...	...	...	...
3220	Musical instruments	...	...	...	...	...	...	...
3230	Sports goods	...	...	...	...	...	...	...
3240	Games and toys	...	...	...	3738	2516	2607	2436
3250	Medical and dental instruments and supplies	...	...	...	3195	3192	3448	3170
3290	Other manufacturing n.e.c.	...	...	...	5945	20539	29787	21881
331	Repair of fabricated metal products/machinery	...	...	...	126470	127646	115056	104018
3311	Repair of fabricated metal products	...	...	...	10586	13410	13717	10915
3312	Repair of machinery	...	...	...	9338	7662	6356	6344
3313	Repair of electronic and optical equipment	...	...	...	2600	2956	...	...
3314	Repair of electrical equipment	...	...	...	8129	6616	7902	7774
3315	Repair of transport equip., excl. motor vehicles	...	...	...	95817	97001	87081	78985
3319	Repair of other equipment	...	...	...	...	...	...	...
3320	Installation of industrial machinery/equipment	...	...	...	...	...	...	...
C	Total manufacturing	...	...	...	4292586	4254957	4494937	4110568

a/ Provisional data.

Panama

ISIC Revision 4 — Index numbers of industrial production (2010=100)

ISIC	Industry	Note	2005	2006	2007	2008	2009	2010	2011	2012	2013	2014	2015	2016
10	Food products	a/	89	93	96	99	100	100	102	105	107	109	113	...
11	Beverages	a/	...	...	...	...	...	...	...	...	...	...	...	...
12	Tobacco products		...	...	...	...	...	...	...	...	...	...	...	...
13	Textiles		372	287	285	222	120	100	92	96	94	89	93	...
14	Wearing apparel		116	106	108	109	113	100	115	107	112	109	121	...
15	Leather and related products		67	79	75	87	84	100	90	108	97	117	107	...
16	Wood products, excluding furniture		104	105	104	101	101	100	101	101	101	101	111	...
17	Paper and paper products		118	128	141	144	111	100	98	106	102	104	112	...
18	Printing and reproduction of recorded media		84	87	86	88	93	100	106	124	104	106	109	...
19	Coke and refined petroleum products		...	...	...	...	...	...	...	...	...	...	...	...
20	Chemicals and chemical products	b/	92	96	99	101	93	100	99	97	97	96	113	...
21	Pharmaceuticals,medicinal chemicals, etc.	b/	...	...	...	...	...	...	...	...	...	...	...	...
22	Rubber and plastics products		100	101	102	99	101	100	100	100	99	100	98	...
23	Other non-metallic mineral products		66	80	94	119	104	100	112	128	135	126	128	...
24	Basic metals		109	108	110	108	100	100	100	91	96	96	99	...
25	Fabricated metal products, except machinery		98	106	112	86	98	100	100	99	97	99	99	...
26	Computer, electronic and optical products	c/	87	65	78	79	91	100	94	97	51	51	43	...
27	Electrical equipment	c/	...	...	...	...	...	...	...	...	...	...	...	...
28	Machinery and equipment n.e.c.		102	99	101	100	100	100	100	100	100	100	100	...
29	Motor vehicles, trailers and semi-trailers		137	123	117	117	95	100	97	99	98	98	98	...
30	Other transport equipment		104	98	101	100	100	100	100	100	100	100	100	...
31	Furniture	d/	91	91	106	104	98	100	97	101	99	101	99	...
32	Other manufacturing	d/	...	...	...	...	...	...	...	...	...	...	...	...
33	Repair and installation of machinery/equipment		...	...	...	...	...	...	...	...	...	...	...	...
C	Total manufacturing		88	93	97	102	100	100	103	109	109	110	113	...

a/ 10 includes 11.
b/ 20 includes 21.
c/ 26 includes 27.
d/ 31 includes 32.

Paraguay

Supplier of information:
Dirección General de Estadísticas, Encuestas y Censos (DGEEC), Asunción.

Basic source of data:
Survey on registered enterprises.

Major deviations from ISIC (Revision 4):
Data presented in accordance with ISIC (Revision 4) were originally classified according to the national classification system (Clasificación Nacional de Actividades Económicas del Paraguay - CNAEP)

Reference period:
Calendar year.

Scope:
All registered enterprises.

Method of data collection:
Mail questionnaires and direct interviews in the field.

Type of enumeration:
Sample survey.

Adjusted for non-response:
Yes.

Concepts and definitions of variables:
Wages and salaries excludes hoursing and family allowances paid directly by the employer; it includes employers' contributions (in respect of their employees) paid to social security, pension and insurance schemes as well as the benefits received by employees under these schemes and severance and termination pay.
Output excludes value of fixed assets produced by the unit for its own use, net change between the beginning and end of the year in the value of stocks of finished goods as well as the value of work in process and stocks and goods to be shipped in the same condition as received; it includes revenue from non-industrial activities.

Related national publications:
Resultados de las Encuestas Económicas (EEE-MyG2015 - EMyPE2016), published by the Dirección General de Estadísticas, Encuestas y Censos (DGEEC), Asunción.

Paraguay

ISIC Revision 4		Number of enterprises					Number of persons engaged					Wages and salaries paid to employees				
			(number)					(number)					(millions of Paraguayan Guaranies)			
ISIC	Industry	Note	2013	2014	2015	2016	Note	2013	2014	2015	2016	Note	2013	2014	2015	2016
C	Total manufacturing		...	7178	...	...		...	124509	...	...		...	3799182	...	...

ISIC Revision 4		Output at producers' prices					Value added					Gross fixed capital formation		
			(millions of Paraguayan Guaranies)					(millions of Paraguayan Guaranies)					(millions of Paraguayan Guaranies)	
ISIC	Industry	Note	2013	2014	2015	2016	Note	2013	2014	2015	2016	Note	2015	2016
C	Total manufacturing		...	44689754	...	...		...	...	...	...		...	...

ISIC Revision 4		Index numbers of industrial production												
			(2010=100)											
ISIC	Industry	Note	2005	2006	2007	2008	2009	2010	2011	2012	2013	2014	2015	2016
C	Total manufacturing		...	...	...	...	...	...	...	...	...	...	...	...

Peru

Supplier of information:
Instituto Nacional de Estadística e Informática (INEI), Lima.

Basic source of data:
Administrative source.

Major deviations from ISIC (Revision 4):
None reported.

Reference period:
Fiscal year.

Scope:
All establishments.

Method of data collection:
Not reported.

Type of enumeration:
Not reported.

Adjusted for non-response:
Not reported.

Concepts and definitions of variables:
No deviations from the standard UN concepts and definitions are reported.

Related national publications:
PERÚ: Serie de Cuentas Nacionales, published by Instituto Nacional de Estadística e Informática (INEI), Lima.

Peru

ISIC	Industry	Output at basic prices (millions of Peruvian New Soles)					Value added at basic prices (millions of Peruvian New Soles)					Gross fixed capital formation (millions of Peruvian New Soles)		
		Note	2013	2014	2015	2016	Note	2013	2014	2015	2016	Note	2015	2016
10	Food products		68313	68764	74093	75645		17563	16586	18463	19315		...	...
11	Beverages	a/	8745	9082	9668	10272	a/	3256	3373	3511	3723		...	...
12	Tobacco products	a/	...	...	...	...	a/	...	...	...	...		...	...
13	Textiles		7293	7416	7309	6932		2674	2609	2604	2482		...	...
14	Wearing apparel		12366	12012	11274	10966		4786	4425	4020	3912		...	...
15	Leather and related products		2505	2459	2489	2509		998	970	945	966		...	...
16	Wood products, excluding furniture		4338	4278	4103	4110		1672	1655	1545	1524		...	...
17	Paper and paper products		5564	5830	6330	6337		2143	2219	2390	2400		...	...
18	Printing and reproduction of recorded media		6011	6091	5845	6372		2627	2642	2401	2831		...	...
19	Coke and refined petroleum products		31102	31305	25456	24812		5579	5898	8091	7745		...	...
20	Chemicals and chemical products		13623	13844	14474	15084		4927	4994	5124	5424		...	...
21	Pharmaceuticals, medicinal chemicals, etc.		2817	2737	2367	2618		1171	1105	901	987		...	...
22	Rubber and plastics products		9743	9893	10175	10063		3179	3102	3346	3485		...	...
23	Other non-metallic mineral products		14259	14920	14760	14937		6357	6610	6449	6593		...	...
24	Basic metals		18449	18303	17184	17029		6232	6243	5707	5111		...	...
25	Fabricated metal products, except machinery		11931	11431	12000	11600		4919	4464	4934	5110		...	...
26	Computer, electronic and optical products		609	589	615	581		192	190	183	174		...	...
27	Electrical equipment		3278	3140	3282	3660		845	893	1069	1326		...	...
28	Machinery and equipment n.e.c.		4868	5617	6146	6396		1935	2319	2597	2704		...	...
29	Motor vehicles, trailers and semi-trailers		...	...	...	...		...	...	...	...		...	...
30	Other transport equipment		4632	4586	4915	5282		1931	2093	2348	2627		...	...
31	Furniture		5607	5548	6079	6366		2378	2346	2599	2740		...	...
32	Other manufacturing		11688	10499	9302	9247		5093	4647	3934	4024		...	...
33	Repair and installation of machinery/equipment		...	...	...	...		...	...	...	...		...	...
C	Total manufacturing	b/	247741	248344	247866	250818	b/	80457	79383	83161	85203		...	...

a/ 11 includes 12.
b/ Sum of available data.

Peru

Index numbers of industrial production

ISIC Revision 4

(2010=100)

ISIC	Industry	Note	2005	2006	2007	2008	2009	2010	2011	2012	2013	2014	2015	2016
10	Food products		77	83	91	98	97	100	113	112	116	106	111	108
11	Beverages		65	74	79	91	93	100	106	110	112	116	119	122
12	Tobacco products		...	...	...	...	...	...	...	...	...	...	...	...
13	Textiles		124	122	129	108	85	100	96	88	84	84	79	74
14	Wearing apparel		88	85	93	91	64	100	112	97	93	88	81	76
15	Leather and related products		60	42	49	70	97	100	78	80	87	73	75	73
16	Wood products, excluding furniture		144	141	131	121	91	100	92	63	50	46	41	39
17	Paper and paper products		57	64	74	101	83	100	104	108	109	114	124	127
18	Printing and reproduction of recorded media		69	72	78	90	87	100	111	112	109	107	89	91
19	Coke and refined petroleum products		64	63	66	69	88	100	96	93	90	93	93	98
20	Chemicals and chemical products		70	79	92	100	93	100	107	112	123	126	127	128
21	Pharmaceuticals, medicinal chemicals, etc.		70	89	101	110	109	100	105	110	99	98	79	85
22	Rubber and plastics products		72	76	84	88	84	100	105	103	117	121	119	116
23	Other non-metallic mineral products		53	60	70	83	82	100	104	115	119	119	117	116
24	Basic metals		117	122	114	125	103	100	105	104	117	112	107	108
25	Fabricated metal products, except machinery		52	62	73	89	77	100	107	113	144	139	142	126
26	Computer, electronic and optical products		...	...	...	...	...	...	...	...	...	...	...	...
27	Electrical equipment		66	82	101	98	78	100	92	125	143	108	109	125
28	Machinery and equipment n.e.c.		97	102	130	136	95	100	139	149	118	117	100	101
29	Motor vehicles, trailers and semi-trailers		37	41	57	84	79	100	103	120	129	122	114	91
30	Other transport equipment		17	24	36	51	60	100	109	108	115	97	94	86
31	Furniture		48	54	67	85	85	100	104	118	130	122	132	139
32	Other manufacturing		67	72	96	97	96	100	90	87	108	102	99	86
33	Repair and installation of machinery/equipment		...	...	...	...	...	...	...	...	...	...	...	...
C	Total manufacturing		73	78	86	94	88	100	106	107	112	108	107	105

Philippines

Supplier of information:
Philippine Statistics Authority, Manila.

Basic source of data:
Annual survey.

Major deviations from ISIC (Revision 4):
Data presented in ISIC (Revision 4) were originally classified according to the Philippine Standard Industrial Classification (PSIC 2009).

Reference period:
Calendar year.

Scope:
Data refer to establishments with average total employment of 20 or more persons engaged.

Method of data collection:
The inquiry is carried out through personal visits of field enumerators.

Type of enumeration:
Sample survey.

Adjusted for non-response:
Yes.

Concepts and definitions of variables:
Wages and salaries is compensation of employees.
Output refers to gross output.
Value added refers to total value added.
Gross fixed capital formation excludes intellectual property products such as products of R&D, computer software, databases, etc.

Related national publications:
None reported.

Philippines

ISIC Revision 4		Note	Number of establishments (number)				Note	Number of employees (thousands)				Wages and salaries paid to employees (millions of Philippine Pesos)			
ISIC	Industry		2012	2013	2014	2015		2012	2013	2014	2015	2012	2013	2014	2015
1010	Processing/preserving of meat		137	131	132	122		21.2	23.4	22.0	20.7	2923	3397	3651	3861
1020	Processing/preserving of fish, etc.		162	141	135	135		24.8	20.1	18.9	18.5	2505	2902	3160	2733
1030	Processing/preserving of fruit,vegetables		93	87	88	82		29.6	28.1	28.9	28.0	11483	12250	7592	9101
1040	Vegetable and animal oils and fats		101	86	94	98		10.6	11.6	17.4	14.8	2102	2121	2849	2709
1050	Dairy products		37	33	33	36		10.4	9.4	10.6	10.6	8890	9474	10113	11309
106	Grain mill products,starches and starch products		197	165	156	141		11.0	9.8	10.0	9.5	3687	2163	2190	2515
1061	Grain mill products		197a/	157	152	137		11.0a/	8.4	8.9	8.3	3687a/	1927	2016	2326
1062	Starches and starch products		...a/	8	4	4		...a/	1.4	1.2	1.1	...a/	236	174	189
107	Other food products		887	818	829	805		75.6	88.7	88.7	96.3	14935	19967	24205	25028
1071	Bakery products		887b/	536	534	511		75.6b/	56.9	56.0	60.2	14935b/	10076	12929	11830
1072	Sugar		...b/	29	30	32		...b/	9.4	9.9	10.5	...b/	2666	3761	3889
1073	Cocoa, chocolate and sugar confectionery		...b/	49	47	51		...b/	4.7	4.9	5.7	...b/	1349	1281	1226
1074	Macaroni, noodles, couscous, etc.		...b/	71	75	71		...b/	7.3	7.2	8.1	...b/	3574	3497	4445
1075	Prepared meals and dishes		...b/	5	4	4		...b/	0.2	0.2	0.3	...b/	101	108	112
1079	Other food products n.e.c.		...b/	128	139	136		...b/	10.1	10.5	11.6	...b/	2201	2629	3526
1080	Prepared animal feeds		116	118	115	120		8.7	7.6	7.6	8.8	1853	1787	1970	2422
110	Beverages		113					18.7				9699			
1101	Distilling, rectifying and blending of spirits		113c/	9	8	9		18.7c/	1.0	0.6	1.3	9699c/	572	411	658
1102	Wines		...c/	9	9	9		...c/				...c/			
1103	Malt liquors and malt		...c/	9	9	9		...c/	3.9	3.9	4.1	...c/	4136	2341	2346
1104	Soft drinks,mineral waters,other bottled waters		...c/	89	79	77		...c/	11.3	10.8	11.1	...c/	4784	4783	4358
1200	Tobacco products		15	14	17	14		8.5	6.9	6.4	10.3	3585	5594	5930	6618
131	Spinning, weaving and finishing of textiles		82	64	59	65		6.5	6.0	5.8	6.6	943	935	989	1057
1311	Preparation and spinning of textile fibres	d/	82	64	59	65	d/	6.5	6.0	5.8	6.6	943	935	989	1057
1312	Weaving of textiles	d/					d/								
1313	Finishing of textiles	d/					d/								
139	Other textiles		133	127	130	123		14.8	17.9	16.8	20.0	2136	2410	2410	2984
1391	Knitted and crocheted fabrics		133e/	13	13	13		14.8e/	0.7	0.7	0.7	2136e/	115	92	93
1392	Made-up textile articles, except apparel		...e/	53	55	46		...e/	12.8	11.3	14.0	...e/	1685	1568	2093
1393	Carpets and rugs		...e/	10	10	11		...e/	0.7	0.7	0.9	...e/	78	85	95
1394	Cordage, rope, twine and netting		...e/	15	14	16		...e/	2.0	2.4	2.6	...e/	351	436	489
1399	Other textiles n.e.c.		...e/	36	38	37		...e/	1.7	1.8	1.7	...e/	181	229	214
1410	Wearing apparel, except fur apparel		678	586	596	545		104.5	94.5	96.6	95.0	13932	14051	14465	14724
1420	Articles of fur														
1430	Knitted and crocheted apparel		29	28	25	22		4.8	4.6	4.3	3.6	568	785	786	586
151	Leather;luggage,handbags,saddlery,harness;fur		61	61	66	63		10.3	10.1	15.7	20.0	1291	1322	1882	2847
1511	Tanning/dressing of leather; dressing of fur		61f/	3	3	3		10.3f/	0.2	0.2	0.2	1291f/	24	20	16
1512	Luggage,handbags,etc.;saddlery/harness		...f/	58	63	60		...f/	9.9	15.5	19.8	...f/	1298	1862	2831
1520	Footwear		116	98	95	96		7.4	6.4	6.4	8.2	692	676	716	889
1610	Sawmilling and planing of wood		39	34	36	32		1.7	1.5	1.6	2.4	118	154	135	222

Code	Description												
162	Wood products, cork, straw, plaiting materials	164	150	148	139	19.5	18.5	15.3	15.1	2162	2236	2155	2183
1621	Veneer sheets and wood-based panels	164g/	38	40	37	19.5g/	6.9	5.6	5.0	2162g/	642	612	692
1622	Builders' carpentry and joinery	...g/	17	16	17	...g/	6.7	5.1	5.5	...g/	1027	1019	952
1623	Wooden containers	...g/	18	14	17	...g/	0.8	0.7	0.8	...g/	78	69	71
1629	Other wood products;articles of cork,straw	...g/	77	78	68	...g/	4.2	3.9	3.8	...g/	489	455	468
170	Paper and paper products	218	216	224	217	18.1	22.6	22.9	22.7	3241	4153	4371	4678
1701	Pulp, paper and paperboard	218h/	57	60	56	18.1h/	6.7	6.6	6.3	3241h/	1388	1461	1584
1702	Corrugated paper and paperboard	...h/	89	87	83	...h/	8.3	8.2	8.2	...h/	1430	1258	1388
1709	Other articles of paper and paperboard	...h/	70	77	78	...h/	7.6	8.1	8.3	...h/	1335	1652	1706
181	Printing and service activities related to printing	363	357	350	337	17.0	19.3	17.7	17.2	2584	2736	2754	3248
1811	Printing	363i/	332	327	317	17.0i/	17.7	16.6	16.3	2584i/	2494	2544	3107
1812	Service activities related to printing	...i/	25	23	20	...i/	1.6	1.1	0.9	...i/	242	210	141
1820	Reproduction of recorded media	...	:	:	3	:	:	:	0.4	...	:	:	48
1910	Coke oven products	:	:	:	:	:	:	:	:	:	:	:	:
1920	Refined petroleum products	13	11	16	11	1.9	2.1	2.6	3.0	3231	3890	4062	4978
201	Basic chemicals,fertilizers, etc.	182	158	117	100	16.0	14.7	9.1	8.7	4529	3885	3529	3641
2011	Basic chemicals	182j/	86	87	74	16.0j/	6.8	5.9	6.1	4529j/	2171	2153	2656
2012	Fertilizers and nitrogen compounds	...j/	13	12	9	...j/	1.8	2.0	1.4	...j/	613	997	593
2013	Plastics and synthetic rubber in primary forms	...j/	59	18	17	...j/	6.2	1.2	1.2	...j/	1101	379	392
202	Other chemical products	209	204	206	202	21.8	21.3	19.2	21.3	7627	7825	7965	7358
2021	Pesticides and other agrochemical products	209k/	12	14	11	21.8k/	1.5	1.2	0.9	7627k/	653	687	448
2022	Paints,varnishes;printing ink and mastics	...k/	58	62	60	...k/	5.4	4.8	5.2	...k/	1017	1232	1274
2023	Soap,cleaning and cosmetic preparations	...k/	89	90	94	...k/	10.2	9.5	10.6	...k/	4564	4630	4279
2029	Other chemical products n.e.c.	...k/	45	40	37	...k/	4.2	3.8	4.6	...k/	1591	1416	1357
2030	Man-made fibres	:	:	:	:	:	:	:	:	:	:	:	:
2100	Pharmaceuticals,medicinal chemicals, etc.	87	90	87	87	13.4	13.1	13.5	14.1	6710	7555	7130	6530
221	Rubber products	109	104	93	89	10.5	12.1	11.2	13.0	1994	2571	2668	2904
2211	Rubber tyres and tubes	109m/	16	13	10	10.5m/	4.0	3.3	3.9	1994m/	1110	1093	1279
2219	Other rubber products	...m/	88	80	79	...m/	8.1	7.9	9.1	...m/	1461	1575	1625
2220	Plastics products	453	448	497	490	38.9	40.7	48.2	47.1	6604	7531	8494	9509
2310	Glass and glass products	48	49	45	39	4.4	4.7	4.2	4.3	1250	1265	1405	1709
239	Non-metallic mineral products n.e.c.	238	201	:	185	28.2	27.5	:	26.3	7405	7084	:	8287
2391	Refractory products	238n/	3	:	3	28.2n/	0.2	0.2	0.2	7405n/	72	72	49
2392	Clay building materials	...n/	14	14	10	...n/	3.8	4.3	2.9	...n/	490	619	382
2393	Other porcelain and ceramic products	...n/	18	18	16	...n/	10.0	8.2	9.6	...n/	1620	1102	1772
2394	Cement, lime and plaster	...n/	24	22	23	...n/	4.4	4.4	4.5	...n/	3069	3222	4308
2395	Articles of concrete, cement and plaster	...n/	114	116	107	...n/	6.5	6.5	6.9	...n/	1340	1088	1348
2396	Cutting, shaping and finishing of stone	...n/	10	10	8	...n/	0.6	0.6	0.6	...n/	99	115	124
2399	Other non-metallic mineral products n.e.c.	...n/	22	21	18	...n/	2.0	1.9	1.5	...n/	394	376	304
2410	Basic iron and steel	157	141	148	135	12.3	12.0	13.2	12.1	3355	3256	3855	3650
2420	Basic precious and other non-ferrous metals	25	18	21	19	3.3	2.6	2.6	2.6	1618	1299	1451	1341
243	Casting of metals	48	43	42	37	4.9	4.2	4.0	4.2	1050	870	788	1011
2431	Casting of iron and steel	48p/	18	18	18	4.9p/	1.0	1.0	1.3	1050p/	198	217	281
2432	Casting of non-ferrous metals	...p/	25	24	19	...p/	3.2	3.0	3.0	...p/	672	571	730
251	Struct.metal products, tanks, reservoirs	179	171	165	162	17.3	16.0	16.0	18.3	3982	3455	3730	4031

continued

Philippines

ISIC	Industry	Number of establishments (number)					Number of employees (thousands)					Wages and salaries paid to employees (millions of Philippine Pesos)			
		Note	2012	2013	2014	2015	Note	2012	2013	2014	2015	Note	2012	2013	2014	2015
2511	Structural metal products		179q/	145	140	140		17.3q/	13.6	13.5	15.7		3982q/	2911	3151	3119
2512	Tanks, reservoirs and containers of metal		...q/	18	19	16		...q/	1.0	1.3	1.3		...q/	134	219	468
2513	Steam generators, excl. hot water boilers		...q/	8	6	6		...q/	1.4	1.2	1.3		...q/	410	360	444
2520	Weapons and ammunition		5	6	4	5		1.1	1.3	0.8	1.0		424	522	490	495
259	Other metal products;metal working services		288	301	301	302		29.1	31.8	32.0	32.3		5912	5761	6744	6667
2591	Forging,pressing,stamping,roll-forming of metal		288r/	65	65	66		29.1r/	7.1	6.9	6.8		5912r/	1651	1861	1768
2592	Treatment and coating of metals; machining		...r/	22	23	24		...r/	1.4	1.8	1.3		...r/	292	361	313
2593	Cutlery, hand tools and general hardware		...r/	35	32	26		...r/	3.9	4.3	4.3		...r/	591	646	583
2599	Other fabricated metal products n.e.c.		...r/	179	181	186		...r/	19.4	19.0	19.9		...r/	3227	3876	4003
2610	Electronic components and boards		148	139	145	145		142.5	138.5	147.0	150.6		35963	42074	41504	45930
2620	Computers and peripheral equipment		40	46	44	42		56.8	54.0	59.0	72.9		13058	12967	13458	14633
2630	Communication equipment		8	8	11	12		1.7	4.8	7.4	5.2		227	1912	2020	756
2640	Consumer electronics		26	29	26	22		11.5	13.3	13.5	12.9		1777	2106	2337	2517
265	Measuring,testing equipment; watches, etc.		13	10	11	11		3.6	3.4	3.8	2.7		806	735	861	718
2651	Measuring/testing/navigating equipment,etc.		13s/	6	7	8		3.6s/	0.5	0.9	0.6		806s/	90	156	106
2652	Watches and clocks		...s/	4	4	3		...s/	2.8	2.9	2.1		...s/	645	705	612
2660	Irradiation/electromedical equipment,etc.		36	28	29	30		12.0	11.1	10.2	14.0		3656	2457	2763	2804
2670	Optical instruments and photographic equipment		...	...	...	...		...	...	...	...		...	...	...	...
2680	Magnetic and optical media		...	...	...	...		...	...	...	...		...	...	...	...
2710	Electric motors,generators,transformers,etc.		41	44	47	43		4.1	6.8	8.2	8.1		554	1628	1593	1030
2720	Batteries and accumulators		4	5	7	6		0.2	0.4	1.7	3.2		74	71	854	1475
273	Wiring and wiring devices		39t/			3		7.0t/			0.8		1496t/			163
2731	Fibre optic cables		...t/	28	30	27		...t/	5.7	6.5			...t/	1504	1804	1617
2732	Other electronic and electric wires and cables		...t/	3	4			...t/	0.2	0.2			...t/	26	29	
2733	Wiring devices		28	26	28	28		5.1	5.4	5.8	5.9		1166	1029	792	874
2740	Electric lighting equipment		28	25	19	21		2.5	3.2	2.8	2.8		694	936	821	940
2750	Domestic appliances		17	14	17	18		4.3	8.1	7.5	7.7		1428	2754	1998	2169
2790	Other electrical equipment		76					7.8					2620			
281	General-purpose machinery		76u/					7.8u/					2620u/			
2811	Engines/turbines,excl.aircraft,vehicle engines		...u/	4	3	3		...u/	0.5	0.4	0.4		...u/	103	115	104
2812	Fluid power equipment		...u/	5	5	5		...u/	2.1	2.1	2.1		...u/	579	645	1019
2813	Other pumps, compressors, taps and valves		...u/	6	6	5		...u/	0.6	0.6	0.4		...u/	157	240	220
2814	Bearings, gears, gearing and driving elements		...u/	6	7	6		...u/	1.2	1.0	1.2		...u/	405	260	299
2815	Ovens, furnaces and furnace burners		...u/					...u/					...u/			
2816	Lifting and handling equipment		...u/	12	11	13		...u/	1.0	0.7	0.8		...u/	204	160	191
2817	Office machinery, excl.computers,etc.		...u/			4		...u/			4.2		...u/			654
2818	Power-driven hand tools		...u/					...u/					...u/			
2819	Other general-purpose machinery		...u/	34	33	32		...u/	2.7	2.6	2.7		...u/	1300	1584	1661
282	Special-purpose machinery		90					6.9					1326			
2821	Agricultural and forestry machinery		90v/	7	8	8		6.9v/	0.5	0.5	0.6		1326v/	34	66	103
2822	Metal-forming machinery and machine tools		...v/	20	20	18		...v/	1.5	1.5	1.1		...v/	374	358	302

ISIC Revision 4

2823	Machinery for metallurgy	730	675	641	...v/	3.7	2.8	3.9	...v/	34	30	27	...v/
2824	Mining, quarrying and construction machinery	76	30	...	...v/	0.4	0.3	0.7	...v/	4	3	9	...v/
2825	Food/beverage/tobacco processing machinery	113	93	126	...v/	0.8	0.6	...	...v/	10	9	9	...v/
2826	Textile/apparel/leather production machinery	...	...	...	...v/	...	...	...	...v/	...	...	...	...v/
2829	Other special-purpose machinery	129	175	130	...v/	0.8	1.0	1.1	...v/	10	13	11	...v/
2910	Motor vehicles	4411	4259	3709	3055	6.6	7.4	6.6	7.1	33	35	36	33
2920	Automobile bodies, trailers and semi-trailers	287	358	412	186	1.3	1.3	1.8	1.1	16	15	17	18
2930	Parts and accessories for motor vehicles	17420	15419	14657	13068	73.8	60.6	65.6	59.4	100	90	99	101
301	Building of ships and boats	...	...	...	3843	...	...	...	19.5	...	...	...	13
3011	Building of ships and floating structures	4063	1257	3066	3843w/	19.9	16.0	17.3	19.5w/	31	10	10	13w/
3012	Building of pleasure and sporting boats	...	...	...	...w/	...	...	...	...w/	...	...	...	...w/
3020	Railway locomotives and rolling stock	...	...	...	...	...	...	...	...	...	...	...	...
3030	Air and spacecraft and related machinery	3727	2315	122	2267	3.9	3.0	0.3	3.2	9	9	9	10
3040	Military fighting vehicles	...	...	...	...	...	...	...	...	...	...	...	...
309	Transport equipment n.e.c.	...	...	...	2219	...	...	...	8.7	...	...	...	35
3091	Motorcycles	2319	662	2356	2219x/	6.0	2.8	6.9	8.7x/	25	18	26	35x/
3092	Bicycles and invalid carriages	...	...	...	...x/	...	...	1.8	...x/	...	...	5	...x/
3099	Other transport equipment n.e.c.	...	...	206	...x/	...	...	...	...x/	...	...	...	...x/
3100	Furniture	3552	3605	2921	3001	20.8	22.2	22.1	23.4	272	291	285	319
321	Jewellery, bijouterie and related articles	496	529	467	380	3.9	4.6	4.0	3.5	44	46	42	37
3211	Jewellery and related articles	397	443	401	380y/	3.0	3.6	3.2	3.5y/	30	32	31	37y/
3212	Imitation jewellery and related articles	99	86	66	...y/	0.9	0.9	0.7	...y/	14	14	11	...y/
3220	Musical instruments	24	14	...	...	0.2	0.2	...	...	3	3	...	...
3230	Sports goods	545	759	619	645	2.2	3.1	3.2	3.3	10	11	13	14
3240	Games and toys	510	543	327	379	2.7	3.1	1.8	2.4	19	18	17	21
3250	Medical and dental instruments and supplies	1740	1566	1235	1138	10.1	5.4	5.6	4.0	28	31	32	30
3290	Other manufacturing n.e.c.	1324	1214	1329	1084	5.6	6.1	7.4	5.7	69	75	84	89
331	Repair of fabricated metal products/machinery	...	...	...	2128	...	...	...	11.3	...	...	...	176
3311	Repair of fabricated metal products	407	434	412	2128z/	2.9	3.2	2.8	11.3z/	69	66	70	176z/
3312	Repair of machinery	464	389	303	...z/	2.2	2.1	1.9	...z/	46	51	53	...z/
3313	Repair of electronic and optical equipment	...	...	...	...z/	...	...	...	...z/	...	...	...	...z/
3314	Repair of electrical equipment	...	...	121	...z/	...	...	0.2	...z/	...	...	4	...z/
3315	Repair of transport equip., excl. motor vehicles	356	2787	3938	...z/	1.6	6.3	10.6	...z/	16	39	39	...z/
3319	Repair of other equipment	...	...	...	...z/	...	...	...	...z/	...	...	...	...z/
3320	Installation of industrial machinery/equipment	...	...	...	...	...	...	...	...	...	...	...	...
C	Total manufacturing	292815	270629	266252	243281	1132.6	1070.1	1060.1	1045.7	6521	6763	6770	7275

a/ 1061 includes 1062.
b/ 1071 includes 1072, 1073, 1074, 1075 and 1079.
c/ 1101 includes 1102, 1103 and 1104.
d/ 1311 includes 1312 and 1313.
e/ 1391 includes 1392, 1393, 1394 and 1399.
f/ 1511 includes 1512.
g/ 1621 includes 1622, 1623 and 1629.
h/ 1701 includes 1702 and 1709.
i/ 1811 includes 1812.
j/ 2011 includes 2012 and 2013.

k/ 2021 includes 2022, 2023 and 2029.
m/ 2211 includes 2219.
n/ 2391 includes 2392, 2393, 2394, 2395, 2396 and 2399.
p/ 2431 includes 2432.
q/ 2511 includes 2512 and 2513.
r/ 2591 includes 2592, 2593 and 2599.
s/ 2651 includes 2652.
t/ 2731 includes 2732 and 2733.
u/ 2811 includes 2812, 2813, 2814, 2815, 2816, 2817, 2818 and 2819.
v/ 2821 includes 2822, 2823, 2824, 2825, 2826 and 2829.

w/ 3011 includes 3012.
x/ 3091 includes 3092 and 3099.
y/ 3211 includes 3212.
z/ 3311 includes 3312, 3313, 3314, 3315 and 3319.

Philippines

ISIC	Industry (ISIC Revision 4)	Note	Output at producers' prices (millions of Philippine Pesos)				Note	Value added at producers' prices (millions of Philippine Pesos)				Note	Gross fixed capital formation (millions of Philippine Pesos)	
			2012	2013	2014	2015		2012	2013	2014	2015		2014	2015
1010	Processing/preserving of meat		50524	67106	82253	80814		7587	10943	14975	10647		897	1171
1020	Processing/preserving of fish, etc.		44092	53095	50710	46887		6660	7900	7061	6236		422	706
1030	Processing/preserving of fruit,vegetables		81249	73591	52430	59315		18863	17185	13380	15174		1633	1430
1040	Vegetable and animal oils and fats		132006	83652	117491	106792		26164	9229	11235	11380		1109	527
1050	Dairy products		174655	186061	204393	209534		45599	57243	52211	56289		2436	2903
106	Grain mill products,starches and starch products		121476	86710	90673	105470		23095	13431	13562	19959		1776	2414
1061	Grain mill products		121476a/	81543	86280	99395		23095a/	12794	12938	18946		1635	2414
1062	Starches and starch products		...a/	5167	4393	6075		...a/	637	624	1013		141	-
107	Other food products		199534	231778	289685	307779		47260	66799	71903	70842		7212	3795
1071	Bakery products		195334b/	116217	151325	139595		47260b/	33783	36655	32479		4070	705
1072	Sugar		...b/	34478	50279	54491		...b/	10339	14272	13027		2593	1986
1073	Cocoa, chocolate and sugar confectionery		...b/	9913	11378	11060		...b/	2063	2631	2253		210	221
1074	Macaroni, noodles, couscous, etc.		...b/	38470	37122	53797		...b/	10231	9764	11410		131	238
1075	Prepared meals and dishes		...b/	678	786	764		...b/	120	214	281		63	-
1079	Other food products n.e.c.		...b/	32022	38795	48072		...b/	10263	8367	11392		145	645
1080	Prepared animal feeds		59783	76034	65838	78317		6256	9012	6531	7894		1378	2567
110	Beverages		192496	...	...	...		85007	...	...	...		...	...
1101	Distilling, rectifying and blending of spirits		192496c/	47318	45668	52353		85007c/	8573	12881	19375		414	388
1102	Wines		...c/	...	...	...		...c/	...	...	...		...	...
1103	Malt liquors and malt		...c/	70063	74725	83405		...c/	49444	57798	62835		1278	2369
1104	Soft drinks,mineral waters,other bottled waters		...c/	67346	61761	61623		...c/	17686	16032	18127		3886	3291
1200	Tobacco products		79142	122150	120008	150244		41453	80287	87763	109367		4459	2118
131	Spinning, weaving and finishing of textiles		12766	10353	10130	8451		1864	1943	1788	1692		199	370
1311	Preparation and spinning of textile fibres	d/	12766	10353	10130	8451		1864	1943	1788	1692		199d/	370d/
1312	Weaving of textiles	d/	...	...	...	...		...	...	...	...		...d/	...d/
1313	Finishing of textiles	d/	...	...	...	...		...	...	...	...		...d/	...d/
139	Other textiles		9665	15600	15437	19116		3023	3756	4211	5154		100	99
1391	Knitted and crocheted fabrics		9665e/	2709	1330	1087		3023e/	207	137	168		3	-
1392	Made-up textile articles, except apparel		...e/	8833	8659	12354		...e/	2530	2757	3584		10	73
1393	Carpets and rugs		...e/	406	485	592		...e/	122	124	179		-	9
1394	Cordage, rope, twine and netting		...e/	2386	3652	3790		...e/	575	913	950		77	8
1399	Other textiles n.e.c.		...e/	1266	1311	1293		...e/	322	280	273		10	9
1410	Wearing apparel, except fur apparel		60279	51652	59514	53683		21393	21561	21307	21994		886	741
1420	Articles of fur		...	...	...	...		...	...	...	...		...	...
1430	Knitted and crocheted apparel		2953	3521	3728	2628		833	1229	1114	1024		68	21
151	Leather;luggage,handbags,saddlery,harness;fur		10856	10777	19197	24550		2579	3375	5311	6737		231	376
1511	Tanning/dressing of leather; dressing of fur		10856f/	198	225	230		2579f/	29	39	44		20	2
1512	Luggage,handbags,etc.;saddlery/harness		...f/	10579	18972	24320		...f/	3346	5272	6693		211	374
1520	Footwear		5169	5070	5085	5349		1365	1315	1332	1427		33	94
1610	Sawmilling and planing of wood		1118	1462	1525	2228		248	338	348	529		-	9

Code	Description	(1)	(2)	(3)	(4)	(5)	(6)	(7)	(8)	(9)	(10)
162	Wood products, cork, straw, plaiting materials	807	639	6483	10323	7791	7935	37760	37502	38273	37888
1621	Veneer sheets and wood-based panels	151	64	2476	1816	1787	7935g/	9231	7314	7623	37888g/
1622	Builders' carpentry and joinery	563	519	2935	7555	4892	...g/	25139	26716	26538	...g/
1623	Wooden containers	13	11	134	132	167	...g/	528	596	599	...g/
1629	Other wood products;articles of cork,straw	80	45	938	820	945	...g/	2862	2876	3513	...g/
170	Paper and paper products	1284	857	14895	13013	14020	8526	80118	77086	66715	55892
1701	Pulp, paper and paperboard	408	435	4592	4259	5076	8526h/	28229	28720	24277	55892h/
1702	Corrugated paper and paperboard	503	89	5844	4810	5698	...h/	27525	28141	25347	...h/
1709	Other articles of paper and paperboard	373	333	4459	3944	3246	...h/	24364	20225	17091	...h/
181	Printing and service activities related to printing	134	912	7141	5895	5847	6092	26932	26279	22173	22245
1811	Printing	128	885	6857	5465	5472	6092i/	25660	24647	20893	22245i/
1812	Service activities related to printing	6	27	284	430	375	...i/	1272	1632	1280	...i/
1820	Reproduction of recorded media	5	5	120	···	···	···	356	···	···	···
1910	Coke oven products	···	···	···	···	···	···	···	···	···	···
1920	Refined petroleum products	15244	6169	35169	31869	23415	25492	388665	507342	475161	477363
201	Basic chemicals,fertilizers, etc.	4393	1966	14176	17425	18390	13201	99215	86731	90008	112765
2011	Basic chemicals	4120	888	9986	12134	12333	13201j/	67569	54220	44704	112765j/
2012	Fertilizers and nitrogen compounds	130	967	2619	4105	2617	...j/	17170	19712	23267	...j/
2013	Plastics and synthetic rubber in primary forms	143	111	1571	1186	3440	...j/	14476	12799	22037	...j/
202	Other chemical products	1164	996	39176	42566	34833	27577	167610	170783	157473	113477
2021	Pesticides and other agrochemical products	13	50	1593	2340	2765	27577k/	8445	11307	8431	113477k/
2022	Paints,varnishes;printing ink and mastics	394	468	6053	9634	9291	...k/	37630	50859	47479	...k/
2023	Soap,cleaning and cosmetic preparations	554	329	26290	25773	17709	...k/	104352	91582	82662	...k/
2029	Other chemical products n.e.c.	203	149	5240	4819	5068	...k/	17183	17035	18901	...k/
2030	Man-made fibres	-	···	···	···	···	···	···	···	···	···
2100	Pharmaceuticals,medicinal chemicals, etc.	3233	6588	15377	24702	29950	16568	50971	57344	63280	51639
221	Rubber products	2781	4049	6389	6986	6141	4789	28800	24863	23675	26309
2211	Rubber tyres and tubes	2494	3571	5722	4401	2997	4789m/	16833	15005	12877	26309m/
2219	Other rubber products	287	478	667	2585	3144	...m/	11967	9858	10798	...m/
2220	Plastics products	2240	2466	20569	19836	18990	17354	102371	99102	90575	83308
2310	Glass and glass products	543	223	5078	3629	4264	2923	16134	15865	16833	16144
239	Non-metallic mineral products n.e.c.	3792	···	45163	···	57070	41565	144695	···	156202	135754
2391	Refractory products	1	158	12	1343	143	41565n/	245	···	307	135754n/
2392	Clay building materials	377	15	1833	···	1658	...n/	5384	5915	6266	...n/
2393	Other porcelain and ceramic products	594	···	7686	27086	12163	...n/	25293	33626	37092	...n/
2394	Cement, lime and plaster	2201	4146	29704	41323	38397	...n/	87301	98864	88877	...n/
2395	Articles of concrete, cement and plaster	555	311	4585	2570	3274	...n/	21763	12679	17647	...n/
2396	Cutting, shaping and finishing of stone	-	34	435	453	468	...n/	1886	1534	1474	...n/
2399	Other non-metallic mineral products n.e.c.	64	260	908	951	967	...n/	2823	3731	4539	...n/
2410	Basic iron and steel	1321	638	12659	12835	12240	11312	123390	130063	109063	107385
2420	Basic precious and other non-ferrous metals	8343	14155	7014	5151	4019	5959	66359	79181	82076	73306
243	Casting of metals	241	219	2292	1305	1643	2459	10725	10897	11811	17720
2431	Casting of iron and steel	56	20	584	326	310	2459p/	2047	1212	1013	17720p/
2432	Casting of non-ferrous metals	185	199	1708	979	1333	...p/	8678	9685	10798	...p/
251	Struct.metal products, tanks, reservoirs	525	···	7394	8145	8017	6633	25413	24505	30144	21922

continued

Philippines

ISIC	Industry	Note	Output at producers' prices (millions of Philippine Pesos)				Note	Value added at producers' prices (millions of Philippine Pesos)				Note	Gross fixed capital formation (millions of Philippine Pesos)	
			2012	2013	2014	2015		2012	2013	2014	2015		2014	2015
2511	Structural metal products		21922q/	27233	21138	20770		6633q/	7155	6932	5361		991	427
2512	Tanks, reservoirs and containers of metal		...q/	1222	1971	2706		...q/	215	383	757		...	36
2513	Steam generators, excl. hot water boilers		...q/	1689	1396	1937		...q/	647	830	1276		2	62
2520	Weapons and ammunition		2274	3322	2447	2495		878	1089	721	638		63	134
259	Other metal products;metal working services		64977	...	...	...		13973	13263	14417	13821		2285	2080
2591	Forging,pressing,stamping,roll-forming of metal		64977r/	22609	22639	19848		13973r/	4900	4802	3514		440	578
2592	Treatment and coating of metals; machining		...r/	2564	2840	2577		...r/	798	1131	864		218	204
2593	Cutlery, hand tools and general hardware		...r/	6190	8231	7313		...r/	758	973	1312		78	61
2599	Other fabricated metal products n.e.c.		...r/	36530	41555	40522		...r/	6807	7511	8131		1549	1237
2610	Electronic components and boards		749617	538792	410044	441469		321468	149463	145855	133727		33305	17643
2620	Computers and peripheral equipment		246493	206043	217947	213485		114419	43575	44100	43916		2589	1998
2630	Communication equipment		3864	11590	13021	6252		914	4429	4676	1083		21	151
2640	Consumer electronics		43546	56149	50623	55112		3615	11190	5791	15315		470	171
265	Measuring,testing equipment; watches, etc.		2321	1916	3002	2796		1150	882	1294	958		40	45
2651	Measuring/testing/navigating equipment,etc.		2321s/	669	1510	1738		1150s/	86	350	168		7	24
2652	Watches and clocks		...s/	1247	1492	1058		...s/	796	944	790		33	21
2660	Irradiation/electromedical equipment,etc.													
2670	Optical instruments and photographic equipment		33095	22844	25158	22783		7831	5500	6240	6190		110	866
2680	Magnetic and optical media													
2710	Electric motors,generators,transformers,etc.		6892	20926	17982	10379		1681	5463	4550	2790		128	106
2720	Batteries and accumulators		6767	5103	10253	14481		1095	2914	2719	6131		841	108
273	Wiring and wiring devices		34283	...	...	...		5312	...	...	...			
2731	Fibre optic cables		34283t/	...	...	992		5312t/	...	...	225		...	16
2732	Other electronic and electric wires and cables		...t/	20557	21985	26350		...t/	3356	3079	5508		1037	193
2733	Wiring devices		...t/	224	270	-		...t/	92	72	-		2	-
2740	Electric lighting equipment		10209	8729	9319	7696		1975	2352	3397	2629		80	89
2750	Domestic appliances		11034	12799	14883	13933		1230	2112	3215	1929		62	251
2790	Other electrical equipment		48627	37850	41041	48752		10846	8550	9708	10365		1677	1104
281	General-purpose machinery		37345	...	...	...		9022	...	...	...			
2811	Engines/turbines,excl.aircraft,vehicle engines		37345u/	958	949	804		9022u/	341	392	317		-	3
2812	Fluid power equipment		...u/	10977	13118	13701		...u/	2134	6776	2775		174	546
2813	Other pumps, compressors, taps and valves		...u/	4331	4499	3426		...u/	522	728	494		-	84
2814	Bearings, gears, gearing and driving elements		...u/	2948	1781	1944		...u/	869	450	1009		42	-
2815	Ovens, furnaces and furnace burners		...u/	...	...	...		...u/	...	...	...			
2816	Lifting and handling equipment		...u/	2002	952	1195		...u/	577	463	353		17	-
2817	Office machinery, excl.computers,etc.		...u/	...	...	8886		...u/	...	...	1259		...	71
2818	Power-driven hand tools		...u/	...	...	...		...u/	...	...	...			
2819	Other general-purpose machinery		...u/	15121	18603	17137		...u/	4997	5067	4492		86	462
282	Special-purpose machinery		10610	...	...	...		2731	...	...	...			
2821	Agricultural and forestry machinery		10610v/	342	762	1630		2731v/	99	184	237		80	22
2822	Metal-forming machinery and machine tools		...v/	3643	2677	1536		...v/	1306	849	295		93	42

2823	Machinery for metallurgy	...v/	5594	5375	8121	...v/	1928	1525	2957	216	941
2824	Mining, quarrying and construction machinery	...v/	...	430	1607	...v/	...	100	174	-	-
2825	Food/beverage/tobacco processing machinery	...v/	468	440	614	...v/	207	146	169	4	9
2826	Textile/apparel/leather production machinery	...v/	1039	1505	798	...v/	311	667	235	11	14
2829	Other special-purpose machinery	...v/	...	...	...	...v/	...	...	...	...	...
2910	Motor vehicles	93506	108007	176203	200287	7551	30324	92034	104551	704	1192
2920	Automobile bodies, trailers and semi-trailers	1949	2389	2209	3362	482	758	678	786	3	10
2930	Parts and accessories for motor vehicles	154090	160389	166059	183223	36061	35930	50490	39030	3413	6185
301	Building of ships and boats	79148	...	...	...	24563	...	...	...	...	...
3011	Building of ships and floating structures	79148w/	42845	68534	82468	24563w/	10037	13911	15842	60	585
3012	Building of pleasure and sporting boats	...w/	...	...	...	...w/	...	...	...	...	-
3020	Railway locomotives and rolling stock	...	...	...	...	...	...	...	...	...	...
3030	Air and spacecraft and related machinery	7373	1193	8064	20278	3076	362	3906	8001	267	668
3040	Military fighting vehicles	...	...	...	...	...	...	...	...	...	...
309	Transport equipment n.e.c.	46935	...	...	...	8823	...	...	...	...	...
3091	Motorcycles	46935x/	47055	14622	54644	8823x/	7973	1848	8989	79	574
3092	Bicycles and invalid carriages	...x/	1543	...	...	...x/	457	...	...	...	...
3099	Other transport equipment n.e.c.	...x/	...	...	...	...x/	...	...	...	...	...
3100	Furniture	21909	21109	27689	24862	5540	5199	6708	6115	235	307
321	Jewellery, bijouterie and related articles	1618	1889	2313	2567	605	754	851	875	19	24
3211	Jewellery and related articles	1618y/	1725	1947	2241	605y/	662	717	716	19	18
3212	Imitation jewellery and related articles	...y/	164	366	326	...y/	92	134	159	-	6
3220	Musical instruments	...	...	63	72	...	...	31	40	3	1
3230	Sports goods	4221	4717	4745	3247	652	1091	1161	835	28	43
3240	Games and toys	5426	4956	4778	6226	1363	2202	1019	978	54	18
3250	Medical and dental instruments and supplies	7370	7847	10751	11921	2256	2350	5018	3326	352	397
3290	Other manufacturing n.e.c.	8109	11002	9932	9333	2138	3130	2953	2836	165	122
331	Repair of fabricated metal products/machinery	9447	...	...	...	4492	...	...	...	142	33
3311	Repair of fabricated metal products	9447z/	2758	2675	2106	4492z/	894	1169	846	6	140
3312	Repair of machinery	...z/	1512	1935	2368	...z/	702	855	1007	...	...
3313	Repair of electronic and optical equipment	...z/	...	...	...	...z/	...	...	...	...	...
3314	Repair of electrical equipment	...z/	331	...	...	...z/	162	...	...	...	...
3315	Repair of transport equip., excl. motor vehicles	...z/	...	...	...	...z/	...	...	...	...	...
3319	Repair of other equipment	...z/	15501	9105	2317	...z/	6747	4159	800	475	324
3320	Installation of industrial machinery/equipment	...	...	...	...	...	...	...	...	...	...
C	Total manufacturing	4344225	4199387	4354596	4451539	1133408	1005503	1133407	1145599	123687	109305

a/ 1061 includes 1062.
b/ 1071 includes 1072, 1073, 1074, 1075 and 1079.
c/ 1101 includes 1102, 1103 and 1104.
d/ 1311 includes 1312 and 1313.
e/ 1391 includes 1392, 1393, 1394 and 1399.
f/ 1511 includes 1512.
g/ 1621 includes 1622, 1623 and 1629.
h/ 1701 includes 1702 and 1709.
i/ 1811 includes 1812.
j/ 2011 includes 2012 and 2013.

k/ 2021 includes 2022, 2023 and 2029.
m/ 2211 includes 2219.
n/ 2391 includes 2392, 2393, 2394, 2395, 2396 and 2399.
p/ 2431 includes 2432.
q/ 2511 includes 2512 and 2513.
r/ 2591 includes 2592, 2593 and 2599.
s/ 2651 includes 2652.
t/ 2731 includes 2732 and 2733.
u/ 2811 includes 2812, 2813, 2814, 2815, 2816, 2817, 2818 and 2819.
v/ 2821 includes 2822, 2823, 2824, 2825, 2826 and 2829.

w/ 3011 includes 3012.
x/ 3091 includes 3092 and 3099.
y/ 3211 includes 3212.
z/ 3311 includes 3312, 3313, 3314, 3315 and 3319.

Philippines

Index numbers of industrial production

ISIC Revision 4

ISIC	Industry	Note	2005	2006	2007	2008	2009	2010	2011	2012	2013	2014	2015	2016
								(2010=100)						
10	Food products		98	102	97	98	95	100	86	99	101	101	87	105
11	Beverages		105	103	112	131	88	100	124	127	120	155	148	159
12	Tobacco products		368	262	178	185	191	100	80	62	67	65	84	93
13	Textiles		257	225	140	107	92	100	95	95	67	76	83	76
14	Wearing apparel		267	214	171	199	130	100	102	193	162	136	130	125
15	Leather and related products		133	128	136	162	89	100	90	111	124	139	148	27
16	Wood products, excluding furniture		119	93	101	109	91	100	80	98	101	108	94	100
17	Paper and paper products		105	107	106	101	88	100	112	104	91	93	101	107
18	Printing and reproduction of recorded media		134	136	121	104	99	100	99	103	95	279	285	289
19	Coke and refined petroleum products		116	108	107	98	71	100	102	93	81	85	79	81
20	Chemicals and chemical products	a/	...	108	106	108	98	100	122	125	279	284	309	313
21	Pharmaceuticals,medicinal chemicals, etc.	a/	...	...	...	...	...	...	...	...	...	...	...	...
22	Rubber and plastics products		191	76	83	85	86	100	111	112	123	121	119	152
23	Other non-metallic mineral products		96	80	77	82	90	100	108	118	112	102	112	110
24	Basic metals		115	119	97	89	80	100	90	82	114	119	127	156
25	Fabricated metal products, except machinery		56	82	89	92	86	100	105	103	97	130	130	118
26	Computer, electronic and optical products		...	...	...	...	...	...	...	...	...	...	...	...
27	Electrical equipment		107	78	74	74	68	100	96	106	110	112	128	129
28	Machinery and equipment n.e.c.		203	141	135	78	69	100	68	73	102	133	134	176
29	Motor vehicles, trailers and semi-trailers	b/	96	82	85	76	75	100	92	116	97	99	104	127
30	Other transport equipment	b/	...	...	...	...	...	...	...	...	...	...	...	...
31	Furniture		122	116	127	111	95	100	206	318	599	690	682	597
32	Other manufacturing		66	78	82	62	67	100	125	111	67	63	67	65
33	Repair and installation of machinery/equipment		...	...	...	...	...	...	...	...	...	...	...	...
C	Total manufacturing		102	103	100	98	84	100	101	108	119	126	126	135

a/ 20 includes 21.
b/ 29 includes 30.

Poland

Supplier of information:
Central Statistical Office of Poland, Warsaw.
Industrial statistics for the OECD countries are compiled by the OECD secretariat, which
supplies them to UNIDO.

Basic source of data:
Annual surveys; business register.

Major deviations from ISIC (Revision 4):
Data presented in ISIC (Revision 4) were originally classified according to the national
NACE-related classification system.

Reference period:
Calendar year.

Scope:
All enterprises.

Method of data collection:
Mail questionnaires; online survey.

Type of enumeration:
Enterprises with 10 or more persons engaged are completely enumerated; smaller
enterprises are surveyed through sampling.

Adjusted for non-response:
Yes.

Concepts and definitions of variables:
No deviations from the standard UN concepts and definitions are reported.

Related national publications:
None reported.

Poland

ISIC Revision 4			Number of enterprises (number)					Number of employees (thousands)					Wages and salaries paid to employees (millions of Polish Zlotys)			
ISIC	Industry	Note	2013	2014	2015	2016	Note	2013	2014	2015	2016	Note	2013	2014	2015	2016
1010	Processing/preserving of meat		2448	2486	2730	2684		114.8	116.2	114.9	115.8		3651	3834	3951	4243
1020	Processing/preserving of fish, etc.		280	281	301	304		15.8	16.7	17.3	18.0		581	661	701	777
1030	Processing/preserving of fruit,vegetables		928	976	1085	1127		30.6	31.1	31.6	33.6		1233	1255	1334	1481
1040	Vegetable and animal oils and fats		127	133	158	177		5.5	5.3	3.0	2.8		299	319	190	174
1050	Dairy products		523	521	643	667		38.0	38.1	38.3	39.1		1676	1713	1747	1867
106	Grain mill products,starches and starch products		525	534	590	560		9.2	9.7	9.7	10.6		388	424	413	481
1061	Grain mill products		511	520	576	545		8.2	8.7	8.7	9.6		341	377	366	427
1062	Starches and starch products		14	14	14	15		1.0	1.0	1.0	1.1		47	48	47	55
107	Other food products		6935	7276	7985	7680		139.9	143.4	146.9	149.8		4899	5139	5473	5783
1071	Bakery products		5325	5572	5986	5549		86.3	90.2	90.6	91.5		2275	2491	2605	2736
1072	Sugar		9	8	9	9		3.4	3.4	3.3	3.3		235	230	227	245
1073	Cocoa, chocolate and sugar confectionery		272	287	334	345		19.4	18.0	18.4	19.1		941	893	900	958
1074	Macaroni, noodles, couscous, etc.		328	325	369	374		4.4	4.6	4.6	4.7		135	127	149	161
1075	Prepared meals and dishes		288	330	425	466		2.1	2.2	2.4	3.0		47	51	59	88
1079	Other food products n.e.c.		713	754	862	937		24.3	25.1	27.5	28.2		1266	1347	1535	1595
1080	Prepared animal feeds		365	384	446	472		10.5	11.2	12.1	12.6		614	677	737	765
110	Beverages		500	507	601	654		24.2	24.1	24.2	22.9		1533	1550	1638	1581
1101	Distilling, rectifying and blending of spirits		99	97	115	114		4.3	4.5	4.6	4.2		276	278	294	288
1102	Wines		57	59	65	75		:	:	:	:		:	:	:	:
1103	Malt liquors and malt		77	91	128	164		8.1	8.1	8.2	8.2		603	588	618	640
1104	Soft drinks,mineral waters,other bottled waters		267	260	293	301		10.5	10.2	10.1	9.1		597	614	652	581
1200	Tobacco products		30	39	39	43		5.3	5.5	5.6	5.8		422	439	480	491
131	Spinning, weaving and finishing of textiles		1219	1285	1274	1329		11.4	11.5	12.1	12.7		331	346	371	412
1311	Preparation and spinning of textile fibres		97	100	97	99		2.8	2.6	2.9	3.1		91	87	92	110
1312	Weaving of textiles		142	153	143	166		3.4	3.6	3.8	4.1		103	116	124	140
1313	Finishing of textiles		980	1032	1034	1064		5.2	5.3	5.4	5.5		137	142	154	163
139	Other textiles		3272	3614	3766	4094		31.5	33.6	35.9	38.7		950	1046	1154	1331
1391	Knitted and crocheted fabrics		207	210	194	203		3.0	2.9	2.8	2.9		87	87	89	94
1392	Made-up textile articles, except apparel		2124	2404	2568	2825		16.4	17.8	19.3	20.4		460	521	593	654
1393	Carpets and rugs		51	57	64	64		1.4	1.6	1.8	:		47	54	60	:
1394	Cordage, rope, twine and netting		100	109	114	122		1.0	0.9	1.0	1.0		34	35	38	40
1399	Other textiles n.e.c.		790	834	826	880		9.7	10.4	11.0	:		321	349	374	:
1410	Wearing apparel, except fur apparel		10337	10923	10872	11735		67.7	67.1	66.7	66.8		1485	1554	1568	1659
1420	Articles of fur		290	290	246	261		0.5	0.4	0.4	0.4		10	11	13	14
1430	Knitted and crocheted apparel		867	879	826	871		8.8	8.7	8.3	8.3		214	225	221	234
151	Leather;luggage,handbags,saddlery,harness;fur		931	1133	1027	1021		5.6	5.9	5.5a/	5.9		146	165	170a/	182
1511	Tanning/dressing of leather; dressing of fur		180	209	176	166		1.9	1.9	...a/	1.6		52	60	...a/	56
1512	Luggage,handbags,etc.;saddlery/harness		751	924	851	855		3.8	4.0	...a/	4.3		93	105	...a/	127
1520	Footwear		1651	1935	1729	1636		15.7	16.5	15.7	16.1		403	439	436	482
1610	Sawmilling and planing of wood		4860	5221	5308	5304		27.0	29.4	29.8	31.2		737	816	851	914

162	Wood products, cork, straw, plaiting materials	10647	11233	11537	11685	69.1	72.6	75.3	78.0	2181	2351	2497	2654
1621	Veneer sheets and wood-based panels	212	235	261	264	11.5	11.9	12.3	13.0	505	548	573	586
1622	Builders' carpentry and joinery	5700	6039	6221	6283	33.5	35.4	36.4	38.1	1027	1102	1169	1281
1623	Wooden containers	1464	1539	1559	1594	9.1	9.5	9.9	10.2	247	261	273	288
1629	Other wood products;articles of cork,straw	3271	3420	3496	3544	15.0	15.8	16.6	16.7	403	440	481	499
170	Paper and paper products	2704	2949	2618	2830	52.0	53.7	55.1	55.0	2402	2552	2682	2870
1701	Pulp, paper and paperboard	163	174	164	174	7.3	7.6	7.6	7.7	447	484	508	522
1702	Corrugated paper and paperboard	1143	1269	1140	1227	24.7	25.9	26.7	27.5	1051	1126	1203	1309
1709	Other articles of paper and paperboard	1398	1506	1314	1429	20.0	20.3	20.7	19.8	905	942	972	1040
181	Printing and service activities related to printing	8629	8254	8423	8820	34.3	35.3	38.4	38.6	1374	1519	1587	1690
1811	Printing	5181	4993	5055	5274	29.6	30.7	32.7	33.0	1230	1353	1400	1487
1812	Service activities related to printing	3448	3261	3368	3546	4.7	4.6	5.7	5.6	145	166	187	203
1820	Reproduction of recorded media	366	342	309	324	2.5	2.2	2.3	2.4	216	210	224	265
1910	Coke oven products	18	17	16	20	4.0	3.9	4.1	3.7	264	274	265	240
1920	Refined petroleum products	157	158	160	183	9.0	9.2	9.3	9.7	895	931	956	1005
201	Basic chemicals,fertilizers, etc.	727	741	766	858	28.8	28.5	29.3	30.4	1693	1727	1859	1993
2011	Basic chemicals	372	367	376	422	⋮	⋮	⋮	⋮	⋮	⋮	⋮	⋮
2012	Fertilizers and nitrogen compounds	103	116	125	157	9.6	9.9	10.1	10.3	609	644	703	739
2013	Plastics and synthetic rubber in primary forms	252	258	265	279	⋮	⋮	⋮	⋮	⋮	⋮	⋮	⋮
202	Other chemical products	1384	1447	1442	1573	42.1	44.4	45.6	46.5	2236	2364	2428	2553
2021	Pesticides and other agrochemical products	45	43	41	48	1.2	1.0	1.0	1.1	65	57	59	62
2022	Paints,varnishes;printing ink and mastics	311	334	322	337	7.6	8.0	8.5	8.7	473	491	520	565
2023	Soap,cleaning and cosmetic preparations	659	677	705	774	23.6	25.2	26.2	25.9	1241	1349	1378	1358
2029	Other chemical products n.e.c.	369	393	374	414	9.8	10.2	10.0	10.9	456	467	472	567
2030	Man-made fibres	15	14	13	13	1.1	1.1	1.1	1.5	48	50	50	69
2100	Pharmaceuticals,medicinal chemicals, etc.	330	341	329	372	21.3	21.3	22.7	23.0	1444	1468	1603	1692
221	Rubber products	901	884	898	888	35.3	37.5	37.9	40.7	1614	1765	1836	2062
2211	Rubber tyres and tubes	202	192	194	191	10.6	10.9	11.0	11.2	620	644	672	717
2219	Other rubber products	699	692	704	697	24.7	26.6	27.0	29.6	995	1121	1164	1345
2220	Plastics products	7133	7012	7473	7497	129.3	136.9	142.6	151.9	5012	5522	6016	6638
2310	Glass and glass products	1025	992	1028	1025	31.8	33.8	35.9	37.0	1343	1496	1605	1711
239	Non-metallic mineral products n.e.c.	7815	7774	8162	8115	83.0	83.9	84.3	86.1	3583	3773	3854	4204
2391	Refractory products	80	85	94	98	2.5	2.6	2.7	2.8	123	129	137	144
2392	Clay building materials	324	304	316	295	10.4	10.0	9.7	10.0	441	429	428	476
2393	Other porcelain and ceramic products	499	490	513	522	⋮	⋮	⋮	⋮	⋮	⋮	⋮	⋮
2394	Cement, lime and plaster	67	69	72	71	6.4	6.3	6.0	6.1	470	481	476	480
2395	Articles of concrete, cement and plaster	3200	3156	3234	3200	⋮	⋮	⋮	⋮	⋮	⋮	⋮	⋮
2396	Cutting, shaping and finishing of stone	3358	3373	3618	3586	7.9	8.0	8.6	7.9	179	192	200	213
2399	Other non-metallic mineral products n.e.c.	287	297	315	343	7.4	7.5	7.7	8.9	369	396	418	513
2410	Basic iron and steel	533	555	587	614	32.1	31.9	31.9	32.4	1759	1815	1877	1948
2420	Basic precious and other non-ferrous metals	278	285	306	347	9.9	10.7	11.6	12.9	509	567	626	720
243	Casting of metals	452	456	470	468	17.9	17.8	17.5	19.7	747	816	836	977
2431	Casting of iron and steel	200	195	201	193	11.4	11.2	10.7	11.7	453	480	476	537
2432	Casting of non-ferrous metals	252	261	269	275	6.5	6.7	6.8	7.9	294	336	360	440
251	Struct.metal products, tanks, reservoirs	7637	8333	9037	9793	105.7	112.1	114.6	121.3	4611	5053	5311	5671

continued

Poland

		Number of enterprises (number)					Number of employees (thousands)					Wages and salaries paid to employees (millions of Polish Zlotys)				
ISIC	Industry (ISIC Revision 4)	Note	2013	2014	2015	2016	Note	2013	2014	2015	2016	Note	2013	2014	2015	2016
2511	Structural metal products		6867	7530	8192	8934		81.9	88.6	89.9	97.5		3526	3921	4149	4510
2512	Tanks, reservoirs and containers of metal		707	733	770	782		17.4	17.3	18.6	17.9		753	777	794	804
2513	Steam generators, excl. hot water boilers		63	70	75	77		6.4	6.2	6.0	5.9		332	354	369	356
2520	Weapons and ammunition		40	36	39	45		5.4	4.9	5.0	5.3		263	240	251	281
259	Other metal products;metal working services		21139	22698	24645	26466		141.5	148.4	150.4	162.2		5441	5930	6321	6954
2591	Forging,pressing,stamping,roll-forming of metal		666	683	693	730		7.4	7.8	7.6	8.8		299	321	326	411
2592	Treatment and coating of metals; machining		16050	17470	19305	21012		63.3	67.5	70.0	76.9		2168	2420	2687	2976
2593	Cutlery, hand tools and general hardware		789	822	888	896		14.0	14.4	14.8	16.1		579	618	666	734
2599	Other fabricated metal products n.e.c.		3634	3723	3759	3828		56.8	58.7	57.9	60.3		2395	2573	2642	2833
2610	Electronic components and boards		642	664	623	693		16.0	17.3	18.4	17.4		619	691	768	778
2620	Computers and peripheral equipment		757	737	625	663		4.7	4.6	4.4	4.3		238	231	228	242
2630	Communication equipment		281	283	256	266		10.2	10.3	11.0	11.4		547	582	626	692
2640	Consumer electronics		230	242	230	271		8.7	8.3	7.9	6.2		352	343	341	269
265	Measuring,testing equipment; watches, etc.		679	665	616	669		10.5	13.3	13.7	16.3		477	681	736	948
2651	Measuring/testing/navigating equipment,etc.		645	633	587	639		10.3	13.2	13.5	16.1		472	677	732	944
2652	Watches and clocks		34	32	29	30		0.2	0.1	0.1	0.1		5	5	5	4
2660	Irradiation/electromedical equipment,etc.		90	92	80	93		0.4	0.5	0.4	0.4		15	21	18	21
2670	Optical instruments and photographic equipment		418	431	376	380		1.2	1.3	1.3	1.2		42	48	50	50
2680	Magnetic and optical media		5	6	4	3		0.1	0.1	0.1	0.1		4	5	5	3
2710	Electric motors,generators,transformers,etc.		954	857	859	903		31.3	31.3	32.3	34.1		1569	1672	1726	1863
2720	Batteries and accumulators		58	48	55	60		3.1	3.2	3.5	3.8		167	180	198	226
273	Wiring and wiring devices		191	182	182	203		10.9	11.9	12.0	12.3		462	510	524	559
2731	Fibre optic cables		14	11	13	13		0.2	0.2	0.3	0.3		8	9	11	13
2732	Other electronic and electric wires and cables		84	82	81	97		8.0	8.6	8.9	9.0		353	380	397	428
2733	Wiring devices		93	89	88	93		2.7	3.0	2.8	2.9		100	121	115	118
2740	Electric lighting equipment		648	582	619	679		12.8	13.3	14.7	15.9		580	587	709	796
2750	Domestic appliances		169	149	154	152		25.3	25.3	26.9	27.5		1212	1252	1360	1483
2790	Other electrical equipment		395	365	367	406		10.4	11.5	11.6	11.5		493	566	587	577
281	General-purpose machinery		2663	2641	2829	3074		59.3	60.1	61.8	64.8		2891	3124	3304	3559
2811	Engines/turbines,excl.aircraft,vehicle engines		113	112	121	139		7.9	7.0	7.1	7.1		504	482	502	512
2812	Fluid power equipment		208	224	261	293		2.5	3.0	3.4	3.5		98	145	170	180
2813	Other pumps, compressors, taps and valves		191	194	196	195		8.0	8.4	8.7	9.1		374	426	459	476
2814	Bearings, gears, gearing and driving elements		109	109	115	132		10.1	10.0	10.3	10.8		475	505	539	575
2815	Ovens, furnaces and furnace burners		184	194	207	226		3.1	3.1	3.1	3.0		157	161	159	156
2816	Lifting and handling equipment		488	468	483	507		9.1	9.4	9.1	9.7		433	489	492	539
2817	Office machinery, excl.computers,etc.		49	49	47	50		0.4	0.5	0.4	0.4		24	24	22	24
2818	Power-driven hand tools		64	58	64	68		0.7	0.7	0.7	0.7		26	29	29	28
2819	Other general-purpose machinery		1257	1233	1335	1464		17.4	17.9	18.8	20.6		800	864	930	1069
282	Special-purpose machinery		1973	1974	2179	2364		57.2	56.5	58.8	57.6		2673	2709	2887	2886
2821	Agricultural and forestry machinery		465	479	529	563		16.4	16.7	17.5	17.2		686	744	779	768
2822	Metal-forming machinery and machine tools		213	213	256	284		6.1	5.8	6.0	6.1		265	267	277	292

Code	Description												
2823	Machinery for metallurgy	29	28	27	35	1.7	1.4	1.3	1.1	95	70	64	58
2824	Mining, quarrying and construction machinery	243	231	241	248	14.9	13.8	14.8	13.3	781	725	807	740
2825	Food/beverage/tobacco processing machinery	331	333	352	358	7.0	7.1	7.1	7.1	356	372	379	387
2826	Textile/apparel/leather production machinery	57	52	51	54	0.7	0.7	0.6	0.8	25	27	26	35
2829	Other special-purpose machinery	635	638	723	822	10.5	10.8	11.5	12.0	464	505	556	605
2910	Motor vehicles	93	113	119	126	30.0	30.6	31.1	32.0	2207	2381	2473	2636
2920	Automobile bodies, trailers and semi-trailers	264	328	328	326	9.3	9.7	10.3	11.5	377	415	457	538
2930	Parts and accessories for motor vehicles	775	920	882	846	122.4	129.7	135.6	142.8	5668	6168	6726	7436
301	Building of ships and boats	664	914	930	939	9.1	9.0	9.1	9.8	484	568	536	569
3011	Building of ships and floating structures	415	593	615	633	5.5	5.0	4.3	4.4	338	393	324	308
3012	Building of pleasure and sporting boats	249	321	315	306	3.6	4.0	4.7	5.4	146	175	212	260
3020	Railway locomotives and rolling stock	82	106	93	100	11.2	11.1	11.1	10.7	571	625	674	633
3030	Air and spacecraft and related machinery	69	82	99	102	15.4	15.8	15.9	15.7	846	923	969	1022
3040	Military fighting vehicles	4	3	4	4	1.3	...	1.3	1.4	73	...	79	90
309	Transport equipment n.e.c.	241	315	307	319	4.9	...	5.0	5.6	148	...	167	197
3091	Motorcycles	35	45	48	52	0.3	0.2	0.3	0.3	11	10	10	12
3092	Bicycles and invalid carriages	148	206	194	198	3.9	4.3	4.1	4.3	118	139	137	149
3099	Other transport equipment n.e.c.	58	64	65	69	0.7	...	0.6	1.0	20	...	20	36
3100	Furniture	14390	14802	16105	17137	134.7	145.0	156.1	163.8	4173	4763	5300	5805
321	Jewellery, bijouterie and related articles	3059	3105	2953	3010	3.6	4.0	3.5	3.9	109	113	109	120
3211	Jewellery and related articles	2445	2495	2343	2392	...	4.0b/	3.5b/	3.9b/	...	113b/	109b/	120b/
3212	Imitation jewellery and related articles	614	610	610	618	0.4	...b/	...b/	...b/	7	...b/	...b/	...b/
3220	Musical instruments	251	258	235	255	0.3	0.3	0.3	0.3	8	10	9	11
3230	Sports goods	317	338	350	391	1.4	1.5	1.3	1.4	46	49	45	52
3240	Games and toys	596	657	677	732	2.8	3.1	3.0	3.3	99	113	117	134
3250	Medical and dental instruments and supplies	5683	6076	5809	5979	15.8	17.1	16.7	17.9	617	677	696	778
3290	Other manufacturing n.e.c.	3343	3486	3345	3363	14.7	15.2	16.4	17.2	442	459	533	590
331	Repair of fabricated metal products/machinery	22631	22384	23155	24546	73.2	74.3	75.9	79.9	3524	3824	4014	4247
3311	Repair of fabricated metal products	1903	1918	2036	2215	5.4	5.3	5.9	8.8	244	247	281	473
3312	Repair of machinery	11138	11090	11460	12105	37.0	35.9	36.2	37.9	1737	1754	1836	1885
3313	Repair of electronic and optical equipment	2704	2600	2577	2677	5.4	5.7	5.9	5.1	285	359	367	322
3314	Repair of electrical equipment	3357	3300	3371	3525	5.5	6.4	7.1	7.2	216	290	352	342
3315	Repair of transport equip., excl. motor vehicles	3027	2957	3164	3415	18.7	19.9	19.7	19.7	982	1128	1128	1163
3319	Repair of other equipment	502	519	547	609	1.1	1.1	1.1	1.3	58	46	50	62
3320	Installation of industrial machinery/equipment	3781	3896	4045	4458	20.3	20.2	20.7	20.5	1208	1248	1311	1277
C	Total manufacturing	174414	180639	187374	196067	2150.5	2226.3	2285.0	2372.0	90149	96813	102414	110155

a/ 1511 includes 1512.
b/ 3211 includes 3212.

Poland

ISIC	Industry	Output (valuation not defined) (millions of Polish Zlotys)					Value added at factor values (millions of Polish Zlotys)					Gross fixed capital formation (millions of Polish Zlotys)		
		Note	2013	2014	2015	2016	Note	2013	2014	2015	2016	Note	2015	2016
1010	Processing/preserving of meat		55525	56381	58348	61866		7644	8597	8644	8872		2142	2024
1020	Processing/preserving of fish, etc.		7888	8437	8962	10562		1198	1542	1567	1370		295	278
1030	Processing/preserving of fruit,vegetables		15173	14899	16650	17967		3149	3283	3658	3882		933	1004
1040	Vegetable and animal oils and fats		5705	4971	4277	4188		982	984	629	532		85	96
1050	Dairy products		28292	28974	26186	26869		3844	3554	3761	4194		985	959
106	Grain mill products,starches and starch products		6383	6069	6271	6818		1059	1111	1247	1405		241	449
1061	Grain mill products		6047	5680	5910	6306		953	988	1124	1229		215	407
1062	Starches and starch products		336	390	361	512		107	123	123	177		26	42
107	Other food products		47254	46702	44333	47567		13729	12890	13973	15164		3677	3815
1071	Bakery products		15991	17894	15607	16034		5152	5699	5945	6264		1379	1542
1072	Sugar		5526	3994	3473	4852		2147	936	1090	1871		199	224
1073	Cocoa, chocolate and sugar confectionery		10463	9364	8141	8653		2760	2400	2464	2329		787	689
1074	Macaroni, noodles, couscous, etc.		1436	1210	1240	1314		379	328	377	395		105	180
1075	Prepared meals and dishes		424	500	432	631		89	107	116	192		22	31
1079	Other food products n.e.c.		13414	13740	15441	16083		3200	3419	3982	4114		1185	1148
1080	Prepared animal feeds		14320	15118	15626	17247		2083	2180	2313	2644		639	566
110	Beverages		30714	28346	30479	30264		4921	5307	5642	5953		1000	1194
1101	Distilling, rectifying and blending of spirits		10847	9021	9932	10666		1085	958	976	1229		166	161
1102	Wines		...	...	...	...		...	...	...	...		...	...
1103	Malt liquors and malt		11851	11118	11846	11749		2231	2457	2563	2641		426	498
1104	Soft drinks,mineral waters,other bottled waters		7003	7192	7674	6860		1403	1692	1906	1887		365	502
1200	Tobacco products		10349	10359	11047	11415		1256	1422	1624	1687		895	1535
131	Spinning, weaving and finishing of textiles		2398	2582	2715	2840		715	793	835	947		156	184
1311	Preparation and spinning of textile fibres		627	669	721	799		185	206	213	233		46	67
1312	Weaving of textiles		816	885	959	998		228	260	277	317		32	58
1313	Finishing of textiles		956	1028	1035	1042		302	328	345	398		79	59
139	Other textiles		7704	8698	9308	10826		2065	2285	2558	2919		397	609
1391	Knitted and crocheted fabrics		669	651	674	682		192	202	206	220		35	41
1392	Made-up textile articles, except apparel		3596	4254	4400	4658		928	1048	1210	1332		154	227
1393	Carpets and rugs		371	459	498	...		97	122	148	...		8	...
1394	Cordage, rope, twine and netting		302	305	315	329		75	75	82	100		11	13
1399	Other textiles n.e.c.		2766	3029	3421	...		773	839	911	...		189	...
1410	Wearing apparel, except fur apparel		5941	6176	6634	7068		2602	2757	2754	2890		177	187
1420	Articles of fur		82	79	98	76		32	28	46	33		6	3
1430	Knitted and crocheted apparel		1120	1110	1136	1251		430	433	411	428		33	38
151	Leather;luggage,handbags,saddlery,harness;fur		1525	1684	1867	2011		365	424	465	435		56	50
1511	Tanning/dressing of leather; dressing of fur		491	530	1867a/	533		117	136	465a/	135		56a/	18
1512	Luggage,handbags,etc.;saddlery/harness		1034	1154	...a/	1478		248	289	...a/	300		...a/	32
1520	Footwear		2490	2792	2575	2821		884	990	921	1002		119	92
1610	Sawmilling and planing of wood		6638	7631	8108	7751		1569	1749	1660	1782		504	665

162	Wood products, cork, straw, plaiting materials	1757	2256	7005	6631	6314	5674	25480	25594	24534	22510
1621	Veneer sheets and wood-based panels	848	1081	2472	2412	2201	1929	9096	9228	8886	8551
1622	Builders' carpentry and joinery	629	831	2826	2500	2490	2248	9771	9297	9307	8287
1623	Wooden containers	94	178	665	637	596	570	3012	3071	2550	2312
1629	Other wood products;articles of cork,straw	185	167	1043	1081	1026	928	3601	3997	3790	3359
170	Paper and paper products	3230	3259	9610	8959	8705	8250	37366	35643	33395	31943
1701	Pulp, paper and paperboard	780	1318	3119	3000	2871	2818	12532	12019	11332	10988
1702	Corrugated paper and paperboard	1047	820	3605	3267	3160	2942	14426	13444	12381	11748
1709	Other articles of paper and paperboard	1403	1122	2886	2690	2673	2490	10408	10181	9682	9206
181	Printing and service activities related to printing	772	821	4269	4053	3993	3517	12865	12479	11901	11068
1811	Printing	716	746	3738	3568	3508	3097	11573	11154	10616	9775
1812	Service activities related to printing	56	74	531	485	485	420	1292	1326	1285	1292
1820	Reproduction of recorded media	9	13	437	518	315	333	765	928	526	568
1910	Coke oven products	189	238	503	681	711	774	3814	4046	4178	4445
1920	Refined petroleum products	2720	2383	10275	6581	2486	3390	76423	81377	95135	103443
201	Basic chemicals,fertilizers, etc.	2622	3039	8036	7637	6247	6210	31684	32736	31639	32886
2011	Basic chemicals	:	745	2240	2495	1990	1818	8386	9348	8905	8944
2012	Fertilizers and nitrogen compounds	1032	:	:	:	:	:	:	:	:	:
2013	Plastics and synthetic rubber in primary forms	:	:	:	:	:	:	:	:	:	:
202	Other chemical products	1272	1221	7559	6721	6597	6283	28101	26690	25819	23718
2021	Pesticides and other agrochemical products	34	28	168	209	178	188	593	586	526	632
2022	Paints,varnishes;printing ink and mastics	237	231	1512	1445	1331	1214	5492	5272	5254	4959
2023	Soap,cleaning and cosmetic preparations	679	649	4375	3810	3832	3602	14276	14028	13670	13396
2029	Other chemical products n.e.c.	321	313	1505	1256	1256	1278	7740	6805	6369	4730
2030	Man-made fibres	15	16	154	103	98	105	416	352	351	387
2100	Pharmaceuticals,medicinal chemicals, etc.	523	616	4683	4873	4218	5479	15495	15641	13776	14155
221	Rubber products	951	964	5520	5121	5191	4666	18379	17104	17340	16509
2211	Rubber tyres and tubes	410	432	2223	2223	2425	2197	8160	8041	8359	8532
2219	Other rubber products	541	532	3297	2898	2766	2469	10219	9064	8980	7977
2220	Plastics products	4533	4495	17519	15715	14553	13405	63339	58313	54701	50555
2310	Glass and glass products	1369	1368	4596	3906	3881	3206	13080	11897	11454	10123
239	Non-metallic mineral products n.e.c.	3184	2516	11509	10930	10763	9822	36184	34377	34445	31571
2391	Refractory products	41	51	349	295	357	268	1281	1256	1286	1162
2392	Clay building materials	450	325	1425	1208	1154	1191	3782	3529	3514	3589
2393	Other porcelain and ceramic products	:	:	:	:	:	:	:	:	:	:
2394	Cement, lime and plaster	342	296	2158	2172	2352	2242	5929	5864	6171	5921
2395	Articles of concrete, cement and plaster	65	102	373	368	433	374	1260	1433	1854	1582
2396	Cutting, shaping and finishing of stone	:	:	:	:	:	:	:	:	:	:
2399	Other non-metallic mineral products n.e.c.	484	241	1607	1242	1180	1073	5118	4119	4026	3767
2410	Basic iron and steel	1069	903	6113	5091	5276	4409	28577	28998	29497	28545
2420	Basic precious and other non-ferrous metals	494	398	2118	1590	1468	1151	10907	10251	9042	8118
243	Casting of metals	641	502	2076	1798	1586	1529	6609	5851	5489	5173
2431	Casting of iron and steel	254	264	1179	1048	928	894	3567	3253	3212	3009
2432	Casting of non-ferrous metals	387	238	898	750	658	636	3042	2597	2277	2165
251	Struct.metal products, tanks, reservoirs	1635	2172	12184	11884	11012	10223	41422	39034	35764	31486

continued

Poland

ISIC	Industry	Note	Output (valuation not defined) (millions of Polish Zlotys)				Note	Value added at factor values (millions of Polish Zlotys)				Note	Gross fixed capital formation (millions of Polish Zlotys)	
			2013	2014	2015	2016		2013	2014	2015	2016		2015	2016
2511	Structural metal products		24223	27706	29578	31779		7745	8477	8865	9551		1787	1308
2512	Tanks, reservoirs and containers of metal		5387	5425	5612	5558		1738	1761	1838	1872		317	290
2513	Steam generators, excl. hot water boilers		1876	2632	3844	4084		740	775	1181	761		68	36
2520	Weapons and ammunition		1085	970	1085	1310		517	492	523	465		94	95
259	Other metal products;metal working services		41776	44736	45952	49166		13767	15108	15936	17520		3337	3152
2591	Forging,pressing,stamping,roll-forming of metal		2697	2895	2894	3696		696	783	694	1028		150	178
2592	Treatment and coating of metals; machining		16774	18429	18909	20272		5507	6271	6824	7423		1179	1220
2593	Cutlery, hand tools and general hardware		2704	2947	3167	3518		1291	1399	1477	1651		360	440
2599	Other fabricated metal products n.e.c.		19601	20465	20982	21679		6273	6654	6941	7417		1649	1315
2610	Electronic components and boards		7387	9308	8836	8911		1483	1654	1679	1651		288	264
2620	Computers and peripheral equipment		1538	1751	1831	1726		543	604	573	586		44	59
2630	Communication equipment		5975	6992	7863	7900		1383	1440	1531	1349		189	128
2640	Consumer electronics		13696	12997	13284	12430		1151	372	459	200		185	120
265	Measuring,testing equipment; watches, etc.		2495	3549	3726	6163		1029	1490	1618	1998		223	281
2651	Measuring/testing/navigating equipment,etc.		2465	3521	3706	6145		1019	1480	1610	1990		223	281
2652	Watches and clocks		30	28	21	17		10	10	7	9		1	-
2660	Irradiation/electromedical equipment,etc.		115	141	126	127		37	53	43	55		3	7
2670	Optical instruments and photographic equipment		330	421	264	303		102	146	115	137		20	15
2680	Magnetic and optical media		16	19	22	17		12	13	8	10		-	1
2710	Electric motors,generators,transformers,etc.		10551	11006	11983	12323		3426	3506	3574	3639		529	656
2720	Batteries and accumulators		2243	2394	2876	3363		359	415	427	538		59	185
273	Wiring and wiring devices		6329	7798	8044	7990		940	1292	1359	1435		222	181
2731	Fibre optic cables		38	40	49	56		16	15	21	22		1	1
2732	Other electronic and electric wires and cables		5706	7062	7393	7302		704	1006	1095	1158		171	136
2733	Wiring devices		585	697	602	632		220	270	244	256		51	44
2740	Electric lighting equipment		5902	6041	7396	7123		1729	1688	2198	1875		279	249
2750	Domestic appliances		18591	17663	20013	20937		3082	2948	3479	3543		960	980
2790	Other electrical equipment		3430	3832	4020	3409		1208	1329	1356	1159		210	219
281	General-purpose machinery		19484	22298	23782	25283		5797	6245	5409	6316		1257	1274
2811	Engines/turbines,excl.aircraft,vehicle engines		3890	4297	4431	4989		276	197	-907	-390		179	251
2812	Fluid power equipment		628	1036	1356	1460		217	337	447	448		55	57
2813	Other pumps, compressors, taps and valves		2123	2709	2767	2970		849	971	958	1012		198	213
2814	Bearings, gears, gearing and driving elements		2799	2983	3145	3400		1048	1130	1137	1285		256	322
2815	Ovens, furnaces and furnace burners		1017	1138	1221	1131		341	371	391	345		62	37
2816	Lifting and handling equipment		2597	3615	3805	4145		952	1042	1065	1177		166	121
2817	Office machinery, excl.computers,etc.		179	167	169	185		69	70	70	64		3	3
2818	Power-driven hand tools		134	125	130	112		53	51	53	52		5	3
2819	Other general-purpose machinery		6117	6228	6760	6890		1993	2075	2195	2323		333	267
282	Special-purpose machinery		17355	17923	19090	17928		5963	5899	6321	6083		1118	862
2821	Agricultural and forestry machinery		5625	6105	6387	5509		1697	1779	1800	1590		349	304
2822	Metal-forming machinery and machine tools		1629	1642	1824	1934		611	577	638	670		112	129

Code	Description										
2823	Machinery for metallurgy	338	268	264	241	183	113	119	94	8	2
2824	Mining, quarrying and construction machinery	4681	4266	4407	4149	1586	1387	1490	1440	273	180
2825	Food/beverage/tobacco processing machinery	2176	2378	2442	2213	846	889	905	845	156	82
2826	Textile/apparel/leather production machinery	152	149	171	229	49	51	66	84	7	12
2829	Other special-purpose machinery	2753	3116	3595	3653	993	1103	1302	1361	213	152
2910	Motor vehicles	46060	45987	50189	55819	6969	6824	7142	7510	3207	3956
2920	Automobile bodies, trailers and semi-trailers	3217	3544	4167	5249	821	876	1033	1371	135	206
2930	Parts and accessories for motor vehicles	61639	65813	73342	81120	14358	15212	16611	18830	4477	5341
301	Building of ships and boats	3991	3961	4691	5003	1122	1116	1106	1157	200	201
3011	Building of ships and floating structures	3086	2995	3469	3458	827	818	727	655	104	96
3012	Building of pleasure and sporting boats	905	966	1223	1545	295	298	378	502	96	105
3020	Railway locomotives and rolling stock	4620	5073	7136	5051	1243	1244	1575	1126	343	247
3030	Air and spacecraft and related machinery	6007	6420	7074	8005	2134	2304	2368	2896	592	731
3040	Military fighting vehicles	717	...	741	788	232	...	238	258	34	21
309	Transport equipment n.e.c.	1346	...	1699	1971	324	...	318	447	67	71
3091	Motorcycles	63	48	43	94	5	6	8	12	4	7
3092	Bicycles and invalid carriages	1187	1390	1536	1679	288	312	270	362	59	49
3099	Other transport equipment n.e.c.	97	...	119	198	31	...	40	72	5	14
3100	Furniture	30746	34525	37695	41017	8787	9958	10991	12269	1941	1963
321	Jewellery, bijouterie and related articles	1109	1170	969	1383	277	392	248	363	50	55
3211	Jewellery and related articles	...	1170b/	969b/	1383b/	...	392b/	248b/	363b/	50b/	55b/
3212	Imitation jewellery and related articles	70	...b/	...b/	...b/	24	...b/	...b/	...b/	...b/	...b/
3220	Musical instruments	56	88	103	70	20	29	36	22	2	2
3230	Sports goods	235	308	311	353	92	115	97	106	17	21
3240	Games and toys	610	664	722	864	251	265	266	331	54	55
3250	Medical and dental instruments and supplies	3616	4394	3999	4460	1410	1636	1669	1881	286	287
3290	Other manufacturing n.e.c.	3848	4265	4903	5174	1181	1333	1291	1503	221	197
331	Repair of fabricated metal products/machinery	18191	21123	23605	22296	7820	8522	8957	8715	705	772
3311	Repair of fabricated metal products	1206	1350	1622	2137	542	568	561	886	35	65
3312	Repair of machinery	8565	9132	9697	9788	3792	3791	4043	3982	272	372
3313	Repair of electronic and optical equipment	1676	1803	2127	1678	656	767	824	627	66	65
3314	Repair of electrical equipment	1511	1806	2159	2009	601	742	757	809	49	48
3315	Repair of transport equip., excl. motor vehicles	4923	6681	7510	6270	2090	2528	2649	2272	262	210
3319	Repair of other equipment	309	352	490	414	138	126	125	139	21	12
3320	Installation of industrial machinery/equipment	7542	8700	12006	8792	2515	2694	2929	2552	158	191
C	Total manufacturing	1028552	1068021	1109480	1154138	229034	241540	258985	280203	61025	63776

a/ 1511 includes 1512.
b/ 3211 includes 3212.

Poland

Index numbers of industrial production

ISIC Revision 4

(2010=100)

ISIC	Industry	Note	2005	2006	2007	2008	2009	2010	2011	2012	2013	2014	2015	2016
10	Food products		76	84	89	91	93	100	106	112	115	115	119	126
11	Beverages		85	88	97	100	111	100	102	104	103	103	103	101
12	Tobacco products		160	149	160	109	107	100	96	112	118	128	140	155
13	Textiles		89	97	107	98	91	100	111	119	125	139	147	168
14	Wearing apparel		110	116	117	111	98	100	108	109	113	112	115	120
15	Leather and related products		90	97	115	104	92	100	118	118	127	134	139	143
16	Wood products, excluding furniture		79	86	95	92	91	100	103	107	115	124	129	133
17	Paper and paper products		74	77	86	81	86	100	108	114	120	128	133	139
18	Printing and reproduction of recorded media		70	80	88	86	90	100	112	120	130	134	143	147
19	Coke and refined petroleum products		89	100	98	103	95	100	101	99	98	98	98	95
20	Chemicals and chemical products		77	86	91	84	82	100	101	110	107	105	110	113
21	Pharmaceuticals,medicinal chemicals, etc.		62	71	75	86	93	100	88	83	86	90	92	95
22	Rubber and plastics products		65	74	84	88	87	100	113	113	120	129	137	146
23	Other non-metallic mineral products		67	80	90	91	86	100	116	110	111	119	123	131
24	Basic metals		97	112	120	115	87	100	117	114	111	118	118	118
25	Fabricated metal products, except machinery		64	76	89	93	87	100	119	126	130	138	147	160
26	Computer, electronic and optical products		32	46	56	59	68	100	93	91	85	92	96	102
27	Electrical equipment		44	52	67	78	84	100	105	112	122	130	145	148
28	Machinery and equipment n.e.c.		73	85	99	109	99	100	94	98	93	101	105	109
29	Motor vehicles, trailers and semi-trailers		67	81	92	99	87	100	114	107	113	119	131	141
30	Other transport equipment		95	104	107	116	104	100	129	144	158	147	174	163
31	Furniture		88	100	108	106	104	100	119	108	115	134	145	163
32	Other manufacturing		63	72	78	92	98	100	124	126	133	136	149	164
33	Repair and installation of machinery/equipment		69	72	85	93	83	100	100	109	120	138	165	131
C	Total manufacturing		70	81	89	92	89	100	108	109	112	117	124	129

Portugal

Supplier of information:
National Institute of Statistics, Lisbon.
Industrial statistics for the OECD countries are compiled by the OECD secretariat, which supplies them to UNIDO.

Basic source of data:
Annual surveys; administrative data.

Major deviations from ISIC (Revision 4):
Data presented in ISIC (Revision 4) were originally classified according to the national NACE-related classification system.

Reference period:
Calendar year.

Scope:
All enterprises.

Method of data collection:
Simplified Business Information (IES): enterprises report, by electronic means, obligations on annual data of accounting, fiscal and statistical nature.

Type of enumeration:
Complete enumeration (mainly administrative sources).

Adjusted for non-response:
Not reported.

Concepts and definitions of variables:
No deviations from the standard UN concepts and definitions are reported.

Related national publications:
"Empresas em Portugal", published by National Institute of Statistics, Lisbon.

Portugal

ISIC	Industry	Note	Number of enterprises (number)				Note	Number of employees (number)				Note	Wages and salaries paid to employees (millions of Euros)			
			2013	2014	2015	2016		2013	2014	2015	2016		2013	2014	2015	2016
1010	Processing/preserving of meat		630	627	654	678		15304	15532	16346	16777		166	168	175	182
1020	Processing/preserving of fish, etc.		154	153	157	160		6414	6790	6936	7244		75	77	80	86
1030	Processing/preserving of fruit,vegetables		285	338	372	391		3669	4078	4519	4850		46	52	56	66
1040	Vegetable and animal oils and fats		511	512	478	456		1876	1916	2178	2177		31	32	40	41
1050	Dairy products		400	388	406	426		5948	6020	6010	6155		90	93	89	92
106	Grain mill products,starches and starch products		217	202	186	189		1587	1641	1641	1681		28	28	29	30
1061	Grain mill products		214	199	183	186		1474	1523	1521	1555		25	25	26	27
1062	Starches and starch products		3	3	3	3		113	118	120	126		3	3	3	3
107	Other food products		6695	6953	6969	6885		45638	46282	46854	47781		465	479	491	510
1071	Bakery products		6311	6330	6310	6202		37839	38139	38476	39322		328	337	347	363
1072	Sugar		7	6	6	7		636	609	583	502		13	12	12	10
1073	Cocoa, chocolate and sugar confectionery		132	147	151	165		900	930	937	919		11	12	12	12
1074	Macaroni, noodles, couscous, etc.		5	10	8	13		469	467	454	480		6	7	7	8
1075	Prepared meals and dishes		121	125	129	140		733	754	831	983		7	8	8	10
1079	Other food products n.e.c.		319	335	365	358		5061	5383	5573	5575		99	103	106	108
1080	Prepared animal feeds		116	116	115	111		3282	3361	3449	3444		52	54	57	57
110	Beverages		1441	1659	1754	1793		13724	13899	14184	14221		246	249	256	260
1101	Distilling, rectifying and blending of spirits		336	338	343	352		324	369	390	419		4	5	5	6
1102	Wines		1025	1230	1302	1302		...	...	...	...		...	...	...	...
1103	Malt liquors and malt		25	39	60	87		...	...	...	...		...	...	...	...
1104	Soft drinks,mineral waters,other bottled waters		55	52	49	52		3094	2992	3000	2988		58	56	57	57
1200	Tobacco products		6	6	5	6		587	577	628	664		18	19	20	20
131	Spinning, weaving and finishing of textiles		763	768	799	825		18097	18389	18679	19360		196	207	213	226
1311	Preparation and spinning of textile fibres		107	98	102	107		2497	2479	2584	2651		26	26	28	28
1312	Weaving of textiles		234	227	242	245		7473	7450	7364	7657		81	86	86	91
1313	Finishing of textiles		422	443	455	473		8127	8460	8731	9052		89	95	99	107
139	Other textiles		2673	2615	2681	2692		20843	21577	22246	23713		229	239	249	273
1391	Knitted and crocheted fabrics		203	194	190	192		2551	2566	2701	2871		30	31	33	36
1392	Made-up textile articles, except apparel		922	944	1007	1038		7775	8120	8381	8958		77	81	86	93
1393	Carpets and rugs		121	101	98	94		1193	1196	1253	1356		13	13	14	16
1394	Cordage, rope, twine and netting		38	37	35	38		2510	2651	2643	2692		32	32	32	34
1399	Other textiles n.e.c.		1389	1339	1351	1330		6814	7044	7268	7836		77	81	84	95
1410	Wearing apparel, except fur apparel		7921	7951	8060	8183		72046	74836	76637	78474		601	642	668	713
1420	Articles of fur		24	21	25	24		44	47	49	49		-	-	-	-
1430	Knitted and crocheted apparel		536	520	509	503		6754	7415	7532	7496		61	71	73	76
151	Leather;luggage,handbags,saddlery,harness;fur		412	399	401	402		3357	3705	3959	4337		38	42	44	50
1511	Tanning/dressing of leather; dressing of fur		105	104	98	107		2068	2300	2272	2462		27	30	29	32
1512	Luggage,handbags,etc.;saddlery/harness		307	295	303	295		1289	1405	1687	1875		11	12	15	17
1520	Footwear		2629	2730	2781	2832		42882	45142	46251	46560		400	432	451	470
1610	Sawmilling and planing of wood		667	629	622	582		4548	4879	4871	4761		46	51	52	52

162	Wood products, cork, straw, plaiting materials	4859	4629	4586	4465	20704	20487	20873	21315	259	264	281	290
1621	Veneer sheets and wood-based panels	38	36	39	37	1545	1587	1735	1673	28	27	32	34
1622	Builders' carpentry and joinery	3032	2822	2774	2673	7584	7459	7743	8045	72	73	79	83
1623	Wooden containers	143	139	141	144	1245	1270	1345	1424	13	13	14	16
1629	Other wood products;articles of cork,straw	1646	1632	1632	1611	10330	10171	10050	10173	146	150	156	157
170	Paper and paper products	602	592	572	571	10793	9661	9947	9917	195	166	171	167
1701	Pulp, paper and paperboard	39	40	38	38	3561	2293	2159	1656	89	57	54	44
1702	Corrugated paper and paperboard	249	242	238	249	4865	5071	5447	5806	72	74	81	86
1709	Other articles of paper and paperboard	314	310	296	284	2367	2297	2341	2455	34	34	35	37
181	Printing and service activities related to printing	2519	2467	2451	2415	14251	14135	14437	14132	194	196	202	201
1811	Printing	1429	1429	1447	1462	10930	10730	10932	10701	155	153	158	156
1812	Service activities related to printing	1090	1038	1004	953	3321	3405	3505	3431	40	42	44	45
1820	Reproduction of recorded media	40	42	49	38	75	70	79	88	1	1	1	2
1910	Coke oven products	–	–	–	–	–	–	–	–	–	–	–	–
1920	Refined petroleum products	17	17	18	15	1982	1785	1825	1786	87	84	89	90
201	Basic chemicals,fertilizers, etc.	183	187	193	194	3993	3945	4024	4140	114	113	116	116
2011	Basic chemicals	110	116	120	123	1976	1834	1855	1893	50	49	47	48
2012	Fertilizers and nitrogen compounds	26	27	28	26	578	600	602	633	14	15	15	15
2013	Plastics and synthetic rubber in primary forms	47	44	45	45	1439	1511	1567	1614	50	50	53	53
202	Other chemical products	568	569	574	585	7052	7091	…	7659	129	131	…	143
2021	Pesticides and other agrochemical products	5	3	2	4	401	391	…	482	10	10	…	13
2022	Paints,varnishes;printing ink and mastics	133	134	119	121	3072	3066	3134	3179	63	64	66	67
2023	Soap, cleaning and cosmetic preparations	214	220	234	251	1990	1970	2074	2208	28	28	29	31
2029	Other chemical products n.e.c.	216	212	219	209	1589	1664	1728	1790	28	29	30	33
2030	Man-made fibres	11	11	12	12	413	420	…	442	8	8	…	9
2100	Pharmaceuticals,medicinal chemicals, etc.	127	131	134	141	6033	6181	6247	6678	147	156	160	171
221	Rubber products	141	139	141	131	5104	5261	5388	5399	94	100	102	105
2211	Rubber tyres and tubes	22	21	22	18	2397	2398	2373	2420	59	61	63	65
2219	Other rubber products	119	118	119	113	2707	2863	3015	2979	35	38	40	40
2220	Plastics products	919	913	933	941	18208	18697	19407	20174	268	280	296	315
2310	Glass and glass products	407	405	391	381	5691	5658	5781	6004	102	103	105	106
239	Non-metallic mineral products n.e.c.	3618	3525	3527	3450	31080	31096	31563	32301	418	419	432	450
2391	Refractory products	22	20	20	19	215	219	199	204	3	3	3	3
2392	Clay building materials	194	184	187	180	5246	5057	5020	4960	78	76	78	78
2393	Other porcelain and ceramic products	918	923	950	937	…	…	…	…	…	…	…	…
2394	Cement, lime and plaster	23	22	21	19	…	…	1020	1075	…	…	35	36
2395	Articles of concrete, cement and plaster	588	563	556	536	5279	4893	4866	4856	80	75	75	75
2396	Cutting, shaping and finishing of stone	1790	1731	1712	1674	8701	8609	8570	8712	91	90	92	97
2399	Other non-metallic mineral products n.e.c.	83	82	81	85	1225	1215	1253	1337	21	22	23	25
2410	Basic iron and steel	101	100	118	121	2831	2820	3031	3135	58	59	63	63
2420	Basic precious and other non-ferrous metals	85	88	78	75	1788	1666	1638	1730	29	27	27	29
243	Casting of metals	150	140	139	135	3407	3384	2959	3008	51	56	46	48
2431	Casting of iron and steel	33	30	28	25	1986	2000	1474	1507	33	35	24	24
2432	Casting of non-ferrous metals	117	110	111	110	1421	1384	1485	1501	18	20	23	23
251	Struct.metal products, tanks, reservoirs	5083	5080	5112	5178	30277	30753	31318	32827	395	408	429	441

continued

Portugal

<table>
<thead>
<tr><th colspan="2" rowspan="3">ISIC Revision 4</th><th colspan="5">Number of enterprises</th><th colspan="5">Number of employees</th><th colspan="5">Wages and salaries paid to employees</th></tr>
<tr><th rowspan="2">Note</th><th colspan="4">(number)</th><th rowspan="2">Note</th><th colspan="4">(number)</th><th rowspan="2">Note</th><th colspan="4">(millions of Euros)</th></tr>
<tr><th>2013</th><th>2014</th><th>2015</th><th>2016</th><th>2013</th><th>2014</th><th>2015</th><th>2016</th><th>2013</th><th>2014</th><th>2015</th><th>2016</th></tr>
<tr><th>ISIC</th><th>Industry</th></tr>
</thead>
<tbody>
<tr><td>2511</td><td>Structural metal products</td><td></td><td>4949</td><td>4944</td><td>4975</td><td>5041</td><td></td><td>27622</td><td>27892</td><td>28171</td><td>29619</td><td></td><td>347</td><td>356</td><td>368</td><td>383</td></tr>
<tr><td>2512</td><td>Tanks, reservoirs and containers of metal</td><td></td><td>120</td><td>124</td><td>123</td><td>122</td><td></td><td>2132</td><td>2349</td><td>2645</td><td>2687</td><td></td><td>36</td><td>40</td><td>49</td><td>45</td></tr>
<tr><td>2513</td><td>Steam generators, excl. hot water boilers</td><td></td><td>14</td><td>12</td><td>14</td><td>15</td><td></td><td>523</td><td>512</td><td>502</td><td>521</td><td></td><td>13</td><td>12</td><td>12</td><td>13</td></tr>
<tr><td>2520</td><td>Weapons and ammunition</td><td></td><td>7</td><td>6</td><td>8</td><td>10</td><td></td><td>414</td><td>477</td><td>434</td><td>410</td><td></td><td>7</td><td>8</td><td>8</td><td>8</td></tr>
<tr><td>259</td><td>Other metal products;metal working services</td><td></td><td>6594</td><td>6364</td><td>6317</td><td>6320</td><td></td><td>40528</td><td>41579</td><td>43269</td><td>44957</td><td></td><td>581</td><td>605</td><td>644</td><td>675</td></tr>
<tr><td>2591</td><td>Forging,pressing,stamping,roll-forming of metal</td><td></td><td>987</td><td>936</td><td>905</td><td>870</td><td></td><td>1523</td><td>1708</td><td>1811</td><td>1916</td><td></td><td>16</td><td>18</td><td>20</td><td>21</td></tr>
<tr><td>2592</td><td>Treatment and coating of metals;machining</td><td></td><td>2268</td><td>2195</td><td>2246</td><td>2300</td><td></td><td>11344</td><td>11641</td><td>12029</td><td>12380</td><td></td><td>151</td><td>164</td><td>171</td><td>176</td></tr>
<tr><td>2593</td><td>Cutlery, hand tools and general hardware</td><td></td><td>1769</td><td>1702</td><td>1662</td><td>1643</td><td></td><td>14985</td><td>15571</td><td>16479</td><td>17304</td><td></td><td>242</td><td>252</td><td>275</td><td>295</td></tr>
<tr><td>2599</td><td>Other fabricated metal products n.e.c.</td><td></td><td>1570</td><td>1531</td><td>1504</td><td>1507</td><td></td><td>12676</td><td>12659</td><td>12950</td><td>13357</td><td></td><td>172</td><td>171</td><td>179</td><td>183</td></tr>
<tr><td>2610</td><td>Electronic components and boards</td><td></td><td>158</td><td>150</td><td>141</td><td>132</td><td></td><td>1405</td><td>1428</td><td>1312</td><td>1297</td><td></td><td>23</td><td>23</td><td>22</td><td>22</td></tr>
<tr><td>2620</td><td>Computers and peripheral equipment</td><td></td><td>39</td><td>36</td><td>34</td><td>39</td><td></td><td>981</td><td>958</td><td>966</td><td>892</td><td></td><td>20</td><td>19</td><td>20</td><td>20</td></tr>
<tr><td>2630</td><td>Communication equipment</td><td></td><td>57</td><td>48</td><td>52</td><td>45</td><td></td><td>1634</td><td>1421</td><td>1393</td><td>1403</td><td></td><td>29</td><td>28</td><td>28</td><td>28</td></tr>
<tr><td>2640</td><td>Consumer electronics</td><td></td><td>18</td><td>13</td><td>12</td><td>15</td><td></td><td>3068</td><td>3281</td><td>3483</td><td>3824</td><td></td><td>58</td><td>64</td><td>69</td><td>75</td></tr>
<tr><td>265</td><td>Measuring,testing equipment; watches, etc.</td><td></td><td>63</td><td>60</td><td>60</td><td>61</td><td></td><td>1047</td><td>1235</td><td>1285</td><td>1407</td><td></td><td>15</td><td>18</td><td>19</td><td>22</td></tr>
<tr><td>2651</td><td>Measuring/testing/navigating equipment,etc.</td><td></td><td>46</td><td>45</td><td>49</td><td>52</td><td></td><td>614</td><td>708</td><td>754</td><td>882</td><td></td><td>10</td><td>12</td><td>13</td><td>16</td></tr>
<tr><td>2652</td><td>Watches and clocks</td><td></td><td>17</td><td>15</td><td>11</td><td>9</td><td></td><td>433</td><td>527</td><td>531</td><td>525</td><td></td><td>5</td><td>6</td><td>6</td><td>6</td></tr>
<tr><td>2660</td><td>Irradiation/electromedical equipment,etc.</td><td></td><td>19</td><td>17</td><td>21</td><td>21</td><td></td><td>...</td><td>...</td><td>...</td><td>...</td><td></td><td>...</td><td>...</td><td>...</td><td>...</td></tr>
<tr><td>2670</td><td>Optical instruments and photographic equipment</td><td></td><td>11</td><td>11</td><td>12</td><td>10</td><td></td><td>555</td><td>567</td><td>548</td><td>598</td><td></td><td>9</td><td>8</td><td>9</td><td>9</td></tr>
<tr><td>2680</td><td>Magnetic and optical media</td><td></td><td>2</td><td>2</td><td>2</td><td>2</td><td></td><td>...</td><td>...</td><td>...</td><td>...</td><td></td><td>...</td><td>...</td><td>...</td><td>...</td></tr>
<tr><td>2710</td><td>Electric motors,generators,transformers,etc.</td><td></td><td>182</td><td>174</td><td>185</td><td>173</td><td></td><td>6884</td><td>6824</td><td>7243</td><td>7220</td><td></td><td>137</td><td>151</td><td>157</td><td>162</td></tr>
<tr><td>2720</td><td>Batteries and accumulators</td><td></td><td>2</td><td>2</td><td>2</td><td>2</td><td></td><td>...</td><td>...</td><td>...</td><td>...</td><td></td><td>...</td><td>...</td><td>...</td><td>...</td></tr>
<tr><td>273</td><td>Wiring and wiring devices</td><td></td><td>35</td><td>35</td><td>35</td><td>35</td><td></td><td>3505</td><td>3409</td><td>3865</td><td>3953</td><td></td><td>63</td><td>47</td><td>68</td><td>49</td></tr>
<tr><td>2731</td><td>Fibre optic cables</td><td></td><td>1</td><td>1</td><td>2</td><td>2</td><td></td><td>...</td><td>...</td><td>...</td><td>...</td><td></td><td>...</td><td>...</td><td>...</td><td>...</td></tr>
<tr><td>2732</td><td>Other electronic and electric wires and cables</td><td></td><td>21</td><td>21</td><td>20</td><td>19</td><td></td><td>3210</td><td>3135</td><td>3505</td><td>3598</td><td></td><td>57</td><td>41</td><td>61</td><td>43</td></tr>
<tr><td>2733</td><td>Wiring devices</td><td></td><td>13</td><td>13</td><td>13</td><td>14</td><td></td><td>...</td><td>...</td><td>...</td><td>...</td><td></td><td>...</td><td>...</td><td>...</td><td>...</td></tr>
<tr><td>2740</td><td>Electric lighting equipment</td><td></td><td>188</td><td>185</td><td>177</td><td>177</td><td></td><td>...</td><td>...</td><td>1988</td><td>2061</td><td></td><td>...</td><td>...</td><td>29</td><td>30</td></tr>
<tr><td>2750</td><td>Domestic appliances</td><td></td><td>106</td><td>103</td><td>107</td><td>107</td><td></td><td>3484</td><td>3573</td><td>3598</td><td>3726</td><td></td><td>52</td><td>55</td><td>57</td><td>61</td></tr>
<tr><td>2790</td><td>Other electrical equipment</td><td></td><td>114</td><td>117</td><td>102</td><td>111</td><td></td><td>1366</td><td>1423</td><td>...</td><td>...</td><td></td><td>21</td><td>23</td><td>...</td><td>...</td></tr>
<tr><td>281</td><td>General-purpose machinery</td><td></td><td>862</td><td>808</td><td>789</td><td>785</td><td></td><td>10484</td><td>10936</td><td>11489</td><td>11445</td><td></td><td>163</td><td>172</td><td>185</td><td>186</td></tr>
<tr><td>2811</td><td>Engines/turbines,excl.aircraft,vehicle engines</td><td></td><td>42</td><td>35</td><td>38</td><td>34</td><td></td><td>1343</td><td>1384</td><td>1379</td><td>1398</td><td></td><td>24</td><td>24</td><td>24</td><td>24</td></tr>
<tr><td>2812</td><td>Fluid power equipment</td><td></td><td>25</td><td>23</td><td>26</td><td>24</td><td></td><td>120</td><td>133</td><td>142</td><td>146</td><td></td><td>2</td><td>2</td><td>2</td><td>2</td></tr>
<tr><td>2813</td><td>Other pumps, compressors, taps and valves</td><td></td><td>57</td><td>56</td><td>55</td><td>56</td><td></td><td>2191</td><td>2226</td><td>2271</td><td>2291</td><td></td><td>34</td><td>35</td><td>36</td><td>38</td></tr>
<tr><td>2814</td><td>Bearings, gears, gearing and driving elements</td><td></td><td>19</td><td>18</td><td>13</td><td>17</td><td></td><td>614</td><td>623</td><td>694</td><td>769</td><td></td><td>11</td><td>12</td><td>14</td><td>15</td></tr>
<tr><td>2815</td><td>Ovens, furnaces and furnace burners</td><td></td><td>31</td><td>31</td><td>30</td><td>33</td><td></td><td>192</td><td>182</td><td>185</td><td>197</td><td></td><td>3</td><td>3</td><td>3</td><td>3</td></tr>
<tr><td>2816</td><td>Lifting and handling equipment</td><td></td><td>91</td><td>93</td><td>89</td><td>85</td><td></td><td>1491</td><td>1562</td><td>1653</td><td>1662</td><td></td><td>26</td><td>27</td><td>28</td><td>30</td></tr>
<tr><td>2817</td><td>Office machinery, excl.computers,etc.</td><td></td><td>8</td><td>4</td><td>3</td><td>1</td><td></td><td>14</td><td>12</td><td>4</td><td>...</td><td></td><td>-</td><td>-</td><td>-</td><td>...</td></tr>
<tr><td>2818</td><td>Power-driven hand tools</td><td></td><td>30</td><td>26</td><td>22</td><td>26</td><td></td><td>39</td><td>42</td><td>48</td><td>...</td><td></td><td>-</td><td>-</td><td>1</td><td>...</td></tr>
<tr><td>2819</td><td>Other general-purpose machinery</td><td></td><td>559</td><td>522</td><td>513</td><td>509</td><td></td><td>4480</td><td>4772</td><td>5113</td><td>4926</td><td></td><td>63</td><td>70</td><td>77</td><td>73</td></tr>
<tr><td>282</td><td>Special-purpose machinery</td><td></td><td>756</td><td>748</td><td>734</td><td>766</td><td></td><td>9377</td><td>9925</td><td>10252</td><td>10774</td><td></td><td>147</td><td>158</td><td>164</td><td>176</td></tr>
<tr><td>2821</td><td>Agricultural and forestry machinery</td><td></td><td>174</td><td>171</td><td>157</td><td>155</td><td></td><td>1238</td><td>1611</td><td>1625</td><td>1609</td><td></td><td>16</td><td>21</td><td>22</td><td>22</td></tr>
<tr><td>2822</td><td>Metal-forming machinery and machine tools</td><td></td><td>91</td><td>78</td><td>79</td><td>89</td><td></td><td>1137</td><td>1070</td><td>1093</td><td>1145</td><td></td><td>20</td><td>18</td><td>19</td><td>20</td></tr>
</tbody>
</table>

Code	Description												
2823	Machinery for metallurgy	22	21	21	29	202	283	305	309	3	3	4	4
2824	Mining, quarrying and construction machinery	70	66	63	62	796	833	839	862	13	14	13	14
2825	Food/beverage/tobacco processing machinery	88	92	91	95	1534	1403	1323	1377	25	25	24	25
2826	Textile/apparel/leather production machinery	52	54	47	48	1209	1202	1241	1304	19	20	20	22
2829	Other special-purpose machinery	259	266	276	288	3261	3523	3826	4168	51	57	62	69
2910	Motor vehicles	25	26	28	30	5610	5395	5333	5329	113	121	124	116
2920	Automobile bodies, trailers and semi-trailers	168	163	172	171	2457	2251	2334	2315	33	29	30	30
2930	Parts and accessories for motor vehicles	516	496	484	484	22015	23331	25456	25557	341	357	400	419
301	Building of ships and boats	131	132	130	124	1118	1213	1323	1460	18	20	21	30
3011	Building of ships and floating structures	74	77	70	68	676	799	856	863	11	13	14	17
3012	Building of pleasure and sporting boats	57	55	60	56	442	414	467	597	7	7	7	13
3020	Railway locomotives and rolling stock	4	4	4	4	...	78	71	74	...	2	2	2
3030	Air and spacecraft and related machinery	19	18	22	27	499	557	850	976	7	9	13	18
3040	Military fighting vehicles	1	-	-	-	...	-	-	-	...	-	-	-
309	Transport equipment n.e.c.	49	51	50	56	1656	1825	2062	2252	21	23	26	31
3091	Motorcycles	14	18	14	16	282	327	318	357	3	4	4	5
3092	Bicycles and invalid carriages	26	28	30	34	1222	1354	1588	1732	16	18	20	24
3099	Other transport equipment n.e.c.	9	5	6	6	152	144	156	163	2	2	2	2
3100	Furniture	4573	4489	4446	4414	25807	26224	27240	28619	240	252	267	292
321	Jewellery, bijouterie and related articles	939	959	1006	1038	1910	1710	1811	1928	20	19	21	22
3211	Jewellery and related articles	679	648	663	680	1638	1584	1621	1689	17	18	19	19
3212	Imitation jewellery and related articles	260	311	343	358	272	126	190	239	3	1	2	3
3220	Musical instruments	36	44	43	45	122	147	158	157	1	2	2	2
3230	Sports goods	69	76	80	88	267	298	307	333	4	4	5	4
3240	Games and toys	48	51	53	67	218	169	183	187	2	2	2	2
3250	Medical and dental instruments and supplies	958	966	981	1028	4162	4143	4319	4561	54	58	57	67
3290	Other manufacturing n.e.c.	797	825	855	831	4778	4794	5344	5523	55	55	63	67
331	Repair of fabricated metal products/machinery	2768	2977	3128	3281	12947	14048	15059	14903	231	261	277	281
3311	Repair of fabricated metal products	139	151	160	160	975	1173	1230	1253	18	20	21	21
3312	Repair of machinery	1815	1958	2061	2168	6173	6631	7141	7664	97	116	127	137
3313	Repair of electronic and optical equipment	107	106	118	135	244	232	252	258	4	4	4	4
3314	Repair of electrical equipment	247	266	279	286	825	1124	1340	742	15	20	19	14
3315	Repair of transport equip., excl. motor vehicles	324	345	344	362	4513	4659	4796	4649	95	98	103	101
3319	Repair of other equipment	136	151	166	170	217	229	300	337	2	3	3	4
3320	Installation of industrial machinery/equipment	399	423	455	468	4131	3990	3651	3595	90	83	78	75
C	Total manufacturing	66423	66201	66729	66953	605054	618797	637772	654140	7925	8215	8608	8961

Portugal

ISIC	Industry	Note	Output (valuation not defined) (millions of Euros) 2013	2014	2015	2016	Note	Value added at factor values (millions of Euros) 2013	2014	2015	2016	Note	Gross fixed capital formation (millions of Euros) 2015	2016
1010	Processing/preserving of meat		2023	2107	2082	2124		306	326	343	360		67	72
1020	Processing/preserving of fish, etc.		921	915	940	969		168	172	174	182		83	28
1030	Processing/preserving of fruit,vegetables		554	688	732	827		121	142	141	169		45	46
1040	Vegetable and animal oils and fats		1040	960	1075	831		98	101	124	111		48	60
1050	Dairy products		1421	1497	1361	1350		220	215	202	212		41	54
106	Grain mill products,starches and starch products		523	493	480	487		68	67	60	64		16	30
1061	Grain mill products		483	461	450	454		60	62	55	59		15	30
1062	Starches and starch products		40	32	31	33		8	5	5	6		1	1
107	Other food products		2841	2728	2719	2814		852	869	888	954		183	189
1071	Bakery products		1400	1437	1447	1516		526	548	575	614		110	113
1072	Sugar		383	214	180	194		35	5	-5	7		6	3
1073	Cocoa, chocolate and sugar confectionery		64	68	67	66		20	22	23	22		3	4
1074	Macaroni, noodles, couscous, etc.		103	100	107	103		21	20	24	24		2	8
1075	Prepared meals and dishes		45	45	47	68		13	11	12	16		8	6
1079	Other food products n.e.c.		846	865	871	868		239	262	260	271		54	55
1080	Prepared animal feeds		1415	1347	1353	1316		143	137	143	146		41	25
110	Beverages		2856	2947	2981	3023		685	721	769	797		184	198
1101	Distilling, rectifying and blending of spirits		67	60	60	71		23	20	18	23		5	4
1102	Wines		...	...	...	...		...	...	...	...		...	...
1103	Malt liquors and malt		...	...	...	...		...	...	...	...		...	...
1104	Soft drinks,mineral waters,other bottled waters		665	706	677	696		154	172	178	188		30	26
1200	Tobacco products		563	680	776	756		331	409	480	463		24	14
131	Spinning, weaving and finishing of textiles		1227	1266	1308	1365		352	373	396	439		105	126
1311	Preparation and spinning of textile fibres		202	204	204	205		46	46	49	54		9	9
1312	Weaving of textiles		562	594	632	674		134	149	166	185		44	55
1313	Finishing of textiles		464	468	472	487		172	178	180	200		52	62
139	Other textiles		1776	1857	1976	2055		431	497	539	587		90	128
1391	Knitted and crocheted fabrics		367	379	399	423		61	64	71	83		13	29
1392	Made-up textile articles, except apparel		498	470	498	512		117	129	150	160		20	27
1393	Carpets and rugs		72	79	84	90		22	29	26	27		6	9
1394	Cordage, rope, twine and netting		279	309	316	312		64	79	76	81		17	19
1399	Other textiles n.e.c.		560	620	679	718		167	196	217	236		34	44
1410	Wearing apparel, except fur apparel		2714	2983	3109	3330		909	1011	1039	1116		95	121
1420	Articles of fur		2	3	3	3		1	1	1	1		-	-
1430	Knitted and crocheted apparel		308	377	371	394		96	111	114	121		17	28
151	Leather/luggage,handbags,saddlery,harness;fur		300	349	349	372		69	76	83	97		8	12
1511	Tanning/dressing of leather; dressing of fur		249	294	288	309		49	53	57	69		6	9
1512	Luggage,handbags,etc.;saddlery/harness		51	55	61	63		20	22	25	28		2	3
1520	Footwear		2211	2371	2367	2385		667	730	751	759		100	92
1610	Sawmilling and planing of wood		341	403	426	394		87	94	104	98		26	25

Code	Description										
162	Wood products, cork, straw, plaiting materials	133	133	624	577	537	527	2424	2428	2278	2165
1621	Veneer sheets and wood-based panels	27	32	65	56	54	55	341	365	353	339
1622	Builders' carpentry and joinery	26	27	148	144	129	126	398	390	357	340
1623	Wooden containers	4	7	35	34	31	29	118	116	104	92
1629	Other wood products;articles of cork,straw	76	67	376	342	324	318	1568	1557	1464	1394
170	Paper and paper products	374	398	839	883	708	805	3902	3933	3633	3626
1701	Pulp, paper and paperboard	290	326	573	632	466	575	2796	2874	2612	2671
1702	Corrugated paper and paperboard	40	40	191	180	170	159	759	719	688	639
1709	Other articles of paper and paperboard	44	32	75	71	73	71	347	341	334	317
181	Printing and service activities related to printing	75	76	399	408	391	394	959	988	963	948
1811	Printing	60	56	316	324	310	318	768	793	769	766
1812	Service activities related to printing	15	19	83	84	81	76	191	195	194	182
1820	Reproduction of recorded media	-	-	2	2	2	2	10	10	11	11
1910	Coke oven products	-	-	-	-	-	-	-	-	-	-
1920	Refined petroleum products	95	92	592	551	118	240	5993	7056	8336	9459
201	Basic chemicals,fertilizers, etc.	80	69	493	473	334	285	2371	2548	2711	2824
2011	Basic chemicals	34	34	156	154	139	152	715	774	815	1053
2012	Fertilizers and nitrogen compounds	8	7	31	40	45	39	191	274	303	279
2013	Plastics and synthetic rubber in primary forms	38	28	306	279	151	95	1465	1500	1593	1491
202	Other chemical products	59	...	344	...	296	282	1594	...	1416	1423
2021	Pesticides and other agrochemical products	4	15	34	...	24	27	138	...	123	118
2022	Paints,varnishes;printing ink and mastics	17	17	141	139	129	125	509	532	515	495
2023	Soap,cleaning and cosmetic preparations	16	15	66	63	61	52	226	219	211	217
2029	Other chemical products n.e.c.	22	33	103	83	81	78	722	671	568	593
2030	Man-made fibres	4	...	11	...	12	16	102	...	121	126
2100	Pharmaceuticals,medicinal chemicals, etc.	104	76	436	437	391	406	1065	1064	971	1028
221	Rubber products	112	72	517	516	436	436	1114	1104	1037	1062
2211	Rubber tyres and tubes	88	51	424	429	350	359	864	864	798	838
2219	Other rubber products	23	21	93	87	86	76	250	241	239	224
2220	Plastics products	229	223	763	706	641	583	2829	2696	2536	2353
2310	Glass and glass products	51	60	335	322	318	322	876	869	852	835
239	Non-metallic mineral products n.e.c.	187	157	929	856	819	782	2696	2704	2587	2504
2391	Refractory products	1	1	7	6	5	5	15	15	14	13
2392	Clay building materials	24	25	154	140	138	137	443	442	438	437
2393	Other porcelain and ceramic products	...	...	...	...	...	...	...	...	...	...
2394	Cement, lime and plaster	27	21	117	104	...	...	427	504	...	...
2395	Articles of concrete, cement and plaster	26	22	146	148	133	118	553	563	515	487
2396	Cutting, shaping and finishing of stone	46	39	182	171	158	161	511	489	463	459
2399	Other non-metallic mineral products n.e.c.	20	9	67	61	56	49	210	185	185	171
2410	Basic iron and steel	72	37	234	183	150	147	1531	1642	1681	1670
2420	Basic precious and other non-ferrous metals	11	9	69	55	49	49	449	395	354	493
243	Casting of metals	55	56	94	90	110	98	302	290	355	320
2431	Casting of iron and steel	6	8	45	48	69	63	129	134	221	198
2432	Casting of non-ferrous metals	49	49	49	42	41	35	172	156	134	122
251	Struct.metal products, tanks, reservoirs	133	129	766	724	677	632	2350	2275	2210	2075

continued

Portugal

	ISIC Revision 4		Output (valuation not defined) (millions of Euros)					Value added at factor values (millions of Euros)					Gross fixed capital formation (millions of Euros)	
ISIC	Industry	Note	2013	2014	2015	2016	Note	2013	2014	2015	2016	Note	2015	2016
2511	Structural metal products		1765	1875	1925	2023		552	590	633	671		110	111
2512	Tanks, reservoirs and containers of metal		230	263	279	247		62	73	77	81		15	10
2513	Steam generators, excl. hot water boilers		81	72	71	80		18	15	14	15		4	13
2520	Weapons and ammunition		48	55	50	48		14	14	14	13		2	2
259	Other metal products;metal working services		2940	3188	3418	3565		1096	1191	1273	1383		272	389
2591	Forging,pressing,stamping,roll-forming of metal		94	98	107	110		32	36	39	43		6	25
2592	Treatment and coating of metals; machining		662	734	806	851		289	319	334	362		67	82
2593	Cutlery, hand tools and general hardware		1063	1204	1321	1430		455	502	540	591		131	206
2599	Other fabricated metal products n.e.c.		1121	1152	1185	1174		320	334	360	387		68	76
2610	Electronic components and boards		105	90	79	91		55	43	34	38		7	25
2620	Computers and peripheral equipment		135	169	166	314		38	45	47	29		4	1
2630	Communication equipment		226	238	233	231		55	55	54	57		6	6
2640	Consumer electronics		754	743	844	1116		121	128	134	169		51	92
265	Measuring,testing equipment; watches, etc.		60	75	82	95		27	33	33	39		6	9
2651	Measuring/testing/navigating equipment,etc.		48	60	66	80		19	25	24	30		4	7
2652	Watches and clocks		13	14	16	14		8	9	9	9		2	2
2660	Irradiation/electromedical equipment,etc.		...	...	...	...		...	...	...	...		...	...
2670	Optical instruments and photographic equipment		53	52	49	52		17	16	17	18		3	4
2680	Magnetic and optical media		...	...	...	...		...	...	...	...		...	...
2710	Electric motors,generators,transformers,etc.		987	925	947	954		272	256	266	285		34	41
2720	Batteries and accumulators		...	...	...	...		...	...	...	...		...	...
273	Wiring and wiring devices		847	817	877	852		131	113	145	116		20	53
2731	Fibre optic cables		...	...	...	...		...	...	...	...		...	...
2732	Other electronic and electric wires and cables		811	784	841	819		116	100	131	102		18	51
2733	Wiring devices		...	...	...	...		...	...	...	...		...	...
2740	Electric lighting equipment		...	...	134	138		...	...	51	53		10	11
2750	Domestic appliances		489	500	517	519		124	131	138	140		20	27
2790	Other electrical equipment		117	119	...	...		43	39	...	...		...	...
281	General-purpose machinery		1478	1720	1530	1598		414	465	441	484		59	67
2811	Engines/turbines,excl.aircraft,vehicle engines		578	709	456	496		153	168	121	155		3	3
2812	Fluid power equipment		21	22	19	21		3	4	4	4		-	1
2813	Other pumps, compressors, taps and valves		261	267	284	299		65	68	71	76		13	17
2814	Bearings, gears, gearing and driving elements		73	75	84	93		21	21	27	32		9	5
2815	Ovens, furnaces and furnace burners		11	13	13	13		5	4	5	5		-	1
2816	Lifting and handling equipment		148	162	162	175		43	49	49	56		5	6
2817	Office machinery, excl.computers,etc.		1	-	-	...		1	1	1	...		-	...
2818	Power-driven hand tools		2	2	3	...		...	...	...	...		-	...
2819	Other general-purpose machinery		384	469	510	496		124	149	163	155		27	35
282	Special-purpose machinery		778	830	830	883		287	323	333	351		61	67
2821	Agricultural and forestry machinery		89	116	108	103		29	39	37	37		11	7
2822	Metal-forming machinery and machine tools		101	83	93	103		40	35	38	44		6	9

Code		1	2	3	4	5	6	7	8	9	10
2823	Machinery for metallurgy	15	18	20	21	6	7	8	8	1	1
2824	Mining, quarrying and construction machinery	77	78	64	71	27	29	24	27	3	3
2825	Food/beverage/tobacco processing machinery	132	123	112	117	47	48	45	47	3	8
2826	Textile/apparel/leather production machinery	75	78	86	95	38	42	50	56	16	11
2829	Other special-purpose machinery	291	335	348	374	101	123	131	134	21	28
2910	Motor vehicles	2298	2433	2430	2189	302	313	274	233	84	125
2920	Automobile bodies, trailers and semi-trailers	187	174	181	171	52	44	47	49	5	9
2930	Parts and accessories for motor vehicles	3701	3895	4645	4883	681	753	860	851	150	271
301	Building of ships and boats	70	64	97	161	27	29	35	49	6	16
3011	Building of ships and floating structures	30	35	57	90	18	18	21	27	3	2
3012	Building of pleasure and sporting boats	40	30	40	70	10	11	14	22	3	14
3020	Railway locomotives and rolling stock	...	5	6	5	...	2	2	3	-	-
3030	Air and spacecraft and related machinery	34	63	113	136	1	2	30	31	32	43
3040	Military fighting vehicles	...	-	-	-	...	-	-	-	-	-
309	Transport equipment n.e.c.	142	174	183	441	42	52	57	80	18	30
3091	Motorcycles	16	19	21	23	6	7	8	9	1	4
3092	Bicycles and invalid carriages	118	148	153	403	34	43	46	65	16	26
3099	Other transport equipment n.e.c.	9	8	9	15	2	2	3	6	-	-
3100	Furniture	1284	1400	1527	1590	415	451	495	545	90	118
321	Jewellery, bijouterie and related articles	111	97	112	112	33	33	36	38	3	5
3211	Jewellery and related articles	100	91	102	94	27	30	32	32	3	4
3212	Imitation jewellery and related articles	11	6	10	19	6	3	4	7	-	1
3220	Musical instruments	4	5	6	5	2	3	3	3	-	-
3230	Sports goods	146	191	216	15	9	11	13	6	3	-
3240	Games and toys	5	5	5	4	2	2	2	2	1	1
3250	Medical and dental instruments and supplies	292	297	298	330	112	116	115	123	15	21
3290	Other manufacturing n.e.c.	336	360	422	450	106	115	134	144	38	32
331	Repair of fabricated metal products/machinery	952	1021	1132	1138	374	417	480	479	44	55
3311	Repair of fabricated metal products	61	77	75	64	26	22	31	30	2	1
3312	Repair of machinery	415	445	492	522	155	186	211	232	25	29
3313	Repair of electronic and optical equipment	13	13	13	14	6	6	7	7	-	-
3314	Repair of electrical equipment	40	49	47	41	23	31	29	22	3	2
3315	Repair of transport equip., excl. motor vehicles	411	425	490	478	158	166	196	180	14	20
3319	Repair of other equipment	13	14	16	20	5	6	7	9	1	3
3320	Installation of industrial machinery/equipment	529	494	405	348	169	137	135	143	18	19
C	Total manufacturing	75262	76429	77841	78036	16684	17425	19227	20136	3909	4571

Portugal

ISIC Revision 4 — Index numbers of industrial production (2010=100)

ISIC	Industry	Note	2005	2006	2007	2008	2009	2010	2011	2012	2013	2014	2015	2016
10	Food products		86	89	93	92	94	100	99	100	104	102	102	102
11	Beverages		123	129	130	124	130	100	87	81	76	83	80	80
12	Tobacco products		...	...	...	...	...	...	...	...	...	...	...	...
13	Textiles		131	125	118	109	102	100	94	95	100	103	106	105
14	Wearing apparel		120	119	119	109	100	100	95	98	105	109	110	115
15	Leather and related products		143	137	131	120	99	100	107	100	108	108	101	101
16	Wood products, excluding furniture		114	115	119	112	98	100	108	112	110	113	118	118
17	Paper and paper products		92	92	93	94	97	100	105	108	107	109	112	111
18	Printing and reproduction of recorded media		115	117	115	113	104	100	94	86	83	81	84	78
19	Coke and refined petroleum products		...	...	...	...	...	...	...	...	...	...	...	...
20	Chemicals and chemical products		105	104	109	99	84	100	99	88	92	94	98	95
21	Pharmaceuticals,medicinal chemicals, etc.		96	101	102	111	107	100	92	95	99	102	120	120
22	Rubber and plastics products		93	95	103	94	91	100	101	95	95	105	112	118
23	Other non-metallic mineral products		128	124	130	118	104	100	100	95	87	87	88	85
24	Basic metals		83	92	95	93	90	100	102	97	99	103	113	116
25	Fabricated metal products, except machinery		100	108	110	112	102	100	97	98	95	96	98	97
26	Computer, electronic and optical products		102	97	93	92	63	100	103	115	78	66	58	66
27	Electrical equipment		130	136	128	128	104	100	99	89	90	83	88	88
28	Machinery and equipment n.e.c.		107	107	108	106	102	100	101	101	101	103	108	106
29	Motor vehicles, trailers and semi-trailers		380	332	285	227	102	100	96	89	92	104	107	106
30	Other transport equipment		130	132	127	120	100	100	96	85	86	70	73	74
31	Furniture		130	122	117	108	89	100	104	97	100	97	91	84
32	Other manufacturing		183	186	178	155	100	100	94	93	88	89	90	90
33	Repair and installation of machinery/equipment		121	128	125	120	99	100	96	89	82	83	83	80
C	Total manufacturing		125	124	122	114	99	100	98	96	97	98	101	100

Qatar

Supplier of information:
Ministry of Development Planning and Statistics, Doha.

Basic source of data:
Annual industrial survey.

Major deviations from ISIC (Revision 4):
None reported.

Reference period:
Calendar year.

Scope:
All registered establishments.

Method of data collection:
Direct interview in the field and E-Mail questionnaires.

Type of enumeration:
Complete enumeration of establishments with 10 or more employees and a sample of smaller establishments.

Adjusted for non-response:
Yes.

Concepts and definitions of variables:
Number of employees includes working proprietors.
Wages and salaries excludes renumeration for time not worked.
Output excludes value of fixed assets produced by the unit for its own use and includes revenues from non-industrial activities.

Related national publications:
Annual Bulletin of Industry and Energy Statistics, published by the Ministry of Development Planning and Statistics, Doha.

Qatar

ISIC Revision 4		Number of establishments (number)					Number of employees (number)					Wages and salaries paid to employees (millions of Qatari Riyals)				
ISIC	Industry	Note	2013	2014	2015	2016	Note	2013	2014	2015	2016	Note	2013	2014	2015	2016
10	Food products		...	211	272	269		...	6013	7699	7736		...	184.7	266.0	280.7
11	Beverages		...	11	11	12		...	2019	2277	2630		...	93.3	105.6	140.4
12	Tobacco products		...	...	...	...		...					...			...
13	Textiles		...	25	26	27		...	641	691	579		...	14.2	14.5	14.6
14	Wearing apparel		...	1002	1455	1476		...	7887	11942	11749		...	168.8	241.0	262.7
15	Leather and related products		...	4	5	4		...	110	122	104		...	3.3	1.9	1.5
16	Wood products, excluding furniture		...	150	240	216		...	4194	5860	6163		...	129.5	173.6	188.2
17	Paper and paper products		...	8	9	9		...	552	620	687		...	15.7	18.4	19.6
18	Printing and reproduction of recorded media		...	58	87	62		...	4045	4473	4333		...	318.9	366.5	301.3
19	Coke and refined petroleum products		...	3	3	3		...	1074	836	846		...	499.8	461.3	426.0
20	Chemicals and chemical products		...	36	37	33		...	8480	8504	8382		...	2545.0	2570.3	2685.5
21	Pharmaceuticals, medicinal chemicals, etc.		...	1	1	1		...	270	216	216		...	2.3	2.7	2.7
22	Rubber and plastics products		...	57	51	95		...	4768	6074	6132		...	191.9	251.7	265.8
23	Other non-metallic mineral products		...	148	201	204		...	20442	27074	26039		...	892.3	1069.8	1103.3
24	Basic metals		...	8	8	8		...	4823	4468	5142		...	1213.8	1171.5	1161.0
25	Fabricated metal products, except machinery		...	439	578	629		...	21901	28759	27821		...	581.0	823.0	867.5
26	Computer, electronic and optical products		...	...	...	...		...					...		...	...
27	Electrical equipment		...	20	19	23		...	1155	1393	1472		...	62.1	62.9	91.3
28	Machinery and equipment n.e.c.		...	5	4	3		...	1303	1634	1840		...	38.8	45.5	58.9
29	Motor vehicles, trailers and semi-trailers		...	8	11	7		...	522	543	559		...	10.5	12.6	12.3
30	Other transport equipment		...	1	2	2		...	776	573	564		...	89.4	87.3	62.3
31	Furniture		...	184	206	205		...	3383	4278	4420		...	107.3	134.4	155.4
32	Other manufacturing		...	3	5	4		...	78	134	144		...	4.1	6.2	8.8
33	Repair and installation of machinery/equipment		...	3	32	95		...	14	700	1255		...	0.5	36.0	121.0
C	Total manufacturing		...	2385	3263	3387		...	94450	118870	118813		...	7167.3	7922.7	8231.0

Qatar

| ISIC Revision 4 | | | Output at producers' prices | | | | | | Value added at producers' prices | | | | | | Gross fixed capital formation | |
| | | | (millions of Qatari Riyals) | | | | | | (millions of Qatari Riyals) | | | | | | (millions of Qatari Riyals) | |
ISIC	Industry	Note	2013	2014	2015	2016	Note	2013	2014	2015	2016	Note	2015	2016
10	Food products		...	1271.2	1675.3	1814.7		...	448.6	639.3	690.7		...	...
11	Beverages		...	556.7	622.5	810.1		...	213.9	267.2	318.4		...	...
12	Tobacco products		...	...	...	...		...	...	...	...		...	...
13	Textiles		...	107.8	78.2	80.7		...	45.5	41.5	37.9		...	...
14	Wearing apparel		...	1062.6	1386.8	1496.6		...	712.6	882.7	798.7		...	...
15	Leather and related products		...	24.6	16.2	25.6		...	15.6	8.4	12.5		...	...
16	Wood products, excluding furniture		...	689.2	909.7	912.7		...	346.8	501.7	495.2		...	...
17	Paper and paper products		...	113.7	108.5	111.6		...	48.1	42.6	47.2		...	...
18	Printing and reproduction of recorded media		...	1208.1	1326.0	1126.8		...	824.9	868.0	724.8		...	...
19	Coke and refined petroleum products		...	29016.5	18546.8	17429.6		...	9007.8	5925.4	6336.4		...	...
20	Chemicals and chemical products		...	60599.1	40880.7	35265.1		...	47734.3	28818.5	23145.5		...	...
21	Pharmaceuticals,medicinal chemicals, etc.		...	30.2	20.8	23.0		...	14.0	5.9	7.7		...	...
22	Rubber and plastics products		...	1533.7	2648.4	2142.0		...	567.3	1225.3	871.7		...	...
23	Other non-metallic mineral products		...	9636.6	11093.4	11796.3		...	377.9	4448.1	4508.0		...	...
24	Basic metals		...	16464.5	13649.3	11597.2		...	5781.5	4717.4	3516.8		...	...
25	Fabricated metal products, except machinery		...	4377.5	6751.2	7380.7		...	1909.1	3008.3	3087.3		...	...
26	Computer, electronic and optical products		...	...	...	...		...	...	...	...		...	...
27	Electrical equipment		...	1365.2	1630.2	2065.5		...	155.3	177.4	692.9		...	...
28	Machinery and equipment n.e.c.		...	230.1	331.2	354.2		...	75.1	91.5	101.5		...	...
29	Motor vehicles, trailers and semi-trailers		...	82.6	94.1	78.6		...	49.9	46.0	54.3		...	...
30	Other transport equipment		...	417.8	345.8	320.3		...	134.6	143.7	138.0		...	...
31	Furniture		...	609.7	751.6	865.0		...	404.9	419.4	388.4		...	...
32	Other manufacturing		...	16.9	22.3	21.2		...	-2.9	0.2	7.6		...	...
33	Repair and installation of machinery/equipment		...	2.2	172.0	1892.6		...	1.5	96.1	1672.3		...	...
C	Total manufacturing		...	129416.4	103061.2	97610.0		...	72266.4	52374.6	47653.8		...	...

Republic of Korea

Supplier of information:
Statistics Korea, Daejeon.
Industrial statistics for the OECD countries are compiled by the OECD secretariat, which supplies them to UNIDO.

Basic source of data:
Mining and manufacturing survey; economic census.

Major deviations from ISIC (Revision 4):
Data presented in ISIC (Revision 4) were originally classified according to the national NACE-related classification system (KSIC).

Reference period:
Calendar year.

Scope:
All establishments.

Method of data collection:
Not reported.

Type of enumeration:
Census covers all establishments in years ending with 3 or 8. For other years, establishments with five or more employees are covered by survey; establishments below that threshold are sampled.

Adjusted for non-response:
Not reported.

Concepts and definitions of variables:
Estimates for output are not adjusted for goods purchased and sold in the same condition during the year; works in progress and own-account capital production are not included.

Related national publications:
Korea Statistical Yearbook, published by Statistics Korea, Daejeon.

Republic of Korea

ISIC	Industry	Establishments Note	Est. 2012	Est. 2013	Est. 2014	Est. 2015	Employees Note	Emp. 2012	Emp. 2013	Emp. 2014	Emp. 2015	Wages Note	Wage 2012	Wage 2013	Wage 2014	Wage 2015
			(number)					(thousands)					(billions of Korean Won)			
1010	Processing/preserving of meat		702	…	…	…		283.0 a/	286.9 a/	34.9	40.9		743	792	889	1088
1020	Processing/preserving of fish, etc.		815	…	…	…		…a/	…a/	25.7	35.5		442	450	531	730
1030	Processing/preserving of fruit,vegetables		436	…	…	…		…a/	…a/	15.7	21.7		264	297	344	460
1040	Vegetable and animal oils and fats		57	…	…	…		…a/	…a/	1.8	2.7		57	60	62	84
1050	Dairy products		107	…	…	…		…a/	…a/	9.9	10.4		357	381	411	434
106	Grain mill products,starches and starch products		261	…	…	…		…a/	…a/	8.0	14.7		246	252	265	450
1061	Grain mill products		236	…	…	…		…	…	6.8	12.8		199	199	211	383
1062	Starches and starch products		25	…	…	…		…	…	1.2	1.8		47	52	55	68
107	Other food products		1555	…	…	…		…a/	…a/	70.7	99.1		1712	1843	2069	2729
1071	Bakery products		369	…	…	…		…	…	18.9	32.1		411	448	534	863
1072	Sugar		2	…	…	…		…	…	…	0.3		…	…	…	19
1073	Cocoa, chocolate and sugar confectionery		86	…	…	…		…	…	3.9	7.9		110	…	116	271
1074	Macaroni, noodles, couscous, etc.		78	…	…	…		…	…	6.8	18.3		197	224	231	448
1075	Prepared meals and dishes		338	…	…	…		…	…	13.3	40.5		300	293	341	1128
1079	Other food products n.e.c.		682	…	…	…		…	…	27.6	10.4		677	746	829	394
1080	Prepared animal feeds		240	…	…	…		…a/	…a/	7.9	10.4		299	298	313	394
110	Beverages		250	…	…	…		16.5	16.5	13.1	16.8		506	511	550	678
1101	Distilling, rectifying and blending of spirits		30	…	…	…		16.5 b/	16.5 b/	2.8	3.1		111	112	126	139
1102	Wines		59	…	…	…		…b/	…b/	1.6	2.7		46	48	50	76
1103	Malt liquors and malt		6	…	…	…		…b/	…b/	1.8	2.2		100	99	98	122
1104	Soft drinks,mineral waters,other bottled waters		155	…	…	…		…b/	…b/	7.0	8.7		249	252	276	341
1200	Tobacco products		8	…	…	…		2.0	2.0	2.1	2.1		115	116	132	144
131	Spinning, weaving and finishing of textiles		1968	…	…	…		147.5 c/	150.1 c/	56.0	71.6		1529	1553	1649	2119
1311	Preparation and spinning of textile fibres		336	…	…	…		…	…	11.9	15.4		308	323	340	454
1312	Weaving of textiles		709	…	…	…		…	…	16.4	22.3		468	463	491	668
1313	Finishing of textiles		923	…	…	…		…	…	27.8	33.8		754	767	818	997
139	Other textiles		1208	…	…	…		…c/	…c/	33.8	56.2		850	906	993	1571
1391	Knitted and crocheted fabrics		132	…	…	…		…	…	2.7	5.4		79	86	85	159
1392	Made-up textile articles, except apparel		546	…	…	…		…	…	15.7	28.8		327	354	404	714
1393	Carpets and rugs		14	…	…	…		…	…	0.6	1.0		18	13	17	30
1394	Cordage, rope, twine and netting		102	…	…	…		…	…	2.3	4.2		59	64	67	114
1399	Other textiles n.e.c.		414	…	…	…		…	…	12.5	16.8		368	389	420	554
1410	Wearing apparel, except fur apparel		2246	…	…	…		149.8 d/	144.3 d/	53.2	89.3		1364	1316	1398	2227
1420	Articles of fur		50	…	…	…		…d/	…d/	0.8	1.9		29	26	26	52
1430	Knitted and crocheted apparel		450	…	…	…		…d/	…d/	11.0	19.4		252	267	270	454
151	Leather;luggage,handbags,saddlery,harness;fur		267	…	…	…		35.9 e/	36.9 e/	7.9	14.0		199	222	228	368
1511	Tanning/dressing of leather; dressing of fur		109	…	…	…		…	…	3.8	4.7		109	110	116	147
1512	Luggage,handbags,etc.;saddlery/harness		158	…	…	…		…	…	4.1	9.3		90	112	113	221
1520	Footwear		531	…	…	…		…e/	…e/	10.3	15.8		245	245	255	380
1610	Sawmilling and planing of wood		260	…	…	…		34.1 f/	35.3 f/	4.5	8.4		114	116	132	245

Code	Description										
162	Wood products, cork, straw, plaiting materials	510	...	...f/	...f/	13.0	24.0	357	388	414	727
1621	Veneer sheets and wood-based panels	90	...	:	:	3.6	5.3	124	138	140	186
1622	Builders' carpentry and joinery	119	...	:	:	3.0	6.6	74	78	86	185
1623	Wooden containers	244	...	:	:	5.4	9.0	136	148	164	284
1629	Other wood products;articles of cork,straw	57	...	:	:	1.0	3.1	23	24	23	71
170	Paper and paper products	1584	...	69.8	73.7	56.4	72.6	1689	1863	1993	2491
1701	Pulp, paper and paperboard	252	...	69.8g/	73.7g/	15.5	16.7	634	701	716	741
1702	Corrugated paper and paperboard	902	...	...g/	...g/	26.1	35.3	654	727	796	1083
1709	Other articles of paper and paperboard	430	...	...g/	...g/	14.8	20.6	402	435	480	667
181	Printing and service activities related to printing	1241	...	72.1h/	69.9h/	27.0	53.9	778	775	838	1615
1811	Printing	909	...	:	:	19.4	41.1	569	569	617	1240
1812	Service activities related to printing	332	...	:	:	7.5	12.7	210	206	222	375
1820	Reproduction of recorded media	15	...	...h/	...h/	0.6	0.6	16	15	18	19
1910	Coke oven products	38	...	12.5l/	10.9l/	0.8	0.8	23	27	27	32
1920	Refined petroleum products	93	...	...l/	...l/	9.5	10.6	852	820	816	899
201	Basic chemicals,fertilizers, etc.	1107	...	142.1j/	147.0l/	56.3	71.7	2782	2950	3154	3908
2011	Basic chemicals	475	...	:	:	29.5	33.3	1571	1788	1770	2085
2012	Fertilizers and nitrogen compounds	160	...	:	:	3.5	7.0	147	137	140	251
2013	Plastics and synthetic rubber in primary forms	472	...	...j/	...j/	23.2	31.5	1064	1025	1245	1572
202	Other chemical products	1302	...	:	:	59.3	74.7	1842	2015	2267	2815
2021	Pesticides and other agrochemical products	50	...	:	:	2.1	2.5	68	88	87	97
2022	Paints,varnishes;printing ink and mastics	247	...	:	:	12.6	15.1	456	507	534	658
2023	Soap,cleaning and cosmetic preparations	467	...	...i/	...	20.0	28.1	498	561	625	877
2029	Other chemical products n.e.c.	538	...	:	:	24.6	28.9	819	859	1022	1183
2030	Man-made fibres	53	...	32.8	34.8	6.3	6.4	281	309	311	317
2100	Pharmaceuticals,medicinal chemicals, etc.	428	...	258.9k/	265.4k/	31.8	39.7	1037	1071	1179	1473
221	Rubber products	770	...	:	:	43.8	49.9	1478	1537	1570	1850
2211	Rubber tyres and tubes	45	...	:	:	16.2	16.3	716	694	666	715
2219	Other rubber products	725	...	...k/	...k/	27.7	33.6	763	843	905	1135
2220	Plastics products	4747	...	105.0m/	108.0m/	165.2	217.8	4546	5045	5492	7376
2310	Glass and glass products	413	...	...m/	...m/	23.3	28.0	868	941	935	1097
239	Non-metallic mineral products n.e.c.	1971	...	:	:	53.6	74.4	1737	1888	2031	2754
2391	Refractory products	56	...	:	:	2.8	4.1	108	132	135	188
2392	Clay building materials	64	...	:	:	3.1	3.6	86	94	103	117
2393	Other porcelain and ceramic products	127	...	:	:	5.6	7.2	164	170	169	214
2394	Cement, lime and plaster	72	...	:	:	5.0	5.3	232	253	295	316
2395	Articles of concrete, cement and plaster	1207	...	:	:	26.7	34.8	809	868	947	1236
2396	Cutting, shaping and finishing of stone	92	...	:	:	1.5	5.6	39	59	45	155
2399	Other non-metallic mineral products n.e.c.	353	...	:	:	8.9	13.7	299	312	337	527
2410	Basic iron and steel	1572	...	158.1n/	159.6n/	91.2	100.7	4257	4470	4687	5234
2420	Basic precious and other non-ferrous metals	616	...	...n/	...n/	30.0	35.1	1094	1207	1279	1511
243	Casting of metals	526	...	:	:	18.8	20.8	643	658	704	786
2431	Casting of iron and steel	356	...	:	:	14.2	14.5	503	511	554	578
2432	Casting of non-ferrous metals	170	...	:	:	4.6	6.3	140	147	150	209
251	Struct.metal products, tanks, reservoirs	2203	...	420.8p/	425.7p/	65.8	107.0	2080	2189	2360	3838

continued

Republic of Korea

ISIC Revision 4		Number of establishments (number)					Number of employees (thousands)					Wages and salaries paid to employees (billions of Korean Won)				
ISIC	Industry	Note	2012	2013	2014	2015	Note	2012	2013	2014	2015	Note	2012	2013	2014	2015
2511	Structural metal products		1849	...	...	...		...	...	49.2	85.7		1375	1461	1604	2822
2512	Tanks, reservoirs and containers of metal		299	...	...	...		...	...	10.1	14.8		354	353	379	584
2513	Steam generators, excl. hot water boilers		55	...	...	...		...	...	6.5	6.4		350	374	378	432
2520	Weapons and ammunition		57	...	...	...		..p/	..p/	7.9	9.5		323	327	345	442
259	Other metal products;metal working services		6547	...	...	...		..p/	..p/	187.8	282.9		5191	5581	6193	9432
2591	Forging,pressing,stamping,roll-forming of metal		1120	...	...	...		...	...	35.8	48.6		1027	1109	1190	1650
2592	Treatment and coating of metals;machining		3267	...	...	...		...	...	81.0	136.6		2199	2350	2604	4457
2593	Cutlery, hand tools and general hardware		686	...	...	...		...	...	23.9	31.8		636	722	796	1046
2599	Other fabricated metal products n.e.c.		1474	...	...	...		...	...	47.1	65.9		1329	1400	1602	2280
2610	Electronic components and boards		2186	...	...	...		539.7q/	552.2q/	286.5	310.3		11863	12703	13044	16193
2620	Computers and peripheral equipment		284	...	...	...		..q/	..q/	9.9	12.0		267	276	305	363
2630	Communication equipment		1258	...	...	...		..q/	..q/	71.5	74.1		2827	2807	2652	2998
2640	Consumer electronics		359	...	...	...		..q/	..q/	17.9	23.6		1804	1011	856	1125
265	Measuring,testing equipment; watches, etc.		1051	...	...	...		..q/	..q/	35.4	53.1		1079	1171	1262	1915
2651	Measuring/testing/navigating equipment,etc.		1028	...	...	...		...	...	35.0	52.3		1067	1160	1252	1895
2652	Watches and clocks		23	...	...	...		...	...	0.4	0.8		12	12	9	21
2660	Irradiation/electromedical equipment,etc.		148	...	...	...		..q/	..q/	7.3	9.0		193	207	235	289
2670	Optical instruments and photographic equipment		343	...	...	...		..q/	..q/	14.5	17.7		434	460	445	565
2680	Magnetic and optical media		9	...	...	...		..q/	..q/	0.2	0.3		6	5	4	9
2710	Electric motors,generators,transformers,etc.		1961	...	...	...		215.5r/	218.2r/	81.9	109.7		2612	2715	2956	4001
2720	Batteries and accumulators		95	...	...	...		...	...	14.3	19.7		625	590	676	1049
273	Wiring and wiring devices		460	...	...	...		..r/	..r/	18.5	21.8		597	590	662	770
2731	Fibre optic cables		9	...	...	...		...	...	0.7	0.9		8	10	24	34
2732	Other electronic and electric wires and cables		329	...	...	...		...	...	13.4	15.1		475	460	509	570
2733	Wiring devices		122	...	...	...		...	...	4.5	5.8		114	120	130	165
2740	Electric lighting equipment		656	...	...	...		..r/	..r/	22.5	35.6		571	628	724	1097
2750	Domestic appliances		512	...	...	...		..r/	..r/	27.2	33.9		849	888	977	1446
2790	Other electrical equipment		266	...	...	...		..r/	..r/	7.8	10.8		246	241	265	356
281	General-purpose machinery		4299	...	...	...		407.3s/	421.4s/	156.3	195.5		5357	5598	5811	7369
2811	Engines/turbines,excl.aircraft,vehicle engines		362	...	...	...		...	...	13.6	13.9		577	546	546	577
2812	Fluid power equipment		276	...	...	...		...	...	9.3	12.9		256	312	322	487
2813	Other pumps, compressors, taps and valves		740	...	...	...		...	...	28.0	35.5		939	1005	1042	1323
2814	Bearings, gears, gearing and driving elements		325	...	...	...		...	...	13.4	16.1		438	461	534	659
2815	Ovens, furnaces and furnace burners		134	...	...	...		...	...	2.7	4.6		132	118	114	181
2816	Lifting and handling equipment		1868	...	...	...		...	...	71.7	87.6		2472	2569	2655	3285
2817	Office machinery, excl.computers,etc.		161	...	...	...		...	...	5.0	6.4		185	186	156	203
2818	Power-driven hand tools		33	...	...	...		...	...	1.3	1.4		43	50	51	48
2819	Other general-purpose machinery		400	...	...	...		...	...	11.2	17.0		316	351	391	606
282	Special-purpose machinery		4653	...	...	...		..s/	..s/	155.7	215.4		5156	5620	6065	8232
2821	Agricultural and forestry machinery		238	...	...	...		...	...	7.6	11.4		233	245	268	390
2822	Metal-forming machinery and machine tools		697	...	...	...		...	...	21.6	31.6		796	861	905	1254

Code	Description									
2823	Machinery for metallurgy	45	..	..	1.5	2.3	51	54	58	89
2824	Mining, quarrying and construction machinery	359	..	..	18.4	20.0	777	829	857	980
2825	Food/beverage/tobacco processing machinery	109	..	..	2.1	4.0	69	73	76	139
2826	Textile/apparel/leather production machinery	138	..	..	2.5	4.5	109	88	88	140
2829	Other special-purpose machinery	3067	..	..	102.0	141.6	3121	3471	3811	5239
2910	Motor vehicles	29	319.7t	337.0t	82.8	86.8	6423	7212	7464	7731
2920	Automobile bodies, trailers and semi-trailers	170	..t	..t	5.5	9.1	146	160	175	321
2930	Parts and accessories for motor vehicles	3670	..t	..t	234.6	263.7	7237	8091	9020	10213
301	Building of ships and boats	1275	164.4u	175.8u	138.9	144.4	6254	6277	6711	6921
3011	Building of ships and floating structures	1270	..	..	138.8	144.1	6251	6274	6706	6914
3012	Building of pleasure and sporting boats	5	..	..	0.2	0.3	3	3	4	7
3020	Railway locomotives and rolling stock	75	..u	..u	5.4	5.7	189	217	240	301
3030	Air and spacecraft and related machinery	82	..u	..u	14.1	15.2	533	565	690	787
3040	Military fighting vehicles	20	..u	..u	2.2	1.7	117	122	132	94
309	Transport equipment n.e.c.	60	..u	..u	1.4	2.1	69	60	43	62
3091	Motorcycles	30	..	..	0.7	0.8	44	36	19	23
3092	Bicycles and invalid carriages	12	..	..	0.3	0.5	9	11	10	16
3099	Other transport equipment n.e.c.	18	..	..	0.4	0.8	17	14	13	23
3100	Furniture	1247	64.9	66.9	37.3	61.5	965	1024	1194	1880
321	Jewellery, bijouterie and related articles	131	62.9v	63.8v	3.0	7.7	75	80	85	218
3211	Jewellery and related articles	80	..	..	2.3	5.5	58	61	65	165
3212	Imitation jewellery and related articles	51	..	..	0.7	2.1	17	19	20	52
3220	Musical instruments	44	..v	..v	1.4	1.5	33	34	36	43
3230	Sports goods	168	..v	..v	3.9	6.4	106	99	112	185
3240	Games and toys	70	..v	..v	1.4	3.1	39	37	38	79
3250	Medical and dental instruments and supplies	546	..v	..v	17.5	28.6	407	438	485	782
3290	Other manufacturing n.e.c.	576	..v	..v	14.6	32.2	333	368	402	830
331	Repair of fabricated metal products/machinery	..	..	..	..	43.3	..	..	..	1668
3311	Repair of fabricated metal products	..	..	..	..	..	..	..	..	..
3312	Repair of machinery	..	..	..	..	5.3	..	..	..	183
3313	Repair of electronic and optical equipment	..	..	..	..	..	..	..	..	..
3314	Repair of electrical equipment	..	..	..	..	6.5	..	..	..	252
3315	Repair of transport equip., excl. motor vehicles	..	..	..	..	..	..	..	..	..
3319	Repair of other equipment	..	..	..	..	31.4	..	..	..	1233
3320	Installation of industrial machinery/equipment	..	..	..	..	-	..	..	..	-
C	Total manufacturing	85468	3715.2	3802.2	3898.4	3667.2	..	104023	155587	143112

a/ 1010 includes 1020, 1030, 1040, 1050, 106, 107 and 1080.
b/ 1101 includes 1102, 1103 and 1104.
c/ 131 includes 139.
d/ 1410 includes 1420 and 1430.
e/ 151 includes 1520.
f/ 1610 includes 162.
g/ 1701 includes 1702 and 1709.
h/ 181 includes 1820.
i/ 1910 includes 1920.
j/ 201 includes 202 and 2030.

k/ 221 includes 2220.
m/ 2310 includes 239.
n/ 2410 includes 2420 and 243.
p/ 251 includes 2520 and 259.
q/ 2610 includes 2620, 2630, 2640, 265, 2660, 2670 and 2680.
r/ 2710 includes 2720, 273, 2740, 2750 and 2790.
s/ 281 includes 282.
t/ 2910 includes 2920 and 2930.
u/ 301 includes 3020, 3030, 3040 and 309.
v/ 321 includes 3220, 3230, 3240, 3250 and 3290.

Republic of Korea

ISIC	Industry	Note	Output (valuation not defined) (billions of Korean Won)				Note	Value added (valuation not defined) (billions of Korean Won)				Note	Gross fixed capital formation (billions of Korean Won)	
			2012	2013	2014	2015		2012	2013	2014	2015		2014	2015
1010	Processing/preserving of meat		10821	11183	12571	13539		2844	2875	3089	3259		573	676
1020	Processing/preserving of fish, etc.		4679	4541	4793	5465		1627	1576	1662	1967		280	284
1030	Processing/preserving of fruit,vegetables		2421	2739	2816	2994		962	1090	1176	1247		201	188
1040	Vegetable and animal oils and fats		2382	2155	2015	2108		557	539	474	583		46	47
1050	Dairy products		7449	7542	8011	7975		2917	2849	2839	2808		207	172
106	Grain mill products,starches and starch products		5942	6118	5669	5974		1762	1868	1697	1762		297	238
1061	Grain mill products		4434	4579	4266	4545		1252	1325	1185	1219		271	186
1062	Starches and starch products		1508	1539	1403	1429		509	543	512	544		26	52
107	Other food products		21503	22220	23247	24830		8270	8900	9908	10828		1530	1364
1071	Bakery products		4124	4221	4851	6854		2050	2239	2662	3858		340	449
1072	Sugar		...	...	...	857		...	...	...	184		...	1
1073	Cocoa, chocolate and sugar confectionery		1632	...	1496	...		808	...	825	...		105	...
1074	Macaroni, noodles, couscous, etc.		2413	2653	2701	2914		756	897	945	1116		105	134
1075	Prepared meals and dishes		2991	2715	3074	3458		1278	1209	1397	1511		195	203
1079	Other food products n.e.c.		9449	10077	10242	10747		3265	3584	3892	4159		750	577
1080	Prepared animal feeds		10755	11322	10458	10348		1992	2280	2131	2261		243	270
110	Beverages		9538	9869	10417	10908		5160	5474	5875	6148		599	775
1101	Distilling, rectifying and blending of spirits		2107	2224	2380	2473		1100	1193	1316	1377		96	154
1102	Wines		508	504	499	506		272	294	285	289		20	16
1103	Malt liquors and malt		2105	2278	2554	2333		1409	1571	1720	1586		259	150
1104	Soft drinks,mineral waters,other bottled waters		4818	4863	4984	5596		2379	2415	2553	2896		223	456
1200	Tobacco products		3412	3225	3528	3637		1998	1909	2130	2327		95	48
131	Spinning, weaving and finishing of textiles		12116	11890	11522	11255		4167	4099	4114	4193		809	625
1311	Preparation and spinning of textile fibres		2707	2795	2702	2600		707	728	757	706		270	140
1312	Weaving of textiles		4969	4677	4395	4255		1532	1451	1406	1454		274	217
1313	Finishing of textiles		4440	4418	4425	4400		1927	1920	1951	2033		265	268
139	Other textiles		8777	8931	9139	9088		2875	2942	3089	3185		526	451
1391	Knitted and crocheted fabrics		1082	1092	867	821		303	323	229	228		45	45
1392	Made-up textile articles, except apparel		3153	3192	3729	4147		1047	1051	1276	1487		194	211
1393	Carpets and rugs		329	134	255	222		100	53	86	63		8	8
1394	Cordage, rope, twine and netting		524	572	581	568		179	207	193	202		33	19
1399	Other textiles n.e.c.		3689	3941	3707	3330		1246	1308	1305	1204		246	168
1410	Wearing apparel, except fur apparel		15421	14762	14664	14218		7162	6760	6785	6681		725	616
1420	Articles of fur		314	260	264	292		104	86	98	104		7	8
1430	Knitted and crocheted apparel		2301	2812	2804	2441		856	1243	1062	1045		100	96
151	Leather;luggage,handbags,saddlery,harness;fur		3037	3408	3264	3057		932	1082	1020	1001		102	101
1511	Tanning/dressing of leather; dressing of fur		1627	1610	1642	1561		353	333	313	323		56	60
1512	Luggage,handbags,etc.;saddlery/harness		1410	1798	1622	1496		579	749	706	678		47	41
1520	Footwear		2157	2034	2280	2605		919	862	986	1060		93	84
1610	Sawmilling and planing of wood		1285	1349	1451	1567		385	398	444	495		104	87

Code	Description										
162	Wood products, cork, straw, plaiting materials	3330	3274	3840	4308	1136	1066	1276	1564	303	278
1621	Veneer sheets and wood-based panels	1504	1373	1704	1831	465	385	502	595	80	123
1622	Builders' carpentry and joinery	644	678	799	1138	230	241	285	446	156	93
1623	Wooden containers	1050	1102	1211	1193	378	384	436	463	58	53
1629	Other wood products;articles of cork,straw	132	120	126	145	63	57	54	61	8	9
170	Paper and paper products	21030	21678	21556	21725	7027	7141	7195	7490	1510	1408
1701	Pulp, paper and paperboard	10180	10573	9891	9323	3167	3242	3006	2747	572	519
1702	Corrugated paper and paperboard	6576	6682	6967	6774	2118	2202	2366	2391	633	420
1709	Other articles of paper and paperboard	4275	4423	4698	5628	1742	1696	1824	2352	305	469
181	Printing and service activities related to printing	4151	3944	4246	4442	1951	1873	2016	2163	355	380
1811	Printing	3163	3026	3277	3444	1444	1403	1508	1630	267	300
1812	Service activities related to printing	987	918	969	998	507	470	507	533	88	80
1820	Reproduction of recorded media	98	78	81	66	48	37	44	35	10	1
1910	Coke oven products	246	244	241	219	-17	-43	-28	-21	20	7
1920	Refined petroleum products	157551	145751	137785	94614	22124	19852	19020	16509	3122	1081
201	Basic chemicals,fertilizers, etc.	124035	124346	115951	96933	30444	30229	26836	25690	11239	5794
2011	Basic chemicals	76725	83708	73248	58848	19912	21040	16655	14776	9386	4025
2012	Fertilizers and nitrogen compounds	2482	2179	2209	2169	806	620	657	802	180	82
2013	Plastics and synthetic rubber in primary forms	44829	38459	40494	35915	9727	8568	9524	10113	1673	1688
202	Other chemical products	31141	31028	34079	35479	11414	11611	13447	15071	2110	2017
2021	Pesticides and other agrochemical products	1318	1400	1421	1603	485	515	530	624	51	57
2022	Paints,varnishes;printing ink and mastics	6277	6349	6369	6349	1933	2017	2014	2158	335	452
2023	Soap,cleaning and cosmetic preparations	8851	10016	11194	13104	4604	5025	5855	7087	555	647
2029	Other chemical products n.e.c.	14695	13263	15094	14423	4392	4054	5048	5202	1168	862
2030	Man-made fibres	6326	6508	5480	4245	1426	1503	1247	947	163	159
2100	Pharmaceuticals,medicinal chemicals, etc.	13933	14273	15139	16489	7887	8098	8630	9637	1106	1746
221	Rubber products	14592	14355	14209	13743	5752	5637	5611	5560	1007	978
2211	Rubber tyres and tubes	8320	7885	7850	7222	3550	3361	3321	3087	534	550
2219	Other rubber products	6272	6469	6358	6521	2202	2276	2289	2473	473	428
2220	Plastics products	45349	48525	51377	53540	14744	15996	16993	19174	4234	3946
2310	Glass and glass products	10864	10022	9681	8899	5277	4949	4739	4460	1657	1066
239	Non-metallic mineral products n.e.c.	20762	22002	22723	24683	8362	9209	9610	10733	1505	1660
2391	Refractory products	1314	1406	1253	1321	456	540	504	542	70	62
2392	Clay building materials	545	517	547	586	276	240	257	303	47	62
2393	Other porcelain and ceramic products	674	720	755	776	377	386	414	432	97	44
2394	Cement, lime and plaster	3858	4216	4667	4921	1449	1818	2014	2128	237	225
2395	Articles of concrete, cement and plaster	10948	11744	12312	13755	4420	4787	4972	5694	796	887
2396	Cutting, shaping and finishing of stone	279	555	330	341	137	231	156	159	13	19
2399	Other non-metallic mineral products n.e.c.	3143	2843	2861	2984	1246	1206	1294	1475	245	361
2410	Basic iron and steel	110342	99527	96585	83999	22189	19812	19394	17702	6277	6224
2420	Basic precious and other non-ferrous metals	39941	38005	36039	34955	6157	5682	5333	5189	1787	1545
243	Casting of metals	6567	5995	5945	5464	2078	2039	2053	2101	423	376
2431	Casting of iron and steel	4638	4399	4391	3980	1630	1561	1572	1581	309	264
2432	Casting of non-ferrous metals	1929	1596	1554	1484	448	478	481	520	115	112
251	Struct.metal products, tanks, reservoirs	27495	25952	24830	26428	11714	10902	9886	9914	1692	1897

continued

Republic of Korea

ISIC	Industry	Note	Output (valuation not defined) (billions of Korean Won) 2012	2013	2014	2015	Note	Value added (valuation not defined) (billions of Korean Won) 2012	2013	2014	2015	Note	Gross fixed capital formation (billions of Korean Won) 2014	2015
2511	Structural metal products		15444	15473	15461	16996		4704	4888	4803	5864		1114	1213
2512	Tanks, reservoirs and containers of metal		3775	3105	3453	3948		1235	1132	1159	1516		390	208
2513	Steam generators, excl. hot water boilers		8276	7374	5917	5483		5775	4882	3924	2534		188	477
2520	Weapons and ammunition		2573	2549	2988	4564		984	978	1191	1630		200	177
259	Other metal products;metal working services		40919	41522	44426	43927		15689	16002	17981	18170		4232	3838
2591	Forging,pressing,stamping,roll-forming of metal		11027	11317	11908	11426		3414	3394	3951	3720		1316	1062
2592	Treatment and coating of metals machining		12029	12378	13377	12897		5733	5979	6650	6517		1445	1490
2593	Cutlery, hand tools and general hardware		5009	5028	5502	5672		2108	2110	2279	2517		457	467
2599	Other fabricated metal products n.e.c.		12854	12799	13639	13933		4435	4519	5101	5416		1014	818
2610	Electronic components and boards		167624	171210	167140	163790		82336	83382	82348	87793		18426	31926
2620	Computers and peripheral equipment		3719	3589	3251	2943		1129	1088	1041	1026		158	155
2630	Communication equipment		76356	75705	69011	61334		29770	29816	27398	21525		1007	1164
2640	Consumer electronics		6814	6569	5797	11567		2564	2530	2229	4372		181	246
265	Measuring;testing equipment; watches, etc.		8768	9706	10185	11307		3510	3928	4195	4807		647	626
2651	Measuring/testing/navigating equipment,etc.		8699	9652	10147	11254		3475	3905	4176	4778		646	620
2652	Watches and clocks		70	53	38	53		35	23	18	28		1	6
2660	Irradiation/electromedical equipment,etc.		1833	2051	2139	2326		812	912	958	1123		118	100
2670	Optical instruments and photographic equipment		3386	3756	3216	3403		1407	1684	1431	1492		300	269
2680	Magnetic and optical media		33	24	18	24		16	13	10	13		1	1
2710	Electric motors,generators,transformers,etc.		29034	28484	28603	30120		9177	8898	9088	9926		1836	1940
2720	Batteries and accumulators		7199	6920	6973	10343		3336	3058	3043	3595		652	1379
273	Wiring and wiring devices		11675	9246	10130	8143		1750	1573	2093	1873		417	321
2731	Fibre optic cables		81	93	203	286		16	26	99	146		7	12
2732	Other electronic and electric wires and cables		10463	8184	8898	6849		1375	1263	1655	1383		358	250
2733	Wiring devices		1131	969	1028	1009		359	284	340	345		52	59
2740	Electric lighting equipment		5956	6418	7331	7602		1703	1778	2074	2258		485	658
2750	Domestic appliances		11470	11939	12686	15310		3521	3703	3828	4563		519	439
2790	Other electrical equipment		1943	1745	1902	1883		768	657	740	843		204	239
281	General-purpose machinery		55985	52095	52604	49653		18865	18113	18822	18623		4013	2757
2811	Engines/turbines,excl.aircraft,vehicle engines		7172	4800	4914	4566		2367	1550	1724	1668		564	301
2812	Fluid power equipment		2446	2332	2401	2816		937	867	957	1120		222	159
2813	Other pumps, compressors, taps and valves		8000	8201	8072	8165		3022	3339	3240	3384		566	590
2814	Bearings, gears, gearing and driving elements		3513	3483	3804	3974		1429	1431	1543	1632		435	316
2815	Ovens, furnaces and furnace burners		991	810	669	708		354	299	276	286		51	25
2816	Lifting and handling equipment		28821	27465	28173	24765		8955	8859	9375	8610		1842	1157
2817	Office machinery, excl.computers,etc.		2185	1997	1525	1530		713	604	477	617		104	66
2818	Power-driven hand tools		288	282	295	223		116	111	121	98		25	12
2819	Other general-purpose machinery		2571	2726	2753	2906		974	1053	1109	1208		204	131
282	Special-purpose machinery		46119	47458	49774	50736		17103	17230	18438	20174		3781	3288
2821	Agricultural and forestry machinery		2542	2518	2726	3006		803	761	786	1145		137	122
2822	Metal-forming machinery and machine tools		7684	7455	7583	7864		3004	2918	3073	3138		602	531

Code	Description										
2823	Machinery for metallurgy	389	431	444	408	156	163	178	159	15	19
2824	Mining, quarrying and construction machinery	11529	10717	10503	9504	3310	3211	3107	3340	450	414
2825	Food/beverage/tobacco processing machinery	483	529	435	495	206	225	160	180	41	42
2826	Textile/apparel/leather production machinery	709	544	546	567	283	226	216	248	32	46
2829	Other special-purpose machinery	22784	25263	27538	28891	9340	9726	10917	11965	2505	2114
2910	Motor vehicles	89462	90396	90428	93431	28028	28891	28915	28689	3246	3062
2920	Automobile bodies, trailers and semi-trailers	1411	1603	1822	2544	446	468	502	666	152	204
2930	Parts and accessories for motor vehicles	84347	89258	97336	97639	24684	25172	28768	29886	7362	6888
301	Building of ships and boats	66625	65066	64169	63474	18314	17210	16962	16488	2275	2390
3011	Building of ships and floating structures	66609	65045	64135	63454	18306	17203	16950	16481	2273	2387
3012	Building of pleasure and sporting boats	16	21	34	20	7	7	12	7	3	3
3020	Railway locomotives and rolling stock	3121	2821	2710	2680	1094	1035	946	923	61	32
3030	Air and spacecraft and related machinery	3816	4719	5012	5947	1565	2029	2152	2180	505	653
3040	Military fighting vehicles	1568	1198	1454	934	533	333	377	265	33	174
309	Transport equipment n.e.c.	661	645	284	294	159	136	90	98	25	11
3091	Motorcycles	454	468	106	89	92	74	32	28	15	5
3092	Bicycles and invalid carriages	62	72	88	108	20	24	27	34	6	1
3099	Other transport equipment n.e.c.	145	106	90	97	47	37	31	36	4	5
3100	Furniture	10126	10429	11858	12899	2967	3054	3564	4114	541	628
321	Jewellery, bijouterie and related articles	803	907	1041	1002	281	357	393	328	18	39
3211	Jewellery and related articles	686	759	887	812	237	310	334	260	13	29
3212	Imitation jewellery and related articles	117	148	154	189	44	47	59	67	5	9
3220	Musical instruments	159	168	161	143	68	73	73	63	3	15
3230	Sports goods	754	649	675	761	350	283	294	364	56	58
3240	Games and toys	345	268	268	322	164	127	126	152	8	21
3250	Medical and dental instruments and supplies	2569	2509	2689	2974	1440	1373	1465	1731	326	250
3290	Other manufacturing n.e.c.	2258	2246	2429	2536	978	976	1071	1145	168	174
331	Repair of fabricated metal products/machinery	…	…	…	4607	…	…	…	2861	…	…
3311	Repair of fabricated metal products	…	…	…	…	…	…	…	…	…	…
3312	Repair of machinery	…	…	…	490	…	…	…	315	…	…
3313	Repair of electronic and optical equipment	…	…	…	…	…	…	…	…	…	…
3314	Repair of electrical equipment	…	…	…	759	…	…	…	448	…	…
3315	Repair of transport equip., excl. motor vehicles	…	…	…	…	…	…	…	…	…	…
3319	Repair of other equipment	…	…	…	3357	…	…	…	2098	…	…
3320	Installation of industrial machinery/equipment	…	…	…	-	…	…	…	-	…	…
C	Total manufacturing	1495730	1489213		1433691		479281	484485	498635	97015	100813

Republic of Korea

Index numbers of industrial production

ISIC Revision 4

(2010=100)

ISIC	Industry	Note	2005	2006	2007	2008	2009	2010	2011	2012	2013	2014	2015	2016
10	Food products		95	97	97	95	94	100	102	103	104	105	107	108
11	Beverages		96	95	97	100	95	100	104	108	109	110	113	116
12	Tobacco products		86	96	100	104	104	100	102	106	97	104	96	109
13	Textiles		104	104	103	94	89	100	102	99	98	96	90	87
14	Wearing apparel		80	88	93	98	95	100	101	98	94	88	84	82
15	Leather and related products		121	124	122	120	105	100	101	98	112	110	104	104
16	Wood products, excluding furniture		115	126	123	114	101	100	98	88	93	89	93	89
17	Paper and paper products		94	95	98	97	94	100	102	103	105	107	106	108
18	Printing and reproduction of recorded media		88	90	90	99	88	100	92	91	87	87	84	84
19	Coke and refined petroleum products		95	96	97	98	97	100	107	109	105	110	117	124
20	Chemicals and chemical products		79	81	87	88	93	100	103	107	111	112	114	118
21	Pharmaceuticals,medicinal chemicals, etc.		69	77	84	90	96	100	100	101	103	105	107	114
22	Rubber and plastics products		89	95	101	97	89	100	105	106	110	111	111	109
23	Other non-metallic mineral products		84	90	95	96	95	100	100	95	101	97	103	107
24	Basic metals		84	87	91	92	83	100	106	107	106	110	108	110
25	Fabricated metal products, except machinery		87	92	97	102	92	100	109	118	117	122	116	110
26	Computer, electronic and optical products		49	60	68	74	80	100	107	110	114	112	113	118
27	Electrical equipment		80	81	84	89	91	100	101	99	97	99	96	97
28	Machinery and equipment n.e.c.		67	73	80	81	72	100	109	107	103	103	100	98
29	Motor vehicles, trailers and semi-trailers		78	84	90	87	81	100	115	115	116	119	121	117
30	Other transport equipment		67	72	77	95	107	100	102	107	102	90	82	79
31	Furniture		103	104	104	106	95	100	105	98	97	104	110	110
32	Other manufacturing		115	109	108	92	87	100	102	104	105	105	101	105
33	Repair and installation of machinery/equipment		...	...	...	...	...	...	...	...	...	...	...	...
C	Total manufacturing		71	78	83	86	86	100	106	108	108	109	108	109

Republic of Moldova

Supplier of information:
National Bureau of Statistics of the Republic of Moldova, Chisinau.

Basic source of data:
Census/exhaustive survey.

Major deviations from ISIC (Revision 4):
None reported.

Reference period:
Calendar year.

Scope:
All registered enterprises.

Method of data collection:
Mail questionnaires.

Type of enumeration:
Complete enumeration.

Adjusted for non-response:
Not reported.

Concepts and definitions of variables:
No deviations from the standard UN concepts and definitions are reported.

Related national publications:
None reported.

Republic of Moldova

ISIC	Industry	Note	Number of enterprises (number)				Note	Number of employees (number)				Note	Wages and salaries paid to employees (thousands of Moldovan Lei)			
			2013	2014	2015	2016		2013	2014	2015	2016		2013	2014	2015	2016
1010	Processing/preserving of meat		157	148	146	135		3707	3335	3328	3287		116868	117585	125349	141784
1020	Processing/preserving of fish, etc.		19	17	16	17		300	347	374	442		7732	9697	14618	21226
1030	Processing/preserving of fruit,vegetables		83	82	90	85		2576	2528	2331	2270		102888	113134	116033	120865
1040	Vegetable and animal oils and fats		110	116	115	107		683	1030	947	925		43572	69320	65847	60195
1050	Dairy products		32	31	29	30		2931	3096	3152	3259		164386	195279	213562	227643
106	Grain mill products,starches and starch products		242	231	221	204		707	833	846	826		16736	25038	27160	27975
1061	Grain mill products		240	229	219	203		:	:	:	:		:	:	:	:
1062	Starches and starch products		2	2	2	1		:	:	:	:		:	:	:	:
107	Other food products		378	372	369	358		10009	9797	9454	9770		403847	447694	466743	524017
1071	Bakery products		326	318	319	303		:	:	:	:		:	:	:	:
1072	Sugar		4	4	4	4		:	:	:	:		:	:	:	:
1073	Cocoa, chocolate and sugar confectionery		9	10	9	12		:	:	:	:		:	:	:	:
1074	Macaroni, noodles, couscous, etc.		5	5	6	6		:	:	:	:		:	:	:	:
1075	Prepared meals and dishes		14	13	12	13		:	:	:	:		:	:	:	:
1079	Other food products n.e.c.		20	22	19	20		:	:	:	:		:	:	:	:
1080	Prepared animal feeds		64	59	55	51		202	229	195	178		9033	9025	7239	7037
110	Beverages		166	160	159	154		8255	7227	7074	6760		378898	341239	371054	398216
1101	Distilling, rectifying and blending of spirits		19	20	20	18		1365	1303	1356	1266		62032	57614	63253	66935
1102	Wines		98	93	94	97		5454	4761	4573	4395		193423	177619	191379	213159
1103	Malt liquors and malt		7	8	9	10		497	471	485	478		72139	74264	80479	82426
1104	Soft drinks,mineral waters,other bottled waters		42	39	36	29		939	692	659	621		51305	31743	35943	35696
1200	Tobacco products		8	8	7	6		864	600	484	367		48819	32812	27587	30367
131	Spinning, weaving and finishing of textiles	a/	7	7	8	8	a/	2700	2905	3092	3570	a/	123398	147873	175047	218935
1311	Preparation and spinning of textile fibres		3	3	3	4		:	:	:	:		:	:	:	:
1312	Weaving of textiles		:	:	:	:		:	:	:	:		:	:	:	:
1313	Finishing of textiles		4	4	5	4		:	:	:	:		:	:	:	:
139	Other textiles	a/	67	68	75	76	a/	:	:	:	:	a/	:	:	:	:
1391	Knitted and crocheted fabrics		:	:	:	:		:	:	:	:		:	:	:	:
1392	Made-up textile articles, except apparel		52	53	61	60		:	:	:	:		:	:	:	:
1393	Carpets and rugs		4	4	3	5		:	:	:	:		:	:	:	:
1394	Cordage, rope, twine and netting		:	:	:	:		:	:	:	:		:	:	:	:
1399	Other textiles n.e.c.		11	11	11	11		:	:	:	:		:	:	:	:
1410	Wearing apparel, except fur apparel	b/	238	224	234	238	b/	14125	13933	14405	14802	b/	516983	557071	653060	725141
1420	Articles of fur	b/	3	2	2	2	b/	:	:	:	:	b/	:	:	:	:
1430	Knitted and crocheted apparel	b/	15	14	17	15	b/	:	:	:	:	b/	:	:	:	:
151	Leather;luggage,handbags,saddlery,harness;fur	c/	18	18	13	15	c/	2644	3211	2755	2917	c/	100702	130855	130233	149974
1511	Tanning/dressing of leather; dressing of fur		5	5	3	2		:	:	:	:		:	:	:	:
1512	Luggage,handbags,etc.;saddlery/harness		13	13	10	13		:	:	:	:		:	:	:	:
1520	Footwear	c/	53	52	48	47	c/	:	:	:	:	c/	:	:	:	:
1610	Sawmilling and planing of wood	d/	57	57	58	56	d/	1157	979	996	1035	d/	37121	37952	41785	50593

Code	Description					fn					fn				
162	Wood products, cork, straw, plaiting materials	178	165	207	200										
1621	Veneer sheets and wood-based panels	5	5	...	1										
1622	Builders' carpentry and joinery	80	78	76	68										
1623	Wooden containers	57	49	51	52										
1629	Other wood products;articles of cork,straw	36	33	80	79	d/					d/				
170	Paper and paper products	62	96	101	99		1087	933	1139	987		39070	38204	54086	55190
1701	Pulp, paper and paperboard	1	1	2	3										
1702	Corrugated paper and paperboard	25	28	27	25										
1709	Other articles of paper and paperboard	36	67	72	71										
181	Printing and service activities related to printing	165	128	141	144	e/	1329	1231	1147	1045	e/	65388	60973	68311	64710
1811	Printing	131	91	98	99										
1812	Service activities related to printing	34	37	43	45										
1820	Reproduction of recorded media	1	1	1	1	e/					e/				
1910	Coke oven products	...	...	...	...	f/	88	84	89	60	f/	3693	3523	3933	2926
1920	Refined petroleum products	2	2	2	3	f/					f/				
201	Basic chemicals,fertilizers, etc.	22	26	24	23										
2011	Basic chemicals	14	15	14	14	g/	1114	1039	984	1017	g/	51707	50210	57203	67242
2012	Fertilizers and nitrogen compounds	1	3	2	2										
2013	Plastics and synthetic rubber in primary forms	7	8	8	7										
202	Other chemical products	43	43	46	42										
2021	Pesticides and other agrochemical products	3	4	3	2										
2022	Paints,varnishes;printing ink and mastics	11	11	11	9										
2023	Soap,cleaning and cosmetic preparations	15	13	15	16										
2029	Other chemical products n.e.c.	14	15	17	14										
2030	Man-made fibres	1	1	1	1	g/					g/				
2100	Pharmaceuticals,medicinal chemicals, etc.	29	26	25	23	g/	845	814	736	722	g/	42630	44786	62645	70306
221	Rubber products	15	15	13	13										
2211	Rubber tyres and tubes	4	4	4	5	h/					h/				
2219	Other rubber products	11	11	9	8										
2220	Plastics products	424	401	379	371	h/	3756	3335	3256	3042	h/	133364	135000	147002	155449
2310	Glass and glass products	38	40	39	35	i/					i/				
239	Non-metallic mineral products n.e.c.	337	331	309	294	i/	4263	4083	4402	4515	i/	261476	271882	298387	342193
2391	Refractory products	5	8	6	4										
2392	Clay building materials	3	3	3	3										
2393	Other porcelain and ceramic products	25	22	21	18										
2394	Cement, lime and plaster	254	240	228	222										
2395	Articles of concrete, cement and plaster	30	39	31	30										
2396	Cutting, shaping and finishing of stone	20	19	20	17										
2399	Other non-metallic mineral products n.e.c.	5	4	4	8										
2410	Basic iron and steel	5	4	1	1	j/	404	442	183	121	j/	15904	19507	9942	6632
2420	Basic precious and other non-ferrous metals	...	1	1	1	j/					j/				
243	Casting of metals	5	6	6	4	j/					j/				
2431	Casting of iron and steel	5	6	5	4										
2432	Casting of non-ferrous metals	...	...	1	...										
251	Struct.metal products, tanks, reservoirs	220	208	204	201	k/	2610	2557	2470	2599	k/	107111	117533	124054	145737

continued

Republic of Moldova

ISIC Revision 4

Number of enterprises (number); Number of employees (number); Wages and salaries paid to employees (thousands of Moldovan Lei)

ISIC	Industry	Ent. Note	Ent. 2013	Ent. 2014	Ent. 2015	Ent. 2016	Emp. Note	Emp. 2013	Emp. 2014	Emp. 2015	Emp. 2016	Wages Note	Wages 2013	Wages 2014	Wages 2015	Wages 2016
2511	Structural metal products		210	203	200	195		...	...	...	...		...	...	...	...
2512	Tanks, reservoirs and containers of metal		10	5	4	6		...	...	...	...		...	...	...	...
2513	Steam generators, excl. hot water boilers		...	...	...	...		...	...	...	...		...	...	...	...
2520	Weapons and ammunition	k/	...	1	1	1	k/	...	...	...	...	k/	...	...	...	...
259	Other metal products;metal working services	k/	144	153	158	158	k/	...	...	...	...	k/	...	...	...	...
2591	Forging,pressing,stamping,roll-forming of metal		22	23	25	25		...	...	...	...		...	...	...	...
2592	Treatment and coating of metals; machining		10	9	9	9		...	...	...	...		...	...	...	...
2593	Cutlery, hand tools and general hardware		112	121	124	124		...	...	...	...		...	...	...	...
2599	Other fabricated metal products n.e.c.		...	...	...	...		...	...	...	...		...	...	...	...
2610	Electronic components and boards	m/	4	...	...	...	m/	1344	924	1018	937	m/	74398	56123	70575	73661
2620	Computers and peripheral equipment	m/	5	5	5	5	m/	...	...	...	...	m/	...	...	...	...
2630	Communication equipment	m/	7	3	3	2	m/	...	...	...	...	m/	...	...	...	...
2640	Consumer electronics	m/	5	6	5	4	m/	...	...	...	...	m/	...	...	...	...
265	Measuring,testing equipment; watches, etc.	m/	19	19	21	18	m/	...	...	...	...	m/	...	...	...	...
2651	Measuring/testing/navigating equipment,etc.		19	19	21	18		...	...	...	...		...	...	...	...
2652	Watches and clocks		...	...	...	...		...	...	...	...		...	...	...	...
2660	Irradiation/electromedical equipment,etc.	m/	2	...	...	...	m/	...	...	...	...	m/	...	...	...	...
2670	Optical instruments and photographic equipment	m/	3	1	1	1	m/	...	...	...	...	m/	...	...	...	...
2680	Magnetic and optical media	m/	...	...	...	...	m/	...	...	...	...	m/	...	...	...	...
2710	Electric motors,generators,transformers,etc.	n/	7	9	9	12	n/	3057	2995	3577	3218	n/	202863	223977	264290	281206
2720	Batteries and accumulators	n/	...	...	...	...	n/	...	...	...	...	n/	...	...	...	...
273	Wiring and wiring devices	n/	8	7	7	7	n/	...	...	...	...	n/	...	...	...	...
2731	Fibre optic cables		...	...	...	...		...	...	...	...		...	...	...	...
2732	Other electronic and electric wires and cables		8	7	7	7		...	...	...	...		...	...	...	...
2733	Wiring devices		...	...	...	...		...	...	...	...		...	...	...	...
2740	Electric lighting equipment	n/	3	3	4	7	n/	...	...	...	...	n/	...	...	...	...
2750	Domestic appliances	n/	3	5	4	4	n/	...	...	...	...	n/	...	...	...	...
2790	Other electrical equipment	n/	1	3	2	1	n/	...	...	...	...	n/	...	...	...	...
281	General-purpose machinery	p/	35	32	26	30	p/	1967	1806	1700	1457	p/	102425	99874	106923	107089
2811	Engines/turbines,excl.aircraft,vehicle engines		...	...	...	...		...	...	...	...		...	...	...	...
2812	Fluid power equipment		...	1	1	1		...	...	...	...		...	...	...	...
2813	Other pumps, compressors, taps and valves		6	3	3	3		...	...	...	...		...	...	...	...
2814	Bearings, gears, gearing and driving elements		...	...	...	...		...	...	...	...		...	...	...	...
2815	Ovens, furnaces and furnace burners		2	2	...	1		...	...	...	...		...	...	...	...
2816	Lifting and handling equipment		7	7	6	7		...	...	...	...		...	...	...	...
2817	Office machinery, excl.computers,etc.		...	...	...	...		...	...	...	...		...	...	...	...
2818	Power-driven hand tools		...	...	...	...		...	...	...	...		...	...	...	...
2819	Other general-purpose machinery		20	19	16	18		...	...	...	...		...	...	...	...
282	Special-purpose machinery		47	41	42	44		...	...	...	...		...	...	...	...
2821	Agricultural and forestry machinery	p/	16	14	15	15	p/	...	...	...	...	p/	...	...	...	...
2822	Metal-forming machinery and machine tools		9	6	5	8		...	...	...	...		...	...	...	...

Code	Item	(1)	(2)	(3)	(4)	fn	(5)	(6)	(7)	(8)	fn	(9)	(10)	(11)	(12)	fn
2823	Machinery for metallurgy	3	:	2	2		:	:	:	:		:	:	:	:	
2824	Mining, quarrying and construction machinery	:	1	2	2		:	:	:	:		:	:	:	:	
2825	Food/beverage/tobacco processing machinery	13	12	13	11		:	:	:	:		:	:	:	:	
2826	Textile/apparel/leather production machinery	1	1	1	1		:	:	:	:		:	:	:	:	
2829	Other special-purpose machinery	5	7	6	7		:	:	:	:		:	:	:	:	
2910	Motor vehicles	1	1	1	1	q/	1089	1257	1075	2153	q/	45040	58433	59075	121471	q/
2920	Automobile bodies, trailers and semi-trailers	1	2	:	1	q/	:	:	:	:	q/	:	:	:	:	q/
2930	Parts and accessories for motor vehicles	2	4	5	6	q/	:	:	:	:	q/	:	:	:	:	q/
301	Building of ships and boats	:	:	:	:	r/	66	58	:	38	r/	3748	4612	9963	3312	r/
3011	Building of ships and floating structures	:	:	:	:		:	:	:	:		:	:	:	:	
3012	Building of pleasure and sporting boats	2	:	:	:		:	:	:	:		:	:	:	:	
3020	Railway locomotives and rolling stock	:	2	:	:	r/	:	:	:	:	r/	:	:	:	:	r/
3030	Air and spacecraft and related machinery	:	:	:	:	r/	:	:	:	:	r/	:	:	:	:	r/
3040	Military fighting vehicles	:	:	:	:	r/	:	:	:	:	r/	:	:	:	:	r/
309	Transport equipment n.e.c.	:	:	:	:	r/	:	:	:	:	r/	:	:	:	:	r/
3091	Motorcycles	1	4	3	3	r/	:	:	:	:	r/	:	:	:	:	r/
3092	Bicycles and invalid carriages	1	3	3	3	r/	:	:	:	:	r/	:	:	:	:	r/
3099	Other transport equipment n.e.c.	:	1	:	:		:	:	:	:		:	:	:	:	
3100	Furniture	419	394	388	381		3626	3510	3494	3491		121206	131963	147436	162303	
321	Jewellery, bijouterie and related articles	23	23	22	19	s/	807	799	802	741	s/	24621	33224	35272	35572	s/
3211	Jewellery and related articles	14	13	14	13		:	:	:	:		:	:	:	:	
3212	Imitation jewellery and related articles	9	10	8	6		:	:	:	:		:	:	:	:	
3220	Musical instruments	:	:	:	:	s/	:	:	:	:	s/	:	:	:	:	s/
3230	Sports goods	2	2	3	4	s/	:	:	:	:	s/	:	:	:	:	s/
3240	Games and toys	5	6	7	6	s/	:	:	:	:	s/	:	:	:	:	s/
3250	Medical and dental instruments and supplies	13	9	12	15	s/	:	:	:	:	s/	:	:	:	:	s/
3290	Other manufacturing n.e.c.	12	12	15	19	s/	:	:	:	:	s/	:	:	:	:	s/
331	Repair of fabricated metal products/machinery	289	288	297	294	t/	1836	1961	1969	1655	t/	97031	112684	121960	109473	t/
3311	Repair of fabricated metal products	8	9	9	8		:	:	:	:		:	:	:	:	
3312	Repair of machinery	209	214	215	214		:	:	:	:		:	:	:	:	
3313	Repair of electronic and optical equipment	35	26	34	36		:	:	:	:		:	:	:	:	
3314	Repair of electrical equipment	19	36	37	34		:	:	:	:		:	:	:	:	
3315	Repair of transport equip., excl. motor vehicles	3	3	2	2		:	:	:	:		:	:	:	:	
3319	Repair of other equipment	:	:	:	:		:	:	:	:		:	:	:	:	
3320	Installation of industrial machinery/equipment	15	28	26	29	t/	:	:	:	:	t/	:	:	:	:	t/
C	Total manufacturing	4342	4223	4232	4139		80148	77878	77582	78206		3462655	3697082	4076373	4508441	

a/ 131 includes 139.
b/ 1410 includes 1420 and 1430.
c/ 151 includes 1520.
d/ 1610 includes 162.
e/ 181 includes 1820.
f/ 1910 includes 1920.
g/ 201 includes 202 and 2030.
h/ 221 includes 2220.
i/ 2310 includes 239.
j/ 2410 includes 2420 and 243.

k/ 251 includes 2520 and 259.
m/ 2610 includes 2620, 2630, 2640, 265, 2660, 2670 and 2680.
n/ 2710 includes 2720, 273, 2740, 2750 and 2790.
p/ 281 includes 282.
q/ 2910 includes 2920 and 2930.
r/ 301 includes 3020, 3030, 3040 and 309.
s/ 321 includes 3220, 3230, 3240, 3250 and 3290.
t/ 331 includes 3320.

Republic of Moldova

ISIC Revision 4			Output (valuation not defined) (millions of Moldovan Lei)					Value added (valuation not defined) (millions of Moldovan Lei)					Gross fixed capital formation (millions of Moldovan Lei)	
ISIC	Industry	Note	2013	2014	2015	2016	Note	2013	2014	2015	2016	Note	2015	2016
1010	Processing/preserving of meat		2640.3	3159.6	2997.5	3131.3		557.7	657.6	581.5	598.1		...	...
1020	Processing/preserving of fish, etc.		236.9	280.9	329.5	369.6		49.9	59.0	63.9	70.6		...	...
1030	Processing/preserving of fruit,vegetables		1776.2	2006.2	2089.3	2174.5		374.5	414.7	405.3	415.3		...	...
1040	Vegetable and animal oils and fats		600.5	752.5	1391.7	1767.0		101.9	159.5	270.0	337.5		...	...
1050	Dairy products		1708.2	2003.9	2063.8	2237.5		360.0	403.3	400.4	427.4		...	...
106	Grain mill products,starches and starch products		335.3	300.7	371.3	384.7		65.5	63.4	72.0	73.5		...	...
1061	Grain mill products		334.0	299.6	370.5	383.7		65.2	63.2	71.9	73.3		...	...
1062	Starches and starch products		...	...	...	...		...	...	...	...		...	...
107	Other food products		4007.7	4366.1	4020.3	4494.6		969.7	893.9	779.9	858.5		...	...
1071	Bakery products		1862.4	1919.6	2096.6	2264.3		523.3	391.9	406.7	432.5		...	...
1072	Sugar		1382.6	1662.2	1015.0	1284.3		291.7	335.8	196.9	245.3		...	...
1073	Cocoa, chocolate and sugar confectionery		606.8	644.6	730.3	803.4		121.0	136.7	141.7	153.4		...	...
1074	Macaroni, noodles, couscous, etc.		5.2	7.0	7.5	8.9		...	1.5	1.5	1.7		...	...
1075	Prepared meals and dishes		40.5	56.4	61.8	69.8		0.8	11.8	12.0	13.3		...	...
1079	Other food products n.e.c.		110.2	76.2	109.3	64.0		23.0	16.2	21.2	12.2		...	...
1080	Prepared animal feeds		216.4	237.8	336.7	105.0		42.9	50.2	65.3	20.1		...	...
110	Beverages		4844.4	4574.2	4827.4	4463.6		1114.8	1219.7	1013.8	924.0		...	...
1101	Distilling, rectifying and blending of spirits		1072.3	999.8	788.6	615.3		218.6	273.9	165.6	127.4		...	...
1102	Wines		2680.0	2404.9	2761.0	2764.5		564.2	625.3	579.8	572.3		...	...
1103	Malt liquors and malt		718.5	720.0	766.2	767.8		233.7	197.3	160.9	158.9		...	...
1104	Soft drinks,mineral waters,other bottled waters		373.6	449.5	511.6	315.9		98.3	123.2	107.4	65.4		...	...
1200	Tobacco products		445.4	332.6	223.5	221.8		110.9	76.8	46.9	50.1		...	...
131	Spinning, weaving and finishing of textiles		71.2	62.6	58.5	39.9		17.1	20.4	12.3	8.7		...	...
1311	Preparation and spinning of textile fibres		69.1	61.1	56.4	38.1		16.9	19.8	11.9	8.3		...	...
1312	Weaving of textiles		...	...	...	...		...	...	...	...		...	...
1313	Finishing of textiles		1.9	1.6	2.1	1.8		0.2	0.5	0.4	0.4		...	...
139	Other textiles		1283.0	1581.5	1865.3	2303.1		314.1	483.5	393.4	499.8		...	...
1391	Knitted and crocheted fabrics		...	...	...	...		...	...	...	...		...	...
1392	Made-up textile articles, except apparel		807.9	1150.8	1556.7	1970.6		196.5	345.2	328.3	427.6		...	...
1393	Carpets and rugs		459.5	418.1	288.8	308.5		113.5	134.2	60.9	66.9		...	...
1394	Cordage, rope, twine and netting		...	...	...	...		...	...	...	...		...	...
1399	Other textiles n.e.c.		15.7	12.6	19.8	24.1		4.0	4.1	4.2	5.2		...	...
1410	Wearing apparel, except fur apparel		1300.6	1652.8	1836.9	2084.5		708.8	402.1	916.0	1125.6		...	...
1420	Articles of fur		...	...	...	...		...	...	...	2.1		...	...
1430	Knitted and crocheted apparel		106.9	111.5	135.6	168.9		64.1	27.8	67.6	91.2		...	...
151	Leather;luggage,handbags,saddlery,harness;fur		100.1	124.2	118.6	133.2		43.3	32.3	63.6	81.1		...	...
1511	Tanning/dressing of leather; dressing of fur		4.3	3.1	4.7	3.4		1.8	0.8	2.5	2.1		...	...
1512	Luggage,handbags,etc.;saddlery/harness		95.7	121.1	114.0	129.7		41.5	31.5	61.1	79.0		...	...
1520	Footwear		278.8	275.3	278.9	370.1		121.3	74.0	149.5	225.4		...	...
1610	Sawmilling and planing of wood		39.3	43.2	57.4	59.2		9.6	10.3	12.7	6.6		...	...

Code	Description								
162	Wood products, cork, straw, plaiting materials	148.0	175.9	244.5	303.5	34.7	42.0	54.0	33.7
1621	Veneer sheets and wood-based panels	0.4	1.4	...	...	0.1	0.3	...	0.1
1622	Builders' carpentry and joinery	48.2	61.4	65.7	65.2	11.2	14.7	14.5	7.2
1623	Wooden containers	61.2	62.3	92.2	131.3	14.7	14.8	20.4	14.6
1629	Other wood products;articles of cork,straw	38.2	50.8	86.6	105.9	8.7	12.1	19.1	11.8
170	Paper and paper products	463.1	507.5	530.2	586.5	106.0	164.0	116.6	162.5
1701	Pulp, paper and paperboard	...	...	...	...	...	...	...	...
1702	Corrugated paper and paperboard	243.1	257.2	230.2	239.4	61.5	82.3	50.6	66.3
1709	Other articles of paper and paperboard	217.6	248.5	296.3	344.2	43.9	81.1	65.2	95.3
181	Printing and service activities related to printing	346.1	394.1	416.1	381.3	120.8	134.3	130.2	104.8
1811	Printing	317.3	359.0	378.2	347.5	114.1	122.1	118.4	95.6
1812	Service activities related to printing	28.8	35.0	37.8	33.8	6.7	12.1	11.8	9.3
1820	Reproduction of recorded media	...	...	...	...	...	...	...	...
1910	Coke oven products	...	...	...	...	...	...	...	...
1920	Refined petroleum products	...	...	...	...	...	...	...	...
201	Basic chemicals,fertilizers, etc.	92.4	102.7	97.6	487.4	23.8	22.2	20.3	87.7
2011	Basic chemicals	57.8	54.3	54.0	444.8	16.5	11.8	11.2	80.1
2012	Fertilizers and nitrogen compounds	4.3	7.2	...	...	0.9	1.5	...	...
2013	Plastics and synthetic rubber in primary forms	30.4	41.1	43.1	42.0	6.4	8.9	9.0	7.6
202	Other chemical products	484.7	696.6	982.4	1029.4	103.0	149.3	204.3	199.5
2021	Pesticides and other agrochemical products	6.2	8.9	5.0	3.4	1.2	1.9	1.0	0.6
2022	Paints,varnishes;printing ink and mastics	392.3	593.0	865.3	902.8	82.4	126.9	180.0	162.5
2023	Soap,cleaning and cosmetic preparations	50.5	52.1	49.3	60.6	12.8	11.3	10.3	10.9
2029	Other chemical products n.e.c.	35.6	42.6	62.7	62.4	6.6	9.2	13.0	25.5
2030	Man-made fibres	...	...	...	...	...	...	...	...
2100	Pharmaceuticals,medicinal chemicals, etc.	464.9	499.2	603.8	595.1	98.7	256.7	126.8	135.1
221	Rubber products	13.3	12.1	9.9	10.9	3.0	2.7	2.7	2.6
2211	Rubber tyres and tubes	8.2	6.6	5.7	6.9	1.9	1.4	1.6	1.7
2219	Other rubber products	5.2	5.4	4.2	4.0	1.1	1.3	1.1	1.0
2220	Plastics products	1421.1	1626.3	1619.9	1752.5	292.5	348.9	439.0	418.9
2310	Glass and glass products	1098.5	1194.2	1211.0	1169.0	218.9	308.2	262.8	278.2
239	Non-metallic mineral products n.e.c.	2561.5	2691.9	2709.8	2230.5	531.8	694.7	588.0	530.9
2391	Refractory products	...	...	...	...	...	...	...	...
2392	Clay building materials	133.8	124.6	130.2	142.4	40.6	32.1	28.3	33.9
2393	Other porcelain and ceramic products	2.3	2.0	2.1	1.9	0.5	0.5	0.5	0.5
2394	Cement, lime and plaster	1112.5	1029.8	1074.8	815.5	226.7	264.4	233.2	194.1
2395	Articles of concrete, cement and plaster	912.3	1000.3	1110.7	1019.8	210.0	259.1	241.0	242.7
2396	Cutting, shaping and finishing of stone	65.7	59.5	62.9	54.0	12.5	15.4	13.6	12.9
2399	Other non-metallic mineral products n.e.c.	334.9	475.6	329.2	196.9	41.5	123.2	71.4	46.9
2410	Basic iron and steel	51.6	64.5	70.7	68.5	16.9	21.2	18.7	12.6
2420	Basic precious and other non-ferrous metals	...	...	...	...	...	...	...	...
243	Casting of metals	13.1	14.0	13.0	11.1	10.6	4.6	3.4	2.1
2431	Casting of iron and steel	13.1	14.0	12.5	11.1	10.6	4.6	3.3	2.1
2432	Casting of non-ferrous metals	...	...	...	...	...	...	...	...
251	Struct.metal products, tanks, reservoirs	445.6	461.9	574.9	552.4	100.3	113.1	118.4	131.5

continued

Republic of Moldova

ISIC	Industry	Output (valuation not defined) (millions of Moldovan Lei)				Note	Value added (valuation not defined) (millions of Moldovan Lei)				Note	Gross fixed capital formation (millions of Moldovan Lei)		Note
		2013	2014	2015	2016		2013	2014	2015	2016		2015	2016	
2511	Structural metal products	368.6	416.4	473.8	420.0		85.5	102.0	97.6	99.9		…	…	
2512	Tanks, reservoirs and containers of metal	77.0	45.5	101.1	132.4		14.8	11.1	20.8	31.5		…	…	
2513	Steam generators, excl. hot water boilers	…	…	…	…		…	…	…	…		…	…	
2520	Weapons and ammunition	…	…	…	…		…	…	…	…		…	…	
259	Other metal products;metal working services	569.5	658.1	724.7	779.2		171.0	160.5	149.3	185.5		…	…	
2591	Forging,pressing,stamping,roll-forming of metal	61.3	67.9	74.6	77.7		25.3	16.7	15.4	18.5				
2592	Treatment and coating of metals; machining	32.0	36.2	25.5	27.4		14.8	8.8	5.3	6.5				
2593	Cutlery, hand tools and general hardware													
2599	Other fabricated metal products n.e.c.	476.2	554.1	624.6	674.1		130.9	134.9	128.7	160.4				
2610	Electronic components and boards						3.8							
2620	Computers and peripheral equipment	44.2	39.1	41.4	42.3		9.0	8.8	9.0	9.5				
2630	Communication equipment	43.7	10.2	4.4			2.6	2.3	1.0	0.2				
2640	Consumer electronics	14.0	16.2	17.9	8.6		3.5	3.6	3.9	1.9				
265	Measuring,testing equipment; watches, etc.	465.9	462.6	492.7	433.9		205.9	104.1	107.4	97.7		…	…	
2651	Measuring/testing/navigating equipment,etc.	465.9	462.6	492.7	433.9		205.9	104.1	107.4	97.6				
2652	Watches and clocks						-							
2660	Irradiation/electromedical equipment,etc.													
2670	Optical instruments and photographic equipment													
2680	Magnetic and optical media													
2710	Electric motors,generators,transformers,etc.	43.7	54.0	67.3	68.7		19.5	24.8	20.6	20.1				
2720	Batteries and accumulators													
273	Wiring and wiring devices	585.5	1196.5	1595.1	1060.7		285.1	551.6	488.1	310.8				
2731	Fibre optic cables													
2732	Other electronic and electric wires and cables	585.5	1196.5	1595.1	1060.7		285.1	551.6	488.1	310.8				
2733	Wiring devices													
2740	Electric lighting equipment	5.2	2.9	11.8	17.7		0.6	1.4	3.6	5.2				
2750	Domestic appliances	1.6	1.8	1.9	1.9		0.3	0.8	0.6	0.6				
2790	Other electrical equipment	3.4	2.8				0.2	1.3						
281	General-purpose machinery	271.6	311.8	441.7	432.7		143.3	132.3	159.0	192.4				
2811	Engines/turbines,excl.aircraft,vehicle engines													
2812	Fluid power equipment													
2813	Other pumps, compressors, taps and valves	149.0	158.6	290.9	253.5		56.3	67.3	104.7	112.8				
2814	Bearings, gears, gearing and driving elements													
2815	Ovens, furnaces and furnace burners													
2816	Lifting and handling equipment	51.3	67.1	72.8	57.0			28.4	26.2	25.4				
2817	Office machinery, excl.computers,etc.													
2818	Power-driven hand tools													
2819	Other general-purpose machinery	55.8	73.0	66.1	111.7		17.8	31.1	23.8	49.7				
282	Special-purpose machinery	187.8	229.5	132.1	173.9		63.0	97.4	47.5	80.8				
2821	Agricultural and forestry machinery	130.7	150.6	87.9	131.4		45.7	64.0	31.6	58.5				
2822	Metal-forming machinery and machine tools	4.5	3.7	3.2	4.3		3.8	1.5	1.2	1.9		…	…	

2823	Machinery for metallurgy	..	..	..	..	..	..	..	..
2824	Mining, quarrying and construction machinery	..	..	..	..	..	..	..	..
2825	Food/beverage/tobacco processing machinery	33.5	56.6	19.5	16.9	5.7	23.9	7.0	7.5
2826	Textile/apparel/leather production machinery	..	..	..	..	..	..	..	..
2829	Other special-purpose machinery	13.7	15.4	17.4	16.7	5.2	6.5	6.3	7.4
2910	Motor vehicles	..	..	..	..	..	..	..	..
2920	Automobile bodies, trailers and semi-trailers	..	..	..	..	..	..	..	..
2930	Parts and accessories for motor vehicles	65.5	95.5	130.0	739.1	29.3	45.5	28.2	639.9
301	Building of ships and boats	..	..	..	..	..	..	..	..
3011	Building of ships and floating structures	..	..	..	..	..	..	..	..
3012	Building of pleasure and sporting boats	..	..	..	..	..	..	..	..
3020	Railway locomotives and rolling stock	..	..	..	..	..	..	..	..
3030	Air and spacecraft and related machinery	..	..	..	..	..	..	..	..
3040	Military fighting vehicles	..	..	..	..	..	..	..	..
309	Transport equipment n.e.c.	14.3	23.1	10.7	13.0	2.6	8.6	6.2	9.2
3091	Motorcycles	..	..	..	..	..	..	..	..
3092	Bicycles and invalid carriages	6.5	10.1	10.7	13.0	1.8	3.8	6.2	9.2
3099	Other transport equipment n.e.c.	..	..	..	..	..	..	..	..
3100	Furniture	870.5	1034.7	1071.7	1244.2	229.0	302.2	289.3	377.0
321	Jewellery, bijouterie and related articles	17.7	24.5	27.3	20.3	5.4	5.4	16.5	12.2
3211	Jewellery and related articles	10.2	16.2	20.5	12.3	3.7	3.6	12.4	7.4
3212	Imitation jewellery and related articles	7.5	8.3	6.8	7.9	1.8	1.8	4.1	4.8
3220	Musical instruments	..	..	..	..	..	..	..	..
3230	Sports goods	..	..	..	5.2	..	..	..	..
3240	Games and toys	40.6	34.0	37.6	41.1	19.0	7.4	22.7	24.7
3250	Medical and dental instruments and supplies	27.9	30.1	31.7	38.8	14.8	6.5	19.1	23.3
3290	Other manufacturing n.e.c.	2.9	4.5	6.9	7.7	1.3	1.0	4.2	4.6
331	Repair of fabricated metal products/machinery	402.3	457.0	458.4	446.4	127.9	194.3	184.7	151.3
3311	Repair of fabricated metal products	26.5	21.9	23.8	5.7	2.5	9.2	9.6	1.9
3312	Repair of machinery	283.4	328.4	291.2	319.9	78.3	139.9	117.4	108.5
3313	Repair of electronic and optical equipment	24.0	42.7	47.4	47.2	22.2	18.1	19.1	16.0
3314	Repair of electrical equipment	67.7	63.7	68.1	45.9	7.7	26.9	27.5	15.6
3315	Repair of transport equip., excl. motor vehicles	0.7	0.3	..	..	0.3	0.1	..	..
3319	Repair of other equipment	..	..	..	..	16.9	..	..	..
3320	Installation of industrial machinery/equipment	83.4	111.2	130.7	969.6	12.0	46.9	52.7	30.2
C	Total manufacturing	31548.8	35282.5	37706.6	39654.3	8152.2	9152.3	9061.5	10117.0

Republic of Moldova

Index numbers of industrial production

ISIC Revision 4

ISIC	Industry	Note	2005	2006	2007	2008	2009	2010 (2010=100)	2011	2012	2013	2014	2015	2016
10	Food products		∶	∶	∶	∶	∶	100	112	114	124	140	134	134
11	Beverages		∶	∶	∶	∶	∶	100	108	106	103	93	91	85
12	Tobacco products		∶	∶	∶	∶	∶	100	96	101	82	49	25	23
13	Textiles		∶	∶	∶	∶	∶	100	143	109	116	140	135	183
14	Wearing apparel		∶	∶	∶	∶	∶	100	125	124	119	131	158	183
15	Leather and related products		∶	∶	∶	∶	∶	100	114	137	133	139	145	160
16	Wood products, excluding furniture		∶	∶	∶	∶	∶	100	131	111	100	121	143	215
17	Paper and paper products		∶	∶	∶	∶	∶	100	98	132	125	135	132	160
18	Printing and reproduction of recorded media		∶	∶	∶	∶	∶	100	109	109	96	120	110	90
19	Coke and refined petroleum products		∶	∶	∶	∶	∶	100	∶	∶	∶	∶	∶	∶
20	Chemicals and chemical products		∶	∶	∶	∶	∶	100	105	112	94	133	167	198
21	Pharmaceuticals,medicinal chemicals, etc.		∶	∶	∶	∶	∶	100	72	103	170	156	182	179
22	Rubber and plastics products		∶	∶	∶	∶	∶	100	118	104	102	106	113	106
23	Other non-metallic mineral products		∶	∶	∶	∶	∶	100	107	100	122	125	127	115
24	Basic metals		∶	∶	∶	∶	∶	100	118	102	117	133	109	104
25	Fabricated metal products, except machinery		∶	∶	∶	∶	∶	100	120	101	109	106	117	123
26	Computer, electronic and optical products		∶	∶	∶	∶	∶	100	149	101	114	112	112	106
27	Electrical equipment		∶	∶	∶	∶	∶	100	148	104	125	193	259	215
28	Machinery and equipment n.e.c.		∶	∶	∶	∶	∶	100	135	117	102	99	114	121
29	Motor vehicles, trailers and semi-trailers		∶	∶	∶	∶	∶	100	120	186	312	290	328	517
30	Other transport equipment		∶	∶	∶	∶	∶	100	∶	∶	∶	∶	∶	∶
31	Furniture		∶	∶	∶	∶	∶	100	112	103	108	116	120	153
32	Other manufacturing		∶	∶	∶	∶	∶	100	27	19	32	37	58	59
33	Repair and installation of machinery/equipment		∶	∶	∶	∶	∶	100	90	21	129	169	177	148
C	Total manufacturing		∶	∶	∶	∶	∶	100	114	113	125	136	139	142

Romania

Supplier of information:
National Institute of Statistics, Bucharest.

Basic source of data:
Annual survey; administrative source.

Major deviations from ISIC (Revision 4):
Data presented in ISIC (Revision 4) were originally classified according to NACE (Revision 2).

Reference period:
Calendar year.

Scope:
All registered enterprises.

Method of data collection:
Mail questionnaires; electronic questionnaires.

Type of enumeration:
Sample survey.

Adjusted for non-response:
Yes.

Concepts and definitions of variables:
Number of enterprises refers to local units.
Wages and salaries excludes housing and family allowances paid directly by the employer and payments in kind.
Output refers to turnover.

Related national publications:
Results and performances of enterprises in industry and construction, published by the National Institute for Statistics, Bucharest.

Romania

ISIC	Industry	Note	Number of enterprises (number)				Note	Number of employees (thousands)				Note	Wages and salaries paid to employees (millions of Romanian Lei)			
			2013	2014	2015	2016		2013	2014	2015	2016		2013	2014	2015	2016
1010	Processing/preserving of meat		858	860	847	853		45.6	44.7	43.2	43.1		814.6	898.5	961.5	1139.3
1020	Processing/preserving of fish, etc.		31	29	37	31		1.2	1.2	1.3	1.3		19.1	22.3	26.9	31.6
1030	Processing/preserving of fruit,vegetables		293	325	372	417		5.4	5.4	5.6	4.8		139.8	137.7	162.8	147.1
1040	Vegetable and animal oils and fats		155	145	148	137		3.3	3.3	3.5	3.4		124.6	132.6	146.8	153.7
1050	Dairy products		567	601	570	542		14.0	13.8	13.4	13.6		298.9	300.1	319.7	405.3
106	Grain mill products,starches and starch products		806	781	736	706		10.6	10.5	10.0	9.4		187.0	200.0	228.3	235.6
1061	Grain mill products		792	768	718	689		10.2	10.1	9.5	9.1		187.0a/	188.3	196.9	235.6a/
1062	Starches and starch products		14	13	18	17		0.4	0.4	0.4	0.4		…a/	11.7	31.4	…a/
107	Other food products		5306	5498	5543	5512		80.1	80.6	81.0	82.5		1121.5	1234.1	1440.3	1781.4
1071	Bakery products		4602	4765	4814	4753		66.9	66.2	67.0	68.1		766.6	849.5	1030.7	1294.2
1072	Sugar		17	17	14	13		1.6	1.5	1.4	1.4		64.6	62.7	61.1	66.8
1073	Cocoa, chocolate and sugar confectionery		219	222	201	203		4.5	4.5	4.4	4.6		121.7	130.0	130.5	163.9
1074	Macaroni, noodles, couscous, etc.		72	74	78	68		0.8	0.6	0.7	0.6		16.9	12.6	13.4	15.9
1075	Prepared meals and dishes		39	39	44	52		0.3	0.2	0.2	0.2		2.5	1.8	2.9	2.3
1079	Other food products n.e.c.		357	381	392	423		6.1	7.6	7.4	7.5		149.2	177.5	201.7	238.3
1080	Prepared animal feeds		153	159	156	155		2.4	2.4	2.4	2.1		69.1	64.3	71.7	63.3
110	Beverages		748	776	767	750		20.4	18.1	18.6	19.7		691.3	699.1	797.0	949.3
1101	Distilling, rectifying and blending of spirits		117	113	110	103		1.8	1.6	2.0	1.8		39.2	41.2	60.1	62.8
1102	Wines		201	200	217	224		3.3	3.1	3.3	3.6		…	…	…	…
1103	Malt liquors and malt		32	35	38	38		5.3	4.0	4.0	4.1		…	…	…	…
1104	Soft drinks,mineral waters,other bottled waters		398	428	402	385		10.0	9.4	9.4	10.3		336.1	350.5	389.6	484.0
1200	Tobacco products		10	10	12	13		1.6	1.6	1.7	1.8		100.6	111.1	123.8	124.2
131	Spinning, weaving and finishing of textiles		247	245	264	252		9.9	10.1	10.9	10.3		208.9	234.9	234.7	277.6
1311	Preparation and spinning of textile fibres		56	55	61	59		4.4	4.5	4.5	4.5		95.7	103.5	106.8	125.5
1312	Weaving of textiles		94	96	95	90		3.5	3.5	3.5	3.3		73.8	89.8	86.5	89.2
1313	Finishing of textiles		97	94	108	103		2.0	2.1	2.9	2.5		39.4	41.6	41.4	62.9
139	Other textiles		1044	1074	1070	1077		19.7	20.7	20.9	20.8		332.9	382.2	453.2	508.4
1391	Knitted and crocheted fabrics		19	19	19	15		0.2	0.2	0.2	0.2		3.2	4.0	4.3	5.1
1392	Made-up textile articles, except apparel		737	767	759	776		15.2	16.1	16.2	16.1		245.8	282.7	349.2	389.9
1393	Carpets and rugs		23	24	27	25		0.4	0.4	0.3	0.4		7.6	6.5	7.6	8.3
1394	Cordage, rope, twine and netting		24	25	24	23		0.3	0.3	0.3	0.3		5.6	7.2	7.0	8.8
1399	Other textiles n.e.c.		241	239	241	238		3.6	3.7	3.8	3.7		70.7	81.8	85.1	96.3
1410	Wearing apparel, except fur apparel		4071	4282	4455	4538		144.9	146.6	144.7	137.4		2162.2	2444.0	2609.8	2827.6
1420	Articles of fur		48	46	42	41		0.2	0.2	0.1	0.1		1.6	1.5	1.4	2.2
1430	Knitted and crocheted apparel		352	350	353	327		12.9	12.5	11.4	11.2		222.7	231.1	236.7	254.5
151	Leather;luggage,handbags,saddlery,harness;fur		329	344	357	368		8.3	8.5	8.7	8.8		150.6	175.3	199.0	230.4
1511	Tanning/dressing of leather; dressing of fur		48	49	50	50		0.5	0.5	0.5	0.5		8.4	9.2	9.4	11.1
1512	Luggage,handbags,etc.;saddlery/harness		281	295	307	318		7.8	8.0	8.2	8.3		142.2	166.1	189.6	219.3
1520	Footwear		1228	1255	1237	1206		53.0	52.4	49.5	46.2		873.1	916.1	930.2	1003.2
1610	Sawmilling and planing of wood		3051	3068	2906	2735		29.5	28.8	28.7	27.9		324.1	373.6	449.5	506.2

Code	Description												
162	Wood products, cork, straw, plaiting materials	2274	2310	2341	2311	25.5	27.2	27.1	28.1	522.0	579.3	610.6	619.8
1621	Veneer sheets and wood-based panels	134	124	126	122	6.8	7.7	7.7	8.0	...	220.6	231.4	233.4
1622	Builders' carpentry and joinery	1321	1317	1274	1245	11.5	12.1	12.1	12.3	...	229.6	...	256.9
1623	Wooden containers	200	204	217	219	2.3	2.0	2.1	2.3	32.5	26.5	39.1	41.8
1629	Other wood products;articles of cork,straw	619	665	724	725	4.9	5.3	5.2	5.5	86.3	102.6	...	87.7
170	Paper and paper products	742	750	762	783	14.2	12.9	12.6	12.3	272.5	300.1	357.1	471.0
1701	Pulp, paper and paperboard	57	53	49	50	2.3	1.5	1.3	1.3	34.8	39.0	44.9	117.4
1702	Corrugated paper and paperboard	320	338	347	348	7.8	6.4	6.2	5.8	130.0	151.9	186.2	251.8
1709	Other articles of paper and paperboard	365	359	366	385	4.1	5.1	5.0	5.3	107.7	109.2	126.0	101.8
181	Printing and service activities related to printing	1925	1984	2011	1944	15.2	15.2	15.4	15.9	...	333.1	392.6	...
1811	Printing	1462	1520	1571	1525	13.5	13.6	13.6	14.0	...	298.9	365.1	...
1812	Service activities related to printing	463	464	440	419	1.8	1.6	1.8	1.9	21.3	34.2	27.5	33.2
1820	Reproduction of recorded media	85	85	77	76	0.3	0.3	0.2	0.3	6.2	...	...	...
1910	Coke oven products	9	10	9	6	-	-	-	-	...	...	...	...
1920	Refined petroleum products	62	69	65	51	2.4	2.5	2.6	2.5	...	...	...	...
201	Basic chemicals,fertilizers, etc.	307	311	320	294	11.0	13.2	15.1	18.2	680.2	535.8	523.0	434.8
2011	Basic chemicals	214	211	212	186	6.9	8.5	9.3	11.0	450.3	535.8b/	523.0b/	434.8b/
2012	Fertilizers and nitrogen compounds	25	26	31	33	2.6	3.1	4.5	5.6	...	...b/	...b/	...b/
2013	Plastics and synthetic rubber in primary forms	68	74	77	75	1.5	1.6	1.3	1.7	...	...b/	...b/	...b/
202	Other chemical products	607	621	625	580	10.3	9.9	9.5	9.3	...	...	...	...
2021	Pesticides and other agrochemical products	18	22	43	17	0.6	0.5	0.4	0.4	...	...	...	...
2022	Paints,varnishes;printing ink and mastics	179	174	158	138	4.4	4.2	3.9	3.8	104.4	123.8	141.4	165.6
2023	Soap,cleaning and cosmetic preparations	240	252	255	263	3.2	3.4	3.2	3.1	107.4	116.5	119.6	133.9
2029	Other chemical products n.e.c.	170	173	169	162	2.1	1.9	2.0	2.0	43.2	51.4	64.5	70.9
2030	Man-made fibres	12	12	13	10	0.9	0.9	1.0	1.1	...	...	...	...
2100	Pharmaceuticals,medicinal chemicals, etc.	146	148	139	135	9.1	9.2	9.3	9.0	403.8	440.6	446.1	455.1
221	Rubber products	278	282	273	257	17.0	15.9	15.3	14.4	469.4	532.9	609.3	715.2
2211	Rubber tyres and tubes	68	66	64	56	8.7	8.2	8.0	7.7	299.4	336.2	380.2	437.3
2219	Other rubber products	210	216	209	201	8.3	7.7	7.3	6.8	170.0	196.7	229.1	277.9
2220	Plastics products	2511	2545	2515	2514	43.7	40.8	39.2	38.1	816.2	893.4	1038.9	1237.2
2310	Glass and glass products	435	438	440	432	7.0	6.9	6.4	6.5	122.4	130.5	157.1	184.5
239	Non-metallic mineral products n.e.c.	2099	2101	2098	2045	32.3	31.7	31.3	32.2	861.5	893.6	991.5	1128.1
2391	Refractory products	29	30	31	28	0.7	0.7	0.7	0.7	13.6	15.4	15.7	16.2
2392	Clay building materials	169	161	155	148	2.7	2.6	2.6	2.8	...	...	85.2	95.9
2393	Other porcelain and ceramic products	155	159	160	152	6.6	6.5	6.4	6.4	154.1	156.6	173.8	195.2
2394	Cement, lime and plaster	61	59	58	53	2.6	2.4	2.6	2.6	...	161.0	170.6	183.7
2395	Articles of concrete, cement and plaster	1068	1058	1042	1016	14.9	14.5	14.1	14.8	367.7	...	435.0	499.1
2396	Cutting, shaping and finishing of stone	506	521	532	531	2.6	2.5	2.3	2.5	27.3	32.1	35.1	59.4
2399	Other non-metallic mineral products n.e.c.	111	113	120	117	2.3	2.4	2.4	2.5	68.0	68.4	76.1	78.6
2410	Basic iron and steel	178	182	172	154	18.6	19.6	20.3	21.5	803.8	768.9	796.3	778.2
2420	Basic precious and other non-ferrous metals	65	68	73	69	5.7	5.5	5.4	5.4	223.0	232.4	259.0	311.1
243	Casting of metals	180	192	180	156	4.6	4.8	4.7	4.7	103.6	115.5	129.5	139.7
2431	Casting of iron and steel c/	57	60	58	53	1.3	1.5	1.5	1.6	103.6	115.5	129.5	139.7
2432	Casting of non-ferrous metals c/	123	132	122	103	3.4	3.3	3.2	3.1	...	...	...	...
251	Struct.metal products, tanks, reservoirs	3320	3439	3371	3424	42.8	43.9	44.0	44.3	910.8	970.1	1100.3	1226.4

continued

Romania

ISIC Revision 4		Number of enterprises (number)					Number of employees (thousands)					Wages and salaries paid to employees (millions of Romanian Lei)				
ISIC	Industry	Note	2013	2014	2015	2016	Note	2013	2014	2015	2016	Note	2013	2014	2015	2016
2511	Structural metal products		3187	3309	3252	3316		39.2	39.7	39.4	39.3		772.1	848.4	961.3	1112.9
2512	Tanks, reservoirs and containers of metal		117	116	104	97		3.9	3.5	3.5	2.6		102.9	98.3	108.5	81.4
2513	Steam generators, excl. hot water boilers		16	14	15	11		1.2	0.8	0.9	0.9		35.8	23.4	30.5	32.1
2520	Weapons and ammunition	d/	17	17	18	19	d/	...	...	...	...	d/	...	...	...	...
259	Other metal products;metal working services		2289	2375	2421	2513	d/	41.3	43.8	45.6	53.2	d/	968.4	1135.5	1295.7	1477.8
2591	Forging,pressing,stamping,roll-forming of metal		169	171	175	172		3.9	4.1	4.2	4.2		106.5	120.7	131.2	152.5
2592	Treatment and coating of metals machining		1176	1244	1306	1381		15.7	17.2	18.7	19.0		353.3	439.2	526.3	570.9
2593	Cutlery, hand tools and general hardware		234	233	232	238		5.3	5.6	5.7	5.9		136.0	159.7	173.6	196.8
2599	Other fabricated metal products n.e.c.		710	727	708	722		16.4	17.0	17.0	24.1		372.6	415.9	464.6	557.6
2610	Electronic components and boards		168	181	199	199		11.2	12.9	13.9	14.4		347.7	421.1	486.9	566.4
2620	Computers and peripheral equipment		251	251	235	224		2.9	2.8	2.6	2.7		83.0	85.4	92.8	101.7
2630	Communication equipment		70	69	70	60		3.4	4.4	4.8	5.0		107.0	148.5	168.5	199.7
2640	Consumer electronics		25	26	35	32		0.2	0.2	0.1	0.1		...	...	2.4	1.7
265	Measuring,testing equipment; watches, etc.		173	178	181	174	e/	7.4	7.8	9.2	8.9	e/	298.4	318.3	403.6	432.2
2651	Measuring/testing/navigating equipment,etc.		173	178	181	174	e/	7.3	7.8	9.2	8.9	e/	298.4	318.3	403.6	432.2
2652	Watches and clocks		...	...	...	...		...	-	...	...		...	...	...	...
2660	Irradiation/electromedical equipment,etc.		46	46	41	39		0.4	0.3	0.2	0.2		9.5	4.3	11.1	5.2
2670	Optical instruments and photographic equipment		127	119	116	105		0.8	0.7	0.7	0.7		18.7	19.8	21.2	19.2
2680	Magnetic and optical media		1	1	...	1		-	-	...	-		-	-	...	-
2710	Electric motors,generators,transformers,etc.		271	275	262	263		13.0	12.2	12.3	13.0		339.7	338.5	382.5	421.6
2720	Batteries and accumulators		4	4	5	5		0.8	0.8	0.8	0.8		...	...	...	...
273	Wiring and wiring devices		59	64	70	70		5.4	5.9	6.5	6.2		142.7	170.8	...	...
2731	Fibre optic cables		4	4	7	7		-	-	-	0.1		...	...	...	0.1
2732	Other electronic and electric wires and cables		39	42	43	42		3.8	4.2	4.5	4.2		...	130.1	155.3	158.6
2733	Wiring devices		16	18	20	21		1.6	1.7	1.9	1.9		33.1	...	47.7	52.5
2740	Electric lighting equipment		83	89	93	88		2.2	2.4	2.3	2.4		...	...	81.0	85.8
2750	Domestic appliances		69	63	66	62		9.0	9.9	10.2	10.6		230.4	278.5	319.9	390.1
2790	Other electrical equipment		134	135	131	132		6.5	7.0	8.0	9.8		173.2	208.0	261.3	339.0
281	General-purpose machinery		775	749	725	689		31.1	31.1	31.6	31.7		942.6	1013.6	1138.8	1279.3
2811	Engines/turbines,excl.aircraft,vehicle engines		52	47	37	37		8.9	8.5	5.1	4.8		...	...	...	...
2812	Fluid power equipment		...	...	...	...		0.4	0.4	0.5	0.6		...	...	...	...
2813	Other pumps, compressors, taps and valves		105	103	97	87		3.5	3.6	3.6	3.7		89.6	95.8	109.6	116.4
2814	Bearings, gears, gearing and driving elements		63	59	62	56		7.7	7.8	12.3	12.5		241.1	267.1	517.9	585.7
2815	Ovens, furnaces and furnace burners		30	29	29	25		0.8	0.7	0.7	0.7		28.2	27.8	30.1	33.0
2816	Lifting and handling equipment		250	238	227	213		4.5	4.5	3.6	3.1		112.6	121.7	104.9	112.9
2817	Office machinery, excl.computers,etc.		21	21	19	18		0.7	0.7	0.7	0.6		...	...	...	...
2818	Power-driven hand tools		12	11	10	10		0.7	0.7	0.7	0.7		...	...	...	...
2819	Other general-purpose machinery		242	241	244	243		3.9	4.1	4.5	4.9		124.8	129.9	156.6	180.5
282	Special-purpose machinery		521	531	523	518		23.1	21.2	20.0	19.2		653.3	412.4	467.9	690.6
2821	Agricultural and forestry machinery		64	69	64	60		2.2	2.2	2.2	2.2		55.3	53.9	61.1	59.2
2822	Metal-forming machinery and machine tools		145	141	135	135		4.3	4.3	4.3	4.3		123.2	134.7	146.2	164.9

2823	Machinery for metallurgy	17	20	21	19	2.8	2.7	2.5	2.3	66.9	69.2	66.5	62.4
2824	Mining, quarrying and construction machinery	68	75	73	75	0.8	0.7	0.7	0.6	14.6	16.0	18.4	17.0
2825	Food/beverage/tobacco processing machinery	67	65	68	64	0.7	0.6	0.6	0.6	16.7	16.5	18.6	21.7
2826	Textile/apparel/leather production machinery	19	18	18	19	4.3	3.8	4.6	4.8	138.3	…	…	…
2829	Other special-purpose machinery	141	143	144	146	7.9	6.9	5.0	4.4	238.3	…	…	…
2910	Motor vehicles	33	34	37	38	18.3	18.0	17.2	17.2	…	…	…	…
2920	Automobile bodies, trailers and semi-trailers	75	76	85	90	1.5	1.6	1.9	2.0	…	…	…	…
2930	Parts and accessories for motor vehicles	361	387	387	389	117.6	130.2	149.5	155.0	3635.2	4075.5	5132.2	6270.7
301	Building of ships and boats	332	372	346	289	17.4	18.3	18.5	16.0	623.5	681.1	737.7	660.9
3011	Building of ships and floating structures	291	328	311	250	17.2	18.0	18.3	15.8	621.4	677.9	734.2	656.6
3012	Building of pleasure and sporting boats	41	44	35	39	0.2	0.2	0.2	0.2	2.1	3.2	3.5	4.3
3020	Railway locomotives and rolling stock f/	50	48	47	50	6.3	6.5	5.9	5.5	201.2	238.9	403.6	221.6
3030	Air and spacecraft and related machinery	19	18	23	29	4.0	4.2	4.5	4.6	172.7	191.0	215.9	238.7
3040	Military fighting vehicles f/	2	2	1	1	…	…	…	…	…	…	…	…
309	Transport equipment n.e.c.	29	32	31	31	1.5	1.5	1.8	1.8	28.6	31.5	44.5	52.5
3091	Motorcycles g/	5	5	3	4	-	-	-	-	28.6 g/	…	…	…
3092	Bicycles and invalid carriages g/	22	23	24	25	1.5	1.5	1.8	1.8	… g/	31.4	44.3	52.3
3099	Other transport equipment n.e.c. g/	2	4	4	2	-	-	-	-	… g/	…	…	…
3100	Furniture	3342	3394	3488	3564	60.5	60.8	62.9	65.1	989.6	1121.1	1267.1	1509.4
321	Jewellery, bijouterie and related articles	356	358	369	398	2.0	2.0	1.9	2.0	29.3	36.9	40.4	55.4
3211	Jewellery and related articles h/	293	284	286	289	1.7	1.7	1.7	1.7	29.3	36.9	40.4	55.4
3212	Imitation jewellery and related articles h/	63	74	83	109	0.3	0.3	0.3	0.3	…	…	…	…
3220	Musical instruments	42	42	38	44	0.8	0.8	0.8	0.8	12.7	14.0	17.1	20.4
3230	Sports goods	45	44	57	61	1.4	1.9	2.2	2.4	25.1	43.6	52.2	63.1
3240	Games and toys	91	96	111	119	1.5	1.6	1.7	1.8	23.3	31.3	34.6	41.7
3250	Medical and dental instruments and supplies	833	908	981	1070	4.3	5.0	5.3	5.8	62.8	105.5	113.8	133.7
3290	Other manufacturing n.e.c.	587	627	659	697	5.1	5.3	4.5	4.7	89.4	103.5	96.9	108.4
331	Repair of fabricated metal products/machinery	1705	1813	1881	1974	26.0	25.0	25.2	24.6	539.8	684.1	749.2	751.9
3311	Repair of fabricated metal products	102	109	123	126	0.8	0.9	0.8	0.9	15.5	22.3	24.4	32.7
3312	Repair of machinery	724	773	803	886	7.9	6.3	6.1	6.1	129.1	205.3	218.3	201.1
3313	Repair of electronic and optical equipment	207	218	221	215	0.6	0.6	0.6	0.7	12.4	10.1	12.8	12.0
3314	Repair of electrical equipment	188	205	216	220	1.7	1.9	1.9	1.8	51.6	55.6	61.4	70.8
3315	Repair of transport equip., excl. motor vehicles	369	383	391	407	14.5	14.7	15.2	14.7	325.1	380.3	…	422.8
3319	Repair of other equipment	115	125	127	120	0.5	0.6	0.6	0.5	6.1	10.5	…	12.5
3320	Installation of industrial machinery/equipment	408	455	469	475	3.4	3.4	3.4	3.3	95.6	113.0	101.3	118.1
C	Total manufacturing	47925	49274	49557	49413	1157.2	1170.2	1192.4	1196.3	26805.4	29233.9	32919.0	37056.8

a/ 1061 includes 1062.
b/ 2011 includes 2012 and 2013.
c/ 2431 includes 2432.
d/ 2599 includes 2520.
e/ 2651 includes 2652.
f/ 3020 includes 3040.
g/ 3091 includes 3092 and 3099.
h/ 3211 includes 3212.

Romania

ISIC Revision 4		Output at factor values (millions of Romanian Lei)					Value added at factor values (millions of Romanian Lei)					Gross fixed capital formation (millions of Romanian Lei)		
ISIC	Industry	Note	2013	2014	2015	2016	Note	2013	2014	2015	2016	Note	2015	2016
1010	Processing/preserving of meat		12652.0	12370.9	12815.2	13019.2		1953.9	2122.1	684.6	836.5		:	:
1020	Processing/preserving of fish, etc.		341.6	369.0	418.7	472.3		56.6	59.8	43.8	45.8		:	:
1030	Processing/preserving of fruit, vegetables		1884.9	1898.0	2286.4	2038.6		365.4	348.0	356.8	279.1		:	:
1040	Vegetable and animal oils and fats		4432.1	4168.1	4530.3	4495.0		239.0	466.7	388.4	345.1		:	:
1050	Dairy products		4293.2	4555.8	4455.0	4838.9		637.5	685.4	676.1	830.7		:	:
106	Grain mill products,starches and starch products		3093.5	3170.9	3307.5	3036.5		453.9	451.2	279.5	391.3		:	:
1061	Grain mill products		2846.6	2962.9	3116.2	2877.5		453.9a/	435.9	231.4	391.3a/		:	:
1062	Starches and starch products		246.9	208.0	191.3	159.0		...a/	15.3	48.1	...a/		:	:
107	Other food products		11504.7	12005.8	12967.5	13479.6		2322.2	2785.9	2057.6	2687.4		:	:
1071	Bakery products		5737.6	6351.4	7041.8	7671.5		1538.4	1890.5	1120.2	1474.8		:	:
1072	Sugar		2416.8	1831.3	1876.6	1595.2		81.8	27.6	79.4	188.0		:	:
1073	Cocoa, chocolate and sugar confectionery		1177.3	1205.5	1272.0	1407.1		244.3	272.8	265.9	373.1		:	:
1074	Macaroni, noodles, couscous, etc.		137.2	131.4	145.9	145.3		39.4	28.5	29.4	29.9		:	:
1075	Prepared meals and dishes		27.8	21.1	20.1	27.6		4.7	4.1	6.4	4.5		:	:
1079	Other food products n.e.c.		2008.0	2465.1	2611.1	2632.9		413.6	562.4	556.3	617.1		:	:
1080	Prepared animal feeds		1791.1	1591.3	1819.3	1567.3		162.8	194.3	176.1	113.1		:	:
110	Beverages		9569.7	9333.8	10714.8	11432.2		2573.8	2081.2	2385.8	2987.5		:	:
1101	Distilling, rectifying and blending of spirits		450.2	481.4	514.5	510.2		81.2	96.7	109.8	158.3		:	:
1102	Wines		826.4	742.9	1032.8	1054.1		:	:	:	:		:	:
1103	Malt liquors and malt		3931.1	3522.8	4001.1	4144.0		:	:	:	:		:	:
1104	Soft drinks,mineral waters,other bottled waters		4362.0	4586.7	5166.4	5723.9		995.8	937.7	1119.0	1515.9		:	:
1200	Tobacco products		880.5	949.4	1171.7	1250.9		321.2	335.5	-20.9	376.3		:	:
131	Spinning, weaving and finishing of textiles		2300.6	2425.8	2608.4	2841.7		561.1	546.8	607.3	690.5		:	:
1311	Preparation and spinning of textile fibres		1463.2	1468.4	1635.7	1728.6		277.5	270.9	302.8	340.8		:	:
1312	Weaving of textiles		549.6	641.9	668.7	736.7		168.5	171.8	202.0	239.6		:	:
1313	Finishing of textiles		287.8	315.5	304.0	376.4		115.1	104.1	102.5	110.1		:	:
139	Other textiles		2649.2	2973.5	3297.4	3203.6		634.0	777.2	810.0	862.7		:	:
1391	Knitted and crocheted fabrics		19.1	27.5	31.9	33.1		6.2	14.7	13.1	11.6		:	:
1392	Made-up textile articles, except apparel		1739.1	2010.9	2196.4	2344.5		465.3	554.8	598.0	633.6		:	:
1393	Carpets and rugs		25.2	13.9	17.1	19.3		:	9.3	4.9	12.1		:	:
1394	Cordage, rope, twine and netting		36.4	42.9	44.5	48.3		19.8	24.1	13.1	18.8		:	:
1399	Other textiles n.e.c.		829.4	878.3	1007.5	758.4		142.7	174.3	180.9	186.6		:	:
1410	Wearing apparel, except fur apparel		8367.0	9106.6	9457.9	9446.1		3895.7	4102.3	3917.4	4222.5		:	:
1420	Articles of fur		10.1	9.3	10.3	9.3		4.0	2.7	0.8	0.3		:	:
1430	Knitted and crocheted apparel		842.2	842.1	749.3	800.5		391.8	369.7	376.0	412.3		:	:
151	Leather;luggage,handbags,saddlery,harness;fur		659.4	694.6	670.5	760.4		252.3	315.4	330.1	363.8		:	:
1511	Tanning/dressing of leather; dressing of fur		156.8	175.6	129.6	132.3		24.1	41.6	51.1	40.2		:	:
1512	Luggage,handbags,etc.;saddlery/harness		502.6	519.0	540.9	628.1		228.2	273.8	279.0	323.6		:	:
1520	Footwear		4138.3	4450.5	4276.8	4463.8		1418.7	1505.8	1336.5	1434.1		:	:
1610	Sawmilling and planing of wood		4503.1	4784.6	5084.1	4936.0		875.5	993.2	1107.4	901.0		0.4b/	:

Code	Description										
162	Wood products, cork, straw, plaiting materials	..b/	1645.3	1682.0	1917.3	1821.5	8398.0	8478.2	8507.4	8614.8	
1621	Veneer sheets and wood-based panels	..	792.6	780.0	774.1	..	4441.5	4409.1	4376.0	4497.6	
1622	Builders' carpentry and joinery	..	626.9	..	862.3	..	3040.3	3153.3	3214.6	3266.9	
1623	Wooden containers	..	101.6	66.5	70.2	87.4	356.8	331.4	320.0	293.5	
1629	Other wood products;articles of cork,straw	..	124.2	..	210.7	180.6	559.4	584.4	596.8	556.8	
170	Paper and paper products	..	1196.7	910.2	839.3	765.5	5549.1	4298.4	3907.3	3632.4	
1701	Pulp, paper and paperboard	..	319.5	150.8	138.9	125.7	1846.0	703.9	595.2	549.1	
1702	Corrugated paper and paperboard	..	604.3	430.9	376.7	340.4	2443.7	1979.3	1799.7	1677.5	
1709	Other articles of paper and paperboard	..	272.9	328.5	323.7	299.4	1259.4	1615.2	1512.4	1405.8	
181	Printing and service activities related to printing	..	..	1069.9	1175.8	..	3367.3	3296.9	3275.4	3001.4	
1811	Printing	..	..	997.7	1102.8	..	3150.3	3097.5	3071.4	2813.5	
1812	Service activities related to printing	..	81.3	72.2	73.0	49.0	217.0	199.4	204.0	187.9	
1820	Reproduction of recorded media	..	..	..	..	23.6	48.6	43.6	60.1	74.0	
1910	Coke oven products	..	..	..	..	..	4.1	6.7	7.6	9.6	
1920	Refined petroleum products	..	866.9	1335.7	1320.8	1760.9	13916.1	14993.5	21088.4	19095.0	
201	Basic chemicals,fertilizers, etc.	..	866.9c/	1335.7c/	1320.8c/	1025.5	5625.8	6320.5	5943.9	6569.3	
2011	Basic chemicals	..	..c/	..c/	..c/	..c/	3058.5	3448.0	3196.3	3208.7	
2012	Fertilizers and nitrogen compounds	..	..c/	..c/	..c/	..c/	1640.1	1908.9	2016.9	1945.1	
2013	Plastics and synthetic rubber in primary forms	..	..	..	..	611.2	927.2	963.6	730.7	1414.9	
202	Other chemical products	..	..	..	..	..	4172.8	3542.3	3367.2	2935.5	
2021	Pesticides and other agrochemical products	..	..	..	..	..	475.9	381.9	341.1	294.2	
2022	Paints,varnishes;printing ink and mastics	..	392.8	393.6	363.2	290.5	1529.2	1471.2	1381.5	1236.1	
2023	Soap,cleaning and cosmetic preparations	..	331.3	311.2	293.4	262.3	1236.3	924.0	797.0	726.9	
2029	Other chemical products n.e.c.	..	179.9	139.0	126.0	58.4	931.4	765.2	847.6	678.3	
2030	Man-made fibres	..	..	76.3	..	..	456.0	459.1	497.2	488.8	
2100	Pharmaceuticals,medicinal chemicals, etc.	..	1417.1	1304.9	1300.1	1258.4	3336.8	3807.6	3628.6	3437.1	
221	Rubber products	0.4d/	3046.0	2440.0	2355.4	2063.0	9528.3	9059.7	8660.0	8278.0	
2211	Rubber tyres and tubes	..	2404.1	1857.1	1783.6	1575.1	7086.3	6730.8	6512.9	6389.6	
2219	Other rubber products	..	641.9	582.9	571.8	487.9	2442.0	2328.9	2147.1	1888.4	
2220	Plastics products	..d/	2918.9	2687.5	2454.1	2114.9	12900.5	11904.5	10699.4	10090.6	
2310	Glass and glass products	8.4e/	437.0	386.8	331.3	310.9	1707.4	1523.4	1259.2	1199.7	
239	Non-metallic mineral products n.e.c.	..e/	3190.2	2985.4	2956.0	2630.1	11367.3	11181.6	10287.7	9724.9	
2391	Refractory products	..	29.5	26.6	36.1	26.7	90.0	110.9	94.4	98.4	
2392	Clay building materials	..	254.9	223.2	..	..	787.0	746.0	684.2	685.9	
2393	Other porcelain and ceramic products	..	297.9	295.4	285.5	271.9	810.8	798.5	729.4	680.1	
2394	Cement, lime and plaster	..	1107.1	965.3	1039.3	..	2910.3	2988.7	2730.6	2590.7	
2395	Articles of concrete, cement and plaster	..	1172.8	1070.0	923.4	923.4	5610.1	5266.0	4909.5	4525.1	
2396	Cutting, shaping and finishing of stone	..	105.1	89.1	79.8	88.0	301.2	321.0	256.3	244.8	
2399	Other non-metallic mineral products n.e.c.	..	222.9	315.8	270.0	274.7	857.9	950.5	883.3	899.9	
2410	Basic iron and steel	..	1352.4	1563.4	2927.8	1443.0	10201.1	11777.9	12447.7	11807.6	
2420	Basic precious and other non-ferrous metals	..	749.7	603.9	562.1	503.7	4041.8	4184.7	3696.8	3598.5	
243	Casting of metals	..	283.8	483.8	337.4	248.9	1252.4	1346.7	1299.5	1245.8	
2431	Casting of iron and steel	..	283.8	483.8	337.4	248.9	170.1	200.7	207.3	225.6	f/
2432	Casting of non-ferrous metals	..	..	..	..	..	1082.3	1146.0	1092.2	1020.2	f/
251	Struct.metal products, tanks, reservoirs	481.8g/	2235.1	2081.2	2077.7	1911.4	8075.1	8116.9	7421.0	7438.8	

continued

Romania

ISIC	Industry	Output at factor values Note	Output 2013 (millions of Romanian Lei)	Output 2014	Output 2015	Output 2016	Value added Note	VA 2013 (millions of Romanian Lei)	VA 2014	VA 2015	VA 2016	GFCF Note	GFCF 2015 (millions of Romanian Lei)	GFCF 2016
2511	Structural metal products		6737.8	6810.2	7434.2	7491.4		1666.5	1844.7	1827.6	2048.8		...	...
2512	Tanks, reservoirs and containers of metal		592.9	561.2	584.6	458.9		209.3	213.4	201.5	155.5		...	...
2513	Steam generators, excl. hot water boilers		108.1	49.6	98.1	124.8		35.6	19.6	52.1	30.8		...	...
2520	Weapons and ammunition	h/	...	...	...	...	h/	...	...	...	...		..g/	...
259	Other metal products;metal working services	h/	8292.5	9142.5	9686.6	10792.1	h/	2318.8	3604.5	2788.1	2690.6		...g/	...
2591	Forging,pressing,stamping,roll-forming of metal		1309.0	1441.2	1460.3	1473.5		272.0	329.9	279.1	326.2		...	...
2592	Treatment and coating of metals; machining		3157.8	3353.1	3722.3	3774.6		918.7	1070.7	1238.1	1237.2		...	...
2593	Cutlery, hand tools and general hardware		815.5	919.8	1005.8	1066.1		241.1	298.2	325.5	348.7		...	...
2599	Other fabricated metal products n.e.c.	h/	3010.2	3428.4	3498.2	4477.9	h/	887.0	1905.7	945.4	-			
2610	Electronic components and boards		2176.3	2688.8	3098.3	3451.8		650.7	749.9	830.0	927.8		6659.3l/	
2620	Computers and peripheral equipment		1685.6	1574.0	1718.4	1986.9		186.0	187.7	241.3	275.9		..l/	
2630	Communication equipment		1019.8	1448.5	1439.1	1443.1		247.5	329.1	315.1	377.6		..l/	
2640	Consumer electronics		27.6	10.5	13.8	12.2		...	...	4.0	4.4		..l/	
265	Measuring,testing equipment; watches, etc.		1931.7	2082.6	2738.1	2263.9	j/	680.6	707.6	722.6	804.0		...l/	
2651	Measuring/testing/navigating equipment,etc.		1929.9	2080.4	2734.6	2262.6	j/	680.6	707.6	722.6	804.0		...	
2652	Watches and clocks		1.8	2.2	3.5	1.3							...	
2660	Irradiation/electromedical equipment,etc.		89.5	33.5	45.3	51.8		31.3	12.3	6.0	16.5		..l/	
2670	Optical instruments and photographic equipment		62.5	67.1	78.8	88.4		21.7	32.6	41.0	41.1		..l/	
2680	Magnetic and optical media		0.6	0.5	-	-		...	...	...	-		..l/	
2710	Electric motors,generators,transformers,etc.		3446.1	3166.7	3445.7	3557.5		754.1	708.6	793.2	831.1		3826.0k/	
2720	Batteries and accumulators		350.2	339.2	367.7	413.5		...	...	...	...		..k/	
273	Wiring and wiring devices		3695.7	4306.5	5149.5	3809.2		421.9	495.6	623.5	...		..k/	
2731	Fibre optic cables		5.4	3.9	4.4	6.8		...	...	...	...			
2732	Other electronic and electric wires and cables		3369.9	3946.6	4809.4	3431.9		...	414.0	541.3	381.2		...	
2733	Wiring devices		320.4	356.0	335.7	370.5		70.2	...	...	93.8		..k/	
2740	Electric lighting equipment		459.2	475.8	501.8	525.1		...	...	166.3	192.8		..k/	
2750	Domestic appliances		2990.2	3500.2	4270.8	4831.2		589.6	673.8	830.0	990.9		..k/	
2790	Other electrical equipment		1846.3	2329.0	2693.0	4747.7		417.4	556.7	540.2	842.8		..k/	
281	General-purpose machinery		8216.9	9315.6	10273.6	11208.3		2443.9	2988.6	2775.4	3108.3		32482.2m/	
2811	Engines/turbines,excl.aircraft,vehicle engines		3382.1	3485.3	2191.9	2274.0		...	...	...	...		...	
2812	Fluid power equipment		67.0	65.5	61.8	72.9		...	...	...	...		...	
2813	Other pumps, compressors, taps and valves		539.5	758.7	998.4	1201.4		159.0	209.1	235.5	316.3		...	
2814	Bearings, gears, gearing and driving elements		1411.0	1851.5	3918.4	4330.8		544.2	639.2	1213.3	1300.2		...	
2815	Ovens, furnaces and furnace burners		150.1	187.4	123.7	129.5		64.1	59.5	49.0	58.2		...	
2816	Lifting and handling equipment		836.4	1084.5	894.0	1043.5		264.1	298.4	235.1	269.7		...	
2817	Office machinery, excl.computers,etc.		104.6	122.3	130.2	102.0		...	...	...	...		...	
2818	Power-driven hand tools		492.9	497.9	431.7	510.1		...	...	...	...		...	
2819	Other general-purpose machinery		1233.3	1262.5	1523.5	1544.1		272.6	294.1	312.6	322.6		...	
282	Special-purpose machinery		4051.3	4424.3	4352.0	4194.2		1498.8	863.0	868.2	1419.4		...m/	
2821	Agricultural and forestry machinery		409.6	437.5	428.6	459.5		125.6	133.0	128.8	100.0		...	
2822	Metal-forming machinery and machine tools		625.4	694.6	703.2	714.9		276.0	309.5	301.3	319.1		...	

Code	Industry		(1)	(2)	(3)	(4)	(5)	(6)	(7)	(8)	(9)
2823	Machinery for metallurgy		228.5	288.8	255.1	182.3	86.1	102.5	81.5	52.5	…
2824	Mining, quarrying and construction machinery		150.3	136.4	129.1	120.9	37.3	39.5	40.0	39.0	…
2825	Food/beverage/tobacco processing machinery		62.4	59.2	68.0	81.2	30.2	33.4	34.4	40.4	…
2826	Textile/apparel/leather production machinery		707.2	669.8	841.7	986.1	283.5	…	…	…	…
2829	Other special-purpose machinery		1867.9	2138.0	1926.3	1649.3	660.1	…	…	…	…
2910	Motor vehicles		23364.0	22970.7	23040.6	24560.8	…	…	…	…	21861.3n/
2920	Automobile bodies, trailers and semi-trailers		273.6	495.2	581.9	708.9	…	…	…	…	…n/
2930	Parts and accessories for motor vehicles		31534.8	35119.9	44884.7	49743.7	7129.3	8439.2	9833.2	12266.6	…n/
301	Building of ships and boats		3762.1	3195.3	4585.7	3960.1	1050.2	885.7	1050.0	1045.4	331.4p/
3011	Building of ships and floating structures		3733.8	3163.0	4540.7	3910.3	1046.4	875.0	1043.5	1033.3	…
3012	Building of pleasure and sporting boats		28.3	32.3	45.0	49.8	3.8	10.7	6.5	12.1	…
3020	Railway locomotives and rolling stock		1348.5	1786.7	1406.0	1518.3	407.8	557.4	366.7	397.1	…p/
3030	Air and spacecraft and related machinery	q/	818.7	908.3	1034.3	1162.0	379.5	466.6	478.2	482.0	…p/
3040	Military fighting vehicles		…	…	…	…	…	…	…	…	…p/
309	Transport equipment n.e.c.	q/	621.0	695.3	790.4	893.4	73.2	76.9	100.1	110.9	…p/
3091	Motorcycles		0.1	0.2	0.1	0.3	73.2r/	…	…	…	…
3092	Bicycles and invalid carriages		620.3	656.3	786.6	892.6	…r/	76.1	99.1	110.6	…
3099	Other transport equipment n.e.c.		0.6	38.8	3.7	0.5	…r/	…r/	…	…	…
3100	Furniture		7316.1	8095.7	8857.1	9667.6	2005.3	2266.4	2130.2	2551.2	1802.5
321	Jewellery, bijouterie and related articles	t/	142.0	180.5	263.5	300.5	68.6	78.9	91.2	106.9	0.1s/
3211	Jewellery and related articles	t/	123.4	158.4	243.7	273.8	68.6	78.9	91.2	106.9	…
3212	Imitation jewellery and related articles		18.6	22.1	19.8	26.7	…	…	…	…	…
3220	Musical instruments		55.4	62.1	72.3	74.6	24.5	30.7	33.9	36.6	…s/
3230	Sports goods		192.0	232.1	245.8	281.7	72.2	78.9	87.2	112.1	…s/
3240	Games and toys		125.4	146.9	166.6	175.0	45.7	47.9	55.4	64.3	…s/
3250	Medical and dental instruments and supplies		396.5	661.6	828.4	821.0	160.4	245.1	331.1	376.3	…s/
3290	Other manufacturing n.e.c.		649.3	705.7	606.0	668.1	211.4	228.3	206.9	203.7	…s/
331	Repair of fabricated metal products/machinery		2364.8	2625.4	2796.6	2790.7	953.5	1202.4	1242.9	1254.4	573.0u/
3311	Repair of fabricated metal products		68.7	139.0	152.2	105.3	25.7	41.2	51.4	44.3	…
3312	Repair of machinery		714.3	802.3	829.5	820.6	227.4	347.8	343.8	324.3	…
3313	Repair of electronic and optical equipment		65.7	94.7	102.2	137.2	23.7	28.6	40.0	42.8	…
3314	Repair of electrical equipment		207.5	209.8	208.9	201.7	96.4	92.5	95.3	98.6	…
3315	Repair of transport equip., excl. motor vehicles		1253.9	1305.8	1430.4	1450.6	563.3	664.5	664.5	716.3	…
3319	Repair of other equipment		54.7	73.8	73.4	75.3	17.0	27.8	…	28.1	…
3320	Installation of industrial machinery/equipment		1764.9	1603.6	1088.9	797.5	274.2	251.5	239.6	239.1	…u/
C	Total manufacturing	v/	290226.1	306144.7	326104.6	337541.2	61700.7	70489.7	68270.0	76085.3	68026.8

a/ 1061 includes 1062.
b/ 1610 includes 162.
c/ 2011 includes 2012 and 2013.
d/ 221 includes 2220.
e/ 2310 includes 239.
f/ 2431 includes 2432.
g/ 251 includes 2520 and 259.
h/ 2599 includes 2520.
i/ 2610 includes 2620, 2630, 2640, 265, 2660, 2670 and 2680.
j/ 2651 includes 2652.

k/ 2710 includes 2720, 273, 2740, 2750 and 2790.
m/ 281 includes 282.
n/ 2910 includes 2920 and 2930.
p/ 301 includes 3020, 3030, 3040 and 309.
q/ 3020 includes 3040.
r/ 3091 includes 3092 and 3099.
s/ 321 includes 3220, 3230, 3240, 3250 and 3290.
t/ 3211 includes 3212.
u/ 331 includes 3320.
v/ Sum of available data.

Romania

Index numbers of industrial production

ISIC Revision 4

(2010=100)

ISIC	Industry	Note	2005	2006	2007	2008	2009	2010	2011	2012	2013	2014	2015	2016
10	Food products		80	84	103	108	107	100	104	105	112	117	123	126
11	Beverages		83	97	102	114	106	100	97	99	94	91	100	103
12	Tobacco products		88	80	101	124	123	100	132	143	131	156	187	187
13	Textiles		128	122	129	118	92	100	111	113	125	127	116	118
14	Wearing apparel		189	191	168	134	100	100	102	100	107	108	100	94
15	Leather and related products		147	150	141	122	96	100	104	97	101	106	101	95
16	Wood products, excluding furniture		61	75	82	75	89	100	112	122	137	133	130	129
17	Paper and paper products		98	110	117	110	99	100	118	116	129	164	178	193
18	Printing and reproduction of recorded media		86	88	83	105	110	100	92	88	82	91	88	93
19	Coke and refined petroleum products		136	131	129	128	113	100	100	94	99	113	113	122
20	Chemicals and chemical products		89	93	94	109	91	100	107	103	111	114	108	104
21	Pharmaceuticals, medicinal chemicals, etc.		89	87	96	112	93	100	130	130	136	134	132	125
22	Rubber and plastics products		56	71	90	100	93	100	119	119	127	134	145	140
23	Other non-metallic mineral products		92	105	135	152	105	100	124	116	129	135	168	182
24	Basic metals		141	143	145	123	79	100	108	100	92	96	100	98
25	Fabricated metal products, except machinery		74	93	108	125	109	100	109	104	108	109	119	119
26	Computer, electronic and optical products		97	130	127	133	100	100	88	98	101	155	160	156
27	Electrical equipment		42	56	59	66	76	100	115	115	138	157	170	193
28	Machinery and equipment n.e.c.		99	105	134	129	106	100	119	130	146	151	132	128
29	Motor vehicles, trailers and semi-trailers		49	56	68	70	77	100	114	116	132	137	151	165
30	Other transport equipment		142	160	182	184	152	100	94	115	135	161	158	148
31	Furniture		105	119	123	119	102	100	99	103	114	117	126	134
32	Other manufacturing		151	160	174	126	112	100	112	122	125	146	129	119
33	Repair and installation of machinery/equipment		100	104	112	92	93	100	113	138	152	148	139	116
C	Total manufacturing		78	87	98	101	94	100	108	110	121	130	134	138

Russian Federation

Supplier of information:
Federal State Statistics Service (Rosstat), Moscow.

Basic source of data:
Survey on registered enterprises; administrative sources.

Major deviations from ISIC (Revision 3):
Data originally classified according to the national classification of economic activities (OKVED) were harmonized with ISIC (Revision 3).

Reference period:
Calendar year.

Scope:
All registered enterprises.

Method of data collection:
Mail and e-mail questionnaires.

Type of enumeration:
Complete enumeration for large and medium enterprises; sample survey for small enterprises.

Adjusted for non-response:
No.

Concepts and definitions of variables:
Wages and salaries was computed by UNIDO from reported monthly average wages and salaries per employee.
Output includes revenue from non-industrial activities.
Value added includes cost of non-industrial activities.

Related national publications:
Monthly reports "Social and economic situation in Russia", published by Rosstat, Moscow.

Russian Federation

ISIC	Industry	Number of enterprises (number)					Number of employees (thousands)					Wages and salaries paid to employees (millions of Russian Roubles)				
	ISIC Revision 3	Note	2013	2014	2015	2016	Note	2013	2014	2015	2016	Note	2013	2014	2015	2016
151	Processed meat,fish,fruit,vegetables,fats		8380	8471	8314	9697		359.2	358.3	361.4	369.1		96283	103880	113336	124277
1511	Processing/preserving of meat		4436	4514	4420	5099		236.2	239.2	244.8	252.3		59594	65854	71370	79022
1512	Processing/preserving of fish		1937	1999	1902	2199		55.3	50.8	49.9	48.8		18000	18005	22075	24581
1513	Processing/preserving of fruit & vegetables		1223	1200	1229	1533		31.0	30.3	27.2	30.1		8467	8701	7755	8233
1514	Vegetable and animal oils and fats		784	758	763	866		36.8	37.9	39.4	37.9		10222	11318	12134	12439
1520	Dairy products		2627	2630	2786	3098		157.1	152.2	158.0	154.0		40940	44341	49055	51298
153	Grain mill products; starches; animal feeds		2657	2576	2424	2912		85.1	83.8	83.2	82.8		22546	24538	26920	28028
1531	Grain mill products		1677	1618	1490	1663		45.8	44.7	44.1	44.3		10148	10815	11607	12072
1532	Starches and starch products		70	68	94	109		5.5	5.4	4.7	4.6		1243	1354	1259	1774
1533	Prepared animal feeds		910	890	840	1140		33.8	33.6	34.5	33.9		10914	12062	13733	14182
154	Other food products		9867	10174	10678	12017		466.0	453.6	443.8	433.1		121529	127183	131913	138739
1541	Bakery products		7358	7593	7570	8523		291.2	234.8	225.7	214.6		64881	56758	57314	57676
1542	Sugar		181	181	150	161		39.1	36.1	37.7	37.7		8589	9206	10260	11441
1543	Cocoa, chocolate and sugar confectionery		668	683	667	742		73.6	72.5	69.5	68.3		26567	26779	26805	28073
1544	Macaroni, noodles & similar products		267	269	254	283		17.0	16.4	13.9	13.2		4813	5193	5080	5248
1549	Other food products n.e.c.		1393	1447	2037	2308		19.4	21.1	20.9	24.4		5735	6072	6253	8229
155	Beverages		3577	3762	3903	4655		140.0	133.9	130.7	127.6		51533	50623	51512	54721
1551	Distilling, rectifying & blending of spirits		486	499	334	378		43.3	41.1	38.0	34.6		11986	11607	11483	11758
1552	Wines		217	238	223	259		11.9	12.4	15.0	15.8		3120	3485	4121	4857
1553	Malt liquors and malt		603	631	1008	1201		42.1	39.2	39.1	40.9		19206	18224	19049	22177
1554	Soft drinks; mineral waters		2271	2395	2338	2817		42.6	41.2	38.5	36.2		17222	17306	16860	15929
1600	Tobacco products		50	57	56	95		9.1	8.7	8.3	7.7		7664	7740	8369	8469
171	Spinning, weaving and finishing of textiles		848	829	760	1045		42.1	37.4	36.1	35.5		7398	7643	7984	8594
1711	Textile fibre preparation; textile weaving		649	626	538	746		37.8	33.1	30.9	30.2		6742	6899	6974	7310
1712	Finishing of textiles		199	203	222	299		4.4	4.3	5.1	5.3		656	743	1134	1283
172	Other textiles		3150	3309	3515	4147		43.7	41.9	42.3	42.0		9326	9627	10901	11700
1721	Made-up textile articles, except apparel		2093	2244	2375	2813		25.6	25.6	26.9	26.3		4052	4201	5105	6185
1722	Carpets and rugs		54	55	64	73		1.0	1.1	1.3	1.1		221	240	271	238
1723	Cordage, rope, twine and netting		165	166	176	206		4.6	3.1	2.6	2.2		880	707	747	778
1729	Other textiles n.e.c.		838	844	900	1055		12.5	12.1	12.2	12.4		2470	2511	2916	3202
1730	Knitted and crocheted fabrics and articles		798	812	766	890		16.7	14.3	13.5	12.8		2824	2606	2541	2657
1810	Wearing apparel, except fur apparel		7808	7889	8013	9537		184.2	175.3	161.6	153.3		27825	27896	27547	27359
1820	Dressing & dyeing of fur; processing of fur		369	350	336	412		5.7	4.6	4.2	3.5		892	795	697	667
191	Tanning, dressing and processing of leather		516	492	492	578		14.3	13.5	13.0	12.2		2601	2846	3088	3190
1911	Tanning and dressing of leather		86	82	81	102		5.8	5.9	5.9	5.8		1217	1463	1691	1846
1912	Luggage, handbags, etc.; saddlery & harness		430	410	411	476		8.5	7.7	7.1	6.4		1384	1383	1397	1345
1920	Footwear		845	821	798	949		35.9	33.8	31.4	31.3		6267	6328	6392	7169
2010	Sawmilling and planing of wood		9480	9214	9059	10130		106.4	97.7	93.1	90.4		18613	19405	20696	22729
202	Products of wood, cork, straw, etc.		7593	7538	7605	9121		138.8	132.3	127.4	127.3		31251	32021	33189	35727
2021	Veneer sheets, plywood, particle board, etc.		597	616	637	760		58.8	57.0	57.6	59.7		16607	17757	19511	21617
2022	Builders' carpentry and joinery		5230	5129	5074	6105		64.9	61.5	56.2	53.1		12561	12202	11236	11248
2023	Wooden containers		748	750	805	983		8.4	7.5	7.3	8.1		1228	1204	1376	1770
2029	Other wood products; articles of cork/straw		1018	1043	1089	1273		6.7	6.4	6.3	6.4		855	857	1065	1093
210	Paper and paper products		2533	2594	2590	2963		108.5	104.6	102.6	105.1		35788	37495	40593	45443
2101	Pulp, paper and paperboard		374	367	326	388		50.9	47.4	45.3	45.6		18674	19074	20254	22955
2102	Corrugated paper and paperboard		1028	1062	1087	1235		33.9	33.8	34.0	34.2		9459	10251	11236	12260
2109	Other articles of paper and paperboard		1131	1165	1177	1340		23.7	23.5	23.2	25.3		6621	7400	7702	10228
221	Publishing		11508	10928	10342	12510		107.2	102.6	96.8	91.2		44278	42567	37903	36952
2211	Publishing of books and other publications		3487	3284	3398	4182		15.0	11.2	13.1	13.0		10014	7416	7805	5868
2212	Publishing of newspapers, journals, etc.		5621	5369	4938	5860		89.3	87.0	79.1	73.5		32848	33512	28399	28953
2213	Publishing of recorded media		178	167	230	282		0.2	0.2	1.0	1.4		102	106	257	300
2219	Other publishing		2222	2108	1776	2186		2.7	4.2	3.5	3.3		1314	1533	1442	1832

Code	Description												
222	Printing and related service activities	10034	9981	10649	12467	102.6	93.8	90.4	89.7	29777	27179	28299	28665
2221	Printing	7996	7945	8651	10120	96.1	88.1	85.0	83.9	27861	25517	26518	26808
2222	Service activities related to printing	2038	2036	1998	2347	6.5	5.7	5.4	5.9	1916	1662	1782	1857
2230	Reproduction of recorded media	190	156	127	177	0.7	0.6	0.4	0.7	212	177	201	387
2310	Coke oven products												
2320	Refined petroleum products	18	13	11	21	14.4	13.8	13.4	12.5	6084	6213	6493	6594
2330	Processing of nuclear fuel	760	733	704	863	99.0	105.2	108.6	110.8	82061	101568	113024	123957
241	Basic chemicals	2285	2390	2419	2996	225.9	217.7	221.1	222.4	89014	96269	109396	118346
2411	Basic chemicals, except fertilizers	1445	1522	1540	1914	103.6	105.1	107.3	110.4	38607	44181	48517	53160
2412	Fertilizers and nitrogen compounds	288	302	290	363	57.6	53.5	55.0	52.8	25795	26753	30343	33782
2413	Plastics in primary forms; synthetic rubber	552	565	589	719	64.7	59.1	61.6	62.4	25409	26867	30536	33230
242	Other chemicals	4272	4400	4756	5971	156.6	155.1	154.7	165.4	61056	66768	72104	84594
2421	Pesticides and other agro-chemical products	101	105	145	173	1.9	2.3	2.8	3.2	659	920	1461	1826
2422	Paints, varnishes, printing ink and mastics	1066	1062	1087	1265	21.9	21.4	21.3	21.2	6560	7320	8155	8779
2423	Pharmaceuticals, medicinal chemicals, etc.	1101	1097	1106	1409	70.2	69.6	71.0	79.0	29529	32628	36072	44180
2424	Soap, cleaning & cosmetic preparations	1013	1077	1215	1657	31.1	32.5	32.5	33.1	13006	14662	15183	16647
2429	Other chemical products n.e.c.	991	1059	1203	1467	31.4	29.3	27.1	29.0	11303	11238	11234	13163
2430	Man-made fibres	93	93	98	122	7.8	7.9	7.7	8.5	2173	2378	2542	3053
251	Rubber products	1256	1334	1363	1694	57.8	53.7	51.4	50.8	16286	16699	17392	18714
2511	Rubber tyres and tubes	224	239	226	280	25.8	23.1	22.1	23.1	8238	8532	9192	10412
2519	Other rubber products	1032	1095	1137	1414	31.8	30.5	29.3	27.7	7993	8125	8221	8303
2520	Plastic products	11117	11309	11353	12906	189.5	184.8	181.8	185.1	47817	49913	52584	59306
2610	Glass and glass products	1690	1734	1689	1993	62.5	58.2	54.8	52.2	18764	18570	19256	19127
269	Non-metallic mineral products n.e.c.	14618	15443	15710	17974	488.5	541.1	512.1	472.1	149573	178046	171468	163774
2691	Pottery, china and earthenware	429	430	394	482	18.7	17.5	16.4	16.1	5168	5348	5746	6324
2692	Refractory ceramic products	222	217	232	286	22.4	20.1	18.3	18.0	6795	6403	6778	7074
2693	Struct.non-refractory clay; ceramic products	1641	1664	1562	1674	73.6	72.4	68.7	58.9	19410	20994	20625	18333
2694	Cement, lime and plaster	386	391	353	455	48.8	48.8	47.1	44.2	17446	17998	18214	18032
2695	Articles of concrete, cement and plaster	8832	9544	9782	11131	259.5	260.9	243.6	220.1	80006	86479	78620	70683
2696	Cutting, shaping & finishing of stone	1442	1509	1669	1990	10.8	11.0	11.2	10.8	2410	2752	3205	2914
2699	Other non-metallic mineral products n.e.c.	1666	1688	1718	1956	54.7	52.2	52.0	51.9	16748	17169	17419	21285
2710	Basic iron and steel	1298	1300	1173	1497	316.9	324.1	296.8	286.7	128985	139979	135954	138599
2720	Basic precious and non-ferrous metals	522	528	533	662	131.7	125.3	123.3	122.6	60772	62675	68639	76082
273	Casting of metals	451	473	547	557	49.2	45.0	42.6	40.1	13859	13451	13442	13726
2731	Casting of iron and steel	323	338	390	395	44.6	40.4	37.7	35.5	12256	11688	11472	11633
2732	Casting of non-ferrous metals	128	135	157	162								
281	Struct.metal products;tanks;steam generators	12293	12833	13153	15800	241.3	232.4	215.9	211.8	68965	70149	70073	72355
2811	Structural metal products	10720	11242	11564	13932	183.1	177.2	162.5	158.7	49284	50193	49013	49995
2812	Tanks, reservoirs and containers of metal	1094	1115	1112	1356	29.8	27.2	25.7	26.4	8275	7869	8359	8510
2813	Steam generators	479	476	477	512	29.8	28.0	27.6	26.6	11937	12086	13322	13849
289	Other metal products; metal working services	10930	11487	12908	14741	252.0	246.1	247.6	249.7	66150	69941	79415	84863
2891	Metal forging/pressing/stamping/roll-forming	1008	1034	1084	1278	20.9	17.2	16.5	16.3	5530	4912	5293	5552
2892	Treatment & coating of metals	4954	5360	6188	7183	106.0	109.8	115.7	117.2	29531	33153	40200	42341
2893	Cutlery, hand tools and general hardware	698	672	741	821	34.8	31.9	30.8	30.2	8399	8170	8465	9346
2899	Other fabricated metal products n.e.c.	4270	4421	4895	5459	90.3	87.3	84.5	86.0	22690	23706	25457	27624
291	General purpose machinery	16745	16901	18517	20981	477.6	470.9	458.6	436.1	173716	181802	186981	194215
2911	Engines & turbines (not for transport equipment)	867	840	805	928	42.4	42.7	43.6	44.3	18625	23643	23982	24659
2912	Pumps, compressors, taps and valves	2103	2065	2117	2426	106.0	104.4	98.4	100.1	35585	38145	38572	43567
2913	Bearings, gears, gearing & driving elements	321	311	273	314	25.7	23.5	21.2	21.5	7149	6648	6758	6906
2914	Ovens, furnaces and furnace burners	366	377	426	475	17.0	17.7	17.5	15.4	4151	4990	4807	4595
2915	Lifting and handling equipment	3557	3608	4211	4768	73.5	70.8	69.0	62.0	24201	24704	24663	24304
2919	Other general purpose machinery	9531	9701	10685	12070	165.9	159.0	156.2	145.0	68796	66339	69381	71738
292	Special purpose machinery	6658	6518	6712	7613	285.6	256.8	238.3	225.8	86120	83505	83359	88532
2921	Agricultural and forestry machinery	1376	1305	1224	1349	45.1	39.0	38.1	37.3	10430	10020	10855	12763
2922	Machine tools	1351	1333	1315	1666	30.1	26.8	26.4	23.0	7616	7364	7518	7184
2923	Machinery for metallurgy	155	152	174	198	44.2	40.5	32.9	30.9	15253	14598	13212	13361
2924	Machinery for mining & construction	646	645	790	861	85.8	75.9	68.7	62.3	26218	24136	23100	23563
2925	Food/beverage/tobacco processing machinery	436	428	523	576	11.7	10.6	11.2	10.9	3121	3114	3700	3659
2926	Machinery for textile, apparel and leather	119	117	87	95	1.9	1.8	1.9	1.6	337	362	400	421
2927	Weapons and ammunition												
2929	Other special purpose machinery	2575	2538	2598	2868	65.4	60.9	58.1	58.9	22791	23512	24129	27265

continued

Russian Federation

ISIC	Industry	Note	Number of enterprises (number) 2013	2014	2015	2016	Note	Number of employees (thousands) 2013	2014	2015	2016	Note	Wages and salaries paid to employees (millions of Russian Roubles) 2013	2014	2015	2016
2930	Domestic appliances n.e.c.		327	311	333	381		29.6	26.6	24.2	23.9		8710	8676	8710	9174
3000	Office, accounting and computing machinery		1260	1215	1131	1464		20.6	18.9	18.7	18.8		9011	9410	11295	12683
3110	Electric motors, generators and transformers		1843	1794	1834	2053		77.1	74.2	73.5	69.5		26041	27535	29538	29975
3120	Electricity distribution & control apparatus		3006	3166	3539	3853		85.1	90.1	95.3	92.9		27786	32052	36116	37179
3130	Insulated wire and cable		353	363	377	450		35.6	34.1	31.8	31.0		11936	12169	12367	13504
3140	Accumulators, primary cells and batteries		81	81	96	108		11.0	10.5	10.6	10.9		3467	3558	3874	4377
3150	Lighting equipment and electric lamps		635	679	818	1002		16.7	16.4	15.6	16.8		3747	4236	4425	5205
3190	Other electrical equipment n.e.c.		3384	3389	4060	4485		79.4	72.6	69.0	70.5		23104	23786	25329	26669
3210	Electronic valves, tubes, etc.	a/	...	...	...	...	a/	...	...	...	...	a/	...	...	...	...
3220	TV/radio transmitters; line comm. apparatus	a/	...	...	...	...	a/	...	...	...	...	a/	...	...	...	...
3230	TV and radio receivers and associated goods	a/	1185	1229	1517	1715	a/	...	...	...	...	a/	...	...	...	...
331	Medical, measuring, testing appliances, etc.		5020	5263	6922	6840		279.9	278.6	283.8	294.9		106277	117362	134612	152233
3311	Medical, surgical and orthopaedic equipment		2148	2218	2535	3173		46.6	44.4	39.3	37.7		17180	16968	17256	16421
3312	Measuring/testing/navigating appliances,etc.		2398	2586	3869	3096		211.7	214.4	224.3	234.3		80987	92197	107968	124996
3313	Industrial process control equipment		474	459	518	571		5.5	4.7	4.7	5.0		1984	1848	2068	2190
3320	Optical instruments & photographic equipment		318	299	373	390		14.8	13.9	14.0	15.2		5148	5582	6422	7702
3330	Watches and clocks		123	103	113	141		1.3	1.1	1.4	2.7		316	277	457	925
3410	Motor vehicles		550	556	501	588		229.1	213.9	186.1	170.6		86090	86267	77959	76933
3420	Automobile bodies, trailers & semi-trailers		250	264	290	351		18.1	17.2	16.9	16.6		5098	5253	5317	5708
3430	Parts/accessories for automobiles		1265	1192	1250	1424		109.6	105.5	98.9	91.3		28912	30865	31550	32486
351	Building and repairing of ships and boats	a/	...	...	...	...	a/	...	...	...	...	a/	...	...	...	...
3511	Building and repairing of ships	a/	...	...	...	...	a/	...	...	126.6	131.9	a/	...	...	68494	78288
3512	Building/repairing of pleasure/sport. boats	a/	...	...	...	...	a/	...a/	...	...	...		...	...	...	...
3520	Railway/tramway locomotives & rolling stock	a/	792	822	849	954		243.9	224.6	208.4	201.6		89303	86515	81648	84651
3530	Aircraft and spacecraft	a/	...	...	...	...		...a/	...a/	325.1	323.5		...a/	...a/	152728	167160
359	Transport equipment n.e.c.		...	...	...	...		...	...	2.1	2.4		...	...	427	614
3591	Motorcycles		21	27	26	28		1.1	0.8	0.8	0.8		186	183	143	169
3592	Bicycles and invalid carriages		37	42	58	68		0.9	1.2	0.8	0.8		219	278	138	200
3599	Other transport equipment n.e.c.		50	42	55	61		0.7	0.7	0.6	0.7		139	163	145	245
3610	Furniture		11364	11377	11636	13852		155.2	146.0	139.6	131.5		31726	31169	32292	30682
369	Manufacturing n.e.c.		3787	3793	4148	4925		62.7	60.4	58.8	59.8		14745	14829	15529	16888
3691	Jewellery and related articles		1522	1467	1486	1850		26.4	24.8	23.4	23.7		7558	7109	7141	7650
3692	Musical instruments		43	48	46	59		0.5	0.5	0.4	0.3		84	93	87	66
3693	Sports goods		338	352	378	458		3.4	3.4	3.2	3.4		853	963	910	1076
3694	Games and toys		370	368	426	531		7.9	7.8	7.3	6.9		1548	1590	1663	1747
3699	Other manufacturing n.e.c.		1514	1558	1812	2027		24.5	23.9	24.5	25.5		4701	5074	5728	6349
3710	Recycling of metal waste and scrap		3174	3178	3181	3896		42.5	40.9	42.2	40.3		12035	12566	14060	13440
3720	Recycling of non-metal waste and scrap		1834	1847	2039	2545		7.7	8.5	9.0	10.2		1768	1943	2598	2628
D	Total manufacturing		211509	214378	224043	259165		7531.0	7309.6	7159.2	7032.5		2444111	2588566	2741404	2911224

a/ Data suppressed due to confidentiality rules.

Russian Federation

ISIC Revision 3

ISIC	Industry	Note	Output at basic prices (billions of Russian Roubles)				Note	Value added at basic prices (billions of Russian Roubles)				Note	Gross fixed capital formation (billions of Russian Roubles)	
			2013	2014	2015	2016		2013	2014	2015	2016		2015	2016
151	Processed meat,fish,fruit,vegetables,fats		2053.3	2269.5	2437.4	2612.3		371.1	376.2	376.9	480.6		...	...
1511	Processing/preserving of meat		1386.6	1532.0	1569.9	1675.8		209.8	183.7	201.5	257.9		...	...
1512	Processing/preserving of fish		237.2	272.0	275.8	311.7		81.5	95.8	94.5	120.7		...	...
1513	Processing/preserving of fruit & vegetables		145.6	152.8	168.5	160.0		36.6	38.5	39.3	42.4		...	...
1514	Vegetable and animal oils and fats		283.9	312.7	423.1	464.8		43.1	58.2	41.6	59.6		...	...
1520	Dairy products		702.3	818.6	886.9	972.0		169.8	173.3	183.0	194.0		...	...
153	Grain mill products; starches; animal feeds		482.4	542.2	687.7	628.6		115.2	116.1	144.6	105.0		...	...
1531	Grain mill products		...	...	...	...		...	...	...	...		...	...
1532	Starches and starch products		276.4	316.8	452.1	400.9		61.4	65.0	85.6	53.3		...	...
1533	Prepared animal feeds		1205.5	1344.8	1553.4	1807.7		360.9	395.4	430.1	429.4		...	...
154	Other food products		428.5	468.5	537.4	531.0		164.0	177.3	187.5	185.5		...	...
1541	Bakery products		142.9	167.3	228.3	242.6		28.9	47.3	70.3	62.2		...	...
1542	Sugar		...	...	...	...		...	...	...	...		...	...
1543	Cocoa, chocolate and sugar confectionery		...	...	...	...		...	...	...	...		...	...
1544	Macaroni, noodles & similar products		...	...	...	...		...	...	...	...		...	...
1549	Other food products n.e.c.		...	...	...	...		...	...	...	...		...	...
155	Beverages		731.2	742.5	799.0	907.1		286.4	249.7	264.3	312.0		...	...
1551	Distilling, rectifying & blending of spirits		...	...	...	...		...	...	...	...		...	...
1552	Wines		...	...	...	...		...	...	...	...		...	...
1553	Malt liquors and malt		...	...	...	...		...	...	...	...		...	...
1554	Soft drinks; mineral waters		...	...	...	...		...	...	...	...		...	...
1600	Tobacco products		197.2	204.8	270.4	304.6		95.7	90.1	107.7	106.8		...	...
171	Spinning, weaving and finishing of textiles	a/	168.5	177.4	224.0	236.4	a/	46.2	51.1	63.4	64.9		...	...
1711	Textile fibre preparation; textile weaving		...	...	...	...		...	...	...	...		...	...
1712	Finishing of textiles		...	...	...	...		...	...	...	...		...	...
172	Other textiles	a/	...	...	...	...	a/	...	...	...	...		...	...
1721	Made-up textile articles, except apparel		...	...	...	...		...	...	...	...		...	...
1722	Carpets and rugs	a/	...	...	...	...	a/	...	...	...	...		...	...
1723	Cordage, rope, twine and netting		...	...	...	...		...	...	...	...		...	...
1729	Other textiles n.e.c.		...	...	...	...		...	...	...	...		...	...
1730	Knitted and crocheted fabrics and articles		...	...	...	...		...	...	...	...		...	...
1810	Wearing apparel, except fur apparel	b/	188.7	217.5	213.8	223.9	b/	82.8	85.3	86.4	85.4		...	...
1820	Dressing & dyeing of fur; processing of fur	b/	...	...	...	...	b/	...	...	...	...		...	...
191	Tanning, dressing and processing of leather	c/	69.9	71.3	75.3	87.4	c/	26.4	24.7	25.2	32.7		...	...
1911	Tanning and dressing of leather		...	...	...	...		...	...	...	...		...	...
1912	Luggage, handbags, etc.; saddlery & harness		...	...	...	...		...	...	...	...		...	...
1920	Footwear	c/	...	...	...	...	c/	...	...	...	...		...	...
2010	Sawmilling and planing of wood		186.0	219.9	253.7	263.3		65.2	77.7	86.7	90.0		...	...
202	Products of wood, cork, straw, etc.		285.9	303.3	338.2	361.2		87.3	97.8	109.3	112.0		...	...
2021	Veneer sheets, plywood, particle board, etc.		...	...	...	...		...	...	...	...		...	...
2022	Builders' carpentry and joinery		...	...	...	...		...	...	...	...		...	...
2023	Wooden containers		...	...	...	...		...	...	...	...		...	...
2029	Other wood products; articles of cork/straw		...	...	...	...		...	...	...	...		...	...
210	Paper and paper products		522.8	518.1	680.5	766.1		150.4	168.3	230.9	273.0		...	...
2101	Pulp, paper and paperboard		...	...	...	...		...	...	...	...		...	...
2102	Corrugated paper and paperboard		...	...	...	...		...	...	...	...		...	...
2109	Other articles of paper and paperboard		...	...	...	...		...	...	...	...		...	...
221	Publishing		172.0	175.5	192.6	186.7		70.6	67.4	88.2	80.9		...	...
2211	Publishing of books and other publications		...	...	...	...		...	...	...	...		...	...
2212	Publishing of newspapers, journals, etc.		...	...	...	...		...	...	...	...		...	...
2213	Publishing of recorded media		...	...	...	...		...	...	...	...		...	...
2219	Other publishing		...	...	...	...		...	...	...	...		...	...

continued

Russian Federation

ISIC	Industry	Output at basic prices (billions of Russian Roubles) Note	2013	2014	2015	2016	Value added at basic prices (billions of Russian Roubles) Note	2013	2014	2015	2016	Gross fixed capital formation (billions of Russian Roubles) Note	2015	2016
222	Printing and related service activities		189.3	250.1	273.8	285.5		52.1	75.6	80.3	79.6		...	...
2221	Printing		...	...	...	...		...	...	...	...		...	...
2222	Service activities related to printing		...	...	...	...		...	...	...	...		...	...
2230	Reproduction of recorded media		4.4	4.1	4.6	4.6		3.1	3.1	3.5	3.5		...	...
2310	Coke oven products		70.9	74.5	101.1	109.7		13.0	11.1	22.4	18.9		...	...
2320	Refined petroleum products	d/	6476.0	6957.7	7081.4	7131.9		1829.4	1836.7	1570.2	1385.7		...	...
2330	Processing of nuclear fuel		...	...	...	...		...	...	...	...		...	...
241	Basic chemicals		1995.9	2229.6	3090.4	3175.1		589.6	743.4	1156.0	1082.6		...	...
2411	Basic chemicals, except fertilizers		...	...	...	...		...	...	...	...		...	...
2412	Fertilizers and nitrogen compounds		...	...	...	...		...	...	...	...		...	...
2413	Plastics in primary forms; synthetic rubber		...	...	...	...		...	...	...	...		...	...
242	Other chemicals		631.9	689.4	890.2	1030.4		172.8	210.0	312.1	339.1		...	...
2421	Pesticides and other agro-chemical products		...	...	...	...		...	...	...	...		...	...
2422	Paints, varnishes, printing ink and mastics		78.2	93.2	105.7	114.6		17.6	21.8	27.0	24.9		...	...
2423	Pharmaceuticals, medicinal chemicals, etc.		263.5	279.2	366.1	439.1		90.7	114.4	161.6	171.4		...	...
2424	Soap, cleaning & cosmetic preparations		180.0	193.4	303.3	348.0		40.9	49.3	95.3	115.8		...	...
2429	Other chemical products n.e.c.		110.2	123.5	115.1	128.7		23.5	24.5	28.2	27.0		...	...
2430	Man-made fibres		14.8	17.9	21.4	20.5		4.7	7.2	6.0	5.3		...	...
251	Rubber products	e/	713.4	753.3	907.4	978.4	e/	171.0	155.6	194.8	210.1		...	...
2511	Rubber tyres and tubes		...	...	...	...		...	...	...	...		...	...
2519	Other rubber products		...	...	...	...		...	...	...	...		...	...
2520	Plastic products	e/	...	...	...	...	e/	...	...	...	...		...	...
2610	Glass and glass products		165.4	148.2	167.9	194.3		37.6	37.7	44.9	57.4		...	...
269	Non-metallic mineral products n.e.c.		1169.2	1225.6	1246.4	1154.5		355.9	374.8	373.1	361.2		...	...
2691	Pottery, china and earthenware		...	...	...	...		...	...	...	...		...	...
2692	Refractory ceramic products		...	...	...	...		...	...	...	...		...	...
2693	Struct.non-refractory clay; ceramic products		239.5	232.6	208.9	201.2		71.3	69.8	57.9	66.3		...	...
2694	Cement, lime and plaster		...	...	...	...		...	...	...	...		...	...
2695	Articles of concrete, cement and plaster		...	...	...	...		...	...	...	...		...	...
2696	Cutting, shaping & finishing of stone		...	...	...	...		...	...	...	...		...	...
2699	Other non-metallic mineral products n.e.c.		...	...	...	...		...	...	...	...		...	...
2710	Basic iron and steel		2080.1	2352.8	2731.4	2752.8		375.1	549.6	716.8	693.7		...	...
2720	Basic precious and non-ferrous metals		1504.1	1851.0	2333.9	2371.5		552.4	723.9	1001.7	1018.5		...	...
273	Casting of metals		50.0	45.3	51.3	55.6		16.3	15.2	14.8	17.9		...	...
2731	Casting of iron and steel		...	...	...	...		...	...	...	...		...	...
2732	Casting of non-ferrous metals		...	...	...	...		...	...	...	...		...	...
281	Struct.metal products;tanks;steam generators		466.6	500.3	588.9	629.6		124.7	127.0	157.9	163.8		...	...
2811	Structural metal products		...	...	...	...		...	...	...	...		...	...
2812	Tanks, reservoirs and containers of metal		...	...	...	...		...	...	...	...		...	...
2813	Steam generators		...	...	...	...		...	...	...	...		...	...
289	Other metal products; metal working services		445.3	517.8	632.7	628.0		134.0	132.6	166.5	181.4		...	...
2891	Metal forging/pressing/stamping/roll-forming		...	...	...	...		...	...	...	...		...	...
2892	Treatment & coating of metals		...	...	...	...		...	...	...	...		...	...
2893	Cutlery, hand tools and general hardware		...	...	...	...		...	...	...	...		...	...
2899	Other fabricated metal products n.e.c.		...	...	...	...		...	...	...	...		...	...
291	General purpose machinery		925.5	995.2	1069.8	997.1		347.7	357.1	371.6	342.4		...	...
2911	Engines & turbines (not for transport equipment)		...	...	...	...		...	...	...	...		...	...
2912	Pumps, compressors, taps and valves		...	...	...	...		...	...	...	...		...	...
2913	Bearings, gears, gearing & driving elements		...	...	...	...		...	...	...	...		...	...
2914	Ovens, furnaces and furnace burners		...	...	...	...		...	...	...	...		...	...
2915	Lifting and handling equipment		...	...	...	...		...	...	...	...		...	...
2919	Other general purpose machinery		...	...	...	...		...	...	...	...		...	...

Code	Description					Note				
292	Special purpose machinery	465.5	435.7	496.6	515.7		161.5	148.8	178.8	164.7
2921	Agricultural and forestry machinery	…	…	…	…		…	…	…	…
2922	Machine tools	…	…	…	…		…	…	…	…
2923	Machinery for metallurgy	…	…	…	…		…	…	…	…
2924	Machinery for mining & construction	…	…	…	…		…	…	…	…
2925	Food/beverage/tobacco processing machinery	…	…	…	…		…	…	…	…
2926	Machinery for textile, apparel and leather	…	…	…	…		…	…	…	…
2927	Weapons and ammunition	…	…	…	…		…	…	…	…
2929	Other special purpose machinery	…	…	…	…	d/	…	…	…	…
2930	Domestic appliances n.e.c.	132.1	136.1	134.2	140.7		11.1	37.1	35.8	32.6
3000	Office, accounting and computing machinery	76.5	82.9	94.7	96.0		22.6	25.9	30.6	31.8
3110	Electric motors, generators and transformers	…	…	…	…	f/	…	…	…	…
3120	Electricity distribution & control apparatus	295.8	308.9	352.7	354.8	f/	97.7	105.5	120.0	120.2
3130	Insulated wire and cable	160.3	158.5	202.9	203.9		21.6	20.1	30.3	21.8
3140	Accumulators, primary cells and batteries	…	…	…	…	g/	…	…	…	…
3150	Lighting equipment and electric lamps	…	…	…	…	g/	…	…	…	…
3190	Other electrical equipment n.e.c.	215.8	226.2	242.3	262.2	g/	70.2	76.7	81.6	85.6
3210	Electronic valves, tubes, etc.	…	…	…	…	d/	…	…	…	…
3220	TV/radio transmitters; line comm. apparatus	…	…	…	…	d/	…	…	…	…
3230	TV and radio receivers and associated goods	…	…	…	…	d/	…	…	…	…
331	Medical, measuring, testing appliances, etc.	439.8	524.6	692.7	723.0		211.1	248.9	326.2	299.4
3311	Medical, surgical and orthopaedic equipment	…	…	…	…		…	…	…	…
3312	Measuring/testing/navigating appliances,etc.	…	…	…	…		…	…	…	…
3313	Industrial process control equipment	…	…	…	…		…	…	…	…
3320	Optical instruments & photographic equipment	20.0	32.6	36.0	57.4	h/	9.2	14.5	16.0	26.3
3330	Watches and clocks	1750.5	1776.1	1514.8	1779.5	h/	217.2	245.3	200.6	231.2
3410	Motor vehicles	…	…	…	…	i/	…	…	…	…
3420	Automobile bodies, trailers & semi-trailers	…	…	…	…	i/	…	…	…	…
3430	Parts/accessories for automobiles	…	…	…	…		…	…	…	…
351	Building and repairing of ships and boats	…	…	…	…	d/	…	…	…	…
3511	Building and repairing of ships	…	…	…	…	d/	…	…	…	…
3512	Building/repairing of pleasure/sport. boats	…	…	…	…	d/	…	…	…	…
3520	Railway/tramway locomotives & rolling stock	427.6	405.1	420.0	468.5		102.2	108.3	147.0	113.6
3530	Aircraft and spacecraft	…	…	…	…	d/	…	…	…	…
359	Transport equipment n.e.c.	…	…	…	…	d/	…	…	…	…
3591	Motorcycles	…	…	…	…		…	…	…	…
3592	Bicycles and invalid carriages	…	…	…	…		…	…	…	…
3599	Other transport equipment n.e.c.	…	…	…	…		…	…	…	…
3610	Furniture	278.0	304.1	332.9	288.9		79.5	85.7	110.8	86.3
369	Manufacturing n.e.c.	215.6	237.8	196.6	184.1		43.6	64.5	52.2	39.3
3691	Jewellery and related articles	159.5	170.4	124.6	115.4		28.4	46.4	31.6	20.1
3692	Musical instruments	…	…	…	…		…	…	…	…
3693	Sports goods	…	…	…	…		…	…	…	…
3694	Games and toys	…	…	…	…		…	…	…	…
3699	Other manufacturing n.e.c.	…	…	…	…		…	…	…	…
3710	Recycling of metal waste and scrap	253.6	305.3	375.9	275.3		54.8	79.0	83.3	48.7
3720	Recycling of non-metal waste and scrap	13.9	27.2	32.2	24.9		4.8	9.7	12.9	8.7
D	Total manufacturing	29881.7	32703.7	36772.7	38342.5		8279.4	9184.5	10546.9	10422.7

a/ 171 includes 172 and 1730.
b/ 1810 includes 1820.
c/ 191 includes 1920.
d/ Data suppressed due to confidentiality rules.
e/ 251 includes 2520.
f/ 3120 includes 3110.
g/ 3190 includes 3140 and 3150.
h/ 3320 includes 3330.
i/ 3410 includes 3420.

Russian Federation

ISIC Revision 3

Index numbers of industrial production (2010=100)

ISIC	Industry	Note	2005	2006	2007	2008	2009	2010	2011	2012	2013	2014	2015	2016
15	Food and beverages	a/	82	88	95	97	97	100	104	108	109	112	114	116
16	Tobacco products	a/	...	...	...	...	...	...	...	...	...	...	...	...
17	Textiles	b/	104	116	116	110	92	100	101	102	106	103	91	96
18	Wearing apparel, fur	b/	...	...	...	...	...	...	...	...	...	...	...	...
19	Leather, leather products and footwear		68	83	85	85	83	100	106	104	99	96	85	90
20	Wood products (excl. furniture)		103	106	115	115	88	100	110	106	114	108	105	108
21	Paper and paper products	c/	100	106	115	115	97	100	107	113	107	107	100	101
22	Printing and publishing	c/	...	...	...	...	...	...	...	...	...	...	...	...
23	Coke,refined petroleum products,nuclear fuel		84	90	92	95	94	100	104	107	109	116	116	113
24	Chemicals and chemical products		90	94	100	96	90	100	110	114	120	120	128	135
25	Rubber and plastics products		49	60	75	92	80	100	111	126	133	143	138	145
26	Non-metallic mineral products		109	124	135	131	87	100	107	119	117	119	109	102
27	Basic metals	d/	95	104	109	106	89	100	107	112	112	113	105	103
28	Fabricated metal products	d/	...	...	...	...	...	...	...	...	...	...	...	...
29	Machinery and equipment n.e.c.		92	103	131	130	87	100	111	114	110	102	90	94
30	Office, accounting and computing machinery	e/	104	120	133	123	84	100	112	119	118	117	108	107
31	Electrical machinery and apparatus	e/	...	...	...	...	...	...	...	...	...	...	...	...
32	Radio,television and communication equipment	e/	...	...	...	...	...	...	...	...	...	...	...	...
33	Medical, precision and optical instruments	e/	...	...	...	...	...	...	...	...	...	...	...	...
34	Motor vehicles, trailers, semi-trailers	f/	101	106	114	115	79	100	117	129	132	143	131	127
35	Other transport equipment	f/	...	...	...	...	...	...	...	...	...	...	...	...
36	Furniture; manufacturing n.e.c.		90	99	103	102	83	100	105	108	103	106	99	93
37	Recycling		...	...	...	...	...	...	...	...	...	...	...	...
D	Total manufacturing		89	96	106	107	90	100	108	114	114	116	110	110

a/ 15 includes 16.
b/ 17 includes 18.
c/ 21 includes 22.
d/ 27 includes 28.
e/ 30 includes 31, 32 and 33.
f/ 34 includes 35.

Saudi Arabia

Supplier of information:
General Authority for Statistics, Riyadh.

Basic source of data:
Annual survey.

Major deviations from ISIC (Revision 4):
None reported.

Reference period:
Calendar year.

Scope:
All establishments.

Method of data collection:
Direct interview in the field and online survey.

Type of enumeration:
Sample survey.

Adjusted for non-response:
Yes.

Concepts and definitions of variables:
Wages and salaries includes employers' contributions (in respect of their employees) paid to social security, pension and insurance schemes as well as the benefits received by employees under these schemes and severance and termination pay; it excludes housing and family allowances paid directly by the employer.
Output excludes value of fixed assets produced by the unit for its own use, net change between the beginning and end of the year in the value of stocks of finished goods as well as the value of work in process and stocks and goods to be shipped in the same condition as received.

Related national publications:
Annual Economic Establishments Survey, published by the General Authority for Statistics, Riyadh.

Saudi Arabia

ISIC Revision 4

ISIC	Industry	Number of establishments (number)				Note	Number of employees (number)				Note	Wages and salaries paid to employees (millions of Saudi Riyals)				Note
		2013	2014	2015	2016		2013	2014	2015	2016		2013	2014	2015	2016	
1010	Processing/preserving of meat	640	656	665	687		6895	7624	8134	8258		272.1	307.5	335.9	346.2	
1020	Processing/preserving of fish, etc.	33	34	35	36		363	401	441	438		14.3	16.2	18.2	18.4	
1030	Processing/preserving of fruit,vegetables	520	533	542	559		7415	8197	8476	8803		292.6	330.7	350.1	368.0	
1040	Vegetable and animal oils and fats	123	126	131	133		1154	1275	1330	1373		45.5	51.4	54.9	57.4	
1050	Dairy products	253	259	266	272		21941	24253	26061	26325		865.7	978.4	1076.4	1104.2	
106	Grain mill products,starches and starch products	...					...					...				
1061	Grain mill products	1190	1219	1230	1276		4054	4481	4719	4837		160.0	180.8	194.9	202.5	
1062	Starches and starch products	23	23	24	25		88	97	103	105		3.5	3.9	4.3	4.4	
107	Other food products	...					...					...				
1071	Bakery products	6992	7166	7183	7487		37516	41470	43401	44685		1480.2	1672.9	1792.5	1869.9	
1072	Sugar	30	31	32	33		832	920	955	989		32.8	37.1	39.4	41.4	
1073	Cocoa, chocolate and sugar confectionery	841	862	877	904		9157	10122	11303	11107		361.3	408.3	466.8	467.5	
1074	Macaroni, noodles, couscous, etc.	71	73	75	77		1842	2036	2088	2182		72.7	82.1	86.2	91.1	
1075	Prepared meals and dishes	3	3	3	3		190	210	231	230		7.5	8.5	9.5	9.6	
1079	Other food products n.e.c.	225	230	241	243		1505	1664	1697	1780		59.4	67.1	70.1	74.3	
1080	Prepared animal feeds	65	66	68	70		780	862	891	926		30.8	34.8	36.8	38.7	
110	Beverages	...					...					...				
1101	Distilling, rectifying and blending of spirits	...					...					...				
1102	Wines	...					...					...				
1103	Malt liquors and malt	...					...					...				
1104	Soft drinks,mineral waters,other bottled waters	888	935	963	1011		23521	26650	28774	29184		1070.7	1241.6	1329.8	1351.9	
1200	Tobacco products	66	75	75	80		177	205	220	225		3.8	4.6	5.0	5.1	
131	Spinning, weaving and finishing of textiles	...					...					...				
1311	Preparation and spinning of textile fibres	19	20	21	21		782	931	1015	1021		20.2	25.0	27.7	28.5	
1312	Weaving of textiles	34	34	34	36		220	262	321	298		5.7	7.0	8.8	8.4	
1313	Finishing of textiles	4	5	5	5		32	38	43	42		0.8	1.0	1.2	1.2	
139	Other textiles	...					...					...				
1391	Knitted and crocheted fabrics	7	7	8	8		17	21	26	24		0.4	0.6	0.7	0.7	
1392	Made-up textile articles, except apparel	2037	2091	2109	2194		7540	8977	9717	9823		195.0	241.2	265.0	273.6	
1393	Carpets and rugs	68	70	73	74		8374	9970	10675	10876		216.6	267.9	291.2	302.6	
1394	Cordage, rope, twine and netting	15	15	16	16		153	182	198	200		4.0	4.9	5.4	5.6	
1399	Other textiles n.e.c.	16	16	16	17		196	233	257	256		5.1	6.3	7.0	7.2	
1410	Wearing apparel, except fur apparel	30648	31263	31452	32629		67707	75819	80754	82675		1200.0	1407.8	1522.2	1537.8	
1420	Articles of fur	5	6	7	6		64	72	80	79		1.1	1.3	1.5	1.5	
1430	Knitted and crocheted apparel	14	14	15	15		70	77	91	87		1.2	1.4	1.7	1.6	
151	Leather;luggage,handbags,saddlery,harness;fur	...					...					...				
1511	Tanning/dressing of leather; dressing of fur	28	32	33	34		1275	1443	1539	1547		31.6	37.4	40.4	40.9	
1512	Luggage,handbags,etc.;saddlery/harness	5	5	5	6		46	49	55	54		1.1	1.3	1.4	1.4	
1520	Footwear	83	94	96	101		493	556	598	598		12.2	14.4	15.7	15.8	
1610	Sawmilling and planing of wood	94	96	99	100		762	832	921	906		17.4	19.6	22.0	21.8	

162	Wood products, cork, straw, plaiting materials	...	...	...	...	...	...	...	...	...	...	...	...
1621	Veneer sheets and wood-based panels	40	41	41	43	20266	22124	23303	23764	463.9	521.7	556.4	570.1
1622	Builders' carpentry and joinery	4275	4370	4382	4531	1416	1546	1652	1667	32.4	36.5	39.4	40.0
1623	Wooden containers	215	220	223	229	666	727	787	787	15.2	17.1	18.8	18.9
1629	Other wood products;articles of cork,straw	78	79	80	82	1109	1211	1303	1308	25.4	28.6	31.1	31.4
170	Paper and paper products	...	...	...	...	...	...	...	...	...	...	...	...
1701	Pulp, paper and paperboard	73	84	88	93	3490	4000	4223	4318	213.9	247.3	262.0	270.0
1702	Corrugated paper and paperboard	128	147	165	166	7016	8040	8601	8712	430.0	497.0	533.6	545.4
1709	Other articles of paper and paperboard	68	78	82	86	3107	3561	3848	3870	190.4	220.1	238.7	242.4
181	Printing and service activities related to printing	...	...	...	...	...	...	...	...	...	...	...	...
1811	Printing	1203	1274	1300	1363	15251	16894	17926	18449	638.1	717.4	767.5	780.8
1812	Service activities related to printing	8	8	9	9	120	133	148	147	5.0	5.6	6.3	6.3
1820	Reproduction of recorded media	38	40	41	43	201	223	255	249	8.4	9.5	10.9	10.6
1910	Coke oven products	6	7	7	8	6	6	7	7	1.8	1.8	2.2	2.2
1920	Refined petroleum products	93	112	111	121	15616	16417	18345	18769	4804.5	5054.6	5708.9	5855.7
201	Basic chemicals,fertilizers, etc.	...	...	...	...	...	...	...	...	...	...	...	...
2011	Basic chemicals	166	184	199	206	39848	46078	57174	53020	4678.4	5487.9	6850.8	6452.1
2012	Fertilizers and nitrogen compounds	13	14	15	16	3038	3513	3999	3936	356.7	418.4	479.2	475.6
2013	Plastics and synthetic rubber in primary forms	548	607	642	674	16292	18839	20747	20905	1912.8	2243.7	2486.0	2518.5
202	Other chemical products	...	...	...	...	...	...	...	...	...	...	...	...
2021	Pesticides and other agrochemical products	20	22	24	25	2432	2812	3281	3174	285.5	334.9	393.1	384.3
2022	Paints,varnishes;printing ink and mastics	188	208	219	231	8103	9371	1007	7661	951.3	1116.1	120.7	829.6
2023	Soap,cleaning and cosmetic preparations	244	270	283	299	3493	4039	4757	4573	410.1	481.0	570.0	554.0
2029	Other chemical products n.e.c.	39	43	47	48	1526	1765	1951	1961	179.2	210.2	233.8	236.3
2030	Man-made fibres	13	14	15	16	1177	1361	1578	1533	138.2	162.1	189.1	185.5
2100	Pharmaceuticals,medicinal chemicals, etc.	74	82	89	94	5632	6572	7104	7283	373.3	441.5	479.4	494.4
221	Rubber products	...	...	...	...	...	...	...	...	...	...	...	...
2211	Rubber tyres and tubes	25	28	31	30	280	321	367	360	9.5	11.2	13.0	12.7
2219	Other rubber products	45	51	55	55	2427	2789	3111	3102	82.3	97.1	109.8	109.4
2220	Plastics products	583	650	681	700	19256	22123	23788	24351	653.2	770.3	839.8	855.6
2310	Glass and glass products	564	601	611	634	17836	19539	20642	20882	727.8	813.3	867.8	905.7
239	Non-metallic mineral products n.e.c.	...	...	...	...	...	...	...	...	...	...	...	...
2391	Refractory products	132	140	149	150	8088	8861	9511	9511	330.0	368.8	399.8	413.1
2392	Clay building materials	245	261	269	276	7430	8140	8482	8666	303.2	338.8	356.6	375.4
2393	Other porcelain and ceramic products	41	44	47	47	1068	1170	1277	1262	43.6	48.7	53.7	54.9
2394	Cement, lime and plaster	193	206	216	219	14341	15711	16538	16774	585.2	653.9	695.2	727.3
2395	Articles of concrete, cement and plaster	2390	2547	2608	2692	51398	56308	60161	60363	2097.2	2343.7	2529.1	2620.7
2396	Cutting, shaping and finishing of stone	517	551	563	582	13239	14503	15569	15568	540.2	603.7	654.5	676.2
2399	Other non-metallic mineral products n.e.c.	34	36	39	39	664	727	772	778	27.1	30.3	32.5	33.8
2410	Basic iron and steel	272	307	328	344	25334	28953	31115	31309	2001.7	2325.0	2515.3	2559.7
2420	Basic precious and other non-ferrous metals	83	93	101	105	5820	6651	7216	7212	459.8	534.1	583.3	590.1
243	Casting of metals	...	...	...	...	...	...	...	...	...	...	...	...
2431	Casting of iron and steel	89	101	113	114	6949	7941	8350	8535	549.0	637.7	675.0	696.5
2432	Casting of non-ferrous metals	31	34	38	39	822	939	994	1011	64.9	75.4	80.4	82.6
251	Struct.metal products, tanks, reservoirs	...	...	...	...	...	...	...	...	...	...	...	...

continued

Saudi Arabia

ISIC	Industry	Number of establishments (number)					Number of employees (number)					Wages and salaries paid to employees (millions of Saudi Riyals)				
		Note	2013	2014	2015	2016	Note	2013	2014	2015	2016	Note	2013	2014	2015	2016
2511	Structural metal products		16370	17178	17231	18062		85228	98182	104757	107376		2214.6	2593.6	2792.5	2857.9
2512	Tanks, reservoirs and containers of metal		174	182	195	195		5079	5852	6302	6416		132.0	154.6	168.0	170.9
2513	Steam generators, excl. hot water boilers		2	2	3	2		25	28	31	31		0.7	0.7	0.8	0.8
2520	Weapons and ammunition		1	1	1	1		9	10	11	11		0.2	0.3	0.3	0.3
259	Other metal products;metal working services		...	...	...	...		...	...	...	...		...	...	...	...
2591	Forging,pressing,stamping,roll-forming of metal		69	72	76	77		1316	1517	1597	1653		34.2	40.1	42.6	43.9
2592	Treatment and coating of metals,machining		1438	1509	1533	1592		8508	9801	10550	10746		221.1	258.9	281.2	286.2
2593	Cutlery, hand tools and general hardware		856	899	921	950		1783	2054	2207	2251		46.3	54.3	58.8	59.9
2599	Other fabricated metal products n.e.c.		220	231	244	246		7993	9210	9912	10097		207.7	243.3	264.2	268.9
2610	Electronic components and boards		17	19	21	22		737	841	904	926		22.9	26.9	29.3	30.5
2620	Computers and peripheral equipment		8	9	10	10		217	248	280	277		6.7	7.9	9.1	9.1
2630	Communication equipment		22	25	26	28		342	390	421	430		10.6	12.5	13.6	14.2
2640	Consumer electronics		9	10	10	11		46	53	62	60		1.4	1.7	2.0	2.0
265	Measuring,testing equipment; watches, etc.		...	...	...	...		...	...	...	...		...	...	...	...
2651	Measuring/testing/navigating equipment,etc.		19	22	23	25		461	527	556	577		14.3	16.9	18.0	19.0
2652	Watches and clocks		20	23	25	26		35	40	44	44		1.1	1.3	1.4	1.5
2660	Irradiation/electromedical equipment,etc.		6	6	7	7		156	178	201	199		4.8	5.7	6.5	6.6
2670	Optical instruments and photographic equipment		3	4	4	4		13	15	18	17		0.4	0.5	0.6	0.6
2680	Magnetic and optical media		6	6	7	7		225	258	281	285		7.0	8.3	9.1	9.4
2710	Electric motors,generators,transformers,etc.		299	335	349	362		5511	6236	6706	6902		234.9	271.7	295.1	303.7
2720	Batteries and accumulators		9	10	11	11		622	704	760	780		26.5	30.7	33.4	34.3
273	Wiring and wiring devices		...	...	...	...		...	...	...	...		...	...	...	...
2731	Fibre optic cables		3	4	4	4		280	317	352	354		11.9	13.8	15.5	15.6
2732	Other electronic and electric wires and cables		36	40	43	44		4249	4808	5192	5328		181.1	209.5	228.5	234.5
2733	Wiring devices		48	54	56	58		2720	3077	3303	3405		116.0	134.1	145.3	149.8
2740	Electric lighting equipment		20	22	23	24		1503	1701	1840	1886		64.1	74.1	81.0	83.0
2750	Domestic appliances		73	82	85	88		2736	3095	3334	3428		116.6	134.8	146.7	150.8
2790	Other electrical equipment		17	19	22	21		591	668	712	738		25.2	29.1	31.3	32.4
281	General-purpose machinery		...	...	...	...		...	...	...	...		...	...	...	...
2811	Engines/turbines,excl.aircraft,vehicle engines		1	1	1	1		80	84	89	92		3.8	4.0	4.3	4.4
2812	Fluid power equipment		-	-	-	-		-	-	-	-		-	-	-	-
2813	Other pumps, compressors, taps and valves		53	57	60	61		1660	1778	1797	1925		78.3	85.3	86.7	91.3
2814	Bearings, gears, gearing and driving elements		4	5	5	5		383	411	464	458		18.1	19.7	22.4	22.0
2815	Ovens, furnaces and furnace burners		1	1	1	1		9	10	10	11		0.4	0.5	0.5	0.5
2816	Lifting and handling equipment		24	26	29	28		1515	1623	1701	1774		71.4	77.8	82.1	84.4
2817	Office machinery, excl.computers,etc.		10	10	11	11		169	181	190	198		8.0	8.7	9.2	9.4
2818	Power-driven hand tools		2	2	2	2		222	238	244	259		10.5	11.4	11.8	12.3
2819	Other general-purpose machinery		81	87	90	93		15654	16775	18113	18483		738.0	804.3	874.3	881.9
282	Special-purpose machinery		...	...	...	...		...	...	...	...		...	...	...	...
2821	Agricultural and forestry machinery		29	31	33	33		688	737	767	804		32.4	35.3	37.0	38.2
2822	Metal-forming machinery and machine tools		49	53	52	56		639	685	699	743		30.1	32.8	33.7	35.3

ISIC Revision 4

Code	Description	(1)	(2)	(3)	(4)	(5)	(6)	(7)	(8)	(9)	(10)	(11)	(12)
2823	Machinery for metallurgy	2	2	3	2	115	123	140	138	6.6	6.8	5.9	5.4
2824	Mining, quarrying and construction machinery	14	15	17	16	479	513	555	565	27.0	26.8	24.6	22.6
2825	Food/beverage/tobacco processing machinery	28	30	33	33	148	159	167	174	8.3	8.1	7.6	7.0
2826	Textile/apparel/leather production machinery	7	8	8	8	69	73	78	80	3.8	3.8	3.5	3.3
2829	Other special-purpose machinery	16	17	17	18	667	715	776	789	37.7	37.5	34.3	31.4
2910	Motor vehicles	139	157	164	172	2809	3117	3374	3401	122.8	121.0	109.9	96.6
2920	Automobile bodies, trailers and semi-trailers	72	81	84	89	1315	1458	1571	1589	57.4	56.3	51.4	45.2
2930	Parts and accessories for motor vehicles	57	64	66	70	2462	2731	2861	2953	106.3	102.6	96.3	84.7
301	Building of ships and boats	...	...	...	...	...	...	...	...	...	...	...	...
3011	Building of ships and floating structures	11	12	13	14	1481	1643	1760	1793	72.0	69.3	64.0	56.2
3012	Building of pleasure and sporting boats	3	4	4	4	263	291	324	321	12.9	12.8	11.3	10.0
3020	Railway locomotives and rolling stock	11	12	13	14	67	75	90	84	3.4	3.5	2.9	2.5
3030	Air and spacecraft and related machinery	-	-	-	-	-	-	-	-	-	-	-	-
3040	Military fighting vehicles	2	2	2	2	377	418	432	452	18.1	17.0	16.3	14.3
309	Transport equipment n.e.c.	...	...	...	...	...	...	...	...	...	...	...	...
3091	Motorcycles	1	1	1	1	1	1	1	1	-	-	-	-
3092	Bicycles and invalid carriages	8	8	9	9	15	16	17	18	0.7	0.7	0.6	0.6
3099	Other transport equipment n.e.c.	2	2	2	2	167	185	193	201	8.0	7.6	7.2	6.3
3100	Furniture	9161	9648	9742	9975	49776	53609	57034	58310	1357.4	1328.9	1229.0	1096.1
321	Jewellery, bijouterie and related articles	...	...	...	...	...	...	...	...	...	...	...	...
3211	Jewellery and related articles	176	197	202	208	2620	2959	3136	3220	103.8	98.8	92.2	79.2
3212	Imitation jewellery and related articles	32	36	38	38	86	97	108	107	3.5	3.4	3.0	2.6
3220	Musical instruments	1	1	1	1	1	1	1	1	-	-	-	-
3230	Sports goods	3	4	5	4	30	34	37	37	1.2	1.2	1.1	0.9
3240	Games and toys	10	11	12	12	250	283	299	307	9.9	9.4	8.8	7.6
3250	Medical and dental instruments and supplies	143	160	164	169	1504	1700	1797	1848	59.5	56.6	52.9	45.5
3290	Other manufacturing n.e.c.	66	74	77	78	1759	1988	2197	2188	70.8	69.2	61.9	53.2
331	Repair of fabricated metal products/machinery	...	...	...	...	...	...	...	...	...	...	...	...
3311	Repair of fabricated metal products	312	337	342	355	4133	4656	5147	5136	124.4	123.9	110.0	95.8
3312	Repair of machinery	10066	10871	10900	11412	27741	31245	32857	33984	819.8	791.1	738.4	642.9
3313	Repair of electronic and optical equipment	74	80	84	85	207	233	271	261	6.3	6.5	5.5	4.8
3314	Repair of electrical equipment	345	372	379	392	2730	3075	3412	3396	82.3	82.1	72.7	63.3
3315	Repair of transport equip., excl. motor vehicles	32	35	37	37	800	901	1003	996	24.1	24.1	21.3	18.5
3319	Repair of other equipment	11	12	13	13	17	19	21	21	0.5	0.5	0.4	0.4
3320	Installation of industrial machinery/equipment	66	71	75	76	16946	19086	20572	20903	505.3	495.3	451.0	392.7
C	Total manufacturing	98684	102974	104031	108045	800358	897573	959642a/	977944	49136.5	49198.2	44057.4	38657.7

a/ Sum of available data.

Saudi Arabia

ISIC Revision 4		Note	Output at producers' prices (millions of Saudi Riyals)				Note	Value added at producers' prices (millions of Saudi Riyals)				Note	Gross fixed capital formation (millions of Saudi Riyals)	
ISIC	Industry		2013	2014	2015	2016		2013	2014	2015	2016		2015	2016
1010	Processing/preserving of meat		4633.3	5024.6	5622.5	5397.3		2098.3	2282.4	33300.0a/	2471.5		339.8	101.9
1020	Processing/preserving of fish, etc.		243.9	264.3	295.5	283.9		110.5	120.1	...a/	130.1		19.8	16.7
1030	Processing/preserving of fruit,vegetables		4982.7	5402.3	5875.5	5743.4		2256.6	2454.0	...a/	2657.7		372.3	135.5
1040	Vegetable and animal oils and fats		775.5	840.3	895.7	887.1		351.2	381.7	...a/	413.5		60.9	67.8
1050	Dairy products		14743.9	15984.1	17284.6	16958.7		6677.2	7260.8	...a/	7863.6		1111.6	1022.0
106	Grain mill products,starches and starch products		...	...	...	...		1260.5	1370.5	...a/	...		...	...
1061	Grain mill products		2724.2	2953.2	3000.5	3065.2		1233.7	1341.5	...	1452.9		239.4	190.2
1062	Starches and starch products		59.1	63.9	88.7	74.8		26.8	29.0	...	31.4		4.8	1.2
107	Other food products		...	...	...	...		15533.4	...	...a/	...		...	...
1071	Bakery products		25209.9	27331.1	28827.4	28740.5		11417.1	12415.2	...	13445.9		2085.7	3121.7
1072	Sugar		559.1	606.3	657.6	643.9		253.2	275.4	...	298.2		35.8	20.4
1073	Cocoa, chocolate and sugar confectionery		6153.3	6671.0	6987.7	6997.9		2786.7	3030.3	...	3281.9		538.3	425.9
1074	Macaroni, noodles, couscous, etc.		1237.8	1341.8	1654.3	1495.5		560.6	609.5	...	660.1		103.5	7.5
1075	Prepared meals and dishes		127.7	138.4	157.0	149.4		57.8	62.9	...	68.1		9.7	7.1
1079	Other food products n.e.c.		1011.3	1096.7	1342.6	1218.8		458.0	498.2	...	539.5		77.0	72.1
1080	Prepared animal feeds		524.1	568.1	602.6	598.6		237.4	258.1	...a/	279.6		45.3	15.4
110	Beverages		...	...	...	...		...	...	5505.8	5411.2		...	...
1101	Distilling, rectifying and blending of spirits		...	...	...	...		...	...	...	...		...	...
1102	Wines		...	...	...	...		...	...	...	...		...	...
1103	Malt liquors and malt		...	...	...	...		...	...	...	...		...	...
1104	Soft drinks,mineral waters,other bottled waters		9494.4	10315.7	11019.4	10672.6		4920.5	5310.3	...	5411.2		1118.5	702.4
1200	Tobacco products		25.7	27.8	31.1	27.8		9.5	10.2	11.5	10.3		1.4	0.6
131	Spinning, weaving and finishing of textiles		...	...	...	...		...	...	5473.2b/	...		...	...
1311	Preparation and spinning of textile fibres		400.0	432.8	463.2	456.4		213.3	234.0	...	241.2		30.7	19.1
1312	Weaving of textiles		112.5	121.8	144.8	142.6		60.0	65.8	...	67.8		10.3	5.7
1313	Finishing of textiles		16.4	17.7	18.5	18.3		8.7	9.6	...	9.9		1.6	0.4
139	Other textiles		...	...	...	...		4441.4	4871.2	...b/	...		...	...
1391	Knitted and crocheted fabrics		8.7	9.8	10.2	10.1		4.6	5.3	...	5.3		0.9	0.7
1392	Made-up textile articles, except apparel		3856.5	4173.1	4455.3	4389.1		2057.0	2256.0	...	2325.5		285.7	288.4
1393	Carpets and rugs		4283.0	4634.7	5320.3	5241.3		2284.5	2505.6	...	2582.7		537.7	494.9
1394	Cordage, rope, twine and netting		78.3	84.6	88.8	87.4		41.7	45.7	...	47.2		7.6	1.6
1399	Other textiles n.e.c.		100.2	108.3	117.9	116.1		53.5	58.6	...	60.4		10.8	12.0
1410	Wearing apparel, except fur apparel		8418.2	9197.2	9468.7	9606.5		4906.5	5398.9	5517.8c/	5586.7		797.0	607.1
1420	Articles of fur		8.0	8.7	92.9	94.3		4.6	5.1	...c/	5.3		0.7	0.7
1430	Knitted and crocheted apparel		8.7	9.3	94.6	95.9		5.1	5.5	...c/	5.7		0.8	0.1
151	Leather;luggage,handbags,saddlery,harness;fur		...	...	...	...		...	...	367.8d/	...		...	...
1511	Tanning/dressing of leather; dressing of fur		392.7	424.0	454.4	430.0		229.7	249.7	...	243.6		85.6	28.1
1512	Luggage,handbags,etc.;saddlery/harness		14.2	14.4	14.8	14.0		8.3	8.5	...	8.5		1.9	1.0
1520	Footwear		151.9	163.4	172.0	162.8		88.8	96.2	...d/	94.0		33.7	8.1
1610	Sawmilling and planing of wood		207.1	218.2	220.0	222.5		103.1	109.2	3499.4e/	110.3		21.7	9.2

162	Wood products, cork, straw, plaiting materials	...	...	...	...	3172.8	...e/	3362.5	3397.6	...	...
1621	Veneer sheets and wood-based panels	181.0	190.6	202.1	204.4	90.1	...	95.5	96.5	19.1	3.6
1622	Builders' carpentry and joinery	5508.0	5800.9	6126.1	6194.2	2741.2	...	2905.1	2935.3	456.2	672.1
1623	Wooden containers	384.9	405.4	421.4	426.1	191.5	...	203.0	205.1	28.6	19.2
1629	Other wood products;articles of cork,straw	301.4	317.5	350.7	354.6	150.0	...	159.0	160.7	19.7	1.8
170	Paper and paper products	...	...	...	...	...	9754.6	...	...	...	...
1701	Pulp, paper and paperboard	3689.9	3952.6	4242.7	4323.1	2132.9	...	2271.0	2533.6	203.7	43.7
1702	Corrugated paper and paperboard	7417.9	7944.8	8669.0	8833.3	4287.8	...	4564.8	5093.2	409.2	112.2
1709	Other articles of paper and paperboard	3285.0	3518.8	3998.8	4074.6	1898.9	...	2021.8	2255.7	195.3	197.2
181	Printing and service activities related to printing	...	...	...	...	...	3601.9f/	...	...	...	...
1811	Printing	6815.8	7305.1	7641.3	7721.9	3157.0	...	3376.2	3533.3	522.3	199.3
1812	Service activities related to printing	53.6	57.5	62.5	63.2	24.8	...	26.6	27.8	4.9	3.4
1820	Reproduction of recorded media	89.8	96.4	104.8	105.9	41.6	...f/	44.6	46.6	8.2	5.5
1910	Coke oven products	45.1	45.1	46.6	47.7	26.0	53622.3g/	25.9	21.0	2.4	0.8
1920	Refined petroleum products	117452.5	123519.3	113720.7	116467.4	67603.7	86847.3h/	70937.8	54579.1	4440.3	5161.4
201	Basic chemicals,fertilizers, etc.	...	...	...	...	...	...	...	...	...	...
2011	Basic chemicals	72176.3	78942.1	86907.3	88632.8	38218.6	...	41291.7	46341.1	15527.0	20578.9
2012	Fertilizers and nitrogen compounds	5502.7	6018.6	6601.5	6732.5	2913.8	...	3148.1	3532.8	1533.0	2640.6
2013	Plastics and synthetic rubber in primary forms	29509.6	32275.5	35742.0	36451.7	15625.8	...h/	16882.1	18946.7	7697.5	9801.5
202	Other chemical products	...	...	...	...	14918.0	...	16118.6	...	...	...
2021	Pesticides and other agrochemical products	4405.1	4817.6	5388.0	5494.9	2332.6	...	2519.9	2828.0	1234.9	851.7
2022	Paints,varnishes;printing ink and mastics	14676.9	16054.7	17853.0	18207.4	7771.7	...	8397.6	9423.9	3170.7	2501.7
2023	Soap,cleaning and cosmetic preparations	6326.8	6919.7	7522.4	7671.8	3350.2	...	3619.5	4061.9	1838.5	713.9
2029	Other chemical products n.e.c.	2764.0	3023.8	3401.5	3469.0	1463.6	...h/	1581.7	1775.0	777.9	34.7
2030	Man-made fibres	2131.9	2331.7	2604.8	2656.5	1128.9	...	1219.6	1368.5	512.3	221.3
2100	Pharmaceuticals,medicinal chemicals, etc.	2625.7	2883.6	3157.3	3197.0	1018.6	1161.0	1085.2	1155.4	159.4	122.3
221	Rubber products	...	...	...	...	...	9495.3i/	...	...	...	...
2211	Rubber tyres and tubes	197.5	216.8	237.5	239.3	109.7	...	120.8	122.0	5.8	2.3
2219	Other rubber products	1711.8	1883.9	2154.9	2171.5	951.3	...	1049.8	1059.1	40.7	10.8
2220	Plastics products	13581.4	14943.5	15578.4	15698.7	7547.6	...i/	8327.6	8401.6	410.1	97.0
2310	Glass and glass products	5066.6	5483.2	5874.5	5941.2	2497.7	18516.1i/	2684.0	2901.8	1314.4	1011.2
239	Non-metallic mineral products n.e.c.	...	...	...	...	13475.5	...j/	14481.4	...	...	...
2391	Refractory products	2297.5	2486.7	2710.2	2741.0	1132.6	...	1217.2	1316.0	1060.4	1141.8
2392	Clay building materials	2110.6	2284.3	2558.8	2587.8	1040.5	...	1118.2	1208.8	836.3	490.6
2393	Other porcelain and ceramic products	303.4	328.3	368.0	372.2	149.6	...	160.7	173.7	98.2	14.8
2394	Cement, lime and plaster	4073.8	4409.0	4902.5	4958.1	2008.3	...	2158.2	2333.3	1404.5	1276.9
2395	Articles of concrete, cement and plaster	14600.5	15801.8	16455.9	16642.6	7197.6	...	7734.9	8362.4	5363.1	4405.9
2396	Cutting, shaping and finishing of stone	3760.8	4070.0	4412.1	4462.2	1854.0	...	1992.3	2153.9	1675.0	1053.4
2399	Other non-metallic mineral products n.e.c.	188.6	204.0	212.6	215.0	93.0	...	99.9	108.0	87.4	93.4
2410	Basic iron and steel	16881.0	18402.8	19151.6	19364.4	7720.2	13242.7k/	8384.6	8611.6	197.3	162.0
2420	Basic precious and other non-ferrous metals	3878.1	4227.4	4782.6	4835.7	1773.6	...k/	1926.1	1978.3	59.7	0.5
243	Casting of metals	...	...	...	...	2368.1	...k/	2571.6	...	...	...
2431	Casting of iron and steel	4630.4	5047.4	5595.0	5657.1	2117.6	...	2299.7	2362.1	83.4	30.3
2432	Casting of non-ferrous metals	547.7	596.8	646.5	653.6	250.5	...	271.9	279.4	8.0	3.3
251	Struct.metal products, tanks, reservoirs	...	...	...	...	...	16962.5m/	...	...	...	...

continued

Saudi Arabia

ISIC	Industry	Note	Output at producers' prices (millions of Saudi Riyals)				Note	Value added at producers' prices (millions of Saudi Riyals)				Note	Gross fixed capital formation (millions of Saudi Riyals)	
			2013	2014	2015	2016		2013	2014	2015	2016		2015	2016
2511	Structural metal products		21203.2	22899.8	24323.7	22478.8		11537.0	12250.6	...	12085.2		732.9	585.0
2512	Tanks, reservoirs and containers of metal		1263.6	1364.9	1526.5	1410.7		687.5	730.2	...	720.3		43.1	41.8
2513	Steam generators, excl. hot water boilers		6.2	6.5	69.9	64.6		3.4	3.5	...	3.5		0.4	0.3
2520	Weapons and ammunition		2.2	2.3	2.6	2.4		1.2	1.2	...m/	1.3		0.1	0.1
259	Other metal products;metal working services		...	...	...	...		2653.3	2817.6	...m/	...		...	...
2591	Forging,pressing,stamping,roll-forming of metal		327.4	353.8	388.0	358.6		178.1	189.3	...	186.7		11.7	5.9
2592	Treatment and coating of metals; machining		2116.6	2286.0	2687.5	2483.6		1151.7	1222.9	...	1206.4		75.5	18.2
2593	Cutlery, hand tools and general hardware		443.6	479.1	535.4	494.8		241.4	256.3	...	252.8		12.1	13.8
2599	Other fabricated metal products n.e.c.		1988.8	2148.1	2414.2	2231.1		1082.1	1149.2	...	1133.6		71.4	51.7
2610	Electronic components and boards		226.0	247.1	253.5	239.7		106.5	117.0	341.2n/	105.2		50.0	8.6
2620	Computers and peripheral equipment		66.5	72.9	77.5	73.3		31.4	34.5	...n/	31.0		8.1	2.1
2630	Communication equipment		104.9	114.6	116.5	110.2		49.4	54.3	...n/	48.8		12.0	11.5
2640	Consumer electronics		14.1	15.6	16.2	15.3		6.6	7.4	...n/	6.6		3.2	1.3
265	Measuring,testing equipment; watches, etc.		...	...	...	...		71.7	78.9	...n/	...		...	...
2651	Measuring/testing/navigating equipment,etc.		141.4	154.8	161.5	152.7		66.6	73.3	...	65.9		20.4	7.5
2652	Watches and clocks		10.7	11.8	12.0	11.3		5.1	5.6	...	5.0		2.4	2.1
2660	Irradiation/electromedical equipment,etc.		47.8	52.3	56.9	53.8		22.5	24.8	...n/	22.3		10.7	7.3
2670	Optical instruments and photographic equipment		4.0	4.4	4.8	4.5		1.9	2.1	...n/	1.8		0.8	0.1
2680	Magnetic and optical media		69.0	75.8	81.8	77.4		32.5	35.9	...n/	32.2		15.3	6.8
2710	Electric motors,generators,transformers,etc.		6842.7	7322.7	8083.9	7425.1		3094.8	3270.3	11373.8p/	3132.8		261.1	127.0
2720	Batteries and accumulators		772.3	826.7	835.7	767.6		349.3	369.2	...p/	353.7		29.3	21.2
273	Wiring and wiring devices		...	...	...	...		4070.8	4301.3	...p/	...		...	...
2731	Fibre optic cables		347.7	372.2	415.9	382.0		157.2	166.2	...	159.2		9.4	10.8
2732	Other electronic and electric wires and cables		5275.7	5645.9	5899.7	5418.9		2386.1	2521.4	...	2415.5		197.9	144.9
2733	Wiring devices		3377.3	3613.2	3800.1	3490.4		1527.5	1613.6	...	1546.1		82.7	70.0
2740	Electric lighting equipment		1866.2	1997.4	2325.5	2136.0		844.0	892.0	...p/	854.6		69.4	4.9
2750	Domestic appliances		3397.1	3634.3	4025.4	3697.4		1536.5	1623.1	...p/	1555.2		62.2	64.0
2790	Other electrical equipment		733.8	784.4	812.5	746.3		331.9	350.3	...p/	335.8		16.1	12.4
281	General-purpose machinery		...	...	...	...		...	...	6267.5q/	...		...	...
2811	Engines/turbines,excl.aircraft,vehicle engines		43.4	45.7	48.5	44.0		20.9	22.5	...	19.8		2.6	2.8
2812	Fluid power equipment		...	...	...	...		...	...	-	...		...	...
2813	Other pumps, compressors, taps and valves		899.7	967.2	1045.8	948.1		434.5	477.0	...	419.1		55.9	61.9
2814	Bearings, gears, gearing and driving elements		207.6	223.6	244.6	221.7		100.2	110.3	...	96.8		12.3	0.4
2815	Ovens, furnaces and furnace burners		4.9	5.4	6.0	5.4		2.4	2.7	...	2.3		0.3	0.1
2816	Lifting and handling equipment		821.2	882.9	937.1	849.6		396.5	435.4	...	382.6		55.4	64.5
2817	Office machinery, excl.computers, etc.		91.6	98.5	113.5	102.9		44.2	48.6	...	42.6		6.7	14.9
2818	Power-driven hand tools		120.3	129.5	144.9	131.3		58.1	63.9	...	56.1		5.7	4.4
2819	Other general-purpose machinery		8484.7	9125.6	9098.4	8248.2		4097.0	4500.6	...	3954.1		445.4	414.1
282	Special-purpose machinery		...	...	...	...		734.1	806.2	...q/	...		...	...
2821	Agricultural and forestry machinery		372.9	400.9	437.0	396.1		180.1	197.7	...	173.7		20.5	11.7
2822	Metal-forming machinery and machine tools		346.3	372.6	392.8	356.1		167.2	183.8	...	161.5		14.3	0.4

ISIC Revision 4

Code	Description										
2823	Machinery for metallurgy	62.3	66.9	65.8	59.6	30.1	33.0	...	29.0	2.6	20.6
2824	Mining, quarrying and construction machinery	259.6	279.1	288.2	261.2	125.4	137.6	...	120.9	13.2	9.0
2825	Food/beverage/tobacco processing machinery	80.2	86.5	87.2	79.1	38.7	42.7	...	37.5	4.6	4.4
2826	Textile/apparel/leather production machinery	37.4	39.7	41.4	37.5	18.1	19.6	...	17.3	2.1	0.3
2829	Other special-purpose machinery	361.5	389.0	412.2	373.6	174.6	191.8	...	168.5	22.5	15.0
2910	Motor vehicles	1828.0	1919.9	2031.1	1824.8	1031.3	1078.0	2528.3r/	963.4	100.3	115.7
2920	Automobile bodies, trailers and semi-trailers	855.8	898.1	910.5	818.0	482.8	504.3	..r/	450.9	33.6	10.2
2930	Parts and accessories for motor vehicles	1602.2	1682.2	1745.9	1568.5	903.9	944.5	..r/	844.3	72.3	88.0
301	Building of ships and boats	...	...	...	...	...	...	966.3s/	...	...	...
3011	Building of ships and floating structures	1453.3	1512.9	1658.6	1452.1	562.8	568.4	...	523.0	194.7	135.2
3012	Building of pleasure and sporting boats	258.1	268.0	281.5	246.4	99.9	100.7	...	92.7	35.0	37.7
3020	Railway locomotives and rolling stock	65.7	69.1	72.5	63.4	25.5	25.9	..s/	23.8	9.4	8.5
3030	Air and spacecraft and related machinery	-	-	-	-	-	-	..s/	-	-	-
3040	Military fighting vehicles	370.0	384.9	400.0	350.2	143.3	144.6	..s/	133.1	51.3	49.9
309	Transport equipment n.e.c.	...	...	...	...	69.5	69.9	..s/	...	...	...
3091	Motorcycles	1.0	0.9	1.0	0.9	0.4	0.3	...	0.3	0.1	0.1
3092	Bicycles and invalid carriages	14.7	14.7	15.1	13.2	5.7	5.5	...	5.2	2.0	0.8
3099	Other transport equipment n.e.c.	163.9	170.4	182.5	159.8	63.5	64.0	...	58.9	12.7	9.7
3100	Furniture	12873.1	13326.7	14233.2	14056.0	5530.6	5633.5	5894.8	5742.0	1622.0	983.8
321	Jewellery, bijouterie and related articles	...	...	...	...	...	...	647.9t/	...	...	...
3211	Jewellery and related articles	603.6	647.0	651.9	583.4	262.8	278.6	..t/	241.4	104.1	101.7
3212	Imitation jewellery and related articles	19.8	21.2	22.7	20.4	8.6	9.1	..t/	7.9	4.4	2.8
3220	Musical instruments	0.2	0.2	0.2	0.2	0.1	0.1	..t/	0.1	0.1	-
3230	Sports goods	6.9	7.4	8.0	7.1	3.0	3.2	..t/	2.8	2.2	1.3
3240	Games and toys	57.6	61.9	66.6	59.6	25.1	26.6	..t/	23.1	12.3	12.8
3250	Medical and dental instruments and supplies	346.5	371.7	401.2	359.0	150.9	160.0	..t/	138.6	69.9	83.8
3290	Other manufacturing n.e.c.	405.2	434.7	455.8	407.9	176.5	187.2	..t/	162.1	79.3	24.5
331	Repair of fabricated metal products/machinery	...	...	...	...	...	...	3629.1u/	...	...	...
3311	Repair of fabricated metal products	539.0	577.3	621.5	629.2	263.4	279.2	...	286.6	289.3	132.9
3312	Repair of machinery	3617.7	3874.1	4062.4	4113.0	1768.3	1873.6	...	1923.6	2707.0	1538.2
3313	Repair of electronic and optical equipment	27.0	28.9	31.6	32.0	13.2	14.0	...	14.4	14.6	7.7
3314	Repair of electrical equipment	356.0	381.3	423.0	428.3	174.0	184.4	...	189.3	257.5	193.5
3315	Repair of transport equip., excl. motor vehicles	104.3	111.7	117.8	119.3	51.0	54.0	...	55.5	5.1	0.4
3319	Repair of other equipment	2.2	2.4	2.5	2.5	1.1	1.1	...	1.2	2.6	3.2
3320	Installation of industrial machinery/equipment	2209.9	2366.5	2514.8	2546.1	1080.2	1144.3	..u/	1175.0	1718.4	2153.7
C	Total manufacturing	540360.2	581788.7	609086.3v/	608215.5	280285.6	300031.8	298528.0v/	297705.3	69258.2v/	68606.3

a/ 1010 includes 1020, 1030, 1040, 1050, 106, 107 and 1080.
b/ 131 includes 139.
c/ 1410 includes 1420 and 1430.
d/ 151 includes 1520.
e/ 1610 includes 162.
f/ 181 includes 1820.
g/ 1910 includes 1920.
h/ 201 includes 202 and 2030.
i/ 221 includes 2220.
j/ 2310 includes 239.

k/ 2410 includes 2420 and 243.
m/ 251 includes 2520 and 259.
n/ 2610 includes 2620, 2630, 2640, 265, 2660, 2670 and 2680.
p/ 2710 includes 2720, 273, 2740, 2750 and 2790.
q/ 281 includes 282.
r/ 2910 includes 2920 and 2930.
s/ 301 includes 3020, 3030, 3040 and 309.
t/ 321 includes 3220, 3230, 3240, 3250 and 3290.
u/ 331 includes 3320.
v/ Sum of available data.

Saudi Arabia

Index numbers of industrial production

ISIC Revision 4

(2010=100)

ISIC	Industry	Note	2005	2006	2007	2008	2009	2010	2011	2012	2013	2014	2015	2016
10	Food products		...	...	...	...	...	...	...	...	...	...	...	...
11	Beverages		...	...	...	...	...	...	...	...	...	...	...	...
12	Tobacco products		...	...	...	...	...	...	...	...	...	...	...	...
13	Textiles		...	...	...	...	...	...	...	...	...	...	...	...
14	Wearing apparel		...	...	...	...	...	...	...	...	...	...	...	...
15	Leather and related products		...	...	...	...	...	...	...	...	...	...	...	...
16	Wood products, excluding furniture		...	...	...	...	...	...	...	...	...	...	...	...
17	Paper and paper products		...	...	...	...	...	...	...	...	...	...	...	...
18	Printing and reproduction of recorded media		...	...	...	...	...	...	...	...	...	...	...	...
19	Coke and refined petroleum products		...	...	...	...	...	...	...	...	...	...	...	...
20	Chemicals and chemical products		...	...	...	...	...	...	...	...	...	...	...	...
21	Pharmaceuticals, medicinal chemicals, etc.		...	...	...	...	...	...	...	...	...	...	...	...
22	Rubber and plastics products		...	...	...	...	...	...	...	...	...	...	...	...
23	Other non-metallic mineral products		...	...	...	...	...	...	...	...	...	...	...	...
24	Basic metals		...	...	...	...	...	...	...	...	...	...	...	...
25	Fabricated metal products, except machinery		...	...	...	...	...	...	...	...	...	...	...	...
26	Computer, electronic and optical products		...	...	...	...	...	...	...	...	...	...	...	...
27	Electrical equipment		...	...	...	...	...	...	...	...	...	...	...	...
28	Machinery and equipment n.e.c.		...	...	...	...	...	...	...	...	...	...	...	...
29	Motor vehicles, trailers and semi-trailers		...	...	...	...	...	...	...	...	...	...	...	...
30	Other transport equipment		...	...	...	...	...	...	...	...	...	...	...	...
31	Furniture		...	...	...	...	...	...	...	...	...	...	...	...
32	Other manufacturing		...	...	...	...	...	...	...	...	...	...	...	...
33	Repair and installation of machinery/equipment		...	...	...	...	...	...	...	...	...	...	...	...
C	Total manufacturing		...	...	...	...	...	100	109	113	117	128	137	141

Serbia

Supplier of information:
Statistical Office of the Republic of Serbia, Belgrade.

Basic source of data:
Annual survey; administrative source.

Major deviations from ISIC (Revision 4):
Data presented in ISIC (Revision 4) were originally classified according to NACE (Revision 2).

Reference period:
Calendar year.

Scope:
All enterprises.

Method of data collection:
Data for output and value added are derived from the financial statements of the National Bank of Serbia; other data are collected by mail questionnaires.

Type of enumeration:
Complete enumeration for large and medium enterprises; sample survey for small enterprises with less than 50 employees.

Adjusted for non-response:
Yes.

Concepts and definitions of variables:
Output refers to gross output.
Value added refers to total value added.

Related national publications:
Statistical Release: Gross domestic product of the Republic of Serbia, published by the Statistical Office of the Republic of Serbia, Belgrade.

Serbia

ISIC Revision 4		Note	Output at basic prices (billions of Serbian Dinars)				Note	Value added at basic prices (billions of Serbian Dinars)				Note	Gross fixed capital formation (billions of Serbian Dinars)	
ISIC	Industry		2013	2014	2015	2016		2013	2014	2015	2016		2015	2016
10	Food products		541.4	550.2	578.8	611.3		134.3	128.6	131.4	136.7		...	...
11	Beverages		92.4	93.3	102.5	100.4		29.7	29.8	35.0	30.5		...	...
12	Tobacco products		25.4	27.6	37.7	49.4		3.2	4.1	5.3	9.7		...	...
13	Textiles		26.6	22.7	32.5	28.1		7.9	6.7	7.7	6.8		...	...
14	Wearing apparel		67.5	66.7	70.4	74.2		25.5	26.6	25.7	27.5		...	...
15	Leather and related products		24.2	24.1	24.5	23.6		10.3	10.9	8.2	8.3		...	...
16	Wood products, excluding furniture		45.2	54.1	51.1	50.8		12.9	15.0	14.8	16.0		...	...
17	Paper and paper products		58.4	59.8	75.7	79.5		14.5	14.0	16.5	19.2		...	...
18	Printing and reproduction of recorded media		36.7	36.1	37.8	41.4		11.1	11.3	11.0	12.2		...	...
19	Coke and refined petroleum products		210.6	196.6	168.1	146.1		82.2	70.2	50.6	39.3		...	...
20	Chemicals and chemical products		141.0	130.4	143.0	155.4		23.5	28.2	39.1	44.5		...	...
21	Pharmaceuticals,medicinal chemicals, etc.		39.0	39.3	42.0	40.8		14.6	14.6	13.5	13.2		...	...
22	Rubber and plastics products		138.1	141.0	157.1	173.2		43.1	42.6	46.8	54.6		...	...
23	Other non-metallic mineral products		71.3	75.6	76.3	81.2		24.2	25.7	26.2	29.7		...	...
24	Basic metals		112.0	119.7	151.2	159.9		11.5	14.7	15.1	18.6		...	...
25	Fabricated metal products, except machinery		164.5	134.2	163.9	186.7		55.2	45.1	49.2	54.3		...	...
26	Computer, electronic and optical products		35.3	39.1	40.4	46.1		13.7	14.6	14.0	14.2		...	...
27	Electrical equipment		71.8	71.4	88.5	96.9		15.5	16.5	17.5	20.4		...	...
28	Machinery and equipment n.e.c.		55.2	69.1	77.5	78.4		21.1	24.5	27.9	28.9		...	...
29	Motor vehicles, trailers and semi-trailers		243.1	231.5	226.1	209.3		36.2	38.2	42.1	44.2		...	...
30	Other transport equipment		7.1	6.8	6.0	9.0		2.5	2.4	2.6	3.0		...	...
31	Furniture		40.9	39.5	42.0	46.9		13.4	13.1	12.1	14.0		...	...
32	Other manufacturing		20.8	19.6	27.4	29.8		8.2	8.2	9.4	10.6		...	...
33	Repair and installation of machinery/equipment		22.6	19.1	20.4	20.9		8.8	7.7	9.7	9.7		...	...
C	Total manufacturing		2291.0	2267.5	2440.8	2539.3		623.3	613.4	631.6	666.1		162.1	170.9

Serbia

ISIC Revision 4 — Index numbers of industrial production (2010=100)

ISIC	Industry	Note	2005	2006	2007	2008	2009	2010	2011	2012	2013	2014	2015	2016
10	Food products		97	100	106	105	99	100	97	98	93	97	97	103
11	Beverages		97	112	119	117	102	100	103	106	98	98	102	102
12	Tobacco products		88	98	95	95	93	100	92	86	79	78	122	150
13	Textiles		196	194	157	130	88	100	88	87	85	68	85	72
14	Wearing apparel		148	139	140	131	101	100	104	115	110	110	104	111
15	Leather and related products		132	131	128	124	102	100	101	89	82	72	62	59
16	Wood products, excluding furniture		221	216	268	221	125	100	110	132	132	148	138	136
17	Paper and paper products		86	83	92	95	91	100	112	118	118	120	127	126
18	Printing and reproduction of recorded media		69	74	83	87	92	100	95	95	92	87	97	111
19	Coke and refined petroleum products		116	120	116	114	103	100	86	82	121	119	128	129
20	Chemicals and chemical products		100	99	115	110	82	100	100	81	101	88	92	106
21	Pharmaceuticals,medicinal chemicals, etc.		94	113	105	121	101	100	107	121	126	127	147	147
22	Rubber and plastics products		118	113	122	123	99	100	98	116	106	106	115	127
23	Other non-metallic mineral products		123	131	131	124	100	100	105	97	84	87	89	95
24	Basic metals		93	114	112	116	83	100	96	51	47	51	62	67
25	Fabricated metal products, except machinery		92	96	104	114	93	100	109	122	129	97	104	112
26	Computer, electronic and optical products		398	209	183	177	140	100	124	122	67	73	57	65
27	Electrical equipment		77	77	97	100	90	100	108	108	120	117	120	131
28	Machinery and equipment n.e.c.		152	126	128	155	113	100	109	113	75	97	115	113
29	Motor vehicles, trailers and semi-trailers		230	211	206	174	105	100	124	145	346	336	321	297
30	Other transport equipment		54	53	80	124	118	100	55	44	29	28	24	36
31	Furniture		79	134	139	155	98	100	80	82	81	78	78	87
32	Other manufacturing		152	135	182	119	123	100	92	94	118	109	151	165
33	Repair and installation of machinery/equipment		135	115	116	103	104	100	79	71	71	60	64	66
C	Total manufacturing		105	110	115	116	97	100	100	99	104	102	108	113

Singapore

Supplier of information:
Research and Statistics Unit, Economic Development Board, Singapore.

Basic source of data:
Annual census of manufacturing activities.

Major deviations from ISIC (Revision 4):
Data presented in ISIC (Revision 4) were originally classified according to the Singapore Standard Industrial Classification System (SSIC).

Reference period:
Calendar year.

Scope:
All establishments.

Method of data collection:
The census was based on information obtained through mail questionnaires and online surveys.

Type of enumeration:
Not reported.

Adjusted for non-response:
Yes.

Concepts and definitions of variables:
Wages and salaries is compensation of employees.
Output refers to gross output.
Value added refers to total value added.

Related national publications:
Report on the Census of Manufacturing Activities, published by the Economic Development Board, Singapore.

Singapore

ISIC	Industry	Note	Number of establishments (number) 2013	2014	2015	2016	Note	Number of persons engaged (number) 2013	2014	2015	2016	Note	Wages and salaries paid to employees (millions of Singapore Dollars) 2013	2014	2015	2016
1010	Processing/preserving of meat		86	82	82	87		3263	3360	3586	3438		87	97	102	103
1020	Processing/preserving of fish, etc.		40	37	37	39		1470	1468	1393	1346		40	44	40	41
1030	Processing/preserving of fruit,vegetables		13	15	14	18		282	364	400	468		8	9	10	13
1040	Vegetable and animal oils and fats		12	12	10	11		732	762	628	659		36	37	30	32
1050	Dairy products		16	17	16	17		2786	2918	2907	3048		188	194	196	208
106	Grain mill products,starches and starch products	a/	...	...	...	...	a/	...	...	...	...	a/	...	...	...	...
1061	Grain mill products		...	...	...	...		...	...	...	...		...	...	...	...
1062	Starches and starch products		...	...	...	...		...	...	...	...		...	...	...	...
107	Other food products		642	663	649	738		17929	18351	18682	18538		544	595	621	630
1071	Bakery products		260	279	278	339		7839	7514	8348	8183		200	201	226	227
1072	Sugar	a/	...	...	...	...	a/	...	...	...	...	a/	...	...	...	...
1073	Cocoa, chocolate and sugar confectionery		10	11	13	13		640	688	746	773		34	39	46	46
1074	Macaroni, noodles, couscous, etc.		50	46	41	42		1259	1298	1364	1381		38	39	41	42
1075	Prepared meals and dishes		143	140	135	146		3526	3681	3487	3144		92	97	102	98
1079	Other food products n.e.c.	a/	179	187	182	198	a/	4665	5170	4737	5057	a/	179	220	206	216
1080	Prepared animal feeds		7	8	10	11		385	372	630	612		26	29	64	64
110	Beverages		32	31	29	27		2503	2510	2324	1518		138	141	146	98
1101	Distilling, rectifying and blending of spirits	b/	32	31	29	27	b/	2503	2510	2324	1518	b/	138	141	146	98
1102	Wines	b/	...	...	...	...	b/	...	...	...	...	b/	...	...	...	...
1103	Malt liquors and malt	b/	...	...	...	...	b/	...	...	...	...	b/	...	...	...	...
1104	Soft drinks,mineral waters,other bottled waters	b/	...	...	...	...	b/	...	...	...	...	b/	...	...	...	...
1200	Tobacco products	a/	...	...	...	...	a/	...	...	...	...	a/	...	...	...	...
131	Spinning, weaving and finishing of textiles	c/	...	...	...	...	c/	...	...	...	...	c/	...	...	...	...
1311	Preparation and spinning of textile fibres		...	...	...	...		...	...	...	...		...	...	...	...
1312	Weaving of textiles		...	...	...	...		...	...	...	...		...	...	...	...
1313	Finishing of textiles		...	...	...	...		...	...	...	...		...	...	...	...
139	Other textiles		...	...	...	...		...	...	...	...		...	...	...	...
1391	Knitted and crocheted fabrics		...	...	...	...		...	...	...	...		...	...	...	...
1392	Made-up textile articles, except apparel	c/	99	90	89	100	c/	717	722	688	686	c/	16	20	17	16
1393	Carpets and rugs		...	...	...	...		...	...	...	...		...	...	...	...
1394	Cordage, rope, twine and netting		...	...	...	...		...	...	...	...		...	...	...	...
1399	Other textiles n.e.c.	c/	...	...	...	...	c/	...	...	...	...	c/	...	...	...	...
1410	Wearing apparel, except fur apparel	d/	412	384	362	394	d/	2950	2203	2106	1985	d/	69	58	64	57
1420	Articles of fur	d/	...	...	...	...	d/	...	...	...	...	d/	...	...	...	...
1430	Knitted and crocheted apparel	d/	...	...	...	...	d/	...	...	...	...	d/	...	...	...	...
151	Leather;luggage,handbags,saddlery,harness;fur	e/	10	11	10	9	e/	501	507	523	428	e/	25	25	26	24
1511	Tanning/dressing of leather; dressing of fur	e/	10	11	10	9	e/	501	507	523	428	e/	25	25	26	24
1512	Luggage,handbags,etc.;saddlery/harness	e/	...	...	...	...	e/	...	...	...	...	e/	...	...	...	...
1520	Footwear		13	9	8	6		172	118	82	52		5	3	2	1
1610	Sawmilling and planing of wood		8	7	6	7		73	73	71	78		2	2	2	2

Code	Description												
162	Wood products, cork, straw, plaiting materials	139	136	129	140	2645	2696	2445	2492	77	79	78	81
1621	Veneer sheets and wood-based panels	10	11	11	9	221	204	191	176	8	7	6	5
1622	Builders' carpentry and joinery	57	60	57	70	1078	1203	1068	1164	28	32	31	32
1623	Wooden containers	46	43	39	39	1179	1144	1042	1002	37	35	38	38
1629	Other wood products;articles of cork,straw	26	22	22	22	167	145	144	150	5	5	4	6
170	Paper and paper products	101	99	91	88	3587	3638	3556	3326	159	167	167	161
1701	Pulp, paper and paperboard	7	6	…f/	…f/	37	12	…f/	…f/	2	-	…f/	…f/
1702	Corrugated paper and paperboard	74	74	70	66	2775	2870	2719	2509	120	130	128	124
1709	Other articles of paper and paperboard	20	19	21f/	22f/	775	756	837f/	817f/	38	37	40f/	37f/
181	Printing and service activities related to printing	918	902	875	866	14998	15361	15055	13523	661	733	723	673
1811	Printing	826	820	797	789	14263	14625	14291	12992	638	705	697	656
1812	Service activities related to printing	92	82	78	77	735	736	764	531	23	28	26	17
1820	Reproduction of recorded media	9	9	7	8	442	379	333	308	16	14	12	12
1910	Coke oven products	…	…	…	…	…	…	…	…	…	…	…	…
1920	Refined petroleum products	14	16	17	17	4073	4302	4404	4369	581	800	866	752
201	Basic chemicals,fertilizers, etc.	82	82	83	84	7698	7852	7699	7682	695	762	786	806
2011	Basic chemicals	22	21	23	24	2237	2042	2092	2124	160	152	173	180
2012 g/	Fertilizers and nitrogen compounds	60	61	60	60	5461	5810	5607	5558	535	610	612	626
2013 g/	Plastics and synthetic rubber in primary forms	202	191	181	198	10909	10684	10518	10419	987	1001	1015	1040
202	Other chemical products	…	…	…	…	…	…	…	…	…	…	…	…
2021 h/	Pesticides and other agrochemical products	31	27	27	29	1880	1735	1635	1617	129	125	118	125
2022	Paints,varnishes;printing ink and mastics	63	57	53	67	2764	2610	2704	2789	293	284	315	349
2023	Soap,cleaning and cosmetic preparations	108	107	101	102	6265	6339	6179	6013	565	592	582	567
2029 h/	Other chemical products n.e.c.	…	…	…	…	…	…	…	…	…	…	…	…
2030 h/	Man-made fibres	…	…	…	…	…	…	…	…	…	…	…	…
2100	Pharmaceuticals,medicinal chemicals, etc.	49	50	51	53	5339	6096	6624	6943	529	621	693	711
221	Rubber products	51	54	50	48	2481	2412	2073	1959	119	117	103	108
2211 i/	Rubber tyres and tubes	51	54	50	48	2481	2412	2073	1959	119	117	103	108
2219 i/	Other rubber products	…	…	…	…	…	…	…	…	…	…	…	…
2220	Plastics products	254	244	233	231	9270	8837	8421	7900	327	325	324	316
2310	Glass and glass products	40	41	36	34	960	980	980	849	33	27	27	26
239 j/	Non-metallic mineral products n.e.c.	101	93	95	96	5875	4267	3788	3905	212	168	158	147
2391	Refractory products	…	…	…	…	…	…	…	…	…	…	…	…
2392	Clay building materials	…	…	…	…	…	…	…	…	…	…	…	…
2393 j/	Other porcelain and ceramic products	…	…	…	…	…	…	…	…	…	…	…	…
2394 j/	Cement, lime and plaster	…	…	…	…	…	…	…	…	…	…	…	…
2395	Articles of concrete, cement and plaster	19	15	16	18	2449	1573	1638	1683	103	70	74	74
2396	Cutting, shaping and finishing of stone	30	30	30	31	634	559	404	407	13	13	11	11
2399 j/	Other non-metallic mineral products n.e.c.	52	48	49	47	2792	2135	1746	1815	97	85	69	63
2410	Basic iron and steel	12	13	13	36k/	1850	1821	1850	2199k/	75	81	77	99k/
2420 j/	Basic precious and other non-ferrous metals	16	17	17	…k/	651	656	670	…k/	29	34	31	…k/
243	Casting of metals	5m/	6m/	6m/	…k/	141m/	141m/	124m/	…k/	6m/	5m/	6m/	…k/
2431	Casting of iron and steel	…m/	6m/	6m/	…	141m/	141m/	124m/	…	6m/	5m/	6m/	…
2432	Casting of non-ferrous metals	…m/	…m/	…	…	…m/	…m/	…m/	…	…m/	…m/	…m/	…
251	Struct.metal products, tanks, reservoirs	454	446	438	440	17123	16820	16310	15974	563	588	577	581

continued

Singapore

ISIC	ISIC Revision 4 — Industry	Establishments Note	Est 2013	Est 2014	Est 2015	Est 2016	Persons Note	Persons 2013	Persons 2014	Persons 2015	Persons 2016	Wages Note	Wages 2013	Wages 2014	Wages 2015	Wages 2016
		(number)						(number)					(millions of Singapore Dollars)			
2511	Structural metal products		422	416	408	410		15307	15186	14799	14657		490	513	513	520
2512	Tanks, reservoirs and containers of metal		21	19	19	19		1275	1099	1019	828		48	48	40	35
2513	Steam generators, excl. hot water boilers		11	11	11	11		541	535	492	489		26	26	24	26
2520	Weapons and ammunition	n/	...	...	...	...	n/	...	...	...	...	n/	...	...	...	...
259	Other metal products;metal working services		869	845	814	806	n/	25875	25051	23763	23321		1063	1053	1005	995
2591	Forging,pressing,stamping,roll-forming of metal		48	42	38	37		2895	2270	2076	2010		126	109	99	99
2592	Treatment and coating of metals; machining		150	146	138	139		3779	3625	3525	3681		136	130	128	139
2593	Cutlery, hand tools and general hardware		20	18	17	17		412	450	500	471		17	20	22	23
2599	Other fabricated metal products n.e.c.	n/	651	639	621	613	n/	18789	18706	17662	17159	n/	784	794	757	735
2610	Electronic components and boards	p/	155	151	146	148	p/	59276	56604	56592	55215	p/	3407	3471	3574	3477
2620	Computers and peripheral equipment		28	22	21	21		13178	11874	11243	10331		726	722	696	704
2630	Communication equipment		31	31	30	30		3275	3218	3235	3783		239	259	263	299
2640	Consumer electronics		10	8	8	9		490	208	182	184		29	8	8	8
265	Measuring, testing equipment; watches, etc.	q/	88	92	94	100	q/	8320	8090	7788	7610	q/	545	562	576	563
2651	Measuring/testing/navigating equipment,etc.	q/	88	92	94	100	q/	8320	8090	7788	7610	q/	545	562	576	563
2652	Watches and clocks	q/	...	...	...	...	q/	...	...	...	...	q/	...	...	...	...
2660	Irradiation/electromedical equipment,etc.	p/	15	13	14	14	p/	2523	2500	2597	2537	p/	119	118	125	141
2680	Magnetic and optical media	p/	...	...	...	...	p/	...	...	...	...	p/	...	...	...	...
2710	Electric motors,generators,transformers,etc.		165	155	150	151		4257	3934	4142	4264		194	194	211	221
2720	Batteries and accumulators	r/	...	...	...	...	r/	...	...	...	...	r/	...	...	...	...
273	Wiring and wiring devices		36	36	31	32		1059	1106	1067	1008		51	56	53	54
2731	Fibre optic cables		...	...	...	...		...	...	...	...		...	...	...	...
2732	Other electronic and electric wires and cables		...	...	31	...		...	...	1067	...		...	...	53	...
2733	Wiring devices		...	...	...	...		...	...	...	...		...	...	...	...
2740	Electric lighting equipment		21	16	15	15		268	186	137	272		9	5	6	11
2750	Domestic appliances		8	8	8	9		121	104	80	82		5	5	5	6
2790	Other electrical equipment	r/	31	32	26	28	r/	2303	2605	2556	2568	r/	142	154	133	136
281	General-purpose machinery	s/	492	499	485	504	s/	16027	18702	17570	17180	s/	799	902	889	892
2811	Engines/turbines,excl.aircraft,vehicle engines		48	51	56	60		2125	2220	2226	1921		116	114	115	111
2812	Fluid power equipment		59	60	55	59		1242	1302	1191	1481		77	85	80	102
2813	Other pumps, compressors, taps and valves		...	...	...	...		...	...	...	...		...	...	...	...
2814	Bearings, gears, gearing and driving elements		15	17	15	12		1231	1289	1287	1309		54	58	59	63
2815	Ovens, furnaces and furnace burners		6	6	6	7		132	78	77	78		6	4	3	3
2816	Lifting and handling equipment		141	137	134	139		4948	5412	5185	5014		266	256	270	268
2817	Office machinery, excl.computers,etc.		9	8	7	11		32	53	25	41		1	1	-	1
2818	Power-driven hand tools		...	...	...	...		...	...	...	...		...	...	...	...
2819	Other general-purpose machinery		214	220	212	216		6317	8348	7579	7336		280	385	360	344
282	Special-purpose machinery	s/	968	935	895	881	s/	51122	46944	45880	37312	s/	2626	2842	2749	2200
2821	Agricultural and forestry machinery	t/	...	...	...	...	t/	...	...	...	...	t/	...	...	...	...
2822	Metal-forming machinery and machine tools		531	503	476	467		9638	7968	7889	8476		357	335	329	374

Code	Description													
2823	Machinery for metallurgy		...	...	...	...	...	...	...	...	...	...	...	...
2824	Mining, quarrying and construction machinery		218	211	204	201	30771	28316	26933	17661	1589	1799	1666	1043
2825	Food/beverage/tobacco processing machinery		14	16	17	17	307	279	345	339	14	14	28	28
2826	Textile/apparel/leather production machinery		5	5	5	...	212	217	208	...	10	10	10	...
2829	Other special-purpose machinery	t/	200	200	193	196	10194	10164	10505	10836	657	684	716	755
2910	Motor vehicles	u/	...	...	...	...	...	...	...	...	...	...	...	...
2920	Automobile bodies, trailers and semi-trailers		30	27	29	29	775	863	813	943	24	27	26	30
2930	Parts and accessories for motor vehicles	u/	40	38	36	38	2011	2013	2035	1922	115	116	114	116
301	Building of ships and boats		999	983	931	908	57345	56496	51607	46379	1598	1642	1426	1291
3011	Building of ships and floating structures		954	943	890	868	55988	54964	50005	45086	1552	1583	1373	1245
3012	Building of pleasure and sporting boats		45	40	41	40	1357	1532	1602	1293	46	59	53	46
3020	Railway locomotives and rolling stock		...	...	...	...	...	...	...	...	...	...	...	...
3030	Air and spacecraft and related machinery		62	65	63	67	19925	19539	19131	19505	1442	1417	1438	1509
3040	Military fighting vehicles	v/	...	...	...	...	...	...	...	...	...	...	...	...
309	Transport equipment n.e.c.	v/	12	10	8	6	2785	2768	2592	2542	197	207	194	202
3091	Motorcycles		...	...	...	...	...	...	...	...	...	...	...	...
3092	Bicycles and invalid carriages		...	...	...	...	...	...	...	...	...	...	...	...
3099	Other transport equipment n.e.c.		...	...	...	...	...	...	...	...	...	...	...	...
3100	Furniture		638	624	608	604	10524	8926	8015	8005	306	252	221	234
321	Jewellery, bijouterie and related articles		90	89	82	85	1116	1125	1048	965	40	42	42	40
3211	Jewellery and related articles	w/	90	89	82	85	1116	1125	1048	965	40	42	42	40
3212	Imitation jewellery and related articles	w/	...	...	...	...	...	...	...	...	...	...	...	...
3220	Musical instruments		...	...	...	...	...	...	...	...	...	...	...	...
3230	Sports goods	x/	...	...	...	...	...	...	...	...	...	...	...	...
3240	Games and toys	x/	...	...	...	...	...	...	...	...	...	...	...	...
3250	Medical and dental instruments and supplies		98	96	93	96	10222	11051	11422	12383	461	582	592	673
3290	Other manufacturing n.e.c.	x/	316	316	304	330	3595	4416	4635	4804	128	149	167	178
331	Repair of fabricated metal products/machinery		...	...	...	...	...	...	...	...	...	...	...	...
3311	Repair of fabricated metal products		...	...	...	...	...	...	...	...	...	...	...	...
3312	Repair of machinery		...	...	...	...	...	...	...	...	...	...	...	...
3313	Repair of electronic and optical equipment		...	...	...	...	...	...	...	...	...	...	...	...
3314	Repair of electrical equipment		...	...	...	...	...	...	...	...	...	...	...	...
3315	Repair of transport equip., excl. motor vehicles		...	...	...	...	...	...	...	...	...	...	...	...
3319	Repair of other equipment		...	...	...	...	...	...	...	...	...	...	...	...
3320	Installation of industrial machinery/equipment		264	250	243	274	6308	7413	6286	6907	202	242	204	217
C	Total manufacturing		9303	9106	8778	8988	424505	416406	403286	384726	20722	21806	21678	20996

a/ 1079 includes 1061, 1072 and 1200.
b/ 1101 includes 1102, 1103 and 1104.
c/ 1392 includes 131 and 1399.
d/ 1410 includes 1420 and 1430.
e/ 1511 includes 1512.
f/ 1709 includes 1701.
g/ 2013 includes 2012.
h/ 2029 includes 2021 and 2030.
i/ 2211 includes 2219.
j/ 2399 includes 2391, 2393 and 2394.

k/ 2410 includes 2420 and 243.
m/ 2431 includes 2432.
n/ 2599 includes 2520.
p/ 2610 includes 2660 and 2680.
q/ 2651 includes 2652.
r/ 2790 includes 2720.
s/ 281 and 282 include both manufacturing and repair activities.
t/ 2829 includes 2821.
u/ 2930 includes 2910.
v/ 309 includes 3040.

w/ 3211 includes 3212.
x/ 3290 includes 3230 and 3240.

Singapore

ISIC	Industry	Output Note	Output 2013	Output 2014	Output 2015	Output 2016	VA Note	VA 2013	VA 2014	VA 2015	VA 2016	GFCF Note	GFCF 2015	GFCF 2016
	ISIC Revision 4		Output at basic prices (millions of Singapore Dollars)					Value added at basic prices (millions of Singapore Dollars)					Gross fixed capital formation (millions of Singapore Dollars)	
1010	Processing/preserving of meat		588	652	649	700		144	168	176	192		26	18
1020	Processing/preserving of fish, etc.		201	214	199	210		64	66	60	60		4	26
1030	Processing/preserving of fruit,vegetables		38	40	40	52		13	13	14	19		1	1
1040	Vegetable and animal oils and fats		613	655	503	449		74	82	81	87		8	3
1050	Dairy products		2334	2695	2525	2410		764	1062	1155	1216		124	65
106	Grain mill products,starches and starch products	a/	...	...	...	...	a/	...	...	...	...	a/	...	...
1061	Grain mill products		...	...	...	...		...	...	...	...		...	...
1062	Starches and starch products		...	...	...	...		...	...	...	...		...	...
107	Other food products	a/	4013	4000	4030	3957	a/	934	1010	1063	1077		181	194
1071	Bakery products		866	910	938	962		309	317	347	355		44	50
1072	Sugar	a/	...	...	...	...	a/	...	...	...	...	a/	...	...
1073	Cocoa, chocolate and sugar confectionery		607	722	741	801		37	76	88	108		17	24
1074	Macaroni, noodles, couscous, etc.		186	177	182	183		64	62	64	65		12	7
1075	Prepared meals and dishes		400	417	405	424		157	173	176	184		26	52
1079	Other food products n.e.c.	a/	1953	1774	1764	1587	a/	368	382	388	365	a/	82	61
1080	Prepared animal feeds		219	204	859	764		76	69	405	331		20	121
110	Beverages		1805	1893	1793	1608		807	944	809	799		72	54
1101	Distilling, rectifying and blending of spirits	b/	1805	1893	1793	1608	b/	807	944	809	799	b/	72	54
1102	Wines	b/	...	...	...	...	b/	...	...	...	...	b/	...	...
1103	Malt liquors and malt	b/	...	...	...	...	b/	...	...	...	...	b/	...	...
1104	Soft drinks,mineral waters,other bottled waters	b/	...	...	...	...	b/	...	...	...	...	b/	...	...
1200	Tobacco products	a/	...	...	...	...	a/	...	...	...	...	a/	...	...
131	Spinning, weaving and finishing of textiles	c/	...	...	...	...	c/	...	...	...	...	c/	...	...
1311	Preparation and spinning of textile fibres		...	...	...	...		...	...	...	...		...	...
1312	Weaving of textiles		...	...	...	...		...	...	...	...		...	...
1313	Finishing of textiles		...	...	...	...		...	...	...	...		...	...
139	Other textiles		...	...	...	...		...	...	...	...		...	...
1391	Knitted and crocheted fabrics		...	...	...	...		...	...	...	...		...	...
1392	Made-up textile articles, except apparel	c/	62	50	54	59	c/	21	18	21	23	c/	3	2
1393	Carpets and rugs		...	...	...	...		...	...	...	...		...	...
1394	Cordage, rope, twine and netting		...	...	...	...		...	...	...	...		...	...
1399	Other textiles n.e.c.	c/	...	...	...	...	c/	...	...	...	...	c/	...	...
1410	Wearing apparel, except fur apparel	d/	478	354	259	227	d/	110	93	92	81	d/	5	1
1420	Articles of fur	d/	...	...	...	...	d/	...	...	...	...	d/	...	...
1430	Knitted and crocheted apparel	d/	...	...	...	...	d/	...	...	...	...	d/	...	...
151	Leather;luggage,handbags,saddlery,harness;fur	e/	154	152	163	146	e/	63	60	60	57	e/	6	1
1511	Tanning/dressing of leather; dressing of fur	e/	154	152	163	146	e/	63	60	60	57	e/	6	1
1512	Luggage,handbags,etc.;saddlery/harness	e/	...	...	...	...	e/	...	...	...	...	e/	...	...
1520	Footwear		17	7	4	3		7	4	2	1		-	-
1610	Sawmilling and planing of wood		9	9	8	9		6	6	6	6		-	-

162	Wood products, cork, straw, plaiting materials		341	358	341	341	118	126	125	127		19	10
1621	Veneer sheets and wood-based panels		54	45	39	20	10	9	8	8		1	1
1622	Builders' carpentry and joinery		110	133	115	126	41	51	48	45		2	6
1623	Wooden containers		164	167	175	183	59	60	62	67		12	4
1629	Other wood products;articles of cork,straw		13	13	12	12	8	7	6	7		4	-
170	Paper and paper products		1104	1143	1124	1086	242	252	239	232		38	18
1701	Pulp, paper and paperboard		9	-	...f/	...f/	3	-	...f/	...f/		...f/	...f/
1702	Corrugated paper and paperboard		886	948	927	861	195	208	197	186		34	15
1709	Other articles of paper and paperboard		209	194	196f/	225f/	45	44	42f/	46f/		4f/	3f/
181	Printing and service activities related to printing		2292	2336	2216	1915	1167	1188	1117	985		100	112
1811	Printing		2239	2276	2167	1878	1135	1154	1090	967		99	108
1812	Service activities related to printing		53	60	49	37	32	35	26	18		2	3
1820	Reproduction of recorded media		60	41	35	31	29	19	17	15		-	-
1910	Coke oven products		...	...	...	...	...	...	...	...		...	...
1920	Refined petroleum products		51027	46359	32483	26987	57	33	2412	2034		781	834
201	Basic chemicals,fertilizers, etc.		37969	43837	33341	29438	1508	2456	4259	7890		917	1638
2011	Basic chemicals		1453	1338	1334	1350	454	491	533	536		164	198
2012	Fertilizers and nitrogen compounds	g/											
2013	Plastics and synthetic rubber in primary forms	g/	36516	42499	32007	28088	1054	1966	3725	7354	g/	753	1440
202	Other chemical products		12050	11504	11576	11771	3693	3164	3734	4502	g/	417	471
2021	Pesticides and other agrochemical products	h/				774	233	229	236	225	h/	20	25
2022	Paints,varnishes;printing ink and mastics		828	844	860								
2023	Soap,cleaning and cosmetic preparations		3827	3420	3487	3664	1385	1211	1301	1618		154	36
2029	Other chemical products n.e.c.	h/	7395	7240	7229	7334	2074	1724	2197	2658	h/	243	411
2030	Man-made fibres	h/									h/		
2100	Pharmaceuticals,medicinal chemicals, etc.		16920	16891	16721	17745	9032	9506	10417	11052		548	338
221	Rubber products		436	473	380	350	189	204	169	173		17	16
2211	Rubber tyres and tubes	i/	436	473	380	350	189	204	169	173	i/	17	16
2219	Other rubber products	i/									i/		
2220	Plastics products		1584	1538	1477	1505	512	516	540	554		58	64
2310	Glass and glass products		203	107	111	91	51	44	39	38		12	5
239	Non-metallic mineral products n.e.c.	j/	2428	2061	2010	1650	488	390	352	316	j/	63	49
2391	Refractory products	j/	...	...	...	...	...	...	...	...	j/	...	...
2392	Clay building materials		...	...	...	...	...	...	...	...		...	...
2393	Other porcelain and ceramic products	j/	...	...	...	...	...	...	...	...	j/	...	...
2394	Cement, lime and plaster	j/	...	...	...	...	...	...	...	...	j/	...	...
2395	Articles of concrete, cement and plaster		1862	1562	1513	1177	290	180	157	125		31	36
2396	Cutting, shaping and finishing of stone		51	53	52	40	19	21	20	17		1	1
2399	Other non-metallic mineral products n.e.c.	j/	516	447	444	433	179	188	175	174	j/	31	12
2410	Basic iron and steel		742	813	652	1108k/	98	58	94	178k/		25	42k/
2420	Basic precious and other non-ferrous metals		280	549	488	...k/	57	63	61	...k/		20	...k/
243	Casting of metals		23	25	21	...k/	2	6	8	...k/		1	...k/
2431	Casting of iron and steel		23m/	25m/	21m/		2m/	6m/	8m/			1m/	...
2432	Casting of non-ferrous metals		...m/	...m/	...m/		...m/	...m/	...m/			...m/	...
251	Struct.metal products, tanks, reservoirs		3113	3189	2961	2699	1017	950	947	904		165	109

continued

Singapore

ISIC	Industry	Note	Output at basic prices (millions of Singapore Dollars)				Note	Value added at basic prices (millions of Singapore Dollars)				Note	Gross fixed capital formation (millions of Singapore Dollars)	
	ISIC Revision 4		2013	2014	2015	2016		2013	2014	2015	2016		2015	2016
2511	Structural metal products		2822	2831	2698	2485		923	852	861	826		152	104
2512	Tanks, reservoirs and containers of metal		197	262	177	139		64	67	57	50		9	3
2513	Steam generators, excl. hot water boilers		93	96	86	75		30	31	30	28		4	2
2520	Weapons and ammunition	n/	...	...	...	...	n/	...	...	...	...	n/	...	...
259	Other metal products;metal working services		6527	6465	5959	5609		1783	1826	1718	1678		216	264
2591	Forging,pressing,stamping,roll-forming of metal		752	671	615	519		187	175	154	141		18	15
2592	Treatment and coating of metals; machining		543	424	378	379		249	218	210	217		26	32
2593	Cutlery, hand tools and general hardware		105	147	131	127		50	69	62	61		3	3
2599	Other fabricated metal products n.e.c.	n/	5126	5223	4835	4583	n/	1297	1364	1292	1259	n/	170	215
2610	Electronic components and boards	p/	55076	56501	58433	65788	p/	12727	14053	15565	12788	p/	4066	7142
2620	Computers and peripheral equipment		27806	26388	31781	25567		4617	4056	3681	3154		386	238
2630	Communication equipment		1174	1174	1112	1474		271	280	262	335		25	59
2640	Consumer electronics		110	45	39	32		44	12	10	9		2	1
265	Measuring,testing equipment; watches, etc.	q/	8898	4510	6371	6227	q/	1353	1239	1309	1302	q/	60	123
2651	Measuring/testing/navigating equipment,etc.	q/	8898	4510	6371	6227	q/	1353	1239	1309	1302	q/	60	123
2652	Watches and clocks	p/	...	...	...	...	p/	...	...	...	...	p/	...	...
2660	Irradiation/electromedical equipment,etc.		...	...	...	...		...	...	...	...		...	...
2670	Optical instruments and photographic equipment		874	846	890	711		382	360	390	262		27	108
2680	Magnetic and optical media	p/	...	...	...	...	p/	...	...	...	...	p/	...	...
2710	Electric motors,generators,transformers,etc.		1241	1122	1232	1235		373	313	336	322		40	18
2720	Batteries and accumulators	r/	...	...	...	...	r/	...	...	...	...	r/	...	...
273	Wiring and wiring devices		488	520	460	491		139	147	125	138		9	9
2731	Fibre optic cables		...	...	...	...		...	...	...	...		...	...
2732	Other electronic and electric wires and cables		...	...	460	...		...	...	125	...		...	...
2733	Wiring devices		27	26	21	69		10	7	8	26		4	1
2740	Electric lighting equipment		20	18	35	35		7	6	7	7		-	2
2750	Domestic appliances		...	...	...	...		...	...	...	...		61	100
2790	Other electrical equipment	r/	890	1082	966	1065	r/	297	335	339	362	r/	118	155
281	General-purpose machinery	s/	4680	4957	5180	4442	s/	1417	1600	1685	1405	s/	12	6
2811	Engines/turbines,excl.aircraft,vehicle engines		421	424	424	414		201	192	205	193		8	9
2812	Fluid power equipment		420	437	407	429		129	143	140	135			
2813	Other pumps, compressors, taps and valves		...	...	...	...		...	...	...	...		5	11
2814	Bearings, gears, gearing and driving elements		232	255	262	281		88	110	120	142		-	-
2815	Ovens, furnaces and furnace burners		11	10	6	6		8	5	4	3		8	16
2816	Lifting and handling equipment		1198	1276	1274	983		411	404	449	397		-	-
2817	Office machinery, excl.computers,etc.		3	3	2	4		1	1	-	1		84	113
2818	Power-driven hand tools		...	...	...	...		...	...	...	...		671	333
2819	Other general-purpose machinery		2395	2551	2805	2325		578	745	765	532			
282	Special-purpose machinery	s/	23739	28254	24826	21866	s/	5613	6715	5280	4869	s/	48	56
2821	Agricultural and forestry machinery	t/	...	...	...	...	t/	...	...	...	...	t/		
2822	Metal-forming machinery and machine tools		1183	1207	1168	1324		488	495	490	565			

Code	Description													
2823	Machinery for metallurgy		14101	16766	12317	5927		3457	4171	2631	1662		521	144
2824	Mining, quarrying and construction machinery		48	64	119	103		9	15	31	24		2	1
2825	Food/beverage/tobacco processing machinery		52	49	51	…		21	21	21	…		1	…
2826	Textile/apparel/leather production machinery		…	…	…	…		…	…	…	…		…	…
2829	Other special-purpose machinery	t/	8355	10168	11171	14512	t/	1638	2013	2108	2618	t/	99	131
2910	Motor vehicles	u/	…	…	…	…	u/	…	…	…	…	u/	…	…
2920	Automobile bodies, trailers and semi-trailers		181	138	120	120		45	49	49	47		3	5
2930	Parts and accessories for motor vehicles	u/	840	951	1059	1118	u/	302	307	302	350	u/	34	65
301	Building of ships and boats		7501	8101	7110	6765		2773	2927	2267	1917		209	132
3011	Building of ships and floating structures		7123	7629	6724	6445		2668	2791	2167	1832		203	130
3012	Building of pleasure and sporting boats		379	472	386	321		106	136	100	85		6	2
3020	Railway locomotives and rolling stock		…	…	…	…		…	…	…	…		…	…
3030	Air and spacecraft and related machinery		8910	8310	8385	8971		3087	2989	3175	3340		460	262
3040	Military fighting vehicles	v/	…	…	…	…	v/	…	…	…	…	v/	…	…
309	Transport equipment n.e.c.	v/	1146	1145	1142	988	v/	408	470	450	371	v/	11	36
3091	Motorcycles		…	…	…	…		…	…	…	…		…	…
3092	Bicycles and invalid carriages		…	…	…	…		…	…	…	…		…	…
3099	Other transport equipment n.e.c.		…	…	…	…		…	…	…	…		…	…
3100	Furniture		1301	969	917	857		476	343	312	323		17	91
321	Jewellery, bijouterie and related articles		978	983	1015	943		86	96	97	85		4	2
3211	Jewellery and related articles	w/	978	983	1015	943	w/	86	96	97	85	w/	4	2
3212	Imitation jewellery and related articles	w/	…	…	…	…	w/	…	…	…	…	w/	…	…
3220	Musical instruments		…	…	…	…		…	…	…	…		…	…
3230	Sports goods	x/	…	…	…	…	x/	…	…	…	…	x/	…	…
3240	Games and toys	x/	…	…	…	…	x/	…	…	…	…	x/	…	…
3250	Medical and dental instruments and supplies		4707	10402	9175	10248		1904	2347	2508	3280		134	249
3290	Other manufacturing n.e.c.	x/	838	893	885	890	x/	314	391	392	426	x/	32	22
331	Repair of fabricated metal products/machinery		…	…	…	…		…	…	…	…		…	…
3311	Repair of fabricated metal products		…	…	…	…		…	…	…	…		…	…
3312	Repair of machinery		…	…	…	…		…	…	…	…		…	…
3313	Repair of electronic and optical equipment		…	…	…	…		…	…	…	…		…	…
3314	Repair of electrical equipment		…	…	…	…		…	…	…	…		…	…
3315	Repair of transport equip., excl. motor vehicles		…	…	…	…		…	…	…	…		…	…
3319	Repair of other equipment		…	…	…	…		…	…	…	…		…	…
3320	Installation of industrial machinery/equipment		569	694	555	712		267	308	262	298		23	23
C	Total manufacturing		299624	306642	284691	273533		60042	63748	69001	70044		10247	13634

a/ 1079 includes 1061, 1072 and 1200.
b/ 1101 includes 1102, 1103 and 1104.
c/ 1392 includes 131 and 1399.
d/ 1410 includes 1420 and 1430.
e/ 1511 includes 1512.
f/ 1709 includes 1701.
g/ 2013 includes 2012.
h/ 2029 includes 2021 and 2030.
i/ 2211 includes 2219.
j/ 2399 includes 2391, 2393 and 2394.

k/ 2410 includes 2420 and 243.
m/ 2431 includes 2432.
n/ 2599 includes 2520.
p/ 2610 includes 2660 and 2680.
q/ 2651 includes 2652.
r/ 2790 includes 2720.
s/ 281 and 282 include both manufacturing and repair activities.
t/ 2829 includes 2821.
u/ 2930 includes 2910.
v/ 309 includes 3040.

w/ 3211 includes 3212.
x/ 3290 includes 3230 and 3240.

Singapore

Index numbers of industrial production

ISIC Revision 4

ISIC	Industry	Note	(2010=100)											
			2005	2006	2007	2008	2009	2010	2011	2012	2013	2014	2015	2016
10	Food products	a/	79	82	91	98	94	100	104	107	107	109	110	114
11	Beverages	a/	...	...	...	...	...	...	...	...	...	...	...	...
12	Tobacco products	a/	...	...	...	...	...	...	...	...	...	...	...	...
13	Textiles		227	191	159	148	119	100	82	84	71	61	60	55
14	Wearing apparel		480	433	378	271	171	100	81	75	63	40	19	16
15	Leather and related products		185	185	185	157	97	100	122	120	134	117	110	98
16	Wood products, excluding furniture		135	153	143	127	98	100	96	94	103	107	100	95
17	Paper and paper products		86	89	96	95	90	100	94	92	97	97	93	91
18	Printing and reproduction of recorded media		111	115	118	114	97	100	97	90	83	78	73	62
19	Coke and refined petroleum products		121	117	117	118	101	100	105	104	98	89	97	101
20	Chemicals and chemical products		81	85	91	87	82	100	102	103	107	117	121	119
21	Pharmaceuticals,medicinal chemicals, etc.		50	64	63	58	65	100	133	146	142	154	140	160
22	Rubber and plastics products		117	116	116	107	90	100	89	86	83	83	76	69
23	Other non-metallic mineral products		148	142	126	104	99	100	108	107	105	89	98	88
24	Basic metals		83	98	89	107	91	100	98	89	75	96	97	103
25	Fabricated metal products, except machinery		93	101	103	98	88	100	97	101	102	102	95	89
26	Computer, electronic and optical products		80	85	88	82	75	100	88	80	83	84	79	90
27	Electrical equipment		58	66	67	66	70	100	81	80	87	98	100	101
28	Machinery and equipment n.e.c.		56	71	85	83	73	100	127	143	146	158	134	108
29	Motor vehicles, trailers and semi-trailers		...	...	109	82	72	100	116	114	140	150	165	174
30	Other transport equipment		69	86	100	109	102	100	106	113	114	110	103	104
31	Furniture		60	75	75	84	91	100	88	93	91	81	79	68
32	Other manufacturing		83	76	92	89	90	100	109	116	127	135	159	176
33	Repair and installation of machinery/equipment		...	...	...	...	...	...	...	...	...	...	...	...
C	Total manufacturing		71	79	84	80	77	100	108	108	110	113	107	111

a/ 10 includes 11 and 12.

Slovakia

Supplier of information:
Statistical Office of the Slovak Republic, Bratislava.
Industrial statistics for the OECD countries are compiled by the OECD secretariat, which
supplies them to UNIDO.

Basic source of data:
Annual surveys; business register.

Major deviations from ISIC (Revision 4):
Data presented in ISIC (Revision 4) were originally classified according to the national
NACE-related classification system.

Reference period:
Calendar year.

Scope:
All enterprises.

Method of data collection:
Not reported.

Type of enumeration:
Data have been collected via three business surveys: for enterprises with 20 or more
employees; for enterprises with less than 20 employees; and for entrepreneurs not
registered in the register of companies.

Adjusted for non-response:
Not reported.

Concepts and definitions of variables:
No deviations from the standard UN concepts and definitions are reported.

Related national publications:
None reported.

Slovakia

ISIC Revision 4		Number of enterprises					Number of employees					Wages and salaries paid to employees				
		Note	(number)				Note	(number)				Note	(millions of Euros)			
ISIC	Industry		2013	2014	2015	2016		2013	2014	2015	2016		2013	2014	2015	2016
1010	Processing/preserving of meat		264	305	299	384		6460	6565	7174	7064		49.8	54.1	63.7	66.2
1020	Processing/preserving of fish, etc.		10	...	...	...		576	...	...	...		5.3	...	...	...
1030	Processing/preserving of fruit,vegetables		157	173	215	337		1118	1285	1749	1714		9.3	9.6	12.6	14.2
1040	Vegetable and animal oils and fats		18	...	...	...		287	...	...	...		2.8	...	...	...
1050	Dairy products		189	180	176	174		3037	2894	2962	3090		33.3	32.0	32.8	36.0
106	Grain mill products,starches and starch products		84	119	115	162		1039	992	994	1198		13.4	14.1	13.9	16.3
1061	Grain mill products		84a/	114	112	162a/		1039a/	641	646	1198a/		13.4a/	5.8	5.9	16.3a/
1062	Starches and starch products		...a/	5	3	...a/		...a/	351	348	...a/		...a/	8.3	8.1	...a/
107	Other food products		1526	1500	1492	1619		17420	17554	18532	19282		145.1	146.7	160.1	174.6
1071	Bakery products		1157	1120	1070	1061		12618	12528	13276	13572		93.4	89.6	99.8	107.3
1072	Sugar		10	14	19	30		348	354	368	378		6.2	6.7	6.5	6.4
1073	Cocoa, chocolate and sugar confectionery		62	74	66	81		1470	1559	1481	1465		14.1	17.0	16.2	17.8
1074	Macaroni, noodles, couscous, etc.		69	61	60	67		572	524	510	539		3.9	4.2	4.0	4.3
1075	Prepared meals and dishes		9	26	36	64		-	40	70	243		-	0.1	0.3	1.7
1079	Other food products n.e.c.		219	205	241	316		2412	2549	2827	3085		27.4	29.0	33.3	37.1
1080	Prepared animal feeds		99	104	59	127		591	653	395	487		6.0	7.2	5.1	5.0
110	Beverages		419	497	492	619		4606	4848	4719	4574		61.3	63.5	62.2	61.0
1101	Distilling, rectifying and blending of spirits		103	107	101	112		554	722	691	724		7.4	6.7	6.9	7.6
1102	Wines		...	23	23	48		...	...	...	...		...	...	...	...
1103	Malt liquors and malt		19	23	23	48		1639	1489	1536	1493		27.1	27.2	26.8	27.7
1104	Soft drinks,mineral waters,other bottled waters		130	188	186	251		1563	1747	1570	1280		19.4	21.2	19.5	15.3
1200	Tobacco products		...	...	...	...		...	...	...	...		...	...	...	...
131	Spinning, weaving and finishing of textiles		109	...	164	299		890	...	1156	1352		9.7	...	13.0	15.1
1311	Preparation and spinning of textile fibres		31	...	20	22		205	...	320	319		2.3	...	3.4	3.4
1312	Weaving of textiles		22	49	90	216		620	681	782	891		7.1	7.9	9.3	10.8
1313	Finishing of textiles		56		54	61		65	...	54	142		0.3	...	0.3	0.9
139	Other textiles		1077	1064	1109	1112		4548	4654	4951	4817		33.7	38.3	41.5	40.5
1391	Knitted and crocheted fabrics		46	35	29	31		818	828	785	704		7.1	8.1	7.5	7.3
1392	Made-up textile articles, except apparel		595	524	458	436		2329	2172	2030	2133		15.2	15.2	14.4	15.6
1393	Carpets and rugs		24	17	15	21		166	185	166	159		1.2	1.6	1.5	1.6
1394	Cordage, rope, twine and netting		16	17	18	18		397	420	385	400		3.6	4.4	4.2	4.6
1399	Other textiles n.e.c.		396	471	589	606		838	1049	1585	1421		6.8	9.1	14.0	11.3
1410	Wearing apparel, except fur apparel		3668	3287	3208	3245		11963	11519	11032	11781		67.9	68.6	68.2	76.3
1420	Articles of fur		51	62	66	78		65	29	39	46		0.3	0.2	0.2	0.1
1430	Knitted and crocheted apparel		193	146	134	125		2497	2337	2119	2248		15.6	15.6	14.4	15.4
151	Leather;luggage,handbags,saddlery,harness;fur		147	120	110	167		1355	1533	1796	2268		10.6	13.0	15.9	20.3
1511	Tanning/dressing of leather; dressing of fur		38	24	21	43		323	371	398	534		3.8	4.3	4.7	6.3
1512	Luggage,handbags,etc.;saddlery/harness		109	96	89	124		1032	1162	1398	1734		6.8	8.8	11.2	14.0
1520	Footwear		223	219	200	170		8581	8576	8393	8427		64.5	68.1	68.8	71.2
1610	Sawmilling and planing of wood		5659	5332	5079	5033		4349	5425	6477	4274		26.1	37.0	43.7	29.0

162	Wood products, cork, straw, plaiting materials	5511	5592	5566	6111	5456	7887	8643	7838	36.8	55.0	60.3	59.1
1621	Veneer sheets and wood-based panels	208	187	155	182	1282	1331	1632	1569	12.4	13.2	17.0	17.3
1622	Builders' carpentry and joinery	2842	3005	3233	3478	2402	3419	4216	3642	14.9	22.4	25.1	25.2
1623	Wooden containers	339	308	285	289	646	683	683	768	3.7	4.7	4.8	5.7
1629	Other wood products;articles of cork,straw	2122	2092	1893	2162	1126	2454	2112	1859	5.7	14.8	13.4	10.8
170	Paper and paper products	272	277	289	340	6499	6670	6732	6760	84.0	86.4	90.7	92.3
1701	Pulp, paper and paperboard	...	...	...	...	...	...	...	...	...	...	...	...
1702	Corrugated paper and paperboard	102	108	108	109	1940	1998	2073	2101	22.7	23.5	25.3	25.7
1709	Other articles of paper and paperboard	...	...	...	...	...	...	...	...	...	...	...	...
181	Printing and service activities related to printing	1302	1402	1535	1675	5322	5249	5024	4698	53.9	48.4	48.9	45.7
1811	Printing	1302b/	966	877	831	5322b/	4504	4141	3531	53.9b/	43.4	41.8	37.8
1812	Service activities related to printing	...b/	436	658	844	...b/	745	883	1167	...b/	5.1	7.1	8.0
1820	Reproduction of recorded media	138	114	106	144	31	45	29	3	0.1	0.2	0.2	-
1910	Coke oven products	...	...	...	...	...	...	...	...	...	...	...	...
1920	Refined petroleum products	...	...	...	...	...	...	...	...	...	...	...	...
201	Basic chemicals,fertilizers, etc.	128	166	175	196	6150	5935	5449	5594	80.7	84.2	81.6	85.7
2011	Basic chemicals	...	...	...	...	...	...	...	...	...	...	...	...
2012	Fertilizers and nitrogen compounds	...	...	...	...	...	...	...	...	...	...	...	...
2013	Plastics and synthetic rubber in primary forms	50	62	72	78	2646	2384	1798	2014	32.6	31.5	26.6	27.9
202	Other chemical products	154	...	...	...	2064	...	...	...	23.8	...	...	...
2021	Pesticides and other agrochemical products	9	...	...	...	7	...	...	...	0.1	...	...	...
2022	Paints,varnishes;printing ink and mastics	30	31	40	43	537	523	541	576	5.9	5.7	6.3	6.8
2023	Soap,cleaning and cosmetic preparations	...	...	...	...	...	...	...	...	...	...	...	...
2029	Other chemical products n.e.c.	...	...	...	...	...	...	...	...	...	...	...	...
2030	Man-made fibres	7	...	...	...	664	...	...	...	7.5	...	...	...
2100	Pharmaceuticals,medicinal chemicals, etc.	24	28	30	32	2007	2163	2217	2235	27.2	29.4	31.0	31.9
221	Rubber products	229	235	288	370	7803	8114	8744	10126	99.9	107.2	118.9	140.5
2211	Rubber tyres and tubes	113	116	101	98	4092	4063	4101	4201	64.3	67.3	70.6	76.2
2219	Other rubber products	116	119	187	272	3711	4051	4643	5925	35.5	39.8	48.4	64.3
2220	Plastics products	1282	1257	1149	1228	20133	21050	22122	23065	211.9	224.7	246.4	260.3
2310	Glass and glass products	250	234	255	281	4405	4386	4356	4485	53.8	55.4	56.9	62.4
239	Non-metallic mineral products n.e.c.	2305	2151	2043	2145	10098	10263	10036	10729	119.3	124.5	127.0	140.0
2391	Refractory products	12	9	11	10	1817	1841	1736	1618	18.0	18.3	19.9	19.3
2392	Clay building materials	18	19	24	17	306	335	399	347	3.1	3.5	4.5	4.3
2393	Other porcelain and ceramic products	...	...	...	...	...	...	...	...	...	...	...	...
2394	Cement, lime and plaster	16	18	18	17	2018	1894	1879	1915	36.5	36.5	34.7	33.5
2395	Articles of concrete, cement and plaster	...	...	...	...	...	...	...	...	...	...	...	...
2396	Cutting, shaping and finishing of stone	735	696	685	680	1027	869	676	894	3.5	4.0	3.2	5.0
2399	Other non-metallic mineral products n.e.c.	...	...	...	63	...	...	...	949	...	...	...	15.3
2410	Basic iron and steel	206	189	...	...	17698	17568	...	...	285.3	293.0	...	...
2420	Basic precious and other non-ferrous metals	24	18	...	...	1745	1755	...	...	26.2	27.4	...	...
243	Casting of metals	62	57	53	53	3556	3897	3586	3708	40.4	44.8	43.3	47.7
2431	Casting of iron and steel	20	19	17	18	1218	1530	1123	1116	13.0	16.5	13.3	14.5
2432	Casting of non-ferrous metals	42	38	36	35	2338	2367	2463	2592	27.3	28.3	30.0	33.2
251	Struct.metal products, tanks, reservoirs	...	...	...	2150	...	...	...	11690	...	...	...	140.1

continued

Slovakia

ISIC	Industry	Number of enterprises (number)					Number of employees (number)					Wages and salaries paid to employees (millions of Euros)				
		Note	2013	2014	2015	2016	Note	2013	2014	2015	2016	Note	2013	2014	2015	2016
2511	Structural metal products		1949	1783	1648	1912		8066	8173	9307	8288		84.6	88.8	102.6	95.6
2512	Tanks, reservoirs and containers of metal		153	142	142	225		2713	2635	2705	2653		30.1	30.4	32.8	32.2
2513	Steam generators, excl. hot water boilers		...	...	...	13		...	...	...	749		...	...	...	12.3
2520	Weapons and ammunition		...	...	...	25		...	...	...	530		...	...	...	5.8
259	Other metal products;metal working services		21952	24150	24473	25319		28867	32096	36596	34925		289.5	336.5	397.0	387.4
2591	Forging,pressing,stamping,roll-forming of metal		171	145	135	136		2369	2428	2923	3039		27.6	29.6	35.7	38.0
2592	Treatment and coating of metals; machining		12486	12673	12406	12200		12391	14608	16646	15153		118.9	140.3	164.0	153.8
2593	Cutlery, hand tools and general hardware		3830	4160	4130	4257		2587	2567	2461	2452		24.3	24.9	25.9	25.7
2599	Other fabricated metal products n.e.c.		5465	7172	7802	8726		11520	12493	14566	14281		118.7	141.7	171.4	170.0
2610	Electronic components and boards		198	204	171	168		4074	4374	4734	4564		40.6	46.1	52.1	50.2
2620	Computers and peripheral equipment		134	165	177	216		1173	1094	712	609		11.6	11.1	8.8	10.4
2630	Communication equipment		142	168	...	458		1665	1079	...	1435		18.4	10.4	...	13.9
2640	Consumer electronics		56	51	56	73		5866	5764	4927	4865		75.6	78.1	67.4	68.6
265	Measuring,testing equipment, watches, etc.		162	177	171	178		2235	2366	2394	2496		26.9	28.1	31.4	32.8
2651	Measuring/testing/navigating equipment,etc.		162	177 c/	171	178		2235	2366 c/	2394	2496		26.9	28.1 c/	31.4	32.8
2652	Watches and clocks		-	... c/	-	-		-	...	-	-		-	... c/	-	-
2660	Irradiation/electromedical equipment,etc.		9	9	11	44		41	54	107	169		0.6	0.9	1.5	2.2
2670	Optical instruments and photographic equipment		24	20	20	37		70	62	70	356		0.5	0.4	0.5	3.8
2680	Magnetic and optical media		10	12	...	5		125	-	...	-		0.1	-	...	-
2710	Electric motors,generators,transformers,etc.		447	515	546	662		10406	9808	10097	10172		144.9	140.5	150.2	146.7
2720	Batteries and accumulators		6	6	...	...		55	22	...	...		0.5	0.2	...	...
273	Wiring and wiring devices		158	150	...	...		3343	6148	...	...		30.7	61.8	...	...
2731	Fibre optic cables		7	7	...	...		309	306	...	...		4.0	4.0	...	...
2732	Other electronic and electric wires and cables		49	49	51	43		2735	5397	5229	5895		24.3	51.6	52.0	59.5
2733	Wiring devices		102	94	85	83		299	445	630	732		2.4	6.3	8.6	10.5
2740	Electric lighting equipment		72	77	88	77		6155	6974	7446	8275		68.6	80.6	90.8	109.3
2750	Domestic appliances		182	167	156	156		2684	2778	2985	2951		29.0	31.4	35.0	34.2
2790	Other electrical equipment		539	489	433	441		3945	4323	4580	4516		45.9	50.9	53.4	56.2
281	General-purpose machinery		1095	1070	1069	1179		26889	28201	28677	30811		345.9	370.2	387.7	436.2
2811	Engines/turbines,excl.aircraft,vehicle engines		18	14	14	16		324	304	272	212		3.4	3.4	3.0	2.4
2812	Fluid power equipment		11	11	11	10		1073	1029	936	873		14.2	14.7	13.9	13.3
2813	Other pumps, compressors, taps and valves		72	73	80	99		4451	4439	4526	4642		53.0	49.3	53.8	57.8
2814	Bearings, gears, gearing and driving elements		28	28	30	30		12533	13343	13914	14514		172.9	195.0	208.2	227.8
2815	Ovens, furnaces and furnace burners		26	30	32	35		683	737	713	737		8.3	9.7	8.6	9.2
2816	Lifting and handling equipment		136	171	178	202		2118	2643	2952	3175		26.5	32.4	36.6	45.4
2817	Office machinery, excl.computers,etc.		...	176	158	162		...	311	278	408		...	3.3	3.8	3.7
2818	Power-driven hand tools		...	4	4	7		...	59	38	5		...	0.6	0.5	0.1
2819	Other general-purpose machinery		624	563	562	618		5241	5336	5048	6245		63.0	61.8	59.3	76.6
282	Special-purpose machinery		316	293	302	369		11639	11430	11551	11743		141.1	143.0	151.1	163.3
2821	Agricultural and forestry machinery		44	45	41	47		1381	1420	1354	1336		14.2	15.0	15.4	16.2
2822	Metal-forming machinery and machine tools		52	52	53	52		2333	2408	2813	2832		27.6	29.6	35.5	38.8

2823	Machinery for metallurgy	17	16	15	17	3043	2809	2479	2486	34.4	34.2	30.5	30.3
2824	Mining, quarrying and construction machinery	30	26	22	33	1023	1047	1080	1135	14.7	14.8	14.9	18.3
2825	Food/beverage/tobacco processing machinery	...	...	...	...	...	...	...	...	...	...	...	...
2826	Textile/apparel/leather production machinery	...	...	...	...	...	...	...	...	...	...	...	...
2829	Other special-purpose machinery	...	...	...	...	...	...	...	...	...	...	...	...
2910	Motor vehicles	54	58	129	140	16706	16498	17051	18692	328.8	343.4	366.4	403.2
2920	Automobile bodies, trailers and semi-trailers	39	41	37	41	1406	1409	1381	1592	18.3	18.3	17.6	21.4
2930	Parts and accessories for motor vehicles	175	179	200	206	43646	43158	47892	49840	518.5	528.2	570.0	645.3
301	Building of ships and boats	18	...	16	17	123	...	97	88	0.9	...	0.7	0.5
3011	Building of ships and floating structures	11	13	12	17d/	48	28	33	88d/	0.3	0.2	0.2	0.5d/
3012	Building of pleasure and sporting boats	7	...	4	..d/	75	64	64	..d/	0.6	...	0.5	..d/
3020	Railway locomotives and rolling stock	13	13	11	8	3160	3438	3346	2918	35.6	41.8	41.0	37.5
3030	Air and spacecraft and related machinery	5	...	...	5	233	...	...	292	2.8	...	...	4.1
3040	Military fighting vehicles	6	...	...	5	553	...	209	209	5.9	...	...	2.8
309	Transport equipment n.e.c.	31	24	24	35	120e/	144	211	226	1.0	1.3	1.8	2.0
3091	Motorcycles	31e/	24e/	24e/	6	120e/	...	211e/	...	1.0e/	...	1.8e/	-
3092	Bicycles and invalid carriages	...e/	...	...e/	26	...e/	...	-	170	...e/	...	...e/	1.5
3099	Other transport equipment n.e.c.	...e/	-	...e/	3	...e/	-	...e/	56	...e/	-	...e/	0.5
3100	Furniture	1404	1263	1200	1345	12606	13250	13483	12793	107.9	118.8	130.5	125.9
321	Jewellery, bijouterie and related articles	878	...	943	1003	563	...	653	741	4.0	...	4.5	5.4
3211	Jewellery and related articles	878f/	631	943f/	1003f/	563f/	653f/	653f/	741f/	4.0f/	...	4.5f/	5.4f/
3212	Imitation jewellery and related articles	..f/	...	..f/	..f/	..f/	126	..f/	..f/	..f/	1.2	..f/	..f/
3220	Musical instruments	77	73	79	106	2	27	23	36	-	0.1	0.2	0.1
3230	Sports goods	60	60	58	52	617	641	756	678	6.3	6.9	8.6	8.1
3240	Games and toys	126	162	160	211	468	468	434	476	4.3	4.6	4.3	4.6
3250	Medical and dental instruments and supplies	1021	...	981	1018	2920	...	3560	3282	28.9	...	36.8	35.4
3290	Other manufacturing n.e.c.	827	803	763	604	1300	639	851	987	8.7	3.9	5.6	7.3
331	Repair of fabricated metal products/machinery	4271	4078	3965	4387	7952	7386	7536	8916	100.2	97.7	101.7	122.6
3311	Repair of fabricated metal products	1196	1105	1021	1000	490	486	501	316	7.0	7.4	7.0	3.3
3312	Repair of machinery	1452	1496	1459	1668	3756	3364	3533	5133	45.7	44.1	48.3	72.5
3313	Repair of electronic and optical equipment	158	161	162	201	311	166	154	167	4.4	1.6	1.6	1.9
3314	Repair of electrical equipment	1401	1262	1266	1429	685	611	578	633	5.8	6.6	6.9	8.5
3315	Repair of transport equip., excl. motor vehicles	42	36	35	46	2681	2730	2736	2627	37.0	37.4	37.2	35.8
3319	Repair of other equipment	22	18	22	43	29	29	34	40	0.4	0.5	0.7	0.6
3320	Installation of industrial machinery/equipment	770	722	669	722	5919	5369	5487	6306	92.9	86.6	90.6	92.7
C	Total manufacturing	63208	64297	63969	68413	385430	397063	413488	422194	4440.6	4692.3	5000.7	5309.5

a/ 1061 includes 1062.
b/ 1811 includes 1812.
c/ 2651 includes 2652.
d/ 3011 includes 3012.
e/ 3091 includes 3092 and 3099.
f/ 3211 includes 3212.

Slovakia

ISIC Revision 4			Output (valuation not defined)					Value added at factor values					Gross fixed capital formation		
			(millions of Euros)					(millions of Euros)					(millions of Euros)		
ISIC	Industry	Note	2013	2014	2015	2016	Note	2013	2014	2015	2016	Note	2015	2016	
1010	Processing/preserving of meat		594.4	595.2	614.0	654.6		82.5	97.9	122.2	99.1		29.9	46.3	
1020	Processing/preserving of fish, etc.		34.0	...	...	...		1.5	...	...	...		...	...	
1030	Processing/preserving of fruit, vegetables		126.5	128.7	133.2	131.1		24.9	25.3	21.5	11.8		9.7	8.6	
1040	Vegetable and animal oils and fats		178.3	...	...	...		8.3	...	...	...		...	...	
1050	Dairy products		586.1	583.2	529.8	517.1		68.6	64.6	67.7	81.6		21.6	29.5	
106	Grain mill products, starches and starch products		285.5	258.6	239.2	243.5		43.0	67.6	53.9	48.6		20.0	12.6	
1061	Grain mill products		285.5a/	94.0	85.2	243.5a/		43.0a/	26.4	19.1	48.6a/		14.8	12.6a/	
1062	Starches and starch products		...a/	164.6	154.0	...a/		...a/	41.2	34.8	...a/		5.2	...a/	
107	Other food products		1024.4	974.0	1002.3	1044.6		305.6	291.8	301.9	348.2		87.7	80.2	
1071	Bakery products		513.8	500.3	494.4	513.1		179.2	177.3	178.4	198.2		50.6	49.4	
1072	Sugar		148.1	87.5	100.4	101.8		30.4	2.0	10.1	20.6		2.1	5.1	
1073	Cocoa, chocolate and sugar confectionery		109.6	128.2	121.0	114.9		35.7	44.4	39.5	40.8		3.8	9.8	
1074	Macaroni, noodles, couscous, etc.		24.5	24.1	23.3	24.9		1.6	3.6	1.7	1.6		3.8	1.7	
1075	Prepared meals and dishes		0.2	1.1	2.7	10.1		0.1	0.5	0.6	2.3		0.1	0.6	
1079	Other food products n.e.c.		228.1	232.9	260.4	279.7		58.5	64.0	71.7	84.7		27.4	13.7	
1080	Prepared animal feeds		100.7	91.6	74.6	71.4		18.4	22.1	13.3	3.5		1.3	3.2	
110	Beverages		668.2	671.2	653.9	626.3		157.9	170.0	168.0	162.3		68.6	54.9	
1101	Distilling, rectifying and blending of spirits		66.7	66.6	62.4	76.3		9.5	12.2	11.5	-0.2		23.6	14.0	
1102	Wines		...	...	...	...		...	...	...	...		...	...	
1103	Malt liquors and malt		292.2	270.0	281.8	297.1		77.3	75.2	72.9	88.7		21.2	15.8	
1104	Soft drinks,mineral waters,other bottled waters		213.2	231.0	209.5	145.8		48.0	54.3	56.1	44.0		14.7	8.7	
1200	Tobacco products		...	...	...	...		...	...	...	...		...	...	
131	Spinning, weaving and finishing of textiles		60.2	...	73.4	88.3		20.1	...	26.1	30.5		6.4	8.1	
1311	Preparation and spinning of textile fibres		7.8	...	12.6	11.7		4.3	...	6.9	6.6		3.2	1.0	
1312	Weaving of textiles		50.5	54.6	57.7	65.5		15.0	17.1	18.2	22.7		3.0	6.1	
1313	Finishing of textiles		1.9	...	3.1	11.1		0.8	...	1.0	1.2		0.2	1.0	
139	Other textiles		236.2	252.1	277.2	265.1		74.5	83.5	92.4	89.7		11.5	11.6	
1391	Knitted and crocheted fabrics		67.7	70.8	79.1	76.7		21.0	22.1	23.2	22.4		1.0	2.1	
1392	Made-up textile articles, except apparel		78.7	83.6	79.4	81.2		29.4	31.3	30.8	33.2		4.1	4.7	
1393	Carpets and rugs		14.3	12.4	10.5	11.4		1.9	2.5	2.3	2.3		0.5	0.6	
1394	Cordage, rope, twine and netting		23.2	25.4	27.9	27.5		4.9	6.8	7.9	8.4		0.7	0.8	
1399	Other textiles n.e.c.		52.4	59.9	80.3	68.3		17.4	20.7	28.2	23.2		5.2	3.3	
1410	Wearing apparel, except fur apparel		253.5	262.5	254.3	286.3		114.1	125.0	117.5	133.9		16.8	11.4	
1420	Articles of fur		1.0	0.7	0.9	0.8		0.7	0.5	0.5	0.4		-		
1430	Knitted and crocheted apparel		77.9	75.8	70.9	73.1		24.1	23.4	19.9	21.9		1.5	0.9	
151	Leather;luggage,handbags,saddlery,harness;fur		64.7	74.5	87.4	98.3		24.0	29.0	29.9	41.2		11.8	11.8	
1511	Tanning/dressing of leather; dressing of fur		22.2	25.0	24.5	30.2		11.4	12.2	11.7	15.3		6.9	6.7	
1512	Luggage,handbags,etc.;saddlery/harness		42.4	49.5	62.9	68.1		12.6	16.9	18.2	26.0		4.9	5.0	
1520	Footwear		489.3	528.4	498.1	503.0		113.4	124.7	111.9	118.9		13.8	9.3	
1610	Sawmilling and planing of wood		363.0	500.5	536.3	397.6		98.6	130.8	124.3	94.7		70.8	22.9	

Code	Description										
162	Wood products, cork, straw, plaiting materials	440.6	649.3	681.5	623.9	108.1	148.4	164.3	142.5	60.9	31.8
1621	Veneer sheets and wood-based panels	188.8	225.6	253.8	254.4	37.4	43.7	48.5	55.0	7.6	14.1
1622	Builders' carpentry and joinery	137.1	219.8	232.2	201.7	38.0	64.4	69.0	60.3	33.4	10.4
1623	Wooden containers	53.1	50.1	47.7	58.0	7.8	9.9	9.6	10.7	3.1	2.2
1629	Other wood products;articles of cork,straw	61.6	153.8	147.7	109.8	24.9	30.4	37.3	16.6	16.7	5.1
170	Paper and paper products	1286.9	1183.9	1268.3	1265.4	281.5	290.6	328.4	334.2	64.1	68.6
1701	Pulp, paper and paperboard	...	...	...	...	...	...	...	...	...	...
1702	Corrugated paper and paperboard	170.7	170.8	180.7	188.5	44.7	43.2	48.1	52.6	15.1	22.3
1709	Other articles of paper and paperboard	...	...	...	...	...	...	...	...	...	...
181	Printing and service activities related to printing	371.0	354.5	365.3	351.0	107.3	101.8	111.5	100.5	23.4	17.5
1811	Printing	371.0b/	322.7	320.0	289.9	107.3b/	88.3	95.1	80.7	14.9	15.0
1812	Service activities related to printing	..b/	31.8	45.3	61.1	..b/	13.3	16.5	19.7	8.5	2.6
1820	Reproduction of recorded media	2.1	5.1	2.7	6.5	1.2	1.9	0.9	2.4	0.1	0.1
1910	Coke oven products	...	...	...	...	...	...	...	...	...	...
1920	Refined petroleum products	...	...	...	...	...	...	...	...	...	...
201	Basic chemicals,fertilizers, etc.	1212.7	1095.6	1031.5	929.0	164.7	121.3	256.0	219.2	132.6	193.6
2011	Basic chemicals	...	...	...	...	...	...	...	...	...	...
2012	Fertilizers and nitrogen compounds	...	...	...	...	...	...	...	...	...	...
2013	Plastics and synthetic rubber in primary forms	511.4	466.6	334.8	333.1	9.3	-25.4	44.3	61.6	33.8	17.5
202	Other chemical products	413.4	...	...	...	54.6	...	...	...	...	...
2021	Pesticides and other agrochemical products	0.8	...	...	...	0.2	...	...	...	...	...
2022	Paints,varnishes;printing ink and mastics	58.6	64.3	69.3	73.7	8.7	9.0	9.9	13.1	2.1	4.4
2023	Soap,cleaning and cosmetic preparations	...	...	...	...	...	...	...	...	...	...
2029	Other chemical products n.e.c.	...	...	...	...	...	...	...	...	...	...
2030	Man-made fibres	98.9	...	...	...	13.4	...	...	...	...	...
2100	Pharmaceuticals,medicinal chemicals, etc.	186.2	189.6	191.8	173.3	65.4	58.7	54.7	62.5	20.8	13.3
221	Rubber products	1574.2	1627.4	1725.3	2017.9	483.9	551.4	601.6	673.3	88.6	122.6
2211	Rubber tyres and tubes	1292.3	1282.9	1316.6	1357.7	406.7	447.9	486.2	514.9	63.1	80.5
2219	Other rubber products	281.9	344.5	408.7	660.2	77.2	103.5	115.4	158.4	25.5	42.1
2220	Plastics products	2125.6	2192.3	2272.9	2296.6	474.9	550.5	556.9	595.3	153.1	154.8
2310	Glass and glass products	400.6	390.8	406.7	437.2	126.6	118.1	140.5	156.8	20.6	25.9
239	Non-metallic mineral products n.e.c.	939.1	986.4	1058.1	1164.1	273.4	300.8	309.5	331.5	92.1	78.4
2391	Refractory products	116.2	119.5	107.5	98.0	38.6	39.0	36.9	34.1	1.5	1.8
2392	Clay building materials	19.4	23.6	24.9	26.7	4.8	5.4	7.4	6.8	1.0	0.6
2393	Other porcelain and ceramic products	...	...	...	...	...	...	...	...	...	...
2394	Cement, lime and plaster	308.6	319.5	329.4	325.8	99.7	98.4	102.1	102.9	31.1	32.4
2395	Articles of concrete, cement and plaster	...	...	...	...	...	...	...	...	...	...
2396	Cutting, shaping and finishing of stone	37.5	32.1	35.0	37.7	9.8	9.4	10.7	12.5	1.0	2.2
2399	Other non-metallic mineral products n.e.c.	...	...	...	150.4	...	...	...	42.6	...	12.0
2410	Basic iron and steel	3138.0	3072.3	...	...	466.8	550.7	...	...	...	...
2420	Basic precious and other non-ferrous metals	510.7	570.2	...	...	113.4	89.8	...	...	...	...
243	Casting of metals	270.9	302.9	326.0	357.4	79.5	89.4	91.6	124.2	29.0	60.6
2431	Casting of iron and steel	71.9	88.7	80.8	84.0	15.9	20.7	20.9	23.0	2.4	3.5
2432	Casting of non-ferrous metals	199.0	214.2	245.2	273.3	63.6	68.7	70.7	101.2	26.6	57.0
251	Struct.metal products, tanks, reservoirs	...	...	...	1514.1	...	...	...	305.5	...	66.0

continued

Slovakia

ISIC	Industry	Note	Output (valuation not defined) (millions of Euros) 2013	2014	2015	2016	Note	Value added at factor values (millions of Euros) 2013	2014	2015	2016	Note	Gross fixed capital formation (millions of Euros) 2015	2016
2511	Structural metal products		577.9	701.6	857.6	870.7		162.8	192.5	197.0	200.2		65.0	38.2
2512	Tanks, reservoirs and containers of metal		621.6	628.5	654.9	604.9		105.0	102.2	99.4	94.2		16.7	27.5
2513	Steam generators, excl. hot water boilers		…	…	…	38.5		…	…	…	11.1		…	0.2
2520	Weapons and ammunition		…	…	…	26.3		…	…	…	9.4		…	2.9
259	Other metal products;metal working services		2721.9	3407.3	3513.5	3397.1		768.9	991.6	1076.9	1046.3		425.8	247.4
2591	Forging,pressing,stamping,roll-forming of metal		235.1	241.9	282.3	299.7		67.8	71.3	94.9	94.6		37.6	32.3
2592	Treatment and coating of metals; machining		991.3	1362.2	1304.2	1158.2		336.1	440.3	450.4	413.9		236.2	114.9
2593	Cutlery, hand tools and general hardware		191.2	235.4	237.1	227.8		71.6	88.2	88.9	87.4		18.2	9.8
2599	Other fabricated metal products n.e.c.		1304.5	1567.7	1689.9	1711.3		293.5	391.8	442.6	450.4		133.8	90.5
2610	Electronic components and boards		515.7	571.6	531.6	538.8		95.5	117.4	108.5	108.3		19.3	19.4
2620	Computers and peripheral equipment		99.5	128.7	134.9	158.6		28.2	28.7	21.4	17.0		0.9	1.1
2630	Communication equipment		116.4	57.1	…	72.3		23.5	18.3	…	28.6		…	6.1
2640	Consumer electronics		4565.1	4682.9	4353.4	4319.3		343.6	355.1	457.5	236.2		57.9	102.7
265	Measuring,testing equipment; watches, etc.		243.3	333.3	485.1	515.4		78.2	108.0	114.9	96.5		16.0	22.8
2651	Measuring/testing/navigating equipment,etc.		243.3	333.3c/	485.1	515.4		78.2	108.0c/	114.9	96.5		16.0	22.8
2652	Watches and clocks		-	…c/	-	-		-	…c/	-	-		-	0.1
2660	Irradiation/electromedical equipment,etc.		2.4	3.2	7.4	11.5		0.9	1.8	2.4	3.8		0.2	0.1
2670	Optical instruments and photographic equipment		5.1	6.2	7.8	17.6		1.2	1.6	1.7	7.1		0.1	1.9
2680	Magnetic and optical media		0.5	0.2	…	0.1		0.2	-	…	0.1		…	…
2710	Electric motors,generators,transformers,etc.		1192.8	1170.5	1174.9	1012.6		281.2	264.9	312.5	268.4		53.1	33.9
2720	Batteries and accumulators		6.4	1.2	…	…		2.8	0.4	…	…		…	…
273	Wiring and wiring devices		245.5	444.9	…	…		50.8	99.3	…	…		…	…
2731	Fibre optic cables		19.6	18.8	…	…		7.9	7.3	…	…		…	…
2732	Other electronic and electric wires and cables		214.3	396.7	405.6	413.7		38.8	83.3	88.9	99.7		32.8	25.8
2733	Wiring devices		11.6	29.4	38.8	50.3		4.1	8.7	14.1	17.6		0.8	1.1
2740	Electric lighting equipment		643.5	704.7	797.3	948.2		174.8	175.9	174.4	196.7		80.0	98.3
2750	Domestic appliances		358.9	398.2	435.4	465.9		-43.7	-55.8	50.8	69.0		14.1	17.5
2790	Other electrical equipment		416.7	442.3	467.7	490.8		121.5	96.7	104.9	112.0		11.5	14.3
281	General-purpose machinery		2691.5	2834.2	3102.6	3377.4		705.4	773.9	843.0	908.1		216.4	232.3
2811	Engines/turbines,excl.aircraft,vehicle engines		29.8	27.2	23.1	18.2		5.3	5.6	4.4	3.4		0.5	2.0
2812	Fluid power equipment		118.9	107.0	93.5	96.8		32.5	26.8	26.9	25.7		3.3	5.5
2813	Other pumps, compressors, taps and valves		527.9	522.3	556.2	552.1		100.9	102.8	109.5	116.7		33.7	24.6
2814	Bearings, gears, gearing and driving elements		1186.5	1295.3	1394.1	1493.5		331.7	372.0	405.7	451.0		97.6	118.6
2815	Ovens, furnaces and furnace burners		72.1	82.6	75.7	71.4		14.3	20.2	16.0	17.6		2.9	2.4
2816	Lifting and handling equipment		161.2	249.1	348.7	415.6		56.6	95.0	126.0	118.1		44.5	28.6
2817	Office machinery, excl.computers,etc.		…	17.0	16.5	24.9		…	7.2	6.3	8.8		1.1	0.6
2818	Power-driven hand tools		…	1.4	1.3	0.6		…	0.8	0.8	0.2		0.1	-
2819	Other general-purpose machinery		575.8	532.1	593.5	704.3		155.6	143.7	147.4	166.5		32.5	50.1
282	Special-purpose machinery		929.9	1030.7	1064.6	1111.4		256.4	280.4	269.9	285.6		70.6	49.6
2821	Agricultural and forestry machinery		160.0	176.7	191.6	209.7		27.5	37.2	24.5	32.0		12.3	6.6
2822	Metal-forming machinery and machine tools		148.4	172.6	194.0	199.2		49.8	53.4	64.5	68.1		17.2	20.0

2823	Machinery for metallurgy	...	3.6	50.4	42.6	58.7	53.8	155.8	160.0	224.2	192.2
2824	Mining, quarrying and construction machinery	3.2	5.7	29.9	31.8	36.8	34.1	171.5	170.0	151.6	138.4
2825	Food/beverage/tobacco processing machinery	3.2	...	...	...	...	...	...	...	...	...
2826	Textile/apparel/leather production machinery	...	...	...	...	...	...	...	...	...	...
2829	Other special-purpose machinery	...	...	...	...	...	...	...	...	...	...
2910	Motor vehicles	761.2	614.6	1334.1	1487.7	1287.8	1087.5	15695.6	14717.1	12807.9	13215.6
2920	Automobile bodies, trailers and semi-trailers	5.1	11.0	41.0	35.1	37.4	32.0	194.5	181.4	203.2	200.5
2930	Parts and accessories for motor vehicles	367.3	359.7	1505.4	1359.2	1109.6	1075.0	9575.8	9288.9	7797.4	7510.6
301	Building of ships and boats	0.1	1.5	1.3	0.4	...	1.4	3.0	3.1	3.1	7.5
3011	Building of ships and floating structures	0.1d	1.2	1.3d	0.6	0.3	0.4	3.0d	1.5	3.8	4.3
3012	Building of pleasure and sporting boats	...d	0.2	...d	-0.2	...	1.0	...d	1.6	...	3.2
3020	Railway locomotives and rolling stock	6.8	5.2	63.7	73.7	69.4	54.6	239.6	310.4	315.7	230.3
3030	Air and spacecraft and related machinery	0.4	...	5.3	...	...	4.0	16.8	...	...	12.2
3040	Military fighting vehicles	0.1	...	5.6	...	5.4	3.3	17.1	...	...	24.7
309	Transport equipment n.e.c.	1.1	1.0	7.1	6.5	...	1.7	29.2	28.3	15.4	7.5
3091	Motorcycles	1.0	1.0e	-0.1	6.5e	...	1.7e	-	28.3e	...	7.5e
3092	Bicycles and invalid carriages	-	...e	6.5	...e	...e	...e	20.6	...e	...e	...e
3099	Other transport equipment n.e.c.	0.1	...e	0.6	...e	-	...	8.7	...e	...e	...
3100	Furniture	94.2	54.7	241.9	201.7	173.0	199.8	828.9	866.1	805.2	710.8
321	Jewellery, bijouterie and related articles	3.0	1.8	13.1	11.9	...	8.0	38.3	49.0	...	52.5
3211	Jewellery and related articles	3.0f	1.8f	13.1f	11.9f	...	8.0f	38.3f	49.0f	...	52.5f
3212	Imitation jewellery and related articles	...f	...f	...f	...f	4.6	...f	...f	...f	12.9	...f
3220	Musical instruments	0.2	0.3	0.6	0.8	1.4	0.5	1.7	2.0	2.0	1.0
3230	Sports goods	1.3	3.1	16.0	15.4	17.3	13.7	55.3	61.7	58.4	51.8
3240	Games and toys	2.2	2.4	12.4	9.1	10.8	8.3	42.2	20.4	23.1	16.4
3250	Medical and dental instruments and supplies	16.2	12.3	81.0	84.4	71.6	71.6	230.6	241.3	...	173.5
3290	Other manufacturing n.e.c.	7.2	1.6	17.5	12.8	13.9	34.4	39.6	31.1	30.4	72.0
331	Repair of fabricated metal products/machinery	36.1	38.9	214.3	171.4	177.2	170.8	760.6	720.6	648.8	612.1
3311	Repair of fabricated metal products	1.3	1.1	13.3	20.2	23.3	19.7	44.1	51.9	55.0	45.9
3312	Repair of machinery	13.9	23.6	132.6	96.0	81.7	83.9	424.9	358.0	294.3	281.9
3313	Repair of electronic and optical equipment	0.5	0.3	5.9	4.5	4.8	8.2	16.6	11.8	11.5	20.0
3314	Repair of electrical equipment	3.1	1.3	38.4	32.1	38.6	29.8	93.5	89.8	97.6	84.7
3315	Repair of transport equip., excl. motor vehicles	17.2	12.5	22.5	17.4	27.6	28.4	178.6	206.5	187.9	177.1
3319	Repair of other equipment	0.1	0.1	1.6	1.1	1.1	0.8	2.8	2.8	2.5	2.6
3320	Installation of industrial machinery/equipment	14.0	12.6	166.0	174.5	168.4	178.0	520.0	577.7	535.6	483.6
C	Total manufacturing	3562.2	3558.6	12901.4	12758.6	11327.2	10109.7	68366.8	67279.5	63461.3	61848.5

a/ 1061 includes 1062.
b/ 1811 includes 1812.
c/ 2651 includes 2652.
d/ 3011 includes 3012.
e/ 3091 includes 3092 and 3099.
f/ 3211 includes 3212.

Slovakia

Index numbers of industrial production

ISIC Revision 4

ISIC	Industry	Note	(2010=100)											
			2005	2006	2007	2008	2009	2010	2011	2012	2013	2014	2015	2016
10	Food products	a/	...	...	...	110	103	100	106	103	101	98	99	99
11	Beverages	a/	...	...	...	...	...	...	...	...	...	...	...	...
12	Tobacco products	a/	...	...	...	...	...	...	...	...	...	...	...	...
13	Textiles	b/	...	...	...	105	94	100	75	91	92	96	91	91
14	Wearing apparel	b/	...	...	...	...	...	...	...	...	...	...	...	...
15	Leather and related products	b/	...	...	...	...	...	...	...	...	...	...	...	...
16	Wood products, excluding furniture	c/	...	...	...	106	97	100	97	100	101	104	109	112
17	Paper and paper products	c/	...	...	...	...	...	...	...	...	...	...	...	...
18	Printing and reproduction of recorded media	c/	...	...	...	...	...	...	...	...	...	...	...	...
19	Coke and refined petroleum products		...	...	...	105	107	100	110	98	95	86	102	99
20	Chemicals and chemical products		...	...	...	97	90	100	113	110	116	109	123	116
21	Pharmaceuticals,medicinal chemicals, etc.		...	...	...	91	86	100	86	83	57	53	59	58
22	Rubber and plastics products	d/	...	...	...	106	89	100	106	107	113	120	125	132
23	Other non-metallic mineral products	d/	...	...	...	...	...	...	...	...	...	...	...	...
24	Basic metals	e/	...	...	...	107	86	100	106	113	119	131	131	137
25	Fabricated metal products, except machinery	e/	...	...	...	...	...	...	...	...	...	...	...	...
26	Computer, electronic and optical products		...	...	...	86	87	100	85	98	96	98	97	95
27	Electrical equipment		...	...	...	100	90	100	110	113	118	134	145	159
28	Machinery and equipment n.e.c.		...	...	...	101	70	100	107	116	113	116	124	132
29	Motor vehicles, trailers and semi-trailers	f/	...	...	...	98	75	100	118	146	156	163	179	191
30	Other transport equipment	f/	...	...	...	...	...	...	...	...	...	...	...	...
31	Furniture	g/	...	...	...	109	96	100	102	112	119	120	139	137
32	Other manufacturing	g/	...	...	...	...	...	...	...	...	...	...	...	...
33	Repair and installation of machinery/equipment	g/	...	...	...	...	...	...	...	...	...	...	...	...
C	Total manufacturing		...	...	...	102	87	100	105	114	117	121	129	134

a/ 10 includes 11 and 12.
b/ 13 includes 14 and 15.
c/ 16 includes 17 and 18.
d/ 22 includes 23.
e/ 24 includes 25.
f/ 29 includes 30.
g/ 31 includes 32 and 33.

Slovenia

Supplier of information:
Statistical Office of the Republic of Slovenia, Ljubljana.
Industrial statistics for the OECD countries are compiled by the OECD secretariat, which supplies them to UNIDO.

Basic source of data:
Annual census/exhaustive survey; administrative source.

Major deviations from ISIC (Revision 4):
Data presented in ISIC (Revision 4) were originally classified according to the national NACE-related classification system.

Reference period:
Calendar year.

Scope:
All registered enterprises.

Method of data collection:
Mail questionnaires, but data are mainly derived from administrative and secondary statistical sources.

Type of enumeration:
Complete enumeration (mainly administrative sources).

Adjusted for non-response:
Yes.

Concepts and definitions of variables:
No deviations from the standard UN concepts and definitions are reported.

Related national publications:
Performance of enterprises by activity (and cohesion region, detailed data), Slovenia, published by the Statistical Office of the Republic of Slovenia, Ljubljana.

Slovenia

ISIC	Industry	Number of enterprises (number)					Number of employees (number)					Wages and salaries paid to employees (millions of Euros)				
		Note	2013	2014	2015	2016	Note	2013	2014	2015	2016	Note	2013	2014	2015	2016
1010	Processing/preserving of meat		254	294	307	339		4162	4069	4276	4428		64.3	64.2	68.5	73.5
1020	Processing/preserving of fish, etc.		4	5	6	6		...	...	...	...		1.7	...	...	...
1030	Processing/preserving of fruit,vegetables		296	338	356	362		710	625	622	655		12.3	11.6	11.6	11.9
1040	Vegetable and animal oils and fats		63	70	74	120		...	...	...	156		2.6	...	...	2.9
1050	Dairy products		167	192	208	236		1193	1203	1252	1329		22.4	23.3	25.4	26.7
106	Grain mill products,starches and starch products		55	65	72	82		582	560	535	...		9.7	9.3	8.8	...
1061	Grain mill products		52	62	70	82		548	530	535a/	...		8.9	8.6	8.8a/	...
1062	Starches and starch products		3	3	2	-		33	30	...a/	...a/		0.8	0.7	...a/	...a/
107	Other food products		921	990	1026	1055		5785	5755	5963	6567		92.2	95.9	98.7	114.9
1071	Bakery products		736	780	796	813		4524	4483	4597	5190		66.7	68.9	70.9	85.6
1072	Sugar		1	2	2	2		-	...	...	...		...	...	...	...
1073	Cocoa, chocolate and sugar confectionery		19	21	23	22		287	296	310	288		4.9	5.1	5.3	4.9
1074	Macaroni, noodles, couscous, etc.		25	29	29	30		67	67	68	77		1.0	1.0	1.1	1.3
1075	Prepared meals and dishes		7	7	11	15		118	121	173	156		1.7	1.8	...	2.4
1079	Other food products n.e.c.		133	151	165	173		789	...	...	...		...	...	...	...
1080	Prepared animal feeds		15	17	17	22		439	448	457	472		8.8	9.1	9.5	9.7
110	Beverages		165	189	193	201		1554	1528	1460	1415		35.9	35.9	35.3	42.5
1101	Distilling, rectifying and blending of spirits		71	91	90	86		26	...	...	17		0.3	0.2	0.2	0.2
1102	Wines		59	58	53	55		399	...	332	...		...	...	...	...
1103	Malt liquors and malt		18	21	32	41		729	751	...	...		19.9	21.1	...	...
1104	Soft drinks,mineral waters,other bottled waters		17	19	18	19		400	385	374	397		8.5	8.2	8.2	8.8
1200	Tobacco products		-	-	-	-		-	-	-	-		-	-	-	-
131	Spinning, weaving and finishing of textiles		71	59	53	50		...	724	...	...		13.2	12.6	...	...
1311	Preparation and spinning of textile fibres		9	8	8	8		555	573	584	586		9.3	9.9	9.9	10.2
1312	Weaving of textiles		15	11	10	7		...	84	...	...		2.6	1.6	...	...
1313	Finishing of textiles		47	40	35	35		...	67	...	...		1.3	1.1	...	...
139	Other textiles		291	279	281	272		2439	2404	2041	2044		41.2	42.0	37.8	40.2
1391	Knitted and crocheted fabrics		13	10	10	9		175	186	181	188		2.7	2.9	...	...
1392	Made-up textile articles, except apparel		159	158	158	159		1349	1290	874	839		20.6	20.2	14.5	15.4
1393	Carpets and rugs		5	5	5	6		48	44	...	...		0.9	1.1	...	...
1394	Cordage, rope, twine and netting		10	8	9	8		61	64	...	...		0.9	0.9	0.9	0.6
1399	Other textiles n.e.c.		104	98	99	90		808	819	864	908		15.9	16.9	18.2	19.7
1410	Wearing apparel, except fur apparel		658	644	643	644		2998	3327b/	2161	1929		39.6	28.8	27.0	27.8
1420	Articles of fur		4	4	4	3		...	...b/	...	...		-	-	-	-
1430	Knitted and crocheted apparel		82	83	89	78		...	...b/	...	...		12.4	13.2	13.0	...
151	Leather;luggage,handbags,saddlery,harness;fur		67	71	70	68		1910	2064	2276	2460		27.9	29.9	...	...
1511	Tanning/dressing of leather; dressing of fur		11	11	11	11		323	318	2276c/	2460c/		6.3	6.2	6.3	5.8
1512	Luggage,handbags,etc.;saddlery/harness		56	60	59	57		1588	1746	...c/	...c/		21.5	23.7	...	...
1520	Footwear		80	81	81	72		1359	1373	1336	1143		19.5	20.4	...	...
1610	Sawmilling and planing of wood		649	705	705	704		1396	1412	1539	1774		20.6	22.0	24.7	30.0

Code	Product														
162	Wood products, cork, straw, plaiting materials	1283	1291	1292	1291	1313	5450	5510	5419	5419	5335	86.1	88.0	89.2	93.0
1621	Veneer sheets and wood-based panels	38	41	40	41	37	1248	1293	1307	1307	1149	21.0	22.0	21.7	21.5
1622	Builders' carpentry and joinery	591	615	602	602	623	3197	3119	2955	2955	2931	50.9	50.2	50.4	52.4
1623	Wooden containers	160	160	164	164	165	385	443	480	480	467	5.5	6.5	6.9	7.0
1629	Other wood products;articles of cork,straw	494	475	486	486	488	620	654	678	678	787	8.8	9.4	10.3	12.0
170	Paper and paper products	178	177	177	177	173	4558	4323	4219	4219	4199	86.9	88.9	88.1	92.0
1701	Pulp, paper and paperboard	13	18	14	14	13	..	..	..	..	..	..	..	..	..
1702	Corrugated paper and paperboard	81	77	79	79	76	1523	1233	1126	1126	1129	26.4	25.7	23.6	24.9
1709	Other articles of paper and paperboard	84	82	84	84	84	1468	..	1540	1540	1570	24.7	28.0	28.0	29.8
181	Printing and service activities related to printing	1179	1189	1183	1183	1182	3759	3647	3631	3631	3653	67.4	66.9	..	71.6
1811	Printing	568	571	564	564	574	2991	2915	2861	2861	2874	55.4	55.0	..	57.9
1812	Service activities related to printing	611	618	619	619	608	769	732	770	770	779	12.0	12.0	12.9	13.7
1820	Reproduction of recorded media	19	14	18	18	13	21	21	18	18	15	0.3	0.3	..	0.3
1910	Coke oven products	-	-	-	-	-	-	-	-	-	-	-	-	-	-
1920	Refined petroleum products	7	4	5	5	2	33	..	26	26	..	0.6	..	..	..
201	Basic chemicals,fertilizers, etc.	50	47	49	49	43	2092	1881	1786	1786	1741	50.8	45.9	44.4	44.2
2011	Basic chemicals	27	27	29	29	25	1811	1881d/	..	..	..	44.5	45.9d/	..	0.5
2012	Fertilizers and nitrogen compounds	9	10	10	10	9	..	..d/	28	28	28	..d/	..d/	0.5	0.5
2013	Plastics and synthetic rubber in primary forms	14	10	10	10	9	..	..d/	..	..	..	..	..d/	..	..
202	Other chemical products	133	150	144	144	162	..	..	..	..	..	..	..	..	..
2021	Pesticides and other agrochemical products	7	7	7	7	7	..	..	..	..	..	..	..	4.1	..
2022	Paints,varnishes;printing ink and mastics	20	20	21	21	22	1476	1480	1509	1509	1573	34.9	34.8	36.7	38.9
2023	Soap,cleaning and cosmetic preparations	62	74	69	69	83	1238	1127	1095	1095	1067	25.5	24.0	..	23.8
2029	Other chemical products n.e.c.	44	49	47	47	50	..	..	..	..	..	..	..	..	..
2030	Man-made fibres	1	1	1	1	1	..	..	..	..	..	..	..	..	..
2100	Pharmaceuticals,medicinal chemicals, etc.	23	23	25	25	24	..	..	..	..	..	282.2	308.3	..	..
221	Rubber products	109	108	109	109	106	3109	3198	3190	3190	3303	75.7	81.0	81.9	86.9
2211	Rubber tyres and tubes	20	20	22	22	20	1360	1351	3190e/	3190e/	3303e/	36.7	38.9	81.9e/	86.9e/
2219	Other rubber products	89	88	87	87	86	1749	1848	..e/	..e/	..e/	39.1	42.1	..e/	..e/
2220	Plastics products	911	891	898	898	875	9801	9663	10231	10231	10895	182.1	186.9	201.6	220.5
2310	Glass and glass products	75	66	67	67	54	1886	1845	1903	1903	1909	34.8	33.6	36.4	37.9
239	Non-metallic mineral products n.e.c.	521	518	510	510	507	5223	5049	4966	4966	4824	106.3	108.4	107.3	107.6
2391	Refractory products	14	16	15	15	15	87	90	102	102	112	2.0	2.2	2.6	3.0
2392	Clay building materials	15	13	15	15	13	..	299	..	..	..	..	6.2	..	..
2393	Other porcelain and ceramic products	65	58	56	56	53	124	..	..	..	..	..	..	..	..
2394	Cement, lime and plaster	6	7	6	6	8	..	..	..	..	..	..	..	..	..
2395	Articles of concrete, cement and plaster	147	138	138	138	131	702	716	688	688	681	10.8	11.3	10.9	11.5
2396	Cutting, shaping and finishing of stone	238	248	244	244	251	2127	2032	..	..	..	48.5	49.4	..	49.9
2399	Other non-metallic mineral products n.e.c.	36	38	36	36	36	..	..	..	..	..	..	..	..	..
2410	Basic iron and steel	26	24	24	24	25	..	..	..	..	..	..	..	..	..
2420	Basic precious and other non-ferrous metals	8	9	9	9	7	510	522	950	950	..	12.3	13.1	19.6	..
243	Casting of metals	88	78	84	84	75	4135	4293	4200	4200	5852	84.9	93.0	90.5	132.4
2431	Casting of iron and steel	20	18	19	19	17	1763	1752	1388	1388	1399	31.8	34.1	26.9	29.3
2432	Casting of non-ferrous metals	68	60	65	65	58	2372	2541	2812	2812	4453	53.1	59.0	63.7	103.2
251	Struct.metal products, tanks, reservoirs	741	757	758	758	786	..	7485	7485	7485	7723	137.5	..	146.4	160.5

continued

Slovenia

ISIC	Industry	Number of enterprises (number) 2013	2014	2015	2016	Number of employees (number) 2013	2014	2015	2016	Wages and salaries paid to employees (millions of Euros) 2013	2014	2015	2016
2511	Structural metal products	694	710	708	738	6896	6635	6924	7165	125.0	123.5	134.8	148.6
2512	Tanks, reservoirs and containers of metal	41	41	42	40	607	...	546	546	11.2	...	10.7	11.7
2513	Steam generators, excl. hot water boilers	6	7	7	8	...	20	17	12	1.3	...	0.9	0.3
2520	Weapons and ammunition	16	17	15	15	...	...	6	12	0.2	...	0.1	0.2
259	Other metal products;metal working services	3399	3442	3520	3517	20396	...	21495	22662	373.4	389.0	417.9	458.2
2591	Forging,pressing,stamping,roll-forming of metal	113	115	112	98	3117	...	3231	3430	61.1	65.9	68.7	77.8
2592	Treatment and coating of metals; machining	2139	2215	2307	2366	7559	8045	8667	9205	128.3	140.0	155.4	169.5
2593	Cutlery, hand tools and general hardware	381	375	380	369	4181	4198	4410	4657	83.6	86.8	94.2	103.4
2599	Other fabricated metal products n.e.c.	766	737	721	684	5540	5088	5188	5372	100.5	96.3	99.7	107.4
2610	Electronic components and boards	131	125	128	129	1829	1542	1579	1511	30.7	24.9	28.1	28.1
2620	Computers and peripheral equipment	26	28	31	29	183	223	221	244	4.4	5.5	5.5	7.0
2630	Communication equipment	22	24	23	21	881	785	787	707	25.0	22.3	23.4	21.1
2640	Consumer electronics	41	48	52	52	386	436	495	555	7.8	8.9	10.2	12.2
265	Measuring,testing equipment; watches, etc.	75	80	83	80	1537	...	...	1468	32.6	...	...	34.2
2651	Measuring/testing/navigating equipment,etc.	74	79	82	79	1537	...	...	1468f/	32.6f/	...	...	34.2f/
2652	Watches and clocks	1	1	1	1	-	...	...	...f/	...f/	...	...	...f/
2660	Irradiation/electromedical equipment,etc.	3	3	5	8	...	...	...	...	...	...	...	...
2670	Optical instruments and photographic equipment	13	14	13	14	138	...	94	...	...	...	1.9	...
2680	Magnetic and optical media	-	-	-	-	-	-	-	-	-	-	-	-
2710	Electric motors,generators,transformers,etc.	114	121	122	118	6901	6876	7035	7105	134.4	141.0	145.2	151.1
2720	Batteries and accumulators	3	4	3	3	...	...	...	...	...	...	...	...
273	Wiring and wiring devices	51	50	52	47	...	...	...	...	...	...	23.1	24.8
2731	Fibre optic cables	5	4	4	3	...	...	...	...	...	...	...	...
2732	Other electronic and electric wires and cables	29	28	30	27	36	61	47	51	0.6	...	...	...
2733	Wiring devices	17	18	18	17	1284	1331	1357	1397	19.6	21.1	21.9	23.5
2740	Electric lighting equipment	63	64	65	68	1510	1849	1872	2065	34.1	43.4	...	...
2750	Domestic appliances	43	45	44	43	7294	7350	7142	7315	142.5	146.9	148.6	152.2
2790	Other electrical equipment	127	126	118	114	1546	1997	1976	1882	30.1	39.5	40.2	39.5
281	General-purpose machinery	400	394	401	393	7893	7181	7246	7307	162.3	157.0	162.7	168.5
2811	Engines/turbines,excl.aircraft,vehicle engines	13	11	11	11	709	690	674	676	17.9	17.7	18.4	19.2
2812	Fluid power equipment	22	25	26	26	507	550	599	609	11.0	12.2	13.7	14.4
2813	Other pumps, compressors, taps and valves	45	46	42	41	1920	1139	992	944	34.7	24.8	21.5	20.1
2814	Bearings, gears, gearing and driving elements	28	27	27	28	781	806	877	938	14.7	15.6	17.7	20.0
2815	Ovens, furnaces and furnace burners	35	36	33	34	169	...	173	176	3.7	...	3.8	...
2816	Lifting and handling equipment	81	76	81	81	1880	1864	2001	2013	41.4	41.6	46.1	46.5
2817	Office machinery, excl.computers,etc.	1	1	1	1	...	...	...	...	...	...	...	...
2818	Power-driven hand tools	5	6	6	5	...	...	...	...	...	...	...	...
2819	Other general-purpose machinery	170	166	174	166	1766	1811	1837	1887	36.5	38.7	39.9	42.5
282	Special-purpose machinery	344	350	350	343	5791	5757	6156	6234	123.3	127.1	140.2	149.6
2821	Agricultural and forestry machinery	56	59	57	56	1201	1259	1323	1345	22.6	24.5	26.0	27.7
2822	Metal-forming machinery and machine tools	93	94	97	97	1218	1174	1351	1390	26.0	26.5	32.0	35.1

2823	Machinery for metallurgy	10	10	9	11	685	662	672	566	15.1	14.9	15.8	14.9
2824	Mining, quarrying and construction machinery	16	18	20	20	317	316	317	317	5.9	6.1	6.2	6.4
2825	Food/beverage/tobacco processing machinery	62	59	56	43	698	722	788	809	15.7	17.2	19.7	21.1
2826	Textile/apparel/leather production machinery	5	5	5	6	237	252	268	279	4.5	4.7	5.2	5.5
2829	Other special-purpose machinery	102	105	106	110	1435	1373	...	...	33.4	33.2	...	...
2910	Motor vehicles	22	19	16	17	2286	2411	2428	2497	44.4	52.2	...	...
2920	Automobile bodies, trailers and semi-trailers	33	35	34	40	1444	1485	1641	2184	29.1	31.1	...	...
2930	Parts and accessories for motor vehicles	110	118	123	126	8460	9149	8637	7869	164.1	181.7	189.0	165.0
301	Building of ships and boats	58	54	60	63	...	131	133	159	2.6	2.3	1.6	3.0
3011	Building of ships and floating structures	14	12	13	14	...	26	43	19	0.4	0.3	0.5	0.4
3012	Building of pleasure and sporting boats	44	42	47	49	130	105	90	139	2.2	2.0	1.0	2.6
3020	Railway locomotives and rolling stock	3	3	2	2	...	...	...	...	...	...	...	...
3030	Air and spacecraft and related machinery	19	20	18	22	152	...	182	227	3.5	3.9	4.3	5.6
3040	Military fighting vehicles	-	-	-	-	-	-	-	-	-	-	-	-
309	Transport equipment n.e.c.	20	22	19	20	167	161	...	43	...	3.2	...	...
3091	Motorcycles	5	7	5	6	14	17	...	43g/	...	0.6	...	...
3092	Bicycles and invalid carriages	15	15	13	13	153	144	...	...g/	2.6	2.5	...	0.4
3099	Other transport equipment n.e.c.	-	-	1	1	-	-	...	...g/	-	...	...	...
3100	Furniture	1099	1114	1116	1131	5315	5114	5060	5189	81.4	81.0	82.1	88.1
321	Jewellery, bijouterie and related articles	157	154	156	157	386	366	369	368	5.4	5.2	5.7	5.8
3211	Jewellery and related articles	142	140	146	146	379	356	369h/	368h/	5.4	5.1	5.5	5.7
3212	Imitation jewellery and related articles	15	14	10	11	8	10	...h/	...h/	0.1	0.1	0.1	0.1
3220	Musical instruments	33	45	44	40	52	45	51	24	0.6	0.6	...	...
3230	Sports goods	48	45	53	51	592	578	621	645	10.5	10.1	...	...
3240	Games and toys	29	34	35	40	215	234	265	449	4.6	5.0	5.7	9.7
3250	Medical and dental instruments and supplies	316	331	327	341	1992	2090	2018	2072	31.5	32.8	32.9	33.8
3290	Other manufacturing n.e.c.	198	199	190	176	567	568	605	629	10.1	10.0	10.7	11.9
331	Repair of fabricated metal products/machinery	1519	1529	1582	1621	5066	5116	5121	4952	111.0	120.9	123.3	125.5
3311	Repair of fabricated metal products	84	86	89	96	99	103	...	...	1.4	1.3	...	1.3
3312	Repair of machinery	968	966	997	1007	2113	2183	2194	2155	42.1	44.9	43.8	45.9
3313	Repair of electronic and optical equipment	90	92	87	79	61	...	67	...	1.0	1.2	1.3	1.8
3314	Repair of electrical equipment	195	188	191	183	281	292	318	209	5.4	6.0	6.5	4.3
3315	Repair of transport equip., excl. motor vehicles	159	173	189	224	...	...	...	...	60.9	67.2	...	...
3319	Repair of other equipment	23	24	29	32	...	...	...	...	0.2	0.3	0.2	0.2
3320	Installation of industrial machinery/equipment	419	465	521	571	3080	3333	3720	3697	55.5	63.6	69.1	83.0
C	Total manufacturing	18148	18561	18853	19074	177671	177302	180271	185341	3496.2	3630.0	3775.4	4019.4

a/ 1061 includes 1062.
b/ 1410 includes 1420 and 1430.
c/ 1511 includes 1512.
d/ 2011 includes 2012 and 2013.
e/ 2211 includes 2219.
f/ 2651 includes 2652.
g/ 3091 includes 3092 and 3099.
h/ 3211 includes 3212.

Slovenia

ISIC	Industry	Note	Output (valuation not defined) (millions of Euros)				Note	Value added at factor values (millions of Euros)					Note	Gross fixed capital formation (millions of Euros)	
			2013	2014	2015	2016		2013	2014	2015	2016			2015	2016
1010	Processing/preserving of meat		522.7	544.3	562.8	578.7		100.9	110.3	115.8	115.2			12.0	19.5
1020	Processing/preserving of fish, etc.		11.3	...	...	...		2.1	...	...	...			...	0.2
1030	Processing/preserving of fruit,vegetables		78.5	85.2	87.2	91.4		24.7	28.0	31.0	30.8			4.9	4.3
1040	Vegetable and animal oils and fats		27.3	...	...	31.6		4.6	...	...	5.8			...	1.1
1050	Dairy products		280.1	294.0	277.7	283.6		43.3	48.9	60.2	62.4			10.0	11.6
106	Grain mill products,starches and starch products		52.5	54.8	53.2	...		15.8	16.1	14.3	...			2.4	0.4
1061	Grain mill products		48.8	50.5	53.2a/	...		14.6	14.9	14.3a/	...			2.4a/	0.4a/
1062	Starches and starch products		3.8	4.3	...a/	-		1.1	1.3	...a/	-			...a/	...a/
107	Other food products		468.9	481.1	497.4	558.4		158.6	164.2	177.8	204.5			22.8	27.9
1071	Bakery products		261.0	266.2	279.5	336.5		93.1	98.8	107.7	130.2			13.7	16.7
1072	Sugar		...	...	...	...		...	...	...	...			-	-
1073	Cocoa, chocolate and sugar confectionery		34.2	35.7	35.2	32.4		8.9	10.9	11.3	10.4			1.7	1.0
1074	Macaroni, noodles, couscous, etc.		3.5	3.5	3.9	4.3		1.6	1.6	1.9	2.0			0.5	0.3
1075	Prepared meals and dishes		9.5	9.6	...	12.5		1.7	1.2	...	3.4			...	0.6
1079	Other food products n.e.c.		...	...	...	...		...	...	...	...			...	...
1080	Prepared animal feeds		93.5	92.3	88.7	87.9		12.9	18.9	19.9	20.0			3.4	2.5
110	Beverages		252.2	243.8	242.9	227.1		76.9	76.9	76.2	78.3			18.0	13.6
1101	Distilling, rectifying and blending of spirits		2.9	3.3	2.5	2.0		0.9	0.8	1.5	0.7			...	13.6b/
1102	Wines		167.8	165.5	...	...		50.8	54.6	...	...			1.1	..b/
1103	Malt liquors and malt		167.8	165.5	...	...		50.8	54.6	...	...			...	..b/
1104	Soft drinks,mineral waters,other bottled waters		52.1	50.9	50.7	55.6		13.9	15.9	16.0	17.2			4.5	..b/
1200	Tobacco products		-	-	-	-		-	-	-	-			-	-
131	Spinning, weaving and finishing of textiles		92.8	81.8	...	...		21.0	26.0	...	...			...	...
1311	Preparation and spinning of textile fibres		73.2	63.5	62.5	64.2		15.6	18.5	20.1	17.3			3.2	...
1312	Weaving of textiles		11.7	12.0	...	...		3.0	6.0	...	...			...	...
1313	Finishing of textiles		7.9	6.3	...	...		2.4	1.5	...	...			...	0.1
139	Other textiles		234.0	244.3	218.5	232.3		72.0	80.3	78.8	89.5			19.3	9.6
1391	Knitted and crocheted fabrics		8.0	8.5	...	...		4.1	4.4	...	...			...	0.5
1392	Made-up textile articles, except apparel		96.7	90.2	55.5	59.1		26.1	25.7	23.3	24.1			1.9	2.0
1393	Carpets and rugs		4.5	8.6	...	...		0.7	2.0	...	...			...	...
1394	Cordage, rope, twine and netting		3.6	5.0	5.3	2.9		0.8	1.3	1.3	0.9			0.1	...
1399	Other textiles n.e.c.		121.1	131.9	139.0	150.5		40.3	46.9	47.1	56.7			...	6.0
1410	Wearing apparel, except fur apparel		83.2	81.9	76.5	88.3		40.5	40.9	37.1	42.3			1.4	1.9
1420	Articles of fur		0.1	0.1	0.1	0.1		-	-	-	-			...	-
1430	Knitted and crocheted apparel		45.9	46.0	46.3	...		17.4	19.0	16.6	...			...	...
151	Leather;luggage,handbags,saddlery,harness;fur		149.4	166.3	...	...		39.7	46.1	...	...			11.1	...
1511	Tanning/dressing of leather; dressing of fur		35.1	33.1	31.8	30.2		8.4	9.7	9.1	8.3			11.1c/	...
1512	Luggage,handbags,etc.;saddlery/harness		114.4	133.3	...	...		31.4	36.4	...	...			...c/	...
1520	Footwear		90.4	104.6	...	...		23.1	28.3	...	...			1.3	...
1610	Sawmilling and planing of wood		156.6	172.5	202.5	222.1		47.5	51.5	65.7	67.0			16.6	17.9

ISIC	Industry									
162	Wood products, cork, straw, plaiting materials	453.4	473.3	490.8	497.4	138.0	146.2	155.4	160.4	18.3	23.0
1621	Veneer sheets and wood-based panels	148.5	172.0	180.7	152.9	34.4	42.3	42.8	38.5	4.0	4.6
1622	Builders' carpentry and joinery	232.1	219.4	224.6	251.4	76.5	73.4	79.5	83.7	…	…
1623	Wooden containers	27.0	31.9	32.2	32.4	9.2	10.6	11.2	11.5	…	…
1629	Other wood products;articles of cork,straw	45.8	50.1	53.3	60.7	18.0	19.9	22.0	26.8	4.3	7.3
170	Paper and paper products	696.4	730.6	745.1	755.8	164.8	177.5	172.8	169.7	30.3	32.4
1701	Pulp, paper and paperboard	…	…	…	…	…	…	…	…	18.6	12.6
1702	Corrugated paper and paperboard	155.2	148.4	143.6	153.2	50.2	47.3	45.4	47.1	8.1	13.0
1709	Other articles of paper and paperboard	139.8	…	163.4	166.9	38.8	…	45.8	46.2	3.7	…
181	Printing and service activities related to printing	388.4	391.7	401.6	…	127.4	125.9	134.3	…	…	…
1811	Printing	321.9	323.0	327.7	…	102.8	101.1	105.0	…	…	…
1812	Service activities related to printing	66.4	68.6	70.7	73.8	24.6	24.9	26.9	29.3	…	6.1
1820	Reproduction of recorded media	1.4	1.4	1.1	…	0.4	0.5	0.3	…	…	…
1910	Coke oven products	-	-	-	-	-	-	-	-	-	-
1920	Refined petroleum products	1.7	…	…	…	0.5	…	…	…	…	…
201	Basic chemicals,fertilizers, etc.	357.7	325.1	320.7	314.6	100.3	103.6	99.3	102.5	21.1	18.9
2011	Basic chemicals	299.8	325.1d/	…d/	…d/	86.3	103.6d/	…d/	…d/	…	18.9d/
2012	Fertilizers and nitrogen compounds	…	…	2.4	2.1	…	0.9	…	0.7	0.2	…d/
2013	Plastics and synthetic rubber in primary forms	…d/	…d/	…d/	…	…d/	…d/	…d/	…d/	…	…d/
202	Other chemical products	…	…	…	…	…	…	…	…	…	…
2021	Pesticides and other agrochemical products	…	…	…	12.8	…	4.5	…	…	…	…
2022	Paints,varnishes;printing ink and mastics	336.7	335.1	324.3	310.7	63.7	73.0	80.2	88.6	5.2	9.1
2023	Soap,cleaning and cosmetic preparations	277.8	259.5	…	110.3	97.6	85.3	…	42.9	3.7	…
2029	Other chemical products n.e.c.	…	…	…	…	…	…	…	…	…	…
2030	Man-made fibres	…	…	…	…	…	…	…	…	…	…
2100	Pharmaceuticals,medicinal chemicals, etc.	1785.7	1836.5	…	…	730.5	805.3	…	…	…	…
221	Rubber products	346.2	354.6	352.9	368.7	142.5	146.6	153.6	165.9	20.6	21.6
2211	Rubber tyres and tubes	107.9	115.9	352.9e/	368.7e/	59.1	63.6	153.6e/	165.9e/	20.6e/	21.6e/
2219	Other rubber products	238.2	238.7	…e/	…e/	83.4	82.9	…e/	…e/	…e/	…e/
2220	Plastics products	1065.8	1122.2	1182.0	1296.0	313.8	345.2	372.9	408.5	90.8	98.7
2310	Glass and glass products	124.1	124.1	151.6	149.6	45.0	47.5	69.1	67.6	12.2	7.4
239	Non-metallic mineral products n.e.c.	653.3	658.3	655.1	658.0	204.6	215.5	210.9	219.0	…	…
2391	Refractory products	25.5	27.6	37.3	40.4	6.4	7.5	9.0	10.7	…	…
2392	Clay building materials	…	24.5	…	…	…	8.5	…	…	…	…
2393	Other porcelain and ceramic products	…	…	…	…	…	…	…	…	…	…
2394	Cement, lime and plaster	…	…	…	…	…	…	…	…	…	…
2395	Articles of concrete, cement and plaster	…	…	…	…	…	…	…	…	…	…
2396	Cutting, shaping and finishing of stone	50.3	52.3	45.0	48.9	19.7	21.2	20.3	21.3	2.0	3.5
2399	Other non-metallic mineral products n.e.c.	314.4	334.6	…	337.7	98.5	107.0	104.7	104.7	…	…
2410	Basic iron and steel	…	…	…	…	…	…	…	…	…	…
2420	Basic precious and other non-ferrous metals	358.3	383.4	426.0	…	5.7	32.1	31.3	…	…	…
243	Casting of metals	416.8	470.3	948.8	1087.3	137.0	170.4	179.8	298.8	…	49.6
2431	Casting of iron and steel	159.2	172.9	132.0	139.0	41.2	56.9	46.6	52.3	…	49.6f/
2432	Casting of non-ferrous metals	257.5	297.4	816.8	948.2	95.8	113.5	133.3	246.5	43.7	…f/
251	Struct.metal products, tanks, reservoirs	756.4	…	737.9	814.5	230.9	…	254.6	286.2	…	…

continued

Slovenia

ISIC	Industry	Note	Output (valuation not defined) (millions of Euros)				Note	Value added at factor values (millions of Euros)				Note	Gross fixed capital formation (millions of Euros)	
			2013	2014	2015	2016		2013	2014	2015	2016		2015	2016
2511	Structural metal products		630.1	616.0	696.4	775.6		209.7	218.8	238.7	271.6		35.5	39.9
2512	Tanks, reservoirs and containers of metal		47.4	...	40.4	38.3		19.5	15.4	15.4	14.7		...	...
2513	Steam generators, excl. hot water boilers		78.9	...	1.1	0.5		1.8	...	0.4	-0.2		-	...
2520	Weapons and ammunition		1.8	-	2.6	3.0		0.4	0.8	0.8	0.6		...	...
259	Other metal products;metal working services		2127.0	2246.5	1933.5	2055.2		645.4	727.4	743.1	826.5		137.2	159.8
2591	Forging,pressing,stamping,roll-forming of metal		727.8	787.4	351.5	362.8		99.7	140.3	105.4	120.6		9.2	9.8
2592	Treatment and coating of metals; machining		521.0	566.2	638.3	691.9		233.1	250.4	281.1	309.7		46.6	51.4
2593	Cutlery, hand tools and general hardware		332.4	357.1	401.1	441.1		140.6	155.8	169.7	190.7		40.6	59.2
2599	Other fabricated metal products n.e.c.		545.9	535.7	542.5	559.7		172.0	180.9	186.8	205.4		40.8	
2610	Electronic components and boards		167.8	147.7	172.8	159.6		50.6	47.9	54.4	55.0		7.2	7.9
2620	Computers and peripheral equipment		25.1	28.2	31.5	40.3		6.7	11.7	11.9	15.0		0.6	0.8
2630	Communication equipment		74.1	96.0	92.4	82.1		24.2	29.2	33.8	27.4		...	
2640	Consumer electronics		48.9	56.5	64.5	83.0		15.6	17.0	19.9	27.9		...	
265	Measuring,testing equipment; watches, etc.		135.5	...	...	145.8		57.7	...	...	62.5		4.4	7.0
2651	Measuring/testing/navigating equipment,etc.		135.5g/	...	...	145.8g/		57.7g/	...	...	62.5g/		4.4g/	7.0g/
2652	Watches and clocks		...g/	...	...	...g/		...g/	...	...	...g/		...g/	...g/
2660	Irradiation/electromedical equipment,etc.		...	...	...	...		...	...	...	...		...	
2670	Optical instruments and photographic equipment		...	...	6.8	...		...	...	2.9	...		0.3	...
2680	Magnetic and optical media		-	-	-	-		-	-	-	-		-	-
2710	Electric motors,generators,transformers,etc.		765.3	818.5	827.5	856.9		238.3	261.4	272.1	286.3		41.7	58.8
2720	Batteries and accumulators		...	...	...	...		...	...	...	...		...	
273	Wiring and wiring devices		...	...	65.5	71.2		...	...	33.3	34.9		2.6	3.3
2731	Fibre optic cables		...	...	...	...		...	...	...	...		...	-
2732	Other electronic and electric wires and cables		3.6	...	...	...		1.1	...	...	...		...	0.3
2733	Wiring devices		49.0	54.3	57.9	62.6		26.4	28.8	30.3	32.6		2.4	3.0
2740	Electric lighting equipment		229.5	264.4	...	...		50.8	60.4	...	...		...	...
2750	Domestic appliances		958.6	902.5	882.8	905.1		266.0	245.5	237.7	252.8		54.3	51.7
2790	Other electrical equipment		154.1	247.6	285.4	253.0		49.0	77.9	84.8	79.4		16.9	10.2
281	General-purpose machinery		832.1	800.6	827.5	862.4		256.4	265.6	283.2	312.1		50.9	56.2
2811	Engines/turbines,excl.aircraft,vehicle engines		75.0	81.2	86.3	96.5		32.3	36.5	42.8	47.2			
2812	Fluid power equipment		47.2	55.6	60.3	64.9		17.6	20.5	22.9	23.3		3.6	5.3
2813	Other pumps, compressors, taps and valves		173.0	119.1	102.1	95.4		41.0	38.1	38.4	37.0		...	
2814	Bearings, gears, gearing and driving elements		100.3	99.6	111.5	123.2		32.3	31.6	36.7	42.4		13.3	10.0
2815	Ovens, furnaces and furnace burners		21.0	...	19.6	...		7.9	...	7.4	...		1.0	1.4
2816	Lifting and handling equipment		246.2	245.0	265.8	270.4		70.0	67.6	68.9	81.5		7.9	8.9
2817	Office machinery, excl.computers,etc.		...	...	...	...		...	...	...	...		...	
2818	Power-driven hand tools		...	...	...	...		...	...	...	...		...	
2819	Other general-purpose machinery		163.2	170.8	175.2	184.4		55.6	60.5	64.0	69.3		5.8	11.4
282	Special-purpose machinery		541.1	588.3	632.3	681.0		192.0	216.6	233.1	259.8		30.4	39.0
2821	Agricultural and forestry machinery		115.7	131.3	132.9	142.4		40.2	52.3	47.4	55.9		7.7	8.3
2822	Metal-forming machinery and machine tools		97.3	112.7	131.9	143.8		34.0	40.5	49.4	55.5		4.2	10.2

2823	Machinery for metallurgy	65.9	61.0	73.2	73.7	24.8	22.0	26.5	24.6	1.7	4.2
2824	Mining, quarrying and construction machinery	21.7	25.2	25.5	26.0	7.4	9.0	9.0	9.1	...	2.4
2825	Food/beverage/tobacco processing machinery	76.3	87.6	93.5	107.6	25.9	30.7	33.1	40.3	3.1	2.8
2826	Textile/apparel/leather production machinery	15.3	16.3	18.5	19.2	6.7	7.8	9.0	9.6	...	...
2829	Other special-purpose machinery	148.9	154.1	...	...	53.1	54.3	...	...	...	...
2910	Motor vehicles	687.0	899.2	...	...	125.6	132.7	...	...	...	...
2920	Automobile bodies, trailers and semi-trailers	339.1	366.2	...	...	50.1	57.7	...	...	...	...
2930	Parts and accessories for motor vehicles	1049.7	1113.5	1067.2	967.8	298.9	314.4	332.5	315.8	61.2	60.2
301	Building of ships and boats	20.0	11.1	11.4	20.2	5.8	3.3	4.4	7.1	1.6	1.6
3011	Building of ships and floating structures	1.3	1.4	1.5	1.1	0.6	0.7	0.6	0.4	1.6h/	1.6h/
3012	Building of pleasure and sporting boats	18.7	9.7	9.9	19.1	5.3	2.7	3.8	6.6	...h/	...h/
3020	Railway locomotives and rolling stock	...	...	...	...	...	...	...	...	-	-
3030	Air and spacecraft and related machinery	16.0	17.5	20.0	25.8	7.1	7.1	8.4	11.0	0.8	1.3
3040	Military fighting vehicles	-	-	-	-	-	-	-	-	-	-
309	Transport equipment n.e.c.	...	12.8	...	...	...	3.9	...	...	...	0.2
3091	Motorcycles	...	3.8	...	...	...	0.9	...	...	...	0.2i/
3092	Bicycles and invalid carriages	10.2	9.0	...	1.4	3.5	3.0	...	0.2	...	...i/
3099	Other transport equipment n.e.c.	-	-	...	...	-	-	...	...	...	...i/
3100	Furniture	311.6	351.4	355.2	383.0	102.8	124.5	125.0	138.4	17.3	22.1
321	Jewellery, bijouterie and related articles	30.2	31.0	28.4	30.2	10.3	12.3	11.8	13.0	...	...
3211	Jewellery and related articles	29.9	30.7	28.1	29.9	10.2	12.1	11.7	12.8	...	...
3212	Imitation jewellery and related articles	0.2	0.3	0.3	0.3	0.1	0.2	0.2	0.2	-	-
3220	Musical instruments	2.2	2.9	...	...	1.2	1.4	...	...	...	...
3230	Sports goods	50.9	51.9	...	...	14.8	16.5	...	...	...	2.5
3240	Games and toys	32.0	37.5	46.1	118.3	11.1	11.6	14.6	45.4	1.5	6.4
3250	Medical and dental instruments and supplies	122.2	134.6	128.3	137.2	53.1	57.4	55.5	62.3	6.2	5.6
3290	Other manufacturing n.e.c.	48.1	52.9	56.7	61.9	16.3	18.3	19.3	22.1	1.9	4.4
331	Repair of fabricated metal products/machinery	322.1	327.2	339.5	337.7	161.3	179.8	186.1	197.2	12.3	11.0
3311	Repair of fabricated metal products	7.4	7.5	...	...	3.2	2.8	...	...	0.4	1.1
3312	Repair of machinery	150.5	144.4	137.3	139.1	65.6	75.2	77.1	78.4	5.2	5.6
3313	Repair of electronic and optical equipment	5.7	7.1	8.0	9.7	2.1	3.5	3.9	3.9	0.3	0.8
3314	Repair of electrical equipment	32.6	37.2	42.0	19.7	10.8	12.9	13.0	8.7	4.0	0.7
3315	Repair of transport equip., excl. motor vehicles	124.9	129.9	...	-	79.1	84.7	...	-	...	...
3319	Repair of other equipment	0.9	1.0	1.1	1.1	0.5	0.6	0.7	0.6	...	...
3320	Installation of industrial machinery/equipment	326.0	333.6	282.7	326.6	102.1	114.2	119.0	133.7	8.2	8.2
C	Total manufacturing	21418.4	22438.2	23218.3	24013.6	6290.7	6888.2	7159.7	7651.9	1298.2	1417.6

a/ 1061 includes 1062.
b/ 1101 includes 1102, 1103 and 1104.
c/ 1511 includes 1512.
d/ 2011 includes 2012 and 2013.
e/ 2211 includes 2219.
f/ 2431 includes 2432.
g/ 2651 includes 2652.
h/ 3011 includes 3012.
i/ 3091 includes 3092 and 3099.

Slovenia

Index numbers of industrial production

(2010=100)

ISIC Revision 4

ISIC	Industry	Note	2005	2006	2007	2008	2009	2010	2011	2012	2013	2014	2015	2016
10	Food products		117	116	115	106	99	100	105	100	99	99	103	106
11	Beverages		119	120	118	109	105	100	103	96	94	92	84	86
12	Tobacco products		...	...	...	...	...	...	...	...	...	...	...	...
13	Textiles		262	246	237	201	99	100	93	90	104	97	85	89
14	Wearing apparel		203	199	192	172	100	100	103	102	84	78	74	78
15	Leather and related products		136	143	113	117	88	100	116	89	91	101	107	109
16	Wood products, excluding furniture		118	122	135	126	95	100	95	88	78	73	79	83
17	Paper and paper products		125	124	122	109	98	100	100	94	100	103	102	100
18	Printing and reproduction of recorded media		112	110	111	122	107	100	99	97	92	92	114	121
19	Coke and refined petroleum products		...	336	878	262	206	100	...	...	...	...	...	...
20	Chemicals and chemical products		85	91	99	103	87	100	99	93	94	95	87	79
21	Pharmaceuticals, medicinal chemicals, etc.		...	...	...	...	...	...	...	...	...	...	...	...
22	Rubber and plastics products		81	86	93	103	86	100	77	71	68	73	85	102
23	Other non-metallic mineral products		121	129	137	140	101	100	91	86	84	88	98	97
24	Basic metals		143	171	182	125	88	100	112	111	114	122	123	123
25	Fabricated metal products, except machinery		83	89	97	123	95	100	107	105	102	105	115	136
26	Computer, electronic and optical products		75	81	87	122	97	100	114	132	123	143	173	250
27	Electrical equipment		78	87	92	97	82	100	104	101	100	112	116	126
28	Machinery and equipment n.e.c.		134	142	163	134	94	100	111	116	110	109	115	124
29	Motor vehicles, trailers and semi-trailers		88	85	98	92	87	100	95	85	77	89	99	98
30	Other transport equipment		135	151	169	179	144	100	67	48	35	28	56	66
31	Furniture		212	217	207	156	103	100	92	79	69	68	69	73
32	Other manufacturing		162	133	129	137	100	100	93	85	85	108	105	124
33	Repair and installation of machinery/equipment		100	113	121	130	103	100	104	103	104	107	106	126
C	Total manufacturing		97	103	111	114	93	100	101	99	97	101	107	116

South Africa

Supplier of information:
Statistics South Africa, Pretoria.

Basic source of data:
Survey; administrative source.

Major deviations from ISIC (Revision 3):
None reported.

Reference period:
Calendar year.

Scope:
Not reported.

Method of data collection:
Mail questionnaires.

Type of enumeration:
Sample survey.

Adjusted for non-response:
Not reported.

Concepts and definitions of variables:
No deviation from the standard UN concepts and definitions are reported.

Related national publications:
Manufacturing production and sales, published by Statistics South Africa, Pretoria.

South Africa

ISIC	Industry	Establishments Note	Est 2013	Est 2014	Est 2015	Est 2016	Employees Note	Emp 2013	Emp 2014	Emp 2015	Emp 2016	Wages 2013	Wages 2014	Wages 2015	Wages 2016
	ISIC Revision 3	**Number of establishments (number)**					**Number of employees (thousands)**					**Wages and salaries paid to employees (millions of South African Rand)**			
151	Processed meat,fish,fruit,vegetables,fats		1337	1340	…	…		53.1	54.1	54.3	59.7	4547	4724	5423	6541
1511	Processing/preserving of meat		831	835	…	…		…	…	…	…	…	…	…	…
1512	Processing/preserving of fish		150	148	…	…		…	…	…	…	…	…	…	…
1513	Processing/preserving of fruit & vegetables		265	263	…	…		…	…	…	…	…	…	…	…
1514	Vegetable and animal oils and fats		91	94	…	…		18.7	18.4	22.1	23.2	2784	2747	3255	3547
1520	Dairy products		271	291	…	…		10.8	11.1	27.0	28.4	1123	1425	5228	5573
153	Grain mill products; starches; animal feeds		613	622	…	…		…	…	…	…	…	…	…	…
1531	Grain mill products		367	374	…	…		…	…	…	…	…	…	…	…
1532	Starches and starch products		4	3	…	…		…	…	…	…	…	…	…	…
1533	Prepared animal feeds		242	245	…	…		…	…	…	…	…	…	…	…
154	Other food products		2830	2879	…	…		90.6	91.5	75.9	88.0	13256	14059	12338	13663
1541	Bakery products		1188	1201	…	…		…	…	…	…	…	…	…	…
1542	Sugar		34	43	…	…		…	…	…	…	…	…	…	…
1543	Cocoa, chocolate and sugar confectionery		168	175	…	…		…	…	…	…	…	…	…	…
1544	Macaroni, noodles & similar products		3	5	…	…		…	…	…	…	…	…	…	…
1549	Other food products n.e.c.		1437	1455	…	…		…	…	…	…	…	…	…	…
155	Beverages	a/	1850	1877	…	…	a/	37.5	39.9	40.1	42.1	9637	9350	10410	12520
1551	Distilling, rectifying & blending of spirits		572 b/	573 b/	…	…		…	…	…	…	…	…	…	…
1552	Wines		… b/	… b/	…	…		…	…	…	…	…	…	…	…
1553	Malt liquors and malt		954	974	…	…		…	…	…	…	…	…	…	…
1554	Soft drinks; mineral waters		324	330	…	…		…	…	…	…	…	…	…	…
1600	Tobacco products	a/	86	95	…	…	a/	…	…	…	…	…	…	…	…
171	Spinning, weaving and finishing of textiles		162	168	…	…		7.8	7.6	10.5	8.8	784	828	1048	1014
1711	Textile fibre preparation; textile weaving		143	148	…	…		…	…	…	…	…	…	…	…
1712	Finishing of textiles		19	20	…	…		…	…	…	…	…	…	…	…
172	Other textiles		1612	1623	…	…		23.9	23.5	21.4	23.4	2053	2196	2409	2720
1721	Made-up textile articles, except apparel		421	440	…	…		…	…	…	…	…	…	…	…
1722	Carpets and rugs		172	173	…	…		…	…	…	…	…	…	…	…
1723	Cordage, rope, twine and netting		62	64	…	…		…	…	…	…	…	…	…	…
1729	Other textiles n.e.c.		957	946	…	…		…	…	…	…	…	…	…	…
1730	Knitted and crocheted fabrics and articles		274	271	…	…		4.8	5.0	4.7	4.7	300	331	374	405
1810	Wearing apparel, except fur apparel	c/	2161	2193	…	…	c/	42.7	40.8	41.0	39.5	2670	2821	3337	3651
1820	Dressing & dyeing of fur; processing of fur	c/	44	44	…	…	c/	4.2	4.0	4.7	5.2	419	469	558	660
191	Tanning, dressing and processing of leather		474	465	…	…		…	…	…	…	…	…	…	…
1911	Tanning and dressing of leather		147	152	…	…		…	…	…	…	…	…	…	…
1912	Luggage, handbags, etc.; saddlery & harness		327	313	…	…		…	…	…	…	…	…	…	…
1920	Footwear		487	483	…	…		10.9	11.0	8.8	8.5	814	850	831	832
2010	Sawmilling and planing of wood		488	488	…	…		14.3	14.9	16.7	17.0	936	1022	1209	1392
202	Products of wood, cork, straw, etc.		1277	1301	…	…		20.8	21.7	27.6	27.7	2012	2275	2693	2851
2021	Veneer sheets, plywood, particle board, etc.		31	32	…	…		…	…	…	…	…	…	…	…
2022	Builders' carpentry and joinery		295	323	…	…		…	…	…	…	…	…	…	…
2023	Wooden containers		124	132	…	…		…	…	…	…	…	…	…	…
2029	Other wood products; articles of cork/straw		827	814	…	…		…	…	…	…	…	…	…	…
210	Paper and paper products		1124	1145	…	…		29.6	31.1	38.2	37.1	5947	6911	7911	8166
2101	Pulp, paper and paperboard		135	137	…	…		…	…	…	…	…	…	…	…
2102	Corrugated paper and paperboard		450	466	…	…		…	…	…	…	…	…	…	…
2109	Other articles of paper and paperboard		539	542	…	…		…	…	…	…	…	…	…	…
221	Publishing		2298	2320	…	…		25.4	24.8	24.4	26.0	5686	5614	6142	6362
2211	Publishing of books and other publications		596	603	…	…		…	…	…	…	…	…	…	…
2212	Publishing of newspapers, journals, etc.		805	818	…	…		…	…	…	…	…	…	…	…
2213	Publishing of recorded media		7	7	…	…		…	…	…	…	…	…	…	…
2219	Other publishing		890	892	…	…		…	…	…	…	…	…	…	…

Code	Description												
222	Printing and related service activities	1576	1636	d/	27.4	28.8	22.7	23.9	d/	4442	4343	3809	3538
2221	Printing	1468	1523		...	...	...	...		...	...	...	...
2222	Service activities related to printing	108	113		...	...	...	...		...	...	...	...
2230	Reproduction of recorded media	32	34		...	...	...	...		...	...	...	...
2310	Coke oven products	24	26	e/	...	...	...	...	e/	...	...	...	...
2320	Refined petroleum products	889	888	e/	22.3	25.6	28.3	27.9	e/	11934	13471	14518	13283
2330	Processing of nuclear fuel	2	2	e/	...	...	...	...	e/	...	...	...	...
241	Basic chemicals	917	930		21.1	22.8	17.5	17.5		6497	6460	5036	4293
2411	Basic chemicals, except fertilizers	458	463		...	...	...	...		...	...	...	...
2412	Fertilizers and nitrogen compounds	227	233		...	...	...	...		...	...	...	...
2413	Plastics in primary forms; synthetic rubber	232	234		...	...	...	...		...	...	...	...
242	Other chemicals	2067	2127	f/	57.6	55.5	48.5	49.8	f/	15809	14249	11786	10761
2421	Pesticides and other agro-chemical products	248	252		...	...	...	...		...	...	...	...
2422	Paints, varnishes, printing ink and mastics	500	496		...	...	...	...		...	...	...	...
2423	Pharmaceuticals, medicinal chemicals, etc.	303	319		...	...	...	...		...	...	...	...
2424	Soap, cleaning & cosmetic preparations	698	733		...	...	...	...		...	...	...	...
2429	Other chemical products n.e.c.	318	327		...	...	...	...		...	...	...	...
2430	Man-made fibres	-	-	f/	...	...	...	...	f/	...	...	...	...
251	Rubber products	442	446		11.6	11.4	12.1	12.5		3381	3037	2791	2757
2511	Rubber tyres and tubes	167	169		...	...	...	...		...	...	...	...
2519	Other rubber products	275	277		...	...	...	...		...	...	...	...
2520	Plastic products	1649	1703		42.0	41.8	37.2	38.2		6763	6346	5434	4989
2610	Glass and glass products	642	640		8.2	8.6	9.8	9.9		1732	1665	1661	1623
269	Non-metallic mineral products n.e.c.	1480	1504		48.4	48.8	47.0	48.4		8092	7867	6629	6250
2691	Pottery, china and earthenware	57	60		...	...	...	...		...	...	...	...
2692	Refractory ceramic products	344	333		...	...	...	...		...	...	...	...
2693	Struct.non-refractory clay; ceramic products	136	139		...	...	...	...		...	...	...	...
2694	Cement, lime and plaster	297	286		...	...	...	...		...	...	...	...
2695	Articles of concrete, cement and plaster	380	407		...	...	...	...		...	...	...	...
2696	Cutting, shaping & finishing of stone	72	83		...	...	...	...		...	...	...	...
2699	Other non-metallic mineral products n.e.c.	194	196		...	...	...	...		...	...	...	...
2710	Basic iron and steel	1441	1459		30.1	32.8	45.8	46.8		9000	8306	10615	10979
2720	Basic precious and non-ferrous metals	1469	1447		17.8	20.9	18.5	18.7		5642	6643	4721	4371
273	Casting of metals	129	130		5.2	5.0	3.4	3.2		1131	1102	661	495
2731	Casting of iron and steel	108	108		...	...	...	...		...	...	...	...
2732	Casting of non-ferrous metals	21	22		...	...	...	...		...	...	...	...
281	Struct.metal products;tanks;steam generators	1325	1400		38.0	42.2	39.2	39.7		7280	7822	7590	6653
2811	Structural metal products	1150	1217		...	...	...	...		...	...	...	...
2812	Tanks, reservoirs and containers of metal	85	92		...	...	...	...		...	...	...	...
2813	Steam generators	90	91		...	...	...	...		...	...	...	...
289	Other metal products; metal working services	6037	6071		59.1	62.5	64.1	63.2		11570	11851	10464	9774
2891	Metal forging/pressing/stamping/roll-forming	42	45		...	...	...	...		...	...	...	...
2892	Treatment & coating of metals	3423	3460		...	...	...	...		...	...	...	...
2893	Cutlery, hand tools and general hardware	314	310		...	...	...	...		...	...	...	...
2899	Other fabricated metal products n.e.c.	2258	2256		...	...	...	...		...	...	...	...
291	General purpose machinery	3214	3276		43.2	42.5	48.1	45.8		12734	11684	11341	10225
2911	Engines & turbines (not for transport equipment)	108	102		...	...	...	...		...	...	...	...
2912	Pumps, compressors, taps and valves	693	725		...	...	...	...		...	...	...	...
2913	Bearings, gears, gearing & driving elements	64	69		...	...	...	...		...	...	...	...
2914	Ovens, furnaces and furnace burners	37	39		...	...	...	...		...	...	...	...
2915	Lifting and handling equipment	535	541		...	...	...	...		...	...	...	...
2919	Other general purpose machinery	1777	1800		...	...	...	...		...	...	...	...
292	Special purpose machinery	3835	3872		54.6	53.9	58.1	59.0		15560	14673	13836	13198
2921	Agricultural and forestry machinery	694	696		...	...	...	...		...	...	...	...
2922	Machine tools	354	358		...	...	...	...		...	...	...	...
2923	Machinery for metallurgy	7	6		...	...	...	...		...	...	...	...
2924	Machinery for mining & construction	875	921		...	...	...	...		...	...	...	...
2925	Food/beverage/tobacco processing machinery	78	86		...	...	...	...		...	...	...	...
2926	Machinery for textile, apparel and leather	78	78		...	...	...	...		...	...	...	...
2927	Weapons and ammunition	13	15		...	...	...	...		...	...	...	...
2929	Other special purpose machinery	1743	1718		...	...	...	...		...	...	...	...

continued

South Africa

ISIC	Industry	Note	Number of establishments (number) 2013	2014	2015	2016	Note	Number of employees (thousands) 2013	2014	2015	2016	Note	Wages and salaries paid to employees (millions of South African Rand) 2013	2014	2015	2016
2930	Domestic appliances n.e.c.		449	447	…	…		7.0	7.1	6.7	7.0		1024	1076	1137	1292
3000	Office, accounting and computing machinery		1583	1538	…	…		6.7	6.4	4.0	4.6		1494	1482	1079	1215
3110	Electric motors, generators and transformers		179	201	…	…		4.9	5.1	16.2	16.3		930	1333	3842	4169
3120	Electricity distribution & control apparatus		189	201	…	…		12.0	12.3	6.9	7.0		2378	2104	1399	1437
3130	Insulated wire and cable		133	143	…	…		4.6	4.4	4.9	5.1		878	919	1049	1167
3140	Accumulators, primary cells and batteries		102	102	…	…		2.6	3.2	3.1	3.2		584	755	724	836
3150	Lighting equipment and electric lamps		120	119	…	…		2.6	2.7	3.1	2.9		418	453	592	540
3190	Other electrical equipment n.e.c.		1064	1066	…	…		11.2	10.4	10.0	10.9		1689	1989	1864	2158
3210	Electronic valves, tubes, etc.	g/	87	94	…	…	g/	5.1	5.6	4.5	4.4	g/	1057	1108	1132	1162
3220	TV/radio transmitters; line comm. apparatus	g/	135	140	…	…	g/	2.1	2.2	2.0	2.4	g/	353	346	514	566
3230	TV and radio receivers and associated goods		194	194	…	…		7.0	7.1	8.0	8.9		1610	1814	2675	3040
331	Medical, measuring, testing appliances, etc.		732	740	…	…										
3311	Medical, surgical and orthopaedic equipment		536	539	…	…										
3312	Measuring/testing/navigating appliances,etc.		177	178	…	…										
3313	Industrial process control equipment		19	23	…	…										
3320	Optical instruments & photographic equipment	h/	185	178	…	…	h/	2.5	2.4	2.4	2.3	h/	406	427	564	582
3330	Watches and clocks	h/	31	31	…	…	h/					h/				
3410	Motor vehicles		1653	1619	…	…		32.0	31.0	28.7	31.3		7265	8082	9407	11408
3420	Automobile bodies, trailers & semi-trailers		450	481	…	…		9.4	8.9	14.6	14.5		1148	1342	2185	2185
3430	Parts/accessories for automobiles		3979	3982	…	…		45.2	44.8	47.0	48.3		7205	8104	9497	10771
351	Building and repairing of ships and boats		124	129	…	…		3.8	4.8	4.5	4.9		650	789	818	957
3511	Building and repairing of ships		77	81	…	…										
3512	Building/repairing of pleasure/sport. boats		47	48	…	…										
3520	Railway/tramway locomotives & rolling stock	i/	95	102	…	…	i/	7.2	7.1	7.4	7.9	i/	1675	1676	2039	2291
3530	Aircraft and spacecraft		236	246	…	…										
359	Transport equipment n.e.c.	i/	350	344	…	…	i/	3.7	3.6	2.9	3.6	i/	553	533	362	435
3591	Motorcycles		152	147	…	…										
3592	Bicycles and invalid carriages		16	16	…	…										
3599	Other transport equipment n.e.c.		182	181	…	…										
3610	Furniture		2560	2561	…	…		32.9	29.9	29.3	28.1		2605	2533	3075	3447
369	Manufacturing n.e.c.		6629	6618	…	…		24.9	25.4	25.0	27.7		3375	3520	3576	4138
3691	Jewellery and related articles		748	749	…	…										
3692	Musical instruments		67	67	…	…										
3693	Sports goods		173	170	…	…										
3694	Games and toys		127	141	…	…										
3699	Other manufacturing n.e.c.		5514	5491	…	…										
3710	Recycling of metal waste and scrap	j/	56	63	…	…	j/	17.2	16.5	12.7	118.6	j/	3603	2734	1244	1193
3720	Recycling of non-metal waste and scrap	j/	115	123	…	…	j/					j/				
D	Total manufacturing	k/	65995	66664	…	…		1144.1	1140.4	1164.1	1286.1		197057	209633	231458	246453

a/ 155 includes 1600.
b/ 1551 includes 1552.
c/ 1810 includes 1820.
d/ 222 includes 2230.
e/ 2320 includes 2310 and 2330.
f/ 242 includes 2430.
g/ 3210 includes 3220.
h/ 3320 includes 3330.
i/ 3520 includes 3530.
j/ 3710 includes 3720.

k/ Sum of available data.

South Africa

Index numbers of industrial production

(2010=100)

ISIC	ISIC Revision 3 — Industry	Note	2005	2006	2007	2008	2009	2010	2011	2012	2013	2014	2015	2016
15	Food and beverages		86	86	90	94	96	100	102	104	108	110	113	113
16	Tobacco products		...	...	...	...	...	...	...	...	...	...	...	...
17	Textiles		141	142	142	134	109	100	94	89	86	85	85	88
18	Wearing apparel, fur		116	119	126	128	112	100	96	99	101	102	100	96
19	Leather, leather products and footwear		100	102	105	107	97	100	102	101	109	113	110	106
20	Wood products (excl. furniture)		116	122	123	116	95	100	102	103	103	106	114	121
21	Paper and paper products		88	95	96	107	91	100	98	99	100	104	103	105
22	Printing and publishing		116	122	124	117	100	100	105	110	109	103	93	94
23	Coke,refined petroleum products,nuclear fuel		108	102	105	103	103	100	95	104	102	102	99	106
24	Chemicals and chemical products		83	88	97	109	91	100	104	108	112	114	117	121
25	Rubber and plastics products		82	90	96	96	92	100	106	110	109	104	103	102
26	Non-metallic mineral products		108	114	120	119	103	100	103	104	106	99	98	96
27	Basic metals		113	122	122	111	92	100	103	95	101	99	92	94
28	Fabricated metal products		98	107	121	123	100	100	103	109	110	109	108	108
29	Machinery and equipment n.e.c.		122	124	131	125	99	100	105	111	109	103	102	95
30	Office, accounting and computing machinery		...	...	...	...	...	...	...	...	...	...	...	...
31	Electrical machinery and apparatus		82	86	89	99	96	100	102	101	104	102	109	107
32	Radio,television and communication equipment	a/	106	102	109	112	104	100	112	123	126	138	131	140
33	Medical, precision and optical instruments	a/	...	...	...	...	...	...	...	...	...	...	...	...
34	Motor vehicles, trailers, semi-trailers		107	120	120	112	80	100	109	112	110	110	114	114
35	Other transport equipment		87	91	98	102	108	100	102	99	97	96	101	99
36	Furniture; manufacturing n.e.c.		109	114	123	127	103	100	102	102	97	99	92	90
37	Recycling		...	...	...	...	...	...	...	...	...	...	...	...
D	Total manufacturing		102	107	111	111	96	100	103	105	106	107	107	107

a/ 32 includes 33.

Spain

Supplier of information:
Instituto Nacional de Estadística (I.N.E.), Ministerio de Economía y Hacienda, Madrid. Industrial statistics for the OECD countries are compiled by the OECD secretariat, which supplies them to UNIDO.

Basic source of data:
Annual industrial survey; business register.

Major deviations from ISIC (Revision 4):
Data presented in ISIC (Revision 4) were originally classified according to the national NACE-related classification system.

Reference period:
Calendar year (exception for companies that operate by seasons or campaigns that comprise two different years).

Scope:
All enterprises.

Method of data collection:
Mail questionnaires; electronic questionnaires.

Type of enumeration:
Complete enumeration for enterprises exceeding employment or turnover threshold; sample survey for enterprises below threshold values.

Adjusted for non-response:
Not reported.

Concepts and definitions of variables:
No deviations from the standard UN concepts and definitions are reported.

Related national publications:
None reported.

Spain

ISIC	Industry	Number of enterprises (number)					Number of employees (thousands)					Wages and salaries paid to employees (millions of Euros)				
		Note	2013	2014	2015	2016	Note	2013	2014	2015	2016	Note	2013	2014	2015	2016
1010	Processing/preserving of meat		3297	3455	3656	3715		79.5	81.1	83.6	89.2		1745	1760	1844	1955
1020	Processing/preserving of fish, etc.		640	542	598	601		18.1	18.2	18.8	20.3		338	336	350	402
1030	Processing/preserving of fruit,vegetables		1370	1226	1363	1426		29.4	30.5	32.1	34.0		617	653	673	683
1040	Vegetable and animal oils and fats		1580	1501	1544	1567		12.3	11.9	11.4	12.3		322	336	317	307
1050	Dairy products		1539	1540	1503	1507		22.5	22.5	22.8	24.1		700	619	637	650
106	Grain mill products,starches and starch products		490	385	409	415		5.9	5.7	5.7	6.2		181	174	181	182
1061	Grain mill products		481	377	391	400		5.3	5.1	5.1	5.5		155	147	154	155
1062	Starches and starch products		9	8	18	15		0.6	0.6	0.6	0.7		25	27	27	27
107	Other food products		12934	13061	12389	12543		111.5	111.3	114.8	125.3		2565	2517	2574	2666
1071	Bakery products		10561	10407	9784	9891		66.1	65.6	68.1	74.6		1305	1209	1292	1342
1072	Sugar		33	30	37	25		1.7	1.6	1.4	1.5		63	68	58	61
1073	Cocoa, chocolate and sugar confectionery		645	636	638	598		16.6	15.7	15.6	12.2		498	500	467	296
1074	Macaroni, noodles, couscous, etc.		71	67	85	88		1.3	1.0	1.3	1.3		33	26	31	31
1075	Prepared meals and dishes		108	178	167	182		4.0	4.2	5.1	6.9		95	101	119	153
1079	Other food products n.e.c.		1516	1743	1677	1761		21.9	23.1	23.3	28.7		571	614	606	783
1080	Prepared animal feeds		769	737	752	764		11.6	11.4	11.3	12.3		339	332	336	357
110	Beverages		4500	4889	4761	4908		43.0	42.1	44.1	47.5		1466	1399	1488	1542
1101	Distilling, rectifying and blending of spirits		378	219	309	296		3.0	2.8	3.1	3.2		94	93	103	109
1102	Wines		...	...	3847	...		...	...	23.6	...		...	...	633	...
1103	Malt liquors and malt		...	...	323	...		...	...	6.6	...		...	...	353	...
1104	Soft drinks,mineral waters,other bottled waters		293	272	282	261		11.4	10.6	10.9	11.5		437	387	398	401
1200	Tobacco products		45	52	49	54		2.5	2.2	2.1	2.1		161	89	95	173
131	Spinning, weaving and finishing of textiles		1522	1433	1504	1545		14.3	14.3	15.0	16.1		328	325	341	358
1311	Preparation and spinning of textile fibres		410	399	402	417		4.3	4.2	4.3	4.7		102	96	94	102
1312	Weaving of textiles		342	397	387	371		5.0	5.3	5.0	5.0		114	122	118	119
1313	Finishing of textiles		770	637	715	757		5.0	4.8	5.6	6.4		112	108	128	137
139	Other textiles		4265	4150	4508	4469		20.6	20.5	21.3	22.1		434	433	450	458
1391	Knitted and crocheted fabrics		190	635	264	222		1.7	1.6	1.6	1.5		37	36	39	34
1392	Made-up textile articles, except apparel		2914	2555	3168	3131		11.0	11.0	11.6	11.9		208	206	211	214
1393	Carpets and rugs		56	55	78	89		0.8	0.8	0.9	1.0		21	21	24	25
1394	Cordage, rope, twine and netting		649	215	351	347		1.5	1.4	1.4	1.5		30	25	26	28
1399	Other textiles n.e.c.		455	691	648	679		5.7	5.7	5.8	6.3		138	144	150	157
1410	Wearing apparel, except fur apparel		8220	7942	7914	7869		34.5	32.1	32.4	33.0		647	589	602	596
1420	Articles of fur		203	160	165	154		0.3	0.3	0.3	0.2		6	5	5	4
1430	Knitted and crocheted apparel		604	694	552	533		4.7	4.3	4.4	4.6		96	81	88	89
151	Leather;luggage,handbags,saddlery,harness;fur		1158	1053	1190	1165		8.1	8.5	8.7	8.7		171	176	183	178
1511	Tanning/dressing of leather; dressing of fur		290	266	288	259		3.1	3.1	3.0	3.1		73	73	75	73
1512	Luggage,handbags,etc.;saddlery/harness		868	787	902	906		5.1	5.3	5.6	5.6		98	103	108	105
1520	Footwear		3052	3203	3636	3531		25.0	27.3	29.5	28.9		390	432	474	458
1610	Sawmilling and planing of wood		1000	1063	1005	1026		6.2	5.8	6.0	6.1		116	111	113	116

Code	Industry	(1)	(2)	(3)	(4)	(5)	(6)	(7)	(8)	(9)	(10)	(11)	(12)
162	Wood products, cork, straw, plaiting materials	736	726	702	749	35.6	34.5	33.3	35.6	8574	8936	9470	9095
1621	Veneer sheets and wood-based panels	191	184	175	170	7.6	7.3	7.0	6.9	293	291	303	309
1622	Builders' carpentry and joinery	279	283	282	323	15.0	14.9	14.6	16.5	5686	6022	6539	6671
1623	Wooden containers	170	161	148	151	8.0	7.4	6.9	7.0	907	869	866	856
1629	Other wood products;articles of cork,straw	96	99	97	106	5.0	4.8	4.8	5.1	1689	1753	1761	1259
170	Paper and paper products	1305	1290	1321	1427	42.2	41.7	40.8	43.4	1652	1651	1608	1716
1701	Pulp, paper and paperboard	370	373	396	402	9.1	9.4	9.0	9.7	169	184	166	201
1702	Corrugated paper and paperboard	596	589	575	593	21.3	20.6	20.1	19.9	793	787	749	629
1709	Other articles of paper and paperboard	339	328	351	432	11.8	11.7	11.8	13.7	690	680	692	886
181	Printing and service activities related to printing	1206	1160	1201	1214	50.1	49.6	48.7	49.1	12380	12340	13649	14041
1811	Printing	1012	932	963	941	41.0	39.3	38.1	37.6	9571	9491	11183	10896
1812	Service activities related to printing	194	229	238	274	9.0	10.3	10.5	11.5	2810	2849	2466	3144
1820	Reproduction of recorded media	20	22	23	34	0.9	0.8	1.0	1.3	1076	1139	330	342
1910	Coke oven products a/	610	567	623	532	8.9	8.5	8.6	8.9	18	14	10	14
1920	Refined petroleum products a/	:	:	:	:	:	:	:	:	:	:	:	:
201	Basic chemicals,fertilizers, etc.	1336	1247	1234	1220	31.3	28.7	28.2	28.6	1064	1019	973	1055
2011	Basic chemicals	712	674	568	612	16.2	15.0	13.3	14.5	413	404	306	299
2012	Fertilizers and nitrogen compounds	151	131	121	116	4.7	3.9	3.6	3.5	316	297	192	475
2013	Plastics and synthetic rubber in primary forms	473	443	546	492	10.4	9.8	11.3	10.5	336	318	475	282
202	Other chemical products	1798	1789	1705	1687	53.2	51.2	48.7	49.0	2309	2366	2217	2234
2021	Pesticides and other agrochemical products	87	80	70	70	2.2	2.1	1.8	2.0	75	82	74	86
2022	Paints,varnishes;printing ink and mastics	444	425	418	447	13.0	12.3	12.0	13.0	437	433	434	460
2023	Soap,cleaning and cosmetic preparations	824	821	792	722	25.7	24.5	23.3	21.9	1053	1080	999	981
2029	Other chemical products n.e.c.	444	464	425	448	12.3	12.3	11.7	12.2	744	772	709	707
2030	Man-made fibres	65	67	66	63	2.0	2.1	2.1	1.9	36	34	34	33
2100	Pharmaceuticals,medicinal chemicals, etc.	1768	1731	1676	1643	41.0	39.0	38.4	36.6	351	343	345	344
221	Rubber products	732	707	699	700	22.9	21.2	20.6	21.1	706	667	675	711
2211	Rubber tyres and tubes	426	420	418	424	11.2	10.3	10.3	10.6	119	107	153	159
2219	Other rubber products	306	287	281	276	11.6	10.9	10.3	10.5	587	560	522	552
2220	Plastics products	1885	1869	1769	1808	68.7	67.5	63.7	65.5	3635	3717	3559	3647
2310	Glass and glass products	500	475	474	488	17.6	16.7	16.1	16.5	962	981	993	1117
239	Non-metallic mineral products n.e.c.	1964	1858	1889	2055	68.2	64.4	65.5	69.9	7054	7296	7034	7468
2391	Refractory products	63	63	77	73	2.0	1.9	2.3	2.2	65	65	56	68
2392	Clay building materials	487	477	472	477	16.3	16.1	15.9	15.9	527	546	509	477
2393	Other porcelain and ceramic products	119	107	114	114	4.4	4.3	4.3	4.4	790	819	786	912
2394	Cement, lime and plaster	276	276	283	331	6.2	6.2	6.3	6.8	136	146	154	167
2395	Articles of concrete, cement and plaster	461	438	439	529	18.6	17.1	17.3	19.8	1983	2022	1853	1914
2396	Cutting, shaping and finishing of stone	354	331	338	376	15.5	14.2	14.7	16.1	3276	3412	3403	3635
2399	Other non-metallic mineral products n.e.c.	203	166	167	154	5.1	4.7	4.8	4.6	278	284	272	293
2410	Basic iron and steel	1134	1110	1115	1164	30.6	29.4	30.0	30.5	486	512	456	468
2420	Basic precious and other non-ferrous metals	418	416	417	420	12.9	12.0	12.0	11.3	195	195	222	232
243	Casting of metals	452	487	479	476	14.4	15.6	15.4	15.3	489	504	524	518
2431	Casting of iron and steel	242	298	302	294	7.5	9.3	9.5	9.3	137	141	184	150
2432	Casting of non-ferrous metals	210	189	177	182	7.0	6.3	5.9	5.9	352	363	340	368
251	Struct.metal products, tanks, reservoirs	2007	1910	1850	1930	86.6	81.6	80.2	82.2	18828	18862	19384	19638

continued

Spain

ISIC	Industry	Number of enterprises (number)				Number of employees (thousands)				Wages and salaries paid to employees (millions of Euros)			
		2013	2014	2015	2016	2013	2014	2015	2016	2013	2014	2015	2016
2511	Structural metal products	18612	18485	17995	18035	68.9	67.3	68.3	72.8	1543	1476	1523	1609
2512	Tanks, reservoirs and containers of metal	969	844	809	734	11.6	11.4	11.7	12.1	331	324	332	342
2513	Steam generators, excl. hot water boilers	57	55	57	58	1.8	1.5	1.6	1.7	55	50	55	57
2520	Weapons and ammunition	51	52	42	39	1.6	1.9	1.9	2.1	51	60	65	67
259	Other metal products;metal working services	15385	13936	14142	13993	119.6	115.1	119.5	124.3	3409	3308	3383	3514
2591	Forging,pressing,stamping,roll-forming of metal	1689	1515	1517	1491	22.0	20.6	21.6	23.2	652	635	648	708
2592	Treatment and coating of metals; machining	7469	6607	6851	7064	49.6	48.3	50.4	53.9	1372	1310	1374	1459
2593	Cutlery, hand tools and general hardware	3142	2833	2831	2670	18.8	17.2	17.1	17.1	544	522	501	494
2599	Other fabricated metal products n.e.c.	3086	2982	2943	2768	29.1	29.0	30.4	30.1	841	841	860	853
2610	Electronic components and boards	551	542	550	575	6.3	6.3	7.1	8.2	188	186	215	241
2620	Computers and peripheral equipment	672	655	717	657	1.5	1.4	1.2	1.0	42	42	34	25
2630	Communication equipment	116	173	177	172	4.9	4.4	4.8	4.0	160	143	150	137
2640	Consumer electronics	76	70	81	86	1.1	0.9	0.9	1.4	31	28	30	43
265	Measuring,testing equipment; watches, etc.	755	714	680	684	9.8	8.2	7.2	7.7	347	269	230	246
2651	Measuring/testing/navigating equipment,etc.	725	692	594	596	9.6	8.0	6.8	7.3	342	265	217	235
2652	Watches and clocks	30	22	86	88	0.2	0.1	0.4	0.4	5	4	13	11
2660	Irradiation/electromedical equipment,etc.	145	135	120	129	1.9	1.7	1.7	1.9	62	58	60	64
2670	Optical instruments and photographic equipment	45	34	...	...	0.7	0.6	...	...	18	15	...	...
2680	Magnetic and optical media	-	-	...	...	-	-	...	...	-	...	...	...
2710	Electric motors,generators,transformers,etc.	854	763	752	743	23.5	23.7	25.8	26.3	903	861	940	994
2720	Batteries and accumulators	32	31	21	21	2.1	2.0	2.0	2.2	75	75	76	74
273	Wiring and wiring devices	172	169	169	197	5.7	6.0	6.3	6.6	198	205	223	211
2731	Fibre optic cables	7	7	11	7	0.4	0.4	0.5	0.4	13	14	14	13
2732	Other electronic and electric wires and cables	127	126	124	157	4.2	4.4	4.4	4.8	143	146	159	153
2733	Wiring devices	38	35	34	34	1.1	1.2	1.4	1.3	42	46	51	46
2740	Electric lighting equipment	379	492	453	459	8.0	8.1	8.7	9.6	226	228	242	269
2750	Domestic appliances	227	200	219	212	9.2	9.6	9.3	9.7	278	290	293	293
2790	Other electrical equipment	280	361	341	346	7.3	6.9	9.2	9.2	204	194	229	236
281	General-purpose machinery	2143	2196	2306	2372	55.3	56.0	56.4	57.6	1828	1874	1829	1859
2811	Engines/turbines,excl.aircraft,vehicle engines	49	45	60	66	2.9	3.8	3.1	3.2	100	130	115	120
2812	Fluid power equipment	70	71	103	100	2.0	1.9	2.5	2.5	62	60	78	77
2813	Other pumps, compressors, taps and valves	234	289	230	238	6.8	6.7	6.5	6.7	223	225	218	222
2814	Bearings, gears, gearing and driving elements	191	147	162	152	4.2	4.2	4.0	3.4	148	147	143	116
2815	Ovens, furnaces and furnace burners	41	48	48	67	0.7	0.8	0.9	0.8	21	23	28	22
2816	Lifting and handling equipment	384	349	416	399	19.9	18.9	19.8	20.3	701	673	669	700
2817	Office machinery, excl.computers,etc.	35	26	23	25	0.4	0.2	0.1	0.1	9	6	2	3
2818	Power-driven hand tools	32	34	30	29	0.3	0.2	0.2	0.2	9	7	5	6
2819	Other general-purpose machinery	1109	1186	1235	1295	18.1	19.3	19.2	20.5	557	602	572	594
282	Special-purpose machinery	2862	3078	3022	3055	39.4	39.1	40.6	43.3	1222	1212	1290	1327
2821	Agricultural and forestry machinery	667	701	709	749	7.2	6.7	7.3	8.0	210	187	203	207
2822	Metal-forming machinery and machine tools	305	450	398	419	6.9	6.9	7.2	7.8	229	232	257	257

ISIC Revision 4

2823	Machinery for metallurgy	62	66	64	60	1.9	2.1	2.1	1.8	152	142	132	125
2824	Mining, quarrying and construction machinery	102	105	102	111	3.3	3.3	3.2	3.6	256	270	220	446
2825	Food/beverage/tobacco processing machinery	264	257	235	234	8.8	8.3	7.7	7.8	622	673	619	500
2826	Textile/apparel/leather production machinery	57	50	47	47	1.8	1.7	1.7	1.6	180	182	284	168
2829	Other special-purpose machinery	380	352	346	330	11.6	10.7	10.7	10.4	676	648	672	649
2910	Motor vehicles	2532	2424	2289	2125	71.5	67.7	63.6	59.7	117	133	113	108
2920	Automobile bodies, trailers and semi-trailers	234	223	196	199	9.4	9.2	7.9	8.0	718	667	681	819
2930	Parts and accessories for motor vehicles	2335	2116	1992	2008	72.2	65.5	63.4	63.1	803	841	805	820
301	Building of ships and boats	..	..	..	362	..	..	..	10.0	..	..	..	387
3011	Building of ships and floating structures	339	340	331	347	9.0	8.8	8.8	9.4	292	324	248	337
3012	Building of pleasure and sporting boats	..	..	..	16	..	..	..	0.6	..	..	..	50
3020	Railway locomotives and rolling stock b/	457	464	495	472	11.3	10.8	10.8	11.1	77	70	81	55
3030	Air and spacecraft and related machinery b/	1067	1033	964	924	23.0	22.2	20.7	19.2	103	111	82	76
3040	Military fighting vehicles	..	..	..	..	..	..	..	..	..	..	..	..
309	Transport equipment n.e.c.	55	49	51	..	1.9	1.7	1.8	..	202	192	184	..
3091	Motorcycles	27	24	25	30	1.0	0.9	1.0	1.1	115	108	61	69
3092	Bicycles and invalid carriages	23	20	23	24	0.7	0.6	0.6	0.6	48	43	78	34
3099	Other transport equipment n.e.c.	5	5	4	..	0.2	0.2	0.2	..	38	41	45	..
3100	Furniture	972	949	956	1048	48.6	46.1	46.3	51.3	11802	11882	12355	12611
321	Jewellery, bijouterie and related articles b/	111	109	106	112	5.2	5.3	4.9	5.2	2380	2409	2321	2590
3211	Jewellery and related articles b/	111	109	106	112	5.2	5.3	4.9	5.2	2380	2409	2321	2590
3212	Imitation jewellery and related articles b/	..	..	..	..	..	..	..	..	..	..	..	..
3220	Musical instruments	14	14	13	14	0.7	0.7	0.6	..	256	239	563	77
3230	Sports goods	35	34	33	31	1.5	1.5	1.3	1.3	193	189	233	106
3240	Games and toys	87	82	82	81	3.1	2.8	2.9	2.7	379	324	260	183
3250	Medical and dental instruments and supplies	387	367	333	329	16.5	15.6	14.4	13.9	5289	5243	4711	4521
3290	Other manufacturing n.e.c.	141	151	156	146	6.9	6.8	6.8	6.7	1492	1469	966	1272
331	Repair of fabricated metal products/machinery	1595	1503	1356	1250	57.8	53.8	48.7	44.8	11042	10556	10381	10267
3311	Repair of fabricated metal products	39	46	51	53	1.4	1.8	2.0	2.1	137	120	140	165
3312	Repair of machinery	792	731	644	659	30.6	28.3	24.6	23.4	8006	7775	7847	8648
3313	Repair of electronic and optical equipment	51	42	38	39	1.8	1.5	1.4	1.5	174	136	135	141
3314	Repair of electrical equipment	123	113	101	106	4.0	3.6	3.2	3.6	321	259	205	234
3315	Repair of transport equip., excl. motor vehicles	580	562	513	384	19.5	18.2	17.1	13.9	2251	2129	1872	1020
3319	Repair of other equipment	10	9	10	9	0.5	0.4	0.4	0.4	153	136	182	59
3320	Installation of industrial machinery/equipment	445	461	437	442	13.4	13.6	13.0	12.7	403	335	401	309
C	Total manufacturing	49573	47836	46476	47167	1748.9	1664.9	1612.1	1628.3	166984	166936	166589	168935

a/ 1910 includes 1920.
b/ 3211 includes 3212.

Spain

			Output (valuation not defined)					Value added at factor values					Gross fixed capital formation	
ISIC Revision 4			(millions of Euros)					(millions of Euros)					(millions of Euros)	
ISIC	Industry	Note	2013	2014	2015	2016	Note	2013	2014	2015	2016	Note	2015	2016
1010	Processing/preserving of meat		21400	21684	23867	23591		3424	4171	3920	3960		678	752
1020	Processing/preserving of fish, etc.		4309	4370	4742	5407		772	792	742	822		92	83
1030	Processing/preserving of fruit,vegetables		7771	8890	9048	9392		1600	1571	1617	1687		367	322
1040	Vegetable and animal oils and fats		8934	11143	11244	10047		1127	1078	835	793		246	216
1050	Dairy products		8748	8973	8510	8426		1542	1538	1607	1584		228	258
106	Grain mill products,starches and starch products		3347	3048	3378	3100		470	471	447	434		68	107
1061	Grain mill products		2945	2699	3035	2751		386	388	367	348		61	103
1062	Starches and starch products		403	350	343	349		84	83	80	86		7	4
107	Other food products		17886	17974	18920	19442		5207	5141	5228	5396		845	938
1071	Bakery products		6646	6539	7165	7551		2362	2387	2467	2512		382	389
1072	Sugar		979	799	659	481		288	116	67	113		12	14
1073	Cocoa, chocolate and sugar confectionery		3978	4088	4114	2570		993	992	1011	612		143	102
1074	Macaroni, noodles, couscous, etc.		347	239	358	333		81	66	80	79		25	18
1075	Prepared meals and dishes		1351	1479	1674	1989		254	270	294	350		62	68
1079	Other food products n.e.c.		4585	4831	4949	6518		1230	1311	1310	1730		221	349
1080	Prepared animal feeds		9063	8921	8844	10868		942	948	805	980		176	168
110	Beverages		15355	14861	15560	16092		3943	4011	4112	4196		991	1011
1101	Distilling, rectifying and blending of spirits		1236	1043	1052	988		304	332	312	286		52	37
1102	Wines		...	...	6594	...		...	...	1742	...		634	...
1103	Malt liquors and malt		...	...	3277	...		...	...	1188	...		137	...
1104	Soft drinks,mineral waters,other bottled waters		4660	4512	4637	4664		960	1001	871	920		168	266
1200	Tobacco products		1008	999	840	812		273	457	382	376		11	10
131	Spinning, weaving and finishing of textiles		2217	2229	2344	2415		581	608	643	688		80	84
1311	Preparation and spinning of textile fibres		861	769	793	747		215	188	196	206		24	30
1312	Weaving of textiles		844	983	1009	1074		182	229	231	250		30	29
1313	Finishing of textiles		512	477	542	594		184	191	216	232		26	25
139	Other textiles		2786	2869	2991	2989		802	812	849	862		89	95
1391	Knitted and crocheted fabrics		316	291	263	238		65	77	69	68		8	9
1392	Made-up textile articles, except apparel		1128	1232	1304	1308		359	360	380	382		35	40
1393	Carpets and rugs		134	142	170	170		40	38	48	48		5	7
1394	Cordage, rope, twine and netting		194	176	183	194		59	54	53	56		5	5
1399	Other textiles n.e.c.		1014	1029	1072	1079		279	284	300	308		35	34
1410	Wearing apparel, except fur apparel		3956	3611	3957	4069		1125	958	1035	1024		62	61
1420	Articles of fur		22	19	18	18		10	8	7	6		-	-
1430	Knitted and crocheted apparel		644	572	601	551		154	154	148	140		12	16
151	Leather;luggage,handbags,saddlery,harness;fur		1147	1224	1261	1142		323	335	332	312		31	27
1511	Tanning/dressing of leather; dressing of fur		617	647	662	575		134	139	139	118		22	17
1512	Luggage,handbags,etc.;saddlery/harness		530	577	599	567		189	196	194	194		9	9
1520	Footwear		2731	3098	3295	3232		743	827	851	805		62	47
1610	Sawmilling and planing of wood		710	729	778	793		190	214	216	211		58	50

Code	Description											Notes
162	Wood products, cork, straw, plaiting materials	4289	4560	5110	5189	1282	1242	1392	1434	172	303	
1621	Veneer sheets and wood-based panels	1413	1575	1812	1850	312	321	405	451	59	191	
1622	Builders' carpentry and joinery	1282	1252	1390	1468	495	441	471	467	34	35	
1623	Wooden containers	951	1066	1204	1213	278	291	312	326	52	51	
1629	Other wood products;articles of cork,straw	643	667	703	658	198	188	204	190	27	26	
170	Paper and paper products	12197	11489	12146	12041	3103	2710	3044	3124	563	576	
1701	Pulp, paper and paperboard	4755	4305	4622	4531	1123	881	1180	1145	164	210	
1702	Corrugated paper and paperboard	4484	4501	4778	4712	1136	1106	1146	1197	245	241	
1709	Other articles of paper and paperboard	2958	2683	2745	2798	844	723	718	781	155	126	
181	Printing and service activities related to printing	5513	5576	5559	5576	2171	2209	2124	2108	286	346	
1811	Printing	4377	4656	4651	4822	1743	1813	1720	1788	237	302	
1812	Service activities related to printing	1136	921	908	754	428	396	404	320	49	44	
1820	Reproduction of recorded media	122	98	104	108	57	40	11	33	3	5	
1910	Coke oven products	:	:	:	:	:	:	:	:	:	:	a/
1920	Refined petroleum products	44811	41710	31508	27499	1600	993	2957	3441	525	619	a/
201	Basic chemicals,fertilizers, etc.	20633	21526	20710	19495	2728	3131	3702	4177	604	691	
2011	Basic chemicals	9602	9844	10441	9605	1539	1650	1872	2160	357	423	
2012	Fertilizers and nitrogen compounds	1544	1401	1508	1563	294	307	335	321	48	72	
2013	Plastics and synthetic rubber in primary forms	9486	10280	8762	8327	895	1175	1495	1696	199	196	
202	Other chemical products	14106	13919	14849	15204	3814	3795	4027	4147	578	527	
2021	Pesticides and other agrochemical products	764	795	924	941	160	175	208	211	19	23	
2022	Paints,varnishes;printing ink and mastics	3421	3035	3127	3285	972	860	886	952	130	95	
2023	Soap,cleaning and cosmetic preparations	6007	6355	6740	6955	1692	1804	1876	1899	248	278	
2029	Other chemical products n.e.c.	3914	3734	4058	4023	990	955	1058	1085	181	132	
2030	Man-made fibres	401	402	404	375	146	148	147	143	26	21	
2100	Pharmaceuticals,medicinal chemicals, etc.	12758	12793	13043	13080	4159	4920	4595	4783	526	555	
221	Rubber products	4557	4426	4534	4450	1581	1585	1658	1668	253	252	
2211	Rubber tyres and tubes	2954	2811	2788	2744	1060	1045	1068	1077	176	169	
2219	Other rubber products	1603	1615	1746	1707	521	540	591	591	77	83	
2220	Plastics products	12854	13092	14216	13820	3698	3783	4058	4058	712	652	
2310	Glass and glass products	2860	2873	3017	3204	939	942	975	1064	120	149	
239	Non-metallic mineral products n.e.c.	11943	12253	12795	13069	3491	3706	3872	4096	431	542	
2391	Refractory products	549	549	493	467	169	173	163	145	22	22	
2392	Clay building materials	2845	3057	3134	3383	927	1003	1076	1187	138	202	
2393	Other porcelain and ceramic products	458	486	525	580	183	201	224	259	20	36	
2394	Cement, lime and plaster	1821	1817	1923	1818	613	649	630	641	70	76	
2395	Articles of concrete, cement and plaster	2557	2616	2791	2789	596	665	691	716	71	71	
2396	Cutting, shaping and finishing of stone	1784	1598	1692	1832	652	608	606	632	59	79	
2399	Other non-metallic mineral products n.e.c.	1930	2130	2238	2201	352	408	482	517	52	56	
2410	Basic iron and steel	14594	14860	13584	12458	1852	2030	2129	2265	253	321	
2420	Basic precious and other non-ferrous metals	9595	9524	10058	9127	1064	1345	1359	1381	190	178	
243	Casting of metals	3057	3218	3291	2960	887	927	945	857	151	147	
2431	Casting of iron and steel	1839	1987	1886	1464	562	609	594	469	74	80	
2432	Casting of non-ferrous metals	1217	1231	1405	1495	325	318	351	388	76	68	
251	Struct.metal products, tanks, reservoirs	8584	9158	9773	9987	3155	3308	3337	3441	359	314	

continued

Spain

ISIC	Industry	Output (valuation not defined) (millions of Euros)					Value added at factor values (millions of Euros)					Gross fixed capital formation (millions of Euros)		
		Note	2013	2014	2015	2016	Note	2013	2014	2015	2016	Note	2015	2016
2511	Structural metal products		6791	7435	7928	8196		2472	2647	2683	2787		263	246
2512	Tanks, reservoirs and containers of metal		1530	1489	1596	1532		580	565	559	557		89	61
2513	Steam generators, excl. hot water boilers		263	235	248	259		104	97	96	98		8	7
2520	Weapons and ammunition		390	492	533	636		121	162	155	183		17	17
259	Other metal products;metal working services		18183	18735	19926	20113		6095	6233	6497	6722		1015	923
2591	Forging,pressing,stamping,roll-forming of metal		5173	5463	5973	6291		1213	1222	1309	1453		332	251
2592	Treatment and coating of metals machining		5407	5458	5854	6009		2342	2368	2479	2623		340	340
2593	Cutlery, hand tools and general hardware		2153	2194	2374	2284		896	944	928	920		121	105
2599	Other fabricated metal products n.e.c.		5451	5621	5725	5528		1644	1699	1782	1726		223	228
2610	Electronic components and boards		822	909	1135	1196		282	319	379	401		59	45
2620	Computers and peripheral equipment		234	274	285	123		77	83	73	47		11	4
2630	Communication equipment		581	606	769	721		242	240	269	245		31	12
2640	Consumer electronics		119	105	129	353		40	37	50	85		4	11
265	Measuring,testing equipment; watches, etc.		1387	1206	1153	1261		587	507	450	485		38	42
2651	Measuring/testing/navigating equipment,etc.		1372	1194	1100	1220		579	502	429	469		38	41
2652	Watches and clocks		15	12	53	41		7	5	21	16		-	1
2660	Irradiation/electromedical equipment,etc.		253	262	289	292		102	95	106	109		5	6
2670	Optical instruments and photographic equipment		98	82	:	:		46	29	:	:		:	:
2680	Magnetic and optical media		-	-	:	:		-	-	:	:		:	:
2710	Electric motors,generators,transformers,etc.		5471	5868	6837	6791		1440	1532	1621	1784		202	106
2720	Batteries and accumulators		846	777	839	872		122	124	155	158		9	16
273	Wiring and wiring devices		1996	2072	2186	2100		265	354	373	389		60	46
2731	Fibre optic cables		89	118	92	80		17	27	27	24		3	2
2732	Other electronic and electric wires and cables		1705	1752	1849	1748		171	244	246	268		45	30
2733	Wiring devices		202	202	245	273		77	82	100	97		12	14
2740	Electric lighting equipment		1559	1837	2054	2401		423	510	550	623		49	90
2750	Domestic appliances		2200	2236	2252	2123		624	578	594	555		86	80
2790	Other electrical equipment		1018	885	1038	1076		381	360	434	421		41	53
281	General-purpose machinery		10137	11088	10859	10729		3337	3763	3544	3500		293	282
2811	Engines/turbines,excl.aircraft,vehicle engines		1193	1609	1162	989		184	445	242	221		37	22
2812	Fluid power equipment		339	367	434	470		127	134	159	154		13	15
2813	Other pumps, compressors, taps and valves		1344	1421	1373	1388		432	457	409	400		38	45
2814	Bearings, gears, gearing and driving elements		868	1014	921	698		298	327	278	223		47	51
2815	Ovens, furnaces and furnace burners		87	101	150	105		31	45	53	38		1	1
2816	Lifting and handling equipment		3360	3424	3538	3684		1363	1396	1376	1394		76	63
2817	Office machinery, excl.computers,etc.		35	22	11	13		13	10	4	4		-	-
2818	Power-driven hand tools		38	25	19	23		15	11	8	7		1	1
2819	Other general-purpose machinery		2874	3106	3251	3359		874	939	1017	1062		81	85
282	Special-purpose machinery		6622	6628	6982	7309		2287	2363	2401	2450		255	236
2821	Agricultural and forestry machinery		1313	1155	1195	1185		477	420	394	401		51	37
2822	Metal-forming machinery and machine tools		1381	1379	1560	1669		381	458	505	500		30	42

2823	Machinery for metallurgy	297	395	373	323	101	113	115	109	11	10
2824	Mining, quarrying and construction machinery	575	523	498	477	181	168	171	166	67	27
2825	Food/beverage/tobacco processing machinery	1215	1219	1387	1440	456	458	497	510	39	49
2826	Textile/apparel/leather production machinery	224	267	283	282	88	92	100	107	4	5
2829	Other special-purpose machinery	1617	1690	1688	1933	602	655	618	659	54	68
2910	Motor vehicles	32189	36461	42084	43241	4241	5535	5722	5712	2165	1896
2920	Automobile bodies, trailers and semi-trailers	1148	1352	1582	1910	293	371	398	471	29	52
2930	Parts and accessories for motor vehicles	15547	16201	17809	18937	3815	3976	4060	4589	500	615
301	Building of ships and boats	1991	...	...	...	366	...	...	...	...	...
3011	Building of ships and floating structures	1926	1601	1843	1663	348	583	349	290	47	59
3012	Building of pleasure and sporting boats	65	...	...	...	18	...	...	...	...	...
3020	Railway locomotives and rolling stock	2652	2710	2902	2971	956	717	871	943	73	33
3030	Air and spacecraft and related machinery	6696	7569	9538	9661	2006	1953	2298	2102	240	284
3040	Military fighting vehicles	...	...	...	...	...	...	...	...	...	...
309	Transport equipment n.e.c.	...	334	317	383	...	87	80	80	15	15
3091	Motorcycles	109	124	112	164	40	39	35	33	7	11
3092	Bicycles and invalid carriages	164	187	175	193	35	41	36	40	6	4
3099	Other transport equipment n.e.c.	22	22	30	26	...	6	9	8	2	-
3100	Furniture	4495	4569	4743	5014	1566	1540	1606	1642	111	144
321	Jewellery, bijouterie and related articles b/	695	789	626	634	216	203	193	194	13	15
3211	Jewellery and related articles b/	695	789	626	634	216	203	193	194	13	15
3212	Imitation jewellery and related articles	...	...	...	...	...	...	...	...	...	...
3220	Musical instruments	39	50	48	48	21	28	22	21	2	2
3230	Sports goods	196	196	222	215	63	66	61	60	7	10
3240	Games and toys	475	516	526	523	163	177	135	155	24	19
3250	Medical and dental instruments and supplies	1342	1427	1570	1697	669	716	748	761	70	110
3290	Other manufacturing n.e.c.	660	711	704	656	242	274	256	229	21	33
331	Repair of fabricated metal products/machinery	4365	4843	5916	6132	2265	2453	2638	2661	189	280
3311	Repair of fabricated metal products	156	161	148	141	82	85	72	62	5	2
3312	Repair of machinery	2287	2340	2768	2943	1242	1193	1299	1333	68	114
3313	Repair of electronic and optical equipment	123	119	139	158	67	60	68	78	7	8
3314	Repair of electrical equipment	316	277	320	358	174	158	174	193	7	6
3315	Repair of transport equip., excl. motor vehicles	1447	1910	2508	2492	686	941	1009	979	102	148
3319	Repair of other equipment	36	35	33	41	14	16	17	18	1	2
3320	Installation of industrial machinery/equipment	1540	1496	1673	1524	729	668	681	657	35	36
C	Total manufacturing	421277	431706	444491	443663	93134	97577	101928	105310	15573	16022

a/ 1910 includes 1920.
b/ 3211 includes 3212.

Spain

Index numbers of industrial production

ISIC Revision 4

(2010=100)

ISIC	Industry	Note	2005	2006	2007	2008	2009	2010	2011	2012	2013	2014	2015	2016
10	Food products		97	98	100	99	98	100	100	97	96	100	101	103
11	Beverages		109	110	111	112	106	100	98	97	94	98	98	99
12	Tobacco products		141	120	123	119	105	100	103	103	100	96	81	62
13	Textiles		154	149	142	118	93	100	95	90	91	93	98	103
14	Wearing apparel		158	154	151	139	111	100	92	86	89	83	78	86
15	Leather and related products		155	146	133	123	98	100	103	94	91	94	94	90
16	Wood products, excluding furniture		185	189	183	143	108	100	94	79	76	79	84	87
17	Paper and paper products		104	105	107	105	95	100	100	100	98	98	101	103
18	Printing and reproduction of recorded media		120	121	128	114	99	100	92	82	74	73	74	72
19	Coke and refined petroleum products		106	108	107	111	99	100	99	105	105	106	113	117
20	Chemicals and chemical products		99	100	103	97	95	100	101	94	93	97	101	103
21	Pharmaceuticals, medicinal chemicals, etc.		72	79	85	91	91	100	101	100	103	101	105	111
22	Rubber and plastics products		120	122	125	111	93	100	99	90	91	96	101	105
23	Other non-metallic mineral products		183	190	188	149	105	100	91	76	70	71	75	76
24	Basic metals		119	126	127	119	90	100	101	94	92	96	96	98
25	Fabricated metal products, except machinery		141	148	154	139	107	100	98	83	82	81	86	86
26	Computer, electronic and optical products		115	120	128	132	97	100	89	72	68	77	84	81
27	Electrical equipment		132	146	150	141	103	100	97	88	83	85	88	86
28	Machinery and equipment n.e.c.		124	143	156	143	105	100	108	108	109	104	106	110
29	Motor vehicles, trailers and semi-trailers		133	140	145	124	89	100	105	93	99	107	122	129
30	Other transport equipment		113	114	122	129	113	100	89	87	79	79	76	80
31	Furniture		172	187	196	157	110	100	91	76	66	64	68	72
32	Other manufacturing		119	123	123	113	95	100	96	94	100	106	111	113
33	Repair and installation of machinery/equipment		94	144	136	148	123	100	94	82	79	78	85	86
C	Total manufacturing		122	127	130	120	99	100	98	91	90	92	95	98

Sri Lanka

Supplier of information:
Department of Census and Statistics, Colombo.

Basic source of data:
Annual survey.

Major deviations from ISIC (Revision 4):
None reported.

Reference period:
Calendar year.

Scope:
Establishments with 25 or more persons engaged; from reference year 2014 onwards, the frame is the register of industrial establishments, which is a product of Economic Census 2013/2014.

Method of data collection:
Mail questionnaires; direct interview in the field.

Type of enumeration:
Sample survey.

Adjusted for non-response:
Yes.

Concepts and definitions of variables:
Wages and salaries includes employers' contributions (in respect of their employees) paid to social security, pension and insurance schemes as well as the benefits received by employees under these schemes and severance and termination pay.
Output includes revenue from non-industrial activities.
Value added includes cost of non-industrial activities.

Related national publications:
Annual Survey of Industries, published by the Department of Census and Statistics, Colombo.

Sri Lanka

		Number of establishments (number)					Number of employees (number)					Wages and salaries paid to employees (millions of Sri Lankan Rupees)				
ISIC	Industry	Note	2012	2013	2014	2015	Note	2012	2013	2014	2015	Note	2012	2013	2014	2015
1010	Processing/preserving of meat		...	116	5	8		...	94722	2745	2303		...	33242	1940	987
1020	Processing/preserving of fish, etc.		...	11	7	8		...	695	679	622		...	195	191	103
1030	Processing/preserving of fruit,vegetables		...	44	82	116		...	6829	9708	11595		...	1576	2221	2954
1040	Vegetable and animal oils and fats		...	13	53	45		...	1082	7311	3153		...	442	2040	853
1050	Dairy products		...	10	15	62		...	943	2470	12586		...	554	952	3789
106	Grain mill products,starches and starch products		...	53	70	72		...	4299	7166	5639		...	1606	1725	1229
1061	Grain mill products		...	51	70	70		...	3833	7166	5483		...	1346	1725	1147
1062	Starches and starch products		...	2	-	2		...	466	...	155		...	261	...	82
107	Other food products		...	575	1185	1532		...	80080	160368	219064		...	18231	35152	45685
1071	Bakery products		...	95	86	142		...	10194	7119	8845		...	3517	1986	2353
1072	Sugar		...	3	2	1		...	5737	5700	6309		...	851	962	947
1073	Cocoa, chocolate and sugar confectionery		...	51	41	13		...	5049	3508	2912		...	1452	1176	1095
1074	Macaroni, noodles, couscous, etc.		...	21	15	10		...	1537	1624	1401		...	348	352	257
1075	Prepared meals and dishes		...	-	-	-		...	-	...	-		...	-	...	-
1079	Other food products n.e.c.		...	405	1041	1365		...	57563	142417	199597		...	12062	30676	41034
1080	Prepared animal feeds		...	13	8	10		...	940	947	775		...	358	393	334
110	Beverages		...	58	45	66		...	8977	5118	6432		...	2952	1795	3012
1101	Distilling, rectifying and blending of spirits		...	23	5	16		...	3139	405	2198		...	1161	247	921
1102	Wines		...	4	...	...		...	120	...	...		...	21	...	...
1103	Malt liquors and malt		...	2	9	1		...	418	408	248		...	322	44	275
1104	Soft drinks,mineral waters,other bottled waters		...	29	31	48		...	5300	4305	3986		...	1449	1504	1816
1200	Tobacco products		...	22	89	75		...	5348	14601	15702		...	1997	2365	5285
131	Spinning, weaving and finishing of textiles		...	186	212	259		...	21591	16642	23410		...	5794	3228	5105
1311	Preparation and spinning of textile fibres		...	123	120	192		...	11198	8540	16623		...	2696	1807	3816
1312	Weaving of textiles		...	33	30	24		...	2802	1624	1856		...	669	276	385
1313	Finishing of textiles		...	30	62	43		...	7591	6478	4931		...	2430	1145	904
139	Other textiles		...	92	89	73		...	12131	8371	6502		...	5800	3210	2146
1391	Knitted and crocheted fabrics		...	3	2	1		...	1350	355	228		...	1124	77	39
1392	Made-up textile articles, except apparel		...	20	2	16		...	3749	1081	1303		...	1604	280	267
1393	Carpets and rugs		...	...	2	10		...	...	115	783		...	...	36	185
1394	Cordage, rope, twine and netting		...	26	28	33		...	1140	1118	1533		...	165	353	404
1399	Other textiles n.e.c.		...	43	55	12		...	5892	5702	2655		...	2906	2465	1252
1410	Wearing apparel, except fur apparel		...	774	1467	1675		...	386566	444849	491189		...	105456	110711	137417
1420	Articles of fur		...	-	-	-		...	-	-	-		...	-	-	-
1430	Knitted and crocheted apparel		...	15	32	4		...	4734	12232	1722		...	1268	4207	544
151	Leather;luggage,handbags,saddlery,harness;fur		...	24	8	15		...	1227	261	833		...	214	15	158
1511	Tanning/dressing of leather; dressing of fur		...	-	-	-		...	-	-	-		...	-	...	-
1512	Luggage,handbags,etc.;saddlery/harness		...	24	8	15		...	1227	261	833		...	214	15	158
1520	Footwear		...	38	46	63		...	3995	5013	5452		...	941	1564	1442
1610	Sawmilling and planing of wood		...	17	251	114		...	471	14408	28592		...	89	1372	2917

Code	Description										
162	Wood products, cork, straw, plaiting materials	...	46	196	57	3815	23608	5341	1054	934	1241
1621	Veneer sheets and wood-based panels	...	15	23	18	2006	1691	1375	630	51	453
1622	Builders' carpentry and joinery	...	6	128	3	240	9897	983	51	431	173
1623	Wooden containers	...	8			565			122		
1629	Other wood products;articles of cork,straw	...	17	45	36	1004	12020	2983	252	452	615
170	Paper and paper products	...	57	50	66	6685	6398	6468	2401	2125	2713
1701	Pulp, paper and paperboard	...	10	2	1	904	244	141	270	14	30
1702	Corrugated paper and paperboard	...	36	31	56	3374	2084	4011	1221	794	1678
1709	Other articles of paper and paperboard	...	11	17	9	2407	4070	2316	909	1318	1006
181	Printing and service activities related to printing	...	218	250	126	21295	22027	22859	10796	10254	11662
1811	Printing	...	212	250	126	20987	22027	22859	10630	10254	11662
1812	Service activities related to printing	...	6	-	-	308	-	-	165	-	-
1820	Reproduction of recorded media	...	-	-	-	-	-	-	-	-	-
1910	Coke oven products	...	-	-	-	-	-	-	-	-	-
1920	Refined petroleum products	...	3	2	7	2816	2783	3120	2029	2000	2092
201	Basic chemicals,fertilizers, etc.	...	91	156	193	7445	16174	26415	2385	7081	11684
2011	Basic chemicals	...	7	19	8	561	1223	1867	129	275	899
2012	Fertilizers and nitrogen compounds	...	10	...	7	887	...	490	445	...	250
2013	Plastics and synthetic rubber in primary forms	...	74	137	178	5997	14951	24058	1811	6806	10534
202	Other chemical products	...	124	187	99	30492	20263	15804	9473	6603	5823
2021	Pesticides and other agrochemical products	...	-	-	-	-	-	-	-	-	-
2022	Paints,varnishes;printing ink and mastics	...	22	94	41	3303	6934	4139	1241	2679	1508
2023	Soap,cleaning and cosmetic preparations	...	57	33	9	12790	4358	2348	6314	1588	1346
2029	Other chemical products n.e.c.	...	45	60	48	14399	8971	9317	1918	2336	2970
2030	Man-made fibres	...	...	11	2	-	714	106	-	23	44
2100	Pharmaceuticals,medicinal chemicals, etc.	...	26	24	21	2915	2101	1974	1140	552	703
221	Rubber products	...	123	187	142	31707	27061	29847	13551	11177	11192
2211	Rubber tyres and tubes	...	34	30	23	13856	1844	16019	7544	824	7439
2219	Other rubber products	...	89	157	119	17851	25217	13828	6007	10353	3752
2220	Plastics products	...	37	57	101	3911	9236	7466	1319	6347	3799
2310	Glass and glass products	...	4	23	1	1251	8409	414	1245	6028	197
239	Non-metallic mineral products n.e.c.	...	215	87	90	21016	13473	19437	9456	6923	11042
2391	Refractory products	...	57	...	...	6612	...	...	4326	...	...
2392	Clay building materials	...	43	14	13	5480	5434	2935	1420	2465	1507
2393	Other porcelain and ceramic products	...	11	2	5	1101	783	918	288	279	425
2394	Cement, lime and plaster	...	2	12	3	1324	1327	678	793	1014	366
2395	Articles of concrete, cement and plaster	...	65	33	52	3995	3375	14010	2104	2753	8480
2396	Cutting, shaping and finishing of stone	...	11	2	10	621	67	393	208	27	152
2399	Other non-metallic mineral products n.e.c.	...	26	24	6	1883	2487	504	318	385	112
2410	Basic iron and steel	...	8	5	9	1107	1009	787	551	942	531
2420	Basic precious and other non-ferrous metals	...	2	...	6	72	...	963	2	...	636
243	Casting of metals	...	10	8	-	570	608	-	116	100	-
2431	Casting of iron and steel	...	10	2	-	570	134	-	116	12	-
2432	Casting of non-ferrous metals	...	...	6	-	...	474	-	...	88	-
251	Struct.metal products, tanks, reservoirs	...	57	34	52	6570	2322	3617	1903	1830	1100

continued

Sri Lanka

ISIC	Industry	Number of establishments (number) Note	2012	2013	2014	2015	Number of employees (number) Note	2012	2013	2014	2015	Wages and salaries paid to employees (millions of Sri Lankan Rupees) Note	2012	2013	2014	2015
2511	Structural metal products		...	57	34	52		...	6570	2322	3617		...	1903	1830	1100
2512	Tanks, reservoirs and containers of metal		...	-	-	-		...	-	-	-		...	-	-	-
2513	Steam generators, excl. hot water boilers		...	-	-	-		...	-	-	-		...	-	-	-
2520	Weapons and ammunition		...	-	-	-		...	-	-	-		...	-	-	-
259	Other metal products;metal working services		...	...	118	148		...	...	11653	12202		...	...	4118	5023
2591	Forging,pressing,stamping,roll-forming of metal		...	3	7	3		...	213	473	244		...	44	263	93
2592	Treatment and coating of metals; machining		...	9	23	17		...	468	824	582		...	135	70	158
2593	Cutlery, hand tools and general hardware		...	17	32	14		...	1351	4650	1478		...	453	1819	407
2599	Other fabricated metal products n.e.c.		...	31	56	114		...	4598	5706	9897		...	1577	1966	4365
2610	Electronic components and boards		...	7	11	4		...	1685	2676	1546		...	495	661	396
2620	Computers and peripheral equipment		...	-	-	-		...	-	-	-		...	-	-	-
2630	Communication equipment		...	3	...	5		...	412	...	1375		...	132	...	326
2640	Consumer electronics		...	-	-	-		...	-	-	-		...	-	-	-
265	Measuring,testing equipment; watches, etc.		...	-	-	-		...	-	-	-		...	-	-	-
2651	Measuring/testing/navigating equipment,etc.		...	-	-	-		...	-	-	-		...	-	-	-
2652	Watches and clocks		...	-	-	-		...	-	-	-		...	-	-	-
2660	Irradiation/electromedical equipment,etc.		...	-	-	-		...	-	-	-		...	-	-	-
2670	Optical instruments and photographic equipment		...	-	2	2		...	-	25	108		...	-	-	58
2680	Magnetic and optical media		...	-	-	-		...	-	-	-		...	-	-	-
2710	Electric motors,generators,transformers,etc.		...	6	...	5		...	2418	...	753		...	957	...	417
2720	Batteries and accumulators		...	3	3	1		...	319	467	290		...	375	186	186
273	Wiring and wiring devices		...	21	5	12		...	4378	5335	6573		...	2344	2123	3220
2731	Fibre optic cables		...	-	-	-		...	-	-	-		...	-	-	-
2732	Other electronic and electric wires and cables		...	11	2	8		...	1828	1846	2375		...	1236	1192	1098
2733	Wiring devices		...	10	3	4		...	2550	3489	4198		...	1108	931	2122
2740	Electric lighting equipment		...	3	2	11		...	160	199	691		...	23	30	224
2750	Domestic appliances		...	12	9	8		...	2067	1864	1174		...	1179	1256	549
2790	Other electrical equipment		...	2	4	2		...	1926	2184	1666		...	361	828	516
281	General-purpose machinery		...	21	8	1		...	3496	758	243		...	1413	60	159
2811	Engines/turbines,excl.aircraft,vehicle engines		...	-	-	-		...	-	-	-		...	-	-	-
2812	Fluid power equipment		...	-	-	-		...	-	-	-		...	-	-	-
2813	Other pumps, compressors, taps and valves		...	8	8	...		...	2608	758	...		...	909	60	...
2814	Bearings, gears, gearing and driving elements		...	-	-	-		...	-	-	-		...	-	-	-
2815	Ovens, furnaces and furnace burners		...	-	-	-		...	-	-	-		...	-	-	-
2816	Lifting and handling equipment		...	-	-	-		...	-	-	-		...	-	-	-
2817	Office machinery, excl.computers,etc.		...	-	-	-		...	-	-	-		...	-	-	-
2818	Power-driven hand tools		...	-	-	-		...	-	-	-		...	-	-	-
2819	Other general-purpose machinery		...	13	...	...		...	888	...	...		...	503	...	...
282	Special-purpose machinery		...	7	20	4		...	463	4094	381		...	102	1803	123
2821	Agricultural and forestry machinery		...	3	8	3		...	221	1998	222		...	29	282	33
2822	Metal-forming machinery and machine tools		...	-	-	-		...	-	-	-		...	-	-	-

ISIC Revision 4

Code	Description									
2823	Machinery for metallurgy	...	2	1	...	1515	159	...	853	90
2824	Mining, quarrying and construction machinery	...	-	-	96	581	...	28	668	-
2825	Food/beverage/tobacco processing machinery	2	10	...	...	...	...	...	...	...
2826	Textile/apparel/leather production machinery	2	-	...	146	...	...	45	...	-
2829	Other special-purpose machinery	...	...	...	...	...	...	...	...	...
2910	Motor vehicles	6	...	1	810	1767	381	477	1050	274
2920	Automobile bodies, trailers and semi-trailers	6	14	-	318	1903	932	12	1316	511
2930	Parts and accessories for motor vehicles	16	21	6	2334	...	...	1592	...	...
301	Building of ships and boats	12	27	13	3522	3871	2825	4186	3981	1132
3011	Building of ships and floating structures	12	27	13	3522	3871	2825	4186	3981	1132
3012	Building of pleasure and sporting boats	-	-	-	-	-	-	-	-	-
3020	Railway locomotives and rolling stock	-	-	-	-	-	-	-	-	-
3030	Air and spacecraft and related machinery	-	-	-	-	-	-	-	-	-
3040	Military fighting vehicles	-	-	-	-	-	-	-	-	-
309	Transport equipment n.e.c.	5	5	8	1439	2546	1151	294	1750	373
3091	Motorcycles	-	-	-	-	-	-	-	-	-
3092	Bicycles and invalid carriages	5	5	8	1439	2546	1151	294	1750	373
3099	Other transport equipment n.e.c.	-	-	-	...	...	...	...	...	...
3100	Furniture	51	70	75	7905	2592	9094	2719	1878	2823
321	Jewellery, bijouterie and related articles	34	34	14	3609	2680	2516	944	801	1164
3211	Jewellery and related articles	34	34	14	3609	2680	2516	944	801	1164
3212	Imitation jewellery and related articles	-	-	-	-	-	-	-	-	-
3220	Musical instruments	...	...	2	...	...	95	...	...	22
3230	Sports goods	...	...	1	...	...	216	...	...	46
3240	Games and toys	9	25	24	5589	7623	2213	1503	462	924
3250	Medical and dental instruments and supplies	2	2	2	142	...	139	33	...	23
3290	Other manufacturing n.e.c.	17	49	53	2622	11113	5954	934	3762	2479
331	Repair of fabricated metal products/machinery	5	6	2	155	198	64	83	110	9
3311	Repair of fabricated metal products	-	-	-	-	-	-	-	-	-
3312	Repair of machinery	...	6	-	...	198	...	...	110	-
3313	Repair of electronic and optical equipment	-	-	-	-	-	-	-	-	-
3314	Repair of electrical equipment	-	-	-	-	-	-	-	-	-
3315	Repair of transport equip., excl. motor vehicles	-	-	-	-	-	-	-	-	-
3319	Repair of other equipment	5	...	2	155	...	64	83	...	9
3320	Installation of industrial machinery/equipment	-	-	2	-	62	62	-	-	16
C	Total manufacturing	3390	5374	5576	828696	933002	1032830	260504	262636	299412

Sri Lanka

ISIC	Industry	Note	Output 2012	Output 2013	Output 2014	Output 2015	Note	VA 2012	VA 2013	VA 2014	VA 2015	Note	GFCF 2014	GFCF 2015
			(millions of Sri Lankan Rupees)					(millions of Sri Lankan Rupees)					(millions of Sri Lankan Rupees)	
1010	Processing/preserving of meat		...	391004	23628	9289		...	127481	3523	2779		440	582
1020	Processing/preserving of fish, etc.		...	2634	3611	848		...	648	1545	682		17	32
1030	Processing/preserving of fruit,vegetables		...	19750	26170	30727		...	7302	5182	8911		1208	996
1040	Vegetable and animal oils and fats		...	14447	16474	16527		...	4518	3479	3950		2707	642
1050	Dairy products		...	6022	47488	37558		...	1369	15163	11273		2234	1175
106	Grain mill products,starches and starch products		...	41220	132518	73145		...	9901	69904	36623		3498	939
1061	Grain mill products		...	39172	132518	72206		...	9364	69904	36240		3498	920
1062	Starches and starch products		...	2047	...	939		...	537	...	383		...	20
107	Other food products		...	173505	820893	954197		...	83018	291941	208288		27974	15243
1071	Bakery products		...	38205	26972	22385		...	13637	602	7580		7899	1787
1072	Sugar		...	4424	5701	1693		...	3254	203	748		241	191
1073	Cocoa, chocolate and sugar confectionery		...	14208	20852	11944		...	8474	3368	3741		948	571
1074	Macaroni, noodles, couscous, etc.		...	3440	6397	2666		...	1672	217	1049		224	176
1075	Prepared meals and dishes		...	-	-	-		...	-	-	-		-	-
1079	Other food products n.e.c.		...	113228	760971	915508		...	55981	287551	195170		18662	12517
1080	Prepared animal feeds		...	11636	16937	32270		...	1148	1493	3016		2028	1343
110	Beverages		...	115739	61581	80737		...	81069	11535	17918		4752	5495
1101	Distilling, rectifying and blending of spirits		...	43780	18959	53979		...	37388	133	6911		26	1989
1102	Wines		...	249	-	-		...	83	...	...		...	...
1103	Malt liquors and malt		...	26539	1757	3237		...	18961	1203	1737		481	392
1104	Soft drinks,mineral waters,other bottled waters		...	45171	40865	23520		...	24637	10198	9271		4245	3115
1200	Tobacco products		...	93551	73696	73316		...	89009	68451	54770		3020	2049
131	Spinning, weaving and finishing of textiles		...	48386	47089	65705		...	16661	16536	24047		1625	5667
1311	Preparation and spinning of textile fibres		...	30949	26290	39145		...	10197	10292	11069		888	5227
1312	Weaving of textiles		...	5371	3380	1480		...	2406	1201	735		240	213
1313	Finishing of textiles		...	12067	17419	25080		...	4058	5043	12244		497	226
139	Other textiles		...	51942	63224	38963		...	22182	24921	17576		720	1080
1391	Knitted and crocheted fabrics		...	13067	236	59		...	4161	87	46		203	16
1392	Made-up textile articles, except apparel		...	13262	7286	11267		...	4379	1668	4487		150	157
1393	Carpets and rugs		...	...	1848	6602		...	...	1160	4620		20	199
1394	Cordage, rope, twine and netting		...	752	25305	4096		...	210	18194	2627		116	52
1399	Other textiles n.e.c.		...	24862	28549	16939		...	13433	3813	5797		232	657
1410	Wearing apparel, except fur apparel		...	933158	889341	975862		...	396100	383127	358550		21692	24227
1420	Articles of fur		...	-	-	-		...	-	-	-		-	-
1430	Knitted and crocheted apparel		...	7137	44237	4528		...	3222	17382	2364		3308	1122
151	Leather;luggage,handbags,saddlery,harness;fur		...	1961	38	1168		...	1718	21	702		22	57
1511	Tanning/dressing of leather; dressing of fur		...	-	-	-		...	-	-	-		-	-
1512	Luggage,handbags,etc.;saddlery/harness		...	1961	38	1168		...	1718	21	702		22	57
1520	Footwear		...	7335	11938	12679		...	4501	5325	5213		1347	1401
1610	Sawmilling and planing of wood		...	266	11780	3219		...	120	4387	2890		87	45

Code	Description								
162	Wood products, cork, straw, plaiting materials	133	737	1287	1228	3806	12438	4167	13618
1621	Veneer sheets and wood-based panels	20	611	-114	93	2619	10421	200	11102
1622	Builders' carpentry and joinery	31	1	21	409	72	41	2899	125
1623	Wooden containers	...	...	...	...	659	...	...	988
1629	Other wood products;articles of cork,straw	82	125	1381	727	456	1976	1069	1403
170	Paper and paper products	954	1420	14496	15701	17456	31945	34348	32374
1701	Pulp, paper and paperboard	11	15	25	25	1990	66	140	3349
1702	Corrugated paper and paperboard	286	1001	10846	12594	12329	24631	20871	20206
1709	Other articles of paper and paperboard	657	405	3626	3083	3136	7248	13337	8820
181	Printing and service activities related to printing	4258	7726	32098	14594	44158	73297	56567	93915
1811	Printing	4258	7726	32098	14594	43187	73297	56567	92687
1812	Service activities related to printing	-	-	-	-	971	-	-	1228
1820	Reproduction of recorded media	-	-	-	-	-	-	-	-
1910	Coke oven products	-	-	-	-	-	-	-	-
1920	Refined petroleum products	52	1017	192730	72061	3416	202900	268227	204779
201	Basic chemicals,fertilizers, etc.	542	5908	27646	6742	8909	47534	47640	29554
2011	Basic chemicals	48	530	11989	483	975	21548	769	1617
2012	Fertilizers and nitrogen compounds	...	343	1095	...	3537	2154	...	8286
2013	Plastics and synthetic rubber in primary forms	494	5035	14562	6258	4398	23833	46871	19651
202	Other chemical products	1466	1717	42981	47703	63983	125594	99629	234351
2021	Pesticides and other agrochemical products	-	-	-	-	-	-	-	-
2022	Paints,varnishes;printing ink and mastics	263	98	5998	40848	8476	10326	71548	17585
2023	Soap,cleaning and cosmetic preparations	284	616	3705	1248	34781	9579	6119	100739
2029	Other chemical products n.e.c.	919	1003	33279	5607	20725	105690	21963	116026
2030	Man-made fibres	47	-	-	4	...	1	9	...
2100	Pharmaceuticals,medicinal chemicals, etc.	49	300	5075	4185	2323	7491	7391	7260
221	Rubber products	5833	10521	53528	41088	64131	100485	63768	135435
2211	Rubber tyres and tubes	459	5005	32368	3151	37652	50375	12180	79275
2219	Other rubber products	5374	5516	21161	37937	26479	50110	51588	56160
2220	Plastics products	1405	2931	25081	23120	3582	56218	84709	12581
2310	Glass and glass products	652	837	2461	22111	5494	5395	85954	15393
239	Non-metallic mineral products n.e.c.	3116	2563	37716	40921	109304	184248	112707	158637
2391	Refractory products	...	...	2534	9249	59389	11678	21836	63840
2392	Clay building materials	1572	1415	1632	529	8456	2857	1806	16936
2393	Other porcelain and ceramic products	120	68	16748	13104	2834	62063	67326	4078
2394	Cement, lime and plaster	1292	641	15569	16183	27266	105096	17691	43163
2395	Articles of concrete, cement and plaster	61	249	590	41	7249	1514	262	21145
2396	Cutting, shaping and finishing of stone	3	120	643	1816	3186	1040	3786	6228
2399	Other non-metallic mineral products n.e.c.	68	72	3221	643	924	8625	...	3248
2410	Basic iron and steel	908	205	2968	8789	4701	31534	40024	21909
2420	Basic precious and other non-ferrous metals	...	532	...	...	3	...	...	19
243	Casting of metals	10	...	...	427	5626	...	490	11617
2431	Casting of iron and steel	5	...	...	46	5626	...	95	11617
2432	Casting of non-ferrous metals	5	...	...	381	...	...	395	...
251	Struct.metal products, tanks, reservoirs	356	2122	6226	5256	11287	13190	14038	38336

continued

Sri Lanka

ISIC	Industry	Output at basic prices (millions of Sri Lankan Rupees)					Value added at basic prices (millions of Sri Lankan Rupees)					Gross fixed capital formation (millions of Sri Lankan Rupees)		
		Note	2012	2013	2014	2015	Note	2012	2013	2014	2015	Note	2014	2015
2511	Structural metal products		...	38336	14038	13190		...	11287	5256	6226		356	2122
2512	Tanks, reservoirs and containers of metal		...	-	-	-		...	-	-	-		-	-
2513	Steam generators, excl. hot water boilers		...	-	-	-		...	-	-	-		-	-
2520	Weapons and ammunition		...	-	-	-		...	-	-	-		-	-
259	Other metal products;metal working services		...	...	41120	43045		...	...	13781	9957		559	3102
2591	Forging,pressing,stamping,roll-forming of metal		...	1221	9838	4413		...	257	1924	2143		54	77
2592	Treatment and coating of metals;machining		...	231	1338	542		...	123	338	211		78	19
2593	Cutlery, hand tools and general hardware		...	2999	3790	964		...	1033	139	399		17	101
2599	Other fabricated metal products n.e.c.		...	26963	26154	37126		...	13926	11380	7205		410	2906
2610	Electronic components and boards		...	3880	5359	2760		...	2710	2686	1688		11	796
2620	Computers and peripheral equipment		...	-	-	-		...	-	-	-		-	-
2630	Communication equipment		...	471	...	906		...	103	...	485		...	243
2640	Consumer electronics		...	-	-	-		...	-	-	-		-	-
265	Measuring,testing equipment; watches, etc.		...	-	-	-		...	-	-	-		-	-
2651	Measuring/testing/navigating equipment,etc.		...	-	-	-		...	-	-	-		-	-
2652	Watches and clocks		...	-	-	-		...	-	-	-		-	-
2660	Irradiation/electromedical equipment,etc.		...	-	-	-		...	-	-	-		-	-
2670	Optical instruments and photographic equipment		...	-	-	687		...	-	-	509		-	129
2680	Magnetic and optical media		...	-	-	-		...	-	-	-		-	-
2710	Electric motors,generators,transformers,etc.		...	6480	...	2299		...	3567	...	1308		...	298
2720	Batteries and accumulators		...	3089	...	2387		...	-192	...	702		...	153
273	Wiring and wiring devices		...	31712	35419	52819		...	8584	10402	24889		259	1941
2731	Fibre optic cables		...	-	-	-		...	-	-	-		-	-
2732	Other electronic and electric wires and cables		...	23129	27290	39904		...	5357	8099	17214		65	761
2733	Wiring devices		...	8583	8130	12915		...	3227	2303	7675		194	1181
2740	Electric lighting equipment		...	196	166	1532		...	82	63	761		-	124
2750	Domestic appliances		...	16025	16013	7983		...	4098	4472	1716		114	200
2790	Other electrical equipment		...	5691	4039	2676		...	3742	620	91		301	156
281	General-purpose machinery		...	13163	1187	1603		...	6929	731	923		49	87
2811	Engines/turbines,excl.aircraft,vehicle engines		...	-	-	-		...	-	-	-		-	-
2812	Fluid power equipment		...	-	-	-		...	-	-	-		-	-
2813	Other pumps, compressors, taps and valves		...	7705	1187	...		...	3708	731	...		49	...
2814	Bearings, gears, gearing and driving elements		...	-	-	-		...	-	-	-		-	-
2815	Ovens, furnaces and furnace burners		...	-	-	-		...	-	-	-		-	-
2816	Lifting and handling equipment		...	-	-	-		...	-	-	-		-	-
2817	Office machinery, excl.computers,etc.		...	-	-	-		...	-	-	-		-	-
2818	Power-driven hand tools		...	-	-	-		...	-	-	-		-	-
2819	Other general-purpose machinery		...	5457	12777	733		...	3222	6516	277		107	34
282	Special-purpose machinery		...	292	2798	207		...	140	526	87		20	6
2821	Agricultural and forestry machinery		...	70	-	-		...	...	-	-		...	-
2822	Metal-forming machinery and machine tools		...	-	-	-		...	-	-	-		-	-

Code	Description							
2823	Machinery for metallurgy	…	9176	526	…	5808	190	47	28
2824	Mining, quarrying and construction machinery	120	803	-	62	182	-	40	-
2825	Food/beverage/tobacco processing machinery	-	-	…	…	-	-	-	…
2826	Textile/apparel/leather production machinery	102	…	…	70	…	…	…	…
2829	Other special-purpose machinery	…	…	…	…	…	…	…	…
2910	Motor vehicles	9071	…	20049	588	…	2999	176	185
2920	Automobile bodies, trailers and semi-trailers	506	6237	…	100	178	…	…	…
2930	Parts and accessories for motor vehicles	8825	15501	2058	5272	7739	591	1133	377
301	Building of ships and boats	21455	16013	25740	6928	4411	8443	1751	95
3011	Building of ships and floating structures	21455	16013	25740	6928	4411	8443	1751	95
3012	Building of pleasure and sporting boats	-	-	-	-	-	-	-	-
3020	Railway locomotives and rolling stock	-	-	-	-	-	-	-	-
3030	Air and spacecraft and related machinery	-	-	-	-	-	-	-	-
3040	Military fighting vehicles	-	-	-	-	-	-	-	-
309	Transport equipment n.e.c.	4384	11280	4388	913	2706	618	948	112
3091	Motorcycles	-	-	-	-	-	-	-	-
3092	Bicycles and invalid carriages	4384	11280	4388	913	2706	618	948	112
3099	Other transport equipment n.e.c.	-	-	-	-	-	-	-	-
3100	Furniture	26235	20310	17976	8776	14095	4477	398	677
321	Jewellery, bijouterie and related articles	14259	6186	18848	8595	2420	2745	79	980
3211	Jewellery and related articles	14259	6186	18848	8595	2420	2745	79	980
3212	Imitation jewellery and related articles	-	-	49	…	…	34	…	…
3220	Musical instruments	…	…	284	…	…	52	…	…
3230	Sports goods	…	…	…	…	…	…	…	5
3240	Games and toys	5198	9825	4405	2751	3596	2530	123	138
3250	Medical and dental instruments and supplies	97	…	42	68	…	2	…	2
3290	Other manufacturing n.e.c.	5088	11162	10965	1638	6954	4497	43	605
331	Repair of fabricated metal products/machinery	223	68	50	130	16	38	…	1
3311	Repair of fabricated metal products	…	68	-	…	16	-	…	-
3312	Repair of machinery	-	-	-	-	-	-	-	-
3313	Repair of electronic and optical equipment	-	-	-	-	-	-	-	-
3314	Repair of electrical equipment	-	-	-	-	-	-	-	-
3315	Repair of transport equip., excl. motor vehicles	-	-	-	-	-	-	-	-
3319	Repair of other equipment	223	-	50	130	…	38	…	1
3320	Installation of industrial machinery/equipment	-	-	16	…	…	3	…	18
C	Total manufacturing	3137222	3429030	3535935	1279010	1311486	1277401	102702	111090

Sri Lanka

Index numbers of industrial production

ISIC Revision 4

(2010=100)

ISIC	Industry	Note	2005	2006	2007	2008	2009	2010	2011	2012	2013	2014	2015	2016
10	Food products	a/	...	...	...	...	...	100	112	117	117	118	122	122
11	Beverages	a/	...	...	...	...	...	...	...	...	...	...	...	...
12	Tobacco products	a/	...	...	...	...	...	...	...	...	...	...	...	...
13	Textiles	b/	...	...	...	...	...	100	90	92	100	104	107	109
14	Wearing apparel	b/	...	...	...	...	...	...	...	...	...	...	...	...
15	Leather and related products	b/	...	...	...	...	...	...	...	...	...	...	...	...
16	Wood products, excluding furniture	c/	...	...	...	...	...	100	120	89	96	88	104	120
17	Paper and paper products	c/	...	...	...	...	...	100	106	95	96	96	106	117
18	Printing and reproduction of recorded media	c/	...	...	...	...	...	...	...	...	...	...	...	...
19	Coke and refined petroleum products	d/	...	...	...	...	...	100	159	130	123	129	130	140
20	Chemicals and chemical products	d/	...	...	...	...	...	100	97	109	118	118	120	125
21	Pharmaceuticals,medicinal chemicals, etc.	d/	...	...	...	...	...	...	...	...	...	...	...	...
22	Rubber and plastics products		...	...	...	...	...	100	120	132	130	114	120	140
23	Other non-metallic mineral products		...	...	...	...	...	100	109	110	102	99	95	85
24	Basic metals	e/	...	...	...	...	...	100	83	78	84	79	91	114
25	Fabricated metal products, except machinery	e/	...	...	...	...	...	...	...	...	...	...	...	...
26	Computer, electronic and optical products	f/	...	...	...	...	...	100	94	86	86	89	108	126
27	Electrical equipment	f/	...	...	...	...	...	...	...	...	...	...	...	...
28	Machinery and equipment n.e.c.	f/	...	...	...	...	...	...	...	...	...	...	...	...
29	Motor vehicles, trailers and semi-trailers	f/	...	...	...	...	...	...	...	...	...	...	...	...
30	Other transport equipment	f/	...	...	...	...	...	...	...	...	...	...	...	...
31	Furniture	g/	...	...	...	...	...	100	95	113	120	147	168	174
32	Other manufacturing	g/	...	...	...	...	...	100	71	86	91	115	141	150
33	Repair and installation of machinery/equipment	g/	...	...	...	...	...	...	...	...	...	...	...	...
C	Total manufacturing		...	...	...	...	...	100	103	107	109	112	118	121

a/ 10 includes 11 and 12.
b/ 13 includes 14 and 15.
c/ 17 includes 18.
d/ 20 includes 21.
e/ 24 includes 25.
f/ 26 includes 27, 28, 29 and 30.
g/ 32 includes 33.

State of Palestine

Supplier of information:
Palestinian Central Bureau of Statistics, Ramallah.

Basic source of data:
Annual survey.

Major deviations from ISIC (Revision 4):
None reported.

Reference period:
Calendar year.

Scope:
All privately owned enterprises.

Method of data collection:
Direct interview in the field.

Type of enumeration:
Sample survey.

Adjusted for non-response:
Yes.

Concepts and definitions of variables:
Wages and salaries is compensation of employees.

Related national publications:
Economic Surveys Series, published by the Palestinian Central Bureau of Statistics, Ramallah.

State of Palestine

ISIC	Industry	Note	Number of enterprises (number)				Note	Number of employees (number)				Note	Wages and salaries paid to employees (thousands of US Dollars)			
			2013	2014	2015	2016		2013	2014	2015	2016		2013	2014	2015	2016
10	Food products		2128	2239	2273	2506		14698	9581	10761	13638		72570	58787	69377	82076
11	Beverages		50	53	56	53		711	1054	1066	930		6651	9680	9140	8181
12	Tobacco products		18	19	23	23		149	192	136	237		3575	1085	702	2816
13	Textiles		386	406	448	503		1230	899	1027	1339		3362	4671	5202	7031
14	Wearing apparel		1580	1662	1591	1668		11505	7019	7994	9046		45406	36243	42814	45340
15	Leather and related products		412	433	454	478		2352	2238	2961	2219		11245	14343	17529	14223
16	Wood products, excluding furniture		773	813	795	894		2150	1234	1504	1336		7364	7163	9087	7571
17	Paper and paper products		64	82	78	84		696	831	833	1198		3978	6905	5602	8623
18	Printing and reproduction of recorded media		427	449	408	469		1882	1487	1590	1570		12194	12012	11185	11911
19	Coke and refined petroleum products	a/	145	152	150	200	a/	846	861	899	919	a/	4316	5526	5042	5949
20	Chemicals and chemical products	a/	...	...	...	...	a/	...	...	...	...	a/	...	...	...	...
21	Pharmaceuticals, medicinal chemicals, etc.		9	9	14	14		689	1144	1327	1713		7698	11533	23172	25678
22	Rubber and plastics products		238	251	208	252		1592	2604	2087	3482		10219	17803	12211	20638
23	Other non-metallic mineral products		2128	2238	2279	2442		12455	12604	13638	13364		62032	83156	90783	89904
24	Basic metals		13	14	24	20		53	45	103	139		141	224	765	1129
25	Fabricated metal products, except machinery		3656	3846	4178	4412		9456	6501	5757	6641		32143	46904	35678	39216
26	Computer, electronic and optical products		8	8	17	29		279	257	262	409		2082	2504	2381	3371
27	Electrical equipment		52	55	68	82		164	340	373	332		630	1400	1758	1818
28	Machinery and equipment n.e.c.		47	50	75	93		308	272	253	272		987	1305	1569	2137
29	Motor vehicles, trailers and semi-trailers		22b/	23b/	32	72		...	270b/	229	525		...	1283b/	1154	3459
30	Other transport equipment		...b/	...b/	6	6		...	...b/	...	...		...	...b/	...	...
31	Furniture		2769	2913	3068	3187		10111	9610	9561	9191		45509	56797	57558	56101
32	Other manufacturing		243	255	332	346		895	601	564	668		3826	3699	3140	3550
33	Repair and installation of machinery/equipment		472	496	727	751		1193	688	992	739		2534	3075	4354	3352
C	Total manufacturing	c/	15640	16466	17304	18584	c/	73441	60332	63917	69907	c/	338526	386095	410201	444074

a/ 19 includes 20.
b/ 29 includes 30.
c/ Sum of available data.

State of Palestine

ISIC Revision 4		Output (valuation not defined) (thousands of US Dollars)					Value added (valuation not defined) (thousands of US Dollars)					Gross fixed capital formation (thousands of US Dollars)		
ISIC	Industry	Note	2013	2014	2015	2016	Note	2013	2014	2015	2016	Note	2015	2016
10	Food products		909782	773672	725112	802068		350189	364628	295405	315787		13376	6323
11	Beverages		131713	181714	123151	126132		37658	64823	20801	23095		165	1854
12	Tobacco products		146429	123347	55830	65706		137111	92686	44469	50894		191	301
13	Textiles		27222	37807	55147	83974		11010	16425	21494	39984		128	91
14	Wearing apparel		118915	86448	108777	120771		72931	52877	70685	78081		1316	729
15	Leather and related products		85991	52623	79223	63477		40276	22095	30042	30912		13	1775
16	Wood products, excluding furniture		62417	51088	75814	57357		24669	21292	29792	25580		632	295
17	Paper and paper products		50557	97835	57008	88543		18752	34057	20684	38515		236	1854
18	Printing and reproduction of recorded media		67027	49779	56001	55570		26647	21520	24225	24789		440	1611
19	Coke and refined petroleum products	a/	62504	51582	71459	46855	a/	28029	21849	28271	19196		717	580
20	Chemicals and chemical products	a/	...	...	...	...	a/	...	...	...	...	a/	...	...
21	Pharmaceuticals,medicinal chemicals, etc.		78366	96143	91673	161322		61272	54724	55612	103752		4419	5237
22	Rubber and plastics products		139198	165424	125394	164813		63628	72344	43333	56932		2204	2648
23	Other non-metallic mineral products		654644	635586	853400	937996		197926	241518	272292	403467		3024	10230
24	Basic metals		1446	7880	7301	12215		551	3194	2231	3812		58	4
25	Fabricated metal products, except machinery		325776	364148	358712	389445		128047	169005	132357	155718		845	666
26	Computer, electronic and optical products		12015	14979	12100	18577		4892	6566	4536	7241		162	66
27	Electrical equipment		5680	11504	14608	15084		2840	5332	5742	6187		31	2
28	Machinery and equipment n.e.c.		11082	12035	13309	18731		5135	6005	5698	9060		22	-73
29	Motor vehicles, trailers and semi-trailers		...	23607b/	7295	18681		...	15987b/	2683	6775		15	19
30	Other transport equipment		...	...b/	77	72		...	...b/	25	41		-	-
31	Furniture		302224	329987	452287	404011		111702	120500	185685	178927		344	4582
32	Other manufacturing		47853	15399	21580	30172		21039	7240	10012	12882		28	489
33	Repair and installation of machinery/equipment		17359	17899	20824	20495		8851	10128	10114	11074		443	25
C	Total manufacturing	c/	3258588	3200484	3386080	3702065	c/	1353273	1424795	1316187	1602697	c/	28807	39306

a/ 19 includes 20.
b/ 29 includes 30.
c/ Sum of available data.

Suriname

Supplier of information:
General Bureau of Statistics, Paramaribo.

Basic source of data:
Survey.

Major deviations from ISIC (Revision 3):
None reported.

Reference period:
Calendar year.

Scope:
All enterprises.

Method of data collection:
Mail questionnaires.

Type of enumeration:
Complete enumeration.

Adjusted for non-response:
No.

Concepts and definitions of variables:
No deviations from the standard UN concepts and definitions are reported.

Related national publications:
Economic Statistics, published by General Bureau of Statistics, Paramaribo.

Suriname

ISIC Revision 3			Establishments (number)				Number of employees (number)					Wages and salaries paid to employees (millions of Surinamese Dollars)				
ISIC	Industry	Note	2013	2014	2015	2016	Note	2013	2014	2015	2016	Note	2013	2014	2015	2016
D	Total manufacturing		...	...	...	...		6158	6352	6532	6269		256.2	269.1	277.8	327.9

ISIC Revision 3			Output (millions of Surinamese Dollars)				Value added at basic prices (millions of Surinamese Dollars)					Gross fixed capital formation (millions of Surinamese Dollars)		
ISIC	Industry	Note	2013	2014	2015	2016	Note	2013	2014	2015	2016	Note	2015	2016
D	Total manufacturing		...	...	...	...		3190.3	2828.2	1619.4	2552.0		...	...

ISIC Revision 3			Index numbers of industrial production (2010=100)											
ISIC	Industry	Note	2005	2006	2007	2008	2009	2010	2011	2012	2013	2014	2015	2016
D	Total manufacturing		...	...	...	...	...	...	...	...	...	...	...	...

Sweden

Supplier of information:
Statistics Sweden, Stockholm.
Industrial statistics for the OECD countries are compiled by the OECD secretariat, which supplies them to UNIDO.

Basic source of data:
Annual surveys; administrative data; business register.

Major deviations from ISIC (Revision 4):
Data presented in ISIC (Revision 4) were originally classified according to the national NACE-related classification system.

Reference period:
Calendar year.

Scope:
All enterprises.

Method of data collection:
Mainly electronic data collection (to some extent directly from enterprises' accounting systems) and administrative data.

Type of enumeration:
System of different statistical surveys in combination with the use of administrative data.

Adjusted for non-response:
Not reported.

Concepts and definitions of variables:
No deviations from the standard UN concepts and definitions are reported.

Related national publications:
Structural business statistics, published by Statistics Sweden, Stockholm,

Sweden

			Number of enterprises (number)					Number of employees (number)					Wages and salaries paid to employees (millions of Swedish Kronor)			
ISIC	Industry	Note	2013	2014	2015	2016	Note	2013	2014	2015	2016	Note	2013	2014	2015	2016
1010	Processing/preserving of meat		533	545	563	550		10900	11429	11349	11430		3373	3628	3727	3734
1020	Processing/preserving of fish, etc.		223	225	224	213		...	2076	1803	1794		...	570	508	507
1030	Processing/preserving of fruit, vegetables		282	308	344	352		4077	3957	4952	3514		1498	1479	1846	1342
1040	Vegetable and animal oils and fats		49	51	49	52		...	731	846	824		...	352	402	380
1050	Dairy products		172	196	219	241		6214	5960	5808	5768		1971	1923	1961	1985
106	Grain mill products, starches and starch products		119	115	116	120		1590	1491	1450	1467		586	529	563	585
1061	Grain mill products		114	110	110	114		1308	1165	1127	1126		481	419	429	446
1062	Starches and starch products		5	5	6	6		282	326	323	341		105	110	133	139
107	Other food products		2075	2122	2163	2211		23556	22786	22352	24724		6996	7056	7078	8033
1071	Bakery products		1459	1471	1485	1483		14630	14438	14008	14457		3985	4114	4081	4248
1072	Sugar		6	...	4	4										
1073	Cocoa, chocolate and sugar confectionery		234	242	238	244		2524	2133	2214	2176		896	772	801	807
1074	Macaroni, noodles, couscous, etc.		12	10	11	13		52	48	52	54		11	12	9	11
1075	Prepared meals and dishes		84	100	107	120		1550	1599	1506	3383		462	475	465	1141
1079	Other food products n.e.c.		280	...	318	347										
1080	Prepared animal feeds		92	97	99	97		773	957	986	890		247	389	351	339
110	Beverages		275	349	441	510		4735	4552	4447	4436		1873	1880	1836	1861
1101	Distilling, rectifying and blending of spirits	a/	47	349	58	56	a/	4735	4552	4447	4436	a/	1873	1880	1836	1861
1102	Wines	a/	31	...	41	47	a/					a/				
1103	Malt liquors and malt	a/	144	...	280	334	a/					a/				
1104	Soft drinks, mineral waters, other bottled waters	a/	53	...	62	73	a/					a/				
1200	Tobacco products		24	...	22	25		...	...	...	...		...	...	...	...
131	Spinning, weaving and finishing of textiles		359	356	335	319		686	653	601	581		184	191	171	167
1311	Preparation and spinning of textile fibres		31	35	34	38		39	40	40	43		8	9	9	9
1312	Weaving of textiles		93	93	88	88		302	288	271	256		98	96	86	82
1313	Finishing of textiles		235	228	213	193		345	325	290	282		79	86	76	75
139	Other textiles		1786	1799	1795	1804		4113	4069	4037	4038		1297	1349	1394	1372
1391	Knitted and crocheted fabrics		41	39	42	40		522	355	353	314		167	120	126	117
1392	Made-up textile articles, except apparel		819	809	798	789		1439	1382	1344	1400		388	384	391	412
1393	Carpets and rugs		36	34	35	35		264	253	275	274		89	98	97	102
1394	Cordage, rope, twine and netting		40	40	41	40		...	241	245	224		...	90	94	91
1399	Other textiles n.e.c.		850	...	879	900		...	...	1820	1825		...	...	686	650
1410	Wearing apparel, except fur apparel		1856	1865	1878	1881		999	1017	956	997		261	277	258	276
1420	Articles of fur		49	49	48	47		25	22	21	19		5	5	5	6
1430	Knitted and crocheted apparel		73	86	90	86		88	85	128	107		25	24	38	34
151	Leather; luggage, handbags, saddlery, harness; fur		384	403	409	413		516	490	499	538		153	146	153	174
1511	Tanning/dressing of leather; dressing of fur		40	38	38	38		516 b/	224	235	260		153 b/	68	75	86
1512	Luggage, handbags, etc.; saddlery/harness		344	365	371	375		... b/	266	264	278		... b/	78	79	88
1520	Footwear		94	...	88	88		234	...	...	172		62	...	...	46
1610	Sawmilling and planing of wood		1319	1295	1280	1244		11329	11654	12515	10375		3795	4075	4552	3746

Code	Description												
162	Wood products, cork, straw, plaiting materials	6350	5896	5655	5405	18993	17966	17687	17431	3886	3965	4050	4082
1621	Veneer sheets and wood-based panels	...	...	328	...	...	...	912	...	57	63	67	69
1622	Builders' carpentry and joinery	...	...	4251	...	...	...	13134	...	2372	2387	2436	2472
1623	Wooden containers	611	590	602	587	1879	1927	2004	1993	325	342	351	340
1629	Other wood products;articles of cork,straw	485	504	473	519	1534	1615	1636	1782	1132	1173	1196	1201
170	Paper and paper products	14139	12987	12687	12717	30393	28375	28675	29730	391	393	433	458
1701	Pulp, paper and paperboard	10586	9573	9225	9280	21967	19901	19736	20627	103	104	126	134
1702	Corrugated paper and paperboard	1468	1408	1500	1497	3789	3877	4252	4234	116	118	130	137
1709	Other articles of paper and paperboard	2085	2005	1962	1941	4636	4597	4687	4870	172	171	177	187
181	Printing and service activities related to printing	4295	4616	4484	4602	11718	12935	12933	13609	2782	2821	2896	2946
1811	Printing	3746	3968	3931	4049	10214	11069	11279	11917	1983	1984	2044	2086
1812	Service activities related to printing	549	647	553	552	1505	1865	1653	1692	799	837	852	860
1820	Reproduction of recorded media	31	36	43	37	113	147	145	142	113	124	136	138
1910	Coke oven products	...	1384c/	...	...	...	2576c/	...	...	...	...	1	2
1920	Refined petroleum products	...	...c/	...	...	...	...c/	...	...	...	33	36	38
201	Basic chemicals,fertilizers, etc.	5348	5267	4519	4534	10011	10116	9016	9394	223	231	232	233
2011	Basic chemicals	...	...	...	...	...	...	...	...	136	139	...	142
2012	Fertilizers and nitrogen compounds	303	290	265	210	712	708	636	560	43	44	47	44
2013	Plastics and synthetic rubber in primary forms	...	1960	...	...	...	3675	...	...	43	45	...	48
202	Other chemical products	3789	3640	3716	3391	8650	8380	8856	8556	590	589	589	581
2021	Pesticides and other agrochemical products	12	15	15	16	42	46	42	49	18	18	18	17
2022	Paints,varnishes;printing ink and mastics	1429	1454	1487	1280	3252	3265	3540	3459	125	125	125	126
2023	Soap,cleaning and cosmetic preparations	704	545	646	608	1894	1555	1827	1787	265	259	265	263
2029	Other chemical products n.e.c.	1645	...	1568	1488	3462	...	3448	3261	182	187	183	175
2030	Man-made fibres	7	7	5	5	25	24	21	21	8	8	7	8
2100	Pharmaceuticals,medicinal chemicals, etc.	6165	6611	...	6734	11836	11891	...	12256	151	146	...	148
221	Rubber products	1809	1839	1829	1858	4471	4643	4674	4925	210	216	210	214
2211	Rubber tyres and tubes	118	125	126	133	356	372	388	418	65	69	65	72
2219	Other rubber products	1690	1714	1703	1725	4115	4271	4286	4508	145	147	145	142
2220	Plastics products	5936	5804	5646	5490	15862	15847	16033	15965	1320	1330	1355	1341
2310	Glass and glass products	1341	1034	981	1161	3286	2891	2764	3228	329	335	336	344
239	Non-metallic mineral products n.e.c.	5904	5783	5608	...	14988	14674	14853	...	1661	1655	1675	1690
2391	Refractory products	226	260	227	224	684	672	632	574	31	32	31	32
2392	Clay building materials	22	...	...	...	64	...	...	...	19	20	19	23
2393	Other porcelain and ceramic products	...	...	...	...	...	...	...	...	862	879	862	900
2394	Cement, lime and plaster	...	...	...	...	...	...	...	...	16	16	17	17
2395	Articles of concrete, cement and plaster	...	...	...	...	...	962	904	...	329	336	336	364
2396	Cutting, shaping and finishing of stone	306	295	274	...	976	...	...	...	325	328	328	332
2399	Other non-metallic mineral products n.e.c.	...	1068	1166	1197	...	2430	2897	2956	44	45	50	57
2410	Basic iron and steel	11098	...	9408	9056	24724	...	22589	22602	231	224	245	244
2420	Basic precious and other non-ferrous metals	1872	...	2248	2403	4369	...	5357	5835	85	94	91	93
243	Casting of metals	740	761	718	765	2041	2169	2125	2277	85	110	121	125
2431	Casting of iron and steel	330	328	328	353	871	917	926	983	49	54	53	57
2432	Casting of non-ferrous metals	411	434	389	412	1170	1252	1199	1294	61	66	68	68
251	Struct.metal products, tanks, reservoirs	4766	4703	4715	4470	13061	13106	13412	13258	1148	1147	1148	1161

continued

Sweden

ISIC Revision 4		Number of enterprises (number)					Number of employees (number)					Wages and salaries paid to employees (millions of Swedish Kronor)				
ISIC	Industry	Note	2013	2014	2015	2016	Note	2013	2014	2015	2016	Note	2013	2014	2015	2016
2511	Structural metal products		1015	1005	1013	1017		11993	12186	12149	12149		4019	4252	4345	4436
2512	Tanks, reservoirs and containers of metal		140	135	126	125		1173	1143	870	829		411	427	319	291
2513	Steam generators, excl. hot water boilers		6	8	8	6		90	83	86	83		41	36	39	38
2520	Weapons and ammunition		75	69	70	67		2293	2074	2014	2112		1043	974	935	980
259	Other metal products;metal working services		9611	9502	9405	9346		56149	54741	50420	49948		18737	18747	17378	17642
2591	Forging,pressing,stamping,roll-forming of metal		647	609	598	590		2199	2075	2011	2016		682	676	684	696
2592	Treatment and coating of metals; machining		6861	6807	6731	6711		29529	29124	28603	28827		9148	9241	9302	9532
2593	Cutlery, hand tools and general hardware		793	786	763	742		12631	12241	8279	7701		4849	4870	3281	3249
2599	Other fabricated metal products n.e.c.		1310	…	1313	1303		…	…	…	…		…	…	…	…
2610	Electronic components and boards		370	…	413	443		3184	…	2549	3478		1088	…	966	1340
2620	Computers and peripheral equipment		175	170	160	147		1422	1453	1308	1371		618	630	567	601
2630	Communication equipment		253	…	253	252		…	…	3588	1935		…	…	1633	886
2640	Consumer electronics		164	175	170	174		533	537	951	919		192	216	438	402
265	Measuring,testing equipment; watches, etc.		493	495	493	495		9571	9255	5933	5121		4533	4328	2641	2390
2651	Measuring/testing/navigating equipment,etc.		471	473	466	461		9468	9146	5821	5008		4499	4291	2603	2351
2652	Watches and clocks		22	22	27	34		103	108	112	113		35	37	39	39
2660	Irradiation/electromedical equipment,etc.		66	64	72	71		771	532	…	679		375	261	…	…
2670	Optical instruments and photographic equipment		77	79	71	71		545	567	580	…		213	237	258	302
2680	Magnetic and optical media		17	16	15	15		…	34	…	…		…	11	…	…
2710	Electric motors,generators,transformers,etc.		377	376	368	361		…	14382	13714	12942		…	6516	6376	6271
2720	Batteries and accumulators		19	…	18	19		…	…	…	…		…	…	…	…
273	Wiring and wiring devices		79	80	84	80		2598	2732	2742	2560		893	1048	1061	1025
2731	Fibre optic cables		11	11	14	13		…	185	…	…		…	50	…	…
2732	Other electronic and electric wires and cables		51	51	50	45		1962	1956	1933	1656		666	774	757	685
2733	Wiring devices		17	18	20	22		…	590	…	…		…	223	…	…
2740	Electric lighting equipment		262	257	254	247		2665	2586	2464	2419		908	908	873	957
2750	Domestic appliances		85	87	84	86		2178	1697	…	…		805	580	…	…
2790	Other electrical equipment		147	…	148	156		2321	…	1723	1877		1059	…	690	811
281	General-purpose machinery		1501	1499	1487	1478		44640	43514	44268	44401		17603	17608	18740	19309
2811	Engines/turbines,excl.aircraft,vehicle engines		82	84	81	75		4978	4517	4519	4486		2224	2112	2260	2276
2812	Fluid power equipment		69	83	84	73		3657	3567	3329	3116		1303	1325	1302	1258
2813	Other pumps, compressors, taps and valves		128	122	121	126		5623	4496	5230	5269		1974	1651	2071	2083
2814	Bearings, gears, gearing and driving elements		79	81	79	80		4337	5056	4343	4144		1960	2208	1967	2070
2815	Ovens, furnaces and furnace burners		71	…	75	73		583	…	…	…		221	…	…	…
2816	Lifting and handling equipment		337	332	336	332		9166	8950	8938	9296		3433	3447	3419	3560
2817	Office machinery, excl.computers,etc.		25	26	25	22		…	276	244	…		…	98	107	…
2818	Power-driven hand tools		24	…	24	25		…	…	…	…		…	…	…	…
2819	Other general-purpose machinery		686	678	662	672		13111	13187	14057	14229		5145	5209	5917	6198
282	Special-purpose machinery		1653	1628	1622	1590		27557	25456	24176	23574		11012	10641	10377	10521
2821	Agricultural and forestry machinery		211	201	206	206		4527	4090	3519	3426		1826	1728	1465	1452
2822	Metal-forming machinery and machine tools		398	394	382	363		2981	2827	2964	2913		1094	1113	1210	1229

Code	Description													
2823	Machinery for metallurgy	17	16	16	13	431	431	378	339	187	185	173	149
2824	Mining, quarrying and construction machinery	162	161	164	158	9710	9118	8512	8190	4021	4009	3948	3856
2825	Food/beverage/tobacco processing machinery	105	102	103	106	755	744	410	508	292	308	139	179
2826	Textile/apparel/leather production machinery	35	33	32	32	866	878	872	889	315	325	328	347
2829	Other special-purpose machinery	725	721	719	712	8286	7367	7520	7309	3278	2974	3113	3309
2910	Motor vehicles	178	174	175	182	42424	42320	45177	46895	19005	19569	20869	22309
2920	Automobile bodies, trailers and semi-trailers	258	269	267	263	3180	3467	3540	3604	1094	1159	1223	1291
2930	Parts and accessories for motor vehicles	634	629	608	605	17195	17411	17382	18685	6175	6685	6891	7551
301	Building of ships and boats	665	672	663	677	2459	2297	2361	2356	885	871	915	915
3011	Building of ships and floating structures	137	143	146	156	1371	1380	1337	1305	570	596	593	562
3012	Building of pleasure and sporting boats	528	529	517	521	1088	917	1025	1051	315	275	323	353
3020	Railway locomotives and rolling stock	37	39	40	37	…	1996	…	2424	…	945	…	1306
3030	Air and spacecraft and related machinery	41	…	44	46	… d/	…	…	… d/	…	…	…	…
3040	Military fighting vehicles	2	…	2	2	… d/	…	…	… d/	…	…	…	…
309	Transport equipment n.e.c.	157	159	155	163	1768	1869	1592	1622	646	685	571	631
3091	Motorcycles	35	…	30	35	…	…	32	26	…	…	7	6
3092	Bicycles and invalid carriages	77	80	81	81	1323	1349	1300	1311	478	492	476	524
3099	Other transport equipment n.e.c.	45	…	44	47	…	…	259	285	…	…	89	101
3100	Furniture	2290	2319	2361	2396	13863	13464	13579	13710	4494	4498	4605	4857
321	Jewellery, bijouterie and related articles	1402	1433	1418	1436	502	517	512	538	121	129	132	145
3211	Jewellery and related articles	1155	1433 d/	1179	1199	502	517	512	538	121	129	132	145
3212	Imitation jewellery and related articles	247	… d/	239	237	…	…	…	147	…	…	…	…
3220	Musical instruments	248	261	254	257	156	140	145	147	45	47	48	50
3230	Sports goods	332	341	341	355	680	706	618	623	223	230	205	208
3240	Games and toys	216	209	211	224	153	153	147	156	40	44	41	49
3250	Medical and dental instruments and supplies	1087	1078	1050	1033	8012	7809	7146	6963	3098	3165	3043	2958
3290	Other manufacturing n.e.c.	1165	1188	1193	1193	2024	2092	1977	1967	643	691	651	658
331	Repair of fabricated metal products/machinery	5317	5460	5526	5642	15815	15330	15318	15523	5515	5441	5680	5887
3311	Repair of fabricated metal products	186	191	192	204	1108	1007	886	859	396	394	357	339
3312	Repair of machinery	3583	3701	3743	3857	8305	8257	8260	8661	2824	2841	2963	3194
3313	Repair of electronic and optical equipment	116	112	112	104	466	426	383	349	162	159	152	118
3314	Repair of electrical equipment	151	156	161	155	466	420	667	591	155	151	262	235
3315	Repair of transport equip., excl. motor vehicles	1174	1187	1193	1188	4999	4970	4835	4728	1835	1813	1849	1893
3319	Repair of other equipment	107	113	125	134	471	251	287	334	144	83	96	107
3320	Installation of industrial machinery/equipment	618	628	630	658	2525	2372	2404	2547	966	891	967	1043
C	Total manufacturing	53681	53896	53712	53795	567669	555150	535572	535824	219364	221721	216013	220685

a/ 1101 includes 1102, 1103 and 1104.
b/ 1511 includes 1512.
c/ 1910 includes 1920.
d/ 3211 includes 3212.

Sweden

ISIC Revision 4			Output (valuation not defined) (millions of Swedish Kronor)					Value added at factor values (millions of Swedish Kronor)					Gross fixed capital formation (millions of Swedish Kronor)		
Note	ISIC	Industry	Note	2013	2014	2015	2016	Note	2013	2014	2015	2016	Note	2015	2016
	1010	Processing/preserving of meat		36064	36366	36898	38333		5480	6523	6702	6738		967	966
	1020	Processing/preserving of fish, etc.		...	5212	4278	4471		...	1309	903	874		94	158
	1030	Processing/preserving of fruit,vegetables		10629	9852	13934	10431		2505	2480	3926	1759		573	225
	1040	Vegetable and animal oils and fats		...	6510	6592	6844		...	999	1080	1094		174	119
	1050	Dairy products		22888	23386	21523	21262		4658	4769	4562	4670		893	744
	106	Grain mill products,starches and starch products		5518	5051	5037	5107		1412	1247	1022	1239		395	457
	1061	Grain mill products		4558	3992	3814	3821		1227	1036	788	972		314	371
	1062	Starches and starch products		960	1058	1223	1286		185	211	235	267		81	86
	107	Other food products		39958	39404	38550	46462		13181	13344	13103	16240		1603	1973
	1071	Bakery products		16747	17449	17177	18409		6538	7047	6952	7262		704	762
	1072	Sugar		...	...	...	...		...	...	...	...		...	...
	1073	Cocoa, chocolate and sugar confectionery		5528	4539	4999	5265		1768	1680	1928	2134		134	200
	1074	Macaroni, noodles, couscous, etc.		42	42	39	42		18	17	13	14		2	3
	1075	Prepared meals and dishes		2617	2788	2488	7479		882	989	832	2678		350	496
	1079	Other food products n.e.c.													
	1080	Prepared animal feeds		6878	7116	4536	4332		835	169	631	643		114	694
	110	Beverages		17186	16081	16551	17130		5764	5985	6503	6438		600	937
a/	1101	Distilling, rectifying and blending of spirits	a/	17186	16081	16551	17130	a/	5764	5985	6503	6438	a/	600	937
a/	1102	Wines	a/	...	...	...	...	a/	...	...	...	...	a/	...	...
a/	1103	Malt liquors and malt	a/	...	...	...	...	a/	...	...	...	...	a/	...	...
a/	1104	Soft drinks,mineral waters,other bottled waters	a/	...	...	...	...	a/	...	...	...	...	a/	...	...
	1200	Tobacco products		...	...	...	...		...	...	...	...		...	...
	131	Spinning, weaving and finishing of textiles		781	779	747	718		247	260	266	261		12	25
	1311	Preparation and spinning of textile fibres		42	45	49	51		13	14	15	16		4	2
	1312	Weaving of textiles		399	378	377	358		119	117	128	122		6	16
	1313	Finishing of textiles		340	356	322	309		114	129	123	123		3	7
	139	Other textiles		6329	6756	7037	7454		2449	2574	2681	2841		222	228
	1391	Knitted and crocheted fabrics		953	679	734	711		331	235	266	264		22	10
	1392	Made-up textile articles, except apparel		1982	1990	2086	2178		711	731	742	787		48	46
	1393	Carpets and rugs		474	489	521	504		173	195	202	198		15	5
	1394	Cordage, rope, twine and netting		...	421	395	398		...	181	172	194		7	15
	1399	Other textiles n.e.c.		...	...	3301	3663		...	...	1297	1399		132	151
	1410	Wearing apparel, except fur apparel		1816	1948	1923	2017		555	618	603	609		45	37
	1420	Articles of fur		48	54	55	53		11	15	13	12		1	2
	1430	Knitted and crocheted apparel		139	138	160	146		36	36	51	52		5	1
	151	Leather;luggage,handbags,saddlery,harness;fur		983	869	904	1068		244	256	284	374		16	21
	1511	Tanning/dressing of leather; dressing of fur		983b/	476	499	544		244b/	125	135	169		5	9
	1512	Luggage,handbags,etc.;saddlery/harness		...b/	393	405	524		...b/	131	150	205		11	12
	1520	Footwear		308	...	...	287		99	...	...	75		...	4
	1610	Sawmilling and planing of wood		42951	49005	45910	43262		6631	9385	8625	7661		1814	2060

162	Wood products, cork, straw, plaiting materials	31311	34374	37628	41321	9363	9972	11091	12103	1078	1218
1621	Veneer sheets and wood-based panels	...	2117	...	...	...	612	...	...	...	...
1622	Builders' carpentry and joinery	...	24779	...	...	...	7294	...	...	...	...
1623	Wooden containers	3523	3812	3726	3846	1136	1158	1148	1194	180	92
1629	Other wood products;articles of cork,straw	4312	3665	3661	3943	978	906	994	996	162	206
170	Paper and paper products	119669	126314	128250	125749	29253	33903	35800	36010	10804	12125
1701	Pulp, paper and paperboard	96382	102352	104016	102761	22136	26912	28842	29600	10012	11125
1702	Corrugated paper and paperboard	9319	9156	8072	8176	2771	2744	2431	2581	285	209
1709	Other articles of paper and paperboard	13968	14807	16162	14811	4346	4247	4527	3829	507	791
181	Printing and service activities related to printing	21781	21105	22714	19942	7699	7422	8004	7556	595	420
1811	Printing	19901	19243	20376	18067	6739	6500	6953	6605	541	383
1812	Service activities related to printing	1879	1861	2338	1876	959	922	1050	952	54	38
1820	Reproduction of recorded media	137	174	169	132	64	80	60	51	4	1
1910	Coke oven products	...	...	91008c/	...	...	...	7675c/	...	1652c/	...
1920	Refined petroleum products	...	...	...c/	...	...	...	...c/	...	...c/	...
201	Basic chemicals,fertilizers, etc.	41128	42596	49743	50673	13976	14854	19488	15860	3935	4146
2011	Basic chemicals	...	...	...	...	...	...	...	...	...	...
2012	Fertilizers and nitrogen compounds	2814	3225	3018	3215	814	1089	933	938	597	553
2013	Plastics and synthetic rubber in primary forms	...	...	19177	...	...	...	9816	...	1431	...
202	Other chemical products	28226	29148	28131	27938	8481	9437	9464	9918	912	1166
2021	Pesticides and other agrochemical products	89	87	92	86	23	28	29	36	-	4
2022	Paints,varnishes;printing ink and mastics	11200	11421	11105	10204	2843	3285	3185	2988	256	266
2023	Soap,cleaning and cosmetic preparations	4629	4549	3058	4001	1348	1348	907	1283	113	80
2029	Other chemical products n.e.c.	12308	13083	13649	...	4266	4768	5610	...	...	816
2030	Man-made fibres	27	21	25	21	10	11	9	8	-	-
2100	Pharmaceuticals,medicinal chemicals, etc.	72717	90041	86852	...	35536	40033	...	39686	2935	3594
221	Rubber products	9703	10042	9850	...	3023	3382	3736	3563	218	194
2211	Rubber tyres and tubes	685	675	589	629	211	205	194	194	12	11
2219	Other rubber products	9018	9316	9261	9414	2812	3176	3546	3369	206	183
2220	Plastics products	30494	32388	35365	34358	10161	10564	10961	11209	1580	1644
2310	Glass and glass products	6661	5766	8078	6073	2090	2189	2133	2938	175	452
239	Non-metallic mineral products n.e.c.	...	36956	40146	37791	...	11411	12260	12336	1485	1704
2391	Refractory products	1017	1038	1051	1190	448	433	464	416	36	49
2392	Clay building materials	...	...	118	...	...	...	...	37	...	1
2393	Other porcelain and ceramic products	...	...	...	...	...	...	...	...	...	...
2394	Cement, lime and plaster	...	...	...	...	...	...	...	...	...	...
2395	Articles of concrete, cement and plaster	...	...	...	...	...	...	...	...	...	...
2396	Cutting, shaping and finishing of stone	...	1064	1277	1241	...	469	536	562	67	58
2399	Other non-metallic mineral products n.e.c.	8156	8520	...	7817	2316	2247	2366	...	313	...
2410	Basic iron and steel	70495	76091	75461	...	15410	18278	...	24680	...	2385
2420	Basic precious and other non-ferrous metals	38226	36073	36094	...	4781	5334	...	4377	...	377
243	Casting of metals	3531	3415	3550	3865	1281	1293	1391	1402	131	140
2431	Casting of iron and steel	1530	1528	1429	1610	559	559	557	542	34	48
2432	Casting of non-ferrous metals	2000	1887	2120	2255	722	734	833	860	97	91
251	Struct.metal products, tanks, reservoirs	24050	26149	27063	25701	7680	8558	8263	8801	716	712

continued

Sweden

			Output (valuation not defined) (millions of Swedish Kronor)					Value added at factor values (millions of Swedish Kronor)					Gross fixed capital formation (millions of Swedish Kronor)	
ISIC	Industry	Note	2013	2014	2015	2016	Note	2013	2014	2015	2016	Note	2015	2016
2511	Structural metal products		21972	23463	23750	25115		6983	7447	7575	8148		667	663
2512	Tanks, reservoirs and containers of metal		1940	2529	1769	1763		632	1044	607	574		46	47
2513	Steam generators, excl. hot water boilers		138	156	181	185		63	68	80	80		2	1
2520	Weapons and ammunition		5056	4223	4469	5614		1948	1647	1800	1976		57	57
259	Other metal products:metal working services		92146	94269	88897	89401		36070	37268	35126	35316		3426	3732
2591	Forging,pressing,stamping,roll-forming of metal		3647	3588	3771	3695		1239	1216	1240	1234		93	97
2592	Treatment and coating of metals; machining		39649	39851	41306	42706		16091	16034	16465	16840		1482	1634
2593	Cutlery, hand tools and general hardware		24834	26516	19140	18806		11223	12486	9759	9454		1065	1121
2599	Other fabricated metal products n.e.c.		...	...	...	...		...	...	...	...		...	...
2610	Electronic components and boards		5420	...	7467	9577		1743	...	2630	4917		53	174
2620	Computers and peripheral equipment		2589	2851	2725	2967		1103	1244	1096	1166		39	49
2630	Communication equipment		...	...	7806	5026		...	...	4977	1574		274	162
2640	Consumer electronics		705	747	1903	1997		92	62	811	762		111	125
265	Measuring,testing equipment; watches, etc.		20942	21559	14637	12097		10035	10403	5719	5517		230	298
2651	Measuring/testing/navigating equipment,etc.		20831	21435	14501	11953		9981	10338	5650	5448		229	297
2652	Watches and clocks		110	124	137	144		54	65	69	68		1	1
2660	Irradiation/electromedical equipment,etc.		1713	1004	...	...		700	341	485	659		...	...
2670	Optical instruments and photographic equipment		1043	1098	1287	1692		279	351	...	...		41	72
2680	Magnetic and optical media		...	37	...	...		...	7	...	...		...	...
2710	Electric motors,generators,transformers,etc.		...	41445	42201	38644		...	10501	12307	12254		1167	1021
2720	Batteries and accumulators		...	...	...	...		...	...	...	...		...	...
273	Wiring and wiring devices		7262	8412	8347	7966		1631	2039	2095	2154		114	179
2731	Fibre optic cables		...	311	...	...		...	127	...	...		...	...
2732	Other electronic and electric wires and cables		6182	7025	6750	6127		1230	1505	1523	1479		80	116
2733	Wiring devices		...	1075	...	...		...	407	...	...		...	...
2740	Electric lighting equipment		4282	4290	4535	4656		1545	1678	1613	1742		105	117
2750	Domestic appliances		3943	2846	...	...		1231	650	1148	1303		...	...
2790	Other electrical equipment		4036	...	3254	3573		1616	...	...	...		52	90
281	General-purpose machinery		103828	102309	112367	111520		38593	36697	40851	41248		2648	2590
2811	Engines/turbines,excl.aircraft,vehicle engines		15876	16071	19027	18202		5542	5421	6201	5382		461	345
2812	Fluid power equipment		5524	5088	5055	4822		2313	2344	2279	2116		80	175
2813	Other pumps, compressors, taps and valves		11313	8904	9976	10204		3762	3366	3876	3874		197	285
2814	Bearings, gears, gearing and driving elements		14002	11928	11365	10000		6065	2998	2588	2598		414	222
2815	Ovens, furnaces and furnace burners		1135	...	...	...		377	...	...	...		...	...
2816	Lifting and handling equipment		21110	21381	22875	23412		6765	6856	7762	7334		478	499
2817	Office machinery, excl.computers,etc.		...	600	602	...		...	245	241	...		7	...
2818	Power-driven hand tools		...	...	...	...		...	...	...	...		...	...
2819	Other general-purpose machinery		26926	27578	31140	31599		9904	10508	11776	12471		596	686
282	Special-purpose machinery		76330	68887	67471	69370		20055	18871	21587	22887		1269	1346
2821	Agricultural and forestry machinery		10032	9735	8452	8518		2968	3135	2893	2877		179	145
2822	Metal-forming machinery and machine tools		5628	5286	5813	6053		1964	1924	2203	2400		151	131

Code												
2823	Machinery for metallurgy	11	10	145	111	92	186	520	662	852	869	
2824	Mining, quarrying and construction machinery	638	639	9820	9854	7275	8228	30353	30759	31437	37944	
2825	Food/beverage/tobacco processing machinery	31	17	350	298	569	506	1158	875	1700	1709	
2826	Textile/apparel/leather production machinery	60	36	732	700	631	606	2113	2010	1832	1754	
2829	Other special-purpose machinery	330	239	6565	5528	5246	5598	20655	18899	18046	18396	
2910	Motor vehicles	14711	14958	54262	54180	33817	30255	219899	201027	167799	160040	
2920	Automobile bodies, trailers and semi-trailers	149	177	2126	2121	1780	1644	7183	6654	6061	5718	
2930	Parts and accessories for motor vehicles	1915	1871	13695	12346	10705	10358	54862	48701	44069	42036	
301	Building of ships and boats	219	157	1528	1706	1367	1516	4793	4565	3588	4198	
3011	Building of ships and floating structures	126	50	1021	1215	908	970	2811	2801	2124	2435	
3012	Building of pleasure and sporting boats	93	109	508	490	459	546	1982	1763	1464	1762	
3020	Railway locomotives and rolling stock	53	...	2833	...	1765	...	7316	...	6010	...	
3030	Air and spacecraft and related machinery	...	...	...	...	...	...	...	...	...	...	
3040	Military fighting vehicles	...	...	...	...	...	...	...	...	...	...	
309	Transport equipment n.e.c.	87	84	1446	1332	1575	1303	4020	3597	4013	3621	
3091	Motorcycles	1	2	10	16	...	...	48	65	...	...	
3092	Bicycles and invalid carriages	81	72	1252	1158	1216	996	3503	3128	3065	2866	
3099	Other transport equipment n.e.c.	6	9	184	158	...	...	469	404	...	...	
3100	Furniture	796	634	8711	8133	7709	7593	24990	24478	23826	24033	
321	Jewellery, bijouterie and related articles	18	9	307	297	283	234	968	909	845	811	d/
3211	Jewellery and related articles	18	9	307	297	283	234	968	909	845	811	d/
3212	Imitation jewellery and related articles	...	...	...	...	...	...	...	...	...	...	
3220	Musical instruments	1	2	153	146	118	111	345	324	278	266	
3230	Sports goods	15	17	374	424	469	460	1255	1202	1272	1146	
3240	Games and toys	7	7	106	127	119	75	292	319	319	205	
3250	Medical and dental instruments and supplies	633	591	6713	6192	6066	5341	15233	14492	14649	13982	
3290	Other manufacturing n.e.c.	164	160	1422	1401	1558	1476	3605	3497	3701	3596	
331	Repair of fabricated metal products/machinery	564	535	9858	9910	9426	9523	23841	23539	22535	22421	
3311	Repair of fabricated metal products	27	25	541	596	661	656	1203	1240	1335	1578	
3312	Repair of machinery	320	327	5391	5187	5001	5070	12039	11869	11723	11516	
3313	Repair of electronic and optical equipment	12	13	210	272	280	288	450	528	555	556	
3314	Repair of electrical equipment	11	11	402	450	252	268	1015	1066	560	580	
3315	Repair of transport equip., excl. motor vehicles	183	151	3119	3239	3092	3031	8718	8442	8029	7717	
3319	Repair of other equipment	12	7	195	165	137	209	415	395	333	472	
3320	Installation of industrial machinery/equipment	57	44	1774	1653	1489	1621	4234	3773	3639	3908	
C	Total manufacturing	70942	67699	506855	499847	471524	455590	1650361	1636722	1654298	1607366	

a/ 1101 includes 1102, 1103 and 1104.
b/ 1511 includes 1512.
c/ 1910 includes 1920.
d/ 3211 includes 3212.

Sweden

Index numbers of industrial production

ISIC Revision 4

(2010=100)

ISIC	Industry	Note	2005	2006	2007	2008	2009	2010	2011	2012	2013	2014	2015	2016
10	Food products		98	99	98	100	102	100	93	90	88	87	84	84
11	Beverages		100	105	110	108	101	100	101	102	111	78	61	58
12	Tobacco products		...	...	...	...	...	...	...	...	...	...	...	...
13	Textiles		...	...	...	...	...	...	...	...	...	...	...	...
14	Wearing apparel		...	...	...	...	...	...	...	...	...	...	...	...
15	Leather and related products		...	...	...	...	...	...	...	...	...	...	...	...
16	Wood products, excluding furniture		113	115	123	116	101	100	98	89	84	86	97	104
17	Paper and paper products		98	102	102	100	93	100	99	96	95	94	98	99
18	Printing and reproduction of recorded media		93	97	96	90	90	100	99	95	87	85	85	79
19	Coke and refined petroleum products		100	100	89	105	102	100	96	106	85	97	100	97
20	Chemicals and chemical products		101	106	107	104	91	100	97	...	...	...	...	97
21	Pharmaceuticals, medicinal chemicals, etc.		119	132	106	99	96	100	118	...	...	...	...	...
22	Rubber and plastics products		98	100	111	105	87	100	108	99	94	96	95	97
23	Other non-metallic mineral products		103	109	117	123	96	100	113	112	106	112	115	116
24	Basic metals		136	131	132	123	84	100	105	97	92	92	110	122
25	Fabricated metal products, except machinery		113	117	125	119	86	100	106	101	94	92	89	89
26	Computer, electronic and optical products		81	89	99	101	90	100	55	53	47	45	49	50
27	Electrical equipment		118	121	123	118	100	100	111	111	108	101	104	103
28	Machinery and equipment n.e.c.		116	127	141	140	91	100	117	109	98	94	95	94
29	Motor vehicles, trailers and semi-trailers		135	141	155	144	73	100	123	102	106	103	119	147
30	Other transport equipment		143	145	142	133	104	100	118	108	101	99	103	95
31	Furniture		130	133	143	114	94	100	99	94	86	91	95	96
32	Other manufacturing		86	87	94	94	93	100	95	88	85	83	98	106
33	Repair and installation of machinery/equipment		99	104	109	107	100	100	85	83	77	69	78	76
C	Total manufacturing		109	114	118	114	92	100	103	98	94	92	95	98

Switzerland

Supplier of information:
Federal Statistical Office (FSO), Neuchâtel.
Industrial statistics for the OECD countries are compiled by the OECD secretariat, which supplies them to UNIDO.

Basic source of data:
Annual survey; business register.

Major deviations from ISIC (Revision 4):
Data presented in ISIC (Revision 4) were originally collected using the national classification system (NOGA).

Reference period:
Calendar year.

Scope:
The number of enterprises is derived from the business register and includes data for all enterprises; other variables are derived from the annual survey that covers all enterprises with two or more employees.

Method of data collection:
Not reported.

Type of enumeration:
Not reported.

Adjusted for non-response:
Not reported.

Concepts and definitions of variables:
No deviations from the standard UN concepts and definitions are reported.

Related national publications:
Statistical Yearbook of Switzerland, published by the Federal Statistical Office, Neuchâtel.

Switzerland

ISIC	Industry	Ent. Note	Number of enterprises (number) 2013	2014	2015	2016	Pers. Note	Number of persons engaged (number) 2013	2014	2015	2016	Wage Note	Wages and salaries paid to employees (millions of Swiss Francs) 2013	2014	2015	2016
1010	Processing/preserving of meat		344	536	403	456		15489	15631	14996	14456		926.2	964.0	959.1	899.9
1020	Processing/preserving of fish, etc.		11	17	13	13		315	243	689	420		17.9	...	43.2	27.8
1030	Processing/preserving of fruit,vegetables		38	33	36	40		1330	1217	1661	2081		84.8	66.3	103.1	128.6
1040	Vegetable and animal oils and fats		14	14	13	12		458	451	442	538		37.3	...	42.9	49.7
1050	Dairy products		536	518	500	503		11871	12219	12734	14093		839.7	850.8	887.6	945.1
106	Grain mill products,starches and starch products	a/	63	61	64	69	a/	1763	1751	1138	1315	a/	109.4	118.1	81.5	89.1
1061	Grain mill products	a/	63	61	64	69	a/	1763	1751	1138	1315	a/	109.4	118.1	81.5	89.1
1062	Starches and starch products		...	...	...	...		...	...	...	...		...	...	...	...
107	Other food products	b/	1220	1326	1397	1450	b/	43867	47921	48075	48992	b/	2648.0	2800.4	2901.4	2942.6
1071	Bakery products	b/	1220	1326	1397	1450	b/	43867	47921	48075	48992	b/	2648.0	2800.4	2901.4	2942.6
1072	Sugar	b/	...	...	...	...	b/	...	...	...	...	b/	...	...	...	...
1073	Cocoa, chocolate and sugar confectionery	b/	...	...	...	...	b/	...	...	...	...	b/	...	...	...	...
1074	Macaroni, noodles, couscous, etc.	b/	...	...	...	...	b/	...	...	...	...	b/	...	...	...	...
1075	Prepared meals and dishes	b/	...	...	...	...	b/	...	...	...	...	b/	...	...	...	...
1079	Other food products n.e.c.	b/	...	...	...	...	b/	...	...	...	...	b/	...	...	...	...
1080	Prepared animal feeds		85	78	64	60		2652	1580	2255	1582		187.7	116.7	127.2	117.1
110	Beverages	c/	234	223	207	232	c/	7253	6519	6030	6120	c/	559.3	497.3	467.5	463.7
1101	Distilling, rectifying and blending of spirits	c/	234	223	207	232	c/	7253	6519	6030	6120	c/	559.3	497.3	467.5	463.7
1102	Wines	c/	...	...	...	...	c/	...	...	...	...	c/	...	...	...	...
1103	Malt liquors and malt	c/	...	...	...	...	c/	...	...	...	...	c/	...	...	...	...
1104	Soft drinks,mineral waters,other bottled waters	c/	...	...	...	...	c/	...	...	...	...	c/	...	...	...	...
1200	Tobacco products		9	10	10	11		2503	2264	2185	2215		...	...	...	...
131	Spinning, weaving and finishing of textiles	d/	87	87	80	82	d/	3484	3563	2971	2858	d/	221.2	227.9	198.4	188.9
1311	Preparation and spinning of textile fibres	d/	87	87	80	82	d/	3484	3563	2971	2858	d/	221.2	227.9	198.4	188.9
1312	Weaving of textiles	d/	...	...	...	...	d/	...	...	...	...	d/	...	...	...	...
1313	Finishing of textiles	d/	...	...	...	...	d/	...	...	...	...	d/	...	...	...	...
139	Other textiles	e/	254	249	239	237	e/	3997	4188	4466	4148	e/	241.9	256.4	286.0	257.3
1391	Knitted and crocheted fabrics	e/	254	249	239	237	e/	3997	4188	4466	4148	e/	241.9	256.4	286.0	257.3
1392	Made-up textile articles, except apparel	e/	...	...	...	...	e/	...	...	...	...	e/	...	...	...	...
1393	Carpets and rugs	e/	...	...	...	...	e/	...	...	...	...	e/	...	...	...	...
1394	Cordage, rope, twine and netting	e/	...	...	...	...	e/	...	...	...	...	e/	...	...	...	...
1399	Other textiles n.e.c.	e/	...	...	...	...	e/	...	...	...	...	e/	...	...	...	...
1410	Wearing apparel, except fur apparel		255	242	239	238		4250	3764	3915	3655		217.0f/	205.9f/	179.3	188.5f/
1420	Articles of fur		5	6	6	4		...	-	...	...		...f/	...f/	...	...f/
1430	Knitted and crocheted apparel		9	10	9	8		330	411	412	253		...f/	...f/	29.9	...f/
151	Leather;luggage,handbags,saddlery,harness;fur	h/	81	83	79	76	h/	1263	1046	1046	897		115.0g/	96.7g/	102.5g/	50.1
1511	Tanning/dressing of leather; dressing of fur	h/	81	83	79	76	h/	1263	1046	1046	897	h/	...	...	...	50.1h/
1512	Luggage,handbags,etc.;saddlery/harness	h/	17	17	16	12	h/	636	627	624	754	h/	...g/	...	...	...h/
1520	Footwear		...	...	...	...		...	...	...	...		...g/	...g/	...g/	50.4
1610	Sawmilling and planing of wood		295	280	266	263		1764	4938	4949	4366		110.2	294.8	311.7	279.1

Code	Industry		(1)	(2)	(3)	(4)		(5)	(6)	(7)	(8)		(9)	(10)	(11)	(12)
162	Wood products, cork, straw, plaiting materials	i/	2861	2881	2852	2779	i/	35076	32218	31739	31662	i/	2245.4	2055.7	2019.8	1889.1
1621	Veneer sheets and wood-based panels	i/	2861	2881	2852	2779	i/	35076	32218	31739	31662	i/	2245.4	2055.7	2019.8	1889.1
1622	Builders' carpentry and joinery	i/	...	...	...	...	i/	...	...	...	...	i/	...	...	...	...
1623	Wooden containers	i/	...	...	...	...	i/	...	...	...	...	i/	...	...	...	...
1629	Other wood products;articles of cork,straw	i/	...	...	...	...	i/	...	...	...	...	i/	...	...	...	...
170	Paper and paper products	j/	156	153	146	137	j/	9587	8981	8864	8208	j/	713.4	675.7	669.9	618.4
1701	Pulp, paper and paperboard	j/	156	153	146	137	j/	9587	8981	8863	8208	j/	713.4	675.7	669.9	618.3
1702	Corrugated paper and paperboard	j/	...	...	...	...	j/	...	...	...	...	j/	...	...	...	...
1709	Other articles of paper and paperboard	j/	...	...	...	...	j/	...	...	...	...	j/	...	...	...	...
181	Printing and service activities related to printing		1286	1238	1156	1131		20523	19407	18663	17442		1406.2 k/	...	...	...
1811	Printing	m/	1286	1238	1156	1131	m/	20523	19407	18663	17442		...	...	...	...
1812	Service activities related to printing	m/	15	12	9	9	m/	52	336	356	233		...	...	...	...
1820	Reproduction of recorded media		...	...	...	...		.. k/	...	...	...		.. k/	...	...	...
1910	Coke oven products		-	-	-	-		-	-	-	-		...	...	...	...
1920	Refined petroleum products		8	9	7	7		914	914	601	623		...	...	...	...
201	Basic chemicals,fertilizers, etc.	n/	85	87	83	79	n/	7573	7035	7322	7250	n/	728.4	687.3	784.1	808.6
2011	Basic chemicals	n/	85	87	83	79	n/	7573	7035	7322	7250	n/	728.4	687.3	784.1	808.6
2012	Fertilizers and nitrogen compounds	n/	...	...	...	...	n/	...	...	...	...	n/	...	...	...	...
2013	Plastics and synthetic rubber in primary forms	n/	...	...	...	...	n/	...	...	...	...	n/	...	...	...	...
202	Other chemical products		365	348	342	349		22375	21627	20850	21333		2324.7	2240.8	2204.3	2381.7
2021	Pesticides and other agrochemical products	p/	365	348	342	349	p/	22375	21627	20850	21333	p/	2324.7	2240.8	2204.3	2381.7
2022	Paints,varnishes;printing ink and mastics	p/	...	...	...	...	p/	...	...	...	...	p/	...	...	...	...
2023	Soap,cleaning and cosmetic preparations	p/	...	...	...	...	p/	...	...	...	...	p/	...	...	...	...
2029	Other chemical products n.e.c.	p/	...	...	...	...	p/	...	...	...	...	p/	...	...	...	...
2030	Man-made fibres		11	11	10	7		505	508	517	531		33.1	34.7	36.2	34.8
2100	Pharmaceuticals,medicinal chemicals, etc.		169	181	179	179		43109	44744	46053	45462		5441.7	5599.4	6029.4	6154.5
221	Rubber products		39	43	40	36		2136	1656	1189	1333		177.0	131.2	95.1	105.9
2211	Rubber tyres and tubes	q/	39	43	40	36	q/	2136	1656	1189	1333	q/	177.0	131.2	95.1	105.9
2219	Other rubber products	q/	...	...	...	...	q/	...	...	...	...	q/	...	...	...	...
2220	Plastics products	q/	536	545	532	516	q/	22431	22337	21748	21227	q/	1625.3	1688.9	1656.5	1604.7
2310	Glass and glass products		92	98	93	91		4312	4123	4636	4401		334.6	315.3	359.3	342.0
239	Non-metallic mineral products n.e.c.		597	579	549	539		14464	13841	12842	13063		1161.3 r/	1168.8	...	...
2391	Refractory products	r/	597	579	549	539	r/	14464	13841	12842	13063	r/	1161.3 r/	1168.8 r/	.. r/	.. r/
2392	Clay building materials	r/	...	...	...	...	r/	...	...	...	...	r/	.. r/	.. r/	.. r/	.. r/
2393	Other porcelain and ceramic products	r/	...	...	...	...	r/	...	...	...	...	r/	.. r/	.. r/	.. r/	.. r/
2394	Cement, lime and plaster	r/	...	...	...	...	r/	...	...	...	...	r/	.. r/	.. r/	.. r/	.. r/
2395	Articles of concrete, cement and plaster	r/	...	...	...	...	r/	...	...	...	...	r/	.. r/	.. r/	.. r/	.. r/
2396	Cutting, shaping and finishing of stone	r/	...	...	...	...	r/	...	...	...	...	r/	.. r/	.. r/	.. r/	.. r/
2399	Other non-metallic mineral products n.e.c.	r/	...	...	...	...	r/	...	...	...	...	r/	.. r/	.. r/	.. r/	.. r/
2410	Basic iron and steel		71	77	73	73		5212	5097	5492	5061		427.3	394.6	430.5	409.6
2420	Basic precious and other non-ferrous metals		48	49	49	47		4095	3720	3720	3294		330.6	313.4	303.6	269.6
243	Casting of metals		82	72	68	63		4186	4048	3460	3742		280.0	275.8	236.4	260.8
2431	Casting of iron and steel	s/	82	72	68	63	s/	4186	4048	3460	3742	s/	280.0	275.8	236.4	260.8
2432	Casting of non-ferrous metals	s/	...	...	...	...	s/	...	...	...	...	s/	...	...	...	...
251	Struct.metal products, tanks, reservoirs		1054	1044	1043	1037		17827	16181	14616	16922		1195.3	1088.2	1034.7	...

continued

Switzerland

ISIC	Industry	Note	Number of enterprises (number) 2013	2014	2015	2016	Note	Number of persons engaged (number) 2013	2014	2015	2016	Note	Wages and salaries paid to employees (millions of Swiss Francs) 2013	2014	2015	2016
2511	Structural metal products	t/	1054	1044	1043	1037	t/	17827	16181	14616	16922		1195.3t/	1088.2t/	1034.7t/	...
2512	Tanks, reservoirs and containers of metal	t/	...	...	...	...	t/	...	...	...	...		...t/	...t/	...t/	...
2513	Steam generators, excl. hot water boilers	t/	13	...	...	13	t/	...	...	...	...		...t/	...t/	...t/	...
2520	Weapons and ammunition		13	14	12	13		3595	3396	1842	1954		304.0	255.9	179.1	193.3
259	Other metal products;metal working services		3289	3299	3173	3104		65046	63998	61874	58484		4491.2	4515.3	4345.5	4153.0
2591	Forging,pressing,stamping,roll-forming of metal	u/	3289	3299	3173	3104	u/	65046	63998	61874	58484	u/	4491.2	4515.3	4345.5	4153.0
2592	Treatment and coating of metals machining	u/	...	...	...	...	u/	...	...	...	...	u/	...	...	...	...
2593	Cutlery, hand tools and general hardware	u/	...	...	...	...	u/	...	...	...	...	u/	...	...	...	...
2599	Other fabricated metal products n.e.c.	u/	...	...	...	...	u/	...	...	...	...	u/	...	...	...	...
2610	Electronic components and boards		342	339	315	302		27505	27802	24168	24206		2276.4	2375.6	2274.7	2139.3
2620	Computers and peripheral equipment		47	47	38	36		880	1049	757	530		81.1	102.0	...	54.8
2630	Communication equipment		77	72	64	61		3451	2873	2264	2579		352.3	277.2	221.1	244.6
2640	Consumer electronics		33	35	31	30		575	312	1068	729		52.8	...	82.0	38.2
265	Measuring,testing equipment; watches, etc.	v/	794	807	803	790	v/	68518	67102	67778	66046	v/	5788.4	5791.9	5841.4	5603.6
2651	Measuring/testing/navigating equipment,etc.	v/	794	807	803	790	v/	68518	67102	67778	66046	v/	5788.4	5791.9	5841.4	5603.6
2652	Watches and clocks															
2660	Irradiation/electromedical equipment,etc.		126	118	106	102		9777	10337	10002	11262		952.5	991.2	950.0	1103.2
2670	Optical instruments and photographic equipment		62	61	58	59		3745	5883	4187	4460		294.5	515.0	395.2	408.0
2680	Magnetic and optical media		4	4	5	5		...	69	61	-		-			-
2710	Electric motors,generators,transformers,etc.		132	130	124	116		14140	13312	12951	11986		1507.4	1432.0	1425.6	1306.3
2720	Batteries and accumulators		9	8	7	10		491	464	523	514		...	...	...	...
273	Wiring and wiring devices		50	46	44	40		5511	5321	5018	4820		...	...	...	...
2731	Fibre optic cables	w/	50	46	44	40	w/	5511	5321	5018	4820		...	...	...	...
2732	Other electronic and electric wires and cables	w/	...	...	...	...	w/	...	...	...	...		...	...	...	...
2733	Wiring devices	w/	...	...	...	...	w/	...	...	...	...		...	...	...	...
2740	Electric lighting equipment		107	115	112	112		2171	2364	1616	1543		179.1	188.4	141.6	127.9
2750	Domestic appliances		42	39	39	38		4652	3350	3058	4551		347.9	284.5	268.5	379.0
2790	Other electrical equipment		237	238	242	236		9196	9533	8994	8562		728.8	800.5	770.1	706.3
281	General-purpose machinery		861	833	805	773		41988	43680	44488	41342		3654.8	3827.3	3819.1	3599.1
2811	Engines/turbines,excl.aircraft,vehicle engines	x/	861	833	805	773	x/	41988	43680	44488	41342	x/	3654.8	3827.3	3819.1	3599.1
2812	Fluid power equipment	x/	...	...	...	...	x/	...	...	...	...	x/	...	...	...	...
2813	Other pumps, compressors, taps and valves	x/	...	...	...	...	x/	...	...	...	...	x/	...	...	...	...
2814	Bearings, gears, gearing and driving elements	x/	...	...	...	...	x/	...	...	...	...	x/	...	...	...	...
2815	Ovens, furnaces and furnace burners	x/	...	...	...	...	x/	...	...	...	...	x/	...	...	...	...
2816	Lifting and handling equipment	x/	...	...	...	...	x/	...	...	...	...	x/	...	...	...	...
2817	Office machinery, excl.computers,etc.	x/	...	...	...	...	x/	...	...	...	...	x/	...	...	...	...
2818	Power-driven hand tools	x/	...	...	...	...	x/	...	...	...	...	x/	...	...	...	...
2819	Other general-purpose machinery	x/	...	...	...	...	x/	...	...	...	...	x/	...	...	...	...
282	Special-purpose machinery		820	789	716	697		40551	39300	36414	37173		3348.7	3205.0	3004.6	3084.2
2821	Agricultural and forestry machinery	y/	820	789	716	697	y/	40551	39300	36414	37173	y/	3348.7	3205.0	3004.6	3084.2
2822	Metal-forming machinery and machine tools	y/	...	...	...	...	y/	...	...	...	...	y/	...	...	...	...

Code	Description	fn												
2823	Machinery for metallurgy	y/	...	...	...		...	...	...		...	...	...	
2824	Mining, quarrying and construction machinery	y/	...	...	...		...	...	...		...	...	...	
2825	Food/beverage/tobacco processing machinery	y/	...	...	...		...	...	...		...	...	...	
2826	Textile/apparel/leather production machinery	y/	...	...	...		...	...	...		...	...	...	
2829	Other special-purpose machinery	y/	...	...	...		...	...	...		...	...	...	
2910	Motor vehicles		33	34	34		1773	1407	1380	1326	128.8	99.7		
2920	Automobile bodies, trailers and semi-trailers		52	50	48		1243	1250	1280	1074	86.1	86.6		
2930	Parts and accessories for motor vehicles		55	57	49		2236	2415	2250	2381	159.7	179.9	183.7	193.7
301	Building of ships and boats	z/	65	67	59		537	503	492	531	30.7	31.7	32.9	31.7
3011	Building of ships and floating structures	z/	65	67	59		537	503	492	531	30.7	31.7	32.9	31.7
3012	Building of pleasure and sporting boats		...	...	...		...	...	...		...	...	...	
3020	Railway locomotives and rolling stock		14	14	12		4127	4159	4075	4150	332.2	340.4	358.2	346.6
3030	Air and spacecraft and related machinery		20	16	17		5931	5794	6130	5954	541.3	565.6	543.9	529.1
3040	Military fighting vehicles		-	-	-		-	-	-	-	-	-	-	-
309	Transport equipment n.e.c.	A/	39	33	32		847	901	882	999	58.1	61.8	65.8	72.2
3091	Motorcycles	A/	39	33	32		847	901	882	999	58.1	61.8	65.8	72.2
3092	Bicycles and invalid carriages	A/	...	...	...		...	...	...		...	...	...	
3099	Other transport equipment n.e.c.	A/	...	...	...		...	...	...		...	...	...	
3100	Furniture		507	496	447		12234	10705	10535	9175	826.3	734.9	739.3	
321	Jewellery, bijouterie and related articles	B/	284	281	266		2859	2505	2448	2715	196.5	167.6	164.3	187.4
3211	Jewellery and related articles	B/	284	281	266		2859	2505	2448	2715	196.5	167.6	164.3	187.4
3212	Imitation jewellery and related articles	B/	...	...	...		...	...	...		...	...	...	
3220	Musical instruments		56	60	54		354	262		1	16.7		12.8	0.1
3230	Sports goods		41	43	40		386	521	304	541	23.4	29.4	39.7	
3240	Games and toys		29	36	32		317	62	862	403	14.3	55.0	3.4	
3250	Medical and dental instruments and supplies		721	708	684		13347	14149	13858	13967	995.1	1107.8	1095.0	1196.5
3290	Other manufacturing n.e.c.		134	136	118		4349	4392	4004	4290	284.0	236.2	254.2	248.6
331	Repair of fabricated metal products/machinery	C/	881	912	969		13774	12689	13233	12951	991.0	972.9	919.3	922.5
3311	Repair of fabricated metal products	C/	881	912	969		13774	12689	13233	12951	991.0	972.9	919.3	922.5
3312	Repair of machinery	C/	...	...	...		...	...	...		...	...	...	
3313	Repair of electronic and optical equipment	C/	...	...	...		...	...	...		...	...	...	
3314	Repair of electrical equipment	C/	...	...	...		...	...	...		...	...	...	
3315	Repair of transport equip., excl. motor vehicles	C/	...	...	...		...	...	...		...	...	...	
3319	Repair of other equipment	C/	...	...	...		...	...	...		...	...	...	
3320	Installation of industrial machinery/equipment		153	155	134		2098	2654	2043	2005	152.3	153.6	200.0	160.4
C	Total manufacturing		21161	21302	20598	20367	685805	679619	662098	653727	54854.2	54871.1	54498.0	53942.8

a/ 1061 includes 1062.
b/ 1071 includes 1072, 1073, 1074, 1075 and 1079.
c/ 1101 includes 1102, 1103 and 1104.
d/ 1311 includes 1312 and 1313.
e/ 1391 includes 1392, 1393, 1394 and 1399.
f/ 1410 includes 1420 and 1430.
g/ 151 includes 1520.
h/ 1511 includes 1512.
i/ 1621 includes 1622, 1623 and 1629.
j/ 1701 includes 1702 and 1709.

k/ 181 includes 1820.
m/ 1811 includes 1812.
n/ 2011 includes 2012 and 2013.
p/ 2021 includes 2022, 2023 and 2029.
q/ 2211 includes 2219.
r/ 2391 includes 2392, 2393, 2394, 2395, 2396 and 2399.
s/ 2431 includes 2432.
t/ 2511 includes 2512 and 2513.
u/ 2591 includes 2592, 2593 and 2599.
v/ 2651 includes 2652.

w/ 2731 includes 2732 and 2733.
x/ 2811 includes 2812, 2813, 2814, 2815, 2816, 2817, 2818 and 2819.
y/ 2821 includes 2822, 2823, 2824, 2825, 2826 and 2829.
z/ 3011 includes 3012.
A/ 3091 includes 3092 and 3099.
B/ 3211 includes 3212.
C/ 3311 includes 3312, 3313, 3314, 3315 and 3319.

Switzerland

ISIC Revision 4

ISIC	Industry	Output Note	Output 2013	Output 2014	Output 2015	Output 2016	VA Note	VA 2013	VA 2014	VA 2015	VA 2016	GFCF Note	GFCF 2015	GFCF 2016
			(millions of Swiss Francs)					(millions of Swiss Francs)					(millions of Swiss Francs)	
1010	Processing/preserving of meat		6777.0	6832.7	6609.3	6673.0		1499.2	1550.0	1580.3	1475.5		184.1	196.8
1020	Processing/preserving of fish, etc.		71.9	...	194.7	108.3		23.3	...	56.8	38.4		0.1	
1030	Processing/preserving of fruit, vegetables		409.3	...	548.5	656.6		136.0	...	178.8	213.1		36.9	47.8
1040	Vegetable and animal oils and fats		486.9	656.2	645.1	698.4		73.9	151.0	144.8	147.7		10.8	
1050	Dairy products		7152.2	7649.7	8035.7	8233.0		1517.1	1590.4	1698.6	1820.1		257.2	336.4
106	Grain mill products,starches and starch products	a/	778.7	919.5	702.1	772.6	a/	191.3	208.4	158.8	165.8	a/	28.6	15.6
1061	Grain mill products	a/	778.7	919.5	702.1	772.6	a/	191.3	208.4	158.8	165.8	a/	28.6	15.6
1062	Starches and starch products													
107	Other food products		14143.1	14901.0	14307.1	14043.6		4716.3	4795.6	4892.8	4974.8		663.2	751.9
1071	Bakery products	b/	14143.1	14901.0	14307.1	14043.6	b/	4716.3	4795.6	4892.8	4974.8	b/	663.2	751.9
1072	Sugar	b/	...	...	...	...	b/	...	...	...	...	b/		
1073	Cocoa, chocolate and sugar confectionery	b/	...	...	...	...	b/	...	...	...	...	b/		
1074	Macaroni, noodles, couscous, etc.	b/	...	...	...	...	b/	...	...	...	...	b/		
1075	Prepared meals and dishes	b/	...	...	...	...	b/	...	...	...	...	b/		
1079	Other food products n.e.c.	b/	...	...	...	...	b/	...	...	...	...	b/		
1080	Prepared animal feeds	b/	1773.4	1139.5	1154.5	991.9	b/	292.6	169.3	202.5	190.7		27.1	23.5
110	Beverages		2780.6	2729.7	2258.4	2231.5		1038.4	975.6	854.3	842.5		143.2	146.2
1101	Distilling, rectifying and blending of spirits	c/	2780.6	2729.7	2258.4	2231.5	c/	1038.4	975.6	854.3	842.5	c/	143.2	146.2
1102	Wines	c/	...	...	...	...	c/	...	...	...	...	c/		
1103	Malt liquors and malt	c/	...	...	...	...	c/	...	...	...	...	c/		
1104	Soft drinks,mineral waters,other bottled waters	c/	...	...	...	...	c/	...	...	...	...	c/		
1200	Tobacco products		...	...	...	...		...	...	...	...			
131	Spinning, weaving and finishing of textiles		665.5	726.1	573.4	557.7		286.1	302.4	248.5	262.5		20.6	18.6
1311	Preparation and spinning of textile fibres	d/	665.5	726.1	573.4	557.7	d/	286.1	302.4	248.5	262.5	d/	20.6	18.6
1312	Weaving of textiles	d/	...	...	...	...	d/	...	...	...	...	d/		
1313	Finishing of textiles	d/	...	...	...	...	d/	...	...	...	...	d/		
139	Other textiles		859.4	962.4	995.2	887.4		360.5	399.4	436.0	376.4		22.4	23.1
1391	Knitted and crocheted fabrics	e/	859.4	962.4	995.2	887.4	e/	360.5	399.4	436.0	376.4	e/	22.4	23.1
1392	Made-up textile articles, except apparel	e/	...	...	...	...	e/	...	...	...	...	e/		
1393	Carpets and rugs	e/	...	...	...	...	e/	...	...	...	...	e/		
1394	Cordage, rope, twine and netting	e/	...	...	...	...	e/	...	...	...	...	e/		
1399	Other textiles n.e.c.	e/	...	...	...	...	e/	...	...	...	...	e/		
1410	Wearing apparel, except fur apparel		1219.9f/	1139.4f/	1081.4	949.2f/		364.8f/	320.3f/	327.6	261.6f/		4.9	8.4f/
1420	Articles of fur		...f/	...f/	-	...f/		...f/	...f/	-	...f/		-	...f/
1430	Knitted and crocheted apparel		...f/	...f/	81.9	...f/		...f/	...f/	42.0	...f/		2.6	...f/
151	Leather;luggage,handbags,saddlery,harness;fur		506.5g/	524.8g/	558.4g/	178.6		151.9g/	134.0g/	...	56.4		...	
1511	Tanning/dressing of leather; dressing of fur		...	...	...	178.6h/		...	...	...	56.4h/			
1512	Luggage,handbags,etc.;saddlery/harness		...	...	...	...h/		...	...	...	...h/			
1520	Footwear		..g/	..g/	..g/	381.7		..g/	..g/	...	58.4			2.9
1610	Sawmilling and planing of wood		451.0	1524.1	1527.5	1379.8		179.6	462.6	518.0	462.7		97.2	159.4

Code	Product		1	2	3	4		5	6	7	8		9	10
162	Wood products, cork, straw, plaiting materials	i/	8403.1	7946.9	7368.9	6710.8	i/	3264.8	3005.8	2941.3	2765.4	i/	354.1	205.3
1621	Veneer sheets and wood-based panels	i/	8403.1	7946.9	7368.9	6710.8	i/	3264.8	3005.8	2941.3	2765.4	i/	354.1	205.3
1622	Builders' carpentry and joinery	i/	...	...	...	...	i/	...	...	...	...	i/	...	...
1623	Wooden containers	i/	...	...	...	...	i/	...	...	...	...	i/	...	...
1629	Other wood products;articles of cork,straw	i/	...	...	...	...	i/	...	...	...	...	i/	...	...
170	Paper and paper products	j/	3444.7	3191.4	2980.7	2968.4	j/	1103.3	1067.1	978.6	946.1	j/	212.7	130.5
1701	Pulp, paper and paperboard	j/	3444.7	3191.4	2980.7	2968.4	j/	1103.3	1067.0	978.6	946.0	j/	212.7	130.5
1702	Corrugated paper and paperboard		...	...	...	...		...	...	...	...		...	...
1709	Other articles of paper and paperboard		...	...	...	...		...	...	...	...		...	...
181	Printing and service activities related to printing		3893.1k/					1991.4k/					215.2	138.2
1811	Printing												215.2m/	138.2m/
1812	Service activities related to printing		...k/					...k/					-	...m/
1820	Reproduction of recorded media													
1910	Coke oven products		...	...	...	...		...	...	...	...		-	-
1920	Refined petroleum products		...	...	...	...		109.7	...	...	...		49.2	18.8
201	Basic chemicals,fertilizers,etc.		3879.6	3602.7	4275.1	5082.9		1429.8	1410.2	1526.0	1684.2		336.1	253.1
2011	Basic chemicals	n/	3879.6	3602.7	4275.1	5082.9	n/	1429.8	1410.2	1526.0	1684.2	n/	336.1	253.1
2012	Fertilizers and nitrogen compounds	n/	...	...	...	...	n/	...	...	...	...	n/	...	...
2013	Plastics and synthetic rubber in primary forms	n/	...	...	...	...	n/	...	...	...	...	n/	...	...
202	Other chemical products		17246.1	17150.4	15496.4	16364.4		4054.4	4072.1	4035.0	4472.3		428.3	785.8
2021	Pesticides and other agrochemical products	p/	17246.1	17150.4	15496.4	16364.4	p/	4054.4	4072.1	4035.0	4472.3	p/	428.3	785.8
2022	Paints,varnishes;printing ink and mastics	p/	...	...	...	...	p/	...	...	...	...	p/	...	...
2023	Soap,cleaning and cosmetic preparations	p/	...	...	...	...	p/	...	...	...	...	p/	...	...
2029	Other chemical products n.e.c.	p/	...	...	...	...	p/	...	...	...	...	p/	...	...
2030	Man-made fibres		48.4		115.9			53.1	51.4	52.9			6.5	8.7
2100	Pharmaceuticals,medicinal chemicals, etc.		73203.8	73866.0	75273.6	80829.7		20899.3	20392.5	23362.1	23732.1		2380.9	2087.2
221	Rubber products		621.2	527.7	379.4	402.2		251.6	189.7	149.1	172.3		13.0	18.8
2211	Rubber tyres and tubes	q/	621.2	527.7	379.4	402.2	q/	251.6	189.7	149.1	172.3	q/	13.0q/	18.8q/
2219	Other rubber products	q/	...	...	...	...	q/	...	...	...	...	q/	...q/	...q/
2220	Plastics products		6959.5	7239.3	6681.7	6402.3		2619.3	2683.8	2584.5	2621.5		296.0	307.5
2310	Glass and glass products		1224.7	1154.1	1237.2	1208.6		533.2	484.6	506.0	490.3		69.7	79.1
239	Non-metallic mineral products n.e.c.		5860.3r/	6687.5r/	...	...		2211.4r/	2354.3r/	...	...		...	...
2391	Refractory products		5860.3r/	6687.5r/	...	...		2211.4r/	2354.3r/	...	...		...	...
2392	Clay building materials		...r/	...r/				...r/	...r/					
2393	Other porcelain and ceramic products		...r/	...r/				...r/	...r/					
2394	Cement, lime and plaster		...r/	...r/				...r/	...r/					
2395	Articles of concrete, cement and plaster		...r/	...r/				...r/	...r/					
2396	Cutting, shaping and finishing of stone		...r/	...r/				...r/	...r/					
2399	Other non-metallic mineral products n.e.c.		...r/	...r/				...r/	...r/					
2410	Basic iron and steel		2444.8	2479.0	2249.2	2031.5		658.3	686.1	656.5	646.8		102.5	133.9
2420	Basic precious and other non-ferrous metals		1903.4	1858.6	1833.5	1740.9		618.0	579.4	532.8	504.8		98.0	65.4
243	Casting of metals		868.3	902.9	697.6	777.7		372.2	370.0	319.8	350.1		32.8	68.2
2431	Casting of iron and steel	s/	868.3	902.9	697.6	777.7	s/	372.2	370.0	319.8	350.1	s/	32.8	68.2
2432	Casting of non-ferrous metals	s/	...	...	...	...	s/	...	...	...	...	s/	...	...
251	Struct.metal products, tanks, reservoirs		4204.5	4196.7	3624.3	...		1670.8	1469.4	1298.5	...		270.3	...

continued

Switzerland

ISIC	Industry	Note	Output (valuation not defined) (millions of Swiss Francs)				Note	Value added at factor values (millions of Swiss Francs)				Note	Gross fixed capital formation (millions of Swiss Francs)	
			2013	2014	2015	2016		2013	2014	2015	2016		2015	2016
2511	Structural metal products		4204.5t/	4196.7t/	3624.3t/	...		1670.8t/	1469.4t/	1298.5t/	...		270.3t/	...
2512	Tanks, reservoirs and containers of metal		..t/	..t/	..t/	...		..t/	..t/	..t/	...		..t/	...
2513	Steam generators, excl. hot water boilers		..t/	..t/	..t/	...		..t/	..t/	..t/	...		..t/	...
2520	Weapons and ammunition		1031.0	957.5	675.4	710.3		369.3	341.9	244.4	261.4		20.1	19.1
259	Other metal products;metal working services		13507.3	13785.0	13111.5	12457.5	u/	7136.6	7226.4	7251.7	6903.7	u/	879.7	767.2
2591	Forging,pressing,stamping,roll-forming of metal		13507.3	13785.0	13111.5	12457.5	u/	7136.6	7226.4	7251.7	6903.7	u/	879.7	767.2
2592	Treatment and coating of metals; machining		...	...	...	...	u/	...	...	...	...	u/	...	...
2593	Cutlery, hand tools and general hardware		...	...	...	...	u/	...	...	...	...	u/	...	...
2599	Other fabricated metal products n.e.c.		...	...	...	...	u/	...	...	...	...	u/	...	...
2610	Electronic components and boards		9873.5	9730.9	9597.0	9524.9		3484.4	3466.6	3634.7	3631.9		209.2	303.1
2620	Computers and peripheral equipment		377.7	417.6	331.5	282.7		137.8	169.4	141.9	101.0		...	...
2630	Communication equipment		1418.5	967.4	769.4	773.3		532.1	346.8	278.4	286.4		...	...
2640	Consumer electronics		173.2	...	...	122.6		66.2	...	...	51.3		...	...
265	Measuring,testing equipment; watches, etc.	v/	34584.1	33298.3	31546.4	28250.5	v/	13477.7	13367.4	12926.0	11110.9	v/	1273.3	1061.3
2651	Measuring/testing/navigating equipment,etc.	v/	34584.1	33298.3	31546.4	28250.5	v/	13477.7	13367.4	12926.0	11110.9	v/	1273.3	1061.3
2652	Watches and clocks		...	...	...	...		...	...	...	...		...	...
2660	Irradiation/electromedical equipment,etc.		13195.5	13786.1	10430.3	11126.3		3572.9	3917.7	1806.0	2315.0		153.1	180.3
2670	Optical instruments and photographic equipment		1030.2	1914.5	1529.2	1682.8		501.7	929.5	708.3	777.5		36.9	48.4
2680	Magnetic and optical media		-	...	-	-		-	...	...	0.1		...	...
2710	Electric motors,generators,transformers,etc.		6766.6	6009.0	5157.6	4881.6		2556.0	2200.9	1789.6	1906.7		126.7	123.4
2720	Batteries and accumulators		...	...	...	...		...	...	...	...		...	14.8
273	Wiring and wiring devices		...	...	...	...		...	...	...	...		...	...
2731	Fibre optic cables		...	...	...	...		...	...	...	...		...	...
2732	Other electronic and electric wires and cables		...	...	...	...		...	...	...	...		...	...
2733	Wiring devices		...	...	...	...		...	...	...	...		...	...
2740	Electric lighting equipment		631.1	593.1	470.8	398.1		266.8	260.5	194.4	177.4		10.3	...
2750	Domestic appliances		1907.2	1348.8	1283.2	2134.4		691.9	548.8	521.2	767.4		64.7	60.4
2790	Other electrical equipment		2511.6	2819.1	4067.0	2622.4		1070.3	1128.2	1186.2	1103.7		172.8	85.6
281	General-purpose machinery	x/	15372.4	16225.5	15771.3	14827.5	x/	6019.6	6367.9	6223.4	5968.2		4192.8w/	...
2811	Engines/turbines,excl.aircraft,vehicle engines	x/	15372.4	16225.5	15771.3	14827.5	x/	6019.6	6367.9	6223.4	5968.2		...	...
2812	Fluid power equipment	x/	...	...	...	...	x/	...	...	...	...		...	...
2813	Other pumps, compressors, taps and valves	x/	...	...	...	...	x/	...	...	...	...		...	...
2814	Bearings, gears, gearing and driving elements	x/	...	...	...	...	x/	...	...	...	...		...	...
2815	Ovens, furnaces and furnace burners	x/	...	...	...	...	x/	...	...	...	...		...	...
2816	Lifting and handling equipment	x/	...	...	...	...	x/	...	...	...	...		...	...
2817	Office machinery, excl.computers,etc.	x/	...	...	...	...	x/	...	...	...	...		...	...
2818	Power-driven hand tools	x/	...	...	...	...	x/	...	...	...	...		...	...
2819	Other general-purpose machinery	x/	...	...	...	...	x/	...	...	...	...		...	...
282	Special-purpose machinery	y/	13640.0	13375.2	12573.3	12827.5	y/	4942.6	4903.1	4682.1	4790.7		...w/	...
2821	Agricultural and forestry machinery	y/	13640.0	13375.2	12573.3	12827.5	y/	4942.6	4903.1	4682.1	4790.7		...	...
2822	Metal-forming machinery and machine tools	y/	...	...	...	...	y/	...	...	...	...		...	...

Code	Description	Notes	(1)	(2)	(3)	(4)	(5)	(6)	(7)	(8)	(9)	(10)
2823	Machinery for metallurgy	y/	...	...	...	...	...	...	...	...	...	...
2824	Mining, quarrying and construction machinery	y/	...	...	...	...	...	...	...	...	...	...
2825	Food/beverage/tobacco processing machinery	y/	...	...	...	...	...	...	...	...	...	...
2826	Textile/apparel/leather production machinery	y/	...	...	...	...	...	...	...	...	...	...
2829	Other special-purpose machinery	y/	...	...	...	...	...	...	...	...	...	...
2910	Motor vehicles		585.9	497.7	...	...	227.8	177.6	227.8	...	20.3	30.5
2920	Automobile bodies, trailers and semi-trailers		345.8	355.8	...	...	117.4	115.4	115.4	...	5.4	8.2
2930	Parts and accessories for motor vehicles		782.2	910.2	841.4	959.5	322.1	368.5	327.3	381.7	36.7	40.6
301	Building of ships and boats	z/	125.6	125.6	112.4	106.5	51.7	48.8	45.3	46.6	...	...
3011	Building of ships and floating structures	z/	125.6	125.6	112.4	106.5	51.7	48.8	45.3	46.6	...	...
3012	Building of pleasure and sporting boats		...	...	...	...	...	...	...	...	...	...
3020	Railway locomotives and rolling stock		2826.2	2401.6	2118.3	2563.4	619.9	621.9	570.9	607.5	58.0	43.0
3030	Air and spacecraft and related machinery		1892.6	2035.5	2117.2	1821.7	912.2	945.7	987.8	818.6	95.1	76.4
3040	Military fighting vehicles		0.1	0.1	0.1	...	0.1	-	-	-0.1	...	...
309	Transport equipment n.e.c.	A/	244.5	345.8	334.9	390.5	48.8	93.3	80.2	100.5	4.1	8.9
3091	Motorcycles	A/	244.5	345.8	334.9	390.5	48.8	93.3	80.2	100.5	4.1	8.9
3092	Bicycles and invalid carriages	A/	...	...	...	...	...	...	...	...	...	...
3099	Other transport equipment n.e.c.	A/	...	...	...	...	...	...	...	...	...	...
3100	Furniture		2921.8	2577.4	2507.3	...	1162.9	1030.1	1053.3	...	424.7	72.7
321	Jewellery, bijouterie and related articles	B/	846.3	727.5	770.4	690.0	335.5	306.4	310.1	285.9	12.9	11.2
3211	Jewellery and related articles	B/	846.3	727.5	770.4	690.0	335.5	306.4	310.1	285.9	12.9	11.2
3212	Imitation jewellery and related articles	B/	...	...	...	...	...	...	...	...	...	...
3220	Musical instruments		40.9	...	...	...	19.2	...	-	...	...	...
3230	Sports goods		86.9	142.5	135.2	...	38.0	64.4	59.6	...	12.9	10.8
3240	Games and toys		47.3	247.1	247.1	...	22.2	92.5	92.5	...	...	...
3250	Medical and dental instruments and supplies		4575.1	5209.1	4529.2	4970.3	2118.8	2311.0	2047.0	2280.9	216.6	227.3
3290	Other manufacturing n.e.c.		932.3	883.4	829.0	858.4	474.6	399.6	393.1	390.1	37.2	32.7
331	Repair of fabricated metal products/machinery	C/	3944.6	3826.7	4350.1	4072.1	1476.8	1406.9	1534.5	1469.8	158.3	323.0
3311	Repair of fabricated metal products	C/	3944.6	3826.7	4350.1	4072.1	1476.8	1406.9	1534.5	1469.8	158.3	323.0
3312	Repair of machinery	C/	...	...	...	...	...	...	...	...	...	...
3313	Repair of electronic and optical equipment	C/	...	...	...	...	...	...	...	...	...	...
3314	Repair of electrical equipment	C/	...	...	...	...	...	...	...	...	...	...
3315	Repair of transport equip., excl. motor vehicles	C/	...	...	...	...	...	...	...	...	...	...
3319	Repair of other equipment	C/	...	...	...	...	...	...	...	...	...	...
3320	Installation of industrial machinery/equipment		548.0	669.5	582.0	581.9	207.2	282.0	208.0	249.7	7.2	8.1
C	Total manufacturing		326422.8	327357.8	312278.9	314050.8	109395.4	108466.0	106667.4	106477.5	15234.2	12785.1

a/ 1061 includes 1062.
b/ 1071 includes 1072, 1073, 1074, 1075 and 1079.
c/ 1101 includes 1102, 1103 and 1104.
d/ 1311 includes 1312 and 1313.
e/ 1391 includes 1392, 1393, 1394 and 1399.
f/ 1410 includes 1420 and 1430.
g/ 151 includes 1520.
h/ 1511 includes 1512.
i/ 1621 includes 1622, 1623 and 1629.
j/ 1701 includes 1702 and 1709.
k/ 181 includes 1820.
m/ 1811 includes 1812.
n/ 2011 includes 2012 and 2013.
p/ 2021 includes 2022, 2023 and 2029.
q/ 2211 includes 2219.
r/ 2391 includes 2392, 2393, 2394, 2395, 2396 and 2399.
s/ 2431 includes 2432.
t/ 2511 includes 2512 and 2513.
u/ 2591 includes 2592, 2593 and 2599.
v/ 2651 includes 2652.

w/ 281 includes 282.
x/ 2811 includes 2812, 2813, 2814, 2815, 2816, 2817, 2818 and 2819.
y/ 2821 includes 2822, 2823, 2824, 2825, 2826 and 2829.
z/ 3011 includes 3012.
A/ 3091 includes 3092 and 3099.
B/ 3211 includes 3212.
C/ 3311 includes 3312, 3313, 3314, 3315 and 3319.

Switzerland

Index numbers of industrial production

ISIC Revision 4

(2010=100)

ISIC	Industry	Note	2005	2006	2007	2008	2009	2010	2011	2012	2013	2014	2015	2016
10	Food products	a/	87	94	97	100	98	100	101	101	101	103	101	102
11	Beverages	a/	...	...	...	...	...	...	...	...	...	...	...	...
12	Tobacco products	a/	...	...	...	...	...	...	...	...	...	...	...	...
13	Textiles	b/	110	116	129	119	99	100	110	102	100	104	95	87
14	Wearing apparel	b/	...	...	...	...	...	...	...	...	...	...	...	...
15	Leather and related products	b/	...	...	...	...	...	...	...	...	...	...	...	...
16	Wood products, excluding furniture	c/	97	99	103	103	96	100	97	92	92	91	89	88
17	Paper and paper products	c/	...	...	...	...	...	...	...	...	...	...	...	...
18	Printing and reproduction of recorded media	c/	...	...	...	...	...	...	...	...	...	...	...	...
19	Coke and refined petroleum products	d/	107	115	117	108	103	100	101	94	104	106	101	105
20	Chemicals and chemical products	d/	...	...	...	...	...	...	...	...	...	...	...	...
21	Pharmaceuticals,medicinal chemicals, etc.		58	68	84	85	94	100	104	115	120	123	124	131
22	Rubber and plastics products	e/	98	103	108	110	95	100	99	93	95	96	95	93
23	Other non-metallic mineral products	e/	...	...	...	...	...	...	...	...	...	...	...	...
24	Basic metals	f/	80	81	93	85	80	100	93	87	85	88	84	83
25	Fabricated metal products, except machinery	f/	...	...	...	...	...	...	...	...	...	...	...	...
26	Computer, electronic and optical products		87	92	103	106	89	100	110	115	113	117	115	110
27	Electrical equipment		65	78	92	100	91	100	102	103	100	101	94	93
28	Machinery and equipment n.e.c.		97	107	118	121	92	100	107	99	94	95	93	93
29	Motor vehicles, trailers and semi-trailers	g/	73	85	97	103	97	100	111	120	126	118	106	101
30	Other transport equipment	g/	...	...	...	...	...	...	...	...	...	...	...	...
31	Furniture	h/	89	95	104	107	97	100	102	106	114	113	115	115
32	Other manufacturing	h/	...	...	...	...	...	...	...	...	...	...	...	...
33	Repair and installation of machinery/equipment	h/	...	...	...	...	...	...	...	...	...	...	...	...
C	Total manufacturing		85	92	101	101	93	100	103	103	104	106	104	105

a/ 10 includes 11 and 12.
b/ 13 includes 14 and 15.
c/ 16 includes 17 and 18.
d/ 19 includes 20.
e/ 22 includes 23.
f/ 24 includes 25.
g/ 29 includes 30.
h/ 31 includes 32 and 33.

The former Yugoslav Republic of Macedonia

Supplier of information:
State Statistical Office of the Republic of Macedonia, Skopje.

Basic source of data:
Annual survey; administrative source.

Major deviations from ISIC (Revision 4):
None reported.

Reference period:
Calendar year.

Scope:
All establishments.

Method of data collection:
Not reported.

Type of enumeration:
Not reported.

Adjusted for non-response:
Not reported.

Concepts and definitions of variables:
No deviations from the standard UN concepts and definitions are reported.

Related national publications:
None reported.

The former Yugoslav Republic of Macedonia

ISIC	Industry	Establishments (number)					Number of employees (number)					Wages and salaries paid to employees (millions of Macedonia Denars)				
		Note	2012	2013	2014	2015	Note	2012	2013	2014	2015	Note	2012	2013	2014	2015
10	Food products		...	...	...	...		16246	17340	17052	17873		4204	3862	4053	4352
11	Beverages		...	...	...	...		2431	2828	2702	2807		1109	1096	1094	1274
12	Tobacco products		...	...	...	...		2503	2717	3937	3094		968	1013	1408	1197
13	Textiles		...	...	...	...		3562	3899	4867	5787		682	804	1102	1429
14	Wearing apparel		...	...	...	...		35213	36387	36882	36085		6412	6835	7430	7461
15	Leather and related products		...	...	...	...		4764	5909	5416	5324		827	978	1043	984
16	Wood products, excluding furniture		...	...	...	...		2326	2428	2584	2476		426	376	434	441
17	Paper and paper products		...	...	...	...		1491	1430	1390	1343		435	374	396	378
18	Printing and reproduction of recorded media		...	...	...	...		2620	2816	3362	3281		810	758	976	936
19	Coke and refined petroleum products		...	...	...	...		712	41a/	42	40		548	9a/	10	11
20	Chemicals and chemical products		...	...	...	...		897	978	726	680		385	386	311	305
21	Pharmaceuticals, medicinal chemicals, etc.		...	...	...	...		1544	1505	1573	1722		1174	1136	1274	1377
22	Rubber and plastics products		...	...	...	...		3972	3951	3383	3447		959	864	840	884
23	Other non-metallic mineral products		...	...	...	...		3189	3308	3229	3212		1476	1229	1294	1251
24	Basic metals		...	...	...	...		5996	5930	6467	5926		2480	2306	2591	2223
25	Fabricated metal products, except machinery		...	...	...	...		6854	6380	6251	6623		1951	1596	1725	1914
26	Computer, electronic and optical products		...	...	...	...		479	581	860	1119		188	218	292	392
27	Electrical equipment		...	...	...	...		2750	2512	2477	2351		933	817	895	872
28	Machinery and equipment n.e.c.		...	...	...	...		1395	1569	1702	1791		557	669	740	813
29	Motor vehicles, trailers and semi-trailers		...	...	...	...		979	3496	7358	9713		351	887	2343	3111
30	Other transport equipment		...	...	...	...		504	455	443	474		220	228	235	237
31	Furniture		...	...	...	...		3776	4540	4313	4569		743	814	860	954
32	Other manufacturing		...	...	...	...		1398	1804	1720	1716		287	428	433	296
33	Repair and installation of machinery/equipment		...	...	...	...		1052	789	783	1022		413	197	209	391
C	Total manufacturing		...	...	...	...		106653	113593	119519	122475		28538b/	27880b/	31988b/	33484

a/ Methodological break in 2013.
b/ Sum of available data.

The former Yugoslav Republic of Macedonia

ISIC Revision 4		Output at basic prices (millions of Macedonia Denars)					Value added at basic prices (millions of Macedonia Denars)					Gross fixed capital formation (millions of Macedonia Denars)	
ISIC	Industry	Note	2012	2013	2014	2015	Note	2012	2013	2014	2015	Note	2014	2015
10	Food products		33610	35618	35561	37792		3881	7170	8241	9158		…	…
11	Beverages		11388	11945	11025	12114		3724	3205	3477	3590		…	…
12	Tobacco products		8936	8439	8212	7339		1891	3441	3279	2134		…	…
13	Textiles		3204	3858	4456	5643		892	1132	1508	2045		…	…
14	Wearing apparel		34947	16693	17828	17081		8162	8705	9452	9124	…	…	…
15	Leather and related products		3112	2433	2555	2421		1016	1118	1245	1238		…	…
16	Wood products, excluding furniture		1756	2133	2098	2215		577	699	683	743		…	…
17	Paper and paper products		2429	2308	2424	2500		714	615	750	767		…	…
18	Printing and reproduction of recorded media		4457	5204	5629	5674		1216	1783	1797	1878		…	…
19	Coke and refined petroleum products		11485	69a/	55	55		1049	12a/	37	22	…	…	…
20	Chemicals and chemical products		1845	1937	1991	2293		646	656	633	708		…	…
21	Pharmaceuticals, medicinal chemicals, etc.		6466	5944	6490	6907		3047	2468	3355	3795		…	…
22	Rubber and plastics products		7069	8010	7922	7981		1531	1483	1852	1962		…	…
23	Other non-metallic mineral products		11434	10893	10818	11049		4131	4063	4149	4264		…	…
24	Basic metals		36806	34429	34388	31261		3868	4463	3318	4648	…	…	…
25	Fabricated metal products, except machinery		7981	7478	8228	9468		2517	2209	2651	2683		…	…
26	Computer, electronic and optical products		728	1255	2077	2814		125	330	542	626		…	…
27	Electrical equipment		8958	9169	9766	11084		2039	1397	1572	1855		…	…
28	Machinery and equipment n.e.c.		31142	40165	58746	76140		4440	1693	4376	7233		…	…
29	Motor vehicles, trailers and semi-trailers		822	3077	9310	14839		281	638	2223	4245	…	…	…
30	Other transport equipment		777	818	1070	1140		59	113	280	388		…	…
31	Furniture		2863	3803	4063	4224		946	1314	1355	1586		…	…
32	Other manufacturing		904	1440	1402	1022		431	639	683	429		…	…
33	Repair and installation of machinery/equipment		1196	792	746	1158		601	342	325	614		…	…
C	Total manufacturing		234315	217910	246860	274217		47784	49758	57783	65735		16691	20105

a/ Methodological break in 2013.

The former Yugoslav Republic of Macedonia

- 770 -

ISIC	Industry	Note	Index numbers of industrial production (2010=100)											
			2005	2006	2007	2008	2009	2010	2011	2012	2013	2014	2015	2016
10	Food products		86	87	93	100	97	100	105	122	120	123	136	132
11	Beverages		89	89	101	111	110	100	86	94	101	92	103	104
12	Tobacco products		84	85	85	86	84	100	121	103	112	119	92	94
13	Textiles		147	143	126	130	87	100	95	89	161	171	197	219
14	Wearing apparel		159	173	149	119	105	100	112	104	118	123	132	122
15	Leather and related products		113	97	97	88	84	100	105	86	90	83	67	57
16	Wood products, excluding furniture		162	151	151	116	68	100	85	87	64	78	94	123
17	Paper and paper products		88	90	93	96	114	100	84	137	114	125	141	139
18	Printing and reproduction of recorded media		60	87	76	120	152	100	87	114	104	102	97	93
19	Coke and refined petroleum products		105	118	115	117	107	100	80	28	9	-	-	-
20	Chemicals and chemical products		121	117	111	125	118	100	106	85	84	93	89	64
21	Pharmaceuticals,medicinal chemicals, etc.		87	91	95	119	103	100	104	111	108	114	119	130
22	Rubber and plastics products		110	89	91	115	113	100	108	129	143	172	164	194
23	Other non-metallic mineral products		118	132	137	133	117	100	110	88	94	99	100	119
24	Basic metals		90	106	141	133	76	100	115	102	92	93	99	88
25	Fabricated metal products, except machinery		61	70	102	155	215	100	107	93	54	57	64	57
26	Computer, electronic and optical products		...	...	...	...	...	...	...	...	...	...	...	...
27	Electrical equipment		188	226	183	234	176	100	133	101	111	144	136	154
28	Machinery and equipment n.e.c.		70	62	101	112	86	100	205	236	295	362	439	536
29	Motor vehicles, trailers and semi-trailers		210	146	107	99	61	100	95	58	27	409	561	854
30	Other transport equipment		111	119	158	129	69	100	180	214	221	257	229	226
31	Furniture		78	60	65	174	124	100	116	117	141	140	158	152
32	Other manufacturing		227	142	88	54	54	100	94	84	76	98	97	95
33	Repair and installation of machinery/equipment		258	413	281	336	173	100	68	50	62	59	43	52
C	Total manufacturing		102	108	114	121	108	100	110	107	110	120	127	134

ISIC Revision 4

Tunisia

Concepts and definitions of variables:
Wages and salaries refers to direct wages and salaries only.

Related national publications:
Statistiques issues du Répertoire National des Entreprises (Entreprises et emploi salarié formel du secteur privé), published by the Institut National de la Statistique, Tunis.

Supplier of information:
Institut National de la Statistique, Tunis.

Basic source of data:
Administrative sources.

Major deviations from ISIC (Revision 4):
Data presented in accordance with ISIC (Revision 4) were originally classified according to the national classification system (NAT2009).

Reference period:
Calendar year.

Scope:
All privately owned enterprises.

Method of data collection:
Information was derived from official administrative data.

Type of enumeration:
Complete enumeration.

Adjusted for non-response:
Not reported.

Tunisia

ISIC Revision 4		Number of enterprises (number)					Number of employees (number)					Wages and salaries paid to employees (millions of Tunisian Dinars)				
ISIC	Industry	Note	2013	2014	2015	2016	Note	2013	2014	2015	2016	Note	2013	2014	2015	2016
10	Food products		12414	12933	13479	14112		54921	55081	57100	56708		429.3	434.6	501.7	541.9
11	Beverages		103	105	108	109		7765	7552	7693	7522		97.2	99.1	108.3	116.5
12	Tobacco products		10	10	10	10		274	253	240	261		2.7	2.8	3.2	3.8
13	Textiles		4379	4438	4523	4495		32112	32648	33644	35020		185.6	199.0	217.2	247.1
14	Wearing apparel		11394	11863	12242	12678		131109	125917	121847	116929		655.6	660.0	680.8	709.6
15	Leather and related products		2574	2610	2631	2666		27555	26897	26700	23568		165.4	168.3	174.9	166.4
16	Wood products, excluding furniture		8382	8618	8927	9273		2796	2893	2897	2919		13.8	14.8	16.5	17.6
17	Paper and paper products		554	597	618	637		7781	8075	8249	8245		78.1	83.0	85.8	93.9
18	Printing and reproduction of recorded media		1488	1555	1645	1716		4285	4150	3989	4175		34.3	33.4	35.2	38.5
19	Coke and refined petroleum products		16	16	19	18		121	114	117	121		2.1	2.7	2.5	2.9
20	Chemicals and chemical products		1774	1878	2000	2094		10071	10355	10451	10399		129.8	139.1	147.5	158.4
21	Pharmaceuticals, medicinal chemicals, etc.		101	106	109	116		5260	5513	5813	6327		78.7	82.1	93.3	103.7
22	Rubber and plastics products		1360	1466	1555	1611		15132	15608	16450	17127		128.3	135.7	153.5	168.8
23	Other non-metallic mineral products		3537	3697	3854	3988		30252	29865	28567	27227		280.0	295.1	310.9	318.0
24	Basic metals		315	343	373	390		2786	2878	2914	2585		29.7	32.6	33.7	34.9
25	Fabricated metal products, except machinery		10774	11311	11935	12525		24528	24843	24001	24577		194.5	208.6	218.7	242.4
26	Computer, electronic and optical products		441	455	452	469		20386	22899	22205	22341		161.5	181.0	191.8	212.5
27	Electrical equipment		799	818	846	854		39294	41575	43690	44901		294.9	318.9	365.0	430.0
28	Machinery and equipment n.e.c.		476	524	569	627		5809	6244	6738	7154		53.6	61.6	73.3	84.4
29	Motor vehicles, trailers and semi-trailers		263	261	262	260		36152	33844	34888	34187		280.5	289.1	316.2	332.8
30	Other transport equipment		231	250	261	268		5053	5382	5599	5708		50.0	56.6	65.2	73.2
31	Furniture		6890	6965	7053	7116		12020	11475	11098	10797		79.1	79.3	82.4	87.2
32	Other manufacturing		3149	3232	3370	3444		6325	6735	6295	6459		39.3	44.9	46.1	50.5
33	Repair and installation of machinery/equipment		3561	3779	3966	4066		5370	5878	5658	6029		51.2	56.3	60.8	66.8
C	Total manufacturing		74985	77830	80807	83542		487155	486674	486839	481284		3515.1	3678.7	3984.5	4301.8

Tunisia

ISIC Revision 4		Output (valuation not defined) (millions of Tunisian Dinars)					Value added (valuation not defined) (millions of Tunisian Dinars)					Gross fixed capital formation (millions of Tunisian Dinars)		
ISIC	Industry	Note	2013	2014	2015	2016	Note	2013	2014	2015	2016	Note	2015	2016
10	Food products		11190.8	11106.0	13252.1	...		2236.8	2220.5	2647.5	...		440.0	...
11	Beverages		...	...	...	...		...	...	...	...		...	...
12	Tobacco products		337.0	354.5	374.6	...		101.2	106.4	112.5	...		22.0	...
13	Textiles		6700.0	6863.8	6548.7	...		1937.7	1977.3	1889.4	...		138.7	...
14	Wearing apparel		...	...	...	...		...	...	...	...		...	...
15	Leather and related products		947.3	1051.4	1013.4	...		267.3	295.9	284.8	...			...
16	Wood products, excluding furniture		760.2	791.6	826.1	...		281.9	293.6	306.3	...		...	...
17	Paper and paper products		916.1	971.9	1185.9	...		251.6	265.6	322.8	...		250.0	...
18	Printing and reproduction of recorded media		...	...	...	...		...	...	...	...		...	...
19	Coke and refined petroleum products		2402.3	2364.9	1202.6	...		59.3	74.5	98.1	...		87.2	...
20	Chemicals and chemical products		5644.2	5370.8	5140.3	...		1161.0	1130.0	1110.5	...		220.0	...
21	Pharmaceuticals, medicinal chemicals, etc.		...	...	...	...		...	...	...	...		...	...
22	Rubber and plastics products		799.2	828.7	834.4	...		258.8	268.3	270.1	...		...	...
23	Other non-metallic mineral products		2599.9	2889.8	2996.1	...		1125.6	1253.3	1311.6	...		205.0	...
24	Basic metals		1173.9	1186.4	1168.3	...		342.3	346.1	341.4	...		420.0	...
25	Fabricated metal products, except machinery		...	...	...	...		...	...	...	...		...	...
26	Computer, electronic and optical products		...	...	...	...		...	...	...	...		...	...
27	Electrical equipment		...	...	...	...		...	...	...	...		...	...
28	Machinery and equipment n.e.c.		708.2	757.7	806.9	...		283.6	306.1	323.5	...		...	...
29	Motor vehicles, trailers and semi-trailers		...	...	...	...		...	...	...	...		...	...
30	Other transport equipment		2834.1	3193.1	3256.0	...		861.8	959.4	976.9	...		...	...
31	Furniture		1521.2	1586.7	1677.9	...		443.3	462.4	488.0	...		...	...
32	Other manufacturing		...	...	...	...		...	...	...	...		...	...
33	Repair and installation of machinery/equipment		716.0	742.5	774.7	...		248.0	257.7	268.5	...		...	...
C	Total manufacturing		40112.2	40987.6	42036.3	...		11266.7	11835.8	12359.7	...		1782.9	...

Tunisia

Index numbers of industrial production

ISIC Revision 4

(2010=100)

ISIC	Industry	Note	2005	2006	2007	2008	2009	2010	2011	2012	2013	2014	2015	2016
10	Food products		:	:	:	:	:	100	103	109	111	113	119	116
11	Beverages		:	:	:	:	:	100	104	118	118	123	119	123
12	Tobacco products		:	:	:	:	:	100	98	94	91	92	105	109
13	Textiles		:	:	:	:	:	100	103	95	94	95	95	93
14	Wearing apparel		:	:	:	:	:	100	99	94	102	100	95	95
15	Leather and related products		:	:	:	:	:	100	104	109	110	99	94	94
16	Wood products, excluding furniture		:	:	:	:	:	100	101	105	106	108	111	111
17	Paper and paper products		:	:	:	:	:	100	107	109	113	127	115	116
18	Printing and reproduction of recorded media		:	:	:	:	:	100	93	92	84	66	87	86
19	Coke and refined petroleum products		:	:	:	:	:	:	:	:	:	:	:	:
20	Chemicals and chemical products		:	:	:	:	:	100	63	76	82	80	70	78
21	Pharmaceuticals, medicinal chemicals, etc.		:	:	:	:	:	100	113	129	137	153	151	152
22	Rubber and plastics products		:	:	:	:	:	100	105	102	102	99	97	86
23	Other non-metallic mineral products		:	:	:	:	:	100	89	95	102	106	106	104
24	Basic metals		:	:	:	:	:	100	98	80	94	99	97	91
25	Fabricated metal products, except machinery		:	:	:	:	:	100	92	90	89	90	88	91
26	Computer, electronic and optical products		:	:	:	:	:	100	101	108	105	108	111	111
27	Electrical equipment		:	:	:	:	:	100	110	109	108	110	109	113
28	Machinery and equipment n.e.c.		:	:	:	:	:	100	100	101	97	97	100	101
29	Motor vehicles, trailers and semi-trailers		:	:	:	:	:	100	105	111	107	113	110	116
30	Other transport equipment		:	:	:	:	:	100	111	79	99	105	103	104
31	Furniture		:	:	:	:	:	100	112	113	106	120	112	113
32	Other manufacturing		:	:	:	:	:	:	:	:	:	:	:	:
33	Repair and installation of machinery/equipment		:	:	:	:	:	:	:	:	:	:	:	:
C	Total manufacturing		:	:	:	:	:	100	96	98	101	102	101	102

Turkey

Supplier of information:
Turkish Statistical Institute, Ankara.

Basic source of data:
Annual surveys; business register.

Major deviations from ISIC (Revision 4):
Data presented in ISIC Revision 4 were originally classified according to NACE revision 2.

Reference period:
Calendar year.

Scope:
All enterprises that are active during the reference period.

Method of data collection:
Web-based electronic questionnaires.

Type of enumeration:
Full enumeration for enterprises with multiple local units or with more than 20 employees; sampling method is used for enterprises having single local unit or with less than 20 employees.

Adjusted for non-response:
Yes.

Concepts and definitions of variables:
No deviations from the standard UN concepts and definitions are reported.

Related national publications:
Annual Industry and Service Statistics, published by the Turkish Statistical Institute, Ankara.

Turkey

ISIC	Industry	Number of enterprises (number)					Number of employees (thousands)					Wages and salaries paid to employees (millions of Turkish Liras)				
		Note	2012	2013	2014	2015	Note	2012	2013	2014	2015	Note	2012	2013	2014	2015
1010	Processing/preserving of meat		501	526	535	559		42.5	41.3	47.2	48.7		800.6	879.0	1062.2	1233.1
1020	Processing/preserving of fish, etc.		65	82	115	117		5.4	6.0	6.6	7.2		89.5	109.6	145.7	163.9
1030	Processing/preserving of fruit,vegetables		1558	1643	1713	1730		49.1	53.3	54.9	58.0		840.5	986.3	1096.7	1300.2
1040	Vegetable and animal oils and fats		908	1005	1087	1140		12.3	13.1	15.0	14.8		271.8	346.5	402.8	463.8
1050	Dairy products		1940	2055	2178	1533		37.2	38.7	39.9	40.1		830.9	774.8	934.3	1101.8
106	Grain mill products,starches and starch products		3469	3073	3102	3143		21.3	22.0	21.0	21.8		348.6	398.3	459.8	511.2
1061	Grain mill products		3456	3056	3085	3126		20.1	20.8	19.7	20.4		316.5	361.0	419.4	461.7
1062	Starches and starch products		13	17	17	17		1.1	1.2	1.3	1.3		32.2	37.2	40.5	49.5
107	Other food products		31399	32444	32895	33401		222.7	238.4	244.1	236.0		4074.1	4734.1	5423.7	5843.7
1071	Bakery products		29752	30617	30815	31334		148.2	160.6	167.9	158.1		1880.6	2279.1	2687.3	2829.6
1072	Sugar		68	14	8	8		18.0	17.0	16.1	16.1		853.4	884.2	895.1	974.9
1073	Cocoa, chocolate and sugar confectionery		1029	1121	1197	1138		25.3	26.8	28.2	27.0		530.9	645.1	752.5	822.7
1074	Macaroni, noodles, couscous, etc.		49	56	65	72		3.3	3.6	4.0	3.8		72.2	86.0	107.0	108.9
1075	Prepared meals and dishes		24	41	60	63		1.6	2.2	2.6	2.9		19.5	30.2	39.5	53.9
1079	Other food products n.e.c.		477	595	750	786		26.3	28.3	25.3	28.0		717.5	809.4	942.3	1053.6
1080	Prepared animal feeds		395	457	405	407		9.2	11.6	10.2	10.2		186.3	268.1	266.3	303.5
110	Beverages		484	509	530	499		13.9	14.6	15.6	15.8		464.7	519.8	609.3	690.2
1101	Distilling, rectifying and blending of spirits		6	9	10	11		...	1.2	...	...		...	33.3	40.1	...
1102	Wines		109	118	128	143		1.1	...	1.6	1.6		23.5	...	...	40.1
1103	Malt liquors and malt		4	3	4	5		...	...	...	...		...	...	...	...
1104	Soft drinks,mineral waters,other bottled waters		365	379	388	340		11.0	11.3	12.0	12.2		309.3	338.8	383.4	453.7
1200	Tobacco products		24	30	28	31		4.9	4.7	4.0	4.2		307.7	338.2	361.2	381.2
131	Spinning, weaving and finishing of textiles		9265	8967	7786	8467		216.1	231.7	246.1	245.0		3221.9	3975.8	4678.3	5402.7
1311	Preparation and spinning of textile fibres		1615	1507	1298	1212		83.1	84.8	90.0	84.5		1152.6	1333.9	1618.8	1804.6
1312	Weaving of textiles		4224	3709	3376	3931		80.9	91.3	98.7	100.7		1362.4	1764.9	2036.4	2400.3
1313	Finishing of textiles		3426	3751	3112	3324		52.1	55.6	57.4	59.8		706.9	877.0	1023.2	1197.8
139	Other textiles		13492	13715	12320	12941		161.9	164.5	171.8	171.1		2323.3	2790.0	3272.9	3679.4
1391	Knitted and crocheted fabrics		888	925	759	705		22.9	24.7	26.3	27.0		317.7	410.0	514.5	628.2
1392	Made-up textile articles, except apparel		8067	8194	7258	7642		72.5	72.1	74.9	75.8		1007.1	1152.1	1340.4	1519.5
1393	Carpets and rugs		643	602	500	518		26.5	28.7	31.8	30.3		360.3	501.1	605.6	658.9
1394	Cordage, rope, twine and netting		151	154	136	158		1.2	1.3	1.1	1.3		19.4	22.8	22.4	22.2
1399	Other textiles n.e.c.		3743	3840	3667	3918		38.7	37.8	37.6	36.8		618.8	704.0	790.1	850.6
1410	Wearing apparel, except fur apparel		49836	50050	48407	48349		437.3	443.6	431.4	433.3		5568.1	6290.7	6832.3	7578.5
1420	Articles of fur		86	90	101	110		2.1	2.1	2.0	1.4		27.4	30.1	31.7	28.0
1430	Knitted and crocheted apparel		3338	3086	3071	2959		43.8	46.1	47.7	46.2		585.6	717.2	829.7	939.1
151	Leather;luggage,handbags,saddlery,harness;fur		2677	2689	2552	2458		19.2	21.6	21.5	17.9		265.0	321.8	378.9	356.2
1511	Tanning/dressing of leather; dressing of fur		1073	987	943	957		10.1	11.7	12.2	9.8		136.7	181.4	222.1	194.9
1512	Luggage,handbags,etc.;saddlery/harness		1604	1702	1609	1501		9.2	9.9	9.2	8.1		128.3	140.5	156.8	161.2
1520	Footwear		4928	5051	4878	4622		38.2	38.5	41.2	38.0		442.6	512.2	607.7	656.1
1610	Sawmilling and planing of wood		4934	3784	3123	3445		8.6	9.6	7.0	6.6		87.9	113.4	89.8	93.7

Code	Description												
162	Wood products, cork, straw, plaiting materials	17821	19393	19750	19515	46.8	44.6	41.2	37.7	1034.5	859.2	699.2	602.6
1621	Veneer sheets and wood-based panels	368	307	350	413	17.5	16.7	15.9	14.5	587.4	490.1	410.5	341.5
1622	Builders' carpentry and joinery	15165	17025	17237	17131	18.7	17.9	16.8	14.9	284.0	231.9	186.8	160.2
1623	Wooden containers	1369	1191	1140	998	8.9	8.3	7.1	7.1	138.5	113.4	85.0	85.9
1629	Other wood products;articles of cork, straw	919	870	1023	973	1.6	1.8	1.4	1.3	24.6	23.8	16.9	15.0
170	Paper and paper products	2676	2501	2409	2201	64.0	61.6	53.3	49.6	1969.1	1710.9	1385.4	1172.1
1701	Pulp, paper and paperboard	268	295	270	236	7.2	7.0	5.6	5.0	254.9	193.1	152.4	128.1
1702	Corrugated paper and paperboard	1370	1248	1197	1138	30.2	30.3	26.4	24.9	870.5	835.5	687.6	578.8
1709	Other articles of paper and paperboard	1038	958	942	827	26.5	24.3	21.3	19.7	843.8	682.2	545.4	465.1
181	Printing and service activities related to printing	10794	11615	12215	12883	41.7a/	47.3	51.3	53.1	940.3a/	848.4	899.2	867.4
1811	Printing	10288	11056	11563	12269	39.7	45.2	48.9	50.5	889.5	804.8	855.1	813.6
1812	Service activities related to printing	506	559	652	614	...	2.1	2.4	2.6	...	43.6	44.0	53.8
1820	Reproduction of recorded media	16	29	31	44	...a/	...	0.1	0.1	...a/	...	1.7	2.1
1910	Coke oven products	5	9	11	14	7.7b/	7.7b/	0.1	0.1	710.1	631.2	561.0	524.3
1920	Refined petroleum products	226	225	260	249	...b/	...b/	7.6	7.5	...	...	...	...
201	Basic chemicals,fertilizers, etc.	958	1092	991	881	19.2	18.8	17.7	17.0	928.0	808.7	675.9	636.0
2011	Basic chemicals	260	298	313	317	6.6	7.0	6.8	6.5	331.0	311.2	250.9	257.5
2012	Fertilizers and nitrogen compounds	...	...	...	...	...	...	...	...	...	...	...	...
2013	Plastics and synthetic rubber in primary forms	698	794	678	564	12.6	11.8	10.9	10.5	597.0	497.4	425.0	378.5
202	Other chemical products	2353	2647	2556	2777	48.3	...	...	43.2	...	...	1269.2	...
2021	Pesticides and other agrochemical products	102	84	76	95	2.2	...	...	2.1	...	...	...	...
2022	Paints,varnishes;printing ink and mastics	624	803	806	960	13.2	13.7	13.8	14.2	595.1	499.4	483.3	440.3
2023	Soap,cleaning and cosmetic preparations	1258	1335	1271	1353	22.4	22.4	20.7	17.8	1027.6	882.3	749.8	507.4
2029	Other chemical products n.e.c.	369	425	403	369	10.4	10.4	9.6	9.2	519.5	435.9	391.7	321.5
2030	Man-made fibres	6	3	3	4	2.7	...	...	2.4	...	...	...	...
2100	Pharmaceuticals,medicinal chemicals, etc.	286	260	307	250	31.3	30.8	29.5	29.1	1951.3	1683.7	1636.2	1566.1
221	Rubber products	1168	1142	1251	1080	44.1	39.4	34.9	33.0	1787.0	1437.7	1145.0	982.2
2211	Rubber tyres and tubes	170	131	222	164	12.1	9.0	8.7	8.3	763.6	621.4	480.7	408.0
2219	Other rubber products	998	1011	1029	916	32.0	30.4	26.2	24.7	1023.4	816.4	664.2	574.2
2220	Plastics products	15440	16803	17493	16512	158.5	154.0	146.4	140.8	3614.1	3107.0	2649.5	2342.1
2310	Glass and glass products	1003	1055	1548	1524	32.0	31.1	33.5	30.6	1193.8	997.1	939.6	867.5
239	Non-metallic mineral products n.e.c.	12785	12833	12254	11949	207.6	205.0	199.3	184.9	5279.7	4660.1	3954.5	3443.5
2391	Refractory products	51	47	42	41	2.6	2.4	2.3	2.1	100.3	81.3	71.2	63.0
2392	Clay building materials	729	628	536	567	37.4	35.8	37.3	35.2	853.3	750.5	633.2	606.9
2393	Other porcelain and ceramic products	728	766	698	654	18.0	17.2	15.5	16.6	513.0	435.4	310.8	315.9
2394	Cement, lime and plaster	205	170	206	144	17.4	17.1	16.8	16.6	869.6	774.3	727.1	683.9
2395	Articles of concrete, cement and plaster	2755	2763	2386	2142	72.7	69.2	64.5	55.1	1713.8	1446.6	1195.7	917.3
2396	Cutting, shaping and finishing of stone	7976	8184	8157	8236	50.9	55.1	55.0	52.7	908.7	901.3	749.1	645.1
2399	Other non-metallic mineral products n.e.c.	341	275	229	165	8.7	8.2	7.9	6.5	320.9	270.8	267.3	211.4
2410	Basic iron and steel	626	598	564	433	72.8	70.0	68.1	65.5	3705.7	3237.0	2875.9	2517.6
2420	Basic precious and other non-ferrous metals	747	701	668	592	31.7	30.2	27.9	25.1	938.7	801.6	694.9	556.0
243	Casting of metals	1594	1627	1497	1384	28.6	29.1	26.3	27.0	940.2	815.5	671.1	600.1
2431	Casting of iron and steel	993	1073	1002	957	21.3	22.4	20.4	20.9	722.1	639.4	524.5	464.0
2432	Casting of non-ferrous metals	601	554	495	427	7.4	6.7	5.8	6.2	218.1	176.1	146.6	136.1
251	Struct.metal products, tanks, reservoirs	28044	27261	28423	28830	119.5	122.3	118.7	107.5	2716.4	2366.3	2094.4	1678.3

continued

Turkey

ISIC Revision 4			Number of enterprises (number)					Number of employees (thousands)					Wages and salaries paid to employees (millions of Turkish Liras)				
ISIC	Industry	Note	Note	2012	2013	2014	2015	Note	2012	2013	2014	2015	Note	2012	2013	2014	2015
2511	Structural metal products			28059	27689	26415	27112		87.0	95.5	99.6	95.9		1229.5	1524.9	1763.9	1985.9
2512	Tanks, reservoirs and containers of metal			727	679	778	852		18.8	21.1	20.7	21.4		413.8	521.0	549.2	674.1
2513	Steam generators, excl. hot water boilers			44	55	68	80		1.7	2.1	2.0	2.2		34.9	48.6	53.2	56.4
2520	Weapons and ammunition			177	222	265	298		12.1	13.0	13.5	14.3		458.3	525.8	569.7	628.3
259	Other metal products;metal working services			25083	26990	28260	29578		146.4	145.3	150.0	153.9		2353.6	2718.3	3143.1	3704.0
2591	Forging,pressing,stamping,roll-forming of metal			464	482	573	659		12.6	13.4	14.6	15.3		272.6	323.1	381.5	458.9
2592	Treatment and coating of metals machining			16126	17386	19197	20516		49.2	46.7	43.9	45.3		658.7	714.5	764.5	895.3
2593	Cutlery, hand tools and general hardware			2720	2776	2716	2652		30.0	30.6	31.6	32.2		523.8	617.2	721.5	855.4
2599	Other fabricated metal products n.e.c.			5773	6346	5774	5751		54.6	54.5	59.8	61.2		898.4	1063.4	1275.6	1494.4
2610	Electronic components and boards			149	198	202	220		3.8	4.1	4.8	4.6		107.9	132.8	149.8	141.4
2620	Computers and peripheral equipment			18	19	20	24		1.4	1.1	1.1	1.0		47.1	26.9	28.5	27.2
2630	Communication equipment			95	151	139	141		3.2	3.8	4.2	4.5		91.7	127.7	141.6	124.5
2640	Consumer electronics			25	39	40	49		7.4	...	...	...		155.3	...	...	...
265	Measuring,testing equipment; watches, etc.			254	287	302	318		10.8	12.6	13.3	13.8		483.5	637.3	731.2	861.7
2651	Measuring/testing/navigating equipment,etc.			247	278	292	306		10.4	12.3	13.0	13.4		479.6	632.9	726.5	855.3
2652	Watches and clocks			7	9	10	12		0.3	0.3	0.3	0.4		3.9	4.4	4.6	6.3
2660	Irradiation/electromedical equipment,etc.			10	11	12	16		...	...	0.3	0.4		...	5.0	5.7	11.7
2670	Optical instruments and photographic equipment			5	8	9	11		...	0.3	0.3	...		...	...	...	...
2680	Magnetic and optical media			14	19	20	24		0.5	0.5	0.6	0.5		9.5	11.4	13.1	13.4
2710	Electric motors,generators,transformers,etc.			1689	1527	1579	1711		30.6	36.1	37.9	39.3		1028.5	1242.9	1449.5	1703.9
2720	Batteries and accumulators			48	52	55	63		2.5	2.5	2.7	2.8		93.3	109.0	116.4	119.1
273	Wiring and wiring devices			433	534	551	591		21.9	22.9	23.3	23.6		490.7	545.7	656.4	726.9
2731	Fibre optic cables			29	30	27	26		2.1	2.1	2.2	2.0		54.2	62.8	70.8	76.0
2732	Other electronic and electric wires and cables			222	199	214	252		11.3	12.1	13.0	12.9		258.4	280.8	378.8	382.6
2733	Wiring devices			182	305	310	313		8.5	8.7	8.2	8.7		178.1	202.2	206.8	268.3
2740	Electric lighting equipment			2842	3240	3315	3414		19.2	19.0	20.0	20.9		318.9	353.3	387.0	431.4
2750	Domestic appliances			1788	1781	1530	1543		49.3	51.2	53.3	56.7		1515.8	1668.9	1938.3	2143.5
2790	Other electrical equipment			350	380	342	337		4.0	4.2	4.2	4.3		88.0	92.1	110.8	131.0
281	General-purpose machinery			5768	6242	6382	6718		100.4	108.2	117.2	121.3		2137.9	2477.5	3165.6	3590.1
2811	Engines/turbines,excl.aircraft,vehicle engines			58	72	84	105		11.6	11.3	13.1	13.2		407.7	433.7	659.4	694.4
2812	Fluid power equipment			163	159	194	230		3.9	4.1	4.5	4.9		94.6	110.1	151.1	164.5
2813	Other pumps, compressors, taps and valves			905	971	889	966		18.0	18.9	20.6	20.2		358.7	425.3	529.2	568.9
2814	Bearings, gears, gearing and driving elements			171	202	246	273		7.3	6.9	8.0	8.2		177.5	184.9	226.3	277.3
2815	Ovens, furnaces and furnace burners			802	848	929	952		5.6	6.4	6.3	5.0		104.9	122.4	129.3	125.9
2816	Lifting and handling equipment			1008	1074	1051	1154		15.3	17.8	19.7	21.4		269.5	324.6	410.2	501.6
2817	Office machinery, excl.computers,etc.			...	...	...	...		...	...	...	...		...	...	...	...
2818	Power-driven hand tools			...	...	...	...		...	...	...	...		...	...	...	...
2819	Other general-purpose machinery			2644	2896	2970	3016		38.5	42.6	44.7	48.1		720.6	869.6	1049.5	1248.8
282	Special-purpose machinery			5913	6228	5934	6356		76.0	80.4	78.4	81.2		1468.7	1703.4	1911.8	2271.8
2821	Agricultural and forestry machinery			1246	1303	1046	1078		15.8	16.5	16.8	19.3		323.5	390.1	478.0	595.0
2822	Metal-forming machinery and machine tools			1157	1218	1176	1230		14.6	15.8	15.2	16.6		297.0	345.6	336.2	449.6

Code	Description											
2823	Machinery for metallurgy	52.5	53.8	54.0	45.2	2.1	2.2	2.3	2.0	140	112	89	72
2824	Mining, quarrying and construction machinery	416.6	398.2	318.6	289.0	13.9	14.8	13.2	13.6	988	824	713	636
2825	Food/beverage/tobacco processing machinery	313.5	260.6	226.3	216.3	12.0	12.6	12.4	11.9	1066	965	1015	1002
2826	Textile/apparel/leather production machinery	191.6	161.5	181.5	140.2	8.3	7.9	11.9	10.1	1074	1105	1197	1149
2829	Other special-purpose machinery	253.0	223.6	187.3	157.6	9.1	9.0	8.4	8.0	780	706	693	651
2910	Motor vehicles	3067.1	2361.2	2138.2	2021.9	46.2	42.3	43.5	43.4	39	34	33	30
2920	Automobile bodies, trailers and semi-trailers	383.0	323.9	261.1	224.8	16.0	16.2	14.8	14.6	1691	1497	1511	1665
2930	Parts and accessories for motor vehicles	4210.1	3469.4	2961.8	2383.4	128.1	118.2	110.6	99.9	2700	2327	2414	2079
301	Building of ships and boats	384.2	377.2	313.6	276.0	9.9	9.8	9.9	9.1	645	637	580	678
3011	Building of ships and floating structures	249.1	261.2	191.3	159.2	6.2	6.6	6.2	5.3	234	224	204	238
3012	Building of pleasure and sporting boats	135.1	116.0	122.2	116.9	3.7	3.3	3.6	3.7	411	413	376	440
3020	Railway locomotives and rolling stock	288.1	249.3	222.7	215.4	4.9	4.7	4.1	4.1	22	18	16	14
3030	Air and spacecraft and related machinery	720.6	597.5	515.0	420.9	9.2	8.6	8.2	7.0	40	34	29	22
3040	Military fighting vehicles	…	…	…	…	…	…	…	…	5	4	5	4
309	Transport equipment n.e.c.	…	…	…	…	…	…	…	…	201	168	141	112
3091	Motorcycles	14.6	19.9	23.4	18.8	0.9	1.1	1.1	1.2	30	26	25	20
3092	Bicycles and invalid carriages	54.8	55.3	43.9	33.6	2.4	2.4	2.3	2.0	129	107	88	70
3099	Other transport equipment n.e.c.	…	…	…	…	…	…	…	…	42	35	28	22
3100	Furniture	3143.8	2681.9	2343.8	2050.6	169.9	161.3	161.5	159.3	34477	33859	37021	39046
321	Jewellery, bijouterie and related articles	340.1	319.3	290.6	230.7	19.0	19.9	19.1	17.7	3991	4399	4346	4510
3211	Jewellery and related articles	…	293.7	260.4	210.8	…	19.0	18.3	17.0	…	4255	4254	4437
3212	Imitation jewellery and related articles	…	…	…	…	…	…	…	…	227	248	…	158
3220	Musical instruments	3.2	3.7	3.1	2.9	0.2	0.3	0.2	0.3	102	104	80	65
3230	Sports goods	33.7	32.6	22.6	18.4	1.4	1.5	1.3	1.0	401	324	284	325
3240	Games and toys	58.9	58.0	41.9	34.1	3.4	3.6	3.1	2.7	3005	2645	2447	2127
3250	Medical and dental instruments and supplies	472.1	389.0	368.0	298.3	21.8	21.1	19.9	18.4	1192	1187	1316	1181
3290	Other manufacturing n.e.c.	261.7	223.9	201.8	149.9	10.9	10.6	10.6	9.4	12354	11419	10385	9594
331	Repair of fabricated metal products/machinery	1442.4	1157.2	803.3	893.9	51.6	50.8	45.3	42.7	118	111	89	83
3311	Repair of fabricated metal products	11.1	13.4	14.5	9.0	0.7	0.8	1.0	0.8	6591	5966	4977	4829
3312	Repair of machinery	236.8	207.4	193.3	158.2	11.3	11.2	12.0	10.8	384	327	326	313
3313	Repair of electronic and optical equipment	22.2	25.9	16.4	18.3	0.8	0.9	0.7	0.8	3474	3212	2659	2261
3314	Repair of electrical equipment	98.5	63.9	62.6	48.7	3.8	3.7	4.1	3.6	1769	1785	2317	2094
3315	Repair of transport equip., excl. motor vehicles	1072.9	845.8	…	651.5	35.0	34.1	27.4	26.1	18	18	17	14
3319	Repair of other equipment	1.0	0.8	…	…	0.1	0.1	-	…	348	353	244	201
3320	Installation of industrial machinery/equipment	110.7	106.0	59.9	59.4	4.4	5.2	3.2	3.0	12354	11419	10385	9594
C	Total manufacturing	92864.1	80804.7	70050.6	60797.1	3427.4	3383.0	3277.9	3126.7	335311	332834	340438	336893

a/ 181 includes 1820.
b/ 1910 includes 1920.

Turkey

ISIC	Industry	Output (valuation not defined) (millions of Turkish Liras)					Value added at factor values (millions of Turkish Liras)					Gross fixed capital formation (millions of Turkish Liras)		
		Note	2012	2013	2014	2015	Note	2012	2013	2014	2015	Note	2014	2015
1010	Processing/preserving of meat		14931	14245	19447	20852		1782	1613	2370	2406		672	700
1020	Processing/preserving of fish, etc.		1116	1513	1903	2510		243	258	411	596		77	132
1030	Processing/preserving of fruit,vegetables		18396	20314	24568	31104		1997	2561	2909	3670		1061	1265
1040	Vegetable and animal oils and fats		11365	12370	14053	15771		700	963	1149	1540		374	448
1050	Dairy products		14492	14789	17434	19095		1927	1965	2116	2390		1111	1028
106	Grain mill products,starches and starch products		11568	14713	14388	16182		1109	1408	1445	1581		510	499
1061	Grain mill products		10712	13501	12957	14568		952	1208	1230	1319		459	422
1062	Starches and starch products		856	1212	1431	1615		157	199	215	261		51	77
107	Other food products		33134	39070	45049	48296		7481	9028	10405	11812		2872	2539
1071	Bakery products		11878	15076	17214	17751		2931	3905	4365	4764		1057	1139
1072	Sugar		5806	5969	6314	6796		1505	1670	1895	1997		...	230
1073	Cocoa, chocolate and sugar confectionery		6684	7899	9588	9933		1471	1582	1778	2160		1036	460
1074	Macaroni, noodles, couscous, etc.		1792	2259	2533	2695		169	201	260	341		107	94
1075	Prepared meals and dishes		251	367	...	449		43	60	71	96		11	18
1079	Other food products n.e.c.		6723	7500	...	10673		1362	1610	2036	2454		...	598
1080	Prepared animal feeds		5544	7917	7405	8502		501	1193	805	1021		243	258
110	Beverages		6550	7053	8111	9117		1562	1500	1760	2010		823	723
1101	Distilling, rectifying and blending of spirits		296	483	487	592		...	...	...	106		...	31
1102	Wines		...	...	...	...		55	44	78	...		35	...
1103	Malt liquors and malt		...	...	...	...		...	...	...	...		...	...
1104	Soft drinks,mineral waters,other bottled waters		4712	5125	6022	6771		896	968	1123	1324		546	441
1200	Tobacco products		4741	4547	5315	6545		1417	1291	1531	1503		314	451
131	Spinning, weaving and finishing of textiles		36669	42362	47605	51638		7132	9404	10828	13305		3890	4040
1311	Preparation and spinning of textile fibres		15777	17885	19730	19936		2713	3530	3866	5020		1842	1697
1312	Weaving of textiles		14528	17185	19700	22684		3078	4203	5047	5990		1414	1666
1313	Finishing of textiles		6363	7293	8176	9018		1341	1672	1915	2295		634	677
139	Other textiles		27372	30133	35546	37684		5233	6350	7696	9106		2476	2567
1391	Knitted and crocheted fabrics		6349	6570	7812	8506		789	978	1245	1550		559	486
1392	Made-up textile articles, except apparel		9861	10803	12636	13246		1992	2373	2822	3335		662	782
1393	Carpets and rugs		5166	5927	7346	8094		1054	1371	1708	2140		808	709
1394	Cordage, rope, twine and netting		166	195	234	266		37	47	54	52		17	16
1399	Other textiles n.e.c.		5831	6639	7519	7572		1362	1582	1866	2029		431	574
1410	Wearing apparel, except fur apparel		42124	47195	53304	56444		8709	10230	11649	12646		1591	2180
1420	Articles of fur		311	365	375	240		49	59	59	47		9	12
1430	Knitted and crocheted apparel		4709	5353	5933	6403		1115	1384	1567	1841		420	428
151	Leather;luggage,handbags,saddlery,harness;fur		2704	3275	3740	3561		485	605	679	696		98	198
1511	Tanning/dressing of leather; dressing of fur		2003	2418	2870	2573		291	382	458	450		77	174
1512	Luggage,handbags,etc.;saddlery/harness		701	857	870	988		195	224	221	245		20	24
1520	Footwear		4043	4760	5054	5315		807	933	1073	1227		222	253
1610	Sawmilling and planing of wood		956	1060	851	945		166	191	173	174		39	57

Code	Description										
162	Wood products, cork, straw, plaiting materials	9100	9986	12184	13300	2126	2163	2702	3106	595	639
1621	Veneer sheets and wood-based panels	6564	7183	8619	9496	1658	1587	2024	2319	419	438
1622	Builders' carpentry and joinery	1375	1676	2187	2235	268	343	405	479	104	111
1623	Wooden containers	1045	1005	1216	1417	171	207	233	272	61	85
1629	Other wood products;articles of cork,straw	116	123	162	153	29	25	41	36	10	5
170	Paper and paper products	15409	18170	22829	26343	3020	3463	4527	5310	2574	2437
1701	Pulp, paper and paperboard	2333	2450	3276	4130	490	555	733	926	348	207
1702	Corrugated paper and paperboard	6832	8175	10143	10738	1356	1576	2062	2091	1134	758
1709	Other articles of paper and paperboard	6244	7545	9410	11475	1174	1332	1732	2293	...	...
181	Printing and service activities related to printing	6973	7878	8152	9569	1543	1837a/	1680	2052a/	424	453a/
1811	Printing	6653	7584	7876	9268	1450	1741	1592	1949	398	434
1812	Service activities related to printing	320	294	276	301	93	...	88	...	26	...
1820	Reproduction of recorded media	20	16	...	...	5	...a/	...	...a/	...	...a/
1910	Coke oven products b/	42172	42199	39521	37821	1872	1939	1531	4346	2575b/	2325b/
1920	Refined petroleum products ..b/	...	...	...	...	...	...	...	...	..b/	..b/
201	Basic chemicals,fertilizers, etc.	13397	14509	16942	18855	1982	2299	2857	3728	1063	1193
2011	Basic chemicals	3385	4013	4537	4864	806	...	...	...	378	...
2012	Fertilizers and nitrogen compounds	...	...	...	...	...	...	...	...	...	...
2013	Plastics and synthetic rubber in primary forms	10012	10497	12405	13991	1177	1369	1737	2451	685	673
202	Other chemical products	18555	...	...	...	3453	...	...	...	...	...
2021	Pesticides and other agrochemical products	18555	18555	...	...	...	...	...	...	...	...
2022	Paints,varnishes;printing ink and mastics	6638	6642	7070	7499	1120	1366	1430	1726	364	402
2023	Soap,cleaning and cosmetic preparations	7041	10928	12019	12438	1346	1751	2211	2834	1009	517
2029	Other chemical products n.e.c.	4876	5608	6400	6921	988	1324	1236	1593	269	414
2030	Man-made fibres	...	...	...	...	...	...	...	...	...	...
2100	Pharmaceuticals,medicinal chemicals, etc.	8114	8465	9452	12246	2610	2719	3132	4280	676	741
221	Rubber products	8914	10058	11503	13543	2233	2906	3365	4106	852	1322
2211	Rubber tyres and tubes	4443	4686	5075	5669	1102	1364	1481	1814	438	800
2219	Other rubber products	4471	5372	6427	7874	1131	1542	1883	2293	414	522
2220	Plastics products	30833	35252	40722	45557	5482	6702	7528	9262	2712	3273
2310	Glass and glass products	5972	7436	8569	9306	1880	1988	2526	2829	647	1107
239	Non-metallic mineral products n.e.c.	36393	45792	51043	56131	8540	11245	12917	15522	5130	7136
2391	Refractory products	634	975	994	1008	100	241	174	248	232	48
2392	Clay building materials	4284	4921	5727	6510	1203	1499	1738	2015	772	706
2393	Other porcelain and ceramic products	2079	2003	2128	2498	653	687	579	1001	191	229
2394	Cement, lime and plaster	9805	12666	12896	13507	2902	4215	4658	5126	1377	2072
2395	Articles of concrete, cement and plaster	13019	17176	20677	23261	1869	2681	3515	4235	1800	3206
2396	Cutting, shaping and finishing of stone	4357	5151	5771	6065	1404	1531	1740	2034	555	645
2399	Other non-metallic mineral products n.e.c.	2214	2899	2851	3282	408	391	514	864	204	230
2410	Basic iron and steel	68585	72867	79802	81387	5850	8582	10403	12612	3740	4045
2420	Basic precious and other non-ferrous metals	17832	18970	21415	23485	2051	2589	2701	3543	1425	1033
243	Casting of metals	5033	5465	6396	6963	1241	1601	1735	2131	607	748
2431	Casting of iron and steel	3963	4224	4968	5239	1001	1306	1394	1696	502	567
2432	Casting of non-ferrous metals	1070	1241	1428	1723	241	295	341	435	105	180
251	Struct.metal products, tanks, reservoirs	17953	20969	22529	26059	3326	4323	4814	5948	1328	1508

continued

Turkey

ISIC	Industry	Note	Output (valuation not defined) (millions of Turkish Liras)				Note	Value added at factor values (millions of Turkish Liras)				Note	Gross fixed capital formation (millions of Turkish Liras)	
			2012	2013	2014	2015		2012	2013	2014	2015		2014	2015
2511	Structural metal products		12538	14969	15699	18262		2221	2944	3272	4087		928	1092
2512	Tanks, reservoirs and containers of metal		5082	5652	6459	7256		1038	1275	1436	1721		356	384
2513	Steam generators, excl. hot water boilers		332	348	371	541		67	105	106	140		44	31
2520	Weapons and ammunition		1864	2213	2469	3030		987	972	1263	1746		306	253
259	Other metal products;metal working services		22491	25830	28454	32894		5028	5962	6827	8173		2149	2469
2591	Forging,pressing,stamping,roll-forming of metal		2586	2735	2932	3416		646	668	768	1030		199	225
2592	Treatment and coating of metals;machining		6512	7362	7744	9147		1354	1590	1758	1832		480	650
2593	Cutlery, hand tools and general hardware		3639	4170	4715	5423		1087	1289	1450	1729		404	448
2599	Other fabricated metal products n.e.c.		9754	11563	13062	14909		1942	2415	2851	3582		1066	1146
2610	Electronic components and boards		627	894	1227	1410		199	247	307	316		71	197
2620	Computers and peripheral equipment		1416	1594	...	...		91	151	...	126		...	4
2630	Communication equipment		508	741	869	939		172	269	293	297		52	55
2640	Consumer electronics		...	...	...	...		290	...	...	...		...	...
265	Measuring,testing equipment; watches, etc.		2661	3541	4110	5082		1004	1262	1429	1927		372	251
2651	Measuring/testing/navigating equipment,etc.		2639	3514	4080	5039		999	1256	1422	1918		371	249
2652	Watches and clocks		22	27	31	43		5	6	7	9		1	2
2660	Irradiation/electromedical equipment,etc.		25	...	55	105		...	12	12	27		...	6
2670	Optical instruments and photographic equipment		...	54	63	61		...	23	23	...		...	...
2680	Magnetic and optical media		66	75	90	109		22	23	24	30		4	3
2710	Electric motors,generators,transformers,etc.		8386	11996	11952	13526		2092	3246	3162	3526		548	649
2720	Batteries and accumulators		1036	1168	1428	1565		234	299	338	420		47	71
273	Wiring and wiring devices		9707	10808	12495	13215		1200	1471	1676	2057		623	388
2731	Fibre optic cables		1480	1645	1741	1755		152	230	238	261		53	28
2732	Other electronic and electric wires and cables		6731	7383	9043	9416		594	737	959	1155		461	272
2733	Wiring devices		1496	1780	1712	2044		454	504	480	641		109	88
2740	Electric lighting equipment		2611	2903	3295	3500		631	716	782	917		200	257
2750	Domestic appliances		16949	19476	21246	24126		3265	4002	4282	5213		892	1007
2790	Other electrical equipment		632	722	839	935		176	160	237	245		63	76
281	General-purpose machinery		18151	22396	26671	30208		4517	5867	7017	8423		2254	2770
2811	Engines/turbines,excl.aircraft,vehicle engines		2695	3238	4280	4818		949	1117	1536	2030		...	188
2812	Fluid power equipment		881	1002	1164	1229		181	255	333	332		74	188
2813	Other pumps, compressors, taps and valves		3207	4138	4982	5256		762	947	1184	1298		202	...
2814	Bearings, gears, gearing and driving elements		1294	1426	1799	2106		376	437	555	687		188	226
2815	Ovens, furnaces and furnace burners		860	1081	1150	973		212	254	150	245			69
2816	Lifting and handling equipment		2578	3211	4055	4562		586	725	913	1056		260	304
2817	Office machinery, excl.computers,etc.		...	...	...	...		...	...	...	...		...	...
2818	Power-driven hand tools													
2819	Other general-purpose machinery		6594	8214	9138	11185		1451	2113	2323	2757		942	874
282	Special-purpose machinery		15154	16179	18273	20916		3637	4342	4522	5430		1675	1546
2821	Agricultural and forestry machinery		4472	5127	5940	7269		1002	1294	1312	1738		491	403
2822	Metal-forming machinery and machine tools		2662	2860	3190	3484		689	803	807	975		457	313

Code	Description										
2823	Machinery for metallurgy	426	418	428	459	89	111	103	110	...	37
2824	Mining, quarrying and construction machinery	3083	2972	3442	3599	714	785	850	945	303	349
2825	Food/beverage/tobacco processing machinery	1856	1803	2309	2777	447	486	614	754	167	195
2826	Textile/apparel/leather production machinery	1507	1553	1316	1465	344	452	332	380	82	98
2829	Other special-purpose machinery	1149	1447	1648	1864	352	412	504	528	...	151
2910	Motor vehicles	34806	42275	44825	56978	5306	5955	4884	8296	6885	2747
2920	Automobile bodies, trailers and semi-trailers	2994	4174	4157	5084	497	626	740	1210	375	226
2930	Parts and accessories for motor vehicles	20486	24444	28893	35181	4633	6486	7480	9315	2146	2658
301	Building of ships and boats	2829	3628	4680	4298	534	469	1044	834	530	746
3011	Building of ships and floating structures	2142	2622	3875	3498	479	504	835	621	374	646
3012	Building of pleasure and sporting boats	686	1007	806	800	56	-35	209	214	156	100
3020	Railway locomotives and rolling stock	711	726	810	...	237	291	350	425	...	99
3030	Air and spacecraft and related machinery	1921	2124	3038	4213	845	919	1420	2232	232	237
3040	Military fighting vehicles	...	...	...	893	...	...	...	...	...	...
309	Transport equipment n.e.c.	...	...	...	...	...	...	...	...	48	13
3091	Motorcycles	223	265	236	255	44	45	45	45	19	13
3092	Bicycles and invalid carriages	334	380	486	550	66	90	86	105	26	25
3099	Other transport equipment n.e.c.	...	...	...	88	...	...	...	...	2	...
3100	Furniture	15963	17669	19268	21772	3485	4147	4480	5301	1109	1209
321	Jewellery, bijouterie and related articles	5129	7133	5557	6057	475	478	545	607	163	140
3211	Jewellery and related articles	4893	6925	5293	...	374	360	420	...	160	...
3212	Imitation jewellery and related articles	...	...	...	...	...	...	...	...	...	...
3220	Musical instruments	14	20	22	17	4	6	6	6	-	1
3230	Sports goods	171	241	240	294	39	57	67	81	34	32
3240	Games and toys	268	389	446	453	68	99	122	120	38	35
3250	Medical and dental instruments and supplies	1921	2213	2489	2658	599	685	840	1008	148	185
3290	Other manufacturing n.e.c.	1319	1581	1802	1947	356	450	512	590	129	120
331	Repair of fabricated metal products/machinery	4335	5800	7237	8976	1515	1367	2152	3203	371	496
3311	Repair of fabricated metal products	39	57	74	57	...	...	28	...	...	3
3312	Repair of machinery	962	1331	1347	1553	312	344	402	462	54	63
3313	Repair of electronic and optical equipment	135	193	234	136	41	41	47	48	6	4
3314	Repair of electrical equipment	334	557	437	470	102	109	114	138	8	12
3315	Repair of transport equip., excl. motor vehicles	2862	3658	5140	6756	1043	849	1559	2536	301	...
3319	Repair of other equipment	4	4	5	5	...	...	2	...	...	...
3320	Installation of industrial machinery/equipment	387	485	705	910	113	129	168	229	29	34
C	Total manufacturing	750398	854138	956836	1062739	132598	162584	184946	227524	64666	66601

a/ 181 includes 1820.
b/ 1910 includes 1920.

Turkey

Index numbers of industrial production

ISIC Revision 4

(2010=100)

ISIC	Industry	Note	2005	2006	2007	2008	2009	2010	2011	2012	2013	2014	2015	2016
10	Food products		80	85	88	91	90	100	107	111	117	122	122	125
11	Beverages		81	83	85	92	90	100	102	110	108	110	112	110
12	Tobacco products		99	109	110	117	115	100	97	117	113	124	136	139
13	Textiles		116	118	117	103	90	100	102	107	110	111	107	108
14	Wearing apparel		105	102	108	98	89	100	99	105	107	107	111	113
15	Leather and related products		90	104	96	91	83	100	103	100	102	92	82	76
16	Wood products, excluding furniture		52	69	78	84	84	100	113	113	113	126	124	124
17	Paper and paper products		79	85	89	90	88	100	110	115	120	128	135	141
18	Printing and reproduction of recorded media		74	80	88	91	94	100	120	124	131	132	138	127
19	Coke and refined petroleum products		111	117	118	119	94	100	108	111	107	102	134	138
20	Chemicals and chemical products		78	86	89	84	83	100	107	109	112	118	122	126
21	Pharmaceuticals,medicinal chemicals, etc.		69	77	91	99	101	100	110	123	117	134	164	187
22	Rubber and plastics products		83	87	94	91	83	100	112	112	115	120	121	121
23	Other non-metallic mineral products		90	99	101	99	87	100	106	107	110	112	110	111
24	Basic metals		86	98	108	106	90	100	111	117	123	123	123	123
25	Fabricated metal products, except machinery		87	95	105	98	83	100	120	127	131	135	138	132
26	Computer, electronic and optical products		185	150	133	114	96	100	107	123	129	142	147	158
27	Electrical equipment		70	82	88	86	86	100	114	116	127	127	127	130
28	Machinery and equipment n.e.c.		90	98	104	99	77	100	129	130	139	143	141	142
29	Motor vehicles, trailers and semi-trailers		84	91	99	106	74	100	118	112	119	122	140	146
30	Other transport equipment		111	127	223	257	141	100	127	108	101	122	140	142
31	Furniture		69	68	86	97	90	100	117	106	118	126	135	121
32	Other manufacturing		63	80	83	98	92	100	108	114	114	105	112	100
33	Repair and installation of machinery/equipment		99	110	168	131	97	100	105	99	107	131	164	179
C	Total manufacturing		87	94	100	99	87	100	111	113	118	121	126	128

Ukraine

Supplier of information:
State Statistics Service of Ukraine, Kiev.

Basic source of data:
Census; sample survey.

Major deviations from ISIC (Revision 4):
None reported.

Reference period:
Calendar year.

Scope:
All registered enterprises.

Method of data collection:
Mail and e-mail questionnaires.

Type of enumeration:
Complete enumeration for medium and large enterprises; sample survey for small enterprises.

Adjusted for non-response:
Yes.

Concepts and definitions of variables:
No deviations from the standard UN concepts and definitions are reported.

Related national publications:
Statistical Yearbook of Ukraine; Activity of Economic Entities; Activity of Small-Scaled Entities, all published by the State Statistics Service of Ukraine, Kiev.

Ukraine

ISIC	Industry	Note	Number of enterprises (number) 2013	2014	2015	2016	Note	Number of employees (number) 2013	2014	2015	2016	Note	Wages and salaries paid to employees (millions of Ukrainian Hryvnias) 2013	2014	2015	2016
1010	Processing/preserving of meat		882	750	762	691		62059	52455	49137	46138		2008	1691	1939	2174
1020	Processing/preserving of fish, etc.		257	193	181	171		7476	5903	4904	6424		169	145	148	235
1030	Processing/preserving of fruit,vegetables		357	335	325	297		21031	19322	15756	14243		903	928	888	986
1040	Vegetable and animal oils and fats		507	471	508	535		24970	26287	25258	27822		1189	1540	1820	2522
1050	Dairy products		467	401	392	355		62506	55232	50172	48889		1958	1985	2035	2430
106	Grain mill products,starches and starch products		748	657	678	651		19396	15421	16063	16906		608	536	760	928
1061	Grain mill products		731	641	659	632		17715	13988	14642	15544		522	452	646	801
1062	Starches and starch products		17	16	19	19		1681	1433	1421	1362		86	84	114	127
107	Other food products		2125	1827	1810	1645		144049	130188	114287	110833		4803	4739	4817	5951
1071	Bakery products		1285	1088	1061	954		82333	72610	67021	61939		2266	2148	2311	2648
1072	Sugar		98	81	75	54		14767	12641	10231	9078		523	519	515	562
1073	Cocoa, chocolate and sugar confectionery		149	126	121	116		26244	20582	15709	16607		1358	1075	1089	1291
1074	Macaroni, noodles, couscous, etc.		77	70	72	53		1599	1470	1507	1472		41	37	45	54
1075	Prepared meals and dishes		82	67	69	59		3522	3550	3118	3731		113	128	144	259
1079	Other food products n.e.c.		434	395	412	409		15584	19335	16701	18006		502	832	713	1138
1080	Prepared animal feeds		270	252	253	236		6396	5686	6537	5410		218	213	330	304
110	Beverages		783	633	583	513		50018	34432	33497	32210		2551	2116	2517	2735
1101	Distilling, rectifying and blending of spirits		103	85	69	58		15029	8123	8930	9478		607	310	565	604
1102	Wines		105	66	64	63		9661	3949	3987	4230		375	134	177	206
1103	Malt liquors and malt		90	83	78	80		13256	11870	11133	10332		1049	1117	1155	1255
1104	Soft drinks,mineral waters,other bottled waters		485	399	372	312		12072	10490	9447	8170		520	555	619	670
1200	Tobacco products		11	9	10	10		4453	4475	3913	3631		674	703	862	806
131	Spinning, weaving and finishing of textiles		107	90	88	66		4160	3644	4080	3601		98	96	130	138
1311	Preparation and spinning of textile fibres		31	29	28	19		1374	586	536	526		35	18	22	27
1312	Weaving of textiles		37	27	28	23		1612	2006	2450	2102		46	61	83	88
1313	Finishing of textiles		39	34	32	24		1174	1052	1094	973		17	17	25	23
139	Other textiles		544	457	467	409		13862	13174	11963	13158		337	366	415	568
1391	Knitted and crocheted fabrics		20	19	18	16		559	589	726	…		11	10	13	…
1392	Made-up textile articles, except apparel		354	290	289	250		9359	8748	7468	8480		235	254	287	411
1393	Carpets and rugs		9	9	12	11		543	533	519	…		20	21	21	…
1394	Cordage, rope, twine and netting		35	28	29	30		485	408	387	412		11	11	13	18
1399	Other textiles n.e.c.		126	111	119	102		2916	2896	2863	2976		59	70	80	101
1410	Wearing apparel, except fur apparel		1949	1682	1663	1432		54351	42972	41672	42638		1104	1041	1417	1848
1420	Articles of fur		31	29	31	25		444	418	336	268		10	6	7	6
1430	Knitted and crocheted apparel		112	114	116	90		3493	3860	3678	3847		88	98	111	151
151	Leather;luggage,handbags,saddlery,harness;fur		126	117	113	93		4943	4519	4781	6118		146	139	220	395
1511	Tanning/dressing of leather; dressing of fur		55	52	48	35		1877	1658	1478	1659		63	48	46	62
1512	Luggage,handbags,etc.;saddlery/harness		71	65	65	58		3066	2861	3303	4459		83	91	174	333
1520	Footwear		320	280	287	226		15330	14331	14328	14787		334	373	465	639
1610	Sawmilling and planing of wood		1496	1392	1473	1273		12483	11222	12896	15298		264	267	407	593

ISIC Revision 4

Code	Description												
162	Wood products, cork, straw, plaiting materials	1259	937	700	659	24704	23705	23275	25457	1315	1566	1557	1728
1621	Veneer sheets and wood-based panels	825	602	430	359	11960	11298	10354	10130	104	108	95	100
1622	Builders' carpentry and joinery	248	190	175	188	7675	7694	8547	10203	668	849	882	1001
1623	Wooden containers	64	52	35	48	1919	1726	1532	1859	169	185	181	198
1629	Other wood products;articles of cork,straw	122	94	61	64	3150	2987	2842	3265	374	424	399	429
170	Paper and paper products	1714	1334	1182	1277	27254	27957	30376	35927	893	946	936	1065
1701	Pulp, paper and paperboard	317	221	407	230	4728	4643	7204	6666	51	52	48	55
1702	Corrugated paper and paperboard	790	598	330	611	11385	11427	10127	14779	286	282	284	299
1709	Other articles of paper and paperboard	606	514	446	436	11141	11887	13045	14482	556	612	604	711
181	Printing and service activities related to printing	990	912	812	775	18471	19337	22890	25116	1547	1751	1771	1978
1811	Printing	920	849	751	674	16491	17054	20589	21436	1196	1336	1358	1484
1812	Service activities related to printing	70	63	55	56	1980	2283	2301	2611	351	415	413	447
1820	Reproduction of recorded media	8	1	7	45	89	49	179	1069	21	32	39	47
1910	Coke oven products	:	1130	984	1047	:	16318	16910	19394	16	14	12	18
1920	Refined petroleum products	:	802	656	808	:	10806	11707	14578	82	111	111	144
201	Basic chemicals,fertilizers, etc.	3174	3043	2701	3625	46397	50839	53023	75867	466	516	494	567
2011	Basic chemicals	1141	1120	749	1435	19457	22366	16795	33620	285	321	308	365
2012	Fertilizers and nitrogen compounds	1743	1715	1681	1908	23329	24758	30104	35519	99	100	93	98
2013	Plastics and synthetic rubber in primary forms	290	209	271	283	3611	3715	6124	6728	82	95	93	104
202	Other chemical products	1398	1045	977	1075	21587	20998	23258	29398	787	851	819	921
2021	Pesticides and other agrochemical products	:	29	22	23	:	583	543	719	41	53	47	54
2022	Paints,varnishes;printing ink and mastics	326	234	210	234	5330	5087	5494	6000	203	215	211	246
2023	Soap,cleaning and cosmetic preparations	501	458	399	369	6777	7013	7506	8169	264	276	265	292
2029	Other chemical products n.e.c.	534	324	346	450	8901	8315	9715	14510	279	307	296	329
2030	Man-made fibres	:	13	6	6	:	358	239	245	11	15	12	14
2100	Pharmaceuticals,medicinal chemicals, etc.	3221	2387	1821	1614	24077	22796	23454	24197	196	229	233	248
221	Rubber products	545	427	442	430	9208	9941	11623	12728	203	211	204	247
2211	Rubber tyres and tubes	:	255	288	266	:	5462	6656	6683	22	20	23	32
2219	Other rubber products	:	171	155	165	:	4479	4967	6045	181	191	181	215
2220	Plastics products	1935	1507	1180	1273	36731	35096	38018	44894	1673	1769	1805	2109
2310	Glass and glass products	695	525	452	508	11208	10350	11325	14225	250	273	263	309
239	Non-metallic mineral products n.e.c.	4288	3458	3042	3198	70398	71393	77097	92356	2281	2625	2637	3125
2391	Refractory products	314	267	271	280	5058	5305	6600	7754	59	59	56	74
2392	Clay building materials	648	556	505	456	14336	14947	15554	17145	415	513	520	582
2393	Other porcelain and ceramic products	161	139	117	134	3077	3466	3597	4324	91	102	93	113
2394	Cement, lime and plaster	650	535	534	570	7095	7261	8463	10289	67	71	70	95
2395	Articles of concrete, cement and plaster	1922	1519	1216	1339	30463	30287	31457	38510	1083	1251	1265	1528
2396	Cutting, shaping and finishing of stone	80	71	78	105	3021	3147	3924	5460	353	406	425	488
2399	Other non-metallic mineral products n.e.c.	514	372	321	315	7348	6980	7502	8874	213	223	208	245
2410	Basic iron and steel	13329	12960	12179	11121	142315	165470	180896	192208	322	325	308	354
2420	Basic precious and other non-ferrous metals	884	843	580	582	13372	13467	12232	13427	104	111	93	116
243	Casting of metals	174	154	166	219	4072	4212	5494	7100	118	125	132	150
2431	Casting of iron and steel	141	127	143	196	3144	3403	4644	6107	79	83	89	100
2432	Casting of non-ferrous metals	33	27	23	23	928	809	850	993	39	42	43	50
251	Struct.metal products, tanks, reservoirs	1006	852	825	1074	22109	23451	26876	34099	1193	1288	1288	1514

continued

Ukraine

ISIC	Industry	Note	Number of enterprises (number)				Note	Number of employees (number)				Note	Wages and salaries paid to employees (millions of Ukrainian Hryvnias)			
			2013	2014	2015	2016		2013	2014	2015	2016		2013	2014	2015	2016
2511	Structural metal products		1267	1081	1075	958		23594	17856	14819	14239		717	505	483	609
2512	Tanks, reservoirs and containers of metal		190	160	171	191		7639	6359	6566	5695		251	216	274	276
2513	Steam generators, excl. hot water boilers		57	47	42	44		2866	2661	2066	2175		107	104	95	122
2520	Weapons and ammunition		30	27	36	42		7261	6428	7547	9628		338	290	440	646
259	Other metal products;metal working services		2063	1776	1852	1760		60507	47690	43775	41260		1938	1748	2044	2396
2591	Forging,pressing,stamping,roll-forming of metal		147	119	121	112		6707	4681	3019	2389		178	124	103	103
2592	Treatment and coating of metals;machining		786	705	727	715		13580	11370	9723	10167		385	423	430	531
2593	Cutlery, hand tools and general hardware		211	185	186	167		7369	5963	5649	4176		198	173	219	191
2599	Other fabricated metal products n.e.c.		919	767	818	766		32851	25676	25384	24528		1178	1029	1292	1571
2610	Electronic components and boards		132	106	97	90		3528	2565	2493	2707		97	87	90	152
2620	Computers and peripheral equipment		126	114	104	77		2973	2841	2665	1890		361	111	118	152
2630	Communication equipment		125	115	113	90		3986	3278	2811	5295		113	109	156	434
2640	Consumer electronics		48	32	33	22		6084	2777	2205	...		217	155	187	...
265	Measuring,testing equipment; watches, etc.		318	311	297	284		20800	19406	15249	15689		636	789	891	1436
2651	Measuring/testing/navigating equipment,etc.		311	305	292	281		20737	19341	15204	...		635	788	890	...
2652	Watches and clocks		7	6	5	3		63	65	45	...		1	1	1	...
2660	Irradiation/electromedical equipment,etc.		83	70	59	44		1158	1078	773	802		36	42	41	60
2670	Optical instruments and photographic equipment		38	36	36	30		2681	3224	2945	3008		73	104	136	194
2680	Magnetic and optical media		7	8	7	7		91	72	54	...		2	1	1	...
2710	Electric motors,generators,transformers,etc.		465	412	450	425		40479	35463	29135	26345		1502	1404	1282	1377
2720	Batteries and accumulators		40	30	24	24		3445	2792	2028	2082		138	114	119	151
273	Wiring and wiring devices		107	108	109	103		9808	9641	8372	8187		379	421	462	545
2731	Fibre optic cables		-	2	2	3		-	...a/	...a/	...a/		-	...a/	...a/	...a/
2732	Other electronic and electric wires and cables		71	73	71	64		6444	6329	5306	5346		263	255	266	365
2733	Wiring devices		36	33	36	36		3364	...a/	...a/	...a/		116	...a/	...a/	...a/
2740	Electric lighting equipment		126	115	122	130		5050	4618	3964	3884		147	140	151	175
2750	Domestic appliances		101	90	93	90		8292	7238	6222	5711		266	222	181	226
2790	Other electrical equipment		183	152	151	136		7187	5700	6780	7807		246	222	363	553
281	General-purpose machinery		1204	1103	1061	1053		97023	86694	73843	70975		3836	3612	3820	4458
2811	Engines/turbines,excl.aircraft,vehicle engines		58	48	41	49		27349	26252	22294	21336		1312	1414	1448	1609
2812	Fluid power equipment		118	105	102	93		7404	5756	4626	4504		261	207	196	246
2813	Other pumps, compressors, taps and valves		119	115	114	117		23777	22707	20235	18768		956	833	971	1062
2814	Bearings, gears, gearing and driving elements		82	70	65	60		6072	5037	4283	4019		236	193	207	265
2815	Ovens, furnaces and furnace burners		43	39	46	48		1860	593	1109	754		71	14	44	44
2816	Lifting and handling equipment		178	174	178	189		9304	9640	7575	7440		330	397	365	448
2817	Office machinery, excl.computers,etc.		13	15	15	15		769	...a/	...a/	...a/		21	...a/	...a/	...a/
2818	Power-driven hand tools		3	2	2	3		215	...a/	...a/	...a/		8	...a/	...a/	...a/
2819	Other general-purpose machinery		590	535	498	479		20273	15984	13069	13584		640	534	559	761
282	Special-purpose machinery		1215	1023	1070	1033		77211	64863	62137	59328		2854	2647	2934	3480
2821	Agricultural and forestry machinery		305	274	287	294		18753	17571	19040	18400		548	559	683	808
2822	Metal-forming machinery and machine tools		144	115	108	99		3828	3379	3188	3192		85	97	113	136

Code	Description												
2823	Machinery for metallurgy	1220	1097	909	841	14618	15981	14841	16166	68	71	68	70
2824	Mining, quarrying and construction machinery	642	527	588	806	10725	11621	14389	21564	188	196	177	246
2825	Food/beverage/tobacco processing machinery	332	236	198	213	5451	5259	5488	6595	141	139	134	161
2826	Textile/apparel/leather production machinery	3	6	3	4	109	113	156	197	8	9	7	10
2829	Other special-purpose machinery	338	273	292	357	6833	6935	9039	10108	235	260	248	279
2910	Motor vehicles	440	369	411	466	8648	8776	12175	16327	42	45	54	61
2920	Automobile bodies, trailers and semi-trailers	93	75	58	50	1820	1942	1902	1996	66	76	66	74
2930	Parts and accessories for motor vehicles	3130	2142	1428	1136	40498	35509	34662	32996	149	159	164	180
301	Building of ships and boats	108	76	111	294	1833	1674	3684	8717	98	130	134	225
3011	Building of ships and floating structures	57	41	84	276	1158	1042	2912	8018	67	84	85	170
3012	Building of pleasure and sporting boats	51	35	26	19	675	632	772	699	31	46	49	55
3020	Railway locomotives and rolling stock	1099	1123	1695	2807	24063	33969	50262	65773	96	106	92	117
3030	Air and spacecraft and related machinery	3296	3100	2574	2524	48576	54895	58232	62491	76	93	82	85
3040	Military fighting vehicles	837	624	328	315	11438	10424	7055	8361	21	20	13	11
309	Transport equipment n.e.c.	45	34	36	51	1002	678	948	1245	23	28	30	32
3091	Motorcycles	...	...	...	...	...a/	...	...	...	-	1	3	2
3092	Bicycles and invalid carriages	43	31	30	46	969	620	807	1107	19	20	20	24
3099	Other transport equipment n.e.c.	2	...a/	...a/	...a/	33	...a/	...a/	...a/	4	7	7	6
3100	Furniture	1614	1275	1031	998	32444	32833	35253	38172	1161	1387	1401	1591
321	Jewellery, bijouterie and related articles	126	99	97	118	4056	3857	4897	6161	232	285	292	345
3211	Jewellery and related articles	126	99	97	118	4050	3843	4883	6147	225	274	283	338
3212	Imitation jewellery and related articles	...	...	...	...	6	14	14	14	7	11	9	7
3220	Musical instruments	3	2	2	2	73	63	80	96	9	10	14	14
3230	Sports goods	134	117	102	86	1801	1956	2073	2191	33	58	58	56
3240	Games and toys	59	36	23	35	1614	1430	1205	1571	71	80	84	95
3250	Medical and dental instruments and supplies	297	240	203	208	5521	5508	5857	6281	198	219	215	232
3290	Other manufacturing n.e.c.	76	103	145	141	2671	3395	4511	4923	177	214	211	258
331	Repair of fabricated metal products/machinery	3237	2565	2380	2173	54177	53446	61000	65149	3491	3842	3818	4584
3311	Repair of fabricated metal products	50	29	33	38	1053	894	1068	1029	110	119	113	127
3312	Repair of machinery	1869	1407	1362	1056	28707	26516	32286	33296	2030	2198	2193	2612
3313	Repair of electronic and optical equipment	145	135	86	126	2166	2219	2631	2990	352	421	415	501
3314	Repair of electrical equipment	370	328	334	278	6684	7212	9612	8826	628	711	708	849
3315	Repair of transport equip., excl. motor vehicles	757	642	508	638	14687	16007	14309	17957	290	293	288	399
3319	Repair of other equipment	46	24	57	36	880	598	1094	1051	81	100	101	96
3320	Installation of industrial machinery/equipment	345	331	290	342	6396	7480	8414	10870	856	1036	1119	1329
C	Total manufacturing	91570	77345	68826	71723	1422291	1470634	1610991	1864589	32435	36000	35878	41446

a/ Data suppressed due to confidentiality rules.

Ukraine

ISIC	Industry	Output Note	Output 2013	2014	2015	2016	VA Note	VA 2013	2014	2015	2016	GFCF Note	GFCF 2015	2016
			(millions of Ukrainian Hryvnias)					(millions of Ukrainian Hryvnias)					(millions of Ukrainian Hryvnias)	
1010	Processing/preserving of meat		31590	32458	42210	43083		5695	6083	6913	6632		1269	1837
1020	Processing/preserving of fish, etc.		2360	2271	2625	3919		535	617	254	559		52	90
1030	Processing/preserving of fruit,vegetables		12410	14931	15670	18476		3368	3792	3212	3269		555	584
1040	Vegetable and animal oils and fats		49050	87708	91295	149757		15968	33836	22587	39656		2945	4240
1050	Dairy products		32734	33367	38432	43242		5311	5961	5637	7554		1315	1671
106	Grain mill products,starches and starch products		9796	9968	16442	20232		2610	3149	4883	5656		504	1141
1061	Grain mill products		7631	7571	13306	16129		1604	1715	3327	3775		388	922
1062	Starches and starch products		2165	2397	3135	4103		1006	1435	1556	1881		116	219
107	Other food products		54148	63837	80476	84683		13555	16761	24098	22294		4750	5090
1071	Bakery products		17635	18260	25582	24270		5412	5706	8271	7049		501	866
1072	Sugar		4739	9119	14234	10774		188	1395	6065	2622		1399	1643
1073	Cocoa, chocolate and sugar confectionery		20279	19669	19234	22634		5703	6507	6236	7485		1745	1413
1074	Macaroni, noodles, couscous, etc.		638	741	1009	1065		97	109	197	151		19	35
1075	Prepared meals and dishes		1088	1332	1922	3233		245	225	466	555		67	141
1079	Other food products n.e.c.		9770	14717	18495	22707		1909	2818	2862	4433		1019	991
1080	Prepared animal feeds		5884	7146	25327	10178		1252	1795	8822	2905		175	302
110	Beverages		40149	31154	41395	46338		3028	8761	12945	12263		1809	2618
1101	Distilling, rectifying and blending of spirits		14433	7353	12112	13247		-2480	1366	3505	3414		250	294
1102	Wines		4692	2697	4443	5356		944	619	1240	1495		106	178
1103	Malt liquors and malt		14835	14551	16680	18663		2235	4436	4504	6085		1189	1256
1104	Soft drinks,mineral waters,other bottled waters		6190	6553	8161	9071		2330	2339	3696	1269		264	890
1200	Tobacco products		12084	15018	20860	20300		-10377	5388	6215	2187		1032	1329
131	Spinning, weaving and finishing of textiles		649	789	1505	1286		180	281	421	389		56	46
1311	Preparation and spinning of textile fibres		257	181	210	264		66	58	66	68		19	11
1312	Weaving of textiles		323	536	1111	846		102	214	305	261		23	26
1313	Finishing of textiles		70	72	184	177		12	9	50	60		14	9
139	Other textiles		3025	4112	5155	6343		891	1559	1774	2042		266	526
1391	Knitted and crocheted fabrics		144	196	392	...		10	65	158	...		42	...
1392	Made-up textile articles, except apparel		1727	2490	2940	3707		611	1057	1069	1282		147	239
1393	Carpets and rugs		387	489	396	...		106	182	125	...		29	...
1394	Cordage, rope, twine and netting		93	86	144	169		15	17	54	50		4	16
1399	Other textiles n.e.c.		673	852	1283	1541		150	238	369	399		46	71
1410	Wearing apparel, except fur apparel		3778	4180	6407	7958		2093	2369	2982	4093		315	469
1420	Articles of fur		134	208	69	102		103	172	39	82		-	-
1430	Knitted and crocheted apparel		570	789	1111	1260		228	330	353	379		71	62
151	Leather,luggage,handbags,saddlery,harness;fur		1102	1125	1656	1910		469	549	749	814		128	507
1511	Tanning/dressing of leather; dressing of fur		776	736	972	942		272	295	302	180		28	36
1512	Luggage,handbags,etc.;saddlery/harness		325	389	683	968		197	254	447	634		100	471
1520	Footwear		1405	2095	3540	3825		642	1275	1923	1932		100	122
1610	Sawmilling and planing of wood		2325	3439	5877	8458		729	1169	1651	2439		414	1743

Code	Description										
162	Wood products, cork, straw, plaiting materials	7793	10723	14781	18284	1817	3466	4487	4992	2232	1427
1621	Veneer sheets and wood-based panels	5053	7185	10576	12683	1005	2376	3350	3465	2035	1064
1622	Builders' carpentry and joinery	1768	2018	2493	3014	474	474	606	843	95	220
1623	Wooden containers	435	694	850	1173	138	194	229	286	40	66
1629	Other wood products;articles of cork,straw	538	826	863	1414	200	423	302	397	63	78
170	Paper and paper products	18569	21894	28984	33763	4356	6440	8059	10409	1237	1397
1701	Pulp, paper and paperboard	3141	6261	4657	5109	566	1462	1081	1152	339	235
1702	Corrugated paper and paperboard	7794	6054	12507	14779	2005	1866	3120	3698	650	701
1709	Other articles of paper and paperboard	7634	9579	11820	13875	1785	3113	3858	5559	248	461
181	Printing and service activities related to printing	7580	9674	10879	13724	2431	3402	3322	4379	190	439
1811	Printing	6929	8930	9782	12786	2036	3123	2953	4036	178	416
1812	Service activities related to printing	651	744	1097	938	192	270	365	319	12	23
1820	Reproduction of recorded media	408	33	12	29	203	10	4	24	-	2
1910	Coke oven products	26626	17680	22294	...	3521	268	117	...	317	...
1920	Refined petroleum products	23082	22469	24604	...	1334	2161	3812	...	259	...
201	Basic chemicals,fertilizers, etc.	48844	40977	57321	39488	10744	13546	19827	6551	1257	917
2011	Basic chemicals	12477	7042	17172	11063	3196	2494	6808	3146	608	339
2012	Fertilizers and nitrogen compounds	33879	31021	37582	24914	7495	10363	12505	2513	609	505
2013	Plastics and synthetic rubber in primary forms	2487	2914	2567	3511	53	689	514	893	40	73
202	Other chemical products	13040	15914	18845	20604	4371	5730	5572	5794	519	681
2021	Pesticides and other agrochemical products	265	317	679	...	106	172	372	...	8	...
2022	Paints,varnishes;printing ink and mastics	2910	3387	4220	5097	747	1034	1156	1157	139	157
2023	Soap,cleaning and cosmetic preparations	6143	8245	8719	8330	2123	3196	2767	2444	261	295
2029	Other chemical products n.e.c.	3722	3964	5227	6337	1396	1329	1278	1974	111	200
2030	Man-made fibres	87	184	214	...	40	154	61	...	18	...
2100	Pharmaceuticals,medicinal chemicals, etc.	13134	15880	21711	26964	5520	7120	8486	10709	1565	1595
221	Rubber products	3251	3482	4060	6463	975	1028	1309	1399	123	275
2211	Rubber tyres and tubes	1731	2040	2110	...	487	529	728	...	52	...
2219	Other rubber products	1520	1443	1950	...	488	499	581	...	72	...
2220	Plastics products	20244	24133	34273	40213	5269	6370	9821	10080	840	2065
2310	Glass and glass products	5352	5763	8081	9729	1103	1166	1562	2130	435	822
239	Non-metallic mineral products n.e.c.	34315	35023	44314	57609	9573	10508	12088	19165	2280	3369
2391	Refractory products	1879	1487	1613	2533	577	196	93	755	31	67
2392	Clay building materials	4697	5340	6168	6960	1419	1724	1660	2481	478	685
2393	Other porcelain and ceramic products	714	823	1029	1042	246	291	333	307	47	46
2394	Cement, lime and plaster	8795	9336	12107	15058	2305	3061	4126	5605	696	925
2395	Articles of concrete, cement and plaster	13913	13801	18016	23671	3672	4080	4975	7499	852	1278
2396	Cutting, shaping and finishing of stone	709	662	444	711	307	319	162	310	28	31
2399	Other non-metallic mineral products n.e.c.	3608	3573	4937	7635	1047	837	738	2209	149	339
2410	Basic iron and steel	185366	231568	261046	279962	17905	46358	41415	44179	10818	11856
2420	Basic precious and other non-ferrous metals	11574	12085	18878	17413	2554	2210	2855	2755	509	772
243	Casting of metals	2862	1078	1228	1440	860	351	350	438	49	71
2431	Casting of iron and steel	1279	865	927	1108	456	286	249	317	37	62
2432	Casting of non-ferrous metals	1584	213	301	332	404	66	101	121	12	9
251	Struct.metal products, tanks, reservoirs	9644	8880	10109	11175	2888	3014	3388	3827	192	333

continued

Ukraine

ISIC Revision 4		Output at factor values (millions of Ukrainian Hryvnias)					Value added at factor values (millions of Ukrainian Hryvnias)					Gross fixed capital formation (millions of Ukrainian Hryvnias)	
ISIC	Industry	Note	2013	2014	2015	2016	Note	2013	2014	2015	2016	Note	2015	2016
2511	Structural metal products		6836	6150	6995	7694		1818	1917	2122	2542		118	231
2512	Tanks, reservoirs and containers of metal		1929	2130	2441	2606		754	877	1001	968		57	63
2513	Steam generators, excl. hot water boilers		879	600	673	876		317	219	265	317		17	40
2520	Weapons and ammunition		2741	1263	1913	2673		593	665	1141	1482		55	71
259	Other metal products;metal working services		15783	15620	19524	22897		5194	5911	6640	8010		1245	1169
2591	Forging,pressing,stamping,roll-forming of metal		1072	850	524	789		352	259	124	271		25	29
2592	Treatment and coating of metals; machining		2841	2639	3044	4594		907	992	866	1536		148	187
2593	Cutlery, hand tools and general hardware		958	872	1277	1221		406	340	552	478		460	62
2599	Other fabricated metal products n.e.c.		10912	11259	14679	16293		3530	4320	5098	5725		612	892
2610	Electronic components and boards		515	524	503	960		215	210	299	497		12	13
2620	Computers and peripheral equipment		1798	1037	651	2491		840	871	242	1608		54	59
2630	Communication equipment		624	619	1285	2231		237	349	503	1374		29	192
2640	Consumer electronics		3314	3334	1798	...		1805	2350	847	...		118	...
265	Measuring,testing equipment; watches, etc.		3092	3571	4417	6638		1231	1778	2134	3362		142	207
2651	Measuring/testing/navigating equipment,etc.		3078	3561	4405	...		1221	1775	2129	...		142	...
2652	Watches and clocks		14	10	12	...		10	3	5	...		-	...
2660	Irradiation/electromedical equipment,etc.		261	232	419	640		83	93	172	199		2	10
2670	Optical instruments and photographic equipment		236	367	512	826		135	200	262	421		15	9
2680	Magnetic and optical media		16	12	14	...		7	4	7	...		-	...
2710	Electric motors,generators,transformers,etc.		11074	8717	9171	10830		4113	3271	2835	3847		174	194
2720	Batteries and accumulators		3462	2029	2427	2523		1648	364	206	107		66	185
273	Wiring and wiring devices		4526	5153	6164	7571		1060	1380	1565	1725		146	234
2731	Fibre optic cables		-	...a/	...a/	...a/		-	...a/	...a/	...a/		-a/	...a/
2732	Other electronic and electric wires and cables		4082	4557	5320	6794		788	990	1003	1279		118	166
2733	Wiring devices		444	...a/	...a/	...a/		273	...a/	...a/	...a/		28a/	...a/
2740	Electric lighting equipment		995	1014	1213	1720		358	341	368	538		38	97
2750	Domestic appliances		2424	3247	3521	4221		702	1365	1136	1584		73	124
2790	Other electrical equipment		2379	2485	3512	3514		593	800	1253	1307		96	226
281	General-purpose machinery		25580	24130	27889	32208		8940	9273	10599	12302		909	1287
2811	Engines/turbines,excl.aircraft,vehicle engines		8120	8038	9736	9855		2751	3511	4570	4659		247	296
2812	Fluid power equipment		1627	1410	1618	2099		601	545	532	715		95	171
2813	Other pumps, compressors, taps and valves		5752	4570	5157	5486		2624	1843	1918	2025		169	253
2814	Bearings, gears, gearing and driving elements		1578	1708	2227	2554		585	785	931	941		82	104
2815	Ovens, furnaces and furnace burners		360	168	292	299		132	58	36	97		13	...
2816	Lifting and handling equipment		1698	2414	2860	3821		460	832	905	1081		45	72
2817	Office machinery, excl.computers,etc.		138	...a/	...a/	...a/		24	...a/	...a/	...a/		3	...a/
2818	Power-driven hand tools		29	...a/	...a/	...a/		12	...a/	...a/	...a/		-	-
2819	Other general-purpose machinery		6278	5747	5837	7952		1752	1669	1623	2717		255	377
282	Special-purpose machinery		17374	16249	20811	26364		6821	6409	7342	9711		1045	1045
2821	Agricultural and forestry machinery		3839	4815	7182	9611		944	1614	1878	2683		442	426
2822	Metal-forming machinery and machine tools		456	650	658	783		187	281	237	330		46	35

Code	Description										
2823	Machinery for metallurgy	3534	3740	5412	6065	1689	1820	2648	2880	369	237
2824	Mining, quarrying and construction machinery	5288	3376	3614	4282	2222	983	1146	1499	74	116
2825	Food/beverage/tobacco processing machinery	1321	1283	2067	2566	506	475	778	977	83	147
2826	Textile/apparel/leather production machinery	20	12	24	31	5	2	10	10	1	2
2829	Other special-purpose machinery	2917	2372	1855	3025	1269	1235	645	1332	31	82
2910	Motor vehicles	6782	5860	5353	5697	1393	1405	1016	1562	53	96
2920	Automobile bodies, trailers and semi-trailers	591	1449	1033	1265	154	451	268	280	23	49
2930	Parts and accessories for motor vehicles	4091	5507	8323	10164	2300	3354	4971	5846	1014	1862
301	Building of ships and boats	2061	1872	955	1035	1091	1549	314	439	73	16
3011	Building of ships and floating structures	1826	1604	499	447	1029	1459	128	222	73	16
3012	Building of pleasure and sporting boats	235	268	456	588	62	90	187	217	-	-
3020	Railway locomotives and rolling stock	25858	11630	6818	6081	7339	3483	2122	1614	347	117
3030	Air and spacecraft and related machinery	19870	19910	24461	24547	11397	9432	12738	14178	1750	1432
3040	Military fighting vehicles	1576	1601	3129	5061	617	481	1090	1690	72	97
309	Transport equipment n.e.c. a/	261	220	261	473	100	79	89	240	3	17
3091	Motorcycles	...	...	...	...	...	...	...	...	...	...
3092	Bicycles and invalid carriages	229	184	235	462	90	68	80	236	3	17
3099	Other transport equipment n.e.c.	...a/	...a/	...a/	11	...a/	...a/	...a/	4	-a/	-a/
3100	Furniture	7858	9881	11617	13950	2695	3593	3561	4310	527	728
321	Jewellery, bijouterie and related articles	440	334	372	379	199	146	145	159	26	9
3211	Jewellery and related articles	439	333	371	377	198	146	144	159	26	9
3212	Imitation jewellery and related articles	1	2	2	2	...	1	1	1	-	-
3220	Musical instruments	7	9	19	16	4	6	10	5	-	-
3230	Sports goods	466	602	740	896	249	338	400	369	21	56
3240	Games and toys	277	296	617	692	151	120	244	240	37	75
3250	Medical and dental instruments and supplies	885	1044	1594	1773	395	478	648	725	43	56
3290	Other manufacturing n.e.c.	938	966	758	682	446	331	230	261	10	17
331	Repair of fabricated metal products/machinery	14632	15519	13178	20087	5600	6296	4976	8606	336	437
3311	Repair of fabricated metal products	313	294	170	375	114	82	55	134	2	8
3312	Repair of machinery	7200	7244	6777	10019	2801	3153	2682	4313	210	219
3313	Repair of electronic and optical equipment	682	654	676	972	272	320	269	547	5	9
3314	Repair of electrical equipment	2662	2538	1847	2905	905	870	615	1109	55	50
3315	Repair of transport equip., excl. motor vehicles	3415	2663	3503	4719	1317	1360	1316	2007	64	101
3319	Repair of other equipment	359	2127	205	1097	191	511	39	495	2	50
3320	Installation of industrial machinery/equipment	3868	3124	2909	3175	1332	1541	1129	1254	56	51
C	Total manufacturing	881614	961457	1169562	1326997	191574	275855	303489	335069	47203	59461

a/ Data suppressed due to confidentiality rules.

Ukraine

Index numbers of industrial production

ISIC	Industry	Note	2005	2006	2007	2008	2009	2010	2011	2012	2013	2014	2015	2016
	ISIC Revision 4							(2010=100)						
10	Food products		..	..	..	..	95	100	107	109	105	110	96	101
11	Beverages		..	..	..	..	96	100	94	93	84	77	68	66
12	Tobacco products		..	..	..	..	111	100	94	92	85	88	95	99
13	Textiles		..	..	..	..	83	100	115	121	113	117	114	119
14	Wearing apparel		..	..	..	..	88	100	104	97	92	94	87	87
15	Leather and related products		..	..	..	..	95	100	105	90	84	70	60	60
16	Wood products, excluding furniture		..	..	..	..	87	100	119	118	118	122	122	128
17	Paper and paper products		..	..	..	..	88	100	101	106	111	105	87	86
18	Printing and reproduction of recorded media		..	..	..	..	108	100	109	101	99	86	74	75
19	Coke and refined petroleum products		..	..	..	..	97	100	96	79	70	55	45	49
20	Chemicals and chemical products		..	..	..	..	81	100	128	123	99	85	72	73
21	Pharmaceuticals,medicinal chemicals, etc.		..	..	..	..	86	100	99	106	118	121	111	116
22	Rubber and plastics products		..	..	..	..	89	100	110	108	107	97	89	97
23	Other non-metallic mineral products		..	..	..	..	88	100	115	106	102	93	87	94
24	Basic metals		..	..	..	..	88	100	110	105	99	85	70	75
25	Fabricated metal products, except machinery		..	..	..	..	83	100	115	114	109	94	82	89
26	Computer, electronic and optical products		..	..	..	..	95	100	102	92	79	62	44	54
27	Electrical equipment		..	..	..	..	61	100	126	111	102	102	92	93
28	Machinery and equipment n.e.c.		..	..	..	..	75	100	110	107	100	89	78	79
29	Motor vehicles, trailers and semi-trailers		..	..	..	..	80	100	122	107	96	86	102	101
30	Other transport equipment		..	..	..	..	62	100	119	122	95	57	44	43
31	Furniture		..	..	..	..	82	100	124	121	125	123	107	114
32	Other manufacturing		..	..	..	..	..	100	..	..	..	..	..	...
33	Repair and installation of machinery/equipment		..	..	..	..	79	100	115	133	117	107	91	91
C	Total manufacturing		..	..	..	..	86	100	110	108	100	90	79	82

United Arab Emirates

Supplier of information:
Federal Competitiveness and Statistics Authority, Dubai.

Basic source of data:
Annual survey.

Major deviations from ISIC (Revision 4):
None reported.

Reference period:
Calendar year.

Scope:
All establishments.

Method of data collection:
Direct interview in the field, mail questionnaires and online survey.

Type of enumeration:
Sample survey.

Adjusted for non-response:
Yes.

Concepts and definitions of variables:
Number of persons engaged includes home workers.
Wages and salaries includes employers' contributions (in respect of their employees) paid to social security, pension and insurance schemes as well as the benefits received by employees under these schemes and severance and termination pay; it excludes housing and family allowances paid directly by the employer and payments in kind.
Output excludes value of goods shipped in the same condition as received less the amount paid for these goods.

Related national publications:
None reported.

United Arab Emirates

ISIC Revision 4

ISIC	Industry	Number of establishments (number)					Number of persons engaged (number)					Wages and salaries paid to employees (millions of United Arab Emirates Dirhams)				
		Note	2013	2014	2015	2016	Note	2013	2014	2015	2016	Note	2013	2014	2015	2016
10	Food products		2457	2551	2740	2842		56885	59748	60841	62371		1932	2047	2188	2534
11	Beverages		146	163	177	194		15938	16635	17341	19912		799	867	947	1018
12	Tobacco products		19	20	20	19		1787	1803	1823	1813		99	81	89	70
13	Textiles		574	607	638	672		11309	9816	9984	10229		311	318	338	334
14	Wearing apparel		10983	11165	11347	11509		76145	77512	79561	80345		1298	1465	1564	1329
15	Leather and related products		19	21	23	23		797	892	946	950		31	30	30	30
16	Wood products, excluding furniture		1096	1112	1145	1169		25804	27923	28082	27351		705	811	868	725
17	Paper and paper products		243	257	279	280		10035	10120	10242	10133		358	379	418	478
18	Printing and reproduction of recorded media		839	847	852	862		20892	21324	21465	22652		1127	1127	1229	1425
19	Coke and refined petroleum products		109	115	118	120		7276	7997	8556	8622		2196	2214	2557	2553
20	Chemicals and chemical products		488	500	519	520		23513	24305	25453	25498		4570	5026	4711	4291
21	Pharmaceuticals,medicinal chemicals, etc.		12	15	16	18		3172	3246	3385	3542		231	236	255	277
22	Rubber and plastics products		441	484	519	648		28735	27743	27282	27744		1090	1112	1197	1371
23	Other non-metallic mineral products		1019	1037	1055	1082		89286	91300	93363	96234		3337	3628	3959	4027
24	Basic metals		194	208	221	231		33911	34774	35122	35971		4085	3954	4054	4005
25	Fabricated metal products, except machinery		5430	5506	5582	5643		125433	128311	136324	138928		5507	5637	6102	6198
26	Computer, electronic and optical products		49	53	57	57		2469	2201	2281	2149		87	105	134	141
27	Electrical equipment		358	369	383	388		16543	16319	16669	16739		878	965	985	1062
28	Machinery and equipment n.e.c.		301	318	327	328		19187	17687	18174	17071		1406	1105	1114	1090
29	Motor vehicles, trailers and semi-trailers		97	100	104	106		8613	8998	9095	9401		194	197	256	302
30	Other transport equipment		308	320	332	334		15756	15986	16646	22270		1321	1347	1384	1377
31	Furniture		1502	1513	1524	1435		34749	35638	36420	39510		1041	1413	1312	1357
32	Other manufacturing		776	793	808	829		7889	8344	8529	8217		264	287	370	368
33	Repair and installation of machinery/equipment		2280	2359	2446	2506		34942	38610	40183	43090		3010	4501	5765	6103
C	Total manufacturing		29740	30433	31232	31815		671066	687232	707767	730742		35877	38852	41826	42465

United Arab Emirates

ISIC Revision 4			Output at producers' prices (millions of United Arab Emirates Dirhams)					Value added at producers' prices (millions of United Arab Emirates Dirhams)					Gross fixed capital formation (millions of United Arab Emirates Dirhams)		
ISIC	Industry	Note	2013	2014	2015	2016	Note	2013	2014	2015	2016	Note	2015	2016	
10	Food products		24154	25944	27638	30637		6199	6584	7571	8175		…	…
11	Beverages		4842	5252	5726	6643		1809	1884	2064	2295		…	…
12	Tobacco products		1431	1489	1670	2033		466	467	512	573		…	…
13	Textiles		2032	2269	2235	2124		576	591	644	620		…	…
14	Wearing apparel		6613	7371	7691	7327		3106	3579	3776	3589		…	…
15	Leather and related products		131	150	156	152		55	59	64	62		…	…
16	Wood products, excluding furniture		4148	4450	4764	4708		1470	1711	1882	1784		…	…
17	Paper and paper products		3598	3548	3775	3882		1103	1126	1176	1230		…	…
18	Printing and reproduction of recorded media		4719	5727	6211	6055		2133	2443	2721	2411		…	…
19	Coke and refined petroleum products		102594	96881	81781	81425		6554	7259	6317	6895		…	…
20	Chemicals and chemical products		46876	50609	43218	41754		22473	24400	20890	19206		…	…
21	Pharmaceuticals, medicinal chemicals, etc.		3703	3850	4042	4469		1685	1539	1685	1928		…	…
22	Rubber and plastics products		11904	11945	11941	11721		2983	3127	3330	3673		…	…
23	Other non-metallic mineral products		36796	37693	41460	43480		11138	11499	12984	13321		…	…
24	Basic metals		42216	44990	42943	41413		12394	13376	12170	12296		…	…
25	Fabricated metal products, except machinery		35725	39611	44046	43235		13965	14350	15523	14733		…	…
26	Computer, electronic and optical products		506	490	500	585		235	216	229	248		…	…
27	Electrical equipment		14052	12476	12299	11461		4439	3533	3373	3166		…	…
28	Machinery and equipment n.e.c.		9925	9261	9800	11108		4254	4057	4167	4476		…	…
29	Motor vehicles, trailers and semi-trailers		1642	1826	2005	2151		576	697	692	753		…	…
30	Other transport equipment		7420	7875	8107	8817		2591	2617	2805	3097		…	…
31	Furniture		7192	7717	8352	8868		2639	2949	3173	3201		…	…
32	Other manufacturing		2137	2210	2395	2195		560	582	658	634		…	…
33	Repair and installation of machinery/equipment		9915	14088	17731	20899		4683	6498	7974	9442		…	…
C	Total manufacturing		384271	397722	390486	397142		108086	115143	116380	117808		…	…

United Kingdom

Supplier of information:
Office for National Statistics, London.
Industrial statistics for the OECD countries are compiled by the OECD secretariat, which supplies them to UNIDO.

Basic source of data:
Annual business survey; business register.

Major deviations from ISIC (Revision 4):
Data presented in ISIC (Revision 4) were originally classified according to the national NACE-related classification system.

Reference period:
Calendar year; however, data given for a financial year are accepted to reduce the burden on survey respondents.

Scope:
All businesses registered for VAT and/or Pay as You Earn (PAYE).

Method of data collection:
Not reported.

Type of enumeration:
Complete enumeration for large enterprises; sample survey for smaller enterprises.

Adjusted for non-response:
Not reported.

Concepts and definitions of variables:
No deviations from the standard UN concepts and definitions are reported.

Related national publications:
None reported.

United Kingdom

ISIC	Industry	Note	Number of enterprises (number)				Note	Number of employees (thousands)				Note	Wages and salaries paid to employees (millions of British Pounds)			
	ISIC Revision 4		2013	2014	2015	2016a/		2013	2014	2015	2016a/		2013	2014	2015	2016a/
1010	Processing/preserving of meat		1017	1022	1013	1014		74.2	79.7	83.2	70.2		1659	1730	1786	2081
1020	Processing/preserving of fish, etc.		323	319	312	309		13.3	14.0	...	...		280	327	333	300
1030	Processing/preserving of fruit,vegetables		555	564	605	606		31.6	32.6	33.5	33.9		829	819	883	1034
1040	Vegetable and animal oils and fats		67	60	62	63		1.4	1.4	1.4	1.4		31	57	63	55
1050	Dairy products		586	612	632	671		25.6	25.1	26.1	26.0		590	634	590	821
106	Grain mill products,starches and starch products		137	143	144	139		10.0	10.1	...	...		381	401	378	328
1061	Grain mill products		137b/	137	144b/	139b/	b/	9.1	9.2	...	...		381	401	378	328
1062	Starches and starch products		..b/	6	..b/	..b/	b/	0.9	1.0	...	...					
107	Other food products		3805	3991	4295	4554		192.9	189.1	188.4	221.3		4152	4199	4445	5011
1071	Bakery products		2379	2425	...	2771		98.3	96.1	95.7	94.7		...	...	...	2155
1072	Sugar		...	...	4	4		2.0	...	1.8	...		...	...	...	104
1073	Cocoa, chocolate and sugar confectionery		363	373	397	396		20.7	19.7	19.9	21.2		476	505	465	734
1074	Macaroni, noodles, couscous, etc.		21	25	...	23		0.7	1.0	0.9	0.8		...	...	...	24
1075	Prepared meals and dishes		...	...	212	211		28.9	...	27.2	...		...	...	...	836
1079	Other food products n.e.c.		891	974	1084	1149		42.3	41.4	42.8	50.1		1011	1043	1135	1159
1080	Prepared animal feeds		399	413	439	455		14.7	15.3	14.5	14.5		419	462	459	468
110	Beverages		1341	1489	1735	1980		...	...	44.0	98.0		1452	1461	1553c/	...
1101	Distilling, rectifying and blending of spirits		152	173	254	337		10.1	...	11.8	7.2		460	404	436	516
1102	Wines		99	93	99	117		...	...	1.7	2.2		63	50	...	...
1103	Malt liquors and malt		859	963	1110	1239		19.3	19.7	17.8	77.2		540	566	546	425
1104	Soft drinks,mineral waters,other bottled waters		231	260	272	287		12.0	...	12.7	11.4		388	441	422	478
1200	Tobacco products		11	11	11	11		...	...	...	0.4		139	128	..c/	...
131	Spinning, weaving and finishing of textiles		1140	1192	1343	1394		...	...	...	...		297	311	295	345
1311	Preparation and spinning of textile fibres		127	123	127	119		2.5	2.9	2.8	2.4		50	61	52	54
1312	Weaving of textiles		203	210	210	223		...	...	...	...		119	129	152	132
1313	Finishing of textiles		810	859	1006	1052		...	...	...	...		129	121	91	159
139	Other textiles		2707	2688	2735	2793		39.1	43.6	34.9	37.5		692	704	699	774
1391	Knitted and crocheted fabrics		80	77	69	62		1.3	1.0	1.1	1.0		24	24	20	28
1392	Made-up textile articles, except apparel		1897	1915	1994	2050		23.9	27.4	21.5	23.6		329	343	347	421
1393	Carpets and rugs		138	122	120	117		5.3	5.8	4.9	5.2		130	150	163	154
1394	Cordage, rope, twine and netting		77	74	78	80		1.0	1.2	0.9	1.1		27	22	14	17
1399	Other textiles n.e.c.		515	500	474	484		7.6	8.1	6.5	6.6		182	165	154	155
1410	Wearing apparel, except fur apparel		...	3199	...	...		32.8d/	...	...	27.3d/		...	403	...	...
1420	Articles of fur		...	7	...	...		..d/	-	-	..d/		...	1	...	...
1430	Knitted and crocheted apparel		221	209	209	202		..d/	...	...	..d/		68	73	70	88
151	Leather;luggage,handbags,saddlery,harness;fur		373	393	403	420		...	...	...	...		79	90	95	100
1511	Tanning/dressing of leather; dressing of fur		44	43	41	39		...	...	...	...		34	35	38	38
1512	Luggage,handbags,etc.;saddlery/harness		329	350	362	381		...	...	...	...		45	55	56	62
1520	Footwear		179	182	177	188		4.2	5.1	...	...		89	84	90	100
1610	Sawmilling and planing of wood		558	550	550	552		7.6	8.8	7.7	8.7		180	174	173	179

162	Wood products, cork, straw, plaiting materials	6770	7082	7699	8463	52.9	66.9	58.9	68.6	1081	1267	1220	1300
1621	Veneer sheets and wood-based panels	...	...	...	...	...	5.1	4.6	4.2	...	...	...	...
1622	Builders' carpentry and joinery	...	...	...	...	...	46.8	41.2	49.9	96	116	105	123
1623	Wooden containers	389	396	393	397	5.8	7.1	6.5	6.5	...	...	...	...
1629	Other wood products;articles of cork,straw	1062	1026	1001	968	6.5	7.9	6.7	7.0	101	123	125	120
170	Paper and paper products	1551	1514	1498	1441	54.0	...	56.2	56.6	1565	1601	1544	1687
1701	Pulp, paper and paperboard	...	...	...	...	54.0e/	...	56.2e/	56.6e/	...	...	...	...
1702	Corrugated paper and paperboard	489	485	464	418	...e/	...	...e/	...e/	722	678	721	795
1709	Other articles of paper and paperboard	812	796	811	786	...e/	...	...e/	...e/	501	594	550	640
181	Printing and service activities related to printing	11973	11608	11400	11208	103.1f/	106.3	110.7f/	...	2380	2377	2376	2350
1811	Printing	9892	9656	9533	9423	...	93.5	...	...	2113	2377g/	2122	2069
1812	Service activities related to printing	2081	1952	1867	1785	...	12.8	...	...	266	...g/	254	280
1820	Reproduction of recorded media	1015	961	922	905	...f/	2.5	...f/	...	73	46	30	44
1910	Coke oven products	134h/	131h/	-	-	...	...	-	-	663h/	610h/	557	697
1920	Refined petroleum products	...h/	...h/	132	120	...	...	...	...	...h/	...h/	...	...
201	Basic chemicals,fertilizers, etc.	744	736	752	751	37.5	34.4	35.4	29.3	1355	1385	1353	1210
2011	Basic chemicals	...	...	...	...	...	22.5	23.9	...	...	...	...	...
2012	Fertilizers and nitrogen compounds	59	55	60	61	2.4	2.3	2.1	2.2	78	78	94	81
2013	Plastics and synthetic rubber in primary forms	...	...	...	...	...	9.6	9.4	...	...	...	...	...
202	Other chemical products	1796	1869	1972	2065	...	...	...	...	2150	2043	2091	2331
2021	Pesticides and other agrochemical products	68	73	67	74	3.0	3.1	2.9	1.9	107	102	102	60
2022	Paints,varnishes;printing ink and mastics	415	409	427	405	...	...	16.9	...	548	538	477	427
2023	Soap,cleaning and cosmetic preparations	694	759	841	929	26.2	20.8	26.1	20.2	786	691	737	1033
2029	Other chemical products n.e.c.	619	...	657	657	...	...	...	...	710	31	13	810
2030	Man-made fibres	15	15	11	10	...	...	...	...	57	13	...	22
2100	Pharmaceuticals,medicinal chemicals, etc.	528	537	574	608	21.7	24.1	22.1	21.4	1954	1884	1750	1377
221	Rubber products	568	564	598	573	6.5	6.4	6.4	6.1	656	627	738	595
2211	Rubber tyres and tubes	48	43	54	46	15.3	17.7	15.7	15.3	229	230	284	235
2219	Other rubber products	520	521	544	527	137.3	149.2	145.4	140.4	427	397	454	360
2220	Plastics products	5131	5151	5223	5206	20.5	21.8	20.6	19.7	3141	3352	3458	3459
2310	Glass and glass products	799	778	778	764	...	...	...	...	551	585	599	589
239	Non-metallic mineral products n.e.c.	2836	2813	2863	2924	...	...	...	...	1612	1548	1710	1866
2391	Refractory products	101	100	97	101	5.2	2.2	...	1.9	84	67	64	62
2392	Clay building materials	205	194	191	188	8.1	...	6.4	...	142	161	200	207
2393	Other porcelain and ceramic products	282	282	272	281	...	...	...	...	...	188	...	...
2394	Cement, lime and plaster	15	...	...	24	...	30.6	27.5	31.2	...	...	...	33
2395	Articles of concrete, cement and plaster	...	...	...	939	6.4	7.3	6.6	7.5	...	...	...	...
2396	Cutting, shaping and finishing of stone	1122	1097	1120	1166	6.9	...	...	...	121	144	137	157
2399	Other non-metallic mineral products n.e.c.	230	233	239	225	69.9i/	71.0i/	...	...	246	238	191	171
2410	Basic iron and steel	680	803	1072	1189	...i/	...i/	21.5	35.0	1024	1152	1080	1120
2420	Basic precious and other non-ferrous metals	335	336	331	353	...i/	...i/	...	...	875	905	996	988
243	Casting of metals	468	456	448	421	80.4	85.9	328.6j/	88.3	388	376	318	325
2431	Casting of iron and steel	229	215	212	194	...	...	...	...	217	193	155	147
2432	Casting of non-ferrous metals	239	241	236	227	...	...	...	...	172	183	163	178
251	Struct.metal products, tanks, reservoirs	4602	4560	4644	4794	...	...	...	...	2104	2167	2430	2004

continued

United Kingdom

ISIC Revision 4		Number of enterprises (number)					Number of employees (thousands)					Wages and salaries paid to employees (millions of British Pounds)				
ISIC	Industry	Note	2013	2014	2015	2016a/	Note	2013	2014	2015	2016a/	Note	2013	2014	2015	2016a/
2511	Structural metal products		4249	4210	4272	4412		68.8	73.8	76.9	76.7		1805	1839	2089	1687
2512	Tanks, reservoirs and containers of metal		269	264	279	286		9.5	9.7	...	10.2		256	271	263	282
2513	Steam generators, excl. hot water boilers		84	86	93	96		2.1	2.3	2.0	1.4		43	57	79	35
2520	Weapons and ammunition		121	124	113	105		...	...	...j/	...		519	508	516	494
259	Other metal products;metal working services		19648	20196	21720	22382		...	...	...j/	...		4465	4604	4582	4755
2591	Forging,pressing,stamping,roll-forming of metal		728	696	631	601		...	18.7	...	19.4		461	463	472	445
2592	Treatment and coating of metals; machining		12604	13319	15100	15808		105.8	110.5	128.1	121.2		2374	2364	2472	2598
2593	Cutlery, hand tools and general hardware		1729	1761	1741	1750		21.7	...	22.9	...		526	610	475	464
2599	Other fabricated metal products n.e.c.		4587	4420	4248	4223		49.5	50.1	54.4	51.6		1104	1167	1163	1248
2610	Electronic components and boards		928	933	919	911		27.6	24.8	23.1	21.0		617	637	516	606
2620	Computers and peripheral equipment		731	706	870	868		...	...	...	...		315	282	246	255
2630	Communication equipment		1313	1288	1202	1189		...	...	...	...		471	516	457	498
2640	Consumer electronics		518	513	508	514		...	...	...	...		110	131	133	205
265	Measuring,testing equipment; watches, etc.		2097	2118	2145	2133		59.6	60.4	...	57.3		1953	1909	2067	2340
2651	Measuring/testing/navigating equipment,etc.		2029	2051	2070	2059		58.8	59.7	...	56.9		...	1898	2059	2332
2652	Watches and clocks		68	67	75	74		0.8	0.7	...	0.3		...	11	8	8
2660	Irradiation/electromedical equipment,etc.		92	104	124	130		4.1	4.7	...	4.2		146	154	183	151
2670	Optical instruments and photographic equipment		...	276	276	298		...	...	...	4.1		...	192	166	132
2680	Magnetic and optical media		...	29	31	35		...	0.2	0.1	0.1		...	1	2	3
2710	Electric motors,generators,transformers.etc.		958	959	948	904		32.9	31.0	33.7	26.7		1019	1069	1016	956
2720	Batteries and accumulators		56	54	53	61		2.1	1.9	2.1	1.9		61	67	58	54
273	Wiring and wiring devices		332	336	352	345		...	...	...	16.3		397	428	429	393
2731	Fibre optic cables		33	36	36	38		...	...	...	1.1		20	12	13	32
2732	Other electronic and electric wires and cables		235	242	247	242		...	...	...	9.4		274	314	301	305
2733	Wiring devices		64	58	69	65		...	...	...	5.9		103	101	115	56
2740	Electric lighting equipment		691	703	696	729		14.2	13.4	...	13.1		411	403	386	432
2750	Domestic appliances		288	298	292	321		...	...	...	...		353	303	346	419
2790	Other electrical equipment		698	704	681	694		9.3	...	...	...		250	224	189	261
281	General-purpose machinery		4544	4572	4515	4511		140.9	181.4k/	137.4	135.5		4543	4698	4408	4567
2811	Engines/turbines,excl.aircraft,vehicle engines		232	270	266	271		27.2	...	27.7	25.0		1398	1464	981	1100
2812	Fluid power equipment		143	153	154	169		7.8	7.8	7.8	7.5		254	257	234	227
2813	Other pumps, compressors, taps and valves		495	472	460	441		24.8	...	22.4	20.2		775	724	809	705
2814	Bearings, gears, gearing and driving elements		228	246	212	209		9.0	...	8.7	8.0		270	256	309	269
2815	Ovens, furnaces and furnace burners		...	168	187	179		...	2.2	2.5	2.0		...	71	50	58
2816	Lifting and handling equipment		875	867	861	867		18.9	17.7	18.6	22.7		393	462	553	487
2817	Office machinery, excl.computers,etc.		110	119	128	123		4.3	4.1	4.2	3.9		169	129	117	137
2818	Power-driven hand tools		...	11	14	12		...	0.5	0.7	0.5		...	20	30	13
2819	Other general-purpose machinery		2282	2266	2233	2240		45.7	41.1	44.8	45.7		1210	1314	1324	1571
282	Special-purpose machinery		3398	3355	3302	3250		...	...k/	54.4	...		1559	1689	1625	1835
2821	Agricultural and forestry machinery		465	479	476	483		...	7.2	7.6	...		169	186	214	218
2822	Metal-forming machinery and machine tools		931	913	905	873		...	...	10.0	...		265	268	281	287

Note: m/ applies to codes 321 and 3211.

Code	Description													
2823	Machinery for metallurgy	15	27	28	15	0.5	0.6	0.6	0.7	11	12	14	15
2824	Mining, quarrying and construction machinery	675	492	489	537	12.6	15.3	14.8	15.7	257	280	279	250
2825	Food/beverage/tobacco processing machinery	161	156	238	155	5.1	5.8	5.3	6.3	448	435	425	419
2826	Textile/apparel/leather production machinery	37	25	38	35	1.4	1.4	1.2	1.5	139	141	136	136
2829	Other special-purpose machinery	440	430	442	383	13.1	13.7	13.2	14.6	1039	1053	1109	1182
2910	Motor vehicles	3842	3707	3188	2952	…	…	…	…	1012	803	731	674
2920	Automobile bodies, trailers and semi-trailers	426	383	465	442	18.9	17.7	18.3	18.8	865	802	781	776
2930	Parts and accessories for motor vehicles	1620	1511	1499	1356	…	…	…	…	1345	1255	1242	1221
301	Building of ships and boats	762	1091	1060	1057	…	…	…	…	1004	976	917	925
3011	Building of ships and floating structures	545	875	838	802	…	…	…	…	508	475	418	394
3012	Building of pleasure and sporting boats	217	216	222	255	5.9	5.1	4.7	4.8	496	501	499	531
3020	Railway locomotives and rolling stock	…	172	188	255	…	…	…	…	119	106	83	65
3030	Air and spacecraft and related machinery	4143	3712	3414	3300	108.3	92.0	92.2	87.0	842	774	709	634
3040	Military fighting vehicles	…	126	116	122	3.2	3.1	3.4	3.4	10	10	10	9
309	Transport equipment n.e.c.	394	86	78	75	…	…	…	…	352	318	317	308
3091	Motorcycles	33	30	28	25	…	…	…	…	97	81	83	71
3092	Bicycles and invalid carriages	349	43	42	43	…	…	…	…	165	133	128	113
3099	Other transport equipment n.e.c.	12	13	8	7	…	…	…	…	90	104	106	124
3100	Furniture	1760	1744	1711	1467	86.0	77.3	69.2	80.8	6222	5998	5937	6019
321	Jewellery, bijouterie and related articles m/	145	119	113	109	…	…	…	…	1415	1420	1395	1402
3211	Jewellery and related articles m/	145	119	113	109	…	…	…	…	1415	1420	1395	1402
3212	Imitation jewellery and related articles	…	…	…	…	…	…	…	…	…	…	…	…
3220	Musical instruments	25	19	17	11	1.1	1.1	…	1.0	268	295	289	274
3230	Sports goods	107	75	81	86	…	5.1	4.5	…	774	736	671	615
3240	Games and toys	119	110	110	90	…	…	…	…	598	564	516	505
3250	Medical and dental instruments and supplies	995	1074	934	1027	36.5	37.9	34.7	36.2	2041	2000	1837	1802
3290	Other manufacturing n.e.c.	428	437	538	548	20.1	21.5	21.5	27.5	4331	4561	4748	5170
331	Repair of fabricated metal products/machinery	2719	2483	2506	2416	98.4	78.4	84.7	88.6	11842	10767	9852	12767
3311	Repair of fabricated metal products	267	249	269	206	7.3	6.9	8.6	8.2	1011	941	849	753
3312	Repair of machinery	1085	968	1000	857	37.0	31.2	33.1	32.6	4384	4006	3562	3123
3313	Repair of electronic and optical equipment	142	124	110	118	5.4	4.2	4.7	3.5	400	377	343	307
3314	Repair of electrical equipment	146	128	129	174	7.0	5.7	6.5	6.1	1031	981	960	974
3315	Repair of transport equip., excl. motor vehicles	1014	998	963	901	37.2	27.1	27.5	25.6	3850	3260	2735	2275
3319	Repair of other equipment	66	16	35	160	4.6	3.4	4.3	12.7	1166	1202	1403	5335
3320	Installation of industrial machinery/equipment	881	677	659	718	23.8	17.2	18.1	16.3	2173	1977	1706	1508
C	Total manufacturing	72619	69492	68505	66781	2554.4	2462.7	2456.4	2441.0	135396	131100	125967	127943

a/ Methodological break in 2016.
b/ 1061 includes 1062.
c/ 110 includes 1200.
d/ 1410 includes 1420 and 1430.
e/ 1701 includes 1702 and 1709.
f/ 181 includes 1820.
g/ 1811 includes 1812.
h/ 1910 includes 1920.
i/ 2410 includes 2420 and 243.
j/ 251 includes 2520 and 259.
k/ 281 includes 282.
m/ 3211 includes 3212.

United Kingdom

ISIC	Industry	Note	Output (valuation not defined) (millions of British Pounds)				Note	Value added at factor values (millions of British Pounds)				Note	Gross fixed capital formation (millions of British Pounds)	
			2013	2014	2015	2016a/		2013	2014	2015	2016a/		2015	2016a/
1010	Processing/preserving of meat		16590	16468	17835	18168		2807	3055	3363	3998		441	485
1020	Processing/preserving of fish, etc.		2770	3009	2834	2776		521	691	587	659		93	113
1030	Processing/preserving of fruit,vegetables		5741	6102	6039	6709		1983	2072	2169	2307		...	274
1040	Vegetable and animal oils and fats		741	699	738	711		160	150	183	126		...	17
1050	Dairy products		7763	8188	7023	7699		1788	2264	2077	2339		247	247
106	Grain mill products,starches and starch products		6555	6364	5924	5270		1335	1419	1406	1450		135	160
1061	Grain mill products	b/	6555	6364	5924	5270	b/	1335	1419	1406	1450	b/	135	160
1062	Starches and starch products	b/					b/					b/		
107	Other food products		25857	25220	25017	29123		9316	8810	9491	10976		1214	1290
1071	Bakery products					887					3879			473
1072	Sugar									142	119			
1073	Cocoa, chocolate and sugar confectionery		3457	3327	3216	5493		1505	1360	1348	2608		167	258
1074	Macaroni, noodles, couscous, etc.										30		...	1
1075	Prepared meals and dishes					4058				1249	1521			
1079	Other food products n.e.c.		7692	7710	7609	7419		2843	2680	2990	2818		426	347
1080	Prepared animal feeds		6229	6347	5906	5324		1801	1681	1758	1388		135	170
110	Beverages		27944c/	27652c/	27298c/			8131c/	7848c/	7917c/			942c/	
1101	Distilling, rectifying and blending of spirits		5140	4701	5173	8648		2633	2360	2760	2643		430	502
1102	Wines													
1103	Malt liquors and malt		7740	7700	7554	6191		2091	2229	2198	2082		210	250
1104	Soft drinks,mineral waters,other bottled waters		4091	4787	4575	5155		1400	1352	1335	2083		227	301
1200	Tobacco products		...c/	...c/	...c/			...c/	...c/	...c/			...c/	
131	Spinning, weaving and finishing of textiles		1613	1667	1612	1737		759	610	756	647		74	58
1311	Preparation and spinning of textile fibres		392	409	398	432		84	83	127	118		5	12
1312	Weaving of textiles		577	563	667	618		251	211	270	237		24	22
1313	Finishing of textiles		644	695	547	688		425	317	358	292		45	24
139	Other textiles		3313	3312	3681	3797		1418	1250	1379	1638		171	122
1391	Knitted and crocheted fabrics		173	130	122	130		71	35	33	52		4	5
1392	Made-up textile articles, except apparel		1520	1599	1964	1977		756	630	795	877		93	64
1393	Carpets and rugs		683	793	814	884		229	279	276	384		31	25
1394	Cordage, rope, twine and netting		120	68	94	81		38	9	31	23		2	2
1399	Other textiles n.e.c.		817	723	688	725		324	296	245	302		41	26
1410	Wearing apparel, except fur apparel			2676					788					
1420	Articles of fur			4					1					
1430	Knitted and crocheted apparel		272	252	319	398		140	89	147	144		11	7
151	Leather;luggage,handbags,saddlery,harness;fur		580	455	397	636		216	147	110	232		23	22
1511	Tanning;dressing of leather; dressing of fur		308	274	238	301		43	52	51	73		3	11
1512	Luggage,handbags,etc.;saddlery/harness		272	181	159	335		173	95	60	159		20	11
1520	Footwear		373	438	393	417		169	234	207	173		8	12
1610	Sawmilling and planing of wood		1147	1204	1224	1292		524	348	420	539		74	84

Code	Description										
162	Wood products, cork, straw, plaiting materials	5513	6377	6586	7059	2022	2344	2763	2910	253	354
1621	Veneer sheets and wood-based panels	...	...	...	...	...	...	...	...	...	...
1622	Builders' carpentry and joinery	464	688	670	577	159	207	272	271	33	28
1623	Wooden containers	507	600	529	592	230	244	273	254	29	28
1629	Other wood products;articles of cork,straw	...	...	...	...	...	...	...	...	...	...
170	Paper and paper products	10293	10127	10850	11162	3582	3714	3992	3891	467	564
1701	Pulp, paper and paperboard	...	...	...	...	...	...	...	...	...	...
1702	Corrugated paper and paperboard	4202	3713	4066	4652	1438	1421	1425	1774	212	275
1709	Other articles of paper and paperboard	3642	3933	4007	4263	1586	1721	1844	1525	181	190
181	Printing and service activities related to printing	9495	9329	10049	9890	4641	4450	4715	4692	600	628
1811	Printing	8735	8546	9129	8827	4185	3960	4187	4142	534	564
1812	Service activities related to printing	760	783	920	1063	456	491	527	550	66	65
1820	Reproduction of recorded media	427	321	245	205	250	193	113	103	15	10
1910	Coke oven products	...	...	...	...	...	...	...	...	-	-
1920	Refined petroleum products	49728d/	41824d/	28933	40280	872d/	695d/	...	3340	527	695
201	Basic chemicals,fertilizers, etc.	13358	13659	13032	12041	3427	3659	3351	3456	685	628
2011	Basic chemicals	...	...	...	...	...	...	...	...	685e/	...
2012	Fertilizers and nitrogen compounds	1579	1651	1457	1193	458	302	154	8	..e/	89
2013	Plastics and synthetic rubber in primary forms	16129	14304	12475	13943	5034	5199	5055	...e/	...e/	...e/
202	Other chemical products	...	...	...	...	...	...	...	...	...	...
2021	Pesticides and other agrochemical products	1064	975	858	566	343	299	248	195	41	49
2022	Paints,varnishes;printing ink and mastics	3314	3299	3142	2643	1095	928	1450	928	...	116
2023	Soap,cleaning and cosmetic preparations	5857	3905	3621	5590	1395	1490	1536	1885	248	215
2029	Other chemical products n.e.c.	5894	...	5144	...	2202	...	...	2048	...	...
2030	Man-made fibres	329	150	69	151	45	25	25	57	...	...
2100	Pharmaceuticals,medicinal chemicals, etc.	13963	12318	12718	7587	6345	5691	5430	3026	1549	484
221	Rubber products	3604	3722	3672	2971	1422	1577	1704	1102	115	148
2211	Rubber tyres and tubes	1748	1694	1540	1357	445	474	498	400	56	148f/
2219	Other rubber products	1855	2029	2132	1614	977	1103	1207	702	59	...f/
2220	Plastics products	16979	18127	18790	18964	6584	6596	7293	7823	882	1248
2310	Glass and glass products	3148	3095	3086	3385	957	977	946	1231	167	177
239	Non-metallic mineral products n.e.c.	8714	8936	11568	11565	2765	2840	4154	3995	679	551
2391	Refractory products	357	344	322	311	124	135	115	113	6	10
2392	Clay building materials	604	747	999	1009	244	318	514	511	66	58
2393	Other porcelain and ceramic products	...	...	...	...	...	223	209	...	47	...
2394	Cement, lime and plaster	540	...	...	268	91	...	...	98	...	...
2395	Articles of concrete, cement and plaster	...	...	...	...	...	...	...	...	...	...
2396	Cutting, shaping and finishing of stone	532	574	503	775	247	275	295	370	23	50
2399	Other non-metallic mineral products n.e.c.	1261	1287	1307	997	395	443	498	322	91	59
2410	Basic iron and steel	8793	9845	8653	8581	1846	1893	2274	1962	269	415
2420	Basic precious and other non-ferrous metals	6519	5847	5573	5701	1730	1669	1549	1476	116	127
243	Casting of metals	1570	1548	1329	1559	633	634	530	573	62	74
2431	Casting of iron and steel	778	778	531	675	319	338	240	240	16	30
2432	Casting of non-ferrous metals	792	770	798	884	314	296	290	333	...	44
251	Struct.metal products, tanks, reservoirs	10571	12195	9804	...	4078	4466	5001	4519	1035	527

continued

United Kingdom

ISIC Revision 4			Output (valuation not defined) (millions of British Pounds)					Value added at factor values (millions of British Pounds)					Gross fixed capital formation (millions of British Pounds)	
ISIC	Industry	Note	2013	2014	2015	2016a/	Note	2013	2014	2015	2016a/	Note	2015	2016a/
2511	Structural metal products		8748	9225	10011	7804		3388	3708	4067	3539		961	469
2512	Tanks, reservoirs and containers of metal		1630	1680	1886	1855		622	658	834	912		69	52
2513	Steam generators, excl. hot water boilers		192	263	299	145		68	100	100	68		5	5
2520	Weapons and ammunition		2927	2769	2649	2594		1028	924	993	1038		68	58
259	Other metal products;metal working services		18341	19667	19404	20231		8882	9894	9404	10080		1217	1422
2591	Forging,pressing,stamping,roll-forming of metal		2190	2252	2168	2257		865	909	799	845		114	117
2592	Treatment and coating of metals; machining		9061	9524	9769	10486		4980	5440	5294	5620		726	820
2593	Cutlery, hand tools and general hardware		1618	2090	1873	1964		879	1122	1020	997		...	136
2599	Other fabricated metal products n.e.c.		5472	5801	5594	5524		2158	2422	2291	2618		...	350
2610	Electronic components and boards		3121	2515	2257	2643		1321	1087	947	1272		88	127
2620	Computers and peripheral equipment		2005	1688	1336	1454		896	808	672	741		41	33
2630	Communication equipment		2595	2596	2506	2457		1385	1119	1267	1310		69	100
2640	Consumer electronics		495	523	437	785		226	253	210	455		11	40
265	Measuring,testing equipment; watches, etc.		7894	8694	9167	9363		3537	3793	4120	4047		306	364
2651	Measuring/testing/navigating equipment,etc.		7850	8661	9126	9337		...	3780	4089	4032		305	362
2652	Watches and clocks		44	33	41	26		...	13	31	15		1	15
2660	Irradiation/electromedical equipment,etc.		1305	1172	1422	963		275	325	472	381		37	28
2670	Optical instruments and photographic equipment		...	793	834	640		...	309	321	318		26	34
2680	Magnetic and optical media		...	10	13	13		...	4	5	6		-	-
2710	Electric motors,generators,transformers,etc.		6186	5584	5466	5087		2071	1905	1677	1791		170	265
2720	Batteries and accumulators		306	370	354	333		136	140	137	124		13	9
273	Wiring and wiring devices		2055	2177	2358	2050		582	706	762	620		92	90
2731	Fibre optic cables		62	56	53	119		31	23	25	61		-	4
2732	Other electronic and electric wires and cables		1547	1716	1855	1678		364	474	506	427		82	69
2733	Wiring devices		446	405	450	253		187	208	230	132		9	16
2740	Electric lighting equipment		1882	1792	1712	2055		814	747	728	1014		40	172
2750	Domestic appliances		2203	1593	1790	2017		680	579	638	744		62	82
2790	Other electrical equipment		1046	1088	1025	1239		474	471	453	540		59	104
281	General-purpose machinery		21830	21987	22455	24678		9141	9378	7362	8872		630	2865
2811	Engines/turbines,excl.aircraft,vehicle engines		6371	6733	6217	7288		2999	3285	1155	2061		93	154
2812	Fluid power equipment		1067	1027	999	932		475	506	388	390		48	47
2813	Other pumps, compressors, taps and valves		3809	3520	3333	2892		1504	1386	1448	1473		195	88
2814	Bearings, gears, gearing and driving elements		1197	1281	1134	2051		517	493	507	584		34	52
2815	Ovens, furnaces and furnace burners		...	344	248	224		...	138	121	109		9	...
2816	Lifting and handling equipment		2607	2713	3017	2460		960	1073	987	903		66	95
2817	Office machinery, excl.computers,etc.		898	822	791	822		232	253	194	252		20	30
2818	Power-driven hand tools		...	147	180	108		...	51	68	26		2	1
2819	Other general-purpose machinery		5460	5398	6537	7902		2272	2193	2494	3074		164	...
282	Special-purpose machinery		10328	10667	9458	10284		3431	3702	3325	3753		319	316
2821	Agricultural and forestry machinery		1978	2109	1905	1932		396	530	567	566		43	39
2822	Metal-forming machinery and machine tools		1198	1502	1051	1230		523	583	519	576		69	69

2823	Machinery for metallurgy	85	97	97	58	27	47	44	26	2	89
2824	Mining, quarrying and construction machinery	4600	4251	3894	4439	1168	1216	1061	1297	97	32
2825	Food/beverage/tobacco processing machinery	868	642	512	588	481	315	216	301	23	6
2826	Textile/apparel/leather production machinery	145	102	184	175	58	49	98	70	14	…
2829	Other special-purpose machinery	1453	1963	1816	1863	779	961	821	917	71	…
2910	Motor vehicles	41873	42406	47212	50438	9627	13618	15847	12944	…	2058
2920	Automobile bodies, trailers and semi-trailers	2539	2871	2601	2751	772	999	731	841	72	119
2930	Parts and accessories for motor vehicles	10585	10764	10440	11735	2706	2845	2855	3444	…	552
301	Building of ships and boats	4424	4747	5204	3576	1390	1812	1892	1630	201	332
3011	Building of ships and floating structures	3588	3965	4399	2833	1200	1589	1585	1384	179	302
3012	Building of pleasure and sporting boats	837	781	805	744	190	224	307	246	21	30
3020	Railway locomotives and rolling stock	1671	1141	1169	…	831	417	404	…	82	…
3030	Air and spacecraft and related machinery	24021	24239	25153	35445	9162	5263	6647	8901	824	1437
3040	Military fighting vehicles	391	343	404	…	149	174	188	…	10	…
309	Transport equipment n.e.c.	517	613	410	758	146	142	152	345	13	29
3091	Motorcycles	…	…	…	208	81	43	62	56	6	13
3092	Bicycles and invalid carriages	…	…	…	479	58	80	67	270	7	10
3099	Other transport equipment n.e.c.	36	64	47	71	7	19	24	19	1	5
3100	Furniture	6524	7195	7578	7745	2741	2778	3089	3299	275	304
321	Jewellery, bijouterie and related articles	937 g/	990 g/	1137	1133	158	302	355	310	36	37
3211	Jewellery and related articles g/	937 g/	990 g/	1137	1133	158	302	355	310	36	37
3212	Imitation jewellery and related articles g/	…	…	…	…	…	…	…	…	2	…
3220	Musical instruments	43	74	63	109	26	38	32	47	14	6
3230	Sports goods	366	414	414	496	185	168	225	257	43	24
3240	Games and toys	474	564	465	601	233	340	274	386	254	40
3250	Medical and dental instruments and supplies	3844	3109	4242	4401	1900	1503	1796	2249	183	336
3290	Other manufacturing n.e.c.	2691	2504	2419	2286	1197	978	1118	1085	…	134
331	Repair of fabricated metal products/machinery	11325	11687	12130	13131	6075	5888	6073	5789	380	370
3311	Repair of fabricated metal products	784	832	712	831	380	554	439	498	19	25
3312	Repair of machinery	3278	3738	3629	4523	1782	2011	2226	2394	124	155
3313	Repair of electronic and optical equipment	379	548	667	538	203	352	273	314	…	25
3314	Repair of electrical equipment	552	567	473	588	292	269	265	331	138	26
3315	Repair of transport equip., excl. motor vehicles	5686	5647	6470	6308	3008	2483	2773	2073	…	121
3319	Repair of other equipment	645	355	180	343	410	219	97	179	45	18
3320	Installation of industrial machinery/equipment	2615	3011	3048	3772	1377	1449	1400	1559	104	480
C	Total manufacturing	488957	483110	477548	507266	151927	152814	161329	165832	21225	24117

a/ Methodological break in 2016.
b/ 1061 includes 1062.
c/ 110 includes 1200.
d/ 1910 includes 1920.
e/ 2011 includes 2012 and 2013.
f/ 2211 includes 2219.
g/ 3211 includes 3212.

United Kingdom

Index numbers of industrial production

(2010=100)

ISIC Revision 4

ISIC	Industry	Note	2005	2006	2007	2008	2009	2010	2011	2012	2013	2014	2015	2016
10	Food products		102	100	100	97	95	100	102	102	99	104	104	105
11	Beverages		...	...	...	...	...	...	...	...	...	...	...	...
12	Tobacco products		...	...	...	...	...	...	...	...	...	...	...	...
13	Textiles		108	105	103	103	96	100	93	92	88	84	76	75
14	Wearing apparel		107	110	107	111	97	100	107	104	94	95	103	98
15	Leather and related products		110	115	118	112	102	100	123	108	118	110	113	112
16	Wood products, excluding furniture		123	120	125	117	98	100	91	83	84	91	93	95
17	Paper and paper products		103	103	106	104	96	100	94	95	94	97	99	94
18	Printing and reproduction of recorded media		116	114	110	105	103	100	97	88	92	89	88	87
19	Coke and refined petroleum products		119	113	112	108	102	100	101	91	89	81	83	82
20	Chemicals and chemical products		113	114	116	116	101	100	107	105	104	106	113	106
21	Pharmaceuticals, medicinal chemicals, etc.		98	104	99	101	108	100	87	81	79	75	76	77
22	Rubber and plastics products		121	126	125	119	103	100	99	101	97	109	105	103
23	Other non-metallic mineral products		111	116	116	111	96	100	101	87	86	99	98	105
24	Basic metals		116	117	119	114	86	100	109	111	111	109	97	85
25	Fabricated metal products, except machinery		116	120	122	117	96	100	103	107	103	105	108	108
26	Computer, electronic and optical products		116	117	116	109	105	100	99	99	97	101	99	99
27	Electrical equipment		111	116	118	116	90	100	96	107	102	98	99	95
28	Machinery and equipment n.e.c.		98	103	106	105	84	100	109	110	97	101	88	87
29	Motor vehicles, trailers and semi-trailers		123	119	124	118	84	100	114	118	128	139	148	155
30	Other transport equipment		66	76	76	75	80	100	106	111	119	115	121	124
31	Furniture		114	113	115	111	98	100	105	94	95	106	110	114
32	Other manufacturing		98	98	101	94	93	100	104	96	100	102	96	107
33	Repair and installation of machinery/equipment		93	100	101	100	97	100	107	103	111	116	116	118
C	Total manufacturing		106	108	109	106	96	100	102	101	100	103	103	103

United Republic of Tanzania

Supplier of information:
National Bureau of Statistics, Dodoma.

Basic source of data:
Annual survey.

Major deviations from ISIC (Revision 4):
None reported.

Reference period:
Calendar year.

Scope:
Establishments with 10 or more employees.

Method of data collection:
Direct interview in the field and mail questionnaires.

Type of enumeration:
Complete enumeration.

Adjusted for non-response:
Yes.

Concepts and definitions of variables:
Wages and salaries refers to direct wages and salaries, bonuses and gratuities only.
Output includes revenue from non-industrial activities.

Related national publications:
Annual Survey of Industrial Production Report, published by the National Bureau of Statistics, Dodoma.

United Republic of Tanzania

ISIC	Industry	Number of establishments (number)					Number of employees (number)					Wages and salaries paid to employees (millions of Tanzanian Shillings)				
		Note	2013	2014	2015	2016	Note	2013	2014	2015	2016	Note	2013	2014	2015	2016
1010	Processing/preserving of meat		10	11	11	12		498	536	578	622		1545	1613	1694	1768
1020	Processing/preserving of fish, etc.		17	18	18	19		3677	3960	4265	4594		11635	12146	12751	13313
1030	Processing/preserving of fruit,vegetables		15	16	17	18		1013	1091	1175	1265		3755	3920	4115	4297
1040	Vegetable and animal oils and fats		56	59	62	65		3566	3841	4137	4455		8235	8597	9025	9423
1050	Dairy products		12	13	13	14		516	556	599	645		3100	3236	3398	3547
106	Grain mill products,starches and starch products		113	119	125	131		4944	5325	5735	6177		25055	26155	27458	28669
1061	Grain mill products		113	119	125	131		4944	5325	5735	6177		25055	26155	27458	28669
1062	Starches and starch products		...	...	...	...		...	...	...	...		...	...	...	...
107	Other food products		148	155	163	171		24186	26050	28057	30219		85381	89132	93570	97698
1071	Bakery products		84	88	93	97		2541	2737	2948	3175		4494	4692	4925	5143
1072	Sugar		16	17	18	19		15136	16303	17559	18912		65330	68200	71596	74754
1073	Cocoa, chocolate and sugar confectionery		1	1	1	1		23	25	27	29		374	391	410	428
1074	Macaroni, noodles, couscous, etc.		...	...	...	...		...	...	...	...		...	...	...	...
1075	Prepared meals and dishes		...	...	...	...		...	...	...	...		...	...	...	...
1079	Other food products n.e.c.		47	49	52	54		6485	6985	7523	8103		15183	15850	16639	17373
1080	Prepared animal feeds		10	11	12	12		462	497	536	577		1527	1594	1674	1748
110	Beverages		48	50	53	55		6808	7333	7898	8506		100997	105433	110683	115566
1101	Distilling, rectifying and blending of spirits		5	5	6	6		769	829	893	961		3784	3950	4147	4330
1102	Wines		6	6	7	7		605	652	702	756		963	1005	1055	1101
1103	Malt liquors and malt		8	8	9	9		1738	1872	2016	2171		72742	75937	79719	83236
1104	Soft drinks,mineral waters,other bottled waters		29	30	32	33		3695	3980	4287	4617		23508	24540	25763	26899
1200	Tobacco products		4	4	4	5		5061	5451	5871	6323		45011	46987	49327	51504
131	Spinning, weaving and finishing of textiles		9	9	10	10		5867	6319	6806	7330		10318	10771	11307	11806
1311	Preparation and spinning of textile fibres		1	1	1	1		243	262	282	304		239	250	262	274
1312	Weaving of textiles		5	5	6	6		5270	5676	6113	6584		9458	9873	10365	10822
1313	Finishing of textiles		3	3	3	3		354	381	411	443		621	648	680	710
139	Other textiles		23	24	25	27		10098	10876	11714	12616		22220	23196	24351	25425
1391	Knitted and crocheted fabrics		3	3	3	3		3516	3787	4079	4393		12062	12592	13219	13802
1392	Made-up textile articles, except apparel		11	12	12	13		1352	1456	1568	1689		2687	2805	2945	3075
1393	Carpets and rugs		2	2	2	2		644	694	747	805		1215	1268	1331	1390
1394	Cordage, rope, twine and netting		6	6	6	7		4539	4888	5265	5671		6050	6316	6631	6923
1399	Other textiles n.e.c.		1	1	1	1		47	51	55	59		205	214	225	235
1410	Wearing apparel, except fur apparel		12	13	13	14		1706	1838	1979	2132		4163	4346	4562	4764
1420	Articles of fur		...	...	...	...		...	...	...	...		8	8	8	9
1430	Knitted and crocheted apparel		1	1	1	1		12	13	14	15		...	...	...	...
151	Leather;luggage,handbags,saddlery,harness;fur		6	6	7	7		222	239	258	278		426	445	467	488
1511	Tanning/dressing of leather; dressing of fur		4	4	4	5		193	208	224	241		370	387	406	424
1512	Luggage,handbags,etc.;saddlery/harness		2	2	2	2		29	31	34	36		56	58	61	64
1520	Footwear		11	12	12	13		907	976	1052	1133		1898	1982	2080	2172
1610	Sawmilling and planing of wood		57	60	63	66		3390	3651	3933	4236		7134	7447	7818	8163

ISIC Revision 4

Code	Description													
162	Wood products, cork, straw, plaiting materials	11	12	12	13	281	302	326	351	1193	1246	1308	1365
1621	Veneer sheets and wood-based panels	1	1	1	1	54	58	63	68	31	32	34	35
1622	Builders' carpentry and joinery	5	5	5	5	104	112	121	130	871	909	955	997
1623	Wooden containers	:	:	:	:	:	:	:	:	:	:	:	:
1629	Other wood products;articles of cork,straw	5	6	6	6	122	132	142	153	291	304	319	333
170	Paper and paper products	12	13	13	14	2221	2392	2576	2775	8018	8370	8787	9174
1701	Pulp, paper and paperboard	2	2	2	2	1631	1757	1892	2038	6064	6331	6646	6939
1702	Corrugated paper and paperboard	9	10	10	11	563	606	653	703	1913	1997	2097	2189
1709	Other articles of paper and paperboard	1	1	1	1	27	29	31	34	40	42	44	46
181	Printing and service activities related to printing	45	48	50	53	2692	2899	3123	3363	14304	14932	15675	16367
1811	Printing	45	48	50	53	2692	2899	3123	3363	14304	14932	15675	16367
1812	Service activities related to printing	-	-	-	-	-	-	-	-	-	-	-	-
1820	Reproduction of recorded media	3	3	3	3	103	111	119	128	962	1004	1054	1100
1910	Coke oven products	:	:	:	:	:	:	:	:	:	:	:	:
1920	Refined petroleum products	3	3	3	3	241	260	280	301	1091	1138	1195	1248
201	Basic chemicals,fertilizers, etc.	8	8	9	9	503	542	584	629	4530	4729	4964	5183
2011	Basic chemicals	7	7	8	8	353	380	409	441	3712	3875	4068	4248
2012	Fertilizers and nitrogen compounds	1	1	1	1	150	162	174	188	818	854	896	936
2013	Plastics and synthetic rubber in primary forms	:	:	:	:	:	:	:	:	:	:	:	:
202	Other chemical products	31	32	34	36	5734	6176	6652	7164	24177	25239	26495	27664
2021	Pesticides and other agrochemical products	1	1	1	1	10	11	12	13	13	14	15	15
2022	Paints,varnishes;printing ink and mastics	8	8	9	9	899	968	1042	1123	3935	4108	4313	4503
2023	Soap,cleaning and cosmetic preparations	19	20	21	22	4392	4731	5095	5488	19671	20535	21558	22509
2029	Other chemical products n.e.c.	3	3	3	3	433	467	503	541	557	581	610	637
2030	Man-made fibres	:	:	:	:	:	:	:	:	:	:	:	:
2100	Pharmaceuticals,medicinal chemicals, etc.	5	5	6	6	774	834	898	968	3829	3998	4197	4382
221	Rubber products	3	3	3	3	161	173	187	201	240	250	262	274
2211	Rubber tyres and tubes	1	1	1	1	16	17	19	20	113	118	124	130
2219	Other rubber products	2	2	2	2	145	156	168	181	126	132	138	144
2220	Plastics products	40	42	44	46	4058	4371	4708	5070	16463	17186	18042	18838
2310	Glass and glass products	6	6	6	7	967	1041	1122	1208	4362	4554	4781	4991
239	Non-metallic mineral products n.e.c.	83	87	91	96	3428	3693	3977	4283	32920	34366	36077	37669
2391	Refractory products	:	:	:	:	:	:	:	:	:	:	:	:
2392	Clay building materials	9	10	10	11	178	192	206	222	496	518	543	567
2393	Other porcelain and ceramic products	:	:	:	:	:	:	:	:	:	:	:	:
2394	Cement, lime and plaster	12	13	13	14	1675	1804	1943	2093	28602	29859	31346	32728
2395	Articles of concrete, cement and plaster	58	61	64	67	1430	1541	1659	1787	3614	3772	3960	4135
2396	Cutting, shaping and finishing of stone	2	2	2	2	134	144	156	168	192	200	210	220
2399	Other non-metallic mineral products n.e.c.	1	1	1	1	11	12	13	14	16	17	18	19
2410	Basic iron and steel	12	13	13	14	2018	2174	2341	2521	4404	4597	4826	5039
2420	Basic precious and other non-ferrous metals	2	2	2	2	130	140	151	163	154	161	169	176
243	Casting of metals	-	-	-	-	-	-	-	-	-	-	-	-
2431	Casting of iron and steel	-	-	-	-	-	-	-	-	-	-	-	-
2432	Casting of non-ferrous metals	:	:	:	:	:	:	:	:	:	:	:	:
251	Struct.metal products, tanks, reservoirs	31	32	34	35	1121	1207	1300	1401	2540	2651	2783	2906

continued

United Republic of Tanzania

ISIC	Industry	Number of establishments (number)					Number of employees (number)					Wages and salaries paid to employees (millions of Tanzanian Shillings)				
		Note	2013	2014	2015	2016	Note	2013	2014	2015	2016	Note	2013	2014	2015	2016
2511	Structural metal products		28	29	30	32		973	1048	1129	1215		1924	2008	2109	2202
2512	Tanks, reservoirs and containers of metal		3	3	3	3		148	159	172	185		616	643	675	705
2513	Steam generators, excl. hot water boilers		...	...	...	...		...	...	...	...		...	...	...	...
2520	Weapons and ammunition		...	...	...	...		...	...	...	...		...	...	...	...
259	Other metal products;metal working services		23	24	25	27		985	1061	1143	1231		3728	3892	4086	4266
2591	Forging,pressing,stamping,roll-forming of metal		...	...	...	...		...	...	...	...		...	...	...	...
2592	Treatment and coating of metals; machining		3	3	3	3		76	82	88	95		287	299	314	328
2593	Cutlery, hand tools and general hardware		5	5	5	5		97	105	113	121		90	94	99	103
2599	Other fabricated metal products n.e.c.		15	16	17	18		812	875	942	1014		3351	3499	3673	3835
2610	Electronic components and boards		1	1	1	1		108	116	125	135		2862	2988	3137	3275
2620	Computers and peripheral equipment		...	...	...	...		...	...	...	...		...	...	...	...
2630	Communication equipment		...	...	...	...		...	...	...	...		...	...	...	...
2640	Consumer electronics		...	...	...	...		...	...	...	...		...	...	...	...
265	Measuring,testing equipment; watches, etc.		...	...	...	...		...	...	...	...		...	...	...	...
2651	Measuring/testing/navigating equipment,etc.		...	...	...	...		...	...	...	...		...	...	...	...
2652	Watches and clocks		...	...	...	...		...	...	...	...		...	...	...	...
2660	Irradiation/electromedical equipment,etc.		...	...	...	...		...	...	...	...		...	...	...	...
2670	Optical instruments and photographic equipment		...	...	...	...		...	...	...	...		...	...	...	...
2680	Magnetic and optical media		...	...	...	...		...	...	...	...		...	...	...	...
2710	Electric motors,generators,transformers,etc.		1	1	1	1		12	13	14	15		47	49	52	54
2720	Batteries and accumulators		1	1	1	1		140	150	162	174		978	1021	1072	1119
273	Wiring and wiring devices		4	4	4	5		419	452	486	524		810	846	888	927
2731	Fibre optic cables		...	...	...	...		...	...	...	...		...	...	...	...
2732	Other electronic and electric wires and cables		4	4	4	5		419	452	486	524		810	846	888	927
2733	Wiring devices		...	...	...	...		...	...	...	...		...	...	...	...
2740	Electric lighting equipment		...	...	...	...		...	...	...	...		...	...	...	...
2750	Domestic appliances		13	14	15	15		319	343	370	398		1013	1058	1110	1159
2790	Other electrical equipment		1	1	1	1		56	60	65	70		451	471	494	516
281	General-purpose machinery		-	-	-	-		-	-	-	-		-	-	-	-
2811	Engines/turbines,excl.aircraft,vehicle engines		...	...	...	...		...	...	...	...		...	...	...	...
2812	Fluid power equipment		...	...	...	...		...	...	...	...		...	...	...	...
2813	Other pumps, compressors, taps and valves		-	-	-	-		-	-	-	-		-	-	-	-
2814	Bearings, gears, gearing and driving elements		...	...	...	...		...	...	...	...		...	...	...	...
2815	Ovens, furnaces and furnace burners		...	...	...	...		...	...	...	...		...	...	...	...
2816	Lifting and handling equipment		...	...	...	...		...	...	...	...		...	...	...	...
2817	Office machinery, excl.computers,etc.		...	...	...	...		...	...	...	...		...	...	...	...
2818	Power-driven hand tools		...	...	...	...		...	...	...	...		...	...	...	...
2819	Other general-purpose machinery		...	...	...	...		...	...	...	...		...	...	...	...
282	Special-purpose machinery		14	15	16	17		342	368	397	427		2277	2377	2496	2606
2821	Agricultural and forestry machinery		5	5	6	6		173	187	201	217		1779	1858	1950	2036
2822	Metal-forming machinery and machine tools		1	1	1	1		17	18	20	21		74	77	81	84

Code		c1	c2	c3	c4	b1	b2	b3	b4	a1	a2	a3	a4
2823	Machinery for metallurgy	1	1	1	1	15	16	17	19	95	99	104	109
2824	Mining, quarrying and construction machinery	1	1	1	1	26	27	30	32	46	48	50	53
2825	Food/beverage/tobacco processing machinery	5	5	6	6	87	94	101	109	247	258	271	283
2826	Textile/apparel/leather production machinery	-	-	-	-	-	-	-	-	-	-	-	-
2829	Other special-purpose machinery	1	1	1	1	24	26	28	30	36	38	40	41
2910	Motor vehicles	-	-	-	-	-	-	-	-	-	-	-	-
2920	Automobile bodies, trailers and semi-trailers	7	7	8	8	371	400	430	464	872	910	956	998
2930	Parts and accessories for motor vehicles	7	7	8	8	897	966	1041	1121	4499	4696	4930	5148
301	Building of ships and boats	1	1	1	1	41	44	48	51	70	73	77	80
3011	Building of ships and floating structures	1	1	1	1	41	44	48	51	70	73	77	80
3012	Building of pleasure and sporting boats	-	-	-	-	-	-	-	-	-	-	-	-
3020	Railway locomotives and rolling stock	:	:	:	:	:	:	:	:	:	:	:	:
3030	Air and spacecraft and related machinery	:	:	:	:	:	:	:	:	:	:	:	:
3040	Military fighting vehicles	-	-	-	-	-	-	-	-	-	-	-	-
309	Transport equipment n.e.c.	1	1	1	1	156	168	181	195	1442	1506	1581	1650
3091	Motorcycles	:	:	:	:	:	:	:	:	:	:	:	:
3092	Bicycles and invalid carriages	:	:	:	:	:	:	:	:	:	:	:	:
3099	Other transport equipment n.e.c.	1	1	1	1	156	168	181	195	1442	1506	1581	1650
3100	Furniture	60	63	66	69	2834	3052	3287	3541	12269	12808	13446	14039
321	Jewellery, bijouterie and related articles	1	1	1	1	13	14	15	16	33	34	36	37
3211	Jewellery and related articles	1	1	1	1	13	14	15	16	33	34	36	37
3212	Imitation jewellery and related articles	:	:	:	:	:	:	:	:	:	:	:	:
3220	Musical instruments	:	:	:	:	:	:	:	:	:	:	:	:
3230	Sports goods	:	:	:	:	:	:	:	:	:	:	:	:
3240	Games and toys	1	1	1	1	38	41	44	48	31	33	34	36
3250	Medical and dental instruments and supplies	-	-	-	-	-	-	-	-	-	-	-	-
3290	Other manufacturing n.e.c.	11	12	12	13	1104	1189	1281	1379	2711	2830	2971	3102
331	Repair of fabricated metal products/machinery	4	4	4	5	317	342	368	396	1765	1843	1935	2020
3311	Repair of fabricated metal products	:	:	:	:	:	:	:	:	-	-	-	-
3312	Repair of machinery	-	-	-	-	-	-	-	-	-	-	-	-
3313	Repair of electronic and optical equipment	:	:	:	:	:	:	:	:	:	:	:	:
3314	Repair of electrical equipment	-	-	-	-	-	-	-	-	-	-	-	-
3315	Repair of transport equip., excl. motor vehicles	:	:	:	:	:	:	:	:	:	:	:	:
3319	Repair of other equipment	4	4	4	5	317	342	368	396	1765	1843	1935	2020
3320	Installation of industrial machinery/equipment	:	:	:	:	:	:	:	:	:	:	:	:
C	Total manufacturing	998	1049a/	1098a/	1155a/	105517	113648a/	122408a/	131835a/	487454	508864a/	533206a/	557773a/

a/ Sum of available data.

United Republic of Tanzania

- 814 -

ISIC	Industry	Note	Output 2013	Output 2014	Output 2015	Output 2016	Note	VA 2013	VA 2014	VA 2015	VA 2016	Note	GFCF 2015	GFCF 2016
			(millions of Tanzanian Shillings)					(millions of Tanzanian Shillings)					(millions of Tanzanian Shillings)	
1010	Processing/preserving of meat		77231	78085	78948	80092		60116	68077	77091	77168		1989	2018
1020	Processing/preserving of fish, etc.		291092	294311	297565	301878		54427	61634	69795	79037		5836	5920
1030	Processing/preserving of fruit,vegetables		112389	113632	114889	116554		39369	44582	50485	57170		302	306
1040	Vegetable and animal oils and fats		761390	769809	778322	789602		254435	288126	326279	369484		43198	43824
1050	Dairy products		103462	104606	105763	107296		33664	38121	43169	48886		1239	1257
106	Grain mill products,starches and starch products		998914	1009960	1021128	1035927		177070	200517	227069	257137		137891	139890
1061	Grain mill products		998914	1009960	1021128	1035927		177070	200517	227069	257137		137891	139890
1062	Starches and starch products		:	:	:	:		:	:	:	:		:	:
107	Other food products		1585651	1603185	1620912	1644404		1137051	1287617	1458119	1485521		151079	153268
1071	Bakery products		84090	85019	85960	87205		31769	35976	40739	46134		9113	9245
1072	Sugar		1249041	1262853	1276817	1295322		983106	1113287	1260705	1261966		124300	126101
1073	Cocoa, chocolate and sugar confectionery		6181	6249	6318	6410		1831	2073	2348	2658		15	15
1074	Macaroni, noodles, couscous, etc.		:	:	:	:		:	:	:	:		:	:
1075	Prepared meals and dishes		:	:	:	:		:	:	:	:		:	:
1079	Other food products n.e.c.		246339	249063	251817	255467		120346	136281	154327	174763		17652	17907
1080	Prepared animal feeds		22945	23199	23456	23796		4089	4631	5244	5938		315	319
110	Beverages		1743089	1762364	1781851	1807676		1019260	1154227	1307067	1480145		231082	234431
1101	Distilling, rectifying and blending of spirits		218441	220857	223299	226535		137551	155766	176392	199749		5854	5939
1102	Wines		45591	46095	46605	47280		19173	21712	24587	27842		549	557
1103	Malt liquors and malt		777040	785632	794319	805831		508655	576010	652283	738657		140888	142930
1104	Soft drinks,mineral waters,other bottled waters		702017	709780	717629	728029		353881	400740	453805	513897		83790	85005
1200	Tobacco products		655603	662852	670182	679895		409867	464141	525601	595200		40998	41593
131	Spinning, weaving and finishing of textiles		152506	154193	155898	158157		57131	64696	73263	82964		8646	8771
1311	Preparation and spinning of textile fibres		4940	4995	5050	5123		186	211	239	270		-262	-266
1312	Weaving of textiles		104634	105791	106961	108511		33738	38205	43264	48993		6843	6943
1313	Finishing of textiles		42932	43407	43887	44523		23207	26280	29760	33701		2065	2095
139	Other textiles		252084	254871	257689	261424		106602	120718	136703	154805		32134	32600
1391	Knitted and crocheted fabrics		133174	134647	136136	138109		54412	61617	69776	79016		6436	6529
1392	Made-up textile articles, except apparel		60766	61438	62117	63017		17318	19611	22208	25148		13613	13810
1393	Carpets and rugs		19157	19369	19583	19867		8394	9506	10764	12190		562	570
1394	Cordage, rope, twine and netting		37153	37564	37979	38530		25767	29179	33042	37418		11523	11690
1399	Other textiles n.e.c.		1834	1854	1874	1902		712	806	913	1034		-	-
1410	Wearing apparel, except fur apparel		24170	24437	24708	25066		9816	11116	12588	14254		1261	1279
1420	Articles of fur		:	:	:	:		:	:	:	:		:	:
1430	Knitted and crocheted apparel		449	454	459	466		234	265	300	339		-	-
151	Leather;luggage,handbags,saddlery,harness;fur		23224	23481	23741	24085		6146	6960	7882	8925		2	2
1511	Tanning/dressing of leather; dressing of fur		22992	23246	23503	23844		6037	6836	7741	8766		2	2
1512	Luggage,handbags,etc.;saddlery/harness		233	235	238	241		109	124	140	159		-	-
1520	Footwear		31818	32170	32525	32997		7819	8855	10027	11355		1599	1622
1610	Sawmilling and planing of wood		116574	117863	119166	120893		63300	71682	81174	91923		2911	2953

Code	Description									
162	Wood products, cork, straw, plaiting materials	7848	7934	8022	8138	4607	5218	5909	6691	245	248
1621	Veneer sheets and wood-based panels	136	137	139	141	45	51	57	65	-	-
1622	Builders' carpentry and joinery	5827	5891	5956	6043	3830	4337	4911	5561	221	225
1623	Wooden containers	...	...	...	...	...	...	...	...	...	...
1629	Other wood products;articles of cork,straw	1885	1906	1927	1955	733	830	940	1065	23	23
170	Paper and paper products	96703	97772	98853	100286	16319	18480	20927	23698	10026	10171
1701	Pulp, paper and paperboard	54323	54924	55531	56336	9072	10274	11634	13175	7902	8016
1702	Corrugated paper and paperboard	41753	42215	42682	43300	7196	8149	9228	10450	2098	2129
1709	Other articles of paper and paperboard	626	633	640	650	50	57	64	73	26	27
181	Printing and service activities related to printing	170310	172193	174097	176620	67715	76681	86835	98334	16554	16794
1811	Printing	170310	172193	174097	176620	67715	76681	86835	98334	16554	16794
1812	Service activities related to printing	-	-	-	-	-	-	-	-	-	-
1820	Reproduction of recorded media	7223	7302	7383	7490	1760	1993	2257	2556	465	471
1910	Coke oven products	...	...	...	...	...	...	...	...	...	...
1920	Refined petroleum products	70052	70827	71610	72648	15060	17054	19312	21869	826	838
201	Basic chemicals,fertilizers, etc.	46571	47086	47606	48296	14590	16522	18709	21187	5799	5883
2011	Basic chemicals	34790	35175	35564	36079	12454	14103	15971	18086	4371	4434
2012	Fertilizers and nitrogen compounds	11781	11911	12043	12217	2135	2418	2738	3101	1428	1448
2013	Plastics and synthetic rubber in primary forms	...	...	...	...	...	...	...	...	...	...
202	Other chemical products	507540	513152	518827	526346	157269	178094	201677	228383	13451	13646
2021	Pesticides and other agrochemical products	207	209	212	215	26	29	33	38	-	-
2022	Paints,varnishes;printing ink and mastics	122584	123939	125310	127126	36493	41325	46797	52994	6070	6158
2023	Soap,cleaning and cosmetic preparations	380819	385030	389287	394929	119222	135009	152886	173131	7335	7441
2029	Other chemical products n.e.c.	3931	3975	4019	4077	1529	1731	1960	2220	46	47
2030	Man-made fibres	...	...	...	...	...	...	...	...	...	...
2100	Pharmaceuticals,medicinal chemicals, etc.	60170	60835	61508	62399	19580	22173	25109	28434	1283	1301
221	Rubber products	2729	2759	2789	2830	711	805	911	1032	76	77
2211	Rubber tyres and tubes	1699	1718	1737	1762	245	278	315	356	10	10
2219	Other rubber products	1029	1041	1052	1067	465	527	597	676	66	67
2220	Plastics products	628813	635766	642796	652112	185332	209874	237664	269135	19912	20200
2310	Glass and glass products	115595	116873	118165	119878	72487	82086	92955	105264	6325	6417
239	Non-metallic mineral products n.e.c.	643633	650750	657946	667482	234498	265550	299868	338729	78121	79254
2391	Refractory products	...	...	...	...	...	...	...	...	...	...
2392	Clay building materials	5173	5231	5288	5365	2688	3044	3447	3904	24	25
2393	Other porcelain and ceramic products	...	...	...	...	...	...	...	...	...	...
2394	Cement, lime and plaster	560502	566700	572967	581271	199447	225857	255764	289632	67646	68626
2395	Articles of concrete, cement and plaster	60015	60678	61349	62238	22329	25286	28634	32426	5780	5864
2396	Cutting, shaping and finishing of stone	11483	11610	11738	11908	4353	4929	5582	6321	4671	4738
2399	Other non-metallic mineral products n.e.c.	6459	6531	6603	6699	5681	6434	6440	6447	-	-
2410	Basic iron and steel	160533	162308	164103	166481	28345	32099	36349	41162	13196	13388
2420	Basic precious and other non-ferrous metals	10274	10388	10503	10655	4244	4806	5443	6163	103	105
243	Casting of metals	-	-	-	-	-	-	-	-	-	-
2431	Casting of iron and steel	-	-	-	-	-	-	-	-	-	-
2432	Casting of non-ferrous metals	...	...	...	...	...	...	...	...	...	...
251	Struct.metal products, tanks, reservoirs	42357	42825	43298	43926	15259	17279	19567	22159	2663	2702

continued

United Republic of Tanzania

ISIC	Industry	Note	Output at factor values (millions of Tanzanian Shillings)				Note	Value added at factor values (millions of Tanzanian Shillings)				Note	Gross fixed capital formation (millions of Tanzanian Shillings)	
	ISIC Revision 4		2013	2014	2015	2016		2013	2014	2015	2016		2015	2016
2511	Structural metal products		34811	35196	35585	36101		11388	12896	14603	16537		2358	2392
2512	Tanks, reservoirs and containers of metal		7546	7629	7714	7825		3871	4384	4964	5622		305	310
2513	Steam generators, excl. hot water boilers		...	...	...	...		...	...	...	...		...	...
2520	Weapons and ammunition		...	...	...	...		...	...	...	...		...	...
259	Other metal products;metal working services		73560	74374	75196	76286		20945	23718	26859	30415		2880	2922
2591	Forging,pressing,stamping,roll-forming of metal													
2592	Treatment and coating of metals; machining		1692	1710	1729	1754		1070	1212	1372	1554		144	146
2593	Cutlery, hand tools and general hardware		6838	6914	6991	7092		759	860	974	1103		386	392
2599	Other fabricated metal products n.e.c.		65030	65749	66476	67440		19115	21647	24513	27759		2350	2384
2610	Electronic components and boards		36456	36859	37267	37807		30967	35068	35103	35138		-4156	-4216
2620	Computers and peripheral equipment		...	...	...	...		...	...	...	...		...	...
2630	Communication equipment		...	...	...	...		...	...	...	...		...	...
2640	Consumer electronics		...	...	...	...		...	...	...	...		...	...
265	Measuring,testing equipment; watches, etc.		...	...	...	...		...	...	...	...		...	...
2651	Measuring/testing/navigating equipment,etc.		...	...	...	...		...	...	...	...		...	...
2652	Watches and clocks		...	...	...	...		...	...	...	...		...	...
2660	Irradiation/electromedical equipment,etc.		...	...	...	...		...	...	...	...		...	...
2670	Optical instruments and photographic equipment		...	...	...	...		...	...	...	...		...	...
2680	Magnetic and optical media		...	...	...	...		...	...	...	...		...	...
2710	Electric motors,generators,transformers,etc.		171	172	174	177		84	95	108	122		-	
2720	Batteries and accumulators		26337	26629	26923	27313		5070	5742	6502	7363		1038	1053
273	Wiring and wiring devices		33844	34219	34597	35098		3496	3959	4483	5077		844	856
2731	Fibre optic cables		...	...	...	...		...	...	...	...		...	...
2732	Other electronic and electric wires and cables		33844	34219	34597	35098		3496	3959	4483	5077		844	856
2733	Wiring devices		...	...	...	...		...	...	...	...		...	...
2740	Electric lighting equipment		...	...	...	...		...	...	...	...		...	...
2750	Domestic appliances		16332	16512	16695	16937		7077	8015	9076	10278		575	584
2790	Other electrical equipment		26283	26574	26868	27257		6588	7460	8448	9566		362	367
281	General-purpose machinery		-			-		-			-		-	
2811	Engines/turbines,excl.aircraft,vehicle engines		...	...	...	...		...	...	...	...		...	...
2812	Fluid power equipment		...	...	...	...		...	...	...	...		...	...
2813	Other pumps, compressors, taps and valves		-	-	-	-		-	-	-	-		-	
2814	Bearings, gears, gearing and driving elements		...	...	...	...		...	...	...	...		...	...
2815	Ovens, furnaces and furnace burners		...	...	...	...		...	...	...	...		...	...
2816	Lifting and handling equipment		...	...	...	...		...	...	...	...		...	...
2817	Office machinery, excl.computers,etc.		...	...	...	...		...	...	...	...		...	...
2818	Power-driven hand tools		...	...	...	...		...	...	...	...		...	...
2819	Other general-purpose machinery		...	...	...	...		...	...	...	...		...	...
282	Special-purpose machinery		10393	10508	10624	10778		4248	4810	5447	6169		306	310
2821	Agricultural and forestry machinery		4707	4759	4811	4881		2701	3059	3464	3922		44	44
2822	Metal-forming machinery and machine tools		497	503	508	515		256	290	329	372		-	

Code	Description										
2823	Machinery for metallurgy	408	413	417	423	190	216	244	276	-	-
2824	Mining, quarrying and construction machinery	520	526	532	540	218	247	280	317	-	-
2825	Food/beverage/tobacco processing machinery	3870	3913	3956	4013	731	828	937	1061	262	266
2826	Textile/apparel/leather production machinery	-	-	-	-	-	-	-	-	-	-
2829	Other special-purpose machinery	391	395	400	405	151	171	193	219	-	-
2910	Motor vehicles	-	-	-	-	-	-	-	-	-	-
2920	Automobile bodies, trailers and semi-trailers	28338	28651	28968	29388	9736	11025	12485	14138	2985	3029
2930	Parts and accessories for motor vehicles	10518	10635	10752	10908	6487	7346	8318	9420	19312	19592
301	Building of ships and boats	1061	1072	1084	1100	88	99	113	128	-	-
3011	Building of ships and floating structures	1061	1072	1084	1100	88	99	113	128	-	-
3012	Building of pleasure and sporting boats	-	-	-	-	-	-	-	-	-	-
3020	Railway locomotives and rolling stock	...	...	...	...	...	...	...	...	...	...
3030	Air and spacecraft and related machinery	...	...	...	...	...	...	...	...	...	...
3040	Military fighting vehicles	...	...	...	...	...	...	...	...	...	...
309	Transport equipment n.e.c.	59419	60076	60741	61621	13796	15622	17691	20034	739	750
3091	Motorcycles	...	...	...	...	...	...	...	...	...	...
3092	Bicycles and invalid carriages	...	...	...	...	...	...	...	...	...	...
3099	Other transport equipment n.e.c.	59419	60076	60741	61621	13796	15622	17691	20034	739	750
3100	Furniture	369046	373126	377252	382720	107416	125975	152103	357777	17494	17748
321	Jewellery, bijouterie and related articles	515	520	526	534	380	430	487	488	-	-
3211	Jewellery and related articles	515	520	526	534	380	430	487	488	-	-
3212	Imitation jewellery and related articles	...	...	...	...	...	...	...	...	...	...
3220	Musical instruments	...	...	...	...	...	...	...	...	...	...
3230	Sports goods	...	...	...	...	...	...	...	...	...	...
3240	Games and toys	482	487	492	499	257	291	330	374	-	-
3250	Medical and dental instruments and supplies	-	-	-	-	-	-	-	-	-	-
3290	Other manufacturing n.e.c.	69305	70071	70846	71873	26046	29495	33400	37823	1306	1325
331	Repair of fabricated metal products/machinery	34946	35332	35723	36240	31864	31928	31960	31992	2	2
3311	Repair of fabricated metal products	...	...	...	...	...	...	...	...	-	-
3312	Repair of machinery	-	-	-	-	-	-	-	-	-	-
3313	Repair of electronic and optical equipment	...	...	...	...	...	...	...	...	...	...
3314	Repair of electrical equipment	-	-	-	-	-	-	-	-	-	-
3315	Repair of transport equip., excl. motor vehicles	...	...	...	...	...	...	...	...	...	...
3319	Repair of other equipment	34946	35332	35723	36240	31864	31928	31960	31992	2	2
3320	Installation of industrial machinery/equipment	...	...	...	...	...	...	...	...	...	...
C	Total manufacturing	10319945	10434060a/	10549438a/	10702331a/	4552716	5155754a/	5838262a/	6621480a/	873214a/	885870a/

a/ Sum of available data.

United Republic of Tanzania

| ISIC Revision 4 | | | Index numbers of industrial production (2010=100) | | | | | | | | | | | |
ISIC	Industry	Note	2005	2006	2007	2008	2009	2010	2011	2012	2013	2014	2015	2016
10	Food products		74	74	79	138	158	100	96	103	104	112	153	...
11	Beverages		84	100	111	161	194	100	112	136	146	154	162	...
12	Tobacco products		73	139	119	103	114	100	108	161	158	110	115	...
13	Textiles		106	168	169	258	179	100	92	140	94	112	87	...
14	Wearing apparel		...	...	...	...	...	...	...	...	...	...	...	...
15	Leather and related products		66	111	174	57	37	100	129	200	243	323	...	...
16	Wood products, excluding furniture		28	26	29	182	132	100	112	153	294	365	358	...
17	Paper and paper products		157	67	...	...	...	100	108	113	97	119	127	...
18	Printing and reproduction of recorded media		...	...	...	...	...	...	...	...	...	...	...	...
19	Coke and refined petroleum products		...	...	...	...	...	...	...	...	...	...	...	...
20	Chemicals and chemical products	a/	17	9	8	8	27	100	181	164	159	169	183	...
21	Pharmaceuticals,medicinal chemicals, etc.	a/	...	...	...	...	...	...	...	...	...	...	...	...
22	Rubber and plastics products		68	65	51	...	...	100	109	105	116	124	124	...
23	Other non-metallic mineral products		62	63	80	93	116	100	102	109	100	117	134	...
24	Basic metals		76	87	98	146	178	100	111	127	119	126	149	...
25	Fabricated metal products, except machinery		106	96	40	85	68	100	99	124	186	233	144	...
26	Computer, electronic and optical products		...	...	...	...	...	100	...	...	...	...	...	...
27	Electrical equipment		33	41	39	64	59	100	183	179	145	136	114	...
28	Machinery and equipment n.e.c.		179	33	23	81	65	100	93	116	47	...	...	...
29	Motor vehicles, trailers and semi-trailers		76	54	71	46	70	100	82	66	114	166	120	...
30	Other transport equipment		76	54	71	46	70	100	82	66	114	166	120	...
31	Furniture		...	...	...	...	...	...	...	...	...	...	...	...
32	Other manufacturing		25	30	39	52	70	100	119	135	155	177	187	...
33	Repair and installation of machinery/equipment		...	...	...	...	...	...	...	...	...	...	...	...
C	Total manufacturing		88	105	109	179	165	100	102	113	117	124	126	...

a/ 20 includes 21.

United States of America

Supplier of information:
Census Bureau, U.S. Department of Commerce, Washington, D.C.

Basic source of data:
Census; annual survey of manufactures and services; administrative data.

Major deviations from ISIC (Revision 4):
Data presented in accordance with ISIC (Revision 4) were originally classified according to the North American Industry Classification System (NAICS).

Reference period:
Calendar year.

Scope:
All manufacturing establishments with one or more paid employees at any time during the reference year.

Method of data collection:
Not reported.

Type of enumeration:
Sample survey.

Adjusted for non-response:
Not reported.

Concepts and definitions of variables:
No deviations from the standard UN concepts and definitions are reported.

Related national publications:
None reported.

United States of America

ISIC Revision 4		Number of enterprises a/ (number)					Number of employees (thousands)					Wages and salaries paid to employees (millions of US Dollars)				
ISIC	Industry	Note	2013	2014	2015	2016	Note	2013	2014	2015	2016	Note	2013	2014	2015	2016
1010	Processing/preserving of meat		2455b/	2534	2489	...		476	472	477	480		15801	16185	16872	17737
1020	Processing/preserving of fish, etc.		80	87	78	...		31	32	32	31		1276	1284	1362	1406
1030	Processing/preserving of fruit,vegetables		1556	1686	1705	...		163	162	162	161		6577	6773	7001	7217
1040	Vegetable and animal oils and fats		206	211	217	...		16	16	16	16		886	904	939	961
1050	Dairy products		831	894	900	...		130	132	132	136		6596	6838	7010	7424
106	Grain mill products,starches and starch products		307	337	338	...		...	...	...	...		...	...	...	...
1061	Grain mill products		...	...	...	...		30	30	30	30		1671	1716	1777	1769
1062	Starches and starch products		...	...	...	...		7	7	7	7		471	496	495	497
107	Other food products		14131	15323	15151	...		...	...	...	...		...	...	...	...
1071	Bakery products		...	...	...	...		246	239	242	252		9507	9572	9748	10417
1072	Sugar		...	...	...	...		13	13	14	13		699	705	739	768
1073	Cocoa, chocolate and sugar confectionery		...	...	...	...		55	54	58	60		2356	2439	2582	2784
1074	Macaroni, noodles, couscous, etc.		...	...	...	...		...	...	...	...		...	...	...	...
1075	Prepared meals and dishes		...	...	...	...		...	...	...	...		...	...	...	...
1079	Other food products n.e.c.		954	1015	1054	...		162	166	178	186		7613	8121	8697	9276
1080	Prepared animal feeds		...	...	...	...		45	44	44	46		2286	2328	2403	2516
110	Beverages		4977	5418	6517	...		136	135	145	154		7199	7536	8389	9067
1101	Distilling, rectifying and blending of spirits		4977b/	5418b/	6517b/	...		7	8	9	9		463	499	565	618
1102	Wines		..b/	..b/	..b/	...		38	38	40	42		1898	2059	2243	2406
1103	Malt liquors and malt		..b/	..b/	..b/	...		27	30	35	40		1658	1883	2222	2488
1104	Soft drinks,mineral waters,other bottled waters		..b/	..b/	..b/	...		64	59	61	62		3180	3095	3360	3554
1200	Tobacco products		94	120	132	...		13	13	13	13		866	822	813	855
131	Spinning, weaving and finishing of textiles		7345	7165	7181	...		...	...	97	97		...	...	4047	4068
1311	Preparation and spinning of textile fibres		...	...	...	...		25	24	24	24		827	809	831	828
1312	Weaving of textiles		...	...	...	...		49	47	46	46		2073	2116	2004	2003
1313	Finishing of textiles		...	...	...	...		29	28	28	28		1198	1200	1212	1238
139	Other textiles		4274	4090	4046	...		110	110	110	110		3814	3987	4067	4172
1391	Knitted and crocheted fabrics		...	...	...	...		24	23	23	23		700	709	721	765
1392	Made-up textile articles, except apparel		...	...	...	...		27	29	29	28		1088	1171	1208	1194
1393	Carpets and rugs		...	...	...	...		5	5	5	5		225	224	242	252
1394	Cordage, rope, twine and netting		...	...	...	...		...	...	...	...		...	...	...	...
1399	Other textiles n.e.c.		...	...	...	...		54	53	53	53		1801	1883	1896	1961
1410	Wearing apparel, except fur apparel		4179	4275	4437	...		85	77	75	71		2402	2303	2313	2237
1420	Articles of fur		2875	3070	3167	...		...	...	...	...		...	...	...	...
1430	Knitted and crocheted apparel		241	239	230	...		12	11	11	10		346	326	321	304
151	Leather;luggage,handbags,saddlery,harness;fur		1021	1049	1040	...		...	...	...	...		...	...	...	...
1511	Tanning/dressing of leather; dressing of fur		...	...	...	...		3	3	3	3		133	141	139	144
1512	Luggage,handbags,etc.;saddlery/harness		...	...	...	...		11	10	10	10		329	331	342	369
1520	Footwear		399	423	413	...		11	11	11	11		394	389	402	398
1610	Sawmilling and planing of wood		5454	5435	5549	...		73	73	77	77		3210	3323	3606	3742

Code	Description				fn					fn				
162	Wood products, cork, straw, plaiting materials	10081	9936	9952		273	279	293	301		10189	10834	11533	12330
1621	Veneer sheets and wood-based panels	...	...	...		63	68	72	73		2786	3006	3171	3380
1622	Builders' carpentry and joinery	...	...	...		99	101	104	105		3824	3996	4185	4374
1623	Wooden containers	...	...	...		49	51	53	55		1480	1654	1773	1903
1629	Other wood products;articles of cork,straw	...	...	...		62	60	64	69		2100	2179	2403	2673
170	Paper and paper products	6775	6984	7165		344	336	334	333		20418	20381	20687	20689
1701	Pulp, paper and paperboard	6775c/	6984c/	7165c/		105	103	102	99		7943	7843	7816	7640
1702	Corrugated paper and paperboard	...c/	...c/	...c/		185	183	183	184		9876	10038	10315	10444
1709	Other articles of paper and paperboard	...c/	...c/	...c/		54	50	49	50		2599	2501	2556	2604
181	Printing and service activities related to printing	9698	9817	10056		432	417	413	416		19875	19595	20275	20801
1811	Printing	...	...	...		406	392	389	394		18625	18357	19064	19644
1812	Service activities related to printing	...	...	...		26	25	24	23		1250	1238	1211	1156
1820	Reproduction of recorded media	418	435	466		...	...	...	...		...	...	...	...
1910	Coke oven products	34	38	42	d/	100	102	103	104	d/	9554	9964	10357	10741
1920	Refined petroleum products	300	308	310	d/	...	...	...	...	d/	...	...	...	...
201	Basic chemicals,fertilizers, etc.	2952	2846	2772		254	250	489e/	489e/		19305	19721	35554e/	36367e/
2011	Basic chemicals	...	...	...		147	146	149	148		11959	12115	12728	13046
2012	Fertilizers and nitrogen compounds	...	...	...		19	17	18	18		1260	1220	1333	1361
2013	Plastics and synthetic rubber in primary forms	5562	5510	5535		88	87	92	91		6086	6386	6992	7124
202	Other chemical products	...	...	...		...	...	...e/	...e/		...	...	...e/	...e/
2021	Pesticides and other agrochemical products	...	...	...		12	11	11	12		782	760	743	763
2022	Paints,varnishes;printing ink and mastics	...	...	...		44	44	44	45		2751	2798	2848	2903
2023	Soap,cleaning and cosmetic preparations	...	...	...		89	87	87	87		5310	5364	5435	5548
2029	Other chemical products n.e.c.	...	...	...		88	88	87	87		5190	5379	5475	5622
2030	Man-made fibres	38	38	37		...	...	...	...e/		...	...	...e/	...e/
2100	Pharmaceuticals,medicinal chemicals, etc.	2059	2018	1977		231	235	253	256		19076	19136	20663	21189
221	Rubber products	1651	1696	1819		129	128	129	128		6286	6449	6586	6659
2211	Rubber tyres and tubes	...	...	...		49	51	50	50		2737	2848	2864	2882
2219	Other rubber products	...	...	...		80	77	79	78		3549	3601	3722	3777
2220	Plastics products	7889	7833	7938		574	584	601	614		25545	26757	27993	28787
2310	Glass and glass products	1478	1506	1499		83	82	86	91		4179	4253	4429	4754
239	Non-metallic mineral products n.e.c.	11328	11127	11033		...	...	...	...		...	...	...e/	...e/
2391	Refractory products	...	...	...	f/	21	20	20	19	f/	954	973	1022	991
2392	Clay building materials	...	...	...	f/	13	12	13	12	f/	...	...	...	...
2393	Other porcelain and ceramic products	...	...	...		13	12	13	12		537	520	538	523
2394	Cement, lime and plaster	...	...	...		12	13	13	13		710	753	810	840
2395	Articles of concrete, cement and plaster	...	...	...	g/	150	157	164	166	g/	7121	7653	8125	8616
2396	Cutting, shaping and finishing of stone	...	...	...	g/	72	72	72	71	g/	3525	3681	3782	3865
2399	Other non-metallic mineral products n.e.c.	...	...	...		...	...	...	...		...	...	...	...
2410	Basic iron and steel	983	970	939		148	147	141	135		10468	10613	10065	9538
2420	Basic precious and other non-ferrous metals	2104	2123	2102		117	114	116	114		6911	6980	7042	6905
243	Casting of metals	1474	1467	1504		123	123	123	116		5983	6280	6274	6065
2431	Casting of iron and steel	...	...	...		67	66	64	58		3391	3498	3364	3152
2432	Casting of non-ferrous metals	...	...	...		56	57	59	57		2593	2781	2910	2912
251	Struct.metal products, tanks, reservoirs	6518	6497	6461	h/	1383	1375	1372	1328	h/	69328	71700	72255	71417

continued

United States of America

ISIC Revision 4		Number of enterprises a/ (number)					Number of employees (thousands)					Wages and salaries paid to employees (millions of US Dollars)				
ISIC	Industry	Note	2013	2014	2015	2016	Note	2013	2014	2015	2016	Note	2013	2014	2015	2016
2511	Structural metal products		...	...	...	...		324	323	328	326		15539	16157	16784	17127
2512	Tanks, reservoirs and containers of metal		...	...	...	...		88	90	88	80		5008	5265	5201	4866
2513	Steam generators, excl. hot water boilers		...	...	...	...		...	...	...	...		...	...	...	...
2520	Weapons and ammunition	h/	414	476	488	...	h/	...	...	...	...	h/	...	...	...	...
259	Other metal products;metal working services		48080	47353	46920	...		...	...	...	...		...	...	...	...
2591	Forging,pressing,stamping,roll-forming of metal		...	...	...	...		111	112	112	107		5708	5893	5875	5697
2592	Treatment and coating of metals;machining		...	...	...	...		123	122	121	120		5466	5739	5862	5768
2593	Cutlery, hand tools and general hardware		...	...	...	...		35	34	35	34		1774	1786	1816	1812
2599	Other fabricated metal products n.e.c.		...	...	...	...		702	694	688	661		35833	36860	36717	36147
2610	Electronic components and boards		3545	3427	3373	...		267	258	255	250		17684	17947	18185	17890
2620	Computers and peripheral equipment		967	985	964	...		48	38	36	36		3478	2837	2775	2751
2630	Communication equipment		517	505	491	...		108	94	94	95		9519	8229	8594	8456
2640	Consumer electronics		573	601	604	...		10	9	10	9		542	530	556	532
265	Measuring,testing equipment; watches, etc.		3923	3907	3872	...		307	298	301	296		25083	25186	26136	25900
2651	Measuring/testing/navigating equipment,etc.		...	...	...	...		...	...	...	...		...	...	...	...
2652	Watches and clocks		...	...	...	...		...	...	...	...		...	...	...	...
2660	Irradiation/electromedical equipment,etc.		680	715	728	...		68	67	67	69		5336	5459	5321	5521
2670	Optical instruments and photographic equipment		458	451	457	...		16	15	20	18		1146	1053	1394	1365
2680	Magnetic and optical media		75	74	77	...		16	15	14	13		749	749	740	662
2710	Electric motors,generators,transformers,etc.		1468	1442	1414	...		115	114	114	109		6480	6655	6677	6463
2720	Batteries and accumulators		1625	1630	1598	...		27	31	31	29		1385	1671	1687	1674
273	Wiring and wiring devices		882	873	862	...		68	65	66	67		3593	3653	3686	3644
2731	Fibre optic cables		...	...	...	...		5	5	5	7		260	274	292	369
2732	Other electronic and electric wires and cables		...	...	...	...		22	21	23	22		1142	1184	1235	1193
2733	Wiring devices		...	...	...	...		42	39	38	37		2190	2195	2160	2082
2740	Electric lighting equipment		996	1024	1026	...		43	40	40	40		2122	2081	2124	2239
2750	Domestic appliances		213	231	241	...		43	46	48	48		1968	2193	2201	2265
2790	Other electrical equipment		2876	2855	2845	...		38	36	53	52		2583	2557	3795	3863
281	General-purpose machinery	i/	11476	11393	11371	...	i/	1035	1016	810	783	i/	59265	60018	48927	47975
2811	Engines/turbines,excl.aircraft,vehicle engines		...	...	...	...		35	34	143	123		2389	2376	9089	8267
2812	Fluid power equipment		...	...	...	...		35	33	34	32		2128	2061	2183	2060
2813	Other pumps, compressors, taps and valves		...	...	...	...		63	64	64	61		3935	4077	4013	3793
2814	Bearings, gears, gearing and driving elements		...	...	...	...		67	65	65	63		3579	3593	3685	3541
2815	Ovens, furnaces and furnace burners		...	...	...	...		11	11	11	10		652	643	677	650
2816	Lifting and handling equipment		...	...	...	...		80	83	83	85		4288	4597	4846	5137
2817	Office machinery, excl.computers,etc.		...	...	...	...		5	5	...	...		315	309	...	...
2818	Power-driven hand tools		...	...	...	...		7	7	7	7		402	397	401	409
2819	Other general-purpose machinery		...	...	...	...		222	214	205	199		11778	11786	11234	11075
282	Special-purpose machinery	i/	8486	8633	8593	...	i/	...	...	...	...	i/	...	...	...	...
2821	Agricultural and forestry machinery		...	...	...	...		81	80	76	70		3950	4101	3873	3707
2822	Metal-forming machinery and machine tools		...	...	...	...		...	...	...	...		...	...	...	...

Code	Description											
2823	Machinery for metallurgy	8472	8575	8304	8089	144	146	143	143	...	...	...
2824	Mining, quarrying and construction machinery	6392	7351	7795	7778	103	121	128	132	...	...	...
2825	Food/beverage/tobacco processing machinery	1036	1022	1004	962	15	16	16	16	...	...	...
2826	Textile/apparel/leather production machinery	...	...	...	...	...	...	...	...	...	...	...
2829	Other special-purpose machinery	9437	9588	8976	9022	138	141	135	139	...	...	...
2910	Motor vehicles	14770	14160	13067	12028	198	190	179	167	874	865	853
2920	Automobile bodies, trailers and semi-trailers	6317	6243	5823	5213	132	131	123	118	18409	18438	18494
2930	Parts and accessories for motor vehicles	29407	28163	26403	24882	540	534	505	483	1331	1364	1361
301	Building of ships and boats	7642	7789	7682	7495	131	133	133	132	3193	3157	3169
3011	Building of ships and floating structures j/	7642	7789	7682	7495	131	133	133	132	...	...	...
3012	Building of pleasure and sporting boats j/	...	...	...	...	...	...	...	...	...	...	...
3020	Railway locomotives and rolling stock	1697	1853	1812	1722	28	34	30	29	339	342	345
3030	Air and spacecraft and related machinery	36599	36815	36789	35256	421	420	425	424	1496	1496	1480
3040	Military fighting vehicles	438	448	399	542	6	6	5	8	43	47	48
309	Transport equipment n.e.c.	1179	1162	1152	1131	23	23	23	23	1297	1305	1314
3091	Motorcycles k/	470	471	470	491	9	9	10	10	...	...	...
3092	Bicycles and invalid carriages k/	...	...	...	...	...	...	...	...	...	...	...
3099	Other transport equipment n.e.c.	708	690	682	640	14	14	14	13	...	...	...
3100	Furniture	15370	14813	13655	13474	354	350	336	342	14505	14812	14968
321	Jewellery, bijouterie and related articles	1085	1126	1100	1081	23	24	24	25	1124	1132	1129
3211	Jewellery and related articles	...	...	...	...	...	...	...	...	...	...	...
3212	Imitation jewellery and related articles	...	...	...	...	...	...	...	...	...	...	...
3220	Musical instruments	548	549	537	496	11	11	11	11	1350	1272	1333
3230	Sports goods	1746	1698	1628	1669	34	35	35	35	462	455	449
3240	Games and toys	252	231	227	230	6	5	6	6	883	823	901
3250	Medical and dental instruments and supplies	16594	16061	15970	17112	257	255	257	281	9015	9277	9484
3290	Other manufacturing n.e.c.	9261	9035	8714	8275	183	182	180	177	7911	7647	7457
331	Repair of fabricated metal products/machinery	...	...	...	...	...	...	...	...	42446	41936	41450
3311	Repair of fabricated metal products	...	...	...	...	...	...	...	...	...	...	...
3312	Repair of machinery	...	...	...	...	...	...	...	...	...	...	...
3313	Repair of electronic and optical equipment	...	...	...	...	...	...	...	...	...	...	...
3314	Repair of electrical equipment	...	...	...	...	...	...	...	...	...	...	...
3315	Repair of transport equip., excl. motor vehicles	...	...	...	...	...	...	...	...	...	...	...
3319	Repair of other equipment	...	...	...	...	...	...	...	...	...	...	...
3320	Installation of industrial machinery/equipment	...	...	...	...	...	...	...	...	25324	24837	24445
C	Total manufacturing	643406	636221	616964	604065	11113	11168	10999	11092	341912	340300	338920

a/ Data were derived from OECD's databases.
b/ 1101 includes 1102, 1103 and 1104.
c/ 1701 includes 1702 and 1709.
d/ 1910 includes 1920.
e/ 201 includes 202 and 2030.
f/ 2391 includes 2392.
g/ 2396 includes 2399.
h/ 251 includes 2520 and 259.
i/ 281 includes 282.
j/ 3011 includes 3012.
k/ 3091 includes 3092.

United States of America

ISIC	Industry	Note	Output (valuation not defined) (billions of US Dollars) 2013	2014	2015	2016	Note	Value added (valuation not defined) (billions of US Dollars) 2013	2014	2015	2016	Note	Gross fixed capital formation (billions of US Dollars) 2015	2016
1010	Processing/preserving of meat		206.3	221.2	215.7	207.7		55.7	58.2	59.1	63.5		4.1	4.2
1020	Processing/preserving of fish, etc.		11.2	12.4	13.4	13.2		4.5	5.0	5.4	5.4		0.3	0.3
1030	Processing/preserving of fruit, vegetables		71.8	72.7	73.7	71.9		33.0	32.4	34.0	33.6		2.2	1.7
1040	Vegetable and animal oils and fats		58.0	55.0	51.3	50.3		9.6	9.2	10.6	11.3		0.6	0.5
1050	Dairy products		112.0	124.8	111.9	111.3		30.7	31.8	31.9	34.2		2.7	3.3
106	Grain mill products,starches and starch products		...	...	...	...		...	...	...	...		...	...
1061	Grain mill products		32.1	31.3	29.3	27.1		11.8	11.7	10.5	10.0		0.6	0.6
1062	Starches and starch products		13.9	11.7	10.5	10.2		4.2	4.1	3.9	3.8		0.3	0.2
107	Other food products		...	...	...	...		...	...	...	...		...	...
1071	Bakery products		66.8	68.7	69.9	70.9		36.9	38.3	39.7	41.5		1.9	2.0
1072	Sugar		10.2	9.3	9.4	9.7		3.6	3.1	3.2	3.7		0.4	0.3
1073	Cocoa, chocolate and sugar confectionery		22.9	23.4	25.1	26.2		11.3	11.9	12.7	13.0		0.8	0.5
1074	Macaroni, noodles, couscous, etc.		...	...	...	...		...	...	...	...		...	...
1075	Prepared meals and dishes		...	...	...	...		...	...	...	...		...	...
1079	Other food products n.e.c.		96.7	104.1	106.6	109.7		47.5	52.0	52.2	54.4		2.4	2.9
1080	Prepared animal feeds		60.8	59.4	57.3	56.5		16.8	16.9	17.6	18.4		1.2	1.4
110	Beverages		106.8	109.7	113.2	112.2		55.2	57.3	59.9	61.6		3.8	4.3
1101	Distilling, rectifying and blending of spirits		10.2	11.0	11.8	12.5		6.7	7.5	8.2	8.6		0.3	0.4
1102	Wines		15.8	18.0	20.0	21.7		8.8	11.1	12.6	13.7		0.9	1.0
1103	Malt liquors and malt		32.0	31.0	31.2	31.2		21.4	20.0	19.9	20.9		1.3	1.6
1104	Soft drinks,mineral waters,other bottled waters		48.7	49.8	50.3	46.8		18.3	18.7	19.2	18.4		1.3	1.4
1200	Tobacco products		40.3	37.3	41.5	42.6		31.9	29.7	33.5	34.4		0.3	0.3
131	Spinning, weaving and finishing of textiles		...	...	29.4	28.1		...	...	11.8	11.4		0.9	0.8
1311	Preparation and spinning of textile fibres		8.0	8.1	7.8	7.2		2.5	2.5	2.5	2.3		0.2	...
1312	Weaving of textiles		15.4	15.1	13.6	13.2		7.1	6.6	6.2	5.9		0.5	0.5
1313	Finishing of textiles		8.1	8.1	8.0	7.8		3.4	3.1	3.1	3.1		0.2	0.2
139	Other textiles		22.9	25.2	24.9	24.7		9.8	10.9	10.9	11.2		0.5	0.4
1391	Knitted and crocheted fabrics		...	...	...	...		...	...	...	...		...	...
1392	Made-up textile articles, except apparel		3.7	4.5	4.6	4.8		1.6	2.3	2.3	2.4		-	...
1393	Carpets and rugs		9.3	9.8	9.8	9.4		3.2	3.2	3.3	3.4		0.2	0.2
1394	Cordage, rope, twine and netting		1.6	1.6	1.6	1.6		0.7	0.6	0.7	0.7		0.1	0.1
1399	Other textiles n.e.c.		8.3	9.3	8.8	8.9		4.3	4.8	4.6	4.7		0.1	0.1
1410	Wearing apparel, except fur apparel		10.3	9.9	9.7	9.4		5.4	5.4	5.3	5.1		0.1	0.1
1420	Articles of fur		...	...	...	...		...	...	...	...		...	...
1430	Knitted and crocheted apparel		1.8	1.6	1.3	1.1		0.9	0.9	0.7	0.5		0.1	-
151	Leather;luggage,handbags,saddlery,harness;fur		...	...	...	...		...	...	...	...		...	...
1511	Tanning/dressing of leather; dressing of fur		1.7	1.9	1.7	1.5		0.4	0.3	0.3	0.4		-	-
1512	Luggage,handbags,etc.;saddlery/harness		1.4	1.4	1.5	1.6		0.8	0.8	0.8	0.8		-	-
1520	Footwear		2.0	1.8	1.8	1.8		1.0	0.9	0.8	0.8		-	-
1610	Sawmilling and planing of wood		26.5	28.2	28.8	30.6		10.0	11.6	10.6	11.7		1.4	1.4

Code												
162	Wood products, cork, straw, plaiting materials		62.1	66.8	68.9	71.5	27.0	28.7	30.3	32.6	2.1	2.3
1621	Veneer sheets and wood-based panels		20.2	20.7	20.9	22.1	8.6	8.3	8.6	9.7	0.8	0.9
1622	Builders' carpentry and joinery		22.8	25.1	25.3	25.2	9.9	10.8	11.5	12.0	0.7	0.6
1623	Wooden containers		7.2	8.3	9.3	9.3	3.3	3.9	4.1	4.0	0.3	0.3
1629	Other wood products;articles of cork,straw		11.9	12.7	13.4	14.9	5.1	5.7	6.2	6.9	0.3	0.4
170	Paper and paper products		185.9	186.9	185.3	181.7	85.6	85.3	85.8	84.5	8.5	8.0
1701	Pulp, paper and paperboard		83.2	82.9	80.5	76.4	43.7	44.2	43.5	41.4	4.9	4.8
1702	Corrugated paper and paperboard		78.8	81.2	81.8	82.5	30.6	30.8	32.0	32.8	2.7	2.5
1709	Other articles of paper and paperboard		23.9	22.9	23.0	22.8	11.4	10.2	10.3	10.3	0.9	0.8
181	Printing and service activities related to printing		82.4	81.6	81.0	82.7	48.9	47.6	47.4	49.2	2.2	2.4
1811	Printing		78.8	78.0	77.6	79.3	46.1	45.0	44.9	46.7	2.1	2.3
1812	Service activities related to printing		3.7	3.6	3.4	3.4	2.8	2.6	2.5	2.5	0.1	0.1
1820	Reproduction of recorded media		...	...	...	...	...	...	...	...	...	...
1910	Coke oven products	a/	852.8	786.3	507.8	430.3	130.0	92.0	101.8	86.0	15.1	14.3
1920	Refined petroleum products	a/	...	...	...	...	...	...	...	...	...	...
201	Basic chemicals,fertilizers, etc.		417.3	399.4	521.6b/	503.4b/	149.0	147.6	237.5b/	245.3b/	26.8b/	27.4b/
2011	Basic chemicals		276.6	259.9	214.3	207.9	100.6	99.6	93.7	98.5	11.7	11.3
2012	Fertilizers and nitrogen compounds		28.0	25.7	19.9	17.2	14.0	12.1	10.9	9.3	5.2	4.0
2013	Plastics and synthetic rubber in primary forms		112.6	113.7	99.7	94.1	34.5	35.9	34.4	35.8	5.1	6.1
202	Other chemical products		...b/	...b/	...b/	...b/	...b/	...b/	...b/	...b/	...b/	...b/
2021	Pesticides and other agrochemical products		17.8	15.9	14.9	15.6	8.9	7.5	6.8	7.0	0.5	0.3
2022	Paints,varnishes;printing ink and mastics		31.0	32.3	32.7	32.5	13.3	14.0	14.7	15.4	0.4	0.5
2023	Soap,cleaning and cosmetic preparations		80.2	85.3	86.1	83.8	45.0	49.4	50.5	52.6	1.9	2.8
2029	Other chemical products n.e.c.		53.3	55.3	54.0	52.3	24.8	25.7	26.6	26.7	2.0	2.4
2030	Man-made fibres		...b/	...b/	...b/	...b/	...b/	...b/	...b/	...b/	...b/	...b/
2100	Pharmaceuticals,medicinal chemicals, etc.		186.0	199.3	215.7	219.9	130.2	136.1	147.0	155.0	7.2	5.7
221	Rubber products		44.3	44.5	44.3	42.5	18.4	19.5	20.5	20.5	1.4	1.8
2211	Rubber tyres and tubes		20.3	20.3	20.3	18.8	7.6	8.1	8.9	8.6	0.8	1.2
2219	Other rubber products		24.0	24.2	24.0	23.7	10.8	11.4	11.7	11.9	0.5	0.6
2220	Plastics products		181.4	189.9	192.2	193.2	86.0	88.2	91.3	97.8	7.1	8.4
2310	Glass and glass products		24.0	24.4	25.5	26.2	13.8	14.0	15.3	15.9	1.4	1.8
239	Non-metallic mineral products n.e.c.		...	...	...	...	...	...	...	...	...	...
2391	Refractory products	c/	5.5	5.6	5.5	5.6	3.2	3.4	3.3	3.4	0.2	0.4
2392	Clay building materials	c/	...	...	...	...	...	...	...	...	...	...
2393	Other porcelain and ceramic products		2.2	2.2	2.2	2.1	1.5	1.5	1.5	1.5	0.1	0.1
2394	Cement, lime and plaster		6.8	7.4	7.5	7.8	3.5	4.0	4.0	4.1	0.5	0.4
2395	Articles of concrete, cement and plaster		44.1	48.7	53.5	57.2	22.9	25.5	28.3	31.3	2.8	2.9
2396	Cutting, shaping and finishing of stone	d/	23.7	24.8	23.9	24.3	14.4	15.2	14.8	15.2	1.0	1.0
2399	Other non-metallic mineral products n.e.c.	d/	...	...	...	...	...	...	...	...	...	...
2410	Basic iron and steel		132.4	134.3	109.4	98.0	42.7	44.4	36.2	35.9	2.5	3.5
2420	Basic precious and other non-ferrous metals		98.8	97.4	86.7	79.1	27.6	28.4	27.3	27.2	2.2	1.9
243	Casting of metals		32.0	33.7	32.3	29.5	17.8	18.7	18.1	16.7	1.2	1.2
2431	Casting of iron and steel		18.8	20.0	18.2	16.2	10.6	11.1	10.2	9.2	0.6	0.5
2432	Casting of non-ferrous metals		13.2	13.7	14.1	13.3	7.2	7.5	7.8	7.6	0.6	0.6
251	Struct.metal products, tanks, reservoirs	e/	347.1	357.5	349.1	335.8	185.7	191.0	186.3	183.0	10.2	10.8

continued

United States of America

		Output (valuation not defined)					Value added (valuation not defined)					Gross fixed capital formation		
		(billions of US Dollars)					(billions of US Dollars)					(billions of US Dollars)		
ISIC	Industry	Note	2013	2014	2015	2016	Note	2013	2014	2015	2016	Note	2015	2016
2511	Structural metal products		78.0	83.0	84.8	84.9		38.4	40.5	41.4	42.8		1.7	1.8
2512	Tanks, reservoirs and containers of metal		35.6	37.1	35.1	31.1		14.5	15.9	14.9	13.2		0.8	0.9
2513	Steam generators, excl. hot water boilers		...	...	...	...		...	...	...	...		...	...
2520	Weapons and ammunition	e/	...	...	...	...	e/	...	...	...	...	e/	...	...
259	Other metal products;metal working services	e/	...	...	...	...	e/	...	...	...	...	e/	...	...
2591	Forging,pressing,stamping,roll-forming of metal		34.7	35.5	33.4	31.4		15.6	15.9	15.2	14.7		1.4	1.4
2592	Treatment and coating of metals; machining		27.5	28.9	26.9	25.7		16.8	17.3	16.0	15.7		0.8	0.9
2593	Cutlery, hand tools and general hardware		10.1	9.9	10.4	9.9		6.5	6.3	6.7	6.4		0.3	0.3
2599	Other fabricated metal products n.e.c.		161.3	163.2	158.5	152.9		93.8	95.0	92.0	90.2		5.2	5.6
2610	Electronic components and boards		86.8	87.8	89.9	87.3		46.2	47.6	49.0	46.3		11.6	7.1
2620	Computers and peripheral equipment		29.4	27.5	26.5	24.4		14.5	13.4	12.6	11.2		0.8	0.6
2630	Communication equipment		44.5	39.3	37.7	36.2		23.4	20.6	20.8	19.9		1.0	1.0
2640	Consumer electronics		3.0	2.9	3.0	3.0		1.7	1.7	1.7	1.7		-	
265	Measuring,testing equipment; watches, etc.		...	...	...	...		...	...	...	...		...	...
2651	Measuring/testing/navigating equipment,etc.		113.7	114.0	110.9	112.8		71.6	71.9	71.2	72.9		2.5	2.2
2652	Watches and clocks		...	...	...	...		...	...	...	...		...	...
2660	Irradiation/electromedical equipment,etc.		28.5	27.7	28.3	27.5		19.3	16.3	16.9	17.1		0.6	0.9
2670	Optical instruments and photographic equipment		4.7	4.2	6.3	6.6		2.7	2.3	3.5	3.9		0.3	0.3
2680	Magnetic and optical media		2.7	2.8	2.8	2.5		1.7	1.6	1.5	1.4		0.1	-
2710	Electric motors,generators,transformers,etc.		39.1	40.1	37.8	36.4		19.3	19.9	18.1	17.3		0.6	0.6
2720	Batteries and accumulators		10.4	11.6	11.7	11.0		5.0	5.6	5.4	5.3		0.6	0.2
273	Wiring and wiring devices		28.5	28.7	28.5	28.0		13.5	13.5	13.6	13.8		0.6	0.7
2731	Fibre optic cables		1.7	2.1	2.4	3.0		0.8	1.0	1.2	1.5		0.1	0.1
2732	Other electronic and electric wires and cables		12.2	12.6	12.2	11.2		4.4	4.4	4.4	4.2		0.2	0.3
2733	Wiring devices		14.6	14.1	14.0	13.7		8.3	8.2	8.0	8.0		0.3	0.3
2740	Electric lighting equipment		12.0	12.2	12.1	12.9		6.5	6.8	6.9	7.4		0.2	0.2
2750	Domestic appliances		19.1	20.1	21.2	22.0		8.4	9.1	9.7	10.6		0.6	0.4
2790	Other electrical equipment		14.5	13.7	19.4	18.9		6.8	6.4	9.6	9.6		0.6	0.5
281	General-purpose machinery	f/	388.8	399.6	273.8	261.6	f/	183.7	199.1	139.1	134.4	f/	6.9	6.4
2811	Engines/turbines,excl.aircraft,vehicle engines		14.9	14.5	65.4	57.7		7.0	5.9	29.3	25.5		1.6	1.5
2812	Fluid power equipment		11.0	11.0	11.1	10.2		5.4	5.4	5.4	4.9		0.3	0.2
2813	Other pumps, compressors, taps and valves		27.7	29.0	27.3	24.9		14.1	15.8	13.9	13.2		0.6	0.6
2814	Bearings, gears, gearing and driving elements		33.5	36.7	35.4	30.3		13.8	15.1	14.7	12.7		0.9	0.8
2815	Ovens, furnaces and furnace burners		2.7	2.8	2.8	2.6		1.5	1.6	1.6	1.5		0.1	0.1
2816	Lifting and handling equipment		28.5	29.6	28.4	28.9		12.5	13.7	12.4	12.5		0.6	0.5
2817	Office machinery, excl.computers,etc.		2.1	1.7	...	...		0.9	1.0	...	...		...	...
2818	Power-driven hand tools		4.0	3.5	3.4	3.4		2.3	1.7	1.7	1.7		0.1	0.1
2819	Other general-purpose machinery		70.7	71.2	67.3	66.8		35.3	36.6	34.0	34.8		1.4	1.2
282	Special-purpose machinery	f/	...	...	...	...	f/	...	...	...	...	f/	...	...
2821	Agricultural and forestry machinery		47.1	47.7	39.8	31.9		16.7	23.3	18.0	13.0		0.9	0.6
2822	Metal-forming machinery and machine tools		...	...	...	...		...	...	...	...		...	...

Code	Description	fn					fn					fn		
2823	Machinery for metallurgy		30.1	31.1	31.3	29.9		18.0	18.8	18.8	18.3		1.3	1.3
2824	Mining, quarrying and construction machinery		66.7	68.5	52.4	43.4		28.9	31.3	21.0	17.8		1.1	0.9
2825	Food/beverage/tobacco processing machinery		4.8	5.3	5.3	5.2		2.6	3.0	3.0	3.0		0.2	0.1
2826	Textile/apparel/leather production machinery		...	...	...	...		...	...	...	...		...	...
2829	Other special-purpose machinery		45.1	46.9	46.5	45.7		24.6	26.0	26.3	25.3		1.1	1.2
2910	Motor vehicles		283.8	313.1	337.1	344.4		64.5	70.8	77.0	82.2		10.0	5.7
2920	Automobile bodies, trailers and semi-trailers		35.2	39.5	42.3	42.0		12.4	13.6	14.2	14.8		0.6	0.6
2930	Parts and accessories for motor vehicles		227.0	247.6	258.5	260.8		74.9	78.9	83.0	84.1		8.5	8.2
301	Building of ships and boats		33.6	33.5	34.3	33.4		20.3	19.9	20.7	20.5		0.9	0.9
3011	Building of ships and floating structures	g/	33.6	33.5	34.3	33.4	g/	20.3	19.9	20.7	20.5	g/	0.9	0.9
3012	Building of pleasure and sporting boats	g/	...	...	...	...	g/	...	...	...	...	g/	...	...
3020	Railway locomotives and rolling stock		20.3	22.8	22.3	16.2		6.8	7.1	6.0	4.0		0.3	0.3
3030	Air and spacecraft and related machinery		223.6	238.5	236.8	234.8		116.4	129.6	129.9	117.3		4.3	4.6
3040	Military fighting vehicles		3.6	2.5	2.6	3.5		2.0	1.1	1.5	2.3		...	0.1
309	Transport equipment n.e.c.		14.0	14.7	15.4	14.3		5.8	5.7	5.6	5.3		0.4	0.4
3091	Motorcycles	h/	6.0	6.1	6.3	6.2	h/	3.1	2.8	2.9	2.9	h/	0.2	0.2
3092	Bicycles and invalid carriages	h/	...	...	...	...	h/	...	...	...	...	h/	...	...
3099	Other transport equipment n.e.c.		7.9	8.6	9.1	8.1		2.7	2.9	2.8	2.5		0.2	0.2
3100	Furniture		68.2	69.7	73.9	74.7		35.6	36.6	39.3	41.1		1.4	1.4
321	Jewellery, bijouterie and related articles		7.9	7.9	7.6	7.3		4.0	4.3	4.2	3.9		0.1	0.1
3211	Jewellery and related articles		...	...	...	...		...	...	...	...		...	...
3212	Imitation jewellery and related articles		...	...	...	...		...	...	...	...		...	...
3220	Musical instruments		1.8	2.0	2.0	2.0		1.2	1.3	1.3	1.2		-	-
3230	Sports goods		10.5	10.4	10.4	10.6		5.9	6.0	6.0	6.2		0.2	0.2
3240	Games and toys		1.4	1.5	1.4	1.5		0.7	0.8	0.7	0.8		-	-
3250	Medical and dental instruments and supplies		95.4	88.8	90.5	92.0		63.7	59.4	59.5	60.5		2.6	2.5
3290	Other manufacturing n.e.c.		38.9	41.1	41.2	41.8		23.4	24.4	24.8	25.3		1.2	1.0
331	Repair of fabricated metal products/machinery		...	...	...	...		...	...	...	...		...	...
3311	Repair of fabricated metal products		...	...	...	...		...	...	...	...		...	...
3312	Repair of machinery		...	...	...	...		...	...	...	...		...	...
3313	Repair of electronic and optical equipment		...	...	...	...		...	...	...	...		...	...
3314	Repair of electrical equipment		...	...	...	...		...	...	...	...		...	...
3315	Repair of transport equip., excl. motor vehicles		...	...	...	...		...	...	...	...		...	...
3319	Repair of other equipment		...	...	...	...		...	...	...	...		...	...
3320	Installation of industrial machinery/equipment		...	...	...	...		...	...	...	...		...	...
C	Total manufacturing		5809.7	5887.6	5527.5	5358.0		2356.0	2387.2	2404.7	2409.0		177.0	168.3

a/ 1910 includes 1920.
b/ 201 includes 202 and 2030.
c/ 2391 includes 2392.
d/ 2396 includes 2399.
e/ 251 includes 2520 and 259.
f/ 281 includes 282.
g/ 3011 includes 3012.
h/ 3091 includes 3092.

United States of America

Index numbers of industrial production

ISIC Revision 4 — (2010=100)

ISIC	Industry	Note	2005	2006	2007	2008	2009	2010	2011	2012	2013	2014	2015	2016
10	Food products		100	101	101	100	100	100	100	100	102	102	104	106
11	Beverages		97	97	103	98	101	100	103	109	112	115	118	116
12	Tobacco products		136	131	120	107	99	100	95	92	90	80	85	83
13	Textiles		168	152	134	118	94	100	98	95	98	100	96	94
14	Wearing apparel		237	230	185	144	103	100	94	91	85	81	77	72
15	Leather and related products		134	134	118	109	89	100	111	97	90	86	83	84
16	Wood products, excluding furniture		157	158	148	126	97	100	100	106	112	115	120	124
17	Paper and paper products		115	114	115	110	98	100	100	103	103	102	101	100
18	Printing and reproduction of recorded media		127	125	128	120	100	100	98	97	97	95	94	96
19	Coke and refined petroleum products		102	104	107	102	101	100	102	102	106	102	100	107
20	Chemicals and chemical products		108	110	116	107	97	100	100	99	95	94	94	93
21	Pharmaceuticals,medicinal chemicals, etc.		111	115	117	114	107	100	100	97	89	87	91	90
22	Rubber and plastics products		124	125	121	110	92	100	101	106	107	110	112	114
23	Other non-metallic mineral products		145	147	146	129	97	100	102	104	110	114	115	116
24	Basic metals		104	107	109	110	81	100	107	105	109	109	102	97
25	Fabricated metal products, except machinery		115	121	127	122	94	100	107	110	112	114	110	106
26	Computer, electronic and optical products		70	79	92	99	88	100	108	117	120	125	126	129
27	Electrical equipment		121	122	127	122	96	100	105	107	107	109	109	108
28	Machinery and equipment n.e.c.		108	113	118	115	90	100	113	122	116	118	108	100
29	Motor vehicles, trailers and semi-trailers		131	129	128	103	75	100	109	121	130	142	149	151
30	Other transport equipment		85	91	106	108	99	100	100	110	114	118	118	110
31	Furniture		163	161	155	140	101	100	103	109	110	110	116	116
32	Other manufacturing		102	105	102	104	97	100	99	97	100	97	97	97
33	Repair and installation of machinery/equipment		…	…	…	…	…	…	…	…	…	…	…	…
C	Total manufacturing		107	110	114	109	94	100	103	106	107	109	108	107

Viet Nam

Supplier of information:
General Statistics Office of Viet Nam, Hanoi.

Basic source of data:
Survey.

Major deviations from ISIC (Revision 4):
None reported.

Reference period:
Fiscal year.

Scope:
All registered enterprises.

Method of data collection:
Mail questionnaires; direct interview in the field.

Type of enumeration:
Complete enumeration.

Adjusted for non-response:
Not reported.

Concepts and definitions of variables:
Number of employees includes home workers.

Related national publications:
Statistical Yearbook of Viet Nam, published by the General Statistics Office of Viet Nam, Hanoi.

Viet Nam

ISIC	Industry	Number of enterprises (number)					Number of employees (thousands)					Wages and salaries paid to employees (billions of Vietnamese Dongs)				
		Note	2013	2014	2015	2016	Note	2013	2014	2015	2016	Note	2013	2014	2015	2016
1010	Processing/preserving of meat		250	297	306	339		13.3	13.8	14.6	14.8		839	927	1024	1325
1020	Processing/preserving of fish, etc.		1123	1181	1196	1239		196.2	200.6	195.0	196.8		9647	10933	11897	13290
1030	Processing/preserving of fruit,vegetables		736	773	844	944		65.9	62.5	61.8	58.9		2920	3273	3510	4052
1040	Vegetable and animal oils and fats		105	99	100	117		5.6	5.5	6.1	5.1		651	587	655	773
1050	Dairy products		155	168	187	211		19.8	19.1	22.8	24.6		2070	2066	2793	3996
106	Grain mill products,starches and starch products		1127	1135	1160	1140		35.6	35.9	37.5	36.3		1625	1825	2337	2207
1061	Grain mill products		956	936	920	885		25.5	25.5	24.6	22.7		1057	1168	1222	1216
1062	Starches and starch products		171	199	240	255		10.0	10.5	13.0	13.5		568	657	1115	991
107	Other food products		1722	1970	2149	2378		131.7	135.2	141.8	144.0		8838	10133	11565	13150
1071	Bakery products		401	463	517	545		36.0	37.1	38.7	35.3		2691	3202	3730	3345
1072	Sugar		49	51	54	50		17.1	15.9	14.6	14.2		1159	1079	1088	1042
1073	Cocoa, chocolate and sugar confectionery		140	147	192	203		12.8	12.6	15.8	17.7		810	958	1285	1796
1074	Macaroni, noodles, couscous, etc.		103	104	103	116		17.4	18.3	18.9	22.0		1473	1610	1839	2273
1075	Prepared meals and dishes		57	87	79	147		1.3	2.0	2.2	3.6		94	141	176	251
1079	Other food products n.e.c.		972	1118	1204	1317		47.2	49.3	51.6	51.2		2611	3144	3446	4443
1080	Prepared animal feeds		602	652	688	769		50.4	54.9	62.6	73.4		4532	5093	7222	7718
110	Beverages		2073	2116	2190	2291		47.1	47.1	49.1	49.3		4512	4456	5532	6293
1101	Distilling, rectifying and blending of spirits		135	137	150	164		2.4	2.1	2.1	1.9		140	126	135	113
1102	Wines		29	27	33	31		0.8	0.8	0.7	0.7		55	54	48	57
1103	Malt liquors and malt		119	116	116	115		14.9	14.7	15.0	15.1		1722	1717	1953	2226
1104	Soft drinks,mineral waters,other bottled waters		1790	1836	1891	1981		29.0	29.4	31.4	31.6		2595	2560	3396	3897
1200	Tobacco products		27	26	26	23		12.8	11.6	11.2	11.1		1772	1541	1785	1661
131	Spinning, weaving and finishing of textiles		969	986	1009	1135		116.5	136.2	138.3	145.4		7843	9528	11246	12744
1311	Preparation and spinning of textile fibres		355	397	411	432		77.2	87.6	91.7	93.6		4987	6240	7531	8089
1312	Weaving of textiles		290	296	283	313		23.7	31.5	29.4	31.8		1917	2118	2339	2901
1313	Finishing of textiles		324	293	315	390		15.6	17.1	17.1	20.1		939	1170	1376	1754
139	Other textiles		-	-	-	2015		-	-	-	133.1		-	-	-	9278
1391	Knitted and crocheted fabrics		-	-	-	308		-	-	-	19.3		-	-	-	1691
1392	Made-up textile articles, except apparel		-	-	-	1086		-	-	-	73.2		-	-	-	4465
1393	Carpets and rugs		-	-	-	60		-	-	-	0.9		-	-	-	40
1394	Cordage, rope, twine and netting		-	-	-	194		-	-	-	13.9		-	-	-	1167
1399	Other textiles n.e.c.		-	-	-	367		-	-	-	25.7		-	-	-	1915
1410	Wearing apparel, except fur apparel		4831	5402	5705	6135		1111.4	1229.8	1318.2	1406.1		60249	71113	85153	99793
1420	Articles of fur		24	23	13	14		1.3	1.4	1.1	0.5		88	98	83	37
1430	Knitted and crocheted apparel		312	284	263	264		18.1	16.8	17.8	20.8		927	964	1163	1344
151	Leather,luggage,handbags,saddlery,harness;fur		612	675	753	852		123.6	158.0	147.7	153.7		6533	8827	10357	11811
1511	Tanning/dressing of leather; dressing of fur		44	50	49	55		6.0	7.2	7.4	8.7		439	573	654	770
1512	Luggage,handbags,etc.;saddlery/harness		568	625	704	797		117.5	150.7	140.3	145.0		6094	8254	9702	11041
1520	Footwear		771	839	931	1056		802.8	908.4	993.1	1055.5		41800	51180	57324	76479
1610	Sawmilling and planing of wood		1545	1482	1561	1701		40.6	35.9	38.3	39.7		1897	1908	2188	2323

Code	Description												
162	Wood products, cork, straw, plaiting materials	6189	5092	4459	3764	94.0	88.1	85.5	82.3	2975	2771	2751	2596
1621	Veneer sheets and wood-based panels	2925	2260	1725	1390	36.2	32.9	29.6	25.7	771	664	604	518
1622	Builders' carpentry and joinery	700	681	591	575	11.8	12.6	11.7	12.6	743	726	696	711
1623	Wooden containers	255	175	166	151	4.1	3.7	3.4	3.1	225	175	164	151
1629	Other wood products;articles of cork,straw	2309	1974	1977	1648	41.8	38.9	40.8	40.8	1236	1206	1287	1216
170	Paper and paper products	9543	8171	7328	6448	114.4	107.9	102.3	106.1	2448	2251	2134	2059
1701	Pulp, paper and paperboard	1155	1143	1323	1105	15.6	17.2	18.0	19.9	388	375	390	373
1702	Corrugated paper and paperboard	5297	4582	4075	3640	65.8	60.8	57.3	59.1	1320	1208	1140	1101
1709	Other articles of paper and paperboard	3090	2447	1930	1703	33.0	29.9	26.9	27.1	740	668	604	585
181	Printing and service activities related to printing	5470	5317	4552	4017	73.3	71.9	67.1	64.5	5590	5168	4847	4398
1811	Printing	3650	3735	3223	2905	47.5	49.6	48.5	46.9	3658	3642	3792	3301
1812	Service activities related to printing	1820	1582	1329	1111	25.8	22.3	18.6	17.6	1932	1526	1055	1097
1820	Reproduction of recorded media	14	13	21	34	0.1	0.2	0.2	0.4	11	15	24	24
1910	Coke oven products	90	71	66	50	1.0	1.0	1.1	1.0	26	18	25	20
1920	Refined petroleum products	789	730	773	656	4.5	5.0	4.6	4.2	98	93	77	76
201	Basic chemicals,fertilizers, etc.	5666	5326	4892	4416	54.7	50.7	50.6	48.6	1297	1173	1089	960
2011	Basic chemicals	1388	1100	1016	911	12.6	10.3	10.7	10.3	310	271	274	251
2012	Fertilizers and nitrogen compounds	3160	3331	3130	2729	29.6	28.8	27.7	25.6	736	682	602	527
2013	Plastics and synthetic rubber in primary forms	1118	895	745	776	12.6	11.6	12.1	12.7	251	220	213	182
202	Other chemical products	9522	7764	6405	5833	75.8	66.9	57.2	56.3	2061	1851	1684	1539
2021	Pesticides and other agrochemical products	1278	981	1001	959	8.7	7.5	8.0	8.8	119	119	104	92
2022	Paints,varnishes;printing ink and mastics	3197	2733	2398	2088	26.6	23.3	21.3	19.8	768	682	649	594
2023	Soap,cleaning and cosmetic preparations	2551	2058	1856	1755	17.9	17.2	16.4	16.6	683	625	540	452
2029	Other chemical products n.e.c.	2496	1991	1151	1032	22.5	18.9	11.4	11.1	491	425	391	401
2030	Man-made fibres	36	35	39	59	0.4	0.5	0.5	1.0	12	14	19	14
2100	Pharmaceuticals,medicinal chemicals, etc.	6233	5146	4413	4263	51.3	48.7	45.6	43.5	484	442	416	393
221	Rubber products	5746	1980a/	1599a/	1419a/	59.5	19.8a/	18.3a/	16.2a/	459	86a/	84a/	83a/
2211	Rubber tyres and tubes	2336	1980	1599	1419	23.1	19.8	18.3	16.2	93	86	84	83
2219	Other rubber products	:	:	:	:	:	:	:	:	:	:	:	:
2220	Plastics products	20283	17596	13875	11889	243.4	221.8	201.0	184.3	4581	4083	3737	3320
2310	Glass and glass products	1606	935	845	767	13.1	11.2	11.3	11.4	211	187	185	192
239	Non-metallic mineral products n.e.c.	22718	19812	17494	16043	281.1	262.4	257.7	262.5	4271	3753	3595	3495
2391	Refractory products	209	180	238	217	2.9	3.0	3.9	3.9	94	85	92	86
2392	Clay building materials	6859	6012	5731	4640	99.4	95.3	93.9	98.3	1265	1164	1146	1135
2393	Other porcelain and ceramic products	2464	2450	2250	2083	33.5	33.2	31.4	31.8	355	335	343	340
2394	Cement, lime and plaster	5583	4937	4628	4878	48.6	48.7	54.5	55.4	226	218	208	213
2395	Articles of concrete, cement and plaster	5461	4477	3150	2939	65.5	54.5	47.7	46.5	1474	1185	1056	964
2396	Cutting, shaping and finishing of stone	1563	1282	1087	908	23.2	20.9	20.0	20.1	631	568	574	571
2399	Other non-metallic mineral products n.e.c.	579	474	410	378	8.1	6.8	6.3	6.5	226	198	176	186
2410	Basic iron and steel	6456	4711	4334	3595	60.6	51.9	52.4	52.1	587	584	599	595
2420	Basic precious and other non-ferrous metals	1878	1610	1507	800	18.9	17.0	16.1	13.7	218	191	168	172
243	Casting of metals	959	1436	574	620	11.7	14.7	13.3	11.5	369	304	289	300
2431	Casting of iron and steel	836	1369	529	575	10.0	13.8	12.4	10.3	302	252	243	257
2432	Casting of non-ferrous metals	122	68	45	45	1.7	0.9	0.9	1.1	67	52	46	43
251	Struct.metal products, tanks, reservoirs	10558	8986	7386	6222	127.8	108.1	100.7	97.5	5951	4980	4520	4520

continued

Viet Nam

ISIC	Industry	Note	Number of enterprises (number)				Note	Number of employees (thousands)				Note	Wages and salaries paid to employees (billions of Vietnamese Dongs)			
ISIC Revision 4			2013	2014	2015	2016		2013	2014	2015	2016		2013	2014	2015	2016
2511	Structural metal products		4227	4215	4657	5593		88.6	91.9	98.1	116.5		5676	6793	8242	9684
2512	Tanks, reservoirs and containers of metal		187	186	196	212		6.7	6.5	7.6	8.5		395	445	564	666
2513	Steam generators, excl. hot water boilers		106	119	127	146		2.2	2.3	2.4	2.9		151	148	180	208
2520	Weapons and ammunition		1	2	2	9		0.8	0.8	0.8	8.1		53	53	53	882
259	Other metal products;metal working services		4825	5578	5990	7105		164.6	176.7	184.8	203.6		10607	13224	15762	17962
2591	Forging,pressing,stamping,roll-forming of metal		126	156	128	143		2.9	2.9	2.0	2.3		229	261	152	173
2592	Treatment and coating of metals; machining		2204	2841	3066	3828		36.6	43.6	46.4	55.1		2274	3453	3518	4045
2593	Cutlery, hand tools and general hardware		428	413	499	558		24.7	34.0	34.3	39.5		1661	2373	2919	3640
2599	Other fabricated metal products n.e.c.		2067	2168	2297	2576		100.3	96.2	102.1	106.8		6443	7138	9172	10105
2610	Electronic components and boards		339	425	486	591		126.2	141.7	167.0	183.2		8461	10054	13080	14936
2620	Computers and peripheral equipment		45	46	33	56		49.2	49.7	49.7	72.4		2246	2714	2620	6186
2630	Communication equipment		161	210	278	321		93.4	151.8	198.3	224.6		8608	9900	19806	28472
2640	Consumer electronics		153	181	191	231		37.5	44.3	59.9	110.1		2891	2818	4194	8417
265	Measuring,testing equipment; watches, etc.		97	116	111	142		2.6	2.8	3.1	7.5		139	282	266	670
2651	Measuring/testing/navigating equipment,etc.		74	90	92	122		1.9	2.1	2.5	4.3		116	235	226	387
2652	Watches and clocks		23	26	19	20		0.7	0.7	0.6	3.2		23	46	40	283
2660	Irradiation/electromedical equipment,etc.		8	7	9	12		2.3	1.5	1.5	1.7		200	155	154	180
2670	Optical instruments and photographic equipment		21	23	26	32		13.1	14.7	13.1	11.3		823	961	722	1121
2680	Magnetic and optical media		15	13	11	14		3.4	4.6	4.3	1.6		222	359	473	121
2710	Electric motors,generators,transformers,etc.		270	303	352	382		43.3	44.7	50.1	49.3		3333	3598	4176	4334
2720	Batteries and accumulators		53	61	58	63		12.7	14.8	18.2	22.5		875	1187	1497	2109
273	Wiring and wiring devices		262	255	274	276		58.1	61.9	65.1	64.7		3962	4990	5431	5964
2731	Fibre optic cables		26	26	27	35		2.1	3.1	5.2	6.0		126	152	435	583
2732	Other electronic and electric wires and cables		171	170	181	177		41.1	44.7	42.7	43.0		2786	3524	3414	3843
2733	Wiring devices		65	59	66	64		14.9	14.2	17.2	15.8		1050	1315	1582	1538
2740	Electric lighting equipment		147	163	180	178		10.9	10.4	10.6	10.8		953	960	1154	668
2750	Domestic appliances		236	237	259	270		17.4	17.0	19.1	22.1		1361	1348	1742	2056
2790	Other electrical equipment		161	199	174	211		7.3	7.4	5.7	9.0		594	564	490	818
281	General-purpose machinery		598	611	686	756		39.0	42.0	42.8	42.3		3057	3500	3996	4251
2811	Engines/turbines,excl.aircraft,vehicle engines		24	22	21	21		2.4	3.0	1.6	1.5		186	272	154	187
2812	Fluid power equipment		22	24	23	30		1.4	1.5	1.8	1.3		104	127	141	114
2813	Other pumps, compressors, taps and valves		96	101	118	120		6.0	6.2	6.2	6.1		425	423	522	627
2814	Bearings, gears, gearing and driving elements		88	78	92	105		3.9	3.7	4.2	5.3		273	286	336	516
2815	Ovens, furnaces and furnace burners		31	25	33	33		0.7	0.6	0.6	0.8		37	32	66	54
2816	Lifting and handling equipment		161	160	190	189		7.2	7.0	7.3	8.6		511	588	603	1285
2817	Office machinery, excl.computers,etc.		29	33	24	25		9.1	11.7	12.7	12.0		721	1003	1200	894
2818	Power-driven hand tools		6	9	10	13		0.1	0.1	0.1	0.1		7	6	9	13
2819	Other general-purpose machinery		141	159	175	220		8.2	8.3	8.4	6.5		792	762	966	562
282	Special-purpose machinery		743	776	879	967		25.8	28.3	30.1	32.2		1691	2093	2544	3063
2821	Agricultural and forestry machinery		136	124	122	144		4.5	3.7	3.9	4.0		260	262	308	375
2822	Metal-forming machinery and machine tools		98	102	149	155		2.1	2.5	3.4	3.5		121	163	214	244

Code	Description												
2823	Machinery for metallurgy	54	34	34	37	0.5	0.4	0.5	0.6	18	10	12	16
2824	Mining, quarrying and construction machinery	182	195	161	142	2.3	2.4	2.5	2.4	107	90	92	84
2825	Food/beverage/tobacco processing machinery	345	302	265	219	3.8	3.5	3.4	3.6	131	118	111	114
2826	Textile/apparel/leather production machinery	566	545	472	251	7.9	7.2	7.5	4.1	52	58	47	37
2829	Other special-purpose machinery	1297	946	736	662	10.1	9.4	8.1	8.4	360	332	288	258
2910	Motor vehicles	2300	2049	1761	1435	18.1	16.0	14.4	13.2	65	53	55	47
2920	Automobile bodies, trailers and semi-trailers	586	448	289	210	5.7	5.4	4.2	3.1	83	62	61	54
2930	Parts and accessories for motor vehicles	9662	7772	6334	5197	104.3	97.0	87.1	80.9	343	320	290	261
301	Building of ships and boats	5028	4184	3591	3002	45.5	36.4	33.9	33.4	409	326	266	256
3011	Building of ships and floating structures	4963	4126	3557	2946	44.6	35.5	33.2	32.7	372	295	234	227
3012	Building of pleasure and sporting boats	65	58	34	56	0.9	0.9	0.7	0.7	37	31	32	29
3020	Railway locomotives and rolling stock	60	60	57	54	0.6	0.6	0.7	0.7	6	3	5	3
3030	Air and spacecraft and related machinery	47	43	26	56	0.4	0.4	0.3	0.6	4	2	1	3
3040	Military fighting vehicles	-	-	-	-	-	-	-	-	-	-	-	-
309	Transport equipment n.e.c.	7550	6246	5496	6149	72.2	68.5	67.9	68.1	318	307	309	294
3091	Motorcycles	6288	5473	4841	5415	58.0	59.3	58.6	57.5	200	210	209	206
3092	Bicycles and invalid carriages	1195	723	611	700	13.0	8.6	8.5	10.0	76	69	71	61
3099	Other transport equipment n.e.c.	66	50	44	34	1.1	0.6	0.9	0.6	42	28	29	27
3100	Furniture	27694	24345	20112	16879	354.5	339.7	313.9	290.5	4172	3677	3400	3247
321	Jewellery, bijouterie and related articles	1404	1197	1011	840	18.7	17.0	19.4	14.0	211	185	161	133
3211	Jewellery and related articles	1041	975	817	694	12.7	12.4	15.2	10.4	154	141	126	106
3212	Imitation jewellery and related articles	363	222	195	146	6.0	4.6	4.2	3.6	57	44	35	27
3220	Musical instruments	54	47	48	48	0.7	0.7	0.8	0.8	18	19	21	22
3230	Sports goods	1623	1703	1291	1021	21.8	25.0	22.9	22.5	88	83	83	76
3240	Games and toys	3715	2491	2009	1439	57.1	46.0	39.8	32.6	251	239	201	188
3250	Medical and dental instruments and supplies	1695	1383	1035	853	19.6	16.2	15.2	13.6	226	189	193	168
3290	Other manufacturing n.e.c.	4597	4321	3463	2987	53.9	57.0	51.9	50.8	951	895	963	683
331	Repair of fabricated metal products/machinery	3147	2323	1965	1454	33.4	25.5	23.8	21.7	1723	1457	1340	1262
3311	Repair of fabricated metal products	60	79	50	40	0.8	0.8	0.8	0.6	58	45	46	44
3312	Repair of machinery	1148	609	483	413	11.5	7.3	6.3	6.0	820	683	603	563
3313	Repair of electronic and optical equipment	245	155	132	151	1.9	1.5	1.4	1.5	69	63	74	75
3314	Repair of electrical equipment	377	393	191	131	3.2	2.8	2.3	2.2	267	217	185	176
3315	Repair of transport equip., excl. motor vehicles	1304	1027	1060	675	15.8	12.7	12.7	10.9	502	430	402	374
3319	Repair of other equipment	11	60	48	44	0.1	0.4	0.4	0.4	7	19	30	30
3320	Installation of industrial machinery/equipment	1757	1637	1291	1112	19.7	16.3	13.4	13.3	595	522	449	363
C	Total manufacturing	555160	448976	373555	320452 b/	6758.0	6097.1	5682.6	5217.2 b/	75351	65383	61355	56935 b/

a/ 221 includes rubber tyres and tubes only.
b/ Sum of available data.

Viet Nam

ISIC	Industry	Note	Output (billions of Vietnamese Dongs) 2013	2014	2015	2016	Note	Value added at producers' prices (billions of Vietnamese Dongs) 2013	2014	2015	2016	Note	Gross fixed capital formation (billions of Vietnamese Dongs) 2015	2016
1010	Processing/preserving of meat		...	...	...	...		1837	2602	2422	2718		2623	2568
1020	Processing/preserving of fish, etc.		...	...	...	...		32170	35235	35009	39060		29352	30857
1030	Processing/preserving of fruit,vegetables		...	...	...	...		7593	10292	10997	15009		6443	6780
1040	Vegetable and animal oils and fats		...	...	...	...		5948	7534	5877	6260		3076	3216
1050	Dairy products		...	...	...	...		10074	13731	12188	13528		12626	13147
106	Grain mill products,starches and starch products		...	...	...	...		20140	19361	22052	22111		25711	23434
1061	Grain mill products		...	...	...	...		15802	14568	16894	17092		15805	13323
1062	Starches and starch products		...	...	...	...		4338	4793	5157	5019		9906	10111
107	Other food products		...	...	...	...		24719	30510	28142	32792		44343	43001
1071	Bakery products		...	...	...	...		5256	6390	6361	5035		12186	8090
1072	Sugar		...	...	...	...		4850	4669	4120	4285		8125	7817
1073	Cocoa, chocolate and sugar confectionery		...	...	...	...		1350	1564	1693	2021		2044	2097
1074	Macaroni, noodles, couscous, etc.		...	...	...	...		3702	4476	3946	4734		4221	4398
1075	Prepared meals and dishes		...	...	...	...		119	171	179	358		253	253
1079	Other food products n.e.c.		...	...	...	...		9442	13240	11843	16358		17514	20345
1080	Prepared animal feeds		...	...	...	...		34194	40285	37846	42998		28808	30978
110	Beverages		...	...	...	...		39710	33997	32401	35747		40354	45486
1101	Distilling, rectifying and blending of spirits		...	...	...	...		512	588	466	277		1081	1099
1102	Wines		...	...	...	...		277	260	181	177		192	221
1103	Malt liquors and malt		...	...	...	...		22049	19411	16987	19500		21727	26221
1104	Soft drinks,mineral waters,other bottled waters		...	...	...	...		16873	13739	14767	15792		17353	17945
1200	Tobacco products		...	...	...	...		14645	5814	6151	6299		3297	3648
131	Spinning, weaving and finishing of textiles		...	...	...	...		20304	29524	29531	32716		80361	93514
1311	Preparation and spinning of textile fibres		...	...	...	...		15710	23242	22443	24513		62936	75697
1312	Weaving of textiles		...	...	...	...		3636	4987	5530	6313		12435	13406
1313	Finishing of textiles		...	...	...	...		958	1296	1558	1890		4990	4410
139	Other textiles		...	...	...	...		-	-	-	-		-	26721
1391	Knitted and crocheted fabrics		...	...	...	...		-	-	-	...		-	9693
1392	Made-up textile articles, except apparel		...	...	...	...		-	-	-	...		-	8325
1393	Carpets and rugs		...	...	...	...		-	-	-	...		-	53
1394	Cordage, rope, twine and netting		...	...	...	...		-	-	-	...		-	2318
1399	Other textiles n.e.c.		...	...	...	...		-	-	-	...		-	6332
1410	Wearing apparel, except fur apparel		...	...	...	...		43762	64439	74123	83087		55930	69920
1420	Articles of fur		...	...	...	...		71	229	209	33		252	41
1430	Knitted and crocheted apparel		...	...	...	...		811	923	1052	1197		2134	2675
151	Leather;luggage,handbags,saddlery,harness;fur		...	...	...	...		6124	9449	10211	10496		8551	7464
1511	Tanning/dressing of leather; dressing of fur		...	...	...	...		1385	2854	2495	2321		2378	2390
1512	Luggage,handbags,etc.;saddlery/harness		...	...	...	...		4739	6595	7716	8175		6173	5074
1520	Footwear		...	...	...	...		39603	54687	59760	70221		54437	61216
1610	Sawmilling and planing of wood		...	...	...	...		9247	8977	9967	10654		7604	8615

Code	Description						
162	Wood products, cork, straw, plaiting materials	8466	11443	10414	12328	14976	14914
1621	Veneer sheets and wood-based panels	3966	5801	5521	6565	9479	9697
1622	Builders' carpentry and joinery	979	1249	1405	1435	1298	1424
1623	Wooden containers	263	354	323	386	318	471
1629	Other wood products;articles of cork,straw	3258	4038	3166	3942	3881	3322
170	Paper and paper products	16955	21823	21026	23667	45578	46482
1701	Pulp, paper and paperboard	3969	4475	4008	4536	16999	16954
1702	Corrugated paper and paperboard	8485	11181	10800	12115	17926	19140
1709	Other articles of paper and paperboard	4501	6167	6218	7016	10653	10388
181	Printing and service activities related to printing	7234	11214	11532	11792	14774	10561
1811	Printing	5343	8770	8172	8048	10893	7290
1812	Service activities related to printing	1891	2445	3360	3744	3881	3271
1820	Reproduction of recorded media	50	50	16	29	10	-7
1910	Coke oven products	505	1411	1062	1468	1839	1857
1920	Refined petroleum products	30616	23705	28704	24599	36146	33593
201	Basic chemicals,fertilizers, etc.	17105	19639	21809	20570	61511	62805
2011	Basic chemicals	2688	3251	3876	4511	11593	11504
2012	Fertilizers and nitrogen compounds	10746	12585	13303	11095	45420	45478
2013	Plastics and synthetic rubber in primary forms	3671	3803	4629	4965	4498	5824
202	Other chemical products	20809	20848	25951	30850	29310	28505
2021	Pesticides and other agrochemical products	3828	3151	3715	4826	2805	2512
2022	Paints,varnishes;printing ink and mastics	5907	6438	8120	8639	5896	7084
2023	Soap,cleaning and cosmetic preparations	7612	7858	9079	10455	10149	8545
2029	Other chemical products n.e.c.	3462	3400	5036	6929	10461	10365
2030	Man-made fibres	203	165	150	61	861	503
2100	Pharmaceuticals,medicinal chemicals, etc.	12520	15535	14650	16024	17869	19579
221	Rubber products	4177a/	4562a/	4705a/	10510	18049a/	29367
2211	Rubber tyres and tubes	4177	4562	4705	5444	18049	19138
2219	Other rubber products				...		...
2220	Plastics products	30927	35894	36949	42554	58388	68715
2310	Glass and glass products	2585	3477	3471	4558	12983	12100
239	Non-metallic mineral products n.e.c.	53075	64967	62760	69953	163845	168842
2391	Refractory products	608	598	741	572	737	647
2392	Clay building materials	10820	12832	12262	12976	28188	31635
2393	Other porcelain and ceramic products	3398	4402	3954	3910	7252	5760
2394	Cement, lime and plaster	24587	29632	25323	27052	99772	101957
2395	Articles of concrete, cement and plaster	10662	12037	15658	19720	19451	18581
2396	Cutting, shaping and finishing of stone	1750	3722	2987	3710	6227	6912
2399	Other non-metallic mineral products n.e.c.	1250	1744	1836	2014	2219	3350
2410	Basic iron and steel	30901	34909	34413	40110	85868	128953
2420	Basic precious and other non-ferrous metals	3583	6372	6304	7998	18639	22471
243	Casting of metals	1021	1310	1022	1463	12507	4372
2431	Casting of iron and steel	625	1230	925	1234	12305	4149
2432	Casting of non-ferrous metals	396	80	97	229	202	224
251	Struct.metal products, tanks, reservoirs	15783	21784	21767	25337	30896	30896

continued

Viet Nam

ISIC	Industry	Output (billions of Vietnamese Dongs)					Value added at producers' prices (billions of Vietnamese Dongs)					Gross fixed capital formation (billions of Vietnamese Dongs)		
		Note	2013	2014	2015	2016	Note	2013	2014	2015	2016	Note	2015	2016
2511	Structural metal products		...	...	...	...		13886	19797	20215	23466		28355	28836
2512	Tanks, reservoirs and containers of metal		...	...	...	...		1179	1335	1277	1527		2095	1821
2513	Steam generators, excl. hot water boilers		...	...	...	...		718	653	275	345		446	239
2520	Weapons and ammunition		...	...	...	...		22	37	24	407		190	3276
259	Other metal products;metal working services		...	...	...	...		23099	29678	30465	33971		56779	59608
2591	Forging,pressing,stamping,roll-forming of metal		...	...	...	...		2084	2130	1306	690		620	665
2592	Treatment and coating of metals; machining		...	...	...	...		5155	6728	7363	8896		13171	11335
2593	Cutlery, hand tools and general hardware		...	...	...	...		1708	3410	3966	4526		7411	8489
2599	Other fabricated metal products n.e.c.		...	...	...	...		14152	17410	17829	19859		35577	39919
2610	Electronic components and boards		...	...	...	...		13397	29101	32937	38122		48567	62759
2620	Computers and peripheral equipment		...	...	...	...		8987	11972	10993	14140		9518	12411
2630	Communication equipment		...	...	...	...		71443	193155	166169	193311		138968	163228
2640	Consumer electronics		...	...	...	...		4655	10809	13701	29484		13393	32232
265	Measuring,testing equipment; watches, etc.		...	...	...	...		265	339	437	847		893	1317
2651	Measuring/testing/navigating equipment,etc.		...	...	...	...		230	267	383	680		798	995
2652	Watches and clocks		...	...	...	...		35	72	53	167		96	321
2660	Irradiation/electromedical equipment,etc.		...	...	...	...		172	183	160	160		334	473
2670	Optical instruments and photographic equipment		...	...	...	...		756	1381	1485	1690		3191	3183
2680	Magnetic and optical media		...	...	...	...		208	390	261	270		3388	1055
2710	Electric motors,generators,transformers,etc.		...	...	...	...		5573	8214	8420	9495		10165	11533
2720	Batteries and accumulators		...	...	...	...		3980	6176	5269	6908		6182	7650
273	Wiring and wiring devices		...	...	...	...		12418	17583	16758	16331		15285	14571
2731	Fibre optic cables		...	...	...	...		644	939	1240	1348		1316	1275
2732	Other electronic and electric wires and cables		...	...	...	...		9439	14555	13092	12596		11730	11508
2733	Wiring devices		...	...	...	...		2335	2089	2426	2387		2239	1787
2740	Electric lighting equipment		...	...	...	...		1245	1866	1551	1548		2250	2416
2750	Domestic appliances		...	...	...	...		3906	4083	4806	4386		4562	5504
2790	Other electrical equipment		...	...	...	...		877	1351	970	1474		1085	2185
281	General-purpose machinery		...	...	...	...		7935	10706	10594	9538		18600	16537
2811	Engines/turbines,excl.aircraft,vehicle engines		...	...	...	...		471	764	317	316		1626	1778
2812	Fluid power equipment		...	...	...	...		236	301	328	252		388	213
2813	Other pumps, compressors, taps and valves		...	...	...	...		793	922	962	1027		2206	2170
2814	Bearings, gears, gearing and driving elements		...	...	...	...		631	678	791	1039		2208	2388
2815	Ovens, furnaces and furnace burners		...	...	...	...		53	65	67	101		90	61
2816	Lifting and handling equipment		...	...	...	...		986	1457	1114	1962		2280	5969
2817	Office machinery, excl.computers,etc.		...	...	...	...		2962	4561	5126	3895		3966	3040
2818	Power-driven hand tools		...	...	...	...		5	-13	11	11		35	32
2819	Other general-purpose machinery		...	...	...	...		1798	1971	1877	935		5800	885
282	Special-purpose machinery		...	...	...	...		3822	4834	5107	6181		7231	6109
2821	Agricultural and forestry machinery		...	...	...	...		780	727	833	968		644	644
2822	Metal-forming machinery and machine tools		...	...	...	...		186	293	349	461		835	871

Code							
2823	Machinery for metallurgy	64	41	80	50	53	84
2824	Mining, quarrying and construction machinery	315	603	468	407	481	348
2825	Food/beverage/tobacco processing machinery	423	492	494	378	481	391
2826	Textile/apparel/leather production machinery	1432	2399	1505	1456	1386	828
2829	Other special-purpose machinery	2361	2217	2205	1634	1413	1206
2910	Motor vehicles	10491	9079	26795	22526	25680	11615
2920	Automobile bodies, trailers and semi-trailers	1348	1030	1445	1186	1303	491
2930	Parts and accessories for motor vehicles	31233	25157	20017	17057	17804	14130
301	Building of ships and boats	25243	23080	10239	8921	11647	9857
3011	Building of ships and floating structures	25142	23014	10107	8765	11470	9758
3012	Building of pleasure and sporting boats	101	66	132	156	177	100
3020	Railway locomotives and rolling stock	44	45	68	54	63	60
3030	Air and spacecraft and related machinery	154	179	44	38	30	137
3040	Military fighting vehicles	-	-	-	-	-	-
309	Transport equipment n.e.c.	20906	2042	34940	32076	35238	29044
3091	Motorcycles	19440	750	33285	30969	34100	28038
3092	Bicycles and invalid carriages	1230	1110	1156	1031	1085	966
3099	Other transport equipment n.e.c.	236	181	498	76	53	40
3100	Furniture	31433	29274	43098	39266	38564	27222
321	Jewellery, bijouterie and related articles	1614	1492	1894	1623	1174	919
3211	Jewellery and related articles	1067	1183	1648	1479	1064	847
3212	Imitation jewellery and related articles	548	309	246	144	109	72
3220	Musical instruments	40	35	49	56	50	38
3230	Sports goods	2517	2317	1785	1856	1518	986
3240	Games and toys	2148	1847	2656	2066	1653	1028
3250	Medical and dental instruments and supplies	5111	4262	4646	3947	3594	2501
3290	Other manufacturing n.e.c.	8951	8642	7248	6628	6296	4330
331	Repair of fabricated metal products/machinery	5423	3228	4908	3750	4195	2756
3311	Repair of fabricated metal products	72	72	158	148	92	54
3312	Repair of machinery	2003	742	1592	1057	1190	1052
3313	Repair of electronic and optical equipment	670	326	482	363	233	110
3314	Repair of electrical equipment	355	322	661	599	940	392
3315	Repair of transport equip., excl. motor vehicles	2589	1761	1899	1549	1702	1114
3319	Repair of other equipment	-266	5	116	36	38	35
3320	Installation of industrial machinery/equipment	1441	762	2958	1936	1442	1866
C	Total manufacturing	1711934	1482999 b/	1300020	1137734	1148802	837204 b/

a/ 221 includes rubber tyres and tubes only.
b/ Sum of available data.

Viet Nam

Index numbers of industrial production

ISIC Revision 4

(2010=100)

ISIC	Industry	Note	2005	2006	2007	2008	2009	2010	2011	2012	2013	2014	2015	2016
10	Food products		⋮	⋮	⋮	⋮	⋮	100	⋮	⋮	130	134	147	158
11	Beverages		⋮	⋮	⋮	⋮	⋮	100	⋮	⋮	147	162	176	199
12	Tobacco products		⋮	⋮	⋮	⋮	⋮	100	⋮	⋮	112	97	105	115
13	Textiles		⋮	⋮	⋮	⋮	⋮	100	⋮	⋮	96	115	134	157
14	Wearing apparel		⋮	⋮	⋮	⋮	⋮	100	⋮	⋮	123	139	152	166
15	Leather and related products		⋮	⋮	⋮	⋮	⋮	100	⋮	⋮	128	163	204	228
16	Wood products, excluding furniture		⋮	⋮	⋮	⋮	⋮	⋮	⋮	⋮	⋮	⋮	⋮	⋮
17	Paper and paper products		⋮	⋮	⋮	⋮	⋮	100	⋮	⋮	124	151	182	191
18	Printing and reproduction of recorded media		⋮	⋮	⋮	⋮	⋮	⋮	⋮	⋮	⋮	⋮	⋮	⋮
19	Coke and refined petroleum products		⋮	⋮	⋮	⋮	⋮	⋮	⋮	⋮	⋮	⋮	⋮	⋮
20	Chemicals and chemical products		⋮	⋮	⋮	⋮	⋮	100	⋮	⋮	123	130	136	137
21	Pharmaceuticals,medicinal chemicals, etc.		⋮	⋮	⋮	⋮	⋮	100	⋮	⋮	122	125	129	132
22	Rubber and plastics products		⋮	⋮	⋮	⋮	⋮	100	⋮	⋮	94	99	108	120
23	Other non-metallic mineral products		⋮	⋮	⋮	⋮	⋮	100	⋮	⋮	97	105	121	138
24	Basic metals		⋮	⋮	⋮	⋮	⋮	100	⋮	⋮	132	147	176	216
25	Fabricated metal products, except machinery		⋮	⋮	⋮	⋮	⋮	100	⋮	⋮	87	101	111	120
26	Computer, electronic and optical products		⋮	⋮	⋮	⋮	⋮	100	⋮	⋮	200	239	287	⋮
27	Electrical equipment		⋮	⋮	⋮	⋮	⋮	100	⋮	⋮	133	136	153	169
28	Machinery and equipment n.e.c.		⋮	⋮	⋮	⋮	⋮	⋮	⋮	⋮	⋮	⋮	⋮	⋮
29	Motor vehicles, trailers and semi-trailers		⋮	⋮	⋮	⋮	⋮	100	⋮	⋮	130	160	205	239
30	Other transport equipment		⋮	⋮	⋮	⋮	⋮	100	⋮	⋮	128	132	137	155
31	Furniture		⋮	⋮	⋮	⋮	⋮	100	⋮	⋮	73	77	86	96
32	Other manufacturing		⋮	⋮	⋮	⋮	⋮	⋮	⋮	⋮	⋮	⋮	⋮	⋮
33	Repair and installation of machinery/equipment		⋮	⋮	⋮	⋮	⋮	⋮	⋮	⋮	⋮	⋮	⋮	⋮
C	Total manufacturing		⋮	⋮	⋮	⋮	⋮	100	⋮	⋮	120	133	150	184

Zambia

Supplier of information:
Central Statistical Office, Lusaka.

Basic source of data:
Annual survey; administrative data.

Major deviations from ISIC (Revision 4):
None reported.

Reference period:
Not reported.

Scope:
All registered establishments.

Method of data collection:
Mail questionnaires.

Type of enumeration:
Not reported.

Adjusted for non-response:
Not reported.

Concepts and definitions of variables:
No deviations from the standard UN concepts and definitions are reported.

Related national publications:
Gross Domestic Product (GDP) Report, published by the Central Statistical Office (CSO), Lusaka.

Zambia

ISIC	Industry	Output (valuation not defined) a/ (millions of Zambian Kwacha)					Value added (valuation not defined) a/ (millions of Zambian Kwacha)					Gross fixed capital formation (millions of Zambian Kwacha)		
		Note	2012	2013	2014	2015	Note	2012	2013	2014	2015	Note	2014	2015
10	Food products	b/	7863.0	8885.5	13048.1	13945.2	b/	3143.4	3358.5	4261.3	4420.5		...	...
11	Beverages	b/	...	...	...	...	b/	...	...	...	...		...	...
12	Tobacco products	b/	...	...	...	...	b/	...	...	...	...		...	...
13	Textiles	c/	775.8	778.4	542.2	578.8	c/	149.9	157.4	144.5	152.8		...	...
14	Wearing apparel		...	...	...	...		...	...	...	...		...	...
15	Leather and related products	c/	...	...	...	...	c/	...	...	...	...		...	...
16	Wood products, excluding furniture		445.2	437.3	434.5	472.1		228.4	227.2	236.9	248.5		...	...
17	Paper and paper products		673.6	590.7	643.2	784.0		222.0	180.2	206.3	245.8		...	...
18	Printing and reproduction of recorded media		...	...	...	...		...	...	...	...		...	...
19	Coke and refined petroleum products	d/	1220.2	1358.5	2417.3	3522.2	d/	762.6	878.5	1263.7	1721.8		...	...
20	Chemicals and chemical products	e/	2385.4	3209.2	3000.2	4065.4	e/	1371.6	928.7	1101.3	1390.9		...	...
21	Pharmaceuticals,medicinal chemicals, etc.							...	...	...	...		...	...
22	Rubber and plastics products	e/	...	...	...	...	e/	...	...	...	...		...	...
23	Other non-metallic mineral products	d/	...	...	...	...	d/	...	...	...	...		...	...
24	Basic metals		8031.9	9351.0	11014.1	11007.2		2284.2	2462.4	2904.6	3925.9		...	...
25	Fabricated metal products, except machinery	f/	3828.5	3454.2	4748.9	5853.7	f/	1126.4	1169.6	1274.4	1688.3		...	...
26	Computer, electronic and optical products	f/	...	...	...	...	f/	...	...	...	...		...	...
27	Electrical equipment		...	...	...	...		...	...	...	...		...	...
28	Machinery and equipment n.e.c.	f/	...	...	...	...	f/	...	...	...	...		...	...
29	Motor vehicles, trailers and semi-trailers	f/	...	...	...	...	f/	...	...	...	...		...	...
30	Other transport equipment		...	...	...	...		...	...	...	...		...	...
31	Furniture		...	...	...	...		...	...	...	...		...	...
32	Other manufacturing		...	...	...	...		...	...	...	...		...	...
33	Repair and installation of machinery/equipment	f/	...	...	...	...	f/	...	...	...	...		...	...
C	Total manufacturing	g/	25223.6	28064.8	35848.5	40228.6	g/	9288.5	9362.5	11393.0	13794.5		...	...

a/ Data were derived from the official website
b/ 10 includes 11 and 12.
c/ 13 includes 15.
d/ 19 includes 23.
e/ 20 includes 22.
f/ 25 includes 26, 28, 29 and 33.
g/ Sum of available data.

Zambia

Index numbers of industrial production

ISIC Revision 4 — (2010=100)

ISIC	Industry	Note	2005	2006	2007	2008	2009	2010	2011	2012	2013	2014	2015	2016
10	Food products	a/	...	...	86	89	93	100	109	117	124	130	131	132
11	Beverages	a/	...	...	...	...	...	...	...	...	...	...	...	...
12	Tobacco products	a/	...	...	...	...	...	...	...	...	...	...	...	...
13	Textiles	b/	...	...	378	289	231	100	45	47	71	35	23	22
14	Wearing apparel	b/	...	...	...	...	...	...	...	...	...	...	...	...
15	Leather and related products	b/	...	...	...	...	...	...	...	...	...	...	...	...
16	Wood products, excluding furniture		...	...	77	86	88	100	106	111	109	110	114	113
17	Paper and paper products		...	...	60	77	82	100	118	135	150	152	145	154
18	Printing and reproduction of recorded media		...	...	...	...	...	...	...	...	...	...	...	...
19	Coke and refined petroleum products		...	...	...	...	...	...	...	...	...	...	...	...
20	Chemicals and chemical products		...	...	...	...	...	...	...	...	...	...	...	...
21	Pharmaceuticals, medicinal chemicals, etc.		...	...	...	...	...	...	...	...	...	...	...	...
22	Rubber and plastics products		...	...	...	...	...	...	...	...	...	...	...	...
23	Other non-metallic mineral products		...	...	76	80	89	100	125	135	137	147	163	196
24	Basic metals		...	...	87	107	102	100	99	113	120	138	151	148
25	Fabricated metal products, except machinery		...	...	101	98	89	100	117	112	108	110	113	109
26	Computer, electronic and optical products		...	...	...	...	...	...	...	...	...	...	...	...
27	Electrical equipment		...	...	...	...	...	...	...	...	...	...	...	...
28	Machinery and equipment n.e.c.		...	...	...	...	...	...	...	...	...	...	...	...
29	Motor vehicles, trailers and semi-trailers		...	...	...	...	...	...	...	...	...	...	...	...
30	Other transport equipment		...	...	...	...	...	...	...	...	...	...	...	...
31	Furniture		...	...	...	...	...	...	...	...	...	...	...	...
32	Other manufacturing		...	...	...	...	...	...	...	...	...	...	...	...
33	Repair and installation of machinery/equipment		...	...	...	...	...	...	...	...	...	...	...	...
C	Total manufacturing		...	...	90	92	94	100	111	117	123	128	132	135

a/ 10 includes 11 and 12.
b/ 13 includes 14 and 15.